CONNECT FEATURES

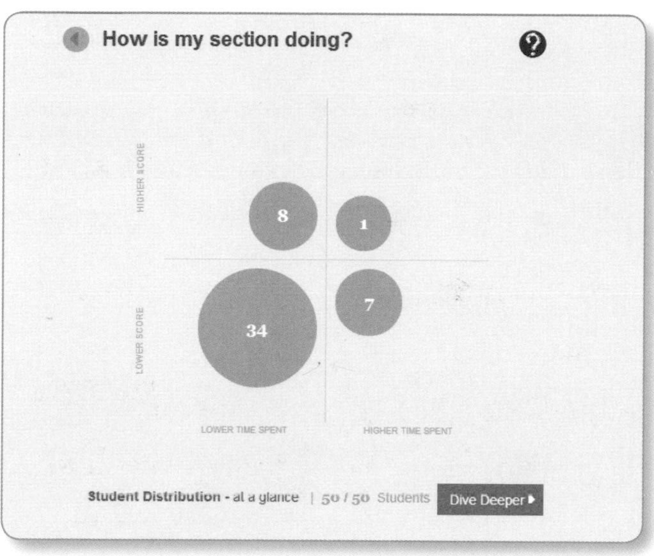

Connect Insight

The first and only analytics tool of its kind, Connect Insight is a series of visual data displays, each of which is framed by an intuitive question and provides at-a-glance information regarding how an instructor's class is performing. Connect Insight is available through Connect titles.

Tax Forms Problems

Updated for the 2016 edition, *Tax Forms Problems* are a set of requirements included in the end-of-chapter material that ask students to complete a tax form. These problems provide valuable experience and practice with filling out forms and are included in *Connect Accounting*. These requirements and their relevant forms are included in *Connect Accounting*.

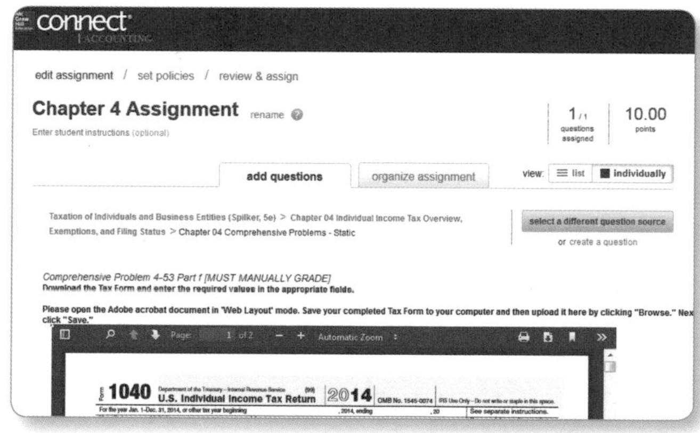

Through November, Tex has received gross income of $120,000. For December, Tex is considering whether to accept one more work engagement for the year. Engagement 1 will generate $7,000 of revenue at a cost of $4,000, which is deductible for AGI. In contrast, engagement 2 will generate $7,000 of revenue at a cost of $3,000, which is deductible as an itemized deduction. Tex files as a single taxpayer. (use the tax rate schedules.)

a. Calculate Tex's taxable income assuming he chooses engagement 1 and assuming he chooses engagement 2. Assume he has no itemized deductions other than those generated by engagement 2.

Description	Engagement 1	Engagement 2
(1) Gross income before new work engagement	$ 120,000	$ 120,000
(2) Income from engagement	7,000	7,000
(3) Additional for AGI deduction	(4,000)	
(4) Adjusted gross income	$ 123,000	$ 127,000
(5) Greater		
(6) Greater of itemized deductions or standard deduction		

End-of-Chapter Material

McGraw-Hill Education redesigned the student interface for our end-of-chapter assessment content. The new interface provides improved answer acceptance to reduce students' frustration with formatting issues (such as rounding) and, for select questions, provides an expanded table that guides students through the process of solving the problem. Many questions have been redesigned to more fully test students' mastery of the content.

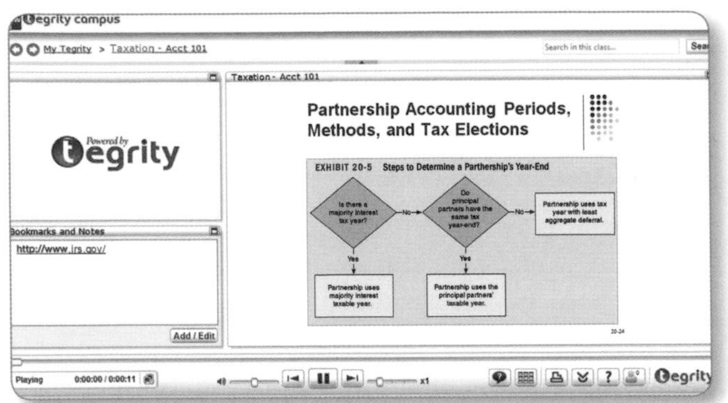

Tegrity

Make your classes available anytime, anywhere. With simple, one-click recording, students can search for a word or phrase and be taken to the exact place in your lecture that they need to review.

EASY TO USE

Learning Management System Integration

McGraw-Hill Campus is a one-stop teaching and learning experience available to use with any learning management system. McGraw-Hill Campus provides single sign-on to faculty and students for all McGraw-Hill material and technology from within the school website. McGraw-Hill Campus also allows instructors instant access to all supplements and teaching materials for all McGraw-Hill products.

Blackboard users also benefit from McGraw-Hill's industry-leading integration, providing single sign-on to access all Connect assignments and automatic feeding of assignment results to the Blackboard grade book.

POWERFUL REPORTING

Connect generates comprehensive reports and graphs that provide instructors with an instant view of the performance of individual students, a specific section, or multiple sections. Since all content is mapped to learning objectives, Connect reporting is ideal for accreditation or other administrative documentation.

At a Glance Insights

Assignment Results & Statistics Reports

Student Performance Reports

Item Analysis Reports

Category Analysis Reports

At-Risk Student Reports

LearnSmart Reports

McGraw-Hill's

Taxation of Business Entities

Brian C. Spilker
Brigham Young University
Editor

Benjamin C. Ayers
The University of Georgia

Edmund Outslay
Michigan State University

Connie D. Weaver
Texas A&M University

John A. Barrick
Brigham Young University

John R. Robinson
The University of Texas–Austin

Ron G. Worsham
Brigham Young University

McGRAW-HILL'S TAXATION OF BUSINESS ENTITIES, 2016 EDITION, SEVENTH EDITION

This book is printed on acid-free paper.

2 3 4 5 6 7 QVS/QVS 19 18 17 16 15

ISBN 978-1-259-42121-1
MHID 1-259-42121-X
ISSN 1946-7737

Senior Vice President, Products & Markets: *Kurt L. Strand*
Vice President, General Manager, Products & Markets: *Marty Lange*
Vice President, Content Design & Delivery: *Kimberly Meriwether David*
Managing Director: *Tim Vertovec*
Marketing Director: *Brad Parkins*
Senior Brand Manager: *Kathleen Klehr*
Director, Product Development: *Rose Koos*
Director of Digital Content: *Patricia Plumb*
Lead Product Developer: *Ann Torbert*
Product Developer: *Danielle Andries*
Digital Product Developer: *Kevin Moran*
Digital Product Analyst: *Xin Lin*
Director, Content Design & Delivery: *Linda Avenarius*
Program Manager: *Daryl Horrocks*
Content Project Managers: *Lori Koetters, Brian Nacik*
Buyer: *Sue Culbertson*
Design: *Matt Diamond*
Content Licensing Specialists: *Keri Johnson, Rita Hingtgen*
Cover Image: *PhotoAlto Photography/Veer*
Compositor: *Aptara®, Inc.*
Printer: *Quad/Graphics*

www.mhhe.com

Dedications

We dedicate this book to:

My children, Braxton, Cameron, Ethan, and Lauren, and to my parents, Ray and Janet. Last but not least, to my wife, Kim, for allowing me to take up valuable kitchen space while I was working on the project. I love you all.

Brian Spilker

My wife, Marilyn, daughters Margaret Lindley and Georgia, son Benjamin, and parents Bill and Linda.

Ben Ayers

My wife, Jill, and my children Annika, Corinne, Lina, Mitch, and Connor.

John Barrick

My family, Jane, Mark, Sarah, Chloe, Lily, and Jeff, and to Professor James E. Wheeler, my mentor and friend.

Ed Outslay

JES, Tommy, and Laura.

John Robinson

My family, Dan, Travis, Alix, and Alan.

Connie Weaver

My wife, Anne, sons Matthew and Daniel, and daughters Whitney and Hayley.

Ron Worsham

About the Authors

Brian Spilker (PhD, University of Texas at Austin, 1993) is the Robert Call/Deloitte Professor in the School of Accountancy at Brigham Young University. He teaches taxation in the graduate and undergraduate programs at Brigham Young University. He received both BS (Summa Cum Laude) and MAcc (tax emphasis) degrees from Brigham Young University before working as a tax consultant for Arthur Young & Co. (now Ernst & Young). After his professional work experience, Brian earned his PhD at the University of Texas at Austin. In 1996, he was selected as one of two nationwide recipients of the Price Waterhouse Fellowship in Tax Award. In 1998, he was a winner of the American Taxation Association and Arthur Andersen Teaching Innovation Award for his work in the classroom; he has also been awarded for his use of technology in the classroom at Brigham Young University. Brian researches issues relating to tax information search and professional tax judgment. His research has been published in journals such as *The Accounting Review, Organizational Behavior and Human Decision Processes, Journal of the American Taxation Association, Behavioral Research in Accounting, Journal of Accounting Education, Journal of Corporate Taxation,* and *Journal of Accountancy.*

Ben Ayers (PhD, University of Texas at Austin, 1996) holds the Earl Davis Chair in Taxation and is the Dean of the Terry College of Business at the University of Georgia. He received a PhD from the University of Texas at Austin and an MTA and BS from the University of Alabama. Prior to entering the PhD program at the University of Texas, Ben was a tax manager at KPMG in Tampa, Florida, and a contract manager with Complete Health, Inc., in Birmingham, Alabama.

Ben teaches tax planning and research courses in the undergraduate and graduate programs at the University of Georgia. He is the recipient of 11 teaching awards at the school, college, and university levels, including the Richard B. Russell Undergraduate Teaching Award, the highest teaching honor for University of Georgia junior faculty members. His research interests include the effects of taxation on firm structure, mergers and acquisitions, and capital markets and the effects of accounting information on security returns. He has published articles in journals such as the *Accounting Review, Journal of Finance, Journal of Accounting and Economics, Contemporary Accounting Research, Review of Accounting Studies, Journal of Law and Economics, Journal of the American Taxation Association,* and *National Tax Journal.* Ben was the 1997 recipient of the American Accounting Association's Competitive Manuscript Award and the 2003 and 2008 recipient of the American Taxation Association's Outstanding Manuscript Award.

John Barrick (PhD, University of Nebraska at Lincoln, 1998) is currently an associate professor in the Marriott School at Brigham Young University. He served as an accountant at the United States Congress Joint Committee on Taxation for the 110th and 111th Congresses. He teaches taxation in the graduate and undergraduate programs at Brigham Young University. He received both BS and MAcc (tax emphasis) degrees from Brigham Young University before working as a tax consultant for Price Waterhouse (now PricewaterhouseCoopers). After his professional work experience, John earned his PhD at the University of Nebraska at Lincoln. He was the 1998 recipient of the American Accounting Association, Accounting, Behavior, and Organization Section's Outstanding Dissertation Award. John researches issues relating to professional tax judgment and tax information search. His research has been published in journals such as *Organizational Behavior and Human Decision Processes, Contemporary Accounting Research,* and *Journal of the American Taxation Association*.

Ed Outslay (PhD, University of Michigan, 1981) is a professor of accounting and the Deloitte/Michael Licata Endowed Professor of Taxation in the Department of Accounting and Information Systems at Michigan State University, where he has taught since 1981. He received a BA from Furman University in 1974 and an MBA and PhD from the University of Michigan in 1977 and 1981. Ed currently teaches graduate classes in corporate taxation, multiunit enterprises, accounting for income taxes, and international taxation. In February 2003, Ed testified before the Senate Finance Committee on the Joint Committee on Taxation's Report on Enron Corporation. MSU has honored Ed with the Presidential Award for Outstanding Community Service, Distinguished Faculty Award, John D. Withrow Teacher-Scholar Award, Roland H. Salmonson Outstanding Teaching Award, Senior Class Council Distinguished Faculty Award, MSU Teacher-Scholar Award, and MSU's 1st Annual Curricular Service-Learning and Civic Engagement Award in 2008. Ed received the Ray M. Sommerfeld Outstanding Tax Educator Award in 2004 and the lifetime Service Award in 2013 from the American Taxation Association. He has also received the ATA Outstanding Manuscript Award twice, the ATA/Deloitte Teaching Innovations Award, and the 2004 Distinguished Achievement in Accounting Education Award from the Michigan Association of CPAs. Ed has been recognized for his community service by the Greater Lansing Chapter of the Association of Government Accountants, the City of East Lansing (Crystal Award), and the East Lansing Education Foundation. He received a National Assistant Coach of the Year Award in 2003 from AFLAC and was named an Assistant High School Baseball Coach of the Year in 2002 by the Michigan High School Baseball Coaches Association.

John Robinson (PhD, University of Michigan, 1981) is the C. Aubrey Smith Professor of Accounting in the McCombs School of Business at the University of Texas at Austin. Prior to joining the faculty at Texas in 1985, he taught at the University of Kansas, where he was the Arthur Young Faculty Scholar from 1982–1984. John served as the Academic Fellow in the Division of Corporation Finance at the Securities and Exchange Commission for 2009–2010. He is the recipient of the Henry A. Bubb Award for outstanding teaching, the Texas Blazer's Faculty Excellence Award, and the MPA Council Outstanding Professor Award. John also received the 2012 Outstanding Service Award from the American Taxation Association (ATA). John conducts research in a broad variety of topics involving financial accounting, mergers and acquisitions, and the influence of taxes on financial structures and performance. His scholarly articles have appeared in *Accounting Review, Journal of Finance, National Tax Journal, Journal of Law and Economics, Journal of the American Taxation Association, The Journal of the American Bar Association,* and *The Journal of Taxation.* In addition, John was the editor of *The Journal of the American Taxation Association,* from 2002 through 2005, and he was a co-author of the articles honored with the 2003 and 2008 ATA Outstanding Manuscript Awards. John received his JD (*cum laude*) from the University of Michigan in 1979, and he was awarded his PhD in accounting from the University of Michigan in 1981. John teaches courses on individual and corporate taxation and advanced accounting at the University of Texas at Austin.

Connie Weaver Connie Weaver (PhD, Arizona State University, 1997) is the KPMG Professor of Accounting at Texas A&M University. She received a PhD from Arizona State University, an MPA from the University of Texas at Arlington, and a BS (chemical engineering) from the University of Texas at Austin. Prior to entering the PhD Program, Connie was a tax manager at Ernst & Young in Dallas, Texas, where she became licensed to practice as a CPA. She teaches taxation in the graduate and undergraduate programs at Texas A&M University. She has also taught undergraduate and graduate students at the University of Wisconsin-Madison and the University of Texas at Austin. She is the recipient of several teaching awards including the 2006 American Taxation Association/Deloitte Teaching Innovations and the David and Denise Baggett Teaching awards both recognizing innovation in teaching taxation. Connie's current research interests include the effects of tax and financial incentives on corporate decisions and reporting. She has published articles in journals such as the *Accounting Review, Contemporary Accounting Research, Journal of the American Taxation Association, Accounting Horizons, Journal of Corporate Finance,* and *Tax Notes*. She serves on the editorial board of Contemporary Accounting Research and Issues in Accounting Education and was the 1998 recipient of the American Taxation Association/Price Waterhouse Outstanding Dissertation award.

Ron Worsham (PhD, University of Florida, 1994) is an associate professor in the School of Accountancy at Brigham Young University. He teaches taxation in the graduate, undergraduate, MBA, and Executive MBA programs at Brigham Young University. He has also taught as a visiting professor at the University of Chicago. He received both BS and MAcc (tax emphasis) degrees from Brigham Young University before working as a tax consultant for Arthur Young & Co. (now Ernst & Young) in Dallas, Texas. While in Texas, he became licensed to practice as a CPA. After his professional work experience, Ron earned his PhD at the University of Florida. He has been honored for outstanding innovation in the classroom at Brigham Young University. Ron has published academic research in the areas of taxpayer compliance and professional tax judgment. He has also published legal research in a variety of areas. His work has been published in journals such as *Journal of the American Taxation Association, The Journal of International Taxation, The Tax Executive, Journal of Accountancy,* and *Practical Tax Strategies.*

TEACHING THE CODE IN CONTEXT

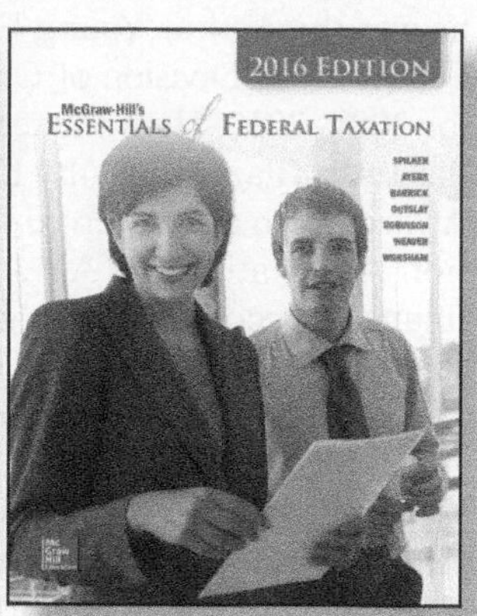

The basic approach to teaching taxation hasn't changed in decades. ***Today's student deserves a new approach.*** McGraw-Hill's Taxation of Individuals and Business Entities *is a bold and innovative series that has been adopted by over 300 schools across the country.*

McGraw-Hill's Taxation is designed to provide a unique, innovative, and engaging learning experience for students studying taxation. The breadth of the topical coverage, **the storyline approach to presenting the material,** the emphasis on the tax and nontax consequences of multiple parties involved in transactions, and the integration of financial and tax accounting topics make this book ideal for the modern tax curriculum.

> **This is the best tax book on the market.** It's very readable, student-friendly, and provides great supplements.
>
> – Ann Esarco, McHenry County College

> A lot of thought and planning went into the structure and content of the text, and a great product was achieved. **One of the most unique and helpful features is the common storyline** throughout each chapter.
>
> – Raymond J. Shaffer, Youngstown State University

Since the first manuscript was written in 2005, 400 professors have contributed 419 book reviews, in addition to 21 focus groups and symposia. Throughout this preface, their comments on the book's organization, pedagogy, and unique features are a testament to the **market-driven nature of *Taxation*'s development.**

> The Spilker text, in many ways, is a more logical approach than any other tax textbook. **The text makes great use of the latest learning technologies through Connect and LearnSmart.**
>
> – Ray Rodriguez, Southern Illinois University – Carbondale

A MODERN APPROACH FOR TODAY'S STUDENT

> **This text provides a new approach to the teaching of the technical material.** The style of the text material is easier to read and understand. The examples and storyline are interesting and informative. The arrangement makes more sense in the understanding of related topics.
>
> – Robert Bertucelli, Long Island University – Post

Spilker's taxation series was built around the following five core precepts:

1. **Storyline Approach:** Each chapter begins with a storyline that introduces a set of characters or a business entity facing specific tax-related situations. Each chapter's examples are related to the storyline, providing students with opportunities to **learn the code in context.**

2. **Conversational Writing Style:** The authors took special care to write *McGraw-Hill's Taxation* that fosters a friendly dialogue between the content and each individual student. The tone of the presentation is intentionally conversational—creating the impression of ***speaking with*** **the student,** as opposed to *lecturing to* the student.

3. **Superior Organization of Related Topics:** *McGraw-Hill's Taxation* takes a fresh approach to taxation by providing two alternative topic sequences. In the *McGraw-Hill's Taxation of Individuals and Business Entities,* topics are grouped in **theme chapters,** including separate chapters on home ownership, compensation, investments, and retirement savings and deferred compensation. However, in the *Essentials of Federal Taxation,* topics follow a more traditional sequence with topics presented in a life-cycle approach.

> I believe it **breaks down complex topics in a way that's easy to understand.** Definitely easier than other tax textbooks that I've had experience with.
>
> – Jacob Gatlin, Athens State University

4. **Real-World Focus:** Students learn best when they see how concepts are applied in the real world. For that reason, real-world examples and articles are included in **"Taxes in the Real World"** boxes throughout the book. These vignettes demonstrate current issues in taxation and show the relevance of tax issues in all areas of business.

5. **Integrated Examples:** The examples used throughout the chapter relate directly to the storyline presented at the beginning of each chapter, so students become familiar with one set of facts and learn how to apply those facts to different scenarios. In addition to providing in-context examples, we provide **"What if"** scenarios within many examples to **illustrate how variations in the facts might or might not change the answers.**

> **Excellent text; love the story line approach and integrated examples.** It's easy to read and understand explanations. The language of the text is very clear and straightforward.
>
> – Sandra Owen, Indiana University – Bloomington

A STORYLINE APPROACH THAT WILL RESONATE WITH STUDENTS

© Image Source

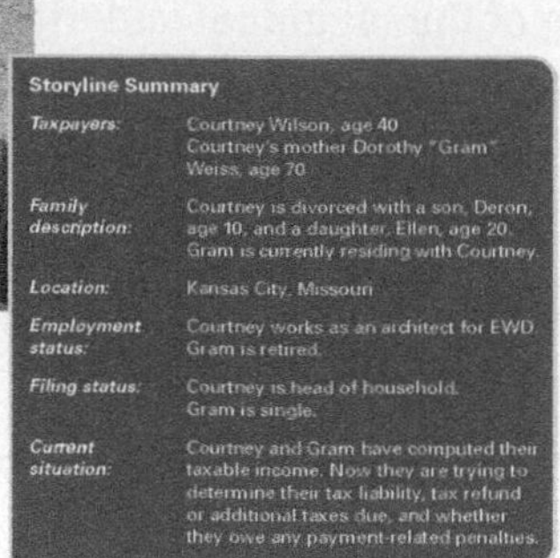

Storyline Summary

Taxpayers:	Courtney Wilson, age 40 Courtney's mother Dorothy "Gram" Weiss, age 70
Family description:	Courtney is divorced with a son, Deron, age 10, and a daughter, Ellen, age 20. Gram is currently residing with Courtney.
Location:	Kansas City, Missouri
Employment status:	Courtney works as an architect for EWD. Gram is retired.
Filing status:	Courtney is head of household. Gram is single.
Current situation:	Courtney and Gram have computed their taxable income. Now they are trying to determine their tax liability, tax refund or additional taxes due, and whether they owe any payment-related penalties.

Courtney has already determined her taxable income. Now she's working on computing her tax liability. She knows she owes a significant amount of regular income tax on her employment and business activities. However, she's not sure how to compute the tax on the qualified dividends she received from General Electric. Courtney is worried that she may be subject to the alternative minimum tax this year because she's heard that an increasing number of taxpayers in her income range must pay the tax. Finally, Courtney knows she owes some self-employment taxes on her business income. Courtney would like to determine whether she is eligible to claim any tax credits such as the child tax credit for her two children and education credits because she paid for a portion of her daughter Ellen's tuition at the University of Missouri–Kansas paid enough in taxes during the year to avoid underpayment penalties. She's planning on filing her tax return and paying her taxes on time.

Gram's tax situation is much more straightforward. She needs to determine the regular income tax on her taxable income. Her income is so low she knows she need not worry about the alternative minimum tax, and she believes she doesn't owe any self-employment tax. Gram didn't prepay any taxes this year, so she is concerned that she might be required to pay an underpayment penalty. She also expects to file her tax return and pay her

Each chapter begins with a storyline that introduces a set of characters facing specific tax-related situations. This revolutionary approach to teaching tax emphasizes real people facing real tax dilemmas. Students learn to apply practical tax information to specific business and personal situations. The characters are brought further to life.

The text provides very useful tools that students can read and understand, making it easier to **break the myth that "tax is hard."**

– Daniel Hoops, Walsh College

I absolutely love this textbook. This textbook makes my job of teaching so much easier.

– Chuck Pier, Angelo State University

Examples

Examples are the cornerstone of any textbook covering taxation. For this reason, *McGraw-Hill's Taxation* authors took special care to create clear and helpful examples that relate to the storyline of the chapter. Students learn to refer to the facts presented in the storyline and apply them to other scenarios—in this way, they build a greater base of knowledge through application. Many examples also include "What if?" scenarios that add more complexity to the example or explore related tax concepts.

Example 2-1

Bill and Mercedes file their 2011 federal tax return on September 6, 2012, after receiving an automatic extension to file their return by October 15, 2012. In 2015, the IRS selects their 2011 tax return for audit. When does the statute of limitations end for Bill and Mercedes's 2011 tax return?

Answer: Assuming the six-year and "unlimited" statute of limitation rules do not apply, the statute of limitations ends on September 6, 2015 (three years after the later of the actual filing date and the *original* due date).

What if: When would the statute of limitations end for Bill and Mercedes for their 2011 tax return if the couple filed the return on March 22, 2012 (before the original due date of April 17, 2012)?

Answer: In this scenario the statute of limitations would end on April 17, 2015, because the later of the actual filing date and the original due date is April 17, 2012.

The **case study approach is excellent** as you follow the taxpayers through the chapters.

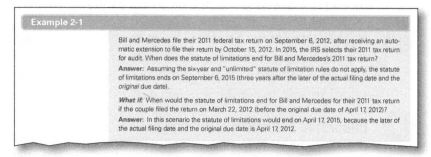

– Irwin Uhr, Hunter College

THE PEDAGOGY YOUR STUDENTS NEED TO PUT THE CODE IN CONTEXT

Taxes in the Real World

Taxes in the Real World are short boxes used throughout the book to demonstrate the real-world use of tax concepts. Current articles on tax issues, real-world application of chapter-specific tax rules, and short vignettes on popular news about tax are some of the issues covered in Taxes in the Real World boxes.

> The Spilker text makes tax easy for students to understand. **It integrates great real-world examples so students can see how topics will be applied in practice.** The integration of the tax form and exhibits of the tax forms in the text are outstanding.
>
> – Kristen Bigbee, Texas Tech University

TAXES IN THE REAL WORLD Republicans vs. Democrats

We often boil down the tax policy of our major political parties into its simplest form: Democrats raise taxes to fund social programs, and Republicans lower taxes to benefit big businesses and the wealthy. Both ideas simplify the policy of each party, yet both ideas are essentially true.

Whether you agree with more government spending or tax breaks for corporations, each party's agenda will affect your taxes.

Political Ideology: Republican

"We believe government should tax only to raise money for its essential functions." The Republicans state their case plainly on the Republican National Convention website. That is, Republicans believe government should spend money only to enforce contracts, maintain basic infrastructure and national security, and protect citizens against criminals.

The literature of the House Republican Conference goes on to illuminate the role of the government and how tax policies affect individuals: "The money the government spends does not belong to the government; it belongs to the taxpayers who earned it. Republicans believe Americans deserve to keep more of their own money to save and invest for the future, and low tax policies help drive a strong and healthy economy."

Tax relief is the Republican route to growing the economy. A Republican government would reduce taxes for businesses to allow businesses to grow and thus hire more employees. Republicans also seek to limit income taxes for individuals so that people can hold on to more disposable income, which they can then spend, save, or invest.

Political Ideology: Democrat

The tax policy for the Democratic Party calls for raising certain taxes to provide money for government spending, which in turn generates business. The party platform asserts that government spending provides "good jobs and will help the economy today."

Many Democrats are adherents to Keynesian economics, or aggregate demand, which holds that when the government funds programs, those programs pump new money into the economy. Keynesians believe that prices tend to stay relatively stable and therefore any kind of spending, whether by consumers or the government, will grow the economy.

Like the Republicans, Democrats believe the government should subsidize vital services that keep cities, states, and the country running: infrastructure such as road and bridge maintenance and repairs for schools. Democrats also call for tax cuts for the middle class. But who benefits most under each platform? The conventional wisdom is that corporations and the wealthy will benefit more with a Republican tax policy, while small businesses and middle-class households will benefit from a Democratic tax policy.

http://www.investopedia.com/articles/economics/09/us-parties-republican-democrat-taxes.asp

The Key Facts

Marginal Key Facts provide quick synopses of the critical pieces of information presented throughout each chapter.

		$11,587.50 = $10,312.50 + 25% × ($80,000 – $74,900).
(3) Taxable income before additional $80,000 of tax deductions	$ 160,000	Example 1-3.
(4) Tax on $160,000 taxable income	$31,851.50	Example 1-3.
Marginal tax rate on additional $80,000 of tax deductions	25.33%	$\frac{\Delta \text{Tax}}{\Delta \text{Taxable income}} = [(2) - (4)]/[(1) - (3)]$

THE KEY FACTS

Different Ways to Measure Tax Rates

- Marginal tax rate
  - The tax that applies to next increment of income or deduction.
  - $= \frac{\Delta \text{Tax}}{\Delta \text{Taxable income}}$

Exhibits

Today's students are visual learners, and *McGraw-Hill's Taxation* delivers by making appropriate use of charts, diagrams, and tabular demonstrations of key material.

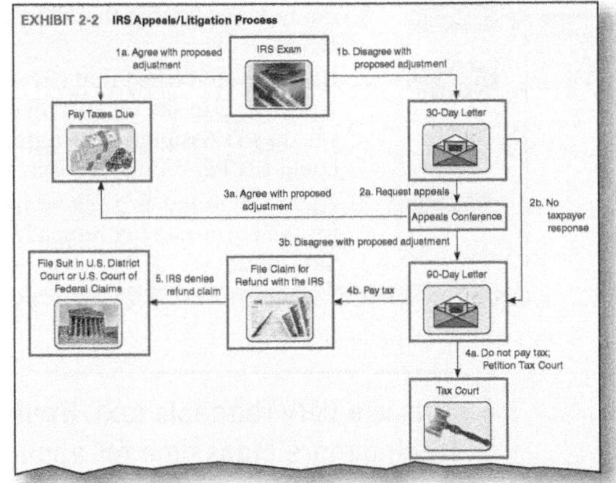

> A good textbook that uses **great examples throughout the chapters** to give a student an understanding of the tax theory and how it applies to the taxpayers.
>
> – Jennifer Wright, Drexel University

> Spilker's use of examples immediately following the concept is a **great way to reinforce the concepts.**
>
> – Karen Wisniewski, County College of Morris

PRACTICE MAKES PERFECT WITH A...

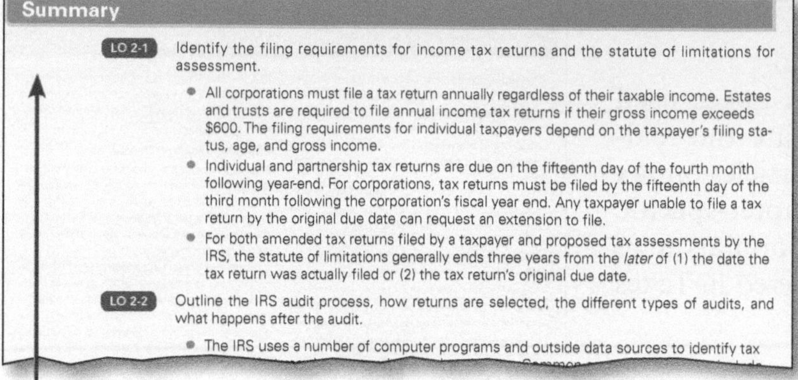

Summary

LO 2-1 Identify the filing requirements for income tax returns and the statute of limitations for assessment.

- All corporations must file a tax return annually regardless of their taxable income. Estates and trusts are required to file annual income tax returns if their gross income exceeds $600. The filing requirements for individual taxpayers depend on the taxpayer's filing status, age, and gross income.
- Individual and partnership tax returns are due on the fifteenth day of the fourth month following year-end. For corporations, tax returns must be filed by the fifteenth day of the third month following the corporation's fiscal year end. Any taxpayer unable to file a tax return by the original due date can request an extension to file.
- For both amended tax returns filed by a taxpayer and proposed tax assessments by the IRS, the statute of limitations generally ends three years from the *later* of (1) the date the tax return was actually filed or (2) the tax return's original due date.

LO 2-2 Outline the IRS audit process, how returns are selected, the different types of audits, and what happens after the audit.

- The IRS uses a number of computer programs and outside data sources to identify tax

Summary

A unique feature of *McGraw-Hill's Taxation* is the end-of-chapter summary organized around learning objectives. Each objective has a brief, bullet-point summary that covers the major topics and concepts for that chapter, including references to critical exhibits and examples.

All end-of-chapter material is tied to learning objectives:

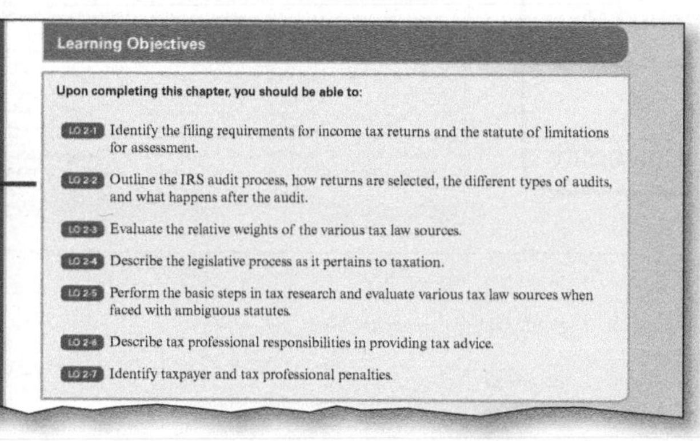

Learning Objectives

Upon completing this chapter, you should be able to:

LO 2-1 Identify the filing requirements for income tax returns and the statute of limitations for assessment.

LO 2-2 Outline the IRS audit process, how returns are selected, the different types of audits, and what happens after the audit.

LO 2-3 Evaluate the relative weights of the various tax law sources.

LO 2-4 Describe the legislative process as it pertains to taxation.

LO 2-5 Perform the basic steps in tax research and evaluate various tax law sources when faced with ambiguous statutes.

LO 2-6 Describe tax professional responsibilities in providing tax advice.

LO 2-7 Identify taxpayer and tax professional penalties.

You can tell the authors of this textbook are still in the classroom and responsible for the day-to-day education of accounting students. Examples are representative of the end-of-chapter problems, and the end-of-chapter summary is an excellent study tool.

– Debra Petrizzo, Franklin University

DISCUSSION QUESTIONS

LO 2-1 1. Name three factors that determine whether a tax return.

LO 2-1 2. Benita is concerned that she will not be able to co April 15. Can she request an extension to file her she do so? Assuming she requests an extension, w could file her return this year without penalty?

LO 2-1 3. Agua Linda Inc. is a calendar-year corporation. for the corporate tax return? What happens if the Saturday?

Discussion Questions are provided for each of the major concepts in each chapter, providing students with an opportunity to review key parts of the chapter and answer evocative questions about what they have learned.

This is a very readable text. **Students will understand it on their own,** generally, freeing more class time for application, practice, and student questions.

– Valrie Chambers,
Texas A&M University – Corpus Christi

...WIDE VARIETY OF ASSIGNMENT MATERIAL

Problems are designed to test the comprehension of more complex topics. Each problem at the end of the chapter is tied to one of that chapter's learning objectives, with multiple problems for critical topics.

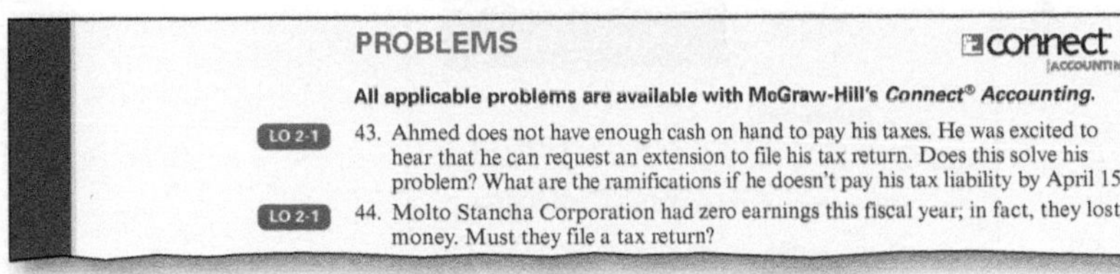

PROBLEMS connect ACCOUNTING

All applicable problems are available with McGraw-Hill's *Connect® Accounting*.

LO 2-1 43. Ahmed does not have enough cash on hand to pay his taxes. He was excited to hear that he can request an extension to file his tax return. Does this solve his problem? What are the ramifications if he doesn't pay his tax liability by April 15?

LO 2-1 44. Molto Stancha Corporation had zero earnings this fiscal year; in fact, they lost money. Must they file a tax return?

Tax Forms Problems are a set of requirements included in the end-of-chapter material of the 2016 edition. These problems require students to complete a tax form (or part of a tax form), providing students with valuable experience and practice with filling out these forms. These requirements—and their relevant forms—are also included in *Connect Accounting.* Each Tax Forms problem includes an icon to differentiate it from regular problems.

> tax forms 70. Shauna Coleman is single. She is employed as an architectural designer for Streamline Design (SD). Shauna wanted to determine her taxable income for this year. She correctly calculated her AGI. However, she wasn't sure how to compute the rest of her taxable income. She provided the following information with hopes that you could use it to determine her taxable income.
>
> a) Shauna paid $4,676 for medical expenses for care from a broken ankle. Also, Shauna's boyfriend, Blake, drove Shauna (in her car) a total of 115 miles to the doctor's office so she could receive care for her broken ankle.
>
> b) Shauna paid a total of $3,400 in health insurance premiums during the year

Research Problems are special problems throughout the end of the chapter assignment material. These require students to do both basic and more complex research on topics outside of the scope of the book. Each Research Problem includes an icon to differentiate it from regular problems.

> LO 2-5 research 72. Matt and Lori recently were divorced. Although grief stricken, Matt was at least partially comforted by his monthly receipt of $10,000 alimony. He was particularly excited to learn from his friend, Denzel, that the alimony was not taxable. Use an available tax service to determine if Denzel is correct. Would your answer change if Matt and Lori continued to live together?
>
> LO 2-5 research 73. Shaun is a huge college football fan. In the past, he has always bought football tickets on the street from ticket scalpers. This year, he decided to join the university's ticket program, which requires a $2,000 contribution to the university

The textbook is comprehensive, uses an integrated approach to taxation, contains clear illustrations and examples in each chapter, and has **a wealth of end-of-chapter assignment material.**

– James P. Trebby, Marquette University

Planning Problems are another unique set of problems, also located at the end of the chapter assignment material. These require students to test their tax planning skills after covering the chapter topics. Each Planning Problem includes an icon to differentiate it from regular problems.

> 56. Jackie has a corporate client that has recently received a 30-day notice from the IRS with a $100,000 tax assessment. Her client is considering requesting an appeals conference to contest the assessment. What factors should Jackie advise her client to consider before requesting an appeals conference? LO 2-2 planning
>
> 57. The IRS recently completed an audit of Shea's tax return and assessed $15,000 additional tax. Shea requested an appeals conference but was unable to settle the case at the conference. She is contemplating which trial court to choose to hear her case. Provide her a recommendation based on the following alternative facts: LO 2-2 planning
>
> a) Shea resides in the 2nd Circuit, and the 2nd Circuit has recently ruled against

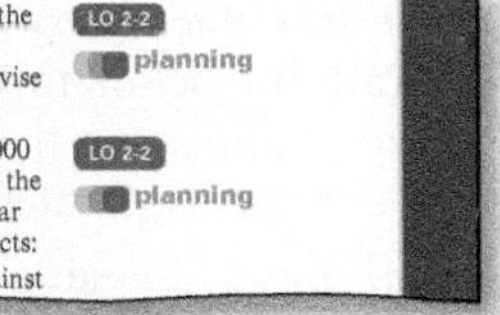

Comprehensive and Tax Return Problems address multiple concepts in a single problem. Comprehensive problems are ideal for cumulative topics; for this reason, they are located at the end of all chapters. In the end-of-book Appendix C, we include Tax Return Problems that cover multiple chapters.

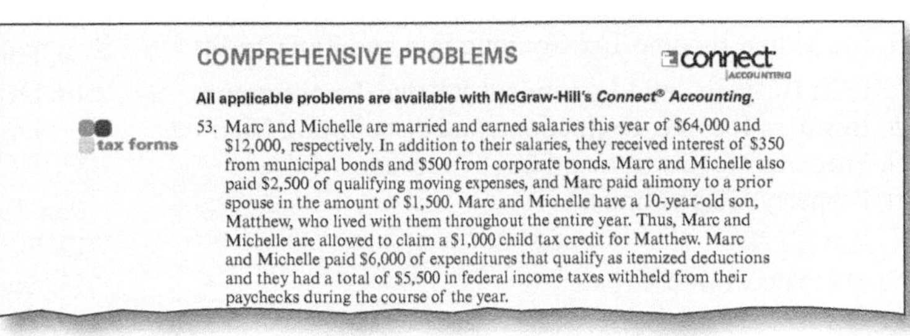

COMPREHENSIVE PROBLEMS connect ACCOUNTING

All applicable problems are available with McGraw-Hill's *Connect® Accounting*.

tax forms 53. Marc and Michelle are married and earned salaries this year of $64,000 and $12,000, respectively. In addition to their salaries, they received interest of $350 from municipal bonds and $500 from corporate bonds. Marc and Michelle also paid $2,500 of qualifying moving expenses, and Marc paid alimony to a prior spouse in the amount of $1,500. Marc and Michelle have a 10-year-old son, Matthew, who lived with them throughout the entire year. Thus, Marc and Michelle are allowed to claim a $1,000 child tax credit for Matthew. Marc and Michelle paid $6,000 of expenditures that qualify as itemized deductions and they had a total of $5,500 in federal income taxes withheld from their paychecks during the course of the year.

Additional Tax Return Problems are also available on the *Connect Library*.

Four Volumes to Fit...

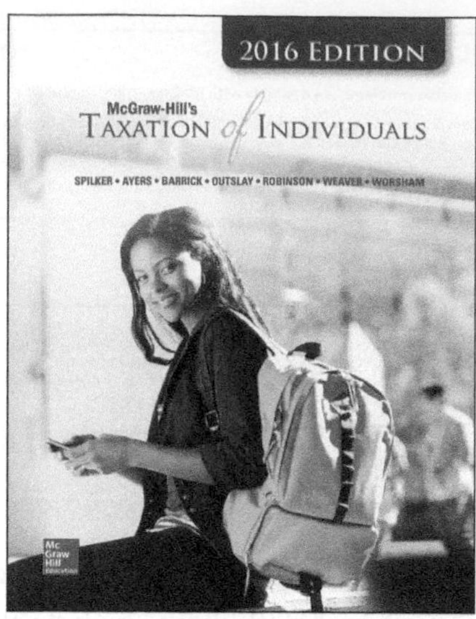

McGraw-Hill's Taxation of Individuals is organized to emphasize topics that are most important to undergraduates taking their first tax course. The first three chapters provide an introduction to taxation and then carefully guide students through tax research and tax planning. Part II discusses the fundamental elements of individual income tax, starting with the tax formula in Chapter 4 and then proceeding to more depth on individual topics in Chapters 5–7. Part III then discusses tax issues associated with business and investment activities. On the business side, it addresses business income and deductions, accounting methods, and tax consequences associated with purchasing assets and property dispositions (sales, trades, or other dispositions). For investments it covers portfolio-type investments such as stocks and bonds and business investments including loss limitations associated with these investments. Part IV is unique among tax textbooks; this section combines related tax issues for compensation, retirement savings, and home ownership.

Part I: Introduction to Taxation
1. An Introduction to Tax
2. Tax Compliance, the IRS, and Tax Authorities
3. Tax Planning Strategies and Related Limitations

Part II: Basic Individual Taxation
4. Individual Income Tax Overview
5. Gross Income and Exclusions
6. Individual Deductions
7. Individual Income Tax Computation and Tax Credits

Part III: Business- and Investment-Related Transactions
8. Business Income, Deductions, and Accounting Methods
9. Property Acquisition and Cost Recovery
10. Property Dispositions
11. Investments

Part IV: Specialized Topics
12. Compensation
13. Retirement Savings and Deferred Compensation
14. Tax Consequences of Home Ownership

McGraw-Hill's Taxation of Business Entities begins with the process for determining gross income and deductions for businesses, and the tax consequences associated with purchasing assets and property dispositions (sales, trades, or other dispositions). Part II provides a comprehensive overview of entities, and the formation, reorganization, and liquidation of corporations. Unique to this series is a complete chapter on accounting for income taxes, which provides a primer on the basics of calculating the income tax provision. Included in the narrative is a discussion of temporary and permanent differences and their impact on a company's book "effective tax rate." Part III provides a detailed discussion of partnerships and S corporations. The last part of the book covers state and local taxation, multinational taxation, and transfer taxes and wealth planning.

Part I: Business- and Investment-Related Transactions
1. Business Income, Deductions, and Accounting Methods
2. Property Acquisition and Cost Recovery
3. Property Dispositions

Part II: Entity Overview and Taxation of C Corporations
4. Entities Overview
5. Corporate Operations
6. Accounting for Income Taxes
7. Corporate Taxation: Nonliquidating Distributions
8. Corporate Formation, Reorganization, and Liquidation

Part III: Taxation of Flow-Through Entities
9. Forming and Operating Partnerships
10. Dispositions of Partnership Interests and Partnership Distributions
11. S Corporations

Part IV: Multijurisdictional Taxation and Transfer Taxes
12. State and Local Taxes
13. The U.S. Taxation of Multinational Transactions
14. Transfer Taxes and Wealth Planning

...Four Course Approaches

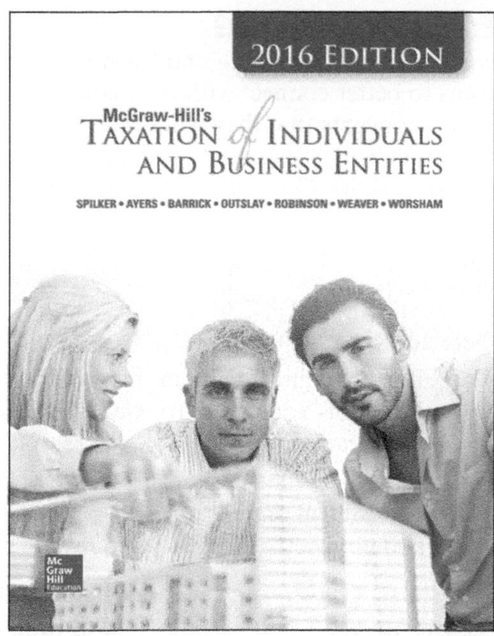

McGraw-Hill's Taxation of Individuals and Business Entities covers all chapters included in the two split volumes in one convenient volume.

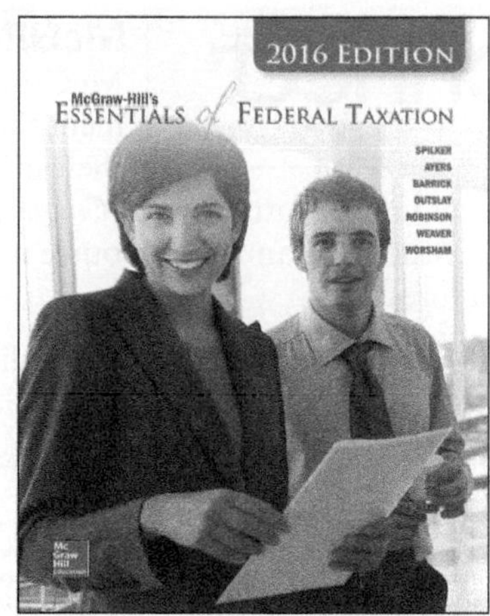

McGraw-Hill's Essentials of Federal Taxation is designed for a one-semester course, covering the basics of taxation of individuals and business entities. To facilitate a one-semester course, *McGraw-Hill's Essentials of Federal Taxation* folds the key topics from the investments, compensation, retirement savings, and home ownership chapters in *Taxation of Individuals* into three individual taxation chapters that discuss gross income and exclusions, for AGI deductions, and from AGI deductions, respectively. The essentials volume also includes a two-chapter C corporation sequence that uses a life-cycle approach covering corporate formations and then corporate operations in the first chapter and nonliquidating and liquidating corporate distributions in the second chapter. This volume is perfect for those teaching a one-semester course and for those who struggle to get through the 25-chapter comprehensive volume.

Part I: Introduction to Taxation

1. An Introduction to Tax
2. Tax Compliance, the IRS, and Tax Authorities
3. Tax Planning Strategies and Related Limitations

Part II: Individual Taxation

4. Individual Income Tax Overview
5. Gross Income and Exclusions
6. Individual for AGI Deductions
7. Individual from AGI Deductions
8. Individual Income Tax Computation and Tax Credits

Part III: Business-Related Transactions

9. Business Income, Deductions, and Accounting Methods
10. Property Acquisition and Cost Recovery
11. Property Dispositions

Part IV: Entity Overview and Taxation of C Corporations

12. Entities Overview
13. Corporate Formations and Operations
14. Corporate Nonliquidating and Liquidating Distributions

Part V: Taxation of Flow-Through Entities

15. Forming and Operating Partnerships
16. Dispositions of Partnership Interests and Partnership Distributions
17. S Corporations

How Can Technology Help...

McGRAW-HILL *CONNECT ACCOUNTING*

McGraw-Hill *Connect Accounting* is a digital teaching and learning environment that gives students the means to better connect with their coursework, their instructors, and the important concepts that they will need to know for success now and in the future. With *Connect Accounting*, instructors can deliver assignments, quizzes, and tests easily online. Students can review course material and practice important skills. *Connect Accounting* provides the following features:

- SmartBook and LearnSmart with additional learning resources.
- Auto-graded Online Homework.
- An integrated media-rich eBook, allowing for anytime, anywhere access to the textbook.
- Dynamic links between the problems or questions you assign to your students and the location in the eBook where that concept is covered.
- A powerful search function to pinpoint and connect key concepts to review.

Through November, Tex has received gross income of $120,000. For December, Tex is considering whether to accept one more work engagement for the year. Engagement 1 will generate $7,000 of revenue at a cost of $4,000, which is deductible for AGI. In contrast, engagement 2 will generate $7,000 of revenue at a cost of $3,000, which is deductible as an itemized deduction. Tex files as a single taxpayer. (use the tax rate schedules.)

a. Calculate Tex's taxable income assuming he chooses engagement 1 and assuming he chooses engagement 2. Assume he has no itemized deductions other than those generated by engagement 2.

	Description	Engagement 1	Engagement 2
(1)	Gross income before new work engagement	$ 120,000	$ 120,000
(2)	Income from engagement	7,000	7,000
(3)	Additional for AGI deduction	(4,000)	
(4)	Adjusted gross income	$ 123,000	$ 127,000
(5)	Greater		
(6)	Greater of itemized deductions or standard deduction		

In short, *Connect Accounting* offers students powerful tools and features that optimize their time and energy, enabling them to focus on learning.

For more information about *Connect Accounting,* go to **www.connect.mheducation.com,** or contact your local McGraw-Hill Higher Education representative.

SMARTBOOK™

SmartBook, powered by LearnSmart

LearnSmart™ is the market-leading adaptive study resource that is proven to strengthen memory recall, increase class retention, and boost grades. LearnSmart allows students to study more efficiently because they are made aware of what they know and don't know.

SmartBook™, which is powered by LearnSmart, is the first and only adaptive reading experience designed to change the way students read and learn. It creates a personalized reading experience by highlighting the most impactful concepts a student needs to learn at that moment in time. As a student engages with SmartBook, the reading experience continuously adapts by highlighting content based on what the student knows and doesn't know. This ensures that the focus is on the content he or she needs to learn, while simultaneously promoting long-term retention of material.

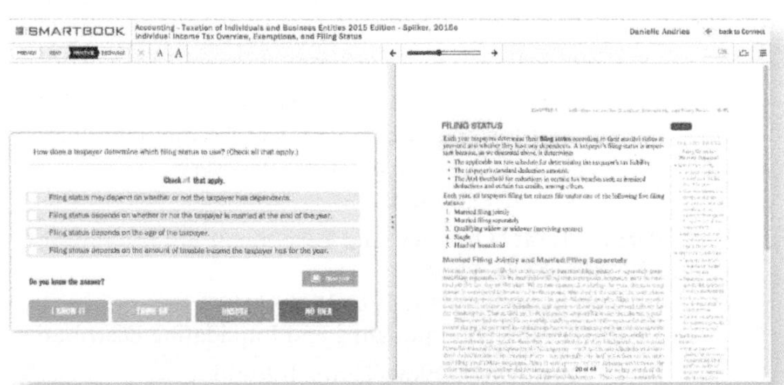

Use SmartBook's real-time reports to quickly identify the concepts that require more attention from individual students—or the entire class. The end result? Students are more engaged with course content, can better prioritize their time, and come to class ready to participate.

...Improve Student Success?

Online assignments

Connect Accounting helps students learn more efficiently by providing feedback and practice material when they need it, where they need it. *Connect* grades homework automatically and gives immediate feedback on any questions students may have missed. Our assignable, gradable end-of-chapter content includes a general journal application that looks and feels like what you would find in a general ledger software package. Also, select questions have been redesigned to test students' knowledge more fully. They now include tables for students to work through rather than requiring that all calculations be done offline.

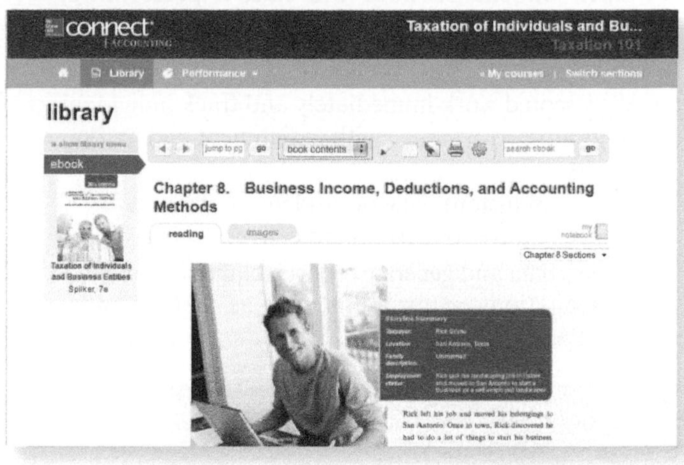

Student Resource Library

The *Connect Accounting* Student Resources give students access to additional resources such as recorded lectures, online practice materials, an eBook, and more.

McGRAW-HILL *CONNECT ACCOUNTING* FEATURES

Connect Accounting offers powerful tools, resources, and features to make managing assignments easier, so faculty can spend more time teaching.

Simple Assignment Management and Smart Grading With *Connect Accounting,* students can engage with their coursework anytime, anywhere, making the learning process more accessible and efficient.

- Create and deliver assignments easily with selectable end-of-chapter questions and test bank items.
- Have assignments scored automatically, giving students immediate feedback on their work and comparisons with correct answers.
- Access and review each response; manually change grades or leave comments for students to review.
- Reinforce classroom concepts with practice assignments, instant quizzes, and exams.

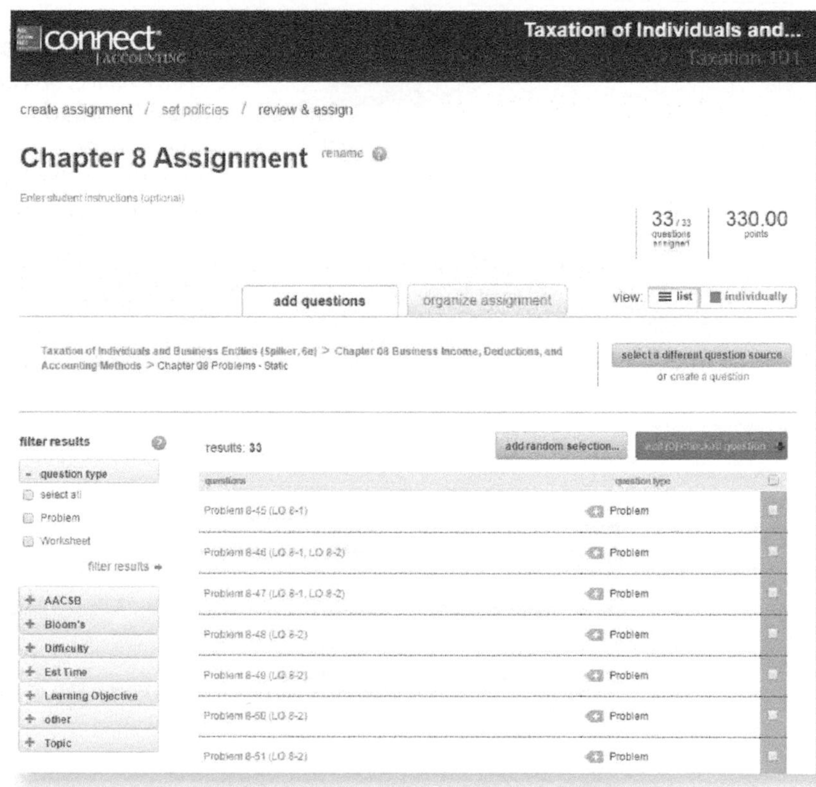

Powerful Instructor and Student Reports

Connect Accounting keeps instructors informed about how each student, section, and class is performing, allowing for more productive use of lecture and office hours. The reports tab enables you to:

- View scored work immediately and track individual or group performance with assignment and grade reports.
- Access an instant view of student or class performance relative to learning objectives.
- Collect data and generate reports required by many accreditation organizations, such as AACSB and AICPA.

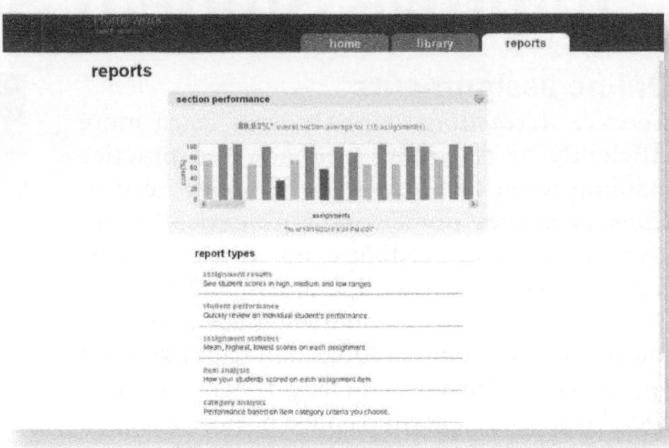

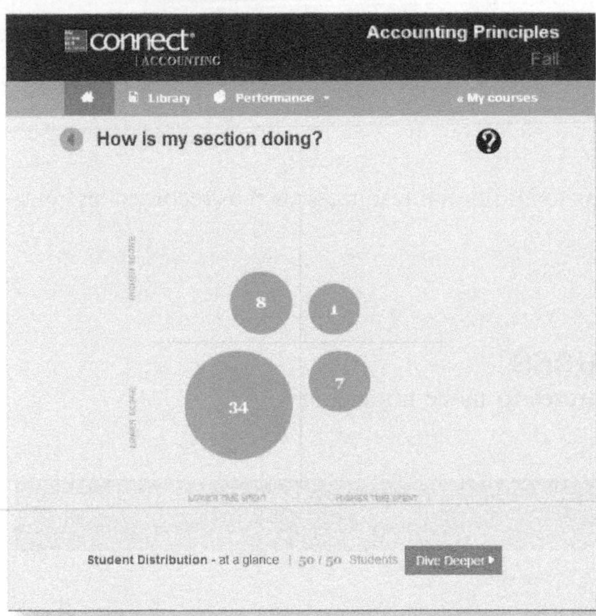

Connect Insight

The first and only analytics tool of its kind, Connect Insight™ is a series of visual data displays—each framed by an intuitive question—to provide at-a-glance information regarding how your class is doing.

Connect Insight™ provides an at-a-glance analysis on five key insights, available at a moment's notice from your tablet device.

- How are my students doing?
- How is my section doing?
- How is this student doing?
- How are my assignments doing?
- How is this assignment going?

Instructor Library

The *Connect Accounting* Instructor Library is your repository for additional resources to improve student engagement in and out of class. You can select and use any asset that enhances your lecture. The *Connect Accounting* Instructor Library includes access to:

- Solutions Manual
- Instructor's Manual
- Test Bank
- Instructor PowerPoint® slides

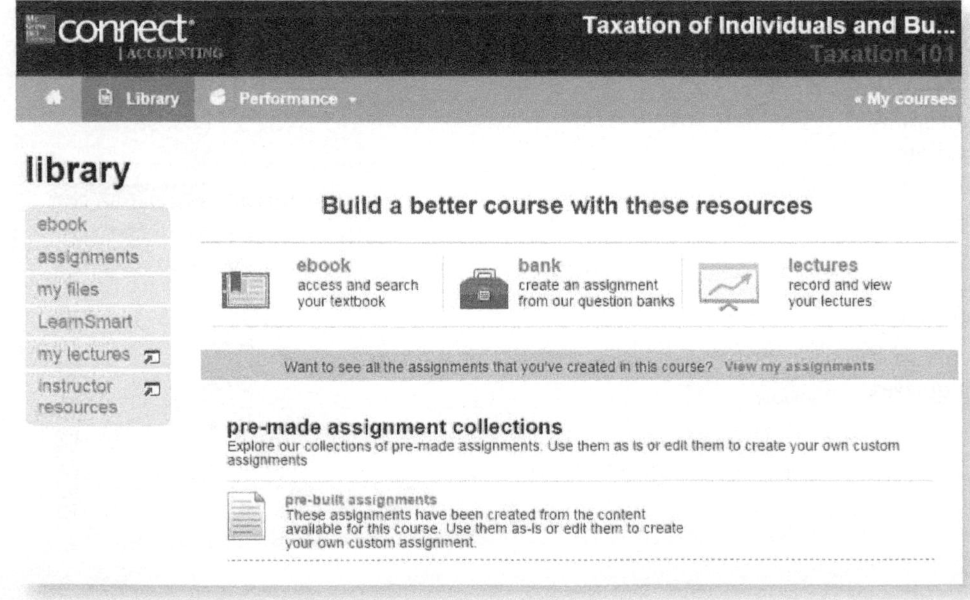

TEGRITY CAMPUS: LECTURES 24/7

Tegrity Campus, is a service that makes class time available 24/7 by automatically capturing every lecture. With a simple one-click start-and-stop process, you capture all computer screens and corresponding audio in a format that is easily searchable, frame by frame. Students can replay any part of any class with easy-to-use browser-based viewing on a PC, Mac, or other mobile device.

Help turn your students' study time into learning moments immediately supported by your lecture. With Tegrity Campus, you also increase intent listening and class participation by easing students' concerns about note-taking. Lecture Capture will make it more likely you will see students' faces, not the tops of their heads. To learn more about Tegrity, watch a 2-minute Flash demo at **http://tegritycampus.mhhe.com.**

McGraw-Hill Campus

McGraw-Hill Campus™ is a new one-stop teaching and learning experience available to users of any learning management system. This institutional service allows faculty and students to enjoy single sign-on (SSO) access to all McGraw-Hill Higher Education materials, including the award-winning McGraw-Hill *Connect Plus* platform, from directly within the institution's website. To learn more about MH Campus, visit **http://mhcampus.mhhe.com.**

Custom Publishing through Create

McGraw-Hill Create™ is a new, self-service website that allows instructors to create custom course materials by drawing upon McGraw-Hill's comprehensive, cross-disciplinary content. Instructors can add their own content quickly and easily and tap into other rights-secured third-party sources as well, then arrange the content in a way that makes the most sense for their course. Instructors can even personalize their book with the course name and information and choose the best format for their students—color print, black-and-white print, or an eBook.

Through Create, instructors can

- Select and arrange the content in a way that makes the most sense for their course.
- Combine material from different sources and even upload their own content.
- Choose the best format for their students—print or eBook.
- Edit and update their course materials as often as they like.

Begin creating now at **www.mcgrawhillcreate.com.**

McGraw-Hill Customer Experience Group Contact Information

At McGraw-Hill, we understand that getting the most from new technology can be challenging. That's why our services don't stop after you purchase our products. You can contact our Product Specialists 24 hours a day to get product training online. Or you can search the knowledge bank of Frequently Asked Questions on our support website. For Customer Support, call **800-331-5094,** or visit **www.mhhe.com/support.** One of our Technical Support Analysts will be able to assist you in a timely fashion.

KAPLAN SIMULATIONS

Apply the knowledge you've gained through *McGraw-Hill's Taxation* with CPA Review simulations from Kaplan and McGraw-Hill Education! Each CPA simulation demonstrates taxation concepts in a Web-based interface, identical to that used in the actual CPA exam. CPA simulations are found in the homework material after the very last case in selected chapters in your book.

TaxACT®

TaxACT *McGraw-Hill's Taxation* can be packaged with tax software from TaxACT, one of the leading preparation software companies in the market today. The 2015 edition includes availability of both Individuals and Business Entities software, including the 1040 forms and TaxACT Preparer's Business 3-Pack (with Forms 1065, 1120, and 1120S).

SUPPLEMENTS FOR INSTRUCTORS

Assurance of Learning Ready

Many educational institutions today are focused on the notion of *assurance of learning*, an important element of many accreditation standards. *McGraw-Hill's Taxation* is designed specifically to support your assurance of learning initiatives with a simple, yet powerful, solution.

Each chapter in the book begins with a list of numbered learning objectives, which appear throughout the chapter as well as in the end-of-chapter assignments. Every Test Bank question for *McGraw-Hill's Taxation* maps to a specific chapter learning objective in the textbook. Each Test Bank question also identifies topic area, level of difficulty, Bloom's Taxonomy level, and AICPA and AACSB skill area. You can use our Test Bank software, *EZ Test Online*, or *Connect Accounting* to easily search for learning objectives that directly relate to the learning objectives for your course. You can then use the reporting features of *EZ Test* to aggregate student results in similar fashion, making the collection and presentation of Assurance of Learning data simple and easy.

AACSB Statement

McGraw-Hill/Irwin is a proud corporate member of AACSB International. Understanding the importance and value of AACSB accreditation, *McGraw-Hill's Taxation* recognizes the curricula guidelines detailed in the AACSB standards for business accreditation by connecting selected questions in the text and the Test Bank to the general knowledge and skill guidelines in the revised AACSB standards.

The statements contained in *McGraw-Hill's Taxation* are provided only as a guide for the users of this textbook. The AACSB leaves content coverage and assessment within the purview of individual schools, the mission of the school, and the faculty. While *McGraw-Hill's Taxation* and the teaching package make no claim of any specific AACSB qualification or evaluation, we have, within the text and test bank, labeled selected questions according to the eight general knowledge and skill areas.

McGraw-Hill's *Connect Accounting*

Connect Accounting offers a number of powerful tools and features to make managing your classroom easier. *Connect Accounting* with *McGraw-Hill's Taxation* offers enhanced features and technology to help both you and your students make the most of your time inside and outside the classroom.

EZ Test Online

This test bank in Word™ format contains multiple-choice questions, essay questions, and short problems. Each test item is coded for level of difficulty, learning objective, AACSB and AICPA skill area, and Bloom's Taxonomy level.

McGraw-Hill's EZ Test Online is a flexible and easy-to-use electronic testing program that allows instructors to create tests from book-specific items. EZ Test Online accommodates a wide range of question types and allows instructors to add their own questions. Multiple versions of the test can be created and any test can be exported for use with course management systems such as BlackBoard/WebCT. EZ Test Online gives instructors a place to easily administer exams and quizzes online. The program is available for Windows and Macintosh environments.

A HEARTFELT THANKS TO THE MANY COLLEAGUES WHO SHAPED THIS BOOK

The version of the book you are reading would not be the same book without the valuable suggestions, keen insights, and constructive criticisms of the list of reviewers below. Each professor listed here contributed in substantive ways to the organization of chapters, coverage of topics, and the use of pedagogy. We are grateful to them for taking the time to read chapters or attend reviewer conferences, focus groups, and symposia in support of the development for the book:

2015 Edition Reviewers

Kevin Baugess, *ICDC College*
Suzon Bridges, *Houston Community College*
Lisa Ekmekjian, *William Paterson University*
Ann Esarco, *Columbia College Columbia*
Robert Gary, *University of New Mexico*
Marcye Hampton, *University of Central Florida*
Melanie Hicks, *Liberty University*
Athena Jones, *University of Maryland University College*
Sandra Kemper, *Regis University*
Jack Lachman, *Brooklyn College*
Stacie Laplante, *University of Wisconsin Madison*
Stephanie Lewis, *Ohio State University Columbus*
Robert Lin, *California State University East Bay*
Anthony Masino, *East Tennessee State University*
Lisa McKinney, *University of Alabama at Birmingham*
Allison McLeod, *University of North Texas*
Frank Messina, *University of Alabama at Birmingham*
Michelle Moshier, *University at Albany*
Leslie Mostow, *University of Maryland, College Park*
Jackie Myers, *Sinclair Community College*
Jeff Paterson, *Florida State University*
James Pierson, *Franklin University*
Anthony Pochesci, *Rutgers University*
Terrie Stolte, *Columbus State Community College*
Marvin Williams, *University of Houston—Downtown*
Massood Yahya-Zadeh, *George Mason University*
Scott Yetmar, *Cleveland State University*

Acknowledgments

We would like to thank the many talented people who made valuable contributions to the creation of this sixth edition. William A. Padley of Madison Area Technical College, and Deanna Sharpe of the University of Missouri—Columbia checked the page proofs, Testbank, and Solutions Manual for accuracy; we greatly appreciate the hours they spent checking tax forms and double-checking our calculations throughout the book. Many thanks also to Jim Young for providing the tax numbers for 2015 well before the IRS made them available. Special thanks to Troy Lewis of Brigham Young University for his sharp eye and valuable feedback throughout the revision process. William A. Padley of Madison Area Technical College, Deanna Sharpe of the University of Missouri, Vivian Paige of Old Dominion University, and Teressa Farough greatly contributed to the accuracy of McGraw-Hill's *Connect Accounting* for the 2016 edition.

We also appreciate the expert attention given to this project by the staff at McGraw-Hill Education, especially Tim Vertovec, Managing Director; Kathleen Klehr, Senior Brand Manager; Danielle Andries, Product Developer; Lori Koetters, Brian Nacik, and Jill Eccher, Content Project Managers; Brad Parkins, Marketing Director; Matthew Diamond, Designer; and Sue Culbertson, Senior Buyer.

Changes in *Taxation of Business Entities*, 2016 Edition

For the 2016 edition of McGraw Hill's *Taxation of Business Entities,* many changes were made in response to feedback from reviewers and focus group participants:

- All **tax forms** have been **updated for the latest available tax form as of January 2015.** In addition, **chapter content** throughout the text has been **updated to reflect tax law changes through January 2015.**

Other notable changes in the 2016 edition include:

Chapter 1

- Updated for 2015 inflation-adjusted limitations.
- Updated for new tax forms.

Chapter 2

- This chapter was formerly chapter 1 in previous editions and updated based on reviewer feedback.
- Updated chapter for legislative changes.
- Added new discussion and footnotes regarding depreciation amounts taken in last year of asset's recovery period.
- Added additional discussion to clarify business income for purposes of the §179 income limitation
- Clarified reporting requirements when taxpayer elects out of bonus depreciation.
- Added two new Taxes in the Real World.
- Added three new problems to end of chapter material.
- Eliminated unnecessary footnotes to streamline chapter.

Chapter 3

- This chapter was formerly chapter 2 in previous editions and updated based on reviewer feedback.
- Updated chapter for legislative changes.
- Revised examples affected by tax law changes.
- Revised discussion of depreciation recapture to clarify the concept

Chapter 4

- Added a footnote highlighting the idea that unincorporated entities taxed as partnerships have more favorable ownership requirements and more favorable tax treatment on nonliquidating and liquidating distributions of noncash property than C or S corporations.
- Edited a footnote to point out that when a shareholder receives interest from a loan to the corporation, the interest income is investment income that could be subject to the 3.8% Net Investment Income Tax.
- Edited footnote indicating that shareholders who hold stock until death may avoid while shareholders may escape the shareholder level of the double tax. However, these shareholders may pay estate tax on the value of the stock held at death.
- Added a row to the entity comparison chart in Exhibit 4-3 that compares across entities the tax consequences of nonliquidating distributions of noncash property.

Chapter 11

- Updated chapter for tax law changes.
- Updated for new tax forms.
- Revised discussion of Net Investment Income tax.

As We Go to Press

The 2016 Edition is current through March 2, 2015. You can go to the *Connect Library* for updates that occur after this date.

Table of Contents

6 Accounting for Income Taxes

9 Forming and Operating Partnerships

10 Dispositions of Partnership Interests and Partnership Distributions

11 S Corporations

12 State and Local Taxes

13 The U.S. Taxation of Multinational Transactions

McGraw-Hill's

Taxation of Business Entities

chapter **1**

Business Income, Deductions, and Accounting Methods

Learning Objectives

Upon completing this chapter, you should be able to:

- **LO 1-1** Describe the general requirements for deducting business expenses and identify common business deductions.
- **LO 1-2** Apply the limitations on business deductions to distinguish between deductible and nondeductible business expenses.
- **LO 1-3** Identify and explain special business deductions specifically permitted under the tax laws.
- **LO 1-4** Explain the concept of an accounting period and describe accounting periods available to businesses.
- **LO 1-5** Identify and describe accounting methods available to businesses and apply cash and accrual methods to determine business income and expense deductions.

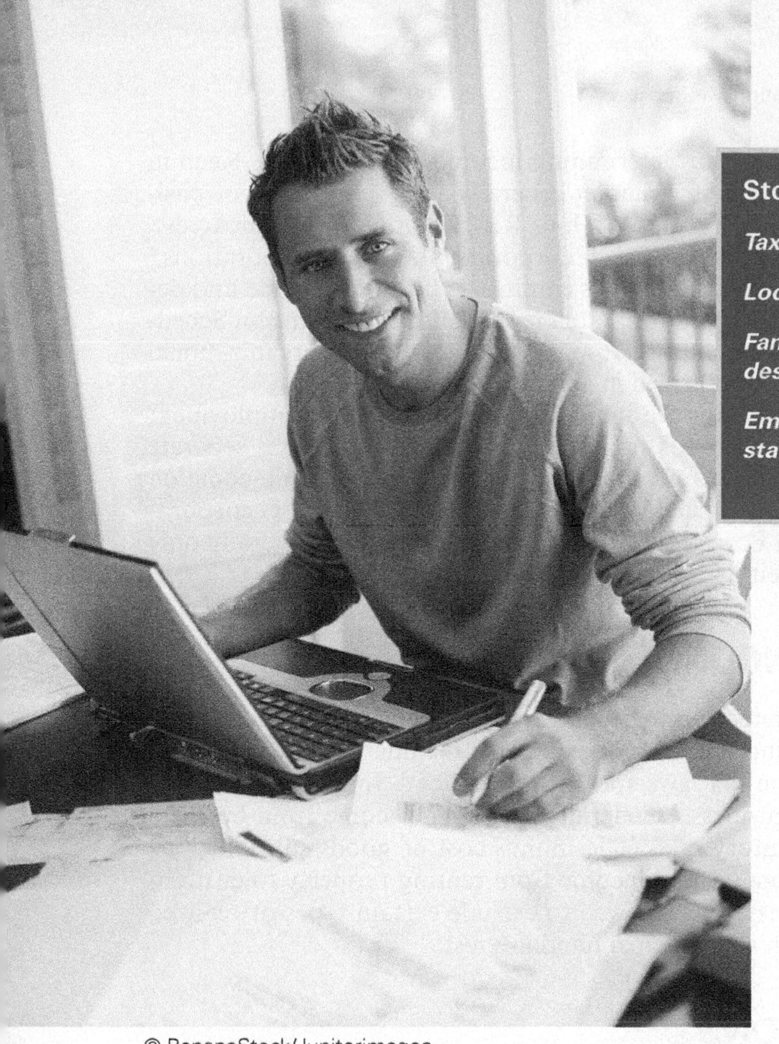
© BananaStock/Jupiterimages

Storyline Summary

Taxpayer:	Rick Grime
Location:	San Antonio, Texas
Family description:	Unmarried
Employment status:	Rick quit his landscaping job in Dallas and moved to San Antonio to start a business as a self-employed landscaper.

Rick Grime graduated from Texas A&M University with a degree in agronomy, and for the past few years he has been employed by a landscape architect in Dallas. Nearly every day that Rick went to work, he shared ideas with his employer about improving the business. Rick finally decided to take his ideas and start his own landscaping business in his hometown of San Antonio, Texas. In mid-April, Rick left his job and moved his belongings to San Antonio. Once in town, Rick discovered he had to do a lot of things to start his business. First, he registered his new business name (Green Acres Landscaping) and established a bank account for the business. Next, he rented a used sport utility vehicle (SUV) and a shop for his place of business. Rick didn't know much about accounting for business activities, so he hired a CPA, Jane Bronson, to help him. Jane and Rick decided that Green Acres would operate as a sole proprietorship, but Jane suggested that as the business grew, he might want to consider organizing it as a different type of legal entity. Operating as a corporation, for instance, would allow him to invite new investors or business partners to help fund future expansion. Rick formally started his business on May 1. He spent a lot of time attracting new customers, and he figured he would hire employees as he needed them.

to be continued . . .

This chapter describes the process for determining income for *businesses*. Keep in mind that the concepts we discuss in this chapter generally apply to all types of business entities including sole proprietorships (such as Rick's company, Green Acres), partnerships, hybrid entities (such as LLCs), S corporations, and C corporations.[1] Because Rick is a sole proprietor, our examples emphasize business income and deductions from his personal perspective. Proprietors report business income on Schedule C of their individual income tax returns. However, the choice of the organizational form is a complex decision that is described in Chapter 4.

Schedule C income is subject to both individual income and self-employment taxes. Entities other than sole proprietorships report income on tax forms separate from the owners' tax returns. For example, partnerships report taxable income on Form 1065, S corporations report taxable income on Form 1120S, and C corporations report taxable income on Form 1120. Of all these entity types, generally only C corporations pay taxes on their income.

BUSINESS GROSS INCOME

In most respects, the rules for determining business gross income are the same as for determining gross income for individuals. Gross income includes "all income from whatever source derived."[2] The tax laws specifically indicate that this definition includes gross income from "business." Generally speaking, income from business includes gross profit from inventory sales (sales minus cost of goods sold), income from services provided to customers, and income from renting property to customers. Just like individuals, businesses are allowed to exclude certain types of realized income from gross income, such as municipal bond interest.

LO 1-1

BUSINESS DEDUCTIONS

THE KEY FACTS

Business Expenses

- Business expenses must be incurred in pursuit of profits, not personal goals.
- Only reasonable amounts are allowed as deductions.
- A deduction must be ordinary and necessary (appropriate and helpful).

Because Congress intended for taxable income to reflect the *net* increase in wealth from a business, it is only fair that businesses be allowed to deduct expenses incurred to generate business income. Typically, Congress provides *specific* statutory rules authorizing deductions. However, as you can see from the following excerpt from IRC §162, the provision authorizing business deductions is relatively broad and ambiguous:

> There shall be allowed as a deduction all the ordinary and necessary expenses paid or incurred during the taxable year in carrying on any trade or business . . .

This provision authorizes taxpayers to deduct expenses for "trade or business" activities.[3] The tax code does not define the phrase "trade or business," but it's clear that the objective of business activities is to make a profit. Thus, the tax law requires that a business expense be made in the pursuit of profits rather than the pursuit of other, presumably personal, motives.

When a taxpayer's activity does not meet the "for profit" requirement, it is treated as a hobby, an activity motivated by personal objectives. A taxpayer engaged in a hobby that generates revenues includes all revenues from the activity in gross

[1]Both S corporations and C corporations are incorporated for state law purposes. However, S corporations are taxed as flow-through entities (S corporation income is taxed to its owners) while C corporations (or taxable corporations) are taxed as separate taxable entities. Hybrid entities may opt to be taxed as either flow-through entities or taxable corporations.

[2]§61(a).

[3]§212 contains a sister provision to §162 allowing deductions for ordinary and necessary expenses incurred for the production of income ("investment expenses") and for the management and maintenance of property (including expenses incurred in renting property in situations when the rental activity is not considered to be a trade or business). A business activity, sometimes referred to as a trade or business, requires a relatively high level of involvement or effort from the taxpayer. Unlike business activities, investments are profit-motivated activities that don't require a high degree of taxpayer involvement or effort.

income and deducts associated expenses to the extent of gross income from the activity as *miscellaneous itemized deductions* (subject to the 2 percent of AGI floor).

Ordinary and Necessary

Business expenditures must be both **ordinary and necessary** to be deductible. An *ordinary* expense is an expense that is normal or appropriate for the business under the circumstances.[4] An expense is *not* necessarily required to be typical or repetitive in nature to be considered ordinary. For example, a business could deduct the legal fees it expends to defend itself in an antitrust suit. Although an antitrust suit would be atypical and unusual for most businesses, defending the suit would probably be deemed ordinary, because it would be expected under the circumstances. A *necessary* expense is an expense that is helpful or conducive to the business activity, but the expenditure need not be essential or indispensable. For example, a deduction for metric tools would qualify as ordinary and necessary even if there was only a small chance that a repairman might need these tools. The "ordinary and necessary" requirements are applied on a case-by-case basis, and while the deduction depends on individual circumstances, the IRS is often reluctant to second-guess business decisions. Exhibit 1-1 presents examples of expenditures that are ordinary and necessary for typical businesses.

EXHIBIT 1-1 Examples of Typical Ordinary and Necessary Business Expenses

- Advertising
- Car and truck expenses
- Depreciation
- Employee compensation and benefits
- Insurance
- Interest
- Legal fees
- Office expenses
- Rent
- Repairs
- Supplies
- Travel
- Utilities
- Wages

Example 1-1

Outside Rick's office is a small waiting room for clients. Rick paid $50 for several books to occupy clients while waiting for appointments. These are hardcover books with photographs and illustrations of landscape designs. Rick believes that the books will inspire new designs and will alleviate boredom for potential clients, and he deducted the $50 cost as a business expense. Is he correct?

Answer: Under the code and regulations, expenses directly connected to a business are deductible if the expenditure is ordinary and necessary. The phrase *ordinary and necessary* is interpreted as *helpful or conducive to business activity.* In Rick's situation, it seems highly unlikely that the IRS or a court would conclude that the cost of these books is not ordinary and necessary. What do you think?

What if: Suppose that Rick's hobby was pre-Columbian Maya civilization. Do you think Rick would be able to deduct the cost of a new treatise on translating Maya script if he placed the book in his waiting room? Why or why not?

ETHICS

Sheri is a lawyer who operates as a sole practitioner. Despite her busy schedule, in the past Sheri found time for her family. This year Sheri took on two new important clients, and she hired a personal assistant to help her manage her schedule and make timely court filings. Occasionally, Sheri asked her assistant to assist her with personal tasks such as having her car serviced or buying groceries. Do you think that Sheri should treat her assistant's entire salary as a business expense? Would your answer be any different if personal assistants commonly perform these tasks for busy attorneys?

[4]*Welch v. Helvering* (1933), 290 US 111.

Reasonable in Amount

Ordinary and necessary business expenses are deductible only *to the extent* they are also **reasonable in amount.** The courts have interpreted this requirement to mean that an expenditure is not reasonable when it is extravagant or exorbitant.[5] If the expenditure is extravagant in amount, the courts presume the excess amount is spent for personal rather than business reasons and is not deductible.

Determining whether an expenditure is reasonable is not an exact science and, not surprisingly, taxpayers and the IRS may have different opinions. Generally, the courts and the IRS test for extravagance by comparing the amount of the expense to a market price or an **arm's length amount.** If the amount of the expense is the amount typically charged in the market by unrelated parties, the amount is considered to be reasonable. The underlying issue is *why* a profit-motivated taxpayer would pay an extravagant amount. Hence, reasonableness is most likely to be an issue when a payment is made to an individual related to the taxpayer, or the taxpayer enjoys some incidental benefit from the expenditure, such as entertainment value.

Example 1-2

During the busy part of the year, Rick could not keep up with all the work. Therefore, he hired four part-time employees and paid them $10 an hour to mow lawns and pull weeds for an average of 20 hours a week. When things finally slowed down in late fall, Rick released his four part-time employees. Rick paid a total of $22,000 in compensation to the four employees. He still needed some extra help now and then, so he hired his brother, Tom, on a part-time basis. Tom performed the same duties as the prior part-time employees (his quality of work was about the same). However, Rick paid Tom $25 per hour because Tom is a college student and Rick wanted to provide some additional support for Tom's education. At year-end, Tom had worked a total of 100 hours and received $2,500 from Rick. What amount can Rick deduct for the compensation he paid to his employees?

Answer: $23,000. Rick can deduct the $22,000 paid to part-time employees. However, he can only deduct $10 an hour for Tom's compensation because the extra $15 per hour Rick paid Tom is unreasonable in amount.[6] The remaining $15 per hour is considered a personal (nondeductible) gift from Rick to Tom. Hence, Rick can deduct a total of $23,000 for compensation expense this year [$22,000 + ($10 × 100)].

TAXES IN THE REAL WORLD What Qualifies as a "Business"?

Richard Bagley earned an MS in accounting from UCLA and was the chief financial manager for TRW's space and technology group. Bagley became aware of false claims made by TRW to the government and discussed these false claims with supervisors. Bagley was subsequently fired. Bagley retained attorneys to help him file a False Claims Act (FCA) suit against his employer.

Over a nine-year period, Bagley exclusively worked on his FCA prosecution activity. Bagley maintained a contemporaneous log of hours that showed he spent over 21,000 hours prosecuting the FCA suits. Besides numerous meetings, Bagley drafted and/or edited at least 73 documents in furtherance of the FCA litigation activity. According to Bagley, he was actively involved with the litigation because the lawyers "weren't accountants and . . . didn't have an in-depth understanding of TRW's accounting system."

Bagley considered himself to be in a trade or business as a "Private Attorney General," but Bagley never filed any business registration or

[5]§162(a) and *Comm. v. Lincoln Electric Co.* (CA-6, 1949), 176 F.2d 815.

[6]In practice, this distinction is rarely cut and dried. Rick may be able to argue for various reasons that Tom's work is worth more than $10 an hour but perhaps not as much as $25 per hour. We use this example to illustrate the issue of reasonable expenses and not to discuss the merits of what actually is reasonable compensation to Tom.

notice anywhere with a city or the state. Furthermore, Bagley did not advertise his business nor did he keep accounting books, but he ultimately received an award of $36,651,295. On his amended federal tax refund claim, Bagley reported the income as attributable to his "trade or business" and deducted $18,477,815 in attorney's fees as ordinary and necessary business expenses. The IRS denied Bagley's refund claim.

The District Court, however, rejected the government's claim that a one-time pursuit of an FCA claim with a large payout was not indicative of a for-profit business. The court held that Bagley's litigation activities, and the regular, continuous way he undertook them, combined with skill and a good-faith effort to make a profit, indicated a trade or business. Further, the individual's litigation expenses were ordinary and necessary expenses paid in relation to his trade or business of prosecuting the FCA lawsuits. Without hiring the attorneys, the individual could not have engaged in his business.

Source: Richard D. Bagley v. U.S. (DC CA), 2013-2 U.S.T.C. 50,462.

LIMITATIONS ON BUSINESS DEDUCTIONS

LO 1-2

For a variety of reasons, Congress specifically prohibits or limits a business's ability to deduct certain expenditures that appear to otherwise meet the general business expense deductibility requirements.

THE KEY FACTS

Limitations on Business Deductions

- No business deductions are allowable for expenditures against public policy (bribes) or political contributions.
- Expenditures that benefit a period longer than 12 months generally must be capitalized.
- No deductions are allowable for expenditures associated with the production of tax-exempt income.
- Personal expenditures are not deductible.

Expenditures against Public Policy

Businesses occasionally incur fines and penalties and may even pay illegal bribes and kickbacks. However, these payments are not deductible for tax purposes.[7] Congress disallows these expenditures under the rationale that allowing them would subsidize illegal activities and frustrate public policy. Interestingly enough, businesses conducting illegal activities (selling stolen goods or conducting illegal gambling activities) are allowed to deduct their cost of goods sold and their ordinary and necessary business expenses in conducting the business activities (note, however, that they are not allowed to deduct fines, penalties, illegal bribes, or illegal kickbacks).[8] Of course, the IRS is probably more concerned that many illegal businesses fail to report *any* income than that illegal businesses overstate deductions.[9]

Political Contributions and Lobbying Costs

Perhaps to avoid the perception that the federal government subsidizes taxpayer efforts to influence politics, the tax laws disallow deductions for political contributions and most lobbying expenses.[10] An exception exists to the prohibition of lobbying expenses. Under §162(e), deductions are allowed for reasonable costs incurred in conjunction with the submission of statements to a local council with respect to proposed legislation of direct interest to the taxpayer.

[7]§162(c) and Reg. §1.162-21. This prohibition applies to fines and penalties imposed by a government or governmental unit. Fines and penalties imposed by other organizations, such as a NASCAR fine, would be fully deductible if the payment otherwise qualified as an ordinary and necessary business expense.

[8]*Comm. v. Sullivan* (1958), 356 US 27.

[9]§280E explicitly prohibits drug dealers from deducting any business expenses associated with this "business" activity. However, drug dealers are able to deduct cost of goods sold because cost of goods sold is technically a reduction in gross income and not a business expense. See Reg. §1.61-3(a).

[10]§162(e).

Example 1-3

In July, the city fined Rick $200 for violating the city's watering ban when he watered a newly installed landscape. Later, Rick donated $250 to the mayor's campaign for reelection. Can Rick deduct these expenditures?

Answer: No. Rick cannot deduct either the fine or the political contribution as a business expense because the tax laws specifically prohibit deductions for these expenditures.

What if: Suppose that Rick had paid $250 for an economist to help Rick prepare a presentation to the city council on a proposed ordinance restricting water usage. Rick's presentation demonstrated to the council how the ordinance on water restrictions could affect area landscapers.

Answer: It is likely that this expenditure would qualify for deduction as a business expense under the exception in §162(e)(2).

Capital Expenditures

Whether a business uses the cash or the accrual method of accounting, it must capitalize expenditures for *tangible* assets such as buildings, machinery and equipment, furniture and fixtures, and similar property that have useful lives of more than one year (12 months).[11] For tax purposes, businesses recover the cost of capitalized tangible assets (other than land) through depreciation.

Businesses also capitalize the cost to create or acquire *intangible* assets such as patents, goodwill, start-up costs, and organizational expenditures.[12] They recover the costs of capitalized intangible assets either through amortization (when the tax laws allow them to do so) or upon disposition of the assets. Prepaid expenses are also subject to capitalization, but there is a special exception that we discuss under accounting methods later in this chapter.[13]

Expenses Associated with the Production of Tax-Exempt Income

Expenses that do not help businesses generate *taxable* income are not allowed to offset taxable income. For example, this restriction disallows interest expense deductions for businesses that borrow money and invest the loan proceeds in municipal (tax-exempt) bonds. It also disallows deductions for life insurance premiums businesses pay on policies that cover the lives of officers or other key employees and compensate the business for the disruption and lost income they may experience due to a key employee's death. Because the death benefit from the life insurance policy is not taxable, the business is not allowed to deduct the insurance premium expense associated with this nontaxable income.

Example 1-4

Rick employs Joan, an arborist who specializes in trimming trees and treating local tree ailments. Joan generates a great deal of revenue for Rick's business, but is in her mid-60s and suffers from diabetes. In November, Rick purchased a "key-employee" term-life insurance policy on Joan's life. The policy cost Rick $720 and will pay Rick (Green Acres) a $20,000 death benefit if Joan passes away during the next 12 months. What amount of life insurance policy premium can Rick deduct?

Answer: $0. Rick cannot deduct the $720 premium on the life insurance policy because the life insurance proceeds from the policy are tax-exempt.

[11]Reg. §1.263(a)-2(d)(4). The act of recording the asset is sometimes referred to as *capitalizing* the expenditure.

[12]Reg. §1.263(a)-4(b). The extent to which expenditures for intangible assets must be capitalized is explored in *Indopco v. Comm.* (1992), 503 US 79.

[13]See §195, §197, and §248 for provisions that allow taxpayers to amortize the cost of certain intangible assets.

What if: Suppose Rick purchased the life insurance policy on Joan's life and allowed Joan to name the beneficiary. The policy cost Rick $720 and will pay the beneficiary a $20,000 death benefit if Joan passes away during the next 12 months. What amount of life insurance policy premium can Rick deduct?

Answer: $720. In this scenario, Rick can deduct the entire premium of $720 as a *compensation* expense because the benefit of the policy inures to Joan and not to Rick's business.

Personal Expenditures

Taxpayers are not allowed to deduct **personal expenses** unless the expenses are "expressly" authorized by a provision in the law.[14] While the tax laws do not define personal expenses, they imply the scope of personal expenses by stating that "personal, living, or family expenses" are not deductible. Therefore, at a minimum, the costs of food, clothing, and shelter are assumed to be personal and nondeductible. Of course, there are the inevitable exceptions when otherwise personal items are specially adapted to business use. For example, taxpayers may deduct the cost of uniforms or special clothing they purchase for use in their business, if the clothing is not appropriate to wear as ordinary clothing outside the place of business. When the clothing is adaptable as ordinary clothing, the cost of the clothing is a nondeductible personal expenditure.[15]

Example 1-5

Rick spent $500 to purchase special coveralls that identify his landscaping service and provide a professional appearance. How much of the cost for the clothing can Rick deduct as a business expense?

Answer: All $500. While the cost of clothing is inherently personal, Rick can deduct the $500 cost of the coveralls because, due to the design and labeling on the coveralls, they are not suitable for ordinary use.

Many business owners, particularly small business owners such as sole proprietors, may be in a position to use business funds to pay for items that are entirely personal in nature. For example, a sole proprietor could use the business checking account to pay for family groceries. These expenditures, even though funded by the business, are not deductible.

Expenditures made by a taxpayer for education, such as tuition and books, are often related to a taxpayer's business aspirations. However, educational expenditures are not deductible as business expenses unless the education: (1) maintains or improves skills required by the individual in his employment or other trade or business, or (2) meets the express requirements of the individual's employer, or the requirements of applicable law or regulations, imposed as a condition to the retention by the individual of an established employment relationship, status, or rate of compensation. Education necessary to meet minimum requirements for an occupation are not deductible. For example, tuition payments for courses to satisfy the education requirement to sit for the CPA exam are not deductible. This is an example of education that qualifies the taxpayer for a new trade or business rather than improving his skills in an existing trade or business.

[14] §262(a).

[15] An employee who purchases clothing for work would go through a similar analysis to determine if the cost of the clothing qualifies as an employee business expense.

THE KEY FACTS

Mixed-Motive Expenditures

- Special limits are imposed on expenditures that have both personal and business benefits.
- Only 50 percent of business meals and entertainment are deductible.
- Contemporaneous written records of business purpose are required.

Mixed-Motive Expenditures

Business owners in general, and owners of small or closely held businesses in particular, often make expenditures that are motivated by *both* business and personal concerns. These **mixed-motive expenditures** are of particular concern to lawmakers and the IRS because of the tax incentive to disguise nondeductible personal expenses as deductible business expenses. Thus, deductions for business expenditures with potential personal motives are closely monitored and restricted. The rules for determining the amount of *deductible* mixed-motive expenditures depend on the type of the expenditure. Here we review the rules for determining the deductible portion of mixed-motive expenditures for meals and entertainment, travel and transportation, and the use of property for both business and personal purposes.

Meals and Entertainment Because everyone needs to eat, even business meals contain a significant personal element. To allow for this personal element, taxpayers may only deduct 50 percent of actual business meals. In addition, to deduct any portion of the cost of a meal as a business expense, (1) the amount must be reasonable under the circumstances, (2) the taxpayer (or an employee) must be present when the meal is furnished, and (3) the meal must be directly associated with the active conduct of the taxpayer's business.

Similar to business meals, entertainment associated with business activities contains a significant element of enjoyment. Hence, only 50 percent of allowable business entertainment may be deducted as a business expense.[16] Further, entertainment deductions are allowable only if (1) "business associates" are entertained, (2) the amounts paid are reasonable in amount, and (3) the entertainment is either "directly related" or "associated with" the active conduct of business.

Business associates are individuals with whom the taxpayer reasonably expects to do business, such as customers, suppliers, employees, or advisors. Entertainment is directly related to business if there is an active discussion aimed at generating revenue or fees or the discussion occurs in a clear business setting (such as a hospitality room). The cost of entertainment that occurs in a setting with little possibility of conducting a business discussion, such as a theater or sports venue, will only be deductible if the entertainment directly precedes or follows a substantial business discussion, thereby satisfying the "associated with" test. In addition, to deduct the cost of meals and entertainment, taxpayers generally must meet strict record-keeping requirements we discuss below.[17]

Example 1-6

Rick went out to dinner with a prospective client to discuss Rick's ideas for landscaping the homeowner's yard. After dinner, Rick and the prospective client attended the theater. Rick paid $190 for the meal and $350 for the tickets, amounts that were reasonable under the circumstances. What amount of these expenditures can Rick deduct as a business expense?

Answer: Rick can deduct $270 [($190 + $350) × 50%], representing half the cost of the meal and entertainment, as a business expense, as long as Rick can substantiate the business purpose and substantial nature of the dinner discussion.

[16]§274 also provides some exceptions to the 50 percent reduction for meals and entertainment, such as meals and entertainment provided for special events or as employee compensation. Taxpayers can also use a *per diem* rate (an automatic, flat amount per meal) in lieu of actual expenditures to determine the amount of the deduction. There are special limits placed on entertainment expenses associated with spouses.

[17]Under §274, there are special limits placed on certain entertainment expenditures, such as those related to spouses, club dues and entertainment facilities, skyboxes, and entertainment associated with corporate officers, directors, and large shareholders.

What if: Suppose that Rick did not discuss business with the client either before, during, or after the meal. What amount of the expenditures can Rick deduct as a business expense?

Answer: $0. In this scenario, Rick cannot deduct the costs of the meal or entertainment because the activity was not directly related to or associated with a substantial business discussion.

Travel and Transportation Under certain conditions, sole proprietors and self-employed taxpayers may deduct the cost of travel and transportation for business purposes. Transportation expenses include the direct cost of transporting the taxpayer to and from business sites. However, the cost of commuting between the taxpayer's home and regular place of business is personal and, therefore, not deductible. If the taxpayer uses a vehicle for business, the taxpayer can deduct the costs of operating the vehicle plus depreciation on the vehicle's tax basis. Alternatively, in lieu of deducting these costs, the taxpayer may simply deduct a standard amount for each business mile driven. The standard mileage rate represents the per-mile cost of operating an automobile (including depreciation or lease payments).[18] For 2015 the standard mileage rate has been set at 57.5 cents per mile. To be deductible, the transportation must be for business reasons. If the transportation is primarily for personal purposes, the cost is not deductible.

Example 1-7

Rick leases an SUV to drive between his shop and various work sites. Rick carefully documents the business use of the SUV (8,100 miles this year) and his $5,335 of operating expenses ($3,935 for gas, oil, and repairs and $1,400 for lease payments). At no time does Rick use the SUV for personal purposes. What amount of these expenses may Rick deduct as business expenses?

Answer: $5,335. Since Rick uses the SUV in his business activities, he can deduct (1) the $5,335 cost of operating and leasing the SUV or (2) $4,658 for the 8,100 business miles he drove (57.5 cents per mile × 8,100 miles). Assuming Rick chooses to deduct operating expenses and lease payments in lieu of using the mileage rate, he can deduct $5,335.

In contrast to transportation expenses, travel expenses are only deductible if the taxpayer is *away from home* overnight while traveling. This distinction is important because, besides the cost of transportation, the deduction for **travel expenses** includes meals (50 percent), lodging, and incidental expenses. A taxpayer is considered to be away from home overnight if the travel is away from the primary place of business and of sufficient duration to require sleep or rest (typically this will be overnight). When a taxpayer travels solely for business purposes, *all* of the costs of travel are deductible (but only 50 percent of meals). When the travel has both business and personal aspects, the deductibility of the transportation costs depends upon whether business is the *primary* purpose for the trip. If the primary purpose of a trip is business, the transportation costs are fully deductible, but meals (50 percent), lodging, and incidental expenditures are limited to those incurred during the business portion of the travel.[19] If the taxpayer's primary purpose for the trip is personal, the taxpayer may not deduct *any* transportation costs to arrive at the location but may deduct meals (50 percent), lodging, transportation, and incidental expenditures for the *business* portion of the trip. The primary purpose of a trip depends upon facts and circumstances and is often the subject of dispute.

[18]This mileage rate is updated periodically (sometimes two or three times within a year) to reflect changes in the cost of operating a vehicle. The mileage option is only available for vehicles not previously depreciated, vehicles previously depreciated on the straight-line method, or for leased vehicles where this method has been used throughout the term of the lease.

[19]Special limitations apply to a number of travel expenses that are potentially abusive, such as luxury water travel, foreign conventions, conventions on cruise ships, and travel expenses associated with taking a companion.

The rule for business travel is modified somewhat if a trip abroad includes both business and personal activities. Like the rule for domestic travel, if foreign travel is primarily for personal purposes, then only those expenses directly associated with business activities are deductible. However, unlike the rule for domestic travel, when foreign travel is primarily for business purposes, a portion of the roundtrip transportation costs is not deductible. The nondeductible portion is typically computed based on a time ratio such as the proportion of personal days to total days (travel days count as business days).[20]

Example 1-8

Rick paid a $300 registration fee for a three-day course in landscape design. The course was held in New York (Rick paid $700 for airfare to attend) and he spent four days in New York. He spent the last day sightseeing. During the trip, Rick paid $150 a night for three nights' lodging, $50 a day for meals, and $70 a day for a rental car. What amount of these travel-related expenditures may Rick deduct as business expenses?

Answer: $1,435 for business travel and $300 for business education. The primary purpose for the trip appears to be business because Rick spent three days on business activities versus one personal day. He can deduct travel costs, computed as follows:

Deductible Travel Costs

Description	Amount	Explanation
Airfare to New York	$ 700	Primary purpose is business.
Lodging in New York	450	3 business days × $150 a day.
Meals	75	3 business days × $50 a day × 50% limit.
Rental car	210	3 business days × $70 a day.
Total business travel expenses	$1,435	

What if: Assume Rick stayed in New York for ten days, spending three days at the seminar and seven days sightseeing. What amount could he deduct?

Answer: In this scenario Rick can deduct $735 for business travel and $300 for business education. Rick would not be able to deduct the $700 cost of airfare because the trip is primarily personal, as evidenced by the seven days of personal activities compared to only three days of business activities.

Deductible Travel Costs

Description	Amount	Explanation
Airfare to New York	$ 0	Primary purpose is personal.
Lodging in New York	450	3 business days × $150 a day.
Meals	75	3 business days × $50 a day × 50% limit.
Rental car	210	3 business days × $70 a day.
Total business travel expenses	$735	

What if: Assume the original facts in the example except Rick traveled to London (rather than New York) for ten days spending six days at the seminar and four days sightseeing. What amount could he deduct?

Answer: In this scenario Rick can deduct $1,890 for travel (computed below) and $300 for business education.

[20]Foreign transportation expense is deductible without prorating under special circumstances authorized in §274(c). For example, the cost of getting abroad is fully deductible if the travel is for one week or less or if the personal activity constitutes less than one-fourth of the travel time.

Deductible Travel Costs

Description	Amount	Explanation
Airfare to London	$ 420	6 business days/10 total days × $700.
Lodging in London	900	6 business days × $150 a day.
Meals	150	6 business days × $50 a day × 50% limit.
Rental car	420	6 business days × $70 a day.
Total business travel expenses	$1,890	

Rick is allowed to deduct $420 of the $700 airfare (60 percent) because he spent 6 of the 10 days on the trip conducting business activities.

Property Use Several types of property may be used for both business and personal purposes. For example, business owners often use automobiles, computers, or cell phones for both business and personal purposes.[21] However, because expenses relating to these assets are deductible only to the extent the assets are used for business purposes, taxpayers must allocate the expenses between the business and personal use portions. The calculation of depreciation on mixed-use assets is discussed in the next chapter and with specific topics, such as the office in the home deduction.

Example 1-9

Rick occasionally uses his personal auto (a BMW) to drive to interviews with prospective clients and to drive back and forth between his shop and various work sites. This year Rick carefully recorded that the BMW was driven 532 miles for business activities and 10,500 miles in total. What expenses associated with the BMW may Rick deduct?

Answer: $306. Based on the standard mileage rate of 57.5 cents per mile, Rick can deduct $306 (532 × 57.5 cents) for business use of his BMW. Alternatively, Rick can track the operating expenses of the BMW (including depreciation) and deduct the business portion [based upon the percentage of business miles driven to total miles driven (532 business miles/10,500 total miles)].

When taxpayers use other business assets for both business and personal purposes, the deductible business expense is determined by prorating the expenses based upon the percentage of the time the asset is used for business purposes. For example, if a full year's expense for a business asset is $1,000, but the asset is only used for business purposes 90 percent of the time, then only $900 of expense can be deducted ($1,000 × 90%). Special rules apply when the business usage for an asset drops below 50 percent. We discuss these issues in the next chapter.

Record Keeping and Other Requirements Because distinguishing business purposes from personal purposes is a difficult and subjective task, the tax laws include provisions designed to help the courts and the IRS determine the business element of mixed-motive transactions. Under these provisions, taxpayers must maintain specific, written, contemporaneous records (of time, amount, and business purpose) for mixed-motive expenses. For example, as we discussed above, the tax laws prohibit any deductions for business meals and entertainment unless substantial business discussions accompany the entertainment activity. Consequently, when taxpayers incur

[21]These types of assets are referred to as "listed property." Note that cell phones are specifically exempted from the definition of listed property (§280F(d)(4)(A), as amended by the 2010 Small Business Act §2043(a)).

meals and entertainment expenses, they must document the business purpose and the extent of the discussion to deduct any of the expenditures.[22]

LO 1-3

SPECIFIC BUSINESS DEDUCTIONS

As we discussed above, the tax code provides general guidelines for determining whether business expenditures are deductible. We learned that to be deductible, business expenditures must be ordinary, necessary, and reasonable in amount. In some cases, however, the tax laws identify specific items businesses are allowed to deduct. We discuss several of these deductions below.

THE KEY FACTS

Domestic Production Activities Deduction

- A subsidy for the cost of producing goods or certain construction services within the United States.
- 9 percent of qualified production activity income.
- Limited to overall income (AGI for individuals) and 50 percent of wages associated with the production.

Domestic Production Activities Deduction

Businesses that manufacture goods are allowed to deduct an *artificial* business deduction for tax purposes called the U.S. **domestic production activities deduction (DPAD).** This deduction is designed to reduce the tax burden on domestic manufacturers to make investments in domestic manufacturing facilities more attractive. The DPAD provides a special tax deduction for businesses, large and small, that "manufacture, produce, grow or extract" tangible products entirely or in significant part within the United States.[23] This deduction is artificial because it does not represent an expenditure per se, but merely serves to reduce the income taxes the business must pay and thereby increase the after-tax profitability of domestic manufacturing.

The formula for computing the DPAD is 9 percent times the *lesser* of (1) the business's taxable income before the deduction (or modified AGI for individuals) or (2) **qualified production activities income (QPAI).**[24] Generally speaking, QPAI is the *net* income from selling or leasing property that was manufactured in the United States. Thus, to compute QPAI, businesses need to determine the amount of revenues, cost of goods sold, and expenses attributable to U.S. production activities. Obviously, the calculation of the income allocable to domestic production can be exceedingly complex, especially in the case of large multinational businesses. The final deduction cannot exceed 50 percent of the wages the business paid to employees for working in qualifying production activities during the year.[25]

Example 1-10

This fall Rick constructed a greenhouse that qualified for the domestic production activities deduction. Rick received $5,000 for the construction project from his client and allocated $4,000 in expenses to the project. These expenses included $2,000 of qualified wages. Thus, the greenhouse project generated $1,000 of qualified production activity income (QPAI) for Rick ($5,000 minus $4,000). What is Rick's domestic production activities deduction for this project?

Answer: $90. Assuming Rick's QPAI of $1,000 is less than his modified AGI, the DPAD is $90, calculated by multiplying 9 percent times $1,000 of QPAI. The entire computation is summarized as follows:

[22]§274 requires substantiation of all elements of travel and entertainment including sufficient corroborating evidence. Although there are a few exceptions to this rule, approximations and estimates are generally not sufficient. Also, taxpayers must maintain records to deduct the business portion of mixed-use assets such as cars used for both business and personal purposes. Note that when the taxpayer is unable to substantiate other deductions, the court may estimate the deductible amount under the Cohan rule (*George Cohan v. Com.*, (1930, CA2), 39 F2d 540).

[23]§199 also allows this deduction for qualifying taxpayers in the domestic film and sound recording industries, those engaged in a construction business in the United States, and engineering and architectural firms providing services for U.S. construction projects. Because the domestic production activities deduction does not represent a real expenditure, the deduction is not an expense for financial accounting purposes.

[24]See §199(d)(2). Modified AGI is AGI before the DPAD and certain other specified deductions.

[25]Taxpayers report the deduction computations on Form 8903.

DPAD Calculation

Description	Amount	Explanation
Qualified domestic gross receipts	$5,000	Must be a qualified activity.
Allocable costs and expenses	−4,000	Allocate to qualified activity.
Qualified production activity income	$1,000	Limited to modified AGI.
Statutory percentage	× 9%	
Domestic production activities deduction	$ 90	Limited to 50% of wages.

The 50 percent wage limitation is $1,000 (50% × $2,000 in wages Rick paid to employees working on the project). Thus, Rick is allowed to deduct the entire $90 domestic production activities deduction even though the $90 deduction doesn't represent a specific liability or payment to anyone.

TAXES IN THE REAL WORLD Decorative Packaging as a Manufacturing Process

Houdini, Inc., designs, assembles, and sells gift baskets and gift "towers" (stacked decorative boxes of food). Houdini has two facilities and maintains about 300 employees and additional temporary workers during the holidays. Houdini selects gift baskets and the items to be placed inside, such as candy or wine, as well as the "void fill" that holds everything together. Houdini's Packaging Department takes food items that are in small, food-safe containers and places them in other packaging, such as a small, colorful box.

Houdini claimed the domestic production activities deduction contending that designing a gift basket is a complicated process that involves steps like determining appropriate container sizes and colors, selecting materials, ensuring quality control, and reviewing packaging. The IRS filed to recover the taxes relating to the DPAD deductions asserting that Houdini merely packaged the items in its gift baskets and towers. To qualify for the deduction, the gift baskets must be items that are "manufactured, produced, grown, or extracted" (MPGE). The regulations hold that "packaging, repackaging, labeling, or minor assembly" doesn't qualify as MPGE but only if the taxpayer engages in no other MPGE activity.

The court determined that Houdini's production qualifies as manufacturing or producing, but also qualifies as packaging or repackaging. To reconcile this contradiction, the court found that Houdini's production process changes "the form of an article" under the regulations. Houdini uses assembly line workers and machines and ultimately produces a final product (i.e., a gift) that is distinct in form and purpose from the individual items inside (i.e., grocery-type items). The court rejected the IRS's argument that Houdini's packaging and repackaging are mere services. The court held that, rather than merely enhancing an existing product, Houdini creates a new product with a different demand.

U.S. v. Dean (DC CA), 112 AFTR 2d 2013-5164.

Losses on Dispositions of Business Property

Besides operating expenses, businesses are generally allowed to deduct losses incurred when selling or disposing of business assets.[26] The calculation of losses from business property dispositions can be complex, but the main idea is that businesses realize and recognize a loss when the asset's tax basis exceeds the sale proceeds. We will discuss the rules governing the tax treatment of gains and losses on asset disposition in more detail in Chapter 3.

[26]In most circumstances businesses may *not* deduct losses on assets sold to related parties. We describe who qualifies as a related party later in this chapter.

Example 1-11

What if: Assume that in late October, Rick purchased a used trailer to transport equipment to work sites. Rick bought the trailer for what he thought was a bargain price of $1,000. However, shortly after Rick acquired it , the axle snapped and was not repairable. Rick was forced to sell the trailer to a parts shop for $325. What amount can Rick deduct as a loss from the trailer sale?

Answer: $675, because the trailer was a business asset (amount realized of $325 minus adjusted basis of $1,000). (Note, as we discuss in the next chapter, Rick is not allowed to deduct depreciation on the trailer because he disposed of it in the same year he acquired it.)

Business Casualty Losses

Besides selling assets, businesses can incur losses when their assets are stolen, damaged, or completely destroyed by a force outside the control of the business. These events are called casualties.[27] Businesses may deduct **casualty losses** in the year the casualty occurs or in the year the theft of an asset is discovered. The amount of the loss deduction depends on whether the asset is (1) completely destroyed or stolen or (2) only partially destroyed. When its asset is *completely* destroyed or stolen, the business calculates the amount of the loss as though it sold the asset for the insurance proceeds, if any. That is, the loss is the amount of insurance proceeds minus the adjusted tax basis of the asset. If the asset is damaged but not completely destroyed, the amount of the loss is the amount of the insurance proceeds minus the *lesser* of (1) the asset's tax basis or (2) the decline in the value of the asset due to the casualty. While individuals deduct business casualty losses and casualty losses associated with rentals and royalties as deductions *for* AGI, casualty and theft losses of assets used for the production of income (investments) and personal-use assets are generally deductible as itemized deductions.[28] We summarize the casualty and theft loss rules for business, production of income, and personal-use assets in Exhibit 1-2, which appears on the following page.

Example 1-12

What if: Suppose Rick acquired a personal-use asset several years ago for $9,000. Suppose further that a casualty event destroyed the asset, and at that time the asset was worth $1,000 and insured for $250. What is the amount of Rick's casualty loss (before applying the per casualty floor and the AGI restriction)?

Answer: $750, computed as follows:

Insurance proceeds		$250
Minus the *lesser* of:		
(1) adjusted tax basis or	$9,000	
(2) value at time of casualty	1,000	−1,000
Casualty loss deduction (before limitations)		($750)

Suppose instead that Rick's asset was a business-use asset and Rick had deducted $4,000 of depreciation expense against the asset. Hence, the asset's tax basis was $5,000 ($9,000 − $4,000). What would be the amount of his business casualty loss?

Answer: $4,750, computed as follows:

Insurance proceeds	$ 250
Minus adjusted tax basis	−5,000
Casualty loss deduction	($4,750)

[27]Casualties are unexpected events driven by forces outside the control of the taxpayer that damage or destroy a taxpayer's property. Section 165 lists "fire, storm, and shipwreck" as examples of casualties.

[28]For example, a taxpayer with a coin collection that is stolen or valuable antique collection that burns is potentially eligible for a casualty loss deduction on assets used for the production of income. Under §165(h)(5), personal casualty losses are allowed to offset personal casualty gains in computing AGI.

EXHIBIT 1-2 Comparison of Casualty and Theft Loss Rules for Property Used in Business, for Production of Income, and for Personal Purposes

	Property Used in Business (including losses from rental and royalty property)	Property Used for the Production of Income	Property Used for Personal Purposes
Amount of loss if property completely destroyed or stolen	Insurance proceeds minus adjusted basis	Same as business	Insurance proceeds minus lesser of (1) adjusted basis or (2) decline in asset's value due to casualty or theft.
Amount of loss if property is not completely destroyed	Insurance proceeds minus lesser of (1) adjusted basis or (2) decline in asset's value	Same as business	Same as business
Loss limitation	None	None	A per casualty floor limitation and 10 percent of AGI floor for total casualty losses for year.
Type of deduction	For AGI	Miscellaneous itemized deduction (not subject to 2 percent floor)	Itemized deduction

ACCOUNTING PERIODS

LO 1-4

So far we've discussed how to determine a business's income and how to determine its deductible business expenses. In this section, we will discuss accounting periods, which affect when taxpayers determine their income and deductions. Businesses must report their income and deductions over a fixed **accounting period** or **tax year.** A full tax year consists of 12 full months. A tax year can consist of a period less than 12 months (a short tax year) in certain circumstances. For instance, a business may report income for such a short year in its first year of existence (for example, it reports income on a calendar year-end and starts business after January 1) or in its final year of existence (for example, a calendar-year business ends its business before December 31). Short tax years in a business's initial or final year are treated the same as full years. A business may also have a short year when it changes its tax year, and this can occur when the business is acquired by new owners. In these situations, special rules may apply for computing the tax liability of the business.[29]

There are three types of tax years, each with different year-ends:

1. A calendar year ends on December 31.
2. A **fiscal year** ends on the last day of a month other than December.
3. A 52/53 week-year ends on the same day of the week every year. In other words, a 52/53 week-year could end on the same day of the week that is the last such day in the month or on the same day of the week nearest the end of the month. For example, a business could adopt a 52/53-week fiscal year that (1) ends on the last Saturday in July each year or (2) ends on the Saturday closest to the end of July (although this Saturday might be in August rather than July).[30]

[29]§443. Discussion of tax consequences associated with these short years is beyond the scope of this text.

[30]Businesses with inventories may benefit from 52/53 year-ends to facilitate an inventory count when the store is closed (e.g., over a weekend).

THE KEY FACTS

Accounting Periods

- Individuals and proprietorships account for income on a calendar year.
- Corporations are allowed to choose a fiscal year.
- Partnerships and other flow-through entities generally use a required year.

Not all types of tax years are available to all types of businesses. The rules for determining the tax years available to the business depends on whether the business is a sole proprietorship, a **flow-through entity,** or a C corporation. These rules are summarized as follows:

- *Sole proprietorships:* Because individual proprietors must report their business income on their individual returns, proprietorships use a calendar year-end to report their business income.[31]
- *Flow-through entities:* Partnerships and S corporations are flow-through entities (partners and S corporation owners report the entity's income directly on their own tax returns), and these entities generally must adopt tax years consistent with the owners' tax years.[32] Because owners are allocated income from flow-through entities on the last day of the entity's taxable year, the tax laws impose the tax year consistency requirement to minimize income tax deferral opportunities for the owners.
- *C corporations:* C corporations are generally allowed to select a calendar, fiscal, or 52/53-week year-end.

A business adopts a calendar year-end or fiscal year-end by filing its initial tax return. In contrast, a business adopts a 52/53-week year-end by filing a special election with the IRS. Once a business establishes its tax year, it generally must receive permission from the IRS to change.

Example 1-13

Rick is a calendar-year taxpayer. What tax year must Rick use to report income from his business Green Acres?

Answer: Calendar year. This is true even though Rick began his business in May of this year. He will calculate income and expense for his landscaping business over the calendar year and include the net business income from May through December of this year on Schedule C of his individual tax return.

What if: Suppose that Rick incorporated Green Acres at the time he began his business. What tax year could Green Acres adopt?

Answer: If Green Acres was operated as a C corporation, it could elect a calendar year-end, a fiscal year-end, or a 52/53-week year-end. If it were an S corporation, it likely would use a calendar year-end.

LO 1-5 ACCOUNTING METHODS

Once a business adopts a tax year, it must determine which items of income and deduction to recognize during a particular year. Generally speaking, the taxpayer's **accounting methods** determine the tax year in which a business recognizes a particular item of income or deduction. Because accounting methods affect the *timing* of when a taxpayer reports income and deductions, these methods are very important for taxpayers using a timing tax strategy to defer income or accelerate deductions.[33]

[31]Virtually all individual taxpayers use a calendar-year tax year.

[32]See §706 for the specific restrictions on year-ends for partnerships and §1378 for restrictions on S corporations. If they can show a business purpose (not easy to do), both partnerships and S corporations may adopt year-ends other than those used by their owners.

[33]Accounting methods do not determine *whether* an item of income is taxable or an expense is deductible. Accordingly, accounting methods generally do not affect the total income or deductions recognized over the lifetime of the business.

Financial and Tax Accounting Methods

Many businesses are required to generate financial statements for nontax reasons. For example, publicly traded corporations must file financial statements with the Securities and Exchange Commission (SEC) based on generally accepted accounting principles (GAAP). Also, privately owned businesses borrowing money from banks are often required to generate financial statements under GAAP, so that the lender can evaluate the business's creditworthiness. In reporting financial statement income, businesses have incentives to select accounting methods permissible under GAAP that accelerate income and defer deductions. In contrast, for tax planning purposes, businesses have incentives to choose accounting methods that *defer income* and *accelerate deductions*. This natural tension between financial reporting incentives and tax reporting incentives may be the reason the tax laws sometimes require businesses to use the same accounting methods for tax purposes that they use for financial accounting purposes. In other words, in many circumstances, if businesses want to defer taxable income, they must also defer book income.[34]

Sometimes the tax laws require businesses to use different, presumably more appropriate, accounting methods for tax purposes. Consequently, for policy and administrative reasons, the tax laws also identify several circumstances when businesses must use specific tax accounting methods to determine taxable income no matter what accounting method they use for financial reporting purposes. We will now turn our attention to accounting methods prescribed by the tax laws. With certain restrictions, businesses are able to select their *overall* accounting methods and accounting methods for *specific* items or transactions. We will cover each of these in turn.

Overall Accounting Method

Businesses must choose an overall method of accounting to track and report their business activities for tax purposes. The overriding requirement for any tax accounting method is that the method must "clearly reflect income" and be applied consistently.[35] The two primary overall methods are the cash method and the accrual method. Businesses may also choose a hybrid method (some accounts on the cash method and others on the accrual method).

Cash Method A taxpayer (or business) using the cash method of accounting recognizes revenue when property or services are actually or constructively received. This is generally true no matter when the business sells the good or performs the service that generates the revenue. Likewise, a business adopting the cash method generally recognizes deductions when the expense is paid. Thus, the timing of the liability giving rise to the expense is usually irrelevant.

Keep in mind that a cash-method business receiving payments in *noncash* form (as property or services) must recognize the noncash payments as gross income. Also, in certain circumstances, a business expending cash on ordinary and necessary business expenses may not be allowed to *currently* deduct the expense at the time of the payment. For example, cash-method taxpayers (and accrual-method taxpayers) are not allowed to deduct prepaid interest expense and cannot usually deduct prepaid expenses or payments that create a tangible or intangible asset.[36] However, the regulations provide a **12-month rule** for prepaid business expenses to simplify the process of determining whether to capitalize or immediately expense payments that create benefits for a relatively brief period of time, such as insurance, security, rent, and

[34]§446(a). Businesses that use different accounting methods for book and tax must typically file a form M-1 that reconciles the results from the two accounting methods.

[35]§446(b).

[36]§461(g).

warranty service contracts. When a business prepays business expenses, it may *immediately* deduct the prepayment if (1) the contract period does not last more than a year *and* (2) the contract period does not extend beyond the end of the taxable year following the tax year in which the taxpayer makes the payment.[37] If the prepaid expense does not meet both of these criteria, the business must capitalize the prepaid amount and amortize it over the length of the contract whether the business uses the cash or accrual method of accounting.[38]

Example 1-14

On July 1 of this year, Rick paid $1,200 for a 12-month insurance policy that covers his business property from accidents and casualties from July 1 of this year, through June 30 of next year. How much of the $1,200 expenditure may Rick deduct this year if he uses the cash method of accounting for his business activities?

Answer: $1,200. Because the insurance coverage does not exceed 12 months and does not extend beyond the end of next year, Rick is allowed to deduct the entire premium payment under the 12-month rule.

What if: Suppose the insurance policy was for 12 months but the policy ran from February 1 of next year, through January 31 of the following year. How much of the expenditure may Rick deduct this year if he uses the cash method of accounting for his business activities?

Answer: $0. Even though the contract period is 12 months or less, Rick is required to capitalize the cost of the prepayment for the insurance policy because the contract period extends beyond the end of next year.

What if: Suppose Rick had paid $1,200 for an *18-month* policy beginning July 1 of this year, and ending December 31 of next year. How much may he deduct this year if he uses the cash method of accounting for his business activities?

Answer: $400. In this scenario, because the policy exceeds 12 months, Rick is allowed to deduct the portion of the premium pertaining to this year. Hence, this year, he would deduct $400 (6 months/18 months × $1,200). He would deduct the remaining $800 in the next year.

Accrual Method Businesses using the accrual method to determine taxable income follow rules similar to GAAP with two basic differences. First, as we discuss below, requirements for recognizing taxable income tend to be structured to recognize income earlier than the recognition rules for financial accounting. Second, requirements for accruing tax deductions tend to be structured to recognize less accrued expenses than the recognition rules for financial reporting purposes. These differences reflect the underlying objectives of financial accounting income and taxable income. The objective of financial accounting is to provide useful information to stakeholders such as creditors, prospective investors, and shareholders. Because financial accounting methods are designed to guard against businesses overstating their profitability to these users, financial accounting tends to bias against *overstating* income. In contrast, the government's main objective for writing tax laws is to collect revenues. Thus, tax accounting rules for accrual-method businesses tend to bias against *understating* income. These differences will become apparent as we describe tax accounting rules for businesses.

[37]This 12-month rule applies to both cash-method and accrual-method taxpayers. However, for accrual-method taxpayers to deduct prepaid expenses, they must meet both the 12-month rule requirements and the economic performance requirements that we discuss in the next section.

[38]Reg. §1.263(a)-4(f).

continued from page 1-1...
Rick's CPA, Jane, informed him that he needs to select an overall method of accounting for Green Acres to compute its taxable income. Jane advised Rick to use the cash method. However, Rick wanted to prepare GAAP financial statements and use the accrual method of accounting. He decided that if Green Acres was going to become a big business, it needed to act like a big business. Finally, after much discussion, Rick and Jane reached a compromise. For the first year, they would track Green Acres's business activities using both the cash *and* the accrual methods. In addition, they would also keep GAAP-based books for financial purposes. When filing time comes, Rick would decide which method to use in reporting taxable income. Jane told Rick that he could wait until he filed his tax return to select the accounting method for tax purposes. ■

Accrual Income

Businesses using the accrual method of accounting generally recognize income when they meet the all-events test.

All-Events Test for Income The all-events test requires that businesses recognize income when (1) all events have occurred that determine or fix their right to receive the income and (2) the amount of the income can be determined with reasonable accuracy.[39] Assuming the amount of income can be determined with reasonable accuracy, businesses meet the all-events requirement on the *earliest* of the following three dates:

1. When they complete the task required to earn the income. Businesses earn income for services as they provide the services, and they generally earn income from selling property when the title of the property passes to the buyer.
2. When the payment for the task is due from the customer.
3. When the business receives payment for the task.

Example 1-15

In early fall, Rick contracted with a dozen homeowners to landscape their yards. Rick agreed to do the work for an aggregate of $11,000. Rick and his crew started in the fall and completed the jobs in December of this year. However, he didn't mail the bills until after the holidays and didn't receive any payments until the following January. When must Rick recognize the income from this work?

Answer: Under the accrual method, Rick must recognize the entire $11,000 as income this year because his right to the income is fixed when Rick and his crew had completed the work by year-end. Under the cash method, however, Rick would not recognize the $11,000 as income until next year when he received it.

Taxation of Advance Payments of Income (Unearned Income)

In some cases, businesses receive income payments *before* they actually earn the income (they receive a prepayment). *When* the business must recognize a prepayment as income depends on the type of income. The rule for interest and rental income is

[39]Reg. §1.451-1(a). The all-events test is sometimes called the "fixed and determinable" test because the right to payment must be fixed and the amount determinable with reasonable accuracy.

relatively strict. Businesses must recognize unearned rental and unearned interest income *immediately* upon receipt (the income is recognized before it is earned). However, businesses are not required to recognize security deposits received from rental customers because they incur a liability to return the deposits when they receive the payments.[40] The income recognition rules are less strict when businesses receive advance payments for services or goods.

THE KEY FACTS

Revenue Recognition Under the Accrual Method

- Income is recognized when earned (all-events) or received (if earlier).
- The all-events test requires that the business has the right to income.
- Taxpayers can generally elect to defer recognition of prepaid income for services (for one year) and goods.

Unearned Service Revenue For financial reporting purposes, a business does not immediately recognize income on payments it receives for services to be provided in the future. For financial reporting purposes, an advance payment for services is recorded as a debit for cash received and a credit to a liability account (unearned income). The business then recognizes the *financial* income from the services as it performs the services. In contrast, for tax purposes, the all-events test generally requires businesses receiving *advance* payments for services to recognize the income when they receive the payment, rather than when they perform the services.

The IRS provides an exception to this immediate recognition general rule. Specifically, businesses receiving advance payments for services may *defer* recognizing the *prepayment* as income until the tax year *following* the year they receive the payment.[41] This one-year deferral does *not* apply (1) if (or the extent to which) the income is actually earned by the end of the year of receipt, (2) if the prepayment was included in financial reporting income, or (3) if the prepayment was for interest or rent (taxpayers must recognize unearned interest and rental income on receipt).

Advance Payment for Goods When an accrual-method business receives an advance payment for *goods* it will provide to customers in the future, the business may account for the prepayment for tax purposes under the **full-inclusion method** or the **deferral method.**[42] A business electing the full-inclusion method will *immediately* recognize an advance payment as income. In contrast, a business using the deferral method will recognize advance payments for goods by the earlier of (1) when the business would recognize the income for tax purposes if it had not received the *advance* payment or (2) when it recognizes the income for financial reporting purposes. Thus, the deferral method is comparable to the deferral allowed for advance payments received for future services. However, unlike the treatment of advance payments for services, advance payments for goods could be deferred for more than a year if the business defers the income for financial reporting purposes for more than a year.

Example 1-16

In late November 2015, Rick received a $7,200 payment from a client for monthly landscaping services from December 1, 2015, through November 30, 2017 ($300 a month for 24 months). When must Rick recognize the income from the advance payment for services?

Answer: Under the accrual method, Rick would initially recognize the $300 income he earned in December 2015. In 2016, he would recognize the remaining $6,900 (rather than only the $3,600

[40]*Comm. v. Indianapolis Power & Light Co.* (1990), 493 US 203. Customer deposits required by a public utility weren't taxable income because the right to keep the deposits depended on events outside of the taxpayer's control, such as the decision to have the deposit applied to future bills.

[41]Rev Proc. 2004-34, 2004-1 CB 991.

[42]Reg. §1.451-5. This exception does not apply to goods held for sale in the ordinary course of business (inventory).

related to 2016) because he is not allowed to defer the prepayments for services for more than a year. Under the cash method, Rick must recognize the entire prepayment, $7,200, as income upon receipt in 2015.

What if: Suppose the $7,200 prepayment was for the delivery of 15 pallets of sod (not inventory) at a cost to Rick of $1,800. Suppose further that five pallets were to be delivered in 2016 and the remainder was to be delivered in 2017. When would Rick recognize the income from the advance payment of goods under the accrual method?

Answer: If Rick elected the full-inclusion method, then he would recognize the entire prepayment of $7,200 as income (minus his cost of goods sold of $1,800) in 2015. However, if Rick elected the deferral method, then he would recognize the income as the sod is delivered, $2,400 in 2016 (minus $600 cost of goods sold) and $4,800 in 2017 (minus $1,200 cost of goods sold).

Inventories

Many businesses generate income by selling products they acquire for resale or products they manufacture. When selling inventory is a material income-producing factor, a business generally must account for gross profit (sales minus cost of goods sold) using the accrual method, even if they are a cash-method taxpayer.

An exception to this general rule is that a cash-method business is allowed to use the cash method to account for gross profit if the average annual gross receipts for the three-year period prior to the current year do not exceed $10 million. In addition, the primary business activity must be to provide services to customers and the sales of products is a secondary or small part of its services.[43] However, the business is not allowed to deduct the cost of the inventory to the extent it has the product at the end of the year. How does this exception benefit a cash-method business if the business is not allowed to fully deduct the cost of inventory until it sells the inventory? It may be beneficial because it allows the business to use the cash method to account for sales revenue. Without the exception, cash-method service businesses would be required to account for sales revenue from inventory sales on the accrual method, which means they may be required to recognize revenue before they actually receive it. With the exception, they are allowed to defer the revenue recognition until they receive the payments from customers.

Businesses selling inventory must determine their inventory costs to accurately compute taxable income. This requires businesses to maintain records of balances for finished goods inventory and, if applicable, for partially finished goods and raw materials. Inventory costs include the purchase price of raw materials (minus any discounts), shipping costs, and any indirect costs it allocates to the inventory under the **uniform cost capitalization rules (UNICAP rules).**[44]

THE KEY FACTS

Inventories

- Businesses must use the accrual method to account for substantial inventories.
- The UNICAP rules require capitalization of most indirect costs of production.
- The LIFO method is allowed if also used for financial reporting purposes.

Uniform Capitalization The tax laws require businesses to capitalize certain direct and indirect costs associated with inventories.[45] Congress enacted these rules primarily for two reasons. First, the rules accelerate tax revenues for the government by deferring deductions for the capitalized costs until the business sells the associated inventory. Thus, there is generally a one-year lag between when businesses initially capitalize the costs and when they deduct them. Second, Congress

[43]Rev. Proc. 2002-28, 2002-1 CB 815. There are other exceptions to this general rule. For example, certain cash-method taxpayers (average annual receipts of $1 million or less) can qualify to account for merchandise for sale as materials and supplies under Rev. Proc. 2001-10, 2001-1 CB 272.

[44]Inventory valuation allowances are generally not allowed, but taxpayers can adopt the lower of cost or market method of inventory valuation. In addition, under certain conditions specific goods not salable at normal prices can be valued at bona fide selling prices less direct cost of disposition.

[45]§263A(a).

designed the "uniform" rules to reduce variation in the costs businesses include in inventory. Congress intended the UNICAP provisions to apply to manufacturers and large resalers. Consequently, businesses that resell personal property are not required to use the UNICAP rules if they report average annual gross receipts of $10 million or less over the three-year period ending with the taxable year prior to the current year.

Under these uniform cost capitalization rules, large businesses are generally required to capitalize more costs to inventory for tax purposes than they capitalize under financial accounting rules. Under GAAP, businesses generally include in inventory only those costs incurred within their production facility. In contrast, the UNICAP rules require businesses to allocate to inventory the costs they incur inside the production facility and the costs they incur outside the facility to support production (or inventory acquisition) activities. For example, under the UNICAP provisions, a business must capitalize at least a portion of the compensation paid to employees in its purchasing department, general and administrative department, and even its information technology department, to the extent these groups provide support for the production process. In contrast, businesses immediately expense these items as period costs for financial accounting purposes. The regulations provide guidance on the costs that must be allocated to inventory. Selling, advertising, and research are specifically identified as costs that do not have to be allocated to inventory under the UNICAP provisions.[46]

Example 1-17

What if: Green Acres sells trees but Rick anticipates selling flowers, shrubs, and other plants in future years. Ken is Rick's employee in charge of purchasing inventory. Ken's compensation this year is $30,000, and Rick estimates that Ken spends about 5 percent of his time acquiring inventory and the remaining time working on landscaping projects. How would Rick allocate Ken's compensation under the UNICAP rules?

Answer: If the UNICAP rules applied to Green Acres, Rick would allocate $1,500 ($30,000 × 5%) of Ken's compensation to the cost of the inventory Green Acres acquired this year. In contrast, Ken's entire salary would be expensed as a period cost for financial accounting purposes. (Note, however, because Green Acres's gross receipts for the year are under $10,000,000, it is not *required* to apply the UNICAP rules.)

Inventory Cost-Flow Methods Once a business determines the cost of its inventory, it must use an inventory cost-flow method to determine its cost of goods sold. Three primary cost-flow methods are (1) first-in, first-out (**FIFO**), (2) last-in, first-out (**LIFO**), and (3) **specific identification.** Businesses might be inclined to use FIFO or LIFO methods when they sell similar, relatively low-cost, high-volume products such as cans of soup or barrels of oil. These methods simplify inventory accounting because the business need not track the individual cost of each item it sells. In contrast, businesses that sell distinct, relatively high-cost, low-volume products might be more likely to adopt the specific identification method. For example, jewelry and used-car businesses would likely use the specific identification method to account for their cost of sales. In general terms, when costs are increasing, a business using the FIFO method will report a higher gross margin than if it used the LIFO method. The opposite is true if costs are decreasing.

[46]Reg. §1.263A–1(e)(3)(iii).

Example 1-18

In late August, Rick purchased 10 oak saplings (immature trees) for a total purchase price of $3,000. In September, he purchased 12 more for a total price of $3,900, and in late October, he purchased 15 more for $5,000. The total cost of each lot of trees was determined as follows:

Purchase Date	Trees	Direct Cost	Other Costs	Total Cost
August 20	10	$ 3,000	$200	$ 3,200
September 15	12	3,900	300	4,200
October 22	15	5,000	400	5,400
Totals	37	$11,900	$900	$12,800

Before the end of the year, Green Acres sold 20 of the oak saplings (5 from the August lot, 5 from the September lot, and 10 from the October lot) for cash. What is Green Acres's gross profit from sales of oak saplings if the sales revenue totaled $14,000 (all collected by year-end), and what is its ending oak sapling inventory under the accrual and the cash method of accounting?

Answer: Under the accrual method, Green Acres's gross profit from sapling sales and its ending inventory balance for the remaining oak saplings under the FIFO, LIFO, and specific identification cost-flow methods is as follows:

	FIFO	LIFO	Specific ID
Sales	$14,000	$14,000	$14,000
Cost of goods sold	−6,700	−7,150	−6,950
Gross profit	$ 7,300	$ 6,850	$ 7,050
Ending inventory:			
August 20 trees	$ 0	$ 3,200	$ 1,600
September 15 trees	700	2,450	2,450
October 22 trees	5,400	0	1,800
Total ending inventory	$ 6,100	$ 5,650	$ 5,850

Using the cash method, the answer is the same as it is under the accrual method. Green Acres is not allowed to deduct the cost of its ending inventory even if it qualifies to use the cash method to account for gross profit under the small business ($10M) exception.

What if: Assume the same original facts except that Green Acres received $10,000 sales revenue from customers this year and the remaining $4,000 early next year. Assuming Green Acres qualifies to use the cash method to account for gross profit under the small business ($10M) exception, what is the amount of Green Acres's gross profit this year if it uses the specific identification method of accounting for its ending inventory?

Answer: $3,050 ($10,000 revenue minus $6,950 cost of goods sold). In this situation Green Acres would be allowed to defer $4,000 of the sales revenue until it collected it next year.

When costs are subject to inflation over time, a business would get the best of both worlds if it adopted the FIFO method for financial reporting purposes and the LIFO method for tax purposes. Not surprisingly, the tax laws require that a business can use LIFO for tax purposes only if it also uses LIFO for financial reporting purposes.[47] While this "conformity" requirement may not matter to entities not required to generate financial reports, it can be very restrictive to publicly traded corporations.

[47]§472(c).

Accrual Deductions

Generally, when accrual-method businesses incur a liability relating to a business expense, they account for it by crediting a liability account (or cash if they pay the liability at the time they incur it) and debiting an expense account. However, to record an expense and the corresponding deduction for tax purposes, the business must meet (1) an **all-events test** for the liability *and* (2) an **economic performance test** with respect to the liability.[48] While the all-events test for recognizing deductions is similar to the all-events test for recognizing income, the additional economic performance requirement makes the deduction recognition rules more stringent than the income recognition rules. The deduction rules generally preclude businesses from deducting estimated expenses or reserves.

All-Events Test for Deductions For a business to recognize a deduction, all events that establish its liability giving rise to the deduction must have occurred, and it must be able to determine the amount of the liability with reasonable accuracy.[49]

Example 1-19

On November of this year, Rick agreed to a one-year $6,000 contract with Ace Advertising to produce a radio ad campaign. Ace agreed that Rick would owe nothing under the contract unless his sales increase a minimum of 25 percent over the next six months. What amount, if any, may Rick deduct this year for this contract under the accrual and cash methods?

Answer: Under the accrual method, Green Acres is not allowed to recognize *any* deduction this year for the liability. Even though Ace will have completed two months of advertising for Green Acres by the end of the year, its guarantee means that Rick's liability is not fixed until and unless his sales increase by 25 percent. Under the cash method, Rick would not deduct any of the cost of the campaign this year because he has not paid anything to Ace.

Economic Performance Even when businesses meet the all-events test, they still must clear the economic performance hurdle to recognize the tax deduction. Congress added the economic performance requirement because in some situations taxpayers claimed current deductions and delayed paying the associated cash expenditures for years. Thus, the delayed payment reduced the real (present value) cost of the deduction. This requirement specifies that businesses may not recognize a deduction for an expense until the underlying activity generating the associated liability has occurred. Thus, an accrual-method business would not be allowed to deduct a prepaid business expense even if it qualified to do so under the 12-month rule (discussed above) unless it also met the economic performance test with respect to the liability associated with the expense.

The specific requirements for the economic performance test differ based on whether the liability arose from

- Receiving goods or services *from* another party.
- Use of property.
- Providing goods or services *to* another party.
- Certain activities creating **payment liabilities.**

THE KEY FACTS

Accrual of Business-Expense Deductions

- Both all-events and economic performance are required for deducting accrued business expenses.
- The all-events test requires that the business be liable for the payment.
- Economic performance generally requires that underlying activity generating liability has occurred in order for the associated expense to be deductible.

[48]§461(h).
[49]§461.

Receiving goods and (or) services from another party. When a business agrees to pay another party for goods or services the other party will provide, the business deducts the expense associated with the liability as the other party provides the goods or services (assuming the all-events test is met for the liability). An exception to this general rule occurs when a business hires another party to provide goods or services, and the business actually *pays* the liability before the other party provides the goods or services. In this circumstance, the business may treat the *actual payment* as economic performance as long as it *reasonably expects* the other party to provide the goods or all of the services within three and one-half months after the payment.[50]

Example 1-20

On December 15, 2015, Rick hires Your New Fence LLC (YNF) to install a concrete wall for one of his clients by paying $1,000 of the cost as a down payment and agreeing to pay the remaining $7,000 when YNF finishes the wall. YNF was not going to start building the wall until early 2016, so as of the end of the year Rick has not billed his client for the wall. Rick expects YNF to finish the wall by the end of April. What amount associated with his liability to YNF is Rick allowed to deduct in 2015 and 2016?

Answer: Under the accrual method, Rick is not entitled to a deduction in 2015. Rick will deduct his full $8,000 cost of the wall in 2016 when YNF builds the wall, because economic performance occurs as YNF provides the services, even though Rick paid for part of the goods and services in 2015. Under the cash method, Rick would deduct $1,000 (his down payment) in 2015 and the remainder in 2016 when he pays the remainder on the contract.

What if: Assume that Rick expected YNF to finish building the wall by the end of January 2016. What amount associated with this liability to YNF is Rick allowed to deduct in 2015 and 2016?

Answer: Under the accrual method, Rick is allowed to deduct $1,000 in 2015 because Rick actually paid this amount in 2015 and he reasonably expected YNF to finish its work on the wall within 3½ months after he made the payment to YNF on December 15. Rick would deduct the remaining $7,000 cost of the wall in 2016 when YNF builds the wall. Under the cash method, Rick deducts the $1,000 down payment in 2015 and the remaining $7,000 when he makes the payment in 2016.

Renting or leasing property from another party. When a business enters into an agreement to rent or lease property from another party, economic performance occurs over the rental period. Thus, the business is allowed to deduct the rental expense over the lease.

Example 1-21

On May 1, 2015, Rick paid $7,200 in advance to rent his shop for 12 months ($600 per month). What amount may Rick deduct for rent in 2015 if he accounts for his business activities using the accrual method?

Answer: $4,800 ($600 × 8 months use). Even though the rent is a prepaid business expense under the 12-month rule (the contract period is for 12 months and the contract period does not extend beyond 2016), he must deduct the rent expense over the term of the lease because that is when economic performance occurs.

What if: Assuming the original facts, what amount of the $7,200 rental payment may Rick deduct in 2015 if he is using the cash method of accounting for his business?

Answer: $7,200. In this case, Rick may deduct the expense under the 12-month rule. He does not have to meet the economic performance requirement to deduct the expense because the economic performance requirements apply to accrual—not cash-method taxpayers.

[50]Reg. §1.461-4(d)(6).

Example 1-22

On November 1, 2015, Rick paid $2,400 to rent a trailer for 24 months. What amount of this payment may Rick deduct and when may he deduct it?

Answer: Under the accrual method, even though Rick paid the entire rental fee in advance, economic performance occurs over the 24-month rental period. Thus, Green Acres deducts $200 for the trailer rental in 2015, $1,200 in 2016, and $1,000 in 2017. Because the rental period exceeds 12 months, the amount and timing of the deductions are the same under the cash method.

Providing goods and services to another party. Businesses liable for providing goods and services to other parties meet the economic performance test as they provide the goods or services that satisfy the liability.

Example 1-23

In the summer, Rick landscaped a city park. As part of this service, Rick agreed to remove a fountain from the park at the option of the city parks committee. In December 2015, the committee decided to have Rick remove the fountain. Rick began the removal in December and completed the removal in the spring of 2016. Rick paid a part-time employee $850 for the removal work in December and an additional $685 to complete the removal the following spring. What is the amount and timing of Rick's deductions for the removal project?

Answer: Under the accrual method, Rick is allowed to deduct his costs as he provides the services. Consequently, in 2015 Rick can deduct $850 for the cost of the services provided by his employee in 2015. In 2016, Rick can deduct the remaining $685 cost of the services provided by his employee in 2016. Under the cash method, the amount and timing of his deductions would be the same as it is under the accrual method.

Payment liabilities. Economic performance occurs for certain liabilities only when the business actually *pays* the liability. Thus, accrual-method businesses incurring payment liabilities are essentially on the *cash method* for deducting the associated expenses. Exhibit 1-3 describes different categories of these payment liabilities.

EXHIBIT 1-3 Categories of Payment Liabilities

Economic performance occurs when taxpayer pays liability associated with:

- Worker's compensation, tort, breach of contract, or violation of law.
- Rebates and refunds.
- Awards, prizes, and jackpots.
- Insurance, warranties, and service contracts provided *to* the business. (Note: This is insurance, warranties, and product service contracts that cover the taxpayer and *not* a warranty that the taxpayer provides to others.)
- Taxes.[51]
- Other liabilities not provided for elsewhere.

Recurring item exception. One of the most common exceptions to economic performance is the **recurring item** exception. This exception is designed to minimize the cost of applying economic performance to relatively small expenses that occur on a regular basis. Under §461(h)(3), accrual method taxpayers can deduct certain accrued

[51]While taxes are generally not deducted until they are paid, §461(c) allows businesses to elect to accrue the deduction for real property taxes ratably over the tax period instead of deducting them when they actually pay them.

expenses even if economic performance has not occurred by year-end. A recurring item is a liability that is expected to persist in future years, and is either not material in amount or deducting the expense currently matches with revenue. In addition, the all-events test must be satisfied at year-end and actual economic performance must occur within a reasonable time after year-end (but prior to the filing of the tax return which could be up to 8½ months with an extension). As a final note, the recurring item exception does not apply to worker's compensation or tort liabilities.

Example 1-24

If clients are not completely satisfied with Green Acres's landscaping work, Rick offers a $200 refund with no questions asked. Near the end of the year, Rick had four clients request refunds. Rick incurred the liability for the refunds this year. However, Rick was busy during the holiday season, so he didn't pay the refunds until January 2016. When should Rick deduct the customer refunds?

Answer: Because refunds are payment liabilities, economic performance does not occur until Rick actually pays the refunds. Consequently, Rick deducts the $800 of refunds in 2016 even though the liability for the refunds met the all-events test in 2015. Under the cash method, Rick would not deduct the refunds until he paid them in 2016.

What if: Suppose that Rick expected that $800 of refunds would typically be accrued at year-end. Under what conditions could Rick deduct the refunds in 2015 if he elects to use accrual accounting?

Answer: If the accrued refunds are not material in amount and Rick expects actual economic performance within a reasonable time after year-end (but not longer than 8½ months or filing of the tax return), then Rick can elect to deduct the refunds in 2015 using the recurring item exception.

Accrual-method taxpayers that prepay business expenses for *payment liabilities* (insurance contracts, warranties, and product service contracts provided to the taxpayer) are allowed to immediately deduct the prepayments subject to the 12-month rule for prepaid expenses. Thus, the deductible amounts for Rick's prepaid insurance contracts in Example 1-14 are the same for both the cash method and accrual method of accounting. Exhibit 1-4 describes the requirements for economic performance for the different types of liabilities.

EXHIBIT 1-4 Economic Performance

Taxpayer incurs liability from	Economic performance occurs
Receiving goods and services *from* another party	When the goods or services are provided to the taxpayer or with payment if the taxpayer reasonably expects actual performance within 3½ months.
Renting or leasing property *from* another party	Ratably over the time period during which the taxpayer is entitled to use the property or money.
Providing goods and services *to* another party	When the taxpayer incurs costs to satisfy the liability or provide the goods and services.
Activities creating "payment" liabilities	When the business actually makes payment.
Interest expense	As accrued. This technically does not fall within the economic performance rules but it is a similar concept.

Bad Debt Expense When accrual method businesses sell a product or a service on credit, they debit accounts receivable and credit sales revenue for both financial and tax purposes. However, because businesses usually are unable to collect the full amount of their accounts receivable, they incur bad debt expense (a customer owes them a debt that the customer will not pay). For financial reporting purposes, the business estimates the amount of the bad debt, debits bad debt expense, and credits an allowance for doubtful accounts. However, for tax purposes, businesses are allowed to deduct bad debt expense only when the debt actually becomes worthless within the taxable year.[52] Consequently, for tax purposes, businesses determine which debts are uncollectible and write them off by debiting bad debt expense and *directly* crediting the actual account receivable account that is uncollectible. This required method of determining bad debt expense for tax purposes is called the **direct write-off method.** In contrast, the method used for financial reporting purposes is called the **allowance method.** Businesses reporting taxable income on the cash method of accounting are *not* allowed to deduct bad debt expenses, because they do not include receivables in taxable income (they do not credit revenue until they actually receive payment).

Example 1-25

At year-end, Rick estimates that about $900 of the receivables from his landscaping services will be uncollectible, but he has identified only one client, Jared, who will definitely not pay his bill. Jared, who has skipped town, owes Rick $280 for landscaping this fall. What amount of bad debt expense may Rick deduct for the year?

Answer: For financial reporting purposes, Rick recognizes a $900 bad debt expense. However, for tax purposes, under the accrual method, Rick can only deduct $280—the amount associated with specifically writing off Jared's receivable. Under the cash method, Rick would not be able to claim any deduction, because he did not receive a payment from Jared and thus did not recognize income on the amount Jared owed him.

Limitations on Accruals to Related Parties To prevent businesses and related parties from working together to defer taxes, the tax laws prevent an accrual-method business from accruing (and deducting) an expense for a liability owed to a related party using the cash method until the related party recognizes the income associated with the payment.[53] For this purpose, related parties include

- Family members including parents, siblings, and spouses.
- Shareholders and C corporations when the shareholder owns more than 50 percent of the corporation's stock.[54]
- Owners of partnerships and S corporations no matter the ownership percentage.[55]

This issue frequently arises in situations in which a business employs the owner or a relative of an owner. The business is not allowed to deduct compensation expense owed to the related party until the year in which the related party includes the compensation in income. However, this related-party limit extends beyond compensation to *any* accrued expense the business owes to a related cash-method taxpayer.

Example 1-26

In December, Rick asked his retired father, Henry, to help him finish a landscaping job. By the end of the year, Rick owed Henry $2,000 of (reasonable) compensation for his efforts, which he paid in January 2016. What amount of this compensation may Rick deduct and when may he deduct it?

Answer: If Rick uses the accrual method and Henry the cash method, Rick will not be able to deduct the $2,000 compensation expense until 2016. Rick is Henry's son, so Rick and Henry are "related" parties for tax purposes. Consequently, Rick can deduct the compensation only when Henry includes the payment in his taxable income in 2016. If Rick uses the cash method, he will deduct the expense when he pays it in January 2016.

[52]§166(a).

[53]§267(a).

[54]Certain constructive ownership rules apply in determining ownership percentages for this purpose. See §267(c).

[55]See §267(b) for related-party definitions.

Comparison of Accrual and Cash Methods

From a business perspective, the two primary advantages of adopting the cash method over the accrual method are that (1) the cash method provides the business with more flexibility to time income and deductions by accelerating or deferring payments (timing tax planning strategy) and (2) bookkeeping for the cash method is easier. For example, a cash-method taxpayer could defer revenue by waiting to bill clients for goods or services until after year-end, thereby increasing the likelihood that customers would send payment after year-end. There are some concerns with this tax strategy. For example, delaying the bills might increase the likelihood that the customers will not pay their bills at all.

The primary advantage of the accrual method over the cash method is that it better matches revenues and expenses. For that reason, external financial statement users who want to evaluate a business's financial performance prefer the accrual method. Consistent with this idea, the cash method is not allowed for financial reporting under GAAP.

Although the cash method is by far the predominate accounting method among sole proprietors, it is less common in other types of businesses. In fact, tax laws generally prohibit C corporations and partnerships with corporate partners from using the cash method of accounting.[56] Exhibit 1-5 details the basic differences in accounting for income and deductions under the accrual and the cash method of accounting.

EXHIBIT 1-5 Comparison of Cash and Accrual Methods

Income or Expense Item	Cash Method	Accrual Method
Income recognition	Actually or constructively received.	Taxable once the all-events test is satisfied.
Unearned rental and interest income	Taxable on receipt.	Taxable on receipt.
Advance payment for services	Taxable on receipt.	Taxed when received or under the deferral method in the following year of receipt if not earned by end of year of receipt.
Advance payment for goods	Taxable on receipt.	Full-inclusion is taxed on receipt but deferral election allows taxation when earned.
Deduction recognition	Deduct when paid; economic performance does not apply.	Deduct once all-events test and economic performance test are both satisfied.
Expenditures for tangible assets with a useful life more than one year	Capitalize and apply cost recovery.	Same as the cash method.
Expenditures for intangible assets other than prepaid business expenses	Capitalize and amortize if provision in code allows it.	Same as the cash method.
Prepaid business expenses	Immediately deductible unless contract period exceeds 12 months or extends beyond the end of the next taxable year.	Same as cash method for payment liabilities; otherwise, apply all-events and economic performance tests to ascertain when to capitalize and amortize.
Prepaid interest expense	Not deductible until interest accrues.	Same as the cash method.
Bad debt expense	Not deductible because sales on account not included in income.	Deduct under direct write-off method.

[56]These entities are able to adopt the cash method if their average annual gross receipts for the three tax years ending with the prior tax year do not exceed $5 million (see §448).

Example 1-27

At year-end, Rick determined that Green Acres had collected a total of $71,000 of service revenue (not described elsewhere in examples). Rick is debating whether to adopt the cash or accrual method. To help him resolve his dilemma, Jane includes these revenues in a calculation of Green Acres's taxable income under the cash and accrual methods (Exhibit 1-6). What are the differences between the two calculations?

Answer: Jane provided the following summary of the differences between taxable income under the cash method and taxable income under the accrual method:

Description	(1) Cash	(2) Accrual	(1) − (2) Difference	Example
Revenue:				
Credit sales	0	11,000	−11,000	8-15
Prepaid revenue	7,200	300	+6,900	8-16
Expenses:				
Prepaid services	−1,000	0	−1,000	8-20
Prepaid rent expense	−7,200	−4,800	−2,400	8-21
Bad debts	0	−280	+280	8-25
Total difference (accrual income > cash income)			**−7,220**	

Jane explains that by comparing the revenue and expenses recognized under the two accounting methods, the selection of the accrual method for Green Acres means that Rick will be taxed on an additional $7,220 of income this year than if Green Acres adopts the cash method.

The business income for Green Acres under the accrual and cash methods is summarized in Exhibit 1-6. After reflecting on these numbers and realizing that he would recognize $7,220 more taxable income (and self-employment income subject to self-employment tax) this year under the accrual method than under the cash method, Rick determined it made sense to adopt the cash method of accounting for Green Acres's first tax return. Meanwhile, he knew he had to include Green Acres's business income on Schedule C of his individual tax return. Exhibit 1-7 presents Rick's Schedule C for Green Acres using the cash method of accounting.

Adopting an Accounting Method

We've seen that businesses use overall accounting methods (cash, accrual, or hybrid) and many specific accounting methods (inventory cost-flow assumption, methods of accounting for prepaid income for goods, and methods for accounting for prepaid expenses, among other methods) to account for their business activities. For tax purposes, it's important to understand how and when a business technically *adopts* an accounting method because once it does so, it must get the IRS's permission to change the method.

Businesses generally elect their accounting methods by using them on their tax returns. However, *when* the business technically adopts a method depends on whether it is a **permissible accounting method** or an **impermissible accounting method.** So far, our discussion has emphasized accounting methods permissible under the tax laws. A business adopts a permissible accounting method by using and reporting the tax results of the method for at least one year. However, businesses may

EXHIBIT 1-6 Green Acres's Net Business Income

Description	Cash	Accrual	Example
Income			
Service revenue:			
Greenhouse construction	$ 5,000	$ 5,000	8-10
December landscape service	0	11,000	8-15
Prepaid landscape services	7,200	300	8-16
Landscaping revenue	71,000	71,000	8-27
Sales of inventory:			
Tree sales	14,000	14,000	8-18
Cost of goods sold (LIFO method)	−7,150	−7,150	8-18
Gross Profit	**$90,050**	**$94,150**	
Car and truck expense:			
SUV operating expense	$ 5,335	$ 5,335	8-7
BMW operating expense	306	306	8-9
Insurance	1,200	1,200	8-14
Rent			
Shop	7,200	4,800	8-21
Trailer	200	200	8-22
Travel, meals, and entertainment:			
Travel to NY seminar	1,435	1,435	8-8
Dinner and theater with client	270	270	8-6
Wages and subcontractor fees:			
Part-time employees	23,000	23,000	8-2
Full time employee (Ken)	30,000	30,000	8-17
Fountain removal (part-time employee)	850	850	8-23
Fence installation (prepaid subcontractor)	1,000	0	8-20
Other expenses:			
Education—meditation class	50	50	8-1
Education—seminar	300	300	8-8
Domestic production activities deduction	90	90	8-10
Uniforms	500	500	8-5
Bad debts	0	280	8-25
Other expenses not in examples:			
Advertising	1,100	1,200	
Depreciation	4,000	4,000	
Interest	300	300	
Legal and professional services	1,100	1,100	
Office expense	1,500	1,500	
Repairs and maintenance	1,975	1,975	
Taxes and licenses	400	400	
Utilities	2,200	2,200	
Total deductions	**$84,311**	**$81,191**	
Net Business Income	**$ 5,739**	**$12,959**	

unwittingly (or intentionally) use impermissible accounting methods. For example, a business using the allowance method for determining bad debt expense for tax purposes is using an impermissible accounting method because the tax laws prescribe the use of the direct write-off method for determining bad debt expense. A business *adopts* an *impermissible* method by using and reporting the results of the method for *two consecutive years*.

EXHIBIT 1-7 Green Acres Schedule C

SCHEDULE C (Form 1040)
Department of the Treasury Internal Revenue Service (99)

Profit or Loss From Business
(Sole Proprietorship)

▶ Information about Schedule C and its separate instructions is at *www.irs.gov/schedulec.*
▶ Attach to Form 1040, 1040NR, or 1041; partnerships generally must file Form 1065.

OMB No. 1545-0074
2014
Attachment Sequence No. **09**

Name of proprietor: RICK GRIME — Social security number (SSN): 000-00-0000

A Principal business or profession, including product or service (see instructions): LANDSCAPER
B Enter code from instructions ▶ 5 7 1 6 3 0

C Business name. If no separate business name, leave blank.: GREEN ACRES LANDSCAPING
D Employer ID number (EIN), (see instr.): 4 6 0 0 0 0 0 0 0

E Business address (including suite or room no.) ▶ BUCKSNORT STREET
City, town or post office, state, and ZIP code: SAN ANTONIO, TEXAS 78208

F Accounting method: **(1)** ☑ Cash **(2)** ☐ Accrual **(3)** ☐ Other (specify) ▶

G Did you "materially participate" in the operation of this business during 2014? If "No," see instructions for limit on losses ☑ Yes ☐ No

H If you started or acquired this business during 2014, check here ▶ ☑

I Did you make any payments in 2014 that would require you to file Form(s) 1099? (see instructions) ☐ Yes ☑ No

J If "Yes," did you or will you file required Forms 1099? ☐ Yes ☐ No

Part I Income

1	Gross receipts or sales. See instructions for line 1 and check the box if this income was reported to you on Form W-2 and the "Statutory employee" box on that form was checked ▶ ☐	1	97,200
2	Returns and allowances	2	
3	Subtract line 2 from line 1	3	
4	Cost of goods sold (from line 42)	4	7,150
5	**Gross profit.** Subtract line 4 from line 3	5	90,050
6	Other income, including federal and state gasoline or fuel tax credit or refund (see instructions)	6	
7	**Gross income.** Add lines 5 and 6 ▶	7	90,050

Part II Expenses. Enter expenses for business use of your home **only** on line 30.

8	Advertising	8	1,100	18	Office expense (see instructions)	18	1,500
9	Car and truck expenses (see instructions)	9	5,641	19	Pension and profit-sharing plans	19	
10	Commissions and fees	10		20	Rent or lease (see instructions):		
11	Contract labor (see instructions)	11	1,000	a	Vehicles, machinery, and equipment	20a	7,400
12	Depletion	12		b	Other business property	20b	
13	Depreciation and section 179 expense deduction (not included in Part III) (see instructions)	13	4,000	21	Repairs and maintenance	21	1,975
				22	Supplies (not included in Part III)	22	
				23	Taxes and licenses	23	400
				24	Travel, meals, and entertainment:		
14	Employee benefit programs (other than on line 19)	14		a	Travel	24a	1,435
15	Insurance (other than health)	15	1,200	b	Deductible meals and entertainment (see instructions)	24b	270
16	Interest:			25	Utilities	25	2,200
a	Mortgage (paid to banks, etc.)	16a	300	26	Wages (less employment credits)	26	58,850
b	Other	16b		27a	Other expenses (from line 48)	27a	940
17	Legal and professional services	17	1,100	b	**Reserved for future use**	27b	

28	**Total expenses** before expenses for business use of home. Add lines 8 through 27a ▶	28	84,311
29	Tentative profit or (loss). Subtract line 28 from line 7	29	5,739
30	Expenses for business use of your home. Do not report these expenses elsewhere. Attach Form 8829 unless using the simplified method (see instructions). **Simplified method filers only:** enter the total square footage of: (a) your home: ____ and (b) the part of your home used for business: ____. Use the Simplified Method Worksheet in the instructions to figure the amount to enter on line 30	30	
31	**Net profit or (loss).** Subtract line 30 from line 29. • If a profit, enter on both **Form 1040, line 12** (or **Form 1040NR, line 13**) and on **Schedule SE, line 2**. (If you checked the box on line 1, see instructions). Estates and trusts, enter on **Form 1041, line 3.** • If a loss, you **must** go to line 32.	31	5,739

32 If you have a loss, check the box that describes your investment in this activity (see instructions).
- If you checked 32a, enter the loss on both **Form 1040, line 12,** (or **Form 1040NR, line 13**) and on **Schedule SE, line 2.** (If you checked the box on line 1, see the line 31 instructions). Estates and trusts, enter on **Form 1041, line 3.**
- If you checked 32b, you **must** attach **Form 6198.** Your loss may be limited.

32a ☑ All investment is at risk.
32b ☐ Some investment is not at risk.

For Paperwork Reduction Act Notice, see the separate instructions. Cat. No. 11334P **Schedule C (Form 1040) 2014**

Changing Accounting Methods

Once a business has adopted an accounting method, it must receive permission to change the method, regardless of whether it is a permissible or an impermissible method. A taxpayer requests permission to change accounting methods by filing Form 3115 with the IRS. The IRS automatically approves certain types of accounting method changes, but for others the business must provide a good business purpose for the change and pay a fee. The IRS also requires permission when a business must change from using an impermissible method; this requirement helps the IRS to certify that the business properly makes the transition to a permissible method. In essence, the IRS requires the business to report its own noncompliance. Why would a business do so? Besides complying with the tax laws, a business might report its own noncompliance to receive leniency from the IRS. Without getting into the details, the IRS is likely to assess fewer penalties and less interest expense for noncompliance when the business reports the noncompliance before the IRS discovers it on its own.

Tax Consequences of Changing Accounting Method When a business changes from one accounting method to another, the business determines its taxable income for the year of change using the new method. Furthermore, the business must make an adjustment to taxable income that effectively represents the *cumulative difference,* as of the beginning of the tax year, between the amount of income (or deductions) recognized under the old accounting method and the amount that would have been recognized for all prior years if the new method had been applied. This adjustment is called a **§481 adjustment.** The §481 adjustment prevents the duplication or omission of items of income or deduction due to a change in accounting method. If the §481 adjustment *increases* taxable income, the taxpayer recognizes it over *four years* beginning with the year of the change (25 percent of the full adjustment each year). If the adjustment *decreases* taxable income, the taxpayer recognizes it *entirely in the year of change.*

Example 1-28

What if: Suppose that at the end of 2015, Green Acres has $24,000 of accounts receivable. Assuming Green Acres uses the cash method of accounting in 2015, it would not include the $24,000 of receivables in income in determining its 2015 taxable income. Suppose further that Rick decides to switch Green Acres to the accrual method of accounting in 2016 by filing a Form 3115 and receiving permission from the IRS. What is Rick's §481 adjustment for his change in accounting method from the cash to the accrual method?

Answer: $24,000 increase to income ($6,000 in 2016 and each of the subsequent three years). Since Rick would use the accrual method in 2016, he would *not* include payments he receives for the $24,000 receivables as income because he earned this income in 2015 (not 2016). Instead, Rick would be required to make a §481 adjustment to ensure that he does not *omit* these items from taxable income. His total §481 adjustment is to increase net income by $24,000. Because this is an income-increasing adjustment, Rick includes $6,000 of the adjustment (25 percent) in Green Acres's taxable income in 2016. He would likewise include a $6,000 §481 adjustment in each of the subsequent three years.

What if: Suppose that at the end of 2015, Green Acres has $4,000 of accounts payable instead of $24,000 of accounts receivable. What is Rick's §481 adjustment for his change in accounting method from the cash to the accrual method?

Answer: In this instance Green Acres would have a negative (income-decreasing) §481 adjustment of $4,000 because the $4,000 of expenses would have accrued in 2015 but would not have been deducted. Hence, Green Acres would be entitled to deduct the full $4,000 as a negative §481 adjustment amount in 2016.

CONCLUSION

This chapter discussed issues relating to business income and deductions. We learned that the income rules for businesses are very similar to those for individuals, and that businesses may deduct only ordinary and necessary business expenses and other business expenses specifically authorized by law. We also described several business expense limitations and discussed the accounting periods and methods businesses may use in reporting taxable income to the IRS. The issues described in this chapter are widely applicable to all types of business entities including sole proprietorships, partnerships, S corporations, and C corporations. In the next chapter, we determine how businesses recover the costs of assets they use in their business activities.

Summary

LO 1-1 Describe the general requirements for deducting business expenses and identify common business deductions.

- Ordinary and necessary business expenses are allowed as deductions to calculate net income from activities entered into with a profit motive.
- Only reasonable amounts are allowed as business expense deductions. Extravagant or excessive amounts are likely to be characterized by personal motives and are disallowed.

LO 1-2 Apply the limitations on business deductions to distinguish between deductible and nondeductible business expenses.

- The law specifically prohibits deducting expenses against public policy (such as fines or bribes) and expenses that produce tax-exempt income.
- Expenses benefiting multiple periods must be capitalized and special limits and record-keeping requirements are applied to business expenses that may have personal benefits, such as entertainment and meals.

LO 1-3 Identify and explain special business deductions specifically permitted under the tax laws.

- Special calculations are necessary for deductions such as bad debt expenses, the domestic production activities deduction, and casualty losses.

LO 1-4 Explain the concept of an accounting period and describe accounting periods available to businesses.

- Accounting periods and methods are chosen at the time of filing the first tax return.
- There are three types of tax years, calendar year, fiscal year, and 52/53-week year, and each tax year is distinguished by year-end.

LO 1-5 Identify and describe accounting methods available to businesses and apply cash and accrual methods to determine business income and expense deductions.

- Under the cash method, taxpayers recognize revenue when they actually or constructively receive property or services and recognize deductions when they actually pay the expense.
- Under the accrual method, the all-events test requires that income be recognized when all the events have occurred that are necessary to fix the right to receive payments and the amount of the payments can be determined with reasonable accuracy.
- The accrual method must be used to account for sales and purchases for businesses where inventories are an income-producing factor.
- Under the accrual method, accrued expenses can only be deducted once both the all-events test and the economic performance tests are met. The application of the economic performance test depends, in part, on the type of business expense.
- Changes in accounting method or accounting period typically require the consent of the IRS and a §481 adjustment to taxable income.

KEY TERMS

12-month rule (1-17)
accounting method (1-16)
accounting period (1-15)
all-events test (1-24)
allowance method (1-28)
arm's length amount (1-4)
casualty losses (1-14)
deferral method (1-20)
direct write-off method (1-28)
domestic production activities deduction (DPAD) (1-12)
economic performance test (1-24)
FIFO (1-22)
fiscal year (1-15)
flow-through entities (1-16)
full-inclusion method (1-20)
impermissible accounting method (1-30)
LIFO (1-22)
mixed-motive expenditures (1-8)
ordinary and necessary (1-3)
payment liabilities (1-24)
permissible accounting method (1-30)
personal expenses (1-7)
qualified production activities income (QPAI) (1-12)
reasonable in amount (1-4)
recurring item (1-26)
§481 adjustment (1-33)
specific identification (1-22)
tax year (1-15)
travel expenses (1-9)
uniform cost capitalization rules (UNICAP rules) (1-21)

DISCUSSION QUESTIONS

1. What is an "ordinary and necessary" business expenditure? LO 1-1
2. Is cost of goods sold deductible as a business expense for a business selling inventory? Explain. LO 1-1
3. Tom is an attorney who often represents individuals injured while working (worker liability claims). This year Tom spent $50 on a book entitled *Plumbing for Dummies* and paid $500 to take a course on plumbing residences and rental housing. Can you imagine circumstances in which these expenditures would be deductible as "ordinary and necessary" for an attorney? Explain. LO 1-1
4. Jake is a professional dog trainer who purchases and trains dogs for use by law enforcement agencies. Last year Jake purchased 500 bags of dog food from a large pet food company at an average cost of $30 per bag. This year, however, Jake purchased 500 bags of dog food from a local pet food company at an average cost of $45 per bag. Under what circumstances would the IRS likely challenge the cost of Jake's dog food as unreasonable? LO 1-1
5. What kinds of deductions are prohibited as a matter of public policy? Why might Congress deem it important to disallow deductions for expenditures against public policy? LO 1-2
6. Provide an example of an expense associated with the production of tax-exempt income, and explain what might happen if Congress repealed the prohibition against deducting expenses incurred to produce tax-exempt income. LO 1-2
7. Jerry is a self-employed rock star and this year he expended $1,000 on special "flashy" clothes and outfits. Jerry would like to deduct the cost of these clothes as work-related because the clothes are not acceptable to Jerry's sense of fashion. Under what circumstances can Jerry deduct the cost of these work clothes? LO 1-2 research
8. Jimmy is a sole proprietor of a small dry cleaning business. This month Jimmy paid for his groceries by writing checks from the checking account dedicated to the dry cleaning business. Why do you suppose Jimmy is using his business checking account rather than his personal checking account to pay for personal expenditures? LO 1-2
9. Tim employs three sales representatives who often take clients to dinner and provide entertainment in order to increase sales. This year Tim reimbursed the representatives $2,500 for the cost of meals and $8,250 for the cost of LO 1-2

entertaining clients. Describe the conditions under which Tim can claim deductions for meals and entertainment.

LO 1-2 10. Jenny uses her car for both business and personal purposes. She purchased the auto this year and drove 11,000 miles on business trips and 9,000 miles for personal transportation. Describe how Jenny will determine the amount of deductible expenses associated with the auto.

LO 1-1 LO 1-2 11. What expenses are deductible when a taxpayer combines both business and personal activities on a trip? How do the rules for international travel differ from the rules for domestic travel?

LO 1-2 12. Clyde lives and operates a sole proprietorship in Dallas, Texas. This year Clyde found it necessary to travel to Fort Worth (about 25 miles away) for legitimate business reasons. Is Clyde's trip likely to qualify as "away from home," and why would this designation matter?

LO 1-2 13. Describe the record-keeping requirements for business deductions expenses including mixed-motive expenditures.

LO 1-3 14. Explain why the domestic production activities deduction is sometimes described as an "artificial" expense and the apparent rationale for this deduction. How might a business begin to determine the domestic portion of revenues and expenses for products that are assembled in the United States from parts made overseas?

LO 1-3 15. Describe the calculation of the domestic production activities deduction.

LO 1-3 16. Describe the limits placed on the domestic production activities deduction, and explain the apparent reason for each limitation.

LO 1-3 17. Explain the difference between calculating a loss deduction for a business asset that was partially damaged in an accident and a loss deduction for a business asset that was stolen or completely destroyed in an accident.

LO 1-3 18. How do casualty loss deductions differ when a business asset is completely destroyed as opposed to the destruction of a personal-use asset?

LO 1-4 19. What is the difference between a full tax year and a short tax year? Describe circumstances in which a business may have a short tax year.

LO 1-4 20. Explain why a taxpayer might choose one tax year over another if given a choice.

LO 1-4 21. Compare and contrast the different year-ends available to sole proprietorships, flow-through entities, and C corporations.

LO 1-4 22. Why does the law generally require partnerships to adopt a tax year consistent with the year used by the partners?

LO 1-4 23. How does an entity choose its tax year? Is it the same process no matter the type of tax year-end the taxpayer adopts?

LO 1-5 24. Explain when an expenditure should be "capitalized" rather than expensed based upon accounting principles. From time to time, it is suggested that all business expenditures should be expensed for tax purposes. Do you agree with this proposition, and if so, why?

LO 1-5 25. Describe the 12-month rule for determining whether and to what extent businesses should capitalize or immediately deduct prepaid expenses such as insurance or security contracts. Explain the apparent rationale for this rule.

LO 1-5 26. Explain why Congress sometimes mandates that businesses use particular accounting methods while other times Congress is content to require businesses to use the same accounting methods for tax purposes that they use for financial accounting purposes.

LO 1-5 27. Why is it not surprising that specific rules differ between tax accounting and financial accounting?

28. Fred is considering using the accrual method for his next business venture. Explain to Fred the conditions for recognizing income for tax purposes under the accrual method. LO 1-5
29. Describe the all-events test for determining income and describe how to determine the date on which the all-events test has been met. LO 1-5
30. Compare and contrast the tax treatment for rental income received in advance and advance payments for services. LO 1-5
31. Compare and contrast the rules for determining the tax treatment of advance payments for services versus advance payments for goods. LO 1-5
32. Jack operates a plumbing business as a sole proprietorship on the cash method. Besides providing plumbing services, Jack also sells plumbing supplies to homeowners and other plumbers. The sales of plumbing supplies constitute less than $20,000 per year, and this is such a small portion of Jack's income that he does not keep physical inventories for the supplies. Describe the conditions in which Jack must account for sales and purchases of plumbing supplies on the accrual method. LO 1-5 research
33. Explain why Congress enacted the UNICAP rules and describe the burdens these rules place on taxpayers. LO 1-5
34. Compare and contrast financial accounting rules with the tax rules under UNICAP (§263A). Explain whether the UNICAP rules tend to accelerate or defer income relative to the financial accounting rules. LO 1-5
35. Compare and contrast the tests for accruing income and those for accruing deductions for tax purposes. LO 1-5
36. Compare and contrast when taxpayers are allowed to deduct amounts for warranties provided by others to the taxpayer and when taxpayers are allowed to deduct expenses associated with warranties they provide to others. LO 1-5
37. Describe when economic performance occurs for the following expenses: LO 1-5

    Worker's compensation

    Rebates and refunds

    Insurance, warranties, and service contracts provided *to* the business

    Taxes
38. On December 31 of the current year, a taxpayer prepays an advertising company to provide advertising services for the next 10 months. Using the 12-month rule and the economic performance rules, contrast when the taxpayer would be able to deduct the expenditure if the taxpayer uses the cash method of accounting versus if the taxpayer uses the accrual method of accounting. LO 1-5
39. Compare and contrast how bad debt expense is determined for financial accounting purposes and how the deduction for bad debts is determined for accrual-method taxpayers. How do cash-method taxpayers determine their bad debt expense for accounts receivable? LO 1-5
40. Describe the related-party limitation on accrued deductions. What tax savings strategy is this limitation designed to thwart? LO 1-5
41. What are the relative advantages of the cash and accrual methods of accounting? LO 1-5
42. Describe how a business adopts a permissible accounting method. Explain whether a taxpayer can adopt an impermissible accounting method. LO 1-5
43. Describe why the IRS might be skeptical of permitting requests for changes in accounting method without a good business purpose. LO 1-5
44. What is a §481 adjustment and what is its purpose? LO 1-5

PROBLEMS

All applicable problems are available with McGraw-Hill's *Connect® Accounting.*

LO 1-1

45. Manny hired his brother's firm to provide accounting services to his business. During the current year, Manny paid his brother's firm $82,000 for services even though other firms were willing to provide the same services for $40,000. How much of this expenditure, if any, is deductible as an ordinary and necessary business expenditure?

LO 1-1 LO 1-2

46. Indicate the amount (if any) that Michael can deduct as ordinary and necessary business deductions in each of the following situations and explain your solution.
    a) From time to time, Michael rents a dump truck for his business. While hauling gravel to a job site, Michael was stopped for speeding. He paid a fine of $125 for speeding and a fine of $80 for carrying an overweight load.
    b) Michael paid a part-time employee $750 to drive his rented dump truck. Michael reimbursed the employee $35 for gasoline for the truck.
    c) Michael gave a member of the city council a new watch, which cost $200. He hopes that the city councilman will "throw" some contracts to his business.

LO 1-1 LO 1-2

47. Indicate the amount (if any) that Josh can deduct as ordinary and necessary business deductions in each of the following situations and explain your solution.
    a) Josh borrowed $50,000 from the First State Bank using his business assets as collateral. He used the money to buy City of Blanksville bonds. Over the course of a year, Josh paid interest of $4,200 on the borrowed funds, but he received $3,500 of interest on the bonds.
    b) Josh purchased a piece of land for $45,000 in order to get a location to expand his business. He also paid $3,200 to construct a new driveway for access to the property.
    c) This year Josh paid $15,000 to employ the mayor's son in the business. Josh would typically pay an employee with these responsibilities about $10,000 but the mayor assured Josh that after his son was hired, some city business would be coming his way.
    d) Josh paid his brother, a mechanic, $3,000 to install a robotic machine for Josh's business. The amount he paid to his brother is comparable to what he would have paid to an unrelated party to do the same work. Once the installation was completed by his brother, Josh began calibrating the machine for operation. However, by the end of the year, he had not started using the machine in his business.

LO 1-2

48. Ralph invited a potential client to dinner and the theater. Ralph paid $250 for the dinner and $220 for the theater tickets in advance. They first went to dinner and then they went to the theater.
    a) What amount can Ralph deduct if, prior to the dinner, he met with the potential client to discuss future business prospects?
    b) What amount can Ralph deduct if he and the client only discussed business during the course of the dinner?
    c) What amount can Ralph deduct if he and the potential client tried to discuss business during the course of the theater performance but did not discuss business at any other time?
    d) What amount can Ralph deduct if the potential client declined Ralph's invitation, so Ralph took his accountant to dinner and the theater to reward his accountant for a hard day at work? At dinner, they discussed the accountant's workload and upcoming assignments.

49. Melissa recently paid $400 for round-trip airfare to San Francisco to attend a business conference for three days. Melissa also paid the following expenses: $250 fee to register for the conference, $300 per night for three nights' lodging, $200 for meals, and $150 for cab fare. LO 1-2

a) What amount of the travel costs can Melissa deduct as business expenses?

b) Suppose that while Melissa was on the coast, she also spent two days sightseeing the national parks in the area. To do the sightseeing, she paid $1,000 for transportation, $800 for lodging, and $450 for meals during this part of her trip, which she considers personal in nature. What amount of the travel costs can Melissa deduct as business expenses?

c) Suppose that Melissa made the trip to San Francisco primarily to visit the national parks and only attended the business conference as an incidental benefit of being present on the coast at that time. What amount of the airfare can Melissa deduct as a business expense?

d) Suppose that Melissa's permanent residence and business was located in San Francisco. She attended the conference in San Francisco and paid $250 for the registration fee. She drove 100 miles over the course of three days and paid $90 for parking at the conference hotel. In addition, she spent $150 for breakfast and dinner over the three days of the conference. She bought breakfast on the way to the conference hotel and she bought dinner on her way home each night from the conference. What amount of the travel costs can Melissa deduct as business expenses?

50. Kimberly is a self-employed taxpayer. She recently spent $1,000 for airfare to travel to Italy. What amount of the airfare is deductible in each of the following alternative scenarios? LO 1-2

a) Her trip was entirely for personal purposes.

b) On the trip, she spent eight days on personal activities and two days on business activities.

c) On the trip, she spent seven days on business activities and three days on personal activities.

d) Her trip was entirely for business purposes.

51. Ryan is self-employed. This year Ryan used his personal auto for several long business trips. Ryan paid $1,500 for gasoline on these trips. His depreciation on the car if he was using it fully for business purposes would be $3,000. During the year, he drove his car a total of 12,000 miles (a combination of business and personal travel). LO 1-2

a) Ryan can provide written documentation of the business purpose for trips totaling 3,000 miles. What business expense amount can Ryan deduct (if any) for these trips?

b) Ryan estimates that he drove approximately 1,300 miles on business trips, but he can only provide written documentation of the business purpose for trips totaling 820 miles. What business expense amount can Ryan deduct (if any) for these trips?

52. Christopher is a cash-method, calendar-year taxpayer, and he made the following cash payments related to his business this year. Calculate the after-tax cost of each payment assuming he has a 30 percent marginal tax rate. LO 1-1 LO 1-2

a) $500 fine for speeding while traveling to a client meeting.

b) $240 of interest on a short-term loan incurred in September and repaid in November. Half of the loan proceeds were used immediately to pay salaries and the other half was invested in municipal bonds until November.

c) $600 for office supplies in May of this year. He used half of the supplies this year and he will use the remaining half by February of next year.

d) $450 for several pairs of work boots. Christopher expects to use the boots about 80 percent of the time in his business and the remainder of the time for hiking. Consider the boots to be a form of clothing.

LO 1-2 research

53. Heather paid $15,000 to join a country club in order to meet potential clients. This year she paid $4,300 in greens fees when golfing with clients. Under what circumstances, if any, can Heather deduct the $15,000 cost of country club dues and the costs of the golf played with clients?

LO 1-1 LO 1-2

54. Assume Sarah is a cash-method, calendar-year taxpayer, and she is considering making the following cash payments related to her business. Calculate the after-tax cost of each payment assuming she has a 25 percent marginal tax rate.

a) $2,000 payment for next year's property taxes on her place of business.

b) $800 to reimburse the cost of meals incurred by employees while traveling for the business.

c) $1,200 for football tickets to entertain out-of-town clients during contract negotiations.

d) $500 contribution to the mayor's re-election campaign.

LO 1-3

55. Renee manufactured and sold a "gadget," a specialized asset used by auto manufacturers that qualifies for the domestic production activities deduction. Renee incurred $15,000 in direct expenses in the project, which includes $2,000 of wages Renee paid to employees in the manufacturing of the gadget. What is Renee's domestic production activities deduction for the gadget in each of the following alternative scenarios?

a) Renee sold the gadget for $25,000 and she reported AGI of $75,000 before considering the manufacturing deduction.

b) Renee sold the gadget for $25,000 and she reported AGI of $5,000 before considering the manufacturing deduction.

c) Renee sold the gadget for $40,000 and she reported AGI of $50,000 before considering the manufacturing deduction.

LO 1-3 planning

56. Andrew is considering starting a business of constructing and selling prefabricated greenhouses. There are three very different methods to constructing these greenhouses, and each method results in different revenue and cost projections. Below, Andrew has projected the qualifying revenue and costs for each method. The selling price includes qualifying receipts. The allocable expenses include wages and allocable expenses are included in total costs.

Method	Selling Price	Qualifying Receipts	Total Cost	Allocable Expenses	Allocable Wages
#1	$13,000	$ 9,000	$6,500	$2,500	$2,000
#2	14,000	9,000	7,400	5,500	1,500
#3	15,000	14,000	8,600	2,000	1,000

a) Estimate the tax benefit from the domestic production activities deduction for each construction technique. You may assume that Andrew has sufficient AGI to utilize the deduction and that his marginal tax rate is 30 percent.

b) Which construction technique should Andrew use if his marginal tax rate is 30 percent?

57. This year Amy purchased $2,000 of equipment for use in her business. However, the machine was damaged in a traffic accident while Amy was transporting the equipment to her business. Note that because Amy did not place the equipment into service during the year, she does not claim any depreciation expense for the equipment. LO 1-3

a) After the accident, Amy had the choice of repairing the equipment for $1,800 or selling the equipment to a junk shop for $300. Amy sold the equipment. What amount can Amy deduct for the loss of the equipment?

b) After the accident, Amy repaired the equipment for $800. What amount can Amy deduct for the loss of the equipment?

c) After the accident, Amy could not replace the equipment so she had the equipment repaired for $2,300. What amount can Amy deduct for the loss of the equipment?

58. In July of this year, Stephen started a proprietorship called ECR (which stands for electric car repair). ECR uses the cash method of accounting and Stephen has produced the following financial information for this year. LO 1-3 tax forms

ECR collected $81,000 in cash for repairs completed during the year and an additional $3,200 in cash for repairs that will commence after year end. Customers owe ECR $14,300 for repairs completed this year, and while Stephen isn't sure which bills will eventually be paid, he expects to collect all but about $1,900 of these revenues next year.

ECR has made the following expenditures:

Interest expense	$ 1,250
Shop rent ($1,500 per month)	27,000
Utilities	1,075
Contract labor	8,250
Compensation	21,100
Liability insurance premiums ($350 per month)	4,200
Term life insurance premiums ($150 per month)	1,800

The interest paid relates to interest accrued on a $54,000 loan made to Stephen in July of this year. Stephen used half of the loan to pay for 18 months of shop rent, and the remainder he used to upgrade his personal wardrobe. In July, Stephen purchased 12 months of liability insurance to protect against liability should anyone be injured in the shop. ECR has only one employee (the remaining workers are contract labor), and this employee thoroughly understands how to repair an electric propulsion system. On November 1 of this year, Stephen purchased a 12-month term-life policy that insures the life of this "key" employee. Stephen paid Gecko Insurance Company $1,800; in return, Gecko promises to pay Stephen a $40,000 death benefit if this employee dies any time during the next 12 months.

Fill out a draft of the front page of Stephen's Schedule C.

59. Nicole is a calendar-year taxpayer who accounts for her business using the cash method. On average, Nicole sends out bills for about $12,000 of her services at the first of each month. The bills are due by the end of the month, and typically 70 percent of the bills are paid on time and 98 percent are paid within 60 days. LO 1-5

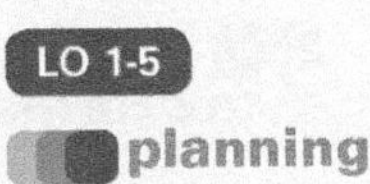

a) Suppose that Nicole is expecting a 2 percent reduction in her marginal tax rate next year. Ignoring the time value of money, estimate the tax savings for Nicole if she postpones mailing of bills for December until January 1 of next year.

b) Describe how the time value of money affects your calculations.

c) Would this tax savings strategy create any additional business risks? Explain.

LO 1-5

60. Jeremy is a calendar-year taxpayer who sometimes leases his business equipment to local organizations. He recorded the following receipts this year. Indicate the extent to which these payments are taxable income to Jeremy this year if Jeremy is (1) a cash-method taxpayer and (2) he is an accrual-method taxpayer.
    a) $1,000 deposit from the Ladies' Club, which wants to lease a trailer. The club will receive the entire deposit back when the trailer is returned undamaged.
    b) $800 from the Ladies' Club for leasing the trailer from December of this year through March of next year ($200 per month).
    c) $300 lease payment received from the Men's Club this year for renting Jeremy's trailer last year. Jeremy billed the club last year but recently he determined that the Men's Club would never pay him, so he was surprised when he received the check.

LO 1-5

61. Brown Thumb Landscaping is a calendar-year, accrual-method taxpayer. In September, Brown Thumb negotiated a $14,000 contract for services it would provide to the city in November of the current year. The contract specifies that Brown Thumb will receive $4,000 in October as a down payment for these services and it will receive the remaining $10,000 in January of next year.
    a) How much income from this $14,000 contract will Brown Thumb recognize in the current year? Explain.
    b) How much income from this $14,000 contract will Brown Thumb recognize in the current year if it uses the cash method of accounting?
    c) Suppose that the total amount to be paid under the contract with the city is estimated at $14,000 but may be adjusted to $12,000 next year during the review of the city budget. What amount from the contract, if any, should Brown Thumb recognize as income this year? Explain.
    d) Suppose that in addition to the basic contract, Brown Thumb will be paid an additional $3,000 if its city landscape design wins the annual design competition next year. Should Brown Thumb accrue $3,000 revenue this year? Why or why not?

LO 1-5

62. In January of year 0, Justin paid $4,800 for an insurance policy that covers his business property for accidents and casualties. Justin is a calendar-year taxpayer who uses the cash method of accounting. What amount of the insurance premium may Justin deduct in year 0 in each of the following alternative scenarios?
    a) The policy covers the business property from April 1 of year 0 through March 31 of year 1.
    b) The policy begins on February 1 of year 1 and extends through January 31 of year 2.
    c) Assume Justin paid $6,000 for a 24-month policy that covers from April 1, year 0 through March 31, year 2.
    d) Assume that instead of paying an insurance premium, Justin paid $4,800 to rent his business property from April 1 of year 0 through March 31 of year 1.

LO 1-5

tax forms

63. Ben teaches golf lessons at a country club under a business called Ben's Pure Swings (BPS). He operates this business as a sole proprietorship on the accrual basis of accounting. Ben's trusty accountant, Brian, has produced the following accounting information for BPS:

    This year BPS billed clients for $86,700 and collected $61,000 in cash for golf lessons completed during the year. In addition, BPS collected an additional $14,500 in cash for lessons that will commence after year-end. Ben hopes to collect about half of the outstanding billings next year but the rest will likely be written off.

    Besides providing private golf lessons, BPS also contracted with the country club to staff the driving range. This year, BPS billed the country club $27,200 for the service. The club paid $17,000 of the amount but disputed the remainder. By year-end, the dispute had not been resolved, and while Ben believes he is entitled to the money, he has still not collected the remaining $10,200.

BPS has accrued the following expenses (explained below):

Advertising (in the clubhouse)	$13,150
Pro Golf Teachers Membership Fees	860
Supplies (golf tees, balls, etc.)	4,720
Club rental	6,800
Malpractice insurance	2,400
Accounting fees	8,820

The expenditures were all paid for this calendar year with several exceptions. First, Ben initiated his golfer's malpractice insurance on June 1 of this year. The $2,400 insurance bill covers the last six months of this calendar year and the first six months of next year. At year-end, Ben had only paid $600, but he has assured the insurance agent he would pay the remaining $1,800 early next year. Second, the amount paid for club rental ($100 per week) represents rental charges for the last 6 weeks of the previous year, for the 52 weeks in this calendar year, and the first 10 weeks of next year. Ben has also mentioned that BPS only pays for supplies that are used at the club. Although BPS could buy the supplies for half the cost elsewhere, Ben likes to "throw some business" to the golf pro shop because it is operated by his brother.

Fill out a draft of the front page of a Schedule C for BPS.

64. On April 1 of year 0 Stephanie received a $9,000 payment for full payment on a three-year service contract (under the contract Stephanie is obligated to provide advisory services for the next three years). LO 1-5
    a) What amount of income should Stephanie recognize in year 0 if she uses the accrual method of accounting (she recognized $2,250 for financial accounting purposes)?
    b) What amount of income will Stephanie recognize in year 1 if she uses the accrual method of accounting?
    c) What amount of income will Stephanie recognize in year 2 if she uses the accrual method of accounting?
    d) What amount of income will Stephanie recognize in year 0 if she recognizes $5,000 of income from the contract for financial statement purposes?

65. In October of year 0, Janine received a $6,000 payment from a client for 25 months of security services she will provide starting on November 1 of year 0. This amounts to $240 per month. LO 1-5
    a) When must Janine recognize the income from the $6,000 advance payment for services if she uses the cash method of accounting?
    b) When must Janine recognize the income from the $6,000 advance payment for services if she uses the accrual method of accounting?
    c) Suppose that instead of services, Janine received the payment for a security system (inventory) that she will deliver and install in year 2. When would Janine recognize the income from the advance payment for inventory sale if she uses the accrual method of accounting and she uses the deferral method for reporting income from advance payments? For financial accounting purposes, she reports the income when the inventory is delivered.
    d) Suppose that instead of services, Janine received the payment for the delivery of inventory to be delivered next year. When would Janine recognize the income from the advance payment for sale of goods if she uses the accrual method of accounting and she uses the full-inclusion method for advance payments?

LO 1-5 66. Nicole's business uses the accrual method of accounting and accounts for inventory with specific identification. In year 0, Nicole received a $4,500 payment with an order for inventory to be delivered to the client early next year. Nicole has the inventory ready for delivery at the end of year 0 (she purchased the inventory in year 0 for $2,300).

a) When does Nicole recognize the $2,200 of gross profit ($4,500 revenue minus $2,300 cost of the inventory) if she uses the full-inclusion method?

b) When does Nicole recognize the $2,200 of gross profit from the inventory sale if she uses the deferral method?

c) How would Nicole account for the inventory-related transactions if she uses the cash method of accounting and her annual sales are usually less than $100,000?

d) How would Nicole account for the inventory-related transactions if she uses the cash method of accounting and her annual sales are usually over $2,000,000 per year?

LO 1-5 67. This year Amber opened a factory to process and package landscape mulch. At the end of the year, Amber's accountant prepared the following schedule for allocating manufacturing costs to the mulch inventory, but her accountant is unsure of what costs need to be allocated to the inventory under UNICAP. Approximately 20 percent of management time, space, and expenses are spent on this manufacturing process.

		Costs	Tax Inventory
Material:	Mulch and packaging	$ 5,000	?
	Administrative supplies	250	?
Salaries:	Factory labor	12,000	?
	Sales & advertising	3,500	?
	Administration	5,200	?
Property taxes:	Factory	4,600	?
	Offices	2,700	?
Depreciation:	Factory	8,000	?
	Offices	1,500	?

a) At the end of the year, Amber's accountant indicated that the business had processed 10,000 bags of mulch but only 1,000 bags remained in the ending inventory. What is Amber's tax basis in her ending inventory after applying the UNICAP rules to allocate indirect costs to inventory? (Assume direct costs are allocated to inventory according to the level of ending inventory. In contrast, indirect costs are first allocated by time spent and then according to level of ending inventory.)

b) Under what conditions could Amber's business avoid having to apply UNICAP to allocate indirect costs to inventory for tax purposes?

LO 1-5 68. Suppose that David adopted the last-in, first-out (LIFO) inventory-flow method for his business inventory of widgets (purchase prices below).

Widget	Purchase Date	Direct Cost	Other Costs	Total Cost
#1	August 15	$2,100	$100	$2,200
#2	October 30	2,200	150	2,350
#3	November 10	2,300	100	2,400

In late December, David sold widget #2 and next year David expects to purchase three more widgets at the following estimated prices:

Widget	Purchase Date	Estimated Cost
#4	Early spring	$2,600
#5	Summer	2,260
#6	Fall	2,400

a) What cost of goods sold and ending inventory would David record if he elects to use the LIFO method this year?
b) If David sells two widgets next year, what will be his cost of goods sold and ending inventory next year under the LIFO method?
c) How would you answer (a) and (b) if David had initially selected the first-in, first-out (FIFO) method instead of LIFO?
d) Suppose that David initially adopted the LIFO method, but wants to apply for a change to FIFO next year. What would be his §481 adjustment for this change, and in what year(s) would he make the adjustment?

69. On November 1 of year 0, Jaxon borrowed $50,000 from Bucksnort Savings and Loan for use in his business. In December, Jaxon paid interest of $4,500 relating to the 12-month period from November of year 0 through October of year 1. LO 1-5
a) How much interest, if any, can Jaxon deduct in year 0 if his business uses the cash method of accounting for tax purposes?
b) How much interest, if any, can Jaxon deduct in year 0 if his business uses the accrual method of accounting for tax purposes?

70. Matt hired Apex Services to repair his business equipment. On November 1 of year 0, Matt paid $2,000 for the repairs that he expects to begin in early March of year 1. LO 1-5
a) What amount of the cost of the repairs can Matt deduct in year 0 if he uses the cash method of accounting for his business?
b) What amount of the cost of the repairs can Matt deduct in year 0 if he uses the accrual method of accounting for his business?
c) What amount of the cost of the repairs can Matt deduct in year 0 if he uses the accrual method and he expects the repairs to be done by early February?
d) What amount of the cost of the repairs can Matt deduct in year 0 if he uses the cash method of accounting and he expects the repairs to be done by early February?

71. Circuit Corporation (CC) is a calendar-year, accrual-method taxpayer. CC manufactures and sells electronic circuitry. On November 15, year 0, CC enters into a contract with Equip Corp (EC) that provides CC with exclusive use of EC's specialized manufacturing equipment for the five-year period beginning on January 1 of year 1. Pursuant to the contract, CC pays EC $100,000 on December 30, year 0. How much of this expenditure is CC allowed to deduct in year 0 and in year 1? LO 1-5

72. This year (year 0) Elizabeth agreed to a three-year service contract with an engineering consulting firm to improve efficiency in her factory. The contract requires Elizabeth to pay the consulting firm $1,500 for each instance that Elizabeth requests their assistance. The contract also provides that Elizabeth only pays the consultants if its advice increases efficiency as measured 12 months from the date of service. This year Elizabeth requested advice on three occasions and she has not yet made any payments to the consultants. LO 1-5

a) How much should Elizabeth deduct in year 0 under this service contract if she uses the accrual method of accounting?

b) How much should Elizabeth deduct in year 0 under this service contract if she uses the cash method of accounting?

LO 1-5

73. Travis is a professional landscaper. He provides his clients with a one-year (12-month) warranty for retaining walls he installs. In June of year 1, Travis installed a wall for an important client, Sheila. In early November, Sheila informed Travis that the retaining wall had failed. To repair the wall, Travis paid $700 cash for additional stone that he delivered to Sheila's location. Travis also offered to pay a mason $800 to repair the wall on November 20 of year 1. Due to some bad weather and the mason's work backlog, the mason agreed to finish the work by the end of January of year 2. Even though Travis expected the mason to finish the project by the end of February, Travis informed the mason that he would pay the mason the $800 when he completed the job.

a) Assuming Travis is an accrual-method taxpayer, how much can he deduct in year 1 from these activities?

b) Assuming Travis is a cash-method taxpayer, how much can he deduct in year 1 from these activities?

LO 1-5

research

74. Adam elects the accrual method of accounting for his business. What amount of deductions does Adam recognize in year 0 for the following transactions?

a) Adam guarantees that he will refund the cost of any goods sold to a client if the goods fail within a year of delivery. In December of year 0, Adam agreed to refund $2,400 to clients, and he expects to make payment in January of year 1.

b) On December 1 of year 0, Adam paid $480 for a one-year contract with CleanUP Services to clean his store. The agreement calls for services to be provided on a weekly basis.

c) Adam was billed $240 for annual personal property taxes on his delivery van. Because this was the first time Adam was billed for these taxes, he did not make payment until January. However, he considers the amounts immaterial.

LO 1-5

75. Rebecca is a calendar-year taxpayer who operates a business. She made the following business-related expenditures in December of year 0. Indicate the amount of these payments that she may deduct in year 0 under both the cash method of accounting and the accrual method of accounting.

a) $2,000 for an accountant to evaluate the accounting system of Rebecca's business. The accountant spent three weeks in January of year 1 working on the evaluation.

b) $2,500 for new office furniture. The furniture was delivered on January 15, year 1.

c) $3,000 for property taxes payable on her factory.

d) $1,500 for interest on a short-term bank loan relating to the period from November 1, year 0 through March 31, year 31.

LO 1-5

76. BCS Corporation is a calendar-year, accrual-method taxpayer. BCS was formed and started its business activities on January 1, year 0. It reported the following information for year 0. Indicate BCS's deductible amount for year 0 in each of the following alternative scenarios.

a) BCS provides two-year warranties on products it sells to customers. For its year 0 sales, BCS estimated and accrued $200,000 in warranty expense for financial accounting purposes. During year 0, BCS actually spent $30,000 repairing its product under the warranty.

b) BCS accrued an expense for $50,000 for amounts it anticipated it would be required to pay under the workers' compensation act. During year 0, BCS actually paid $10,000 for workers' compensation–related liabilities.

c) In June of year 0, a display of BCS's product located in its showroom fell on and injured a customer. The customer sued BCS for $500,000. The case is scheduled to go to trial next year. BCS anticipates that it will lose the case and accrued a $500,000 expense on its financial statements.

d) Assume the same facts as in (c) except that BCS was required to pay $500,000 to a court-appointed escrow fund in year 0. If BCS loses the case in year 1, the money from the escrow fund will be transferred to the customer suing BCS.

e) On December 1 of year 0, BCS acquired equipment from Equip Company. As part of the purchase, BCS signed a warranty agreement with Equip so that Equip would warranty the equipment for two years (from December 1 of year 0 through November 30 of year 2). The cost of the warranty was $12,000. BCS paid Equip for the warranty in January of year 1.

77. This year William provided $4,200 of services to a large client on credit. Unfortunately, this client has recently encountered financial difficulties and has been unable to pay William for the services. Moreover, William does not expect to collect for his services. William has "written off" the account and would like to claim a deduction for tax purposes. LO 1-5

a) What amount of deduction for bad debt expense can William claim this year if he uses the accrual method?

b) What amount of deduction for bad debt expense can William claim this year if he uses the cash method?

78. Dustin has a contract to provide services to Dado Enterprises. In November of year 0, Dustin billed Dado $10,000 for the services he rendered during the year. Dado is an accrual-method proprietorship that is owned and operated by Dustin's father. LO 1-5

a) What amount of revenue must Dustin recognize in year 0 if Dustin uses the cash method and Dado remits payment for the services in December of year 0? What amount can Dado deduct in year 0?

b) What amount of revenue must Dustin recognize in year 0 if Dustin uses the accrual method and Dado remits payment for the services in December of year 0? What amount can Dado deduct in year 0?

c) What amount of revenue must Dustin recognize in year 0 if Dustin uses the cash method and Dado remits payment for the services in January of year 1? What amount can Dado deduct in year 0?

d) What amount of revenue must Dustin recognize in year 0 if Dustin uses the accrual method and Dado remits payment for the services in January of year 1? What amount can Dado deduct in year 0?

79. Nancy operates a business that uses the accrual method of accounting. In December, Nancy asked her brother, Hank, to provide her business with consulting advice. Hank billed Nancy for $5,000 of consulting services in year 0 (a reasonable amount), but Nancy was only able to pay $3,000 of the bill by the end of year 0. However, Nancy paid the remainder of the bill in year 1. LO 1-5

a) How much of the $5,000 consulting services will Hank include in his income in year 0 if he uses the cash method of accounting? What amount can Nancy deduct in year 0 for the consulting services?

b) How much of the $5,000 consulting services will Hank include in his income in year 0 if he uses the accrual method of accounting? What amount can Nancy deduct in year 0 for the consulting services?

LO 1-5

80. Erin is considering switching her business from the cash method to the accrual method at the beginning of next year (year 1). Determine the amount and timing of her §481 adjustment assuming the IRS grants Erin's request in the following alternative scenarios.
    a) At the end of year 0/beginning of year 1, Erin's business has $15,000 of accounts receivables and $18,000 of accounts payables that have not been recorded for tax purposes.
    b) At the end of year 0/beginning of year 1, Erin's business reports $25,000 of accounts receivables and $9,000 of accounts payables that have not been recorded for tax purposes.

COMPREHENSIVE PROBLEMS

All applicable problems are available with McGraw-Hill's *Connect® Accounting.*

81. Joe operates a business that locates and purchases specialized assets for clients, among other activities. Joe uses the accrual method of accounting but he doesn't keep any significant inventories of the specialized assets that he sells. Joe reported the following financial information for his business activities during year 0. Determine the effect of each of the following transactions on the taxable business income.
    a) Joe has signed a contract to sell gadgets to the city. The contract provides that sales of gadgets are dependent upon a test sample of gadgets operating successfully. In December, Joe delivers $12,000 worth of gadgets to the city that will be tested in March. Joe purchased the gadgets especially for this contract and paid $8,500.
    b) Joe paid $180 for entertaining a visiting out-of-town client. The client didn't discuss business with Joe during this visit, but Joe wants to maintain good relations to encourage additional business next year.
    c) On November 1, Joe paid $600 for premiums providing for $40,000 of "key man" insurance on the life of Joe's accountant over the next 12 months.
    d) At the end of year 0, Joe's business reports $9,000 of accounts receivable. Based upon past experience, Joe believes that at least $2,000 of his new receivables will be uncollectible.
    e) In December of year 0, Joe rented equipment to complete a large job. Joe paid $3,000 in December because the rental agency required a minimum rental of three months ($1,000 per month). Joe completed the job before year-end, but he returned the equipment at the end of the lease.
    f) Joe hired a new sales representative as an employee and sent her to Dallas for a week to contact prospective out-of-state clients. Joe ended up reimbursing his employee $300 for airfare, $350 for lodging, $250 for meals, and $150 for entertainment (Joe provided adequate documentation to substantiate the business purpose for the meals and entertainment). Joe requires the employee to account for all expenditures in order to be reimbursed.
    g) Joe uses his BMW (a personal auto) to travel to and from his residence to his factory. However, he switches to a business vehicle if he needs to travel after he reaches the factory. Last month, the business vehicle broke down and he was forced to use the BMW both to travel to and from the factory and to visit work sites. He drove 120 miles visiting work sites and 46 miles driving to and from the factory from his home. Joe uses the standard mileage rate to determine his auto-related business expenses.
    h) Joe paid a visit to his parents in Dallas over the Christmas holidays. While he was in the city, Joe spent $50 to attend a half-day business symposium. Joe paid $200 for airfare, $50 for meals during the symposium, and $20 on cab fare to the symposium.

82. Jack, a geologist, had been debating for years whether or not to venture out on his own and operate his own business. He had developed a lot of solid relationships with clients and he believed that many of them would follow him if he were to leave his current employer. As part of a New Year's resolution, Jack decided he would finally do it. In January, Jack put his business plan together and in February opened his doors for business as a C corporation called Geo-Jack (GJ). Jack is the sole shareholder. Jack reported the following financial information for the year (assume GJ reports on a calendar year and uses the accrual method of accounting).

a) In January, GJ rented a small business office about 12 miles from Jack's home. GJ paid $10,000 which represented a damage deposit of $4,000 and rent for two years ($3,000 annually).

b) GJ earned and collected $290,000 performing geological-related services and selling its specialized digging tool [see part (i)].

c) GJ received $50 interest from municipal bonds and $2,100 interest from other investments.

d) GJ purchased some new equipment in February for $42,500. It claimed depreciation on these assets during the year in the amount of $6,540.

e) GJ paid $7,000 to buy luxury season tickets for Jack's parents for State U football games.

f) GJ paid Jack's father $10,000 for services that would have cost no more than $6,000 if Jack had hired any other local business to perform the services. While Jack's dad was competent, he does not command such a premium from his other clients.

g) In an attempt to get his name and new business recognized, GJ paid $7,000 for a one-page ad in the *Geologic Survey.* It also paid $15,000 in radio ads to be run through the end of December.

h) GJ leased additional office space in a building downtown. GJ paid rent of $27,000 for the year.

i) In August, GJ began manufacturing a special geological digging tool that it sells to wholesalers. GJ's QPAI from the activity for the year is $100,000 [included in revenues reported in part (b)]. GJ paid $10,000 of wages to the employees working on the project during the year and its cost of goods sold on the sales is $15,000. (Assume that taxable income does not limit the amount of the DPAD, and that no wages should be included in cost of goods sold.) Remember that cost of goods sold and wages reduce taxable income.

j) In November, Jack's office was broken into and equipment valued at $5,000 was stolen. The tax basis of the equipment was $5,500. Jack received $2,000 of insurance proceeds from the theft.

k) GJ incurred a $4,000 fine from the state government for digging in an unauthorized digging zone.

l) GJ contributed $3,000 to lobbyists for their help in persuading the state government to authorize certain unauthorized digging zones.

m) On July 1, GJ paid $1,800 for an 18-month insurance policy for its business equipment. The policy covers the period July 1 of this year through December 31 of next year.

n) GJ borrowed $20,000 to help with the company's initial funding needs. GJ used $2,000 of funds to invest in municipal bonds. At the end of the year, GJ paid the $1,200 of interest expense that accrued on the loan during the year.

o) Jack lives 12 miles from the office. He carefully tracked his mileage and drove his truck 6,280 miles between the office and his home. He also drove an additional 7,200 miles between the office and traveling to client sites. Jack did not use the truck for any other purposes. He did not keep track of the specific expenses associated with the truck. However, while traveling to a client site, Jack received a $150 speeding ticket. GJ reimbursed Jack for business mileage and for the speeding ticket.

p) GJ purchased two season tickets (20 games) to attend State U baseball games for a total of $1,100. Jack took existing and prospective clients to the games to maintain contact and find further work. This was very successful for Jack as GJ gained many new projects through substantial discussions with the clients following the games.

q) GJ reimbursed employee-salespersons $3,500 for meals involving substantial business discussion.

r) GJ had a client who needed Jack to perform work in Florida. Because Jack had never been to Florida before, he booked an extra day and night for sightseeing. Jack spent $400 for airfare and booked a hotel for 3 nights ($120/night). (Jack stayed two days for business purposes and one day for personal purposes.) He also rented a car for $45 per day. The client arranged for Jack's meals while Jack was doing business. GJ reimbursed Jack for all expenses.

Required:

A) What is GJ's net business income for tax purposes for the year?

B) As a C corporation, does GJ have a required tax year? If so, what would it be?

C) If GJ were a sole proprietorship, would it have a required tax year-end? If so, what would it be?

D) If GJ were an S corporation, would it have a required tax year-end? If so, what would it be?

83. Rex loves to work with his hands and is very good at making small figurines. Three years ago, Rex opened Bronze Age Miniatures (BAM) for business as a sole proprietorship. BAM produces miniature characters ranging from sci-fi characters (his favorite) to historical characters like George Washington (the most popular). Business has been going very well for him, and he has provided the following information relating to his business. Calculate the business taxable income for BAM.

a) Rex received approval from the IRS to switch from the cash method of accounting to the accrual method of accounting effective January 1 of this year. At year-end of last year, BAM reported accounts receivable that had not been included in income under the accrual method of $14,000 and accounts payable that had not been deducted under the accrual method of $5,000.

b) In March, BAM sold 5,000 miniature historical figures to History R Us Inc. (HRU), a retailer of historical artifacts and figurines, for $75,000.

c) HRU was so impressed with the figurines that it purchased in March that it wanted to contract with BAM to continue to produce the figurines for them for the next three years. HRU paid BAM $216,000 ($12 per figurine) on October 30 of this year, to produce 500 figurines per month for 36 months beginning on November 1 of this year. BAM delivered 500 figurines on November 30 and again on December 30. Rex elects to use the deferral method to account for the transaction.

d) Though the sci-fi figurines were not quite as popular, BAM sold 400 figurines at a sci-fi convention in April. Rex accepted cash only and received $11,000 for these sales.

e) In January, BAM determined that it would not be able to collect on $2,000 of its beginning-of-the-year receivables, so it wrote off $2,000 of specific receivables. BAM sold 100,000 other figurines on credit for $120,000. BAM estimates that it will be unable to collect 5 percent of the sales revenue from these sales but it has not been able to specifically identify any accounts to write off.

f) Assume that BAM correctly determined that its cost of goods sold this year is $54,000.

g) The sci-fi convention in April was held in Chicago, Illinois. Rex attended the convention because he felt it was a good opportunity to gain new customers and to get new ideas for figurines. He paid $350 round-trip airfare, $100 for entrance to the convention, $210 for lodging, $65 for cab fare, and $110 for meals during the trip. He was busy with business activities the entire trip.

h) On August 1, BAM purchased a 12-month insurance policy that covers its business property for accidents and casualties through July 31 of next year. The policy cost BAM $3,600.

i) BAM reported depreciation expense of $8,200 for this year.

j) Rex had previously operated his business out of his garage, but in January he decided to rent a larger space. He entered into a lease agreement on February 1 and paid $14,400 ($1,200 per month) to possess the space for the next 12 months (February of this year through January of next year).

k) Before he opened his doors for business, Rex spent $30,000 investigating and otherwise getting ready to do business. He expensed $5,000 immediately and is amortizing the remainder using the straight-line method over 180 months.

l) In December, BAM agreed to a 12-month $8,000 contract with Advertise-With-Us (AWU) to produce a radio ad campaign. BAM paid $3,000 up front (in December of this year) and AWU agreed that BAM would owe the remaining $5,000 only if BAM's sales increased by 15 percent over the nine-month period after the contract was signed.

m) In November of this year, BAM paid $2,500 in business property taxes (based on asset values) covering the period December 1 of this year through November 30 of next year. In November of last year, BAM paid $1,500 for business property taxes (based on asset values) covering the period December 1 of last year through November 30 of this year.

84. Bryan followed in his father's footsteps and entered into the carpet business. He owns and operates I Do Carpet (IDC). Bryan prefers to install carpet only, but in order to earn additional revenue, he also cleans carpets and sells carpet cleaning supplies. Compute his taxable income for the current year considering the following items:

a) IDC contracted with a homebuilder in December of last year to install carpet in 10 new homes being built. The contract price of $80,000 includes $50,000 for materials (carpet). The remaining $30,000 is for IDC's service of installing the carpet. The contract also stated that all money was to be paid up front. The homebuilder paid IDC in full on December 28 of last year. The contract required IDC to complete the work by January 31 of this year. Bryan purchased the necessary carpet on January 2 and began working on the first home January 4. He completed the last home on January 27 of this year.

b) IDC entered into several other contracts this year and completed the work before year-end. The work cost $130,000 in materials. Bryan billed out $240,000 but only collected $220,000 by year-end. Of the $20,000 still owed to him, Bryan wrote off $3,000 he didn't expect to collect as a bad debt from a customer experiencing extreme financial difficulties.

c) IDC entered into a three-year contract to clean the carpets of an office building. The contract specified that IDC would clean the carpets monthly from July 1 of this year through June 30 three years hence. IDC received payment in full of $8,640 ($240 a month for 36 months) on June 30 of this year.

d) IDC sold 100 bottles of carpet stain remover this year for $5 per bottle (it collected $500). Rex sold 40 bottles on June 1 and 60 bottles on November 2. IDC had the following carpet cleaning supplies on hand for this year and it uses the LIFO method of accounting for inventory under a perpetual inventory system:

Purchase Date	Bottles	Total Cost
November last year	40	$120
February this year	35	112
July this year	25	85
August this year	40	140
Totals	140	$457

e) On August 1 of this year, IDC needed more room for storage and paid $900 to rent a garage for 12 months.

f) On November 30 of this year, Bryan decided it was time to get his logo on the sides of his work van. IDC hired We Paint Anything Inc. (WPA) to do the job. It paid $500 down and agreed to pay the remaining $1,500 upon completion of the job. WPA indicated it wouldn't be able to begin the job until January 15 of next year, but the job would only take one week to complete. Due to circumstances beyond its control, WPA wasn't able to complete the job until April 1 of next year, at which time IDC paid the remaining $1,500.

g) In December, Bryan's son, Aiden, helped him finish some carpeting jobs. IDC owed Aiden $600 (reasonable) compensation for his work. However, Aiden did not receive the payment until January of next year.

h) IDC also paid $1,000 for interest on a short-term bank loan relating to the period from November 1 of this year through March 31 of next year.

85. Hank started a new business in June of last year, Hank's Donut World (HW for short). He has requested your advice on the following specific tax matters associated with HW's first year of operations. Hank has estimated HW's income for the first year as follows:

Revenue:		
Donut sales	$252,000	
Catering revenues	71,550	$323,550
Expenditures:		
Donut supplies	$124,240	
Catering expense	27,910	
Salaries to shop employees	52,500	
Rent expense	40,050	
Accident insurance premiums	8,400	
Other business expenditures	6,850	−259,950
Net Income		$ 63,600

HW operates as a sole proprietorship and Hank reports on a calendar year. Hank uses the cash method of accounting and plans to do the same with HW (HW has no inventory of donuts because unsold donuts are not salable). HW does not purchase donut supplies on credit nor does it generally make sales on credit. Hank has provided the following details for specific first-year transactions.

- A small minority of HW clients complained about the catering service. To mitigate these complaints, Hank's policy is to refund dissatisfied clients 50 percent of the catering fee. By the end of the first year, only two HW clients had complained but had not yet been paid refunds. The expected refunds amount to $1,700, and Hank reduced the reported catering fees for the first year to reflect the expected refund.
- In the first year, HW received a $6,750 payment from a client for catering a monthly breakfast for 30 consecutive months beginning in December. Because the payment didn't relate to last year, Hank excluded the entire amount when he calculated catering revenues.

- In July, HW paid $1,500 to ADMAN Co. for an advertising campaign to distribute fliers advertising HW's catering service. Unfortunately, this campaign violated a city code restricting advertising by fliers, and the city fined HW $250 for the violation. HW paid the fine, and Hank included the fine and the cost of the campaign in "other business" expenditures.
- In July, HW also paid $8,400 for a 24-month insurance policy that covers HW for accidents and casualties beginning on August 1 of the first year. Hank deducted the entire $8,400 as accident insurance premiums.
- On May of the first year, Hank signed a contract to lease the HW donut shop for 10 months. In conjunction with the contract, Hank paid $2,000 as a damage deposit and $8,050 for rent ($805 per month). Hank explained that the damage deposit was refundable at the end of the lease. At this time, Hank also paid $30,000 to lease kitchen equipment for 24 months ($1,250 per month). Both leases began on June 1 of the first year. In his estimate, Hank deducted these amounts ($40,050 in total) as rent expense.
- Hank signed a contract hiring WEGO Catering to help cater breakfasts. At year-end, WEGO asked Hank to hold the last catering payment for the year, $9,250, until after January 1 (apparently because WEGO didn't want to report the income on its tax return). The last check was delivered to WEGO in January after the end of the first year. However, because the payment related to the first year of operations, Hank included the $9,250 in last year's catering expense.
- Hank believes that the key to the success of HW has been hiring Jimbo Jones to supervise the donut production and manage the shop. Because Jimbo is such an important employee, HW purchased a "key-employee" term-life insurance policy on his life. HW paid a $5,100 premium for this policy and it will pay HW a $40,000 death benefit if Jimbo passes away any time during the next 12 months. The term of the policy began on September 1 of last year and this payment was included in "other business" expenditures.
- In the first year, HW catered a large breakfast event to celebrate the city's anniversary. The city agreed to pay $7,100 for the event, but Hank forgot to notify the city of the outstanding bill until January of this year. When he mailed the bill in January, Hank decided to discount the charge to $5,500. On the bill, Hank thanked the mayor and the city council for their patronage and asked them to "send a little more business our way." This bill is not reflected in Hank's estimate of HW's income for the first year of operations.

Required:

A) Hank files his personal tax return on a calendar year, but he has not yet filed last year's personal tax return nor has he filed a tax return reporting HW's results for the first year of operations. Explain when Hank should file the tax return for HW and calculate the amount of taxable income generated by HW last year.

B) Determine the taxable income that HW will generate if Hank chooses to account for the business under the accrual method.

C) Describe how your solution might change if Hank incorporated HW before he commenced business last year.

86. R.E.M., a calendar-year corporation and Athens, Georgia, band, recently sold tickets ($20,000,000) for concerts scheduled in the United States for next year and the following year. For financial statement purposes, R.E.M. will recognize the income from the ticket sales when it performs the concerts. For tax purposes, it uses the accrual method and would prefer to defer the income from the ticket sales until after the concerts are performed. This is the first time that it has sold tickets one or two years in advance. Michael Stipe has asked your advice. Write a memo to Michael explaining your findings. research

chapter **2**

Property Acquisition and Cost Recovery

Learning Objectives

Upon completing this chapter, you should be able to:

LO 2-1 Explain the concept of basis and adjusted basis and describe the cost recovery methods used under the tax law to recover the cost of personal property, real property, intangible assets, and natural resources.

LO 2-2 Determine the applicable cost recovery (depreciation) life, method, and convention for tangible personal and real property and calculate the deduction allowable under basic MACRS.

LO 2-3 Explain the additional special cost recovery rules (§179, bonus, listed property) and calculate the deduction allowable under these rules.

LO 2-4 Explain the rationale behind amortization, describe the four categories of amortizable intangible assets, and calculate amortization expense.

LO 2-5 Explain cost recovery of natural resources and the allowable depletion methods.

© Brand X Pictures/SuperStock

Storyline Summary

Taxpayer:	Teton Mountaineering Technology, LLC (Teton)—a calendar-year single-member LLC (treated as a sole proprietorship for tax purposes)
Location:	Cody, Wyoming
President/ Founder:	Steve Dallimore
Current situation:	Teton must acquire property to start manufacturing operations and wants to understand the tax consequences of property acquisitions.

Two years ago while climbing the Black Ice Couloir (pronounced "cool-wahr") in Grand Teton National Park, Steve Dallimore and his buddy got into a desperate situation. The climbers planned to move fast and light and to be home before an approaching storm reached the Teton. But just shy of the summit, climbing conditions forced them to turn back. Huddled in a wet sleeping bag in a dark snow cave waiting for the tempest to pass, Steve had an epiphany—a design for a better ice-climbing tool. Since that moment, Steve has been quietly consumed with making his dream—designing and selling his own line of climbing equipment—a reality. Although his current sales career is challenging and financially rewarding, Steve has too often found himself watching the clock and dreaming of a more fulfilling and adventurous career based upon his early training as a mechanical engineer. Steve decided to exercise his stock options, leave his current position, and start Teton. The only problem is that Steve has no employees, no business location, and no manufacturing equipment.

to be continued . . .

Steve obviously has many issues to resolve and decisions to make. In this chapter, we focus on the tax issues relating to the assets Steve will acquire for use in his new business. In particular, we explain how Teton will determine its cost recovery (depreciation, amortization, and depletion) deductions for the assets in the year the business begins and in subsequent years.[1] These deductions can generate significant tax savings for companies in capital-intensive industries.

This chapter explores the tax consequences of acquiring new or used property, depreciation methods businesses may use to recover the cost of their assets, and other special cost recovery incentives. Along the way, we compare and contrast the process of computing depreciation for tax purposes and for financial accounting purposes. We also address the tax consequences of using intangible assets and natural resources in business activities.

LO 2-1

COST RECOVERY AND BASIS FOR COST RECOVERY

Most businesses make a significant investment in property, plant, and equipment that is expected to provide benefits over a number of years. For both financial accounting and tax accounting purposes, businesses must capitalize the cost of assets with a useful life of more than one year (on the balance sheet) rather than expense the cost immediately. Businesses are allowed to use various methods to allocate the cost of these assets over time because the assets are subject to wear, tear, and obsolescence.

The method of **cost recovery** depends on the nature of the underlying asset. **Depreciation** is the method of deducting the cost of *tangible* personal and real property (other than land) over a specific time period. **Amortization** is the method of deducting the cost of **intangible assets** over a specific time period. Finally, **depletion** is the method of deducting the cost of natural resources over time. Exhibit 2-1 summarizes these concepts.

Generally, a significant portion of a firm's assets comprises property, plant, equipment, intangibles, or even natural resources. In most cases, this holds true for small businesses like Teton and also for large publicly traded companies. For example, Exhibit 2-2 describes the assets held by Weyerhaeuser, a publicly traded timber company. As indicated in Exhibit 2-2, Weyerhaeuser has almost $3 billion in property and equipment (net of depreciation) and $6 billion in timber (net of depletion), comprising roughly 60 percent of its assets.

Businesses must choose accounting methods for the assets acquired during the year from among the allowable cost recovery alternatives we describe in this chapter. Attention to detail is important because the basis of an asset must be reduced by the

EXHIBIT 2-1 Assets and Cost Recovery

Asset Type	Cost Recovery Method
Personal property is comprised of tangible assets such as automobiles, equipment, and machinery.	Depreciation
Real property is comprised of buildings and land (although land is nondepreciable).	Depreciation
Intangible assets are nonphysical assets such as goodwill and patents.	Amortization
Natural resources are commodities that are considered valuable in their natural form such as oil, coal, timber, and gold.	Depletion

[1]Cost recovery is the common term used to describe the process by which businesses allocate the cost of their fixed assets over the time period in which the assets are used.

EXHIBIT 2-2 Weyerhaeuser Assets

Assets (in millions) per 2012 10-K Statement	2013	2012
Total current assets	$ 2,326	$ 2,407
Property and equipment, net (Note 6)	2,704	2,872
Construction in progress	112	50
Timber and timberlands at cost, less depletion charged to disposals	6,580	3,961
Investments in and advances to equity affiliates (Note 7)	211	213
Goodwill	42	40
Deferred tax assets	41	368
Restricted assets held by special purpose entities (Note 9)	615	615
Other	1,867	2,066
Total Assets	$14,498	$12,592

cost recovery deductions allowed or *allowable*.[2] This means that if a business fails to deduct (by mistake or error) the allowable amount of depreciation expense for the year, the business must still reduce the asset's basis by the depreciation expense the taxpayer could have deducted under the method the business is using to depreciate the asset (this reduces the future depreciation deductions for the asset).

Basis for Cost Recovery

Businesses may begin recouping the cost of purchased business assets (cost basis) once they begin using the asset in their business (place it in service).[3] Once the business establishes its cost basis in an asset, the basis is reduced as the business recovers the cost of the asset through cost recovery deductions such as depreciation, amortization, or depletion. The amount of an asset's cost that has yet to be recovered through cost recovery deductions is called the asset's **adjusted basis** or **tax basis.** An asset's adjusted basis can be computed by subtracting the accumulated depreciation (or amortization or depletion) from the asset's initial cost or historical basis.[4]

For most assets, the initial basis is the cost plus all of the expenses to purchase, prepare it for use, and begin using the asset. These costs may include sales tax, shipping, and installation. The financial accounting and tax rules for computing an asset's basis are very similar. Thus, a purchased asset's initial basis for both tax and book purposes is generally the same.[5]

When a business incurs additional costs associated with an asset after the asset has been placed in service, how are the additional costs treated for tax purposes? In December 2011, the Treasury issued regulations to help guide taxpayers on this question. In general, the answer depends on whether the expense constitutes routine maintenance on the asset or whether it results in a "betterment, restoration, or new or different use for the property."[6] Routine maintenance costs are immediately deductible as ordinary business expenses. For example, Teton would immediately deduct a $35 cost to have a delivery truck's oil changed as routine maintenance. Alternatively, if an additional cost significantly extends an asset's useful life or increases

THE KEY FACTS

Cost Basis

- An asset's cost basis includes all costs needed to purchase the asset, prepare it for use, and begin using it.
- Cost basis is usually the same for book and tax purposes.
- Special basis rules apply when personal use assets are converted to business use and when assets are acquired through nontaxable transactions, gifts, or inheritances.

[2]If a business discovers that it failed to claim allowable depreciation in a previous year, it cannot currently deduct the depreciation attributable to prior years. Rather, the business must file amended returns—assuming the statute of limitations is still open—to claim the depreciation expense. Additionally, Reg. §1.446-1 indicates other situations that will result in an accounting method change.

[3]Cost basis is defined under §1012. The mere purchase of an asset does not trigger cost recovery deductions. A business must begin using the asset for business purposes (place it in service) in order to depreciate the asset. However, because businesses generally acquire and place assets in service at the same time, we refer to these terms interchangeably throughout the chapter.

[4]§1011.

[5]However, special basis rules apply when an asset is acquired through a nontaxable transaction. See discussion in Chapter 3.

[6]Reg. §1.263(a)-1T.

the value of the asset, the expenditure generates a new asset (for cost recovery purposes) separate from the original asset.[7] For example, if Teton spends $3,000 on a rebuilt engine for a delivery truck in an attempt to add 50,000 miles to the truck's useful life, the cost of the engine would be accounted for as a separate, new asset.

When a business acquires multiple assets for one purchase price, the tax laws require the business to determine a cost basis for each separate asset. For example, if Teton were to acquire land and a building on the land, Teton must treat the building and land as separate assets. In these types of acquisitions, businesses determine the cost basis of each asset by allocating a portion of the purchase price to each asset based on that asset's value relative to the total value of all the assets the business acquired in the same purchase. The asset values are generally determined by an appraisal.[8]

Example 2-1

Steve determined that he needed machinery and office furniture for a manufacturing facility and a design studio (located in Cody, Wyoming). During the year, Steve purchased the following assets and incurred the following costs to prepare the assets for business use. His cost basis in each asset is determined as follows:

Asset	Date Acquired	(1) Purchase Price	(2) Business Preparation Costs	(1) + (2) Cost Basis
Office furniture	2/3/15	$ 10,000		$ 10,000
Warehouse	5/1/15	270,000*	$5,000 (minor modifications)	275,000
Land (10 acres)	5/1/15	75,000*		75,000
Machinery	7/22/15	500,000	$10,000 (delivery and setup)	510,000
Delivery truck (used)	8/17/15	15,000		15,000

*Note that the warehouse and the land were purchased together for $345,000. Steve and the seller determined that the value (and cost) of the warehouse was $270,000 and the value (and cost) of the land was $75,000.

Special rules apply when determining the tax basis of assets converted from personal to business use or assets acquired through a nontaxable exchange, gift, or inheritance. If an asset is used for personal purposes and is later converted to business (or rental) use, the basis for cost recovery purposes is the *lesser* of (1) the cost basis of the asset or (2) the fair market value of the asset on the date of conversion to business use.[9] This rule prevents taxpayers from converting a nondeductible personal loss into a deductible business loss. For example, if Steve had purchased a truck for $20,000 several years ago for personal use but decided to use it as a delivery truck when its value had declined to $15,000, his basis in the truck for cost recovery purposes would be $15,000. The $5,000 decline in the truck's value from $20,000 to $15,000 would be a nondeductible personal loss to Steve, and the reduction in basis ensures that he will not be allowed to deduct the loss as a business loss. Assets acquired through a nontaxable exchange such as a like-kind exchange generally take the same basis the taxpayer had in the property the taxpayer transferred in the transaction. Assets acquired by gift have a carryover basis. This means that the taxpayer's basis in property received through a gift is generally the same basis the transferor had in the property.[10] For example, if Steve's parents gave him equipment worth

[7]§168(i)(6).

[8]Reg. §1.167(a)-5.

[9]Reg. §§1.167(g)-1 and 1.168(i)-4(b). However, this rule creates an interesting situation when selling converted assets. The taxpayer uses the lower of the adjusted basis or the fair market value at the time of the conversion for computing loss but uses the adjusted basis to compute a gain when selling converted assets.

[10]§1015. The basis may be increased if the transferor is required to pay gift tax on the transfer [see §1015(d)]. In addition, special dual basis rules apply if the basis in the gifted property at the gift date is greater than its fair market value.

$45,000 to help him start his business and his parents had purchased the equipment 10 years earlier for $25,000, Steve's basis in the equipment would be $25,000 (the same basis his parents had in the equipment). Assets acquired through inheritance generally receive a basis equal to the fair market value on the transferor's date of death.[11] For example, if Steve inherited a building worth $90,000 from his grandfather who originally paid $3,500 for it, Steve's basis would be $90,000 (its fair market value at date of death) because Steve acquired it through an inheritance.

ETHICS

Catherine Travis is starting a new business. She has several assets that she wants to use in her business that she has been using personally. Since she plans to convert several assets from personal to business use, she will need to find out how much each asset is worth so she can determine her basis for depreciating the assets. Catherine has decided to obtain two appraisals and take the better of the two figures for each asset. What do you think of Catherine's strategy for determining her business asset bases?

DEPRECIATION

LO 2-2

THE KEY FACTS

Tax Depreciation

- To depreciate an asset, a business must determine:
  - Original basis
  - Depreciation method
  - Recovery period
  - Depreciation convention

Before 1981, tax depreciation methods closely resembled financial accounting methods. For both financial accounting and tax purposes, businesses were allowed to choose from among a wide range of depreciation methods and **recovery periods.** Computing both tax and financial accounting depreciation required businesses to determine the assets' useful lives and "salvage values." In 1981, tax and financial accounting depreciation methods parted ways when Congress introduced the **Accelerated Cost Recovery System (ACRS)** for computing depreciation expense. Under ACRS, businesses used accelerated depreciation methods to depreciate assets over predetermined, fixed recovery periods.

Today, businesses calculate their tax depreciation using the **Modified Accelerated Cost Recovery System (MACRS)**—which is pronounced "makers" by tax accountants.[12] Compared to financial (book) depreciation, MACRS tax depreciation is quite simple. To compute MACRS depreciation for an asset, the business need only know the asset's *original cost,* the applicable *depreciation method,* the asset's *recovery period* (or depreciable "life"), and the applicable depreciation *convention* (the amount of depreciation deductible in the year of acquisition and the year of disposition). The method, recovery, period, and convention vary based on whether the asset is **personal property** or **real property.** The tax depreciation laws also include several special rules, which we discuss following the basic MACRS rules. We first turn our attention to determining depreciation expense for personal property.

Personal Property Depreciation

Personal property includes all tangible property, such as computers, automobiles, furniture, machinery, and equipment, other than real property. Note that personal property and *personal-use* property are *not* the same thing. Personal property denotes any property that is not real property (e.g., building and land) while personal-use property is any property used for personal purposes (e.g., a personal residence is personal-use property even though it is real property). Personal property is relatively short-lived and subject to obsolescence as compared to real property.

[11]§1014. In certain circumstances, the estate can elect an alternative valuation date six months after death.

[12]IRS Publication 946 provides a useful summary of MACRS depreciation.

Depreciation Method MACRS provides three acceptable methods for depreciating personal property: 200 percent (double) declining balance (DB), 150 percent declining balance, and straight-line.[13] The 200 percent declining balance method is the default method. This method takes twice the straight-line amount of depreciation in the first year and continues to take twice the straight-line percentage on the asset's declining basis until switching to the straight-line method in the year that the straight-line method over the remaining life provides a greater depreciation expense. Fortunately, as we describe below, the IRS provides depreciation tables to simplify the calculations.

Profitable businesses with relatively high marginal tax rates generally choose to use the 200 percent declining balance method because it generates the largest depreciation expense in the early years of the assets' lives and, thus, the highest current year after-tax cash flows. For tax planning purposes, companies that currently have lower marginal tax rates but expect their marginal tax rates to increase in the near future may elect the straight-line method because that method generates less depreciation expense in the early years of the asset's life, relatively, and more depreciation expense in the later years when their marginal tax rates may increase.

Example 2-2

If Teton wants to accelerate its current depreciation deductions to the extent possible, what method should it use to depreciate its office furniture, machinery, and delivery truck?

Answer: The 200 percent declining balance method (default). Teton could elect to use either the 150 percent declining balance or the straight-line method, if it wants a less accelerated method for determining its depreciation deductions.

Each year, businesses elect the depreciation method for the assets placed in service during *that year*. Specifically, businesses elect one depreciation method for all similar assets they acquired that year.[14] Thus, if a business acquires several different machines during the year, it must use the same method to depreciate all of the machines. However, the methods may differ for machines acquired in different tax years.

Depreciation Recovery Period For financial accounting purposes, an asset's recovery period (depreciable life) is based on its taxpayer-determined estimated useful life. In contrast, for tax purposes an asset's recovery period is predetermined by the IRS in Rev. Proc. 87-56. This revenue procedure helps taxpayers categorize each of their assets based upon the property's description. Once the business has determined the appropriate categories for its assets, it can use the Revenue Procedure to identify the recovery period for all assets in a particular category. For example, Teton placed office furniture in service during the year. By examining the excerpt from Rev. Proc. 87-56 provided in Exhibit 2-3, you can see that Category or Asset Class 00.11 includes office furniture and that assets in this category, including Teton's office furniture, have a recovery period of seven years (emphasis in excerpt added through bold text).[15]

[13]For personal property, the 200 percent DB is often referred to as the General Depreciation System (GDS) while the 150 percent DB or straight-line methods are referred to as the Alternative Depreciation System (ADS).

[14]Technically, similar assets are assets in the same asset class. We discuss asset classes below.

[15]The "alternative" recovery period in Rev. Proc. 87-56 refers to an asset's life under the alternative depreciation system (which was discussed earlier under depreciation methods). The Class Life referred to in Rev. Proc. 87-56 refers to the midpoint of asset depreciation range (ADR) applicable under pre-ACRS and has little or no meaning under MACRS.

EXHIBIT 2-3 Excerpt from Revenue Procedure 87-56

Description of Assets Included	Years		
Specific depreciable assets used in all business activities, except as noted:	**Class Life**	**General Recovery Period**	**Alternative Recovery Period**
00.11 Office Furniture, Fixtures, and Equipment: Includes furniture and fixtures that are not a structural component of a building. Includes such assets as desks, files, safes, and communications equipment. Does not include communications equipment that is included in other classes.	10	7	10
00.241 Light General Purpose Trucks: Includes trucks for use over the road (actual unloaded weight less than 13,000 pounds) . . .	4	5	5
34.0 Manufacture of Fabricated Metal Products Special Tools: Includes assets used in the production of metal cans, tinware . . .	12	7	12

While even this small excerpt from Rev. Proc. 87-56 may seem a bit intimidating, you can classify the vast majority of business assets acquired by knowing a few common recovery periods. Exhibit 2-4 lists the most commonly purchased assets and their recovery periods.

EXHIBIT 2-4 Recovery Period for Most Common Business Assets

Asset Description (summary of Rev. Proc. 87-56)	Recovery Period
Cars, light general-purpose trucks, and computers and peripheral equipment.	5-year
Office furniture, fixtures, and equipment.	7-year

To this point, our discussion has emphasized computing depreciation for new assets. Does the process change when businesses acquire used assets? No, it is exactly the same. For example, Teton purchased a *used* delivery truck. The fact that the truck is used does not change its MACRS recovery period. No matter how long the previous owner used the truck, Teton will restart the five-year recovery period for light general purpose trucks (see Exhibit 2-4).

Under MACRS, the tax recovery period for machinery and equipment is seven years. Using Rev. Proc. 87-56, Teton has determined the cost recovery periods for the personal property it purchased and placed in service during the year. Exhibit 2-5 summarizes this information.

EXHIBIT 2-5 Teton Personal Property Summary (Base Scenario)

Asset	Date Acquired	Quarter Acquired	Cost Basis	Recovery Period	Reference
Office furniture	2/3/15	1st	$ 10,000	7	Example 2-1; Exhibit 2-3.
Machinery	7/22/15	3rd	$510,000	7	Example 2-1; Exhibit 2-3.
Delivery truck	8/17/15	3rd	15,000	5	Example 2-1; Exhibit 2-3.
Total personal property			**$535,000**		

Depreciation Conventions Once a business has determined the depreciation methods and recovery periods for the assets it placed in service during the year, it must also determine the applicable depreciation conventions. The depreciation convention specifies the portion of a full year's depreciation the business can deduct for an asset in the year the asset is first placed in service *and* in the year the asset is sold. For *personal property,* taxpayers must use either the **half-year convention** or the **mid-quarter convention.** But, as we discuss below, taxpayers are *not* free to choose between the two conventions. The half-year convention applies most of the time; however, under certain conditions taxpayers will be required to use the mid-quarter convention.

> **THE KEY FACTS**
>
> **Half-Year Convention**
>
> - One-half of a year's depreciation is allowed in the first and the last year of an asset's life.
> - The IRS depreciation tables automatically account for the half-year convention in the acquisition year.
> - If an asset is disposed of before it is fully depreciated, only one-half of the table's applicable depreciation percentage is allowed in the year of disposition.

Half-year convention. The half-year convention allows one-half of a full year's depreciation in the year the asset is placed in service, regardless of when it was actually placed in service. For example, when the half-year convention applies to a calendar-year business, an asset placed in service on either February 3 or August 17 is treated as though it was placed in service on July 1, which is the middle of the calendar year. Thus, under this convention, Teton would deduct one-half of a year's worth of depreciation for the machinery, office furniture, and delivery truck even though it acquired the machinery, delivery truck, and office furniture at various times during the year (see Exhibit 2-5). The half-year convention is built into the depreciation tables provided by the IRS, which simplifies the depreciation calculation for the year the asset is placed into service.

The original ACRS system required the use of the half-year convention for all personal property placed in service during the year. However, Congress believed that many businesses took unfair advantage of the half-year convention by purposely acquiring assets at the end of the year that they otherwise would have acquired at the beginning of the next taxable year. Thus, businesses received one-half of a year's worth of depreciation for assets that they only used for a small portion of the year. Even though the half-year convention is the default convention, policy makers introduced the *mid-quarter convention* under MACRS to limit or prevent this type of opportunistic behavior.

Calculating Depreciation for Personal Property Once a business has identified the applicable method, recovery period, and convention for personal property, tax depreciation is relatively easy to calculate because the Internal Revenue Service provides depreciation percentage tables in Rev. Proc. 87-57. The percentages in the depreciation tables for tangible personal property incorporate the method and convention [accordingly there are separate tables for each combination of depreciation method (200 percent declining balance, 150 percent declining balance, and straight-line) and convention (half-year and mid-quarter; each quarter has its own table)]. To determine the depreciation for an asset for the year, use the following three steps:

Step 1: Locate the applicable table provided in Rev. Proc. 87-57.

Step 2: Select the column that corresponds with the asset's recovery period.

Step 3: Find the row identifying the year of the asset's recovery period.

The tables are constructed so that the intersection of the row and column provides the percentage of the asset's *original basis* that is deductible as depreciation expense for the particular year. Thus, depreciation expense for a particular asset is the product of the percentage from the table and the asset's *original basis.*

Applying the Half-Year Convention Consider Table 1 in the appendix at the end of the chapter that shows the depreciation percentages for MACRS 200 percent declining balance using the half-year convention. If a seven-year asset is placed into service during the current year, the depreciation percentage is 14.29 percent [the intersection of row 1 (year 1) and the seven-year property column].

Notice from Table 1 that the depreciation percentages for five-year property extend for six years and the percentages for seven-year property extend for eight years.

Why does it take six years to fully depreciate an asset with a five-year recovery period and eight years for a seven-year asset? Because the business does not deduct a full year's depreciation in the first year (businesses must use either the half-year or mid-quarter convention), an entire year of depreciation is effectively split between the first and last year. For example, when the half-year convention applies to a five-year asset, the taxpayer deducts one-half of a year's depreciation in year 1 and one-half of a year's depreciation in year 6.

Example 2-3

Teton is using the 200 percent declining balance method and half-year convention to compute depreciation expense on its current year personal property additions. What is Teton's depreciation expense for these assets?

Answer: $77,308, computed as follows:

Asset	Date Placed in Service	(1) Original Basis	(2) Rate	(1) × (2) Depreciation
Office furniture	February 3	$ 10,000	14.29%	$ 1,429
Machinery	July 22	510,000	14.29	72,879
Used delivery truck	August 17	15,000	20.00	3,000
Total				$77,308

Because the office furniture and machinery have a seven-year recovery period and it is the first year for depreciation, the depreciation rate is 14.29 percent (see Table 1). The depreciation rate for the used delivery truck (five-year property) is determined in a similar manner.

Calculating depreciation for assets in years after the year of acquisition is also relatively simple. Again, using Table 1 to compute depreciation for the second year, the taxpayer would multiply the asset's original basis times the rate factor in the *year 2* row and the *year 3* row in the following year and so on.

Example 2-4

What if: Assume that Teton holds the tangible personal property it acquired and placed in service this year until the assets are fully depreciated. Using the IRS provided tables (see Table 1) how would Teton determine its depreciation expense for years 1 through 8?

Answer: See the following table:

Depreciation Over Asset Recovery Period

Year	7-Year Office Furniture	7-Year Machinery	5-Year Delivery Truck	Yearly Total
1	$ 1,429	$ 72,879	$ 3,000	$ 77,308
2	2,449	124,899	4,800	132,148
3	1,749	89,199	2,880	93,828
4	1,249	63,699	1,728	66,676
5	893	45,543	1,728	48,164
6	892	45,492	864	47,248
7	893	45,543	N/A	46,436
8	446	22,746	N/A	23,192
Accumulated Depreciation	$10,000	$510,000	$15,000	$535,000

Half-year convention for year of disposition. Businesses often sell or dispose of assets before they fully depreciate them. Recall that the half-year convention applies in both the year of acquisition and the year of disposition. Note, however, that the tables can't anticipate when a business may dispose of an asset. Accordingly, the tables only provide depreciation percentages for assets assuming the asset won't be disposed of before it is fully depreciated. That is, for each year in the asset's recovery period, the tables provide a percentage for an entire year's worth of depreciation. So, to calculate the depreciation for the year of disposition, the business first calculates depreciation for the *entire year* as if the property had not been disposed of. Then the business applies the half-year convention by multiplying the full year's depreciation by 50 percent (one-half of a year's depreciation). Note, however, that if a business acquires and disposes of an asset in the same tax year, it is not allowed to claim any depreciation on the asset.[16]

Example 2-5

What if: Assume that Teton sells all of its office furniture in year 2 (the year after it buys it). What is Teton's depreciation for the office furniture in the year of disposition (year 2)?

Answer: $1,225, calculated using the MACRS Half-Year Convention Table as follows:

Asset	Amount	Explanation
(1) Office furniture	$10,000	Original basis.
(2) Depreciation percentage	24.49%	Seven-year property, year 2.
(3) Full year of depreciation	$ 2,449	(1) × (2).
(4) Half-year convention percentage	50%	Depreciation limit in year of disposal.
Depreciation in year of disposal	$ 1,225	(3) × (4).

What if: Assume that Teton sold all of its office furniture in year 1 (the year it bought it and placed it in service). How much depreciation expense can Teton deduct for the office furniture in year 1?

Answer: $0. A business is not allowed to claim any depreciation expense for assets it acquires and disposes of in the same year.

Mid-quarter convention. Under the mid-quarter convention, businesses treat assets *as though* they were placed in service during the middle of the *quarter* in which the business actually placed the assets into service. For example, when the mid-quarter convention applies, if a business places an asset in service on December 1 (in the fourth quarter) it must treat the asset as though it was placed in service on November 15, which is the middle of the fourth quarter. Consequently, the business would only be able to deduct one-half of a quarter's worth of depreciation in the year the asset was placed in service (depreciation for the second half of November and the entire month of December). In addition, if the mid-quarter convention applies, businesses must use the convention for all tangible personal property placed in service during the year. The IRS depreciation tables have built in the mid-quarter convention to simplify the calculations.

Businesses must use the mid-quarter convention when *more* than 40 percent of their total *tangible personal property* that they place in service during the year is placed in service during the *fourth* quarter. Thus, the steps to determine whether the mid-quarter convention applies are the following:

Step 1: Sum the total basis of the tangible personal property that was placed in service during the year.

[16]Suppose Teton sells the 5-year delivery truck in year 6 on January 5. What depreciation percentage should Teton use for purposes of determining year 6 depreciation? Teton should take one-half year's depreciation on the truck. The percentage shown in Table 1 for year 6 already reflects the half-year convention, so Teton would take $864 of depreciation regardless of when during year 6 the truck was sold.

Step 2: Sum the total basis of the tangible personal property that was placed in service in the fourth quarter.

Step 3: Divide the outcome of Step 2 by the outcome of Step 1. If the quotient is greater than 40 percent, the business must use the mid-quarter convention to determine the depreciation for all tangible personal property the business placed in service during the year. Otherwise, the business uses the half-year convention for depreciating this property.

In accordance with Reg. §1.168(d)-1(b)(4), property expensed under §179 (discussed later in the chapter) is not included in the numerator or denominator of the mid-quarter test. The mid-quarter test is applied after the §179 expense but before bonus depreciation.

Example 2-6

The following excerpt from the base scenario in Exhibit 2-5 provides the information we need to determine if Teton must use the mid-quarter convention to compute depreciation:

Asset	Date Acquired	Quarter Acquired	Cost Basis
Office furniture	2/3/15	First	$ 10,000
Machinery	7/22/15	Third	510,000
Delivery truck	8/17/15	Third	15,000
Total personal property			**$535,000**

Is Teton required to use the mid-quarter convention to depreciate its personal property?

Answer: No. See computation below.

Description	Amount	Explanation
(1) Total basis of tangible personal property placed in service during year	$535,000	
(2) Total basis of tangible personal property placed in service in fourth quarter	0	
(3) Percentage of basis of total tangible personal property placed in service during fourth quarter	0%	(2)/(1).

Teton is not required to use the mid-quarter convention because it did not place more than 40 percent of its assets in service during the fourth quarter. (In fact, Teton did not place any assets in service in the fourth quarter.) Consequently, Teton will use the half year convention to calculate its depreciation expense.

THE KEY FACTS

Mid-Quarter Convention

- The mid-quarter convention is required when more than 40 percent of a taxpayer's personal property placed in service during the year was placed during the fourth quarter.
- Each quarter has its own depreciation table. Once you begin using a table, you must use the table over the asset's whole life.
- If an asset is disposed of before it is fully depreciated, use the formula given to determine the allowable depreciation in the year of disposition.

Example 2-7

What if: Let's replace the facts from the base scenario presented in Exhibit 2-5 with the following alternative scenario 1 facts. In this alternative set of facts, we assume the machinery was acquired during the fourth quarter on October 25 as follows:

Asset	Date Acquired	Quarter Acquired	Cost Basis
Office furniture	2/3/15	First	$ 10,000
Delivery truck	8/17/15	Third	15,000
Machinery	10/25/15	Fourth	510,000
Total personal property			**$535,000**

(continued on page 2-12)

Under alternative scenario 1, is Teton required to use the mid-quarter convention?

Answer: Yes. Of the personal property it placed in service during the year, it placed 95.3 percent in service in the last quarter (this is greater than 40 percent). See the calculations below:

Description	Amount	Explanation
(1) Cost of all personal property placed in service during current year.	$535,000	
(2) Cost of personal property placed in service in the fourth quarter during current year.	510,000	
(3) Percentage of all personal property placed in service during current year that was placed in service in the fourth quarter.	95.3%	(2)/(1).

What if: Assume that Teton also placed in service on July 1 a building costing $1,000,000. Is Teton subject to the mid-quarter convention?

Answer: Yes. Because the building is real property (not personal property), it is not included in the mid-quarter calculation. The calculation is exactly the same as the calculation in alternative scenario 1 above.

Applying the Mid-Quarter Convention When the mid-quarter convention applies, the process for computing depreciation is the same as it is when the half-year convention applies, except that businesses use a different set of depreciation tables (a separate table for each quarter). After categorizing the assets by recovery period and grouping them into quarters, businesses consult the Mid-Quarter Convention Tables 2a–d in the appendix to this chapter to determine the depreciation rate for each asset group.

The depreciation expense for an asset is the product of the asset's original basis and the percentage from the table.

Example 2-8

What if: For this example, we assume the facts from alternative scenario 1 presented in Example 2-7 (see table below). What is Teton's year 1 depreciation expense for its personal property additions under the alternative scenario 1 presented in Example 2-7?

Answer: $22,957, computed as follows:

Asset	Purchase Date	Quarter	Original Basis	Rate	Depreciation
Office furniture (7-year)	February 3	First	$ 10,000	25.00%	$ 2,500
Delivery truck (5-year)	August 17	Third	15,000	15.00%	2,250
Machinery (7-year)	October 25	Fourth	510,000	3.57%	18,207
					$22,957

The office furniture factor of 25.00 percent is located in Table 2a. See the columns for property placed into service during the first quarter (first two columns), select the 7-year recovery period column (last column), and the year 1 row. The process for determining the rate factor for the delivery truck and machinery follows the same methodology using Tables 2c and 2d, respectively.

Teton's $77,308 depreciation expense under the half-year convention (see Example 2-3) is significantly higher than its $22,957 depreciation expense under the mid-quarter convention (see Example 2-8). Why the big disparity? Because the (high cost) machinery was placed into service during the fourth quarter and thus generated significantly less current depreciation expense (one-half of one quarter's depreciation) than it would have under the half-year convention. It is important to note, however, that when using the mid-quarter convention, assets placed in service in the first or second quarter will generate more depreciation than they would have under the half-year convention (10.5/12ths and 7.5/12ths of a full year, respectively). However, because the mid-quarter convention only applies when a large percentage of the cost of the assets was placed in service in the fourth quarter, the mid-quarter convention tends to generate less overall depreciation expense for new additions than the half-year convention.

The process for calculating depreciation for assets in years after the year of acquisition under the mid-quarter convention is nearly identical to the process we described for making this computation under the half-year convention. The only difference is that the business looks to the MACRS Mid-Quarter Convention Table (Table 2 in the chapter appendix) for the appropriate quarter rather than the MACRS Half-Year Convention Table (Table 1 in the chapter appendix).

Example 2-9

What if: Assume that Teton held and fully depreciated the tangible personal property it placed in service this year under the mid-quarter convention (alternative scenario 1). What would be Teton's depreciation expense for its personal property additions for years 1 through 8 using the mid-quarter tables provided in the appendix at the end of this chapter?

Answer: See table below*:

Year	7-Year Office Furniture 1st Quarter	5-Year Delivery Truck 3rd Quarter	7-Year Machinery 4th Quarter	Yearly Total
1	$ 2,500	$ 2,250	$ 18,207	$ 22,957
2	2,143	5,100	140,505	147,748
3	1,531	3,060	100,368	104,959
4	1,093	1,836	71,706	74,635
5	875	1,695	51,204	53,774
6	874	1,059	44,523	46,456
7	875	N/A	44,523	45,398
8	109	N/A	38,964	39,073
	$10,000	$15,000	$510,000	$535,000

*See Table 2; the depreciation is calculated by multiplying the applicable rate by the cost basis.

Mid-quarter convention for year of disposition. Calculating depreciation expense in the year of sale or disposition is a bit more involved when the mid-quarter convention applies than when it does not. When the mid-quarter convention applies, the asset is treated as though it is sold in the middle of the quarter of which it was actually sold. The process for calculating mid-quarter convention depreciation for the year of sale is exactly the same as the process for using the half-year convention, except that *instead of* multiplying the full year's depreciation by 50 percent, the business multiplies the amount of depreciation it would have been able to claim on the asset if it had not sold the asset (a full year's depreciation) by the applicable percentage in Exhibit 2-6.[17]

[17]Suppose Teton sells the 5-year delivery truck in year 6 on January 5 after using the mid-quarter convention as in example 2-9. What depreciation percentage should Teton use for purposes of determining year 6 depreciation? Teton should be allowed 1/2 of a quarter's depreciation in year 6. The calculation of this amount is complicated by the mid-quarter convention because the 3rd quarter depreciation percentage for a 5-year asset in year 6 using Table 2c shows 7.06 percent. This amount, however, is the depreciation rate for 2 1/2 quarters representing the remaining depreciation in the final year of the asset's recovery period. Teton will be allowed $212 of depreciation in the year of disposition determined as $15,000 multiplied by 1.412 percent (7.06%/2.5 quarters × .5 quarters = 1.412%).

EXHIBIT 2-6 Mid-Quarter Convention Percentage of Full Year's Depreciation in Year of Disposition

Quarter of Disposition	Percentage	Calculation*
First	12.5%	1.5/12
Second	37.5	4.5/12
Third	62.5	7.5/12
Fourth	87.5	10.5/12

*The calculation is the number of months the taxpayer held or is deemed to have held the asset in the year of disposition divided by 12 months in the year.

Example 2-10

What if: Assume that Teton depreciates its personal property under the mid-quarter convention (alternative scenario 1, see Example 2-5) and that it sells its office furniture in the third quarter of year 2. The office furniture ($10,000 original basis) was placed into service during the first quarter of year 1 and has a seven-year recovery period. What depreciation expense can Teton deduct for the office furniture in year 2, the year of sale?

Answer: $1,339. Computed as follows:

Description	Amount	Explanation
(1) Original basis	$10,000	Example 2-7.
(2) Year 2 depreciation percentage	21.43%	Table 2a, mid-quarter, first quarter table, 7-year property, year 2.
(3) Full year 2 depreciation	2,143	(1) × (2).
(4) Percentage of full year's depreciation in year of disposition if mid-quarter convention applies	62.5%	From Exhibit 2-6; asset disposed of in third quarter.
Depreciation in year of disposition	$ 1,339	(3) × (4).

What if: Assume Teton disposed of the office furniture on January 2 of year 2. How much depreciation expense would it be able to claim on the furniture in year 2?

Answer: $268 ($2,143 full year's depreciation × 12.5% from Exhibit 2-6).

THE KEY FACTS

Real Property Depreciation

- Real property is depreciated using the straight-line method.
- Real property uses the mid-month convention.
- Residential property has a recovery period of 27.5 years.
- Nonresidential property placed in service on or after May 13, 1993, has a life of 39 years.

Real Property

For depreciation purposes, real property is classified as land, *residential rental* property, or *nonresidential property*. Land is nondepreciable. Residential rental property consists of dwelling units such as houses, condominiums, and apartment complexes. Residential property has a 27.5-year recovery period. Nonresidential property consists of all other buildings (office buildings, manufacturing facilities, shopping malls, and the like). Nonresidential property placed in service on or after May 13, 1993, has a 39-year recovery period and nonresidential property placed in service after December 31, 1986, and before May 13, 1993, has a 31.5-year recovery period. Exhibit 2-7 summarizes the recovery periods for real property.

If a building is substantially improved (not a minor repair) at some point after the initial purchase, the building addition is treated as a new asset with the same recovery period of the original building. For example, if Teton expanded its warehouse 10 years after the building was placed in service, the expansion or building addition would be depreciated as a *new, separate* asset over 39 years because it is nonresidential property.

EXHIBIT 2-7 Recovery Period for Real Property

Asset Description (summary from Rev. Proc. 87-57)	Recovery Period
Residential	27.5 years
Nonresidential property placed in service on or after May 13, 1993	39 years
Nonresidential property placed in service before May 13, 1993	31.5 years

An important area of tax practice related to real property is cost segregation. This practice attempts to partition or divide the costs of a building into two or more categories. The first category is the building itself, which has a recovery period as noted in Exhibit 2-7. The second category is building components (tangible personal property associated with the building such as electrical and plumbing fixtures that have a shorter recovery period and accelerated depreciation method). Cost segregation utilizes engineers and construction experts who divide the costs between real and tangible personal property. This can generate significant tax savings due to the difference in the present value of the tax savings from the accelerated depreciation deductions associated with personal property relative to real property.

Applicable Method All depreciable real property is depreciated for tax purposes using the straight-line method. This is generally consistent with depreciation methods used for financial accounting purposes.

Applicable Convention All real property is depreciated using the mid-month convention. The **mid-month convention** allows the owner of real property to expense one-half of a month's depreciation for the month in which the property was placed in service (and in the month of the year it is sold as well). This is true regardless of whether the asset was placed in service at the beginning or at the end of the month. For example, if Teton placed its warehouse into service on May 1 (or on *any* other day in May), it would deduct *one-half* a month's depreciation for May and then full depreciation for the months June through December.

Depreciation Tables Just as it does for personal property, the IRS provides depreciation tables for real property. The depreciation tables for 27.5 years, 31.5 years, and 39 years real property are reproduced as Tables 3, 4, and 5, respectively, in this chapter's appendix. The percentage of the asset's original basis that is depreciated in a particular year is located at the intersection of the month the asset was placed in service (column) and the year of depreciation (row—first, second, etc.).

Example 2-11

As indicated in Example 2-1, Teton's basis in the warehouse it purchased on May 1 of year 1 is $275,000. What is Teton's year 1 depreciation on its warehouse?

Answer: $4,414, computed as follows:

Asset	Method	Recovery Period	Date Placed in Service	(1) Basis	(2) Rate*	(1) × (2) Depreciation
Warehouse	SL	39	May 1	$275,000	1.605%	$4,414

(continued on page 2-16)

What if: What would be Teton's year 1 depreciation expense if the building was not a warehouse but was an apartment building that it rented to Teton's employees?

Answer: $6,251, computed as follows:

Asset	Method	Recovery Period	Date Placed in Service	(1) Basis	(2) Rate†	(1) × (2) Depreciation
Apt. Bldg.	SL	27.5	May 1	$275,000	2.273%	$6,251

*The 1.605 percent tax rate factor for the year is found in the 39-year table (Table 5, in the appendix to this chapter) in the fifth column (fifth month) and first row (first year).

†The 2.273 percent tax rate factor for the year is found in the 27.5-year table (Table 4, in the appendix to this chapter) in the fifth column (fifth month) and first row (first year).

When using depreciation tables for real property it is important to stay in the month column corresponding with the month the property was originally placed in service.[18] Thus, to calculate depreciation for a piece of real property placed in service in May (the fifth month), businesses will *always* (for each year of depreciation) find the current year rate factor in the fifth column for that asset. This is true even if the asset is sold in a subsequent year in July (it's easy to make the mistake of using the seventh column to calculate the depreciation for the year of disposition in this situation).

Mid-month convention for year of disposition. Businesses deduct one-half of a month's depreciation in the month they sell or otherwise dispose of real property. For example, if Teton sold its warehouse on March 5 of year 2, it would deduct two and one-half months of depreciation in that year for the warehouse (depreciation for January, February, and one-half of March). Calculating depreciation expense in the year of sale or disposition for mid-month convention assets is similar to the calculation under the mid-quarter convention. When the mid-month convention applies, the asset is treated as though it is sold in the *middle of the month* of which it was actually sold. The simplest process for calculating mid-month convention depreciation for the year of sale consists of the following four steps:

Step 1: Determine the amount of depreciation expense for the asset as if the asset was held for the entire year.

Step 2: Subtract one-half of a month from the month in which the asset was sold (if sold in third month, subtract .5 from 3 to get 2.5). (Subtract half of a month because the business is treated as though the asset was disposed of in the middle of the third month—not the end.)

Step 3: Divide the amount determined in Step 2 by 12 months (2.5/12). This is the fraction of the full year's depreciation the business is eligible to deduct.

Step 4: Multiply the Step 3 outcome by the full depreciation determined in Step 1.

These steps are summarized in the following formula:

Mid-month depreciation for year of disposition

$$= \text{Full year's depreciation} \times \frac{(\text{Month in which asset was disposed of} - .5)}{12}$$

[18]Failure to do so will result in the wrong depreciation expense and is technically a change in accounting method (which requires filing of a Form 3115 with the IRS).

Example 2-12

What if: Assume that Teton sells its warehouse on March 5 in year 2 (the year after Teton buys it). What is Teton's depreciation for the warehouse in the year of disposition (year 2)?

Answer: $1,469, computed using the four-step procedure outlined above as follows.

Step 1: Determine full year's depreciation: $275,000 × 2.564%* = $7,051

Step 2: 3 (month sold) − .5 = 2.5

Step 3: 2.5/12

Step 4: $7,051 × 2.5/12 = $1,469 (see formula above).

*The 2.564 percent rate factor (full year percentage) in Step 1 is obtained from the MACRS Mid-Month Table for 39-year property (Table 5) placed in service during the fifth month (year 2 row).

Special Rules Relating to Cost Recovery

LO 2-3

In addition to the basic MACRS rules, several additional provisions examining the cost recovery of tangible personal property. Congress often uses these special rules for economic stimulus or to curb perceived taxpayer abuses. At the time we went to press, it was unclear whether Congress would extend the higher 2014 limits for these provisions to 2015. If the 2014 limits are not extended to 2015, the limits will decrease significantly. Throughout our main discussion, we assume that the 2014 limits are extended to 2015. However, we also provide examples illustrating how same calculations will be made if Congress does not extend the 2014 limits into 2015.

Immediate Expensing Policy makers created an important tax incentive designed to help small businesses purchasing new or used tangible personal property. This incentive is commonly referred to as the **§179 expense** or *immediate expensing* election.[19] As discussed earlier in the chapter, businesses must generally depreciate assets over the assets' recovery periods. However, under §179, businesses may elect to immediately expense up to $500,000 of tangible personal property placed in service during 2015 (assuming the 2014 limits are extended to 2015).[20,21] Businesses can also use immediate expensing (up to $250,000) for qualified real property (qualified leasehold improvements, qualified retail improvements, and qualified restaurant property). They may also elect to deduct less than the maximum. When businesses elect to deduct a certain amount of §179 expense, they immediately expense all or a portion of an asset's basis or several assets' bases. To reflect this immediate depreciation expense, they must reduce the basis of the asset or assets (to which they applied the expense) *before* they compute the MACRS depreciation expense (from the tables).

Example 2-13

What if: Assume Teton is eligible for and elects to immediately deduct $80,000 of §179 expense against the basis of the machinery. (Note that Teton could have elected to deduct up to $500,000.) What is the amount of Teton's current year depreciation expense, including regular MACRS depreciation and the §179 expense on its machinery (assuming half-year convention applies)?

(continued on page 2-18)

[19]Intangibles and tangible personal property that are used less than 50 percent for business and most real property are not eligible for immediate expensing.

[20]The maximum allowable expense under §179 is indexed for inflation and changes annually. Generally, the annual amount is released in a Revenue Procedure at the beginning of the taxable year. However, in recent years Congress has passed new legislation to enact the expense amounts under §179.

[21]These maximum amounts are per tax return. Thus, if an individual has multiple businesses with asset acquisitions, the taxpayer may only deduct up to these maximum amounts for the combined businesses.

Answer: $141,447, computed as follows:

Description	Amount	Explanation
(1) Machinery	$510,000	Example 2-1.
(2) §179 expense	$ 80,000	
(3) Remaining basis in machinery	$430,000	(1) − (2).
(4) MACRS depreciation rate for 7-year machinery	14.29%	Rate from Table 1.
(5) MACRS depreciation expense on machinery	$ 61,447	(3) × (4).
Total depreciation on machinery	$141,447	(2) + (5).

What if: Assume that Teton was eligible for and elected to claim the maximum amount of §179 expense. What would be its total current-year depreciation expense, including MACRS depreciation and §179 expense (assuming half-year convention applies)?

Answer: $501,429, computed as follows:

Description	Amount	Explanation
(1) Machinery	$510,000	Example 2-1.
(2) §179 expense	$500,000	Maximum expense in 2015.
(3) Remaining basis in machinery	$ 10,000	(1) − (2).
(4) MACRS depreciation rate for 7-year machinery	14.29%	Rate from Table 1.
(5) MACRS depreciation expense on machinery	$ 1,429	(3) × (4).
Total depreciation on machinery	$501,429	(2) + (5).

Limits on immediate expensing. The maximum amount of §179 expense a business may elect to claim for the year is subject to a phase-out limitation. Under the phase-out limitation, businesses must reduce the $500,000 maximum available expense dollar for dollar for the amount of *tangible personal property* purchased and placed in service during 2015 *over* a $2,000,000 threshold (assuming the 2014 limits are extended to 2015).[22] Thus if a business places $2,500,000 ($2,000,000 threshold plus $500,000) or more of tangible personal property into service during 2015, its maximum available §179 expense for the year is $0. The phased-out portion of the maximum expense disappears and does *not* carry over to another year.

Example 2-14

What if: Let's assume that during 2015, Teton placed into service $2,100,000 of machinery (up from the base scenario amount of $510,000), $10,000 of office furniture, and a $15,000 truck for a total of $2,125,000 tangible *personal* property placed in service for the year. What is Teton's maximum §179 expense after applying the phase-out limitation?

[22]The threshold under §179 is indexed for inflation and changes annually. Generally, the annual amount is released in a Revenue Procedure at the beginning of the taxable year.

Answer: $375,000 computed as follows:

Description	Amount	Explanation
(1) Property placed in service in 2015	$2,125,000	
(2) Threshold for §179 phase out	2,000,000	2015 amount [§179(b)(1)].
(3) Phase-out of maximum §179 expense	$ 125,000	(1) − (2) (permanently disallowed).
(4) Maximum §179 expense before phase-out	$ 500,000	§179(b)(2).
(5) Phase-out of maximum §179 expense	125,000	From (3).
Maximum §179 expense after phase-out*	$ 375,000	(4) − (5).

*Note that this is the maximum expense after phase-out but *before* the taxable income limitation we discuss next.

What if: Assume further that Teton acquired and placed in service a warehouse costing $275,000. Taking the warehouse into account, what is Teton's maximum §179 expense after the phase-out?

Answer: $375,000. The same answer as above. The phase-out is based on the amount of tangible personal property placed in service during the year. Because the warehouse is *real property* (not qualified), its acquisition has no effect on Teton's maximum §179 expense.

Businesses may elect to claim the §179 expense for the year up to the maximum amount available (after computing the phase-out—see the previous example). When a business elects to claim a certain amount of §179 expense, it must reduce the basis of the asset(s) to which the expense is applied. It then computes regular depreciation on the remaining basis after reducing the basis of the asset(s) for the §179 expense.

The business's *deductible* §179 expense is limited to the taxpayer's business income after deducting all expenses (including regular depreciation expense) except the §179 expense. Consequently, the §179 expense cannot create or extend a business's net operating loss. Taxpayers' business income includes income from all businesses. For example, a sole-proprietor's business income for purposes of §179 would include not only the income from all Schedules C but also from regular wages. If a business claims more §179 expense than it is allowed to deduct due to the taxable income limitation, it carries the excess forward (indefinitely) and deducts it in a subsequent year, subject to the taxable income limitation (but not the phase-out limitation) in the subsequent year.[23]

Example 2-15

What if: Let's assume the facts of the previous example, where Teton's maximum §179 expense after applying the phase-out limitation is $375,000. Also assume that Teton elects to claim the entire $375,000 expense and it chooses to apply it against the machinery. Further assume that Teton reports $296,503 of taxable income before deducting any §179 expense and depreciation. What amount of total depreciation (including §179 expense) is Teton able to deduct on the machinery for the year?

(continued on page 2-20)

[23]Businesses typically elect only to expense the currently deductible amount since the taxable income limitation may also limit their §179 expense in future years just as it does for the current year.

Answer: $296,503 computed as follows:

Description	Amount	Explanation
(1) Machinery	$2,100,000	Example 2-14.
(2) Elected §179 expense	375,000	
(3) Remaining basis	1,725,000	(1) − (2).
(4) MACRS depreciation rate for 7-year machinery, year 1	14.29%	See Table 1.
(5) MACRS deprecation expense on machinery	$ 246,503	(3) × (4).
(6) Deductible §179 expense	50,000	Taxable income limitation ($296,503 − $249,503).
(7) Total depreciation expense on machinery for the year	296,503	(5) + (6).
(8) Excess §179 expense	325,000	(2) − (6).

What is the amount of Teton's excess §179 expense (elected expense in excess of the deductible amount due to the taxable income limitation), and what does it do with it for tax purposes?

Answer: $325,000. See the above table for the computation (line 8). Teton carries this $325,000 excess §179 expense forward to future years and may deduct it subject to the taxable income limitation. Note that the depreciable basis of the machinery remaining after the §179 expense is $1,725,000 because the depreciable basis is reduced by the full $375,000 of §179 expense claimed even though the deductible §179 expense was limited to $50,000 in the current year.

Effect of Congress not extending the §179 provisions. Our prior discussion assumes Congress will extend the 2014 §179 limits to 2015. However, as of press time, the limits had not been extended. If Congress does not act to extend the 2014 limits to to 2015, the maximum amount businesses would be allowed to immediately expense would drop to $25,000 subject to a property phase-out threshold beginning at $200,000. Example 2-16 illustrates the effect of the reduction of the §179 expensing provision.

Example 2-16

What if: Suppose the maximum §179 expense is $25,000 for 2015, what is Teton's maximum amount of §179 expense on the following assets (same as in Exhibit 2-5) after applying the phase-out limitation of $200,000?

Asset	Date Placed in Service	Original Basis
Office furniture	February 3	$ 10,000
Machinery	July 22	510,000
Used delivery truck	August 17	15,000
Total		$535,000

Answer: $-0-, computed as follows:

Description	Amount	Explanation
(1) Maximum §179 expense for 2015	$ 25,000	Assuming Congress does not extend provision.
(2) Property placed in service in 2015	$535,000	
(3) Threshold for §179 phase-out	200,000	
(4) Phase-out of maximum §179 expense	$ 25,000	Lesser of (1) or (2) − (3).
Maximum §179 expense after phase-out	$ -0-	(1) − (4).

What if: Suppose Teton places only $150,000 of machinery into service on May 12. What would be its total depreciation expense, including MACRS depreciation and §179 expense for the year?

Answer: $42,863, computed as follows:

Description	Amount	Explanation
(1) Machinery	$150,000	
(2) §179 expense	25,000	Not subject to phase-out since machinery placed in service is below threshold amount of $200,000.
(3) Remaining basis in machinery	125,000	(1) − (2).
(4) MACRS depreciation rate for 7-year machinery	14.29%	Rate from Table 1.
(5) MACRS depreciation expense on machinery	17,863	(3) × (4).
Total depreciation on machinery	$ 42,863	(2) + (5).

Choosing the assets to immediately expense. Businesses qualifying for immediate expensing are allowed to choose the asset or assets (from tangible personal property placed in service during the year) they immediately expense under §179. If a business's objective is to maximize its current depreciation expense and the half-year convention applies, it should immediately expense the asset with the lowest first-year cost recovery percentage including bonus depreciation (discussed in the next section). For example, looking at Tables 2a and 2c in the chapter appendix, if a business had to choose between immediately expensing seven-year property placed in service in the first quarter or five-year property placed in service in the third quarter, which asset should it elect to expense under §179 if it wanted to maximize its current year depreciation expense? The five-year asset because its first year depreciation percentage is 15 percent, while the seven-year asset's first year depreciation percentage is 25 percent. Finally, it is important to note that businesses reduce the basis of the assets for the §179 expense before computing whether the mid-quarter convention applies.[24]

THE KEY FACTS

§179 Expenses

- $500,000 of tangible personal property can be immediately expensed in 2015 (assuming 2014 amounts are extended to 2015).
- Businesses are eligible for the full amount of this expense when tangible personal property placed in service is less than $2,000,000 (assuming 2014 amounts are extended to 2015). Beginning at $2,000,000, the §179 expense is phased out, dollar-for-dollar. When assets placed in service reach $2,500,000, no §179 expense can be taken.
- §179 expenses are also limited to a business's taxable income before the §179 expense. §179 expenses cannot create losses.

Example 2-17

What if: Let's assume that Teton placed into service on June 1, five-year property costing $600,000 and seven-year property costing $600,000. Further assume that Teton is not subject to the taxable income limitation for the §179 expense. What is Teton's depreciation expense (including §179 expense) if it elects to apply the full §179 expense against the five-year property (Scenario A)? What is its depreciation expense if it applies it against its seven-year property (Scenario B)? (Assume the 2013 limits are extended to 2015.)

(continued on page 2-22)

[24]Treasury Regulation §1.168(d)-1(b)(4)(i).

Answer: $605,740 if it applies the §179 to the five-year property (Scenario A) and $634,290 if it applies it to the seven-year property (Scenario B). See the computations below:

Description	(Scenario A) §179 Expense on 5-year Property	(Scenario B) §179 Expense on 7-year Property	Explanation
(1) Original basis	$600,000	$600,000	
(2) Elected §179 expense	500,000	500,000	Maximum expense.
(3) Remaining basis	100,000	100,000	(1) − (2).
(4) MACRS depreciation rate	20%	14.29%	See Table 1.
(5) MACRS depreciation expense	$ 20,000	$ 14,290	(3) × (4).
(6) Deductible §179 expense	500,000	500,000	Example 2-14.
(7) MACRS depreciation on other property	85,740	120,000	This is the depreciation on the $600,000 seven-year property in the five-year column and on the $600,000 five-year property in the seven-year column.
Total depreciation expense	$605,740	$634,290	(5) + (6) + (7).

Note that Teton deducts $28,550 more in depreciation expense if it applies the §179 expense to the seven-year property.

What if: Assume the same facts, except that Teton placed the five-year property in service on December 1. Absent any §179 expense, Teton would be subject to the mid-quarter convention because 50 percent of its tangible personal property was placed in service in the fourth quarter. Assuming Teton wanted to avoid the mid-quarter convention, how should it apply its §179 expense?

Answer: It should apply the §179 expense against the five-year property. By doing so, the basis of the assets placed in service in the fourth quarter is $100,000 ($600,000 minus $500,000 §179 expense) and the basis of the assets placed in service in total is $700,000 ($600,000 7-year property + $100,000 5-year property). Thus, the percentage of tangible personal property placed in service in the fourth quarter is 14.3 percent ($100,000/$700,000) and the mid-quarter convention does not apply. If, however, it applies the §179 expense against the seven-year property, the mid-quarter convention would apply because the percentage of tangible personal property placed in service in the fourth quarter increases to 85.7 percent ($600,000/$700,000). Because this exceeds 40 percent, the mid-quarter convention applies. Teton could also expense just enough five-year property to avoid the mid-quarter convention and elect the rest of the §179 expense against the seven-year property to maximize its total depreciation.

Bonus depreciation.[25] To stimulate the economy, policy makers occasionally implement **bonus depreciation.**[26] Taxpayers can immediately expense 50 percent of qualified property. Qualified property must have a recovery period of 20 years or less (no real property) and the original use of the property must commence with the taxpayer (the property must be new rather than used), and the property must be placed in service during 2015.[27] The bonus depreciation is calculated after the §179 expense

[25]Although, as of press time, the bonus depreciation provisions from 2014 were scheduled to expire in 2015, we assume Congress will extend the bonus depreciation rules to 2015 in order to illustrate the tax consequences of bonus depreciation.

[26]§168(k)(2)(6). Bonus depreciation, if applicable, is also allowable for purposes of the AMT.

[27]§168(k)(2)(A)(iv).

but before regular MACRS depreciation.[28] Taxpayers may elect not to take bonus depreciation by attaching a statement to their tax return indicating they are electing to not claim bonus depreciation.

Example 2-18

What if: Assume that Teton elected bonus depreciation for the tangible personal property acquired in Exhibit 2-5.

Asset	Date Acquired	Quarter Acquired	Cost Basis	Recovery Period
Office furniture	2/3/15	1st	$ 10,000	7
Machinery	7/22/15	3rd	510,000	7
Delivery truck	8/17/15	3rd	15,000	5
Total			$535,000	

Assuming Teton elects no §179 expense, what is Teton's bonus depreciation?

Answer: $260,000 computed as follows:

Description	Amount	Explanation
(1) Qualified property	$520,000	
(2) Bonus depreciation rate	50%	§168(k)(1)(A).
Bonus depreciation	$260,000	(1) × (2).

Note that the delivery truck is not eligible for bonus depreciation because it is used property.

What if: Assuming Teton elects the maximum §179 expense, what is Teton's bonus depreciation?

Answer: $17,500 computed as follows:

Description	Amount	Explanation
(1) §179 qualified property	$535,000	
(2) §179 expense	500,000	Maximum expense assuming the 2014 amounts are extended to 2015.
(3) Remaining basis	35,000	(1) − (2).
(4) Remaining amount eligible for bonus depreciation	35,000	Remaining amount relates to the office furniture and machinery. Since the truck is used and not eligible for bonus depreciation, we would apply the §179 expense to the truck to maximize the current year depreciation deduction.
(5) Bonus depreciation rate	50%	§168(k)(1)(A).
(6) Bonus depreciation	$ 17,500	(4) × (5).

What if: Suppose Congress does not extend bonus depreciation to 2015 and that it does not extend the 2014 limits for the §179 provisions to 2015. What is the amount of Teton's total depreciation expense for the year?

Answer: $77,308, computed as follows:

Asset	(1) Original Basis	(2) Rate	(1) × (2) Depreciation
Office furniture	$ 10,000	14.29%	$ 1,429
Machinery	510,000	14.29	72,879
Used delivery truck	15,000	20.00	3,000
Total			$77,308

[28]Reg. §1.168(k)-1(a)(2)(iii) and Reg. §1.168(k)-1(d)(3) Example (2).

THE KEY FACTS

Listed Property

- When an asset is used for both personal and business use, calculate the business-use percentage.
- If the business-use percentage is above 50 percent, the allowable depreciation is limited to the business-use percentage.
- If a listed property's business-use percentage ever falls below 50 percent, depreciation for all previous years is retroactively restated using MACRS straight-line method.

Teton is not eligible for §179 expense because it has placed $535,000 of qualified assets into service during the year. This amount exceeds the threshold amount of $200,000 by more than $25,000 so Teton's §179 is $-0-. In addition, if Congress does not extend the bonus depreciation provision, Teton's depreciation will be limited to MACRS depreciation only.

TAXES IN THE REAL WORLD What a Difference a Day (or Few) Makes

Taxpayers may begin taking depreciation deductions on their tax returns for business assets "placed in service" during the taxable year. As one taxpayer recently found out, determining when an asset is placed in service is not as simple as purchasing and using an asset. Michael Brown, a wealthy insurance salesman, purchased a $22 million Bombardier Challenger 604 airplane for use in his business. He took possession of the plane on December 30, 2003, and flew the plane across the country on business trips before the end of the year. Accordingly, Brown claimed about $11 million of bonus depreciation on his 2003 tax return. In January 2004, the plane was grounded for a period of time while a conference table and a display screen were added at an additional cost of $500,000. These improvements were "needed" and "required" for his insurance business according to Brown.

The IRS challenged Brown's bonus depreciation deduction claiming that the plane was not "placed in service" in 2003. The issue is when the plane was regularly available for use in its specifically intended function. Per Brown's testimony, he insisted on having the conference table and display screen so he could conduct business on the plane. Because of this testimony that determined the plane's specifically intended function, the Tax Court denied the bonus depreciation deduction for 2003.

The outcome of this case illustrates the importance of determining the specific function for an asset and whether seemingly minor (2 percent) upgrades can make the asset substantially unavailable for its specifically intended function. It seems the taxpayer's own testimony of the plane's specifically intended function drove the Tax Court's decision to disallow the bonus depreciation deduction.

Source: Brown, T. C. Memo. 2013-275.

Listed Property Most business-owned assets are used for business rather than personal purposes. For example, Weyerhaeuser employees probably have little or no personal interest in using Weyerhaeuser's timber-harvesting equipment during their free time. In contrast, business owners and employees may find some business assets, such as company automobiles or laptop computers, conducive for personal use.

Business assets that tend to be used for both business and personal purposes are referred to as **listed property.** For example, automobiles, other means of transportation (planes, boats, and recreation vehicles), computer equipment, and even digital cameras are considered to be listed property. The tax law limits the allowable depreciation on listed property to the portion of the asset used for business purposes.

How do taxpayers compute depreciation for listed property? First, they must determine the percentage of business vs. personal use of the asset for the year. If the business-use percentage for the year *exceeds* 50 percent, the deductible depreciation is limited to the full annual depreciation multiplied by the *business-use* percentage for the year. Listed property used in trade or business more than 50 percent is eligible for the §179 expensing election and bonus depreciation (if bonus depreciation is applicable for year asset was placed into service).

Example 2-19

What if: Assume that, in addition to the assets Teton purchased in the base scenario presented in Exhibit 2-5, it also purchased a new computer projector for $2,000 that its employees use for business presentations on weekdays. On weekends, Steve uses the projector as an integral part of his high-definition home theater system. Since the computer projector is listed property, Teton must assess the business-use percentage to properly calculate its deductible depreciation for the projector. Assuming that Teton determines the business-use percentage to be 75 percent, what is Teton's depreciation deduction on the projector for the year (ignoring bonus depreciation and §179 expensing)?

Answer: $300, computed as follows:

Description	Amount	Explanation
(1) Original basis of projector	$2,000	
(2) MACRS depreciation rate	20%	5-year property, year 1, half-year convention.
(3) Full MACRS depreciation expense	$ 400	(1) × (2).
(4) Business-use percentage	75%	
Depreciation deduction for year	$ 300	(3) × (4).

When the business-use percentage of an asset is 50 percent or less, the business must compute depreciation for the asset using the MACRS *straight-line* method over the MACRS ADS (alternative depreciation system) recovery period.[29] For five-year assets such as automobiles and computers, the assets on which the personal use limitation is most common, the MACRS ADS recovery period is also five years. However, for seven-year assets, the ADS recovery period is generally 10 years.[30]

If a business initially uses an asset more than 50 percent of the time for business (and appropriately adopts the 200 percent declining balance method) but subsequently its business use drops to 50 percent or below, the *depreciation expense for all prior years must be recomputed* as if it had been using the straight-line depreciation over the ADS recovery period the entire time. It must then recapture any excess accelerated depreciation it deducted over the straight-line depreciation it should have deducted by adjusting the current year depreciation. In practical terms, the business can use the following five steps to determine its current depreciation expense for the asset:

Step 1: Compute depreciation for the year it drops to 50 percent or below using the straight-line method (this method also applies to all subsequent years).

Step 2: Compute the amount of depreciation the taxpayer would have deducted if the taxpayer had used the straight-line method over the ADS recovery period for all prior years (recall that depreciation is limited to the business-use percentage in those years).

Step 3: Compute the amount of depreciation the taxpayer had actually deducted on the asset for all prior years.

Step 4: Subtract the amount from Step 2 from the amount in Step 3. The difference is the prior year accelerated depreciation in excess of straight-line depreciation.

Step 5: Subtract the excess accelerated depreciation determined in Step 4 from the current year straight-line depreciation in Step 1. This is the business's allowable depreciation expense on the asset for the year. If the prior year excess depreciation from Step 4 exceeds the current year straight-line depreciation in Step 1, the business is not allowed to deduct any depreciation on the asset for the year and must actually recognize additional ordinary income for the amount of the excess.

This five-step process is designed to place the business in the same position it would have been in if it had used straight-line depreciation during all years of the asset's life.

[29]This is the alternative recovery period listed in Rev. Proc. 87-56. See §168(g)(3)(C) and Reg. §1.280F-3T(d)(1).

[30]However, there are exceptions to this general rule. For example, the ADS recovery period for certain machinery for food and beverages is 12 years and the ADS recovery period for machinery for tobacco products is 15 years. Thus, it is important to check Rev. Proc. 87-56 to verify the ADS recovery period in these situations.

Example 2-20

What if: Assume that, consistent with the previous example, in year 1 Teton used the projector 75 percent of the time for business purposes and deducted $300 depreciation expense on the projector. However, in year 2, Teton's business-use percentage falls to 40 percent. What is Teton's depreciation deduction for the projector in year 2?

Answer: $10, computed using the five-step process described above as follows:

Description	Amount	Explanation*
(1) Straight-line depreciation in current year	$160	$2,000/5 years × 40 percent business use percentage (Step 1).
(2) Prior year straight-line depreciation	150	$2,000/5 × 50 percent (half-year convention) × 75 percent business-use percentage (Step 2).
(3) Prior year accelerated depreciation	300	Example 2-19 (prior example) (Step 3).
(4) Excess accelerated depreciation	150	(3) − (2) (Step 4).
Allowable current year depreciation	**$ 10**	(1) − (4) (Step 5).

*Note that the MACRS ADS recovery period (five years) for computers and peripherals (qualified technological equipment) is the same as the standard MACRS recovery period (five years).

What if: Now assume that, in year 1 Teton used the projector 85 percent of the time for business purposes and deducted $340 depreciation expense on the projector. However, in year 2, Teton's business-use percentage falls to 40 percent. What is Teton's depreciation deduction for the projector in year 2?

Answer: $0 depreciation deduction and $10 of ordinary income because excess accelerated depreciation exceeds current year straight-line depreciation, computed as follows:

Description	Amount	Explanation
(1) Straight-line depreciation in current year	$160	$2,000/5 years × 40 percent business use.
(2) Prior year straight-line depreciation	170	$2,000/5 × 50 percent (half-year convention) × 85 percent business-use percentage.
(3) Prior year accelerated depreciation	340	Example 2-19 (prior example, if 85%).
(4) Excess accelerated depreciation	170	(3) − (2).
Allowable current year depreciation (income)	**($10)**	(1) − (4).

TAXES IN THE REAL WORLD Do Depreciation Tax Incentives Work?

U.S. companies have been hoarding cash to the tune of $1.64 trillion as of the 2013 year-end according to a Moody's Investors Services report. One way the government tries to stimulate business spending is through generous depreciation provisions such as bonus depreciation and §179 immediate expensing provisions. So do these provisions really work?

A survey conducted by Bloomberg BNA, a tax and accounting software vendor, says not really. The survey found that just 10 percent of CFOs, controllers, and tax directors of companies with average revenues of $7.5 billion per year expect their 2014 capital expenditures to change because of the expiration of the bonus depreciation and §179 incentives. A majority of respondents to the survey were even more specific by saying that even if the currently available tax incentives could reduce their total cost of capital by 10 percent, their companies would not increase their capital expenditures.

Bloomberg BNA concludes that "Bonus depreciation and Section 179 expensing, while welcomed by the business community, is not viewed by a majority of that same community as an economic stimulus that drives business decisions."

Source: Bloomberg BNA "US Corporate Capital Expenditures: Consciously Uncoupled from Federal Tax Incentives" http://forms.bnasoftware.com/MTC_Common/mtcURLSrv.aspx?ID=13723&Key=ECEDF59D-C244-4682-B6EF-8278126A6F67&URLID=30222&mtcPromotion=20490

Luxury Automobiles As we discussed in Chapter 1, §162 limits business deductions to those considered to be "ordinary, necessary, and reasonable" to prevent subsidizing (giving a tax deduction for) unwarranted business expenses. Although these terms are subject to interpretation, most taxpayers agree that for purposes of simply transporting passengers for business-related purposes, the cost of acquiring and using a Ford Focus is more likely to be ordinary, necessary, and reasonable than the cost of acquiring and using a Ferrari California—although perhaps not as exhilarating. Since either vehicle should be able to transport an employee or business owner from the office to a business meeting, the Ford Focus should be just as effective at accomplishing the business purpose as the Ferrari. If this is true, why should the government help taxpayers pay for expensive cars with tax savings from large depreciation deductions associated with automobiles? Congress decided it shouldn't. Therefore, with certain exceptions we discuss below, the tax laws generally limit the annual depreciation expense for automobiles.[31] Each year, the IRS provides a maximum depreciation schedule for automobiles placed in service during that particular year.[32] For 2010 through 2014, taxpayers are allowed to expense $8,000 of bonus depreciation above the otherwise allowable maximum depreciation (maximum depreciation of $11,160 for automobiles placed in service in 2012 through 2014); however, as of press date the bonus depreciation provisions have not been extended to 2015.[33] Exhibit 2-8 summarizes these schedules for automobiles placed in service for each year from 2015 back to 2012.

THE KEY FACTS

Luxury Vehicles

- Depreciation on automobiles weighing less than 6,000 lbs. is subject to luxury auto provisions.
- Luxury automobiles have a maximum depreciation limit for each year.
- Listed property rules are also applicable to luxury automobiles.

EXHIBIT 2-8 Automobile Depreciation Limits

Recovery Year	Year Placed in Service			
	2015	2014	2013	2012
1	3,160*	3,160*	3,160*	3,160*
2	5,100	5,100	5,100	5,100
3	3,050	3,050	3,050	3,050
4 and after	1,875	1,875	1,875	1,875

*$8,000 additional depreciation is allowed when bonus depreciation is elected. If the 2014 bonus depreciation provisions are not extended to 2015, the $8,000 additional amount would not apply for those years.

Businesses placing automobiles into service during the year determine depreciation expense for the automobiles by first computing the regular MACRS depreciation expense (using the appropriate convention). They then compare it to the maximum depreciation amount for the first year of the recovery period based on the IRS-provided tables. Businesses are allowed to deduct the lesser of the two. If the automobile depreciation limits apply in the first year, the taxpayer must use the IRS maximum automobile depreciation table to compute depreciation for the asset(s) in all

[31]The passenger automobile definition excludes vehicles that charge for transportation such as taxi cabs, limousines, and hearses. It also excludes delivery trucks and vans. The tax law also limits the deduction for leased autos, which closed the leasing loophole that circumvented the luxury auto depreciation rules.

[32]These limitations are indexed for inflation and change annually. Revenue Procedure 2015-19 includes the 2015 limitations for automobiles and also provides slightly higher limits for hybrids, trucks, and SUVs.

[33]§168(k)(2)(F)(i).

subsequent years. In 2015, if the half-year convention applies, the table limits the depreciation on automobiles placed in service during the year costing more than $15,800.[34] Automobiles to which the depreciation limits apply are commonly referred to as **luxury automobiles.**[35] For any two such luxury cars—say, a 2016 Honda Civic and a 2016 Porsche 911—the annual depreciation limit is the same, regardless of the cost of the vehicles. The only difference is the length of time it will take to fully depreciate the vehicle.

Example 2-21

What is the maximum annual depreciation expense available for 2015 (year 1) on a 2016 Honda Civic costing $15,860 and a 2016 Porsche 911 costing $97,400 (ignoring bonus depreciation)?

Answer: $3,160 for both. See the following depreciation schedules for each automobile.

Luxury Auto Depreciation

Year/Make	2016 Honda Civic	2016 Porsche 911
Model	DX 2dr Coupe	Carrera 4S
Price	$15,860	$97,400
Depreciation		
Year 1	$ 3,160	$ 3,160
Year 2	5,100	5,100
Year 3	3,050	3,050
Year 4	1,875	1,875
Year 5	1,875	1,875
Year 6	800	1,875
Years 7–48		1,875
Year 49		1,715

Given the maximum deduction limitations, the depreciation of the Honda and Porsche are identical in years 1–5. However, beginning in year 6 the Porsche is depreciated at a maximum of $1,875 per year until fully depreciated in year 49—however, it is unlikely the business will actually hold the Porsche through year 49.

The luxury automobile limitations don't apply to vehicles weighing more than 6,000 pounds. Thus, businesses owning these vehicles are allowed to claim §179, bonus, and regular MACRS depreciation expense for these vehicles.[36]

Just like businesses using other types of listed property, businesses using luxury automobiles for business and personal purposes may only deduct depreciation on the asset to the extent of business use. Business use is determined by miles driven for business purposes relative to total miles driven for the year.[37] Consequently, if a business places a luxury automobile into service in 2015 and uses the automobile 90 percent of the time for business purposes during the year (9,000 miles for business and 1,000 miles of personal use), the owner's depreciation (ignoring bonus depreciation) on the auto for the year is limited to $2,844 (year 1 full depreciation of $3,160 × 90 percent business use—see Exhibit 2-8).[38] Further, if the business use falls to

[34]In 2015, the full first-year depreciation on an automobile costing $15,800 is $3,160 ($15,800 × 20%). This is the amount of the first year limit for automobiles placed in service in 2015.

[35]Correspondingly, the depreciation limits on automobiles are commonly referred to as the *luxury auto depreciation limits.*

[36]§280F(d)(5)(A).

[37]As an alternative to deducting depreciation expense and other costs of operating an automobile, taxpayers using automobiles for both personal and business purposes may deduct a standard mileage rate for each mile of business use. In 2015 the business mileage rate is 57.5 cents per mile.

[38]Even if the business-use percentage multiplied by the MACRS depreciation is greater than the $3,160 maximum, the depreciation amount is limited to the maximum depreciation amount times the business-use percentage.

50 percent or less in any subsequent year, just as with other listed property, the taxpayer must use the straight-line method of depreciation and reduce depreciation expense by the amount of excess accelerated depreciation (see Example 2-20). However, because straight-line depreciation is also limited by the luxury auto depreciation limits, it may turn out that the business doesn't have any excess accelerated depreciation.

Are businesses allowed to deduct §179 expensing on luxury automobiles? Yes, but the maximum depreciation *including* §179 expense (but excluding the additional $8,000 bonus depreciation) is subject to the luxury auto limits ($3,160 for 2015). Thus, using the §179 expense on a luxury auto is unlikely to provide any tax benefit beyond the regular depreciation for most automobiles. However, businesses may deduct $25,000 of §179 expense for trucks and SUVs weighing over 6,000 pounds. This $25,000 is part of the overall $500,000 maximum §179 amount. Some companies use tax benefits to sell customers on purchasing these types of automobiles.

Depreciation for the Alternative Minimum Tax

Both individuals and corporations are subject to tax under the alternative minimum tax (AMT) system. In determining their alternative minimum taxable income, individuals and corporations may be required to recalculate their depreciation expense. For AMT purposes, the allowable recovery period and conventions are the same for all depreciable assets as they are for regular tax purposes.[39] However, for AMT purposes, businesses are not allowed to use the 200 percent declining balance method to depreciate tangible personal property. Rather, they must choose from the 150 percent declining balance method or the straight-line method to depreciate the property for AMT purposes. The difference between regular tax depreciation and AMT depreciation is an adjustment that is either added to or subtracted from regular taxable income in computing the alternative minimum tax base.[40] In contrast, the §179 expense is equally deductible for both regular tax and AMT purposes. Depreciation of real property is the same for both regular tax and AMT purposes.

Depreciation Summary

Teton's depreciation for the year is summarized in Exhibit 2-9, and Exhibit 2-10 presents Teton's depreciation expense as it would be reported on its tax return on Form 4562 (this assumes Teton elected out of bonus depreciation).

EXHIBIT 2-9 Tax Depreciation Expense Summary

Asset	Original Basis	§179 Expense	Remaining Basis*	Depreciation Expense	Reference
Machinery	$510,000	$80,000	$430,000	$ 61,447	Example 2-13 (What-if scenario).
Office furniture	10,000		10,000	1,429	Example 2-3.
Delivery truck	15,000	0	15,000	3,000	Example 2-3.
Warehouse	275,000	N/A	275,000	4,414	Example 2-11.
Land	75,000	N/A	75,000	0	N/A.
§179 Expense				80,000	Example 2-13.
Total Depreciation Expense				$150,290	

*Note that Teton's remaining basis is the original cost less the §179 expense.

[39]This is true for assets placed in service after 1998.

[40]If the taxpayer elected either the 150 percent declining balance or the straight-line method for regular tax depreciation of tangible personal property, then there is no AMT adjustment with respect to that property.

EXHIBIT 2-10 **Teton's Form 4562 Parts I-IV for Depreciation (Assumes $100,000 of taxable income before the §179 expense)**

Form **4562**

Department of the Treasury
Internal Revenue Service (99)

Depreciation and Amortization
(Including Information on Listed Property)
▶ Attach to your tax return.
▶ Information about Form 4562 and its separate instructions is at *www.irs.gov/form4562.*

OMB No. 1545-0172
2014
Attachment Sequence No. **179**

Name(s) shown on return	Business or activity to which this form relates	Identifying number

Part I **Election To Expense Certain Property Under Section 179**
Note: *If you have any listed property, complete Part V before you complete Part I.*

1	Maximum amount (see instructions)	1	500,000
2	Total cost of section 179 property placed in service (see instructions)	2	535,000
3	Threshold cost of section 179 property before reduction in limitation (see instructions)	3	2,000,000
4	Reduction in limitation. Subtract line 3 from line 2. If zero or less, enter -0-	4	0
5	Dollar limitation for tax year. Subtract line 4 from line 1. If zero or less, enter -0-. If married filing separately, see instructions	5	500,000

6 (a) Description of property	(b) Cost (business use only)	(c) Elected cost
Machinery	510,000	80,000
7 Listed property. Enter the amount from line 29	7	

8	Total elected cost of section 179 property. Add amounts in column (c), lines 6 and 7	8	80,000
9	Tentative deduction. Enter the **smaller** of line 5 or line 8	9	80,000
10	Carryover of disallowed deduction from line 13 of your 2013 Form 4562	10	
11	Business income limitation. Enter the smaller of business income (not less than zero) or line 5 (see instructions)	11	100,000
12	Section 179 expense deduction. Add lines 9 and 10, but do not enter more than line 11	12	80,000
13	Carryover of disallowed deduction to 2015. Add lines 9 and 10, less line 12 ▶ 13		

Note: *Do not use Part II or Part III below for listed property. Instead, use Part V.*

Part II **Special Depreciation Allowance and Other Depreciation (Do not** include listed property.) (See instructions.)

14	Special depreciation allowance for qualified property (other than listed property) placed in service during the tax year (see instructions)	14	
15	Property subject to section 168(f)(1) election	15	
16	Other depreciation (including ACRS)	16	

Part III **MACRS Depreciation (Do not** include listed property.) (See instructions.)

Section A

17	MACRS deductions for assets placed in service in tax years beginning before 2014	17	
18	If you are electing to group any assets placed in service during the tax year into one or more general asset accounts, check here ▶ ☐		

Section B—Assets Placed in Service During 2014 Tax Year Using the General Depreciation System

(a) Classification of property	(b) Month and year placed in service	(c) Basis for depreciation (business/investment use only—see instructions)	(d) Recovery period	(e) Convention	(f) Method	(g) Depreciation deduction
19a 3-year property						
b 5-year property		15,000	5-year	HY	DDB	3,000
c 7-year property		440,000	7-year	HY	DDB	62,876
d 10-year property						
e 15-year property						
f 20-year property						
g 25-year property			25 yrs.		S/L	
h Residential rental property			27.5 yrs.	MM	S/L	
			27.5 yrs.	MM	S/L	
i Nonresidential real property	May 2014	275,000	39 yrs.	MM	S/L	4,414
				MM	S/L	

Section C—Assets Placed in Service During 2014 Tax Year Using the Alternative Depreciation System

20a Class life					S/L	
b 12-year			12 yrs.		S/L	
c 40-year			40 yrs.	MM	S/L	

Part IV **Summary** (See instructions.)

21	Listed property. Enter amount from line 28	21	
22	**Total.** Add amounts from line 12, lines 14 through 17, lines 19 and 20 in column (g), and line 21. Enter here and on the appropriate lines of your return. Partnerships and S corporations—see instructions	22	150,290
23	For assets shown above and placed in service during the current year, enter the portion of the basis attributable to section 263A costs — 23		

For Paperwork Reduction Act Notice, see separate instructions. Cat. No. 12906N Form **4562** (2014)

AMORTIZATION

LO 2-4

Businesses recover the cost of intangible assets through amortization rather than depreciation expense. Intangible assets in the form of capitalized expenditures, such as capitalized **research and experimentation (R&E) costs** or **covenants not to compete,** do not have physical characteristics. Nonetheless, they may have determinable lives. While research and experimentation costs may have an indeterminate life, a covenant not to compete, for example, would have a life equal to the stated term of the contractual agreement. When the life of intangible assets cannot be determined, taxpayers recover the cost of the assets when they dispose of them—unless they are assigned a specific tax recovery period.

For tax purposes, an intangible asset can be placed into one of the following four general categories:

1. §197 purchased intangibles.
2. Start-up expenditures and organizational costs.
3. Research and experimentation costs.
4. Patents and copyrights.

Businesses amortize all intangible assets in these categories using the straight-line method for both book and tax purposes.

Section 197 Intangibles

When a business purchases the *assets* of another business for a single purchase price, the business must determine the basis of each of the assets it acquired in the transaction. To determine basis, the business must allocate a portion of the purchase price to each of the individual assets acquired in the transaction. Generally, under this approach, each asset acquired in the purchase (cash, machinery, and real property, for example) takes a basis equal to its fair market value. However, some of the assets acquired in the transaction may not appear on the seller's balance sheet. In fact, a substantial portion of a business's value may exist in the form of intangible assets such as customer lists, patents, trademarks, trade names, goodwill, going-concern value, covenants not to compete, and so forth. Nearly all of these assets are amortized according to §197 of the Internal Revenue Code—hence, they are often referred to **§197 purchased intangibles.** According to §197, these assets have a recovery period of 180 months (15 years), *regardless of their actual life.*[41] For example, when a business buys an existing business, the owner selling the business often signs a covenant not to compete for a specified period such as five years.[42] Even though a five-year covenant not to compete clearly has a fixed and determinable life, it must be amortized over 180 months (15 years). The **full-month convention** applies to the amortization of purchased intangibles. This convention allows taxpayers to deduct an entire month's worth of amortization for the month of purchase and all subsequent months in the year. The full-month convention also applies in the month of sale or disposition.[43]

THE KEY FACTS

§197 Intangible Assets

- Purchased intangibles are amortized over a period of 180 months, regardless of their explicitly stated lifetimes.
- The full-month convention applies to amortizable assets.

[41]§197 was Congress's response to taxpayers manipulating the valuation and recovery periods assigned to these purchased intangibles.

[42]A covenant not to compete is a contract between the seller of a business and its buyer that the seller will not operate a similar business that would compete with the previous business for a specified period of time.

[43]Reg. §1.197-2(g)(l)(i) illustrates the special rules that apply when a taxpayer sells a §197 intangible or the intangible becomes worthless and the taxpayer's basis in the asset exceeds the sale proceeds (if any). A business may recognize a loss on the sale or disposition only when the business does not hold any other §197 assets that the business acquired in the *same initial transaction.* Otherwise, the taxpayer may not deduct the loss on the sale or disposition until the business sells or disposes of *all* of the other §197 intangibles that it purchased in the same initial transaction. The same loss disallowance rule applies if a §197 intangible expires before it is fully amortized.

Example 2-22

What if: Assume that at the beginning of year 1, Teton acquires a competitor's assets for $350,000.[44] Of the $350,000 purchase price, $125,000 is allocated to tangible assets and $225,000 is allocated to §197 intangible assets (patent, goodwill, and a customer list with a three-year life).[45] For each of the first three years, Teton would deduct one-fifteenth of the basis of each asset as amortization expense. What is Teton's accumulated amortization and remaining basis in each of these §197 intangibles after three years?

Answer: See the table below:

Description	Patent	Goodwill	Customer List
Basis	$25,000	$150,000	$50,000
Accumulated amortization (3/15ths of original basis)	(5,000)	(30,000)	(10,000)
Remaining basis	$20,000	$120,000	$40,000

When a taxpayer sells a §197 intangible for more than its basis, the taxpayer recognizes gain. We describe how to characterize this type of gain in the next chapter.

Organizational Expenditures and Start-Up Costs

Organizational expenditures include expenditures to form and organize a business in the form of a corporation or a partnership.[46] Organizational expenditures typically include costs of organizational meetings, state fees, accounting service costs incident to organization, and legal service expenditures such as document drafting, taking minutes of organizational meetings, and creating terms of the original stock certificates. These costs are generally incurred prior to the starting of business (or shortly thereafter) but relate to creating the business entity. The costs of selling or marketing stock do *not* qualify as organizational expenditures and cannot be amortized.[47]

Example 2-23

What if: Suppose Teton was organized as a corporation rather than a sole proprietorship (recall that sole proprietorships cannot expense organizational expenditures). Steve paid $35,000 of legal costs to Scott, Tang, and Malan to draft the corporate charter and articles of incorporation; $10,000 to Harvey and Stratford for accounting fees related to the organization; and $7,000 for organizational meetings, $5,000 for stock issuance costs, and $1,000 for state fees related to the incorporation. What amounts of these expenditures qualify as organizational costs?

Answer: $53,000 computed as follows (with the exception of the stock issuance costs, each of Teton's expenses qualify as amortizable organizational expenditures):

[44] If a business acquires another business's stock (rather than assets) there is no goodwill assigned for tax purposes, and the purchase price simply becomes the basis of the stock purchased.

[45] A customer base is the value assigned to current customers (i.e., the lists that will allow the new owner to capture future benefits from the current customers).

[46] §248 for corporations and §709 for partnerships. Sole proprietorships cannot deduct organizational expenditures.

[47] These syndication costs are capitalized and deducted on the final tax return a business files.

Description	Qualifying Organizational Expenditures
Legal drafting of corporate charter and articles of incorporation	$35,000
Accounting fees related to organization	10,000
Organizational meetings	7,000
Stock issuance costs	0
State incorporation fees	1,000
Totals	$53,000

THE KEY FACTS

Organizational Expenditures and Start-Up Costs

- Taxpayers may immediately expense up to $5,000 of organizational expenditures and $5,000 of start-up costs.
- The immediate expense rule has a dollar-for-dollar phase-out that begins at $50,000 for organizational expenditures and for start-up costs. Thus, when organizational expenditures or start-up costs exceed $55,000 there is no immediate expensing.

Businesses may *immediately expense* up to $5,000 of organizational expenditures.[48] However, businesses incurring more than $50,000 in organizational expenditures must phase-out (reduce) the $5,000 immediate expense amount dollar for dollar for expenditures exceeding $50,000. Thus, businesses incurring at least $55,000 of organizational expenditures are not allowed to immediately expense any of the expenditures.

Example 2-24

What if: Suppose Teton is a corporation and it wants to maximize its current year organizational expenditure deduction. As described in Example 2-23, Teton incurred $53,000 of organizational expenditures in year 1. How much of the organizational expenditures can Teton immediately expense in year 1?

Answer: $2,000, computed as follows:

Description	Amount	Explanation
(1) Maximum immediate expense	$ 5,000	§248(a)(1).
(2) Total organizational expenditures	53,000	Example 2-23.
(3) Phase-out threshold	50,000	§248(a)(1)(B).
(4) Immediate expense phase-out	3,000	(2) − (3).
(5) Allowable immediate expense	**2,000**	(1) − (4), but not below zero.
Remaining organizational expenditures	$51,000*	(2) − (5).

What if: Assuming that Teton is a corporation and that it incurred $41,000 of organizational expenditures in year 1, how much of the organizational expenditures could Teton immediately expense in year 1?

Answer: $5,000, computed as follows:

Description	Amount	Explanation
(1) Maximum immediate expense	$ 5,000	§248(a)(1).
(2) Total organizational expenditures	41,000	
(3) Phase-out threshold	50,000	§248(a)(1)(B).
(4) Immediate expense phase-out	0	(2) − (3), limit to zero.
(5) Allowable immediate expense	**5,000**	(1) − (4).
Remaining organizational expenditures	$36,000*	(2) − (5).

(continued on page 2-34)

[48]§248(a)(1) for corporations or §709 for partnerships.

What if: Assuming that Teton is a corporation and it incurred $60,000 of organizational expenditures in year 1, how much of the organizational expenditures could Teton immediately expense in year 1?

Answer: $0, computed as follows:

Description	Amount	Explanation
(1) Maximum immediate expense	$ 5,000	§248(a)(1).
(2) Total organizational expenditures	60,000	
(3) Phase-out threshold	50,000	§248(a)(1)(B).
(4) Immediate expense phase-out	10,000	(2) − (3).
(5) Allowable immediate expense	**0**	(1) − (4).
Remaining organizational expenditures	$60,000*	(2) − (5).

*As we discuss below, Teton amortizes the remaining organizational costs.

Businesses amortize organizational expenditures that they do not immediately expense using the straight-line method over a recovery period of 15 years (180 months).

Example 2-25

What if: Assume Teton is a corporation and it amortizes the $51,000 of organizational expenditures remaining after it immediately expenses $2,000 of the costs (see Example 2-24). If Teton began business on February 1 of year 1, how much total cost recovery expense for the organizational expenditures is Teton able to deduct in year 1?

Answer: $5,117, computed as follows:

Description	Amount	Explanation
(1) Total organizational expenditures	$53,000	Example 2-22.
(2) Amount immediately expensed	2,000	Example 2-23.
(3) Expenditures subject to straight-line amortization	$51,000	(1) − (2).
(4) Recovery period in months	180	15 years §248(a)(2).
(5) Monthly straight-line amortization	283.33	(3)/(4).
(6) Teton business months during year 1	× 11	February through December.
(7) Year 1 straight-line amortization	3,117	(5) × (6).
Total year 1 cost recovery expense for organizational expenditures.	**$ 5,117**	(2) + (7).

Start-up costs are costs businesses incur to, not surprisingly, start up a business.[49] Start-up costs apply to all types of business forms.[50] These costs include costs associated with investigating the possibilities of and actually creating or acquiring a trade or business. For example, costs Teton incurs in deciding whether to locate the business in Cody, Wyoming, or Bozeman, Montana, are start-up costs. Start-up costs also include costs that would normally be deductible as ordinary business expenses except that they don't qualify as business expenses because they are incurred before the trade or business activity actually begins. For example, costs Teton incurs to train its employees before the business begins are start-up costs. The rules for immediately expensing and amortizing start-up costs are the same as those for immediately expensing and amortizing organizational expenditures. Consequently, businesses incurring at least $55,000 of start-up costs are not allowed to immediately expense any of the costs. The limitations are computed separately for organizational expenditures and for start-up costs.

[49]§195.

[50]Recall that rules for amortizing organizational expenditures apply only to corporations and partnerships.

Consequently, a business could immediately expense $5,000 of organizational expenditures and $5,000 of start-up costs in its first year of business.

Example 2-26

What if: Assume that in January of year 1 (before it began business on February 1) Teton spent $4,500 investigating the climbing hardware market, creating company logos, and determining the locations for both the office and manufacturing facility. The $4,500 of expenditures qualifies as start-up costs. How much of the $4,500 of start-up costs is Teton allowed to immediately expense?

Answer: All $4,500. Teton is allowed to immediately expense the entire $4,500 because its total start-up costs do not exceed $50,000. Teton could have immediately expensed up to $5,000 of start-up costs as long as its total start-up costs did not exceed $50,000.

Exhibit 2-11 illustrates the timing of organizational expenditures, start-up costs, and normal trade or business expenses.

EXHIBIT 2-11 Summary of Timing for Organizational Expenditures, Start-Up Costs, and Normal Trade or Business Expenses

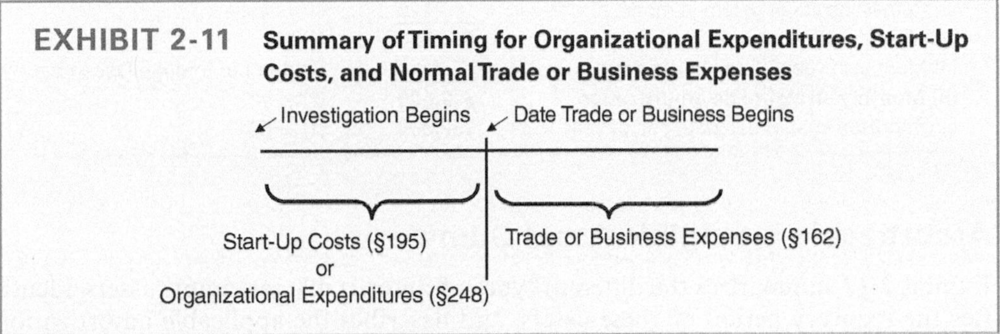

Research and Experimentation Expenditures

To stay competitive, businesses often invest in activities they believe will generate innovative products or significantly improve their current products or processes. These research and experimentation costs include expenditures for research laboratories including salaries, materials, and other related expenses. Businesses may immediately expense these costs or they may *elect* to capitalize these costs and amortize them using the straight-line method over the determinable useful life or, if there is no determinable useful life, over a period of not less than 60 months, beginning in the month benefits are first derived from the research.[51] However, if a business elects to capitalize and amortize the costs, it must stop amortizing the costs if and when the business receives a patent relating to the expenditures. When the business obtains a patent, it adds any remaining basis in the costs to the basis of the patent and it amortizes the basis of the patent over the patent's life (see discussion below).

Patents and Copyrights

The manner in which a business amortizes a patent or copyright depends on whether the business directly purchases the patent or copyright or whether it self-creates the intangibles. Businesses directly purchasing patents or copyrights (not in an asset acquisition to which §197 applies) amortize the cost over the remaining life of the patents or copyrights.[52] Businesses receiving "self-created" patents or copyrights amortize the cost or basis of the self-created intangible assets over their legal lives. The costs included in the basis

[51]See §174. High tax rate taxpayers may choose to deduct these costs while low tax rate taxpayers may prefer to capitalize and amortize them so that they will have more future deductions when they generate more income. There is also the research and experimentation credit which is available to some businesses.

[52]§167(f).

of a self-created patent or copyright include legal costs, fees, and, as we discussed above, unamortized research and experimentation expenditures associated with the creation of the patent or copyright. However, because the patent approval process is slow, the unamortized research and experimentation costs included in the patent's basis are likely to be relatively small because, with a five-year recovery period, the research and experimentation costs would likely be mostly or even fully amortized by the time the patent is approved.

Example 2-27

In September of year 1, Teton purchased a patent with a remaining life of 10 years from Chouinard Equipment for $60,000. What amount of amortization expense is Teton allowed to deduct for the patent in year 1?

Answer: $2,000, computed as follows:

Description	Amount	Explanation
(1) Cost of patent	$60,000	
(2) Remaining life of patent in months	120	10 years.
(3) Monthly amortization	$ 500	(1)/(2).
(4) Months in year 1 Teton held patent	× 4	September through December.
(5) Monthly straight-line amortization	**$ 2,000**	(3) × (4).
Unamortized cost of patent at end of year 1	$58,000	(1) − (5).

Amortizable Intangible Asset Summary

Exhibit 2-12 summarizes the different types of amortizable intangible assets, identifies the recovery period of these assets, and describes the applicable amortization method for each asset. Exhibit 2-12 also identifies the applicable convention for each type of amortizable intangible asset and identifies the financial accounting treatment for recovering the cost of the intangible assets under GAAP.

EXHIBIT 2-12 Summary of Amortizable Assets

Asset Description	Recovery Period (months)	Applicable Method	Applicable Convention	Financial Accounting Treatment
§197 purchased intangibles including goodwill, trademarks, patents, and covenants not to compete.[53]	180	Straight-line	Full-month beginning with month of purchase.	ASC 350 tests for annual impairment.
Organizational expenditures and start-up costs are required to be capitalized.	180	Straight-line	Full-month in month business begins.	AICPA SOP 98-5.
Research and experimentation costs that are capitalized.	Determinable useful life, or 60 (not less than); ceases when patent is issued.	Straight-line	Full-month in first month that benefits from research are obtained.	Expensed.
Self-created patents and copyrights.	Actual life.	Straight-line	Full-month month intangible is obtained.	Expensed.
Purchased patents and copyrights.	Remaining life.	Straight-line	Full-month in month intangible is obtained.	Expensed.

[53]A patent or copyright that is part of a basket purchase (several assets together) is treated as a §197 intangible. A patent or copyright that is purchased separately is simply amortized over its remaining life (§167(f)).

Exhibit 2-13 presents Teton's amortization expense as it would be reported on its tax return on Form 4562 (the exhibit assumes that Teton is a corporation so it can amortize organizational expenditures).

EXHIBIT 2-13 Teton Form 4562, Part VI Amortization of Organizational Expenditures and Patent

Part VI Amortization

(a) Description of costs	(b) Date amortization begins	(c) Amortizable amount	(d) Code section	(e) Amortization period or percentage	(f) Amortization for this year
42 Amortization of costs that begins during your 2014 tax year (see instructions):					
Organizational expenditures	2/1/2015	53,000	243	15 years	5,117
Patents	9/1/2015	60,000	167	10 years	2,000
43 Amortization of costs that began before your 2014 tax year				43	
44 **Total.** Add amounts in column (f). See the instructions for where to report				44	7,117

Form **4562** (2014)

continued from page 2-1 . . .

Teton was developing some additional employee parking on a lot adjacent to the warehouse when the excavation crew discovered a small gold deposit. Steve called his friend Ken, who had some experience in mining precious metals, to see what Ken thought of the find. Ken was impressed and offered Steve $150,000 for the rights to the gold. Steve accepted the offer on Teton's behalf. ■

LO 2-5

DEPLETION

Depletion is the method taxpayers use to recover their capital investment in natural resources. Depletion is a particularly significant deduction for businesses in the mining, oil and gas, and forestry industries. These businesses generally incur depletion expense as they use the natural resource. Specifically, businesses compute annual depletion expense under both the cost and percentage depletion methods and they deduct the larger of the two.[54]

Under **cost depletion,** taxpayers must estimate or determine the number of units or reserves (tons of coal, barrels of oil, board feet of timber, for example) that remain at the beginning of the year and allocate a pro rata share of that basis to each unit that is extracted during the year.[55]

Example 2-28

Ken's cost basis in the gold is the $150,000 he paid for it. Based on a mining engineer's estimate that the gold deposit probably holds 1,000 ounces of gold, Ken can determine his cost depletion. What is Ken's cost depletion for year 1 and year 2, assuming he extracts 300 and 700 ounces of gold in year 1 and year 2, respectively?

(continued on page 2-38)

[54]Depletion of timber and major integrated oil companies must be calculated using only the cost depletion method (no percentage depletion is available).

[55]§612.

THE KEY FACTS

Depletion

- Cost depletion involves estimating resource reserves and allocating a pro-rata share of basis based on the number of units extracted.
- Percentage depletion is determined by a statutory percentage of gross income that is permitted to be expensed each year. Different resources have different statutory percentages (i.e., gold, tin, coal).
- Taxpayers may expense the larger of cost or percentage depletion.

Answer: $45,000 in year 1 and $105,000 in year 2, computed as follows:

Description	Amount	Explanation
(1) Cost basis in gold	$150,000	
(2) Estimated ounces of gold	1,000	
(3) Per ounce cost depletion rate	150	(1)/(2).
(4) Year 1 ounces extracted	300	
(5) Year 1 cost depletion	**$ 45,000**	(3) × (4).
(6) Basis remaining after year 1 depletion	105,000	(1) − (5).
(7) Year 2 ounces extracted	700	
(8) Year 2 cost depletion	**$105,000**	(7) × (3).
Basis remaining after year 2 depletion	$ 0	(6) − (8).

Ken is not eligible for cost depletion after year 2 because as of the end of year 2, his cost basis has been reduced to $0.

Because the cost depletion method of depletion requires businesses to estimate the number of units of the resource they will actually extract, it is possible that their estimate will prove to be inaccurate. If they underestimate the number of units, they will fully deplete the cost basis of the resource before they have fully extracted the resource. Once they have recovered the entire cost basis of the resource, businesses are not allowed to use cost depletion to determine depletion expense. Businesses, however, may continue to use percentage depletion (see discussion below). If a business overestimates the number of units to be extracted, it will still have basis remaining after the resource has been fully extracted. In these situations, the business would deduct the unrecovered basis once it had sold all the remaining units.

The amount of **percentage depletion** for a natural resource business activity is determined by multiplying the *gross income* from the resource extraction activity by a fixed percentage based on the type of natural resource as indicated in Exhibit 2-14.[56]

EXHIBIT 2-14 Applicable Percentage Depletion Rates

Statutory Percentage	Natural Resources (Partial list)
5 percent [§613(b)(6)]	Gravel, pumice, and stone.
14 percent [§613(b)(3)]	Asphalt rock, clay, and other metals.
15 percent [§613(b)(2)]	Gold, copper, oil shale, and silver.
15 percent [§613A(c)(1)]	Domestic oil and gas
22 percent [§613(b)(1)]	Platinum, sulfur, uranium, and titanium.

In many cases, percentage depletion may generate *larger* depletion deductions than does cost depletion. Recall that taxpayers are allowed to deduct the greater of cost or percentage depletion. Businesses reduce their cost basis in the resource when they deduct percentage depletion. However, once the cost basis is exhausted, they are allowed to continue to deduct percentage (but not cost) depletion. This provides a potentially significant governmental subsidy to extraction businesses that have completely recovered their costs in a natural resource.[57]

It is important to note that businesses deduct percentage depletion when they *sell* the natural resource and they deduct cost depletion in the year they *produce* or extract the natural resource. Also, percentage depletion cannot exceed 50 percent (100 percent in the case of oil and gas properties) of the *taxable income* from the

[56]§613.

[57]Percentage depletion in excess of basis is an AMT preference item.

natural resource business activity before considering the depletion expense, while cost depletion has no such limitation.

Example 2-29

In Example 2-28, Ken determined his cost depletion expense for the gold. However, because he is allowed to deduct the greater of cost or percentage depletion each year, he set out to determine his percentage depletion for year 2. Assuming that Ken has gross (taxable) income from the gold mining activity before depletion expense of $200,000 ($50,000), $600,000 ($450,000), and $600,000 ($500,000) in year 1, year 2, and year 3, respectively, what is his percentage depletion expense for each of these three years?

Answer: $25,000, $90,000, and $90,000 for years 1, 2, and 3, respectively, computed as follows:

	Year 1	Year 2	Year 3	Explanation
(1) Taxable income from activity (before depletion expense)	$ 50,000	$450,000	$500,000	
(2) Gross income	$200,000	$600,000	$600,000	
(3) Percentage	× 15%	× 15%	× 15%	Exhibit 2-14.
(4) Percentage depletion expense before limit	$ 30,000	$ 90,000	$ 90,000	(2) × (3).
(5) 50 percent of taxable income limitation	$ 25,000	$225,000	$250,000	(1) × 50%.
Allowable percentage depletion	**$ 25,000**	**$ 90,000**	**$ 90,000**	Lesser of (4) or (5).

Finally, as we discussed above, a business's depletion expense deduction is the greater of either the annual cost or percentage depletion.

Example 2-30

Based on his computations of cost depletion and percentage depletion, Ken was able to determine his deductible depletion expense. Using the cost and percentage depletion computations from Examples 2-28 and 2-29, what is Ken's deductible depletion expense for years 1, 2, and 3?

Answer: $45,000 for year 1, $105,000 for year 2, and $90,000 for year 3, computed as follows:

Tax Depletion Expense	Year 1	Year 2	Year 3	Explanation
(1) Cost depletion	$45,000	$105,000	$ 0	Example 2-28.
(2) Percentage depletion	25,000	90,000	90,000	Example 2-29.
Allowable expense	45,000	105,000	90,000	Greater of (1) or (2).

CONCLUSION

This chapter describes and discusses how businesses recover the costs of their tangible and intangible assets. Cost recovery expenses are important because they represent a significant tax deduction for many businesses. Businesses must routinely make choices that affect the amount and timing of these deductions. Further understanding cost recovery basics helps businesses determine how to compute and characterize gain and loss they recognize when they sell or otherwise dispose of business assets. We address the interaction between cost recovery expenses and gain and loss on property dispositions in the next chapter.

Appendix MACRS Tables

TABLE 1 MACRS Half-Year Convention

	Depreciation Rate for Recovery Period					
Year	3-year	5-year	7-year	10-year	15-year	20-year
1	33.33	20.00	14.29	10.00	5.00	3.750
2	44.45	32.00	24.49	18.00	9.50	7.219
3	14.81	19.20	17.49	14.40	8.55	6.677
4	7.41	11.52	12.49	11.52	7.70	6.177
5		11.52	8.93	9.22	6.93	5.713
6		5.76	8.92	7.37	6.23	5.285
7			8.93	6.55	5.90	4.888
8			4.46	6.55	5.90	4.522
9				6.56	5.91	4.462
10				6.55	5.90	4.461
11				3.28	5.91	4.462
12					5.90	4.461
13					5.91	4.462
14					5.90	4.461
15					5.91	4.462
16					2.95	4.461
17						4.462
18						4.461
19						4.462
20						4.461
21						2.231

TABLE 2a MACRS Mid-Quarter Convention: *For property placed in service during the first quarter*

	Depreciation Rate for Recovery Period	
Year	5-year	7-year
1	35.00%	25.00%
2	26.00	21.43
3	15.60	15.31
4	11.01	10.93
5	11.01	8.75
6	1.38	8.74
7		8.75
8		1.09

TABLE 2b MACRS Mid-Quarter Convention: *For property placed in service during the second quarter*

	Depreciation Rate for Recovery Period	
Year	**5-year**	**7-year**
1	25.00%	17.85%
2	30.00	23.47
3	18.00	16.76
4	11.37	11.97
5	11.37	8.87
6	4.26	8.87
7		8.87
8		3.34

TABLE 2c MACRS Mid-Quarter Convention: *For property placed in service during the third quarter*

	Depreciation Rate for Recovery Period	
Year	**5-year**	**7-year**
1	15.00%	10.71%
2	34.00	25.51
3	20.40	18.22
4	12.24	13.02
5	11.30	9.30
6	7.06	8.85
7		8.86
8		5.53

TABLE 2d MACRS-Mid Quarter Convention: *For property placed in service during the fourth quarter*

	Depreciation Rate for Recovery Period	
Year	**5-year**	**7-year**
1	5.00%	3.57%
2	38.00	27.55
3	22.80	19.68
4	13.68	14.06
5	10.94	10.04
6	9.58	8.73
7		8.73
8		7.64

TABLE 3 Residential Rental Property Mid-Month Convention Straight Line—27.5 Years

	Month Property Placed in Service											
Year	**1**	**2**	**3**	**4**	**5**	**6**	**7**	**8**	**9**	**10**	**11**	**12**
1	3.485%	3.182%	2.879%	2.576%	2.273%	1.970%	1.667%	1.364%	1.061%	0.758%	0.455%	0.152%
2–9	3.636	3.636	3.636	3.636	3.636	3.636	3.636	3.636	3.636	3.636	3.636	3.636
10	3.637	3.637	3.637	3.637	3.637	3.637	3.636	3.636	3.636	3.636	3.636	3.636
11	3.636	3.636	3.636	3.636	3.636	3.636	3.637	3.637	3.637	3.637	3.637	3.637
12	3.637	3.637	3.637	3.637	3.637	3.637	3.636	3.636	3.636	3.636	3.636	3.636
13	3.636	3.636	3.636	3.636	3.636	3.636	3.637	3.637	3.637	3.637	3.637	3.637
14	3.637	3.637	3.637	3.637	3.637	3.637	3.636	3.636	3.636	3.636	3.636	3.636
15	3.636	3.636	3.636	3.636	3.636	3.636	3.637	3.637	3.637	3.637	3.637	3.637
16	3.637	3.637	3.637	3.637	3.637	3.637	3.636	3.636	3.636	3.636	3.636	3.636
17	3.636	3.636	3.636	3.636	3.636	3.636	3.637	3.637	3.637	3.637	3.637	3.637
18	3.637	3.637	3.637	3.637	3.637	3.637	3.636	3.636	3.636	3.636	3.636	3.636
19	3.636	3.636	3.636	3.636	3.636	3.636	3.637	3.637	3.637	3.637	3.637	3.637
20	3.637	3.637	3.637	3.637	3.637	3.637	3.636	3.636	3.636	3.636	3.636	3.636
21	3.636	3.636	3.636	3.636	3.636	3.636	3.637	3.637	3.637	3.637	3.637	3.637
22	3.637	3.637	3.637	3.637	3.637	3.637	3.636	3.636	3.636	3.636	3.636	3.636
23	3.636	3.636	3.636	3.636	3.636	3.636	3.637	3.637	3.637	3.637	3.637	3.637
24	3.637	3.637	3.637	3.637	3.637	3.637	3.636	3.636	3.636	3.636	3.636	3.636
25	3.636	3.636	3.636	3.636	3.636	3.636	3.637	3.637	3.637	3.637	3.637	3.637
26	3.637	3.637	3.637	3.637	3.637	3.637	3.636	3.636	3.636	3.636	3.636	3.636
27	3.636	3.636	3.636	3.636	3.636	3.636	3.637	3.637	3.637	3.637	3.637	3.637
28	1.97	2.273	2.576	2.879	3.182	3.485	3.636	3.636	3.636	3.636	3.636	3.636
29							0.152	0.455	0.758	1.061	1.364	1.667

TABLE 4 **Nonresidential Real Property Mid-Month Convention Straight Line—31.5 Years (for assets placed in service before May 13, 1993)**

	Month Property Placed in Service											
Year	**1**	**2**	**3**	**4**	**5**	**6**	**7**	**8**	**9**	**10**	**11**	**12**
1	3.042%	2.778%	2.513%	2.249%	1.984%	1.720%	1.455%	1.190%	0.926%	0.661%	0.397%	0.132%
2–7	3.175	3.175	3.175	3.175	3.175	3.175	3.175	3.175	3.175	3.175	3.175	3.175
8	3.175	3.174	3.175	3.174	3.175	3.174	3.175	3.175	3.175	3.175	3.175	3.175
9	3.174	3.175	3.174	3.175	3.174	3.175	3.174	3.175	3.174	3.175	3.174	3.175
10	3.175	3.174	3.175	3.174	3.175	3.174	3.175	3.174	3.175	3.174	3.175	3.174
11	3.174	3.175	3.174	3.175	3.174	3.175	3.174	3.175	3.174	3.175	3.174	3.175
12	3.175	3.174	3.175	3.174	3.175	3.174	3.175	3.174	3.175	3.174	3.175	3.174
13	3.174	3.175	3.174	3.175	3.174	3.175	3.174	3.175	3.174	3.175	3.174	3.175
14	3.175	3.174	3.175	3.174	3.175	3.174	3.175	3.174	3.175	3.174	3.175	3.174
15	3.174	3.175	3.174	3.175	3.174	3.175	3.174	3.175	3.174	3.175	3.174	3.175
16	3.175	3.174	3.175	3.174	3.175	3.174	3.175	3.174	3.175	3.174	3.175	3.174
17	3.174	3.175	3.174	3.175	3.174	3.175	3.174	3.175	3.174	3.175	3.174	3.175
18	3.175	3.174	3.175	3.174	3.175	3.174	3.175	3.174	3.175	3.174	3.175	3.174
19	3.174	3.175	3.174	3.175	3.174	3.175	3.174	3.175	3.174	3.175	3.174	3.175
20	3.175	3.174	3.175	3.174	3.175	3.174	3.175	3.174	3.175	3.174	3.175	3.174
21	3.174	3.175	3.174	3.175	3.174	3.175	3.174	3.175	3.174	3.175	3.174	3.175
22	3.175	3.174	3.175	3.174	3.175	3.174	3.175	3.174	3.175	3.174	3.175	3.174
23	3.174	3.175	3.174	3.175	3.174	3.175	3.174	3.115	3.174	3.175	3.174	3.175
24	3.175	3.174	3.175	3.174	3.175	3.174	3.175	3.174	3.175	3.174	3.175	3.174
25	3.174	3.175	3.174	3.175	3.174	3.175	3.174	3.175	3.174	3.175	3.174	3.175
26	3.175	3.174	3.175	3.174	3.175	3.174	3.175	3.174	3.175	3.174	3.175	3.174
27	3.174	3.175	3.174	3.175	3.174	3.175	3.174	3.175	3.174	3.175	3.174	3.175
28	3.175	3.174	3.175	3.174	3.175	3.174	3.175	3.174	3.175	3.174	3.175	3.174
29	3.174	3.175	3.174	3.175	3.174	3.175	3.174	3.175	3.174	3.175	3.174	3.175
30	3.175	3.174	3.175	3.174	3.175	3.174	3.175	3.174	3.175	3.174	3.175	3.174
31	3.174	3.175	3.174	3.175	3.174	3.175	3.174	3.175	3.174	3.175	3.174	3.175
32	1.720	1.984	2.249	2.513	2.778	3.042	3.175	3.174	3.175	3.174	3.175	3.174
33							0.132	0.397	0.661	0.926	1.190	1.455

TABLE 5 **Nonresidential Real Property Mid-Month Convention Straight Line—39 Years (for assets placed in service on or after May 13, 1993)**

	Month property placed in service											
Year	**1**	**2**	**3**	**4**	**5**	**6**	**7**	**8**	**9**	**10**	**11**	**12**
1	2.461%	2.247%	2.033%	1.819%	1.605%	1.391%	1.177%	0.963%	0.749%	0.535%	0.321%	0.107%
2–39	2.564	2.564	2.564	2.564	2.564	2.564	2.564	2.564	2.564	2.564	2.564	2.564
40	0.107	0.321	0.535	0.749	0.963	1.177	1.391	1.605	1.819	2.033	2.247	2.461

Summary

LO 2-1 Explain the concept of basis and adjusted basis and describe the cost recovery methods used under the tax law to recover the cost of personal property, real property, intangible assets, and natural resources.

- Tangible personal and real property (depreciation), intangibles (amortization), and natural resources (depletion) are all subject to cost recovery.
- An asset's basis is the amount that is subject to cost recovery. Generally, an asset's initial basis is its purchase price, plus the cost of any other expenses incurred to get the asset in working condition.
- The taxpayer's basis of assets acquired in a nontaxable exchange is the same basis the taxpayer transferred to acquire the property received.
- Expenditures on an asset are either expensed currently or capitalized as a new asset. Expenditures for routine or general maintenance of the asset are expensed currently. Expenditures that extend the useful life of the asset are capitalized.
- When acquiring a business and purchasing a bundle of property, the basis of each asset is determined as the fair market value of the asset.

LO 2-2 Determine the applicable cost recovery (depreciation) life, method, and convention for tangible personal and real property and calculate the deduction allowable under basic MACRS.

- Tax depreciation is currently calculated under the Modified Accelerated Cost Recovery System (MACRS).
- MACRS for tangible personal property is based upon recovery period (Rev. Proc. 87-56), method (200 percent declining balance, 150 percent declining balance, and straight-line), and convention (half-year or mid-quarter).
- Real property is divided into two groups for tax purposes: residential rental and nonresidential. The recovery period is 27.5 years for residential property and 31.5 years or 39 years for nonresidential property, depending on when the property was placed in service. The depreciation method is straight-line and the convention is mid-month.

LO 2-3 Explain the additional special cost recovery rules (§179, bonus, listed property) and calculate the deduction allowable under these rules.

- §179 allows taxpayers to expense tangible personal property. The expense is limited by the amount of property placed in service and taxable income.
- Bonus depreciation allows taxpayers to immediately expense 50 percent of qualified property in the year of acquisition.
- Listed property includes automobiles, other means of transportation, and computer equipment. Depreciation is limited to the expense multiplied by business-use percentage. Special rules apply if business use is less than 50 percent.
- Additional limitations apply to luxury automobiles.

LO 2-4 Explain the rationale behind amortization, describe the four categories of amortizable intangible assets, and calculate amortization expense.

- Intangible assets (such as patents, goodwill, and trademarks) have their costs recovered through amortization.
- Intangible assets are amortized (straight-line method) using the full-month convention.
- Intangibles are divided into four types (§197 purchased intangibles, start-up costs and organizational expenditures, research and experimentation, and self-created intangibles).

LO 2-5 Explain cost recovery of natural resources and the allowable depletion methods.

- Depletion allows a taxpayer to recover his or her capital investment in natural resources.
- Two methods of depletion are available, and the taxpayer must calculate both and take the one that results in the larger depletion deduction each year.
- Cost depletion allows taxpayers to estimate number of units and then allocate a pro rata share of the basis to each unit extracted during the year.
- Percentage depletion allows the taxpayer to take a statutory determined percentage of gross income as an expense. Deductions are not limited to basis.

KEY TERMS

Accelerated Cost Recovery System (ACRS) (2-5)
adjusted basis (2-3)
amortization (2-2)
bonus depreciation (2-22)
cost depletion (2-37)
cost recovery (2-2)
covenant not to compete (2-31)
depletion (2-2)
depreciation (2-2)
full-month convention (2-31)
half-year convention (2-8)
intangible assets (2-2)
listed property (2-24)
luxury automobile (2-28)
mid-month convention (2-15)
mid-quarter convention (2-8)
Modified Accelerated Cost Recovery System (MACRS) (2-5)
organizational expenditures (2-32)
percentage depletion (2-38)
personal property (2-5)
real property (2-5)
recovery period (2-5)
research and experimentation (R&E) costs (2-31)
§179 expense (2-17)
§197 purchased intangibles (2-31)
start-up costs (2-34)
tax basis (2-3)

DISCUSSION QUESTIONS

1. Explain the reasoning why the tax laws require the cost of certain assets to be capitalized and recovered over time rather than immediately expensed. LO 2-1
2. Explain the differences and similarities between personal property, real property, intangible property, and natural resources. Also, provide an example of each type of asset. LO 2-1
3. Explain the similarities and dissimilarities between depreciation, amortization, and depletion. Describe the cost recovery method used for each of the four asset types (personal property, real property, intangible property, and natural resources). LO 2-1
4. Is an asset's initial or cost basis simply its purchase price? Explain. LO 2-1
5. Compare and contrast the basis of property acquired via purchase, conversion from personal use to business or rental use, a nontaxable exchange, gift, and inheritance. LO 2-1
6. Explain why the expenses incurred to get an asset in place and operable should be included in the asset's basis. LO 2-1
7. Graber Corporation runs a long-haul trucking business. Graber incurs the following expenses: replacement tires, oil changes, and a transmission overhaul. Which of these expenditures may be deducted currently and which must be capitalized? Explain. LO 2-1
8. MACRS depreciation requires the use of a recovery period, method, and convention to depreciate tangible personal property assets. Briefly explain why each is important to the calculation. LO 2-2
9. Can a taxpayer with very little current year income choose to not claim any depreciation expense for the current year and thus save depreciation deductions for the future when the taxpayer expects to be more profitable? LO 2-2
10. What depreciation methods are available for tangible personal property? Explain the characteristics of a business likely to adopt each method. LO 2-2 planning
11. If a business places several different assets in service during the year, must it use the same depreciation method for all assets? If not, what restrictions apply to the business's choices of depreciation methods? LO 2-2
12. Describe how you would determine the MACRS recovery period for an asset if you did not already know it. LO 2-2

research LO 2-2 13. Compare and contrast the recovery periods used by MACRS and those used under generally accepted accounting principles (GAAP).

LO 2-2 14. What are the two depreciation conventions that apply to tangible personal property under MACRS? Explain why Congress provides two methods.

LO 2-2 15. A business buys two identical tangible personal property assets for the same identical price. It buys one at the beginning of the year and one at the end of the year. Under what conditions would the taxpayer's depreciation on each asset be exactly the same? Under what conditions would it be different?

LO 2-2 16. AAA Inc. acquired a machine in year 1. In May of year 3, it sold the asset. Can AAA find its year 3 depreciation percentage for the machine on the MACRS table? If not, what adjustment must AAA make to its full year depreciation percentage to determine its year 3 depreciation?

LO 2-2 17. There are two recovery period classifications for real property. What reasons might Congress have to allow residential real estate a shorter recovery period than nonresidential real property?

LO 2-2 18. Discuss why Congress has instructed taxpayers that real property be depreciated using the mid-month convention as opposed to the half-year or mid-quarter conventions used for tangible personal property.

LO 2-2 research 19. If a taxpayer has owned a building for 10 years and decides that it should make significant improvements to the building, what is the recovery period for the improvements?

LO 2-2 20. Compare and contrast the differences between computing depreciation expense for tangible personal property and depreciation expense for real property under both the regular tax and alternative tax systems.

LO 2-3 21. Discuss why a small business might be able to deduct a greater percentage of the assets it places in service during the year than a larger business.

LO 2-3 22. Explain the two limitations placed on the §179 deduction. How are they similar? How are they different?

LO 2-3 23. Compare and contrast the types of businesses that would benefit from and those that would not benefit from the §179 expense.

LO 2-3 24. What strategies will help a business maximize its current depreciation deductions (including §179)? Why might a taxpayer choose not to maximize its current depreciation deductions?

LO 2-3 25. Why might a business elect only the §179 expense it can deduct in the current year rather than claiming the full amount available?

LO 2-3 26. Describe assets that are considered to be listed property. Why do you think the Internal Revenue Service requires them to be "listed"?

LO 2-3 27. Are taxpayers allowed to claim depreciation expense on assets they use for both business and personal purposes? What are the tax consequences if the business use drops from above 50 percent in one year to below 50 percent in the next?

LO 2-3 28. Discuss why Congress limits the amount of depreciation expense businesses may claim on certain automobiles.

LO 2-3 29. Compare and contrast how a Land Rover SUV and a Mercedes Benz sedan are treated under the luxury auto rules. Also include a discussion of the similarities and differences in available §179 expense.

LO 2-4 30. What is a §197 intangible? How do taxpayers recover the costs of these intangibles? How do taxpayers recover the cost of a §197 intangible that expires (such as a covenant not to compete)?

31. Compare and contrast the tax and financial accounting treatment of goodwill. Are taxpayers allowed to deduct amounts associated with self-created goodwill? LO 2-4
32. Compare and contrast the similarities and differences between organizational expenditures and start-up costs for tax purposes. LO 2-4
33. Discuss the method used to determine the amount of organizational expenditures or start-up costs that may be immediately expensed in the year a taxpayer begins business. LO 2-4
34. Explain the amortization convention applicable to intangible assets. LO 2-4
35. Compare and contrast the recovery periods of §197 intangibles, organizational expenditures, start-up costs, and research and experimentation expenses. LO 2-4
36. Compare and contrast the cost and percentage depletion methods for recovering the costs of natural resources. What are the similarities and differences between the two methods? LO 2-5
37. Explain why percentage depletion has been referred to as a government subsidy. LO 2-5

PROBLEMS

All applicable problems are available with McGraw-Hill's *Connect® Accounting.*

38. Jose purchased a delivery van for his business through an online auction. His winning bid for the van was $24,500. In addition, Jose incurred the following expenses before using the van: shipping costs of $650; paint to match the other fleet vehicles at a cost of $1,000; registration costs of $3,200, which included $3,000 of sales tax and a registration fee of $200; wash and detailing for $50; and an engine tune-up for $250. What is Jose's cost basis for the delivery van? LO 2-1
39. Emily purchased a building to store inventory for her business. The purchase price was $760,000. Beyond this, Emily incurred the following necessary expenses to get the building ready for use: $10,000 to repair the roof (does not extend the roof life), $5,000 to make the interior suitable for her finished goods, and $300 in legal fees. What is Emily's cost basis in the new building? LO 2-1
40. Dennis contributed business assets to a new business in exchange for stock in the company. The exchange did not qualify as a nontaxable exchange. The fair market value of these assets was $287,000 on the contribution date. Dennis's original basis in the assets he contributed was $143,000, and the accumulated depreciation on the assets was $78,000. LO 2-1
    a) What is the business's basis in the assets it received from Dennis?
    b) What would be the business's basis if the transaction qualified as a nontaxable exchange?
41. Brittany started a law practice as a sole proprietor. She owned a computer, printer, desk, and file cabinet she purchased during law school (several years ago) that she is planning to use in her business. What is the depreciable basis that Brittany should use in her business for each asset, given the following information? LO 2-1

Asset	Purchase Price	FMV at Time Converted to Business Use
Computer	$2,500	$ 800
Printer	300	150
Desk	1,200	1,000
File cabinet	200	225

LO 2-1 42. Meg O'Brien received a gift of some small-scale jewelry manufacturing equipment that her father had used for personal purposes for many years. Her father originally purchased the equipment for $1,500. Because the equipment is out of production and no longer available, the property is currently worth $4,000. Meg has decided to begin a new jewelry manufacturing trade or business. What is her depreciable basis for depreciating the equipment?

LO 2-1 43. Gary inherited a Maine summer cabin on 10 acres from his grandmother. His grandparents originally purchased the property for $500 in 1950 and built the cabin at a cost of $10,000 in 1965. His grandfather died in 1980 and when his grandmother recently passed away, the property was appraised at $500,000 for the land and $700,000 for the cabin. Since Gary doesn't currently live in New England, he decided that it would be best to put the property to use as a rental. What is Gary's basis in the land and in the cabin?

LO 2-1 44. Wanting to finalize a sale before year-end, on December 29, WR Outfitters sold to Bob a warehouse and the land for $125,000. The appraised fair market value of the warehouse was $75,000, and the appraised value of the land was $100,000.

a) What is Bob's basis in the warehouse and in the land?

b) What would be Bob's basis in the warehouse and in the land if the appraised value of the warehouse is $50,000, and the appraised value of the land is $125,000?

c) Which appraisal would Bob likely prefer?

LO 2-2 45. At the beginning of the year, Poplock began a calendar-year dog boarding business called Griff's Palace. Poplock bought and placed in service the following assets during the year:

Asset	Date Acquired	Cost Basis
Computer equipment	3/23	$ 5,000
Dog grooming furniture	5/12	7,000
Pickup truck	9/17	10,000
Commercial building	10/11	270,000
Land (one acre)	10/11	80,000

Assuming Poplock does not elect §179 expensing or bonus depreciation, answer the following questions:

a) What is Poplock's year 1 depreciation expense for each asset?

b) What is Poplock's year 2 depreciation expense for each asset?

LO 2-2 46. DLW Corporation acquired and placed in service the following assets during the year:

Asset	Date Acquired	Cost Basis
Computer equipment	2/17	$ 10,000
Furniture	5/12	17,000
Commercial building	11/1	270,000

Assuming DLW does not elect §179 expensing or bonus depreciation, answer the following questions:

a) What is DLW's year 1 cost recovery for each asset?

b) What is DLW's year 3 cost recovery for each asset if DLW sells all of these assets on 1/23 of year 3?

47. At the beginning of the year, Dee began a calendar-year business and placed in service the following assets during the year: LO 2-2

Asset	Date Acquired	Cost Basis
Computer equipment	3/23	$ 5,000
Furniture	5/12	7,000
Pickup truck	11/15	10,000
Commercial building	10/11	270,000

Assuming Dee does not elect §179 expensing or bonus depreciation, answer the following questions:

a) What is Dee's year 1 cost recovery for each asset?

b) What is Dee's year 2 cost recovery for each asset?

48. Evergreen Corporation (calendar-year-end) acquired the following assets during the current year (ignore §179 expense and bonus depreciation for this problem): LO 2-2

Asset	Placed in Service Date	Original Basis
Machinery	October 25	$ 70,000
Computer equipment	February 3	10,000
Used delivery truck*	August 17	23,000
Furniture	April 22	150,000

*The delivery truck is not a luxury automobile.

a) What is the allowable MACRS depreciation on Evergreen's property in the current year?

b) What is the allowable MACRS depreciation on Evergreen's property in the current year if the machinery had a basis of $170,000 rather than $70,000?

49. Convers Corporation (June 30 year-end) acquired the following assets during the current tax year (ignore §179 expense and bonus depreciation for this problem): LO 2-2

Asset	Placed in Service Date	Original Basis
Machinery	October 25	$ 70,000
Computer equipment	February 3	10,000
Used delivery truck*	March 17	23,000
Furniture	April 22	150,000
Total		$253,000

*The delivery truck is not a luxury automobile.

What is the allowable MACRS depreciation on Convers' property in the current year?

50. Harris Corp. is a technology start-up and is in its second year of operations. The company didn't purchase any assets this year but purchased the following assets in the prior year: LO 2-2

Asset	Placed in Service	Basis
Office equipment	August 14	$10,000
Manufacturing equipment	April 15	68,000
Computer system	June 1	16,000
Total		$94,000

Harris did not know depreciation was tax deductible until it hired an accountant this year and didn't claim any depreciation expense in its first year of operation.

a) What is the maximum amount of depreciation expense Harris Corp. can deduct in its second year of operation (ignore bonus and §179 expense)?

b) What is the basis of the office equipment at the end of the second year?

LO 2-2 planning

51. Parley needs a new truck to help him expand Parley's Plumbing Palace. Business has been booming and Parley would like to accelerate his tax deductions as much as possible (ignore §179 expense and bonus depreciation for this problem). On April 1, Parley purchased a new delivery van for $25,000. It is now September 26 and Parley, already in need of another vehicle, has found a deal on buying a truck for $22,000 (all fees included). The dealer tells him if he doesn't buy the truck (Option 1), it will be gone tomorrow. There is an auction (Option 2) scheduled for October 5 where Parley believes he can get a similar truck for $21,500, but there is also a $500 auction fee.

a) Which option allows Parley to generate more depreciation expense deductions this year (the vehicles are not considered to be luxury autos)?

b) Assume the original facts, except that the delivery van was placed in service one day earlier on March 31 rather than April 1. Which option generates more depreciation expense?

LO 2-2

52. Way Corporation disposed of the following tangible personal property assets in the current year. Assume that the delivery truck is not a luxury auto. Calculate Way Corporation's 2015 depreciation expense (ignore §179 expense and bonus depreciation for this problem).

Asset	Date Acquired	Date Sold	Convention	Original Basis
Furniture (7-year)	5/12/11	7/15/15	HY	$ 55,000
Machinery (7-year)	3/23/12	3/15/15	MQ	72,000
Delivery truck* (5-year)	9/17/13	3/13/15	HY	20,000
Machinery (7-year)	10/11/14	8/11/15	MQ	270,000
Computer (5-year)	10/11/15	12/15/15	HY	80,000

*Used 100 percent for business.

LO 2-2

53. On November 10 of year 1 Javier purchased a building, including the land it was on, to assemble his new equipment. The total cost of the purchase was $1,200,000; $300,000 was allocated to the basis of the land and the remaining $900,000 was allocated to the basis of the building.

a) Using MACRS, what is Javier's depreciation expense on the building for years 1 through 3?

b) What would be the year 3 depreciation expense if the building was sold on August 1 of year 3?

c) Answer the question in part (a), except assume the building was purchased and placed in service on March 3 instead of November 10.

d) Answer the question in part (a), except assume that the building is residential property.

e) What would be the depreciation for 2015, 2016, and 2017 if the property were nonresidential property purchased and placed in service November 10, 1998 (assume the same original basis)?

LO 2-2

54. Carl purchased an apartment complex for $1.1 million on March 17 of year 1. $300,000 of the purchase price was attributable to the land the complex sits on. He also installed new furniture into half of the units at a cost of $60,000.

a) What is Carl's allowable depreciation expense for his real property for years 1 and 2?

b) What is Carl's allowable depreciation expense for year 3 if the real property is sold on January 2 of year 3?

55. AMP Corporation (calendar-year-end) has 2015 taxable income of $900,000 before the §179 expense. During 2015, AMP acquired the following assets: LO 2-2 LO 2-3

Asset	Placed in Service	Basis
Machinery	September 12	$1,550,000
Computer equipment	February 10	365,000
Office building	April 2	480,000
Total		$2,395,000

a) What is the maximum amount of §179 expense AMP may deduct for 2015 (assume the 2014 §179 limits are extended to 2015)?
b) What is the maximum total depreciation expense, including §179 expense, that AMP may deduct in 2015 on the assets it placed in service in 2015 assuming no bonus depreciation (assume the 2014 §179 limits are extended to 2015)?

56. Assume that TDW Corporation (calendar-year-end) has 2015 taxable income of $650,000 before the §179 expense and acquired the following assets during 2015: LO 2-2 LO 2-3

Asset	Placed in Service	Basis
Machinery	October 12	$1,270,000
Computer equipment	February 10	263,000
Furniture	April 2	880,000
Total		$2,413,000

a) What is the maximum amount of §179 expense TDW may deduct for 2015 (assume the 2014 §179 limits are extended to 2015)?
b) What is the maximum total depreciation expense, including §179 expense, that TDW may deduct in 2015 on the assets it placed in service in 2015 assuming no bonus depreciation (assume the 2014 §179 limits are extended to 2015)?

57. Assume that Timberline Corporation has 2015 taxable income of $240,000 before the §179 expense (assume the 2014 §179 limits are extended to 2015). LO 2-2 LO 2-3

Asset	Purchase Date	Basis
Furniture (7-year)	December 1	$350,000
Computer equipment (5-year)	February 28	90,000
Copier (5-year)	July 15	30,000
Machinery (7-year)	May 22	480,000
Total		$950,000

a) What is the maximum amount of §179 expense Timberline may deduct for 2015? What is Timberline's §179 carryforward to 2016, if any?
b) What would Timberline's maximum depreciation expense be for 2015 assuming no bonus depreciation?
c) What would Timberline's maximum depreciation expense be for 2015 if the furniture cost $2,000,000 instead of $350,000 and assuming no bonus depreciation?

58. Dain's Diamond Bit Drilling purchased the following assets this year. Assume its taxable income for the year was $53,000 before deducting any §179 expense LO 2-2 LO 2-3

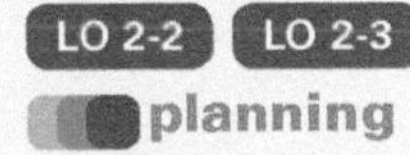

(assume no bonus depreciation but assume that the 2014 §179 limits are extended to 2015).

Asset	Purchase Date	Original Basis
Drill bits (5-year)	January 25	$ 90,000
Drill bits (5-year)	July 25	95,000
Commercial building	April 22	220,000

a) What is the maximum amount of §179 expense Dain may deduct for the year?
b) What is Dain's maximum depreciation expense for the year (including §179 expense)?
c) If the January drill bits' original basis was $2,375,000, what is the maximum amount of §179 expense Dain may deduct for the year?
d) If the January drill bits' basis was $2,495,000, what is the maximum amount of §179 expense Dain may deduct for the year?

59. Assume that ACW Corporation has 2015 taxable income of $1,000,000 before the §179 expense and acquired the following assets during 2015 (assume no bonus depreciation but assume that the 2014 §179 limits are extended to 2015).

Asset	Placed in Service	Basis
Machinery	September 12	$ 470,000
Computer equipment	February 10	70,000
Delivery truck	August 21	93,000
Qualified leasehold improvements	April 2	380,000
Total		$1,013,000

a) What is the maximum amount of §179 expense ACW may deduct for 2015?
b) What is the maximum *total* depreciation expense that ACW may deduct in 2015 on the assets it placed in service in 2015?

60. Chaz Corporation has taxable income in 2015 of $312,000 before the §179 expense and acquired the following assets during the year:

Asset	Placed in Service	Basis
Office furniture	September 12	$1,280,000
Computer equipment	February 10	930,000
Delivery truck	August 21	68,000
Total		$2,278,000

What is the maximum *total* depreciation expense that Chaz may deduct in 2015 (assume that the 2014 §179 limits and bonus depreciation are extended to 2015)?

61. Woolard Inc. has taxable income in 2015 of $150,000 before any depreciation deductions (§179, bonus, or MACRS) and acquired the following assets during the year:

Asset	Placed in Service	Basis
Office furniture (used)	March 20	$600,000

a) If Woolard elects $50,000 of §179, what is Woolard's total depreciation deduction for the year (assume that bonus depreciation and 2014 §179 limits are extended to 2015)?
b) If Woolard elects the maximum amount of §179 for the year, what is the amount of deductible §179 expense for the year? What is the *total* depreciation expense that Woolard may deduct in 2015? What is Woolard's §179 carryforward

amount to next year, if any (assume that bonus depreciation and 2014 §179 limits are extended to 2015)?

c) Woolard is concerned about future limitations on its §179 expense. How much §179 expense should Woolard expense this year if it wants to maximize its depreciation this year and avoid any carryover to future years (assume that bonus depreciation and 2014 §179 limits are extended to 2015)?

62. Assume that Sivart Corporation has 2015 taxable income of $750,000 before the §179 expense and acquired the following assets during 2015: LO 2-2 LO 2-3 planning

Asset	Placed in Service	Basis
Machinery	October 12	$1,440,000
Computer equipment	February 10	70,000
Delivery Truck-used	August 21	93,000
Furniture	April 2	310,000
Total		$1,913,000

a) What is the maximum amount of §179 expense Sivart may deduct for 2015 (assume that bonus depreciation and 2014 §179 limits are extended to 2015)?

b) What is the maximum *total* depreciation expense (§179, bonus, MACRS) that Sivart may deduct in 2015 on the assets it placed in service in 2015 (assume that bonus depreciation and 2014 §179 limits are extended to 2015)?

63. Acorn Construction (calendar year-end C-corporation) has had rapid expansion during the last half of the current year due to the housing market's recovery. The company has record income and would like to maximize its cost recovery deduction for the current year. Acorn provided you with the following information: LO 2-2 LO 2-3 planning

Asset	Placed in Service	Basis
New equipment and tools	August 20	$ 800,000
Used light duty trucks	October 17	1,200,000
Used machinery	November 6	525,000
Total		$2,525,000

a) What is Acorn's maximum cost recovery deduction in the current year assuming that bonus depreciation and 2014 §179 limits are extended to 2015?

b) What planning strategies would you advise Acorn to consider?

64. Phil owns a ranch business and uses four-wheelers to do much of his work. Occasionally, though, he and his boys will go for a ride together as a family activity. During year 1, Phil put 765 miles on the four-wheeler that he bought on January 15 for $6,500. Of the miles driven, only 175 miles were for personal use. Assume four-wheelers qualify to be depreciated according to the five-year MACRS schedule and the four-wheeler was the only asset Phil purchased this year. LO 2-3

a) Calculate the allowable depreciation for year 1 (ignore the §179 expense and bonus depreciation).

b) Calculate the allowable depreciation for year 2 if total miles were 930 and personal use miles were 400 (ignore the §179 expense and bonus depreciation).

65. Assume that Ernesto purchased a laptop computer on July 10 of year 1 for $3,000. In year 1, 80 percent of his computer usage was for his business and 20 percent was for computer gaming with his friends. This was the only asset LO 2-3

he placed in service during year 1. Ignoring any potential §179 expense and bonus depreciation, answer the questions for each of the following alternative scenarios:

a) What is Ernesto's depreciation deduction for the computer in year 1?
b) What would be Ernesto's depreciation deduction for the computer in year 2 if his year 2 usage was 75 percent business and 25 percent for computer gaming?
c) What would be Ernesto's depreciation deduction for the computer in year 2 if his year 2 usage was 45 percent business and 55 percent for computer gaming?
d) What would be Ernesto's depreciation deduction for the computer in year 2 if his year 2 usage was 30 percent business and 70 percent for computer gaming?

LO 2-3

66. Lina purchased a new car for use in her business during 2015. The auto was the only business asset she purchased during the year and her business was extremely profitable. Calculate her maximum depreciation deductions (including §179 expense unless stated otherwise) for the automobile in 2015 and 2016 (Lina doesn't want to take bonus depreciation for 2015 or 2016) in the following alternative scenarios (assuming half-year convention for all and that the 2014 §179 amounts are extended to 2015):

a) The vehicle cost $15,000 and business use is 100 percent (ignore §179 expense).
b) The vehicle cost $40,000, and business use is 100 percent.
c) The vehicle cost $40,000, and she used it 80 percent for business.
d) The vehicle cost $40,000, and she used it 80 percent for business. She sold it on March 1 of year 2.
e) The vehicle cost $40,000, and she used it 20 percent for business.
f) The vehicle cost $40,000, and is an SUV that weighed 6,500 pounds. Business use was 100 percent.

LO 2-2 LO 2-3

67. Burbank Corporation (calendar-year end) acquired the following property this year:

Asset	Placed in Service	Basis
Used copier	February 12	$ 7,800
New computer equipment	June 6	14,000
Furniture	July 15	32,000
New delivery truck	October 28	19,000
Luxury auto	December 31	60,000
Total		$132,800

a) Assuming no bonus or §179 expense, what is Burbank's maximum cost recovery deduction for this year?
b) Assuming Burbank would like to maximize its cost recovery deductions by electing bonus and §179 expense, which assets should Burbank immediately expense? Assume the 2014 §179 expense limits and bonus depreciation are extended to this year.
c) What is Burbank's maximum cost recovery deduction this year assuming it elects §179 expense and bonus depreciation? Assume the 2014 §179 expense limits and bonus depreciation are extended to this year.

LO 2-3

68. Paul Vote purchased the following assets this year (ignore §179 expensing and bonus depreciation when answering the questions below):

Asset	Purchase Date	Basis
Machinery	May 12	$ 23,500
Computers	August 13	20,000
Warehouse	December 13	180,000

a) What is Paul's allowable MACRS depreciation expense for the property?

b) What is Paul's allowable alternative minimum tax (AMT) depreciation expense for the property? You will need to find the AMT depreciation tables to compute the depreciation.

69. After several profitable years running her business, Ingrid decided to acquire the assets of a small competing business. On May 1 of year 1, Ingrid acquired the competing business for $300,000. Ingrid allocated $50,000 of the purchase price to goodwill. Ingrid's business reports its taxable income on a calendar-year basis. LO 2-4
   a) How much amortization expense on the goodwill can Ingrid deduct in year 1, year 2, and year 3?
   b) In lieu of the original facts, assume that Ingrid purchased only a phone list with a useful life of 5 years for $10,000. How much amortization expense on the phone list can Ingrid deduct in year 1, year 2, and year 3?

70. Juliette formed a new business to sell sporting goods this year. The business opened its doors to customers on June 1. Determine the amount of start-up costs Juliette can immediately expense (not including the portion of the expenditures that are amortized over 180 months) this year in the following alternative scenarios: LO 2-4
   a) She incurred start-up costs of $2,000.
   b) She incurred start-up costs of $45,000.
   c) She incurred start-up costs of $53,500.
   d) She incurred start-up costs of $63,000.
   e) How would you answer parts (a) through (d) if she formed a partnership or a corporation and she incurred the same amount of organizational expenditures rather than start-up costs (how much of the organizational expenditures would be immediately deductible)?

71. Nicole organized a new corporation. The corporation began business on April 1 of year 1. She made the following expenditures associated with getting the corporation started: LO 2-4

Expense	Date	Amount
Attorney fees for articles of incorporation	February 10	$32,000
March 1–March 30 wages	March 30	4,500
March 1–March 30 rent	March 30	2,000
Stock issuance costs	April 1	20,000
April 1–May 30 wages	May 30	12,000

   a) What is the total amount of the start-up costs and organizational expenditures for Nicole's corporation?
   b) What amount of the start-up costs and organizational expenditures may the corporation immediately expense in year 1 (excluding the portion of the expenditures that are amortized over 180 months)?
   c) What amount can the corporation deduct as amortization expense for the organizational expenditures and for the start-up costs for year 1 (not including the amount determined in part b)?
   d) What would be the total allowable organizational expenditures, if Nicole started a sole proprietorship instead?

72. Bethany incurred $20,000 in research and experimental costs for developing a specialized product during July of year 1. Bethany went through a lot of trouble and spent $10,000 in legal fees to receive a patent for the product in August of year 3. Bethany expects the patent to have a remaining useful life of 10 years. LO 2-4
   a) What amount of research and experimental expenses for year 1, year 2, and year 3 may Bethany deduct if she elects to amortize the expenses over 60 months?

b) How much *patent* amortization expense would Bethany deduct in year 3 assuming she elected to amortize the research and experimental costs over 60 months?

c) If Bethany chose to capitalize but *not* amortize the research and experimental expenses she incurred in year 1, how much patent amortization expense would Bethany deduct in year 3?

LO 2-5

73. Last Chance Mine (LC) purchased a coal deposit for $750,000. It estimated it would extract 12,000 tons of coal from the deposit. LC mined the coal and sold it, reporting gross receipts of $1 million, $3 million, and $2 million for years 1 through 3, respectively. During years 1–3, LC reported net income (loss) from the coal deposit activity in the amount of ($20,000), $500,000, and $450,000, respectively. In years 1–3, LC actually extracted 13,000 tons of coal as follows:

(1) Tons of Coal	(2) Basis	Depletion (2)/(1) Rate	Tons Extracted per Year Year 1	Year 2	Year 3
12,000	$750,000	$62.50	2,000	7,200	3,800

a) What is Last Chance's cost depletion for years 1, 2, and 3?

b) What is Last Chance's percentage depletion for each year (the applicable percentage for coal is 10 percent)?

c) Using the cost and percentage depletion computations from the previous parts, what is Last Chance's actual depletion expense for each year?

COMPREHENSIVE PROBLEMS

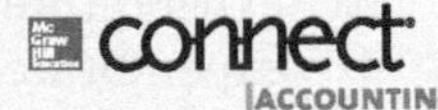

All applicable problems are available with McGraw-Hill's *Connect® Accounting.*

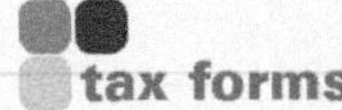

74. Back in Boston, Steve has been busy creating and managing his new company, Teton Mountaineering (TM), which is based out of a small town in Wyoming. In the process of doing so, TM has acquired various types of assets. Below is a list of assets acquired during 2014:

Asset	Cost	Date Placed in Service
Office furniture	$ 10,000	02/03/2014
Machinery	560,000	07/22/2014
Used delivery truck*	15,000	08/17/2014

*Not considered a luxury automobile, thus not subject to the luxury automobile limitations.

During 2014, TM had huge success (and had no §179 limitations) and Steve acquired more assets the next year to increase its production capacity. These are the assets acquired during 2015:

Asset	Cost	Date Placed in Service
Computers & Info. System	$ 40,000	03/31/2015
Luxury Auto†	80,000	05/26/2015
Assembly Equipment	475,000	08/15/2015
Storage Building	400,000	11/13/2015

†Used 100% for business purposes.

TM generated a taxable income in 2015 before any §179 expense of $732,500 (assume bonus depreciation and the 2014 §179 limitations are extended to 2015).

Required

a) Compute maximum 2014 depreciation deductions including §179 expense (ignoring bonus depreciation).
b) Compute maximum 2015 depreciation deductions including §179 expense (ignoring bonus depreciation).
c) Compute maximum 2015 depreciation deductions including §179 expense, but now assume that Steve would like to take bonus depreciation.
d) Ignoring part (c), now assume that during 2015, Steve decides to buy a competitor's assets for a purchase price of $350,000. Compute maximum 2015 cost recovery including §179 expense (ignoring bonus depreciation). Steve purchased the following assets for the lump-sum purchase price.

Asset	Cost	Date Placed in Service
Inventory	$ 20,000	09/15/2015
Office furniture	30,000	09/15/2015
Machinery	50,000	09/15/2015
Patent	98,000	09/15/2015
Goodwill	2,000	09/15/2015
Building	130,000	09/15/2015
Land	20,000	09/15/2015

e) Complete Part I of Form 4562 for part (b). tax forms

75. While completing undergraduate school work in information systems, Dallin Bourne and Michael Banks decided to start a business called ISys Answers, which was a technology support company. During year 1, they bought the following assets and incurred the following fees at start-up:

Year 1 Assets	Purchase Date	Basis
Computers (5-year)	October 30, Y1	$15,000
Office equipment (7-year)	October 30, Y1	10,000
Furniture (7-year)	October 30, Y1	3,000
Start-up costs	October 30, Y1	17,000

In April of year 2, they decided to purchase a customer list from a company started by fellow information systems students preparing to graduate who provided virtually the same services. The customer list cost $10,000 and the sale was completed on April 30. During their summer break, Dallin and Michael passed on internship opportunities in an attempt to really grow their business into something they could do full-time after graduation. In the summer, they purchased a small van (for transportation, not considered a luxury auto) and a pinball machine (to help attract new employees). They bought the van on June 15, Y2, for $15,000 and spent $3,000 getting it ready to put into service. The pinball machine cost $4,000 and was placed in service on July 1, Y2.

Year 2 Assets	Purchase Date	Basis
Van	June 15, Y2	$18,000
Pinball machine (7-year)	July 1, Y2	4,000
Customer list	April 30, Y2	10,000

Assume that ISys Answers does not claim any §179 expense or bonus depreciation.
a) What are the maximum cost recovery deductions for ISys Answers for Y1 and Y2?
b) Complete ISys Answers' Form 4562.
c) What is ISys Answers' basis in each of its assets at the end of Y2?

76. Diamond Mountain was originally thought to be one of the few places in North America to contain diamonds, so Diamond Mountain Inc. (DM) purchased the land for $1,000,000. Later, DM discovered that the only diamonds on the mountain had been planted there and the land was worthless for mining. DM engineers discovered a new survey technology and discovered a silver deposit estimated at 5,000 pounds on Diamond Mountain. DM immediately bought new drilling equipment and began mining the silver.

In years 1–3 following the opening of the mine, DM had net (gross) income of $200,000 ($700,000), $400,000 ($1,100,000), and $600,000 ($1,450,000), respectively. Mining amounts for each year were as follows: 750 pounds (year 1), 1,450 pounds (year 2), and 1,800 pounds (year 3). At the end of year 2, engineers used the new technology (which had been improving over time) and estimated there was still an estimated 6,000 pounds of silver deposits.

DM also began a research and experimentation project with the hopes of gaining a patent for its new survey technology. Diamond Mountain Inc. chooses to capitalize research and experimentation expenditures and amortize the costs over 60 months or until it obtains a patent on its technology. In March of year 1, DM spent $95,000 on research and experimentation. DM spent another $75,000 in February of year 2 for research and experimentation. In September of year 2, DM paid $20,000 of legal fees and was granted the patent in October of year 2 (the entire process of obtaining a patent was unusually fast).

Answer the following questions regarding DM's activities (assume that DM tries to maximize its deductions if given a choice).

a) What is DM's depletion expense for years 1–3?

b) What is DM's research and experimentation amortization for years 1 and 2?

c) What is DM's basis in its patent and what is its amortization for the patent in year 2?

chapter

3 Property Dispositions

Learning Objectives

Upon completing this chapter, you should be able to:

- LO 3-1 Calculate the amount of gain or loss recognized on the disposition of assets used in a trade or business.
- LO 3-2 Describe the general character types of gain or loss recognized on property dispositions.
- LO 3-3 Explain the rationale for and calculate depreciation recapture.
- LO 3-4 Describe the tax treatment of unrecaptured §1250 gains and determine the character of gains on property sold to related parties.
- LO 3-5 Describe the tax treatment of §1231 gains or losses, including the §1231 netting process.
- LO 3-6 Explain common exceptions to the general rule that realized gains and losses are recognized currently.

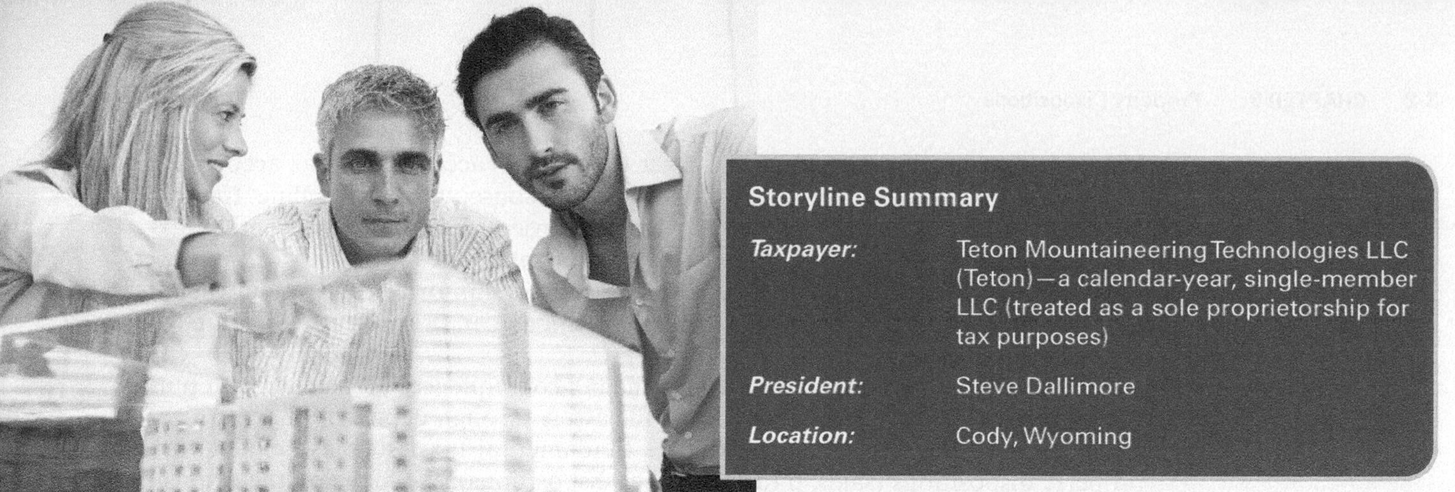

Storyline Summary

Taxpayer:	Teton Mountaineering Technologies LLC (Teton)—a calendar-year, single-member LLC (treated as a sole proprietorship for tax purposes)
President:	Steve Dallimore
Location:	Cody, Wyoming

© BananaStock/Jupiterimages

By most measures, Teton Mountaineering Technologies LLC (Teton) has become a success with sponsored climbers summiting the world's highest peaks, satisfied customers creating brand loyalty, and profitability improving steadily. However, after several years of operation, some of Teton's machinery is wearing out and must be replaced. Further, because Teton has outgrown its manufacturing capacity, Steve is considering whether to expand the company's current facility or sell it and build a new one in a different location. Steve would like to know how any asset dispositions will affect Teton's tax bill.

Steve has found a willing buyer for Teton's machinery, and he has options for trading the equipment. For tax purposes, does it matter whether he sells or trades the equipment? Steve also has questions about how to best manage Teton's acquisitions and dispositions of real property. It all seems a bit overwhelming. . . . He picks up the phone and dials his tax accountant's number. ■

You can imagine why Steve might be eager to reach his accountant. Tax accounting widely impacts business decisions: What are the tax consequences of selling, trading, or even abandoning business assets? Are the tax consequences the same whether taxpayers sell machinery, inventory, or investment assets? Does it matter for tax purposes whether Teton is structured as a sole proprietorship or a corporation when it sells its warehouse? If Steve sells his personal sailboat, car, or furniture, what are the tax consequences?

In the previous chapter we explained the tax consequences associated with purchasing assets and recovering the cost of the assets through depreciation, amortization, or depletion. This chapter explores fundamental tax issues associated with property dispositions (sales, trades, or other dispositions). We focus on the disposition of tangible assets, but the same principles apply to the sale of intangible assets and natural resources.

LO 3-1

DISPOSITIONS

Taxpayers can dispose of assets in many ways. For example, a taxpayer could sell an asset, donate it to charity, trade it for a similar asset, take it to the landfill, or have it destroyed in a natural disaster. No matter how it is accomplished, every asset disposition triggers a realization event for tax purposes. To calculate the amount of gain or loss taxpayers realize when they sell assets, they must determine the amount realized on the sale and the *adjusted basis* of each asset they are selling.

Amount Realized

Simply put, the **amount realized** by a taxpayer from the sale or other disposition of an asset is everything of *value* received from the buyer *less* any selling costs.[1] Although taxpayers typically receive cash when they sell property, they may also accept marketable securities, notes receivable, similar assets, or any combination of these items as payment. Additionally, taxpayers selling assets such as real property subject to loans or mortgages may receive some debt relief and would increase their amount realized by the amount of debt relief (the buyer's assumption of the seller's liability increases the seller's amount realized). The amount realized computation is captured in the following formula:

Amount realized = Cash received + Fair market value of other property
+ Buyer's assumption of liabilities − Seller's expenses

Example 3-1

Teton wants to upgrade its old manufacturing machinery that is wearing out. On November 1 of the current year, Teton sells the old machinery for $130,000 cash and marketable securities valued at $70,500. Teton paid a broker $500 to find a buyer. What is Teton's amount realized on the sale of the machinery?

Answer: $200,000, computed as follows:

Description	Amount	Explanation
(1) Cash received	$130,000	
(2) Marketable securities received	70,500	
(3) Broker commission paid	(500)	
Amount realized	$200,000	(1) + (2) + (3).

[1]*S.C. Chapin*, CA-8, 50-1 USTC ¶9171.

Determination of Adjusted Basis

In the previous chapter, we discussed the basis for cost recovery and focused on purchased assets in which the initial basis is the asset's cost. However, taxpayers may acquire assets without purchasing them. For example a taxpayer may acquire an asset as a gift or as an inheritance. In either case, the taxpayer does not purchase the asset, so the taxpayer's initial basis in the asset must be computed as something other than purchase price. Although there are many situations when an asset's initial basis is not the asset's cost, we focus on three cases: gifts, inherited assets, and property converted from personal use to business use.

Gifts. A gift is defined as a transfer of property proceeding from a detached and disinterested generosity, out of affection, respect, admiration, charity, or like impulses.[2] The initial basis of gift property to a recipient (donee) depends on whether the value of the asset exceeds the donor's basis on the date of the gift. If the fair market value of the asset on the date of the gift is greater than the donor's basis, then the asset's initial basis to the recipient of the gift will be the same as the donor's basis.[3] That is, the donor's basis carries over to the donee.

If the asset has declined in value since the donor acquired it (fair market value at the date of the gift is less than the donor's basis), then special dual basis rules apply. A dual basis means that the gift property has one basis to the donee for determining gains and a different basis for determining losses when the donee disposes of the property. Thus, the basis of gifted property that has declined in value depends on the sales price of the asset subsequent to the gift. The donee uses the carryover basis if the asset is sold for a gain, whereas the donee uses the fair market value at the date of the gift if the asset sells for a loss.[4] If the asset sells at a price between the donor's basis and the fair market value at the date of the gift, then the donee's basis at the time of the sale is assumed to equal the selling price so the donee does not recognize gain or loss on the sale. The dual basis rule prevents the transfer of unrealized losses from one taxpayer to another by gift.

Inherited Property. For inherited property, the general rule is that the heir's basis in property passing from a decedent to the heir is the fair market value on the date of the decedent's death.[5] The holding period of inherited property is deemed to be long-term regardless of how long the heir owns the property.[6]

Property Converted from Personal Use to Business Use. In order to prevent taxpayers from converting nondeductible personal losses to business losses, special basis rules apply when property is converted from personal use to business use. The basis for determining the gain or loss on the sale of converted property depends on whether the property appreciated or declined in value during the time the property was used personally. That is, if the fair market value at the date of the conversion is greater than the taxpayer's basis in the property, then the taxpayer will use the lower taxpayer basis to calculate gain or loss at disposition. However, if the fair market value at the date of conversion is below the taxpayer's basis, the basis for calculating loss will be the fair market value at the date of conversion. After conversion, the taxpayer adjusts the loss

[2]Comr. v. Duberstein, 363 U.S. 278 (1960), rev'g 265 F.2d 28 (6th Cir. 1959), rev'g T. C. Memo 1958–4.

[3]§1015(a). The basis to the donee may be increased if the donor is required to pay gift tax on the gift.

[4]The holding period of the asset also depends on whether the gift property subsequently sells for a gain or loss. If the donor's basis is used to determine the gain, the holding period includes that of the donor. If the fair market value at the date of the gift is used to figure the loss, the holding period starts on the date of the gift.

[5]§1014(a)(1). An alternate valuation date may be used to determine the basis to the heirs if elected by the estate.

[6]§1223(9).

basis and the gain basis for depreciation deductions from the date of conversion to the date of disposition. As discussed in Chapter 2, the taxpayer uses the basis for loss in calculating depreciation deductions. If the property later sells for an amount that falls between the basis for gain and the basis for loss, the basis for the sale is treated as the sales price so that the taxpayer does not recognize gain or loss on the sale.[7]

Example 3-2

Assume that Steve received a desk from his grandfather on January 8. On the date of the gift, the desk was worth $15,000. Steve's grandfather originally purchased the desk 10 years earlier for $10,000. What is Steve's initial basis in the desk?

Answer: Since the desk had appreciated in value while Steve's grandfather owned it, Steve's initial basis is a carryover basis of $10,000.

What if: Assume that on the date of the gift, the fair market value of the desk was $8,000. What is Steve's initial basis in the desk?

Answer: Steve's initial basis depends on the price for which he later sells the desk. If Steve subsequently sells the desk at a price greater than $10,000, his initial basis is the $10,000 carryover basis. If he sells the desk at a price less than $8,000, his basis is $8,000, the fair market value at the date of the gift. If he sells the desk for a price in between $10,000 and $8,000, his basis is the sales price.

What if: Assume that Steve inherited the desk from his grandfather on January 8. What is Steve's initial basis if the fair market value was (a) $15,000 and (b) $8,000 at the time of his grandfather's death?

Answer: Steve's initial basis is the fair market value at the date of his grandfather's death regardless of whether the value is greater or less than his grandfather's original cost. If the fair market value was $15,000, Steve's initial basis is $15,000. If the fair market value is $8,000, Steve's initial basis is $8,000.

What if: Assume Steve owns some mountaineering equipment that he uses personally and purchased two years ago for $4,000. On March 20, he converts the equipment into business use property when the fair market value of the equipment is $5,000. What is Steve's initial basis in the equipment for business purposes?

Answer: Because the equipment appreciated in value before Steve converted it to business use, his basis is his original cost of $4,000. Steve uses the $4,000 as his initial basis for calculating cost recovery and determining his adjusted basis when he sells or otherwise disposes of the equipment.

What if: Assume that the equipment that Steve converts from personal to business use has a fair market value of $3,000 at the date of conversion. What is Steve's initial basis in the equipment for business purposes?

Answer: The equipment declined in value before Steve converted it to business use. In order to prevent Steve from converting his $1,000 personal loss into a business loss, his initial basis for business purposes will depend on whether he subsequently sells the equipment at a gain or loss. His initial basis for loss (and cost recovery) is the $3,000 fair market value at the conversion date. His initial basis for gain is his $4,000 original cost.

What if: Assume that the equipment that Steve converts from personal to business use has a fair market value of $3,000 at the date of conversion. Two years later, after taking $500 of depreciation deductions, he sells the equipment for $3,300. What is Steve's adjusted basis in the equipment for purposes of determining the gain or loss on the disposition?

Answer: Steve's initial basis for loss was the $3,000 fair market value at the conversion date, and his initial basis for gain was $4,000 original cost. At the time of the sale, the adjusted basis for loss is $2,500, and the adjusted basis for gain is $3,500. Because the sales price falls between the adjusted basis for gain and the adjusted basis for loss, the adjusted basis is assumed to be equal to the sales price of $3,300.

[7]Reg. §1.165-9(b)(2) and Reg. §1.167(g)-1.

The **adjusted basis** for determining the gain or loss on the sale of an asset is the initial basis (however determined) reduced by depreciation or other types of cost recovery deductions allowed (or allowable) on the property. The adjusted basis of an asset can be determined using the following formula:

Adjusted basis = Initial basis − Cost recovery allowed (or allowable)

Example 3-3

To determine its realized gain or loss on the sale, Teton must calculate the adjusted basis of the machinery it sold in Example 3-1 for $200,000. Teton originally purchased the machinery for $510,000 three years ago. For tax purposes, Teton depreciated the machinery using MACRS (seven-year recovery period, 200 percent declining balance method, and half-year convention). The machinery's adjusted basis at the time of the sale is $191,173, computed as follows:

Description	Tax	Explanation
(1) Original basis	$510,000	Example 10-1.
(2) Year 1	(72,879)	Example 10-4.
(3) Year 2	(124,899)	Example 10-4.
(4) Year 3	(89,199)	Example 10-4.
(5) Year 4	(31,850)	$63,699 (Example 10-4) × 50% (half-year convention).
(6) Accumulated depreciation	(318,827)	(2) + (3) + (4) + (5).
Adjusted basis	$191,173	(1) + (6).

Because businesses generally use more highly accelerated depreciation methods for tax purposes than they do for book purposes, the tax-adjusted basis of a particular asset is likely to be lower than the book-adjusted basis.

Realized Gain or Loss on Disposition

The amount of gain or loss taxpayers realize on a sale or other disposition of assets is simply the amount they realize minus their adjusted basis in the disposed assets.[8] The formula for computing **realized gain or loss** is as follows:

Gain or (loss) realized = Amount realized − Adjusted basis

Example 3-4

In Example 3-1, we learned that Teton sold machinery for a total amount realized of $200,000, and in Example 3-3 we learned that its basis in the machinery was $191,173. What is Teton's realized gain or loss on the sale of the machinery?

Answer: $8,827, computed as follows:

Description	Amount	Explanation
(1) Amount realized	$200,000	Example 3-1.
(2) Adjusted basis	(191,173)	Example 3-3.
Gain realized	**$ 8,827**	(1) + (2).

Exhibit 3-1 details the important formulas necessary to determine realized tax gains and losses.

[8]§1001(a).

EXHIBIT 3-1 Summary of Formulas for Computing Gain or Loss Realized on an Asset Disposition

- Gain (loss) realized = Amount realized − Adjusted basis; where
  - Amount realized = Cash received + Fair market value of other property + Buyer's assumption of seller's liabilities − Seller's expenses
  - Adjusted basis = Initial basis − Cost recovery deductions

So far, our examples have used one of Teton's asset sales to demonstrate how to compute gain or loss realized when property is sold. However, as we describe in Exhibit 3-2, Teton disposed of several assets during the year. We refer to this exhibit throughout the chapter as a reference point for discussing the tax issues associated with property dispositions.

EXHIBIT 3-2 Teton's Asset Dispositions* Realized Gain (Loss) for Tax Purposes

Asset	(1) Amount Realized	(2) Initial Basis	(3) Accumulated Depreciation	(4) [(2) − (3)] Adjusted Basis	(5) [(1) − (4)] Gain (Loss) Realized
Machinery	$200,000	$510,000	$318,827	$191,173	$ 8,827
Office furniture	12,000	10,000	7,000	3,000	9,000
Delivery truck	2,000	15,000	10,500	4,500	(2,500)
Warehouse	350,000	275,000	15,000	260,000	90,000
Land	175,000	75,000	0	75,000	100,000
Total gain realized					$205,327

*These are the assets initially purchased by Teton in Example 2-1. Chapter 3 generally assumes that Teton has been in business for four years. For simplicity, this chapter assumes Teton did not previously elect any §179 immediate expensing or bonus depreciation.

THE KEY FACTS

- Realized gain or loss.
  - Amount realized less adjusted basis.
- Recognized gain or loss.
  - A realized gain or loss reported on the taxpayer's current year return.

Recognized Gain or Loss on Disposition

As a general rule, taxpayers realizing gains and losses during a year must recognize the gains or losses. **Recognized gains or losses** are gains (losses) that increase (decrease) taxpayers' gross income.[9] Thus, taxpayers must report recognized gains and losses on their tax returns. Although taxpayers must immediately recognize the vast majority of realized gains and losses, in certain circumstances they may be allowed to defer recognizing gains to subsequent periods, or they may be allowed to permanently exclude the gains from taxable income. However, taxpayers may also be required to defer losses to later periods and, in more extreme cases, they may have their realized losses permanently disallowed. We address certain nonrecognition provisions later in the chapter.

LO 3-2

CHARACTER OF GAIN OR LOSS

In order to determine how a recognized gain or loss affects a taxpayer's income tax liability, the taxpayer must determine the *character* or type of gain or loss recognized. Ultimately, every gain or loss is characterized as either ordinary or capital (long-term or short-term). As described below, businesses may recognize certain gains or losses (known as §1231) on property dispositions that require some intermediary steps, but even the §1231 gains or losses are eventually characterized as ordinary or capital (long-term). The character of a gain or loss is important because gains and losses of

[9]When a taxpayer sells an asset, the taxpayer's adjusted basis is a return of capital and not a deductible expense.

different characters are treated differently for tax purposes. For example, ordinary income (loss) is generally taxed at ordinary rates (fully deductible against ordinary income). However, capital gains may be taxed at preferential (lower) rates while deductions for capital losses are subject to certain restrictions. The character of the gains or losses taxpayers recognize when they sell assets depends on the character of the assets they are selling. The character of an asset depends on how the taxpayer used the asset and how long the taxpayer owned the asset (the holding period) before selling it.

In general terms, property may be used in a trade or business, treated as inventory or accounts receivable of a business, held for investment, or used for personal purposes. The holding period may be short-term (one year or less) or long-term (more than a year). Exhibit 3-3 provides a matrix of the character of assets (ordinary, capital, or §1231) depending on how taxpayers used the assets and the length of time they held the property before selling it.

THE KEY FACTS

Character of Assets

- Ordinary assets
  - Assets created or used in a taxpayer's trade or business.
  - Business assets held for one year or less.
- Capital assets
  - Assets held for investment purposes.
  - Assets held for personal-use purposes.
- §1231 assets
  - Depreciable assets and land used in a trade or business held for *more* than one year.

EXHIBIT 3-3 Character of Assets Depending on Property Use and Holding Period

	Property Use		
Holding Period	**Trade or Business**	**Investment or Personal-Use Assets***	**Inventory and Accounts Receivable**
Short-term (one year or less)	Ordinary	Short-term capital	Ordinary
Long-term (more than one year)	§1231†	Long-term capital	Ordinary

*Gains on the sale of personal-use assets are taxable capital gains, but losses on the sale of personal-use assets are not deductible.

†As we describe later in the chapter, gain or loss is eventually characterized as ordinary or capital (long-term).

Ordinary Assets

Ordinary assets are generally assets created or used in a taxpayer's trade or business. For example, inventory is an **ordinary asset** because it is held for sale to customers in the ordinary course of business. Accounts receivable are ordinary assets because receivables are generated from the sale of inventory or business services. Other assets used in a trade or business such as machinery and equipment are also considered to be ordinary assets if they have been used in a business for *one year or less*. For example, if Teton purchased a forklift for the warehouse but sold it six months later, the gain or loss would be ordinary. When taxpayers sell ordinary assets at a gain, they recognize an ordinary gain that is taxed at ordinary rates. When taxpayers sell ordinary assets at a loss, they deduct the loss against other ordinary income.

Capital Assets

A **capital asset** is generally something held for investment (stocks and bonds), for the **production of income** (a for-profit activity that doesn't rise to the level of a trade or business), or for personal use (your car, house, or personal computer).[10] Whether an asset qualifies as a capital asset depends on the purpose for which the taxpayer uses the asset. Thus, the same asset may be considered a capital asset to one taxpayer and an ordinary asset to another taxpayer. For example, a piece of land held as an investment because it is expected to appreciate in value over time is a capital asset to that taxpayer. However, the same piece of land held as inventory by a real estate developer would be an ordinary asset. Finally, the same piece of land would be a §1231 asset if the taxpayer held it for more than one year and used it in a trade or business (e.g., as a parking lot).

[10]§1221 defines what is not a capital asset. Broadly speaking, a *capital asset* is any property *other than* property used in a trade or business (e.g., inventory, manufacturing equipment) or accounts (or notes) receivable acquired in a business from the sale of services or property.

Individual taxpayers generally prefer capital gains to ordinary income because certain capital gains are taxed at lower rates and capital gains may offset capital losses that cannot be deducted against ordinary income. Individuals also prefer ordinary losses to capital losses because ordinary losses are deductible without limit, while individuals may deduct only $3,000 of net capital losses against ordinary income each year. Corporate taxpayers may prefer capital gains to ordinary income because capital gains may offset capital losses that they would not be allowed to offset otherwise. Corporations are not allowed to offset any net capital losses, but they are allowed to carry capital losses back three years and forward five years. Exhibit 3-4 reviews the treatment of capital gains and losses for individuals and corporations.

EXHIBIT 3-4 Review of Capital Gains and Losses

Taxpayer Type	Preferential Rates	Loss Limitations
Individuals	• Net capital gains on assets held more than one year are taxed at 15 percent (0 percent to the extent the gain would have been taxed at a 15 percent or lower rate if it were ordinary income and 20 percent to the extent the gain would have been taxed at 39.6 percent if it were ordinary income). • Unrecaptured §1250 gains on real property held more than one year are taxed at a maximum rate of 25 percent. • Net gains on collectibles held for more than a year are taxed at a maximum rate of 28 percent. • Net capital gains on assets held one year or less are taxed at ordinary rates.	• Individuals may annually deduct up to $3,000 of net capital losses against ordinary income. • Losses carried forward indefinitely but not carried back.
Corporations	• No preferential rates, taxed at ordinary rates.	• No offset against ordinary income. • Net capital losses can generally be carried back three years and forward five years to offset net capital gains in those years.

§1231 Assets

Section 1231 assets are depreciable assets and land used in a trade or business (including rental property) held by taxpayers for *more* than one year.[11] At a general level, when a taxpayer sells a §1231 asset, the taxpayer recognizes a §1231 gain or loss. As discussed above, however, ultimately §1231 gains or losses are characterized as ordinary or capital on a taxpayer's return. When taxpayers sell multiple §1231 assets during the year, they combine or "net" their §1231 gains and §1231 losses together. If the netting results in a net §1231 gain, the net gain is treated as a long-term capital gain. If the netting results in a net §1231 loss, the net loss is treated as an ordinary loss. Because net §1231 gains are treated as capital gains and §1231 losses are treated as ordinary losses, §1231 assets are tax favored relative to other types of assets.

As we discuss below, §1231 gains on individual depreciable assets may be recharacterized as ordinary income under the depreciation recapture rules. However,

[11]As noted above, property used in a trade or business and held for *one year or less* is ordinary income property.

because land is not depreciable, when taxpayers sell or otherwise dispose of land that qualifies as §1231 property, the gain or loss from the sale is always characterized as §1231 gain or loss. Thus, we refer to land as a pure §1231 asset.

Example 3-5

In order to acquire another parcel of land to expand its manufacturing capabilities, Teton sold five acres of land that it has been using in its trade or business for $175,000. Teton purchased the land several years ago for $75,000. What is the amount and character of Teton's gain recognized on the land?

Answer: $100,000 §1231 gain, calculated as follows:

Description	Amount	Explanation
(1) Amount realized	$175,000	
(2) Original basis and current adjusted basis	75,000	
Gain (Loss) realized and recognized	**$100,000**	(1) − (2) §1231 gain.

What if: Assume that Teton sold the land for $50,000. What would be the character of the ($25,000) loss it would recognize?

Answer: §1231 loss.

What if: Assume that the land was the only asset Teton sold during the year. How would the §1231 gain or §1231 loss on the sale ultimately be characterized on its tax return?

Answer: If Teton recognized a §1231 gain on the sale, it would be characterized as a long-term capital gain on its return. If Teton recognized a §1231 loss on the sale, it would be characterized as an ordinary loss.

DEPRECIATION RECAPTURE

LO 3-3

Although Congress intended for businesses to receive favorable treatment on economic gains from the economic *appreciation* of §1231 assets, it did not intend for this favorable treatment to apply to gains that were created artificially through depreciation deductions that offset ordinary income. For example, if a taxpayer purchases an asset for $100 and sells it three years later for the same amount, we would generally agree that there is no economic gain on the disposition of the asset. However, if the taxpayer claimed depreciation deductions of $70 during the three years of ownership, the taxpayer would recognize a $70 gain on the disposition simply because the depreciation deductions reduced the asset's adjusted basis. Depreciation is an ordinary deduction that offsets income that would otherwise be taxed at ordinary rates. Absent tax rules to the contrary, the gain recognized by the taxpayer upon the sale of the asset would be treated as long-term capital gain and would be taxed at a preferential rate (for individuals). Thus, depreciation deductions save taxes at the ordinary rate but the gains created by depreciation would generate income taxed at a preferential rate. This potential asymmetrical treatment led Congress to implement the concept of **depreciation recapture.** Depreciation recapture potentially applies to gains (but not losses) on the sale of depreciable or amortizable business property. When depreciation recapture applies, it changes the character of the gain on the sale of a §1231 asset (all or a portion of the gain) from §1231 gain into ordinary income. Note, however, that depreciation recapture does not affect losses recognized on the disposition of §1231 assets.

The method for computing the amount of depreciation recapture depends on the type of §1231 asset the taxpayer is selling (personal property or real property). As presented in Exhibit 3-5, §1231 assets can be categorized as pure §1231 assets (land), §1245 assets (personal property), or §1250 assets (real property). Whether personal or real property is sold, it is important to understand that depreciation recapture changes only the *character* but not the *amount* of gain recognized.

EXHIBIT 3-5 §1231 Asset Types

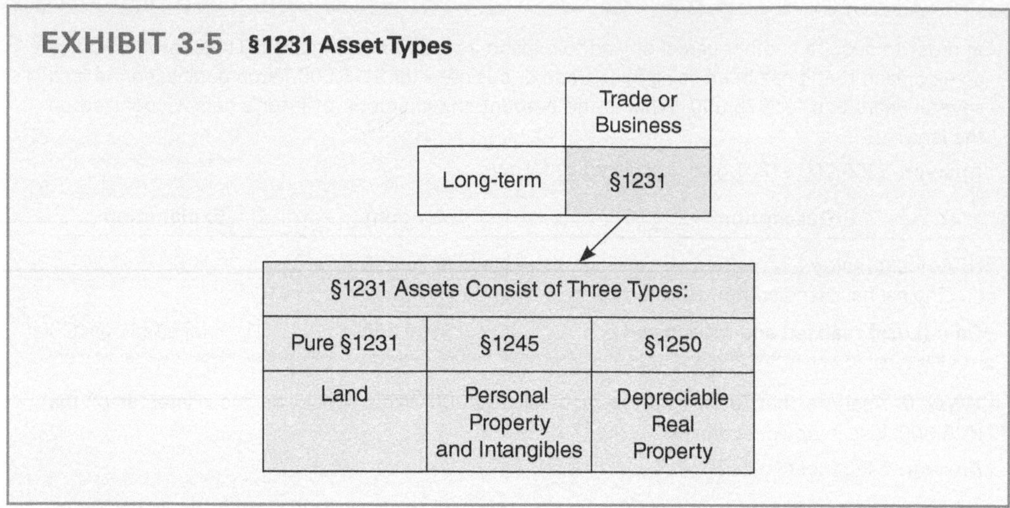

THE KEY FACTS

§1245 Assets

- Personal property and amortizable intangible assets are §1245 assets.
- The lesser of (1) gain recognized or (2) accumulated depreciation is recaptured (characterized) as ordinary income under §1245.
- Any remaining gain is §1231 gain.
- There is no depreciation recapture on assets sold at a loss.

§1245 Property

Tangible personal property (machinery, equipment, and automobiles) and amortizable intangible property (patents, copyrights, and purchased goodwill) are a subset of §1231 property known as **§1245 property.**[12] The gain from the sale of §1245 property is characterized as ordinary income to the extent the gain was created by depreciation or amortization deductions. The amount of *ordinary income* (§1245 depreciation recapture) taxpayers recognize when they sell §1245 property is the lesser of (1) recognized gain on the sale *or* (2) total accumulated depreciation (or amortization) on the asset.[13] The remainder of any recognized gain is characterized as §1231 gain.[14] The sum of the ordinary income (due to depreciation recapture) and the §1231 gain on the sale equals the *total* gain recognized because depreciation recapture changes only the character of the gain, not the amount.

When taxpayers sell or dispose of §1245 property, they encounter one of the following three scenarios involving gain or loss:

Scenario 1: They recognize a gain created solely through depreciation deductions.

Scenario 2: They recognize a gain created through both depreciation deductions and actual asset appreciation.

Scenario 3: They recognize a loss.

[12]An exception in the law is that §1245 property also includes nonresidential real property placed in service between 1981 and 1986 (ACRS) for which the taxpayer elected accelerated depreciation.

[13]§1245 recapture is commonly referred to as "full" depreciation recapture because it may cause a taxpayer to recapture the entire accumulated depreciation amount as ordinary income. §1245 recapture applies notwithstanding any other provision of the Internal Revenue Code (depreciation recapture trumps all other tax rules).

[14]As a practical matter, taxpayers are unlikely to recognize any §1231 gain on the disposition of personal property because the real economic value of most tangible personal property does not increase over time as the property is used.

The following discussion considers each of these scenarios.

Scenario 1: Gain Created Solely through Cost Recovery Deductions Most §1231 assets that experience wear and tear or obsolescence generally do not appreciate in value. Thus, when a taxpayer sells these types of assets at a gain, the gain is usually created because the taxpayer's depreciation deductions associated with the asset reduced the asset's adjusted basis faster than the real decline in the asset's economic value. In other words, the entire gain is artificially generated through depreciation the taxpayer claims before disposing of the asset. That is, absent depreciation deductions, the taxpayer would recognize a loss on the sale of the asset. Therefore, the entire gain on the disposition is recaptured (or characterized) as ordinary income under §1245 (recall that without depreciation recapture the gain would be §1231 gain, which can generate long-term capital gain and could create a double benefit for the taxpayer: ordinary depreciation deductions and capital gain upon disposition).

Example 3-6

As indicated in Exhibit 3-2, Teton sold machinery for $200,000. What is the amount and character of the gain Teton recognizes on the sale?

Answer: $8,827 of ordinary income under the §1245 depreciation recapture rules and $0 of §1231 gain, computed as follows:

Machinery Sale: Scenario 1
(Original scenario sales price = $200,000)

Description	Amount	Explanation
(1) Amount realized	$200,000	Exhibit 3-2.
(2) Original basis	510,000	Exhibit 3-2.
(3) Accumulated depreciation	318,827	Exhibit 3-2.
(4) Adjusted basis	191,173	(2) − (3).
(5) Gain (loss) recognized	8,827	(1) − (4).
(6) Ordinary income (§1245 depreciation recapture)	**$ 8,827**	Lesser of (3) or (5).
§1231 gain	**0**	(5) − (6).

Note that in this situation, because Teton's entire gain is created through depreciation deductions, the entire gain is treated as ordinary income under §1245.

What if: What would be the amount and character of Teton's gain without the depreciation recapture rules?

Answer: $8,827 of §1231 gain. Note that the recapture rules change the character of the gain but not the amount of the gain.

Scenario 2: Gain Due to Both Cost Recovery Deductions and Asset Appreciation Assets subject to cost recovery deductions may actually *appreciate* in value over time. When these assets are sold, the recognized gain must be divided into ordinary gain from depreciation recapture and §1231 gain. The portion of the gain created through cost recovery deductions is **recaptured** as ordinary income. The remaining gain (the gain due to economic appreciation) is §1231 gain.

Example 3-7

What if: Let's assume the same facts as in the previous example and in Exhibit 3-2, except that Teton sells the machinery for $520,000. What is the amount and character of the gain Teton would recognize on this sale?

Answer: $318,827 of ordinary income under the §1245 depreciation recapture rules and $10,000 of §1231 gain due to the asset's economic appreciation, computed as follows:

Machinery Sale: Scenario 2
(Assumed sales price = $520,000)

Description	Amount	Explanation
(1) Amount realized	$520,000	
(2) Original basis	510,000	Exhibit 3-2.
(3) Accumulated depreciation	$318,827	Exhibit 3-2.
(4) Adjusted basis	191,173	(2) − (3).
(5) Gain (loss) recognized	328,827	(1) − (4).
(6) Ordinary income (§1245 depreciation recapture)	**$318,827**	Lesser of (3) or (5).
§1231 gain	**$ 10,000**	(5) − (6).

Note that taxpayers can quickly determine their §1231 gain (if any) when they sell §1245 property by subtracting the asset's *original* basis from the amount realized. In Scenario 2, presented above (Example 3-7), the §1231 gain is $10,000 ($520,000 amount realized less the $510,000 original basis).

Scenario 3: Asset Sold at a Loss Many §1231 assets, such as computer equipment or automobiles, tend to decline in value faster than the corresponding depreciation deductions reduce the asset's adjusted basis. When taxpayers sell or dispose of these assets before the assets are fully depreciated, they recognize a loss on the disposition. Because the depreciation recapture rules don't apply to losses, taxpayers selling §1245 property at a loss recognize §1231 loss.

Example 3-8

What if: Let's assume the same facts as in Example 3-6 and in Exhibit 3-2, except that Teton sells the machinery for $180,000. What is the amount and character of the gain or loss Teton would recognize on this sale?

Answer: A $11,173 §1231 loss, computed as follows:

Machinery Sale: Scenario 3
(Assumed sales price = $180,000)

Description	Amount	Explanation
(1) Amount realized	$180,000	
(2) Original basis	510,000	Exhibit 3-2.
(3) Accumulated depreciation	318,827	Exhibit 3-2.
(4) Adjusted basis	191,173	(2) − (3).
(5) Gain (loss) recognized	(11,173)	(1) − (4).
(6) Ordinary income (§1245 depreciation recapture)	0	Lesser of (3) or (5) (limited to $0).
§1231 (loss)	**($11,173)**	(5) − (6).

Exhibit 3-6 graphically illustrates the §1245 depreciation recapture computations for the machinery sold in Scenarios 1, 2, and 3, presented in Examples 3-6, 3-7, and 3-8, respectively.[15]

EXHIBIT 3-6 Machinery §1245 Depreciation Recapture Scenarios 1, 2, and 3

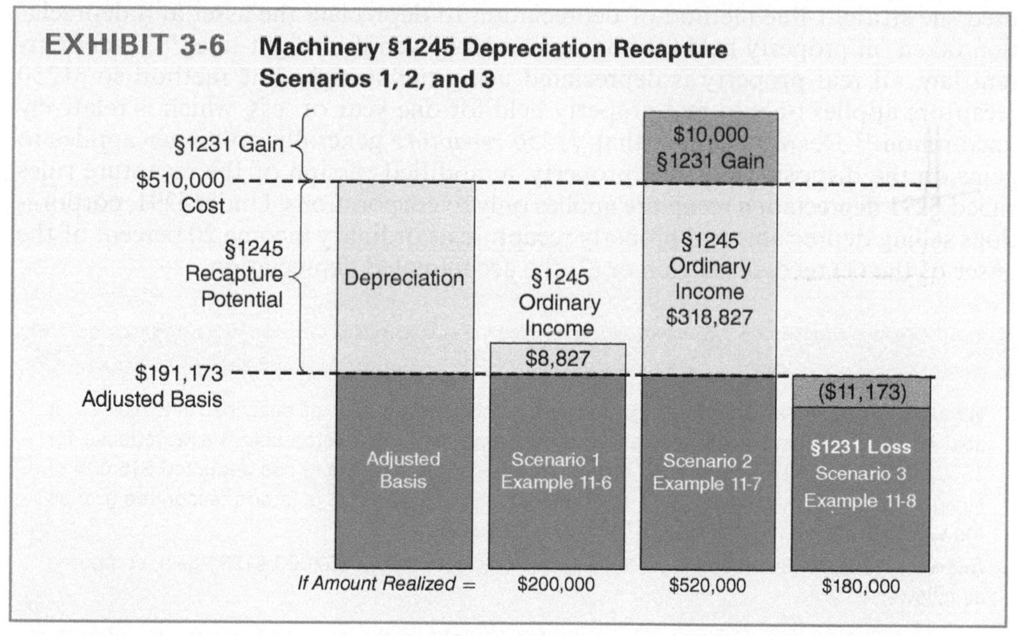

Example 3-9

In Example 3-6 (Scenario 1), we characterized the gain Teton recognized when it sold its machinery. For completeness, let's characterize the gain or loss Teton recognized on the other two §1245 assets it sold during the year (see Exhibit 3-2). Teton sold its office furniture for $12,000 and its delivery truck for $2,000. What is the amount and character of gain or loss Teton recognizes on the sales of the office furniture and delivery truck?

Answer: Office furniture: $7,000 ordinary income and $2,000 §1231 gain. Delivery truck: $2,500 §1231 loss.

The computations supporting the answers are as follows:

Description	Office Furniture	Delivery Truck	Explanation
(1) Amount realized	$12,000	$ 2,000	Exhibit 3-2.
(2) Original basis	10,000	15,000	Exhibit 3-2.
(3) Accumulated depreciation	7,000	10,500	Exhibit 3-2.
(4) Adjusted basis	3,000	4,500	(2) − (3).
(5) Gain (loss) recognized	9,000	(2,500)	(1) − (4).
(6) Ordinary income (§1245 depreciation recapture)	**7,000**	**0**	Lesser of (3) or (5), limited to $0.
§1231 gain (loss)	**2,000**	**(2,500)**	(5) − (6).

§1250 Depreciation Recapture for Real Property

Depreciable real property, such as an office building or a warehouse, sold at a gain is *not* subject to §1245 depreciation recapture. Rather, it is subject to a different type of recapture called §1250 depreciation recapture. Thus, depreciable real property is

[15]The authors thank PwC for allowing us to use these figures.

frequently referred to as **§1250 property.** Under §1250, when depreciable real property is sold at a gain, the amount of gain recaptured as ordinary income is limited to *additional* depreciation, defined as the excess of *accelerated* depreciation deductions on the property over the amount that would have been deducted if the taxpayer had used the straight-line method of depreciation to depreciate the asset and depreciation taken on property held for one year or less (even if straight-line).[16] Under current law, all real property is depreciated using the straight-line method so §1250 recapture applies only to real property held for one year or less, which is relatively uncommon.[17] Despite the fact that *§1250 recapture* generally no longer applies to gains on the disposition of real property, a modified version of the recapture rules called **§291 depreciation recapture** applies only to corporations. Under §291, corporations selling depreciable real property recapture as ordinary income 20 percent of the lesser of the (1) recognized gain or (2) the accumulated depreciation.

Example 3-10

What if: Suppose that Teton was organized as a corporation and that, as described in Exhibit 3-2, it sold its existing warehouse. Let's assume the same facts: that Teton sold the warehouse for $350,000, that it initially purchased the warehouse for $275,000, and has deducted $15,000 of straight-line depreciation deductions as of the date of the sale. What is Teton's recognized gain on the sale and what is the character of its gain on the sale?

Answer: $90,000 gain recognized; $3,000 ordinary income and $87,000 §1231 gain, computed as follows:

Description	Amount	Explanation
(1) Amount realized	$350,000	Exhibit 3-2.
(2) Original basis	275,000	Exhibit 3-2.
(3) Accumulated depreciation	15,000	Exhibit 3-2.
(4) Adjusted basis	260,000	(2) − (3).
(5) Gain (Loss) recognized	90,000	(1) − (4).
(6) Lesser of accumulated depreciation or recognized gain	15,000	Lesser of (3) or (5).
(7) §291 recapture (ordinary income)	$ 3,000	20% × (6).
§1231 gain	$ 87,000	(5) − (7).

LO 3-4

OTHER PROVISIONS AFFECTING THE RATE AT WHICH GAINS ARE TAXED

Other provisions, other than depreciation recapture, may affect the rate at which taxpayer gains are taxed. The first potentially applies when individuals sell §1250 property at a gain, and the second potentially applies when taxpayers sell property to related parties at a gain.

Unrecaptured §1250 Gain for Individuals

Except for assets held 12 months or less, neither corporations nor individuals recognize §1250 recapture on the sale of §1250 property when sold at a gain. Instead,

[16]§1250 recapture is commonly referred to as *partial depreciation recapture.*

[17]Accelerated depreciation was allowed for real property placed in service before 1987. Such property had a maximum recovery period of 19 years, which means that as of 2005 all of this property is now fully depreciated under both the accelerated and straight-line depreciation methods.

corporations recognize §291 recapture as ordinary income on the sale of these assets. Individuals, however, do not recognize ordinary income from the sale of §1250 property when held long term. Rather, individual taxpayers treat a gain resulting from the disposition of §1250 property as a §1231 gain and combine it with other §1231 gains and losses to determine whether a net §1231 gain or a net §1231 loss results for the year.

If, after the §1231 netting process (described below), the gain on the sale of the §1250 property is ultimately determined to be a long-term capital gain, the taxpayer must determine the rate at which the gain will be taxed. Tax policy makers determined that the portion of the gain caused by depreciation deductions reducing the basis (called **unrecaptured §1250 gain**) should be taxed at a maximum rate of 25 percent (taxed at the ordinary rate if the ordinary rate is lower than 25 percent) and not the 0/15/20 percent rate generally applicable to other types of long-term capital gains. Consequently, when an individual sells §1250 property at a gain, the amount of the gain taxed at a maximum rate of 25 percent is the *lesser* of the (1) recognized gain or (2) the accumulated depreciation on the asset.[18] The remainder of the gain is taxed at a maximum rate of 0/15/20 percent.[19]

Example 3-11

Teton bought its warehouse for $275,000, depreciated it $15,000, and sold it for $350,000. What is the amount and character of the gain Teton (and thus Steve) reports on the sale (recall that income of sole proprietorships is taxed directly to the owner of the business)?

Answer: $90,000 of §1231 gain, which includes $15,000 of unrecaptured §1250 gain, computed as follows:

Description	Amount	Explanation
(1) Amount realized	$350,000	
(2) Original basis	275,000	
(3) Accumulated depreciation	15,000	
(4) Adjusted basis	260,000	(2) − (3).
(5) Gain (Loss) recognized	90,000	(1) − (4).
(6) Unrecaptured §1250 gain	15,000	Lesser of (3) or (5).
(7) Remaining §1231 gain	75,000	(5) − (6).
Total §1231 gain	**$ 90,000**	(6) + (7).

What if: Suppose Steve's marginal ordinary tax rate is 35 percent. What amount of tax will he pay on the gain (assuming no other asset dispositions)?

Answer: $15,000, computed as follows:

Description	(1) Gain	(2) Rate	(1) × (2) Tax	Explanation
Long-term capital gain (unrecaptured §1250 gain portion)	$15,000	25%	$ 3,750	This is the gain due to depreciation deductions.
Long-term capital gain (15 percent portion)	75,000	15%	11,250	Taxed at 15 percent because Steve is in the 35% tax bracket.
Totals	$90,000		$15,000	

Because Steve did not sell any other §1231 assets during the year, the entire §1231 gain is treated as a long-term capital gain that is split into a portion taxed at 25 percent and a portion taxed at 15 percent.

THE KEY FACTS

Unrecaptured §1250 Gains

- Depreciable real property sold at a gain is §1250 property but is no longer subject to §1250 recapture unless it is held 12 months or less.
- The lesser of the (1) recognized gain or (2) accumulated depreciation on the assets is called *unrecaptured* §1250 gain.
- Unrecaptured §1250 gain is §1231 gain that, if ultimately characterized as a long-term capital gain, is taxed at a maximum rate of 25 percent.

[18]The amount taxed at a maximum rate of 25 percent cannot exceed the amount of the taxpayer's net §1231 gain.

[19]These rates (25 or 0/15/20 percent) apply to net §1231 gains after a netting process for capital gains.

THE KEY FACTS

§1239 Related-Person Transactions

- All gain recognized from selling property that is a depreciable asset to a related buyer is ordinary income (regardless of the character of the asset to the seller).
- Related persons are defined in §1239 and include
  - An individual and the individual's controlled corporation or partnership.
  - A taxpayer and any trust in which the taxpayer (or spouse) is a beneficiary.

Characterizing Gains on the Sale of Depreciable Property to Related Persons

Under §1239, when a taxpayer sells property to a *related person* and the property is depreciable property to the *buyer,* the entire gain on the sale is characterized as ordinary income to the *seller*.[20] Without this provision, related taxpayers could create tax savings by currently generating capital or §1231 gains through selling appreciated assets to related persons who would receive future ordinary deductions through depreciation expense on the basis of the property (stepped up to fair market value through the sale) acquired in the transaction.

The §1239 recapture provision is different from depreciation recapture in the sense that the seller is required to recognize ordinary income *for depreciation deductions the buyer will receive in the future,* while depreciation recapture requires taxpayers to recognize ordinary income *for depreciation deductions they have received in the past.* In both cases, however, the tax laws are designed to provide symmetry between the character of deductions an asset generates and the character of income the asset generates when it is sold. When depreciation recapture and the §1239 recapture provision apply to the same gain, the depreciation recapture rule applies first.

For purposes of §1239, a related person includes an individual and his or her controlled (more than 50 percent owned) corporation or partnership or a taxpayer and any trust in which the taxpayer (or spouse) is a beneficiary.[21]

Example 3-12

What if: Suppose that Teton is organized as a corporation and Steve is the sole shareholder. Steve sells equipment that he was using for personal purposes to Teton for $90,000 (he originally purchased the equipment for $80,000). The equipment was a capital asset to Steve because he had been using it for personal purposes (he did not depreciate it). What is the amount and character of the gain Steve would recognize on the sale?

Answer: $10,000 of ordinary income (amount realized $90,000 − $80,000 adjusted basis). Even though Steve is selling what is a capital asset to him, because it is a depreciable asset to Teton and because Steve and Teton are considered to be related persons, Steve is required to characterize the entire amount of gain as ordinary under §1239. Without the §1239 provision, Steve would have recognized a capital gain.

Exhibit 3-7 provides a flowchart for determining the character of gains and losses on the taxable sale of assets used in a trade or business.

LO 3-5

CALCULATING NET §1231 GAINS OR LOSSES

Once taxpayers determine the amount and character of gain or loss they recognize on *each* §1231 asset they sell during the year, they still have work to do to determine whether the gains or losses will be treated as ordinary or capital. After recharacterizing §1231 gain as ordinary income under the §1245 and §291 (if applicable) depreciation recapture rules and the §1239 related-person rules, the remaining §1231 gains and losses are netted together.[22] If the gains exceed the losses, the net gain

[20]§1239. §707(b)(2) contains a similar provision for partnerships.

[21]Additional related persons for purposes of §1239 include two corporations that are members of the same controlled group, a corporation and a partnership if the same person owns more than 50 percent of both entities, two S corporations controlled by the same person, and an S corporation and a C corporation controlled by the same person.

[22]If any of the §1231 gains and losses result from casualty or theft, these gains and losses are netted together first. If a net loss results, the net loss from §1231 casualty and theft events are treated as ordinary loss. Net gains from casualty and theft are treated as other §1231 gains and continue through the normal §1231 netting process.

EXHIBIT 3-7

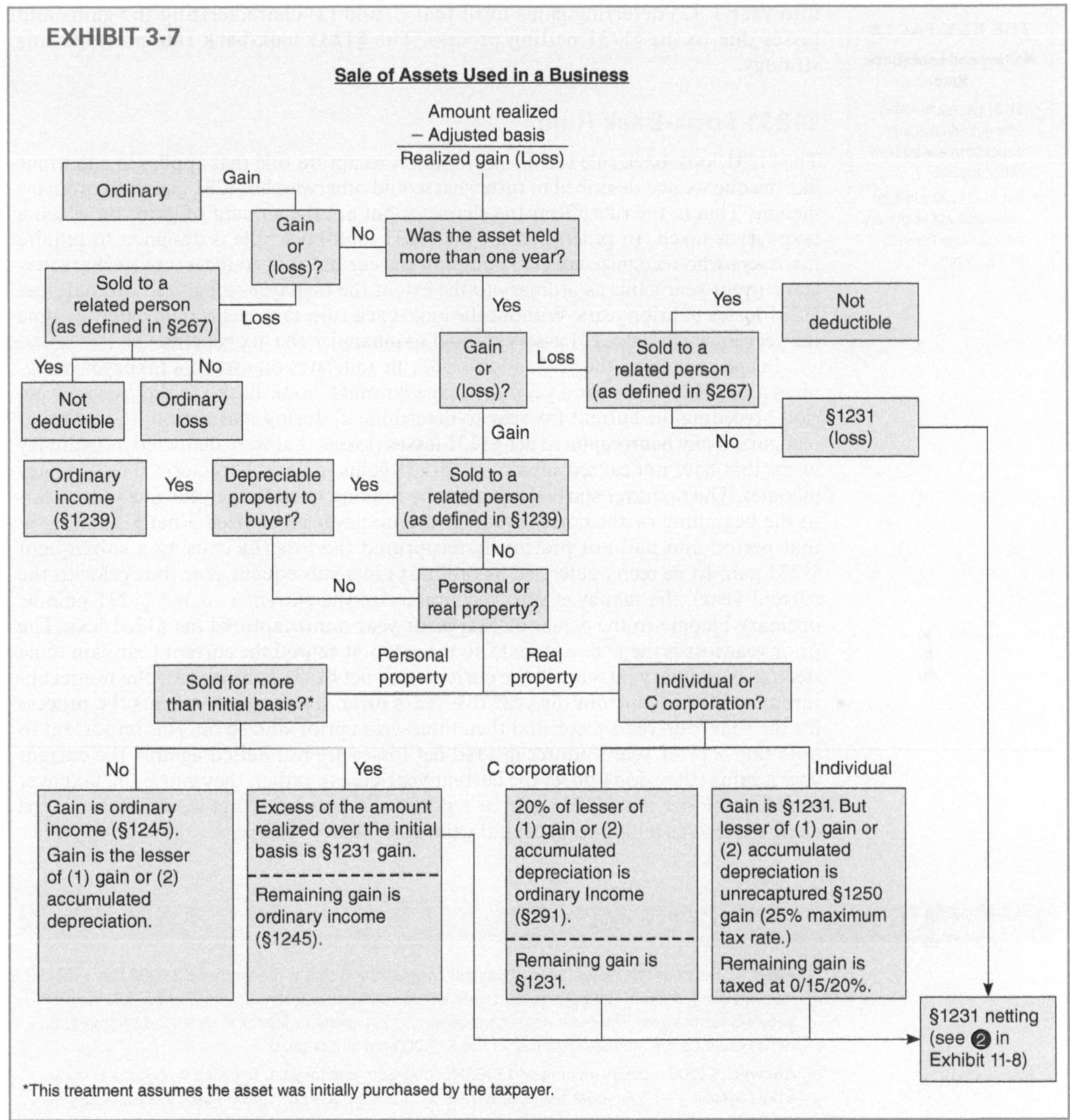

*This treatment assumes the asset was initially purchased by the taxpayer.

becomes a long-term capital gain (a portion of which may be taxed at the maximum rate of 25 percent). If the losses exceed the gains, the net loss is treated as an ordinary loss.

A taxpayer could gain significant tax benefits by discovering a way to have all §1231 gains treated as long-term capital gains and all §1231 losses treated as ordinary losses. The *annual* netting process makes this task impossible for a *particular* year. However, a taxpayer who owns multiple §1231 assets could sell the §1231 loss assets at the end of year 1 and the §1231 gain assets at the beginning of year 2. The taxpayer could benefit from this strategy in three ways: (1) accelerating losses

THE KEY FACTS

Netting and Look-Back Rule

- §1231 gains and losses from individual asset dispositions are annually netted together.
- Net §1231 gains may be recharacterized as ordinary income under the §1231 look-back rule.

into year 1, (2) deferring gains until year 2, and (3) characterizing the gains and losses due to the §1231 netting process. The **§1231 look-back rule** prevents this strategy.

§1231 Look-Back Rule

The §1231 look-back rule is a *nondepreciation* recapture rule that applies in situations like the one we just described to turn what would otherwise be §1231 gain into ordinary income. That is, the rule affects the character but not the amount of gains on which a taxpayer is taxed. In general terms, the §1231 look-back rule is designed to require taxpayers who recognize net §1231 gains in the current year to recapture (recharacterize) current year gains as ordinary to the extent the taxpayer recognized ordinary net §1231 losses in prior years. Without the look-back rule, taxpayers could carefully time the year in which the §1231 assets are sold to maximize the tax benefits.

In specific terms, the §1231 look-back rule indicates that when a taxpayer recognizes a net §1231 gain for a year, the taxpayer must "look-back" to the *five-year* period preceding the current tax year to determine if, during that period, the taxpayer recognized any **nonrecaptured net §1231 losses** (losses that were deducted as ordinary losses that have not caused subsequent §1231 gains to be recharacterized as ordinary income). The taxpayer starts the process by looking back to the year five years prior to the beginning of the current year. If the taxpayer recognized a net §1231 loss in that period and had not previously recaptured the loss (by causing a subsequent §1231 gain to be recharacterized as ordinary) in a subsequent year (but prior to the current year), the taxpayer must recharacterize the *current year* net §1231 gain as ordinary income to the extent of that prior year nonrecaptured net §1231 loss. The prior year loss is then "recaptured," to the extent it caused the current year gain to be treated as ordinary income. If the current year net §1231 gain exceeds the nonrecaptured net §1231 loss from the year five-years prior, the taxpayer repeats the process for the year four-years prior, and then three-years prior, and so on. It is important to note that a prior year's nonrecaptured net losses are not netted against the current year's gains (they don't offset the current year gains); rather, they cause the taxpayer to recharacterize a net §1231 gain or a portion of that gain (that would otherwise be characterized as a long-term capital gain) as ordinary income.[23]

Example 3-13

What if: Suppose that Teton began business in year 1 and that it recognized a $7,000 net §1231 loss in year 1. Assume that the current year is year 6 and that Teton reports a *net* §1231 gain of $25,000 for the year. Teton did not recognize any §1231 gains or losses in years 2–5. For year 6, what would be the ultimate character of the $25,000 net §1231 gain?

Answer: $7,000 ordinary income and $18,000 long-term capital gain. Because it recognized a net §1231 loss in year 1, it must recharacterize $7,000 of its net §1231 gain in year 6 as ordinary income. The remaining $18,000 §1231 gain is taxed as long-term capital gain.

What if: Assume the same facts as above, except that Teton also recognized a $2,000 net §1231 loss in year 5. For year 6, what would be the ultimate character of the $25,000 net §1231 gain?

Answer: $9,000 ordinary income and $16,000 long-term capital gain. Note that the overall gain is still $25,000, but to the extent of the $7,000 loss in year 1 and the $2,000 loss in year 5, the §1231 gain is recharacterized as ordinary income under the §1231 look-back rule.

[23]If the taxpayer's net §1231 gains include unrecaptured §1250 gains and other 0/15/20 percent long-term capital gains, the nonrecaptured net §1231 losses first recharacterize the unrecaptured §1250 gains as ordinary income.

ETHICS

Emma Bean operates a yoga studio and wants to sell some of her business equipment and a piece of land that is used as a parking lot. She expects to realize a $10,000 loss on the equipment and a $15,000 gain on the land. Emma has talked to her accountant and has learned about the look-back rule for §1231 property. To thwart any negative effects, she has decided to game the system and sell the land this year and then sell the equipment early next year. What do you think about her strategy to avoid the look-back rule?

As we've mentioned before, ultimately, all of a taxpayer's §1231 gains and losses must be characterized as ordinary or capital for purposes of determining a taxpayer's tax liability. Exhibit 3-8 summarizes the process of characterizing §1231 gains and losses as ordinary or capital.

EXHIBIT 3-8 §1231 Netting Process

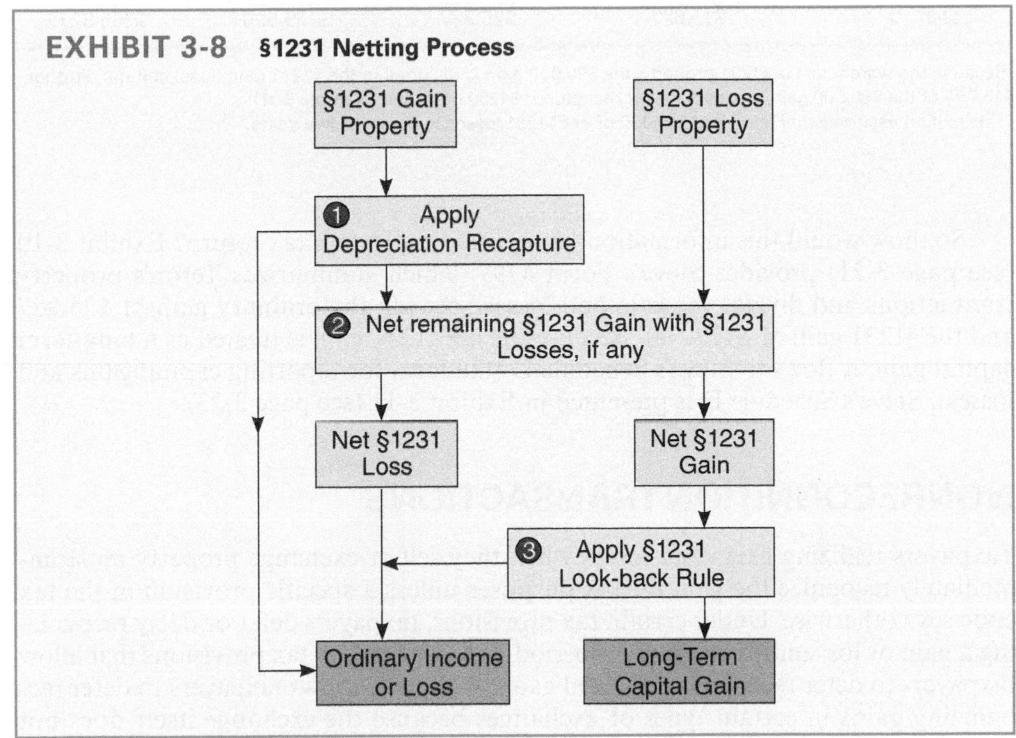

The following provides details on Steps 1–3 from Exhibit 3-8:

Step 1: Apply the *depreciation* recapture rules (and the §1239 recapture rules) to §1231 assets sold at a gain (any recaptured amounts become ordinary).

Step 2: Net the remaining §1231 gains with the §1231 losses. If the netting process yields a §1231 loss, the net §1231 loss becomes an ordinary loss.

Step 3: If the netting process produces a net §1231 gain, the taxpayer applies the §1231 look-back rule to determine if any of the remaining §1231 gain should be recharacterized as ordinary gain. Any gain remaining after applying the look-back rule is treated as long-term capital gain (including unrecaptured §1250 gain). This gain is included in the capital gains netting process.

GAIN OR LOSS SUMMARY

As indicated in Exhibit 3-2, Teton sold several assets during the year. Exhibit 3-9 summarizes the character of the gain or loss Teton (and thus Steve) recognized on each asset sale.

EXHIBIT 3-9 Summary of Teton Gains and Losses on Property Dispositions

Asset	(1) §1245 Ordinary Gain	(2) Total Ordinary Gain	(3) §1231 Gain (Loss)	(2) + (3) Total Gain
Machinery	$ 8,827	$ 8,827	$ 0	$ 8,827
Office furniture	7,000	7,000	2,000	9,000
Delivery truck	0	0	(2,500)	(2,500)
Warehouse	0	0	90,000*	90,000
Land	0	0	100,000	100,000
§1231 look-back		10,000	(10,000)[†]	0
Totals	$15,827	$25,827	$179,500*	$205.327

*Because the warehouse is §1231 property, the $90,000 gain is included in the §1231 gain (loss) column. Further, $15,000 of the $90,000 gain is considered unrecaptured §1250 gain (see Example 3-11).
[†]This exhibit assumes that Teton had $10,000 of net §1231 losses in the prior five years.

So, how would this information be reported on Steve's tax return? Exhibit 3-10 (see page 3-21) provides Steve's Form 4797, which summarizes Teton's property transactions and divides the gain and losses between the ordinary gain of $25,827 and the §1231 gain of $179,500. Because the net §1231 gain is treated as a long-term capital gain, it flows to Steve's Schedule D (the form for reporting capital gains and losses). Steve's Schedule D is presented in Exhibit 3-11 (see page 3-23).

LO 3-6

NONRECOGNITION TRANSACTIONS

Taxpayers realizing gains and losses when they sell or exchange property must immediately recognize the gain for tax purposes unless a specific provision in the tax code says otherwise. Under certain tax provisions, taxpayers defer or delay recognizing a gain or loss until a subsequent period. We first explore tax provisions that allow taxpayers to defer recognizing realized gains. Congress allows taxpayers to defer recognizing gains in certain types of exchanges because the exchange itself does not provide the taxpayers with the wherewithal (cash) to pay taxes on the realized gain if the taxpayers were required to immediately recognize the gain. In particular, we discuss common **nonrecognition transactions** such as like-kind exchanges, involuntary conversions, installment sales, and other business-related transactions such as business formations and reorganizations.

Like-Kind Exchanges

Taxpayers involved in a business may have valid reasons to trade business assets to others for similar business assets. For example, to increase productivity a taxpayer may want to trade machinery used in the business for the latest model. As we discussed earlier in this chapter, taxpayers exchanging property *realize* gains (or losses) on exchanges just as taxpayers do by selling property for cash. However,

EXHIBIT 3-10 Teton's (On Steve's return) Form 4797

Form **4797**

Department of the Treasury
Internal Revenue Service

Sales of Business Property

(Also Involuntary Conversions and Recapture Amounts Under Sections 179 and 280F(b)(2))

▶ Attach to your tax return.
▶ Information about Form 4797 and its separate instructions is at *www.irs.gov/form4797.*

OMB No. 1545-0184

2014

Attachment Sequence No. 27

Name(s) shown on return: Steve Dallimore (Teton Mountaineering Technologies, LLC)

Identifying number

1	Enter the gross proceeds from sales or exchanges reported to you for 2014 on Form(s) 1099-B or 1099-S (or substitute statement) that you are including on line 2, 10, or 20 (see instructions)	1	

Part I **Sales or Exchanges of Property Used in a Trade or Business and Involuntary Conversions From Other Than Casualty or Theft—Most Property Held More Than 1 Year** (see instructions)

2 (a) Description of property	(b) Date acquired (mo., day, yr.)	(c) Date sold (mo., day, yr.)	(d) Gross sales price	(e) Depreciation allowed or allowable since acquisition	(f) Cost or other basis, plus improvements and expense of sale	(g) Gain or (loss) Subtract (f) from the sum of (d) and (e)
Delivery truck	Yr 0	Yr 4	2,000	10,500	15,000	(2,500)
Land	Yr 0	Yr 4	175,000	0	75,000	100,000

3	Gain, if any, from Form 4684, line 39	3	
4	Section 1231 gain from installment sales from Form 6252, line 26 or 37	4	
5	Section 1231 gain or (loss) from like-kind exchanges from Form 8824	5	
6	Gain, if any, from line 32, from other than casualty or theft.	6	92,000
7	Combine lines 2 through 6. Enter the gain or (loss) here and on the appropriate line as follows:	7	189,500
	Partnerships (except electing large partnerships) and S corporations. Report the gain or (loss) following the instructions for Form 1065, Schedule K, line 10, or Form 1120S, Schedule K, line 9. Skip lines 8, 9, 11, and 12 below.		
	Individuals, partners, S corporation shareholders, and all others. If line 7 is zero or a loss, enter the amount from line 7 on line 11 below and skip lines 8 and 9. If line 7 is a gain and you did not have any prior year section 1231 losses, or they were recaptured in an earlier year, enter the gain from line 7 as a long-term capital gain on the Schedule D filed with your return and skip lines 8, 9, 11, and 12 below.		
8	Nonrecaptured net section 1231 losses from prior years (see instructions)	8	10,000
9	Subtract line 8 from line 7. If zero or less, enter -0-. If line 9 is zero, enter the gain from line 7 on line 12 below. If line 9 is more than zero, enter the amount from line 8 on line 12 below and enter the gain from line 9 as a long-term capital gain on the Schedule D filed with your return (see instructions)	9	179,500

Part II **Ordinary Gains and Losses** (see instructions)

10 Ordinary gains and losses not included on lines 11 through 16 (include property held 1 year or less):

11	Loss, if any, from line 7	11	( )
12	Gain, if any, from line 7 or amount from line 8, if applicable	12	10,000
13	Gain, if any, from line 31	13	15,827
14	Net gain or (loss) from Form 4684, lines 31 and 38a	14	
15	Ordinary gain from installment sales from Form 6252, line 25 or 36	15	
16	Ordinary gain or (loss) from like-kind exchanges from Form 8824.	16	
17	Combine lines 10 through 16	17	25,827
18	For all except individual returns, enter the amount from line 17 on the appropriate line of your return and skip lines a and b below. For individual returns, complete lines a and b below:		
a	If the loss on line 11 includes a loss from Form 4684, line 35, column (b)(ii), enter that part of the loss here. Enter the part of the loss from income-producing property on Schedule A (Form 1040), line 28, and the part of the loss from property used as an employee on Schedule A (Form 1040), line 23. Identify as from "Form 4797, line 18a." See instructions . .	18a	
b	Redetermine the gain or (loss) on line 17 excluding the loss, if any, on line 18a. Enter here and on Form 1040, line 14	18b	25,827

For Paperwork Reduction Act Notice, see separate instructions. Cat. No. 13086I Form **4797** (2014)

EXHIBIT 3-10 Teton's (On Steve's return) Form 4797 (*continued*)

Form 4797 (2014) Page 2

Part III **Gain From Disposition of Property Under Sections 1245, 1250, 1252, 1254, and 1255** (see instructions)

19 (a) Description of section 1245, 1250, 1252, 1254, or 1255 property:	(b) Date acquired (mo., day, yr.)	(c) Date sold (mo., day, yr.)
A Machinery	Yr 0	Yr 4
B Office furniture	Yr 0	Yr 4
C Warehouse	Yr 0	Yr 4
D		

These columns relate to the properties on lines 19A through 19D. ▶		Property A	Property B	Property C	Property D
20 Gross sales price (**Note:** *See line 1 before completing.*)	20	200,000	12,000	350,000	
21 Cost or other basis plus expense of sale	21	510,000	10,000	275,000	
22 Depreciation (or depletion) allowed or allowable	22	318,827	7,000	15,000	
23 Adjusted basis. Subtract line 22 from line 21	23	191,173	3,000	260,000	
24 Total gain. Subtract line 23 from line 20	24	8,827	9,000	90,000	
25 If section 1245 property:					
a Depreciation allowed or allowable from line 22	25a	318,827	7,000		
b Enter the **smaller** of line 24 or 25a	25b	8,827	7,000		
26 If section 1250 property: If straight line depreciation was used, enter -0- on line 26g, except for a corporation subject to section 291.					
a Additional depreciation after 1975 (see instructions)	26a				
b Applicable percentage multiplied by the **smaller** of line 24 or line 26a (see instructions)	26b				
c Subtract line 26a from line 24. If residential rental property **or** line 24 is not more than line 26a, skip lines 26d and 26e	26c				
d Additional depreciation after 1969 and before 1976	26d				
e Enter the **smaller** of line 26c or 26d	26e				
f Section 291 amount (corporations only)	26f				
g Add lines 26b, 26e, and 26f	26g			0	
27 If section 1252 property: Skip this section if you did not dispose of farmland or if this form is being completed for a partnership (other than an electing large partnership).					
a Soil, water, and land clearing expenses	27a				
b Line 27a multiplied by applicable percentage (see instructions)	27b				
c Enter the **smaller** of line 24 or 27b	27c				
28 If section 1254 property:					
a Intangible drilling and development costs, expenditures for development of mines and other natural deposits, mining exploration costs, and depletion (see instructions)	28a				
b Enter the **smaller** of line 24 or 28a	28b				
29 If section 1255 property:					
a Applicable percentage of payments excluded from income under section 126 (see instructions)	29a				
b Enter the **smaller** of line 24 or 29a (see instructions)	29b				

Summary of Part III Gains. Complete property columns A through D through line 29b before going to line 30.

30 Total gains for all properties. Add property columns A through D, line 24	30	107,827
31 Add property columns A through D, lines 25b, 26g, 27c, 28b, and 29b. Enter here and on line 13	31	15,827
32 Subtract line 31 from line 30. Enter the portion from casualty or theft on Form 4684, line 33. Enter the portion from other than casualty or theft on Form 4797, line 6	32	92,000

Part IV **Recapture Amounts Under Sections 179 and 280F(b)(2) When Business Use Drops to 50% or Less** (see instructions)

		(a) Section 179	(b) Section 280F(b)(2)
33 Section 179 expense deduction or depreciation allowable in prior years	33		
34 Recomputed depreciation (see instructions)	34		
35 Recapture amount. Subtract line 34 from line 33. See the instructions for where to report	35		

Form **4797** (2014)

EXHIBIT 3-11 **Steve's Schedule D (Assumes Steve had no other capital gains and losses other than those incurred by Teton)**

SCHEDULE D (Form 1040)

Department of the Treasury Internal Revenue Service (99)

Capital Gains and Losses

► Attach to Form 1040 or Form 1040NR.
► Information about Schedule D and its separate instructions is at *www.irs.gov/scheduled*.
► Use Form 8949 to list your transactions for lines 1b, 2, 3, 8b, 9, and 10.

OMB No. 1545-0074

2014

Attachment Sequence No. 12

Name(s) shown on return: Steve Dallimore

Your social security number

Part I **Short-Term Capital Gains and Losses—Assets Held One Year or Less**

See instructions for how to figure the amounts to enter on the lines below. This form may be easier to complete if you round off cents to whole dollars.	(d) Proceeds (sales price)	(e) Cost (or other basis)	(g) Adjustments to gain or loss from Form(s) 8949, Part I, line 2, column (g)	(h) Gain or (loss) Subtract column (e) from column (d) and combine the result with column (g)
1a Totals for all short-term transactions reported on Form 1099-B for which basis was reported to the IRS and for which you have no adjustments (see instructions). However, if you choose to report all these transactions on Form 8949, leave this line blank and go to line 1b				
1b Totals for all transactions reported on Form(s) 8949 with **Box A** checked				
2 Totals for all transactions reported on Form(s) 8949 with **Box B** checked				
3 Totals for all transactions reported on Form(s) 8949 with **Box C** checked				

4 Short-term gain from Form 6252 and short-term gain or (loss) from Forms 4684, 6781, and 8824	4	
5 Net short-term gain or (loss) from partnerships, S corporations, estates, and trusts from Schedule(s) K-1	5	
6 Short-term capital loss carryover. Enter the amount, if any, from line 8 of your **Capital Loss Carryover Worksheet** in the instructions	6	( )
7 Net short-term capital gain or (loss). Combine lines 1a through 6 in column (h). If you have any long-term capital gains or losses, go to Part II below. Otherwise, go to Part III on the back	7	

Part II **Long-Term Capital Gains and Losses—Assets Held More Than One Year**

See instructions for how to figure the amounts to enter on the lines below. This form may be easier to complete if you round off cents to whole dollars.	(d) Proceeds (sales price)	(e) Cost (or other basis)	(g) Adjustments to gain or loss from Form(s) 8949, Part II, line 2, column (g)	(h) Gain or (loss) Subtract column (e) from column (d) and combine the result with column (g)
8a Totals for all long-term transactions reported on Form 1099-B for which basis was reported to the IRS and for which you have no adjustments (see instructions). However, if you choose to report all these transactions on Form 8949, leave this line blank and go to line 8b				
8b Totals for all transactions reported on Form(s) 8949 with **Box D** checked				
9 Totals for all transactions reported on Form(s) 8949 with **Box E** checked				
10 Totals for all transactions reported on Form(s) 8949 with **Box F** checked				

11 Gain from Form 4797, Part I; long-term gain from Forms 2439 and 6252; and long-term gain or (loss) from Forms 4684, 6781, and 8824	11	179,500
12 Net long-term gain or (loss) from partnerships, S corporations, estates, and trusts from Schedule(s) K-1	12	
13 Capital gain distributions. See the instructions	13	
14 Long-term capital loss carryover. Enter the amount, if any, from line 13 of your **Capital Loss Carryover Worksheet** in the instructions	14	( )
15 Net long-term capital gain or (loss). Combine lines 8a through 14 in column (h). Then go to Part III on the back	15	179,500

For Paperwork Reduction Act Notice, see your tax return instructions. Cat. No. 11338H **Schedule D (Form 1040) 2014**

taxpayers exchanging property for property are in a different situation than taxpayers selling the same property for cash. Taxpayers exchanging one piece of business property for another haven't changed their relative economic position in the sense that both before and after the exchange they hold an asset for use in their business. Further, exchanges of property do not generate the wherewithal (cash) for the taxpayers to pay taxes on the gain they realize on the exchanges. While taxpayers selling property for cash must immediately recognize gain on the sale, taxpayers exchanging property for assets other than cash must defer recognizing gain (or loss) realized on the exchange if they meet certain requirements. This type of deferred gain (or loss) transaction is commonly referred to as a **like-kind exchange** or §1031 exchange.[24]

Like-kind exchange treatment can provide taxpayers with significant tax advantages by allowing them to defer gain (and current taxes payable) that would otherwise be recognized immediately.[25] For an exchange to qualify as a like-kind exchange for tax purposes, the transaction must meet the following three criteria:

1. The property is exchanged "solely for like-kind" property.
2. Both the property given up and the property received in the exchange by the taxpayer are either "used in a trade or business" or are "held for investment," by the taxpayer.
3. The "exchange" must meet certain time restrictions.

Below, we discuss each of these requirements in detail.

THE KEY FACTS

Like-Kind Property

- Real property
  - All real property used in a trade or business or held for investment is considered "like-kind" with other real property used in a trade or business or held for investment.
- Personal property
  - Personal property is considered "like-kind" if it has the same general use and is used in a business or held for investment.
- Ineligible property
  - Inventory.
  - Most financial instruments.
  - Partnerships interests.
  - Domestic property exchanged for property used in a foreign country and all property used in a foreign country.

Definition of Like-Kind Property

The definition of like-kind property depends on whether the property exchanged is real property or tangible personal property. Generally, the definition of like-kind *real* property is much less restrictive than it is for like-kind *personal* property.

Real Property

All real property is considered to be "like-kind" with any other type of real property as long as the real property is used in a trade or business or held for investment. For example, from Teton's perspective, its warehouse on 10 acres would be considered to be like-kind with a nearby condominium complex, a 20-acre parcel of raw land for sale across town, or even a Manhattan skyscraper.

Personal Property

Determining what qualifies as like-kind property for tangible personal property is a little more involved. The Treasury regulations explain that tangible personal property qualifies as "like-kind" if the property transferred and the property received in the exchange is in the same general asset class in Rev. Proc. 87-56 (this is the concept we use in the previous chapter to determine the recovery period for MACRS depreciation).[26] In simpler terms, for personal property to qualify as like-kind property the property given in the exchange and the property received in the exchange must have the same general use to the taxpayer. For example, if Teton were to trade some machinery used in its manufacturing operations for some new machinery to be used in its manufacturing process, the transaction would qualify as a like-kind exchange. However, if Teton were to trade some machinery used in its manufacturing operations for a new delivery truck, the exchange would not qualify as a like-kind exchange.

[24]Like-kind exchanges are defined in §1031 of the Internal Revenue Code.

[25]In contrast, financial accounting rules require businesses to recognize (for financial accounting purposes) any gain they realize in a like-kind exchange transaction.

[26]Like-kind is defined in Reg. §1.1031(a)-2(b).

Property Ineligible for Like-Kind Treatment Certain types of property are, by definition, excluded from the definition of like-kind property and thus are not eligible for like-kind treatment.[27] This property includes inventory held for resale (including land held by a developer), most financial instruments (such as stocks, bonds, or notes), domestic property exchanged for foreign property, and partnership interests.[28]

Property Use

Even when property meets the definition of like-kind property, taxpayers can only exchange the property in a qualifying like-kind exchange if the taxpayer used the transferred property in a trade or business or for investment *and* the taxpayer will use the property received in the exchange in a trade or business or for investment. For example, Teton could exchange its warehouse on 10 acres for a 200-acre parcel of land it intends to hold as an investment in a qualifying like-kind exchange because Teton was using the warehouse in its business and it would hold the land as an investment. However, if Steve exchanged his personal-use cabin in Maine for a personal residence in Wyoming, the exchange would not qualify because Steve used the residence for personal purposes, and he would be using the Wyoming property for personal rather than business or investment purposes. In fact, even if Steve was renting his Maine cabin (it qualifies as investment property) when he exchanged it for his principal residence in Wyoming, the exchange would not qualify for like-kind exchange treatment because *both* properties (the property the taxpayer is giving up and the property the taxpayer is receiving in the exchange) must meet the use test (the personal residence does not qualify as business or investment property). Likewise, if Teton exchanged a business computer for Steve's personal use computer, Teton would qualify for like-kind exchange treatment because Teton was using its computer equipment in its business and it will use Steve's computer in its business. However, the exchange would not qualify as a like-kind exchange for Steve because Steve used the computer for personal (not business or investment) purposes. A key takeaway here is that due to the use and other requirements, one party to an exchange may qualify for like-kind treatment and the other party may not. Each party to the exchange must individually determine whether or not the exchange qualifies as a like-kind exchange to her.

Timing Requirements for a Like-Kind Exchange

Many like-kind exchanges involve a simultaneous exchange of like-kind assets. For example, Teton could take its used machinery to a dealer and pick up its new machinery at the same time. However, a simultaneous exchange may not be practical or possible. For example, taxpayers may not always be able to immediately (or even eventually) find another party who is willing to exchange properties with the taxpayer. In these situations taxpayers often use **third-party intermediaries** to facilitate like-kind exchanges. When a third party is involved, the taxpayer transfers the like-kind property to the intermediary and the intermediary sells the property and uses the proceeds to acquire the new property for the taxpayer.[29] Because the third party must sell the taxpayer's old property and locate and purchase suitable replacement property, this process is subject to delay. In these types of situations, does a delay in

THE KEY FACTS

Timing Requirements

- Like-kind property exchanges may involve intermediaries.
- Taxpayers must identify replacement like-kind property within 45 days of giving up their property.
- Like-kind property must be received within 180 days of when the taxpayer transfers property in a like-kind exchange.

[27]§1031(a)(2).

[28]Property used more than 50 percent of the time in a foreign country is not like-kind with domestic or with other foreign property.

[29]Exchanges involving third-party intermediaries are very common with real estate exchanges. For real estate, taxpayers must use a "qualified exchange intermediary," such as a title company, and cannot use a personal attorney (because attorneys are considered to be the taxpayer's agent).

the completion of the exchange disqualify an otherwise allowable like-kind exchange? Not necessarily. The tax laws do not require a simultaneous exchange of assets, but they do impose some timing requirements to ensure that a transaction is completed within a reasonable time in order to qualify as a **deferred** (not simultaneous) **like-kind exchange**—often referred to as a *Starker exchange*.[30]

The two timing rules applicable to like-kind exchanges are (1) the taxpayer must *identify* the like-kind replacement property within 45 days after transferring the property given up in the exchange, and (2) the taxpayer must receive the replacement like-kind property within 180 days (or the due date of the tax return including extensions) after the taxpayer initially transfers property in the exchange.[31] The time limits force the taxpayer to close the transaction within a specified time period, so that the taxpayers can report the tax consequences of the transaction. Exhibit 3-12 provides a diagram of a like-kind exchange involving a third-party intermediary.

EXHIBIT 3-12 Diagram of Deferred or Starker Exchange

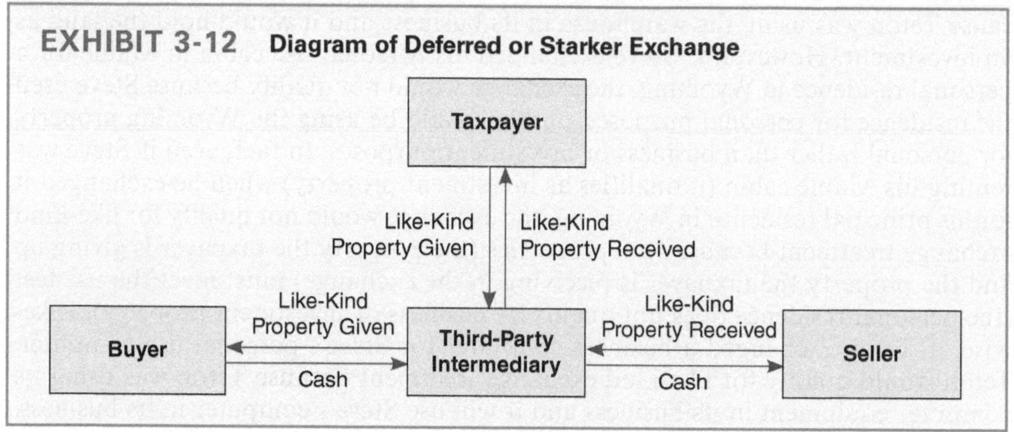

When a taxpayer fails to meet the timing requirements, the exchange fails to qualify for like-kind treatment and is thus fully taxable.

Example 3-14

What if: Suppose that on July 1 of year 1 Steve transferred a parcel of real property that he was holding as an investment to a third-party intermediary with the intention of exchanging the property for another suitable investment property. By what date does Steve need to identify the replacement property?

Answer: August 16 of year 1, which is 45 days after Steve transferred the property to the intermediary.

Assuming Steve identifies the replacement property within the 45-day time period, by what date does he need to receive the replacement property in order to qualify for like-kind exchange treatment?

Answer: December 28 of year 1, which is 180 days from July 1, the date he transferred the property to the intermediary.

[30]The term *Starker exchange* refers to a landmark court case that first allowed deferred exchanges (*T.J. Starker, Appellant v. United States of America,* 79-2 USTC ¶9541). The rules for deferred exchanges are found in §1031(a)(3). The tax laws also allow for reverse like-kind exchanges where replacement property is acquired before the taxpayer transfers the like-kind property.

[31]The taxpayer must identify at least one like-kind asset; however, since failure to obtain the asset disqualifies the transaction from having deferred like-kind exchange status, the taxpayer may identify up to three alternatives to hedge against the inability to obtain the first identified asset. Generally, a taxpayer must obtain only one to facilitate the exchange [see Reg. §1.1031(k)-1(c)(4)].

Tax Consequences When Like-Kind Property Is Exchanged Solely for Like-Kind Property

As we've discussed, when taxpayers exchanging property meet the like-kind exchange requirements, they do not recognize gain or loss on the exchange. They also establish or receive an **exchanged basis** in the like-kind property they receive. That is, they exchange the basis they had in the property given up and transfer it to the basis of the property received.[32]

Example 3-15

Teton would like to trade machinery worth $29,500 (adjusted basis of $18,742), for new machinery worth $29,500. How much gain does Teton recognize on this exchange?

Answer: $0. Teton's exchange qualifies as a like-kind exchange and the $10,758 realized gain ($29,500 amount realized minus $18,742 adjusted basis) is deferred.

What is Teton's basis in the new machinery?

Answer: $18,742, the basis it had in the old machinery it traded in.

Tax Consequences of Transfers Involving Like-Kind and Non-Like-Kind Property (Boot)

THE KEY FACTS

Like-Kind Exchanges Involving Boot

- Non-like-kind property is known as boot.
- When boot is given as part of a like-kind transaction:
  - The asset received is recorded in two parts: property received in exchange for like-kind property and property received in a sale (bought by the boot).
- When boot is received:
  - Boot received usually creates recognized gain.
  - Gain recognized is lesser of gain realized or boot received.

A practical problem with like-kind exchanges is that the value of the like-kind property the taxpayer transfers may differ from the value of the like-kind property the taxpayer receives in the exchange. In these situations the party transferring the lesser-valued asset must also transfer additional property to the other party to equate the values. When this additional property or **"boot"** (non-like-kind property) is transferred, the party receiving it apparently fails the first like-kind exchange requirement that like-kind property be exchanged solely for like-kind property. Nevertheless, if a taxpayer receives boot in addition to like-kind property, the transaction can still qualify for like-kind exchange treatment, but the taxpayer is required to recognize realized gain *to the extent of the boot received.*[33] As a practical matter, this means the taxpayer's recognized gain is the *lesser of* (1) gain realized or (2) boot received.

The reason a taxpayer must recognize gain is that the taxpayer is essentially selling a portion of the like-kind property for the boot in a taxable exchange. The receipt of boot triggers taxable gain (but not a taxable loss) in an otherwise qualifying like-kind exchange. If the taxpayer transfers loss property (adjusted basis is greater than fair market value) in a qualifying like-kind exchange, the taxpayer defers recognition of the loss until the taxpayer sells or disposes of the loss property in a taxable transaction—so it may be important for tax planning purposes to avoid the like-kind exchange rules if the taxpayer wishes to currently recognize the loss.[34] When a taxpayer recognizes gain in a like-kind exchange, the character of the gain depends on the character of the asset transferred by the taxpayer (the depreciation recapture rules apply when characterizing gains).

[32]If the asset is a depreciable asset, the taxpayer continues to depreciate the new asset as if it were the old asset.

[33]§1031(b).

[34]§1031(a) states that no gain or loss is recognized in a qualifying like-kind exchange.

Example 3-16

What if: Suppose that Teton trades its used machinery with a value of $29,500 and an adjusted basis of $18,742 ($30,615 historical cost less $11,873 of accumulated depreciation) to the dealer for new machinery valued at $27,500. To equate the value of the property exchanged, the dealer also pays Teton $2,000. What gain or loss does Teton realize on the exchange and what gain or loss does Teton recognize on the exchange?

Answer: $10,758 realized gain and $2,000 recognized gain, calculated as follows:

Description	Amount	Explanation
(1) Amount realized from machine	$27,500	
(2) Amount realized from boot (cash)	2,000	
(3) Total amount realized	29,500	(1) + (2).
(4) Adjusted basis	18,742	
(5) Gain realized	**10,758**	(3) − (4).
Gain recognized	**$ 2,000**	Lesser of (2) or (5).

What is the character of Teton's $2,000 gain?

Answer: Ordinary income. Because Teton's accumulated depreciation on the asset exceeds its $2,000 gain, Teton must treat the gain as ordinary gain under the §1245 depreciation recapture rules discussed earlier.

What if: Suppose the same facts as above, except that Teton's adjusted basis in the machinery was $29,000. What amount of gain would Teton recognize on the exchange?

Answer: $500. Teton recognizes the lesser of (1) $500 gain realized ($29,500 minus $29,000) or (2) $2,000 boot received.

When taxpayers receive like-kind property and boot in a like-kind exchange, their basis in the like-kind property is computed under §1031(d) using the following formula:

Adjusted basis of like-kind property surrendered
+ Adjusted basis of boot given
+ Gain recognized
− Fair market value of boot received
− Loss recognized
= Basis of like-kind property received

An alternative and simplified method for checking the basis calculation is to begin with the fair market value of the like-kind property received and subtract any deferred gain or add any deferred loss.

The basis of boot received in the exchange is always the boot's fair market value. This formula for computing basis ensures that the taxpayer's deferred gain or loss on the exchange (the gain or loss realized that is not recognized) is captured in the difference between the value and the basis of the new property received. Consequently, taxpayers defer realized gain or loss on qualifying like-kind exchanges; they do not exclude them. Taxpayers will ultimately recognize the gain or loss when they dispose of the new asset in a taxable transaction.[35]

[35]Additionally, the deferred gain is subject to depreciation recapture when the asset is eventually disposed of in a taxable disposition.

Example 3-17

What if: Assume the facts in the previous example where Teton traded its used machinery with a value of $29,500 and an adjusted basis of $18,742 to the dealer for new machinery valued at $27,500 and $2,000 cash. Teton recognized $2,000 on the exchange. What is Teton's basis in the new machinery it received from the dealer?

Answer: $18,742, computed as follows:

Description	Amount	Explanation
(1) Amount realized from machine	$27,500	Fair market value of new machine.
(2) Amount realized from boot (cash)	2,000	
(3) Total amount realized	29,500	(1) + (2).
(4) Adjusted basis of used machinery	18,742	
(5) Gain realized	10,758	(3) − (4).
(6) Gain recognized	$ 2,000	Lesser of (2) or (5).
(7) Deferred gain	8,758	(5) − (6).
Adjusted basis in new property	**$18,742**	(1) − (7).

THE KEY FACTS

Exchanged Basis

- The basis of like-kind property received is the fair market value of the new asset minus deferred gain or plus deferred loss on the exchange (unless boot is given).
  - When no gain is recognized on the exchange, the basis of the new property is the same as taxpayer's basis in the old like-kind property.
- The basis of boot received is the fair market value of the boot.

It is important to note that anything a taxpayer receives in an exchange other than like-kind property is considered boot. This includes cash, other property, or even the amount of a taxpayer's liability transferred to (assumed by) the other party in the exchange. For example, let's return to the previous example. If instead of paying Teton $2,000 of cash, the dealer assumed Teton's $2,000 liability secured by Teton's old machinery, the tax consequences would have been identical. The dealer relieved Teton of $2,000 of debt and the debt relief is treated the same as if the dealer had paid Teton cash and Teton had paid off its $2,000 liability. Generally, when a taxpayer both transfers and receives boot in an otherwise qualifying like-kind exchange, the taxpayer must recognize any realized gain to the extent of the boot received. That is, the taxpayer is not allowed to offset boot received with boot paid.[36] However, when the taxpayer gives and receives boot in the form of liabilities, the taxpayer is allowed to net the boot received and the boot paid.[37]

Reporting Like-Kind Exchanges

Like-kind exchange transactions are reported on Form 8824. Exhibit 3-13 presents the computations from Form 8824 reflecting the like-kind exchange of the machinery in Example 3-15.

Involuntary Conversions

Usually, when taxpayers sell, exchange, or abandon property they intend to do so. However, sometimes taxpayers may involuntarily dispose of property due to circumstances beyond their control. Thus, the tax law refers to these types of property dispositions as **involuntary conversions.**[38] Involuntary conversions occur when property is partially or wholly destroyed by a natural disaster or accident, stolen, condemned, or seized via eminent domain by a governmental agency. Tragic examples of this include the results of the September 11, 2001, terrorist attacks and the Hurricane Katrina-related events in 2005. Even in situations when taxpayers

THE KEY FACTS

Involuntary Conversions

- Gain is deferred when appreciated property is involuntarily converted in an accident or natural disaster.
- Basis of property directly converted is carried over from the old property to the new property.
- In an indirect conversion, gain recognized is the lesser of:
  - Gain realized, or
  - Amount of reimbursement the taxpayer does not reinvest in qualified property.
- Qualified replacement property must be of a similar or related use to the original property.

[36]However, Reg. §1.1031(j)-1 provides an exception where multiple like-kind exchanges are made in a single exchange.

[37]Further details of this important exception are beyond the scope of our discussion. See the examples provided in Reg. §1.1031(d)-2 for further guidance.

[38]§1033.

EXHIBIT 3-13 **Form 8824, Part III (From machine exchange in Example 3-15)**

Form 8824 (2014) Page **2**

Name(s) shown on tax return. Do not enter name and social security number if shown on other side.	**Your social security number**
Steve Dallimore (Teton Mountaineering Technologies, LLC)	

Part III **Realized Gain or (Loss), Recognized Gain, and Basis of Like-Kind Property Received**

Caution: *If you transferred* ***and*** *received* ***(a)*** *more than one group of like-kind properties or* ***(b)*** *cash or other (not like-kind) property, see* **Reporting of multi-asset exchanges** *in the instructions.*

Note: *Complete lines 12 through 14* ***only*** *if you gave up property that was not like-kind. Otherwise, go to line 15.*

12	Fair market value (FMV) of other property given up	12			
13	Adjusted basis of other property given up	13			
14	Gain or (loss) recognized on other property given up. Subtract line 13 from line 12. Report the gain or (loss) in the same manner as if the exchange had been a sale			14	
	Caution: *If the property given up was used previously or partly as a home, see* **Property used as home** *in the instructions.*				
15	Cash received, FMV of other property received, plus net liabilities assumed by other party, reduced (but not below zero) by any exchange expenses you incurred (see instructions)			15	0
16	FMV of like-kind property you received			16	29,500
17	Add lines 15 and 16			17	29,500
18	Adjusted basis of like-kind property you gave up, net amounts paid to other party, plus any exchange expenses **not** used on line 15 (see instructions)			18	18,742
19	**Realized gain or (loss).** Subtract line 18 from line 17			19	10,758
20	Enter the smaller of line 15 or line 19, but not less than zero			20	
21	Ordinary income under recapture rules. Enter here and on Form 4797, line 16 (see instructions)			21	
22	Subtract line 21 from line 20. If zero or less, enter -0-. If more than zero, enter here and on Schedule D or Form 4797, unless the installment method applies (see instructions)			22	
23	**Recognized gain.** Add lines 21 and 22			23	0
24	Deferred gain or (loss). Subtract line 23 from line 19. If a related party exchange, see instructions			24	10,758
25	**Basis of like-kind property received.** Subtract line 15 from the sum of lines 18 and 23			25	18,742

experience a loss of property due to theft, disaster, or other circumstances, they might realize a gain for tax purposes if they receive replacement property or insurance proceeds in excess of their basis in the property that was stolen or destroyed.

Taxpayers may experience a tremendous financial hardship if they were required to recognize the realized gain in these circumstances. For example, let's consider a business that acquired a building for \$100,000. The building appreciates in value and when the building is worth \$150,000 it is destroyed by fire. The building is fully insured at its replacement cost, so the business receives a check from the insurance company for \$150,000. The problem for the business is that it realizes a \$50,000 gain on this involuntary conversion (\$150,000 insurance proceeds minus \$100,000 basis in property without considering depreciation). Assuming the business's income is taxed at a 30 percent marginal rate, it must pay \$15,000 of tax on the insurance money it receives. This leaves the business with only \$135,000 to replace property worth \$150,000. This hardly seems equitable. Congress provides special tax laws to allow taxpayers to defer the gains on such *involuntary* conversions.

Taxpayers may defer realized gains on both direct and indirect involuntary conversions. **Direct conversions** involve taxpayers receiving a direct property replacement for the involuntarily converted property. For example, a municipality that is widening its streets may seize land from a taxpayer through its eminent domain and compensate the taxpayer with another parcel of similar value. In this case, the taxpayer would not recognize gain on the exchange of property and would take an adjusted basis in the new parcel of land equal to the taxpayer's basis in the land that was claimed by the municipality. Just as with like-kind exchanges, an exchanged basis

(basis of old property exchanged for basis of new property) ensures that the gain built into the new property (fair market value minus adjusted basis) includes the same gain that was built into the old property.

Indirect conversions involve taxpayers receiving money for the involuntarily converted property through insurance reimbursement or some other type of settlement. Taxpayers meeting the involuntary conversion requirements may *elect* to either recognize or defer realized gain on the conversions. Indirect conversions are more common than direct conversions. Taxpayers can defer realized gains on indirect conversions *if* they acquire **qualified replacement property** within a prescribed time limit, which is generally two years (three years in case of condemnation) after the close of the tax year in which they receive the proceeds.[39]

For both personal and real property, qualified replacement property for an involuntary conversion is defined more narrowly than is like-kind property in a like-kind exchange. The property must be similar *and* related in service or use to qualify.[40] For example, a bowling alley is not qualified replacement property for a pool hall, even though both are real properties used for entertainment purposes. This is stricter than the like-kind exchange rules that would allow the bowling alley to be exchanged for any other real property including a pool hall. Taxpayers recognize realized gain to the extent that they do not reinvest the reimbursement proceeds in qualified property. However, just as in like-kind exchanges, taxpayers do not recognize more gain than they realize on involuntary conversions. That is, a taxpayer's recognized gain on an involuntary conversion can be determined by the following formula: Recognized gain on involuntary conversion = the *lesser of* (1) the gain realized on the conversion or (2) the amount of reimbursement the taxpayer does *not reinvest* in qualified property.

The character of any gain recognized in an involuntary conversion depends on the nature of the asset that was converted—including depreciation recapture if applicable. The basis of the replacement property in an involuntary conversion is calculated in the same way it is for like-kind exchange property. That is, the basis of the replacement property is the fair market value of the new property minus the deferred gain on the conversion.

Example 3-18

What if: Assume that one of Teton's employees was involved in a traffic accident while driving a delivery van. The employee escaped without serious injury but the van was totally destroyed. Before the accident, Teton's delivery van had a fair market value of $15,000 and an adjusted basis of $11,000 (the cost basis was $15,000 and accumulated depreciation on the van was $4,000). Teton received $15,000 of insurance proceeds to cover the loss. Teton was considering two alternatives for replacing the van: Alternative 1 was to purchase a new delivery van for $20,000 and Alternative 2 was to purchase a used delivery van for $14,000. What gain or loss does Teton recognize under Alternative 1 and Alternative 2?

Answer: $0 gain recognized under Alternative 1 and $1,000 gain recognized under Alternative 2 (see computations below). Teton qualifies for a deferral because the new property (delivery van) has a similar and related use to the old property (delivery van). But it must recognize gain under Alternative 2 because it did not reinvest all of the insurance proceeds in a replacement van.

(continued on page 3-32)

[39]§1033(a)(2)(B). The time period varies depending on the type of property converted. Additionally, the IRS may consent to an extension of the time period for replacement.

[40]The similar and related-use test has been developed through a variety of administrative pronouncements and judicial law.

What is Teton's basis in the replacement property it acquired under Alternative 1 and Alternative 2?

Answer: $16,000 in Alternative 1 and $11,000 in Alternative 2, computed as follows:

Description	Alternative 1 Amount	Alternative 2 Amount	Explanation
(1) Amount realized	$15,000	$15,000	
(2) Adjusted basis	11,000	11,000	
(3) Gain realized	4,000	4,000	(1) − (2).
(4) Insurance proceeds	15,000	15,000	
(5) Proceeds reinvested	15,000	14,000	
(6) Amount not reinvested	0	1,000	(4) − (5).
(7) Gain recognized	**0**	**1,000**	Lesser of (3) or (6).*
(8) Deferred gain	4,000	3,000	(3) − (7).
(9) Value of replacement property	20,000	14,000	
Basis of replacement property	**16,000**	**11,000**	(9) − (8).

*The character of the $1,000 recognized gain is ordinary income under §1245 (lesser of gain recognized or accumulated depreciation).

Involuntary conversions share several similar concepts with like-kind exchanges such as the concept of qualified property, time period restrictions, the method of computing gain recognized (lesser of realized gain or cash received in addition to qualifying property), and basis calculation (gain or loss from old property remains built into new property). However, one important difference between the two is that taxpayers experiencing a loss from involuntary conversion may immediately deduct the loss as a casualty loss (either personal or business depending on the nature of the loss).

TAXES IN THE REAL WORLD Weather Break

Weather conditions across the country have caused hardship to many cattle farmers. Drought in the Southwest or floods in the Plains could cause cattle farmers to sell more of their herds than normal because they may not have enough crops to feed the livestock. To aid these farmers, the IRS offers relief in the form of an election to postpone recognizing gain from the sale of livestock sold due to weather-related conditions. What's the catch? The livestock must be replaced within a two-year period. In essence, the IRS allows cattle farmers to take advantage of the §1033 (involuntary conversion) rules.

As an alternative, if a taxpayer sells livestock because of weather conditions, he or she may be able to defer reporting the sale of the livestock for a one-year period. As a result of these two possibilities, cattle farmers may need to consider whether they will replace the livestock to take advantage of the involuntary conversion provision or whether the one-year deferral will better suit their plans.

THE KEY FACTS

Installment Sales

- Sale of property where the seller receives at least one payment in a taxable year subsequent to the year of disposition of the property.
- Must recognize a portion of gain on each installment payment received.
- Gains from installment sales are calculated as follows:

  Gross profit percentage = Gross profit/Contract price.

  Gain recognized = Gross profit percentage × Payment received in the year.
- Inventory, marketable securities, and depreciation recapture cannot be accounted for under installment sale rules.
- Does not apply to losses.

Installment Sales

In general, when taxpayers sell property for cash and collect the entire sale proceeds in one lump-sum payment, they immediately recognize gain or loss for tax purposes. However, taxpayers selling property don't always collect the sale proceeds in one lump sum from the buyer. For example, the buyer may make a down payment in the year of sale and then agree to pay the remainder of the sale proceeds over a period of time. This type of arrangement is termed an **installment sale.** Technically, an installment sale is any sale of property where the seller receives at least one payment in a taxable year subsequent to the year of disposition of the property.[41] Taxpayers selling property via an installment sale realize gains to the extent the selling price (the amount realized) exceeds their adjusted basis in the property sold. The installment

[41]§453(b)(1).

sale rules stay true to the wherewithal-to-pay concept and allow taxpayers selling property in this manner to use the installment method of recognizing *gain* on the sale over time.[42] The installment method does not apply to property sold at a loss. Under the installment method taxpayers determine the amount of realized gain on the transaction, and they recognize the gain pro rata as they receive the installment payments. So, by the time they have received all of the installment payments, they will have recognized all of the initial realized gain.[43] For financial accounting purposes, businesses selling property on an installment basis generally immediately recognize the realized gain on their financial statements.[44]

To determine the amount of gain the taxpayer (seller) must recognize on each installment payment received, the seller must compute the gross profit percentage on the transaction. The gross profit percentage is calculated as follows:

$$\text{Gross profit percentage} = \frac{\text{Gross profit}}{\text{Contract price}}$$

The gross profit percentage indicates the percentage of the contract price that will ultimately be recognized as gain. Gross profit is calculated as the sales price minus the adjusted basis of the property being sold. The contract price is the sales price less the seller's liabilities that are assumed by the buyer. To determine the portion of a particular payment that is currently recognized as gain, the seller multiplies the amount of the payments received during the year (including the year of sale) by the gross profit percentage (note that once established, the gross profit percentage does not change). Similar to fully taxable transactions, the character of gain taxpayers recognize using the installment method is determined by the character of the asset sold.

Example 3-19

What if: Suppose Teton decides to sell 5 acres of land adjacent to the warehouse for $100,000. The cost basis for the land is $37,500. Teton agrees to sell the property for four equal payments of $25,000—one now (in year 1) and the other three on January 1 of the next three years—plus interest. What amount of gain does Teton realize on the sale and what amount of gain does it recognize in year 1?

Answer: The realized gain on the transaction is $62,500 ($100,000 amount realized less $37,500 adjusted basis), and the year 1 recognized gain is $15,625, computed as follows:

Description	Amount	Explanation
(1) Sales price	$100,000	
(2) Adjusted basis	37,500	
(3) Gross profit	$ 62,500	(1) − (2).
(4) Contract price	$100,000	(1) − assumed liabilities (-0-).
(5) Gross profit percentage	62.5%	(3)/(4).
(6) Payment received in year 1	$ 25,000	
Gain recognized in year 1	**$ 15,625**	(5) × (4).

Because Teton used the land in its trade or business and it held the land for more than a year, the character of the gain is §1231 gain.

[42]Technically, a taxpayer selling property on an installment basis at a gain is required to use the installment method of reporting the recognized gain from the transaction. However, taxpayers are allowed to *elect* out of using the installment method §453(d).

[43]Because the seller in an installment sale is essentially lending money to the buyer, the buyer makes the required installment payments to the seller and the buyer pays interest to the seller for the money the buyer is borrowing. Any interest income received by the seller is immediately taxable as ordinary income. Special rules apply regarding interest for installment sales of more than $150,000 (see §453A).

[44]One exception is that the installment sale method similar to the tax installment method is used for financial accounting purposes when there is doubt that the business will collect the receivable.

The formula for determining the basis of an installment note receivable is (1 – gross profit percentage) × remaining payments on note. Because the gross profit percentage reflects the percentage of the installment payments that will be recognized as gain, (1 – gross profit percentage) is the percentage that is not recognized as gain because it reflects a return of capital (basis).

Gains Ineligible for Installment Reporting

Not all gains are eligible for installment sale reporting. Taxpayers selling marketable securities or inventory on an installment basis may not use the installment method to report gain on the sales. Similarly, any depreciation recapture (including §1245, §1250, and §291 depreciation recapture) is not eligible for installment reporting and must be recognized in the year of sale.[45] However, the §1231 gain remaining after the depreciation recapture can be recognized using the installment method. To ensure that any depreciation recapture is not taxed twice (once immediately and then a second time as payments are received), immediately taxable recapture-related gains are *added to* the adjusted basis of the property sold to determine the gross profit percentage. The increase in basis reduces the gain realized, which also reduces the gross profit percentage and the amount of future gain that will ultimately be recognized as the taxpayer receives the installment payments.

Example 3-20

What if: Assume that Teton agrees to sell some of its machinery for $90,000 for two equal payments of $45,000 plus interest. Teton's original basis was $80,000 and accumulated depreciation on the machinery was $30,000. Teton will receive one payment in year 1 (the current year) and the other payment in year 2. What is the amount and character of the gain Teton recognizes on the sale in year 1?

Answer: $30,000 ordinary income and $5,000 of §1231 gain, computed as follows:

Description	Amount	Explanation
(1) Sales price	$90,000	
(2) Original basis	80,000	
(3) Accumulated depreciation	(30,000)	
(4) Adjusted basis	50,000	(2) + (3).
(5) Realized gain (loss)	$40,000	(1) – (4).
(6) Ordinary income from depreciation recapture (not eligible for installment reporting)	**30,000**	Ordinary income. Lesser of (3) or (5).
(7) Gain eligible for installment reporting	$10,000	(5) – (6).
(8) Contract price	$90,000	(1) – assumed liabilities (-0-)
(9) Gross profit percentage	11.11%	(7)/(8)
(10) Payment received in year 1	$45,000	
Installment gain recognized in year 1	**$ 5,000**	(10) × (9) §1231 gain.

What is the amount and character of the gain Teton recognized upon receipt of the payment in year 2?

Answer: $5,000 of §1231 gain ($45,000 payment received times the gross profit percentage of 11.11 percent).

Other Nonrecognition Provisions

There are several tax law provisions that allow businesses to change the form or organization of their business while deferring the realized gains for tax purposes. For

[45]§453(i).

example, a sole proprietor can form his business as a corporation or contribute assets to an existing corporation and defer the gain realized on the exchange of assets for an ownership interest in the business entity.[46] Without the nonrecognition provision, the tax cost of forming a corporation may be large enough to deter taxpayers from doing so. Nonrecognition rules also apply to taxpayers forming partnerships or contributing assets to partnerships.[47] In still other corporate transactions, such as mergers, divisions (spin-offs or split-ups), or reorganizations, corporations can often do so in tax deferred transactions.[48] While these transactions generally result in deferred gain or loss for the involved parties, the specific details of these topics can easily fill chapters worth of material, and are not considered further in this chapter.

THE KEY FACTS

Related-Person Losses

- Related persons are defined in §267 and include certain family members, related corporations, and other entities.
- Losses on sales to related persons are not deductible by the seller.
- The related person may deduct the previously disallowed loss *to the extent of the gain* on the sale to the unrelated third person.

Related-Person Loss Disallowance Rules

Taxpayers selling business or investment property at a loss to unrelated persons are generally able to deduct the loss.[49] This makes sense in most situations because taxpayers are selling the property for less than their remaining investment (adjusted basis) in the property, and after the sale, the taxpayer's investment in the property is completely terminated. In contrast, when a taxpayer sells property at a loss to a related person, she effectively retains some element of control over the property through the related person. Consistent with this idea, §267(a) disallows recognition of losses on sales to related persons. Under §267, related persons include individuals with family relationships including siblings, spouses, ancestors, and lineal descendants. Related persons also include an individual and a corporation if the individual owns more than 50 percent of the stock of the corporation.[50]

Example 3-21

What if: Suppose Teton is formed as a corporation and Steve is its sole shareholder. Teton is looking to make some long-term investments to fund its anticipated purchase of a new manufacturing facility. Steve currently owns 1,000 shares of stock in his previous company Northeastern Corp., which he intends to sell in the near future. Steve initially paid $40 a share for the stock but the stock is currently valued at $30 a share. While Steve believes the stock has good long-term potential, he needs cash now to purchase a personal residence in Cody, Wyoming. Steve believes selling the shares to Teton makes good sense because he can deduct the loss and save taxes now and Teton can benefit from the expected long-term appreciation of the stock. If Steve sells 1,000 shares of Northeastern Corp. stock to Teton for $30 per share, what amount of loss will he realize and what amount of loss will he recognize for tax purposes?

Answer: $10,000 loss realized and $0 loss recognized, determined as follows:

Description	Amount	Explanation
(1) Amount realized on sale	$30,000	(1,000 × $30).
(2) Adjusted basis in stock	40,000	(1,000 × $40).
(3) Loss realized on sale	**($10,000)**	(1) − (2).
Loss recognized on sale	**$ 0**	Losses on sales to related persons are disallowed.

Because Steve owns more than 50 percent of Teton (he owns 100 percent), Steve and Teton are considered to be related persons. Consequently, Steve is not allowed to recognize any loss on the sale.

[46]§351.

[47]§721.

[48]§368 contains the numerous variations and requirements of these tax-deferred reorganizations.

[49]Capital losses are subject to certain limitations for individuals and corporate taxpayers (§1211).

[50]§267(a). The related-person rules include both direct ownership as well as indirect ownership (ownership attributed to the taxpayer from related persons). See §267(c) for a description of the indirect ownership rules.

Although taxpayers are not allowed to immediately deduct losses when they sell property to the related person, the related-person buyer may be able to subsequently deduct the disallowed loss by selling the property to an *unrelated* third party at a gain. The rules follow:

- If the related buyer sells the property at a gain (the related-person buyer sells it for more than she purchased it for) greater than the disallowed loss, the entire loss that was disallowed for the related-person seller is deductible by the buyer.
- If the related-person buyer subsequently sells the property and the related-person seller's disallowed loss exceeds the related person's gain on the subsequent sale, the related-person buyer may only deduct or offset the previously disallowed loss *to the extent of the gain* on the sale to the unrelated third party—the remaining disallowed loss expires unused.
- If the related-person buyer sells the property for less than her purchase price from the related seller, the disallowed loss expires unused.

Example 3-22

What if: Let's return to the previous example where Steve sold 1,000 shares of Northeastern Corp. stock to Teton (a corporation) for $30,000. As we discovered in that example, Steve realized a $10,000 loss on the sale, but he was not allowed to deduct it because Steve and Teton are related persons. Let's assume that a few years after Teton purchased the stock from Steve, Teton sells the Northeastern Corp. stock to an unrelated third party. What gain or loss does *Teton* recognize when it sells the stock in each of three scenarios, assuming it sells the stock for $37,000 in Scenario 1, $55,000 in Scenario 2, and $25,000 in Scenario 3?

Answer: $0 gain or loss in Scenario 1, $15,000 gain in Scenario 2, and $5,000 loss in Scenario 3, computed as follows:

Description	Scenario 1	Scenario 2	Scenario 3	Explanation
(1) Amount realized	$37,000	$55,000	$25,000	
(2) Adjusted basis	30,000	30,000	30,000	Example 3-21 (Teton's purchase price).
(3) Realized gain (loss)	7,000	25,000	(5,000)	(1) − (2).
(4) Benefit of Steve's ($10,000) disallowed loss	(7,000)	(10,000)	0	Loss benefit limited to realized gain.
Recognized gain (loss)	**$ 0**	**$15,000**	**($5,000)**	(3) + (4).

In Scenario 1 $3,000 of Steve's $10,000 remaining disallowed loss expires unused. In Scenario 3, Steve's entire $10,000 disallowed loss expires unused.

CONCLUSION

This chapter describes and discusses the tax consequences associated with sales and other types of property dispositions. We've learned how to determine the amount of gain or loss taxpayers recognize when they sell or otherwise dispose of property, and we've learned how to determine the character of these gains and losses. Tax accountants who understand the rules and concepts of property dispositions are able to comply with the tax law and advise clients of potential tax-planning opportunities and avoid pitfalls associated with various nonrecognition provisions.

Summary

Calculate the amount of gain or loss recognized on the disposition of assets used in a trade or business. LO 3-1

- Dispositions occur in the form of sales, trades, or other realization events.
- Gain realized is the amount realized less the adjusted basis of an asset.
- Amount realized is everything of value received in the transaction less any selling costs.
- Adjusted basis is the historical cost or basis of an asset less any cost recovery deductions applied against the asset.
- Gain realized on asset dispositions is not always recognized.

Describe the general character types of gain or loss recognized on property dispositions. LO 3-2

- Recognized gains must be characterized as ordinary, capital, or §1231. An asset's character is a function of the asset's use and holding period.
- Ordinary assets are derived from normal transactions of the business (revenues and accounts receivable), sale of short-term trade or business assets, and depreciation recapture.
- Capital assets are assets that are held either for investment or for personal use (a taxpayer's principal residence).
- §1231 assets consist of property used in a taxpayer's trade or business that has been held for more than one year.
- Net §1231 gains are treated as long-term capital gains and net §1231 losses are treated as ordinary losses.

Explain the rationale for and calculate depreciation recapture. LO 3-3

- §1231 assets, other than land, are subject to cost recovery deductions (depreciation), which generate ordinary deductions.
- Gains that are created through depreciation deductions are subject to depreciation recapture. Any remaining gain is §1231 gain.
- Depreciation recapture does not change the amount of the gain but simply converts or recharacterizes the gain from §1231 to ordinary.
- Different recapture rules apply to tangible personal property (§1245) and real property (§291 for corporations only and §1250).

Describe the tax treatment of unrecaptured §1250 gains and determine the character of gains on property sold to related parties. LO 3-4

- When individuals sell §1250 property at a gain, the portion of the gain generated by depreciation deductions is called unrecaptured §1250 gain.
- This gain is a §1231 gain that, if treated as a capital gain after the §1231 netting process, flows into the capital gain/loss process (Chapter 3) and is taxed at a maximum rate of 25 percent.
- If a taxpayer sells an asset at a gain to a related person and the asset is a depreciable asset to the related person, the seller must characterize the entire gain as ordinary income.

Describe the tax treatment of §1231 gains or losses, including the §1231 netting process. LO 3-5

- After applying the depreciation recapture rules, taxpayers calculate the net §1231 gain or loss.
- If a net §1231 loss results, the loss will become ordinary and offset ordinary income.
- If a net §1231 gain results, the §1231 look-back rule must be applied.
- After applying the look-back rule, any remaining net §1231 gain is a long-term capital gain.

Explain common exceptions to the general rule that realized gains and losses are recognized currently. LO 3-6

- Like-kind exchanges involve trading or exchanging business assets for similar business assets. The gain is deferred unless boot or non-like-kind property is received.

- Involuntary conversions are the losses on property through circumstances beyond taxpayers' control. Reasons include natural disasters, accidents, theft, or condemnation.
- Installment sales occur when any portion of the amount realized is received in a year subsequent to the disposition.
- §267 related-person losses are disallowed but the related-person buyer may be able to deduct the disallowed loss if she subsequently sells the property at a gain.

KEY TERMS

adjusted basis (3-5)
amount realized (3-2)
boot (3-27)
capital asset (3-7)
deferred like-kind exchange (3-26)
depreciation recapture (3-9)
direct conversion (3-30)
exchanged basis (3-27)
indirect conversion (3-31)
installment sale (3-32)
involuntary conversion (3-29)
like-kind exchange (3-24)
nonrecaptured net §1231 losses (3-18)
nonrecognition transaction (3-20)
ordinary asset (3-7)
production of income (3-7)
qualified replacement property (3-31)
realized gain or loss (3-5)
recapture (3-11)
recognized gain or loss (3-6)
§291 depreciation recapture (3-14)
§1231 assets (3-8)
§1231 look-back rule (3-18)
§1245 property (3-10)
§1250 property (3-14)
third-party intermediaries (3-25)
unrecaptured §1250 gain (3-15)

DISCUSSION QUESTIONS

LO 3-1 1. Compare and contrast different ways in which a taxpayer triggers a realization event by disposing of an asset.

LO 3-1 2. Potomac Corporation wants to sell a warehouse that it has used in its business for 10 years. Potomac is asking $450,000 for the property. The warehouse is subject to a mortgage of $125,000. If Potomac accepts Wyden Inc.'s offer to give Potomac $325,000 in cash and assume full responsibility for the mortgage on the property, what amount does Potomac realize on the sale?

LO 3-1 3. Montana Max sells a 2,500-acre ranch for $1,000,000 in cash, a note receivable of $1,000,000, and debt relief of $2,400,000. He also pays selling commissions of $60,000. In addition, Max agrees to build a new barn on the property (cost $250,000) and spend $100,000 upgrading the fence on the property before the sale. What is Max's amount realized on the sale?

LO 3-1 4. Hawkeye sold farming equipment for $55,000. It bought the equipment four years ago for $75,000, and it has since claimed a total of $42,000 in depreciation deductions against the asset. Explain how to calculate Hawkeye's adjusted basis in the farming equipment.

LO 3-1 5. When a taxpayer sells an asset, what is the difference between realized and recognized gain or loss on the sale?

LO 3-2 6. What does it mean to characterize a gain or loss? Why is characterizing a gain or loss important?

LO 3-2 7. Explain the difference between ordinary, capital, and §1231 assets.

LO 3-2 8. Discuss the reasons why individuals generally prefer capital gains over ordinary gains. Explain why corporate taxpayers might prefer capital gains over ordinary gains.

LO 3-2 9. Dakota Conrad owns a parcel of land he would like to sell. Describe the circumstances in which the sale of the land would generate §1231 gain or loss, ordinary gain or loss, or capital gain or loss. Also, describe the circumstances where Dakota would not be allowed to deduct a loss on the sale.

10. Lincoln has used a piece of land in her business for the past five years. The land qualifies as §1231 property. It is unclear whether Lincoln will have to recognize a gain or loss when she eventually sells the asset. She asks her accountant how the gain or loss would be characterized if she decides to sell. Her accountant said that selling §1231 assets gives sellers "the best of both worlds." Explain what her accountant means by "the best of both worlds." LO 3-2
11. Explain Congress's rationale for depreciation recapture. LO 3-3
12. Compare and contrast §1245 recapture and §1250 recapture. LO 3-3
13. Why is depreciation recapture not required when assets are sold at a loss? LO 3-3
14. What are the similarities and differences between the tax benefit rule and depreciation recapture? LO 3-3
15. Are both corporations and individuals subject to depreciation recapture when they sell depreciable real property at a gain? Explain. LO 3-3 LO 3-4
16. How is unrecaptured §1250 gain for individuals similar to depreciation recapture? How is it different? LO 3-4
17. Explain why gains from depreciable property sold to a related taxpayer are treated as ordinary income under §1239. LO 3-4
18. Bingaman Resources sold two depreciable §1231 assets during the year. One asset resulted in a large gain (the asset was sold for more than it was purchased for) and the other in a small loss. Describe the §1231 netting process for Bingaman. LO 3-5
19. Jeraldine believes that when the §1231 look-back rule applies, the taxpayer deducts a §1231 loss in a previous year against §1231 gains in the current year. Explain whether Jeraldine's description is correct. LO 3-5
20. Explain the purpose behind the §1231 look-back rule. LO 3-5
21. Does a taxpayer apply the §1231 look-back rule in a year when the taxpayer recognizes a net §1231 loss? Explain. LO 3-5
22. Describe the circumstances in which an individual taxpayer with a net §1231 gain will have different portions of the gain taxed at different rates. LO 3-4 LO 3-5
23. Rocky and Bullwinkle Partnership sold a parcel of land during the current year and realized a gain of $250,000. Rocky and Bullwinkle did not recognize gain related to the sale of the land on its tax return. Is this possible? Explain how a taxpayer could realize a gain but not recognize it. LO 3-6
24. Why does the tax code allow taxpayers to defer gains on like-kind exchanges? How do the tax laws ensure that the gains (or losses) are deferred and not permanently excluded from a taxpayer's income? LO 3-6
25. Compare and contrast the like-kind property requirements for real property and for personal property for purposes of qualifying for a like-kind exchange. Explain whether a car held by a corporation for delivering documents will qualify as like-kind property with a car held by an individual for personal use. LO 3-6
26. Salazar Inc., a Colorado company, is relocating to a nearby town. It would like to trade its real property for some real property in the new location. While Salazar has found several prospective buyers for its real property and has also located several properties that are acceptable in the new location, it cannot find anyone that is willing to trade Salazar Inc. for its property in a like-kind exchange. Explain how a third-party intermediary could facilitate Salazar's like-kind exchange. LO 3-6
27. Minuteman wants to enter into a like-kind exchange by exchanging its old New England manufacturing facility for a ranch in Wyoming. Minuteman is using a third-party intermediary to facilitate the exchange. The purchaser of the manufacturing facility wants to complete the transaction immediately but, for various reasons, the ranch transaction will not be completed for three to four months. Will this delay cause a problem for Minuteman's desire to accomplish this through a like-kind exchange? Explain. LO 3-6

LO 3-6 28. Olympia Corporation, of Kittery, Maine, wants to exchange its manufacturing machinery for Bangor Company's machinery. Both parties agree that Olympia's machinery is worth $100,000 and that Bangor's machinery is worth $95,000. Olympia would like the transaction to qualify as a like-kind exchange. What could the parties do to equalize the value exchanged but still allow the exchange to qualify as a like-kind exchange? How would the necessary change affect the tax consequences of the transaction?

LO 3-6 29. Compare and contrast the similarities and differences between like-kind exchanges and involuntary conversions for tax purposes.

LO 3-6 30. What is an installment sale? How do the tax laws ensure that taxpayers recognize all the gain they realize on an installment sale? How is depreciation recapture treated in an installment sale? Explain the gross profit ratio and how it relates to gains recognized under installment method sales.

LO 3-6 31. Mr. Kyle owns stock in a local publicly traded company. Although the stock price has declined since he purchased it two years ago, he likes the long-term prospects for the company. If Kyle sells the stock to his sister because he needs some cash for a down payment on a new home, is the loss deductible? If Kyle is right and the stock price increases in the future, how is his sister's gain computed if she sells the stock?

PROBLEMS

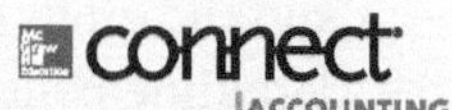

All applicable problems are available with McGraw-Hill's *Connect*® *Accounting*.

LO 3-1 32. Rafael sold an asset to Jamal. What is Rafael's amount realized on the sale in each of the following alternative scenarios?

a) Rafael received $80,000 of cash and a vehicle worth $10,000. Rafael also pays $5,000 in selling expenses.

b) Rafael received $80,000 of cash and was relieved of a $30,000 mortgage on the asset he sold to Jamal. Rafael also paid a commission of $5,000 on the transaction.

c) Rafael received $20,000 of cash, a parcel of land worth $50,000, and marketable securities of $10,000. Rafael also paid a commission of $8,000 on the transaction.

LO 3-1 33. Alan Meer inherits a hotel from his grandmother, Mary, on February 11 of the current year. Mary bought the hotel for $730,000 three years ago. Mary deducted $27,000 of cost recovery on the hotel before her death. The fair market of the hotel in February is $725,000. (Assume that the alternative valuation date is not used.)

a) What is Alan's adjusted basis in the hotel?

b) If the fair market value of the hotel at the time of Mary's death was $500,000, what is Alan's basis?

LO 3-1 34. Shasta Corporation sold a piece of land to Bill for $45,000. Shasta bought the land two years ago for $30,600. What gain or loss does Shasta realize on the transaction?

LO 3-1 35. Lassen Corporation sold a machine to a machine dealer for $25,000. Lassen bought the machine for $55,000 and has claimed $15,000 of depreciation expense on the machine. What gain or loss does Lassen realize on the transaction?

LO 3-1 LO 3-2 36. Hannah Tywin owns 100 shares of MM Inc. stock. She sells the stock on December 11 for $25 per share. She received the stock as a gift from her Aunt Pam on March 20 of this year when the fair market value of the stock was $18 per share. Aunt Pam originally purchased the stock seven years ago at a price of $12 per share. What is the amount and character of Hannah's recognized gain on the stock?

37. On September 30 of last year, Rex received some investment land from Holly as a gift. Holly's adjusted basis was $50,000 and the land was valued at $40,000 at the time of the gift. Holly acquired the land five years ago. What is the amount and character of Rex's recognized gain (loss) if he sells the land on May 12 this year at the following prices? LO 3-1 LO 3-2
a) $32,000
b) $70,000
c) $45,000

38. Franco converted a building from personal to business use in May 2013 when the fair market value was $55,000. He purchased the building in July 2010 for $80,000. On December 15 of this year, Franco sells the building for $40,000. On the date of sale, the accumulated depreciation on the building was $5,565. What is Franco's recognized gain or loss on the sale? LO 3-1 LO 3-2

39. Identify each of White Corporation's following assets as an ordinary, capital, or §1231 asset. LO 3-2
a) Two years ago, White used its excess cash to purchase a piece of land as an investment.
b) Two years ago, White purchased land and a warehouse. It uses these assets in its business.
c) Manufacturing machinery White purchased earlier this year.
d) Inventory White purchased 13 months ago but is ready to be shipped to a customer.
e) Office equipment White has used in its business for the past three years.
f) 1,000 shares of stock in Black corporation that White purchased two years ago because it was a good investment.
g) Account receivable from a customer with terms 2/10 net 30.
h) Machinery White held for three years and then sold at a loss of $10,000.

40. In year 0, Canon purchased a machine to use in its business for $56,000. In year 3, Canon sold the machine for $42,000. Between the date of the purchase and the date of the sale, Canon depreciated the machine by $32,000. LO 3-3 LO 3-4
a) What is the amount and character of the gain Canon will recognize on the sale, assuming that it is a partnership?
b) What is the amount and character of the gain Canon will recognize on the sale, assuming that it is a corporation?
c) What is the amount and character of the gain Canon will recognize on the sale, assuming that it is a corporation and the sale proceeds were increased to $60,000?
d) What is the amount and character of the gain Canon will recognize on the sale, assuming that it is a corporation and the sale proceeds were decreased to $20,000?

41. In year 0, Longworth Partnership purchased a machine for $40,000 to use in its business. In year 3, Longworth sold the machine for $35,000. Between the date of the purchase and the date of the sale, Longworth depreciated the machine by $22,000. LO 3-3 LO 3-4
a) What is the amount and character of the gain (loss) Longworth will recognize on the sale?
b) What is the amount and character of the gain (loss) Longworth will recognize on the sale if the sale proceeds were increased to $45,000?
c) What is the amount and character of the gain (loss) Longworth will recognize on the sale if the sale proceeds were decreased to $15,000?

LO 3-3 LO 3-4

42. On August 1 of year 0, Dirksen purchased a machine for $20,000 to use in its business. On December 4 of year 0, Dirksen sold the machine for $18,000.
    a) What is the amount and character of the gain or loss Dirksen will recognize on the sale?
    b) What is the amount and character of the gain or loss Dirksen will recognize on the sale if the machine was sold on January 15 of year 1 instead?

LO 3-3 LO 3-4

43. Rayburn Corporation has a building that it bought during year 0 for $850,000. It sold the building in year 5. During the time it held the building Rayburn depreciated it by $100,000. What is the amount and character of the gain or loss Rayburn will recognize on the sale in each of the following alternative situations?
    a) Rayburn receives $840,000.
    b) Rayburn receives $900,000.
    c) Rayburn receives $700,000.

LO 3-3 LO 3-4

44. Moran owns a building he bought during year 0 for $150,000. He sold the building in year 6. During the time he held the building he depreciated it by $32,000. What is the amount and character of the gain or loss Moran will recognize on the sale in each of the following alternative situations?
    a) Moran received $145,000.
    b) Moran received $170,000.
    c) Moran received $110,000.

LO 3-3 LO 3-4 LO 3-5 planning

45. Hart, an individual, bought an asset for $500,000 and has claimed $100,000 of depreciation deductions against the asset. Hart has a marginal tax rate of 30 percent. Answer the questions presented in the following alternative scenarios (assume Hart had no property transactions other than those described in the problem):
    a) What is the amount and character of Hart's recognized gain if the asset is tangible personal property sold for $450,000? What effect does the sale have on Hart's tax liability for the year?
    b) What is the amount and character of Hart's recognized gain if the asset is tangible personal property sold for $550,000? What effect does the sale have on Hart's tax liability for the year?
    c) What is the amount and character of Hart's recognized gain if the asset is tangible personal property sold for $350,000? What effect does the sale have on Hart's tax liability for the year?
    d) What is the amount and character of Hart's recognized gain if the asset is a nonresidential building sold for $450,000? What effect does the sale have on Hart's tax liability for the year?
    e) Now assume that Hart is a corporation. What is the amount and character of its recognized gain if the asset is a nonresidential building sold for $450,000? What effect does the sale have on Hart's tax liability for the year (assume the same 30 percent marginal tax rate)?
    f) Now assuming that the asset is real property, which entity type should be used to minimize the taxes paid on real estate gains?

LO 3-4

46. Luke sold a building and the land on which the building sits to his wholly owned corporation, Studemont Corp. at fair market value. The fair market value of the building was determined to be $325,000; Luke built the building several years ago at a cost of $200,000. Luke had claimed $45,000 of depreciation expense on the building. The fair market value of the land was determined to be $210,000 at the time of the sale; Luke purchased the land many years ago for $130,000.
    a) What is the amount and character of Luke's recognized gain or loss on the building?
    b) What is the amount and character of Luke's recognized gain or loss on the land?

47. Buckley, an individual, began business two years ago and has never sold a §1231 asset. Buckley owned each of the assets since he began the business. In the current year, Buckley sold the following business assets: LO 3-5

Asset	Original Cost	Accumulated Depreciation	Gain/Loss
Computers	$ 6,000	$ 2,000	($3,000)
Machinery	10,000	4,000	(2,000)
Furniture	20,000	12,000	7,000
Building	100,000	10,000	(1,000)

Assuming Buckley's marginal ordinary income tax rate is 35 percent, answer the questions for the following alternative scenarios:

a) What is the character of Buckley's gains or losses for the current year? What effect do the gains and losses have on Buckley's tax liability?

b) Assume that the amount realized increased so that the building was sold at a $6,000 gain instead. What is the character of Buckley's gains or losses for the current year? What effect do the gains and losses have on Buckley's tax liability?

c) Assume that the amount realized increased so that the building was sold at a $15,000 gain instead. What is the character of Buckley's gains or losses for the current year? What effect do the gains and losses have on Buckley's tax liability?

48. Lily Tucker (single) owns and operates a bike shop as a sole proprietorship. This year, she sells the following long-term assets used in her business: LO 3-3 LO 3-4 LO 3-5

Asset	Sales Price	Cost	Accumulated Depreciation
Building	$230,000	$200,000	$52,000
Equipment	80,000	148,000	23,000

Lily's taxable income before these transactions is $160,500. What are Lily's taxable income and tax liability for the year?

49. Shimmer Inc. is a calendar-year-end, accrual-method corporation. This year, it sells the following long-term assets: LO 3-3 LO 3-4 LO 3-5

Asset	Sales Price	Cost	Accumulated Depreciation
Building	$650,000	$642,000	$37,000
Sparkle Corporation stock	130,000	175,000	n/a

Shimmer does not sell any other assets during the year, and its taxable income before these transactions is $800,000. What are Shimmer's taxable income and tax liability for the year?

50. Aruna, a sole proprietor, wants to sell two assets that she no longer needs for her business. Both assets qualify as §1231 assets. The first is machinery and will generate a $10,000 §1231 loss on the sale. The second is land that will generate a $7,000 §1231 gain on the sale. Aruna's ordinary marginal tax rate is 30 percent. LO 3-5 planning

a) Assuming she sells both assets in December of year 1 (the current year), what effect will the sales have on Aruna's tax liability?

b) Assuming that Aruna sells the land in December of year 1 and the machinery in January of year 2, what effect will the sales have on Aruna's tax liability for each year?

c) Explain why selling the assets in separate years will result in greater tax savings for Aruna.

LO 3-5

51. Bourne Guitars, a corporation, reported a $157,000 net §1231 gain for year 6.
    a) Assuming Bourne reported $50,000 of nonrecaptured net §1231 losses during years 1–5, what amount of Bourne's net §1231 gain for year 6, if any, is treated as ordinary income?
    b) Assuming Bourne's nonrecaptured net §1231 losses from years 1–5 were $200,000, what amount of Bourne's net §1231 gain for year 6, if any, is treated as ordinary income?

LO 3-5
planning

52. Tonya Jefferson, a sole proprietor, runs a successful lobbying business in Washington, DC. She doesn't sell many business assets, but she is planning on retiring and selling her historic townhouse, from which she runs her business, in order to buy a place somewhere sunny and warm. Tonya's townhouse is worth $1,000,000 and the land is worth another $1,000,000. The original basis in the townhouse was $600,000, and she has claimed $250,000 of depreciation deductions against the asset over the years. The original basis in the land was $500,000. Tonya has located a buyer that would like to finalize the transaction in December of the current year. Tonya's marginal ordinary income tax rate is 35 percent.
    a) What amount of gain or loss does Tonya recognize on the sale? What is the character of the gain or loss? What effect does the gain or loss have on her tax liability?
    b) In addition to the original facts, assume that Tonya reports the following nonrecaptured net §1231 loss:

Year	Net §1231 Gains/(Losses)
Year 1	($200,000)
Year 2	0
Year 3	0
Year 4	0
Year 5	0
Year 6 (current year)	?

    What amount of gain or loss does Tonya recognize on the sale? What is the character of the gain or loss? What effect does the gain or loss have on her year 6 (the current year) tax liability?
    c) As Tonya's tax advisor, you suggest that Tonya sell the townhouse in year 7 in order to reduce her taxes. What amount of gain or loss does Tonya recognize on the sale in year 7?

LO 3-5

53. Morgan's Water World (MWW), an LLC, opened several years ago and reports the following net §1231 gains and losses since it began business.

Year	Net §1231 Gains/(Losses)
Year 1	($11,000)
Year 2	5,000
Year 3	(21,000)
Year 4	(4,000)
Year 5	17,000
Year 6	(43,000)
Year 7 (current year)	113,000

    What amount, if any, of the year 7 $113,000 net §1231 gain is treated as ordinary income?

54. Hans runs a sole proprietorship. Hans reported the following net §1231 gains and losses since he began business: LO 3-5

Year	Net §1231 Gains/(Losses)
Year 1	($65,000)
Year 2	15,000
Year 3	0
Year 4	0
Year 5	10,000
Year 6	0
Year 7 (current year)	50,000

a) What amount, if any, of the year 7 (current year) $50,000 net §1231 gain is treated as ordinary income?

b) Assume that the $50,000 net §1231 gain occurs in year 6 instead of year 7. What amount of the gain would be treated as ordinary income in year 6?

55. Independence Corporation needs to replace some of the assets used in its trade or business and is contemplating the following exchanges: LO 3-6

Exchange	Asset Given Up by Independence	Asset Received by Independence
a	Band saw	Band saw
b	Machinery used in textiles	Machinery used for wood working
c	Passenger automobile used for deliveries	Heavy duty van that seats two and has a large cargo box
d	Large warehouse on two acres	Small warehouse on twenty-two acres
e	Office building in Green Bay, WI, used in the business	Apartment complex in Newport Beach, CA, that will be held as an investment

Determine whether each exchange qualifies as a like-kind exchange. Also, explain the rationale for why each qualifies or does not qualify as a like-kind exchange.

56. Kase, an individual, purchased some property in Potomac, Maryland, for $150,000 approximately 10 years ago. Kase is approached by a real estate agent representing a client who would like to exchange a parcel of land in North Carolina for Kase's Maryland property. Kase agrees to the exchange. What is Kase's realized gain or loss, recognized gain or loss, and basis in the North Carolina property in each of the following alternative scenarios? LO 3-6

a) The transaction qualifies as a like-kind exchange and the fair market value of each property is $675,000.

b) The transaction qualifies as a like-kind exchange and the fair market value of each property is $100,000.

57. Longhaul Trucking traded two small trucks (each had a 10,000-pound gross weight) for one large truck (18,000-pound gross weight). Do the trucks qualify as like-kind property? (*Hint:* Because the trucks are tangible personal property they must be the same asset class to be like-kind assets. Use Rev. Proc. 87-56 to determine the asset classes for the trucks.) LO 3-6

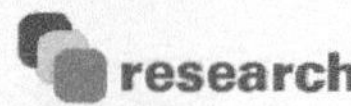

58. Twinbrook Corporation needed to upgrade to a larger manufacturing facility. Twinbrook first acquired a new manufacturing facility for $2,100,000 cash, and then transferred the facility it was using (building and land) to White Flint Corporation for $2,000,000 three months later. Does the exchange qualify for like-kind exchange treatment? (*Hint:* Examine Revenue Procedures 2000-37 and 2004-51.) If not, can you propose a change in the transaction that will allow it to qualify? LO 3-6

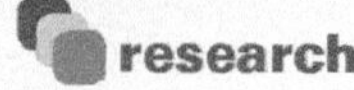

LO 3-6

research

59. Woodley Park Corporation currently owns two parcels of land (parcel 1 and parcel 2). It owns a warehouse facility on parcel 1. Woodley needs to acquire a new and larger manufacturing facility. Woodley was approached by Blazing Fast Construction (who specializes in prefabricated warehouses) about acquiring Woodley's existing warehouse on parcel 1. Woodley indicated that it prefers to exchange its existing facility for a new and larger facility in a qualifying like-kind exchange. Blazing Fast indicated that it could construct a new manufacturing facility on parcel 2 to Woodley's specification within four months. Woodley and Blazing Fast agreed to the following arrangement. First, Blazing Fast would construct the new warehouse on parcel 2 and then relinquish the property to Woodley within four months. Woodley would then transfer the warehouse facility and land parcel 1 to Blazing Fast. All of the property exchanged in the deal was identified immediately and the construction was completed within 180 days. Does the exchange of the new building for the old building and parcel 1 qualify as a like-kind exchange (see *DeCleene v. Commissioner*, 115 TC 457)?

LO 3-6

60. Metro Corp. traded machine A for machine B. Metro originally purchased machine A for $50,000 and machine A's adjusted basis was $25,000 at the time of the exchange. What is Metro's realized gain or loss, recognized gain or loss, and adjusted basis in machine B in each of the following alternative scenarios?
   a) The fair market value of machine A and of machine B is $40,000 at the time of the exchange. The exchange does not qualify as a like-kind exchange.
   b) The fair market value of machine A and of machine B is $40,000. The exchange qualifies as a like-kind exchange.
   c) The fair market value of machine A is $35,000 and machine B is valued at $40,000. Metro exchanges machine A and $5,000 cash for machine B. Machine A and machine B are like-kind property.
   d) The fair market value of machine A is $45,000 and Metro trades machine A for machine B valued at $40,000 and $5,000 cash. Machine A and machine B are like-kind property.

LO 3-6

61. Prater Inc. enters into an exchange in which it gives up its warehouse on 10 acres of land and receives a tract of land. A summary of the exchange is as follows:

Transferred	FMV	Original Basis	Accumulated Depreciation
Warehouse	$300,000	$225,000	$45,000
Land	50,000	50,000	
Mortgage on warehouse	30,000		
Cash	20,000	20,000	

Assets Received	FMV
Land	$340,000

What is Prater's realized and recognized gain on the exchange and its basis in the assets it received in the exchange?

LO 3-6

62. Baker Corporation owned a building located in Kansas. Baker used the building for its business operations. Last year a tornado hit the property and completely destroyed it. This year, Baker received an insurance settlement. Baker had originally purchased the building for $350,000 and had claimed a total of $100,000 of depreciation deductions against the property. What is Baker's realized and recognized gain or (loss) on this transaction and what is its basis in the new building in the following alternative scenarios?
   a) Baker received $450,000 in insurance proceeds and spent $450,000 rebuilding the building during the current year.

b) Baker received $450,000 in insurance proceeds and spent $500,000 rebuilding the building during the current year.
c) Baker received $450,000 in insurance proceeds and spent $400,000 rebuilding the building during the current year.
d) Baker received $450,000 in insurance proceeds and spent $450,000 rebuilding the building during the next three years.

63. Russell Corporation sold a parcel of land valued at $400,000. Its basis in the land was $275,000. For the land, Russell received $50,000 in cash in year 0 and a note providing that Russell will receive $175,000 in year 1 and $175,000 in year 2 from the buyer. LO 3-6
a) What is Russell's realized gain on the transaction?
b) What is Russell's recognized gain in year 0, year 1, and year 2?

64. In year 0, Javens Inc. sold machinery with a fair market value of $400,000 to Chris. The machinery's original basis was $317,000 and Javens's accumulated depreciation on the machinery was $50,000, so its adjusted basis to Javens was $267,000. Chris paid Javens $40,000 immediately (in year 0) and provided a note to Javens indicating that Chris would pay Javens $60,000 a year for six years beginning in year 1. What is the amount and character of the gain that Javens will recognize in year 0? What amount and character of the gain will Javens recognize in years 1 through 6? LO 3-6

65. Ken sold a rental property for $500,000. He received $100,000 in the current year and $100,000 each year for the next four years. $400,000 of the sales price was allocated to the building and the remaining $100,000 was allocated to the land. Ken purchased the property several years ago for $300,000. When he initially purchased the property, he allocated $225,000 of the purchase price to the building and $75,000 to the land. Ken has claimed $25,000 of depreciation deductions over the years against the building. Ken had no other sales of §1231 or capital assets in the current year. For the year of the sale, determine Ken's recognized gain or loss, the character of Ken's gain, and calculate Ken's tax due because of the sale (assuming his marginal ordinary tax rate is 35 percent). (*Hint:* See the examples in Reg. §1.453-12.) LO 3-6 research

66. Hillary is in the leasing business and faces a marginal tax rate of 35 percent. She has leased equipment to Whitewater Corporation for several years. Hillary bought the equipment for $50,000 and claimed $20,000 of depreciation deductions against the asset. The lease term is about to expire and Whitewater would like to acquire the equipment. Hillary has been offered two options to choose from: LO 3-6 planning

Option	Details
Like-kind exchange	Whitewater would provide Hillary with like-kind equipment. The like-kind equipment has a fair market value of $35,000.
Installment sale	Whitewater would provide Hillary with two payments of $19,000. She would use the proceeds to purchase equipment that she could also lease.

Ignoring time value of money, which option provides the greatest after-tax value for Hillary, assuming she is indifferent between the proposals based on nontax factors?

67. Deirdre sold 100 shares of stock to her brother, James, for $2,400. Deirdre purchased the stock several years ago for $3,000. LO 3-6
a) What gain or loss does Deirdre recognize on the sale?
b) What amount of gain or loss does James recognize if he sells the stock for $3,200?
c) What amount of gain or loss does James recognize if he sells the stock for $2,600?
d) What amount of gain or loss does James recognize if he sells the stock for $2,000?

COMPREHENSIVE PROBLEMS

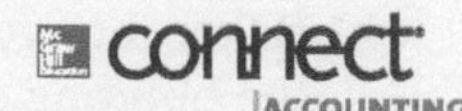

All applicable problems are available with McGraw-Hill's *Connect® Accounting.*

68. Two years ago, Bethesda Corporation bought a delivery truck for $30,000 (not subject to the luxury auto depreciation limits). Bethesda used MACRS 200 percent declining balance and the half-year convention to recover the cost of the truck, but it did not elect §179 expensing or any eligible bonus depreciation. Answer the questions for the following alternative scenarios.
    a) Assuming Bethesda used the truck until March of year 3, what depreciation expense can it claim on the truck for years 1 through 3?
    b) Assume that Bethesda claimed $18,500 of depreciation expense on the truck before it sold it in year 3. What is the amount and character of the gain or loss if Bethesda sold the truck in year 3 for $17,000, and incurred $2,000 of selling expenses on the sale?
    c) Assume that Bethesda claimed $18,500 of depreciation expense on the truck before it sold it in year 3. What is the amount and character of the gain or loss if Bethesda sold the truck in year 3 for $35,000, and incurred $3,000 of selling expenses on the sale?
69. Hauswirth Corporation sold (or exchanged) some manufacturing equipment in year 0. Hauswirth bought the machinery several years ago for $65,000 and it has claimed $23,000 of depreciation expense against the equipment.
    a) Assuming that Hauswirth receives $50,000 in cash for the equipment, compute the amount and character of Hauswirth's recognized gain or loss on the sale.
    b) Assuming that Hauswirth receives like-kind equipment with a fair market value of $50,000 in exchange for its equipment, compute Hauswirth's gain realized, gain recognized, deferred gain, and basis in the new equipment.
    c) Assuming that Hauswirth receives $20,000 in cash in year 0 and a $50,000 note receivable that is payable in year 1, compute the amount and character of Hauswirth's gain in year 0 and in year 1.

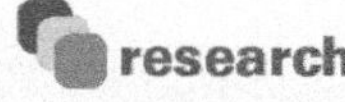

70. Fontenot Corporation sold some machinery to its majority owner Gray (an individual who owns 60 percent of Fontenot). Fontenot purchased the machinery for $100,000 and has claimed a total of $40,000 of depreciation expense deductions against the property. Gray will provide Fontenot with $10,000 of cash today and provide a $100,000 note that will pay Fontenot $50,000 one year from now and $50,000 two years from now.
    a) What gain does Fontenot realize on the sale?
    b) What is the amount and character of the gain that Fontenot must recognize in the year of sale (if any) and each of the two subsequent years? (*Hint:* Use the Internal Revenue Code and start with §453; please give appropriate citations.)

tax forms

71. Moab Inc. manufactures and distributes high-tech biking gadgets. It has decided to streamline some of its operations so that it will be able to be more productive and efficient. Because of this decision it has entered into several transactions during the year.

    Part (1) Determine the gain/loss realized and recognized in the current year for each of these events. Also determine whether the gain/loss recognized will be §1231, capital, or ordinary.
    a) Moab Inc. sold a machine that it used to make computerized gadgets for $27,300 cash. It originally bought the machine for $19,200 three years ago and has taken $8,000 depreciation.
    b) Moab Inc. held stock in ABC Corp., which had a value of $12,000 at the beginning of the year. That same stock had a value of $15,230 at the end of the year.
    c) Moab Inc. sold some of its inventory for $7,000 cash. This inventory had a basis of $5,000.

d) Moab Inc. disposed of an office building with a fair market value of $75,000 for another office building with a fair market value of $55,000 and $20,000 in cash. It originally bought the office building seven years ago for $62,000 and has taken $15,000 in depreciation.

e) Moab Inc. sold some land held for investment for $28,000. It originally bought the land for $32,000 two years ago.

f) Moab Inc. sold another machine for a note payable in four annual installments of $12,000. The first payment was received in the current year. It originally bought the machine two years ago for $32,000 and has claimed $9,000 in depreciation expense against the machine.

g) Moab Inc. sold stock it held for eight years for $2,750. It originally purchased the stock for $2,100.

h) Moab Inc. sold another machine for $7,300. It originally purchased this machine six months ago for $9,000 and has claimed $830 in depreciation expense against the asset.

Part (2) From the recognized gains/losses determined in part 1, determine the net §1231 gain/loss and the net ordinary gain/loss Moab will recognize on its tax return. Moab Inc. also has $2,000 of nonrecaptured net §1231 losses from previous years.

Part (3) Complete Moab Inc.'s Form 4797 for the year.

72. Vertovec Inc., a large local consulting firm in Utah, hired several new consultants from out of state last year to help service their expanding list of clients. To aid in relocating the consultants, Vertovec Inc. purchased the consultants' homes in their prior location if the consultants were unable to sell their homes within 30 days of listing them for sale. Vertovec Inc. bought the homes from the consultants for 5 percent less than the list price and then continued to list the homes for sale. Each home Vertovec Inc. purchased was sold at a loss. By the end of last year, Vertovec had suffered a loss totaling $250,000 from the homes. How should Vertovec treat the loss for tax purposes? Write a memo to Vertovec Inc. explaining your findings and any planning suggestions that you may have if Vertovec Inc. continues to offer this type of relocation benefit to newly hired consultants.

73. WAR (We Are Rich) has been in business since 1982. WAR is an accrual method sole proprietorship that deals in the manufacturing and wholesaling of various types of golf equipment. Hack & Hack CPAs have filed accurate tax returns for WAR's owner since WAR opened its doors. The managing partner of Hack & Hack (Jack) has gotten along very well with the owner of WAR – Mr. Someday Woods (single). However, in early 2015, Jack Hack and Someday Woods played a round of golf and Jack, for the first time ever, actually beat Mr. Woods. Mr. Woods was so upset that he fired Hack & Hack and has hired you to compute his 2015 taxable income. Mr. Woods was able to provide you with the following information from prior tax returns. The taxable income numbers reflect the results from all of Mr. Wood's activities *except for the items separately stated.* You will need to consider how to handle the separately stated items for tax purposes. Also, note that the 2010–2014 numbers do not reflect capital loss carryovers.

	2010	2011	2012	2013	2014
Ordinary taxable income	$4,000	$ 2,000	$94,000	$170,000	$250,000
Other items not included in ordinary taxable income					
Net gain (loss) on disposition of §1231 assets	$3,000	10,000		($6,000)	
Net long-term capital gain (loss) on disposition of capital assets	($15,000)	$ 1,000	($7,000)		($7,000)

In 2015, Mr. Woods had taxable income in the amount of $460,000 *before* considering the following events and transactions that transpired in 2015:

a) On January 1, 2015, WAR purchased a plot of land for $100,000 with the intention of creating a driving range where patrons could test their new golf equipment. WAR never got around to building the driving range; instead, WAR sold the land on October 1, 2015, for $40,000.

b) On August 17, 2015, WAR sold its golf testing machine, "Iron Byron" and replaced it with a new machine "Iron Tiger." "Iron Byron" was purchased and installed for a total cost of $22,000 on February 5, 2011. At the time of sale, "Iron Byron" had an adjusted tax basis of $4,000. WAR sold "Iron Byron" for $25,000.

c) In the months October through December 2015, WAR sold various assets to come up with the funds necessary to invest in WAR's latest and greatest invention–the three dimple golf ball. Data on these assets are provided below:

Asset	Placed in Service (or purchased)	Sold	Initial Basis	Accumulated Depreciation	Selling Price
Someday's black leather sofa (used in office)	4/4/14	10/16/15	$ 3,000	$ 540	$ 2,900
Someday's office chair	3/1/13	11/8/15	$ 8,000	$3,000	$ 4,000
Marketable securities	2/1/12	12/1/15	$12,000	$ 0	$20,000
Land held for investment	7/1/14	11/29/15	$45,000	$ 0	$48,000
Other investment property	11/30/13	10/15/15	$10,000	$ 0	$ 8,000

d) Finally, on May 7, 2015, WAR decided to sell the building where they tested their plutonium shaft, lignite head drivers. WAR purchased the building on January 5, 2003, for $190,000 ($170,000 for the building, $20,000 for the land). At the time of the sale, the accumulated depreciation on the building was $50,000. WAR sold the building (with the land) for $300,000. The fair market value of the land at the time of sale was $45,000.

Part 1: Compute Mr. Woods's taxable income *after* taking into account the transactions described above.

Part 2: Compute Mr. Woods's tax liability for the year. (Ignore any net investment income tax for the year.)

Part 3: Complete Mr. Woods's Form 8949, Schedule D, and Form 4797 (use the most current version of these schedules) to be attached to his Form 1040. Assume that asset bases are not reported to the IRS.

74. Fizbo Corporation is in the business of breeding and racing horses. Fizbo has taxable income of $5,000,000 other than from these transactions. It has nonrecaptured §1231 losses of $10,000 from 2011 and $13,000 from 2009.

Consider the following transactions that occur during 2015:

a) A building with an adjusted basis of $300,000 is totally destroyed by fire. Fizbo receives insurance proceeds of $400,000, but does not plan to replace the building. The building was built 12 years ago at a cost of $420,000 and was used to provide lodging for employees.

b) Fizbo sells four acres of undeveloped farmland (used for grazing) for $50,000. Fizbo purchased the land 15 years ago for $15,000.

c) Fizbo sells a racehorse for $250,000. The racehorse was purchased four years ago for $200,000. Total depreciation taken on the racehorse was $160,000.

d) Fizbo exchanges equipment that was purchased three years ago for $300,000 for $100,000 of IBM common stock. The adjusted basis of the equipment is

$220,000. If straight-line depreciation had been used, the adjusted basis would be $252,000.

e) On November 1, Fizbo sold XCON stock for $50,000. Fizbo had purchased the stock on December 12, 2014 for $112,000.

Part 1: After ALL netting is complete, what is Fizbo's total amount of income from these transactions to be treated as ordinary income or loss? What is its capital gain or loss?

Part 2: What is Fizbo's taxable income for the year after including the effects of these transactions?

chapter

4 Entities Overview

Learning Objectives

Upon completing this chapter, you should be able to:

LO 4-1 Discuss the legal and nontax characteristics of different types of legal entities.

LO 4-2 Describe the different types of entities for tax purposes.

LO 4-3 Identify fundamental differences in tax characteristics across entity types.

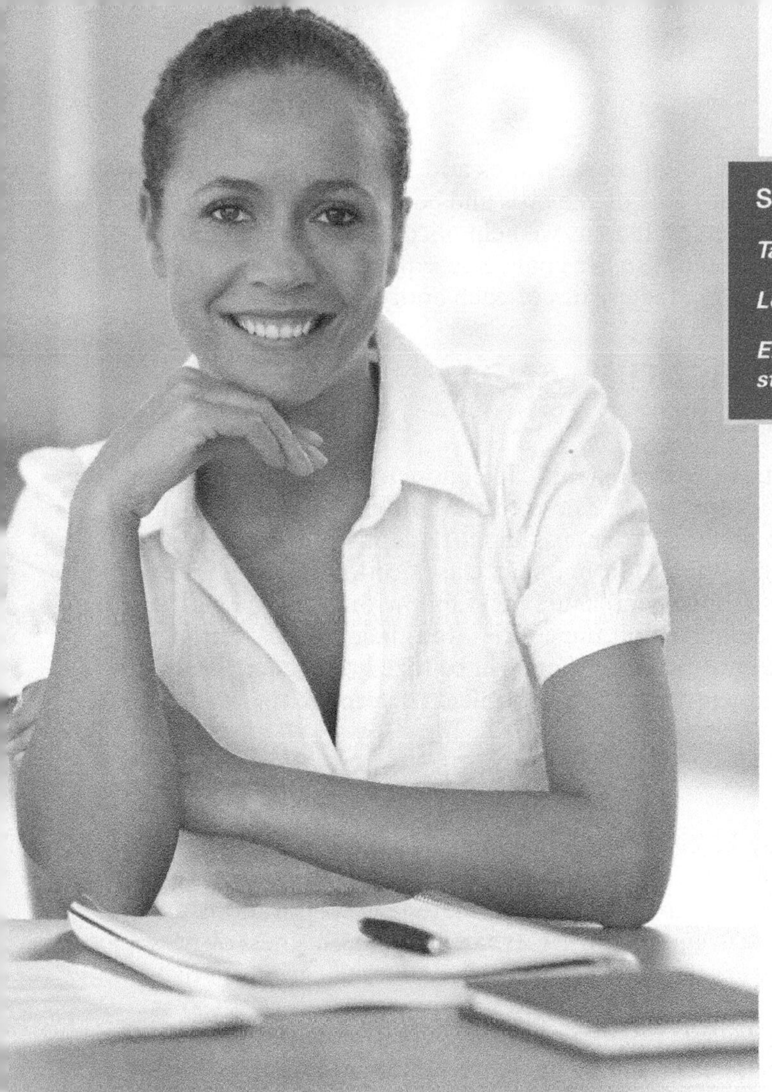

© PhotoAlto

Storyline Summary

Taxpayer:	Nicole Johnson
Location:	Salt Lake City, Utah
Employment status:	State government employee with entrepreneurial ambitions

Nicole Johnson is currently employed by the Utah Chamber of Commerce in Salt Lake City, Utah. While she enjoys the relatively short workweeks, she eventually would like to work for herself rather than for an employer. In her current position, she deals with a lot of successful entrepreneurs who have become role models for her. Nicole has also developed an extensive list of contacts that should serve her well when she starts her own business. It has taken a while, but Nicole believes she has finally developed a viable new business idea. Her idea is to design and manufacture bed sheets that have various colored patterns and are made of unique fabric blends. The sheets look great and are extremely comfortable whether the bedroom is warm or cool. She has had several friends try out her prototype sheets and they have consistently given the sheets rave reviews. With this encouragement, Nicole started giving serious thought to making "Color Comfort Sheets" a moneymaking enterprise.

Nicole has enough business background to realize that she is embarking on a risky path, but one, she hopes, with significant potential rewards in the future. After creating some initial income projections, Nicole realized that it will take a few years for the business to become profitable.

While Nicole's original plan was to start the business by herself, she is considering seeking out another equity owner for the business so that she can add financial resources and business experience to the venture. Nicole felt like she had a grasp on her business plan, but she still needed to determine how to organize the business for tax purposes. After doing some research, Nicole learned that she should consider many factors in order to determine the "best" entity type for her business. Each type of entity has advantages and disadvantages from both tax and nontax perspectives, and the best entity for a business depends on the goals, outlook, and strategy for that particular business and its owners. She realized she had more work to do to make an informed decision.

to be continued . . .

This chapter explores the various types of legal entities and then discusses entities available for tax purposes. We outline some of the pros and cons of each entity type, emphasizing both nontax and tax perspectives as we help Nicole determine how she will organize her business to best accomplish her goals. Subsequent chapters provide additional detail concerning the tax characteristics of each entity type.

LO 4-1

ENTITY LEGAL CLASSIFICATION AND NONTAX CHARACTERISTICS

THE KEY FACTS

Legal Classification and Nontax Characteristics of Entities

- State law generally classifies entities as either corporations, limited liability companies, general partnerships, limited partnerships, or sole proprietorships.
- Corporations and limited liability companies shield all of their owners against the entity's liabilities.
- Corporations are less flexible than other entities but are generally better suited for going public.

When forming new business ventures, entrepreneurs can choose to house their operations under one of several basic entity types. These entities differ in terms of their legal and tax considerations. In fact, as we discuss in more depth below, the legal classification of a business may be different from its tax classification. These entities differ in terms of the formalities that entrepreneurs must follow to create them, the legal rights and responsibilities conferred on the entities and their owners, and the tax rules that determine how the entities and owners will be taxed on income generated by the entities. CPAs are frequently asked to help clients determine the best entity choice for their businesses.

Legal Classification

Generally, a business entity may be classified as a **corporation,** a **limited liability company** (LLC), a **general partnership** (GP), a **limited partnership** (LP), or a **sole proprietorship** (that is not formed as an LLC).[1] Under state law, corporations are recognized as legal entities separate from their owners (shareholders). Business owners legally form corporations by filing **articles of incorporation** with the state in which they organize the business. State laws also recognize limited liability companies (LLCs) as legal entities separate from their owners (members). Business owners create limited liability companies by filing **articles of organization** with the state in which they are organizing the businesses.

Partnerships are formed under state partnership statutes and the degree of formality required depends on the type of partnership being formed. General partnerships may be formed by written agreement among the partners, called a **partnership agreement,** or may be formed informally without a written agreement when two or more owners join together in an activity to generate profits. Although general partners are not required to file partnership agreements with the state, general partnerships are still considered to be legal entities separate from their owners under state laws. Unlike general partnerships, limited partnerships are usually organized by written agreement and must typically file a **certificate of limited partnership** to be recognized by the state.[2]

Finally, for state law purposes, sole proprietorships are *not* treated as legal entities separate from their individual owners. As a result, sole proprietors are not required to formally organize their businesses with the state, and they hold title to business assets in their own names rather than in the name of their businesses.

Nontax Characteristics

The different legal entity types may differ from or share similarities with other legal entity types with respect to certain nontax characteristics. Rather than identify and discuss all possible nontax entity characteristics, we compare and contrast several prominent characteristics across the different legal entity types.

[1]Variations of these entities include Limited Liability Partnerships (LLPs), Limited Liability Limited Partnerships (LLLPs), Professional Limited Liability Companies (PLLCs), and Professional Corporations (PCs).

[2]Similar to limited partnerships, LLPs, LLLPs, PLLCs, and PCs must register with the state to receive formal recognition.

Responsibility for Liabilities Whether the entity or the owner(s) is ultimately responsible for paying the liabilities of the business depends on the type of entity. Under state law, a corporation is solely responsible for its liabilities.[3] Similarly, LLCs and not their members are responsible for the liabilities of the business.[4] For entities formed as partnerships, all general partners are ultimately responsible for the liabilities of the partnership. In contrast, limited partners are not responsible for the partnership's liabilities.[5] However, limited partners are not allowed to actively participate in the activities of the business.

Finally, if a business is conducted as a sole proprietorship, the individual owner rather than the sole proprietorship is responsible for the liabilities of the business. It is important to note, however, that individual business owners may also organize their businesses as single-member LLCs. In exchange for observing the formalities of organizing as an LLC, they receive the liability protection afforded LLC members.[6]

Rights, Responsibilities, and Legal Arrangement among Owners State corporation laws specify the rights and responsibilities of corporations and their shareholders. For example, to retain limited liability protection for shareholders, corporations must create, regularly update, and comply with their bylaws (internal rules governing how the corporation is run). They must have a board of directors. They must have regular board meetings and regular (at least annual) shareholder meetings, and they must keep minutes of these meetings. They must also issue shares of stock to owners (shareholders) and maintain a stock ledger reflecting stock ownership. They must also comply with annual filing requirements specified by the state of incorporation, pay required filing fees, and pay required corporate taxes, if any. Consequently, shareholders have no flexibility to alter their legal treatment with respect to one another, with respect to the corporation, and with respect to outsiders. In contrast, while state laws provide *default* provisions specifying rights and responsibilities of LLCs and their members, members have the *flexibility to alter* their arrangement by spelling out, through an operating agreement, the management practices of the entity and the rights and responsibilities of the members consistent with their wishes. Thus, LLCs allow more flexible business arrangements than do corporations.

Similar to LLC statutes, state partnership laws provide default provisions specifying the partners' legal rights and responsibilities for dealing with each other absent an agreement to the contrary. Because partners have the flexibility to depart from the default provisions, they frequently craft partnership agreements that are consistent with their preferences.

Although in many instances having the flexibility to customize business arrangements is desirable, sometimes inflexible governance rules mandated by state statute are needed to limit the participation of owners in management when their participation becomes impractical. For example, when businesses decide to "go public" with an **initial public offering** (IPO) on one of the public securities exchanges, they usually solicit a vast pool of potential investors to become *corporate*

[3]Payroll tax liabilities are an important exception to this general rule. Shareholders of closely held corporations may be held responsible for these liabilities.

[4]When closely held corporations and LLCs borrow from banks or other lenders, shareholders or members are usually asked to personally guarantee the debt. To the extent they do this, they become personally liable to repay the loan in the event the corporation or LLC is unable to repay it.

[5]Limited liability limited partnerships (LLLPs) are limited partnerships in which the general partners are protected from the liabilities of the entity. Also, professional service businesses such as accounting firms and law firms are generally not allowed to operate as corporations, LLCs, or limited partnerships. These businesses are frequently organized as limited liability partnerships (LLPs), professional limited liability companies (PLLCs), or as professional corporations (PCs). An owner of PLLCs and PCs are protected from liabilities other than liabilities stemming from the owner's negligence. LLPs do not provide protection against liabilities stemming from a partner's own malpractice or from the LLP's contractual liabilities.

[6]Shareholders of corporations and LLC members are responsible for liabilities stemming from their own negligence.

shareholders.[7] As shareholders, state corporation laws prohibit them from directly amending corporate governance rules and from directly participating in management—they only have the right to vote for corporate directors or officers. In comparison, LLC members generally have the right to amend the LLC operating agreement, provide input, and manage LLCs. Obviously, managing a publicly traded business would be next to impossible if thousands of owners had the legal right to change operating rules and to directly participate in managing the enterprise.

Exhibit 4-1 summarizes several nontax characteristics of different types of legal entities.

EXHIBIT 4-1 Business Types: Legal Entities and Nontax Characteristics

Nontax Characteristics	Corporation	LLC	General Partnership	Limited Partnership	Sole Proprietorship
Must formally organize with state	Yes	Yes	No	Yes	No*
Responsibility for liabilities of business	Entity	Entity	General partner(s)	General partner(s)	Owner†
Legal arrangement among owners	Not flexible	Flexible	Flexible	Flexible	Not applicable
Suitable for initial public offering	Yes	No	No	No	No

*Sole proprietor must organize with state if she forms a single-member LLC.
†Owner is not responsible for the liabilities of the business if sole proprietorship is organized as an LLC. However, owner is responsible for liabilities stemming from her own negligence.

As summarized in Exhibit 4-1, corporations and LLCs have the advantage in liability protection, LLCs and partnerships have an advantage over other entities in terms of legal flexibility, and corporations have the advantage when owners want to take a business public.

continued from page 4-1 . . .

As an initial step in the process of selecting an entity to house CCS, Nicole began to research nontax issues that might be relevant to her decision. Early on in her research she realized that the nontax benefits unique to traditional corporations were relevant primarily to large, publicly traded corporations. Although Nicole was very optimistic about CCS's prospects, she knew it would likely be a long time, if ever, before it went public. However, she remained concerned about limiting her own and other potential investors' liability in the new venture so she began to dig a little deeper. As she perused the Utah state Web site, she learned that corporations and LLCs are the only legal entities that can completely shield her and future investors from liabilities. Although Nicole doesn't anticipate any trouble from her future creditors, she decides to limit her choice of legal entity to either a corporation or LLC.

At this point in her information-gathering process, Nicole is leaning toward the LLC option because she is not sure if she wants to deal with board meetings and all the other formalities of operating a corporation; however, she decides to assemble a five-year forecast of CCS's expected operating results and to learn a little more about the way corporations and LLCs are taxed before narrowing her options any further.

to be continued . . .

[7]The vast majority of IPOs involve corporate shares; however, limited partnership interests are occasionally sold in IPOs. Like shareholders, limited partners are typically not allowed to participate in management. Limited partnerships are used for public offerings in lieu of corporations when they qualify for favorable partnership tax treatment available to some publicly traded partnerships.

ENTITY TAX CLASSIFICATION

LO 4-2

A business's legal form may be different from its tax form. We discussed the legal form of business entities above. We now discuss the tax form of business entities. In general terms, for tax purposes business entities can be classified as either separate taxpaying entities or as **flow-through entities.** Separate taxpaying entities pay tax on their own income. In contrast, flow-through entities generally don't pay taxes because income from these entities flows through to their business owners who are responsible for paying tax on the income.

How do we determine whether a particular business entity is treated as a separate taxpaying entity or as a flow-through entity for tax purposes? According to Treasury Regulations, commonly referred to as the "check-the-box" regulations, entities that are legal corporations under state law are, by default, treated as **C corporations** for tax purposes. These corporations and their shareholders are subject to tax provisions in Subchapter C (and not Subchapter S) of the Internal Revenue Code.[8] C corporations report their taxable income to the IRS on Form 1120. However, shareholders of *legal* corporations may qualify to make a special tax election known as an "S" election permitting the corporation to be taxed as a flow-through entity called an **S corporation.**[9] S corporations and their shareholders are subject to tax provisions in Subchapter S of the Internal Revenue Code. S corporations report the results of their operations to the IRS on Form 1120S.

Also under the check-the-box regulations, unincorporated entities are, by default, treated as flow-through entities.[10] However, owners of an unincorporated entity can still elect to have their business taxed as a C corporation instead of as the default flow-through entity.[11] In fact, the owner(s) of an unincorporated entity could elect to have the business taxed as a C corporation and then make a second election to have the "C corporation" taxed as an S corporation (provided that it meets the S corporation eligibility requirements). Before making such elections, however, the business owner(s) would need to be convinced that the move makes sense from a tax perspective.[12] The nontax considerations do not change because these elections do not affect the legal classification of the entity.

Finally, unincorporated flow-through entities (all flow-through entities except S corporations) are treated (for tax purposes) as either partnerships, sole proprietorships, or **disregarded entities** (an entity that is considered to be the same entity as the owner).[13] Unincorporated entities (including LLCs) with more than one owner are treated as partnerships.[14] Partnerships report their operating results to the IRS on Form 1065. Unincorporated entities (including LLCs) with only one *individual* owner such as sole proprietorships and **single-member LLCs** are treated as sole proprietorships.[15] Income from businesses taxed as sole proprietorships is reported on Schedule C of Form 1040. Similarly, unincorporated entities with only one *corporate* owner, typically a single-member LLC, are disregarded for tax purposes. Thus, income and losses from this single, corporate-member LLC is reported as if it had originated from a division of the corporation and is reported directly on the single-member corporation's return. Exhibit 4-2 provides a flowchart for determining the tax form of a business entity under the check the box regulations. Taxpayers check the box by filing Form 8832.

THE KEY FACTS

Tax Classification of Legal Entities

- Corporations are C corporations unless they make a valid S election.
- Unincorporated entities are taxed as partnerships if they have more than one owner.
- Unincorporated entities are taxed as sole proprietorships if held by a single individual or as disregarded entities if held by a single entity.
- Unincorporated entities may elect to be treated as C corporations. They then could make an S election if eligible.

[8]Reg. §301.7701-3(a).

[9]§1362(a). Because §1361 limits the number and type of shareholders of corporations qualifying to make an S election, some corporations are ineligible to become S corporations.

[10]Reg. §301.7701-3(b). However, §7704 mandates that unincorporated publicly traded entities be taxed as corporations unless their income predominately consists of certain types of passive income.

[11]Reg. §301.7701-3(a).

[12]As presented in Exhibit 4-3, compared to corporations, unincorporated entities taxed as partnerships have more favorable ownership requirements and more favorable tax treatment on nonliquidating and liquidating distributions of noncash property.

[13]Reg. §301.7701-3(a).

[14]Reg. §301.7701-3(b)(i).

[15]Reg. §301.7701-3(b)(ii).

EXHIBIT 4-2

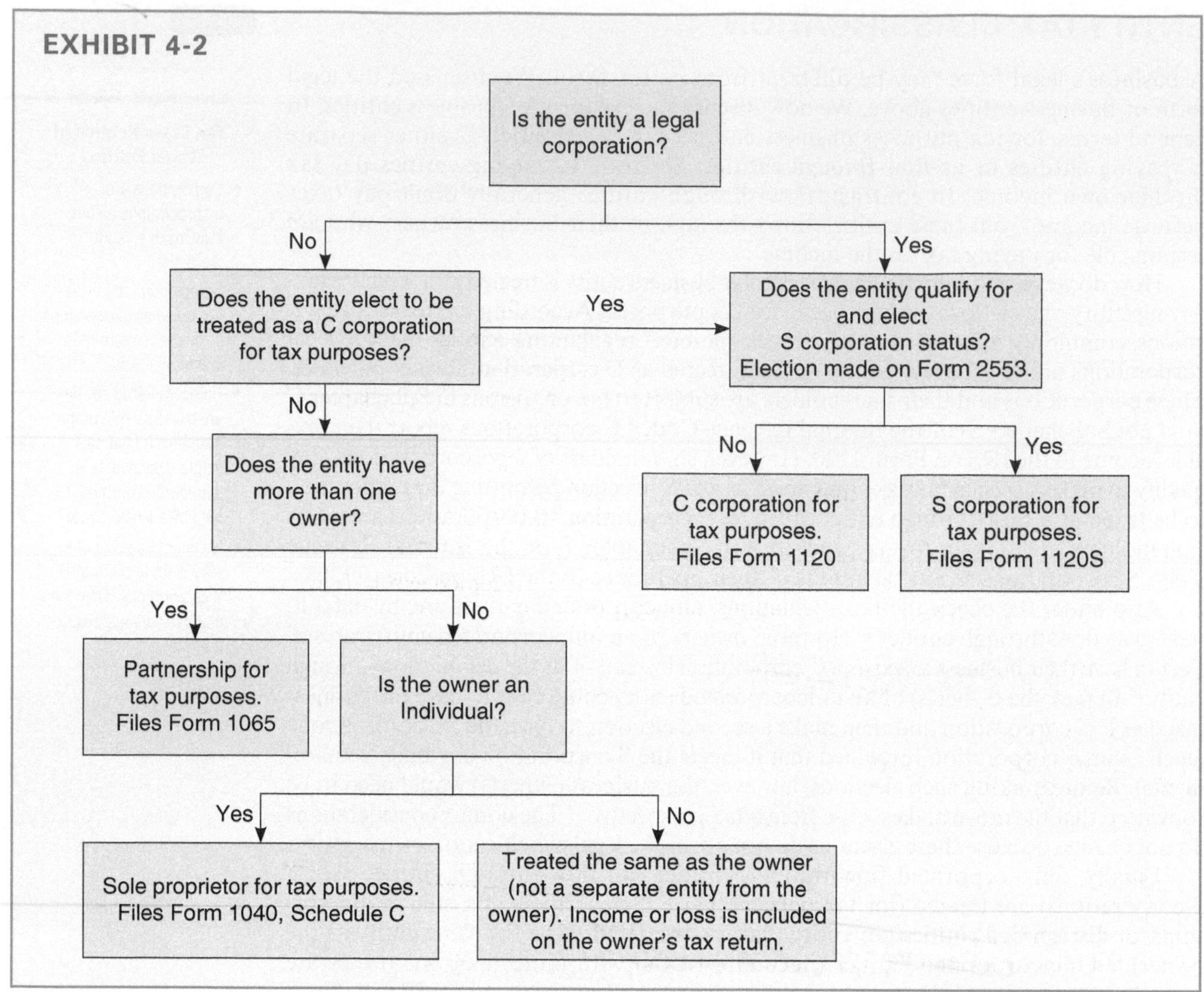

To summarize, although there are other types of legal entities, there are really only four categories of business entities recognized by the U.S. tax system, as follows:

1. C corporation (separate taxpaying entity; income reported on Form 1120)
2. S corporation (flow-through entity; income reported on Form 1120S)
3. Partnership (flow-through entity; income reported on Form 1065)
4. Sole proprietorship (flow-through entity; income reported on Form 1040, Schedule C)

Example 4-1

What if: Assume Nicole legally forms CCS as a corporation (with only common stock) by filing articles of incorporation with the state. What are Nicole's options for classifying CCS for tax purposes if she is the only shareholder of CCS?

Answer: Nicole may treat CCS as either a C corporation or as an S corporation. The default tax classification of legal corporations is as a C corporation for tax purposes. In addition, certain eligible corporations may elect to be treated as S corporations. Given the facts provided, CCS is eligible to make an S election.[16]

[16]§1361(b).

What if: Assume Nicole legally forms CCS as an LLC (with only one class of ownership rights) by filing articles of organization with the state. What are Nicole's options for classifying CCS for tax purposes if she is the only member of CCS?

Answer: The default classification for CCS is a sole proprietorship because CCS is unincorporated with one individual member. However, Nicole may elect to have CCS treated as a C corporation or as an S corporation. CCS can be treated as a C corporation because unincorporated entities may elect to be taxed as corporations. Further, eligible entities taxed as corporations can elect to be treated as S corporations. Given the facts provided, CCS is eligible to make an S election after first electing to be treated as a corporation.

What if: Assume Nicole legally forms CCS as an LLC and allows other individuals or businesses to become members in return for contributing their cash, property, or services to CCS. What is the default tax classification of CCS under these assumptions?

Answer: Partnership. The default tax classification for unincorporated entities with more than one owner is a partnership.

It might seem at this point that owners of businesses classified as flow-through entities would be treated the same for tax purposes; however, that is only true in a general sense. We see in this and in other chapters that there are some subtle, and some not so subtle, differences in how the owners of ventures classified as S corporations, partnerships, and sole proprietorships are taxed.[17]

ENTITY TAX CHARACTERISTICS

LO 4-3

In deciding among the available options for taxing business ventures, owners and their advisors must carefully consider whether tax rules that apply to a particular tax classification would be either more or less favorable than tax rules under other alternative tax classifications. The specific tax rules they must compare and contrast are unique to their situations; however, certain key differences in the tax rules tend to be relevant in many scenarios. We turn our attention to the taxation (or double taxation) of entity

TAXES IN THE REAL WORLD Comparing Entities Selected

In its Statistics of Income Tax report for 2008 (the most recent report posted when this book went to press), the Internal Revenue Service reported the following information relating to tax entity selection by business owners. Sole proprietorships are most common but C corporations by far generate the most business receipts and net income.

	Number of Entities	Business Receipts	Net Income (including deficits)
Totals for all Entities	31,607,710	$30,379,435,786	$1,784,099,872
Entity Type	**Percentage**	**Percentage**	**Percentage**
C corporations	5.64%	61.57%	21.79%
S corporations	12.81	19.79	17.77
General partnerships	2.26	2.07	9.46
Limited partnerships	1.69	4.51	3.07
LLCs (taxed as partnerships)	6.01	7.72	14.07
Sole proprietorships (nonfarm)	71.55	4.34	14.83
Other*	.05	0	19.93

*Other includes Real Estate Investment Trusts (REITs) and Regulated Investment Companies (RICs). Neither type of entity has business receipts.

Source: http://www.irs.gov/uac/SOI-Tax-Stats-Integrated-Business-Data Table 3: Selected financial data on businesses Tax Year 2008.

[17]Chapter 2 explains how sole proprietors are taxed, and Chapters 9 through 11 explain how partners and S corporation shareholders are taxed.

income and the tax treatment of entity losses because these are two of the most important tax characteristics to consider when selecting how to organize a business for tax purposes. Later in the chapter we preview other tax factors that differ between entities and we identify the chapters where each factor is discussed in detail.

Double Taxation

Under our current system of tax rates, flow-through entities are generally considered to be superior to corporations for tax purposes because they generate income that is taxed only once while corporations produce income that is taxed twice. Flow-through entity income retains its character (such as ordinary, short-term capital gain, or long-term capital gain) and is allocated to or "flows through" to entity owners. The owners include their share of the income on their own tax returns and pay tax on the income as if they had earned it themselves.

C corporations (or entities taxed as C corporations) pay the first level of tax on their taxable income. The marginal rate for the first level of tax depends on where the corporation's taxable income falls in the corporate tax rate schedule (provided inside the back cover of this text).[18] The current lowest marginal tax rate for corporations is 15 percent and the top marginal rate is 39 percent. The most profitable corporations are taxed at a flat 35 percent rate.

Corporate taxable income is subject to **double taxation** because shareholders pay a second level of tax on corporate income. The applicable rate for the second level of tax depends on whether corporations retain their after-tax earnings and on the type of shareholder(s). We first discuss the second level of tax that shareholders pay if corporations distribute their after-tax earnings and then we discuss the second level of tax if they retain the earnings.

After-Tax Earnings Distributed Assuming a C corporation distributes its after-tax earnings, the second level of tax depends on whether the corporation's shareholders are individuals, other corporations, **institutional shareholders,** tax-exempt, or foreign entities.

Individual shareholders. Individual shareholders receiving distributions from C corporations pay the second tax on the dividends they receive generally at a 15 percent tax rate. However, to the extent the dividends would be taxed at 39.6 percent if they were ordinary income, they are taxed at 20 percent and to the extent they would be taxed at 15 percent or less as ordinary income, they are taxed at 0 percent. Also, taxpayers with (modified) AGI in excess of a threshold amount pay an additional 3.8 percent net investment income tax on dividends. The threshold amount is $250,000 for married taxpayers filing jointly and surviving spouses, $125,000 for married taxpayers filing separately, and $200,000 for all other taxpayers.[19,20]

Example 4-2

What if: Assume that Nicole did some income projections to help her in her quest to determine the taxable form of her business. She makes the following assumptions:

- CCS earns taxable income of $335,000.
- CCS will pay out all of its after-tax earnings annually as a dividend.
- Her ordinary marginal tax rate is 33 percent and her dividend rate is 18.8 percent (including the 3.8 percent net investment income tax).

[18]C corporations that qualify as personal service corporations (PSCs) are taxed at a flat 35 percent rate (not eligible for graduated corporate rates). In general, a personal service corporation is a corporation whose shareholders perform professional services such as law, engineering, and accounting. See §448(d)(2) for more detail.

[19]Distributions to shareholders of C corporations are taxed as dividends to the extent they come from the "earnings and profits" (similar to economic income) of corporations.

[20]See §1(h) and §1411.

Given these assumptions, if Nicole organizes CCS as a C corporation, what would be the overall tax rate on CCS's income [(corporate-level tax + shareholder-level tax)/taxable income]?

Answer: 46.41 percent, computed as follows:

Description	Amount	Explanation
(1) Taxable income	$335,000	
(2) Corporate tax rate	34%	From tax table, inside back cover.
(3) Corporate-level tax	**$113,900**	(1) × (2) [first level of tax].
(4) Income remaining after taxes and distributed as a dividend	$221,100	(1) − (3).
(5) Dividend tax rate	18.8%	
(6) Shareholder-level tax on dividend	**$ 41,567**	(4) × (5) [second level of tax].
(7) Total tax paid on corporate taxable income	**$155,467**	(3) + (6).
Overall tax rate on corporate taxable income	**46.41%**	(7)/(1).

Note that the overall rate is not 52.8 percent (34 percent corporate rate + 18.8 percent shareholder rate) because the amount of corporate-level tax ($340,000) is not taxed twice (it is paid to the government, not to the shareholders).

What if: Given the same assumptions, what would be the overall tax rate on CCS's income if Nicole forms CCS as an S corporation (a flow-through entity)?

Answer: 33 percent, computed as follows:

Description	Amount	Explanation
(1) Taxable income	$335,000	
(2) Nicole's marginal individual tax rate	33%	
(3) Owner-level tax	$110,550	(1) × (2) [first and only level of tax].
Overall tax rate on CCS income	**33%**	(3)/(1).

Under these assumptions, CCS's income is subject to a 13.41 percent higher overall tax rate if it is organized as a C corporation rather than as an S corporation (46.41% − 33%).

Although corporate income is subject to a double tax, there may be circumstances in which the overall tax rate for corporate income is lower than the tax rate for flow-through income. With recent increases in individual tax rates, including the net investment income tax, and proposed legislation to reduce corporate tax rates, this situation may become increasingly more common.

Example 4-3

What if: Assume that Nicole made the following assumptions when projecting CCS's income:

- CCS's taxable income is $50,000.
- CCS pays out all of its after-tax earnings.
- Nicole's ordinary marginal tax rate is 33 percent and her dividend tax rate is 18.8 percent (including the 3.8 percent net investment income tax).

Given these assumptions, if Nicole organizes CCS as a C corporation, what would be the overall tax rate on CCS's income?

Answer: 30.98 percent, computed as follows:

(continued on page 4-10)

Description	Amount	Explanation
(1) Taxable income	$50,000	
(2) Corporate tax rate	15%	From tax table, inside back cover.
(3) Corporate-level tax	**$ 7,500**	(1) × (2) [first level of tax].
(4) Income remaining after taxes and amount distributed as a dividend	$42,500	(1) − (3).
(5) Dividend tax rate	18.8%	
(6) Shareholder-level tax on dividend	**$ 7,990**	(4) × (5) [second level of tax].
(7) Total tax paid on corporate taxable income	**$15,490**	(3) + (6).
Overall tax rate on corporate taxable income	**30.98%**	(7)/(1).

What if: Under the revised assumptions presented in this example, if Nicole forms CCS as an S corporation (flow-through entity), what would be the overall tax rate on CCS's income?

Answer: 33 percent. CCS's income would flow through to Nicole and be taxed at her 33 percent marginal ordinary income tax rate. Under the assumptions provided in this example, CCS's income is subject to a 2.02 percent *lower* overall tax rate if it is organized as a C corporation rather than as an S corporation (33% − 30.98%).

Examples 4-2 and 4-3 highlight the importance for business owners to accurately estimate their corporate marginal tax rate and their own individual marginal tax rates when deciding whether to have an entity taxed as a corporation or flow-through entity. These examples also suggest that individual business owners' overall tax rates will be higher with a corporation when the corporation's marginal tax rate is expected to be higher than or equal to the owners' marginal tax rates. Moreover, they suggest that overall tax rates may be lower with corporations when corporate marginal rates are substantially lower than individual shareholder marginal rates.

Corporate shareholders. Corporate shareholders receiving dividends are not entitled to the reduced dividend tax rate available to individual shareholders. That is, dividends received by a C corporation are subject to the corporation's ordinary tax rates. Further, dividends received by a corporation are potentially subject to another (third) level of tax when the corporation receiving the dividend distributes its earnings as dividends to its shareholders. This potential for more than two levels of tax on the same before-tax earnings prompted Congress to allow corporations to claim the **dividends received deduction** (DRD). In the next chapter, we discuss the DRD in detail but the underlying concept is that a corporation *receiving* a dividend is allowed to deduct a certain percentage of the dividend from its taxable income to offset the potential for additional layers of taxation on the dividend when the dividend-receiving corporation distributes the dividend to its shareholders. The dividends received deduction percentage is 70, 80, or 100 percent of the dividend received depending on the extent of the recipient corporation's ownership in the dividend-paying corporation. Thus, the DRD partially mitigates the tax burden associated with *more than two levels* of tax on corporate income.

Example 4-4

What if: Assume that Nicole invites a corporation with a 35 percent marginal tax rate to invest in exchange for a 10 percent share in CCS. Nicole makes the following assumptions as part of her calculations:

- CCS is a C corporation.
- CCS earns taxable income of $335,000.
- CCS will pay out all of its after-tax earnings annually as a dividend.

Given these assumptions, what would be the overall tax rate on the corporate investor's share of CCS's income [(corporate-level tax + shareholder-level tax)/taxable income] given that the corporation would be eligible for a 70 percent dividends received deduction?

Answer: 40.9 percent, computed as follows:

Description	Amount	Explanation
(1) Taxable income	$335,000	
(2) Corporate tax rate	34%	From tax table, inside back cover.
(3) Entity-level tax	$113,900	(1) × (2) [first level of tax].
(4) After-tax income	$221,100	(1) − (3).
(5) Corporate investor's dividend	$ 22,110	(4) × 10%.
(6) Taxable dividend	$ 6,633	(5) × (1 − 70% DRD).
(7) Corporate investor's share of entity-level tax	$ 11,390	(3) × 10% investor's share.
(8) Corporate investor's tax on dividend	$ 2,322	(6) × 35% assumed investor tax rate [second level of tax].
(9) Total tax paid on corporate taxable income	$ 13,712	(7) + (8).
Overall tax rate on corporate taxable income	**40.9%**	(9)/[(1) × 10% investor's share].

Institutional shareholders. Pension and retirement funds are some of the largest institutional shareholders of corporations. However, these entities do not pay shareholder-level tax on the dividends they receive. Ultimately, retirees pay the second tax on this income when they receive retirement distributions from these funds. While retirees pay the second tax at ordinary rates, not the reduced dividend rates, they are able to defer the tax until they receive fund distributions.

Tax-exempt and foreign shareholders. Tax-exempt organizations such as churches and universities are exempt from tax on their investment income, including dividend income from investments in corporate stock. Similarly, foreign investors may be eligible for reduced rates on dividend income depending on the tax treaty, if any, their country of residence has signed with the United States.

Some or All After-Tax Earnings Retained We've already determined that a double tax on corporate income arises when corporations pay tax on their income, and shareholders pay a second level of tax when they receive dividends. Can corporations avoid the second level of tax entirely by not paying dividends? The answer is no for two reasons. First, corporations that retain earnings may be required to pay a penalty tax in addition to income tax on their earnings. With certain exceptions, unless corporations have a business reason to retain earnings, they are subject to a 20 percent **accumulated earnings tax** on the retained earnings.[21] Also, **personal holding companies** (closely held corporations generating primarily investment income) are subject to a 20 percent **personal holding company tax** on their undistributed income.[22] These penalty taxes remove the tax incentive for corporations to retain earnings. Second, shareholders also pay a second level of tax when corporations *retain* their after-tax earnings. Keep in mind that shareholders should experience an increase in the value of their shares to reflect any undistributed earnings (increase in assets). Individual shareholders generally pay the second tax at capital gains rates on this undistributed income when they realize the appreciation in their stock (from the retained earnings) by selling their shares. These long-term capital gains are generally taxed at 15 percent, However, to the extent the (long-term) capital gains would be taxed at 39.6 percent if they were ordinary income, they are taxed at 20 percent and to the extent they would be taxed at 15 percent or less as ordinary income, they are

[21]See §531 and §532.

[22]See §541.

taxed at 0 percent. Also, taxpayers with (modified) AGI in excess of a threshold amount pay an additional 3.8 percent net investment income tax on net capital gains. The threshold amount is $250,000 for married taxpayers filing jointly and surviving spouses, $125,000 for married taxpayers filing separately, and $200,000 for all other taxpayers.[23] Because shareholders *defer* paying this portion of the second tax until they sell their shares, taxes on capital gains must be discounted to reflect their present value.

Note, however, that other types of shareholders will face different tax consequences when they sell their shares. If a corporation with corporate shareholders retains after-tax earnings, corporate shareholders are taxed on capital gains at ordinary rates (there is no preferential tax rate on capital gains for corporations) when they eventually sell the stock. Consequently, a corporate shareholder's income from capital appreciation may be subject to *more* than two levels of taxation because income from capital appreciation doesn't qualify for the dividends received deduction. Also, institutional shareholders don't pay tax when they sell their stock and recognize capital gains. However, retirees generally pay tax on the gains at ordinary rates when they receive distributions from their retirement accounts. Finally, tax-exempt shareholders do not pay tax on capital gains from selling stock and foreign investors are generally not subject to U.S. tax on their capital gains from selling corporate stock.

Mitigating the Double Tax While corporate taxable income is subject to double taxation, corporations and shareholders have options for mitigating the double tax by taking steps to reduce the corporate-level tax and/or the shareholder-level tax. These options are particularly relevant when corporations are not eligible to make an S election or when the tax and nontax costs of converting to some other legal entity are prohibitive. Let's first focus on strategies to reduce the corporate-level tax.

Reducing the corporate-level tax. When a C corporation's marginal tax rate exceeds its *individual* shareholders' marginal tax rates the overall tax rate on corporate income will exceed the flow-through tax rate even if shareholders can defer the second tax indefinitely. In these situations, it makes sense for closely held corporations and their shareholders to consider strategies to shift income from the corporation to shareholders. These strategies are all designed to move earnings out of the corporations and to shareholders with payments that are *deductible* (dividends are not deductible payments) by the corporation and (generally) taxable to shareholders. Making tax-deductible payments to shareholders accomplishes two objectives. First, it shifts income away from (relatively) high tax rate corporations to (relatively) low tax rate shareholders. Second, the deduction shields income from the corporate-level tax. Strategies that shift income from corporations to shareholders include:

- Paying salaries to shareholders (salaries are deductible only to the extent they are reasonable).
- Paying fringe benefits to shareholders (generally taxable to shareholders unless benefits are specifically excluded from taxation).[24]
- Leasing property from shareholders.
- Paying interest on loans from shareholders.[25]

[23]See §1(h) and §1411.

[24]Common fringe benefits excluded from taxation are medical insurance, group-term life insurance, dependent care assistance, tuition benefits, and so forth.

[25]If the shareholder is an individual, depending on the shareholder's income level, rental income and interest income may be subject to the 3.8 percent net investment income tax.

Example 4-5

What if: Assume Nicole uses her own funds to purchase the equipment required to manufacture the color comfort sheets. She leases the equipment to CCS corporation for $12,000 per year, the fair rental value for the equipment. What are the tax consequences to CCS and to Nicole of this leasing arrangement?

Answer: CCS deducts the $12,000 paid to Nicole each year for the use of the equipment, shielding $12,000 of its earnings from the corporate-level tax. Nicole is taxed on the $12,000 lease payments at her ordinary rate. In the end, Nicole and the corporation have achieved their objective of getting earnings out of CCS and into Nicole's hands with only one level of tax on the earnings.

THE KEY FACTS

Double Taxation

- Most profitable C corporations are taxed at a 35 percent rate.
- Individual C corporation shareholders are generally taxed at a 15 percent rate on dividends when received (20 percent for high income taxpayers). Further, certain taxpayers may be charged a 3.8 percent net investment income tax on dividends and capital gains.
- C corporation shareholders that are C corporations are generally eligible to receive a 70 percent or greater dividends received deduction.
- C corporation shareholders who are individuals generally pay capital gains taxes when shares are sold at a gain.
- The double tax is mitigated when income is shifted from C corporations to shareholders and when dividends are deferred or not paid.

ETHICS

Troy is the CEO and sole shareholder of BQT. BQT is a very profitable C corporation. Until this year, Troy's salary was in line with the salaries of other comparable CEOs. However, early this year it came to Troy's attention that another CEO for a similarly sized firm in the same industry was receiving a salary almost two times what Troy was receiving. Wanting to mitigate the double tax on his corporation's income, Troy decided to give himself a 75 percent raise. Do you think Troy's decision is ethical? Why or why not?

Reducing the shareholder-level tax. Shareholders generally pay the second tax immediately when they receive dividends or in the future when they sell their stock and pay capital gains tax. For *individual* shareholders, the tax rate applicable to both dividend income and (long-term) capital gains is generally 15 or 20 percent depending on the taxpayer's income level. Further, high-income taxpayers may be charged an additional 3.8 percent net investment income tax on dividends and capital gains. However, because individual shareholders defer paying the second tax on capital gains until they sell their stock, the present value of the second tax is a function of the (1) percentage of after-tax earnings the corporation retains rather than currently distributing as dividends and (2) the length of time shareholders hold the stock before selling. By retaining after-tax earnings, corporations defer the second level of tax until the shareholder sells the stock. The longer a shareholder holds stock in a corporation that retains earnings, the lower the present value of the shareholder-level tax on the corporation's earnings. Individuals who make lifetime gifts of appreciated stock to their children utilize this basic strategy. The concept is that by deferring the second level of tax until children sell the shares many years into the future, the double tax becomes very small on a present value basis.[26] Alternatively, the donor could have sold the shares, paid the resulting capital gains tax, and given the remainder to her children, but this would have immediately triggered the shareholder tax leaving her children with less after-tax wealth on a present value basis.

It is important to note that the length of time a shareholder holds stock before selling and the percentage of earnings retained are not always under the shareholder's or corporation's control. For example, a shareholder may need cash for reasons unrelated to the business and therefore may need to sell the stock before recognizing the deferral benefits of holding the stock. Also, as we discussed above, the accumulated

[26]Shareholders who wait until death to bequeath stock along with their heirs escape the shareholder tax entirely because the tax basis of inherited shares is stepped up to fair market value on the date of death. These shareholders may pay estate tax on the value of the shares held at death, however.

earnings tax and personal holding company tax may force corporations to distribute rather than retain earnings.

In spite of the fact that the double tax can be reduced by careful planning at both the corporate and shareholder level, some element of the double tax will likely remain, leaving corporations disadvantaged relative to flow-through entities under our current system of individual and corporate tax rates.

Deductibility of Entity Losses

When C corporations are reporting losses for tax purposes, double taxation (or even single taxation) is not a concern. Losses generated by C corporations are called **net operating losses** (NOLs). While NOLs provide no tax benefit to a corporation in the year the corporation experiences the NOL, they may be used to reduce corporate taxes in other years. Generally, C corporations with an NOL for the year can carry back the loss to offset the taxable income reported in the two preceding years and carry it forward for up to 20 years.

Under this approach, losses from C corporations are *not* available to offset their shareholders' personal income. In contrast, losses generated by flow-through entities are generally available to offset the owners' personal income, subject to certain restrictions. For example, the owner of a flow-through entity may only deduct losses from the entity to the extent of the owner's basis in her ownership interest in the flow-through entity. In addition, deductibility of losses from flow-through entities may be further limited by the "at-risk" and passive activity loss limitations. The at-risk limitation is similar to the basis limitation but slightly more restrictive. The passive activity loss limitations typically apply to individual investors who do little, if any, work for the business activities of the flow-through entity (referred to as "passive" activities to the individual investors). In these circumstances, the taxpayer can only deduct such losses to the extent they have income from other passive activities. Due to the complex nature of these limitations, we defer detailed discussion of these limitations until we discuss partnerships in Chapter 9. The ability to deduct flow-through losses against other sources of income can be a significant issue for owners of new businesses because new businesses tend to report losses early on as the businesses get established. If owners form a new business as a C corporation, the corporate-level losses provide no current tax benefits to the shareholders. The fact that C corporation losses are trapped at the corporate level effectively imposes a higher tax cost for shareholders initially doing business as a C corporation relative to a flow-through entity such as an S corporation or partnership because the flow-through entity owners, subject to the limits mentioned above, can use the losses to offset other sources of income.

Example 4-6

What if: Assume that Nicole organizes CCS as a C corporation and that, in spite of her best efforts as CEO of the company, CCS reports a tax loss of $50,000 in its first year of operation (year 1). Also, assume Nicole's marginal tax rate is 33 percent and assume she will have ordinary taxable income of $200,000 from her husband's salary in year 1. How much tax will CCS pay in year 1 and how much tax will Nicole (and her husband) pay on the $200,000 of other taxable income if CCS is organized as a C corporation?

Answer: CCS will pay $0 in taxes because it reports a loss for tax purposes. Because Nicole may not use the CCS loss to offset her other income, she must pay $66,000 in taxes. See the computations in the table below.

What if: Suppose CCS is organized as an S corporation and Nicole's stock basis in CCS before the year 1 loss is $100,000. How much tax will CCS pay in year 1, and how much tax will Nicole (and her husband) pay on the $200,000 of other income?

Answer: CCS pays $0 taxes (S corporations are not taxpaying entities) and Nicole pays $49,500 in taxes. See the computations in table below:

Description	C Corporation	S Corporation (flow-through)	Explanation
(1) Taxable income (loss)	($50,000)	($50,000)	
(2) CCS corporate-level tax	**$ 0**	**$ 0**	No taxable income.
(3) Nicole's other income	$200,000	$200,000	
(4) CCS loss available to offset Nicole's other income	$ 0	($50,000)	$0 if C corp. (1) if flow-through entity (S corporation).
(5) Nicole's other income reduced by entity loss	$200,000	$150,000	(3) + (4).
(6) Nicole's marginal ordinary tax rate	33%	33%	
Nicole's tax on other income	**$ 66,000**	**$ 49,500**	(5) × (6).

What if: Suppose CCS is organized as an S corporation and Nicole's stock basis before the $50,000 year 1 loss is $100,000. Further, assume that Nicole does not participate in CCS's business activities; that is, assume she is a passive investor in the business entity. How much tax will Nicole (and her husband) pay on the $200,000 of other income?

Answer: $66,000. Because Nicole is a passive investor, she is not allowed to deduct the loss allocated to her this year. She must carry it over and use it in future years (this assumes neither Nicole nor her husband have income from other investments in which they are passive investors).

As the example above illustrates, owners' ability to immediately use start-up losses from flow-through entities to offset income from other sources further enhances the tax advantages of flow-through entities relative to corporations in many situations.

OTHER TAX CHARACTERISTICS

The taxation of entity income and the tax treatment of entity losses are two important factors to consider when comparing tax entities. There are many other tax characteristics that differ across entities and could influence the entity selection decision. Factors that are most important to the decision also depend on the facts and circumstances of the particular situation. Exhibit 4-3 provides an overview of many of these tax characteristics. The exhibit describes the general rules for each tax characteristic as it relates to C corporations, S corporations, entities taxed as partnerships, and sole proprietorships and it ranks the entities on each characteristic (1 is most tax favorable). Finally, the exhibit indicates the chapters where detail on these tax characteristics can be found. Because this is an overview chapter, details on each factor are provided elsewhere in the text.

Converting to Other Entity Types

As we discuss previously, C corporations can take steps to mitigate the double tax. For example, deductible compensation, rent, and interest payments, to the extent they are reasonable, provide a mechanism for shifting income to their shareholders. Depending on the total amount of these deductible shareholder payments relative to a corporation's income before the payments, they effectively convert or partially convert C corporations into flow-through entities in the sense that these payments are taxed at the owner level and not at the corporate level. If this is true, why not avoid the constraints associated with deductible shareholder payments and accomplish the same result more directly by converting an existing corporation into a flow-through entity?

Besides making deductible payments to their shareholders, existing corporations really only have two options for converting into flow-through entities. First, shareholders of C corporations could make an S election to treat the corporation as an S corporation (flow-through entity), if they are eligible to do so. This option is not available for many corporations due to the tax rule restrictions prohibiting certain corporations from operating as S corporations. The only other option is for the shareholders to liquidate the corporation and form the business as a partnership or LLC. This may not be a viable option, however, because the taxes imposed on liquidating corporations with appreciated assets can be very punitive. As described in Exhibit 4-3, liquidating corporations are taxed on the appreciation in the assets they distribute to their shareholders as part of the liquidation. Further, shareholders of liquidating corporations are also taxed on the difference between the fair market value of the assets they receive from the liquidating corporation and their tax basis in their stock. Effectively, the total double-tax cost of liquidating a corporation can swamp the expected tax savings from operating as a flow-through entity.

Example 4-7

What if: Assume we are years down the road and that Nicole is the sole shareholder of CCS (a C corporation). CCS's assets have a fair market value of $10 million and adjusted tax basis of $6 million ($4 million built-in gain). Further assume that CCS has a 34 percent marginal tax rate, Nicole's stock basis in CCS is $2 million, and her marginal tax rate on long-term capital gains is 23.8 percent (20 percent capital gains rate + 3.8 percent net investment income tax). How much tax would the CCS and Nicole be required to pay if CCS were to liquidate in order to form an LLC?

Answer: $2,940,320. This is a steep tax price to pay for changing from C corporation to LLC.

Description	Amount	Explanation
(1) FMV of CCS assets	$10,000,000	
(2) Adjusted basis of CCS assets	$6,000,000	
(3) CCS taxable income on liquidation	$4,000,000	(1) − (2).
(4) Corporate tax rate	34%	
(5) Entity-level tax	$1,360,000	(3) × (4).
(6) After-tax assets distributed to Nicole.	$8,640,000	(1) − (5).
(7) Nicole's stock basis	$2,000,000	
(8) Nicole's long-term capital gain on distribution	$6,640,000	(6) − (7).
(9) Nicole's marginal tax rate on gain	23.8%	
(10) Shareholder-level tax	$1,580,320	(8) × (9).
Total entity and shareholder-level tax on liquidation	**$2,940,320**	(5) + (10).

EXHIBIT 4-3 Comparison of Tax Characteristics across Entities

Tax Characteristic	C corporation	Entity Taxed as Partnership	S corporation	Sole Proprietorship	Detail in Chapter	Summary
Owner limits	At least one shareholder.	At least two owners.	Not more than 100; no corporations, partnerships, nonresident aliens, or certain trusts.	N/A	11	Limitations are least strict for C corporations and most strict for S corporations. S corporations are the only entity with significant owner limitations.
Rank[1]	1	2	3	N/A		
Owner contributions of appreciated property to entity	Nontaxable to shareholder if certain requirements are met.	Nontaxable to owner.	Nontaxable to shareholder if certain requirements are met.	N/A	8, 9, and 11	This factor favors entities taxed as partnerships because partners are not required to meet special requirements in order to avoid recognizing gain on the contribution of appreciated property to the partnership, but shareholders of both C and S corporations are required to meet certain requirements to avoid recognizing gain on such contributions to the corporation.
Rank	2	1	2	N/A		
Accounting periods	Generally, any tax year that ends on the last day of any month.[2]	Generally, must use tax year that matches tax year of owners (special rules when not all owners have same tax year-end).	Calendar year.	Generally a calendar year.	2, 9, and 11	C corporations generally have the most flexibility to select their year-end. But because C corporations are not flow-through entities, this is not a real advantage or disadvantage from a tax perspective. Partnerships generally are not free to choose their year-end but they can have a year-end that is a different year-end from some of the owners. Because this allows some partners to defer reporting income, this factor favors partnerships over S corporations. S corporations generally have the same calendar year-end as their shareholders.
Rank	N/A	1	2	N/A		
Overall accounting method	Generally, must use accrual method unless smaller corporation.[3]	Generally, allowed to use cash or accrual method.	Generally, allowed to use cash or accrual method.	Cash or accrual method.	2, 5, 9, and 11	Entities taxed as partnerships, S corporations, and sole proprietorships generally have more flexibility to choose their overall accounting method than do C corporations. The cash method makes it easier for these entities to plan the timing of income and expenses than does the accrual method.
Rank	4	1	1	1		
Allocation of income or loss items to owners	N/A	Allocations based on partnership agreement (can differ from ownership percentages).	Allocations based on stock ownership percentages.	N/A	9 and 11	This factor applies to partnerships and S corporations only. Partnerships have more flexibility than S corporations to determine how to allocate income and loss items to entity owners.
Rank	N/A	1	2	N/A		

(continued on page 4-18)

Tax Characteristic	C corporation	Entity Taxed as Partnership	S corporation	Sole Proprietorship	Detail in Chapter	Summary
FICA and self-employment tax	Employee-owners pay FICA tax on salary.	Compensation received by owners (guaranteed payments) is subject to self-employment tax. Business (operating) income allocation is generally subject to self-employment tax if owner is actively involved in business. It is not otherwise.[4]	Employee-owners pay FICA on salary. But they do not pay FICA/self-employment tax on business income allocations. Owners providing services for the S corporation must receive a reasonable salary for their efforts.[5]	Net income is subject to self-employment tax, including the .9 percent additional Medicare tax depending on the proprietor's income level (see §1401 for details).	9 and 11	This factor tends to favor S corporations because S corporation owners can work for the business and yet receive business income allocations that are not subject to FICA/self-employment tax or the .9 percent additional Medicare tax. In contrast, business income allocations to partners working for partnerships are subject to self-employment tax and potentially the .9 percent additional Medicare tax. Congress is currently considering proposals to reduce this discrepancy in tax treatment between entities.
Rank	2	3	1	4		
Share of flow-through entity debt included in basis of owner's equity interest	N/A	Increase basis in ownership interest by owner's share of entity's debt.	No increase in stock basis for debt of entity (special rules if shareholder lends money to S corporation).	N/A	9 and 11	Partners are allowed to increase the basis in their ownership interest by their share of the partnership's debt; S corporation shareholders generally are not. This factor favors partnerships over S corporations.
Rank	N/A	1	2	N/A		
Nonliquidating distributions of noncash property	Gains recognized on distributions of appreciated property and losses disallowed on distributions of appreciated property.	Generally no gain or loss recognized on noncash property distributions.	Same as C corporation.	N/A	7, 10, and 11	This factor favors partnerships for distributions of appreciated and depreciated property.
Rank	2	1	1	N/A		
Liquidating distributions	Gain and loss (certain losses disallowed).	Generally no gain or loss.	Gain and loss (certain losses disallowed).	N/A	8, 10, and 11	This factor tends to favor partnerships if the liquidating entities have gain assets, and it tends to favor corporations if the entities have loss assets.
Rank	1	1	1	N/A		

[1]"Rank" orders the entities based on the particular characteristic (1 is most favorable).
[2]C corporations that qualify as personal service corporations (PSCs) are generally required to use a calendar year. In general, a personal service corporation is a corporation whose shareholders perform professional services such as law, engineering, and accounting. See §448(d)(2) for more detail.
[3]C corporations that qualify as personal service corporations (PSCs) are required to use the cash method.
[4]Guaranteed payments and income allocations (if the partner is involved in the business) are subject to an additional .9 percent Medicare tax depending on the partner's income level (see §1401 for details). If the partner is not involved in the business, income allocations are subject to the 3.8 percent net investment income tax, depending on the partner's income level.
[5]An S corporation shareholder receiving salary may be be required to pay the .9 percent additional Medicare tax on some or all of the salary depending on the shareholder's income level and other sources of earned income (see §1401 for details). Further, if the S corporation shareholder is not actively involved in the business, income allocations may be subject to the 3.8 percent net investment income tax, depending on the shareholder's income level.

When feasible, S elections or corporate liquidations, like deductible payments to shareholders, are used to convert *existing* corporations into flow-through entities. Why then, didn't shareholders of *existing* corporations initially form the entities as flow-through entities? Perhaps, at the time of formation the corporate form was optimal from purely a tax perspective because corporate marginal tax rates were significantly lower than shareholder marginal tax rates at that time. Or, maybe, the corporations were willing to be treated as C corporations in order to go public but then became closely held when all their outstanding shares were purchased by a small number of shareholders.

As costly as it can be to convert corporations to flow-through entities, it is equally as easy and inexpensive to convert entities taxed as partnerships or sole proprietorships into corporations. Typically, converting entities taxed as partnerships or sole proprietorships into corporations can be accomplished in a tax-deferred transaction without any special tax elections.[27] For this reason, many businesses that plan to eventually go public will operate for a time as entities taxable as partnerships to receive the associated tax benefits and then convert to C corporations when they finally decide to go public.

continued from page 4-4. . .
Nicole's five-year forecast of CCS's expected operating results showed that CCS would generate losses for the first three years and then become very profitable after. With these projections in hand, Nicole then considered the basic question of whether a C corporation or a flow-through entity would minimize her overall tax liability. Nicole's marginal tax rate and CCS's expected marginal tax rate after three years, if it were to operate as a C corporation, led her to conclude that she needed to avoid the double tax by operating CCS as a flow-through entity from the start. Given her initial desire to limit her choice of legal entity to either a corporation or LLC, this left her with the option of operating CCS as either an S corporation or as an LLC taxed as a partnership.

After narrowing her choice down to either an LLC or S corporation, Nicole compared the specific tax rules applicable to LLCs and S corporations before making her final decision. As she compared them, she identified four differences that could sway her decision one way or the other. Supporting a decision to select an LLC, Nicole learned she would likely be able to deduct the projected start-up losses from CCS more quickly with an LLC compared with an S corporation because she could include a share of the LLC's debt in her tax basis (but she would not be able to include a share of the S corporation's debt in the tax basis of her ownership interest). Moreover, she learned that LLC profits and losses can be specially allocated while S corporation profits and losses must be allocated pro rata to the shareholders. Nicole was hoping to have the ability to be a little more creative with profit and loss allocations. Finally, she had hoped to possibly attract corporate investors, but discovered that S corporations are not permitted to have corporate shareholders. She did find however, that S corporations appear to have a compelling advantage over LLCs in reducing the self-employment tax of owners active in managing their businesses.

Ultimately, Nicole decided that she would be willing to incur additional self-employment taxes with an LLC in exchange for the ability to deduct her losses sooner, for the flexibility she might need one day to specially allocate profits or losses, and for the freedom to solicit corporate investors. Given these considerations, she decided to organize CCS as an LLC in the state of Utah.

With this big decision out of the way, Nicole could now focus on applying for a small business loan from her local bank and on having her attorney take the necessary steps to formally organize CCS as a limited liability company. ■

[27]§351 and Rev. Rul. 84-111 1984-2 CB 88.

TAXES IN THE REAL WORLD Best Entity Choice for Small Businesses?

Small businesses generally have the option to be taxed as a flow-through entity (S corporation or partnership). Historically, the obvious tax benefit of a flow-through entity is that the entity's income is taxed once at the owner level. Nevertheless, a recently published study from economists at the Treasury Department indicates that more than 1.6 million small businesses forgo flow-through entity status and are taxed as Subchapter C corporations, subjecting their income to both entity-level and shareholder level tax (Matthew Knittel, Susan Nelson, Jason DeBacker, John Kitchen, James Pearce, and Richard Prisinzano, "Methodology to Identify Small Businesses and Their Owners," Office of Tax Analysis, Technical Paper 4, Aug. 2011, *Doc 2011-17260, 2011 TNT 154-18*). Despite a C corporation's historically bad tax reputation, there are good tax reasons for small businesses to subject themselves to double tax under Subchapter C. For example, graduated corporate rates, the low effective tax rate on corporate dividends (due to the dividends received deduction), and an exemption from payroll taxes (that is, a C corporation is not subject to FICA or self-employment tax on its own earnings) combine to make Subchapter C the most advantageous choice for a lot of small business profits. This is particularly true when a business owner can afford to defer the shareholder level tax by leaving profits inside the corporation. Further, now that the top marginal individual tax rate is higher than the top corporate tax rate, even more small businesses may choose to be taxed as C corporations.

CONCLUSION

Any time a new business is formed and periodically thereafter as circumstances change, business owners must carefully evaluate what type of business entity will maximize the after-tax profits from their business ventures. Many of the key factors to consider in the entity selection decision-making process are outlined in this chapter. When making the entity selection decision, owners must carefully balance the tax and nontax characteristics unique to the entities available to them. This chapter explains how various legal entities are treated for tax purposes and how certain tax characteristics differ between entity types. Moreover, it also identifies some of the more important nontax issues that come to bear on the choice of entity decision. With this understanding, taxpayers and their advisors will be better prepared to face this frequently encountered business decision. In Chapter 9, we return to Nicole and Color Comfort Sheets LLC to examine the tax rules that apply to Nicole and other members in CCS as they form the entity for tax purposes and begin business operations.

Summary

LO 4-1 Discuss the legal and nontax characteristics of different types of legal entities.

- Entities that differ in terms of their legal characteristics include corporations, limited liability companies, general partnerships, limited partnerships, and sole proprietorships.
- Corporations are formally organized by filing articles of incorporation with the state. They are legally separate entities and protect their shareholders from the liabilities of the corporation. State corporation laws dictate interactions between corporations and shareholders. As a result, shareholders have limited flexibility to customize their business arrangements with the corporation and other shareholders. State corporate governance rules do, however, facilitate initial public offerings.
- Limited liability companies are formally organized by filing articles of organization with the state. Like corporations, they are separate legal entities that shield their members from liabilities. In contrast to corporations, state LLC statutes give members a great deal of latitude in customizing their business arrangements with the LLC and other members.

- General partnerships may be organized informally without state approval, but limited partnerships must file a certificate of limited partnership with the state to organize. Although they are considered to be legally separate entities, they provide either limited or no liability protection for partners. While limited partners in limited partnerships have liability protection, general partners are fully exposed to the liabilities of the partnership. General and limited partnerships are given a great deal of latitude in customizing their partnership agreements.
- Sole proprietorships are businesses legally indistinguishable from their sole individual owners. As such, they are very flexible but provide no liability protection. Sole proprietors can obtain liability protection by converting to a single-member LLC.

Describe the different types of entities for tax purposes. LO 4-2

- The four categories of business entities recognized by our tax system include: C corporations, S corporations, partnerships, and sole proprietorships.
- Legal corporations that don't make the S election are treated as C corporations and therefore pay taxes. All other entities recognized for tax purposes are flow-through entities.
- Legal corporations that qualify for and make the S election are treated as S corporations.
- Unincorporated entities with more than one owner are treated as partnerships.
- Unincorporated entities with one owner are treated as sole proprietorships where the sole owner is an individual or as a disregarded entity otherwise.

Identify fundamental differences in tax characteristics across entity types. LO 4-3

- Because C corporations and their shareholders pay taxes, C corporation income is double taxed. Corporations that retain earnings may be subject to the accumulated earnings tax or the personal holding company tax. These taxes eliminate the tax incentive for corporations to retain earnings.
- Shareholders in C corporations are taxed either when they receive dividends or when they sell their shares.
- Tax planning strategies applied at the corporate level to mitigate the double taxation of C corporations include paying salary to shareholder-employees, paying fringe benefits to shareholder-employees, leasing property from a shareholder, and borrowing money from and paying interest to shareholders. All of these strategies provide deductions to the corporation, which reduces corporate-level taxes. Shareholders are generally taxed when they receive these payments except when they receive qualified fringe benefits. In addition, corporations also mitigate the double tax by retaining income rather than paying dividends.
- Shareholders can mitigate the double tax by increasing the time they hold shares before selling.
- C corporation losses are referred to as net operating losses (NOLs). Generally, C corporations may carry an NOL back 2 years and forward up to 20 years to offset taxable income in those years. C corporation losses do not flow through to shareholders.
- Operating losses from S corporations and partnerships flow through to the owners. Owners may deduct these losses only to the extent of the basis in their ownership interest. The losses must also clear "at-risk" limitations and passive activity loss limitations in order for the owners to deduct the loss.
- The at-risk limitation is similar to the basis limitation. The passive activity loss limitations typically apply to individual investors who do little, if any, work relating to the business activities of the flow-through entity (referred to as *passive* activities to the individual investors). In these circumstances, the taxpayer can only deduct such losses to the extent they have income from other passive activities.
- C corporations may have one or many shareholders. S corporations may have one shareholder and as many as 100 unrelated shareholders; but corporations, nonresident aliens, partnerships, and certain trusts may not be S corporation shareholders. Partnerships must have at least two partners but are not restricted to a maximum number of partners. Sole proprietorships may have only one owner.
- Gains and income from contributing appreciated property to business entities are more easily deferred with partnerships compared to C and S corporations.

- S corporations, partnerships, and sole proprietorships are generally required to use tax year-ends conforming to the tax year-ends of their owners. C corporations may use any tax year-end.
- C corporations generally must use the accrual method unless they are a smaller corporation. S corporations may use either the cash or accrual method of accounting. Partnerships generally may use either the cash or accrual method. Sole proprietorships may use either the cash or accrual method.
- Income and losses may be specially allocated to partners based on the partnership agreement. This gives partnerships a great deal of flexibility in determining how the risks and rewards of the enterprise are shared among partners. In contrast, income and losses must be allocated pro rata to S corporation shareholders consistent with their ownership percentages.
- Shareholder-employees of C corporations or S corporations must pay FICA tax on their wages. However, shareholders of S corporations are not required to pay self-employment tax on business income allocated to them from S corporations. Owners providing services for an S corporation must receive a reasonable salary for their efforts.
- Owners of entities taxed as partnerships must pay self-employment taxes on compensation (guaranteed payments) they receive from the entity. Owners of entities taxed as a partnership generally must pay self-employment tax on business (operating) income allocated to them if the owner is actively involved in business.
- Partners, but not S corporation shareholders, may add their share of entity debt to their basis.
- Generally, distributions of appreciated property trigger gain at both the corporate and shareholder level when made to shareholders of C corporations, trigger gain at the corporate level when made to S corporation shareholders, and don't trigger any gain at all when made to partners.
- On liquidation, C and S corporations will generally recognize gains and losses on distributed assets. In contrast, partnerships and their partners generally do not recognize gains or losses on liquidating distributions.
- C corporations wanting to convert to a flow-through entity have two options. They may elect to become an S corporation if eligible, or they may liquidate the corporation and organize as a new entity. Taxes from liquidating C corporations are typically prohibitive when C corporations have appreciated assets.

KEY TERMS

accumulated earnings tax (4-11)
articles of incorporation (4-2)
articles of organization (4-2)
C corporation (4-5)
corporation (4-2)
certificate of limited partnership (4-2)
disregarded entities (4-5)
dividends received deduction (4-10)
double taxation (4-8)
flow-through entities (4-5)
general partnership (4-2)
initial public offering (4-3)
institutional shareholders (4-8)
limited liability company (4-2)
limited partnership (4-2)
net operating losses (4-14)
partnership agreement (4-2)
personal holding company (4-11)
personal holding company tax (4-11)
S corporation (4-5)
single-member LLCs (4-5)
sole proprietorship (4-2)

DISCUSSION QUESTIONS

LO 4-1 1. What are the most common legal entities used for operating a business? How are these entities treated similarly and differently for state law purposes?

LO 4-1 2. How do business owners create legal entities? Is the process the same for all entities? If not, what are the differences?

LO 4-1 3. What is an operating agreement for an LLC? Are operating agreements required for limited liability companies? If not, why might it be important to have one?

4. Explain how legal entities differ in terms of the liability protection they afford their owners. LO 4-1
5. Why are C corporations still popular despite the double tax on their income? LO 4-1
6. Why is it a nontax advantage for corporations to be able to trade their stock on the stock market? LO 4-1
7. How do corporations protect shareholders from liability? If you formed a small corporation, would you be able to avoid repaying a bank loan from your community bank if the corporation went bankrupt? Explain. LO 4-1
8. Other than corporations, are there other legal entities that offer liability protection? Are any of them taxed as flow-through entities? Explain. LO 4-1 LO 4-2
9. In general, how are unincorporated entities classified for tax purposes? LO 4-2
10. Can unincorporated legal entities ever be treated as corporations for tax purposes? Can corporations ever be treated as flow-through entities for tax purposes? Explain. LO 4-2
11. What are the differences, if any, between the legal and tax classification of business entities? LO 4-2
12. What types of business entities does the U.S. tax system recognize? LO 4-2
13. Who pays the first level of tax on a C corporation's income? What is the tax rate applicable to the first level of tax? LO 4-3
14. Who pays the second level of tax on a C corporation's income? What is the tax rate applicable to the second level of tax and when is it levied? LO 4-3
15. Is it possible for shareholders to defer or avoid the second level of tax on corporate income? Briefly explain. LO 4-3
16. How does a corporation's decision to pay dividends affect its overall tax rate [(corporate level tax + shareholder level tax)/taxable income]? LO 4-3
17. Is it possible for the overall tax rate on corporate taxable income to be lower than the tax rate on flow-through entity taxable income? If so, under what conditions would you expect the overall corporate tax rate to be lower? LO 4-3
18. Assume Congress increases individual tax rates on ordinary income while leaving all other tax rates unchanged. How would this change affect the overall tax rate on corporate taxable income? How would this change affect overall tax rates for owners of flow-through entities? LO 4-3
19. Assume Congress increases the dividend tax rate to the ordinary tax rate while leaving all other tax rates unchanged. How would this change affect the overall tax rate on corporate taxable income? LO 4-3
20. Evaluate the following statement: "When dividends and long-term capital gains are taxed at the same rate, the overall tax rate on corporate income is the same whether the corporation distributes its after-tax earnings as a dividend or whether it reinvests the after-tax earnings to increase the value of the corporation." LO 4-3
21. If XYZ corporation is a shareholder of BCD corporation, how many levels of tax is BCD's before-tax income potentially subject to? Has Congress provided any tax relief for this result? Explain. LO 4-3
22. How many times is income from a C corporation taxed if a retirement fund is the owner of the corporation's stock? Explain. LO 4-3
23. List four basic tax planning strategies that corporations and shareholders can use to mitigate double taxation of a C corporation's taxable income. LO 4-3
24. Explain why paying a salary to an employee-shareholder is an effective way to mitigate the double taxation of corporate income. LO 4-3

LO 4-3 25. What limits apply to the amount of deductible salary a corporation may pay to an employee-shareholder?

LO 4-3 26. Explain why the IRS would be concerned that a closely held C corporation only pay its shareholders reasonable compensation.

LO 4-3 research 27. When a corporation pays salary to a shareholder-employee beyond what is considered to be reasonable compensation, how is the salary in excess of what is reasonable treated for tax purposes? Is it subject to double taxation? [*Hint:* See Reg. §1.162-7(b)(1).]

LO 4-3 28. How can fringe benefits be used to mitigate the double taxation of corporate income?

LO 4-3 29. How many levels of taxation apply to corporate earnings paid out as qualified fringe benefits? Explain.

LO 4-3 30. How many levels of taxation apply to corporate earnings paid out as nonqualified fringe benefits? Explain.

LO 4-3 31. How can leasing property to a corporation be an effective method of mitigating the double tax on corporate income?

LO 4-3 32. When a corporation leases property from a shareholder and pays the shareholder at a higher than market rate, how is the excess likely to be classified by the IRS?

LO 4-3 33. How do shareholder loans to corporations mitigate the double tax of corporate income?

LO 4-3 34. Conceptually, what is the overall tax rate imposed on interest paid on loans from shareholders to corporations?

LO 4-3 35. If a corporation borrows money from a shareholder and pays the shareholder interest at a greater than market rate, how will the interest in excess of the market rate be treated by the IRS?

LO 4-3 36. When a C corporation reports a loss for the year, can shareholders use the loss to offset their personal income? Why or why not?

LO 4-3 37. Is a current-year net operating loss of a C corporation available to offset income from the corporation in other years? Explain.

LO 4-3 38. A C corporation has a current year loss of $100,000. The corporation had paid estimated taxes for the year of $10,000 and expects to have this amount refunded when it files its tax return. Is it possible that the corporation may receive a refund larger than $10,000? If so, how is it possible? If not, why not?

LO 4-3 39. What happens to a C corporation's net operating loss carryover after 20 years?

LO 4-3 40. Does a C corporation gain more tax benefit by carrying forward a net operating loss to offset other taxable income two years after the NOL arises or by carrying the NOL back two years? Explain.

LO 4-3 41. In its first year of existence, KES, an S corporation, reported a business loss of $10,000. Kim, KES's sole shareholder, reports $50,000 of taxable income from sources other than KES. What must you know to determine whether she can deduct the $10,000 loss against her other income? Explain.

LO 4-3 42. Why are S corporations less favorable than C corporations and entities taxed as partnerships in terms of owner-related limitations?

LO 4-3 43. Are C corporations or flow-through entities (S corporations and entities taxed as partnerships) more flexible in terms of selecting a tax year-end? Why are the tax rules in this area different for C corporations and flow-through entities?

LO 4-3 44. Which entity types are generally allowed to use the cash method of accounting?

LO 4-3 45. According to the tax rules, how are profits and losses allocated to LLC members? How are they allocated to S corporation shareholders? Which entity permits greater flexibility in allocating profits and losses?

46. Compare and contrast the FICA tax burden of S corporation shareholder-employees and LLC members receiving compensation for working for the entity (guaranteed payments) and business income allocations to S corporation shareholders and LLC members assuming the owners are actively involved in the entity's business activities. How does your analysis change if the owners are not actively involved in the entity's business activities? LO 4-3

47. Explain how liabilities of an LLC or an S corporation affect the amount of tax losses from the entity that limited liability company members and S corporation shareholders may deduct. Do the tax rules favor LLCs or S corporations? LO 4-3

48. Compare the entity level tax consequences for C corporations, S corporations, and partnerships for both nonliquidating and liquidating distributions of noncash property. Do the tax rules tend to favor one entity type more than the others? Explain. LO 4-3

49. If limited liability companies and S corporations are both taxed as flow-through entities for tax purposes, why might an owner prefer one form over the other for tax purposes? List separately the tax factors supporting the decision to operate as either an LLC or S corporation. LO 4-3

50. What are the tax advantages and disadvantages of converting a C corporation into an LLC? LO 4-3

PROBLEMS

All applicable problems are available with McGraw-Hill's *Connect® Accounting.*

51. Visit your state's official Web site and review the information there related to forming and operating business entities in your state. Write a short report explaining the steps for organizing a business in your state and summarizing any tax-related information you found. LO 4-1 research

52. Evon would like to organize SHO as either an LLC or as a C corporation generating an 11 percent annual before-tax return on a $200,000 investment. Assume individual and corporate tax rates are both 35 percent and individual capital gains and dividend tax rates are 15 percent. SHO will pay out its after-tax earnings every year as a dividend if it is formed as a C corporation. Assume Evon is the sole owner of the entity. Ignore self-employment taxes and the net investment income tax. LO 4-3
    a) How much would Evon keep after taxes if SHO is organized as either an LLC or as a C corporation?
    b) What are the overall tax rates if SHO is organized as either an LLC or as a C corporation?

53. Evon would like to organize SHO as either an S corporation or as a C corporation generating a 9 percent annual before-tax return on a $200,000 investment. Assume individual and corporate tax rates are both 35 percent and individual capital gains and dividend tax rates are 20 percent. SHO will pay out its after-tax earnings every year as a dividend if it is formed as a corporation. Assume Evon is the sole owner of the entity and ignore FICA taxes. Finally, assume Evon is actively involved in the business. LO 4-3
    a) How much would Evon keep after taxes if SHO is organized as either an S corporation or as a C corporation?
    b) What are the overall tax rates if SHO is organized as either an S corporation or as a C corporation?

LO 4-3

54. Jack would like to organize PPS as either an LLC or as a C corporation generating an 11 percent annual before-tax return on a $100,000 investment. Assume individual ordinary rates are 35 percent, corporate rates are 15 percent, and individual capital gains and dividends tax rates are 20 percent. PPS will pay out its after-tax earnings every year as a dividend if it is formed as a C corporation. Assume Jack is the sole owner of the entity and is actively involved in the business. Ignore self-employment taxes.
    a) How much would Jack keep after taxes if PPS is organized as either an LLC or as a C corporation?
    b) What are the overall tax rates if PPS is organized as either an LLC or as a C corporation?

LO 4-3 research

55. Using the web as a research tool, determine which countries levy a double tax on corporate income. Based on your research, what seem to be the pros and cons of the double tax?

LO 4-3

tax forms

56. Marathon Inc. (a C corporation) reported $1,000,000 of taxable income in the current year. During the year, it distributed $100,000 as dividends to its shareholders as follows:
    - $5,000 to Guy, a 5 percent individual shareholder.
    - $15,000 to Little Rock Corp. a 15 percent shareholder (C corporation).
    - $80,000 to other shareholders.

    a) How much of the dividend payment did Marathon deduct in determining its taxable income?
    b) Assuming Guy's marginal ordinary tax rate is 35 percent, how much tax will he pay on the $5,000 dividend he received from Marathon Inc.?
    c) Assuming Little Rock Corp.'s marginal tax rate is 34 percent, what amount of tax will it pay on the $15,000 dividend it received from Marathon Inc. (70 percent dividends received deduction)?
    d) Complete Form 1120 Schedule C for Little Rock Corp. to reflect its dividends received deduction.
    e) On what line of Little Rock Corp.'s Form 1120 page 1 is the dividend from Marathon Inc. reported, and on what line of Little Rock Corp.'s Form 1120 is its dividends received deduction reported?

LO 4-3 research

57. After several years of profitable operations, Javell, the sole shareholder of JBD Inc., a C corporation, sold 18 percent of her JBD stock to ZNO Inc., a C corporation in a similar industry. During the current year JBD reports $1,000,000 of after-tax income. JBD distributes all of its after-tax earnings to its two shareholders in proportion to their shareholdings. Assume ZNO's marginal tax rate is 35 percent. How much tax will ZNO pay on the dividend it receives from JBD? What is ZNO's overall tax rate on its dividend income? [*Hint:* See IRC §243(a).]

LO 4-3

58. For the current year, Custom Craft Services Inc. (CCS), a C corporation, reports taxable income of $200,000 before paying salary to Jaron the sole shareholder. Jaron's marginal tax rate on ordinary income is 35 percent and 15 percent on dividend income. Assume CCS's tax rate is 35 percent.
    a) How much total income tax will Custom Craft Services and Jaron pay (combining both corporate and shareholder level taxes) on the $200,000 taxable income for the year if CCS doesn't pay any salary to Jaron and instead distributes all of its after-tax income to Jaron as a dividend (ignore the net investment income tax)?
    b) How much total income tax will Custom Craft Services and Jaron pay (combining both corporate and shareholder level taxes) on the $200,000 of income if CCS pays Jaron a salary of $150,000 and distributes its remaining after-tax earnings to Jaron as a dividend (ignore the net investment income tax)?
    c) Why is the answer to part (b) lower than the answer to part (a)?

59. For the current year, Maple Corporation, a C corporation, reports taxable income of $200,000 before paying salary to its sole shareholder, Diane. Diane's marginal tax rate on ordinary income is 35 percent and 15 percent on dividend income. If Maple pays Diane a salary of $150,000 but the IRS determines that Diane's salary in excess of $80,000 is unreasonable compensation, what is the amount of the overall tax (corporate level + shareholder level) on Maple's $200,000 presalary income (ignore the net investment income tax)? Assume Maple's tax rate is 35 percent and it distributes all after-tax earnings to Diane. LO 4-3

60. Sandy Corp. projects that it will have taxable income of $150,000 for the year before paying any fringe benefits. Assume Karen, Sandy's sole shareholder, has a marginal tax rate of 35 percent on ordinary income and 15 percent on dividend income. Assume Sandy's tax rate is 35 percent. LO 4-3
   a) What is the amount of the overall tax (corporate level + shareholder level) on Sandy's $150,000 of pre-benefit income if Sandy Corp. does not pay out any fringe benefits and distributes all of its after-tax earnings to Karen (ignore the net investment income tax)?
   b) What is the amount of the overall tax on Sandy's $150,000 of pre-benefit income if Sandy Corp. pays Karen's adoption expenses of $10,000 and the payment is considered to be a nontaxable fringe benefit (ignore the net investment income tax)? Sandy Corp. distributes all of its after-tax earnings to Karen.
   c) What is the amount of the overall tax on Sandy's $150,000 of pre-benefit income if Sandy Corp. pays Karen's adoption expenses of $10,000 and the payment is considered to be a taxable fringe benefit (ignore the net investment income tax)? Sandy Corp. distributes all of its after-tax earnings to Karen.

61. Jabar Corporation, a C corporation, projects that it will have taxable income of $300,000 before incurring any lease expenses. Jabar's tax rate is 35 percent. Abdul, Jabar's sole shareholder, has a marginal tax rate of 39.6 percent on ordinary income and 20 percent on dividend income. Jabar always distributes all of its after-tax earnings to Abdul. LO 4-3
   a) What is the amount of the overall tax (corporate level + shareholder level) on Jabar Corp.'s $300,000 prelease expense income if Jabar Corp. distributes all of its after-tax earnings to its sole shareholder, Abdul (include the net investment income tax on dividend and rental income)?
   b) What is the amount of the overall tax on Jabar Corp.'s $300,000 prelease expense income if Jabar leases equipment from Abdul at a cost of $30,000 for the year (include the net investment income tax on dividend and rental income)?
   c) What is the amount of the overall tax on Jabar Corp.'s $300,000 prelease expense income if Jabar Corp. leases equipment from Abdul at a cost of $30,000 for the year but the IRS determines that the fair market value of the lease payments is $25,000 (include the net investment income tax on dividend and rental income)?

62. Nutt Corporation projects that it will have taxable income for the year of $400,000 before incurring any interest expense. Assume Nutt's tax rate is 35 percent. LO 4-3
   a) What is the amount of the overall tax (corporate level + shareholder level) on the $400,000 of preinterest expense earnings if Hazel, Nutt's sole shareholder, lends Nutt Corporation $30,000 at the beginning of the year, Nutt pays Hazel $8,000 of interest on the loan (interest is considered to be reasonable), and Nutt distributes all of its after-tax earnings to Hazel (ignore the net investment income tax)? Assume her ordinary marginal rate is 35 percent and dividend tax rate is 15 percent.
   b) Assume the same facts as in part (a) except that the IRS determines that the fair market value of the interest should be $6,000. What is the amount of

the overall tax on Nutt Corporation's preinterest expense earnings (ignore the net investment income tax)?

LO 4-3 research

63. Ultimate Comfort Blankets Inc. has had a great couple of years and wants to distribute its earnings while avoiding double taxation on its income. It decides to give its sole shareholder, Laura, a salary of $1,500,000 in the current year. What factors would the courts examine to determine if Laura's salary is reasonable? [*Hint:* See Elliotts, Inc. v. Commissioner, 716 F.2d 1241 (9th Cir. 1983)].

LO 4-3

64. Alice, the sole shareholder of QLP, decided that she would purchase a building and then lease it to QLP. She leased the building to QLP for $1,850 per month. However, the IRS determined that the fair market value of the lease payment should only be $1,600 per month. How would the lease payment be treated with respect to both Alice and QLP?

LO 4-3

65. In its first year of existence (year 1), SCC Corporation (a C corporation) reported a loss for tax purposes of $30,000. Using the corporate tax rate table, determine how much tax SCC will pay in year 2 if it reports taxable income from operations of $20,000 in year 2 before any loss carryovers.

LO 4-3

66. In its first year of existence (year 1), Willow Corp. (a C corporation) reported a loss for tax purposes of $30,000. In year 2 it reports a $40,000 loss. For year 3, it reports taxable income from operations of $100,000 before any loss carryovers. Using the corporate tax rate table, determine how much tax Willow Corp. will pay for year 3.

LO 4-3 planning tax forms

67. In its first year of existence (year 1), WCC Corporation (a C corporation) reported taxable income of $170,000 and paid $49,550 of federal income tax. In year 2, WCC reported a net operating loss of $40,000. WCC projects that it will report $800,000 of taxable income from its year 3 activities.

a) Based on its projections, should WCC carry back its year 2 NOL to year 1, or should it forgo the carryback and carry the year 2 NOL forward to year 3?
b) Assuming WCC corporation carries back its year 2 NOL to year 1, prepare a Form 1139 "Corporation Application for Tentative Refund" for WCC Corporation to reflect the NOL carryback. Use reasonable assumptions to fill in missing information.

LO 4-3

68. Damarcus is a 50 percent owner of Hoop (a business entity). In the current year, Hoop reported a $100,000 business loss. Answer the following questions associated with each of the following alternative scenarios.

a) Hoop is organized as a C corporation and Damarcus works full-time as an employee for Hoop. Damarcus has a $20,000 basis in his Hoop stock. How much of Hoop's loss is Damarcus allowed to deduct this year?
b) Hoop is organized as an LLC. Fifty percent of Hoop's loss is allocated to Damarcus. Damarcus works full-time for Hoop (he is not considered to be a passive investor in Hoop). Damarcus has a $20,000 basis in his Hoop ownership interest and he also has a $20,000 at-risk amount in his investment in Hoop. Damarcus does not report income or loss from any other business activity investments. How much of the $50,000 loss allocated to him by Hoop is Damarcus allowed to deduct this year?
c) Hoop is organized as an LLC. Fifty percent of Hoop's loss is allocated to Damarcus. Damarcus does not work for Hoop at all (he is a passive investor in Hoop). Damarcus has a $20,000 basis in his Hoop ownership interest and he also has a $20,000 at-risk amount in his investment in Hoop. Damarcus does not report income or loss from any other business activity investments. How much of the $50,000 loss allocated to him by Hoop is Damarcus allowed to deduct this year?

d) Hoop is organized as an LLC. Fifty percent of Hoop's loss is allocated to Damarcus. Damarcus works full-time for Hoop (he is not considered to be a passive investor in Hoop). Damarcus has a $70,000 basis in his Hoop ownership interest and he also has a $70,000 at-risk amount in his investment in Hoop. Damarcus does not report income or loss from any other business activity investments. How much of the $50,000 loss allocated to him by Hoop is Damarcus allowed to deduct this year?

e) Hoop is organized as an LLC. Fifty percent of Hoop's loss is allocated to Damarcus. Damarcus does not work for Hoop at all (he is a passive investor in Hoop). Damarcus has a $70,000 basis in his Hoop ownership interest and he also has a $70,000 at-risk amount in his investment in Hoop. Damarcus does not report income or loss from any other business activity investments. How much of the $50,000 loss allocated to him by Hoop is Damarcus allowed to deduct this year?

f) Hoop is organized as an LLC. Fifty percent of Hoop's loss is allocated to Damarcus. Damarcus does not work for Hoop at all (he is a passive investor in Hoop). Damarcus has a $20,000 basis in his Hoop ownership interest and he also has a $20,000 at-risk amount in his investment in Hoop. Damarcus reports $10,000 of income from a business activity in which he is a passive investor. How much of the $50,000 loss allocated to him by Hoop is Damarcus allowed to deduct this year?

LO 4-3

research

69. Mickey, Mickayla, and Taylor are starting a new business (MMT). To get the business started, Mickey is contributing $200,000 for a 40 percent ownership interest, Mickayla is contributing a building with a value of $200,000 and a tax basis of $150,000 for a 40 percent ownership interest, and Taylor is contributing legal services for a 20 percent ownership interest. What amount of gain is each owner required to recognize under each of the following alterative situations? [*Hint:* Look at §351 and §721.]

a) MMT is formed as a C corporation.

b) MMT is formed as an S corporation.

c) MMT is formed as a LLC.

LO 4-3

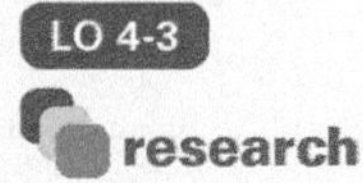

70. Dave and his friend Stewart each own 50 percent of KBS. During the year, Dave receives $75,000 compensation for services he performs for KBS during the year. He performed a significant amount of work for the entity and he was heavily involved in management decisions (he was not a passive investor in KBS). After deducting Dave's compensation, KBS reports taxable income of $30,000. How much FICA and/or self-employment tax is Dave required to pay on his compensation and his share of the KBS income if KBS is formed as a C corporation, S corporation, or a limited liability company (ignore the .9 percent additional Medicare tax)?

LO 4-3

71. Rondo and his business associate, Larry, are considering forming a business entity called R&L but they are unsure about whether to form it as a C corporation, an S corporation or as an LLC. Rondo and Larry would each invest $50,000 in the business. Thus, each owner would take an initial basis in his ownership interest of $50,000 no matter which entity type was formed. Shortly after the formation of the entity, the business borrowed $30,000 from the bank. If applicable, this debt is shared equally between the two owners.

a) After taking the loan into account, what is Rondo's tax basis in his R&L stock if R&L is formed as a C corporation?

b) After taking the loan into account, what is Rondo's tax basis in his R&L stock if R&L is formed as an S corporation?

c) After taking the loan into account, what is Rondo's tax basis in his R&L ownership interest if R&L is formed as an LLC?

LO 4-3

72. Kevin and Bob have owned and operated SOA as a C corporation for a number of years. When they formed the entity, Kevin and Bob each contributed $100,000 to SOA. They each have a current basis of $100,000 in their SOA ownership interest. Information on SOA's assets at the end of year 5 is as follows (SOA does not have any liabilities):

Assets	FMV	Adjusted Basis	Built-in Gain
Cash	$200,000	$200,000	$ 0
Inventory	80,000	40,000	40,000
Land and building	220,000	170,000	50,000
Total	$500,000		

At the end of year 5, SOA liquidated and distributed half of the land, half of the inventory, and half of the cash remaining after paying taxes (if any) to each owner. Assume that, excluding the effects of the liquidating distribution, SOA's taxable income for year 5 is $0. Also, assume that if SOA is required to pay tax, it pays at a flat 30 percent tax rate.

a) What is the amount and character of gain or loss SOA will recognize on the liquidating distribution?

b) What is the amount and character of gain or loss Kevin will recognize when he receives the liquidating distribution of cash and property? Recall that his stock basis is $100,000 and he is treated as having sold his stock for the liquidation proceeds.

COMPREHENSIVE PROBLEMS

73. Dawn Taylor is currently employed by the state Chamber of Commerce. While she enjoys the relatively short workweeks, she eventually would like to work for herself rather than for an employer. In her current position, she deals with a lot of successful entrepreneurs who have become role models for her. Dawn has also developed an extensive list of contacts that should serve her well when she starts her own business.

It has taken a while but Dawn believes she has finally developed a viable new business idea. Her idea is to design and manufacture cookware that remains cool to the touch when in use. She has had several friends try out her prototype cookware and they have consistently given the cookware rave reviews. With this encouragement, Dawn started giving serious thoughts to making "Cool Touch Cookware" (CTC) a moneymaking enterprise.

Dawn has enough business background to realize that she is embarking on a risky path, but one, she hopes, with significant potential rewards down the road. After creating some initial income projections, Dawn realized that it will take a few years for the business to become profitable. After that, she hopes the sky's the limit. She would like to grow her business and perhaps at some point "go public" or sell the business to a large retailer. This could be her ticket to the rich and famous.

Dawn, who is single, decided to quit her job with the state Chamber of Commerce so that she could focus all of her efforts on the new business. Dawn had some savings to support her for a while but she did not have any other source of income. Dawn was able to recruit Linda and Mike to join her as initial equity investors in CTC. Linda has an MBA and a law degree. She was employed as a business consultant when she decided to leave that job and work with Dawn and Mike. Linda's husband earns around $300,000 a year as an engineer (employee). Mike owns a *very* profitable used car business. Because buying and selling used cars takes all his time, he is interested in becoming only a passive investor in CTC. He wanted to get in on the ground floor because he really likes the product and believes CTC will be wildly successful. While CTC originally has three investors, Dawn and Linda have plans to grow the business and seek more owners and capital in the future.

The three owners agreed that Dawn would contribute land and cash for a 30 percent interest in CTC, Linda would contribute services (legal and business advisory) for the first two years for a 30 percent interest, and Mike would contribute cash for a 40 percent interest. The plan called for Dawn and Linda to be actively involved in managing the business while Mike would not be. The three equity owners' contributions are summarized as follows:

Dawn Contributed	FMV	Adjusted Basis	Ownership Interest
Land (held as investment)	$120,000	$70,000	30%
Cash	$ 30,000		
Linda Contributed			
Services	$150,000		30%
Mike Contributed			
Cash	$200,000		40%

Working together, Dawn and Linda made the following five-year income and loss projections for CTC. They anticipate the business will be profitable and that it will continue to grow after the first five years.

Cool Touch Cookware
5-Year Income and Loss Projections

Year	Income (Loss)
1	$(200,000)
2	(80,000)
3	(20,000)
4	60,000
5	180,000

With plans for Dawn and Linda to spend a considerable amount of their time working for and managing CTC, the owners would like to develop a compensation plan that works for all parties. Down the road, they plan to have two business locations (in different cities). Dawn would take responsibility for the activities of one location and Linda would take responsibility for the other. Finally, they would like to arrange for some performance-based financial incentives for each location.

To get the business activities started, Dawn and Linda determined CTC would need to borrow $800,000 to purchase a building to house its manufacturing facilities and its administrative offices (at least for now). Also, in need of additional cash, Dawn and Linda arranged to have CTC borrow $300,000 from a local bank and to borrow $200,000 cash from Mike. CTC would pay Mike a market rate of interest on the loan but there was no fixed date for principal repayment.

Required:

Identify significant tax and nontax issues or concerns that may differ across entity types and discuss how they are relevant to the choice of entity decision for CTC.

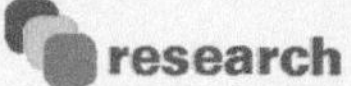

74. Cool Touch Cookware (CTC) has been in business for about 10 years now. Dawn and Linda are each 50 percent owners of the business. They initially established the business with cash contributions. CTC manufactures unique cookware that remains cool to the touch when in use. CTC has been fairly profitable over the years. Dawn and Linda have both been actively involved in managing the business. They have developed very good personal relationships with many customers (both wholesale and retail) that, Dawn and Linda believe, keep the customers coming back.

    On September 30 of the current year, CTC had all of its assets appraised. Below is CTC's balance sheet, as of September 30, with the corresponding appraisals of the fair market value of all of its assets. Note that CTC has several depreciated assets. CTC uses the hybrid method of accounting. It accounts for its gross margin-related items under the accrual method and it accounts for everything else using the cash method of accounting.

Assets	Adjusted Tax Basis	FMV
Cash	$150,000	$150,000
Accounts receivable	20,000	15,000
Inventory*	90,000	300,000
Equipment	120,000	100,000
Investment in XYZ stock	40,000	120,000
Land (used in the business)	80,000	70,000
Building	200,000	180,000
Total assets	$700,000	$935,000†
Liabilities		
Accounts payable	$ 40,000	
Bank loan	60,000	
Mortgage on building	100,000	
Equity	500,000	
Total liabilities and equity	$700,000	

*CTC uses the LIFO method for determining the adjusted basis of its inventory. Its basis in the inventory under the FIFO method would have been $110,000.

†In addition, Dawn and Linda had the entire business appraised at $1,135,000, which is $200,000 more than the value of the identifiable assets.

From January 1 of the current year through September 30, CTC reported the following income:

Ordinary business income	$530,000
Dividends from XYZ stock	12,000
Long-term capital losses	15,000
Interest income	3,000

Dawn and Linda are considering changing the business form of CTC.

Required:

a) Assume CTC is organized as a C corporation. Identify significant tax and nontax issues associated with converting CTC from a C corporation to an S corporation. [*Hint:* See IRC §1374 and §1363(d).]

b) Assume CTC is organized as a C corporation. Identify significant tax and nontax issues associated with converting CTC from a C corporation to an LLC. Assume CTC converts to an LLC by distributing its assets to its shareholders who then contribute the assets to a new LLC. [*Hint:* See IRC §§331, 336, and 721(a).]

c) Assume that CTC is a C corporation with a net operating loss carryforward as of the beginning of the year in the amount of $2,000,000. Identify significant tax and nontax issues associated with converting CTC from a C corporation to an LLC. Assume CTC converts to an LLC by distributing its assets to its shareholders who then contribute the assets to a new LLC. [*Hint:* See IRC §§172(a), 331, 336, and 721(a).]

chapter

5 Corporate Operations

Learning Objectives

Upon completing this chapter, you should be able to:

LO 5-1 Describe the corporate income tax formula, compare and contrast the corporate tax formula to the individual tax formula, and discuss tax considerations relating to corporations' accounting periods and accounting methods.

LO 5-2 Identify common book–tax differences, distinguish between permanent and temporary differences, and compute a corporation's taxable income and regular tax liability.

LO 5-3 Describe a corporation's tax return reporting and estimated tax payment obligations.

LO 5-4 Calculate a corporation's alternative minimum tax liability.

© Sam Edwards/age fotostock

Storyline Summary

Premiere Computer Corporation (PCC)
Medium-sized publicly traded company
Manufactures and sells computer-related equipment
Calendar-year taxpayer

Elise Brandon
Newly hired tax associate for a large public accounting firm
Currently assigned to prepare the federal income tax return for PCC

Today was Elise's first day on the job as a tax associate for a public accounting firm. Shortly after she arrived, Darryl, a tax manager, introduced himself and took Elise around the office to meet some of the people with whom she would be working. After the introductions, Darryl told Elise he would like her to work with him to prepare the tax return for Premiere Computer Corporation (PCC).

PCC is a medium-sized publicly traded taxable corporation (C corporation) that manufactures computers and computer equipment. It has been a client of the firm for several years. Overall, PCC has been a fairly profitable company, but last year it experienced a bit of a setback, incurring its first tax loss in many years.

Elise was excited about her opportunity, and she was confident her accounting education had adequately prepared her to successfully complete the assignment. In fact, her tax class was her favorite class. She had studied hard and learned all about computing corporate taxable income. When Elise spoke with Darryl about the assignment, he advised her to first review PCC's tax return and tax return workpapers from last year to get an idea how to prepare the return. Next, she should start with the audited numbers on the income statement and make book-to-tax adjustments for the items that are accounted for differently for book and tax purposes. Once she makes these adjustments, Elise will input the numbers into the firm's tax preparation software package to produce the return. Because Darryl would be reviewing the return, he told Elise to stay in close contact and let him know if she had any questions.

to be continued . . .

This chapter explores computing and reporting taxable income for taxable corporations (also known as *C corporations*). As we discussed in the previous chapter, C corporations are legal and taxpaying entities separate from their owners. Each year, C corporations are required to compute their taxable income and pay tax on the income. In contrast to individuals, C corporations generally compute their taxable income by starting with their book (financial accounting) income and making adjustments for book–tax differences.

LO 5-1

CORPORATE TAXABLE INCOME FORMULA

The formula for computing corporate taxable income and individual taxable income is similar in some respects and different in others. Exhibit 5-1 presents the corporate income tax formula along with the individual tax formula for comparison purposes.

EXHIBIT 5-1 Corporate and Individual Tax Formulas

	Corporate Tax Formula	Individual Tax Formula
	Gross income	Gross income
Minus:	Deductions	*For* AGI deductions
Equals		Adjusted gross income
Minus:		*From* AGI deductions
		(1) *Greater* of:
		(a) Standard deduction or
		(b) Itemized deductions and
		(2) Personal and dependency exemptions
Equals	Taxable income	Taxable income
Times	Tax rates	Tax rates
Equals	Regular income tax liability	Regular income tax liability
Add	Other taxes	Other taxes
Equals	Total tax	Total tax
Minus	Credits	Credits
Minus	Prepayments	Prepayments
Equals	Taxes due or (refund)	Taxes due or (refund)

THE KEY FACTS

Corporate Taxable Income Formula and Accounting Periods and Methods

- The corporate tax formula is similar to the individual tax formula, but corporations don't itemize deductions or deduct personal and dependency exemptions.
- Corporations with average gross receipts of $5 million or less over the three prior tax years (or a shorter period for new corporations) may use the cash method.

Corporations compute gross income as do other types of business entities and individual taxpayers. However, in contrast to individual taxpayers, corporations do not report adjusted gross income (AGI). Similar to other businesses, corporations are allowed to deduct ordinary and necessary business expenditures (see discussion in Chapter 1). In contrast to individual taxpayers, corporations treat all deductions as related to a trade or business and do not compute adjusted gross income. Corporations do not receive a standard deduction or exemptions. Consequently, the "formula" to compute a corporation's taxable income is relatively straightforward.

Accounting Periods and Methods

In Chapter 1, we discussed accounting periods and methods for all types of business entities. We learned that corporations measure their taxable income over a tax year and that their tax year must be the same as their financial accounting year. Corporations generally elect their tax year when they file their first income tax returns.

The timing of when corporations recognize income and deductions depends on their accounting methods. As we discussed in Chapter 1, accounting methods include overall methods of accounting (accrual method, cash method, or hybrid method) and accounting methods for individual items such as inventory (LIFO vs. FIFO) or depreciation (accelerated vs. straight line). For tax purposes, corporations have some flexibility in choosing methods of accounting for individual items or transactions. However, corporations generally are required to use the accrual overall method of accounting.[1] For tax purposes, corporations with average gross receipts of $5 million or less for the three years prior to the current tax year may use the cash method of accounting.[2] Corporations that have not been in existence for at least three years compute their average gross receipts over the prior periods they have been in existence to determine if they are allowed to use the cash method of accounting.

TAXES IN THE REAL WORLD Choosing Tax Accounting Methods

For certain transaction types, corporations face an interesting choice when choosing from permissible accounting methods. A corporation could choose an accounting method that tends to defer income or accelerate deductions from certain types of transactions or it could choose a method that tends to accelerate income or defer deductions. A research study by accounting professors provides evidence that when faced with this decision, publicly traded corporations tend to select income *accelerating* methods while privately held corporations tend to select income *deferring* methods.[3] Why the difference? Recall that generally speaking, the tax treatment of a transaction follows the book treatment. Publicly traded corporations are generally more concerned with increasing financial statement income to impress stockholders and potential investors. If corporations have to report higher levels of taxable income and pay more taxes as a result, that's OK. Privately held corporations are just the opposite. They don't need to impress the shareholders with accelerated earnings. They would rather reap the benefits of paying less current taxes even if it means reporting lower book income. This research illustrates the fact that nontax considerations may be more important than tax factors in the decision-making process. *After all, a business's objective should not be to minimize taxes but rather to maximize after-tax cash-flows.*

COMPUTING CORPORATE REGULAR TAXABLE INCOME

LO 5-2

To compute taxable income, most corporations start with **book (financial reporting) income** and then make adjustments for book–tax differences to reconcile to the tax numbers.[4] Privately held corporations may use tax accounting rules for book purposes. These corporations need not make adjustments for book–tax differences.

Book–Tax Differences

Many items of income and expense are accounted for differently for book and tax purposes. The following discussion describes several common **book–tax differences** applicable to corporations. Each book–tax difference can be considered to be

[1]See Chapter 1 for a detailed discussion of determining the timing of taxable income and tax deductions under the accrual method.

[2]§448. Other special types of corporations such as qualified family farming corporations and qualified personal service corporations may use the cash method of accounting.

[3]See C. B. Cloyd, J. Pratt, and T. Stock, "The Use of Financial Accounting Choice to Support Aggressive Tax Positions: Public and Private Firms," *Journal of Accounting Research* 34 (Spring 1996), pp. 23–43.

[4]This chapter generally assumes that GAAP is used to determine book income numbers.

"unfavorable" or "favorable" depending on its effect on taxable income relative to book income. Any book–tax difference that requires an add back to book income to compute taxable income is an **unfavorable book–tax difference** because it requires an adjustment that increases taxable income (and taxes payable) relative to book income. Any book–tax difference that requires corporations to subtract the difference from book income in computing taxable income is a **favorable book–tax difference** because it decreases taxable income (and taxes payable) relative to book income.

In addition to the favorable/unfavorable distinction, book–tax differences also can be categorized as permanent or temporary differences. **Permanent book–tax differences** arise from items that are income or deductions during the year for either book purposes or for tax purposes but not both. Permanent differences *do not reverse* over time, so over the long-run the *total* amount of income or deductions for the items is different for book and tax purposes. In contrast, **temporary book–tax differences** are those book–tax differences that reverse over time such that over the long-term, corporations recognize the same amount of income or deductions for the items on their financial statements as they recognize on their tax returns. Temporary book–tax differences arise because the income or deduction items are included in financial accounting income in one year and in taxable income in a different year. It also is important to note that temporary book–tax differences that are *initially* favorable (unfavorable) subsequently will become unfavorable (favorable) in future years when they reverse.

THE KEY FACTS

Computing Corporate Regular Taxable Income

- Corporations reconcile from book income to taxable income.
  - Favorable (unfavorable) book–tax differences decrease (increase) book income relative to taxable income.
  - Permanent book–tax differences arise in one year and never reverse.
  - Temporary book–tax differences arise in one year and reverse in a subsequent year.

Distinguishing between permanent and temporary book–tax differences is important for at least two reasons. First, as we discuss later in the chapter, large corporations are *required to disclose* their permanent and temporary book–tax differences on their tax returns. Second, the distinction is useful for those responsible for computing and tracking book–tax differences. For temporary book–tax differences, it is important to understand how the items were accounted for in previous years to appropriately account for current year reversals. In contrast, for permanent book–tax differences, corporations need only consider current year amounts to determine book–tax differences. Although small corporations may report only a few book–tax differences, large corporations may report hundreds. Below we describe some of the most common book–tax differences.

Common Permanent Book–Tax Differences As we previously described in Chapter 1, businesses, including corporations, are allowed to exclude certain income items from gross income, and they are not allowed to deduct certain expenditures for tax purposes. Because these income items are included in book income, and the expenditures are deductible for financial reporting purposes, they generate permanent book–tax differences. Exhibit 5-2 identifies several permanent book–tax differences associated with items we discuss in Chapter 1, explains their tax treatment, and identifies whether the items create favorable or unfavorable book–tax differences.

Example 5-1

Elise reviewed PCC's prior year tax return and its current year trial balance. She discovered that PCC earned $12,000 of interest income from City of San Diego municipal bonds (bonds issued in 2013), expensed $34,000 for premiums on key employee life insurance policies, expensed $28,000 in meals and entertainment expenses for the year, and reported a domestic production activities deduction of $465,000. What amount of permanent book–tax differences does PCC report from these transactions? Are the differences favorable or unfavorable?

Answer: See Elise's summary of these items below:

Item	Adjustment (Favorable) Unfavorable	Notes
Interest income from City of San Diego municipal bonds (bonds issued in 2013)	($12,000)	Income excluded from gross income. Bond proceeds used to help fund *privately owned* baseball stadium.
Premiums paid for key employee life insurance policies	34,000	Premiums paid to insure lives of key company executives are not deductible for tax purposes.
Meals and entertainment	14,000	$28,000 expense for book purposes, but only 50 percent deductible for tax purposes.
Domestic production activities deduction	(465,000)	$5,166,667 qualified production activities income (QPAI) × 9%.

EXHIBIT 5-2 Common Permanent Book–Tax Differences Associated with Items Discussed in Chapter 1

Description	Explanation	Difference
Interest income from municipal bonds	Income included in book income, excluded from taxable income	Favorable
Death benefit from life insurance on key employees	Income included in book income, excluded from taxable income	Favorable
Interest expense on loans to acquire investments generating tax-exempt income	Deductible for books, but expenses incurred to generate tax-exempt income are not deductible for tax	Unfavorable
Life insurance premiums for which corporation is beneficiary	Deductible for books, but expenses incurred to generate tax-exempt income (life insurance death benefit) are not deductible for tax	Unfavorable
Meals and entertainment expenses	Fully deductible for books, but only 50 percent deductible for tax	Unfavorable
Fines and penalties and political contributions	Deductible for books, but not for tax	Unfavorable
Domestic production activities deduction (DPAD)	Deduction for businesses involved in manufacturing activities in the U.S. equal to the lesser of 9 percent of the company's qualified production activities income (QPAI) or taxable income computed without the DPAD (i.e., the DPAD cannot create a NOL)	Favorable

Federal income tax expense. Corporations deduct federal income tax expense (called a provision for income taxes) in determining their book income [determined under ASC (Accounting Standards Codification) 740 (the codification of FAS 109)]. However, they are not allowed to deduct federal income tax expense for tax purposes.[5] The book–tax provision acts as a permanent difference if the corporation is reconciling after-tax book income with taxable income.

[5]§275(a)(1).

Example 5-2

What if: Assume that PCC's audited financial reporting income statement indicates that its federal income tax provision (expense) is $2,000,000.[6] What is PCC's book–tax difference for the year associated with this expense? Is the difference favorable or unfavorable? Is it permanent or temporary?

Answer: $2,000,000 unfavorable, permanent book–tax difference because PCC is not allowed to deduct federal income tax expense for tax purposes.

Common Temporary Book–Tax Differences Corporations experience temporary book–tax differences because the accounting methods they apply to determine certain items of income and expense for financial reporting purposes differ from those they use for tax purposes. Unlike permanent book–tax differences, temporary book–tax differences balance out over time so that corporations eventually recognize the same amount of income or deduction for the particular item. Exhibit 5-3 identifies

EXHIBIT 5-3 Common Temporary Book–Tax Differences Associated with Items Discussed in Other Chapters

Description	Explanation	Initial Difference*
Depreciation expense (Chapter 2)	Difference between accelerated depreciation expense for tax purposes and straight-line depreciation expense for book purposes.	Favorable
Gain or loss on disposition of depreciable assets (Chapter 3)	Difference between gain or loss for tax and book purposes when corporation sells or disposes of depreciable property. Difference generally arises because depreciation expense, and thus the adjusted basis of the asset, is different for tax and book purposes. This difference is essentially the reversal of the book–tax difference for the depreciation expense on the asset sold or disposed of.	Unfavorable
Bad debt expense (Chapter 1)	Direct write-off method for tax purposes, allowance method for book purposes.	Unfavorable
Unearned rent revenue (Chapter 1)	Taxable on receipt but recognized when earned for book purposes.	Unfavorable
Deferred compensation (Chapter 1)	Deductible when accrued for book purposes, but deductible when paid for tax purposes if accrued but not paid within 2.5 months after year-end. Also, accrued compensation to shareholders owning more than 50 percent of the corporation is not deductible until paid.	Unfavorable
Organizational expenses and start-up costs (Chapter 2)	Immediately deducted for book purposes but capitalized and amortized for tax purposes (limited immediate expensing allowed for tax).	Unfavorable
Warranty expense and other estimated expenses (Chapter 1)	Estimated expenses deducted for book purposes, but actual expenses deducted for tax purposes.	Unfavorable
UNICAP (§263A) (Chapter 1)	Certain expenditures deducted for book purposes, but capitalized to inventory for tax purposes. Difference reverses when inventory is sold.	Unfavorable

*Note that each of the initial book–tax differences will reverse over time [the initially favorable (unfavorable) book–tax differences will reverse to become unfavorable (favorable) book–tax differences in the future].

[6]Note that this example is presented in *what-if* form because this is not the income tax expense PCC will report in its financial statements. We compute PCC's actual income tax expense in Chapter 6.

common book–tax differences associated with items we discuss in other chapters. Exhibit 5-4 summarizes PCC's temporary book–tax differences described in Exhibit 5-3.

EXHIBIT 5-4 PCC's Temporary Book–Tax Differences Associated with Items Discussed in Other Chapters

Item	(1) Books (Dr) Cr	(2) Tax (Dr) Cr	(2) − (1) Difference (Favorable) Unfavorable
Depreciation expense	($2,400,000)	($3,100,000)	($700,000)
Gain on fixed asset disposition	54,000	70,000	16,000
Bad debt expense	(165,000)	(95,000)	70,000
Warranty expense	(580,000)	(410,000)	170,000
Deferred compensation	(300,000)	(450,000)	(150,000)

Dividends. Corporations receiving dividends from other corporations may account for the dividends in different ways for book and tax purposes. For tax purposes, corporations receiving dividends include the dividends in gross income.[7] For financial reporting purposes, accounting for the dividend (and investment in the corporation) depends on the level of ownership in the distributing corporation. The *general* rules for such investments are summarized as follows:

- If the receiving corporation owns less than 20 percent of the stock of the distributing corporation, the receiving corporation includes the dividend in income (same as tax; no book–tax difference).
- If the receiving corporation owns at least 20 percent but not more than 50 percent of the distributing corporation's stock, the receiving corporation includes a pro rata portion of the distributing corporation's earnings in its income under the equity method of accounting and does not include the dividend in its income (temporary favorable or unfavorable book–tax difference for the difference between the pro rata share of income and the amount of the dividend).
- If the receiving corporation owns more than 50 percent of the distributing corporation's stock, the receiving corporation and the distributing corporation consolidate their financial reporting and the intercompany dividend is eliminated (book–tax difference beyond the scope of the text).[8]

Example 5-3

What if: Assume that PCC owns 30 percent of the stock of BCS corporation. During 2015, BCS distributed a $40,000 dividend to PCC. BCS reported $100,000 of net income for 2015. Based on this information, what is PCC's 2015 book–tax difference relating to the dividend and its investment in BCS (ignore the dividends received deduction)? Is the difference favorable or unfavorable?

(continued on page 5-8)

[7]As we discuss later in the chapter, corporations are entitled to deduct a certain percentage of the dividends received based on the level of the receiving corporation's ownership in the distributing corporation.

[8]Note that 80 percent ownership is required to file a consolidated tax return.

Answer: $10,000 unfavorable book–tax difference, computed as follows:

Description	Amount	Explanation
(1) Dividend received in 2015 (included in 2015 taxable income but not in book income)	$ 40,000	
(2) BCS 2015 net income	$100,000	
(3) PCC's ownership in BCS stock	30%	
(4) PCC's book income from BCS investment	$ 30,000	(2) × (3).
Unfavorable book–tax difference associated with dividend	**$ 10,000**	(1) − (4).

What if: Assume the same facts as above, except that PCC owns 10 percent of BCS rather than 30 percent. What would be PCC's 2015 book–tax difference relating to the dividend and its investment in BCS (ignore the dividends received deduction)?

Answer: $0. PCC includes the $40,000 dividend in income for both book and tax purposes.

Goodwill acquired in an asset acquisition. When a corporation acquires the *assets* of another business in a taxable transaction, and it allocates part of the purchase price to goodwill (excess purchase price over the fair market value of identifiable assets acquired), the corporation is allowed to amortize this purchased goodwill on a straight-line basis over 15 years (180 months) for tax purposes.[9] For book purposes, corporations acquiring the assets of another business also allocate part of the purchase price to goodwill. Generally speaking in these asset acquisitions, the amount of goodwill corporations recognize for tax purposes can be the same as, or different from, the amount they recognize for book purposes. Corporations recover the cost of goodwill for book purposes only when and only to the extent goodwill is impaired. Thus, to determine the *temporary* book–tax difference associated with purchased goodwill, corporations generally compare the amount of goodwill they amortize for tax purposes with the goodwill impairment expense for book purposes. If the tax amortization exceeds the book impairment expense, corporations report favorable book–tax differences. If the book impairment expense exceeds the goodwill tax amortization, corporations report unfavorable book–tax differences for goodwill.[10]

Example 5-4

What if: Suppose that on July 1, 2015, PCC acquired the assets of another business in a taxable acquisition. As part of the transaction, PCC recognized $180,000 of goodwill for both financial accounting and tax purposes. During 2015, PCC amortized $6,000 of the goodwill for tax purposes ($180,000/180 months × 6 months during year) and did not impair any of the goodwill for financial accounting purposes. What was PCC's book–tax difference associated with this goodwill in 2015? Is it a favorable or unfavorable difference? Is the difference permanent or temporary?

Answer: $6,000 favorable, temporary book–tax difference. The amount of capitalized goodwill is the same for book and tax purposes and PCC deducted $6,000 of the goodwill for tax purposes and none for book purposes.

What if: Assume that at the end of 2016, PCC determined that the carrying value of the goodwill had been reduced to $150,000. That is, PCC experienced a $30,000 impairment expense to its goodwill. What is PCC's book–tax difference associated with its goodwill during 2016? Is the difference favorable or unfavorable? Is the difference permanent or temporary?

[9]§197. Self-created goodwill is not amortizable for tax purposes.

[10]When corporations acquire the stock of another corporation, they often recognize book goodwill but do not recognize any tax goodwill. When this book goodwill is written off as impaired, it generates a permanent unfavorable book–tax difference. Beginning in 2016, private companies can elect to amortize book goodwill over 10 years or less.

Answer: $18,000 unfavorable, temporary book–tax difference, computed as follows:

Description	Amount	Explanation
(1) Goodwill initially recorded on 7/1/15 acquisition	$180,000	
(2) Goodwill impairment recorded in 2016	$ 30,000	This write-down is expensed for book purposes.
(3) Months over which goodwill amortized for tax purposes.	180	15 years × 12 months = 180 months.
(4) Tax goodwill amortization expense for 2016	$ 12,000	[(1)/(3)] × 12 months.
Unfavorable book–tax temporary difference associated with goodwill in 2016.	**$ 18,000**	(2) − (4).

Corporate-Specific Deductions and Associated Book–Tax Differences

Certain deductions and corresponding limitations apply specifically to corporations. In this section, we introduce these deductions and identify book–tax differences associated with the deductions.

Stock Options Corporations often compensate executives and other employees with stock options. Stock options allow recipients to acquire stock in corporations issuing the options. To acquire the stock, employees exercise the options and pay the **exercise price.** The exercise price is usually the stock price on the day the options are issued to the employee. For example, at a time when a corporation's stock is trading for $10 per share, a corporation might issue (or grant) 100 stock options to an employee that allow the employee to purchase up to 100 shares of the corporation's stock for $10 a share. Employees usually must wait a certain amount of time between when they receive the options and when they are able to exercise them (i.e., they must wait until the options **vest** before they can exercise them). If employees quit working for the corporation before the options vest, they forfeit the options.

Stock options are valuable to employees when the stock price appreciates above the exercise price because, when the options vest, employees can use the options to purchase the stock at a price below the market price. Stock options are a popular form of compensation because they provide incentives for employees receiving the options to work to increase the value of the corporation and thereby benefit themselves and the stockholders.

For tax purposes, the tax treatment to the corporation (and the employee[11]) depends on whether the options are **incentive stock options** (ISOs) (less common, more administrative requirements for the corporation to qualify) or **nonqualified stock options** (NQOs) (more common, options that don't qualify as ISOs).[12] Corporations issuing incentive stock options *never* deduct any compensation expense associated with the options for tax purposes. In contrast, for nonqualified options, corporations deduct the difference between the fair market value of the stock and the exercise price of the option (the **bargain element**) as compensation expense in the year in which employees exercise the stock options.

For financial accounting purposes, corporations generally were not required to expense stock options until 2006. Consequently, corporations do not report a book–tax

[11]Employees do not recognize any income when they exercise incentive stock options. However, for nonqualified options, they recognize ordinary income for the difference between the value of the stock and the exercise price on the date of exercise. This chapter emphasizes the tax treatment of the options from the corporation's perspective.

[12]Requirements for options to qualify as incentive stock options are more restrictive than for nonqualified stock options. The formal requirements for incentive stock options are beyond the scope of this chapter.

difference for *incentive* stock options granted before 2006, and they report favorable, *permanent* book–tax differences for the bargain element of *nonqualified* stock options they granted *before* 2006 (when the options are exercised).

Under ASC 718 (the codification of FAS 123R), corporations are required to recognize *book expense* for stock options they grant after 2005.[13] Corporations granting stock options *after 2005* are required to estimate the value of the options at the time they issue them. They deduct the estimated value of the options over the option **vesting period** as they vest. Book–tax differences for options granted after 2005 may be permanent, temporary, or a combination of both. For incentive stock options, the amount of the permanent difference is the estimated value of the stock that vests during the year. The book–tax difference associated with incentive stock options is always unfavorable.

Example 5-5

What if: Assume that on January 1, 2015, PCC issued 10,000 incentive stock options (ISOs) with an estimated value of $6 per option. Each option entitles the owner to purchase one share of PCC stock for $15 a share (the per share price of PCC stock on January 1, 2015, when the options were granted). The options vest 25 percent a year for four years. What would be PCC's 2015 book–tax difference associated with the incentive stock options? Would the difference be favorable or unfavorable? Would the difference be permanent or temporary?

Answer: $15,000 unfavorable, permanent difference (10,000 options × 25% vesting × $6 estimated value). This is the book deduction for the ISOs. PCC does not deduct anything relating to the ISOs for tax purposes.

Nonqualified options generate temporary book–tax differences. Corporations *initially* recognize *temporary* book–tax differences associated with stock options for the value of options that vest during the year but are not exercised during that year. This initial temporary difference is always *unfavorable* because the corporation deducts the value of the unexercised options that vest during the year for book purposes but not for tax purposes. This initial unfavorable temporary book–tax difference *completely reverses* when employees *actually exercise* the stock options.

When an employee exercises the NQO, the tax deduction (i.e., the difference between the fair market value of the stock purchased less the option price) is likely to differ from the compensation expense recorded on the income statement when the option vested. If the tax deduction exceeds the previously recorded book deduction, the tax benefit from the excess deduction (called a "*windfall tax benefit*") is recorded in shareholders' equity as an addition to paid-in capital (APIC). If the tax deduction is less than the previously recorded book deduction, the tax detriment from the excess book deduction (called a "*shortfall*") reduces the existing windfall tax benefit pool in APIC with any excess charged to the income statement. The tax windfall or shortfall from an NQO exercise acts as a permanent difference, although it generally does not impact the income statement. The FASB is reconsidering whether to treat windfalls and shortfalls as part of the tax provision, which will impact the income statement. A full discussion of this complicated topic is beyond the scope of this chapter.

Example 5-6

On January 1, 2015, PCC granted 20,000 nonqualified options with an estimated $5 value per option ($100,000 total value). Each option entitled the owner to purchase one share of PCC stock for $15 a share (the per share price of PCC stock on January 1, 2015, when the options were granted).

[13]ASC 718 is effective for years beginning after June 15, 2005, for large publicly traded corporations and for years beginning after December 15, 2005, for small publicly traded corporations and nonpublicly traded entities. Corporations could have elected to expense stock options for book purposes before the effective date of ASC 718.

The options vested at the end of the day on December 31, 2015 (employees could not exercise options in 2015). What is PCC's book–tax difference associated with the nonqualified options in 2015? Is the difference favorable or unfavorable? Is it permanent or temporary?

Answer: $100,000 unfavorable, temporary book–tax difference. PCC expensed $100,000 for book purposes and $0 for tax purposes (the options were not exercised).

What if: Assume the same facts as above and that on March 1, 2016, employees exercised all 20,000 options at a time when the PCC stock was trading at $20 per share. What is PCC's book–tax difference associated with the stock options in 2016? Is it a permanent difference or a temporary difference? Is it favorable or unfavorable?

Answer: $100,000 favorable, temporary book–tax difference in 2016. PCC gets a $100,000 tax deduction in 2016, equal to the number of shares exercised times the bargain element of $5 per option exercised. The favorable book–tax difference is a complete reversal of the unfavorable book–tax difference in 2015. The 2015 and 2016 book–tax differences completely offset each other because the estimated value of $5 per option is equal to the bargain element ($20 FMV minus $15 exercise price per share).

What if: Assume that on March 1, 2016, employees exercised all 20,000 options at a time when the PCC stock was trading at $24 per share. What is PCC's book–tax difference associated with the stock options in 2016? Is it a permanent difference or a temporary difference? Is it favorable or unfavorable?

Answer: $180,000 favorable book–tax difference in 2016. The $180,000 difference consists of a $100,000 favorable, temporary difference (the reversal of the prior year unfavorable, temporary difference) and an $80,000 permanent, favorable difference. The permanent difference is the bargain element on the 20,000 options in excess of the estimated value of the options for book purposes [($9 − $5) × 20,000 options]. This "windfall tax benefit" is recorded as an increase in the corporation's additional paid-in capital.

Exhibit 5-5, which appears on the next page, summarizes the book and tax treatment of stock options both before and after ASC 718 became effective.

TAXES IN THE REAL WORLD Facebook's Billion Dollar NQO Tax Benefit

When Facebook filed its Registration Statement for its Initial Public Offering in February 2012, it was revealed that CEO Mark Zuckerberg had been granted nonqualifying stock options (NQOs) to purchase 120 million additional shares of the company for 6 cents per share. The company also informed potential investors that Mr. Zuckerberg intended to exercise these options when the company became a publicly traded company. Mr. Zuckerberg subsequently exercised his option to purchase 60 million additional Facebook shares prior to the IPO at a time when the value of the shares was $2,276,677,500. This transaction simultaneously created a tax deduction for Facebook and compensation income to Mr. Zuckerberg of approximately $2,273 million (fair value of the Facebook stock on the exercise date less the exercise price)! The company's tax benefit of $800 million also created an $800 million tax bill to Mr. Zuckerberg. In total, employees of Facebook exercised 135.5 million NQOs in 2012, resulting in a tax benefit to the company of more than $1 billion, of which $451 million was recovered as a refund for taxes paid in 2010–2011. The cash proceeds received by the company from the employees exercise of the NQOs was only $17 million.

The publicity surrounding the stock option exercise by Mr. Zuckerberg and the subsequent deduction granted to Facebook did not go unnoticed in Congress. Senator Carl Levin of Michigan expressed outrage that a "profitable" U.S. company could eliminate its tax liability because of the tax deduction granted (legally) by the U.S. tax laws. Senator Levin emphasized that Facebook's actions were within the tax law, but exclaimed that "As with so much of our tax code, it's not the law-breaking that shocks the conscience, it's the stuff that's perfectly legal." Of course, Senator Levin neglected to mention that the taxes saved by Facebook were offset by the taxes paid by Mr. Zuckerberg.

Source: All of the information is publicly available on Facebook's Form 10-K and Proxy Statement for 2012.

EXHIBIT 5-5 Book and Tax Treatment of Stock Options Before and After ASC 718 Effective Date

Description	Book Deduction	Tax Deduction	Book–Tax Difference
Pre ASC 718			
Incentive stock option	No deduction	No deduction	None
Nonqualified stock option	No deduction	Bargain element*	Favorable, permanent
Under ASC 718			
Incentive stock option	Initial estimated value of stock options × percentage of options that vest during the year	No deduction	Unfavorable, permanent
Nonqualified stock option (in years before exercise)	Initial estimated value of stock options × percentage of options that vest during the year	No deduction until exercise	Unfavorable, temporary
Nonqualified stock option (in year of exercise)	Initial estimated value of stock options × percentage of options that vest during the year	Bargain element*	Favorable, temporary reversing unfavorable, temporary difference in prior years Favorable, permanent difference if the bargain element exceeds the initial estimated value of stock options, unfavorable permanent difference otherwise

*The bargain element is the difference between the fair market value of the stock and the exercise price on the date the employee exercises the stock options.

Net Capital Losses For corporations, all net capital gains (long- and short-term) are taxed at ordinary income rates. Yet, corporations still generally prefer capital gains to ordinary income because corporations can only deduct capital losses *to the extent they recognize capital gains* in a particular year.[14] That is, corporations cannot deduct net capital losses. In contrast, individuals can deduct up to $3,000 of net capital losses in a year against ordinary income.[15]

When corporations recognize net capital losses for a year, they are permitted to carry the capital losses back three years (called a **net capital loss carryback**) and forward five years (called a **net capital loss carryover**) to offset net capital gains in the three years preceding the current tax year and then to offset net capital gains in the five years subsequent to the current tax year.[16] The capital loss carrybacks and carryovers must be applied in a particular order. If a corporation reports a net capital loss in year 4, it must first carry back the loss to year 1, then year 2, and then year 3. If the net capital loss remains after the carryback period, the corporation carries the loss forward to year 5 first, then year 6, year 7, year 8, and finally year 9. If the capital loss carryover has not been fully absorbed by the end of the fifth year after it was incurred (year 9), the carryover expires unused.

Although corporations may carry back net capital losses, they may not *carry back* a capital loss to a year if doing so creates or increases the net operating loss of

[14]§1211(a).

[15]§1211(b). Individuals are also allowed to carry net capital losses forward indefinitely.

[16]§1212(a).

the corporation (excess of deductions over income) in the year to which it is carried back (see discussion of net operating losses in the next section).[17]

For financial reporting purposes, corporations deduct net capital losses in the year they sell the property. Thus, corporations recognizing net capital losses report unfavorable book–tax differences in the year they recognize the losses and favorable book–tax differences in the year they use capital loss carrybacks or carryovers.

Example 5-7

During 2015, PCC sold Intel stock at a $12,000 gain and also reported a $40,000 capital loss on the disposition of land held for investment. PCC has not recognized a net capital gain or loss since 2010. PCC has a net operating loss carryover from 2014. What is PCC's net capital loss for the year?

Answer: $28,000 loss; [$12,000 + ($40,000)]. Because PCC had not recognized any net capital gains in 2012, 2013, and 2014 it may not carry back the loss (note that it could not carry back the loss to 2014 in any event because it recognized a net operating loss in that year as evidenced by its net operating loss carryover from 2014).

What amount of book–tax difference does this loss trigger? Is the difference favorable or unfavorable? Is it temporary or permanent?

Answer: $28,000 unfavorable, temporary book tax difference.

What if: Assume that in 2015, PCC reported a net capital loss of $28,000 and that it reported a $7,000 net capital gain in 2012, no net capital gain or loss in 2013, and a $4,000 net capital gain in 2014. What is the amount of its net capital loss carryover to 2016? PCC reported a net operating loss in 2014 but did not report a net operating loss in either 2012 or 2013.

Answer: $21,000. PCC first carries back the $28,000 loss to 2012, offsetting the $7,000 net capital gain in that year. PCC then carries the remaining $21,000 loss [($28,000) + $7,000] back to 2014. However, because PCC reported a net operating loss in 2014, it is not allowed to offset the $4,000 net capital gain with the capital loss carryback. Consequently, the $21,000 unused capital loss carryover is carried forward to 2016.

What if: Suppose PCC did not recognize any net capital gains in prior years but that next year (2015) it recognizes a net capital gain of $5,000 (before considering any capital loss carryovers). What will be its book–tax difference associated with capital gains and losses next year? Is it favorable or unfavorable? Is it temporary or permanent?

Answer: Next year, PCC would report a $5,000 favorable, temporary book–tax difference because it would be allowed to deduct $5,000 of its $28,000 capital loss carryover for tax purposes. This is a reversal of $5,000 of the unfavorable $28,000 book–tax difference from the prior year.

Net Operating Losses Compare the tax burden of Corporation A and Corporation B. Corporation A reports $1,000,000 of taxable income and pays $340,000 of tax in year 1 and again in year 2 (see corporate tax rate schedule inside of the back cover). In contrast, Corporation B reports $4,000,000 of taxable income in year 1 and a $2,000,000 loss in year 2. Absent any special tax provisions, Corporation B would pay $1,360,000 of tax in year 1 and no tax in year 2. Over the same two-year period both Corporation A and Corporation B reported $2,000,000 of (net) taxable income, yet Corporation B paid twice the tax Corporation A paid ($1,360,000 vs. $680,000). The problem for Corporation B is that, because it is required to report taxable income on an annual basis, it receives no tax benefit for its $2,000,000 loss (deductions in excess of gross income) in year 2. To ease the tax burden on corporations that aren't consistently profitable (for tax purposes), the tax laws allow corporations that report

[17]§1212(a)(1)(A)(ii). To allow a corporation to carry back a net capital loss to absorb capital gains in a net operating loss year would increase the NOL carry forward by the amount of the net capital loss used to offset the capital gain. This freed-up NOL would have a 20-year carryover rather than the 5-year carryover of the net capital loss.

deductions in excess of gross income in a particular year to carry back or carry over the excess deductions to reduce taxable income and taxes payable in years when gross income exceeds deductions. This excess of deductions over gross income is referred to as a **net operating loss (NOL).** A corporation's net operating loss for the current year is the excess of its deductions over its gross income with the following adjustments:

- A corporation does not deduct a NOL generated in another year in determining its current year NOL.
- A corporation may deduct a capital loss carryover against a net capital gain arising in the current year in determining its NOL but it may not deduct a capital loss carryback against a net capital gain in determining its NOL.
- A corporation does not deduct the domestic production activities deduction in determining its NOL.

Corporations can carry current year net operating losses back **(net operating loss carrybacks)** two years and forward **(net operating loss carryovers)** 20 years to offset taxable income and reduce taxes payable (or already paid) in those years. Corporations that carry back losses to offset taxable income in prior years can file for and receive an immediate refund of taxes they paid on this income. When they carry a loss back, they must first carry it back to the year two years before the current year.

Example 5-8

What if: Assume that in 2015 PCC reported a $300,000 net operating loss. In addition, PCC reported the following taxable income from 2012 through 2014:

	2012	2013	2014
Taxable income	$90,000	$45,000	$250,000

If PCC carries back its NOL, what is its NOL carryover to 2016?

Answer: $5,000 carryover. PCC first carries the 2015 NOL back to 2013 reducing its 2013 taxable income to $0 and reducing the NOL carryback/over to $255,000 ($300,000 – $45,000). PCC receives a refund for taxes it paid in 2013. It then carries the remaining $255,000 NOL back to 2014 reducing 2014 taxable income to $0. PCC receives a refund for tax it paid in 2014. This leaves a $5,000 NOL carryover (from 2015) to 2016 ($255,000 – $250,000).

What If: Assume that in 2015 PCC reported $120,000 of deductions and $90,000 of gross income (including $6,000 of net capital gain). PCC also has a $15,000 NOL carryover from 2014 and an $8,000 capital loss carryover from 2014. What are PCC's net operating loss and capital loss carryovers to 2016 and when do they expire?

Answer: $15,000 net operating loss carryover from 2014 that expires at the end of 2034 if unused, a $36,000 net operating loss carryover from 2015 that expires at the end of 2035 if unused, and a $2,000 capital loss carryover from 2014 that expires at the end of 2019 if unused. PCC's 2014 NOL is unused in 2015 because PCC reports a NOL in 2015 and it does not deduct NOL carryovers in determining its 2015 NOL. In 2015, PCC is able to offset the $6,000 net capital gain included in gross income with $6,000 of the $8,000 capital loss carryover from 2014. This reduces PCC's gross income to $84,000 ($90,000 – $6,000) and increases its deductions in excess of gross income (its current year NOL) to $36,000 ($120,000 – $84,000). Finally, PCC's 2014 capital loss carryover is reduced by the $6,000 absorbed portion to $2,000 ($8,000 minus $6,000 used in 2015).

A corporation with a current net operating loss may elect to forgo the carryback option and instead carry the net operating loss forward to future years. From a tax planning perspective, why would a corporation elect to forgo the carryback if it had taxable income in previous years? In deciding whether to forgo the carryback, corporations must evaluate the tax savings the NOL will generate if they carry the losses back and the tax savings they will generate if they carry them forward. If a carryback will offset income that was taxed at a low marginal tax rate, it may make sense for the corporation to forgo the carryback and carry the NOL forward to offset income that would otherwise be taxed at a higher rate in upcoming years. Tax savings notwithstanding, corporations carrying back losses receive immediate cash while corporations forgoing the carryback do not.

Example 5-9

What if: Suppose that PCC generates a $50,000 net operating loss in the current year (year 1) and that last year (year 0) it reported taxable income of $50,000 and paid $7,500 in taxes. Next year, PCC expects to earn $335,000 of taxable income. How much more tax savings will PCC realize by electing to forgo the NOL carryback (ignore the time value of money)?

Answer: $12,000 [$50,000 × (39% − 15%)]. If PCC carries the loss back, it offsets $50,000 of income that was taxed at 15%. If it decides to forgo the carryback, the carryover to next year will offset $50,000 of income that would be taxed at 39%. Note, however, that PCC will immediately receive the $7,500 if it carries the loss back. It will have to wait to get its tax savings if it elects to forgo the carryback.

For financial reporting purposes, corporations report losses in the year they incur them. Consequently corporations report unfavorable temporary book–tax difference in the year they generate NOLs. However, because corporations do not deduct NOL carrybacks or NOL carryovers in determining book income they report favorable *temporary* book–tax differences in the year they deduct the NOL carrybacks or carryovers for tax purposes. A corporation reports its NOL carryforwards on Schedule K to Form 1120.

Example 5-10

What if: Assume that last year PCC incurred a $24,000 net operating loss. Last year's NOL becomes an NOL carryover to this year that is available to reduce its current year taxable income. What is PCC's current year book–tax difference associated with its NOL carryover? Is the difference favorable or unfavorable? Is it permanent or temporary?

Answer: $24,000 favorable, temporary book–tax difference. The net operating loss carryover from the prior year is deductible for tax purposes but not for book purposes.

Charitable Contributions Similar to individuals, corporations are allowed to deduct charitable contributions to qualified charitable organizations.[18] However, the deduction and timing limitations are a little different for corporations than they are for individual taxpayers. Generally, corporations are allowed to deduct the amount of money they contribute, the fair market value of **capital gain property** they donate (property that would generate long-term capital gain if sold), and the adjusted basis of **ordinary income property** they donate (property that if sold would generate income taxed at ordinary rates). This chapter emphasizes the tax consequences of cash donations by corporations to qualified charities.[19] Generally, corporations are allowed to deduct charitable contributions at the time they make payment to charitable

[18]The IRS has a database of qualifying charities on its website (http://www.irs.gov/Charities-&-Non-Profits/Organizations-Eligible-to-Receive-Tax-Deductible-Charitable-Contributions). Qualifying organizations tend to be those engaging in educational, scientific, governmental, and other public activities.

[19]For more details on the tax consequences of charitable contributions, see §170.

organizations (subject to an overall taxable income limitation we discuss below). However, corporations using the accrual method of accounting can deduct contributions in the year *before* they actually pay the contribution when (1) their board of directors approves the payment and (2) they actually pay the contributions within two and one-half months of their tax year.[20]

Example 5-11

On December 1, 2015, the PCC board of directors approved a $110,000 cash contribution to the American Red Cross (ARC). For financial reporting purposes, PCC accrued and expensed the donation in 2015. PCC transferred the cash to the ARC on March 1, 2016. Does PCC report a book–tax difference associated with the charitable contribution (assume the taxable income limitation does not apply)?

Answer: No book–tax difference. For tax purposes, as an accrual-method taxpayer PCC may deduct the $110,000 contribution in 2015 because it paid the donation to the ARC within two and one-half months after year-end.

What if: Assume the same facts as above, except that PCC transferred the cash to the ARC on March 31, 2016. Does PCC report a book–tax difference associated with the charitable contribution (assume the taxable income limitation does not apply)?

Answer: Yes, it reports a $110,000 unfavorable, temporary book–tax difference in 2015. This will reverse and become a $110,000 favorable, temporary book–tax difference in 2016 when PCC deducts the contribution for tax purposes.

THE KEY FACTS

Charitable Contributions

- Charitable contribution deductions
  - Deductible when they accrue if approved by board of directors and paid within 2.5 months of year-end.
  - Deductions limited to 10 percent of charitable contribution deduction modified taxable income.
  - Contributions in excess of 10 percent limit carried forward up to five years.

A corporation's deductible charitable contributions for the year may not exceed 10 percent of its **charitable contribution limit modified taxable income.** A corporation's charitable contribution limit modified taxable income is its taxable income *before* deducting the following:

1. *Any* charitable contributions.
2. The dividends received deduction (DRD) (discussed below).
3. NOL *carrybacks.*
4. The domestic production activities deduction (DPAD).
5. Capital loss *carrybacks.*

Note that capital loss and NOL *carryovers are deductible* in determining charitable contribution limit modified taxable income. Capital loss and NOL *carrybacks* are *not deductible* for charitable contribution limitation purposes because they are unknown when corporations must determine the limitation (they arise in a future year).

Due to the 10 percent limitation, a corporation's charitable contribution deduction for the year is the *lesser* of (1) the amount of charitable contributions to qualifying charities (including charitable contribution carryovers—discussed below) or (2) 10 percent of charitable contribution limit modified taxable income.

Example 5-12

What if: Assume that PCC's 2015 taxable income before considering the charitable contribution limitation was $100,000. The taxable income computation includes an $18,000 charitable contribution deduction, an $11,000 DRD, a $9,000 DPAD, a $24,000 NOL carryover, a $4,000 capital loss carryover (offsets $4,000 of capital gain), and $25,000 of depreciation expense. Under these circumstances, what would be PCC's 2015 deductible charitable contribution?

[20]§170(a)(2).

Answer: $13,800 deductible charitable contribution, computed as follows:

Description	Amount	Explanation
(1) Taxable income before charitable contribution limitation	$100,000	
(2) Charitable contribution deduction before limitation	$ 18,000	Not deductible in computing limitation.
(3) Dividends received deduction	$ 11,000	Not deductible in computing limitation.
(4) Domestic production activities deduction	$ 9,000	Not deductible in computing limitation.
(5) Charitable contribution limit modified taxable income*	**$138,000**	Sum of (1) through (4).
(6) Tax deduction limitation percentage	10%	§170(b)(2)(A).
(7) Charitable contribution deduction limitation	$ 13,800	(5) × (6).
(8) Charitable contribution deduction for year	**$ 13,800**	Lesser of (2) or (7).
Charitable contribution carryover	$ 4,200	(2) − (8).

*Note that the NOL and capital loss carryover are not added back to compute line (5) because they are deductible in determining the charitable contribution limit modified taxable income.

Corporations making current year charitable contributions in excess of the 10 percent modified taxable limitation may carry forward the excess for up to five years after the year in which the carryover arises. Carryforwards are absorbed on a FIFO basis, and are applied after the current year contribution deduction. They may deduct the carryover in future years to the extent the 10 percent limitation does not restrict deductions for charitable contributions corporations actually make in those years. Unused carryovers expire after five years.

Example 5-13

What if: Under the assumptions provided in the previous example, we determined that PCC had a $4,200 charitable contribution carryover (it was not able to deduct $4,200 of its $18,000 contribution). Assume that in 2016, PCC contributed $10,000 to charity, and its charitable contribution limit modified taxable income was $110,000. What would be PCC's deductible charitable contribution in 2016? What would its charitable contribution carryover be at the end of 2016? When would it expire?

Answer: $11,000 charitable contribution deduction. This is the lesser of the charitable contribution limit of $11,000 ($110,000 × 10%) or $14,200 ($10,000 current year contribution plus $4,200 carryover from prior year). The carryover is $3,200 ($14,200 − $11,000). Because the current year contribution uses the limit first, the $3,200 carryover is from the excess contribution in 2015 and it will expire if it has not been used by the end of 2020.

Corporations report *unfavorable, temporary* book–tax differences to the extent the 10 percent modified taxable income limitation restricts the amount of their tax charitable contribution deduction. That is, they recognize unfavorable, temporary book–tax differences in the amount of the charitable contribution *carryover* they generate for the year. Conversely, corporations report *favorable, temporary* book–tax differences when they deduct charitable contribution carryovers because they deduct the carryovers for tax purposes, but not book purposes.

Example 5-14

In 2015, PCC donated a total of $700,000 of cash to the American Red Cross. Elise knew she still had to apply the 10 percent taxable income limitation to determine the amount PCC could deduct for tax purposes. She had determined that PCC's taxable income before the charitable contribution deduction, NOL carryover ($24,000), DRD ($21,000) (see Example 5-15 below), and DPAD ($465,000) was $6,287,000. What is PCC's charitable contribution deduction for the year? What is its charitable contribution carryover to next year, if any?

Answer: $626,300 charitable contribution deduction and $73,700 charitable contribution carryover, computed as follows:

Description	Amount	Explanation
(1) Taxable income before *any* charitable contribution, NOL carryover from previous year, DRD, and DPAD	$6,287,000	Exhibit 5-7.
(2) NOL *carryover* from previous year	(24,000)	Deductible in determining taxable income limit.
(3) Charitable contribution limit modified taxable income	$6,263,000	(1) + (2).
(4) Total charitable contributions for year	$ 700,000	
(5) Tax deduction limitation percentage	10%	§170(b)(2)(A)
(6) Charitable contribution deduction limitation	$ 626,300	(3) × (5).
(7) Charitable contribution deduction for year	**$ 626,300**	Lesser of (4) or (6).
Charitable contribution carryover*	**$ 73,700**	(4) − (7).

*As we discuss above, the carryover expires if it has not been used during the five-year period after the current year.

What is PCC's book–tax difference associated with its charitable contribution? Is the difference favorable or unfavorable? Is it permanent or temporary?

Answer: $73,700 unfavorable, temporary book–tax difference.

THE KEY FACTS

Dividends Received Deduction

- Dividends received deduction
  - Generally lesser of deduction percentage (70 percent, 80 percent, or 100 percent) based on ownership times DRD modified taxable income.
  - Limitation doesn't apply if full DRD creates or increases a corporation's NOL.
  - Generates favorable permanent difference.

Dividends Received Deduction When corporations receive dividends from other corporations they are taxed on the dividends at their ordinary tax rate, not the preferential 20 percent rate available to individual taxpayers. This isn't all bad news, however, because corporations are allowed a dividends received deduction (DRD) that reduces the actual tax they pay on the dividends.[21] The DRD is designed to mitigate the extent to which corporate earnings are subject to three (or perhaps even more) levels of taxation. Corporate taxable income is subject to triple taxation when a corporation pays tax on its income and then distributes its after-tax income to shareholders that are corporations. Corporate shareholders are taxed on the dividends, creating the second tax. When corporate shareholders distribute their after-tax earnings from the dividends to their shareholders the income is taxed for a third time. The dividends received deduction reduces the amount of the second-level tax and thus reduces the impact of triple taxation (or more) of earnings that corporations distribute as dividends.

Corporations generally compute their dividends received deduction by multiplying the dividend amount by 70 percent, 80 percent, or 100 percent, depending on their level of ownership in the distributing corporation's stock. Exhibit 5-6 summarizes

[21]§243. Also, §246(c) describes certain dividends that are ineligible for the dividends received deduction.

EXHIBIT 5-6 Stock Ownership and Dividends Received Deduction Percentage

Receiving Corporation's Stock Ownership in Distributing Corporation's Stock	Dividends Received Deduction Percentage
Less than 20 percent	70%
At least 20 percent but less than 80 percent	80
80 percent or more[22]	100

the stock ownership thresholds and the corresponding dividends received deduction percentage. Only dividends received from domestic corporations are eligible for the DRD. Dividends received from non-U.S. corporations may be eligible for a foreign tax credit, which is discussed in Chapter 13.

Example 5-15

During 2015, PCC received a $30,000 dividend from IBM. PCC owns less than 1 percent of the IBM stock. What is PCC's DRD associated with the dividend?

Answer: $21,000 ($30,000 × 70%).

What if: Assume PCC's marginal tax rate on the dividend *before* considering the effect of the dividends received deduction is 34 percent. What is PCC's marginal tax rate on the IBM dividend income *after* considering the dividends received deduction?

Answer: 10.2 percent marginal tax rate on dividend income, computed as follows:

Description	Amount	Explanation
(1) Dividend from IBM	$30,000	
(2) DRD percentage	70%	Less than 20 percent ownership in IBM.
(3) Dividends received deduction	**$21,000**	(1) × (2).
(4) Dividend subject to taxation after DRD	$ 9,000	(1) − (3).
(5) Marginal ordinary tax rate	34%	
(6) Taxes payable on dividend *after* DRD	$ 3,060	(4) × (5).
Marginal tax rate on dividend *after* DRD	**10.20%**	(6)/(1).

Deduction limitation. The dividends received deduction is limited to the product of the applicable dividends received deduction percentage (see Exhibit 5-6) and **DRD modified taxable income.**[23] DRD modified taxable income is the dividend receiving corporation's taxable income *before* deducting the following:

- The DRD.
- *Any* NOL deduction (carryover or carryback).
- Capital loss *carrybacks.*
- The domestic production activities deduction (DPAD).[24]

[22]To qualify for the 100 percent dividends received deduction, the receiving and distributing corporations must be in the same affiliated group as described in §1504. The 80 percent ownership requirement is the minimum ownership level required for inclusion in the same affiliated group.

[23]When corporations receive dividends from multiple corporations with different deduction percentages, according to §246(b)(3), the limitations first apply to the 80 percent dividends received deduction and then the 70 percent dividends received deduction.

[24]§246(b)(1).

Example 5-16

What if: Suppose that during 2015, PCC received a $30,000 dividend from IBM and that PCC owns less than 1 percent of the IBM stock. Further assume that PCC's taxable income before the dividends received deduction was $50,000 in Scenario A and $25,000 in Scenario B. To arrive at the taxable income under both scenarios (before the DRD), PCC deducted a $2,000 NOL carryover, a $4,000 capital loss carryover, and a $1,000 DPAD. What is PCC's dividends received deduction associated with the dividend in Scenario A and in Scenario B?

Answer: $21,000 in Scenario A and $19,600 in Scenario B, computed as follows:

Description	Scenario A	Scenario B	Explanation
(1) Taxable income before the dividends received deduction (includes dividend income)	$50,000	$25,000	
(2) NOL carryover	2,000	2,000	
(3) DPAD	1,000	1,000	
(4) DRD modified taxable income	$53,000	$28,000	(1) + (2) + (3).
(5) Dividend income	$30,000	$30,000	
(6) Dividends received deduction percentage based on ownership	70%	70%	§243(a).
(7) Dividends received deduction before limitation	$21,000	$21,000	(5) × (6).
(8) Dividends received deduction limitation	$ 37,100	$19,600	(4) × (6).
Deductible DRD	**$21,000**	**$19,600**	Lesser of (7) or (8).

Note that the capital loss carryover is deductible in determining the DRD modified taxable income so it is not added back to taxable income to arrive at DRD modified taxable income.

The modified taxable income limitation *does not apply* if after deducting the *full* dividends received deduction (dividend × DRD percentage) a corporation reports a current year net operating loss. That is, if after deducting the full dividends received deduction, the corporation has a net operating loss, the corporation is allowed to deduct the *full* dividends received deduction no matter what the modified taxable income limitation is.[25] As the following example illustrates, this rule can cause some unusual results.

Example 5-17

What if: Let's assume that PCC reports gross income of $80,000, *including* $30,000 of dividend income from TOU Corp. PCC owns 25 percent of TOU Corp. stock so its applicable DRD percentage is 80 percent (see Exhibit 5-6). Finally, let's consider two alternative scenarios. In Scenario A, PCC reports $56,000 of business expenses deductible in determining its DRD modified taxable income. In Scenario B, PCC reports $57,000 of business expenses deductible in determining its DRD modified taxable income. For each scenario, what is PCC's DRD modified taxable income? For each scenario, what is PCC's dividends received deduction?

[25]§246(b)(2).

Scenario A Answer: $24,000 DRD modified taxable income; $19,200 dividends received deduction (see computation below).

Scenario B Answer: $23,000 DRD modified taxable income; $24,000 dividends received deduction, computed as follows:

Description	Scenario A	Scenario B	Explanation
(1) Gross income other than dividends	$50,000	$50,000	
(2) Dividend income	30,000	30,000	
(3) Gross income	$80,000	$80,000	(1) + (2).
(4) Business expenses deductible in determining the DRD modified taxable income	56,000	57,000	
(5) DRD modified taxable income (note this is taxable income before the DRD)	**$24,000**	**$23,000**	(3) − (4).
(6) Full dividends received deduction	$24,000	$24,000	(2) × 80%.
(7) DRD modified taxable income limitation	19,200	18,400	(5) × 80%.
(8) Taxable income (loss) after deducting full DRD	0	(1,000)	(5) − (6).
Deductible DRD	**19,200**	**24,000**	Lesser of (6) or (7) unless (8) is negative, then (6).

Compare the results in Scenario A and Scenario B in the previous example. In Scenario B, PCC's DRD is $4,800 larger than it is in Scenario A ($24,000 − $19,200) despite the fact that the only difference in the two scenarios is that PCC reports $56,000 of business expenses in Scenario A and $57,000 of business expenses in Scenario B. Interestingly, the tax laws allow a corporation to increase its DRD by $4,800 for a $30,000 dividend simply by incurring $1,000 more in expenses (or even $1 more).

Because the dividends received deduction is strictly a tax deduction and not a book deduction, *any* dividends received deduction creates a *favorable, permanent* book–tax difference.

Example 5-18

From her review of PCC's dividend income computations, Elise discovered that the only dividend PCC received during the year was a $30,000 dividend from IBM, a U.S. corporation. Because PCC owns a very small percentage of IBM stock (less than 1 percent) Elise determined that PCC was entitled to a 70 percent dividends received deduction. What is PCC's book–tax difference associated with its dividends received deduction? Is the difference favorable or unfavorable? Is it permanent or temporary?

(continued on page 5-22)

Answer: $21,000 favorable, permanent book–tax difference, computed as follows:

Description	Amount	Explanation
(1) Taxable income before NOL, DRD and DPAD (DRD modified taxable income)	$5,660,700	Exhibit 5-7 ($5,636,700 + 24,000 NOL).
(2) Dividend income	$ 30,000	Exhibit 5-7.
(3) Applicable DRD percentage	70%	Own less than 20 percent of IBM.
(4) Full dividends received deduction	$ 21,000	(2) × (3).
(5) Dividends received deduction taxable income limitation	$3,962,490	(1) × (3).
(6) Book deductible dividends received deduction	0	No book DRD.
(7) Tax deductible dividends received deduction	$ 21,000	Lesser of (4) or (5).
(Favorable) permanent book–tax difference	**($21,000)**	(6) − (7).

Taxable Income Summary

Exhibit 5-7 presents Elise's template for reconciling PCC's book and its taxable income. Note that the template does not follow the typical financial accounting format because it organizes the information to facilitate the taxable income computation. In particular, it puts the deductions in the *sequence they are deducted for tax purposes.*

Regular Tax Liability

When corporations determine their taxable income, they can compute their tax liability from the corporate tax rate schedule. The corporate tax rate schedule is not indexed for inflation like the individual tax rate schedules are. Consequently, unlike the individual tax rate schedules, the corporate tax rate schedule does not change every year. The lowest marginal corporate tax rate bracket is 15 percent and the highest marginal tax rate bracket is 39 percent. Corporations with over $18,333,333 of taxable income pay tax at a flat 35 percent rate.

Example 5-19

Elise determined that PCC's taxable income is $5,150,700. What is its regular income tax liability?

Answer: $1,751,238, computed as follows:

Description	Amount	Explanation
(1) Taxable income	$5,150,700	Exhibit 5-7.
(2) Tax on first $335,000	$ 113,900	Corporate tax rate schedule (for taxable income between $335K and $10M).
(3) Taxable income above $335,000	$4,815,700	(1) − $335,000.
(4) Marginal tax rate for fifth bracket	34%	Tax rate schedule.
(5) Tax on income above $335,000	$1,637,338	(3) × (4).
Regular tax liability	**$1,751,238**	(2) + (5).

EXHIBIT 5-7 PCC Book–Tax Reconciliation Template

Description	Book Income (Dr) Cr	Book–Tax Adjustments (Dr)†	Book–Tax Adjustments Cr†	Taxable Income (Dr) Cr
Revenue from sales	$60,000,000			$60,000,000
Cost of goods sold	(38,000,000)			(38,000,000)
Gross profit	$22,000,000			$22,000,000
Other income:				
Dividend income	30,000			30,000
Interest income	120,000	(12,000)[ex. 1]		108,000
Capital gains (losses)	(28,000)		28,000[ex. 7]	0
Gain on fixed asset dispositions	54,000		16,000[exh. 4]	70,000
Gross income	$22,176,000			$22,208,000
Expenses:				
Compensation	(9,868,000)			(9,868,000)
Deferred compensation	(300,000)	(150,000)[exh. 4]		(450,000)
Stock option compensation	(100,000)		100,000[ex. 6]	0
Bad debt expense	(165,000)		70,000[exh. 4]	(95,000)
Charitable contributions	Moved below			
Depreciation	(2,400,000)	(700,000)[exh. 4]		(3,100,000)
Advertising	(1,920,000)			(1,920,000)
Warranty expenses	(580,000)		170,000[exh. 4]	(410,000)
Meals and entertainment	(28,000)		14,000[ex. 1]	(14,000)
Life insurance premiums	(34,000)		34,000[ex. 1]	0
Other expenses	(64,000)			(64,000)
Federal income tax expense	(2,000,000)*		2,000,000[ex. 2]	0
Total expenses *before* charitable contribution, NOL, DRD, and DPAD	(17,459,000)			(15,921,000)
Income *before* charitable contribution, NOL, DRD, and DPAD	4,717,000			$ 6,287,000
NOL carryover from prior year		(24,000)[ex. 10]		(24,000)
Taxable income for charitable contribution limitation purposes				6,263,000
Charitable contributions	(700,000)		73,700[ex. 14]	(626,300)
Taxable income before DRD and DPAD				5,636,700
Dividends received deduction (DRD)		(21,000)[ex. 18]		(21,000)
Domestic production activities deduction (DPAD)		(465,000)[ex. 1]		(465,000)
Book/taxable income	**$ 4,017,000**			**$ 5,150,700**

*This number is used only for illustrative purposes. In Chapter 6, we compute the correct federal income tax expense (also referred to as the federal income tax provision).

†Note that the superscript by each book–tax difference identifies the example (ex) or exhibit (exh) where the adjustment is calculated. Also note that the numbers in the debit column are favorable book–tax adjustments while numbers in the credit column are unfavorable book–tax adjustments.

Why do corporate marginal tax rates increase from 15 percent to 25 percent to 34 percent to 39 percent and then drop to 34 percent and then increase again to 35 percent and then to 38 percent before settling in at 35 percent? This doesn't really look like a truly progressive tax rate schedule, does it? It turns out that the rate schedule is progressive with some modifications. When the apparent marginal rate increases to

39 percent, the marginal tax rate is really 34 percent but the tax laws impose a 5 percent add-on tax that is designed to eliminate the benefit of the rates lower than 34 percent (15 percent and 25 percent). Consequently, by the time the marginal rate from the schedule drops back down to 34 percent at $335,000 of taxable income, the entire amount of taxable income is taxed at a flat 34 percent rate. Therefore, taxable income between $335,000 and $10,000,000, is taxed at a flat 34 percent rate (verify this by referring to the previous example and dividing PCC's tax liability by its taxable income). The marginal rate then jumps to 35 percent and then to 38 percent. The 3 percent increase from 35 percent to 38 percent is also an add-on tax designed to phase-out the benefit of the 34 percent tax rate relative to the 35 percent rate. As a result, by the time taxable income hits $18,333,333, a corporation's taxable income is taxed at a flat 35 percent tax rate. In effect, the 15 percent and 25 percent rate brackets are reserved for "small" corporations.

Controlled Groups Corporate shareholders interested in reducing a corporation's overall tax burden may be tempted to split up an existing profitable corporation into several smaller corporations. By doing this, the group of corporations may earn the same taxable income in the aggregate but will pay less in taxes because each corporation will benefit from the low end of the corporate tax rate schedule. In the extreme, shareholders could split a corporation into enough separate corporations such that each separate corporation will report taxable income of $50,000 or lower and, consequently, pay tax on all of its income at the lowest marginal tax rate of 15 percent. Congress was concerned about this possibility and other similar abuses so they implemented special rules for **controlled groups.**

Essentially, a controlled group is a group of corporations that is controlled or owned by the same taxpayer or group of taxpayers. A controlled group could be a **parent-subsidiary controlled group,** a **brother-sister controlled group,** or a **combined controlled group.**[26] Exhibit 5-8 summarizes, in general terms, the definition of each of these controlled group types.

EXHIBIT 5-8 Controlled Group Definitions

Type	Definition	Reference
Parent-Subsidiary	One corporation (the parent) owns at least 80 percent of the voting power or stock value of another corporation (the subsidiary) on the last day of the year.	§1563(a)(1)
Brother-Sister	Two or more corporations of which five or fewer individuals collectively own more than 50 percent of the voting power or stock value of each corporation on the last day of the year, taking into account each individual's minimum ownership in each corporation in the group.	§1563(a)(2)
Combined	Three or more corporations, each of which is a member of either a parent-subsidiary or brother-sister controlled group and one of the corporations is the parent in the parent-subsidiary controlled group and also is in a brother-sister controlled group.	§1563(a)(3)

The tax laws impose complex rules for determining whether corporations meet the stock ownership requirements for controlled groups described in Exhibit 5-8.[27]

[26]§1563(a). The definition of a controlled group also includes certain insurance companies [§1563(a)].

[27]The ownership rules include direct and indirect (or constructive) ownership and the concept of identical ownership in each corporation in a brother-sister controlled group. For example, an individual is treated as owning the stock owned by a spouse, children under age 21, and parents, grandparents, and children age 21 or older, but only if the individual owns more than 50 percent of the corporation's stock. The details of these rules are beyond the scope of this text. See §1563 for more detail.

No matter the type, a controlled group of corporations may use only one 15 percent tax bracket and one 25 percent tax bracket among all the corporations in the group. That is, the controlled group is treated as one corporation for purposes of using the tax rate schedules.[28] In general, the tax provisions associated with controlled groups are designed to eliminate the benefit of splitting large corporations into smaller commonly controlled entities to take advantage of multiple tax benefits allowable to smaller corporations because the controlled group rules treat the entire group as though it is one entity.[29]

Example 5-20

What if: Assume that PCC and ACC are privately held corporations with calendar year-ends. On December 31, Jordan Michaels owns 50 percent of the stock of PCC and 50 percent of the stock of ACC. Sally Perkins owns the remaining shares of PCC and ACC. Are PCC and ACC a controlled group?

Answer: Yes, two individuals (Jordan and Sally) own more than 50 percent of the stock of both PCC and ACC on the last day of the year (they own 100 percent of the stock of both corporations).

Assuming PCC reported $45,000 of taxable income for the year and ACC reported $40,000 of taxable income, what is the combined tax liability of PCC and ACC (given that they comprise a controlled group)?

Answer: $17,150 [$13,750 + 34% × (85,000 − 75,000)].

What if: Assume the same taxable income for PCC and for ACC but that PCC and ACC have the same ten owners and that each owner owns 10 percent of each corporation. What would be the combined tax liability of PCC and ACC?

Answer: $12,750 [PCC: $6,750 ($45,000 × 15%) + ACC: $6,000 ($40,000 × 15%)]. PCC and ACC are *not* part of a controlled group, so both corporations are allowed to take advantage of the 15 percent corporate tax bracket.

In this example, the controlled group rules would extract an additional $4,400 of tax ($17,150 − $12,750) from the entities because the rules essentially treat the two entities as one.

COMPLIANCE

LO 5-3

Corporations report their taxable income on Form 1120. Exhibit 5-9 presents the front page of PCC's current year Form 1120 through the tax liability.

Form 1120 includes a schedule for corporations to report their book–tax differences and reconcile their book and taxable income. Corporations with total assets of less than $10,000,000 report their book–tax differences on Schedule M-1. Corporations with total assets of $10,000,000 or more are required to report their book–tax differences on Schedule M-3.[30] Because corporations report book–tax differences as adjustments to book income to compute taxable income on either Schedule M-1 or M-3, these book-to-tax adjustments are often referred to as **Schedule M adjustments, M adjustments,** and even "Ms" (plural version of M).

[28]§1561(a).

[29]The controlled group provisions require corporations in the group to share other tax benefits such as the AMT exemption discussed below. A potential benefit of having a controlled group is that if the group files a consolidated tax return, the losses of one corporation in the group can offset income from other corporations in the group. The apportionment of tax benefits between a controlled group is reported on Schedule O to Form 1120.

[30]Corporations with at least $10 million but less than $50 million in total assets at tax year-end are permitted to file Schedule M-1 in place of Schedule M-3, Parts II and III. Schedule M-3, Part I, lines 1–12 continue to be required for these taxpayers. Corporations with $10 million to $50 million in total assets may voluntarily file Schedule M-3 Parts II and III rather than Schedule M-1.

EXHIBIT 5-9 PCC Form 1120 page 1, through tax refund

Form **1120**
Department of the Treasury
Internal Revenue Service

U.S. Corporation Income Tax Return

For calendar year 2014 or tax year beginning __________, 2014, ending __________, 20 ___

▶ Information about Form 1120 and its separate instructions is at *www.irs.gov/form1120*.

OMB No. 1545-0123

2014

A Check if:
1a Consolidated return (attach Form 851) ☐
b Life/nonlife consolidated return ☐
2 Personal holding co. (attach Sch. PH) ☐
3 Personal service corp. (see instructions) ☐
4 Schedule M-3 attached ☐

TYPE OR PRINT

Name
Premier Computer Corporation
Number, street, and room or suite no. If a P.O. box, see instructions.
1533 East Crown Drive
City or town, state, or province, country and ZIP or foreign postal code
Denver, CO 80239

B Employer identification number 12-3456789
C Date incorporated 01/01/1998
D Total assets (see instructions) $ 9,500,000

E Check if: **(1)** ☐ Initial return **(2)** ☐ Final return **(3)** ☐ Name change **(4)** ☐ Address change

Income	1a	Gross receipts or sales	1a	60,000,000		
	b	Returns and allowances	1b			
	c	Balance. Subtract line 1b from line 1a			1c	60,000,000
	2	Cost of goods sold (attach Form 1125-A)			2	38,000,000
	3	Gross profit. Subtract line 2 from line 1c			3	22,000,000
	4	Dividends (Schedule C, line 19)			4	30,000
	5	Interest			5	108,000
	6	Gross rents			6	
	7	Gross royalties			7	
	8	Capital gain net income (attach Schedule D (Form 1120))			8	
	9	Net gain or (loss) from Form 4797, Part II, line 17 (attach Form 4797)			9	70,000
	10	Other income (see instructions—attach statement)			10	
	11	**Total income.** Add lines 3 through 10 ▶			11	22,208,000
Deductions (See instructions for limitations on deductions.)	12	Compensation of officers (see instructions—attach Form 1125-E) ▶			12	1,500,000
	13	Salaries and wages (less employment credits)			13	8,818,000
	14	Repairs and maintenance			14	
	15	Bad debts			15	95,000
	16	Rents			16	
	17	Taxes and licenses			17	
	18	Interest			18	
	19	Charitable contributions			19	626,300
	20	Depreciation from Form 4562 not claimed on Form 1125-A or elsewhere on return (attach Form 4562)			20	3,100,000
	21	Depletion			21	
	22	Advertising			22	1,920,000
	23	Pension, profit-sharing, etc., plans			23	
	24	Employee benefit programs			24	
	25	Domestic production activities deduction (attach Form 8903)			25	465,000
	26	Other deductions (attach statement)			26	488,000
	27	**Total deductions.** Add lines 12 through 26 ▶			27	17,012,300
	28	Taxable income before net operating loss deduction and special deductions. Subtract line 27 from line 11			28	5,195,700
	29a	Net operating loss deduction (see instructions)	29a	24,000		
	b	Special deductions (Schedule C, line 20)	29b	21,000		
	c	Add lines 29a and 29b			29c	45,000
Tax, Refundable Credits, and Payments	30	**Taxable income.** Subtract line 29c from line 28 (see instructions)			30	5,150,700
	31	Total tax (Schedule J, Part I, line 11)			31	1,751,238
	32	Total payments and refundable credits (Schedule J, Part II, line 21)			32	1,813,333
	33	Estimated tax penalty (see instructions). Check if Form 2220 is attached ▶ ☐			33	
	34	**Amount owed.** If line 32 is smaller than the total of lines 31 and 33, enter amount owed			34	
	35	**Overpayment.** If line 32 is larger than the total of lines 31 and 33, enter amount overpaid			35	62,095
	36	Enter amount from line 35 you want: **Credited to 2015 estimated tax** ▶		**Refunded** ▶	36	62,095

Sign Here

Under penalties of perjury, I declare that I have examined this return, including accompanying schedules and statements, and to the best of my knowledge and belief, it is true, correct, and complete. Declaration of preparer (other than taxpayer) is based on all information of which preparer has any knowledge.

▶ Signature of officer | Date | ▶ Title

May the IRS discuss this return with the preparer shown below (see instructions)? ☐ **Yes** ☐ **No**

Paid Preparer Use Only

Print/Type preparer's name	Preparer's signature	Date	Check ☐ if self-employed	PTIN
Firm's name ▶			Firm's EIN ▶	
Firm's address ▶			Phone no.	

For Paperwork Reduction Act Notice, see separate instructions. Cat. No. 11450Q Form **1120** (2014)

EXHIBIT 5-10 Form 1120, Schedule M-1

Schedule M-1 Reconciliation of Income (Loss) per Books With Income per Return
Note: The corporation may be required to file Schedule M-3 (see instructions).

1	Net income (loss) per books	4,017,000	7	Income recorded on books this year not included on this return (itemize): Tax-exempt interest $ 12,000	12,000
2	Federal income tax per books	2,000,000			
3	Excess of capital losses over capital gains	28,000			
4	Income subject to tax not recorded on books this year (itemize): gain on disposition of fixed assets	16,000	8	Deductions on this return not charged against book income this year (itemize):	
5	Expenses recorded on books this year not deducted on this return (itemize):		a	Depreciation $ 700,000	
a	Depreciation $		b	Charitable contributions $	
b	Charitable contributions $ 73,700			deferred comp. 150,000	
c	Travel and entertainment $ 14,000			dom. prod. act. ded. 465,000	1,315,000
	Other (see Statement 1) 374,000	461,700	9	Add lines 7 and 8	1,327,000
6	Add lines 1 through 5	6,522,700	10	Income (page 1, line 28)—line 6 less line 9	5,195,700

Schedule M-1
Statement 1
Other expenses recorded on books this year not deducted on this return

Compensation expense (stock options)	$100,000
Bad debt expense	70,000
Warranty expense	170,000
Life insurance premiums	34,000
Total other expenses	$374,000

Because PCC's total assets are $9,500,000 (see Exhibit 5-9, line D), it may complete a Schedule M-1 rather than a Schedule M-3. Exhibit 5-10 presents PCC's completed Schedule M-1 based on the information provided in Exhibit 5-7 (the 2014 form is used because the 2015 form was unavailable at the time the book went to press). As you can see, Schedule M-1 is a relatively short schedule, and it does not require corporations to provide much detail about the nature of their book–tax differences.

The schedule begins on line 1 with book income after taxes. The left-hand column includes all unfavorable book–tax differences (add-backs to book income to arrive at taxable income). In general, the top part of the left column is for income items and the bottom part is for expense items. The right-hand column consists of all favorable book–tax differences. The top part of the right column is for income items and the bottom part includes expense items.

Finally, it is important to note that Schedule M-1 (and Schedule M-3) reconcile to taxable income *before* the net operating loss deduction and the dividends received deduction.[31] Consequently, to fully reconcile book and taxable income, corporations must deduct net operating loss carryovers and dividends received deductions from line 10 on Schedule M-1 (or the amount on line 30d on Schedule M-3).

Example 5-21

In reviewing her work on PCC's tax return, Elise wanted to check to make sure that she could reconcile from the bottom line of the Schedule M-1 to PCC's taxable income. She noted that line 10 of PCC's Schedule M-1 was $5,195,700. How should Elise reconcile from this number to PCC's taxable income?

(continued on page 5-28)

[31]Schedule M-1 (and the Schedule M-3) reconcile to line 28 on the Form 1120. Line 28 is taxable income before the net operating loss and special deductions (the dividends received deduction).

Answer: Start with the amount on line 10 and subtract PCC's NOL carryover and its DRD, as illustrated below:

Description	Amount	Explanation
(1) Schedule M-1 taxable income reconciliation total	$5,195,700	Form 1120, Schedule M-1, line 10.
(2) Net operating loss deduction	(24,000)	Exhibit 5-7.
(3) Dividends received deduction	(21,000)	Exhibit 5-7.
Taxable income	**$5,150,700**	(1) + (2) + (3).

Schedule M-3 requires corporations to report significantly more information than Schedule M-1 does. For example, Schedule M-3 includes more than 60 specific types of book–tax differences, while Schedule M-1 includes only ten summary lines. Furthermore, Schedule M-3 requires corporations to identify each book–tax difference as either temporary or permanent. The IRS created Schedule M-3 in hopes of providing a better and more efficient starting point for agents to identify and scrutinize large dollar compliance issues.

Form 1120 also requires corporations to complete Schedule M-2, which provides a reconciliation of the corporation's beginning and ending balance in its unappropriated retained earning from its financial accounting balance sheet (reported on Schedule L). Corporations with total receipts and total assets less than $250,000 are not required to complete Schedules L, M-1, and M-2.

ETHICS

Elizabeth (Liz) Young, senior manager in the tax group in the Cleveland office of Tics & Tax, an international professional services firm, was reviewing the workpapers related to the tax return to be filed by her biggest client, General Inertia. She was intrigued by one of the items listed under *"other deductions"* (line 26 of Form 1120), which was described as a *"settlement amount"* of $100 million. After consulting with the director of taxes at General Inertia, Dee Ductit, Liz discovered the amount related to a settlement with the Department of Justice (DOJ) for violation of the False Claims Act. Dee described the settlement as a *"penalty"* (her words) the firm had to pay to the federal government because one of its divisions billed the Department of Defense (DOD) for work that was not performed in relation to a contract to provide helicopters to the DOD.

Dee's use of the term *"penalty"* caused Liz to question whether such a payment was deductible for tax purposes (the company also deducted the payment on its financial statements). In particular, she remembered that Code *§162(f)* specifically prohibits the deduction of *"any fine or similar penalty paid to a government for the violation of any law."* When Liz asked to see the settlement letter from the DOJ, she was told that the client's legal department considered the terms of the letter to be confidential, but that the company's reason for deducting the amount was that the letter did not describe the settlement as a "penalty" and specifically stated that "nothing in the agreement characterizes the payments for federal income tax purposes."

General Inertia is a long-term client that provides the firm with $10 million in audit and tax fees annually. Dee informed Liz that the company was willing to take the "risk" in deducting the full amount of the settlement payment because its IRS auditors were unlikely to question the item and the "tax refund" from deducting the settlement ($35 million) would help alleviate some short-term cash flow problems the company was having. In fact, the company hoped to use the "refund" to pay off parts suppliers that were threatening to take the company to court over nonpayment. The company also preferred not to provide any further disclosure or description of the deduction in the tax return so as not to alert the IRS to a potential tax audit issue.

What do you think of the tax director's approach to filing the company's tax return? What would you do if you were in Liz's position?[32]

[32]See S. Convery and E. Outslay, "Assessing Professional Ethics in Tax: A Case on Uncertain Tax Positions," *Journal of Accounting Education* 30 (March 2012), pp. 80–99.

Consolidated Tax Returns An affiliated group of corporations may elect to file a **consolidated tax return** in which the group files a tax return as if it were one entity for tax purposes. An **affiliated group** exists when one corporation owns at least 80 percent of (1) the total voting power and (2) the total stock value of another corporation.[33] Filing a consolidated tax return allows the losses of one group member to offset income of other members. Further, income from certain intercompany transactions is deferred until realized through a transaction outside of the affiliated group. However, losses from certain intercompany transactions are deferred until realized through a transaction outside of the affiliated group.

Affiliated groups cannot file a consolidated tax return unless they elect to do so. Because the election is binding on subsequent years, it should be made with care. Consolidated tax returns may impose additional administrative and compliance costs on the taxpayers. The consolidated tax return laws are very complex and beyond the scope of this text. Further, the rules for consolidated reporting for financial statement purposes are different from the tax rules.

Corporate Tax Return Due Dates and Estimated Taxes

The tax return due date for a C corporation is two and one-half months after the corporation's year-end. Thus, a calendar-year corporation's unextended tax return due date is March 15. Corporations requesting an extension can extend the due date for filing their tax returns (not for paying the taxes) for six months (September 15 for calendar-year corporations).

Corporations with a federal income tax liability of $500 or more (including the alternative minimum tax—discussed below) are required to pay their tax liability for the year in quarterly estimated installments.[34] The installments are due on the 15th day of the 4th, 6th, 9th, and 12th months of their tax year.[35] When corporations file their tax returns, they determine whether they must pay estimated tax underpayment penalties. Generally, corporations are subject to underpayment penalties if they did not pay in 25 percent, 50 percent, 75 percent, and 100 percent of their *required annual payment* with their first, second, third, and fourth installment payments, respectively.[36] The required annual payment is the *least* of:

1. 100 percent of the tax liability on the prior year's return, but only if there was a positive tax liability on the return and the prior year return covered a 12-month period (however, see discussion of "large" corporations below).
2. 100 percent of the current year tax liability (corporations usually don't rely on this method to determine the required payment because they won't know what this is until they complete their tax returns—after the estimated tax due dates).
3. 100 percent of the estimated current year tax liability using the annualized income method (discussed below).[37]

From a cash management perspective (time value of money) it generally makes sense for corporations to make the *minimum* required estimated payment installments for each quarter. Thus, as each estimated tax due date approaches, corporations will generally compute the required estimated payment under the prior year tax method (if available) and under the annualized method and pay the lesser of the two.

THE KEY FACTS

Tax Compliance

- Corporations report taxable income on Form 1120.
- Corporations with total assets of less than $10M report book–tax differences on Schedule M-1 of Form 1120. Otherwise, they are required to report book–tax differences on Schedule M-3.
- Tax return due date is 2.5 months after year-end.
    - Extensions of filing return (not paying taxes) for six additional months after year-end.
- An affiliated group may file a consolidated tax return.
- Corporations pay expected annual tax liability through estimated tax payments.
    - Installments due in 4th, 6th, 9th, and 12th months of their taxable year.
- Underpayment penalties apply if estimated tax payments are inadequate.

[33]§1504(a).

[34]§6655; §6655(e).

[35]§6655(c).

[36]§6665(d).

[37]§6655(e). Corporations may also use the adjusted seasonal income method of determining their required estimated tax payments. This method is similar in concept to the annualized method but is less common and is beyond the scope of this text.

The **annualized income method** is perhaps the most popular method of determining estimated tax payments (particularly for corporations that can't use the prior year tax liability to determine their current year estimated tax payment obligations) because corporations can use this method as a safe harbor to avoid estimated payment penalties. Under this method, corporations determine their taxable income as of the end of each quarter and then annualize (project) the amounts to determine their estimated taxable income and tax liability for the year. The estimated annual tax liability is used at the end of each quarter to determine the minimum required estimated payment for that quarter. Corporations use the first quarter taxable income to project their annual tax liability for the *first and second quarter* estimated tax payments. They use taxable income at the end of the second quarter to determine the third quarter estimated tax payment requirement, and taxable income at the end of the third quarter to determine their fourth quarter payment requirement. Exhibit 5-11 shows the formula for computing estimated taxable income under the annualized income method.

EXHIBIT 5-11 Estimated Taxable Income Computation under Annualized Income Method

Installment	(1) Taxable Income (first __ months of year)	(2) Annualization Factor	(1) × (2) Annual Estimated Taxable Income
First quarter	3	12/3 = 4	
Second quarter	3	12/3 = 4	
Third quarter	6	12/6 = 2	
Fourth quarter	9	12/9 = 1.3333	

Example 5-22

PCC determined its taxable income at the close of the first, second, and third quarters as follows:

Quarter-end	Cumulative Taxable Income
First	$1,000,000
Second	3,200,000
Third	4,000,000

What is its annual estimated taxable income for estimated tax purposes as of the end of the first, second, third, and fourth quarters respectively?

Answer: $4,000,000 for the first and second quarters, $6,400,000 for the third quarter, and $5,333,333 for the fourth quarter, computed as follows:

Installment	(1) Taxable Income	(2) Annualization Factor	(1) × (2) Annual Estimated Taxable Income
First quarter	$1,000,000	12/3 = 4	**$4,000,000**
Second quarter	1,000,000	12/3 = 4	**4,000,000**
Third quarter	3,200,000	12/6 = 2	**6,400,000**
Fourth quarter	4,000,000	12/9 = 1.333	**5,333,333**

Once corporations have determined their annual estimated taxable income for each quarter, they can use the formulas in Exhibit 5-12 to compute the required estimated tax installments for each quarter under the annualized income method.

EXHIBIT 5-12 Estimated Taxable Income Computation under Annualized Income Method

Installment	(1) Annual Estimated Taxable Income	(2) Tax on Estimated Taxable Income	(3) Percentage of Tax Required to Be Paid	(4) (2) × (3) Required Cumulative Payment	(5) Prior Cumulative Payments	(4) – (5) Required Estimated Tax Payment
First quarter			25%			
Second quarter			50			
Third quarter			75			
Fourth quarter			100			

Example 5-23

Based on the estimated taxable income in the previous example, what are PCC's required estimated tax payments for the year under the annualized income method?

Answer: $340,000 for the first and second quarters, $952,000 for the third quarter, and $181,333 for the fourth quarter, computed as follows:

Installment	(1) Annual Estimated Taxable Income	(2) Tax on Estimated Taxable Income (flat 34 percent)	(3) Percentage of Tax Required to Be Paid	(4) (2) × (3) Required Cumulative Payment	(5) Prior Cumulative Payments	(4) – (5) Required Estimated Tax Payment
First quarter	$4,000,000	$1,360,000	25%	$ 340,000	$ 0	**$340,000**
Second quarter	4,000,000	1,360,000	50	680,000	340,000	**340,000**
Third quarter	6,400,000	2,176,000	75	1,632,000	680,000	**952,000**
Fourth quarter	5,333,333	1,813,333	100	1,813,333	1,632,000	**181,333**

Can PCC use its prior year tax liability to determine its current year estimated tax payments?

Answer: No. PCC reported a net operating loss last year and did not pay taxes so it may not use its prior year tax liability to determine its current year estimated tax payments.

Can PCC use its current year tax liability to determine its current year estimated tax payments?

Answer: Yes. As we determined in Example 5-19, PCC's actual tax liability for the year is $1,751,238. So, PCC could have avoided estimated tax penalties by paying in $437,810 each quarter ($1,751,238 × 25%). However, it did not know this amount when it was required to make its estimated tax payments so it would likely have used the annualized income method of determining its estimated tax payments to protect itself from penalties.

"Large" corporations, defined as corporations with over $1,000,000 of taxable income in *any* of the three years prior to the current year,[38] may use the prior year tax liability to determine their *first quarter* estimated tax payments only. If they use the prior year tax liability to determine their first quarter payment, their second quarter payment must "catch up" their estimated payments. That is, the second quarter payment must be large enough for the sum of their first and second quarter payments to equal or exceed 50 percent of their projected current year tax liability.[39]

[38]§6655(g)(2).
[39]§6655(d).

Example 5-24

What if: Assume that last year PCC reported taxable income of $2,000,000 and a tax liability of $680,000. Further, PCC determined its required estimated tax payments under the annualized method as described in the previous example. What would be PCC's required minimum estimated tax payments for each quarter for the current year (ignore the current year tax requirement because PCC is unsure what its current year tax will be)?

Answer: $170,000 for the first quarter, $510,000 for the second quarter, $952,000 for the third quarter, and $181,333 for the fourth quarter, computed as follows:

Installment	(1) Estimated Tax Payment under Prior Year Tax Exception	(2) Estimated Tax Payment under Annualized Method	(3) Required Cumulative Payment for Quarter × [sum of the lesser of (1) or (2) through quarter]	(4) Prior Cumulative Payments	(5) (3) − (4) Required Estimated Tax Payment
First quarter	$170,000*	$340,000	$ 170,000	$ 0	**$170,000**
Second quarter	Not applicable*	340,000	680,000	170,000	**510,000**
Third quarter	Not applicable*	952,000	1,632,000	680,000	**952,000**
Fourth quarter	Not applicable*	181,333	1,813,333	1,632,000	**181,333**

*Because PCC is a large corporation, it may determine its first quarter estimated tax payment using its prior year liability ($680,000 × 25% = $170,000). However, it must use the annualized method to determine its second, third, and fourth quarter required payments.

With its second installment, PCC must have paid in $680,000. Because it only paid in $170,000 with the first quarter installment, it must pay $510,000 with its second quarter payment.

What if: Assume the same facts as above, except that last year PCC paid $200,000 in tax and PCC is not a large corporation. What would be PCC's required minimum estimated tax payments for each quarter (ignore the current year tax requirement)?

Answer: $50,000 for the first quarter, $50,000 for the second quarter, $50,000 for the third quarter, and $50,000 for the fourth quarter, computed as follows:

Installment	(1) Estimated Tax Payment under Prior Year Tax Exception ($200,000/4)	(2) Estimated Tax Payment under Annualized Method	(3) Required Cumulative Payment for Quarter × [sum of the lesser of (1) or (2) through quarter ×]	(4) Prior Cumulative Payments	(5) (3) − (4) Required Estimated Tax Payment
First quarter	$50,000	$340,000	$ 50,000	$ 0	**$50,000**
Second quarter	50,000	340,000	100,000	50,000	**50,000**
Third quarter	50,000	952,000	150,000	100,000	**50,000**
Fourth quarter	50,000	181,333	200,000	150,000	**50,000**

PCC can use the prior year tax to determine its minimum required estimated tax payments.

Corporations that have underpaid their estimated taxes for any quarter must pay an underpayment penalty determined on Form 2220. The amount of the penalty is based on the underpayment rate (or interest rate), the amount of the underpayment, and the period of the underpayment. The interest rate is generally the federal short-term interest rate plus 3 percent. The period of the underpayment is the due date for the installment through the earlier of (1) the date the payment is made or (2) the 15th day of the third month after the close of the tax year. The penalties are not deductible.[40]

[40]§6655(b)(2).

continued from page 5-1...
Elise figured she was done when she sat down to discuss PCC's tax return with Darryl. Darryl only had a few review comments. One of the comments sounded pretty important, though. Darryl asked Elise if PCC owed any alternative minimum tax. Elise told Darryl she would get back to him on that one. She left Darryl's office and immediately started researching the alternative minimum tax. ■

CORPORATE ALTERNATIVE MINIMUM TAX

LO 5-4

Back in the early 1980s Congress was concerned that many large corporations were reporting positive financial income to shareholders, but reporting tax losses or minimal taxable income to the IRS and, as a result, not paying what the voting public perceived as their fair share of taxes. A common perception was that big businesses (and wealthy individuals) had the ability and sophistication to avoid paying taxes while middle-class taxpayers were carrying a disproportionate amount of the country's tax burden. Congress decided to do something about this perceived inequity by enacting the corporate (and individual) **alternative minimum tax** as part of the Tax Reform Act of 1986. The alternative minimum tax is a tax on a base broader than the regular tax base. The alternative minimum tax is designed to require corporations to pay some minimum level of tax even when they have low or no regular taxable income due to certain tax breaks they gain from the tax code.

Small corporations are exempt from the AMT. For this purpose, small corporations are those with average annual gross receipts *less than* $7.5 million for the three years prior to the current tax year. New corporations are automatically exempt from the AMT in their first year of existence, and they are exempt from the AMT for their first three years of existence as long as their average annual gross receipts are below $5 million during the three-year period. Once a corporation fails the AMT gross-receipts test, it is no longer exempt from the AMT.

Corporations compute their alternative minimum tax by multiplying their AMT base by the 20 percent AMT rate and then subtracting their regular tax liability from the product of the base and rate.[41] To determine their AMT base, corporations start with regular taxable income, add preference items, add or subtract certain adjustments, and then subtract an exemption amount. Exhibit 5-13 presents the corporate AMT formula.

Preference Items

When computing alternative minimum taxable income, corporations *add* preference items to taxable income. These items represent tax breaks that corporations received for regular tax purposes, but that Congress chose to eliminate for alternative minimum tax purposes. Common preference items include percentage depletion in excess of cost basis and tax-exempt interest income from a **private activity bond** (a municipal bond used to fund a nonpublic activity—if the bond is for a public purpose, the interest is not a preference item). Tax exempt interest on private activity bonds issued in 2009 or 2010 is not an AMT tax preference item.[42]

[41]§55(a).

[42]§56(a)(5)(C)(vi).

EXHIBIT 5-13 Corporate AMT Formula

Taxable income or loss before NOL deduction
Add: Preference items
Add or subtract: Adjustments
Preadjustment AMT income
Add or subtract: ACE adjustment
Subtract: AMT NOL deduction
Alternative minimum taxable income (AMTI)
Subtract: Exemption
AMT base
× 20%
Gross AMT
− AMT foreign tax credit
Tentative minimum tax
Subtract: Regular income tax
Alternative minimum tax if positive

Example 5-25

Elise reviewed PCC's book–tax reconciliation provided in Exhibit 5-7 to determine if it had any preference items during the year. What preference items if any should PCC report for alternative minimum tax purposes?

Answer: $12,000 tax-exempt interest income from the San Diego municipal bond issued in 2013. The bond is a private activity bond because proceeds from the bond were used to fund a privately owned and used baseball stadium.

What if: Assume the San Diego municipal bond proceeds were used to construct public roads. Would the interest represent an AMT preference item?

Answer: No, because the bond was not a private activity bond.

Adjustments

Corporations may add or subtract alternative minimum tax adjustments to regular taxable income in computing alternative minimum taxable income.[43] Whether the adjustment is positive (unfavorable) or negative (favorable) for a particular item depends on the way the corporation accounts for the item for regular taxable income purposes and the way it accounts for the item for AMT purposes. In general, the most common AMT adjustments for corporations are (1) depreciation, (2) gain or loss on sale of depreciable assets, and (3) adjusted current earnings (ACE).

Depreciation Adjustment Corporations with fixed assets may benefit from the highly accelerated depreciation methods allowed under the regular taxable income system. For alternative minimum tax purposes, assets aren't depreciated as quickly.[44] Consequently, in the early years of an asset's depreciable life, regular tax depreciation exceeds alternative minimum tax depreciation, and corporations must make positive adjustments to regular taxable income to compute the AMT base. However,

[43]§56.

[44]Chapter 2 describes the regular tax and alternative minimum tax depreciable lives and methods.

after corporations fully depreciate assets for regular tax purposes they may still have basis left to depreciate for AMT purposes. In these situations, corporations make negative AMT depreciation adjustments to regular taxable income to compute the AMT base.

Example 5-26

Elise reviewed the tax depreciation calculations. She discovered that although PCC deducted $3,100,000 of depreciation expense for regular tax purposes, it was entitled to deduct only $2,500,000 for AMT purposes. What is the amount of PCC's depreciation AMT adjustment? Is the adjustment positive or negative?

Answer: $600,000 positive or unfavorable adjustment, computed as follows:

Description	Amount	Explanation
(1) Regular tax depreciation	$3,100,000	Exhibit 5-7.
(2) AMT depreciation	2,500,000	
Positive or unfavorable AMT adjustment	**$ 600,000**	(1) – (2).

Gain or Loss on Disposition of Depreciable Assets Depreciation differences for regular tax and AMT purposes cause differences in the adjusted basis of the assets for regular tax purposes and AMT purposes. Consequently, when corporations sell or dispose of depreciable assets before they completely depreciate them, they will likely recognize a different gain or loss for regular tax purposes than they recognize for AMT purposes. If the regular tax gain is greater than the AMT gain, due to accelerated depreciation, corporations make negative adjustments to regular taxable income to compute the AMT base.

Example 5-27

Elise discovered that while PCC's regular tax gain on fixed asset dispositions for the year was $70,000, its AMT gain on fixed asset dispositions was only $55,000. What is the amount of PCC's fixed asset dispositions AMT adjustment? Is the adjustment positive or negative?

Answer: $15,000 negative (favorable), computed as follows:

Description	Amount	Explanation
(1) AMT gain on fixed asset dispositions	$55,000	
(2) Regular tax gain on fixed asset dispositions	70,000	Exhibit 5-7.
Negative or (favorable) AMT adjustment	**($15,000)**	(1) – (2).

ACE Adjustment The ACE **(adjusted current earnings)** adjustment is designed to capture various sources of economic income not otherwise included in the alternative minimum tax base. Consequently, unlike other adjustments, the ACE adjustment is not tied to any one item. To calculate the ACE adjustment, a corporation must first compute its adjusted current earnings. Adjusted current earnings is computed by making certain modifications (designed to reflect economic income) to AMTI (discussed below). Once the corporation has computed its ACE it determines its ACE *adjustment* by subtracting AMTI (before the ACE adjustment) from ACE

THE KEY FACTS

Alternative Minimum Tax

- Corporations with average annual gross receipts less than $7.5M for three years prior to the current year are exempt from tax.
  - Corporations are exempt from tax in their first year of existence.
  - For first three years, exempt if annual average gross receipts are below $5M.
  - Once fail gross receipts test, no longer exempt.
- Common preference items are tax-exempt interest from private activity

(continued)

bonds (unless issued in 2009 or 2010) and percentage depletion in excess of cost basis.

- Common adjustments are for depreciation, gain or loss on sale of depreciable assets, and adjusted current earnings.
  - ACE adjustment is sum of ACE adjustment items times 75 percent.

and multiplying the difference by 75 percent [(ACE – AMTI) × 75%].[45] Exhibit 5-14 describes several of the more common modifications to AMTI in computing ACE and indicates whether each modification is added to or subtracted from AMTI to determine ACE.

EXHIBIT 5-14 Common Modifications to AMTI to Determine ACE

Description	Modification to AMTI
Tax-exempt interest income from tax-exempt bond that funds a public *activity* (as opposed to private activity). If bond was issued in 2009 or 2010 it is not a modification.[46]	+
Difference between AMT depreciation and ACE depreciation*	+ or –
Difference between AMT and ACE gain or loss on asset disposition	+ or –
Death benefit from life insurance contracts	+
70 percent dividends received deduction (not the 80 percent or 100 percent deduction)	+
Organizational expenditures that were expensed during the year	+
Difference between gain reported under the installment method and gain otherwise reported (installment method not allowed for ACE purposes)	+ or –

*This adjustment may apply only for assets placed in service after 1989 and before 1994.

As a practical matter, the amount of the ACE adjustment can be determined by multiplying the sum of the modifications to AMTI in computing ACE by 75 percent. If the sum of the modifications is negative, the ACE adjustment may also be negative. However, negative ACE adjustments in excess of cumulative positive prior year ACE adjustments are not allowed.[47]

Example 5-28

Finally, Elise focused on the ACE adjustment. She discovered that the only modification to AMTI for computing ACE was the $21,000 (70 percent) dividends received deduction. What is PCC's ACE adjustment?

Answer: $15,750, positive adjustment, computed as follows:

Description	Amount	Explanation
(1) Dividends received deduction	$21,000	70 percent dividends received deduction is not deductible in determining ACE.
(2) ACE adjustment percentage	75%	§56(g)(1).
Positive or unfavorable ACE adjustment	**$15,750**	(1) × (2).

What if: Assume that PCC did not receive any dividends and that the San Diego bond generating $12,000 of tax-exempt interest is *not* a private activity bond. Further, assume that PCC reported $5,000 of organizational expenses this year and it reported $20,000 of gain this year from an installment sale it executed two years ago. Assuming PCC's cumulative ACE adjustment as of the beginning of the year is $100,000, what is its current year ACE adjustment under these circumstances?

[45]§56(g)(1).
[46]§56(g)(4)(B)(iv).
[47]§56(g)(2).

Answer: $2,250 negative ACE adjustment.

Description	Amount	Explanation
(1) Tax-exempt interest	$12,000	Public activity bond.
(2) Organizational expenses	5,000	Not deductible for ACE.
(3) Installment gain	(20,000)	Negative modification because all gain was already included in ACE in year of sale (prior year).
(4) Total modification items	($3,000)	(1) + (2) + (3).
(5) ACE adjustment percentage	75%	§56(g)(1).
Negative or favorable ACE adjustment	**($2,250)**	(4) × (5). Not limited because prior year cumulated ACE adjustment is positive $100,000.

What if: Assume the same facts as above except that PCC's cumulative positive ACE adjustment at the beginning of the year was $1,000 rather than $100,000. What would be PCC's ACE adjustment in these circumstances?

Answer: $1,000 negative ACE adjustment. PCC's current year negative ACE adjustment is limited to the cumulative positive ACE adjustment at the beginning of the year.

AMT NOL Deduction (ATNOLD) If the deductions allowed in computing AMTI exceed the income included in AMTI, the excess becomes an AMT net operating loss (ATNOL). The ATNOL can be carried back two years (elective) and carried forward 20 years, similar to a regular tax NOL. The AMT NOL deduction (AMTNOLD) is limited to 90 percent of AMTI computed without regard to the ATNOLD and the domestic production activities deduction.

Alternative Minimum Taxable Income (AMTI) Corporations compute their alternative minimum taxable income by adding their preference items and adding or subtracting their adjustments from regular taxable income. The alternative minimum taxable income is an important number because corporations use it to determine the amount of the AMT exemption (discussed next) they are allowed to deduct to compute their AMT base.

Example 5-29

After computing PCC's preference items and adjustments Elise had all the information she needed to compute PCC's AMTI. What is PCC's AMTI?

Answer: $5,763,450, computed as follows:

Description	Amount	Explanation
(1) Regular taxable income	$5,150,700	Exhibit 5-7.
(2) Preference items	12,000	Example 5-25.
(3) Depreciation adjustment	600,000	Example 5-26.
(4) Fixed asset disposition adjustment	(15,000)	Example 5-27.
(5) ACE adjustment	15,750	Example 5-28.
Alternative minimum taxable income (AMTI)	$5,763,450	Sum of (1) through (5).

Note, the NOL deduction of $24,000 is less than the 90 percent limitation applied to modified AMTI. The limitation is $5,627,205, computed as 90 percent × (5,763,450 + 24,000 + 465,000 DPAD).

AMT Exemption Much like individual taxpayers are allowed to deduct standard deductions and personal exemptions in computing their taxable income, corporations are allowed to deduct a certain exemption amount in computing their alternative minimum tax base. The exemption is subject to an AMTI-based phase-out. The full exemption amount for corporations is $40,000. The exemption is phased out by 25 percent of the amount that AMTI exceeds $150,000 and is completely phased out for corporations with AMTI of at least $310,000.[48] Thus, the exemption is fully phased out for only moderately profitable large corporations. However, the exemption protects many small corporations from paying the alternative minimum tax.

Example 5-30

Because PCC's AMTI exceeds $310,000, Elise determined that PCC's deductible AMT exemption amount is $0.

What if: If PCC's AMTI was $200,000, what exemption amount would it deduct?

Answer: $27,500, computed as follows:

Description	Amount	Explanation
(1) Full exemption amount	$ 40,000	§55(d)(2).
(2) Assumed AMTI	200,000	
(3) Exemption phase-out threshold	150,000	§55(d)(3).
(4) AMTI over exemption threshold)	$ 50,000	(2) − (3).
(5) Phase-out percentage	25%	§55(d)(3).
(6) Exemption phase-out amount	$ 12,500	(4) × (5).
Deductible exemption	**$ 27,500**	(1) − (6).

THE KEY FACTS

Alternative Minimum Tax

- AMT full exemption amount is $40,000.
  - Phase-out 25 percent for each $1 of AMTI in excess of $150,000.
- AMT rate is 20 percent.
- AMT equals excess of TMT over regular tax liability.
- Tentative minimum tax credit reduces regular tax down to TMT in year corporation doesn't owe AMT.

Alternative Minimum Tax To determine their alternative minimum tax, corporations next compute their **tentative minimum tax** (TMT) by multiplying their AMT base (AMTI minus exemption amount) by a flat 20 percent rate. Then they compare their TMT to their regular tax liability. If a corporation's regular tax liability is greater than the TMT, it does not owe any alternative minimum tax. If its TMT is greater than its regular tax liability, it must pay its regular tax liability and the excess of the TMT over its regular tax liability. This excess is the alternative minimum tax. Corporations are allowed to reduce the gross AMT by any foreign tax credits they have for regular tax purposes.

Example 5-31

Elise had enough information to compute PCC's alternative minimum tax. She knew the tax software would compute the AMT but she wanted to calculate it independent from the program to ensure the results were accurate. What is PCC's alternative minimum tax, if any?

Answer: $0, computed as follows:

Description	Amount	Explanation
(1) AMTI	$5,763,450	Example 5-29.
(2) Deductible exemption	0	Example 5-30.
(3) AMT base	$5,763,450	(1) + (2).
(4) AMT rate	20%	§55(b)(3)(D).
(5) Tentative minimum tax	$1,152,690	(3) × (4).
(6) Regular tax	$1,751,238	Example 5-19.
Alternative minimum tax	**$ 0**	(5) − (6), but not less than $0.

[48]§55(d)(2).

What if: If PCC's regular tax liability had been $1,000,000, what would be the amount of its AMT?

Answer: $152,690, which is the excess of the $1,152,690 TMT over the $1,000,000 regular tax liability. PCC would pay its $1,000,000 regular tax liability and $152,690 of AMT.

When corporations owe the alternative minimum tax, they generate a **minimum tax credit** that they can carry forward *indefinitely* to offset their regular tax liability down to their tentative minimum tax in years when their regular tax exceeds their tentative minimum tax. That is, they can use the tentative minimum tax credit in years when they do not owe the alternative minimum tax.

Example 5-32

What if: Assume that in year 1, PCC has a TMT of $1,152,690 and a regular tax liability of $1,000,000. PCC would owe $152,690 of AMT and $1,000,000 of regular tax. It would also generate a $152,690 minimum tax credit. Further, assume that in year 2 PCC reports a tentative minimum tax of $900,000 and a regular tax liability of $1,000,000. What is PCC's tax liability after applying the minimum tax credit?

Answer: $900,000 tax liability and $52,690 minimum tax credit carryover, computed as follows:

Description	Amount	Explanation
(1) Year 1 minimum tax credit	$ 152,690	
(2) Year 2 tentative minimum tax	900,000	
(3) Year 2 regular tax liability	1,000,000	
(4) Year 2 AMT	0	(2) − (3), but not less than $0.
(5) Limit on year 2 minimum tax credit	100,000	(3) − (2).
(6) Year 2 minimum tax credit	100,000	Lesser of (1) and (5).
(7) Total tax liability for year	**900,000**	(3) − (6).
Minimum tax credit carryover	**52,690**	(1) − (6).

Exhibit 5-15 presents PCC's Form 4626: Alternative Minimum Tax—Corporations.

CONCLUSION

A taxable or C corporation is a separate legal and taxpaying entity from its stockholders. Consequently, it must determine and report its own taxable income to the IRS. This chapter discussed and described the process of computing a corporation's taxable income and the associated tax liability for C corporations. We learned that book income is the starting point for determining taxable income. Corporations adjust their book income for book–tax differences that arise because they account for many items of income and deduction differently for book purposes than they do for tax purposes. Some of these book–tax differences are temporary (the differences balance out over time) and some are permanent in nature (they don't balance out over the long-term). As we discover in the next chapter, the distinction between temporary and permanent book–tax differences is critical for corporations computing their income tax expense or benefit for financial accounting purposes.

EXHIBIT 5-15 PCC's Form 4626

Form **4626** | Department of the Treasury Internal Revenue Service

Alternative Minimum Tax—Corporations

▶ Attach to the corporation's tax return.
▶ Information about Form 4626 and its separate instructions is at *www.irs.gov/form4626*.

OMB No. 1545-0123 | 2014

Name	Employer identification number
Premier Computer Corporation	12-3456789

Note: *See the instructions to find out if the corporation is a small corporation exempt from the alternative minimum tax (AMT) under section 55(e).*

1	Taxable income or (loss) before net operating loss deduction			1	5,150,700
2	**Adjustments and preferences:**				
a	Depreciation of post-1986 property			2a	600,000
b	Amortization of certified pollution control facilities			2b	
c	Amortization of mining exploration and development costs			2c	
d	Amortization of circulation expenditures (personal holding companies only)			2d	
e	Adjusted gain or loss			2e	(15,000)
f	Long-term contracts			2f	
g	Merchant marine capital construction funds			2g	
h	Section 833(b) deduction (Blue Cross, Blue Shield, and similar type organizations only)			2h	
i	Tax shelter farm activities (personal service corporations only)			2i	
j	Passive activities (closely held corporations and personal service corporations only)			2j	
k	Loss limitations			2k	
l	Depletion			2l	
m	Tax-exempt interest income from specified private activity bonds			2m	12,000
n	Intangible drilling costs			2n	
o	Other adjustments and preferences			2o	
3	Pre-adjustment alternative minimum taxable income (AMTI). Combine lines 1 through 2o			3	5,747,700
4	**Adjusted current earnings (ACE) adjustment:**				
a	ACE from line 10 of the ACE worksheet in the instructions	4a	5,768,700		
b	Subtract line 3 from line 4a. If line 3 exceeds line 4a, enter the difference as a negative amount (see instructions)	4b	21,000		
c	Multiply line 4b by 75% (.75). Enter the result as a positive amount	4c	15,750		
d	Enter the excess, if any, of the corporation's total increases in AMTI from prior year ACE adjustments over its total reductions in AMTI from prior year ACE adjustments (see instructions). **Note:** *You **must** enter an amount on line 4d (even if line 4b is positive).*	4d			
e	ACE adjustment. • If line 4b is zero or more, enter the amount from line 4c • If line 4b is less than zero, enter the **smaller** of line 4c or line 4d as a negative amount			4e	15,750
5	Combine lines 3 and 4e. If zero or less, stop here; the corporation does not owe any AMT			5	5,763,450
6	Alternative tax net operating loss deduction (see instructions)			6	
7	**Alternative minimum taxable income.** Subtract line 6 from line 5. If the corporation held a residual interest in a REMIC, see instructions			7	5,763,450
8	**Exemption phase-out** (if line 7 is $310,000 or more, skip lines 8a and 8b and enter -0- on line 8c):				
a	Subtract $150,000 from line 7 (if completing this line for a member of a controlled group, see instructions). If zero or less, enter -0-	8a			
b	Multiply line 8a by 25% (.25)	8b			
c	Exemption. Subtract line 8b from $40,000 (if completing this line for a member of a controlled group, see instructions). If zero or less, enter -0-			8c	0
9	Subtract line 8c from line 7. If zero or less, enter -0-			9	5,763,450
10	Multiply line 9 by 20% (.20)			10	1,152,690
11	Alternative minimum tax foreign tax credit (AMTFTC) (see instructions)			11	
12	Tentative minimum tax. Subtract line 11 from line 10			12	1,562,290
13	Regular tax liability before applying all credits except the foreign tax credit			13	1,751,238
14	**Alternative minimum tax.** Subtract line 13 from line 12. If zero or less, enter -0-. Enter here and on Form 1120, Schedule J, line 3, or the appropriate line of the corporation's income tax return			14	0

For Paperwork Reduction Act Notice, see separate instructions. Cat. No. 12955I Form **4626** (2014)

Summary

Describe the corporate income tax formula, compare and contrast the corporate to the individual tax formula, and discuss tax considerations relating to corporations' accounting periods and accounting methods. LO 5-1

- A corporation's taxable income is gross income minus deductions.
- The corporate tax formula is similar to the individual formula except that corporations don't itemize deductions or deduct standard deductions. Corporations also don't deduct personal and dependency exemptions.
- Corporations may generally elect any tax year for reporting their taxable income, but the year must coincide with their financial accounting year.
- The timing of a corporation's income and deductions depends on the corporation's overall accounting method and its methods for specific transactions.
- Corporations are generally required to use the accrual overall method of accounting. However, smaller corporations may be allowed to use the cash method.

Identify common book–tax differences, distinguish between permanent and temporary differences, and compute a corporation's taxable income and regular tax liability. LO 5-2

- Corporations typically compute taxable income by starting with book income and adjusting for book–tax differences.
- Book–tax differences are favorable when they reduce taxable income relative to book income and unfavorable when they increase it.
- Book–tax differences are permanent when the amount of income or deduction items is different for book and tax purposes and the amount will not reverse in the future.
- Book–tax differences are temporary when the amount of income or deduction item is different for book and tax purposes in the current year but the same for book and tax purposes over the long-term. That is, temporary book–tax differences reverse over time.
- Common permanent book–tax differences include interest from municipal bonds (favorable), life insurance premiums on policies covering key employees (unfavorable), and one-half of meals and entertainment expense, among others.
- Nonqualified stock options granted before ASC 718's effective date generate favorable permanent book–tax differences when employees exercise them. The amount of the difference is the bargain element of the options that is deductible for tax but not for books.
- Common temporary book–tax differences include depreciation expense, gain or loss on sale of depreciable assets, bad-debt expense, purchased goodwill amortization, and warranty expense, among others.
- Stock options granted when ASC 718 applies can generate temporary and permanent book–tax differences.
- Corporations may not deduct net capital losses for tax purposes. However, they may carry them back three years and forward five years to offset capital gains in those other years.
- When computing their net operating losses for the year, corporations may not deduct net operating losses from other years or net capital losses from other years.
- Subject to limitation, corporations can deduct as the amount of money, the fair market value of capital gain property, and the adjusted basis of ordinary income property they donate to charity.
- The charitable contribution deduction for the year is limited to 10 percent of taxable income before deducting the charitable contribution, the dividends received deduction, NOL carrybacks, the domestic production activities deduction, and capital loss carrybacks. Amounts in excess of the limitation can be carried forward for up to five years.
- Corporations are allowed a deduction for dividends received to help mitigate potential triple taxation of the income distributed as a dividend. The amount of the deduction depends on the corporation's ownership in the distributing corporation. The deduction is 70 percent if the ownership is less than 20 percent; the deduction is 80 percent if the ownership is at least 20 percent but less than 80 percent; and finally, the deduction is 100 percent if the ownership is 80 percent or more.

- The dividends received deduction (DRD) is subject to a taxable income limitation. This limitation does not apply if the full DRD extends or creates a net operating loss for the corporation in the current year.
- A corporation's marginal tax rates range from 15 percent to 39 percent. High-income corporations are taxed at a flat 35 percent tax rate.
- Controlled groups are groups of corporations with common ownership. Special rules apply to limit the tax benefits (including lower marginal tax rates) of splitting large corporations into smaller corporations. Controlled groups can be parent-subsidiary controlled groups, brother-sister controlled groups, or combined groups.

LO 5-3 Describe a corporation's tax return reporting and estimated tax payment obligations.

- Corporations file their tax returns on Form 1120, which are due two and one-half months after the corporation's year-end. Corporations can apply for an extension of the due date for filing the return for six months.
- Small corporations report their book–tax differences on Schedule M-1 of Form 1120. Large corporations (assets of $10 million or more) report them on Schedule M-3. Schedule M-3 requires much more detail than Schedule M-1.
- Corporations pay income taxes through estimated tax payments. Each payment should be 25 percent of their required annual payment. The installments are due on the 15th day of the 4th, 6th, 9th, and 12th months of the corporation's taxable year.
- Corporations' required annual payment is the least of (1) 100 percent of their current year tax liability, (2) 100 percent of their prior year tax liability (but only if they had a positive tax liability in the prior year), or (3) 100 percent of the estimated current year tax liability using the annualized income method. Large corporations may rely on (2) only to compute their first quarter estimated payment requirement.

LO 5-4 Calculate a corporation's alternative minimum tax liability.

- The alternative minimum tax is a tax on a broader base than the regular tax. It ensures that corporations are not able to avoid taxes entirely by receiving tax-advantaged treatment for regular income tax items. The alternative minimum tax rate is a flat 20 percent for corporations.
- To compute alternative minimum taxable income, corporations start with regular taxable income and add preferences, add or subtract adjustments, and subtract an exemption amount. The AMT base is taxed at 20 percent to provide a tentative minimum tax. The AMT is the excess of the tentative minimum tax over the regular tax.
- Corporations receive a minimum tax credit in the amount of the alternative minimum tax they pay for the year. This credit can offset the corporation's regular tax liability to the extent it exceeds the tentative minimum tax in a future year.

KEY TERMS

adjusted current earnings (ACE) (5-35)
affiliated group (5-29)
alternative minimum tax (5-33)
annualized income method (5-30)
bargain element (5-9)
book (financial reporting) income (5-3)
book–tax differences (5-3)
brother-sister controlled group (5-24)
capital gain property (5-15)
charitable contribution limit modified taxable income (5-16)
combined controlled group (5-24)
controlled groups (5-24)
consolidated tax return (5-29)
DRD modified taxable income (5-19)
exercise price (5-9)
favorable book–tax difference (5-4)
incentive stock options (5-9)
M adjustments (5-25)
minimum tax credit (5-39)
net capital loss carryback (5-12)
net capital loss carryover (5-12)
net operating loss (NOL) (5-14)
net operating loss carryback (5-14)
net operating loss carryover (5-14)
nonqualified stock options (5-9)
ordinary income property (5-15)
parent-subsidiary controlled group (5-24)
permanent book–tax differences (5-4)
private activity bond (5-33)
Schedule M adjustments (5-25)
temporary book–tax differences (5-4)
tentative minimum tax (5-38)
unfavorable book–tax difference (5-4)
vest (5-9)
vesting period (5-10)

DISCUSSION QUESTIONS

1. In general terms, identify the similarities and differences between the corporate taxable income formula and the individual taxable income formula. LO 5-1
2. Is a corporation's choice of its tax year independent from its year-end for financial accounting purposes? LO 5-1
3. Can C corporations use the cash method of accounting? Explain. LO 5-1
4. Briefly describe the process of computing a corporation's taxable income assuming the corporation must use GAAP to determine its book income. How might the process differ for corporations not required to use GAAP for book purposes? LO 5-2
5. What role does a corporation's audited financial statements play in determining its taxable income? LO 5-2
6. What is the difference between favorable and unfavorable book–tax differences? LO 5-2
7. What is the difference between permanent and temporary book–tax differences? LO 5-2
8. Why is it important to be able to determine whether a particular book–tax difference is permanent or temporary? LO 5-2
9. Describe the relation between the book–tax differences associated with depreciation expense and with gain or loss on disposition of depreciable assets. LO 5-2
10. When a corporation receives a dividend from another corporation, does the dividend generate a book–tax difference to the dividend-receiving corporation (ignore the dividends received deduction)? Explain. LO 5-2
11. Describe how goodwill recognized in an asset acquisition leads to temporary book–tax differences. LO 5-2
12. Describe the book–tax differences that arise from incentive stock options and nonqualified stock options granted before ASC 718 (the codification of FAS 123R) became effective. LO 5-2
13. Describe the book–tax differences that arise from incentive stock options granted after ASC 718 (the codification of FAS 123R) became effective. LO 5-2
14. Describe the book–tax differences that arise from nonqualified stock options granted after ASC 718 (the codification of FAS 123R) became effective. LO 5-2
15. How do corporations account for capital gains and losses for tax purposes? How is this different from the way individuals account for capital gains and losses? LO 5-2
16. What are the common book–tax differences relating to accounting for capital gains and losses? Do these differences create favorable or unfavorable book-to-tax adjustments? LO 5-2
17. What is the carryback and carryover period for a net operating loss? Does it depend on the size of the corporation? Explain. LO 5-2
18. Is a corporation allowed to carry a net operating loss forward if it has income in prior years that it could offset with a carryback? Explain. LO 5-2
19. What must a decision maker consider when deciding whether to carry back a net operating loss or to elect to forgo the carryback? LO 5-2
20. A corporation commissioned an accounting firm to recalculate the way it accounted for leasing transactions. With the new calculations, the corporation was able to file amended tax returns for the past few years that increased the corporation's net operating loss carryover from $3,000,000 to $5,000,000. Was the corporation wise to pay the accountants for their work that led to the increase in the NOL carryover? What factors should be considered in making this determination? LO 5-2
21. Compare and contrast the general rule for determining the amount of the charitable contribution if the corporation contributes capital gain property versus ordinary income property. LO 5-2

LO 5-2 22. Which limitations might restrict a corporation's deduction for a cash charitable contribution? Explain how to determine the amount of the limitation.

LO 5-2 23. For tax purposes, what happens to a corporation's charitable contributions that are not deducted in the current year because of the taxable income limitation?

LO 5-2 24. What are common book–tax differences relating to corporate charitable contributions? Are these differences favorable or unfavorable?

LO 5-2 25. Why does Congress provide the dividends received deduction for corporations receiving dividends?

LO 5-2 26. How does a corporation determine the percentage for its dividends received deduction? Explain.

LO 5-2 27. What limitations apply to the amount of the allowable dividends received deduction?

LO 5-2 28. Why do the marginal rates in the corporate tax rate schedule increase and then decrease before increasing again?

LO 5-2 29. Explain the controlled group rules in very general terms and indicate what type of behavior the rules are attempting to prevent in terms of computing a corporation's tax liability.

LO 5-2 30. Describe the three types of controlled groups.

LO 5-3 31. How is the Schedule M-1 similar to and different from a Schedule M-3? How does a corporation determine whether it must complete Schedule M-1 or Schedule M-3 when it completes its tax return?

LO 5-3 32. What is the due date for the corporation tax return Form 1120? Is it possible to extend the due date? Explain.

LO 5-3 33. How does a corporation determine the minimum amount of estimated tax payments it must make to avoid underpayment penalties? How are these rules different for large corporations than they are for other corporations?

LO 5-3 34. Describe the annualized income method for determining a corporation's required estimated tax payments. What advantages does this method have over other methods?

LO 5-4 35. Are any corporations exempt from the AMT? Briefly explain.

LO 5-4 36. Briefly describe the process of computing a corporation's AMT.

LO 5-4 37. What is the conceptual difference between adjustments and preference items for AMT purposes?

LO 5-4 38. What does the ACE adjustment attempt to capture? How does a corporation determine its ACE adjustment?

LO 5-4 39. What is the corporate AMT exemption? Is it available to all corporations? Briefly explain.

LO 5-4 40. How is it possible that a corporation's marginal AMT rate is greater than 20 percent if the stated AMT rate is 20 percent?

LO 5-4 41. Does a corporation pay the AMT in addition to or instead of the regular tax? Briefly explain.

LO 5-4 42. How does a corporation compute its minimum tax credit? How does a minimum tax credit benefit a corporation?

LO 5-4 planning 43. What basic tax planning strategies might a corporation that is expected to owe AMT this year but not next year engage in? How would those strategies change if the corporation expected to be in AMT next year but not in the current year?

PROBLEMS

connect ACCOUNTING

All applicable problems are available with McGraw-Hill's *Connect® Accounting*.

44. LNS corporation reports book income of $2,000,000. Included in the $2,000,000 is $15,000 of tax-exempt interest income. LNS reports $1,345,000 in ordinary and necessary business expenses. What is LNS corporation's taxable income for the year? LO 5-1

45. ATW corporation currently uses the FIFO method of accounting for its inventory for book and tax purposes. Its beginning inventory for the current year was $8,000,000. Its ending inventory for the current year was $7,000,000. If ATW had been using the LIFO method of accounting for its inventory, its beginning inventory would have been $7,000,000 and its ending inventory would have been $5,500,000. Assume ATW corporation's marginal tax rate is 34 percent. LO 5-1
    a) How much more in taxes did ATW corporation pay for the current year because it used the FIFO method of accounting for inventory than it would have paid if it had used the LIFO method?
    b) Why would ATW use the FIFO method of accounting if doing so causes it to pay more taxes on a present value basis? (Note that the tax laws don't allow corporations to use the LIFO method of accounting for inventory unless they also use the LIFO method of accounting for inventory for book purposes.)

46. ELS corporation is about to begin its sixth year of existence. Assume that ELS reported gross receipts for each of its first five years of existence for Scenarios A, B, and C as follows: LO 5-1

Year of Existence	Scenario A	Scenario B	Scenario C
1	$4,000,000	$3,000,000	$5,500,000
2	5,000,000	5,000,000	5,000,000
3	5,900,000	7,500,000	4,750,000
4	6,000,000	6,000,000	5,000,000
5	4,500,000	4,500,000	5,250,000

    a) In what years is ELS allowed to use the cash method of accounting under Scenario A?
    b) In what years is ELS allowed to use the cash method of accounting under Scenario B?
    c) In what years is ELS allowed to use the cash method of accounting under Scenario C?

47. On its year 1 financial statements, Seatax Corporation, an accrual-method taxpayer, reported federal income tax expense of $570,000. On its year 1 tax return, it reported a tax liability of $650,000. During year 1, Seatax made estimated tax payments of $700,000. What book–tax difference, if any, associated with its federal income tax expense should Seatax have reported when computing its year 1 taxable income? Is the difference favorable or unfavorable? Is it temporary or permanent? LO 5-2

48. Assume Maple Corp. has just completed the third year of its existence (year 3). The table below indicates Maple's ending book inventory for each year and the additional §263A costs it was required to include in its ending inventory. Maple immediately expensed these costs for book purposes. In year 2, Maple sold all of its year 1 ending inventory, and in year 3 it sold all of its year 2 ending inventory. LO 5-2

	Year 1	Year 2	Year 3
Ending book inventory	$2,400,000	$2,700,000	$2,040,000
Additional §263A costs	60,000	70,000	40,000
Ending tax inventory	$2,460,000	$2,770,000	$2,080,000

a) What book–tax difference associated with its inventory did Maple report in year 1? Was the difference favorable or unfavorable? Was it permanent or temporary?

b) What book–tax difference associated with its inventory did Maple report in year 2? Was the difference favorable or unfavorable? Was it permanent or temporary?

c) What book–tax difference associated with its inventory did Maple report in year 3? Was the difference favorable or unfavorable? Was it permanent or temporary?

LO 5-2 49. JDog corporation owns stock in Oscar Inc. JDog received a $10,000 dividend from Oscar Inc. What temporary book–tax difference associated with the dividend will JDog report for the year in the following alternative scenarios (income difference only—ignore the dividends received deduction)?

a) JDog owns 5 percent of the Oscar Inc. stock. Oscar's income for the year was $500,000.

b) JDog owns 40 percent of the Oscar Inc. stock. Oscar's income for the year was $500,000.

LO 5-2 50. On July 1 of year 1, Riverside Corp. (RC), a calendar-year taxpayer, acquired the assets of another business in a taxable acquisition. When the purchase price was allocated to the assets purchased, RC determined it had purchased $1,200,000 of goodwill for both book and tax purposes. At the end of year 1, RC determined that the goodwill had not been impaired during the year. In year 2, however, RC concluded that $200,000 of the goodwill had been impaired, and they required RC to write down the goodwill by $200,000 for book purposes.

a) What book–tax difference associated with its goodwill should RC report in year 1? Is it favorable or unfavorable? Is it permanent or temporary?

b) What book–tax difference associated with its goodwill should RC report in year 2? Is it favorable or unfavorable? Is it permanent or temporary?

LO 5-2 51. Assume that on January 1, year 1, ABC Inc. issued 5,000 stock options with an estimated value of $10 per option. Each option entitles the owner to purchase one share of ABC stock for $25 a share (the per share price of ABC stock on January 1, year 1, when the options were granted). The options vest 50 percent at the end of the day on December 31, year 1, and 50 percent at the end of the day on December 31, year 2. All 5,000 stock options were exercised in year 3 when the ABC stock was valued at $31 per share. Identify ABC's year 1, 2, and 3 tax deductions and book–tax differences (indicate whether permanent and/or temporary) associated with the stock options under the following alternative scenarios:

a) The stock options are incentive stock options and ASC 718 (the codification of FAS 123R) does not apply to the options.

b) The stock options are nonqualified stock options and ASC 718 does not apply to the options.

c) The stock options are incentive stock options and ASC 718 applies to the options.

d) The stock options are nonqualified stock options and ASC 718 applies to the options.

LO 5-2 52. Assume that on January 1, year 1, XYZ Corp. issued 1,000 nonqualified stock options with an estimated value of $4 per option. Each option entitles the owner to purchase one share of XYZ stock for $14 a share (the per share price of XYZ stock on January 1, year 1, when the options were granted). The options vest 25 percent a year (on December 31) for four years (beginning with year 1). All

500 stock options that had vested to that point were exercised in year 3 when the XYZ stock was valued at $20 per share. No other options were exercised in year 3 or year 4. Identify XYZ's year 1, 2, 3, and 4 tax deductions and book–tax difference (identify as permanent and/or temporary) associated with the stock options under the following alternative scenarios:

a) ASC 718 does not apply to the stock options.
b) ASC 718 applies to the stock options.

53. What book–tax differences in year 1 and year 2 associated with its capital gains and losses would ABD Inc. report in the following alternative scenarios? Identify each book–tax difference as favorable or unfavorable and as permanent or temporary. LO 5-2

a)

	Year 1	Year 2
Capital gains	$20,000	$5,000
Capital losses	8,000	0

b)

	Year 1	Year 2
Capital gains	$ 8,000	$ 5,000
Capital losses	20,000	0

c)

	Year 1	Year 2
Capital gains	$ 0	$50,000
Capital losses	25,000	30,000

d)

	Year 1	Year 2
Capital gains	$ 0	$40,000
Capital losses	25,000	0

e) Answer for year 6 only.

	Year 1	Years 2–5	Year 6
Capital gains	$ 0	$ 0	$15,000
Capital losses	10,000	0	0

f) Answer for year 7 only.

	Year 1	Years 2–6	Year 7
Capital gains	$ 0	$ 0	$15,000
Capital losses	10,000	0	0

54. What book–tax differences in year 1 and year 2 associated with its capital gains and losses would DEF Inc. report in the following alternative scenarios? Identify each book–tax difference as favorable or unfavorable and as permanent or temporary. LO 5-2

a) In year 1, DEF recognized a loss of $15,000 on land that it had held for investment. In year 1, it also recognized a $30,000 gain on equipment it had purchased a few years ago. The equipment sold for $50,000 and had an adjusted basis of $20,000. DEF had deducted $40,000 of depreciation on the equipment. In year 2, DEF recognized a capital loss of $2,000.
b) In year 1, DEF recognized a loss of $15,000 on land that it had held for investment. It also recognized a $20,000 gain on equipment it had purchased a few years ago. The equipment sold for $50,000 and had an adjusted basis of $30,000. DEF had deducted $15,000 of tax depreciation on the equipment.

LO 5-2 55. MWC Corp. is currently in the sixth year of its existence (2015). In 2010–2014, it reported the following income and (losses) (before net operating loss carryovers or carrybacks).

2010:	($ 70,000)
2011:	(30,000)
2012:	60,000
2013:	140,000
2014:	(25,000)
2015:	300,000

a) Assuming the original facts and that MWC elects to not carry back NOLs, what was MWC's 2013 taxable income?

b) If MWC does not elect to forgo any NOL carrybacks, what is its 2015 taxable income after the NOL deduction?

c) If MWC always elects to forgo NOL carrybacks, what is its 2015 taxable income after the NOL deduction? What is its 2015 book–tax difference associated with its NOL? Is it favorable or unfavorable? Is it permanent or temporary?

LO 5-2 56. WCC Inc. has a current year (2015) net operating loss of $100,000. It is trying to determine whether it should carry back the loss or whether it should elect to forgo the carryback. How would you advise WCC in each of the following alternative situations (ignore the time value of money in your computations)?

a)

	2013	2014	2016
Taxable income	$ 30,000	$ 0	$ 300,000

b)

	2013	2014	2016
Taxable income	$900,000	$60,000	$ 100,000

c)

	2013	2014	2016
Taxable income	$900,000	$60,000	$5,000,000

d)

	2013	2014	2016
Taxable income	$ 50,000	$20,000	$2,000,000

LO 5-2 57. Assume that in year 1 Hill Corporation reported a net operating loss of $10,000 that it carried forward to year 2. In year 1, Hill also reported a net capital loss of $3,000 that it carried forward to year 2. In year 2, ignoring any carryovers from other years, Hill reported a loss for tax purposes of $50,000. The current year loss includes a $12,000 net capital gain. What is Hill's year 2 net operating loss?

LO 5-2 58. Golf Corp. (GC), a calendar-year accrual-method corporation, held its directors' meeting on December 15 of year 1. During the meeting the board of directors authorized GC to pay a $75,000 charitable contribution to the World Golf Foundation, a qualifying charity.

a) If GC actually pays $50,000 of this contribution on January 15 of year 2 and the remaining $25,000 on March 15 of year 2, what book–tax difference will it report associated with the contribution in year 1 (assume the 10 percent limitation does not apply)? Is it favorable or unfavorable? Is it permanent or temporary?

b) Assuming the same facts as in part (a), what book–tax difference will GC report in year 2 (assuming the 10 percent limitation does not apply)? Is it favorable or unfavorable?

c) If GC actually pays $50,000 of this contribution on January 15 of year 2 and the remaining $25,000 on April 15 of year 2, what book–tax difference will it report associated with the contribution in year 1 (assume the 10 percent limitation does not apply)? Is it favorable or unfavorable? Is it permanent or temporary?

d) Assuming the same facts as in part (c), what book–tax difference will GC report in year 2 (assuming the 10 percent limitation does not apply)? Is it favorable or unfavorable?

59. In year 1 (the current year), OCC Corp. made a charitable donation of $200,000 to the Phil and Amy Mickelson Foundation (a qualifying charity). For the year, OCC reported taxable income of $1,500,000 before deducting any charitable contributions, before deducting its $20,000 dividends received deduction, and before deducting its $40,000 NOL carryover from last year. LO 5-2
   a) What amount of the $200,000 donation is OCC allowed to deduct for tax purposes in year 1?
   b) In year 2, OCC did not make any charitable contributions. It reported taxable income of $300,000 before any charitable contribution deductions and before a $15,000 dividends received deduction. What book–tax difference associated with the charitable contributions will OCC report in year 2? Is the difference favorable or unfavorable? Is it permanent or temporary?
   c) Assume the original facts and those provided in part (b). In years 3, 4, and 5, OCC reported taxable losses of $50,000. Finally, in year 6 it reported $1,000,000 in taxable income before any charitable contribution deductions. It did not have any dividends received deduction. OCC did not actually make any charitable donations in year 6. What book–tax difference associated with charitable contributions will OCC report in year 6?

60. In year 1 (the current year), LAA Inc. made a charitable donation of $100,000 to the American Red Cross (a qualifying charity). For the year, LAA reported taxable income of $550,000, which included a $100,000 charitable contribution deduction (before limitation), a $50,000 dividends received deduction, a $20,000 domestic production activities deduction, and a $10,000 net operating loss carryover from year 0. What is LAA Inc.'s charitable contribution deduction for year 1? LO 5-2

61. Coattail Corporation (CC) manufactures and sells women's and children's coats. This year, CC donated 1,000 coats to a qualified public charity. The charity distributed the coats to needy women and children throughout the region. At the time of the contribution, the fair market value of each coat was $80. Determine the amount of CC's charitable contribution (the taxable income limitation does not apply) for the coats assuming the following: LO 5-2 research
   a) CC's adjusted basis in each coat was $30.
   b) CC's adjusted basis in each coat was $10.

62. Maple Corp. owns several pieces of highly valued paintings that are on display in the corporation's headquarters. This year, it donated one of the paintings valued at $100,000 (adjusted basis of $25,000) to a local museum for the museum to display. What is the amount of Maple Corp.'s charitable contribution deduction for the painting (assuming income limitations do not apply)? What would be Maple's deduction if the museum sold the painting one month after it received it from Maple? LO 5-2 research

63. Riverbend Inc. received a $200,000 dividend from stock it held in Hobble Corporation. Riverbend's taxable income is $2,100,000 before deducting the dividends received deduction (DRD), a $40,000 NOL carryover, a $10,000 domestic production activities deduction, and a $100,000 charitable contribution. LO 5-2
   a) What is Riverbend's deductible DRD assuming it owns 10 percent of Hobble Corporation?
   b) Assuming the facts in part (a), what is Riverbend's marginal tax rate on the dividend?
   c) What is Riverbend's DRD assuming it owns 60 percent of Hobble Corporation?

d) Assuming the facts in part (c), what is Riverbend's marginal tax rate on the dividend?

e) What is Riverbend's DRD assuming it owns 85 percent of Hobble Corporation (and is part of the same affiliated group)?

f) Assuming the facts in part (e), what is Riverbend's marginal tax rate on the dividend?

LO 5-2

64. Wasatch Corp. (WC) received a $200,000 dividend from Tager Corporation (TC). WC owns 15 percent of the TC stock. Compute WC's deductible DRD in each of the following situations:

a) WC's taxable income (loss) without the dividend income or the DRD is $10,000.

b) WC's taxable income (loss) without the dividend income or the DRD is ($10,000).

c) WC's taxable income (loss) without the dividend income or the DRD is ($59,000).

d) WC's taxable income (loss) without the dividend income or the DRD is ($61,000).

e) WC's taxable income (loss) without the dividend income or the DRD is ($500,000).

f) What is WC's book–tax difference associated with its DRD in part (a)? Is the difference favorable or unfavorable? Is it permanent or temporary?

LO 5-2

65. Compute SWK Inc.'s tax liability for each of the following scenarios:

a) SWK's taxable income is $60,000.

b) SWK's taxable income is $275,000.

c) SWK's taxable income is $15,500,000.

d) SWK's taxable income for the year is $50,000,000.

LO 5-2

66. ABC's taxable income for the year is $200,000 and CBA's taxable income for the year is $400,000. Compute the combined tax liability of the two corporations assuming the following:

a) Amanda, Jermaine, and O'Neil each own one-third of the stock of ABC and CBA.

b) Amanda, Jermaine, and O'Neil each own one-third of the stock of ABC and Amanda and Dustin each own 50 percent of the stock of CBA.

c) ABC owns 85 percent of CBA's stock on the last day of the year. ABC and CBA file separate (as opposed to consolidated) tax returns.

LO 5-2

67. ABC's taxable income for the year is $25,000 and CBA's taxable income for the year is $10,000,000. Compute the combined tax liability of the two corporations assuming the following:

a) Amanda, Jermaine, and O'Neil each own one-third of the stock of ABC and CBA.

b) Amanda, Jermaine, and O'Neil each own one-third of the stock of ABC and Amanda and Dustin each own 50 percent of the stock of CBA.

LO 5-3

68. Last year, TBA Corporation, a calendar-year taxpayer, reported a tax liability of $100,000. TBA confidently anticipates a current year tax liability of $240,000. What minimum estimated tax payments should TBA make for the first, second, third, and fourth quarters respectively (ignore the annualized income method) assuming the following:

a) TBA is not considered to be a large corporation for estimated tax purposes.

b) TBA is considered to be a large corporation for estimated tax purposes.

69. Last year, BTA Corporation, a calendar-year taxpayer, reported a net operating loss of $10,000 and a $0 tax liability. BTA confidently anticipates a current year tax liability of $240,000. What minimum estimated tax payments should BTA make for the first, second, third, and fourth quarters, respectively (ignore the annualized income method), assuming the following: LO 5-3

a) BTA is not considered to be a large corporation for estimated tax purposes.

b) BTA is considered to be a large corporation for estimated tax purposes.

70. For the current year, LNS corporation reported the following taxable income at the end of its first, second, and third quarters. What are LNS's minimum first, second, third, and fourth quarter estimated tax payments determined using the annualized income method? LO 5-3

Quarter-End	Cumulative Taxable Income
First	$1,000,000
Second	1,600,000
Third	2,400,000

71. Last year, JL Corporation's tax liability was $900,000. For the current year, JL Corporation reported the following taxable income at the end of its first, second, and third quarters (see table below). What are JL's minimum required first, second, third, and fourth quarter estimated tax payments (ignore the actual current year tax safe harbor)? LO 5-3 planning

Quarter-End	Cumulative Taxable Income
First	$ 500,000
Second	1,250,000
Third	2,250,000

72. Last year, Cougar Corp. (CC) reported a net operating loss of $25,000. In the current year, CC expected its current year tax liability to be $440,000 so it made four equal estimated tax payments of $110,000 each. Cougar closed its books at the end of each quarter. The following schedule reports CC's taxable income at the end of each quarter: LO 5-3

Quarter-End	Cumulative Taxable Income
First	$ 300,000
Second	700,000
Third	1,000,000
Fourth	1,470,588

CC's current year tax liability on $1,470,588 of taxable income is $500,000. Does CC owe underpayment penalties on its estimated tax payments? If so, for which quarters does it owe the penalty?

73. For the current year, CCP Inc. received the following interest income: LO 5-2 LO 5-4

- $12,000 interest from Irvine City bonds: Bonds issued in 2012 and proceeds used to fund public schools.
- $20,000 interest from Fluor Corporation bonds.
- $8,000 interest from Mission Viejo City: Bonds issued in 2013 and proceeds used to lure new business to the area.
- $6,000 interest from U.S. Treasury notes.

a) What amount of this interest income is taxable to CCP?

b) What amount of interest should CCP report as a preference item when calculating its alternative minimum tax liability?

LO 5-4

74. On January 2 of year 1, XYZ Corp. acquired a piece of machinery for $50,000. The recovery period for the assets is seven years for both regular tax and AMT purposes. XYZ uses the double declining balance method to compute its tax depreciation on this asset, and it uses 150 percent declining balance to determine its depreciation for AMT purposes. The following schedule projects the tax and AMT depreciation on the asset until it is fully depreciated:

	Tax		AMT	
Year	**Depreciation**	**Basis at End of Year**	**Depreciation**	**Basis at End of Year**
1	$ 7,145	$42,855	$5,355	$44,645
2	12,245	30,610	9,565	35,080
3	8,745	21,865	7,515	27,565
4	6,245	15,620	6,125	21,440
5	4,465	11,155	6,125	15,315
6	4,460	6,695	6,125	9,190
7	4,465	2,230	6,125	3,065
8	2,230	0	3,065	0

a) What AMT adjustment relating to depreciation on the equipment will XYZ make for year 1? Is the adjustment positive (unfavorable) or negative (favorable)?

b) What AMT adjustment relating to depreciation on the equipment will XYZ make for year 5? Is the adjustment positive or negative?

c) If XYZ sells the equipment for $30,000 at the beginning of year 3, what AMT adjustment will it make in year 3 to reflect the difference in the gain or loss for regular tax and for AMT purposes on the sale (assume no year 3 depreciation)? Is the adjustment positive or negative?

LO 5-4

75. During the current year, CRS Inc. reported the following tax-related information:

- $10,000 tax-exempt interest from public activity bonds issued in 2013.
- $16,000 tax-exempt interest from private activity bonds issued in 2013.
- $150,000 death benefit from life insurance policies on officers' lives.
- $6,000 70 percent dividends received deduction.
- $12,000 80 percent dividends received deduction.
- $50,000 bad debt expense.
- $20,000 tax amortization expense relating to organizational expenditures.
- $80,000 gain included in taxable income under the installment method (sale occurred in previous year).

What is CRS's current year ACE adjustment?

LO 5-4

76. During the current year, ELS Corporation reported the following tax-related information:

- $5,000 tax-exempt interest from public activity bonds issued in 2008.
- $45,000 gain included in taxable income under the installment method. The installment sale occurred two years ago.

a) What is ELS Corp.'s current year ACE adjustment assuming its cumulative ACE adjustment as of the beginning of the year is a positive $12,000?

b) What is ELS Corp.'s current year ACE adjustment assuming its cumulative ACE adjustment as of the beginning of the year is a positive $80,000?

77. During the current year, FTP Corporation reported regular taxable income of $500,000. FTP used the following information in its tax-related computations: LO 5-4
   - $12,000 interest from Irvine City bonds: Bonds issued in 2013 and proceeds used to fund public schools.
   - $20,000 interest from Fluor Corporation bonds.
   - $8,000 interest from Mission Viejo City bonds: Bonds issued in 2012 and proceeds used to lure new business to the area.
   - $6,000 interest from U.S. Treasury notes.
   - $30,000 dividends received from General Electric Corporation (FTP owns less than 1 percent of GE stock).
   - $10,000 dividends received from Hobble Inc. (FTP owns 25 percent of Hobble Inc.).
   - $25,000 charitable contribution to the World Golf Foundation.
   - $60,000 AMT depreciation (regular tax depreciation was $70,000).
   - $50,000 ACE depreciation.
   - $7,000 AMT gain on disposition of assets (regular tax gain on the disposition of assets was $8,000).
   - $5,000 ACE gain on disposition of assets.

   a) What is FTP's ACE adjustment for the current year? Is it positive or negative?
   b) What is FTP's alternative minimum tax base?
   c) What is FTP's alternative minimum tax liability, if any?

78. What is WSS Corporation's AMT base in each of the following alternative scenarios? LO 5-4
   a) WSS's AMTI is $50,000.
   b) WSS's AMTI is $175,000.
   c) WSS's AMTI is $300,000.
   d) WSS's AMTI is $1,000,000.

79. Assume CDA corporation must pay the AMT for the current year. It is considering entering into a transaction that will generate $20,000 of income for the current year. What is CDA's after-tax benefit of receiving this income in each of the following alternative scenarios? LO 5-4 planning
   a) CDA's AMTI before the transaction is $50,000.
   b) CDA's AMTI before the transaction is $140,000.
   c) CDA's AMTI before the transaction is $200,000.
   d) CDA's AMTI before the transaction is $1,000,000.

80. Assume JJ Inc. must pay the AMT for the current year. Near the end of the year, JJ is considering making a charitable contribution of $20,000. What is its after-tax cost of the contribution under each of the following alternative scenarios? LO 5-4 planning
   a) JJ's AMTI before the transaction is $50,000.
   b) JJ's AMTI before the transaction is $160,000.
   c) JJ's AMTI before the transaction is $200,000.
   d) JJ's AMTI before the transaction is $1,000,000.

81. Compute ACC Inc.'s tentative minimum tax (TMT), alternative minimum tax (AMT), and minimum tax credit (MTC) in each of the following alternative scenarios: LO 5-4
   a) ACC's alternative minimum tax base is $500,000 and its regular tax liability is $80,000.
   b) ACC's alternative minimum tax base is $300,000 and its regular tax liability is $80,000.
   c) ACC's alternative minimum tax base is $1,000,000 and its regular tax liability is $250,000.

LO 5-4

82. In year 1, GSL Corp.'s alternative minimum tax base was $2,000,000 and its regular tax liability is $350,000.
    a) What is GSL's total tax liability for years 1, 2, 3, and 4 (by year) assuming the following?
       Year 2: AMT base $600,000; Regular tax liability $100,000.
       Year 3: AMT base $500,000; Regular tax liability $160,000.
       Year 4: AMT base $1,000,000; Regular tax liability $150,000.
    b) What, if any, minimum tax credit does GSL have at the end of year 4?

LO 5-4
research

83. In year 1, Lazy Corporation reported a $500,000 net operating loss for regular tax purposes and a $450,000 net operating loss for alternative minimum tax purposes (called an *alternative tax net operating loss*). In year 2, Lazy reported $450,000 of taxable income before deducting its net operating loss carryover from year 1 (it elected to forgo the net operating loss carryback). It also reported $450,000 of alternative minimum taxable income before taking the alternative tax net operating loss carryover into account (it did not report any preference or adjustments in year 2). (Note that, subject to certain limitations, alternative tax NOLs are deducted from AMTI in the process of determining the alternative minimum tax.) What is Lazy Corporation's year 2 tax liability? Assume Lazy did not have any MTC carryover from a prior year.

COMPREHENSIVE PROBLEMS

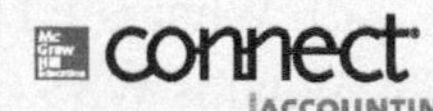

All applicable problems are available with McGraw-Hill's *Connect® Accounting*.

84. Compute MV Corp.'s 2015 taxable income given the following information relating to its year 1 activities. Also, compute MV's Schedule M-1 assuming that MV's federal income tax expense for book purposes is $100,000.
    - Gross profit from inventory sales of $500,000 (no book–tax differences).
    - Dividends MV received from 25 percent-owned corporation of $100,000 (assume this is also MV's pro rata share of the distributing corporation's earnings).
    - Expenses *other than* DRD, charitable contribution (CC), net operating loss (NOL), and domestic production activities deduction (DPAD) are $350,000 (no book–tax differences).
    - NOL carryover from prior year of $10,000.
    - Cash charitable contribution of $120,000.
    - Domestic production activities deduction of $5,000 (wage limitation does not apply).

85. Compute HC Inc.'s current year taxable income given the following information relating to its 2015 activities. Also, compute HC's Schedule M-1 assuming that HC's federal income tax expense for book purposes is $30,000.
    - Gross profit from inventory sales of $310,000 (no book–tax differences).
    - Dividends HC received from 28 percent-owned corporation of $120,000 (this is also HC's pro rata share of the corporation's earnings).
    - Expenses *other than* DRD, charitable contribution (CC), net operating loss (NOL), and domestic production activities deduction (DPAD) are $300,000 (no book–tax differences).
    - NOL carryover from prior year of $12,000.
    - Cash charitable contribution of $50,000.
    - Domestic production activities deduction of $4,000 (wage limitation does not apply).

86. Timpanogos Inc. is an accrual-method calendar-year corporation. For 2015, it reported financial statement income after taxes of $1,149,000. Timpanogos provided the following information relating to its 2015 activities:

Life insurance proceeds as a result of CEO's death	$ 200,000
Revenue from sales (for both book and tax purposes)	2,000,000
Premiums paid on the key-person life insurance policies. The policies have no cash surrender value.	21,000
Charitable contributions	180,000
Overhead costs that were expensed for book purposes but are included in ending inventory for tax purposes under §263A	50,000
Overhead costs that were expensed for book purposes in 2014 but were included in 2014 ending inventory. All 2014 ending inventory was sold in 2015.	60,000
Cost of goods sold for book purposes	300,000
Interest income on private activity tax-exempt bonds issued in 2014	40,000
Interest paid on loan obtained to purchase tax-exempt bonds	45,000
Rental income payments received and earned in 2015	15,000
Rental income payments received in 2014 but earned in 2015	10,000
Rental income payments received in 2015 but not earned by year-end	30,000
MACRS depreciation	55,000
Book depreciation	25,000
Alternative minimum tax depreciation	50,000
Net capital loss	45,000
Federal income tax expense for books in 2015	500,000

Timpanogos did not qualify for the domestic production activities deduction.

Required:

a) Reconcile book income to taxable income for Timpanogos Inc. Be sure to start with book income and identify all of the adjustments necessary to arrive at taxable income.

b) Identify each book–tax difference as either permanent or temporary.

c) Complete Schedule M-1 for Timpanogos.

d) Compute Timpanogos Inc.'s regular tax liability for 2015.

e) Determine Timpanogos's alternative minimum tax, if any.

87. XYZ is a calendar-year corporation that began business on January 1, 2015. For 2015, it reported the following information in its current year audited income statement. Notes with important tax information are provided below.

Required:

Identify the book-to-tax adjustments for XYZ.

a) Reconcile book income to taxable income and identify each book–tax difference as temporary or permanent.

b) Compute XYZ's regular income tax liability.

c) Complete XYZ's Schedule M-1.

d) Complete XYZ's Form 1120, page 1 (use 2014 form if 2015 form is unavailable). Ignore estimated tax penalties when completing this form.

e) Compute XYZ's alternative minimum tax, if any.

f) Complete Form 4626 for XYZ (use 2014 form if 2015 form is unavailable).

g) Determine the quarters for which XYZ is subject to underpayment of estimated taxes penalties (see estimated tax information below).

XYZ Corp. Income Statement for Current Year	Book Income	Book to Tax Adjustments (Dr.)	Cr.	Taxable Income
Revenue from sales	$40,000,000			
Cost of goods sold	(27,000,000)			
Gross profit	$13,000,000			
Other income:				
Income from investment in corporate stock	300,000[1]			
Interest income	20,000[2]			
Capital gains (losses)	(4,000)			
Gain or loss from disposition of fixed assets	3,000[3]			
Miscellaneous income	50,000			
Gross Income	$13,369,000			
Expenses:				
Compensation	(7,500,000)[4]			
Stock option compensation	(200,000)[5]			
Advertising	(1,350,000)			
Repairs and maintenance	(75,000)			
Rent	(22,000)			
Bad debt expense	(41,000)[6]			
Depreciation	(1,400,000)[7]			
Warranty expenses	(70,000)[8]			
Charitable donations	(500,000)[9]			
Meals and entertainment	(18,000)			
Goodwill impairment	(30,000)[10]			
Organizational expenditures	(44,000)[11]			
Other expenses	(140,000)[12]			
Total expenses	($11,390,000)			
Income before taxes	$ 1,979,000			
Provision for income taxes	(720,000)[13]			
Net Income after taxes	$ 1,259,000[14]			

Notes:

1. XYZ owns 30 percent of the outstanding Hobble Corp. (HC) stock. Hobble Corp. reported $1,000,000 of income for the year. XYZ accounted for its investment in HC under the equity method and it recorded its pro rata share of HC's earnings for the year. HC also distributed a $200,000 dividend to XYZ.
2. Of the $20,000 interest income, $5,000 was from a City of Seattle bond (issued in 2013) that was used to fund public activities, $7,000 was from a Tacoma City bond (issued in 2012) used to fund private activities, $6,000 was from a fully taxable corporate bond, and the remaining $2,000 was from a money market account.
3. This gain is from equipment that XYZ purchased in February and sold in December (i.e., it does not qualify as §1231 gain).
4. This includes total officer compensation of $2,500,000 (no one officer received more than $1,000,000 compensation).
5. This amount is the portion of incentive stock option compensation that vested during the year (recipients are officers).
6. XYZ actually wrote off $27,000 of its accounts receivable as uncollectible.
7. Regular tax depreciation was $1,900,000 and AMT (and ACE) depreciation was $1,700,000.
8. In the current year, XYZ did not make any actual payments on warranties it provided to customers.
9. XYZ made $500,000 of cash contributions to qualified charities during the year.
10. On July 1 of this year XYZ acquired the assets of another business. In the process it acquired $300,000 of goodwill. At the end of the year, XYZ wrote off $30,000 of the goodwill as impaired.
11. XYZ expensed all of its organizational expenditures for book purposes. It expensed the maximum amount of organizational expenditures allowed for tax purposes.
12. The other expenses do not contain any items with book–tax differences.
13. This is an estimated tax provision (federal tax expense) for the year. (In a subsequent class period, we will learn how to compute the correct tax provision.) Assume that XYZ is not subject to state income taxes.
14. XYZ calculated that its domestic production activities deduction (DPAD) is $90,000. This amount is not included on the audited income statement numbers.

Estimated Tax Information:

XYZ made four equal estimated tax payments totaling $480,000. Assume for purposes of estimated tax liabilities, XYZ was in existence in 2014 and it reported a tax liability of $800,000. During 2015, XYZ determined its taxable income at the end of each of the four quarters as follows:

Quarter-End	Cumulative Taxable Income (Loss)
First	$ 350,000
Second	800,000
Third	1,000,000

Finally, assume that XYZ is not a large corporation for purposes of estimated tax calculations.

KAPLAN CPA SIMULATION

KAPLAN CPA REVIEW

Please visit the *Connect Library* to access the following Kaplan CPA Simulation:

The simulation for **Investment Inc.** covers several corporate tax issues.

chapter

6 Accounting for Income Taxes

Learning Objectives

Upon completing this chapter, you should be able to:

LO 6-1 Explain the objectives behind FASB ASC Topic 740, *Income Taxes,* and the income tax provision process.

LO 6-2 Calculate the current and deferred income tax expense or benefit components of a company's income tax provision.

LO 6-3 Recall what a valuation allowance represents and describe the process by which it is determined.

LO 6-4 Explain how a company accounts for its uncertain income tax positions under FASB ASC Topic 740.

LO 6-5 Recognize the different components of a company's disclosure of its income tax accounts in the financial statements and footnotes, and comprehend how a company computes and discloses the components of its "effective tax rate."

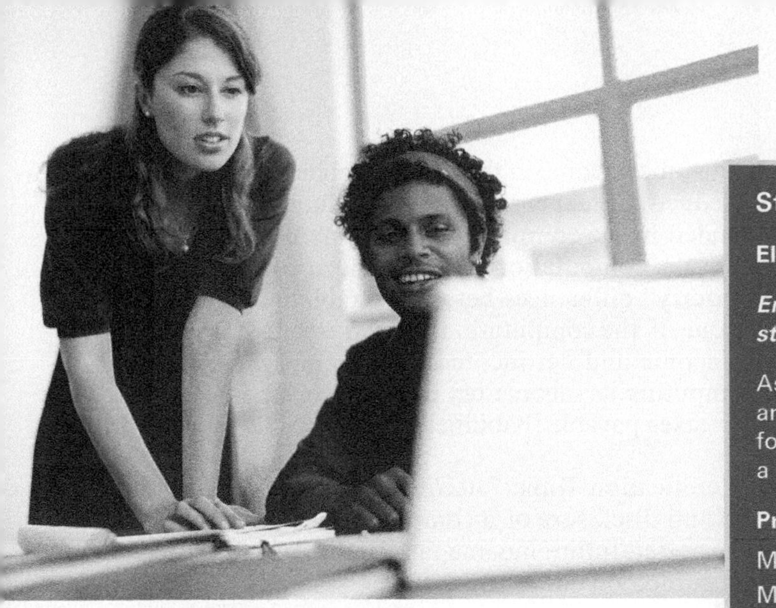

© Sam Edwards/age fotostock

Storyline Summary

Elise Brandon

Employment status:	Tax associate for a large public accounting firm.

Assigned to prepare the federal income tax provision and income-tax-related balance sheet accounts and footnote disclosures for Premiere Computer Corporation, a nonaudit client.

Premiere Computer Corporation

Medium-sized publicly traded company.

Manufactures and sells computer-related equipment.

Calendar-year taxpayer.

Marginal tax rate:	34 percent, unless otherwise stated.

Elise felt a great sense of accomplishment when she completed the federal income tax return for Premiere Computer Corporation (PCC). She was glad the return was filed on time and did not need to be extended. With the tax return filed, Elise was assigned to help the PCC tax department compute the federal income tax provision for the company's soon to be published income statement and to determine the correct amounts in the company's income-tax-related balance sheet accounts. She also was given the responsibility to help prepare the income tax note to the financial statements.[1]

Elise was aware that, as a result of more stringent independence requirements imposed by the Sarbanes-Oxley Act, her colleagues in the tax department were getting a lot of new engagements to help prepare the income tax provision for nonaudit clients. In fact, her firm now considered accounting for income taxes to be a "core competency" for all tax staff. Elise even heard that individuals who understood the nuances of accounting for income taxes were being called the new "rock stars" of accounting.[2] Having recently attended firm training on accounting for income taxes, which was now required of all tax staff, Elise was eager to apply her new knowledge to an actual client situation. She knew that developing her skill set in this complex topic would make her more valuable to her firm and her clients.[3]

to be continued . . .

[1]Publicly traded companies usually file their financial statements (Form 10-K) with the Securities and Exchange Commission well before they file their income tax returns with the Internal Revenue Service, often by as much as six months. The company must estimate its current year income tax liability when it files its financial statements and then adjust for any "provision to return" differences in the quarter (Form 10-Q) in which the tax return is filed. In today's post–Sarbanes-Oxley environment, staff from public accounting firms that are not a company's auditors often are hired to help prepare the company's income tax provision under ASC 740 because many companies do not have staff with the expertise to make this calculation.

[2]Kris Frieswick, "Too Taxing," *CFO Magazine* (November 1, 2005).

[3]An international tax services partner at a major public accounting firm recently testified before members of Congress that her firm spent more than 7,000 hours auditing a client's accounting for income taxes for its 2011 Form 10-K. See Beth Carr, "Written Testimony for Senate Permanent Subcommittee on Investigations," September 20, 2012, available at http://www.hsgac.senate.gov/

As you learned in computing PCC's taxable income in the previous chapter, many of the items of income (revenue) and deductions (expenses) that are included in a company's taxable income also are included in the company's net income before taxes. Not all of these items are included in the computations in the same accounting period, however, which creates "temporary" differences between taxable income and net income. Other items affect only one of the computations, which creates "permanent" differences between taxable income and net income. A company must take these differences into account in computing its income tax provision on the income statement and its "deferred" income taxes payable (liabilities) or refundable (assets) on the balance sheet.

FASB Accounting Standards Codification Topic 740, *Income Taxes* (hereafter, ASC 740), governs the computation and disclosure of a company's income tax provision (expense or benefit) and its expected future income tax liabilities or benefits related to "events" that have been recorded on either the financial statement or the tax return. ASC 740 codifies the majority of accounting and reporting guidance related to income taxes, primarily FAS 109. Accounting for income taxes guidance related to accounting for investments under the equity method, stock compensation, business combinations, foreign currency translation, and industry subtopics such as real estate, entertainment, and oil and gas is embedded within the ASC topic that deals with that issue. The Emerging Issues Task Force (EITF)[4] and the Securities and Exchange Commission continue to provide guidance on issues related to accounting for income taxes.

A company's failure to accurately compute the income tax provision and related balance sheet accounts can lead to the issuance of a material weakness statement by the auditor and, in some cases, a restatement of the financial statements. Not surprisingly, individuals who understand these complex and sometimes counterintuitive rules are in great demand by public accounting firms and industry.

This chapter discusses the basic rules for how a company computes and discloses its current year income tax provision and its future income taxes payable or refundable using the facts related to Premiere Computer Corporation in the previous chapter. We focus on the portion of the provision that relates to federal income taxes.

LO 6-1 OBJECTIVES OF ACCOUNTING FOR INCOME TAXES AND THE INCOME TAX PROVISION PROCESS

In addition to filing its federal, state and local, and non-U.S. income tax returns, Premiere Computer Corporation, along with all other U.S. publicly traded corporations and many privately held corporations, must prepare financial statements in accordance with generally accepted accounting principles (GAAP) issued by the FASB. Under GAAP, a company must include as part of its income statement a "provision" for the income tax expense or benefit that is associated with the pretax net income or loss reported on the income statement. The income tax provision includes not only current year taxes payable or refundable, but also any changes to future income taxes payable or refundable that result from differences in the timing of when an item is reported on the tax return compared to the financial statement. The company records these future income taxes payable or refundable on its balance sheet as the amount the company expects to pay (**deferred tax liability**) or recover (**deferred tax asset**) in a future accounting period.

[4]The Emerging Issues Task Force is a committee of accounting practitioners who assist the FASB in providing timely guidance on emerging issues and the implementation of existing standards.

TAXES IN THE REAL WORLD Weatherford International's $500 Million Material Weakness Related to Accounting for Income Taxes

On March 1, 2011, Weatherford International informed its shareholders that it would be late in issuing its Form 10-K because of a material weakness in internal control over the company's financial reporting for income taxes. As a result, management cautioned its investors not to rely on any of its financial statements issued for the years 2007–2010. Management estimated the total financial reporting error to be around $500 million. At a press conference the next day, the CEO made the following statement:

> To a degree, the discipline of tax within our Company is a two-headed animal–one, planning, and two, process. Both pieces must work well in order for us to be able to maximize the value of our multinational status. This mistake, the embarrassment of which is difficult, if not impossible to quantify, highlights that we have work to do on strengthening the process piece. We will work hard to make sure this happens with all appropriate speed and effectiveness.[1]

The company remediated the deficiencies during 2013, although the SEC and the U.S. Department of Justice are now investigating the circumstances surrounding the material weakness and restatements of the company's financial statements. The company restated its 2009–2011 financial statements in December 2012. During 2012, the company hired a new vice president of taxes and 25 additional "qualified tax professionals." In addition, the company spent considerable resources engaging third-party tax advisors and consultants to assist with enhancing internal controls over financial reporting for income taxes and developing and implementing a remediation plan; revising the process for the quarterly and annual tax provisions; recruiting positions within the tax and financial reporting departments; and providing income tax accounting training to tax and financial personnel. The magnitude of these expenditures was published in the company's Proxy Statement in June 2013 as follows:

> When our tax accounting issues were first identified, we brought in external experts to assist with the restatement and realignment of our tax accounting. We engaged experts in tax accounting, international taxes and internal controls, including professionals with substantial knowledge of processes of large multinational organizations. Our outside advisors have provided over 272,000 hours of time to the restatement and remediation at a cost of over $100 million to Weatherford to help ensure that we addressed the issues fully and appropriately.[2]

[1]Final transcript of Weatherford International to adjust 2007–2010 results due to "material weakness" in its income tax reporting—Conference Call. Available at http://www.sec.gov.

[2]See Weatherford International's *2013 Proxy Statement*, p. vi. Available at http://www.weatherford.com.

Why Is Accounting for Income Taxes So Complex?

ASC 740 provides the general rules that apply to the computation of a company's income tax provision. The basic principles that underlie these rules are fairly straightforward, but the application of the rules themselves can be very complex. Much of the complexity is due to the fact that the U.S. tax laws are complex and often ambiguous. In addition, companies frequently prepare their financial statements (Form 10-K) much earlier than when they file their corresponding tax returns. For example, a calendar-year corporation generally files its Form 10-K with the SEC in February or early March, but the company might not file its federal income tax return (Form 1120) with the Internal Revenue Service (IRS) until August or September.[5] As a result, a company often must exercise a high degree of judgment in estimating its income tax return positions currently and in future years when a tax return position might be challenged by the tax authorities. After the tax return is filed, it may take five years or more before the tax return is audited by the IRS and the final tax liability is determined.[6]

[5]The due date for a federal income tax return filed by a calendar-year corporation is March 15, but corporations can request a six-month extension to September 15 by filing Form 7004 and paying any remaining tax liability.

[6]Although the statute of limitations for a filed income tax return is three years, large corporations often agree to extend the statute for a longer period of time to allow the IRS to audit the return. As a result, a corporation's tax return may not be audited for five or more years from the date it is filed.

For example, General Electric (GE) mentions in its Form 10-K for 2013 that the IRS currently was auditing its U.S. income tax returns for 2010–2011. GE also notes that it files more than 5,800 income tax returns in over 250 global taxing jurisdictions!

Objectives of ASC 740

ASC 740 applies only to *income* taxes levied by the U.S. federal government, U.S. state and local governments, and non-U.S. ("foreign") governments. The FASB defines an *income tax* as a tax *based on income.* This definition excludes property taxes, excise taxes, sales taxes, and value-added taxes. Companies report nonincome taxes as expenses in the computation of their net income before taxes.

ASC 740 has two primary objectives. One objective is to "recognize the amount of taxes payable or refundable in the current year" (referred to as the **current tax liability or asset**).[7] A second objective is to "recognize deferred tax liabilities and assets for the future tax consequences of events that have been recognized in an entity's financial statements or tax returns."[8] Both objectives relate to reporting a company's income tax amounts on the *balance sheet,* not the *income statement*. The FASB refers to this method as the "asset and liability approach" to accounting for income taxes.[9] The FASB chose this approach because it felt it is most consistent with the definitions in FASB Concepts Statement No. 6, *Elements of Financial Statements,* and produces the most useful and understandable information.[10]

To compute the deferred tax liability or asset, a company must calculate the future tax effects attributable to temporary differences and **tax carryforwards.**[11] As you learned in the previous chapter, temporary differences generally can be thought of as revenue (income) or expenses (deductions) that will appear on both the income statement and the tax return but in different accounting periods. Temporary differences that are cumulatively favorable create deferred tax liabilities, while temporary differences that are cumulatively unfavorable create deferred tax assets.

Example 6-1

Before she began the income tax provision process, Elise knew she needed to get the ending balances in PCC's deferred tax accounts from the prior year. Accordingly, she retrieved PCC's prior year balance sheet (Exhibit 6-1) and the deferred tax component of the company's income tax note (Exhibit 6-2).

Looking at Exhibit 6-1, what income tax accounts appear on PCC's balance sheet from the prior year?

Answer: There are three deferred tax accounts on PCC's prior year balance sheet: current deferred tax assets of $271,660, noncurrent deferred tax assets of $408,000, and noncurrent deferred tax liabilities of $3,400,000.

Looking at Exhibit 6-2, is PCC in a net deferred tax asset or net deferred tax liability position at the end of the prior year (gross deferred tax assets less gross deferred tax liabilities)?

Answer: PCC ended the prior year with a net deferred tax liability of $2,720,340.

Since its inception, has PCC had net favorable or unfavorable temporary differences (i.e., has PCC's cumulative pretax net income been greater or less than its taxable income)?

Answer: PCC's net deferred tax liability indicates that the company has had net cumulative favorable temporary differences, which indicates its cumulative pretax net income has exceeded its cumulative taxable income.

[7]ASC 740-10-10-1(a).

[8]ASC 740-10-10-1(b).

[9]FAS 109, ¶63. (This paragraph was not codified in ASC 740.)

[10]FAS 109, ¶63.

[11]ASC 740-10-25-2(b).

EXHIBIT 6-1 PCC Balance Sheet at 12/31/2014

Assets	
Current Assets	
Cash	$10,722,380
Municipal bonds	300,000
Accounts receivable	17,250,000
Less: Allowance for bad debts	(345,000)
Accounts receivable (net)	16,905,000
Inventory	4,312,500
Deferred tax assets	271,660
Total Current Assets	$32,511,540
Noncurrent Assets	
Fixed assets	$60,000,000
Less: Accumulated depreciation	(12,000,000)
Fixed assets (net)	48,000,000
Life insurance (cash surrender value)	1,100,000
Investments	497,960
Goodwill	180,000
Deferred tax assets	408,000
Total Noncurrent Assets	50,185,960
Total Assets	$82,697,500
Liabilities and Shareholders' Equity	
Current Liabilities	
Accounts payable	$20,013,000
Reserve for warranties	430,000
Deferred tax liabilities	—
Total Current Liabilities	$20,443,000
Noncurrent Liabilities	
Long-term debt	$40,000,000
Deferred compensation	1,200,000
Deferred tax liabilities	3,400,000
Total Noncurrent Liabilities	$44,600,000
Total Liabilities	$65,043,000
Shareholders' Equity	
Common stock (par value = $1)	$ 500,000
Additional paid-in-capital	5,000,000
Retained earnings	12,154,500
Total Shareholders' Equity	$17,654,500
Total Liabilities and Shareholders' Equity	$82,697,500

EXHIBIT 6-2 PCC Deferred Tax Accounts at 12/31/2014

Deferred Tax Assets	
Allowance for bad debts	$ 117,300
Reserve for warranties	146,200
Net operating loss carryforward	8,160
Current deferred tax assets	$ 271,660
Deferred compensation	408,000
Capital loss carryforward	—
Contribution carryforward	—
Noncurrent deferred tax assets	$ 408,000
Total deferred tax assets	$ 679,660
Valuation allowance for deferred tax assets	—
Deferred tax assets, net of valuation allowance	$ 679,660
Deferred tax liabilities	
Depreciation	(3,400,000)
Total deferred tax liabilities	($3,400,000)
Net deferred tax liabilities	($2,720,340)

The Income Tax Provision Process

A company computes the two components of its income tax provision (current and deferred) separately (independently) for each category of income tax (U.S. federal, U.S. state and local, and international) and then combines the components to produce the total income tax provision. The "formula" to compute a company's total income tax provision can be summarized as:

Total income tax provision = Current income tax expense (benefit)
+ Deferred income tax expense (benefit)

There are six steps in the computation of a company's federal income tax provision. These steps are:

1. Adjust pretax net income or loss for all permanent differences.
2. Identify all temporary differences and tax carryforward amounts.
3. Calculate the current income tax expense or benefit (refund).
4. Determine the ending balances in the balance sheet deferred tax asset and liability accounts.
5. Evaluate the need for a valuation allowance for gross deferred tax assets.
6. Calculate the deferred income tax expense or benefit.

CALCULATING THE CURRENT AND DEFERRED INCOME TAX EXPENSE OR BENEFIT COMPONENTS OF A COMPANY'S INCOME TAX PROVISION

continued from page 6-1...

Elise gathered the financial statement and tax return data she needed to get started beginning with the workpaper template she used to compute PCC's taxable income (Exhibit 6-3 reproduces the book–tax reconciliation template from Exhibit 5-7, excluding the book federal income tax expense of $2,000,000). She identified each of the book–tax adjustments as being either permanent (P) or temporary (T). Elise was ready to begin the process of computing PCC's federal income tax provision using the six-step method she had learned at firm training.

to be continued...

Step 1: Adjust Pretax Net Income for All Permanent Differences

As you learned in the previous chapter, not all book–tax differences meet the definition of a temporary difference. Some differences will appear only on the income statement or the tax return, but not on both. Examples of the former include tax-exempt interest income and nondeductible fines. Examples of the latter include the dividends received deduction and the domestic production activities deduction. Although not defined as such in ASC 740, most accounting professionals refer to these types of book–tax differences as **permanent differences.**

A company does not take permanent differences into account in computing its balance sheet deferred tax assets and liabilities (and consequently, the deferred component of its income tax provision). Permanent differences enter into the company's computation of taxable income, and thus affect the current tax expense or benefit,

EXHIBIT 6-3 PCC Book–Tax Reconciliation Template

Premiere Computer Corporation				
		Book–Tax Adjustments		
Income Statement for Current Year	**Book Income**	**(Dr)**	**Cr**	**Taxable Income**
Revenue from sales	$60,000,000			$60,000,000
Cost of goods sold	(38,000,000)			(38,000,000)
Gross profit	$22,000,000			$22,000,000
Other income:				
Dividend income	30,000			30,000
Interest income (P)	120,000	(12,000)		108,000
Capital gains (losses) (T)	(28,000)		28,000	0
Gain on fixed asset dispositions (T)	54,000		16,000	70,000
Gross Income	$ 22,176,000			$22,208,000
Expenses:				
Compensation	(9,868,000)			(9,868,000)
Deferred compensation (T)	(300,000)	(150,000)		(450,000)
Stock option compensation (T)	(100,000)		100,000	0
Bad debt expense (T)	(165,000)		70,000	(95,000)
Charitable contributions (T)	(700,000)		73,700	(626,300)
Depreciation (T)	(2,400,000)	(700,000)		(3,100,000)
Advertising	(1,920,000)			(1,920,000)
Warranty expenses (T)	(580,000)		170,000	(410,000)
Meals and entertainment (P)	(28,000)		14,000	(14,000)
Life insurance premiums (P)	(34,000)		34,000	0
Other expenses	(64,000)			(64,000)
Total expenses *before* NOL, DRD, DPAD	$(16,159,000)			$16,547,300
Income *before* NOL, DRD, DPAD	$ 6,017,000			$ 5,660,700
NOL carryforward from prior year (T)	0	(24,000)		(24,000)
Dividends received deduction (P)	0	(21,000)		(21,000)
Domestic production activities deduction (P)	0	(465,000)	0	(465,000)
Book/Taxable income	**$ 6,017,000**	**(1,372,000)**	**505,700**	**$ 5,150,700**

either increasing or decreasing it. As a result, permanent differences usually affect a company's **effective tax rate** (income tax provision/pretax net income) and appear as part of the company's reconciliation of its effective tax rate with its statutory U.S. tax rate (34 percent in PCC's case).[12] We discuss ASC 740 disclosure requirements in a subsequent section of this chapter.

Exhibit 6-4 provides a list of common permanent differences you will encounter in practice.

EXHIBIT 6-4 Common Permanent Differences

Life insurance proceeds	Disallowed meals and entertainment expenses
Tax-exempt interest income	Disallowed premiums on officers' life insurance
Nondeductible tax penalties and fines	Dividends received deduction
Tax credits	Domestic production activities deduction
Political contributions	

[12]The windfall tax benefit from a nonqualified stock option deduction that is not treated as a temporary difference is recorded in additional paid-in capital (refer back to the previous discussion of stock option deductions in Chapter 5).

Example 6-2

Elise went back to the template she used to compute PCC's taxable income and identified the book–tax adjustments that were considered permanent in nature. What are PCC's permanent differences and are they favorable or unfavorable?

Answer: A net favorable permanent difference of $450,000, computed as follows:

Permanent Differences	(Favorable) Unfavorable
Tax-exempt interest income	$ (12,000)
Meals and entertainment	14,000
Life insurance premiums	34,000
Dividends received deduction	(21,000)
Domestic production activities deduction	(465,000)
Net favorable permanent difference	$(450,000)

Example 6-3

Elise used the net favorable permanent difference of $450,000 to adjust PCC's pretax net income. What is PCC's pretax net income adjusted for permanent differences?

Answer: $5,567,000, computed as follows:

PCC pretax net income	$6,017,000
Net favorable permanent difference	(450,000)
PCC pretax net income adjusted for permanent differences	$5,567,000

Elise remembered that her instructor at ASC 740 training referred to this intermediate computation as a company's **book equivalent of taxable income.** That is, this amount represents the book income that ultimately will be taxable, either currently or in the future.

Step 2: Identify All Temporary Differences and Tax Carryforward Amounts

ASC 740 formally defines a *temporary difference* as

> A difference between the tax basis of an asset or liability . . . and its reported amount in the financial statements that will result in taxable or deductible amounts in future years when the reported amount of the asset or liability is recovered or settled, respectively.[13]

As you learned in Chapter 5, temporary differences commonly arise in four instances.

Revenues or Gains That Are Taxable after They Are Recognized in Financial Income An example of such a "favorable" book–tax adjustment is gain from an installment sale that is recognized for financial accounting purposes in the year of sale but is recognized over the collection period for tax purposes.[14]

Expenses or Losses That Are Deductible after They Are Recognized in Financial Income Examples of such "unfavorable" book–tax adjustments include bad debt expenses, warranty expenses, and accrued compensation and vacation pay that are recorded using the reserve method for financial accounting purposes but

[13]ASC 740-10-20 Glossary.

[14]Consistent with the terminology introduced in Chapter 5, a "favorable" book–tax adjustment is one that reduces current year taxable income compared to current year net income.

can only be deducted when paid on the tax return.[15] Capitalized inventory costs under §263A also fall into this category, as do nonqualified stock option compensation expenses that are recorded at the grant date for financial reporting purposes under ASC 718 but do not become tax deductible until the exercise date.

Revenues or Gains That Are Taxable before They Are Recognized in Financial Income An example of such an "unfavorable" book–tax adjustment is a prepayment that is recognized in the year received for tax purposes but is not recognized for financial accounting purposes until the revenue is earned.

Expenses or Losses That Are Deductible before They Are Recognized in Financial Income A common example of such a "favorable" book–tax adjustment is the excess of tax depreciation over financial reporting depreciation.

Temporary differences also can arise from items that cannot be associated with a particular asset or liability for financial accounting purposes but produce revenue (income) or expense (deduction) that has been recognized in the financial statement and will result in taxable or deductible amounts in future years. For example, a net operating loss carryover and a net capital loss carryover create unfavorable temporary differences in the year they arise without being associated with a specific asset or liability.

Exhibit 6-5 lists common temporary differences.

EXHIBIT 6-5 Common Temporary Differences

Depreciation	Reserves for bad debts (uncollectible accounts)
Accrued vacation pay	Inventory costs capitalized under §263A
Prepayments of income	Warranty reserves
Installment sale income	Stock option expense under ASC 718
Pension plan deductions	Accrued bonuses and other compensation
Accrued contingency losses	Net operating loss and net capital loss carryovers

Identifying Taxable and Deductible Temporary Differences

Taxable Temporary Difference A temporary difference that is cumulatively *favorable* (i.e., an item that has cumulatively decreased taxable income relative to book income) gives rise to what ASC 740 refers to as a **taxable temporary difference.**[16] This category of temporary difference gets its name from the fact that when the difference reverses in a future period it will *increase taxable income* relative to book income.

Taxable temporary differences generally arise when (1) revenues or gains are taxable *after* they are recognized in net income (e.g., gross profit from an installment sale) and (2) expenses or losses are deductible on the tax return *before* they reduce net income (e.g., excess tax depreciation over financial accounting depreciation). From a balance sheet perspective, a taxable temporary difference generally arises when the financial reporting basis of an asset exceeds its corresponding tax basis or when the financial reporting basis of a liability is less than its corresponding tax basis. Subsequent "recovery" of the balance sheet basis of the asset or "payment" of the balance sheet liability will cause taxable income to exceed book income, either by creating a tax gain or reducing a tax deduction. The future tax cost associated with a taxable temporary difference is recorded on the balance sheet as a deferred tax liability.

Deductible Temporary Difference A temporary difference that is cumulatively *unfavorable* (i.e., an item that has cumulatively increased taxable income relative to book income) gives rise to what ASC 740 refers to as a **deductible temporary**

THE KEY FACTS

Identifying Taxable and Deductible Temporary Differences

- ASC 740 defines a temporary difference as a difference between the financial reporting and tax basis of an asset or liability that will create a future tax liability or benefit when the difference reverses.
- A temporary difference that cumulatively is *favorable* gives rise to a net taxable temporary difference.
- The future tax cost associated with a taxable temporary difference is recorded on the balance sheet as a deferred tax liability.
- A temporary difference that cumulatively is *unfavorable* gives rise to a net deductible temporary difference.
- The future tax benefit associated with a deductible temporary difference is recorded on the balance sheet as a deferred tax asset.

[15]Consistent with the terminology introduced in Chapter 5, an "unfavorable" book–tax adjustment is one that increases current year taxable income compared to current year net income.

[16]ASC 740-10-25-23.

difference.[17] This category of temporary difference gets its name from the fact that when the difference reverses in a future period it will *decrease taxable income* relative to book income.

Deductible temporary differences generally arise when (1) revenues or gains are taxable *before* they are recognized in net income (e.g., prepayments of subscriptions) and (2) expenses or losses are deductible on the tax return *after* they reduce net income (e.g., reserves for product warranty or uncollectible accounts). From a balance sheet perspective, a deductible temporary difference generally arises when the financial reporting basis of an asset is less than its corresponding tax basis or the financial reporting basis of a liability exceeds its corresponding tax basis. Subsequent "recovery" of the balance sheet basis of the asset or "payment" of the balance sheet liability will cause taxable income to be less than book income, either by creating a tax loss or increasing a tax deduction. The future tax benefit associated with a deductible temporary difference is recorded on the balance sheet as a deferred tax asset.

Unfavorable temporary differences that do not have balance sheet accounts, such as net operating loss carryovers, net capital loss carryovers, and charitable contribution carryovers, must be tracked to ensure that the appropriate adjustment is made to a company's deferred tax asset accounts when the carryover is used on a future tax return.

Example 6-4

Elise decided to separate PCC's temporary differences as being cumulatively favorable or cumulatively unfavorable (see Exhibit 6-3). What are PCC's taxable (cumulatively favorable) temporary differences?

Answer: PCC has one taxable temporary difference that arises in the current year—the excess of tax depreciation over book depreciation in the amount of $684,000. The gain on the sale of the fixed asset appears as an unfavorable difference, but it actually represents the reversal of a previously recorded favorable difference, the excess of tax over book depreciation. This "drawdown" of a previously recorded taxable temporary difference reduces the cumulatively favorable temporary differences arising in the current year. Elise summarized the taxable temporary differences as follows:

Taxable Temporary Differences	Amount
Excess of tax over book depreciation	($700,000)
Gain on fixed asset dispositions	16,000
Total taxable temporary differences	($684,000)

What are PCC's deductible (cumulatively unfavorable) temporary differences?

Answer: The deduction of previously accrued deferred compensation and PCC's use of its net operating loss carryover appear as favorable temporary differences in 2015, but they are actually reversals of prior year unfavorable temporary differences and reduce the cumulatively unfavorable temporary differences. PCC has net deductible temporary differences of $267,700, computed as follows:

Deductible Temporary Differences	Amount
Net capital loss carryforward	$ 28,000
Deferred compensation	(150,000)
Stock option compensation	100,000
Bad debt expense	70,000
Charitable contribution carryforward	73,700
Warranty expense	170,000
NOL carryforward from prior year	(24,000)
Total deductible temporary differences	$267,700

For the year, PCC has a net taxable (favorable) temporary difference of $(416,300) [($684,000) + $267,700].

[17]ASC 740-10-25-23.

Step 3: Compute the Current Income Tax Expense or Benefit

In many respects, the computation of the current portion of a company's tax provision appears to be straightforward. ASC 740 defines the **current income tax expense or benefit** as

> The amount of income taxes paid or payable (or refundable) for a year as determined by applying the provisions of the enacted tax law to the taxable income or excess of deductions over revenues for that year.[18]

To be sure, the major component of a company's current income tax expense or benefit is the income tax liability or refund from its current year operations. However, there are other items that enter into the computation that do not appear on the company's income tax return (Form 1120), which adds to the complexity of the computation.

In practice, the computation of a company's current income tax expense or benefit rarely equals the actual taxes paid on the company's current year tax returns. In particular, the current component of PCC's income tax provision also can be impacted by prior year income tax refunds from current year carrybacks of a net operating loss or net capital loss,[19] IRS audit adjustments from prior year tax returns,[20] windfall tax benefits from the exercise of nonqualified stock options, and changes in the company's **uncertain tax positions** (a company's reserve for taxes it has not paid but could pay in the future for positions taken on the current and prior year income tax returns).[21]

Example 6-5

Elise used her summary of permanent and temporary differences to verify her previous computation of PCC's taxable income. Does using Elise's summary of PCC's permanent and temporary differences verify her previous computation of PCC's taxable income?

Answer: Yes!

PCC pretax net income	$6,017,000
Net favorable permanent differences (from Example 6-2)	(450,000)
Net favorable temporary differences (from Example 6-4)	(416,300)
PCC taxable income	$5,150,700

What is PCC's current income tax expense, assuming a tax rate of 34 percent?

Answer: $1,751,238, computed as follows:

PCC taxable income	$5,150,700
	× 34%
PCC federal income tax payable	$1,751,238

What tax accounting journal entry does PCC make to record its current tax expense?

Answer:

Current income tax expense	1,751,238	
Current income taxes payable (or cash)		1,751,238

THE KEY FACTS

Computing the Deferred Income Tax Expense or Benefits

- Identify current year changes in taxable and deductible temporary differences.
- Determine ending balances in each deferred tax asset and liability balance sheet account.
- Identify carryovers (net operating loss, capital loss, charitable contributions) not on the balance sheet.
- The current year deferred income tax expense or benefit is the difference between the deferred tax asset and liability balances at the beginning of the year to the end of the year as well as changes in tax carryovers.

[18]ASC 740-10-20 Glossary.

[19]Requested on Form 1139 or Form 1120X.

[20]Agreed to on Form 5701.

[21]Calculated in the uncertain tax position workpapers.

Step 4: Determine the Ending Balances in the Balance Sheet Deferred Tax Asset and Liability Accounts

continued from page 6-6. . .
Having calculated the current portion of PCC's income tax provision, Elise turned her attention to computing the deferred piece of PCC's income tax provision. She knew from training that the technically correct method to compute PCC's deferred tax provision would be to compare the financial accounting basis of each asset and liability with its corresponding tax basis. Elise had the financial accounting basis of each account from the balance sheet but, like most companies, PCC did not keep a formal **tax accounting balance sheet.**[22] She would need to use an alternative method to calculate the change in the cumulative book–tax basis differences for each account she identified as being a temporary difference.

to be continued . . .

The FASB could have decided that a company report only the "as-paid" income taxes on its income statement. Investors and policymakers might favor this approach because it would disclose the actual income taxes paid or refunded (cash outflow or inflow) in the current year. Reporting only income taxes currently payable ignores one of the basic premises underlying financial accounting, which is that the accrual method of accounting provides more relevant information to investors and creditors than the cash method of accounting.[23]

The deferred income tax expense or benefit portion of a company's income tax provision reflects the change during the year in a company's balance sheet deferred tax liabilities or assets.[24] This information provides investors and other interested parties with a measure of a company's expected future income tax-related cash inflows or outflows resulting from book–tax differences that are *temporary* in nature or from tax carryovers.

ASC 740 takes an "asset and liability" or balance sheet approach to the computation of the deferred tax expense or benefit. The computations are based on the change in the *cumulative* differences between the financial accounting basis of an asset or liability and its corresponding tax basis from the beginning of the year to the end of the year. Under GAAP, the company is presumed to recover these basis differences over time, resulting in future sacrifices of a company's resources (in the case of liabilities) or future recoveries of a company's resources (in the case of assets). These expected future recoveries of assets or future sacrifices of assets to settle liabilities give rise to future (deferred) tax payments or refunds that are recorded in the income tax provision in the year the differences arise rather than in the year in which the future taxes are paid or recovered.

The future tax cost of a taxable (cumulatively favorable) temporary difference is recorded on the balance sheet as a deferred tax liability. The company computes the deferred tax liability using the **enacted tax rate** that is expected to apply to taxable income in the period(s) in which the deferred tax liability is expected to be settled.[25]

[22]Schedule L to Form 1120 requests that the taxpayer report its financial statement balance sheet. An increasing number of corporations are finding that a "best practice" is to maintain a tax basis balance sheet separate from the financial accounting balance sheet.

[23]ASC 230, *Statement of Cash Flows,* requires an enterprise to separately disclose income taxes paid as part of the statement itself or in a note to the financial statements (usually the income taxes note or a supplemental cash flow note).

[24]ASC 740-10-20 Glossary.

[25]ASC 740-10-30-2. For federal income tax provision purposes, a corporation applies the regular tax rate in computing its deferred tax assets and liabilities. The alternative minimum tax is treated as a prepaid income tax and reported as a deferred tax asset on the balance sheet.

Example 6-6

Lacking a formal tax-basis balance sheet, Elise identified the current year temporary differences and adjusted ("rolled forward") the cumulative differences at the beginning of the year to get the end of the year cumulative book–tax basis differences. She used this change in the cumulative book–tax basis difference to compute the deferred tax expense or benefit for the current year. Elise reviewed her schedules of favorable and unfavorable temporary differences (from Example 6-3). She identified one favorable temporary difference related to an asset recorded on the balance sheet—the excess of tax depreciation over book depreciation. Elise retrieved the fixed asset workpaper and recorded the changes in the financial accounting and tax accumulated depreciation balances of PCC's fixed assets from the beginning of the year to the end of the year related to current year depreciation.

Financial accounting change in accumulated depreciation	
Beginning of the year	$12,000,000
End of the year	14,400,000
Net change	$ 2,400,000
*Tax accounting change in accumulated depreciation**	
Beginning of the year	$22,000,000
End of the year	25,100,000
Net change	$ 3,100,000

*Not given in the original facts; assumed for purposes of this example.

The net increase in tax accounting accumulated depreciation over the corresponding financial accounting depreciation created a current year $700,000 favorable (taxable) temporary difference (i.e., the difference between the financial accounting basis of the fixed assets increased by $700,000 over their corresponding tax basis). This increase in the cumulative favorable temporary difference requires an *increase* in PCC's deferred tax liabilities.

By what amount will PCC increase its deferred tax liabilities as a result of the increase in the book over tax basis in these assets from the beginning of the year to the end of the year?

Answer: $238,000, computed as $700,000 × 34 percent.

What tax accounting journal entry does PCC record related to this transaction?

Answer:

Deferred income tax expense	238,000	
Deferred income tax liability		238,000

What if: Assume current year book depreciation exceeded current year tax depreciation by $700,000. What adjustment to the balance sheet would PCC be required to make?

Answer: PCC would *decrease* its deferred tax liability on the balance sheet by $238,000.

Example 6-7

Elise also saw that accumulated depreciation decreased as a result of PCC's sale of a fixed asset during the year (see Exhibit 6-3). She observed from the workpapers that PCC sold the fixed asset for $100,000, its original cost (not given in the original facts, assumed for purposes of this example). The book basis of the asset was $46,000, resulting in a book gain of $54,000. The tax gain on the sale was $70,000, which corresponds to a decrease in accumulated tax depreciation of $70,000 (i.e., the tax basis of the asset was $30,000). The excess of the reduction in accumulated tax

(continued on page 6-14)

depreciation over accumulated book depreciation of $16,000 corresponds to the excess of the tax gain over the book gain on the sale.

Financial accounting change in accumulated depreciation on the fixed asset sold	
Beginning of the year	$54,000
End of the year	0
Net change	$54,000
Tax accounting change in accumulated depreciation on the fixed asset sold	
Beginning of the year	$70,000
End of the year	0
Net change	$70,000

By what amount will PCC *decrease* its deferred tax liabilities as a result of the decrease in the tax over book basis in this asset from the beginning of the year to the end of the year?

Answer: $5,440, computed as $16,000 × 34%

What tax accounting journal entry does PCC record *related to this transaction*?

Answer:

Deferred income tax liability	5,440	
Deferred income tax benefit		5,440

This "drawdown" of the excess of tax accumulated depreciation over book accumulated depreciation requires a reduction in the previously recorded deferred tax liability that resulted from the book–tax difference created by the excess of tax depreciation over book depreciation in prior periods.

By what amount will PCC increase its current income tax expense as a result of this transaction (the tax gain was $70,000)?

Answer: $23,800, computed as $70,000 × 34%

What tax accounting journal entry does PCC record *related to this transaction*?

Answer:

Current income tax expense	23,800	
Income taxes payable		23,800

What is the net impact of this transaction on PCC's income tax provision?

Answer: A net increase of $18,360, computed as:

Current income tax expense	$23,800
Deferred income tax benefit	(5,440)
Net increase in PCC's income tax provision	$18,360

What do these journal entries accomplish?

Answer: The $18,360 provision reflects the tax expense related to the book gain of $54,000, computed as follows:

Book gain on sale of the fixed asset	$54,000
	× 34%
Net increase in PCC's income tax provision	$18,360

The recording of a deferred tax liability for years in which tax depreciation exceeded book depreciation anticipated the difference in the book and tax gain that would result when the fixed asset eventually was recovered, either through sale or depreciation of the entire basis.

Example 6-8

Using her cumulative temporary differences template, Elise recorded the cumulative taxable temporary differences and the corresponding deferred tax liability at the beginning of the year (BOY) and the end of the year (EOY) to determine the change in the deferred tax liability related to accumulated depreciation.

Premiere Computer Corporation
Temporary Difference Scheduling Template

Taxable Temporary Differences	BOY Cumulative T/D	Beginning Deferred Taxes (@ 34%)	Current Year Change	EOY Cumulative T/D	Ending Deferred Taxes (@ 34%)
Noncurrent					
Accumulated Depreciation	(10,000,000)*	**(3,400,000)**	(684,000)	(10,684,000)	**(3,632,560)**

*$22,000,000 − $12,000,000, from Example 6-6.

What is the net increase in PCC's deferred tax liability related to fixed assets for 2015?

Answer: $232,560, the change in the cumulative deferred tax liability from the beginning of the year ($3,400,000) to the end of the year ($3,632,560).

This amount corresponds to the increase in the deferred tax liability due to the current year change in the book–tax difference related to depreciation ($700,000) less the reduction in the deferred tax liability due to the change in the book–tax difference related to accumulated depreciation written off on the sale of the fixed asset ($16,000).

What tax accounting journal entry does PCC record related to the change in total deferred tax liabilities from the beginning of the year to the end of the year?

Answer:

Deferred income tax expense	232,560	
Deferred income tax liability		232,560

Using a template that tracks the cumulative changes in the book–tax differences related to balance sheet accounts becomes especially important when a company's enacted tax rate changes. For example, if PCC's federal income tax rate increased from 34 percent to 35 percent as a result of an increase in its taxable income, and PCC expects to maintain that tax rate in future periods, the company would tax-effect its year-end cumulative book–tax difference related to fixed assets at the new tax rate, 35 percent. The increase in the deferred tax expense related to adjusting the balance sheet will reflect the current year change in the book–tax difference and also an adjustment to revalue the cumulative book–tax difference at the beginning of the year. This discussion points to the fact that the focus of ASC 740 is to have the balance sheet deferred tax accounts reflect the tax that will be due or refunded when the underlying temporary differences reverse in a future period.

Example 6-9

What if: Assume PCC's tax rate increased from 34 percent in 2014 to 35 percent in 2015. By what amount would PCC increase or decrease its balance sheet deferred tax liability related to the fixed asset account?

(continued on page 6-16)

Answer: PCC *increases* its deferred tax liability related to fixed assets by $339,400, calculated as follows:

Premiere Computer Corporation Temporary Difference Scheduling Template					
Taxable Temporary Differences	**BOY Cumulative T/D**	**Beginning Deferred Taxes (@ 34%)**	**Current Year Change**	**EOY Cumulative T/D**	**Ending Deferred Taxes (@ 35%)**
Noncurrent					
Accumulated Depreciation	(10,000,000)	(3,400,000)	(684,000)	(10,684,000)	**(3,739,400)**

PCC would use a tax rate of 35 percent to compute the ending balance in its deferred tax liability related to fixed assets. The net increase in the deferred tax liability related to accumulated depreciation is now $339,400 ($3,739,400 − $3,400,000).

What tax accounting journal entry does PCC record *related to fixed assets?*

Answer:

Deferred income tax expense	339,400	
Deferred income tax liability		339,400

This amount no longer corresponds to the increase in the deferred income tax liability due to the current year net change in the book–tax difference related to depreciation of $684,000 times the new applicable tax rate of 35 percent ($684,000 × 35% = $239,400). The $100,000 difference results from increasing the beginning of the year cumulative temporary difference of $10,000,000 times the change in the tax rate of 1 percent ($10,000,000 × 1% = $100,000).

Example 6-10

Returning to her temporary differences template, Elise recorded the deductible (cumulatively unfavorable) temporary differences and the corresponding deferred tax assets at the beginning of the year (BOY) and the end of the year (EOY) to determine the change in PCC's deferred tax assets during the current year.

Premiere Computer Corporation Temporary Difference Scheduling Template					
Deductible Temporary Differences	**BOY Cumulative T/D**	**Beginning Deferred Taxes (@ 34%)**	**Current Year Change**	**EOY Cumulative T/D**	**Ending Deferred Taxes (@ 34%)**
Current					
Allowance for bad debts	$ 345,000	$ 117,300	$ 70,000	$ 415,000	$141,100
Reserve for warranties	430,000	146,200	170,000	600,000	204,000
Net operating loss	24,000	8,160	(24,000)	0	0
Total current	**$ 799,000**	**$271,660**	**$ 216,000**	**$1,015,000**	**$345,100**
Noncurrent					
Deferred compensation	$1,200,000	$408,000	($150,000)	$1,050,000	$357,000
Stock option compensation	0	0	100,000	100,000	34,000
Net capital loss carryover	0	0	28,000	28,000	9,520
Contribution carryover	0	0	73,700	73,700	25,058
Total noncurrent	**$1,200,000**	**$408,000**	**$ 51,700**	**$1,251,700**	**$425,578**
Total	**$1,999,000**	**$679,660**	**$ 267,700**	**$2,266,700**	**$770,678**

What is the net increase in PCC's total deferred income tax assets for 2015?

Answer: $91,018, the change in the cumulative deferred tax asset from the beginning of the year balance of $679,660 to the end of the year balance of $770,678.

What tax accounting journal entry does PCC record *related to deferred tax assets?*

Answer:

Deferred income tax assets	91,018	
Deferred income tax benefit		91,018

Example 6-11

What if: Assume PCC's tax rate increased from 34 percent in 2014 to 35 percent in 2015. By what amount would PCC increase or decrease its *total* balance sheet deferred income tax assets?

Answer: PCC *increases* its total deferred tax asset balance by $113,685, calculated as follows:

Premiere Computer Corporation
Temporary Difference Scheduling Template

Deductible Temporary Differences	BOY Cumulative T/D	Beginning Deferred Taxes (@ 34%)	Current Year Change	EOY Cumulative T/D	Ending Deferred Taxes (@ 35%)
Current					
Allowance for bad debts	$ 345,000	$ 117,300	$ 70,000	$ 415,000	$145,250
Reserve for warranties	430,000	146,200	170,000	600,000	210,000
Net operating loss	24,000	8,160	(24,000)	0	0
Total current	**$ 799,000**	**$271,660**	**$ 216,000**	**$1,015,000**	**$355,250**
Noncurrent					
Deferred compensation	$1,200,000	$408,000	($150,000)	$1,050,000	$367,500
Stock option compensation	0	0	100,000	100,000	35,000
Net capital loss carryover	0	0	28,000	28,000	9,800
Contribution carryover	0	0	73,700	73,700	25,795
Total noncurrent	**$1,200,000**	**$408,000**	**$ 51,700**	**$1,251,700**	**$438,095**
Total	**$1,999,000**	**$679,660**	**$ 267,700**	**$2,266,700**	**$793,345**

PCC would use a tax rate of 35 percent to compute the ending balance in each of its deferred tax asset accounts. The net increase in total deferred tax assets is now $113,685 ($793,345 − $679,660).

What tax accounting journal entry does PCC record to reflect the change in its *total* deferred tax assets?

Answer:

Deferred income tax assets	113,685	
Deferred income tax benefit		113,685

This amount no longer corresponds to the increase in total deferred tax assets due to the current year change in cumulative deductible temporary differences of $267,700 times the new applicable tax rate of 35 percent ($267,700 × 35% = $93,695). The $19,990 difference results from increasing the beginning of the year cumulative temporary difference of $1,999,000 times the change in the tax rate of 1 percent ($1,999,000 × 1% = $19,990).

LO 6-3

DETERMINING WHETHER A VALUATION ALLOWANCE IS NEEDED

THE KEY FACTS

Determining if a Valuation Allowance Is Needed

- A valuation allowance is required if it is more likely than not that some or all of the deferred tax asset will not be realized in the future.
- To make this determination, a company must determine its sources of future (or past) taxable income.
  - Taxable income in carryback years.
  - Reversing taxable temporary differences in future years.
  - Expected taxable income in future years from other than reversing taxable temporary differences.
  - Expected taxable income in future taxable years from implementing tax planning strategies.
- A company must evaluate (weigh) positive and negative evidence in deciding whether a valuation allowance is needed.
- A company must monitor whether increases or decreases should be made to the valuation allowance account every quarter.

Step 5: Evaluate the Need for a Valuation Allowance for Gross Deferred Tax Assets

ASC 740 specifically precludes PCC or any company from discounting (recording the present value of) the deferred tax liability or asset related to a temporary difference based on when the asset is expected to be recovered or the liability settled. The FASB debated whether discounting deferred tax assets and liabilities would provide more relevant information to investors, but ultimately it decided that the complexity and cost of making the computation outweighed any benefits investors and creditors might receive from the computation.[26]

In lieu of discounting, ASC 740 requires that a company evaluate each of its gross deferred tax assets on the balance sheet and assess the likelihood the expected tax benefit will be realized in a future period. The income tax benefits reflected in the deferred tax assets can only be *realized* (converted into cash) if the company expects to have sufficient taxable income or tax liability in the future or carryback period to absorb the unused tax deductions or credits before they expire.

Determining the Need for a Valuation Allowance

Under ASC 740, if a company determines that it is *more likely than not* (a likelihood greater than 50 percent) that some portion or all of the deferred tax assets will not be realized in a future period, it must offset the deferred tax assets with a **valuation allowance** to reflect the amount the company does not expect to realize in the future.[27] Valuation allowances operate as *contra accounts* to the deferred tax assets on the balance sheet, much like the allowance for bad debts a company must estimate for its accounts receivable. Companies usually disclose the amount of the valuation allowance in the income tax footnote to the financial statements.

Management must assess whether it is more likely than not that a deferred tax asset will *not* be realized in the future based on all available evidence, both positive and negative. ASC 740 identifies four sources of potential future taxable income, two of which are objective and two of which are subjective (i.e., determined by management judgment).[28] The objective sources include (1) future reversals of existing taxable temporary differences and (2) taxable income in prior carryback year(s). The subjective sources include (1) expected future taxable income exclusive of reversing temporary differences and carryforwards and (2) tax planning strategies.

Future Reversals of Existing Taxable Temporary Differences Existing taxable (cumulatively favorable) temporary differences provide taxable income when they are recovered in a future period. For example, the recovery of the excess of an asset's financial accounting basis over its tax basis, whether through sale or depreciation, will cause taxable income to be higher than net income in the periods in which the excess financial accounting basis is recovered. If the reversing taxable temporary differences provide sufficient future taxable income to absorb the reversing

[26] FAS 109, ¶¶198–199. (These paragraphs were not codified in ASC 740.)
[27] ASC 740-10-30-5(e).
[28] ASC 740-10-30-18.

deductible temporary differences, the company does not record a valuation allowance against the deferred tax asset.

Taxable Income in Prior Carryback Year(s) The company does not record a valuation allowance if the tax benefit from the realization of a deferred tax asset can be carried back to a prior year that has sufficient taxable income (or capital gain net income in the case of a net capital loss carryback) to absorb the realized tax benefit.

Expected Future Taxable Income Exclusive of Reversing Temporary Differences and Carryforwards ASC 740 allows a company to consider taxable income it expects to earn in future periods in determining whether a valuation allowance is necessary. The company might support its predictions of future taxable income with evidence of existing contracts or a sales backlog that will produce enough taxable income to realize the deferred tax asset when it reverses. In addition, the company might demonstrate that it has a strong earnings history if a deferred tax asset arises from a loss that could be considered out of the ordinary and not from a continuing condition. Cyclical industries such as automobile manufacturers and airlines traditionally have cited a history of past income as evidence of expected future income.

Tax Planning Strategies The most subjective source of future taxable income to support the realization of a deferred tax asset involves the company's ability and willingness to employ tax strategies in those future periods to create the taxable income needed to absorb the deferred tax asset. ASC 740 allows a company to consider actions it might take to create sufficient taxable income to absorb a deferred tax asset, provided such actions (1) are prudent and feasible; (2) are actions an enterprise might not take, but would take to prevent an operating loss or tax credit carryforward from expiring unused; and (3) would result in realization of the deferred tax assets. The company does not have to implement the strategy to avoid recording a valuation allowance, but management must be willing and able to execute the strategy if the need arises. Tax planning strategies could include (1) selling and leasing back operating assets, (2) changing inventory accounting methods (e.g., from LIFO to FIFO), (3) refraining from making voluntary contributions to the company pension plan, (4) electing to capitalize certain expenditures (e.g., research and development costs) rather than deduct them currently, (5) selling noncore assets, and (6) electing the alternative depreciation system (straight line instead of declining balance).

Negative Evidence That a Valuation Allowance Is Needed ASC 740 requires that a company consider *negative evidence* as well as *positive evidence* in determining whether it is more likely than not that a deferred tax asset will not be realized in the future. Negative evidence could include (1) cumulative (book) losses in recent years, (2) a history of net operating (capital) losses and credits expiring unused, (3) an expectation of losses in the near future, and (4) unsettled circumstances that, if resolved unfavorably, will result in losses from continuing operations in future years (e.g., the loss of a patent on a highly profitable drug).[29] As a general rule, public accounting firms interpret "recent years" with regard to cumulative book losses as a rolling 12 quarters (i.e., three years). As with all general rules, there are exceptions depending on the industry.

[29]ASC 740-10-30-21.

TAXES IN THE REAL WORLD AIG's $17.7 Billion "Fantasy" Profit

On February 23, 2012, American International Group, Inc. (AIG) announced net income of $19.8 billion for the full year 2011. Closer inspection of the announcement revealed that $17.7 billion of the amount was due to the company's release of a portion of its valuation allowance related to its deferred tax assets. The company's CEO stated that, "In 2011, we began to prosper once again. We have a high degree of confidence in our future earnings prospects, which is a critical element in our assessment supporting the release of the deferred tax asset valuation allowance."[a] In its Form 10-K, the company explained the rationale for releasing the valuation allowance as follows:

> The evaluation of the recoverability of the deferred tax asset and the need for a valuation allowance requires AIG to weigh all positive and negative evidence to reach a conclusion that it is more likely than not that all or some portion of the deferred tax asset will not be realized. The weight given to the evidence is commensurate with the extent to which it can be objectively verified. The more negative evidence that exists, the more positive evidence is necessary and the more difficult it is to support a conclusion that a valuation allowance is not needed. During 2011, AIG's level of profitability, excluding the $3.3 billion loss on extinguishment of debt in January confirmed its return to sustainable operating profit for the full year. This, together with the emergence from cumulative losses in recent years and projections of sufficient future taxable income, represent significant positive evidence. As of December 31, 2011, the cumulative positive evidence outweighed the historical negative evidence regarding the likelihood that the deferred tax asset for AIG's U.S. consolidated income tax group (other than the life-insurance-business capital loss carryforwards) will be realized.[b]

Not everyone was impressed with AIG's "whopping" profit. A writer for the *New York Times* referred to the profit as "pure fantasy." What do you think?[c]

[a]Form 8-K, issued 2/23/12. Available at http://www.sec.gov.
[b]Form 10-K, page 357. Available at http://www.sec.gov.
[c]Andrew Ross Sorkin, "Bending the Tax Code, and Lifting A.I.G.'s Profit," *New York Times*, February 23, 2012, (blog).

Example 6-12

Elise created a workpaper that listed PCC's ending balances in its deferred tax assets and liabilities at December 31, 2015 (from Examples 6-8 and 6-10), as follows:

PCC Deferred Tax Accounts at 12/31/2015

Deferred Tax Assets	
Allowance for bad debts	$ 141,100
Reserve for warranties	204,000
Net operating loss carryforward	0
Deferred compensation	357,000
Stock option compensation	34,000
Capital loss carryforward	9,520
Contribution carryforward	25,058
Total deferred tax assets	**$ 770,678**
Deferred tax liabilities	
Depreciation	(3,632,560)
Total deferred tax liabilities	$ (3,632,560)
Net deferred tax liabilities	**$(2,861,882)**

What *positive* evidence should Elise consider in her evaluation as to whether PCC should record a valuation allowance against some or all of the deferred tax assets?

Answer: PCC has an excess of deferred tax liabilities over deferred tax assets of $2,861,882. When the book–tax depreciation difference reverses in the future, this will provide PCC with enough taxable income to absorb the reversing deferred tax assets.

What *negative* evidence should Elise consider in her evaluation as to whether PCC should record a valuation allowance against some or all of the deferred tax assets?

Answer: The deferred tax asset related to the charitable contribution carryover has a short carryover expiration date (five years). Elise may need to schedule out when the depreciation differences will reverse to determine if the reversals alone will provide PCC with enough taxable income to absorb the contribution carryover within the next five years.

More problematic, the net capital loss carryover has both a short carryover expiration date (five years) and requires PCC to recognize net capital gains in future periods to absorb the net capital loss. A reversal of the book–tax depreciation temporary difference will not provide PCC with net capital gain to absorb the net capital loss carryover.

What other sources of *positive* evidence should Elise consider in her evaluation as to whether PCC should record a valuation allowance against the deferred tax asset related to the net capital loss carryover?

Answer: Two additional sources of positive evidence are management's projections of future taxable income from sources other than reversing taxable temporary differences and future taxable income from tax planning strategies. Because PCC is in the business of manufacturing and selling computer-related equipment, any additional taxable income it generates from selling additional equipment will produce ordinary income. The company likely will have to rely on an assertion that management has a "prudent" *tax planning strategy* it would be willing to use to generate net capital gain in the future. An example of such a strategy might be management's willingness to sell a parcel of land held for investment to generate a capital gain sufficient to absorb the net capital loss.

Example 6-13

What if: Assume PCC has had net book losses of $5,000,000 and $2,500,000 in 2013 and 2014, respectively. How might this additional fact influence Elise's assessment about the need for a valuation allowance?

Answer: PCC would have a cumulative book loss of $1,483,000 over the past 12 quarters at December 31, 2015 (combined book losses of $7,500,00 in excess of 2015 book income of $6,017,000 from Exhibit 6-3). ASC 740 states that a cumulative loss "in recent years" is considered objective negative evidence that may be hard to overcome. Elise would have to consider other sources of positive evidence that will outweigh the "significant" negative evidence in this situation.

Example 6-14

What if: Assume PCC just lost a big account to its competitor, but the company had reported cumulative net income in the current and prior two years. How might this additional fact influence Elise's assessment about the need for a valuation allowance?

Answer: Expectations of future events can outweigh historic results. In this case, Elise would have to seriously consider whether a valuation allowance would be required to the extent that reversing taxable temporary differences would not absorb expected future losses.

Step 6: Calculate the Deferred Income Tax Expense or Benefit

Example 6-15

After discussing with management its assessment of the company's sources of future taxable income, Elise concurred with management that the company did not need to record a valuation allowance for 2015. Elise now had the pieces to determine PCC's deferred income tax expense or benefit for 2015. What is PCC's deferred income tax provision for 2015 (use the solutions from Examples 6-8 and 6-10)?

Answer: $141,542 net deferred tax expense, computed as follows:

Gross deferred tax expense	$232,560	[Example 6-8]
Gross deferred tax benefit	(91,018)	[Example 6-10]
Net deferred tax expense	$141,542	

What is PCC's total income tax provision for 2015? (also use the solution from Example 6-5).

Answer: $1,892,780 income tax expense, computed as follows:

Current tax expense	$1,751,238	[Example 6-5]
Gross deferred tax expense	232,560	
Gross deferred tax benefit	(91,018)	
Income tax expense	$1,892,780	

There is a straightforward "back-of-the-envelope" method of verifying the ASC 740 approach to calculating PCC's total tax provision. Under the assumption that all temporary differences will appear on a tax return in a current or future period, the total tax provision should reflect the tax that ultimately will be paid on pretax net income adjusted for *permanent differences.* Remember from Example 6-3 that this amount is sometimes referred to as a company's book equivalent of taxable income. The total income tax provision should equal the company's tax rate times its book equivalent of taxable income. We would emphasize that this approach to computing a company's income tax provision is not in accordance with GAAP and will not provide the correct answer when there are changes in a company's income tax rate.

Example 6-16

Elise retrieved her computation of PCC's book equivalent of taxable income (from Example 6-3), as follows:

PCC pretax net income	$6,017,000
Net favorable permanent difference	(450,000)
PCC book equivalent to taxable income	$5,567,000

What is PCC's total tax provision using book equivalent of taxable income as a base?

Answer: $1,892,780, computed as follows:

PCC book equivalent to taxable income	$5,567,000
	× 34%
PCC book equivalent to taxable income	$1,892,780

This computation confirms the computation made under ASC 740 from Example 6-15.

ACCOUNTING FOR UNCERTAINTY IN INCOME TAX POSITIONS

LO 6-4

continued from page 6-12...
Elise recalled from her calculation of PCC's taxable income that there had been some discussion about the appropriate tax treatment of certain items on the tax return. In particular, she and PCC's tax director had debated whether certain income qualified for the domestic production activities deduction. In particular, there was some uncertainty as to whether $1,000,000 of the company's QPAI would be allowed by the IRS on audit. This amount of QPAI provided the company with a domestic production activities deduction of $90,000 (9% × $1,000,000). The tax director felt "comfortable" in taking the tax return position that the income met the definition of qualified production activity income (QPAI). Elise decided she needed to know more about how to deal with accounting for this tax uncertainty. ■

As you have learned in your study of the U.S. income tax laws, the answer to every tax question is not always certain. Taxpayers and the IRS can differ in their opinions as to whether an expenditure is deductible or must be capitalized or whether income is taxable or is deferred or exempt from taxation. When irresolvable disputes arise, the taxpayer can petition the courts to resolve the tax treatment of a transaction. Taxpayers and the IRS can appeal decisions of the lower courts to the appellate courts and ultimately to the Supreme Court. Taxpayers also take tax positions that can be disputed by state and local taxing authorities and international tax authorities. For example, the taxpayer and a state (international) tax authority may differ on whether the taxpayer has earned income in that jurisdiction and should pay tax on such income. The courts may not resolve this issue for many years after the original transaction takes place. If the courts do not resolve the issue in the taxpayer's favor, the taxpayer will be subject to interest and possible penalties on the tax owed.

For financial accounting purposes, a company must determine whether it can record the current or future tax benefits from an "uncertain" tax position in its financial statement for the period in which the transaction takes place, knowing that the ultimate resolution of the tax position may not be known until some time in the future.

FAS 109 as originally written provided no specific guidance on how to deal with uncertain tax positions. As a result, companies generally applied the principles of FAS 5, *Accounting for Contingencies* (codified as ASC 450), to uncertain tax positions. The FASB became concerned that companies were not applying FAS 5 uniformly, leading to diversity in practice and financial statements that were not comparable. After much debate, the FASB issued FASB Interpretation (FIN) No. 48, *Accounting for Uncertainty in Income Taxes—An Interpretation of FASB Statement No. 109,* in July 2006, effective for years beginning after December 15, 2006. FIN 48 has been codified in ASC 740. The objective of FIN 48 is to provide a uniform approach to recording and disclosing tax benefits resulting from tax positions that are considered to be uncertain.

ASC 740 (FIN 48) applies a two-step process to evaluating tax positions. ASC 740 refers to the first step as *recognition.*[30] A company must determine whether it is *more likely than not* (a greater than 50 percent probability) that a tax position will be sustained on examination by the IRS or other taxing authority, including resolution of any appeals within the court system, based on the technical merits of the position. In making this determination, the company must presume that the taxing authority (IRS) will examine the tax position with full knowledge of all relevant information.

THE KEY FACTS

Accounting for Uncertain Tax Positions

- ASC 740 requires a two-step process in determining if a tax benefit can be recognized in the financial statements.
  - A company first determines if it is more likely than not that its tax position on a particular account will be sustained on IRS examination based on its technical merits.
  - A company then determines the amount it expects to be able to recognize.
- The measurement process requires the company to make a cumulative probability assessment of all likely outcomes of the audit and litigation process.
  - The company recognizes the amount that has a greater than 50 percent probability of being sustained on examination and subsequent litigation.
  - The amount not recognized is recorded as a liability on the balance sheet.

[30]ASC 740-10-25-5 through 25-7.

In other words, the company cannot take into account the possibility that the taxing authority will not audit the uncertain tax position (play the "audit lottery").

The second step is referred to as *measurement*.[31] If the tax position meets the more-likely-than-not threshold (a subjective determination), the company must determine the amount of the benefit to record in the financial statements, or from an ASC 740 perspective, how much of its claimed tax benefit the company is not allowed to recognize. (ASC 740 refers to this unclaimed amount as "unrecognized tax benefits.") Under ASC 740, the company records the largest amount of the benefit, as calculated on a cumulative probability basis, which is more likely than not to be realized on the ultimate settlement of the tax position.

Application of ASC 740 to Uncertain Tax Positions

ASC 740 applies to all *tax positions* dealing with income taxes. As a result, ASC 740 pertains to tax positions taken on a current or previously filed tax return or a tax position that will be taken on a future tax return that is reflected in the financial statements as a deferred tax asset or liability. ASC 740 also applies to tax positions that result in permanent differences (e.g., the domestic production activities deduction and credits) and to decisions not to file a tax return in a particular jurisdiction. For example, assume a company deducts an expenditure on its current tax return, which the IRS may challenge on audit in a future period. The deduction produces a net operating loss that will be carried forward and offset against future taxable income. ASC 740 addresses whether the company can *recognize* the deferred tax asset related to the NOL carryforward on its balance sheet. Once the recognition hurdle is overcome, the company must then evaluate whether it is more likely than not that the deferred tax asset will be *realized* in the future period (i.e., whether a valuation allowance should be recorded).

Step 1: Recognition A company first must determine if it is more likely than not that its tax position on a particular account will be sustained on IRS examination based on its technical merits. If the company believes this threshold has been met, the company can record (recognize) the tax benefit of the tax position on its financial statements as a reduction in its current tax expense or an increase in its deferred tax benefit. The company must presume that the IRS will examine this tax position with full knowledge of all relevant information. However, in determining if the more-likely-than-not threshold has been met, the company can take into account how the tax position might be resolved if litigated. This requires the company to evaluate the sources of authority that address this issue (i.e., the tax law, regulations, legislative history, IRS rulings, and court opinions).

Step 2: Measurement After the company determines that the more-likely-than-not recognition threshold has been met, it must compute the amount of the tax benefit to recognize in its financial statements. ASC 740 states that the tax position is to be measured as

> the largest amount of tax benefit that is greater than 50 percent likely of being realized upon ultimate settlement with a taxing authority that has full knowledge of all relevant information.[32]

This measurement process requires the company to make a cumulative probability assessment of all likely outcomes of the audit and litigation process. The company then recognizes the amount that has a greater than 50 percent probability of being sustained on examination and subsequent litigation.

The amount of the tax benefit that is not recognized ("unrecognized tax benefit") is recorded as a liability on the balance sheet (usually labeled as "Income Taxes

[31] ASC 740-10-30-7.

[32] ASC 740-10-30-7.

Payable"). The corresponding "debit" to record the balance sheet liability is to *current* income tax expense (or a decrease in income tax benefit). If the company expects the uncertain tax position to be resolved in the next 12 months, the balance sheet payable is characterized as current. Otherwise, the payable is characterized as being noncurrent. The increase in tax expense is added to the current portion of the provision under the theory that this is an on-demand liability.

Example 6-17

Elise saw in the domestic production activities deduction (DPAD) workpapers that PCC claimed $465,000 of DPAD on its tax return, computed as 9 percent times $5,166,667 of qualified production activity income (from Example 5-1). She noted that there was mention in the uncertain tax position (UTP) workpapers that there was uncertainty as to whether $1,000,000 of the $5,166,667 met the definition of qualified production activity income (QPAI). This tax position provided PCC with a current year tax benefit of $30,600 ($1,000,000 × 9% × 34%).

What threshold must be met before PCC can *recognize* any of the tax benefit from the "uncertain" portion of the DPAD on its financial statements?

Answer: PCC must determine that it is more likely than not that its tax position on the DPAD will be sustained by the IRS on examination based on its technical merits.

Example 6-18

PCC determined that it was more likely than not that the tax position would be sustained on audit and litigation. The tax department calculated the probability of receiving a full or partial benefit after resolution of the issue as follows:

Potential Estimated Tax Benefit	Individual Probability of Being Realized	Cumulative Probability of Being Realized
$30,600	60%	60%
22,500	25	85
18,000	10	95
0	5	100

Based on these probabilities, how much of the uncertain tax benefit of $30,600 can PCC recognize?

Answer: $30,600. PCC can recognize all $30,600 of the DPAD tax benefit because this amount is the largest amount that has a greater than 50 percent cumulative probability of being realized on the ultimate settlement of the tax position.

Example 6-19

What if: Assume PCC's tax department had assessed the cumulative probabilities of sustaining the DPAD tax benefit as follows:

Potential Estimated Tax Benefit	Individual Probability of Being Realized	Cumulative Probability of Being Realized
$30,600	40%	40%
22,500	30	70
18,000	20	90
0	10	100

Based on these probabilities, how much of the uncertain tax benefit of $30,600 can PCC recognize?

(continued on page 6-26)

Answer: $22,500. PCC can recognize $22,500 of the DPAD tax benefit because this amount is the largest amount that has a greater than 50 percent cumulative probability of being realized on the ultimate settlement of the tax position. This translates into management believing that $735,294 of the uncertain DPAD will be sustained on audit ($22,500/.09/.34).

What would be PCC's journal entry to record the portion of the tax benefit that cannot be recognized?

Answer: PCC would establish a liability for the $8,100 difference between the amount of the benefit received on the current year tax return ($30,600) and the amount the company ultimately expects to receive ($22,500). PCC would record the following journal entry:

Current income tax expense	8,100	
Income taxes payable		8,100

The income taxes payable account is characterized as noncurrent on the balance sheet if PCC does not expect the UTP to be resolved within the next 12 months. The uncertain tax benefit is recorded as a current tax expense because this is the additional amount of taxes PCC would pay if it prepared its tax return by deducting only $735,294 of the uncertain DPAD instead of $1,000,000.

Subsequent Events

ASC 740 requires a company to monitor subsequent events (e.g., the issuance of new regulations, rulings, court opinions) that might change the company's assessment that a tax position will be sustained on audit and litigation. As facts and circumstances change, a company must reevaluate the tax benefit amount they expect to realize in the future. For example, the Treasury might issue a regulation or ruling that clarifies its tax position on a particular item. This regulation could change a company's assessment that its tax position meets the more-likely-than-not threshold required for recognition.

In its 2009 Annual Report, Cisco Systems Inc. disclosed that it took a tax charge of approximately $174 million in the fourth quarter of fiscal 2009 after the U.S. Court of Appeals for the Ninth Circuit overturned a 2005 U.S. Tax Court ruling in *Xilinx, Inc. v. Commissioner*. The company increased its unrecognized tax benefits even though it was not named as a party to the case because it had the same issue on its tax returns (the deduction of share-based compensation expenses for the purpose of determining intangible development costs under a company's research and development cost sharing arrangement). This increase in the company's prior period unrecognized tax benefits increased its effective tax rate by 2.3 percentage points in fiscal 2009.

In its 2010 Annual Report, Cisco reported that the Ninth Circuit withdrew its prior holding and reaffirmed the 2005 U.S. Tax Court ruling in *Xilinx, Inc. v. Commissioner*. As a result of this final decision, the company decreased the amount of gross unrecognized tax benefits by approximately $220 million and decreased the amount of accrued interest by $218 million. This adjustment decreased Cisco's effective tax rate by 1.7 percentage points.

Interest and Penalties

ASC 740 requires a company to accrue interest and any applicable penalties on liabilities it establishes for potential future tax obligations. The interest (net of the tax benefit from deducting it on a future tax return when paid) and penalties (which are not tax deductible) can be treated as part of the company's UTP-related income tax expense and income tax payable or can be recognized as interest or penalties separate from the UTP-related income tax expense. ASC 740 only requires that the company apply its election consistently from period to period. This election creates the potential for diversity in practice. For example, General Motors

Corporation treats accrued interest and penalties on its uncertain tax positions as part of its selling, general, and administrative expenses, while Ford Motor Company treats accrued interest and penalties on its uncertain tax positions as part of its income tax provision.

Disclosures of Uncertain Tax Positions

One of the most controversial aspects of ASC 740 is its expansion of the disclosure requirements related to liabilities recorded due to uncertain tax positions. ASC 740 requires the company to roll forward all unrecognized tax benefits (UTBs) on a worldwide aggregated basis. Specific line items must disclose (1) the gross amounts of increases and decreases in liabilities related to uncertain tax positions as a result of tax positions taken during a prior period, (2) the gross amounts of increases and decreases in liabilities related to uncertain tax positions as a result of tax positions taken during the current period, (3) the amounts of decreases in liabilities related to uncertain tax positions relating to settlements with taxing authorities, and (4) reductions in liabilities related to uncertain tax positions as a result of a lapse of the applicable statute of limitations (the taxing authority can no longer audit the tax return on which the tax position was taken). The UTP disclosure by Microsoft Corporation is illustrated in Exhibit 6-6.

EXHIBIT 6-6 The UTP Disclosure of Microsoft Corporation

The aggregate changes in the balance of unrecognized tax benefits were as follows:

	(In millions)		
Year Ended June 30,	**2014**	**2013**	**2012**
Balance, beginning of year	**$8,648**	$ 7,202	$6,935
Decreases related to settlements	**(583)**	(30)	(16)
Increases for tax positions related to the current year	**566**	612	481
Increases for tax positions related to prior years	**217**	931	118
Decreases for tax positions related to prior years	**(95)**	(65)	(292)
Decreases due to lapsed statutes of limitations	**(39)**	(2)	(24)
Balance, end of year	**$8,714**	$8,648	$ 7,202

FIN 48 became effective for years beginning after December 15, 2006. The FASB required adopters to record their initial FIN 48 cumulative effect adjustment (in the first quarter after adoption) to retained earnings or other balance sheet account rather than to the income tax provision. Subsequent adjustments must be reported as part of the income tax provision.

Opponents of FIN 48 worried that the FIN 48 disclosures would provide a "roadmap" to the IRS to a company's uncertain tax positions.[33] The FIN 48 disclosures have not provided the IRS with the hoped-for details because the UTP disclosure does not identify the tax jurisdictions to which the uncertain tax positions relate.

Schedule UTP (Uncertain Tax Position Statement)

In January 2010, Commissioner Shulman announced that the IRS would begin asking large corporations to report their financial statement uncertain tax positions

[33] Jesse Drucker, "Lifting the Veil on Tax Risk—New Accounting Rule Lays Bare a Firm's Liability if Transaction Is Later Disallowed by the IRS," *The Wall Street Journal,* May 25, 2007.

on new Schedule UTP beginning in tax year 2010. The commissioner stated that the goals of the new schedule would be to increase transparency and efficiency in identifying audit issues and help the IRS prioritize the selection of issues and taxpayers for audit. Schedule UTP requires corporations to report any federal income tax position for which an unrecognized tax benefit has been recorded in an audited financial statement. A corporation must identify the IRC section or sections relating to the position, indicate whether the position involves a temporary or permanent difference, identify whether the tax position is a major tax position (10 percent or more of the total), rank the tax positions by size, and provide a "concise" description of the UTP. Corporations with assets of $10 million or more must file Schedule UTP. An analysis of the tax year 2012 filed Schedule UTPs revealed that 2,333 taxpayers filed the schedule and reported 5,807 issues. The top three issues involved transfer pricing (22%), the research credit (24%), capitalization (4%), and the domestic production activities deduction (4%).[34]

ETHICS

Pete Cooper, senior manager in the tax group in the Boston office of Bean Counters LLP, an international professional services firm, was reviewing the workpapers related to the uncertain tax positions prepared by his biggest client, Pro Vision Inc. Pete noticed that the client took the position that it did not need to record an uncertain tax benefit for a significant transaction because it had a "should level" opinion from its law firm. (A "should level" tax opinion means that the law firm believes there is a 70 to 90 percent probability that the tax benefit from the transaction will be allowed if litigated.) When Pete asked to see the tax opinion, he was told by the firm's tax director that the company did not want to disclose the item for fear the IRS also would ask to see the opinion. Pete has always had a good working relationship with the tax staff at Pro Vision and trusts their integrity.

Should Pete take the tax director's word when auditing the company's reserve for uncertain tax positions? What would you do if you were in Pete's position?

LO 6-5

FINANCIAL STATEMENT DISCLOSURE AND THE COMPUTATION OF A CORPORATION'S EFFECTIVE TAX RATE

Balance Sheet Classification

ASC 740 requires publicly traded and privately held companies to disclose their deferred tax assets and liabilities on their balance sheets and classify them as either current or noncurrent.[35] A company classifies its deferred tax assets and liabilities based on the classification of the asset or liability to which the deferred tax account relates. For example, a deferred tax liability related to a long-term asset (e.g., depreciation of a fixed asset) is classified as noncurrent because the related asset is classified as noncurrent on the balance sheet. Deferred tax liabilities and assets not related to a specific asset (e.g., a net operating loss carryover or organizational expenditures capitalized for tax purposes) are classified based on the expected reversal date of the temporary difference.

[34]http://www.irs.gov/Businesses/Corporations/UTPFilingStatistics

[35]ASC 740-10-45-4.

ASC 740 requires companies to net deferred tax assets and liabilities based on their classification (current with current, noncurrent with noncurrent) and present the net amount on the balance sheet.[36] ASC 740 does not permit netting of deferred tax assets and liabilities that are attributable to different tax jurisdictions. For example, PCC cannot offset a noncurrent deferred tax asset related to a net operating loss incurred in Germany against a noncurrent deferred tax liability arising from depreciation of fixed assets within the United States. Exhibit 6-7 provides the balance sheet classification for common deferred tax assets and liabilities.

EXHIBIT 6-7 Classification of Common Deferred Tax Assets and Liabilities

Current Deferred Account	**Related Balance Sheet Account**
Allowance for Bad Debts	Accounts Receivable
Reserve for Warranties	Warranty Payable (liability)
Inventory §263A Adjustment	Inventory
Revenue Recognition	Unearned Revenue (liability)
Noncurrent Deferred Account	**Related Balance Sheet Account**
Accumulated Depreciation	Fixed Assets
Amortization	Goodwill or Other Intangible
Deferred Compensation	Deferred Compensation (liability)

Deferred tax assets related to net operating loss carryovers, net capital loss carryovers, and charitable contribution are classified based on when the temporary difference is expected to reverse (be deducted on a future tax return).

Example 6-20

Elise reviewed her temporary difference templates (see Examples 6-8 and 6-10). What will be the ending balance in PCC's net current deferred tax assets or liabilities at December 31, 2015?

Answer: $345,100 net current deferred tax assets. PCC does not have any current deferred tax liabilities to offset against its current deferred tax assets.

What will be the ending balance in PCC's net noncurrent deferred tax assets or liabilities at December 31, 2015?

Answer: ($3,206,982) net noncurrent deferred tax liability.

Because PCC's deferred tax accounts relate to the same tax jurisdiction (United States), PCC can net the noncurrent deferred tax liabilities of $3,632,560 with the noncurrent deferred tax assets of $425,578, resulting in a net noncurrent deferred tax liability of $3,206,982.

Example 6-21

What if: Assume the noncurrent deferred tax asset related to deferred compensation arose in Canada. What will be the ending balance in PCC's net noncurrent deferred tax assets or liabilities at December 31, 2015?

Answer: $357,000 noncurrent deferred tax asset and $3,563,982 net noncurrent deferred tax liability ($3,632,560 − $68,578).

PCC cannot net the deferred tax asset that relates to Canada with the other noncurrent deferred tax accounts that relate to the United States.

[36]ASC 740-10-45-6. The FASB has proposed simplifying ASC 740 by treating all deferred tax accounts as noncurrent beginning in 2017.

Income Tax Footnote Disclosure

In addition to the above balance sheet disclosure requirements, ASC 740 mandates that a company disclose the components of the net deferred tax assets and liabilities reported on its balance sheet and the total valuation allowance recognized for deferred tax assets.[37] Most companies provide this information in a footnote to the financial statements (often referred to as the *income tax footnote*). Publicly traded companies must disclose the approximate "tax effect" of each type of temporary difference and carryforward that gives rise to a *significant* portion of the net deferred tax liabilities and deferred tax assets.[38] Privately held (nonpublic) companies only need to disclose the types of significant temporary differences without disclosing the tax effects of each type. ASC 740 does not define the term *significant,* although the SEC requires a publicly traded company to disclose separately the components of its total deferred tax assets and liabilities that are 5 percent or more of the total balance.[39] Exhibit 6-8 provides the disclosure of PCC's deferred tax accounts in its income tax footnote.

ASC 740 also requires publicly traded companies to disclose the significant components of its income tax provision (expense or benefit) attributable to continuing operations in either the financial statements or a note thereto.[40] These components include the (1) current tax expense or benefit, (2) deferred tax expense or benefit, (3) the benefits of operating loss carryforwards, (4) adjustments of a deferred tax liability or asset for enacted changes in tax laws or rates, and (5) adjustments of the beginning-of-the-year balance of a valuation allowance because of a change in circumstances that causes a change in management's judgment about the realizability of the recognized deferred tax assets.

Computation and Reconciliation of the Income Tax Provision with a Company's *Hypothetical* Tax Provision ASC 740 requires a company to reconcile its (a) reported income tax provision attributable to continuing operations with (b) the amount of income tax expense that would result from applying its U.S. statutory tax rate to its pretax net income or loss from continuing operations.[41] Alternatively, a company can present the reconciliation in terms of tax rates, comparing its statutory tax rate with its effective tax rate (income tax provision/pretax income from continuing operations).

Differences between a company's income tax provision and its hypothetical tax provision can arise from several sources. Income taxes paid to a state or municipality increase a company's total income tax provision over its hypothetical income tax expense. Income taxes paid to a jurisdiction outside the United States can increase or decrease a company's total income tax provision over its hypothetical income tax expense depending on whether the jurisdiction taxes the company's income at more or less than the U.S. statutory rate. Permanent differences also affect the computation of PCC's income tax provision. Favorable permanent differences (e.g., tax-exempt income) decrease the income tax provision relative to the hypothetical income tax provision. Unfavorable permanent differences (e.g., nondeductible fines and penalties) increase the income tax provision relative to the hypothetical income tax provision.

[37]ASC 740-10-50-2.

[38]ASC 740-10-50-6.

[39]ASC 740-10-50-8 and SEC Regulation S-X, §210.4-08(h).

[40]ASC 740-10-50-9.

[41]ASC 740-10-50-12. The income tax provision computed using the statutory tax rate is often referred to as the *hypothetical* income tax expense.

EXHIBIT 6-8 PCC's Income Tax Note to Its Financial Statements

NOTE 5 INCOME TAXES

The Company's income (loss) from continuing operations before the income tax provision by taxing jurisdiction is as follows:

	2015
United States	$6,017,000

The provision (benefit) for income taxes is as follows:

Current tax provision (benefit)	
Federal (U.S.)	$1,751,238
Deferred tax expense (benefit)	
Federal (U.S.)	141,542
Income tax provision	$1,892,780

Deferred tax assets and liabilities are classified as current or noncurrent according to the classification of the related asset or liability. The significant components of the Company's deferred tax assets and liabilities as of December 31, 2015, are as follows:

	2015
Deferred tax *assets*	
Allowance for bad debts	$ 141,100
Reserve for warranties	204,000
Deferred compensation	357,000
Stock option compensation	34,000
Capital loss carryover	9,520
Contribution carryforward	25,058
Total deferred tax assets	$ 770,678
Valuation allowance	0
Net deferred tax assets	$ 770,678
Deferred tax *liabilities*	
Depreciation	($3,632,560)
Total deferred tax liabilities	($3,632,560)
Net deferred tax liabilities	($2,861,882)

The capital loss carryforward and the contribution carryforward expire in 2020 if unused.

A reconciliation of income taxes computed by applying the statutory U.S. income tax rate to the Company's income before income taxes to the income tax provision is as follows:

	2015
Amount computed at the statutory U.S. tax rate (34 percent)	$2,045,780
Tax-exempt income	(4,080)
Nondeductible meals and entertainment	4,760
Nondeductible life insurance premiums	11,560
Dividends received deduction	(7,140)
Domestic production activities deduction	(158,100)
Income tax provision	$1,892,780

Cash amounts paid during 2015 for income taxes, net of refunds, was $1,751,238.

ASC 740 requires a publicly traded company to disclose the estimated amount and nature of each significant reconciling item, which the SEC defines as an amount equal to or greater than 5 percent of the hypothetical provision. The SEC requires nonpublicly traded companies to disclose the nature of significant reconciling items but not the reconciling amount.

Example 6-22

Elise used her schedule of permanent differences (from Example 6-2) to reconcile PCC's income tax provision ($1,892,780, from Example 6-15) with the company's hypothetical income tax provision. The permanent differences from Example 6-2 are reproduced below:

Permanent Differences	(Favorable) Unfavorable
Tax exempt interest income	$ (12,000)
Meals and entertainment	14,000
Life insurance premiums	34,000
Dividends received deduction	(21,000)
Domestic production activities deduction	(465,000)

PCC's pretax net income from continuing operations in 2015 is $6,017,000.

What is PCC's *hypothetical* income tax provision for 2015?

Answer: $2,045,780, computed as $6,017,000 × 34 percent.

What is PCC's *effective tax rate* for 2015?

Answer: 31.5 percent, computed as $1,892,780/$6,017,000.

Provide a reconciliation of PCC's hypothetical income tax provision with its actual income tax provision in 2015. The tax cost or benefit from each permanent difference is computed by multiplying the permanent difference (from above) times 34 percent.

Answer:

	2015
Amount computed at statutory U.S. tax rate (34%)	$2,045,780
Tax-exempt income	(4,080)
Nondeductible meals and entertainment	4,760
Nondeductible life insurance premiums	11,560
Dividends received deduction	(7,140)
Domestic production activities deduction	(158,100)
Income tax provision	$1,892,780

The SEC requires its registrants to separately disclose only those components of their effective tax rate reconciliations that equal or exceed 5 percent of the "hypothetical" tax expense. In the above reconciliation, PCC would only be required to separately disclose the items that equal or exceed $102,289 ($2,045,780 × 5%), which, in this example, would be the domestic production activities deduction. The other items could be netted in the reconciliation.

Provide a reconciliation of PCC's statutory income tax rate (34 percent) with its actual effective tax rate (31.5 percent) in 2015. The percentage effect of each permanent difference is computed by dividing the tax cost or benefit from the item (from above) by PCC's pretax net income ($6,017,000).

Answer:

	2015
Statutory U.S. tax rate	34.0%
Tax-exempt income	(0.0)
Nondeductible meals and entertainment	0.0
Nondeductible life insurance premiums	0.2
Dividends received deduction	(0.1)
Domestic production activities deduction	(2.6)
Effective tax rate	31.5%

Exhibit 6-8 provides the disclosure of PCC's reconciliation of its effective tax rate in its income tax footnote.

Importance of a Company's Effective Tax Rate The effective tax rate often serves as a benchmark for companies in the same industry. However, nonrecurring events can sometimes have a significant impact on the effective tax rate. To mitigate the impact of such aberrational events, companies and their investors may use (at least for internal purposes) a different measure of effective tax rate that backs out one-time and nonrecurring events. This effective tax rate is referred to as the company's **structural tax rate.** The structural effective tax rate often is viewed as more representative of the company's effective tax rate from its normal (recurring) operations. In our example, PCC does not appear to have any nonrecurring reconciling items, which would make its effective tax rate and its structural tax rate the same.

Analysts often compute a company's **cash tax rate** (cash taxes paid divided by pretax book income) in their evaluation of the company's tax status. As the name implies, the cash tax rate excludes deferred taxes. PCC's cash tax rate in 2015 is 29.1 percent ($1,751,238/$6,017,000). Companies earning income in low-tax jurisdictions outside the United States or that have significant favorable permanent differences can have a cash tax rate that is much lower than their accounting effective tax rate. For example, Amazon.com Inc. reported an accounting effective tax rate of 31.1 percent and a cash tax rate of 3.5 percent in 2011!

Interim Period Effective Tax Rates

In addition to annual reports (Form 10-K), PCC also must report earnings on a quarterly basis (Form 10-Q). ASC 740-270, *Interim Reporting,* governs the preparation of these quarterly statements. ASC 740-270-30-6, states that *"at the end of each interim period the entity should make its best estimate of the effective tax rate expected to be applicable for the full fiscal year"* and apply this rate to the income reported in the quarterly statement. A company must reconsider its estimate of the annual rate each quarter. When the estimate changes, the company must adjust the cumulative tax provision for the year-to-date earnings to reflect the new expected annual rate. The adjusting amount becomes the company's income tax provision for the quarter.

CONVERGENCE OF ASC 740 WITH INTERNATIONAL FINANCIAL REPORTING STANDARDS

In 2002, the FASB and the International Accounting Standards Board (IASB) announced they would work together to develop common accounting standards for the world's capital markets. Included in this project was an effort to converge ASC 740 with its International Financial Reporting Standards (IFRS) counterpart, IAS 12, *Income Taxes*. The convergence project was put on hold by the FASB after the SEC announced that it was considering allowing the adoption of all IFRS standards by U.S. companies. In March 2009, the IASB issued a proposed revision of IAS 12 that incorporated some convergence with ASC 740. IAS 12 and ASC 740 share many commonalities. The differences relate primarily to issues beyond the scope of this chapter, although there are some disclosure and measurement differences (e.g., IAS 12 does not separate deferred tax accounts between current and noncurrent and does not specifically address accounting for uncertain tax positions). The FASB and IASB have not announced a resumption of the convergence project, and the IASB withdrew its proposed revision of IAS 12. The European Financial Reporting Advisory Group recently issued a thoughtful discussion paper on improving the financial reporting of income taxes.[42]

[42]European Financial Reporting Advisory Group, Improving the *Financial Reporting of Income Taxes,* Discussion Paper, December 2011. Available at http://www.efrag.org.

CONCLUSION

In this chapter we discussed the basic rules that govern the computation of a company's U.S. income tax provision. As a result of increased SEC and PCAOB scrutiny, the need for individuals who understand these rules has increased dramatically. The FASB requires a company to take a balance sheet approach to computing its current and future (deferred) tax liabilities or benefits (assets). The income tax provision that appears on a company's income statement becomes the amount necessary to adjust the beginning balances of these accounts to their appropriate ending balances. The FASB and SEC also impose disclosure requirements for how a company reports its tax accounts in the financial statement amounts and notes to the financial statements.

Summary

LO 6-1 Explain the objectives behind FASB ASC Topic 740, *Income Taxes,* and the income tax provision process.

- Objectives of ASC 740:
  - To recognize a current income tax liability or asset for the company's taxes payable or refundable in the current year.
  - To recognize a deferred income tax liability or asset for the income tax effects of the company's temporary differences and carryovers.
- The income tax provision process consists of six steps:
  - Adjust net income before income taxes for all permanent differences.
  - Identify all temporary differences and tax carryforward amounts.
  - Calculate the current income tax expense or benefit (refund).
  - Determine the ending balances in the balance sheet deferred tax asset and liability accounts.
  - Evaluate the need for a valuation allowance for gross deferred tax assets.
  - Calculate the deferred income tax expense or benefit.

LO 6-2 Calculate the current and deferred income tax expense or benefit components of a company's income tax provision.

- The company first adjusts its pretax net income or loss for permanent and temporary book–tax differences to compute taxable income or loss. The company then applies the appropriate tax rate to taxable income (loss) to compute the tax return current tax expense or benefit.
- The company adjusts its tax return income tax liability or benefit for audit refunds or deficiencies from prior year tax returns, and income tax benefits from stock option exercises treated as permanent differences.
- A company computes its deferred income tax expense or benefit by applying the applicable tax rate to the change in the cumulative balance sheet temporary differences between the financial accounting basis of an asset or liability and its corresponding tax basis from the beginning of the year to the end of the year.
- The future tax benefits from deductible (cumulatively unfavorable) temporary differences are recorded as deferred tax assets.
- The future tax costs of favorable taxable (cumulatively favorable) temporary differences are recorded as deferred tax liabilities.

LO 6-3 Recall what a valuation allowance represents and describe the process by which it is determined.

- If a company determines that it is more likely than not (a greater than 50 percent probability) that some portion or all of the deferred tax assets will not be realized in a future period, it must offset the deferred tax assets with a valuation allowance to reflect the amount the company does not expect to realize in the future.

- The determination as to whether it is more likely than not that a deferred tax asset will not be realized in the future must be based on all available evidence, both positive and negative.
- ASC 740 identifies four sources of prior and future taxable income to consider: (1) future reversals of existing taxable temporary differences, (2) taxable income in prior carryback year(s), (3) expected future taxable income exclusive of reversing temporary differences and carryforwards, and (4) expected income from tax strategies.

Explain how a company accounts for its uncertain income tax positions under FASB ASC 740. LO 6-4

- A company must determine whether it can record the tax benefits from an "uncertain" tax position in its financial statement for the period in which the transaction takes place, knowing that the ultimate resolution of the tax position may not be known until some future period.
- ASC 740 applies a two-step process to evaluating uncertain tax positions:
  - Recognition: A company must determine whether it is more likely than not (a greater than 50 percent probability) that a tax position will be sustained upon examination by the IRS or other taxing authority, including resolution of any appeals within the court system, based on the technical merits of the position.
  - Measurement: If the tax position meets the more-likely-than-not threshold (a subjective determination), the company must determine the amount of the benefit to record in the financial statements.
- Under ASC 740, the amount to be recorded is the largest amount of the benefit, as calculated on a cumulative probability basis, which is more likely than not to be realized on the ultimate settlement of the tax position.

Recognize the different components of a company's disclosure of its income tax accounts in the financial statements and footnotes, and comprehend how a company computes and discloses the components of its "effective tax rate." LO 6-5

- ASC 740 requires a company to disclose and separate its deferred tax liabilities and assets into a current amount and a noncurrent amount on its balance sheet.
- A company also is required to present the "significant" components of the income tax provision (expense or benefit) attributable to continuing operations.
- ASC 740 requires publicly traded companies to reconcile their reported income tax expense (benefit) from continuing operations with the *hypothetical* tax expense that would have resulted from applying the domestic federal statutory rate to pretax income from continuing operations. Alternatively, the company can compute an *effective tax rate* from its continuing operations and reconcile it with the domestic federal statutory rate (34 percent or 35 percent).
- A company computes its effective tax rate by dividing its income tax provision (benefit) from continuing operations by its pretax net income from continuing operations.
- Items that cause the effective tax rate to differ from the statutory tax rate include permanent differences, audit adjustments, state and local taxes, and international taxes.

KEY TERMS

book equivalent of taxable income (6-8)
cash tax rate (6-33)
current income tax expense or benefit (6-11)
current tax liability or asset (6-4)
deductible temporary difference (6-9)
deferred tax asset (6-2)
deferred tax liability (6-2)
effective tax rate (6-7)
enacted tax rate (6-12)
permanent differences (6-6)
structural tax rate (6-33)
tax accounting balance sheet (6-12)
tax carryforwards (6-4)
taxable temporary difference (6-9)
uncertain tax positions (6-11)
valuation allowance (6-18)

DISCUSSION QUESTIONS

LO 6-1 1. Identify some of the reasons why accounting for income taxes is complex.

LO 6-1 2. True or False: ASC 740 applies to all taxes paid by a corporation. Explain.

LO 6-1 3. True or False: ASC 740 is the sole source for the rules that apply to accounting for income taxes. Explain.

LO 6-1 4. How does the fact that most corporations file their financial statements several months before they file their income tax returns complicate the income tax provision process?

LO 6-1 5. What distinguishes an *income tax* from other taxes?

LO 6-1 6. Briefly describe the six-step process by which a company computes its income tax provision.

LO 6-2 7. What are the two components of a company's income tax provision? What does each component represent about a company's income tax provision?

LO 6-2 8. True or False: All differences between book and taxable income, both permanent and temporary, affect a company's effective tax rate. Explain.

LO 6-2 9. When does a temporary difference resulting from an expense (deduction) create a taxable temporary difference? A deductible temporary difference?

LO 6-2 10. When does a temporary difference resulting from income create a taxable temporary difference? A deductible temporary difference?

LO 6-2 11. Briefly describe what is meant by the *asset and liability* or *balance sheet* approach taken by ASC 740 with respect to computing a corporation's deferred tax provision.

LO 6-2 12. Why are cumulatively favorable temporary differences referred to as taxable temporary differences?

LO 6-2 13. Why are cumulatively unfavorable temporary differences referred to as deductible temporary differences?

LO 6-2 14. In addition to the current year tax return taxes payable or refundable, what other transactions can affect a company's current income tax provision?

LO 6-2 LO 6-4 15. What is an unrecognized tax benefit and how does it affect a company's current income tax expense?

LO 6-2 16. True or False: When Congress changes the corporate tax rates, only the current year book–tax temporary differences are measured using the new rates. Explain.

LO 6-2 17. True or False: All temporary differences have a financial accounting basis. Explain.

LO 6-3 18. What is the purpose behind a valuation allowance as it applies to deferred tax assets?

LO 6-3 19. What is the difference between *recognition* and *realization* as it applies to the recording of a deferred tax asset on a balance sheet?

LO 6-3 20. Briefly describe the four sources of taxable income a company evaluates in determining if a valuation allowance is necessary.

LO 6-3 21. Which of the four sources of taxable income are considered objective and which are considered subjective? Which of these sources generally receives the most weight in analyzing whether a valuation allowance is necessary?

LO 6-3 22. What are the elements that define a tax planning strategy as it applies to determining if a valuation allowance is necessary? Provide an example where a tax planning strategy may be necessary to avoid recording a valuation allowance.

LO 6-3 23. When does a company remove a valuation allowance from its balance sheet?

24. What is a company's *book equivalent of taxable income* and how does this computation enter into the income tax provision process? LO 6-3
25. What motivated the FASB to issue FIN 48? LO 6-4
26. Briefly describe the two-step process a company must undertake when it evaluates whether it can record the tax benefit from an uncertain tax position under ASC 740. LO 6-4
27. Distinguish between *recognition* and *measurement* as they relate to the computation of unrecognized tax benefits under ASC 740. LO 6-4
28. What is a *tax position* as it relates to the application of ASC 740 to uncertain tax positions? LO 6-4
29. True or False: A company determines its unrecognized tax benefits with respect to a transaction only at the time the transaction takes place; subsequent events are ignored. Explain. LO 6-4
30. True or False: ASC 740 requires that a company treat potential interest and penalties related to an unrecognized tax benefit as part of its income tax provision. Explain. LO 6-4
31. Where on the balance sheet does a company report its unrecognized tax benefits? LO 6-4
32. Why did many companies oppose FIN 48 when it was first proposed? LO 6-4
33. How does a company determine if a deferred tax asset or liability should be classified as current or noncurrent on its balance sheet? LO 6-5
34. Under what conditions can a company net its current deferred tax assets with its current deferred tax liabilities on the balance sheet? LO 6-5
35. True or False: A publicly traded company must disclose all of the components of its deferred tax assets and liabilities in a footnote to the financial statements. Explain. LO 6-5
36. What is a company's *hypothetical* income tax provision and what is its importance in a company's disclosure of its income tax provision in the tax footnote? LO 6-5
37. Briefly describe the difference between a company's effective tax rate, cash tax rate, and structural tax rate. LO 6-5

PROBLEMS

connect ACCOUNTING

All applicable problems are available with McGraw-Hill's *Connect*® *Accounting*.

38. Which of the following taxes is *not* accounted for under ASC 740? LO 6-1
    a) Income taxes paid to the U.S. government.
    b) Income taxes paid to the French government.
    c) Income taxes paid to the city of Detroit.
    d) Property taxes paid to the city of Detroit.
    e) All of the above taxes are accounted for under ASC 740.
39. Which of the following organizations can issue rules that govern accounting for income taxes? LO 6-1
    a) FASB.
    b) SEC.
    c) IRS.
    d) a and b above.
    e) All of the above organizations.

LO 6-1 research

40. Find the paragraph(s) in ASC 740 that deal with the following items (you can access ASC 740 on the FASB website, www.fasb.org, and then clicking on "Standards"). You will need a password from your instructor.
    a) The objectives and basic principles that underlie ASC 740.
    b) Examples of book–tax differences that create temporary differences.
    c) The definition of a *tax planning strategy.*
    d) Examples of positive evidence in the valuation allowance process.
    e) Rules relating to financial statement disclosure.

LO 6-2

41. Woodward Corporation reported pretax book income of $1,000,000. Included in the computation were favorable temporary differences of $200,000, unfavorable temporary differences of $50,000, and favorable permanent differences of $100,000. Assuming a tax rate of 34 percent, compute the company's current income tax expense or benefit.

LO 6-2

42. Cass Corporation reported pretax book income of $10,000,000. During the current year, the reserve for bad debts increased by $100,000. In addition, tax depreciation exceeded book depreciation by $200,000. Cass Corporation sold a fixed asset and reported book gain of $50,000 and tax gain of $75,000. Finally, the company received $250,000 of tax-exempt life insurance proceeds from the death of one of its officers. Assuming a tax rate of 34 percent, compute the company's current income tax expense or benefit.

LO 6-2

43. Grand Corporation reported pretax book income of $600,000. Tax depreciation exceeded book depreciation by $400,000. In addition, the company received $300,000 of tax-exempt municipal bond interest. The company's prior year tax return showed taxable income of $50,000. Assuming a tax rate of 34 percent, compute the company's current income tax expense or benefit.

LO 6-2

44. Chandler Corporation reported pretax book income of $2,000,000. Tax depreciation exceeded book depreciation by $500,000. During the year the company capitalized $250,000 into ending inventory under §263A. Capitalized inventory costs of $150,000 in beginning inventory were deducted as part of cost of goods sold on the tax return. Assuming a tax rate of 34 percent, compute the company's taxes payable or refundable.

LO 6-2

45. Davison Company determined that the book basis of its office building exceeded the tax basis by $800,000. This basis difference is properly characterized as:
    a) A permanent difference.
    b) A taxable temporary difference.
    c) A deductible temporary difference.
    d) A favorable book–tax difference.
    e) Both b and d above are correct.

LO 6-2

46. Abbot Company determined that the book basis of its allowance for bad debts is $100,000. There is no corresponding tax basis in this account. The basis difference is properly characterized as:
    a) A permanent difference.
    b) A taxable temporary difference.
    c) A deductible temporary difference.
    d) A favorable book–tax difference.
    e) Both b and d above are correct.

LO 6-2

47. Which of the following items is *not* a temporary book–tax basis difference?
    a) Warranty reserve accruals.
    b) Accelerated depreciation.

c) Capitalized inventory costs under §263A.
d) Nondeductible stock option compensation from exercising an ISO.
e) All of the above are temporary differences.

48. Which of the following book–tax differences does *not* create a favorable temporary book–tax basis difference? LO 6-2
   a) Tax depreciation for the period exceeds book depreciation.
   b) Bad debts charged off in the current period exceed the bad debts accrued in the current period.
   c) Inventory costs capitalized under §263A deducted as part of current year tax cost of goods sold are less than the inventory costs capitalized in ending inventory.
   d) Vacation pay accrued for tax purposes in a prior period is deducted in the current period.
   e) All of the above create a favorable temporary book–tax difference.

49. Lodge Inc. reported pretax book income of $5,000,000. During the year, the company increased its reserve for warranties by $200,000. The company deducted $50,000 on its tax return related to warranty payments made during the year. What is the impact on taxable income compared to pretax book income of the book–tax difference that results from these two events? LO 6-2
   a) Favorable (decreases taxable income).
   b) Unfavorable (increases taxable income).
   c) Neutral (no impact on taxable income).

50. Which of the following book–tax basis differences results in a deductible temporary difference? LO 6-2
   a) Book basis of a fixed asset exceeds its tax basis.
   b) Book basis of a pension-related liability exceeds its tax basis.
   c) Prepayment of income included on the tax return but not on the income statement (the transaction is recorded as a liability on the balance sheet).
   d) All of the above result in a deductible temporary difference.
   e) Both (b) and (c) result in a deductible temporary difference.

51. Shaw Corporation reported pretax book income of $1,000,000. Included in the computation were favorable temporary differences of $200,000, unfavorable temporary differences of $50,000, and favorable permanent differences of $100,000. Assuming a tax rate of 34 percent, compute the company's deferred income tax expense or benefit. LO 6-2

52. Shaw Inc. reported pretax book income of $10,000,000. During the current year, the reserve for bad debts increased by $100,000. In addition, tax depreciation exceeded book depreciation by $200,000. Shaw Inc. sold a fixed asset and reported book gain of $50,000 and tax gain of $75,000. Finally, the company received $250,000 of tax-exempt life insurance proceeds from the death of one of its officers. Assuming a tax rate of 34 percent, compute the company's deferred income tax expense or benefit. LO 6-2

53. Harrison Corporation reported pretax book income of $600,000. Tax depreciation exceeded book depreciation by $400,000. In addition, the company received $300,000 of tax-exempt municipal bond interest. The company's prior year tax return showed taxable income of $50,000. Assuming a tax rate of 34 percent, compute the company's deferred income tax expense or benefit. LO 6-2

LO 6-2

54. Identify the following items as creating a temporary book–tax difference, permanent book–tax difference, or no book–tax difference.

Item	Temporary Difference	Permanent Difference	No Difference
Reserve for warranties			
Accrued pension liability			
Goodwill not amortized for tax purposes but subject to impairment under ASC 350			
Meal and entertainment expenses			
Life insurance proceeds			
Net capital loss carryover			
Nondeductible fines and penalties			
Accrued vacation pay liability paid within the first two and one-half months of the next tax year			

LO 6-2

55. Which of the following items is *not* a permanent book–tax difference?
   a) Tax-exempt interest income.
   b) Tax-exempt insurance proceeds.
   c) Domestic production activities deduction.
   d) Nondeductible meals and entertainment expense.
   e) First-year expensing under §179.

LO 6-2

56. Ann Corporation reported pretax book income of $1,000,000. Included in the computation were favorable temporary differences of $200,000, unfavorable temporary differences of $50,000, and favorable permanent differences of $100,000. Compute the company's book equivalent of taxable income. Use this number to compute the company's total income tax provision or benefit, assuming a tax rate of 34 percent.

LO 6-2

57. Burcham Corporation reported pretax book income of $600,000. Tax depreciation exceeded book depreciation by $400,000. In addition, the company received $300,000 of tax-exempt municipal bond interest. The company's prior year tax return showed taxable income of $50,000. Compute the company's book equivalent of taxable income. Use this number to compute the company's total income tax provision or benefit, assuming a tax rate of 34 percent.

LO 6-3

58. Adams Corporation has total deferred tax assets of $3,000,000 at year-end. Management is assessing whether a valuation allowance must be recorded against some or all of the deferred tax assets. What level of assurance must management have, based on the weight of available evidence, that some or all of the deferred tax assets will not be realized before a valuation allowance is required?
   a) Probable.
   b) More likely than not.
   c) Realistic possibility.
   d) Reasonable.
   e) More than remote.

LO 6-3

59. Which of the following evidence would *not* be considered positive in determining whether Adams Corporation needs to record a valuation allowance for some or all of its deferred tax assets?
   a) The company forecasts future taxable income because of its backlog of orders.
   b) The company has unfavorable temporary differences that will create future taxable income when they reverse.

c) The company has tax planning strategies that it can implement to create future taxable income.
d) The company has cumulative net income over the current and prior two years.
e) The company had a net operating loss carryover expire in the current year.

60. As of the beginning of the year, Gratiot Company recorded a valuation allowance of $200,000 against its deferred tax assets of $1,000,000. The valuation allowance relates to a net operating loss carryover from the prior year. During the year, management concludes that the valuation allowance is no longer necessary because it forecasts sufficient taxable income to absorb the NOL carryover. What is the impact of management's reversal of the valuation allowance on the company's effective tax rate? LO 6-3
a) Increases the effective tax rate
b) Decreases the effective tax rate
c) No impact on the effective tax rate

61. Which of the following evidence would be considered negative in determining whether Gratiot Corporation needs to record a valuation allowance for some or all of its deferred tax assets? LO 6-3
a) The company forecasts future taxable income because of its backlog of orders.
b) The company has a cumulative net loss over the current and prior two years.
c) The company has unfavorable temporary differences that will create future taxable income when they reverse.
d) The company had a net operating loss carryover expire in the current year.
e) Both (b) and (d) constitute negative evidence in assessing the need for a valuation allowance.

62. Saginaw Inc. completed its first year of operations with a pretax loss of $500,000. The tax return showed a net operating loss of $600,000, which the company will carry forward. The $100,000 book–tax difference results from excess tax depreciation over book depreciation. Management has determined that they should record a valuation allowance equal to the net deferred tax asset. Assuming the current tax expense is zero, prepare the journal entries to record the deferred tax provision and the valuation allowance. LO 6-3

63. Access Ford Motor Company's Annual Report for 2011 from the company's website (www.ford.com). What amount of valuation allowance against its deferred tax assets did the company release in 2011? What reasons did management give for releasing the valuation allowance? (*Hint:* Read management's discussion and analysis section and the income taxes footnote.) What impact, if any, did release of the valuation allowance have on the company's effective tax rate for 2011? Why did the valuation allowance release affect (or not affect) the company's ETR? LO 6-3 research

64. Montcalm Corporation has total deferred tax assets of $3,000,000 at year-end. Of that amount, $1,000,000 results from the current expensing of an expenditure that the IRS might assert must be capitalized on audit. Management is trying to determine if it should not recognize the deferred tax asset related to this item under ASC 740. What confidence level must management have that the item will be sustained on audit before it can recognize any portion of the deferred tax asset under ASC 740? LO 6-4
a) Probable.
b) More likely than not.
c) Realistic possibility.
d) Reasonable.
e) More than remote.

LO 6-4 65. Which of the following statements about uncertain tax positions (UTP) is correct?

a) UTP applies only to tax positions accounted for under ASC 740 taken on a filed tax return.
b) UTP applies to all tax positions accounted for under ASC 740, regardless of whether the item is taken on a filed tax return.
c) UTP deals with both the recognition and realization of deferred tax assets.
d) If a tax position meets the more-likely-than-not standard, the entire amount of the deferred tax asset or current tax benefit related to the tax position can be recognized under ASC 740.
e) Statements (b), (c), and (d) are correct.

LO 6-4 66. Cadillac Square Corporation determined that $1,000,000 of its domestic production activities deduction on its current year tax return was uncertain, but that it was more likely than not to be sustained on audit. Management made the following assessment of the company's potential tax benefit from the deduction and its probability of occurring.

Potential Estimated Benefit (000s)	Individual Probability of Occurring	Cumulative Probability of Occurring
$340,000	40%	40%
272,000	25	65
170,000	20	85
0	15	100

What amount of the tax benefit related to the uncertain tax position from the domestic production activities deduction can Cadillac Square Corporation recognize in calculating its income tax provision in the current year?

LO 6-4 67. How would your answer to Problem 66 change if management determined that there was only a 50/50 chance any portion of the $1,000,000 DPAD would be sustained on audit?

LO 6-4 68. As part of its UTP assessment, Penobscot Company records interest and penalties related to its unrecognized tax benefit of $500,000. Which of the following statements about recording this amount is most correct?

a) Penobscot must include the amount in its income tax provision.
b) Penobscot must record the amount separate from its income tax provision.
c) Penobscot can elect to allocate a portion of the amount to both its income tax provision and its general and administrative expenses provided the company discloses which option it chose.
d) Penobscot can elect to record the entire amount as part of its income tax provision or separate from its income tax provision, provided the company discloses which option it chose.
e) Statements (c) and (d) above are both correct.

LO 6-5 research 69. What was IBM's accounting effective tax rate for 2013? What items caused the company's accounting effective tax rate to differ from the "hypothetical" tax rate of 35 percent? What was the company's cash effective tax rate for 2013? What factors cause a company's cash tax rate to differ from its accounting effective tax rate? You can access IBM's annual report for 2013 at www.ibm.com.

LO 6-5 70. Beacon Corporation recorded the following deferred tax assets and liabilities:

Current deferred tax assets	$ 650,000
Current deferred tax liabilities	(400,000)
Noncurrent deferred tax assets	1,000,000
Noncurrent deferred tax liabilities	(2,500,000)
Net deferred tax liabilities	$(1,250,000)

All of the deferred tax accounts relate to temporary differences that arose as a result of the company's U.S. operations. Which of the following statements describes how Beacon should disclose these accounts on its balance sheet?

a) Beacon reports a net deferred tax liability of $1,250,000 on its balance sheet.
b) Beacon nets the deferred tax assets and the deferred tax liabilities and reports a net deferred tax asset of $1,650,000 and a net deferred tax liability of $2,900,000 on its balance sheet.
c) Beacon can elect to net the current deferred tax accounts and the noncurrent tax accounts and report a net current deferred tax asset of $250,000 and a net deferred tax liability of $1,500,000 on its balance sheet.
d) Beacon is required to net the current deferred tax accounts and the noncurrent tax accounts and report a net current deferred tax asset of $250,000 and a net deferred tax liability of $1,500,000 on its balance sheet.

71. ASC 740 requires a company to disclose those components of its deferred tax assets and liabilities that are considered LO 6-5
a) Relevant.
b) Significant.
c) Important.
d) Major.

72. Which of the following temporary differences creates a current deferred tax asset? LO 6-5
a) Allowance for bad debts.
b) Goodwill amortization.
c) Accumulated depreciation.
d) Inventory capitalization under §263A.
e) Both (a) and (d) above create a current deferred tax asset.

73. Which formula represents the calculation of a company's effective tax rate? LO 6-5
a) Income taxes paid/Taxable income.
b) Income taxes paid/Pretax income from continuing operations.
c) Income tax provision/Taxable income.
d) Income tax provision/Pretax income from continuing operations.

74. Which of the following items is *not* a reconciling item in the income tax footnote? LO 6-5
a) State income taxes.
b) Foreign income taxes.
c) Accrued pension liabilities.
d) Dividends received deduction.
e) Tax-exempt municipal bond interest.

75. Randolph Company reported pretax net income from continuing operations of $800,000 and taxable income of $500,000. The book–tax difference of $300,000 was due to a $200,000 favorable temporary difference relating to depreciation, an unfavorable temporary difference of $80,000 due to an increase in the reserve for bad debts, and a $180,000 favorable permanent difference from the receipt of life insurance proceeds. Randolph Company's applicable tax rate is 34 percent. LO 6-5
a) Compute Randolph Company's current income tax expense.
b) Compute Randolph Company's deferred income tax expense or benefit.

c) Compute Randolph Company's effective tax rate.
d) Provide a reconciliation of Randolph Company's effective tax rate with its hypothetical tax rate of 34 percent.

LO 6-5

76. Which of the following pronouncements should a company consult in computing its quarterly income tax provision?
a) ASC 740.
b) ASC 230.
c) ASC 718.
d) ASC 810.
e) SarbOX 404.

COMPREHENSIVE PROBLEMS

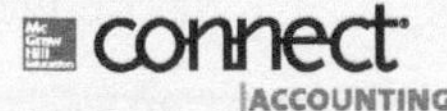

All applicable problems are available with McGraw-Hill's *Connect® Accounting.*

77. You have been assigned to compute the income tax provision for Motown Memories Inc. (MM) as of December 31, 2015. The company's federal income tax rate is 34 percent. The company's income statement for 2015 is provided below:

Motown Memories Inc. Statement of Operations at December 31, 2015	
Net sales	$50,000,000
Cost of sales	28,000,000
Gross profit	$22,000,000
Compensation	$ 2,000,000
Selling expenses	1,500,000
Depreciation and amortization	4,000,000
Other expenses	500,000
Total operating expenses	$ 8,000,000
Income from operations	$14,000,000
Interest and other income	1,000,000
Income before income taxes	$15,000,000

You identified the following permanent differences:

Interest income from municipal bonds:	$ 50,000
Nondeductible meals and entertainment expenses:	$ 20,000
Domestic production activities deduction:	$250,000
Nondeductible fines:	$ 5,000

MM prepared the following schedule of temporary differences from the beginning of the year to the end of the year:

Motown Memories Inc. Temporary Difference Scheduling Template					
Taxable Temporary Differences	**BOY Cumulative T/D**	**Beginning Deferred Taxes (@ 34%)**	**Current Year Change**	**EOY Cumulative T/D**	**Ending Deferred Taxes (@ 34%)**
Noncurrent					
Accumulated depreciation	(8,000,000)	(2,720,000)	(1,000,000)	(9,000,000)	**(3,060,000)**

Deductible Temporary Differences	BOY Cumulative T/D	Beginning Deferred Taxes (@ 34%)	Current Year Change	EOY Cumulative T/D	Ending Deferred Taxes (@ 34%)
Current					
Allowance for bad debts	200,000	68,000	50,000	250,000	85,000
Reserve for warranties	100,000	34,000	20,000	120,000	40,800
Inventory §263A adjustment	240,000	81,600	60,000	300,000	102,000
Total current	**540,000**	**183,600**	**130,000**	**670,000**	**227,800**
Noncurrent					
Deferred compensation	50,000	17,000	10,000	60,000	20,400
Accrued pension liabilities	3,000,000	1,020,000	250,000	3,250,000	1,105,000
Total noncurrent	**3,050,000**	**1,037,000**	**260,000**	**3,310,000**	**1,125,400**
Total	**3,590,000**	**1,220,600**	**390,000**	**3,980,000**	**1,353,200**

Required:

a) Compute MM's current income tax expense or benefit for 2015.
b) Compute MM's deferred income tax expense or benefit for 2015.
c) Prepare a reconciliation of MM's total income tax provision with its hypothetical income tax expense in both dollars and rates.

78. You have been assigned to compute the income tax provision for Tulip City Flowers Inc. (TCF) as of December 31, 2015. The company's federal income tax rate is 34 percent. The company's income statement for 2015 is provided below:

Tulip City Flowers Inc. Statement of Operations at December 31, 2015	
Net sales	$20,000,000
Cost of sales	12,000,000
Gross profit	$ 8,000,000
Compensation	$ 500,000
Selling expenses	750,000
Depreciation and amortization	1,250,000
Other expenses	1,000,000
Total operating expenses	$ 3,500,000
Income from operations	$ 4,500,000
Interest and other income	25,000
Income before income taxes	$ 4,525,000

You identified the following permanent differences:

Interest income from municipal bonds	$10,000
Nondeductible stock compensation	5,000
Domestic production activities deduction	8,000
Nondeductible fines	1,000

TCF prepared the following schedule of temporary differences from the beginning of the year to the end of the year:

Tulip City Flowers Inc.
Temporary Difference Scheduling Template

Taxable Temporary Differences	BOY Cumulative T/D	Beginning Deferred Taxes (@ 34%)	Current Year Change	EOY Cumulative T/D	Ending Deferred Taxes (@ 34%)
Noncurrent					
Accumulated depreciation	(5,000,000)	(1,700,000)	(500,000)	(5,500,000)	(1,870,000)

Deductible Temporary Differences	BOY Cumulative T/D	Beginning Deferred Taxes (@ 34%)	Current Year Change	EOY Cumulative T/D	Ending Deferred Taxes (@ 34%)
Current					
Allowance for bad debts	100,000	34,000	10,000	110,000	37,400
Prepaid income	0	0	20,000	20,000	6,800
Total current	**100,000**	**34,000**	**30,000**	**130,000**	**44,200**
Noncurrent					
Deferred compensation	50,000	17,000	10,000	60,000	20,400
Accrued pension liabilities	500,000	170,000	100,000	600,000	204,000
Total noncurrent	**550,000**	**187,000**	**110,000**	**660,000**	**224,400**
Total	**650,000**	**221,000**	**140,000**	**790,000**	**268,600**

Required:

a) Compute TCF's current income tax expense or benefit for 2015.
b) Compute TCF's deferred income tax expense or benefit for 2015.
c) Prepare a reconciliation of TCF's total income tax provision with its hypothetical income tax expense in both dollars and rates.
d) Assume TCF's tax rate increased to 35 percent in 2015. Recompute TCF's deferred income tax expense or benefit for 2015 using the following template:

Tulip City Flowers Inc.
Temporary Difference Scheduling Template

Taxable Temporary Differences	BOY Cumulative T/D	Beginning Deferred Taxes (@ 34%)	Current Year Change	EOY Cumulative T/D	Ending Deferred Taxes (@ 35%)
Noncurrent					
Accumulated depreciation	(5,000,000)	(1,700,000)	(500,000)	(5,500,000)	

Deductible Temporary Differences	BOY Cumulative T/D	Beginning Deferred Taxes (@ 34%)	Current Year Change	EOY Cumulative T/D	Ending Deferred Taxes (@ 35%)
Current					
Allowance for bad debts	100,000	34,000	10,000	110,000	
Prepaid income	0	0	20,000	20,000	
Total current	**100,000**	**34,000**	**30,000**	**130,000**	
Noncurrent					
Deferred compensation	50,000	17,000	10,000	60,000	
Accrued pension liabilities	500,000	170,000	100,000	600,000	
Total noncurrent	**550,000**	**187,000**	**110,000**	**660,000**	
Total	**650,000**	**221,000**	**140,000**	**790,000**	

79. Access the 2013 Annual Report for Google and answer the following questions. You can access the annual report at www.google.com.

Required:

a) Using information from the company's income statement and income taxes footnote, what was the company's effective tax rate for 2013? Show how the rate is calculated.
b) Using information from the statement of cash flows, calculate the company's cash tax rate.
c) What does the company's income taxes note tell you about where the company earns its international income? Why does earning income in these countries cause the effective tax rate to decrease?
d) What item creates the company's largest deferred tax asset? Explain why this item creates a deductible temporary difference.
e) What item creates the company's largest deferred tax liability? Explain why this item creates a taxable temporary difference.
f) How does the company classify its income taxes payable related to its unrecognized tax benefits on the balance sheet?
g) How does the company treat interest and penalties related to its unrecognized tax benefits?

80. Spartan Builders Corporation is a builder of high-end housing with locations in major metropolitan areas throughout the Midwest. At June 30, 2015, the company has deferred tax assets totaling $10 million and deferred tax liabilities of $5 million, all of which relate to U.S. temporary differences. Reversing taxable temporary differences and taxable income in the carryback period can be used to support approximately $2 million of the $10 million gross deferred tax asset. The remaining $8 million of gross deferred tax assets will have to come from future taxable income.

The company has historically been profitable. However, significant losses were incurred in fiscal years 2013 and 2014. These two years reflect a cumulative loss of 10 million, with losses of $3 million expected in 2015. $7 million of the losses was due to a write-down of inventory. Beginning in fiscal 2016, management decided to get out of the metropolitan Chicago market, which had become oversaturated with new houses.

Evaluate the company's need to record a valuation allowance for the $10 million of gross deferred tax assets. What positive and negative evidence would you weigh?

chapter

7 Corporate Taxation: Nonliquidating Distributions

Learning Objectives

Upon completing this chapter, you should be able to:

- LO 7-1 Explain the framework that applies to the taxation of property distributions from a corporation to a shareholder.
- LO 7-2 Compute a corporation's earnings and profits and a shareholder's dividend income.
- LO 7-3 Identify when a corporation may be deemed to have paid a "constructive dividend" to a shareholder.
- LO 7-4 Explain the taxation of stock dividends.
- LO 7-5 Comprehend the tax consequences of stock redemptions.
- LO 7-6 Describe the tax consequences of a partial liquidation to the corporation and its shareholders.

© Jupiterimages Corporation

Storyline Summary

Taxpayer:	Jim Wheeler
Location:	East Lansing, Michigan
Employment status:	Co-owner of Spartan Cycle and Repair (75 percent)
Filing status:	Married filing jointly
Dependents:	One child
Marginal tax rate:	30 percent
Taxpayer:	Ginny Gears
Location:	East Lansing, Michigan
Employment status:	Co-owner of Spartan Cycles and Repair (25 percent)
Filing status:	Unmarried
Marginal tax rate:	25 percent

Jim Wheeler and Ginny Gears are old friends who met at the Mid-Michigan Cycling Club. They often discussed their shared dream of owning and operating a high-end bicycle shop in East Lansing, Michigan. Many of their friends in the club often remarked how difficult it was to get parts and have their bicycles repaired locally. Jim found himself repairing his friends' bicycles using the knowledge he gained while working at a bicycle shop during his undergraduate days at the University of Colorado. Ginny majored in marketing at Michigan State University (MSU) and was eager to put her marketing and management skills to work in her own business.

A few years ago, Jim and Ginny fulfilled their dream by launching Spartan Cycles and Repair (SCR). Their business had humble beginnings, as most start-up companies do. They raised the $50,000 capital they needed to purchase inventory and the necessary repair tools by borrowing from Jim's father, Walt. They also leased a vacant building on Grand River Avenue. On the advice of their accountant and lawyer, Jim and Ginny organized their company as a C corporation, with Jim owning 75 percent of the corporation's stock and Ginny owning the remaining 25 percent. Jim's responsibilities include doing the bicycle repairs and deciding which bicycle brands to carry, while Ginny is responsible for managing and marketing the business. Jim works approximately 10 hours per week at the store, and he currently receives a modest salary of $15,000 per year. Ginny works half-time at the store and currently receives a salary of $25,000 per year.

Since the company's inception, Jim and Ginny used most of the company's profits to pay back the loan to Jim's father and expand the store's inventory and marketing activities. By the end of this year, SCR had become very successful, as evidenced by the significant amount of cash ($300,000) in the company's bank accounts. Jim and Ginny made many sacrifices, both financially and socially, to make the business successful. Over a café latte at the local gourmet coffee shop, Jim and Ginny decided it was time to think about distributing some of the company's profits to reward their hard work. Jim admitted he had his eye on a dark green BMW 528i Sedan, which retailed for approximately $48,000, fully loaded. Ginny was a bit more restrained, hoping she could put a down payment on a condominium in the newly developed Evergreen Commons being constructed near their store. She estimated she would need approximately $16,000 for the down payment.

Jim and Ginny considered several options for distributing cash from SCR. One alternative was to increase their salaries. Another option was to pay a year-end bonus, while a third alternative was for SCR to pay a $64,000 dividend at year-end ($48,000 to Jim and $16,000 to Ginny). They decided to call their tax accountant, Louis Tully, to ask for his recommendation.

to be continued . . .

At some point during the life of a company, especially in the case of a closely held business, the shareholders will likely want to distribute some of the company's accumulated profits. If the business is operated as a C corporation, the company can distribute its *after-tax* profits to its shareholders in the form of a **dividend, stock redemption,** or, in rare cases, a **partial liquidation.** Alternatively, if a shareholder also serves in some other capacity in the business (e.g., as an employee, creditor, or lessor), the company may be able to distribute its *before-tax* profits to this person in the form of compensation (salary or bonus), interest, or rent.

This chapter addresses the tax consequences to the corporation and its shareholders when making distributions to its shareholders in these various ways. Because Jim and Ginny have chosen to operate through a C corporation, they must confront the potential double taxation if the company's earnings are distributed as a dividend. If Jim and Ginny elected to operate their business through an S corporation or partnership, the entity-level taxation of the company's earnings would be eliminated. The tax consequences of these two flow-through entity choices are discussed in more detail in subsequent chapters.

LO 7-1 TAXATION OF PROPERTY DISTRIBUTIONS

The characterization of a distribution from a corporation to a shareholder has important tax consequences to both the shareholders and the corporation. If the tax law characterizes the distribution as a dividend, the corporation may not deduct the amount paid in computing its taxable income. In addition, the shareholder must include the gross amount of the dividend received in gross income. The nondeductibility of the distribution by the corporation, coupled with the taxation of the distribution to the shareholder, creates *double taxation* of the corporation's income, first at the corporate level and then at the shareholder level. The double taxation of distributed corporate income has been a fundamental principle of the U.S. income tax since 1913.

Historically, tax planning focused on eliminating or mitigating the second level of taxation on C corporation earnings.[1] For example, if the distribution can instead be characterized as salary, bonus, interest, or rent, the corporation can deduct the amount paid in computing its taxable income. However, the Internal Revenue Service (IRS) can assert that the distribution is a **constructive dividend.** In such a case, the corporation cannot deduct the amount recharacterized as a dividend.

DETERMINING THE DIVIDEND AMOUNT FROM EARNINGS AND PROFITS

LO 7-2

Overview

When a corporation distributes property to shareholders *in their capacity as shareholders,* the shareholders will characterize the distribution either as dividend income or a return of capital. They include the portion characterized as dividend income in their gross income. In contrast, a return of capital is not considered income, but rather a reduction in the shareholder's tax basis in the stock. If the return of capital exceeds the tax basis of the stock, then the excess distribution (above basis) is taxed as a capital gain from the sale of the shares.[2]

Corporate distributions of "property" usually take the form of cash, but distributions can also consist of other tangible or intangible property. Special rules apply when a corporation distributes its own stock **(stock dividends)** to its shareholders.[3]

Dividends Defined

A dividend is any distribution of property made by a corporation to its shareholders out of its earnings and profits (E&P) account. Congress intended earnings and profits to be a measure of the corporation's *economic earnings* available for distribution to its shareholders. Hence, earnings and profits is similar in concept to financial accounting retained earnings, but the computation of E&P can be very different.

Corporations keep two separate E&P accounts: one for the current year **(current earnings and profits)** and one for undistributed earnings and profits accumulated in all prior years **(accumulated earnings and profits).** Distributions are designated as dividends in the following order:

1. Distributions are dividends up to the balance of current E&P.
2. Distributions in excess of current E&P are dividends up to the balance in accumulated E&P.

Current E&P not distributed to shareholders is added to accumulated E&P at the beginning of the next taxable year. Distributions reduce E&P but cannot produce (or extend) a deficit (negative balance) in E&P. That is, dividend treatment requires positive E&P, but E&P can have a deficit balance if losses exceed income. In other words, a corporation cannot distribute E&P if there is a deficit in E&P, and only losses can create a deficit in E&P. A corporation that makes a distribution in excess of its total E&P (i.e., a return of capital) must report the distribution on Form 5452 and include a calculation of its E&P balance to support the tax treatment.

[1]Taxable corporations are referred to as *C corporations* because Subchapter C (§§ 301–385) describes the tax consequences of distributions between a corporation and its shareholders.

[2]§301(c).

[3]§317.

Example 7-1

Jim owns 75 percent of the SCR stock, while Ginny owns the remaining 25 percent. Jim has a tax basis in his Spartan Cycles and Repair (SCR) stock of $24,000. Ginny's tax basis in her SCR stock is $10,000.

What if: Assume SCR has current earnings and profits (CE&P) of $30,000, and no accumulated earnings and profits. At year-end, SCR makes a $64,000 distribution, a $48,000 distribution to Jim and a $16,000 distribution to Ginny.

What is the tax treatment of the distribution to Jim and Ginny?

Answer: Only $30,000 of the $64,000 distribution is treated as a dividend. The distribution in excess of E&P is treated as a return of capital.

Jim treats the $48,000 distribution for tax purposes as follows:

- $22,500 is treated as a dividend (to the extent of his 75 percent share of current E&P).
- $24,000 is a nontaxable reduction in his stock tax basis (return of capital).
- $1,500 is treated as gain from the deemed sale of his stock (capital gain).

Note that a distribution cannot reduce a shareholder's stock basis below zero.

Ginny treats the $16,000 distribution for tax purposes as follows:

- $7,500 is treated as a dividend (to the extent of her 25 percent share of current E&P).
- $8,500 is a nontaxable reduction in her stock tax basis (return of capital).

What is Jim and Ginny's tax basis in their SCR stock after the distribution?

Answer: Jim has a zero basis in his SCR stock, while Ginny has a remaining tax basis of $1,500 ($10,000 − $8,500) in her SCR stock.

Computing Earnings and Profits

Earnings and profits has been part of the tax laws since 1916, but Congress has never provided a precise definition of this term. Hence, the calculation of E&P is somewhat counterintuitive. For example, E&P includes both taxable and nontaxable income indicating that Congress intended E&P to represent a corporation's economic income. As a result, shareholders may be taxed on distributions of income not subject to tax at the corporate level.

A corporation begins the computation of current E&P with taxable income or loss. It then makes adjustments required by the IRC or the accompanying regulations and IRS rulings. These adjustments fall into four broad categories:

1. Certain nontaxable income is included in E&P.
2. Certain deductions do not reduce E&P.
3. Certain nondeductible expenses reduce E&P.
4. The timing of certain items of income and deduction is modified for E&P calculations because separate accounting methods are required for E&P purposes.[4]

Nontaxable Income Included in E&P Tax exempt income has economic value when distributed to shareholders and, thus, increases E&P. Common examples of tax-exempt income included in E&P are tax-exempt municipal interest and tax-exempt life insurance proceeds. Other types of exempt income, such as gifts, bequests, and contributions to capital, are not included in E&P.

Example 7-2

SCR reported current earnings and profits of $100,000 related to taxable income. The company also earned $5,000 of tax-exempt interest from its investment in City of East Lansing municipal bonds. If SCR distributes all of its current year E&P to Jim and Ginny, what amount will they report as dividend income in the current year?

[4]§312 and the related regulations describe these adjustments.

Answer: $105,000. SCR must include the $5,000 of tax-exempt interest in the computation of current E&P. The portion of the E&P that represents the tax-exempt interest will be treated as a taxable dividend even though Jim and Ginny would not have included the interest in gross income had they earned it directly.

What if: Assume Jim and Ginny operated SCR as a partnership. How would that have changed your answer to the previous example?

Answer: Jim and Ginny would have reported their share of the tax-exempt interest on their individual tax returns as being tax-exempt and would not have been taxed on the amount.

Deductible Expenses That Do Not Reduce E&P Deductions that require no cash outlay by the corporation or are carryovers from another tax year do not represent current economic outflows and cannot be used to reduce E&P. Examples include the dividends received deduction, the domestic production activities deduction, net capital loss carryovers from a different tax year, net operating loss carryovers from a different tax year, and charitable contribution carryovers from a prior tax year. Note, however, that the deduction allowed for employee exercises of nonqualified stock options reduces E&P even though no cash flow is required.

Nondeductible Expenses That Reduce E&P A corporation reduces its current E&P for certain items that are not deductible in computing its taxable income but require a cash outflow. Examples of such expenses include:

- Federal income taxes (regular or alternative minimum tax) paid or accrued (depending on the corporation's method of accounting).
- Expenses incurred in earning tax-exempt income (such income is included in E&P).
- Current year charitable contributions in excess of 10 percent of taxable income (there is no 10 percent limitation for E&P purposes).
- Premiums on life insurance contracts in excess of the increase in the policy's cash surrender value.
- Current year net capital loss (there is no limit on capital losses).
- Meals and entertainment expenses disallowed (generally 50 percent of the total).
- Nondeductible lobbying expenses and political contributions.
- Penalties and fines.

Timing Items Requiring Separate Accounting Methods for E&P Purposes A corporation must generally use the same accounting method for computing E&P and taxable income. For example, a gain or loss deferred for tax purposes under the like-kind exchange rules or the involuntary conversion rules is also deferred for E&P purposes. A corporation using the accrual method for regular income tax purposes generally must use the accrual method for E&P purposes. However, some types of income deferred from inclusion in the computation of current year taxable income must be included in the computation of current E&P in the year in which the transaction occurs. For example, if a corporation uses the installment sales method for tax purposes, the deferred gain from current year sales must be included in current E&P.

In addition, certain expenses currently deducted in the computation of taxable income are deferred in computing E&P.[5] Organizational expenditures, which can

[5]§312(n). Section 312(n) was added in 1984 to "ensure that a corporation's earnings and profits more closely conform to its economic income."

be deducted currently or amortized for income tax purposes, must be capitalized for E&P purposes. Depreciation must be computed using the prescribed E&P method. For property acquired after 1986, the alternative depreciation system must be used. This system requires that assets be depreciated using a straight-line method over the asset's *"mid-point class life"* (40 years in the case of realty).[6] Amounts expensed under §179 (first year expensing) must be amortized over five years for E&P purposes.

The IRC does not impose a statute of limitations on the computation of earnings and profits. Hence, for many corporations (public and private), the initial computation of E&P only comes after years of operations and often requires significant resources because the annual adjustments to taxable income were not well documented. Exhibit 7-1 provides a summary of common adjustments made to compute current E&P.

EXHIBIT 7-1 Template for Computing Current Earnings and Profits

Taxable Income (Net Operating Loss)

Add: **Exclusions from Taxable Income**
- Tax-exempt bond interest.
- Life insurance proceeds.
- Federal tax refunds (if a cash-basis taxpayer).

Add: **Deductions Allowed for Tax Purposes but Not for E&P**
- Dividends received deduction.
- NOL deduction carrybacks and carryforwards.
- Net capital loss carrybacks and carryforwards.
- Contribution carryforwards.
- Domestic production activities deduction.

Add: **Income Deferred for Tax Purposes but Not for E&P**
- Deferred gain on installment sales.
- Deferred gain on completed contract method of accounting.
- Increase in cash surrender value of corporate-owned life insurance policies.

Add: **Deductions Deferred for E&P Purposes**
- Regular tax depreciation in excess of E&P depreciation.
- Percentage depletion in excess of cost depletion.
- Capitalized construction period interest, taxes, and carrying charges.
- Amortized intangible costs of oil and gas wells over 60 months.
- Amortized mineral exploration and development costs over 120 months.
- Capitalized circulation expenditures and organizational expenditures.
- Capitalized first-year expensing and amortize over five years.
- Increases in the LIFO recapture amount (FIFO over LIFO ending inventory).

Less: **Deductions Allowed for E&P Purposes but Not for Tax**
- Federal income taxes paid or accrued.
- Expenses of earning tax-exempt income.
- Current year charitable contributions in excess of the 10 percent limitation.
- Nondeductible premiums on life insurance policies.
- Current year net capital loss.
- E&P depreciation in excess of regular tax depreciation.
- Penalties and fines.
- Decreases in the LIFO recapture amount (LIFO over FIFO ending inventory).
- Disallowed entertainment expenses.
- Disallowed lobbying expenses, dues, and political contributions.

Equals: **Current Earnings and Profits**

[6]§168(g)(2).

Example 7-3

This year, SCR reported taxable income of $500,000 and paid federal income tax of $170,000. SCR reported the following items of income and expense:

- $50,000 of depreciation.
- $7,000 dividends received deduction.
- $10,000 net operating loss from the prior year.
- $5,000 of tax-exempt interest.
- $6,000 of nondeductible meals and entertainment expense.
- $4,000 net capital loss from the current year.

For E&P purposes, depreciation computed under the alternative depreciation method is $30,000.

What is SCR's current E&P?

Answer: $362,000, computed as follows:

Taxable income	$500,000
Add:	
Tax-exempt interest	5,000
Dividends received deduction	7,000
NOL carryover	10,000
Excess of regular tax deprecation over E&P depreciation	20,000
Subtract:	
Federal income taxes	(170,000)
Nondeductible meals and entertainment	(6,000)
Net capital loss for the current year	(4,000)
Current E&P	$362,000

What if: Assume SCR also reported a tax-deferred gain of $100,000 as the result of a §1031 exchange and deferred $75,000 of gain from an installment sale during the year. What is SCR's current E&P under these circumstances?

Answer: Current E&P would equal $437,000 ($362,000 + $75,000). Deferred gains from §1031 (like-kind) exchanges are not included in the computation of current E&P, but all gain from current year installment sales is included in current E&P. In future years, SCR would back out any deferred gain recognized in taxable income from the installment sale in its computation of current E&P.

What if: Assume SCR did not report any gains and instead reported a $400,000 loss from a sale of property. What is SCR's current E&P under these circumstances?

Answer: Current E&P would be a deficit balance of $38,000 ($362,000 − $400,000). The balance of E&P can be negative, but E&P cannot be driven below zero by distributions.

Ordering of E&P Distributions

As we noted above, a corporation must maintain two separate E&P accounts: current E&P and accumulated E&P. Whether a distribution is characterized as a dividend depends on whether the balances in these accounts are positive or negative. There are four possible scenarios:

1. Positive current E&P, positive accumulated E&P.
2. Positive current E&P, negative accumulated E&P.
3. Negative current E&P, positive accumulated E&P.
4. Negative current E&P, negative accumulated E&P.

Positive Current E&P and Positive Accumulated E&P Corporate distributions are deemed to be paid out of current E&P first. If distributions exceed current E&P, the amount distributed out of current E&P is allocated pro rata to all of the distributions made during the year. Any distribution out of accumulated E&P is allocated to the recipients in the chronological order in which the distributions were made.[7] This ordering of distributions is necessary only when distributions exceed current E&P and either the identity of the shareholders receiving the distributions changes or a shareholder's percentage ownership changes during the year.

Example 7-4

What if: Assume SCR reported current E&P of $40,000, and the balance in accumulated E&P was $16,000. On December 31, SCR distributed $48,000 to Jim and $16,000 to Ginny. What amount of dividend income do Jim and Ginny report, and what is the balance of E&P for SCR at the beginning of next year?

Answer: $42,000 and $14,000 of dividend income to Jim and Ginny, respectively. The distribution is first deemed to be paid from current E&P to each shareholder in proportion to their ownership interests on the date of the distribution, $30,000 to Jim (equal to $40,000 times 75%) and $10,000 to Ginny (equal to $40,000 times 25%). The distribution in excess of current E&P ($64,000 – $40,000 equals $24,000) is then deemed to be paid from accumulated E&P ($16,000) in proportion to ownership interests ($12,000 to Jim and $4,000 to Ginny). The remaining distribution of $8,000 ($64,000 total minus $40,000 current E&P and $16,000 accumulated E&P) is a return of capital. Hence, Jim will reduce his stock basis by $6,000 and Ginny will reduce her stock basis by $2,000.

SCR has a zero balance in accumulated E&P at the beginning of the next year because all current and accumulated E&P was distributed during the year.

What if: Assume that SCR's current E&P is $40,000 and its accumulated E&P is $15,000. Also, assume that Jim was the sole shareholder of SCR and he received a $45,000 distribution on June 1. Assume that after the June distribution Jim sold all his SCR shares to Ginny who received a $15,000 dividend on December 31. What is the amount and the character of each distribution?

Answer: Jim has a $45,000 dividend. Ginny has a $10,000 dividend and a $5,000 return of capital. Of the $40,000 of current E&P, $30,000 is allocated to Jim's distribution and $10,000 is allocated to Ginny's distribution. Current E&P is allocated between the two distributions in proportion to the total distributions (June 1 is $40,000 times $45,000/$60,000). However, because Jim's distribution took place before Ginny's distribution, the accumulated E&P is allocated to Jim's distribution ($15,000), leaving $0 in remaining accumulated E&P to be allocated to Ginny's distribution. Ginny is allocated only $10,000 of E&P, leaving her with an excess distribution of $5,000 ($15,000 – $10,000). This excess distribution is treated as a nontaxable reduction of her basis in the SCR stock. Current E&P is determined on the last day of the tax year before deduction for current year distributions.

Positive Current E&P and Negative Accumulated E&P Distributions deemed paid out of current E&P are taxable as dividends. Distributions in excess of current E&P in this scenario would first be treated as nontaxable reductions in the shareholders' tax basis in their stock. Any excess received over their stock basis would be treated as a (capital) gain from sale of the stock.

Example 7-5

What if: Assume SCR reported current E&P of $60,000. The balance in accumulated E&P at the beginning of the year was negative $20,000. On December 31, SCR distributed $48,000 to Jim and $16,000 to Ginny. Jim has a tax basis in his SCR stock of $24,000. Ginny's tax basis in her SCR stock is $10,000. What amount of income will Jim and Ginny report?

Answer: $45,000 and $15,000 of dividend income to Jim and Ginny, respectively. The distribution is first deemed to be paid from current E&P ($45,000 to Jim and $15,000 to Ginny). No additional amount is treated as a dividend because SCR has negative accumulated E&P.

[7]Reg. §1.316-2(b) and Rev. Rul. 74-164, 1974-1 C.B. 74.

What tax basis will Jim and Ginny have in their SCR stock after the distribution?

Answer: The amount in excess of current E&P ($3,000 to Jim, $1,000 to Ginny) would be treated as a nontaxable return of capital because Jim and Ginny have enough tax basis in their SCR stock to absorb the amount paid in excess of E&P. Jim's tax basis in his SCR stock after the distribution would be $21,000 ($24,000 − $3,000), and Ginny's tax basis in her SCR stock after the distribution would be $9,000 ($10,000 − $1,000).

What is SCR's remaining balance in accumulated E&P at the end of the year?

Answer: SCR has a $20,000 deficit (negative) balance in accumulated E&P.

Negative Current E&P and Positive Accumulated E&P When current E&P is negative, the tax status of a dividend is determined by total E&P on the *date of the distribution*. This requires the corporation to prorate the negative current E&P to the distribution date and add it to accumulated E&P at the beginning of the year to determine total E&P at the distribution date. Distributions in excess of total E&P in this scenario are treated as reductions in the shareholders' tax basis in their stock. Any excess over their stock basis would be treated as a capital gain.

Example 7-6

What if: Assume SCR reported current E&P of negative $20,000. The balance in accumulated E&P at the beginning of the year was $60,000. On June 30, SCR distributed $48,000 to Jim and $16,000 to Ginny. Jim has a tax basis in his SCR stock of $24,000. Ginny's tax basis in her SCR stock is $10,000. What amount of dividend income do Jim and Ginny report?

Answer: $37,500 to Jim and $12,500 to Ginny. Because current E&P is negative, SCR must determine its total E&P on the distribution date. SCR prorates the full year negative current E&P to June 30 [6 months/12 months × ($20,000) = ($10,000)]. The negative current E&P of $10,000 is added to the beginning balance in accumulated E&P of $60,000 to get total E&P as of July 1 of $50,000. Because their distributions were made at the same time, Jim is allocated 75 percent of the total E&P and Ginny is allocated the remaining 25 percent.

What tax basis do Jim and Ginny have in their SCR stock after the distribution?

Answer: The amount in excess of total E&P ($10,500 to Jim, $3,500 to Ginny) is treated first as a nontaxable return of capital. Jim reduces the basis in his SCR stock to $13,500 ($24,000 − $10,500). Ginny reduces the basis in her SCR stock to $6,500 ($10,000 − $3,500).

What is SCR's remaining balance in accumulated E&P at the end of the year?

Answer: Negative $10,000, computed as follows:

Beginning balance	$60,000
Prorated negative current E&P, 1/1–6/30	(10,000)
Dividends	(50,000)
Prorated negative current E&P, 7/1–12/31	(10,000)
Ending balance	($10,000)

Negative Current E&P and Negative Accumulated E&P When current E&P and accumulated E&P are both negative, none of the distribution is treated as a dividend. Distributions in this scenario would first be treated as reductions in the shareholders' tax basis in their stock. Any excess over their stock basis would be treated as a capital gain.

Example 7-7

What if: Assume SCR reported current E&P of negative $50,000. The balance in accumulated E&P at the beginning of the year was negative $60,000. Jim has a tax basis in his SCR stock of $24,000. Ginny's tax basis in her SCR stock is $10,000. On December 31 of this year, SCR distributed $48,000 to Jim and $16,000 to Ginny. What amount of dividend income do Jim and Ginny report this year?

Answer: $0 to Jim and $0 to Ginny. Because current E&P and accumulated E&P are negative, the entire distribution would be treated as either a return of capital or capital gain.

What are Jim and Ginny's tax bases in their SCR stock after the distribution?

Answer: The amount in excess of total E&P ($48,000 to Jim, $16,000 to Ginny) is treated first as a nontaxable return of capital. Jim reduces the basis in his SCR stock to $0 ($24,000 − $48,000, limited to $0). Ginny reduces the basis in her SCR stock to $0 ($10,000 − $16,000, limited to $0).

What amount of capital gain do Jim and Ginny report as a result of the distribution?

Answer: Jim has a capital gain of $24,000, the amount by which the distribution exceeds the tax basis in his SCR stock ($48,000 − $24,000). Ginny has a capital gain of $6,000, the amount by which the distribution exceeds the tax basis in her SCR stock ($16,000 − $10,000).

What is SCR's remaining balance in accumulated E&P at the end of the year?

Answer: A deficit (negative) balance of $110,000, the sum of accumulated E&P of negative $60,000 plus current E&P of negative $50,000.

Exhibit 7-2 summarizes the rules for determining whether a distribution represents dividend income. When both balances are negative, the distribution is treated as a return of capital (tax-free to the extent of the shareholder's tax basis in their stock and capital gain in excess of this amount), and the deficits in E&P are unaffected. When both balances are positive, the distribution is treated as a dividend to the extent of current E&P at year-end and then to the extent of the balance of accumulated E&P. A distribution in excess of current and accumulated E&P is treated as a return of capital. When current E&P is negative and accumulated E&P is positive, distributions are dividend income to extent of accumulated E&P after netting against deficit in current E&P (up to the date of the distribution). The distribution reduces accumulated E&P but not below zero. Finally, when accumulated E&P is negative and current E&P is positive, distributions are dividend income to extent of current E&P.

EXHIBIT 7-2 Summary of E&P Status and Taxability of Cash Distributions

	Balance in Accumulated E&P at the Time of the Distribution	
Balance in Current E&P at the Time of the Distribution	**Negative**	**Positive**
Negative	Distributions are a return of capital.	Distributions are dividend income to extent of accumulated E&P after netting against deficit in current E&P.
Positive	Distributions are dividend income to extent of current E&P.	Distributions are dividend income to extent of current E&P and the balance of accumulated E&P.

Distributions of Noncash Property to Shareholders

On occasion, a shareholder will receive property other than cash in the form of a dividend. When noncash property is received, the shareholder determines the amount distributed as follows:

	Money received
+	Fair market value of other property received
−	Liabilities assumed by the shareholder on property received
	Amount distributed[8]

Example 7-8

What if: Assume Ginny elected to receive $15,000 in cash and a Fuji custom touring bike that had a fair market value of $1,000. SCR has current E&P of $100,000 and no accumulated E&P. What amount of dividend income will Ginny report this year?

Answer: $16,000. Ginny would include the $15,000 plus the $1,000 fair market value of the bicycle in her gross income as a dividend.

As a general rule, a shareholder's tax basis in noncash property received as a dividend equals the property's fair market value.[9] No downward adjustment is made for liabilities assumed by the shareholder (these are considered part of the property's cost). The shareholder determines fair market value as of the date of the distribution.

Example 7-9

What is Ginny's tax basis in the bicycle she received as a dividend in the previous example?

Answer: $1,000. Ginny has a tax basis in the bicycle of $1,000, the bicycle's fair market value. Ginny would pay an income tax of $150 on receipt of the bicycle (assuming the dividend qualifies for the preferential 15 percent tax rate).

Example 7-10

What if: Assume Jim elected to receive a parcel of land SCR had previously purchased for possible expansion instead of cash. The land has a fair market value of $60,000 and a remaining mortgage of $12,000 attached to it. SCR has a tax basis in the land of $20,000. Jim will assume the mortgage on the land. SCR has current E&P of $100,000 and no accumulated E&P. How much dividend income does Jim recognize on the distribution?

Answer: $48,000. Jim recognizes dividend income in an amount equal to the land's fair market value of $60,000 less the mortgage he assumes on the land in the amount of $12,000.

What is Jim's tax basis in the land he receives?

Answer: $60,000. Jim receives a tax basis equal to the land's fair market value. Jim has a $60,000 basis in the land because he recognized $48,000 of income and assumed $12,000 of debt.

[8]§301(b).
[9]§301(d).

Corporate Tax Consequences of Noncash Distributions Gains (but not losses) are recognized by a corporation on the distribution of noncash property.[10] Specifically, to the extent the fair market value of property distributed exceeds the corporation's tax basis in the property, the corporation recognizes a taxable gain on the distribution. This gain increases current E&P because it increases taxable income. In contrast, if the fair market value of the property distributed is less than the corporation's tax basis in the property, the corporation does not recognize a deductible loss on the distribution. E&P is subsequently reduced by the distributed property's fair market value if the property is appreciated (gain is recognized) and by the property's E&P basis if the property is depreciated (loss is not recognized).

Example 7-11

What if: Assume SCR had a tax basis of $650 in the Fuji custom touring bike that it distributed to Ginny (see the facts in Example 7-8). How much gain, if any, does SCR recognize when it distributes the bicycle to Ginny as a dividend?

Answer: $350. SCR recognizes a taxable gain of $350 on the distribution of the bicycle to Ginny ($1,000 − $650). Because the bike is considered inventory, SCR would characterize the gain as ordinary income. Assuming a tax rate of 34 percent, SCR would pay a corporate level tax of $119 on the distribution (34% × $350). The total tax paid by SCR and Ginny would be $269 ($150 + $119). This is a high tax cost to pay to transfer the $1,000 bicycle to Ginny in the form of a dividend.

What if: Assume SCR had a tax basis of $1,200 in the Fuji custom touring bike that it distributed to Ginny. The bicycle's fair market value declined to $1,000 because it was an outdated model. How much loss, if any, does SCR recognize when it distributes the bicycle to Ginny as a dividend?

Answer: $0. SCR is not permitted to recognize a loss on the distribution of the bicycle to Ginny.

What if: Suppose SCR *sold* the bicycle to Ginny for $1,000. How much loss, if any, could SCR recognize if it sold the bicycle to Ginny?

Answer: $200. SCR is permitted to recognize a loss on the sale of property to a shareholder provided it does not run afoul of the related-person loss rules found in §267. To be a related person, Ginny must own *more than* 50 percent of SCR, which she does not in this scenario.

Liabilities If the property's fair market value is less than the amount of the liability assumed, the property's fair market value is deemed to be the amount of the liability assumed by the shareholder.[11] If the liability assumed is less than the property's fair market value, the gain recognized on the distribution is the excess of the property's fair market value over its tax basis (i.e., the liability is ignored).

Example 7-12

What if: Assume Jim received a parcel of land the company had previously purchased for possible expansion. The land has a fair market value of $60,000 and a remaining mortgage of $12,000 attached to it. SCR has a tax basis in the land of $20,000. Jim will assume the mortgage on the land. SCR has current E&P of $100,000 and no accumulated E&P. How much gain, if any, does SCR recognize when it distributes the land to Jim as a dividend?

Answer: $40,000 ($60,000 − $20,000). Because the mortgage assumed by Jim is less than the land's fair market value, SCR recognizes gain in an amount equal to the excess of the land's fair market value of $60,000 over its tax basis of $20,000.

[10]§311. Congress made distributions of appreciated property taxable to the distributing corporation in 1986 to prevent corporations from avoiding the double taxation of corporate income by distributing appreciated property to shareholders in the form of a dividend.

[11]§311(b)(2) refers to §336(b).

What if: Assume the mortgage assumed by Jim was $75,000 instead of $12,000. The land has a fair market value of $60,000, and SCR has a tax basis in the land of $20,000. Jim will assume the mortgage on the land. SCR has current E&P of $100,000. How much gain, if any, does SCR recognize when it distributes the land to Jim as a dividend?

Answer: $55,000 ($75,000 − $20,000). Because the mortgage assumed by Jim exceeds the land's fair market value, SCR treats the land's fair market value as $75,000 and recognizes gain in an amount equal to the excess of the mortgage assumed of $75,000 over its tax basis of $20,000.

THE KEY FACTS

Adjustments to Taxable Income (Loss) to Compute Current E&P

- A corporation makes the following adjustments to taxable income to compute current E&P:
  - Include certain income that is excluded from taxable income.
  - Disallow certain expenses that are deducted in computing taxable income.
  - Deduct certain expenses that are excluded from the computation of taxable income.
  - Defer deductions or accelerate income due to separate accounting methods required for E&P purposes.
- The amount distributed as a dividend equals:
  - Cash received.
  - Fair market value of noncash property received.
  - Reduced by any liabilities assumed by the shareholder on property received.
- E&P is reduced by distributions treated as dividends as follows:
  - Cash distributed.
  - E&P basis of noncash property with a fair market value less than or equal to its E&P basis.
  - Fair market value of noncash appreciated property reduced by any liabilities assumed by the shareholder on property received.

Effect of Noncash Property Distributions on E&P Gain recognized by a corporation on a distribution of appreciated property increases current E&P because it increases taxable income. In contrast, if the fair market value of the property distributed is less than the corporation's tax basis in the property, the corporation does not recognize a deductible loss on the distribution. E&P is subsequently reduced by the distributed property's fair market value if the property is appreciated (gain is recognized) and by the property's E&P basis if the property is depreciated (loss is not recognized).[12]

When appreciated property is distributed by the corporation, the corporation recognizes gain to the extent the property's fair market value exceeds the corporation's E&P tax basis in the property. The corporation then reduces E&P by the property's fair market value and adds back any mortgage or other liability assumed by the shareholders in the distribution.

Exhibit 7-3 provides a template for computing the effect of distributions on current E&P.

EXHIBIT 7-3 Template to Compute the Effect of Distributions on E&P

	Current E&P (computed before any distributions but including gain recognized on distribution of appreciated property)
−	Money distributed
−	E&P adjusted basis of unappreciated property distributed
−	Fair market value of appreciated property distributed
+	Liabilities assumed by the shareholders
−	Tax on gain recognized
	Undistributed current E&P (added to accumulated E&P from prior years)

In the case where a property's fair market value or E&P basis exceeds current E&P, the excess amount reduces any accumulated E&P at the beginning of the year. Note, however, that a distribution of property can only reduce E&P to the extent E&P is positive. Recall that a distribution cannot create negative E&P or increase already existing negative E&P that results from operations.

Example 7-13

What if: Assume the same facts as in Example 7-12. SCR distributed land to Jim that has a fair market value of $60,000 and a remaining mortgage of $12,000 attached to it. SCR has a tax and E&P basis in the land of $20,000. Jim assumed the mortgage on the land. SCR has current E&P of $100,000, which includes the net gain of $26,400 from distribution of the land ($40,000 gain less a related tax liability of $13,600 assuming a tax rate of 34 percent), and accumulated E&P at the beginning of the year of $500,000. What is SCR's beginning balance in accumulated E&P at January 1 of next year, as a result of the distribution of the land to Jim?

(continued on page 7-14)

[12]§312.

Answer: $552,000, computed as follows:

Accumulated E&P, this year	$500,000
Current E&P	100,000
Fair market value of land distributed	(60,000)
Liability assumed by Jim	12,000
Beginning balance, AE&P, next year	$552,000

What if: Assume SCR has current E&P of $40,000, which includes the net gain of $26,400 from distribution of the land ($40,000 gain less a related tax liability of $13,600 assuming a tax rate of 34 percent), and accumulated E&P of $500,000. What is SCR's beginning balance in accumulated E&P at January 1 of next year, as a result of the distribution of the land to Jim?

Answer: $492,000, computed as follows:

Accumulated E&P, this year	$500,000
Current E&P	40,000
Fair market value of land distributed	(60,000)
Liability assumed by Jim	12,000
Beginning balance, AE&P, next year	$492,000

What if: Assume the land distributed to Jim had a tax and E&P basis to SCR of $75,000 instead of $20,000. SCR has current E&P of $100,000, which does not include the disallowed loss of $15,000 on the distribution ($60,000 fair market value less $75,000 tax basis). SCR has accumulated E&P at the beginning of the year of $500,000. What is SCR's beginning balance in accumulated E&P at January 1 of next year, as a result of the distribution of the land to Jim?

Answer: $537,000, computed as follows:

Accumulated E&P, this year	$500,000
Current E&P	100,000
E&P basis of land distributed	(75,000)
Liability assumed by Jim	12,000
Beginning balance, AE&P, next year	$537,000

LO 7-3

CONSTRUCTIVE DIVIDENDS

THE KEY FACTS

Examples of Disguised Dividends

- Unreasonable compensation.
- Bargain sales to shareholders.
- Shareholder use of corporate assets without an arm's-length payment.
- Loans from shareholders at unreasonable interest rates.
- Corporate payments made on behalf of the shareholder.

Dividend distributions result in double taxation to the parties to the transaction because the corporation making the distribution cannot deduct dividends paid in computing its taxable income. Corporations can avoid this second level of taxation by making a distribution to a shareholder in a nonshareholder capacity. For example, the corporation might characterize the distribution as a payment of salary, interest, or rent to a shareholder who also is an employee, creditor, or lessor to the corporation, respectively. The corporation can deduct these types of payments, thus eliminating the double tax imposed on the distribution at the corporate level. From the recipient's perspective, the amount included in gross income no longer qualifies for preferential tax rates and would be taxed at the recipient's marginal tax rate. Payments designated to be compensation are subject to Social Security and Medicare payroll taxes.

The incentive for a corporation to make payments to shareholders that are deductible typically arises in close corporations, where the shareholders act in other capacities, such as managers, creditors, and lessors. In this setting, the shareholders are likely to consider the combined tax to be paid by the corporation and themselves rather than just the tax they pay individually.

The IRS has the ability to recharacterize the form of a transaction between a corporation and its shareholders into what the IRS considers to be the transaction's substance. In effect, the IRS can recharacterize what the corporation calls a deductible payment (e.g., compensation) into a nondeductible *constructive* dividend distribution. Common examples of constructive dividends include:

- Excess (*unreasonable*) compensation paid to shareholder/employees.
- Bargain sales of property by the corporation to shareholders.
- A bargain lease or uncompensated use of corporate property by a shareholder (e.g., a company car or corporate jet used for personal reasons).
- Excess rent paid to a shareholder/lessor by the corporation.
- Payments to a shareholder/creditor where the corporation is undercapitalized or the loan has an unreasonably high rate of interest.
- Corporate payments on a shareholder's behalf (e.g., legal fees paid to defend a sole shareholder of criminal charges).

The most frequent causes of disputes between corporations and the IRS over the characterization of deductible payments made to shareholders involve compensation and interest payments. To determine if compensation paid to a shareholder/employee is *reasonable,* the IRS usually looks to factors that include the individual's duties and responsibilities, what individuals performing in comparable capacities at other corporations are paid, whether the corporation has a formal compensation policy, and what the individual's return on his or her investment is as a shareholder of the company.[13]

Corporate payments made on behalf of shareholders are often the subject of litigation. In one case, the Tax Court held that a corporation's payment of a seat license fee to purchase season tickets to Houston Texans football games, to be used exclusively by the sole shareholder, was a constructive dividend to the shareholder.[14]

Example 7-14

What if: Assume SCR has current E&P of $200,000. Jim and Ginny would like to withdraw $48,000 and $16,000, respectively, from the company to fulfill some personal dreams (a BMW and a condominium, respectively). If SCR pays the amounts to Jim and Ginny as dividends, it will not be able to deduct the payments in computing its taxable income. What is the total tax cost (entity and shareholder level) of distributing a dividend to Jim and Ginny?

Answer: $31,360. The nondeductibility of the dividend payments will increase SCR's tax liability by $21,760 ($64,000 × 34%). Jim and Ginny will be eligible for a reduced dividend tax rate of 15 percent on the distributions, causing them to pay a shareholder-level tax of $7,200 and $2,400, respectively. The total tax cost to this strategy will be $31,360.

What if: Assume SCR declared a year-end bonus (additional compensation) of $48,000 and $16,000 to Jim and Ginny, respectively, to reward them for their hard work as employees. What is the total tax cost (entity and shareholder level) of paying a bonus to Jim and Ginny?

(*continued on page 7-16*)

[13]*Thomas A. Curtis, M.D., Inc.*, 67 T.C.M. 1958 (1994).

[14]*Kerns v. Comm.*, T.C. Memo 2004-63. See also *U.S. vs. Boulware* (9th CA, 2009) 558 F.3d. 971, and *William F. Bruecher III,* TC Summary 2005-52.

Answer: $23,200. By converting the dividend into compensation, SCR can deduct the $64,000 payment in computing its taxable income, saving $21,760 in taxes in the process ($64,000 × 34%). Jim and Ginny will no longer be eligible for the preferential dividend tax rate and will have to pay tax at their marginal tax rates (30 percent and 25 percent, respectively). Jim's tax cost will increase to $14,400 while Ginny's tax cost will increase to $4,000, for a combined tax cost of $18,400. This is still $12,960 less than the combined cost of the dividend strategy ($31,360).

What other tax costs will SCR and Jim and Ginny incur as a result of converting the dividend into a bonus?

Answer: Social Security and Medicare taxes, and perhaps, net investment income taxes. SCR and Jim and Ginny will have to pay Social Security and Medicare taxes on the $64,000 of compensation payments. Net investment income taxes are imposed on dividends but the tax rate depends on the level of the taxpayer's modified adjusted gross income.

What if: If Jim and Ginny go through with the bonus compensation alternative, would the strategy be vulnerable to IRS scrutiny?

Answer: Possibly. The IRS could argue that the bonus is really a constructive dividend. Key facts in the determination would be Jim and Ginny's contribution to the business, the compensation paid to individuals doing similar jobs at comparable businesses, whether SCR paid any dividends, and whether SCR had a formal compensation policy for determining year-end bonuses. For example, would Jim, who works only part-time, be able to justify why his contributions as an employee are valued at four times the bonus paid to Ginny, who works full-time?

Example 7-15

What if: Assume SCR sold Ginny a Fuji custom touring bike for its cost of $650. The selling price of the bicycle to customers was $1,000. What tax issues might arise in this transaction?

Answer: Two tax issues arise here. The transaction meets the definition of a *bargain purchase* by Ginny of the bicycle. The IRS could argue that Ginny received property worth $1,000 for $650 and thus had a constructive dividend of $350. Because the bicycle is inventory to SCR, the sale could qualify as a nontaxable fringe benefit under the employee discount rules.[15] Assuming this "discount" is available to all SCR employees, Ginny would not have taxable income (compensation) for the bargain portion of the sale in an amount equal to SCR's gross profit percentage times the price it normally charges nonemployee customers for the bicycle. SCR's gross profit percentage is 35 percent ($350/$1,000). The maximum employee discount that would be tax-free is $350 (35% × $1,000). Ginny would not have to report any compensation in this bargain purchase under the fringe benefit rules.

What if: Assume SCR sold the bicycle to Ginny for $500 (i.e., below cost). How might your answer change?

Answer: Ginny would now have taxable compensation of $150 at the very least. Depending on the circumstances, the IRS could assert that she had a constructive dividend of $500.

The Motivation to Pay Dividends

Many publicly traded corporations regularly pay out a portion of their earnings to shareholders as a dividend. Why corporate managers would willingly pay out cash that could be reinvested in the corporation has long intrigued corporate finance theorists. Several possible reasons have been offered to explain this "dividend puzzle" such as signaling earnings persistence.

Closely held corporations are the alter egos of their shareholders. As a result, their dividend policies are much less likely to be structured. Rather, dividends may be a function of the shareholders' cash needs. The double taxation of corporate earnings plus the higher corporate tax rates provide an incentive for closely held

[15]§132(c).

corporations to pay out earnings in tax deductible ways, the additional payroll tax cost of a compensation strategy might outweigh the double tax imposed on the dividend. It makes sense to retain earnings in the corporation if the after-tax rate of return earned by the corporation exceeds the rate that could be earned by the individual shareholders. Paying dividends rather than salary can be a way to avoid Social Security taxes (in which case, the IRS may argue the dividend is really compensation). Closely held corporations also run the risk of paying a penalty tax called the *accumulated earnings tax* if they accumulate earnings in excess of $250,000 without having a documented business purpose for retaining the excess.[16]

ETHICS

Karla Heyne is the sole shareholder of XYZ Corporation. This past year Karla paid her retired father, Paul, $10,000 from the company's checking account because he was having financial trouble. XYZ files as a C corporation, and Karla noticed that her accountant erroneously deducted this payment as salary on XYZ's return. What would you do with this information if you were in Karla's shoes?

STOCK DIVIDENDS

LO 7-4

Rather than distribute cash dividends to its shareholders, a corporation may instead distribute additional shares of its own stock or rights to acquire additional shares. Publicly held corporations are likely to issue stock dividends to promote shareholder goodwill (i.e., a stock dividend allows the corporation to retain cash and still provide shareholders with tangible evidence of their interest in corporate earnings) or reduce the market price of its outstanding shares. A stock dividend increases the number of shares outstanding and thereby reduces the price per share and makes the stock more accessible to a wider range of shareholders. For example, a 5 percent stock dividend would increase the number of shares outstanding by 5 percent. Hence, a shareholder holding 100 shares would own 105 shares after a 5 percent stock dividend. While stock dividends are relatively rare, stock splits are more common. In a **stock split,** the number of shares outstanding is increased by the ratio of the split. For example, a 2-for-1 stock split would double the number of shares outstanding. Hence, a shareholder holding 100 shares would own 200 shares after a 2-for-1 stock split. Stock dividends and stock splits are used by many firms to keep stock prices accessible to a diverse group of investors.

Tax Consequences to Shareholders Receiving a Stock Dividend

Nontaxable Stock Dividends Stock dividends generally do not provide shareholders with any increase in value. In other words, the shareholders' interest in the corporation remains unchanged except that they now own more pieces of paper (stock) than before. As a result, a stock dividend usually is not included in the shareholders' gross income.[17]

[16]§§531–535. Under certain conditions, accumulated earnings can also trigger the personal holding company tax. See §§541–547.

[17]§305(a).

For the nontaxable general rule to apply, the stock distribution must meet two conditions: (1) it must be made with respect to the corporation's common stock, and (2) it must be pro rata with respect to all shareholders (i.e., the shareholders' relative equity positions do not change as a result of the distribution).

The recipient of a nontaxable stock dividend allocates a portion of the tax basis from the stock on which the stock dividend was issued to the newly issued stock based on the relative fair market values (FMV) of the stock.[18] In the case of a simple dividend of common stock or stock split where the stock distributed is identical to the stock from which the distribution is made (same class and same fair market value), the new per share tax basis is the original tax basis divided by the total number of shares held (including the new shares).

For example, assume a shareholder owns 100 shares of Acme Corporation stock, for which she paid $3,000. Acme declares a 100 percent stock dividend and sends the shareholder an additional 100 shares of stock. The shareholder will now own 200 shares of stock with the same tax basis of $3,000. The basis of each share of stock decreases from its original $30 per share ($3,000/100) to $15 per share ($3,000/200). The holding period of the new stock includes the holding period for which the shareholder held the old stock.[19]

Example 7-16

Jim has a tax basis in his SCR stock of $24,000. Ginny's tax basis in her SCR stock is $10,000. Jim owns 75 of the 100 shares of outstanding SCR stock, while Ginny owns the remaining 25 shares.

What if: Assume for estate and gift tax purposes, their tax accountant, Louis Tully, suggested that SCR declare a 100 percent stock dividend. As a result, Jim would own 150 shares of SCR stock and Ginny would own the remaining 50 shares.

Is the stock dividend taxable to Jim and Ginny?

Answer: No. The stock dividend to Jim and Ginny is nontaxable because it is made equally (pro rata) to the shareholders.

What is the tax basis of each share of SCR stock now held by Jim and Ginny?

Answer: Jim's original tax basis of $24,000 is divided among 150 shares. Hence, each one of Jim's shares has a basis of $160. Ginny's original tax basis of $10,000 is divided among 50 shares. Hence, each one of Ginny's shares has a basis of $200.

THE KEY FACTS

Tax Consequences of Stock Dividends

- Pro rata distributions generally are nontaxable.
- Shareholders allocate basis from the "old" stock to the "new" stock based on relative fair market value.
- Non-pro rata stock dividends usually are taxable as dividends.

Taxable Stock Dividends Non-pro rata stock dividends usually are included in the shareholder's gross income as taxable dividends to the extent of the distributing corporation's E&P.[20] This makes sense because the recipient has now received something of value: an increase in the shareholder's claim on the corporation's income and assets. For example, a corporation may give its shareholders the choice between a cash dividend or a stock dividend. In this case, shareholders who elect the stock dividend in lieu of money will have a taxable dividend equal to the fair market value of the stock received. Because the stock dividend is taxable, the recipient will have a

[18]§307. Technically, the shares received in the distribution are allocated a portion of the original basis determined by the ratio of FMVs. This computation is necessary when the stock dividend includes a different class of shares (e.g., preferred stock).

[19]§1223(4).

[20]§305(b).

tax basis in the stock equal to its fair market value. A technical discussion of all of the rules that apply to determine if a stock dividend is taxable is beyond the scope of this text.

STOCK REDEMPTIONS

LO 7-5

continued from page 7-2...

In the original storyline, Jim and Ginny raised some of the initial capital they needed to start SCR by borrowing $50,000 from Jim's father, Walt. An alternative strategy would have been to issue 25 additional shares of SCR stock to Walt in return for $50,000. This change in facts would reduce Jim's ownership percentage in SCR to 60 percent (75 shares/125 shares). Ginny's ownership percentage would decrease to 20 percent (25 shares/125 shares). Walt would own the remaining 20 percent. We will assume this change in facts to continue the storyline.

Walt does not participate in the management of the company. In fact, Walt was hoping to cash out of SCR when it became profitable and use the money to put a down payment on a condominium in The Villages, a retirement community near Orlando, Florida. With the SCR stock valued at $5,000 per share ($125,000 in total), Walt saw this as an opportunity to realize his retirement dream. Jim and Ginny saw this as an opportunity to own all of the company's stock, eliminating a potential source of discord should Jim's father disapprove of the way Jim and Ginny were managing the company.

By the end of this year, the company expects to have sufficient cash to buy back some or all of Walt's shares of SCR stock. Jim and Ginny were wondering about the potential tax consequences to SCR and Walt under various redemption plans. In particular, Jim and Ginny wanted to know if there was a tax difference in (1) buying back five of Walt's shares this year, and the remaining 20 shares equally over the next four years (five shares per year), or (2) buying back all 25 shares this year using an installment note that would pay him 20 percent of the purchase price in each of the next five years plus interest. Once again, they turned to their trusted tax accountant, Louis Tully, for advice. ■

Publicly held corporations buy back (redeem) their stock from existing shareholders for many and varied reasons. For example, a corporation may have excess cash and limited investment opportunities, or management may feel the stock is undervalued. Management may see a large redemption as a way to get analysts to take a closer look at their company (this action sometimes is referred to as *signaling*). Reducing the number of outstanding shares also increases earnings per share (by reducing the number of shares in the denominator of the calculation) and potentially increases the stock's market price. Moreover, corporations are not taxed on gains or losses resulting from transactions in their own stock.[21] Stock redemptions can also be used to selectively buy-out dissenting shareholders who have become disruptive to the company.

[21]§1032.

TAXES IN THE REAL WORLD An (Un)fortunate Redemption

There are many reasons that companies choose to redeem stock, but sometimes the timing of the transactions is questionable. For example, Netflix (the online movie company, symbol NFLX) is a company that has a policy of returning "excess" cash to shareholders in the form of buybacks. However, in September 2011, Netflix proposed a rate change that was supposed to increase average revenue per subscriber. Netflix proposed to separate its DVD-by-mail service from movie streaming and increase fees. This proposal would have required subscribers who wanted both DVDs and movie streaming to have separate accounts for each service.

This proposal made finding entertainment more complicated and triggered a revolt by subscribers. Instead of paying more, an estimated 800,000 Netflix subscribers dropped their subscription. More bad news followed when, in late October, Netflix announced that the expected costs of expanding into Ireland and the United Kingdom were likely to generate a quarterly deficit rather than the $7 per share earnings expected in the first-quarter 2012. Altogether, these changes caused shares in Netflix to plummet from $300 to around $42.

Unfortunately during the third quarter Netflix continued to redeem shares, spending $39.6 million to repurchase approximately 182,000 shares at an average cost of $218 per share. Without more information, it is difficult to determine if any single sale would qualify as substantially disproportionate under §302(b)(2). However, because Netflix is publicly held (no individual or corporation owns more than 5 percent of the stock), it is likely that these redemptions were treated as sales because they would meet the not essentially equivalent to a dividend test under §302(b)(1). Hence, many former shareholders benefited from participating in redemptions at historically high prices and having the redemptions taxed as sales. However, Netflix could not recognize any of the losses associated with transactions in its own stock.

Source: Netflix Shareholder letter Q3 2011, October 24, 2011.

Privately held corporations engage in stock redemptions for reasons that are different from publicly traded corporations. These corporations often use stock redemptions to shift ownership control between family members (usually the older generation to the younger generation) when the acquiring family members do not have the resources to purchase shares directly from the other family members. They also use redemptions to buy out dissatisfied, disinterested, or deceased shareholders (e.g., a child who does not want to continue in the family business or a family member who has become disruptive in the management of the company). In addition, redemptions of an ex-spouse's stock can provide liquidity in a divorce agreement and eliminate the individual from management or ownership in the company. Finally, redemptions can be used to provide cash to satisfy estate taxes imposed on the estate of a deceased shareholder of the company.

The Form of a Stock Redemption

A stock redemption is an acquisition by a corporation of its stock from a shareholder in exchange for property, whether or not the stock so acquired is cancelled, retired, or held as treasury stock.[22] The term *property* has the same meaning as it did for dividend transactions (i.e., cash and noncash property).

Stock redemptions take the form of an *exchange* where the shareholders exchange their stock in the corporation for property, usually cash. If the *form* of the transaction is respected, shareholders compute gain or loss (usually capital) by comparing the amount realized (money and the fair market value of other property received) with their tax basis in the stock exchanged.

Without any tax law restrictions, a sole shareholder of a corporation could circumvent the dividend rules by structuring distributions to have the form of an exchange (i.e., a stock redemption). For example, rather than have the corporation

[22]§317(b).

make a $100,000 dividend distribution, the shareholder could have the corporation buy back $100,000 of stock from the shareholder. If the shareholder had a tax basis of $60,000 in the stock redeemed, the amount of income reported on the shareholder's tax return would decrease from $100,000 (dividend) to $40,000 (capital gain). At present, both amounts would be taxed at the same preferential tax rate (generally 15 percent), assuming the shareholder held the stock for more than a year. Similar to a dividend, however, the sole shareholder would continue to own 100 percent of the corporation before and after the stock redemption.

Form is not always respected in a redemption, however. The tax law may determine (or the IRS may argue that) the transaction is, in substance, a property distribution, the tax consequences of which should be determined under the previously discussed dividend rules.

The IRC provides both "bright line" and subjective tests to distinguish when a redemption should be treated as an exchange or a potential dividend.[23] The result is an intricate set of rules that must be navigated carefully by the corporation and its shareholders to ensure that the shareholders receive the tax treatment they desire.[24] This is especially true in closely held, family corporations, where the majority of stock is held by people related to each other through birth or marriage.

While individual shareholders prefer sale treatment, corporate shareholders generally have more incentive for dividend treatment. Dividends from domestic corporations are eligible for the dividends received deduction (usually 70 or 80 percent), whereas a capital gain is taxed at the corporation's marginal tax rate (as high as 35 percent). Again, a corporation might prefer exchange treatment if the redemption results in a loss or its stock tax basis as a percentage of the redemption price exceeds the dividends received deduction ratio.

Redemptions That Reduce a Shareholder's Ownership Interest

The IRC allows a shareholder to treat a redemption as an exchange if the transaction meets one of three change-in-stock-ownership tests.[25] These stock ownership tests look at the redemption from the shareholder's perspective.

Redemptions That Are Substantially Disproportionate The IRC states that a redemption will be treated as an exchange if the redemption is *"substantially disproportionate with respect to the shareholder."*[26] A shareholder meets this requirement by satisfying three mechanical ("bright line") *stock ownership tests:*

1. Immediately after the exchange, the shareholder owns less than 50 percent of the total combined voting power of all classes of stock entitled to vote.
2. The shareholder's percentage ownership of voting stock after the redemption is less than 80 percent of his or her percentage ownership before the redemption.
3. The shareholder's percentage ownership of the aggregate fair market value of the corporation's common stock (voting and nonvoting) after the redemption is less than 80 percent of his or her percentage ownership before the redemption.

[23]§302. The IRC also defines when sale treatment is appropriate in some special circumstances. For example, §303 defines when sale treatment is allowed for redemptions of stock to pay death taxes.

[24]Not all taxpayers have the same tax incentives in a redemption. Corporate shareholders may desire dividend treatment to capture the dividends received deduction. Individuals, on the other hand, may desire exchange treatment to lessen the amount of gain recognized (by reducing the amount received by the basis of the stock exchanged) or to report a capital loss.

[25]§302(b)(1), (b)(2), and (b)(3).

[26]§302(b)(2).

For example, if a shareholder owns 60 percent of a corporation's stock, she must own less than 48 percent of the stock after a stock redemption to have the redemption treated as an exchange (60% × 80% = 48%, which is less than 50 percent). If the shareholder owns 70 percent of the stock, she must own less than 50 percent of the stock after the redemption to have the transaction treated as an exchange (70% × 80% = 56%, which is greater than 50 percent).

The determination as to whether a shareholder meets the 50 percent and 80 percent tests is evaluated on a shareholder-by-shareholder basis. As a result, some shareholders can satisfy the test while others do not. If a shareholder owns multiple classes (voting and nonvoting) of common stock, the less-than-80-percent of fair market value test is applied to the shareholder's aggregate ownership of the common stock rather than on a class-by-class basis.

Example 7-17

What if: Assume Walt is not related to either Jim or Ginny. This year, SCR redeemed five shares of his stock in exchange for $25,000. Walt has a tax basis in the five shares of SCR stock of $10,000 ($2,000 per share). What is the tax treatment of the stock redemption to Walt under §302(b)(2)?

Answer: $25,000 dividend. Prior to the redemption, Walt owned 20 percent of SCR (25/125 shares). After the redemption, his ownership percentage in SCR drops to 16.67 percent (20/120 shares). This redemption does not satisfy the substantially disproportionate test, which would treat the redemption as an exchange. After the redemption, Walt owns less than 50 percent of SCR stock, but his ownership percentage after the redemption (16.67 percent) does not fall below 80 percent of their ownership percentage prior to the redemption (80% × 20% = 16%). Walt will not be able to treat the redemption as an exchange under this change-in-ownership test. Unless he can satisfy one of the other change-in-ownership tests, Walt will have a $25,000 dividend, assuming SCR has sufficient E&P, rather than a $15,000 capital gain ($25,000 − $10,000).

How many shares of stock would SCR have to redeem from Walt to guarantee exchange treatment under the substantially disproportionate test?

Answer: Six shares. For Walt to meet the 80 percent test, SCR must redeem six shares of stock. The computation is made as follows:

$$\frac{25 - x}{125 - x} < 16\%, \text{ where } x \text{ is the number of shares to be redeemed}$$

Using some algebra, we can compute x to be 5.95, rounded up to six shares.[27] If SCR redeems six shares from Walt, his ownership percentage after the redemption will be 15.97 percent (19/119 shares), which now meets the 80 percent test. The redemption of this one additional share transforms the transaction from a $30,000 dividend (6 shares × $5,000) to an $18,000 capital gain ($30,000 − $12,000).

In determining whether Walt meets the 50 percent and 80 percent tests, he must take into account the **constructive ownership** (stock attribution) rules found in subchapter C.[28] These tax law rules force stock owned by other persons (individuals and entities) to be treated as owned by (attributed to) the shareholder for purposes of determining whether the shareholder has met the change-in-stock-ownership tests. The purpose of the attribution rules is to prevent shareholders from dispersing stock ownership to either family members who have similar economic interests or entities controlled by the shareholder to avoid having stock redemptions recharacterized as dividends.

[27]Multiply both sides by $(125 - x)$, we get $25 - x = 20 - .16x$. Moving x to the right side of the equation and the integers to the left side of the equation, we get $5 = .84x$. Solving for x we get 5.95.

[28]§318.

Family attribution. Individuals are treated as owning the shares of stock owned by their spouse, children, grandchildren, and parents. Stock owned constructively through the family attribution rule cannot be reattributed to another family member through the family attribution rule (this is known as *double family attribution*).

Example 7-18

Return to the original storyline facts, where Walt is Jim's father. This year, SCR redeemed six shares of stock from them in exchange for $30,000. Walt has a tax basis in the six shares of stock redeemed of $12,000 ($2,000 per share). What is the tax treatment of the stock redemption to Walt under §302(b)(2)?

Answer: $30,000 dividend.

Prior to the redemption, Walt owned 20 percent of SCR (25/125 shares) directly. Under the family attribution rules, he is treated as constructively owning the shares of SCR stock owned by his son Jim (75 shares). In applying the substantially disproportionate change-in-stock-ownership tests, Walt is treated as owning 100 shares of SCR stock (25 + 75), or 80 percent of the SCR stock (100/125 shares). After the redemption, his ownership percentage in SCR drops to 79 percent (94/119 shares). This redemption does not satisfy the substantially disproportionate test because Walt is deemed to own more than 50 percent of the SCR stock after the redemption. As a result, he will have a $30,000 dividend, assuming SCR has sufficient E&P, rather than an $18,000 capital gain ($30,000 − $12,000).

An interesting question arises as to what happens to the tax basis of stock redeemed that is not used in determining the shareholder's tax consequences. This occurs in a redemption treated as a dividend, where the tax basis of the stock redeemed is not subtracted from the amount received from the corporation. Under the current rules, the tax basis of the stock redeemed is added back to the tax basis of any shares still held by the shareholder.[29] If the shareholder no longer holds any shares, the tax basis transfers to the stock held by those persons who caused the shareholder to have dividend treatment under the attribution rules.

Example 7-19

In the prior example, SCR redeemed six shares of stock from Walt for $30,000, and the transaction was treated as a dividend because of the application of the family attribution rules. Walt had a tax basis in the six shares of stock redeemed of $12,000 ($2,000 per share), but this tax basis was not used in determining their taxable income from the transaction.

What is Walt's tax basis in the remaining 19 shares of SCR stock?

Answer: $50,000. Walt adds back the unused $12,000 tax basis in the six shares redeemed to the tax basis of their remaining 19 shares. The tax basis in these remaining shares increases to $50,000, the original tax basis of the 25 shares.

Attribution from entities to owners or beneficiaries. Owners or beneficiaries of entities can be deemed to own shares of stock owned by the entity itself. Under these rules, partners are deemed to own a pro rata share of their partnership's stock holdings (i.e., a partner who has a 10 percent interest in a partnership is deemed to own 10 percent of any stock owned by the partnership). Beneficiaries are deemed to own a pro rata share of the stock owned by the trust or estate of which they are a beneficiary. Shareholders are deemed to own a pro rata share of their corporation's stock

[29]Reg. §1.302-2.

holdings, but only if they own at least 50 percent of the value of the corporation's stock. Other attribution rules, such as family attribution, apply in determining if this 50 percent test is met.

For example, assume an individual owns 100 shares of a corporation's stock directly. In addition, she is a 50 percent partner in a partnership that owns 100 shares of stock in the same corporation. Under the entity-to-owner attribution rules, the individual is deemed to own 50 percent of the partnership's 100 shares in the corporation. She is deemed to own 150 shares of stock in the corporation (100 + 50) for purposes of applying any of the change-in-stock-ownership tests in a stock redemption.

Example 7-20

What if: Assume that Walt is not Jim's father, and he is a 50 percent partner in a partnership that owns 25 shares in SCR. The other 50 percent of the partnership is owned by his neighbors, Fred and Ethel, who are unrelated to Walt. How many shares of SCR is treated as constructively owning through the partnership?

Answer: 12.5 shares. Walt is treated as owning a pro rata share of stock owned by the partnership; in this example, 50 percent times 25 shares.

Attribution from owners or beneficiaries to entities. Entities can be deemed to own other stock owned by their owners or beneficiaries. Under these rules, a partnership is deemed to own 100 percent of the shares owned by its partners. A trust or estate is deemed to own 100 percent of the shares owned by its beneficiaries. A corporation is deemed to own 100 percent of the shares owned by its shareholders, but only if the shareholder owns at least 50 percent of the value of the corporation's stock. Stock that is deemed owned by an entity cannot be reattributed to the other owners in the entity under the entity-to-owner rules previously discussed (this is known as *sideways attribution*).

For example, assume an individual owns 100 shares of a corporation's stock directly. In addition, she is a 50 percent partner in a partnership that owns 100 shares of stock in the same corporation. Under the owner-to-entity attribution rules, the partnership is deemed to own 100 percent of the partner's 100 shares in the corporation. The partnership is treated as owning 200 shares of stock in the corporation (100 + 100) for purposes of applying any of the change-in-stock-ownership tests in a stock redemption.

Option attribution. A person having an option to purchase stock is deemed to own the stock that the option entitles the person to purchase.

Complete Redemption of the Stock Owned by a Shareholder The IRC holds that a redemption will be treated as an exchange if the redemption is in *"complete redemption of all of the stock of the corporation owned by the shareholder."*[30] This test seems redundant with the substantially disproportionate test discussed previously; after all, a complete redemption automatically satisfies the 50 percent and 80 percent tests. The difference relates to the application of the stock attribution rules that apply to this form of redemption.

The stock attribution rules previously discussed also apply to a complete redemption. This presents a potential problem in family-owned corporations in which the only (or majority) shareholders are parents, children, and grandchildren. Parents who have all of their stock redeemed will be treated as having received a dividend if their children or grandchildren continue to own the remaining stock in the corporation

[30]§302(b)(3).

because of the operation of the family attribution rules. To provide family members with relief in these situations, the IRC allows shareholders to waive (ignore) the family attribution rules in a complete redemption of their stock.[31] As usual, there are some strings attached.

The first requirement is that the shareholder has no interest in the corporation immediately after the exchange as a *"shareholder, employee, director, officer or consultant."*[32] These relations to the corporation are referred to as prohibited interests. The second requirement is that the shareholder does not acquire a prohibited interest within 10 years after the redemption, unless by inheritance (this is known as the *10-year look-forward rule*). Finally, the shareholder must agree to notify the IRS district director within 30 days if he or she acquires a prohibited interest within 10 years after the redemption. These agreements are referred to as **triple i agreements.**[33] The shareholder can still be a creditor of the corporation (i.e., the parents can receive a corporate note in return for their stock if the corporation does not have the cash on hand to finance the redemption).

Example 7-21

Return to the original storyline facts, where Walt is Jim's father. Assume SCR redeemed all of his 25 shares this year for $125,000. Walt's tax basis in the SCR shares is $50,000 (25 × $2,000). Under the family attribution rules, Walt would still be treated as constructively owning 75 percent of the SCR stock (Jim would own 75 of the remaining 100 shares in SCR). The $125,000 payment would be treated as a taxable dividend.

What happens to the unused $50,000 tax basis in the SCR stock redeemed?

Answer: The tax basis transfers to Jim's stock, giving him a new tax basis in his SCR stock of $74,000 ($24,000 + $50,000).

How can Walt change the tax treatment of the complete redemption?

Answer: Because Walt has all of their shares redeemed, he can waive the family attribution rules provided they file a triple i agreement with the IRS and does not retain a prohibited interest in SCR (e.g., as an employee or consultant). By waiving the family attribution rules, Walt will be able to treat the redemption as an exchange and report a capital gain of $75,000 ($125,000 − $50,000).

Redemptions That Are Not Essentially Equivalent to a Dividend The IRC provides that a redemption will be treated as an exchange if the redemption is *"not essentially equivalent to a dividend."*[34] This is a subjective determination that turns on the facts and circumstances of each case. To satisfy this requirement, the IRS or the court must conclude that there has been a "meaningful" reduction in the shareholder's ownership interest in the corporation as a result of the redemption. The IRS does not provide any mechanical tests to make this determination. As a result, shareholder reliance on this test usually is one of last resort. The Supreme Court has held that the only way for a shareholder to qualify under this test is for the redemption to "result in a meaningful reduction of the shareholder's proportionate interest in the corporation."[35]

Although the courts have held that a shareholder's interest can include the right to vote and exercise control, participate in current and accumulated earnings, or share in net assets on liquidation, the IRS generally looks at the change in voting

[31]§302(c)(2).

[32]§302(c).

[33]The agreement gets its name from the clause in which it is described [§302(c)(2)(A)(*iii*)].

[34]§302(b)(1).

[35]*United States v. Davis,* 397 U.S. 301, at 313 (1970).

power as the key factor. The shareholder's voting power must decrease and be below 50 percent as a result of the exchange before this test can be considered.[36] As before, the stock attribution rules apply to these types of redemptions. Shareholders generally turn to this test to provide exchange treatment for redemptions when they cannot meet the "bright line" tests discussed previously.

Example 7-22

What if: Assume Walt is not related to Jim or Ginny. This year, SCR redeemed five shares of his stock in exchange for $25,000. Walt has a tax basis in the five shares of SCR stock of $10,000 ($2,000 per share).

What is the tax treatment of the stock redemption to Walt under the *not essentially equivalent to a dividend* test?

Answer: $15,000 capital gain.

Prior to the redemption, Walt owned 20 percent of SCR (25/125 shares). After the redemption, his ownership percentage in SCR drops to 16.67 percent (20/120 shares). This redemption does not satisfy the substantially disproportionate test, which would treat the redemption as an exchange. Walt likely has a case that the redemption should be treated as an exchange because it was *not essentially equal to a dividend.* After all, his ownership percentage decreased (20 percent to 16.67 percent) and is below 50 percent after the redemption. However, the result Walt seeks (exchange treatment) is not guaranteed. For peace of mind, he might prefer having SCR redeem one additional share and have the certainty that the redemption will be treated as an exchange.

Example 7-23

What if: Assume Walt is Jim's father, and SCR redeemed five shares of his stock in exchange for $25,000. Walt has a tax basis in the five shares of SCR stock of $10,000 ($2,000 per share). What is the tax treatment of the stock redemption to Walt under the *not essentially equivalent to a dividend* test?

Answer: $25,000 dividend.

Prior to the redemption, Walt is treated as owning 80 percent of SCR (25 shares directly and 75 shares through Jim). After the redemption, his ownership percentage in SCR drops to 79 percent (95/120 shares). This redemption does not satisfy the *not essentially equal to a dividend* test because Walt is treated as owning more than 50 percent of the SCR stock.

Tax Consequences to the Distributing Corporation

The corporation distributing property to shareholders in a redemption generally recognizes gain on distributions of appreciated property, but is not permitted to recognize loss on distribution of property with a fair market value less than its tax basis.[37]

If the shareholder treats the redemption as a *dividend,* the corporation reduces its current E&P by the cash distributed and the fair market value of other property

[36]In Rev. Rul. 76-385, 1976-2 C.B. 92, the IRS held that in the case of a "small, minority shareholder, whose relative stock interest is minimal and who exercises no control over the affairs of the corporation," any reduction in proportionate interest is "meaningful." In this ruling, the shareholder's ownership percentage decreased from .0001118% to .0001081%, which would not be considered a "meaningful" reduction by most standards. Because the reduction in stock ownership did not meet the substantially disproportionate tests of §302(b)(2), the shareholder's only hope for exchange treatment was to qualify under §302(b)(1).

[37]§311(a) and (b).

distributed as described in Exhibit 7-3.[38] If the shareholder treats the redemption as an *exchange,* the corporation reduces current and accumulated E&P at the date of distribution by the percentage of stock redeemed (i.e., if 60 percent of the stock is redeemed, E&P is reduced by 60 percent), not to exceed the fair market value of the property distributed.[39] The distributing corporation reduces its current E&P by any dividend distributions made during the year before reducing its E&P for redemptions treated as exchanges.[40]

The distributing corporation cannot deduct expenses incurred in a stock redemption.[41] The corporation can deduct interest on debt incurred to finance a redemption, however.

Example 7-24

What if: Assume SCR redeemed all of the 25 shares owned by Walt in exchange for $125,000. The stock redeemed represents 20 percent of the total stock outstanding. Walt has a tax basis in his SCR shares of $50,000. Further assume that Walt treated the redemption as an exchange because he waived the family attribution rules and filed a triple i agreement with the IRS.[42] As a result, Walt recognized a capital gain of $75,000 ($125,000 − $50,000). The redemption took place on December 31, on which date SCR had total E&P of $500,000. SCR did not make any dividend payments during the year.

By what amount does SCR reduce its E&P as a result of this redemption?

Answer: $100,000. SCR reduces total E&P by the lesser of (1) $100,000 (20% × $500,000) or (2) $125,000, the amount paid to Walt in the redemption.

What if: Assume total E&P was $1,000,000 at the end of the year. By what amount does SCR reduce its E&P as a result of this redemption?

Answer: $125,000. SCR reduces total E&P by the lesser of (1) $200,000 (20% × $1,000,000) or (2) $125,000, the amount paid to Walt in the redemption.

What if: Assume SCR paid a dividend of $100,000 to its shareholders on June 1. Total E&P was $500,000 at the end of the year, before taking into account the dividend and redemption. By what amount does SCR reduce its E&P as a result of this redemption?

Answer: $80,000. SCR first reduces total E&P by the dividend paid during the year to $400,000 ($500,000 − $100,000). SCR then reduces its E&P for the redemption by the lesser of (1) $80,000 (20% × $400,000) or (2) $125,000, the amount paid to Walt in the redemption.

THE KEY FACTS

Stock Redemptions Treated as Exchanges

- A stock redemption is treated as an exchange if it meets one of the following three tests:
  - Not essentially equivalent to a dividend.
  - Substantially disproportionate with respect to the shareholders.
  - In complete termination of the shareholder's interest.
- The following attribution rules are used to determine if one of the three tests is met:
  - Family attribution.
  - Entity-to-owner attribution (pro rata).
  - Owner-to-entity attribution (100 percent).
  - Options.
- A corporation reduces its E&P as a result of a stock redemption as follows:
  - If the distribution is treated as an exchange, E&P is reduced by the lesser of (1) the amount distributed or (2) the percentage of stock redeemed times AE&P at the redemption date.
  - If the distribution is treated as a dividend, E&P is reduced using the dividend rules.

Trends in Stock Redemptions by Publicly Traded Corporations

Traditionally, publicly traded corporations viewed stock redemptions as a tax-efficient means to return cash to their shareholders. Redemptions allow shareholders to "declare their own dividends" by voluntarily selling shares back to the corporation. Many companies increased their dividends after Congress decreased the dividend tax rate to 15 percent or 5 percent (now 0 percent) for individuals in 2003. On the other hand, the impending dividend tax increase at the end of 2010 motivated other companies, such as Masimo, to declare special dividends to avoid the anticipated higher shareholder tax.

[38]§312(a), and note that E&P cannot be reduced by more than the pro rata percentage of E&P allocated to the redeemed shares.

[39]§312(n)(7).

[40]Rev. Rul. 74-338, 1974-2 C.B. 101 and Rev. Rul. 74-339, 1974-2 C.B. 103.

[41]§162(k).

[42]The requirements for filing the triple i agreement are found in Reg. §1.302-4T.

TAXES IN THE REAL WORLD **Changing Distribution Strategies in Light of Tax Law Changes**

Masimo Board of Directors Declares Special Cash Dividend

Dividend Set at $0.75 Per Share

Irvine, California—November 22, 2010—Masimo (NASDAQ: MASI) announced today that its Board of Directors has declared a special $0.75 per share cash dividend, payable on December 21, 2010, to stockholders of record as of the close of business on December 7, 2010. The total dividend payout is expected to be approximately $44.3 million, based on the current shares outstanding and will be the third instance of a special dividend paid by Masimo in the past four years.

Masimo Founder, CEO, and Chairman of the Board, Joe Kiani, stated, "The special dividend is another step in demonstrating our commitment to enhancing stockholder value. The Board's decision to pay a dividend reflects our strong balance sheet, confidence in our long term outlook and capital structure. In addition, due to the uncertainty over potential changes in tax policy, the timing of this dividend will allow Masimo stockholders to take advantage of the current low dividend tax rate."

Masimo Form 8-K filed November 22, 2010.

Individuals have a tax incentive to participate in a redemption because gain recognized as a result of the redemption is usually capital gain (which is reduced by the basis of the stock redeemed and can absorb capital losses from other investments). Losses produced by the buyback generally can be deducted against capital gains.

LO 7-6

PARTIAL LIQUIDATIONS

Corporations can contract their operations by either distributing the stock of a subsidiary to their shareholders or by selling the business. In the case of a sale, the corporation may distribute the proceeds from the sale to its shareholders in partial liquidation of their ownership interests. The distribution may require the shareholders to tender shares of stock back to the corporation or may be pro rata to all the shareholders without an actual exchange of stock.

The tax treatment of a distribution received in a partial liquidation depends on the identity of the shareholder receiving the distribution.[43] All *noncorporate* shareholders receive exchange treatment. This entitles the individual to capital gain treatment with respect to gain or loss recognized on the actual or deemed exchange. If the shareholder is not required to tender stock to the corporation in return for the property received, the shareholder computes gain or loss recognized on the exchange by calculating the tax basis of the shares that would have been transferred to the corporation had the transaction been a stock redemption.

All *corporate* shareholders are subject to the change-in-stock-ownership rules that apply to stock redemptions. This usually results in dividend treatment because partial liquidations almost always involve pro rata distributions. Corporate shareholders generally prefer dividend treatment because of the availability of the dividends received deduction.

For a distribution to be in partial liquidation of the corporation, it must either be *"not essentially equivalent to a dividend"* (as determined at the corporate level) or the result of the termination of a *"qualified trade or business."*[44] The technical requirements to meet these requirements are beyond the scope of this text.

[43]§302(b)(4).

[44]§302(e).

Partial liquidations can be a tax-efficient way for a corporation to satisfy both its corporate and individual shareholders. For example, in the 1990s, General Dynamics Corporation sold off several of its divisions and distributed the proceeds ($20 per share) to its shareholders in partial liquidation of the corporation. As a result, the company's largest corporate shareholder treated the distribution as a dividend and received a 70 percent dividends received deduction. The company's largest individual shareholders treated the redemption as an exchange and received preferential taxation at the capital gain tax rate. The corporation was able to distribute cash from the sale of its assets in a manner that was tax-efficient to its diverse set of shareholders. Despite their beneficial tax results, partial liquidations are rare in practice.

> **THE KEY FACTS**
>
> **Tax Consequences to Shareholders in a Partial Liquidation of a Corporation**
>
> - Noncorporate shareholders receive exchange treatment.
> - Corporate shareholders determine their tax consequences using the change-in-stock ownership rules that apply to stock redemptions.

CONCLUSION

In this chapter we learned that a corporation can distribute cash and other property to its shareholders in alternative ways. The most common forms are dividend distributions and stock buybacks (redemptions). The form chosen to make such a distribution affects the tax consequences to the recipients (shareholders) as well as the corporation itself. In some cases, the tax laws or the tax administrators can ignore the form of the transaction and assess tax based on the substance of the transaction. This is common in the case of stock redemptions that can be taxed as dividend payments or deductible payments (compensation, interest, rent) that can be treated as constructive dividends (with no deduction for the corporation). The tax rules that apply to make this distinction often are complex and must be evaluated carefully by taxpayers and their tax advisers prior to making a decision.

Summary

LO 7-1

Explain the framework that applies to the taxation of property distributions from a corporation to a shareholder.

- Subchapter C of the Internal Revenue Code provides guidelines and rules for determining the tax status of distributions from a taxable ("C") corporation to its shareholders.
- When a corporation distributes property to persons in their capacity as shareholders without receiving any property or services in return, the shareholder must determine if the amount received is a dividend.
- If the distribution is of property other than cash, the distributing corporation recognizes gain but not loss on the distribution.

LO 7-2

Compute a corporation's earnings and profits and a shareholder's dividend income.

- The IRC defines a dividend as any distribution of property made by a corporation to its shareholders out of its current or accumulated earnings and profits (E&P).
- Earnings and profits is the tax equivalent of financial accounting retained earnings, although the computations can be significantly different.
- A corporation must keep two E&P accounts: current E&P and accumulated E&P.
- The IRC and the related regulations list four basic types of adjustments that a corporation must make to its taxable income to compute current E&P.
  - Inclusion of income that is excluded from taxable income.
  - Disallowance of certain expenses that are deducted in computing taxable income.
  - Deduction of certain expenses that are excluded from the computation of taxable income.
  - Deferral of deductions or acceleration of income due to separate accounting methods required for E&P purposes.

- The shareholder computes the dividend amount to include in gross income as the sum of cash received plus the fair market value of property received less any liabilities assumed.
- The distributing corporation recognizes gain, but not loss, on the distribution of noncash property in a dividend distribution.
- A corporation reduces its E&P by the amount of cash distributed, the E&P basis of unappreciated property distributed, and the fair market value of appreciated property distributed, net of any liability assumed by the shareholders.

LO 7-3 Identify when a corporation may be deemed to have paid a "constructive dividend" to a shareholder.

- A transaction between a shareholder and a corporation that does not take the form of a dividend may be treated by the IRS as a constructive dividend. Examples include:
  - Unreasonable compensation paid to shareholder/employees.
  - A bargain lease or uncompensated use of corporate property by a shareholder.
  - An excess purchase/lease price paid to a shareholder.
  - "Loans" to a shareholder who has no intent to repay the loan.
  - Corporate payments on a shareholder's behalf.
  - Unlawful diversions of corporate income to shareholders.

LO 7-4 Explain the taxation of stock dividends.

- The general rule is that a stock dividend is not taxable.
- The basis of the "new" stock received is computed by allocating basis from the existing stock based on relative fair market value.
- The holding period of the new stock includes the holding period of the existing stock on which the new stock was distributed.
- Non-pro rata stock dividends usually are treated as taxable dividends to the recipients.

LO 7-5 Comprehend the tax consequences of stock redemptions.

- If a redemption is treated as an exchange, the shareholder computes gain or loss by comparing the amount realized (money and property received) with the tax-adjusted basis of the stock surrendered.
  - The character of the gain or loss is capital.
  - The basis of noncash property received is its fair market value.
  - The holding period of the property received begins at the date of receipt.
- If the transaction is treated as a dividend, the shareholder has gross income in an amount equal to the cash and fair market value of other property received to the extent of the corporation's E&P.
  - The basis of the property received is its fair market value.
- The IRC treats redemptions as exchanges in transactions in which the shareholder's ownership interest in the corporation has been "meaningfully" reduced relative to other shareholders as a result of the redemption.
- There are three change-in-stock-ownership tests that entitle the shareholder to exchange treatment in a redemption.
- The IRC states that a redemption will be treated as an exchange if the redemption is "not essentially equivalent to a dividend."
  - This is a facts and circumstances determination (subjective).
  - To satisfy this requirement, the courts or IRS must conclude that there has been a "meaningful" reduction in the shareholder's ownership interest in the corporation as a result of the redemption (usually below 50 percent stock ownership).
- The IRC states that a redemption will be treated as an exchange if the redemption is "substantially disproportionate with respect to the shareholder," defined as follows:
  - Immediately after the exchange the shareholder owns less than 50 percent of the total combined voting power of all classes of stock entitled to vote.

- The shareholder's percentage ownership of voting stock after the redemption is less than 80 percent of his or her percentage ownership before the redemption.
- The shareholder's percentage ownership of the aggregate fair market value of the corporation's common stock (voting and nonvoting) after the redemption is less than 80 percent of his or her percentage ownership before the redemption.

- The IRC holds that a redemption will be treated as an exchange if the redemption is in "complete redemption of all of the stock of the corporation owned by the shareholder."
- In determining whether the change-in-stock-ownership tests are met, each shareholder's percentage change in ownership in the corporation before and after a redemption must take into account constructive ownership (attribution) rules.
- The attribution rules cause stock owned by other persons to be treated as owned by (attributed to) the shareholder for purposes of determining whether the shareholder has met any of the change-in-stock-ownership tests to receive exchange treatment.
  - Family attribution. Individuals are treated as owning the shares of stock owned by their spouse, children, grandchildren, and parents.
  - Attribution from entities to owners or beneficiaries.
    - Partners are deemed to own a pro rata share of their partnership's stock holdings (i.e., a partner who has a 10 percent interest in a partnership is deemed to own 10 percent of any stock owned by the partnership).
    - Shareholders are deemed to own a pro rata share of their corporation's stock holdings, but only if they own at least 50 percent of the value of the corporation's stock.
  - Attribution from owners or beneficiaries to entities.
    - Partnerships are deemed to own 100 percent of stock owned by partners (i.e., a partnership is deemed to own 100 percent of stock owned by a 10 percent partner)
    - Attribution to a corporation only applies to shareholders owning 50 percent or more of the value of the corporation's stock.
  - Option attribution. A person having an option to purchase stock is deemed to own the stock that the option entitles the person to purchase.
- Shareholders can waive the family attribution rules in a complete redemption of their stock if certain conditions are met.
  - The shareholder has not retained a prohibited interest in the corporation immediately after the exchange (e.g., as a shareholder, employee, director, officer, or consultant).
  - The shareholder does not acquire a prohibited interest within 10 years after the redemption, unless by inheritance (the 10-year look-forward rule).
  - The shareholder agrees to notify the IRS district director within 30 days if she acquires a prohibited interest within 10 years (sign a triple i agreement).
- If the redemption is treated as a dividend by the shareholder, the corporation generally reduces its E&P by the cash distributed and the fair market value of other property distributed.
- If the redemption is treated as an exchange by the shareholder, the corporation reduces E&P at the date of distribution by the percentage of stock redeemed (i.e., if 50 percent of the stock is redeemed, E&P is reduced by 50 percent), not to exceed the fair market value of the property distributed.

Describe the tax consequences of a partial liquidation to the corporation and its shareholders. LO 7-6

- For a distribution to be a partial liquidation, it must either be "not essentially equivalent to a dividend" (as determined at the corporate level, not the shareholder level) or is the result of the termination of a "qualified trade or business."
- The tax treatment of a distribution received in partial liquidation of a corporation depends on the identity of the shareholder receiving it.
  - All noncorporate shareholders get exchange treatment.
  - All corporate shareholders are subject to the stock redemption change in ownership rules, which usually results in dividend treatment because partial liquidations are almost always pro rata distributions.

KEY TERMS

accumulated earnings and profits (7-3)
constructive dividend (7-3)
constructive ownership (7-22)
current earnings and profits (7-3)
dividend (7-2)
partial liquidation (7-2)
stock dividend (7-3)
stock redemption (7-2)
stock split (7-17)
triple i agreement (7-25)

DISCUSSION QUESTIONS

LO 7-1 1. What is meant by the term *double taxation of corporate income*?

LO 7-1 2. How does the issue of double taxation arise when a corporation decides between making a distribution to a shareholder-employee as a dividend or compensation?

LO 7-1 3. Why might a shareholder who is also an employee prefer receiving a dividend instead of compensation from a corporation?

LO 7-2 4. What are the three potential tax treatments of a cash distribution to a shareholder? Are these potential tax treatments elective by the shareholder?

LO 7-2 5. In general, what is the concept of earnings and profits designed to represent?

LO 7-2 6. How does *current earnings and profits* differ from *accumulated earnings and profits*? Is there any congressional logic for keeping the two accounts separate?

LO 7-2 7. True or False: A calendar-year corporation has positive current E&P of $100 and accumulated negative E&P of $200. A cash distribution of $100 to the corporation's sole shareholder at year-end will not be treated as a dividend because total E&P is negative $100. Explain.

LO 7-2 8. True or False: A calendar-year corporation has negative current E&P of $100 and accumulated E&P of $100. A cash distribution of $100 to the corporation's sole shareholder on June 30 will not be treated as a dividend because total E&P at December 31 is $0. Explain.

LO 7-2 9. List the four basic adjustments that a corporation makes to taxable income or net loss to compute current E&P. What is the rationale for making these adjustments?

LO 7-2 10. What must a shareholder consider in computing the amount of a noncash distribution to include in her gross income?

LO 7-2 11. What income tax issues must a corporation consider before it makes a noncash distribution to a shareholder?

LO 7-2 12. Will the shareholder's tax basis in noncash property received equal the amount she includes in gross income as a dividend? Under what circumstances will the amounts be different, if any?

LO 7-2 13. A shareholder receives appreciated noncash property from his corporation and assumes a liability attached to the property. How does the assumption of a liability affect the amount of dividend he reports in gross income?

LO 7-2 14. A shareholder receives appreciated noncash property from his corporation and assumes a liability attached to the property. How does this assumption affect the amount of gain the corporation recognizes? From the corporation's perspective, does it matter if the liability assumed by the shareholder exceeds the property's gross fair market value?

LO 7-2 15. A corporation distributes appreciated noncash property to a shareholder as a dividend. What impact does the distribution have on the corporation's earnings and profits?

LO 7-3 16. Amy is the sole shareholder of her corporation. Rather than have the corporation pay her a dividend, Amy decides to have the corporation declare a "bonus" at year-end and pay her tax-deductible compensation. What potential tax issue may arise in this situation? Which parties, Amy or the corporation or both, are affected by the classification of the payment?

LO 7-4 17. Why might a corporation issue a stock dividend to its shareholders?

18. What tax issue arises when a shareholder receives a nontaxable stock dividend? LO 7-4
19. In general, what causes a stock dividend to be taxable to the recipient? LO 7-4
20. What are the potential tax consequences to a shareholder who participates in a stock redemption? LO 7-5
21. What stock ownership tests must be met before a shareholder receives exchange treatment under the substantially disproportionate change-in-stock-ownership test in a stock redemption? Why is a change-in-stock-ownership test used to determine the tax status of a stock redemption? LO 7-5
22. What are the criteria to meet the "not essentially equivalent to a dividend" change-in-stock-ownership test in a stock redemption? LO 7-5
23. When might a shareholder have to rely on the not essentially equivalent to a dividend test in arguing that her stock redemption should be treated as an exchange for tax purposes? LO 7-5
24. Why do you think the tax law imposes constructive stock ownership rules on stock redemptions? LO 7-5
25. Which members of a family are included in the family attribution rules? Is there any rationale for the family members included in the test? LO 7-5
26. Ilya and Olga are brother and sister. Ilya owns 200 shares of stock in Parker Corporation. Is Olga deemed to own Ilya's 200 shares under the family attribution rules that apply to stock redemptions? LO 7-5
27. Maria has all of her stock in Mayan Corporation redeemed. Under what conditions will Maria treat the redemption as an exchange and recognize capital gain or loss? LO 7-5
28. What must a shareholder do to waive the family attribution rules in a complete redemption of stock? LO 7-5
29. How does a corporation's computation of earnings and profits differ based on the tax treatment of a stock redemption to the shareholder (i.e., as either a dividend or exchange)? LO 7-5
30. How does the tax treatment of a partial liquidation differ from a stock redemption? LO 7-6
31. Bevo Corporation experienced a complete loss of its mill as the result of a fire. The company received $2 million from the insurance company. Rather than rebuild, Bevo decided to distribute the $2 million to its two shareholders. No stock was exchanged in return. Under what conditions will the distribution meet the requirements to be a partial liquidation and not a dividend? Why does it matter to the shareholders? LO 7-6

PROBLEMS

All applicable problems are available with McGraw-Hill's *Connect® Accounting.*

32. Gopher Corporation reported taxable income of $500,000 this year. Gopher paid a dividend of $100,000 to its sole shareholder, Sven Anderson. Gopher Corporation is subject to a flat-rate tax of 34 percent. The dividend meets the requirements to be a qualified dividend, and Sven is subject to a tax rate of 15 percent on the dividend. What is the income tax imposed on the corporate income earned by Gopher and the income tax on the dividend distributed to Sven? LO 7-1
33. Bulldog Corporation reported taxable income of $500,000 this year, before any deduction for any payment to its sole shareholder and employee, Georgia Brown. Bulldog chose to pay a bonus of $100,000 to Georgia at year-end. Bulldog Corporation is subject to a flat-rate tax of 34 percent. The bonus meets the requirements to be "reasonable" and is therefore deductible by Bulldog. Georgia is subject to a marginal tax rate of 35 percent on the bonus. What is the income tax imposed on the corporate income earned by Bulldog and the income tax on the bonus paid to Georgia? LO 7-1

LO 7-2 34. Hawkeye Company reports current E&P of $300,000 this year and accumulated E&P at the beginning of the year of $200,000. Hawkeye distributed $400,000 to its sole shareholder, Ray Kinsella, on December 31 of this year. Ray's tax basis in his Hawkeye stock is $75,000.

a) How much of the $400,000 distribution is treated as a dividend to Ray?
b) What is Ray's tax basis in his Hawkeye stock after the distribution?
c) What is Hawkeye's balance in accumulated E&P as of January 1 of next year?

LO 7-2 35. Jayhawk Company reports current E&P of $300,000 and accumulated E&P of negative $200,000. Jayhawk distributed $400,000 to its sole shareholder, Christine Rock, on the last day of the year. Christine's tax basis in her Jayhawk stock is $75,000.

a) How much of the $400,000 distribution is treated as a dividend to Christine?
b) What is Christine's tax basis in her Jayhawk stock after the distribution?
c) What is Jayhawk's balance in accumulated E&P on the first day of next year?

LO 7-2 36. This year, Sooner Company reports current E&P of negative $300,000. Its accumulated E&P at the beginning of the year was $200,000. Sooner distributed $400,000 to its sole shareholder, Boomer Wells, on June 30 of this year. Boomer's tax basis in his Sooner stock is $75,000.

a) How much of the $400,000 distribution is treated as a dividend to Boomer?
b) What is Boomer's tax basis in his Sooner stock after the distribution?
c) What is Sooner's balance in accumulated E&P on the first day of next year?

LO 7-2 37. Blackhawk Company reports current E&P of negative $300,000. Its accumulated E&P at the beginning of the year was a negative $200,000. Blackhawk distributed $400,000 to its sole shareholder, Melanie Rushmore, on June 30 of this year. Melanie's tax basis in her Blackhawk stock is $75,000.

a) How much of the $400,000 distribution is treated as a dividend to Melanie?
b) What is Melanie's tax basis in her Blackhawk stock after the distribution?
c) What is Blackhawk's balance in accumulated E&P on the first day of next year?

LO 7-2 38. This year, Jolt Inc. reported $40,000 of taxable income before any charitable contribution deduction. Jolt contributed $10,000 this year to Goodwill Industries, a public charity. Compute the company's current E&P.

LO 7-2 39. Boilermaker Inc. reported taxable income of $500,000 this year and paid federal income taxes of $170,000. Not included in the company's computation of taxable income is tax-exempt income of $20,000, disallowed meals and entertainment expenses of $30,000, and disallowed expenses related to the tax-exempt income of $1,000. Boilermaker deducted depreciation of $100,000 on its tax return. Under the alternative (E&P) depreciation method, the deduction would have been $60,000. Compute the company's current E&P.

LO 7-2 40. Gator Inc. reported taxable income of $1,000,000 this year and paid federal income taxes of $340,000. Included in the company's computation of taxable income is gain from the sale of a depreciable asset of $50,000. The income tax basis of the asset was $100,000. The E&P basis of the asset using the alternative depreciation system was $175,000. Compute the company's current E&P.

LO 7-2 41. Paladin Inc. reported taxable income of $1,000,000 this year and paid federal income taxes of $340,000. The company reported a capital gain from sale of investments of $150,000, which was partially offset by a $100,000 net capital loss carryover from last year, resulting in a net capital gain of $50,000 included in taxable income. Compute the company's current E&P.

LO 7-2 42. Volunteer Corporation reported taxable income of $500,000 from operations this year. The company paid federal income taxes of $170,000 on this taxable income. During the year, the company made a distribution of land to its sole shareholder, Rocky Topp. The land's fair market value was $75,000 and its tax and E&P basis to Volunteer was $25,000. Rocky assumed a mortgage attached to the land of $15,000. Any gain from the distribution will be taxed at 34 percent. The company had accumulated E&P of $750,000 at the beginning of the year.

a) Compute Volunteer's total taxable income and federal income tax.
b) Compute Volunteer's current E&P.
c) Compute Volunteer's accumulated E&P at the beginning of next year.
d) What amount of dividend income does Rocky report as a result of the distribution?
e) What is Rocky's income tax basis in the land received from Volunteer?

43. Tiger Corporation reported taxable income of $500,000 from operations this year. The company paid federal income taxes of $170,000 on this taxable income. During the year, the company made a distribution of land to its sole shareholder, Mike Woods. The land's fair market value was $75,000 and its tax and E&P basis to Tiger was $125,000. Mike assumed a mortgage attached to the land of $15,000. Any gain from the distribution will be taxed at 34 percent. The company had accumulated E&P of $750,000 at the beginning of the year. LO 7-2

a) Compute Tiger's total taxable income and federal income tax.
b) Compute Tiger's current E&P.
c) Compute Tiger's accumulated E&P at the beginning of next year.
d) What amount of dividend income does Mike report as a result of the distribution?
e) What is Mike's tax basis in the land he received from Tiger?

44. Illini Corporation reported taxable income of $500,000 from operations for this year. The company paid federal income taxes of $170,000 on this taxable income. During the year, the company made a distribution of an automobile to its sole shareholder, Carly Urbana. The auto's fair market value was $30,000 and its tax basis to Illini was $0. The auto's E&P basis was $15,000. Any gain from the distribution will be taxed at 34 percent. Illini had accumulated E&P of $1,500,000. LO 7-2

a) Compute Illini's total taxable income and federal income tax.
b) Compute Illini's current E&P.
c) Compute Illini's accumulated E&P at the beginning of next year.
d) What amount of dividend income does Carly report as a result of the distribution?
e) What is Carly's tax basis in the auto she received from Illini?

45. Beaver Corporation reported taxable income of $500,000 from operations this year. The company paid federal income taxes of $170,000 on this taxable income. During the year, the company made a distribution of land to its sole shareholder, Eugenia VanDam. The land's fair market value was $20,000 and its tax and E&P basis to Beaver was $50,000. Eugenia assumed a mortgage on the land of $25,000. Any gain from the distribution will be taxed at 34 percent. Beaver Corporation had accumulated E&P of $1,500,000. LO 7-2

a) Compute Beaver's total taxable income and federal income tax.
b) Compute Beaver's current E&P.
c) Compute Beaver's accumulated E&P at the beginning of next year.
d) What amount of dividend income does Eugenia report as a result of the distribution?

46. Tiny and Tim each own half of the 100 outstanding shares of Flower Corporation. This year, Flower reported taxable income of $6,000 and was subject to a 25 percent tax rate. In addition, Flower received $20,000 of life insurance proceeds due to the death of an employee (Flower paid $500 in life insurance LO 7-2

research

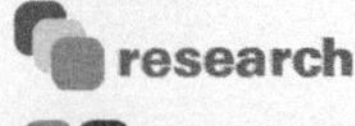

tax forms

premiums this year). Flower had $5,000 of accumulated E&P at the beginning of the year.

a) What is Flower's current E&P?

b) Flower distributed $6,000 on February 15 and $30,000 on August 1. What total amount of dividends will Tiny and Tim report?

c) What amount of capital gain (if any) would Tiny and Tim report on the distributions in part (b) if their stock basis is $2,000 and $10,000, respectively?

d) What form would Flower use to report nondividend distributions?

e) On what form (line) would Tiny and Tim report nondividend distributions?

LO 7-3

47. Nittany Company pays its sole shareholder, Tammy Lion, a salary of $100,000. At the end of each year, the company pays Tammy a "bonus" equal to the difference between the corporation's taxable income for the year (before the bonus) and $75,000. In this way, the company hopes to keep its taxable income at amounts that are taxed at either 15 percent or 25 percent. This year Nittany reported pre-bonus taxable income of $675,000 and paid Tammy a bonus of $600,000. On audit, the IRS determined that individuals working in Tammy's position earned on average $300,000 per year. The company had no formal compensation policy and never paid a dividend.

a) How much of Tammy's bonus might the IRS recharacterize as a dividend?

b) What arguments might Tammy make to counter this assertion?

c) Assuming the IRS recharacterizes $200,000 of Tammy's bonus as a dividend, what additional income tax liability does Nittany Company face?

LO 7-4

48. Hoosier Corporation declared a 2-for-1 stock split to all shareholders of record on March 25 of this year. Hoosier reported current E&P of $600,000 and accumulated E&P of $3,000,000. The total fair market value of the stock distributed was $1,500,000. Barbara Bloomington owned 1,000 shares of Hoosier stock with a tax basis of $100 per share.

a) What amount of taxable dividend income, if any, does Barbara recognize this year? Assume the fair market value of the stock was $150 per share on March 25 of this year.

b) What is Barbara's income tax basis in the new and existing stock she owns in Hoosier Corporation, assuming the distribution is tax-free?

c) How does the stock dividend affect Hoosier's accumulated E&P at the beginning of next year?

LO 7-4

49. Badger Corporation declared a stock dividend to all shareholders of record on March 25 of this year. Shareholders will receive one share of Badger stock for each 10 shares of stock they already own. Madison Cheeseman owns 1,000 shares of Badger stock with a tax basis of $100 per share. The fair market value of the Badger stock was $110 per share on March 25 of this year.

a) What amount of taxable dividend income, if any, does Madison recognize this year?

b) What is Madison's income tax basis in her new and existing stock in Badger Corporation, assuming the distribution is nontaxable?

c) How would you answer parts (a) and (b) if Madison was offered the choice between one share of stock in Badger for each ten shares she owned or $100 cash for each ten shares she owned in Badger?

LO 7-5

50. Wildcat Company is owned equally by Evan Stone and his sister Sara, each of whom hold 1,000 shares in the company. Sara wants to reduce her ownership in the company, and it was decided that the company will redeem 500 of her shares for $25,000 per share on December 31 of this year. Sara's income tax basis in each share is $5,000. Wildcat has current E&P of $10,000,000 and accumulated E&P of $50,000,000.

a) What is the amount and character (capital gain or dividend) recognized by Sara as a result of the stock redemption?
b) What is Sara's income tax basis in the remaining 500 shares she owns in the company?
c) Assuming the company did not make any dividend distributions during this year, by what amount does Wildcat reduce its E&P as a result of the redemption?

51. Flintstone Company is owned equally by Fred Stone and his sister Wilma, each of whom hold 1,000 shares in the company. Wilma wants to reduce her ownership in the company, and it was decided that the company will redeem 250 of her shares for $25,000 per share on December 31 of this year. Wilma's income tax basis in each share is $5,000. Flintstone has current E&P of $10,000,000 and accumulated E&P of $50,000,000. LO 7-5
a) What is the amount and character (capital gain or dividend) recognized by Wilma as a result of the stock redemption, assuming only the "substantially disproportionate with respect to the shareholder" test is applied?
b) Given your answer to part (a), what is Wilma's income tax basis in the remaining 750 shares she owns in the company?
c) Assuming the company did not make any dividend distributions this year, by what amount does Flintstone reduce its E&P as a result of the redemption?
d) What other argument might Wilma make to treat the redemption as an exchange?

52. Acme Corporation has 1,000 shares outstanding. Joan and Bill are married, and they each own 20 shares of Acme. Joan's daughter, Shirley, also owns 20 shares of Acme. Joan is an equal partner with Jeri in the J&J partnership, and this partnership owns 60 shares of Acme. Jeri is not related to Joan or Bill. How many shares of Acme is Shirley deemed to own under the stock attribution rules? LO 7-5

53. Bedrock Inc. is owned equally by Barney Rubble and his wife Betty, each of whom hold 1,000 shares in the company. Betty wants to reduce her ownership in the company, and it was decided that the company will redeem 500 of her shares for $25,000 per share on December 31 of this year. Betty's income tax basis in each share is $5,000. Bedrock has current E&P of $10,000,000 and accumulated E&P of $50,000,000. LO 7-5
a) What is the amount and character (capital gain or dividend) recognized by Betty as a result of the stock redemption, assuming only the "substantially disproportionate with respect to the shareholder" test is applied?
b) Given your answer to part (a), what is Betty's income tax basis in the remaining 500 shares she owns in the company?
c) Assuming the company did not make any dividend distributions this year, by what amount does Bedrock reduce its E&P as a result of the redemption?
d) Can Betty argue that the redemption is "not essentially equivalent to a dividend" and should be treated as an exchange?

54. Assume in problem 53 that Betty and Barney are not getting along and have separated due to marital discord (although they are not legally separated). In fact, they cannot even stand to talk to each other anymore and communicate only through their accountant. Betty wants to argue that she should not be treated as owning any of Barney's stock in Bedrock because of their hostility toward each other. Can family hostility be used as an argument to void the family attribution rules? Consult Rev. Rul. 80-26, 1980-1 C.B. 66, *Robin Haft Trust v. Comm.*, 510 F.2d 43 (CA-1 1975), *Metzger Trust v. Comm.*, 693 F.2d 459 (CA-5 1982), and *Cerone v. Comm.*, 87 TC 1 (1986). LO 7-5 research

LO 7-5

55. Boots Inc. is owned equally by Frank Albert and his daughter Nancy, each of whom hold 1,000 shares in the company. Frank wants to retire from the company, and it was decided that the company will redeem all 1,000 of his shares for $25,000 per share on December 31 of this year. Frank's income tax basis in each share is $500. Boots Inc. has current E&P of $1,000,000 and accumulated E&P of $5,000,000.
   a) What must Frank do to ensure that the redemption will be treated as an exchange?
   b) If Frank remained as the chairman of the board after the redemption, what is the amount and character (capital gain or dividend) of income that Frank will recognize this year?
   c) If Frank treats the redemption as a dividend, what happens to his stock basis in the 1,000 shares redeemed?

LO 7-5
research

56. In the previous problem, Nancy would like to have Frank stay on as a consultant after all of his shares are redeemed. She would pay him a modest amount of $500 per month. Nancy wants to know if there is any *de minimus* rule such that Frank would not be treated as having retained a prohibited interest in the company because he is receiving such a small amount of money. Consult *Lynch v. Comm.*, 801 F.2d 1176 (CA-9 1986), *reversing* 83 T.C. 597 (1984), *Seda,* 82 T.C. 484 (1984), and *Cerone,* 87 T.C. 1 (1986).

LO 7-5
planning

57. Limited Brands recently repurchased 68,965,000 of its shares, paying $29 per share. The total number of shares outstanding before the redemption was 473,223,066. The total number of shares outstanding after the redemption was 404,258,066. Assume your client owned 20,000 shares of stock in The Limited. What is the minimum number of shares she must tender to receive exchange treatment under the "substantially disproportionate with respect to the shareholder" change-in-ownership rules?

LO 7-5

58. Cougar Company is owned equally by Cat Stevens and a partnership that is owned equally by his father and two unrelated individuals. Cat and the partnership each own 3,000 shares in the company. Cat wants to reduce his ownership in the company, and it is decided that the company will redeem 1,500 of his shares for $25,000 per share. Cat's income tax basis in each share is $5,000. What are the income tax consequences to Cat as a result of the stock redemption, assuming the company has earnings and profits of $10 million?

LO 7-5
planning

59. Oriole Corporation, a privately held company, has one class of voting common stock, of which 1,000 shares are issued and outstanding. The shares are owned as follows:

Larry Byrd	400
Paul Byrd (Larry's son)	200
Lady Byrd (Larry's daughter)	200
Cal Rifkin (unrelated)	200
Total	1,000

Larry is considering retirement and would like to have the corporation redeem all of his shares for $400,000.
   a) What must Larry do or consider if he wants to guarantee that the redemption will be treated as an exchange?
   b) Could Larry act as a consultant to the company and still have the redemption treated as an exchange?

LO 7-5
research

60. Using the facts from the previous problem, Oriole Corporation proposes to pay Larry $100,000 and give him an installment note that will pay him $30,000 per year for the next 10 years plus a market rate of interest. Will this

arrangement allow Larry to treat the redemption as an exchange? Consult §453(k)(2)(A).

61. EG Corporation redeemed 200 shares of stock from one of its shareholders in exchange for $200,000. The redemption represented 20 percent of the corporation's outstanding stock. The redemption was treated as an exchange by the shareholder. By what amount does EG reduce its total E&P as a result of the redemption under the following E&P assumptions? LO 7-5
   a) EG's total E&P at the time of the distribution was $2,000,000.
   b) EG's total E&P at the time of the distribution was $500,000.

62. Spartan Corporation redeemed 25 percent of its shares for $2,000 on July 1 of this year, in a transaction that qualified as an exchange under §302(a). Spartan's accumulated E&P at the beginning of the year was $2,000. Its current E&P is $12,000. Spartan made dividend distributions of $1,000 on June 1 and $4,000 on August 31. Determine the beginning balance in Spartan's accumulated E&P at the beginning of the next year. See Rev. Rul. 74-338, 1974-2 C.B. 101 and Rev. Rul. 74-339, 1974-2 C.B. 103 for help in making this calculation. LO 7-5 research

63. Bonnie and Clyde are the only two shareholders in Getaway Corporation. Bonnie owns 60 shares with a basis of $3,000, and Clyde owns the remaining 40 shares with a basis of $12,000. At year-end, Getaway is considering different alternatives for redeeming some shares of stock. Evaluate whether each of the following stock redemption transactions will qualify for sale and exchange treatment. LO 7-5
   a) Getaway redeems 10 of Bonnie's shares for $2,000. Getaway has $20,000 of E&P at year-end and Bonnie is unrelated to Clyde.
   b) Getaway redeems 25 of Bonnie's shares for $4,000. Getaway has $20,000 of E&P at year-end and Bonnie is unrelated to Clyde.
   c) Getaway redeems 10 of Clyde's shares for $2,500. Getaway has $20,000 of E&P at year-end and Clyde is unrelated to Bonnie.

64. Spartan Corporation made a distribution of $500,000 to Rusty Cedar in partial liquidation of the company on December 31 of this year. Rusty, an individual, owns 100 percent of Spartan Corporation. The distribution was in exchange for 50 percent of Rusty's stock in the company. At the time of the distribution, the shares had a fair market value of $200 per share. Rusty's income tax basis in the shares was $50 per share. Spartan had total E&P of $8,000,000 at the time of the distribution. LO 7-6
   a) What is the amount and character (capital gain or dividend) of any income or gain recognized by Rusty as a result of the partial liquidation?
   b) Assuming Spartan made no other distributions to Rusty during the year, by what amount does Spartan reduce its total E&P as a result of the partial liquidation?

65. Wolverine Corporation made a distribution of $500,000 to Jim Har Inc. in partial liquidation of the company on December 31 of this year. Jim Har Inc. owns 100 percent of Wolverine Corporation. The distribution was in exchange for 50 percent of Jim Har Inc.'s stock in the company. At the time of the distribution, the shares had a fair market value of $200 per share. Jim Har Inc.'s income tax basis in the shares was $50 per share. Wolverine had total E&P of $8,000,000 at the time of the distribution. LO 7-6
   a) What is the amount and character (capital gain or dividend) of any income or gain recognized by Jim Har Inc. as a result of the partial liquidation?
   b) Assuming Wolverine made no other distributions to Jim Har Inc. during the year, by what amount does Wolverine reduce its total E&P as a result of the partial liquidation?

COMPREHENSIVE PROBLEMS

All applicable problems are available with McGraw-Hill's *Connect® Accounting*.

66. Lanco Corporation, an accrual-method corporation, reported taxable income of $1,460,000 this year. Included in the computation of taxable income were the following items:

    - MACRS depreciation of $200,000. Straight-line depreciation would have been $120,000.
    - A net capital loss carryover of $10,000 from last year.
    - A net operating loss carryover of $25,000 from last year.
    - $65,000 capital gain from the distribution of land to the company's sole shareholder (see below).

    Not included in the computation of taxable income were the following items:

    - Tax-exempt income of $5,000.
    - Life insurance proceeds of $250,000.
    - Excess current year charitable contribution of $2,500 (to be carried over to next year).
    - Tax-deferred gain of $20,000 on a like-kind exchange.
    - Federal income tax refund from last year of $35,000.
    - Nondeductible life insurance premium of $3,500.
    - Nondeductible interest expense of $1,000 on a loan used to buy tax-exempt bonds.

    Lanco paid federal income taxes this year of $496,400. The company's accumulated E&P at the beginning of the year was $2,400,000. During the year, Lanco made the following distributions to its sole shareholder, Luigi (Lug) Nutt:

    - June 30: $50,000.
    - September 30: Parcel of land with a fair market value of $75,000. Lanco's tax basis in the land was $10,000. Lug assumed an existing mortgage on the property of $15,000.

Required:

a) Compute Lanco's current E&P for this year.
b) Compute the amount of dividend income reported by Lug Nutt this year as a result of the distributions.
c) Compute Lanco's accumulated E&P at the beginning of next year.

67. Petoskey Stone Quarry Inc. (PSQ), a calendar-year, accrual-method C corporation, provides landscaping supplies to local builders in northern Michigan. PSQ has always been a family-owned business and has a single class of voting common stock outstanding. The 500 outstanding shares are owned as follows:

Nick Adams	150
Amy Adams (Nick's sister)	150
Abigail Adams (Nick's daughter)	50
Charlie Adams (Nick's son)	50
Sandler Adams (Nick's father)	100
Total shares	500

Nick Adams serves as president of PSQ, and his father Sandler serves as chairman of the board. Amy is the company's CFO, and Abigail and Charlie work as employees of the company. Sandler would like to retire and sell his shares back to the company. The fair market value of the shares is $500,000. Sandler's tax basis is $10,000. The redemption is tentatively scheduled to take place on December 31 of this year. At the beginning of the year, PSQ had accumulated earnings and profits of $2,500,000. The company projects current E&P of $200,000. The company intends to pay pro rata cash dividends of $300 per share to its shareholders on December 1 of this year.

Required:

a) Assume the redemption takes place as planned on December 31 and no elections are made by the shareholders.
   1. What amount of dividend or capital gain will Sandler recognize as a result of the stock redemption?
   2. How will the tax basis of Sandler's stock be allocated to the remaining shareholders?

b) What must Sandler and the other shareholders do to change the tax results you calculated in part (a)?

c) Compute PSQ's accumulated earnings and profits on January 1 of next year, assuming the redemption is treated as an exchange.

68. Thriller Corporation has one class of voting common stock, of which 1,000 shares are issued and outstanding. The shares are owned as follows:

Joe Jackson	400
Mike Jackson (Joe's son)	200
Jane Jackson (Joe's daughter)	200
Vinnie Price (unrelated)	200
Total	1,000

Thriller Corporation has current E&P of $300,000 for this year and accumulated E&P at January 1 of this year of $500,000. During this year, the corporation made the following distributions to its shareholders:

03/31: Paid a dividend of $10 per share to each shareholder ($10,000 in total).

06/30: Redeemed 200 shares of Joe's stock for $200,000. Joe's basis in the 200 shares redeemed was $100,000.

09/30: Redeemed 60 shares of Vinnie's stock for $60,000. His basis in the 60 shares was $36,000.

12/31: Paid a dividend of $10/share to each shareholder ($7,400 in total).

Required:

a) Determine the tax status of each distribution made this year. (*Hint:* First, consider if the redemptions are treated as dividend distributions or exchanges.)

b) Compute the corporation's accumulated E&P at January 1 of next year.

c) Joe is considering retirement and would like to have the corporation redeem all of his shares for $100,000 plus a 10-year note with a fair market value of $300,000.
   1. What must Joe do or consider if he wants to ensure that the redemption will be treated as an exchange?
   2. Could Joe still act as a consultant to the company?

d) Thriller Corporation must pay attorney's fees of $5,000 to facilitate the stock redemptions. Is this fee deductible?

chapter

8 Corporate Formation, Reorganization, and Liquidation

Learning Objectives

Upon completing this chapter, you should be able to:

LO 8-1 Review the taxation of property dispositions.

LO 8-2 Compute the tax consequences to the parties to a tax-deferred corporate formation.

LO 8-3 Identify the different forms of taxable and tax-deferred acquisitions.

LO 8-4 Determine the tax consequences to the parties to a corporate acquisition.

LO 8-5 Calculate the tax consequences that apply to the parties to a complete liquidation of a corporation.

© Purestock/Superstock

Storyline Summary

Spartan Cycle and Repair

Privately held company located in East Lansing, Michigan

Sells and repairs high-end bicycles

Jim Wheeler

Co-owner of Spartan Cycle and Repair (75 percent)

Filing status:	Married filing jointly
Dependents:	One child
Marginal tax rate:	40 percent

Ginny Gears

Co-owner of Spartan Cycles and Repair (25 percent)

Filing status:	Unmarried
Marginal tax rate:	25 percent

360 Air

Privately held company in East Lansing, Michigan

Sells snowboarding equipment

Al Pine

Owner of 360 Air

Filing status:	Unmarried
Marginal tax rate:	35 percent

Jim Wheeler and Ginny Gears were excited about the growth of their business, Spartan Cycles and Repair (SCR). The business had a solid base of loyal customers and was showing a healthy profit, and Jim and Ginny were ready for some new challenges. They have considered expanding the bicycle business to a new geographic region and branching out into a new line of business. Given the seasonal nature of the demand for bicycle products and repair in Michigan, Jim and Ginny favor a complementary line of business that would provide them with a source of income during the winter months. Ginny was impressed with the growing popularity of snowboarding, especially among young people. Factors that contributed to this growth included low equipment costs (especially compared to skiing), easily attained skills, a "coolness" attractive to young people, and the sport's inclusion in the Olympic games.

Jim and Ginny were aware of a small snowboarding store in East Lansing called 360 Air that was named after a daring snowboarding maneuver. The business was owned and operated by Al Pine, a rather free-spirited individual whose enthusiasm for the sport was not matched by his business acumen.

Jim and Ginny feel that with some additional capital investment and marketing effort, they could turn Al's snowboarding business into a profitable operation. They set up a meeting with Al to discuss how they could become partners in his business enterprise.

After some negotiation, Jim, Ginny, and Al agreed to jointly operate the snowboarding business through a C corporation. Al had been operating his business as a sole proprietorship. As part of the incorporation process, each of the three individuals will make a contribution of property or services to the corporation in return for stock. Al will contribute his existing inventory as well as the building and land on which the building was situated in return for 50 percent of the stock in 360 Air. The corporation would assume the existing mortgage on the property. Jim will contribute cash in exchange for 40 percent of the stock, and Ginny will contribute her marketing services in return for 10 percent of the stock.

Each of the parties wants to know the income tax implications of incorporating Al's ongoing business. In addition, Jim is wondering if the manner in which they are intending to create the corporation is tax efficient, and whether there are other issues they should consider that would lessen the tax burdens of both the corporation and its new shareholders. They turned to their trusted tax accountant, Louis Tully, for his expertise.

to be continued . . .

When creating a business, the owners must choose the organizational form for operating the business. The choice of legal entity affects how (whether) the income or loss generated by the business is taxed at the entity level and the owner level. At some point during the life of a business, the owners may decide to change its tax status. In the case of an ongoing business, such as 360 Air, the decision to change to a corporate tax status will involve the transfer of assets and liabilities by one or more of the owners in return for stock in the corporation. These property transfers raise several tax questions. A transfer of assets or liabilities to a corporation in exchange for stock triggers realization of gains and losses and may cause shareholders to recognize gains in the year of the transfer. In addition, shareholders will need to calculate the tax basis of their stock and the corporation will need to determine the basis of the assets and liabilities received in the transfer.

LO 8-1 REVIEW THE TAXATION OF PROPERTY DISPOSITIONS

This section provides a brief review of tax rules that apply to transfers of property to a corporation in the incorporation process. Before gain or loss is *recognized* (included in taxable income), it must first be *realized*. **Realization** generally occurs when a *transaction* takes place (i.e., an exchange of property rights between two persons).

Exhibit 8-1 provides a template for computing gain or loss realized by a party to a property transaction.

EXHIBIT 8-1 Computing Gain or Loss Realized in a Property Transaction[1]

	Amount realized (received)
−	Adjusted tax basis of the property transferred
	Gain (+) or loss (−) realized

The **amount realized** is computed using the template in Exhibit 8-2.

EXHIBIT 8-2 Computing the Amount Realized in a Property Transaction[2]

	Cash received
+	Fair market value of other property received
+	Liabilities assumed by the transferee on the transferred property
−	Selling expenses incurred in the transaction
−	Liabilities assumed by the transferor on any property received in the exchange
	Amount realized

A property's **adjusted tax basis** is calculated using the template in Exhibit 8-3.

EXHIBIT 8-3 Computing a Property's Adjusted Tax Basis in a Property Transaction[3]

	Acquisition basis
+	Capital improvements
−	Depreciation
	Adjusted tax basis

THE KEY FACTS

Overview of the Taxation of Property Transactions

- Gain or loss is realized when a person engages in a transaction (an exchange of property rights with another person).
- Gain or loss realized is computed by subtracting the transferor's tax-adjusted basis in the property exchanged from the amount realized in the exchange.
- Gain or loss realized is recognized (included in the computation of taxable income) unless exempted or deferred by a provision of the tax laws.

The entire amount of gain or deductible loss realized is recognized unless *otherwise provided* by the Internal Revenue Code.[4] Gain or loss is not recognized if (1) the gain or loss is *excluded* from gross income (the gain or loss will never be recognized) or (2) the gain or deductible loss is *deferred* from gross income (recognition of the gain or deductible loss is postponed to a future period). Transfers of property to a corporation are transactions in which realized gain or loss may be deferred if certain requirements are met.[5] Recognition of a deferred gain or loss is postponed until the property received in the exchange is subsequently disposed of (e.g., recognition of Al's realized gain will be postponed until he sells his stock in 360 Air).

[1]§1001(a).
[2]§1001(b).
[3]§1011.
[4]§1001(c). Realized losses must be deductible to be recognized. Nondeductible losses are never recognized.
[5]§351.

LO 8-2

TAX-DEFERRED TRANSFERS OF PROPERTY TO A CORPORATION

In the formation of a corporation, or in subsequent transfers of property to an existing corporation, shareholders transfer cash and noncash property to the corporation in return for stock in the corporation. The stock can be common or preferred, voting or nonvoting.[6]

Example 8-1

As part of the incorporation of 360 Air, Al Pine will transfer inventory, a building, and land to the corporation in return for 50 percent of the corporation's stock (50 shares). The property has the following fair market values and adjusted bases:

	FMV	Adjusted Basis
Inventory	$ 25,000	$ 15,000
Building	150,000	60,000
Land	200,000	100,000
Total	$375,000	$175,000

The corporation will assume a mortgage of $75,000 attached to the building and land. The fair market value of the 360 Air stock Al will receive in the exchange is $300,000. How much net gain or loss does Al *realize* in the exchange?

Answer: Al realizes a net gain of $200,000 on this transfer, computed as follows:

	Fair market value of 360 Air stock received	$300,000
+	Mortgage assumed by 360 Air	75,000
	Amount realized	$375,000
−	Adjusted tax basis of the property transferred	175,000
	Gain realized	$200,000

THE KEY FACTS

Requirements for Tax Deferral in a Corporate Formation

- Tax deferral only applies to transfers of property to a corporation.
- The persons transferring property to a corporation must receive solely stock in the corporation in return.
- The persons transferring property to a corporation must collectively control the corporation after the transaction.
- Control is defined as ownership of 80 percent or more of the corporation's voting stock and 80 percent or more of each class of nonvoting stock.
- Stock received in exchange for services can be counted in the control test if the transferor also receives stock in exchange for property with a fair market value of 10 percent or more of the services rendered.

Gain or loss deferred in the transfer of property to a corporation in return for stock is reflected in the shareholder's *tax basis* in the stock received in exchange for the transferred property.[7] A deferred gain *decreases* the shareholder's tax basis in the stock to an amount equal to the stock's fair market value less the gain deferred. A deferred loss *increases* the shareholder's tax basis in the stock to an amount equal to the stock's fair market value plus the loss deferred. In essence, the shareholder's tax basis in the stock received reflects the deferred gain or loss.

Congress provides for the deferral of gain or loss on the transfer of property to a corporation in exchange for stock to remove tax consequences as an impediment to forming a corporation and to provide taxpayers with flexibility in choosing their preferred form of doing business. Congress justified tax deferral because shareholders maintained an interest in the property transferred through a different form of ownership (from direct ownership to indirect ownership through stock).

[6]A category of stock with different rights (e.g., voting rights, dividend rights, liquidation rights) is referred to as a *class* of stock.

[7]§358.

Example 8-2

Assume Al meets the tax law requirements to defer recognizing the $200,000 gain realized in the property transfer to 360 Air. The fair market value of the 360 Air stock he receives in the exchange is $300,000. What is Al's tax basis in the stock received?

Answer: $100,000. To reflect the deferral of the gain in his tax basis in the stock, Al's tax basis must be $100,000 ($300,000 − $200,000 gain deferred). If he subsequently sells the stock for $300,000, Al will recognize the $200,000 gain deferred previously ($300,000 − $100,000).

What if: Assume Al realized a $100,000 loss on the exchange of his property for stock in 360 Air. What would be his tax basis in the stock received?

Answer: $400,000. To reflect the deferral of the loss in his tax basis in the stock, Al's tax basis must be $400,000 ($300,000 + $100,000 loss deferred). If he subsequently sells the stock for $300,000, Al will recognize the $100,000 loss deferred previously ($300,000 − $400,000).

Transactions Subject to Tax Deferral

For shareholders to receive tax deferral in a transfer of property to a corporation, the transferors must meet the requirements of IRC §351. Section 351 applies to those transactions in which one or more shareholders transfer property to a corporation in return for stock, and immediately after the transfer, these same shareholders, in the aggregate, control the corporation to which they transferred the property. When the requirements are met, deferral of gain or loss in a §351 transaction is mandatory. Section 351 applies to transfers of property to both C corporations and S corporations.

Section 351 applies only to those **persons** who transfer property to the corporation in exchange for stock (i.e., shareholders). The IRC defines a person for tax purposes as including individuals, corporations, partnerships, and fiduciaries (estates and trusts).[8] Thus, §351 allows individuals like Al to form a corporation and also allows existing corporations such as General Electric to create a subsidiary. The corporation receiving the property in exchange for its own stock is not subject to tax when it receives property.[9]

Meeting the Section 351 Tax Deferral Requirements

The shareholders transferring property to a corporation must meet several requirements for the transfer to be tax deferred. Some of these requirements are not precisely defined in either the IRC or the regulations. As a result, much of what we understand about the parameters of §351 has developed over time as the IRS and the courts have attempted to discern Congressional intent. This incremental approach to understanding the parameters within which §351 operates is prevalent throughout subchapter C of the Internal Revenue Code.[10]

Section 351 Applies Only to the Transfer of Property to the Corporation

Most assets (tangible and intangible) meet the definition of property for purposes of §351. Property includes money, tangible assets, and intangible assets

[8]§7701(a)(1).

[9]§1032. Note, however, that under GAAP a corporation will record contributed property at fair value for book purposes. Hence, a contribution of property under §351 will give rise to book–tax differences because different amounts of depreciation will be recorded for book and tax purposes.

[10]Subchapter C encompasses IRC §§ 301–385 and provides the tax rules for the corporate transactions discussed in this chapter. Tax advisers who specialize in structuring corporate transactions often are referred to as "subchapter C experts."

(e.g., company name, patents, customer lists, trademarks, and logos). Services are excluded from the definition of property. Thus, a person who receives stock in return for services generally has compensation equal to the fair market value of the stock received.[11]

Example 8-3

As part of the incorporation, Ginny received 10 percent of the stock in 360 Air valued at $60,000 in exchange for her services in setting up the corporation. Will Ginny defer recognition of the $60,000 "gain" she realizes on the transaction?

Answer: No. Ginny must report compensation income of $60,000 as a result of this exchange because services are not considered property under §351.

What if: Suppose Ginny received 10 percent of the stock in 360 Air valued at $60,000 in exchange for a catchphrase she created to provide the company with a distinctive logo. Assume her tax basis in the catchphrase is zero because she created it. Will Ginny defer recognition of the $60,000 gain she realizes on the transfer of the catchphrase?

Answer: Yes. Ginny defers recognition of the $60,000 gain realized because intangibles are considered property under §351.

The Property Transferred to the Corporation Must Be Exchanged for Stock of the Corporation When property is transferred to a corporation in exchange for stock and other property, only the portion of the transfer exchanged for stock will qualify for tax deferral. The portion of the transfer relating to other property is referred to as **boot.** The term *boot* derives from a trading expression where a party to an exchange might throw in additional property "*to boot*" to equalize the exchange. The receipt of boot will cause the transferor to recognize gain, but not loss, realized on the exchange. We will discuss the details of this computation later in the chapter.

The type of stock a shareholder can receive in a §351 exchange is quite flexible and includes voting or nonvoting, common or preferred stock. Stock for purposes of §351 does not include stock warrants, rights, or options.[12] Property transferred in exchange for debt of the corporation is not eligible for deferral under §351.

Example 8-4

What if: Suppose Ginny received a five-year note (debt) in 360 Air valued at $60,000 in exchange for machinery. The original cost of the machinery was $70,000 and Ginny has depreciated it to a basis of zero. Will Ginny defer recognition of the $60,000 gain she realizes on the transfer of the machinery?

Answer: No. Section 351 provides for deferral only when the transferor of property receives stock in return. Ginny must recognize the entire $60,000 gain.

The Transferor(s) of Property to the Corporation Must Be in Control, in the Aggregate, of the Corporation Immediately after the Transfer Control for purposes of §351 is defined as the ownership of 80 percent or more of the

[11]An individual who receives stock subject to "restrictions" (e.g., she remains with the company for a certain number of years) does not report compensation income until the restrictions attached to the stock are lifted (§83) unless she elects to value the stock at the date received and report that amount as income (called a "§83(b) election").

[12]§351 precludes nonqualified preferred stock from qualifying as equity eligible for deferral. Nonqualified preferred stock generally has characteristics that cause it to more resemble debt than equity.

total combined *voting power* of all voting stock that is issued and outstanding, and 80 percent or more of the total number of shares of *each class* of nonvoting stock.[13]

Whether the control test is met is based on the collective ownership of the shareholders transferring property to the corporation immediately after the transfer. It is important to reiterate that this group of shareholders is only composed of those who have transferred property (not services) in exchange for stock and the aggregate ownership (not the change in ownership) of these shareholders immediately after the transfer must meet the 80 percent threshold.

ETHICS

Michelle owns appreciated property and she wants to use this property to start a business with her son, Lance. Michelle is considering making a contribution of the property to a newly organized corporation in exchange for 100 percent of the corporate stock. She then contemplates giving half of the stock to Lance in exchange for his promise to manage the business. Do you think this transaction will qualify for §351 treatment? Suppose that Michelle promises that she won't transfer the stock for a month after making the contribution of property. Any difference? Compare Rev. Rul. 54-96, 1954-1 CB 111 and *Intermountain Lumber Co.*, 65 TC 1025 (1976).

Example 8-5

What if: Assume Ginny was hesitant to join with Jim and Al in the incorporation of 360 Air. After six months, she changed her mind and received a 10 percent interest in 360 Air stock in exchange for intangibles that qualified as property under §351. The stock was valued at $60,000, and Ginny's tax basis in the intangibles was zero. Will Ginny defer recognition of the $60,000 gain she realized on the exchange under §351?

Answer: No. Ginny does not control (own 80 percent or more of the stock of) 360 Air immediately after the transfer. As a result, she must recognize the $60,000 gain.

Example 8-6

What if: Suppose Ginny joined with Jim and Al in the incorporation of 360 Air and received 25 percent of the corporation's stock in exchange for services. The stock was valued at $150,000. Al and Jim received the remaining 75 percent of the stock in the company in exchange for appreciated property. Will Al and Jim defer recognition of gain they realize on the exchange of the appreciated property under §351?

Answer: No. Taking into account only the stock received in exchange for property, Al and Jim do not collectively control 360 Air immediately after the transaction. Al and Jim own only 75%, not 80%. Consequently, the transaction is not eligible for deferral under §351, and all gain realized is recognized.

Generally when a shareholder transfers services and property to the corporation in exchange for stock, that shareholder is considered to be a transferor of property for purposes of the control test. However, if the primary purpose for the shareholder's transfer of property (in addition to services) to the corporation is to qualify the exchange of another person under §351, that shareholder would be considered to be a transferor of property only if the value of the stock received for property is not of "relatively small value" compared to the value of the stock received for services.[14] The IRS has stated that for ruling purposes, property will not be of *"relatively small value"* if it equals at least 10 percent of the value of the services provided.[15]

[13]§368(c). Voting power is generally defined as the ability of the shareholders to elect members of the corporation's board of directors.

[14]Reg. §1.351-1(a)(1)(ii).

[15]Rev. Proc. 77-37, 1977-2 C.B. 568.

Example 8-7

What if: Let's say Ginny joined with Jim and Al in the incorporation of 360 Air and received 25 percent of the corporation's stock in exchange for services and intangibles treated as property. The stock was valued at $150,000. The services were valued at $125,000 and the intangibles were valued at $25,000. Al and Jim received the remaining 75 percent of the stock in the company in exchange for appreciated property. Will Al and Jim defer recognition of gain they realize on the exchange of the appreciated property under §351?

Answer: Yes. The stock Ginny received in exchange for the intangibles exceeds 10 percent of the value of the services ($25,000/$125,000 = 20%). For purposes of determining control, Ginny will treat all of the stock she received in 360 Air as having been received for property. Al, Jim, and Ginny will be treated as collectively receiving 100 percent of the 360 Air stock in exchange for property. Hence, Al and Jim will defer gain realized on their exchanges of property for stock. Ginny will recognize compensation of $125,000 on the exchange, but she will defer recognizing any gain realized on the transfer of the intangibles.

What if: Assume Ginny's services were valued at $140,000 and the intangibles were valued at $10,000. Will Al and Jim defer recognition of gain they realize on the exchange of the appreciated property under §351?

Answer: No. The primary purpose of transferring the intangible property was to qualify the transfer for deferral. The fair market value of the intangibles is less than 10 percent of the fair market value of the services ($10,000/$140,000 = 7.14%). As a result, only the stock Ginny receives in exchange for the intangibles is counted in the control test ($10,000/$150,000 × 25% = 1.67%). Al, Jim, and Ginny are treated as having received collectively only 76.67 percent of 360 Air stock in exchange for property. Consequently, §351 does not apply to any of the transferors of the property to 360 Air.

This same rule applies to subsequent transfers of property by an existing shareholder to "accommodate" a new shareholder's transfer of property to an established corporation. The regulations state that stock received for property that is of "relatively small value" in comparison to the value of the stock already owned will not be considered issued in return for property (i.e., the shareholder making the contribution will not be included in the control test) if the "primary purpose" of the transfer is to qualify the exchanges of another person under §351. The IRS has stated that for ruling purposes, an existing shareholder must contribute property that has a fair market value of at least 10 percent of the value of the stock already owned to be included in the control test.[16]

Example 8-8

What if: Assume Jim and Ginny were 100 percent shareholders of SCR and wanted to bring Al on board as a 20 percent shareholder. Al will transfer appreciated property to SCR in return for stock in SCR valued at $100,000. Will Al defer recognizing any gain realized on the transfer under §351?

Answer: No. Al does not control SCR "immediately after" the exchange, taking into account only the stock he owns in SCR.

What if: Suppose Jim agreed to make an additional property contribution to SCR at the same time as Al's transfer in order to help Al qualify his transfer under §351. Jim's 75 percent ownership interest in SCR was valued at $300,000 at the time of Al's transfer. How much property (fair market value) must Jim contribute to SCR to have his ownership of stock in SCR counted in determining if Al qualifies for deferral under §351?

Answer: $30,000. For this "accommodation transfer" by Jim to be respected by the IRS, he must contribute property with a fair market value of 10 percent or more of the fair market value of his existing stock in SCR (10% × $300,000).

[16]Rev. Proc. 77-37, 1977-2 C.B. 568.

Tax Consequences to Shareholders

The tax basis of stock received in a tax-deferred §351 exchange equals the tax basis of the property transferred less any liability assumed by the corporation.[17] The stock is said to have a **substituted basis** (i.e., the basis of the property transferred is substituted for the basis of the property received).[18] Exhibit 8-4 provides a template for computing the tax basis of stock received in a tax-deferred §351 transaction.

EXHIBIT 8-4 Computing the Tax Basis of Stock Received in a Tax-Deferred Section 351 Transaction

	Cash contributed
+	Tax basis of other property contributed
−	Liabilities assumed by the corporation on property contributed
	Tax basis of stock received

Example 8-9

As part of the incorporation of 360 Air, Al transferred inventory, a building, and land to the corporation in return for 50 percent of the corporation's stock (50 shares). The property transferred to the corporation had the following fair market values and adjusted bases:

	FMV	Adjusted Basis
Inventory	$ 25,000	$ 15,000
Building	150,000	60,000
Land	200,000	100,000
Total	$375,000	$175,000

In addition, the corporation assumed a mortgage of $75,000 attached to the building and land. The fair market value of the 360 Air stock Al received in the exchange was $300,000. As we computed in Example 8-1, Al realizes a gain of $200,000 on the transfer, computed as follows:

	Fair market value of 360 Air stock received	$300,000
+	Mortgage assumed by 360 Air	75,000
	Amount realized	$375,000
−	Adjusted tax basis of the property transferred	175,000
	Gain realized	$200,000

Assuming Al meets the requirements under §351 to defer recognizing the $200,000 gain realized, what is his tax basis in the 50 shares of 360 Air stock he receives in the exchange?

Answer: $100,000. Al's tax basis in his stock must reflect the gain he defers in the exchange. He computes his tax basis in his 360 Air stock as follows:

	Adjusted basis of property contributed	$175,000
−	Mortgage assumed by 360 Air	75,000
	Tax basis of 360 Air stock received	$100,000

(continued on page 8-10)

[17]§358(a).
[18]§7701(a)(44) uses the term *exchanged basis property* for this type of property.

If Al subsequently sells his 360 Air stock for its fair market value of $300,000, he would recognize a capital gain of $200,000 ($300,000 − $100,000), an amount equal to the gain he deferred previously. In determining whether the gain is long or short term, Al includes the holding periods of capital assets and §1231 property transferred in exchange for the stock.[19]

Example 8-10

What if: Assume Al did not meet the requirements under §351 and was required to recognize the $200,000 gain realized. What is his tax basis in the 50 shares of 360 Air stock he receives in the exchange?

Answer: $300,000. Al's tax basis in his stock equals its fair market value. If Al subsequently sells his 360 Air stock for its fair market value of $300,000, he would not recognize any further gain.

Tax Consequences When a Shareholder Receives Boot

A shareholder who receives property other than stock (boot) recognizes gain (*but not loss*) in an amount not to exceed the *lesser of* (1) gain realized or (2) the fair market value of the boot received. The amount of gain recognized when boot is received in a §351 transaction is determined by allocating the boot received pro rata to each property using the relative fair market values of the properties.[20] The character of gain recognized (capital gain, §1231 gain, ordinary income) is determined by the type of property to which the boot is allocated.

Example 8-11

What if: Suppose Al received 40 shares of 360 Air stock with a fair market value of $315,000 plus $60,000 in return for his transfer of inventory, a building, and land to the corporation. The property transferred to the corporation had the following fair market values and adjusted bases:

	FMV	Adjusted Basis	Gain Realized
Inventory	$ 25,000	$ 15,000	$ 10,000
Building	150,000	60,000	90,000
Land	200,000	100,000	100,000
Total	$375,000	$175,000	$200,000

What amount of gain does Al recognize on his receipt of the $60,000 boot and what is its character (ordinary or §1231)?

Answer: The $60,000 received by Al constitutes boot received and causes him to recognize some or all of the gain realized on the transfer. He apportions the $60,000 to each of the properties transferred to the corporation based on their relative fair market values. Al recognizes gain on each property transferred in an amount equal to the lesser of the gain realized or the fair market

[19]§1223(1).

[20]Rev. Rul. 68-55, 1968-1 C.B. 140 and Rev. Rul. 85-164, 1985-2 C.B. 117.

value of the boot apportioned to the property. The computation is made for each property separately as follows:

Inventory	
Fair market value of 360 Air stock and cash received	$ 25,000
Less adjusted basis of the inventory transferred	−15,000
(1) Gain realized	$ 10,000
(2) Boot apportioned (25/375 × $60,000)	4,000
Gain recognized: lesser of (1) or (2)	$ 4,000
Character of gain recognized: ordinary	
Building	
Fair market value of 360 Air stock and cash received	$150,000
Less adjusted basis of the building transferred	− 60,000
(1) Gain realized	$ 90,000
(2) Boot apportioned (150/375 × $60,000)	24,000
Gain recognized: lesser of (1) or (2)	$ 24,000
Character of gain recognized: §1231[21]	
Land	
Fair market value of 360 Air stock and cash received	$200,000
Less adjusted basis of the building transferred	− 100,000
(1) Gain realized	$100,000
(2) Boot apportioned (200/375 × $60,000)	32,000
Gain recognized: lesser of (1) or (2)	$ 32,000
Character of gain recognized: §1231	

Al recognizes total gain of $60,000 on this transfer and defers recognition of $140,000 of the $200,000 gain realized ($200,000 − $60,000).

What If: Let's say the land had an adjusted basis of $250,000. What amount of gain or loss does Al now recognize?

Answer: The $60,000 of boot received by Al still must be apportioned among the assets based on relative fair market values. However, Al cannot recognize any of the realized loss on the land because boot only causes gain realized to be recognized. The recomputation for the land is as follows:

Land	
Fair market value of 360 Air stock and cash received	$200,000
Less adjusted basis of the building transferred	− 250,000
(1) Loss realized	$ (50,000)
(2) Boot apportioned (200/375 × $60,000)	32,000
No loss is recognized	

Al recognizes total gain of $28,000 from receipt of the building and inventory ($24,000 + $4,000). Al defers recognition of $72,000 of gain realized ($6,000 + $66,000) from receipt of the building and inventory and all of the $50,000 loss realized from receipt of the land.

Boot received in a §351 transaction receives a tax basis equal to its fair market value.[22] Al must adjust the tax basis in his 360 Air stock to take into account the boot received and the gain recognized. Exhibit 8-5 provides a template for computing stock basis when boot is received in a §351 transaction.

[21] If Al owned more than 50 percent of 360 Air after the transfer, the gain would be treated as ordinary income under §1239(a). Section 1239 converts §1231 gain to ordinary income if the transferor of the property owns more than 50 percent of the corporation and the property is depreciable in the hands of the transferee. The gain also could be unrecaptured §1250 gain subject to a maximum tax rate of 25 percent.

[22] §358(a)(2).

EXHIBIT 8-5 Computing the Tax Basis of Stock in a Section 351 Transaction When Boot Is Received

	Cash contributed
+	Tax basis of other property contributed
+	Gain recognized on the transfer
−	Fair market value of boot received
−	Liabilities assumed by the corporation on property contributed
	Tax basis of stock received

Example 8-12

Return to the original facts in Example 8-11, in which Al received $60,000 and recognized $60,000 gain in the exchange. What is Al's tax basis in his 360 Air stock?

Answer: $175,000. Al computes his tax basis in the 360 Air stock as follows:

	Adjusted basis of property contributed	$175,000
+	Gain recognized on the exchange	60,000
−	Fair market value of boot (cash) received	60,000
	Tax basis of stock received	$175,000

If Al subsequently sells his 360 Air stock for its current fair market value of $315,000, he would recognize a gain of $140,000 ($315,000 − $175,000), an amount equal to the gain he deferred in the exchange.

Assumption of Shareholder Liabilities by the Corporation

When an unincorporated business (e.g., Al's sole proprietorship) is incorporated, the newly created corporation frequently assumes the outstanding liabilities of the business (e.g., accounts payable or mortgages). An important tax issue is whether the assumption of these liabilities by the newly created corporation constitutes boot received by the shareholder transferring the liabilities to the corporation. After all, the shareholder does receive something other than stock in the transaction—that is, relief from debt.

Under the general rule, the corporation's assumption of a shareholder's liability attached to property transferred (e.g., the mortgage attached to the building and land transferred by Al to 360 Air) is *not* treated as boot received by the shareholder.[23] However, there are two important exceptions to this rule.

Tax-Avoidance Transactions If *any* of the liabilities assumed by the corporation are contributed with the purpose of avoiding the federal income tax or if there is no corporate business purpose for the assumption, *all* of the liabilities assumed are treated as boot to the shareholder.[24] The "avoidance" motive may be present where the corporation assumes debt created by the shareholders immediately prior to the contribution of the encumbered assets. This transaction is essentially equivalent to having the corporation pay the shareholder cash in exchange for the property. The "no business purpose" motive can also be present where shareholders have the corporation assume the shareholder's personal liabilities (e.g., grocery bills or alimony).

Liabilities in Excess of Basis Even when liabilities are not treated as boot, the taxpayer is required to recognize gain to the extent the liabilities assumed by the corporation exceed the aggregate tax basis of the properties transferred by the shareholder.[25]

[23]§357(a).

[24]§357(b).

[25]§357(c). A liability assumed by the corporation cannot reduce stock basis below zero.

ETHICS

Lisa is the sole proprietor of a business that manufactures solar panels. This week Lisa was approached to exchange her business assets for shares in Burns Power. As part of the exchange, Lisa is requiring Burns Power to assume the home equity loan on her home. Do you think that Lisa should argue that there is no tax-avoidance motive in this arrangement? Suppose that Lisa established her business five years ago by investing funds from a home equity loan. Any difference?

Example 8-13

What if: Assume Al transferred inventory and a building and land to 360 Air in return for 50 percent of the corporation's stock (50 shares) with a fair market value of $175,000 and the corporation's assumption of a mortgage of $200,000 attached to the land and building. The properties transferred have fair market values and tax bases as follows:

	FMV	Adjusted Basis
Inventory	$ 25,000	$ 15,000
Building	150,000	60,000
Land	200,000	100,000
Total	$375,000	$175,000

Al realizes a gain of $200,000 on the transfer, computed as follows:

	Fair market value of 360 Air stock received	$175,000
+	Mortgage assumed by 360 Air	200,000
	Amount realized	$375,000
−	Adjusted tax basis of the property transferred	175,000
	Gain realized	$200,000

What amount of gain, if any, does Al recognize on the transfer, assuming all of the other requirements of §351 are met?

Answer: $25,000, the excess of the mortgage assumed by 360 Air ($200,000) over the total tax-adjusted basis of the property Al transferred to the corporation ($175,000). Al defers gain of $175,000.

What is Al's tax basis in the 360 Air stock?

Answer: $0, computed as follows:

	Adjusted basis of property contributed	$175,000
+	Gain recognized on the exchange	25,000
−	Mortgage assumed by 360 Air	200,000
	Tax basis of stock received	$ 0

If Al sold his 360 Air stock for $175,000 (its current fair market value), he would recognize a gain of $175,000 ($175,000 − $0), an amount equal to the gain he deferred in the exchange.

There is a special exception for the assumption of liabilities the payment of which would give rise to a deduction. The assumption of such liabilities is disregarded in determining if the liabilities assumed exceed basis.[26] Examples would be where a corporation assumes the accounts payable of a cash-method sole proprietorship or where a subsidiary assumes "payment liabilities" (e.g., accrued vacation pay) of an accrual-method corporation.

[26]357(c)(3). Note that this exception is not available when the liabilities are used to create basis in assets, such as payables related to the purchase of tools.

Example 8-14

What if: Suppose Al transferred inventory and a building and land to 360 Air in return for 50 percent of the corporation's stock (50 shares) with a fair market value of $175,000 and the corporation's assumption of cash-method accounts payable of $200,000. The properties transferred have fair market values and tax bases as follows:

	FMV	Adjusted Basis
Inventory	$ 25,000	$ 15,000
Building	150,000	60,000
Land	200,000	100,000
Total	$375,000	$175,000

Al realizes a gain of $200,000 on the transfer, computed as follows:

	Fair market value of 360 Air stock received	$175,000
+	Payables assumed by 360 Air	200,000
	Amount realized	$375,000
−	Adjusted tax basis of the property transferred	175,000
	Gain realized	$200,000

What amount of gain, if any, does Al recognize in the transfer, assuming all of the other requirements of §351 are met?

Answer: $0. Al defers recognition of the entire gain of $200,000. The assumption of the cash-method payables is disregarded in computing whether the liabilities assumed exceed the aggregate tax basis of the property transferred.

What is Al's tax basis in the 360 Air stock?

Answer: $175,000, computed as follows:

	Adjusted basis of property contributed	$175,000
+	Gain recognized on the exchange	0
−	Payables assumed by 360 Air	0
	Tax basis of stock received	$175,000

If Al subsequently sells his 360 Air stock for $175,000 (its current fair market value), he would recognize a gain of $0 ($175,000 − $175,000). This result seems odd at first glance because the gain deferred previously was $200,000. However, by transferring the payables to 360 Air, Al is forgoing a $200,000 deduction that he would have received if he paid off the liabilities while operating as a sole proprietorship. This $200,000 "loss" exactly offsets the $200,000 gain he realized when 360 Air assumed the payables, resulting in a net gain of $0.

Tax Consequences to the Transferee Corporation

The corporation receiving property in exchange for its stock does not recognize gain or loss realized on the transfer.[27] In transactions that do not qualify for §351, the corporation will have a fair market value tax basis in the property. In a §351 transaction the corporation will have a tax basis in the property that equals the property's tax basis in the transferor's hands.[28] The transferred property is said to have a **carryover basis** (i.e., the corporation "carries over" the shareholder's basis in the property).[29] To the extent the shareholder's tax basis carries over to the

[27]§1032.

[28]§362(a).

[29]§7701(a)(43) refers to this type of property as *transferred basis property*.

corporation and the property is §1231 property or a capital asset, the shareholder's holding period also carries over (it *tacks* to the property).[30] This could be important in determining if subsequent gain or loss recognized on the disposition of the property qualifies as a §1231 gain or loss or a long-term capital gain or loss.

If the shareholder recognizes gain as a result of the property transfer (e.g., because boot is received), the corporation increases its tax basis in the property by the gain recognized. Exhibit 8-6 provides a template for computing the tax basis of property received by the corporation in a §351 transaction.

EXHIBIT 8-6 Computing the Tax Basis of Property Received by the Corporation in a Section 351 Transaction

	Cash contributed by the shareholder
+	Tax basis of other property contributed by the shareholder
+	Gain recognized on the transfer by the shareholder
	Tax basis of property received

Example 8-15

Let's return to the facts in Example 8-11 where Al received 40 shares of 360 Air stock with a fair market value of $315,000 and $60,000 in return for his transfer of inventory, a building, and land to the corporation. The $60,000 received by Al constituted boot received and caused him to recognize gain on the transfer. The $60,000 was allocated to each of the properties transferred to the corporation based on their relative fair market values. Al recognized gain on each property transferred in an amount equal to the lesser of the gain realized or the fair market value of the boot allocated to the property. Al's tax results from this transaction can be summarized as follows:

	Tax Basis	Gain Recognized
Inventory	$ 15,000	$ 4,000
Building	60,000	24,000
Land	100,000	32,000
Total	$175,000	$60,000

What tax basis does 360 Air get in each of the properties it receives from Al in the exchange?

Answer: 360 Air will carry over Al's tax basis in the property transferred and will increase the tax basis by gain recognized by Al on the transfer. The corporation's tax basis in each of the three properties is as follows:

	Tax Basis	Gain Recognized	360 Air Tax Basis
Inventory	$ 15,000	$ 4,000	$ 19,000
Building	60,000	24,000	84,000
Land	100,000	32,000	132,000
Total	$175,000	$60,000	$235,000

360 Air also will carry over Al's holding period in the building and land transferred because they are §1231 assets.

The tax law limits the ability of a shareholder to transfer a "built-in loss" to a corporation in a §351 transaction. In particular, if the *aggregate* adjusted tax basis of property transferred to a corporation by a shareholder in a §351 transfer exceeds the aggregate fair market value of the assets, the aggregate tax basis of the assets in the

[30]§1223(1).

hands of the transferee corporation cannot exceed their aggregate fair market value.[31] The aggregate reduction in tax basis is allocated among the assets transferred in proportion to their respective built-in losses immediately before the transfer. As an alternative, the transferor and transferee can elect to have the transferor reduce her stock basis to fair market value (i.e., the duplicate loss is eliminated at either the corporate or shareholder level).

Example 8-16

What if: Assume Al transferred a building and land to the corporation in return for 50 percent of the corporation's stock (50 shares). The property transferred to the corporation had the following fair market values and adjusted bases:

	FMV	Adjusted Basis
Building	$ 75,000	$100,000
Land	200,000	100,000
Total	$275,000	$200,000

The fair market value of the 360 Air stock Al received in the exchange was $275,000.

Assuming the transfer meets the requirements under §351 to defer recognizing the $75,000 net gain realized, what is Al's tax basis in the 50 shares of 360 Air stock he receives in the exchange?

Answer: $200,000. In this case, the aggregate fair market value of the property transferred to the corporation exceeds the aggregate adjusted basis of the property. As a result, Al's tax basis in the stock he receives equals the aggregate adjusted bases of the property transferred.

What is the adjusted basis of the building and land held by 360 Air?

Answer: The building has a carryover basis of $100,000, and the land has a carryover basis of $100,000. Because the aggregate fair market value of the assets transferred to the corporation exceeds the aggregate adjusted basis of the property, 360 Air applies the general basis carryover rules. The building retains its built-in loss of $25,000 at the corporate level.

Example 8-17

What if: Suppose Al transferred a building and land to the corporation in return for 50 percent of the corporation's stock (50 shares). The property transferred to the corporation had the following fair market values and adjusted bases:

	FMV	Adjusted Basis
Building	$ 75,000	$200,000
Land	200,000	100,000
Total	$275,000	$300,000

The fair market value of the 360 Air stock Al received in the exchange was $275,000.

Assuming the transfer meets the requirements under §351 to defer recognizing the $25,000 net loss realized, what is Al's tax basis in the 50 shares of 360 Air stock he receives in the exchange?

Answer: $300,000. In this case, the aggregate adjusted bases of the property transferred to the corporation exceed the aggregate fair market value of the property. Assuming he doesn't elect to reduce his stock basis to fair market value, Al's tax basis in the stock he receives will equal the adjusted basis of the assets transferred.

[31]§362(e)(2).

What is the adjusted basis of the building and land held by 360 Air?

Answer: An aggregate adjusted basis of $275,000. Because the aggregate fair market value of the property transferred to the corporation is less than the aggregate adjusted bases of the property, 360 Air must reduce the aggregate adjusted bases of the property to their aggregate fair market value. The allocation is made to those assets that have a built-in loss; in this example, only the building. The adjusted basis of the building will be reduced to $175,000 ($200,000 − $25,000 net built-in loss). The adjusted basis of the land will retain its carryover basis of $100,000. This adjustment eliminates the net $25,000 built-in loss at the corporate level.

What alternative election can Al and 360 Air make with respect to these basis reduction rules?

Answer: Al and the corporation can jointly elect to have Al reduce his stock basis to its fair market value of $275,000. The corporation would take a carryover basis of $200,000 in the building and a carryover basis of $100,000 in the land.

Other Issues Related to Incorporating an Ongoing Business

Depreciable Assets Transferred to a Corporation To the extent a property's tax-adjusted basis carries over from the shareholder, the corporation *steps into the shoes* of the shareholder and continues to depreciate the *carryover basis* portion of the property's tax basis using the shareholder's depreciation schedule.[32] Any additional basis (from recognition of gain due to boot received) is treated as a separate asset and is subject to a separate depreciation election (i.e., this one physical asset is treated as two tax assets for depreciation purposes).

Example 8-18

Let's return to the facts in Example 8-15. Recall that Al received 40 shares of 360 Air stock with a fair market value of $315,000 and $60,000 in return for his transfer of inventory, a building, and land to the corporation. The cash received by Al constituted boot received and caused him to recognize $60,000 of gain on the transfer. 360 Air takes Al's tax basis in the property and increases it by the gain recognized by Al on the transfer. The corporation's tax basis in each of the three properties is as follows:

	Tax Basis	Gain Recognized	360 Air Tax Basis
Inventory	$ 15,000	$ 4,000	$ 19,000
Building	60,000	24,000	84,000
Land	100,000	32,000	132,000
Total	$175,000	$60,000	$235,000

360 Air also will carry over Al's holding period in the building and land transferred because they are §1231 assets. How will 360 Air compute the depreciation deduction on the building for the year of the transfer? For this problem, let's assume that the transfer occurs on January 1. Furthermore, let's assume that that Al originally purchased the building for $67,400 in September five years ago and has claimed $7,400 of depreciation using straight-line and midmonth conventions over a 39-year recovery period.

(continued on page 8-18)

[32]§168(i)(7)(B)(ii).

Answer: 360 Air carries over Al's depreciation schedule for the building with respect to the $60,000 original basis, but 360 Air depreciates the additional $24,000 as a new asset. With respect to the carryover basis portion of the building, 360 Air uses Al's original cost of $67,400 in the building to calculate the depreciation computation. Al is entitled to .5 month of depreciation on the building in the year of transfer ($67,400 × .02564 × .5/12 = $72), and the corporation is entitled to the remaining 11.5 months of depreciation of $1,656 ($67,400 × .02564 × 11.5/12 = $1,656). The corporation treats the additional $24,000 of basis as a new asset and applies the proper depreciation rate to calculate the additional depreciation. Because the transfer took place in January, 360 Air would be entitled to 11.5 months of depreciation (recall the mid-month convention). Hence, 360 Air would claim additional depreciation of $591 ($24,000 × .02461 = $591) for a total depreciation deduction of $2,247. This bifurcated computation often is ignored or overlooked in practice.

Practitioners often advise against transferring appreciated property (especially real estate) into a closely held corporation. By transferring the property into the corporation, the shareholder creates two assets with the same built-in gain as the original property (the stock received in the hands of the shareholder and the building owned by the corporation). The federal government can now collect taxes twice on the same gain: once when the corporation sells the property received and a second time when the shareholder sells the stock. You will notice that Congress is not concerned by a duplication of gain result, only a duplication of loss result. By retaining the property outside the corporation, the shareholder can lease the property to the corporation, thereby reducing the corporation's taxable income through rent deductions. Note, however, that there may be valid state tax reasons to own the property inside a corporation, such as lower property taxes.

Contributions to Capital

A **contribution to capital** is a transfer of property to a corporation by a shareholder or nonshareholder for which no stock or other property is received in return. The corporation receiving the property is not taxed on the receipt of the property.[33] If the property is contributed by a shareholder, the corporation takes a carryover tax basis in the property.[34] If the property is contributed by a nonshareholder (e.g., a city contributes land to induce a corporation to locate its operations there), the corporation's tax basis in the property is zero.[35]

A capital contribution generally is not a taxable event to the shareholder because the shareholder does not receive any additional consideration in return for the transfer. A shareholder making a capital contribution gets to increase the tax basis in her existing stock in an amount equal to the tax basis of the property contributed.

Section 1244 Stock

Stock is generally a capital asset in the hands of the shareholders, and gains or losses from sale or exchange are capital in nature. For individuals, long-term capital gains are taxed at a maximum tax rate of 20 percent. Losses can only offset capital gains plus $3,000 of ordinary income per year. Section 1244 allows a shareholder to treat a *loss* on the sale or exchange of stock that qualifies as §1244 stock as an *ordinary* loss.

[33]§118.

[34]§362(a)(2).

[35]§362(c)(1).

Section 1244 applies only to individual shareholders who are the original recipients of the stock. The maximum amount of loss that can be treated as an ordinary loss under §1244 is $50,000 per year ($100,000 in the case of married, filing jointly shareholders). To qualify for this tax benefit, the corporation from which the stock was received must be a "small business corporation" when the stock was issued. The IRC defines a small business corporation as one in which the aggregate amount of money and other property received in return for the stock or as a contribution to capital did not exceed $1 million. In our storyline, 360 Air would qualify as a small business corporation. There is an additional requirement that for the five taxable years preceding the year in which the stock was sold, the corporation must have derived more than 50 percent of its aggregate gross receipts from an *active* trade or business. 360 Air meets this test as well. Section 1244 provides a tax benefit to entrepreneurs who create a risky start-up company that ultimately fails rather than succeeds.

Example 8-19

What if: Assume Al received 50 shares of 360 Air stock (50 percent of the outstanding stock) with a fair market value of $300,000 in return for his transfer of a building and land to the corporation in a transaction that qualified under §351. As a result of the transfer, Al received a tax basis in the 50 shares of $200,000 ($4,000 per share). Suppose that over time, the snowboarding business declined due to a change in weather patterns in Michigan. As a result, Al's 50 shares were worth $50,000 ($1,000 per share). Needing some cash, Al sold all 50 of his shares to Jim for $50,000 and recognized a $150,000 loss [$50,000 − ($4,000 × 50 shares)]. 360 Air qualifies as a small business corporation under §1244. Al has no capital gains in the year of the sale. How much of the loss can Al deduct if he held his stock at least five years, assuming current tax rules and he is married, filing a joint tax return? What is the character of the loss (capital or ordinary)?

Answer: $103,000, $100,000 of which is ordinary loss and $3,000 of which is capital loss that can reduce up to $3,000 of ordinary income. The remaining $47,000 loss is carried forward as a capital loss.

What tax planning advice would you give Al to maximize the tax treatment of his loss from sale of the stock?

Answer: §1244 imposes an annual limit on the amount of the loss that can be treated as ordinary. To maximize the tax value of his loss, Al should sell enough shares of 360 Air stock to generate a $100,000 loss this year and sell the remaining amount to generate a $50,000 loss next year. In that way, the entire $150,000 loss will be treated as ordinary loss. Of course, delaying the sale of shares is risky because the stock could continue to lose value. Al would need to weigh the tax benefits of the delay against the risk of additional loss.

A special rule applies when §1244 stock is issued by a corporation in exchange for property that, immediately before the exchange, has an adjusted basis (for determining loss) in excess of its fair market value (i.e., a "built-in loss"). If §1244 stock is issued in exchange for such property and the taxpayer has elected not to reduce the stock's basis by the built-in loss, then for purposes of §1244 only, the basis of the stock is reduced by an amount equal to the built-in loss at the time of the exchange. For example, assume a taxpayer transfers property with an adjusted basis of $1,000 and a fair market value of $250 in exchange for 10 shares of §1244 stock in a §351 transaction. The total basis of the stock is $1,000, but, solely for purposes of §1244, the total basis of the stock must be reduced by $750, the excess of the adjusted basis of the property exchanged over its fair market value. The total basis of such stock for purposes of §1244 is $250. If the taxpayer sells her 10 shares for $250, she will recognize a loss of $750, all of which must be treated as a capital loss. If she sells the 10 shares for $200, then $50 of her total loss of $800 will be treated as an ordinary loss under §1244 and the remaining $750 will be a capital loss.

LO 8-3

TAXABLE AND TAX-DEFERRED CORPORATE ACQUISITIONS

Storyline Summary

Spartan Cycle and Repair

Privately held company located in East Lansing, Michigan

Sells and repairs high-end bicycles

Jim Wheeler

Co-owner of Spartan Cycle and Repair (75 percent)

Filing status:	Married filing jointly
Dependents:	One child
Marginal tax rate:	40 percent

Ginny Gears

Co-owner of Spartan Cycles and Repair (25 percent)

Filing status:	Unmarried
Marginal tax rate:	25 percent

Wolverine Cycles and Repair

Privately held company in Ann Arbor, Michigan

Sells and repairs high-end bicycles

Pam Peloton

Owner of Wolverine Cycles and Repair

Filing status:	Unmarried
Marginal tax rate:	31 percent

continued from page 8-2...
Jim Wheeler and Ginny Gears were excited about their new business venture with Al Pine. This seemed to solve their need to find a source of revenues during the winter months, when the demand for bicycles declined significantly. With that challenge met, Jim and Ginny turned their attention to expanding their bicycle business to a new geographic region. At the recent Tour de Gaslight race sponsored by the Michigan Bicycle Racing Association, Jim struck up a conversation with Pam Peloton, owner of Wolverine Cycles and Repair (WCR) in Ann Arbor, Michigan. Pam mentioned she was planning to move to Colorado and was looking to sell her business. Jim could see lots of synergies in buying her business. He and Ginny were familiar with the biking community in Ann Arbor, and they understood the economics of operating a business in a college town. Ginny was excited about the possibility of expanding their business to Ann Arbor. Both communities had a large network of bike paths and avid biking clubs.

A meeting was set up with Pam to explore the possible acquisition of her business. Pam operated her business through a C corporation, which gave Jim and Pam the opportunity to consider buying the assets of the business directly or buying Pam's stock in the corporation. If the stock acquisition route is taken, Jim and Ginny need to consider whether they want to operate their new company as a subsidiary of Spartan Cycles and Repair or in a lateral ownership arrangement ("brother-sister" corporations). Operating WCR as a subsidiary of SCR would allow Jim and Ginny to file a consolidated tax return with SCR. Pam is concerned about the tax consequences of each of these options, as are Jim and Ginny. They know they are in over their heads, so a call was made to their tax accountant, Louis Tully, for help in sorting out their options.

to be continued...

At some point in the life of a successful business, the owners likely will consider expanding the scope or geographic locations of their business. Businesses can grow internally through expansion or externally by acquiring an existing business. Jim and Ginny prefer to buy Pam's existing business to expand in a new geographic location. Because Pam operates the business through a C corporation, Jim and Ginny have multiple options. Jim and Ginny first need to consider whether they will personally acquire the stock or assets of WCR or whether SCR will make the acquisition. Second, Jim and Ginny then need to decide whether they should acquire Pam's stock or WCR's assets. Third, Jim and Ginny need to decide what consideration should be used to make the acquisition (e.g., SCR stock or cash). Each of these options can result in different tax consequences to the buyer and the seller. Thus, Jim and Ginny will also need to negotiate the form of the transaction with Pam.

In this section of the chapter, we consider the *basic* ways in which a corporation or its shareholders can acquire the stock or assets of another corporation and the tax consequences that follow the form of the acquisition. This is an extremely complicated and technical area of the tax law. A thorough discussion of all of the variations in which an acquisition can take place likely would take up most or all of a semester. As a result, our discussion is limited to the basic types of corporate acquisitions.

THE KEY FACTS

Tax Model for Corporate Acquisitions

- The acquiring corporation can acquire the target corporation through either a stock or asset acquisition.
- The acquisition can be structured as either taxable or tax-deferred.
- Taxable asset acquisitions allow the acquiring corporation to step-up the tax basis of the assets acquired to fair value.
- In stock acquisitions and tax-deferred asset acquisitions, the tax basis of the target corporation's assets remain at their carryover basis (generally, cost less accumulated depreciation).

The Acquisition Tax Model

When negotiating an acquisition, management of the acquiring corporation must decide whether to acquire the target corporation's assets or stock and what consideration to use (equity, debt, and/or cash). The *form* of the transaction and the consideration will jointly determine the *tax status* of the transaction.[36] Nontax considerations, such as the ease of transferring stock or the existence of contingent liabilities, often dictate the form of an acquisition by a publicly traded corporation. In contrast, privately held corporations are more likely to make tax considerations a priority.

The shareholders of the target company also must decide what consideration to accept in return for their stock or assets in the company. Cash provides liquidity and does not decline in value after the acquisition is announced, but it also causes the transaction to be fully or partially taxable to the seller. Receiving stock in the acquiring corporation may allow shareholders to defer paying tax on gain realized on the exchange, but the sellers must accept the risk that the acquiring corporation's stock will decline in value after the merger is announced or consummated.

The technical tax (and accounting) rules that apply to mergers and acquisitions are extremely complex. Because the statutory language governing reorganizations is sparse, the IRS and courts often must decide whether the *form* of a reorganization transaction meets both the literal language of the statute and the *substance* of the judicial principles that underlie the reorganization provisions. As a result, the reorganization area is heavily laden with administrative and judicial pronouncements. Our goal is to provide you with a basic overview of the most common types of corporate acquisitions that you will see discussed in business periodicals such as *The Wall Street Journal*.

Exhibit 8-7 summarizes the four basic types of transactions that can be used to effect an acquisition of another company. The *buyer* can purchase either stock or assets in a transaction that is either taxable or tax-deferred (in whole or in part) to the seller. Both sides to the transaction must decide which category they desire to be in after the transaction.

EXHIBIT 8-7 Types of Corporate Acquisitions

	Asset Purchase from WCR	Stock Purchase from Pam
Taxable	Any consideration (Cell 1)	Any consideration (Cell 2)
Tax Deferred Reorganization	Type A reorganization using SCR equity (Cell 3)	Type B reorganization using SCR voting equity (Cell 4)

[36]The form of the transaction and the consideration paid to shareholders does not affect the financial accounting treatment of the acquisition—ASC 805-10-25-1 requires that all business combinations be accounted for using the purchase method.

Often the buyer and seller have different tax incentives (i.e., they each want to be in a different cell), which requires both sides to negotiate a compromise arrangement that satisfies both parties. For example, the buyer likely prefers to acquire the target corporation's assets in a taxable transaction (cell 1). By purchasing the target corporation's assets directly, the acquiring corporation gets a "stepped-up" tax basis in the assets equal to fair market value (cost). To the extent the acquiring corporation can allocate the purchase price to depreciable or amortizable assets, this increases future depreciation or amortization deductions on the acquiring corporation's tax return. It is not uncommon in an acquisition involving publicly traded corporations for goodwill to comprise 80 percent to 90 percent of the purchase price. If the acquiring corporation can achieve a tax basis in the goodwill, the basis can be amortized over 15 years.[37] If the acquiring corporation makes the acquisition using a tax-deferred technique, then the tax basis of the acquired assets will not be stepped up to fair value and goodwill will have a zero tax basis. Hence, the acquiring company will be ineligible for increased depreciation deductions, and there is no amortization deduction for goodwill.

The seller likely prefers to sell stock in a tax-deferred transaction (cell 1 or cell 4) because any tax on the appreciation in the stock will be postponed. Alternatively, the seller would prefer to sell the stock in a taxable transaction (cell 2) because any gain on the stock would be taxed at a capital gains tax rate. However, neither of these options provides the acquiring corporation with a stepped-up tax basis in the assets, greatly reducing the future value of the acquisition to the buyer. The seller would likely be reluctant to sell the assets of the corporation in a taxable transaction (cell 1) because the seller would be required to pay both the corporate tax on appreciation of the assets and the individual capital gains tax on the appreciation of the stock. Of course, the buyer might be able to overcome the seller's reluctance by offering a sufficiently high purchase price.

LO 8-4 TAX CONSEQUENCES TO A CORPORATE ACQUISITION

continued from page 8-20. . .

As part of their negotiations with Pam, Jim and Ginny had their tax accountant, Louis Tully, look over WCR's **tax accounting balance sheet** along with a recent valuation of the assets' fair market values. Pam held the WCR stock for 10 years and her tax basis in the stock is $50,000. WCR is an accrual-method taxpayer, and as a result, the payables have a tax basis. That is, the corporation deducted the expenses related to the payables when the expenses were accrued. These facts are summarized as follows:

	FMV	Adjusted Basis	Appreciation
Cash	$ 10,000	$ 10,000	
Receivables	5,000	5,000	
Inventory	20,000	10,000	$ 10,000
Building	80,000	50,000	30,000
Land	120,000	60,000	60,000
Total	$235,000	$135,000	$100,000
Payables	4,000	4,000	
Mortgage*	31,000	31,000	
Total	$ 35,000	$ 35,000	

*The mortgage was attached to the building and land.

[37]§197.

Jim and Ginny agreed to pay Pam $300,000 for her business, an amount that is $100,000 more than the net fair market value of the assets less the liabilities listed on the balance sheet ($235,000 − $35,000). The additional $100,000 reflects an amount to be paid for the company's customer list valued at $25,000, with the remaining $75,000 allocated to goodwill.

With the price settled, Jim, Ginny, and Pam now must agree on the form the transaction will take. Jim and Ginny asked Louis to develop some computations for each of the different ways in which the transaction could take place.

to be continued . . .

Taxable Acquisitions

A corporation can acquire an ongoing business through the purchase of its stock or assets in return for cash, debt, or equity or a combination thereof. Cash purchases of stock are the most common form of acquisition of publicly held corporations. Using cash to acquire another company has several nontax advantages; most notably, the acquiring corporation does not "acquire" the target corporation's shareholders in the transaction and does not increase the denominator in its calculation of earnings per share. There are disadvantages to using cash, particularly if the acquiring corporation incurs additional debt to fund the purchase.

If SCR purchases the assets directly from WCR in return for cash (cell 1), WCR will recognize gain or loss on the sale of each asset individually. WCR may cease to exist as a separate corporation and might completely liquidate by transferring the net after-tax proceeds received from SCR to its shareholder. If WCR liquidates, Pam recognizes gain or loss on the exchange of her WCR stock for the cash received.

Example 8-20

What if: Assume SCR will purchase WCR's assets for $300,000 and assume the company's liabilities of $35,000. WCR will realize $335,000 ($300,000 + $35,000), which it will allocate to each of the assets sold, as follows:

	Allocation	Adjusted Basis	Gain Realized
Cash	$ 10,000	$ 10,000	$ 0
Receivables	5,000	5,000	0
Inventory	20,000	10,000	10,000
Building	80,000	50,000	30,000
Land	120,000	60,000	60,000
Customer list	25,000	0	25,000
Goodwill	75,000	0	75,000
Total	$335,000	$135,000	$200,000

What amount of gain or loss does WCR recognize on the sale of its assets and what is the character of the gain or loss (ordinary, §1231, or capital)?

(continued on page 8-24)

Answer: WCR recognizes total gain of $200,000, and WCR pays a corporate-level tax of $68,000 (assuming a tax rate of 34 percent). The character of the gain will be as follows:

	Gain Recognized	Character
Inventory	$ 10,000	Ordinary
Building	30,000	Ordinary (§291) and §1231
Land	60,000	§1231
Customer list	25,000	§1231
Goodwill	75,000	§1231
Total	$200,000	

What if: Suppose that WRC opts to go out of existence (liquidate) by exchanging the $232,000 net amount realized after taxes ($300,000 − $68,000) to Pam in return for her WCR stock.

What amount of gain or loss will Pam recognize on the exchange of her WCR stock for the after-tax proceeds from the sale ($232,000)?

Answer: Pam recognizes a long-term capital gain of $182,000 ($232,000 − $50,000 stock basis) and pays a shareholder-level tax of $27,300 ($182,000 × 15% assuming Pam's income is not above the trigger for the 20% capital gains tax rate). The total tax paid using this form of acquisition is $95,300. Pam is left with $204,700 after taxes ($300,000 − $68,000 − $27,300).

Although unattractive to Pam, this deal provides SCR (Jim and Ginny) with the maximum tax benefits. The building will have an increased tax basis of $30,000, which SCR can depreciate over 39 years. The customer list and goodwill will have a tax basis of $25,000 and $75,000, respectively, which SCR can amortize over 15 years on a straight-line basis.[38]

If SCR acquires WCR by acquiring Pam's stock for cash (cell 2), WCR retains its tax and legal identity (unless SCR liquidates WCR into itself or merges it into an existing subsidiary). The **tax basis** of WCR's assets, which will carry over, will not reflect SCR's **tax basis** (purchase price) in WCR's stock.

Example 8-21

What if: Suppose instead that SCR purchases the WCR stock from Pam for $300,000. What amount of gain or loss does WCR recognize in this transaction?

Answer: WCR will not recognize gain on this form of acquisition because it has not sold any assets directly to SCR.

What amount and character of gain or loss does Pam recognize in this transaction?

Answer: Pam recognizes long-term capital gain of $250,000 ($300,000 − $50,000 stock basis) and pays a shareholder-level tax of $37,500 ($250,000 × 15%). Pam will be left with $262,500 after taxes ($300,000 − $37,500), which is $57,800 more than a direct asset sale ($262,500 − $204,700).

Although attractive to Pam, this deal will not be as attractive to SCR (Jim and Ginny). The building will retain its carryover tax basis of $50,000, and the customer list and goodwill will have a tax basis of zero. The customer list and goodwill have a zero tax basis to WCR because they are self-created assets. The inside tax bases of WCR's assets remain at $135,000. SCR has an outside tax basis in the WCR stock equal to the purchase price of $300,000.

[38]§197. Note that goodwill is not amortized for financial accounting purposes, and the determination of goodwill for accounting purposes under ASC 805-30-30-1 differs from the determination of goodwill for tax purposes under §1060. Hence, even a taxable acquisition can give rise to a book–tax difference because different amounts of goodwill exist for tax and book purposes.

Tax nirvana would be achieved if Pam can treat the transaction as a stock sale and pay a single level of capital gains tax on the gain recognized from the sale, while SCR can treat the transaction as an asset purchase and receive a step-up in basis of the assets to fair market value. This best of both tax worlds is available in transactions where a corporate taxpayer purchases 80 percent or more of another corporation's stock within a 12-month period. In such cases, SCR can make a **§338 election** to treat the stock purchase as a *deemed asset purchase*.

As with most things that appear too good to be true, this election does not come without some tax costs. The calculation of these costs is extremely technical and beyond the scope of this text. In big-picture terms, WCR is treated as selling its assets prior to the transaction and then repurchasing them at fair market value. This deemed sale of assets causes WCR to recognize gain on assets that have appreciated in value. SCR, as the buyer, bears this tax cost because the fair market value of WCR will be reduced by the tax paid. In almost all cases, this tax cost negates the tax benefits of getting a step-up in basis in WCR's assets and is rarely ever elected. For example, it rarely makes economic sense to pay income taxes on a $100 gain just to increase the basis of an asset by $100. The additional tax on the $100 gain would very likely outweigh the present value of the savings from an additional $100 of future depreciation deductions. However, this election might be tax-efficient if WCR has net operating losses or net capital losses that can be used to offset gain from the deemed sale of its assets.

If the target corporation is a subsidiary of the seller, the acquiring corporation and seller can make a joint **§338(h)(10) election** and have the seller report the gain from the deemed sale of the target corporation's assets on its tax return in lieu of reporting the actual gain from the sale of the target corporation stock. The technical rules that apply to §338(h)(10) elections are beyond the scope of this text. These elections, which are more common than a regular §338 election, often achieve tax savings to both parties to the transaction. For example, the Wm. Wrigley Jr. Company purchased Life Savers® and Altoids® from Kraft Foods. The buyer and seller made a joint §338(h)(10) election, which allowed Wrigley to record a tax basis for the intangibles and goodwill acquired in the transaction. As you can see from the announcement reproduced below, this provided Wrigley with an estimated $300 million in cash tax benefits from being able to amortize the step-up in basis.

TAXES IN THE REAL WORLD Wrigley's "Curiously Refreshing" Tax Benefits from Acquiring Altoids

Wm. Wrigley Jr. Company entered into an agreement to purchase certain confectionery assets of Kraft Foods for $1.48 billion. In order to complete this all-cash transaction, the Company announced that it had received a commitment for $1.5 billion in credit. Of the estimated $1.5 billion in borrowing to complete the Kraft transaction, the Company issued approximately $1.35 billion of long-term debt, with the balance to be funded primarily with commercial paper. At December 31, 2005, indefinite lived intangible assets totaled $368 million consisting of brand names purchased as part of the acquisitions of certain confectionery assets from Kraft Foods. Wrigley was looking for additional diversification in key categories of mints and hard and chewy candy including such brands as Life Savers, Altoids, Creme Savers and Sugus brands. The goodwill from these brands produced over $19 million of amortization deductions in 2005.

Source: Wrigley 2005 form 10-K dated February 16, 2006.

THE KEY FACTS

Forms of a Tax-Deferred Asset Acquisition

- Statutory Type A merger
  - Must meet state law requirements to be a merger or consolidation.
  - Judicial requirements of COI, COBE, and business purpose must be met.
- Forward triangular Type A merger
  - Must meet requirements to be a straight Type A merger.
  - The target corporation merges into an 80 percent or more owned acquisition subsidiary of the acquiring corporation.
  - The acquisition subsidiary must acquire "substantially all" of the target corporation's properties in the exchange.
- Reverse triangular Type A merger
  - Must meet requirements to be a straight Type A merger.
  - The acquisition subsidiary merges into the target corporation.
  - The target corporation must hold "substantially all" of the acquisition subsidiary's properties and its own properties after the exchange.
  - The acquisition subsidiary must receive in the exchange 80 percent or more of the target corporation's stock in exchange for voting stock of the acquiring corporation.

Tax-Deferred Acquisitions

As you learned previously in this chapter, the tax law allows taxpayers to organize a corporation in a tax-deferred manner under §351. The tax laws also allow taxpayers to *reorganize* their corporate structure in a tax-deferred manner. For tax purposes, **reorganizations** encompass acquisitions and dispositions of corporate assets (including the stock of subsidiaries) and a corporation's restructuring of its capital structure, place of incorporation, or company name. The IRC provides tax deferral to the corporation(s) involved in the reorganization (the *parties to the reorganization*) and the shareholders if the transaction meets one of seven statutory definitions[39] and satisfies the judicial principles that underlie the reorganization statutes. As before, tax deferral in corporate reorganizations is predicated on the seller receiving a continuing ownership interest in the assets transferred through the receipt of equity in the acquiring corporation.

The statutory language governing corporate reorganizations is rather sparse. It should not be surprising, then, that the IRS and the courts frequently must interpret how changes in the facts related to a transaction's form affect its tax status. The end result has been the development of a complex and confusing legacy of IRS rulings and court decisions that dictate how a reorganization transaction will be taxed. Corporate reorganizations are best left to the tax experts who have devoted much of their professional lives to understanding their intricacies. Our goal is to acquaint you with the basic principles that underlie all corporate reorganizations and provide you with an understanding of the most common forms of corporate acquisitions that are tax-deferred.

Judicial Principles That Underlie All Tax-Deferred Reorganizations

Continuity of Interest (COI) Tax deferral in a reorganization is based on the presumption that the shareholders of the acquired (target) corporation retain a continuing ownership (equity) interest in the target corporation's assets or historic business through ownership of stock in the acquiring corporation. The IRC does not provide a **bright line test** for when **continuity of interest (COI)** is met, although the regulations provide an example that states that COI is satisfied when the shareholders of the target corporation, in the aggregate, receive equity equal to 40 percent or more of the total value of the consideration received.[40] The proposed acquisition of Marvel Entertainment by The Walt Disney Company involved a combination of cash and equity and was designed to be a tax-deferred reorganization. As you can see by the announcement below, the amount of cash was restricted to 60 percent of the total consideration so as to not violate the continuity of interest rules.

TAXES IN THE REAL WORLD **Disney to Acquire Marvel Entertainment**

In 2009 Disney agreed to exchange stock and cash for Marvel Entertainment. Under the agreement, Marvel shareholders would receive cash of $30 and approximately 0.745 Disney shares for each Marvel share. The ratio of cash and stock was to be adjusted so that the total value of the Disney stock issued would not be less than 40% of the total merger consideration. According to SEC filings, this adjustment was necessary to qualify the transaction as a "reorganization" within the meaning of Section 368(a) of the Internal Revenue Code of 1986.

Continuity of Business Enterprise (COBE) For a transaction to qualify as a tax-deferred reorganization, the acquiring corporation must continue the target corporation's historic business or continue to use a *significant* portion of the target corporation's historic business assets. Whether the historic business assets retained are "significant" is a facts and circumstances test, which adds to the administrative and judicial rulings that are part and parcel of the reorganization

[39]The "forms" of corporate reorganizations are defined in §368(a)(1).

[40]Reg. §1.368-1T(e)(2)(v), Example 10.

landscape. **Continuity of business enterprise (COBE)** does not apply to the historic business or assets of the acquiring corporation; the acquiring corporation can sell off its assets after the reorganization without violating the COBE requirement.

Business Purpose Test As early as 1935, the Supreme Court stated that transactions with "no business or corporate purpose" should not receive tax deferral even if they comply with the statutory requirements.[41] To meet the business purpose test, the acquiring corporation must be able to show a significant nontax avoidance purpose for engaging in the transaction.

Type A Asset Acquisitions

Type A reorganizations (cell 3) are statutory **mergers** or **consolidations.**[42] In a merger, either the acquired corporation or the acquiring corporation will cease to exist. For example, SCR could acquire the assets and liabilities of WCR by transferring SCR shares to Pam in exchange for her WCR stock, and WCR would no longer exist. This type of merger is an *upstream* or *forward* acquisition because the acquired company is merged into the acquiring company. Alternatively, the acquired company could be the surviving entity, and this type of acquisition is a *downstream* or *reverse* acquisition. In a consolidation, SCR and WCR will transfer their assets and liabilities to a newly formed corporation in return for stock in the new corporation, after which SCR and WCR will both cease to exist.

In a Type A reorganization, the target corporation shareholders defer recognition of gain or loss realized on the receipt of stock of the acquiring corporation. Similar to a §351 transaction, if a target corporation shareholder receives money or other property (boot) from the acquiring corporation or its acquisition subsidiary, the shareholder recognizes *gain* to the extent of the money and fair market value of other property received (not to exceed the gain realized). The shareholder's tax basis in the stock received is a *substituted basis* of the stock transferred plus any gain recognized less any money and the fair market value of other property received. The target corporation's assets remain at their carryover (historic) tax basis in a Type A merger.

Exhibit 8-8 provides an illustration of a Type A merger. The consideration that can be paid to Pam is very flexible in a Type A merger; the only limitation being that the transaction satisfy the COI requirement (i.e., at least 40 percent of the consideration must be SCR stock). The stock used to satisfy the COI test can be voting or nonvoting, common or preferred.

EXHIBIT 8-8 Form of a Type A Merger

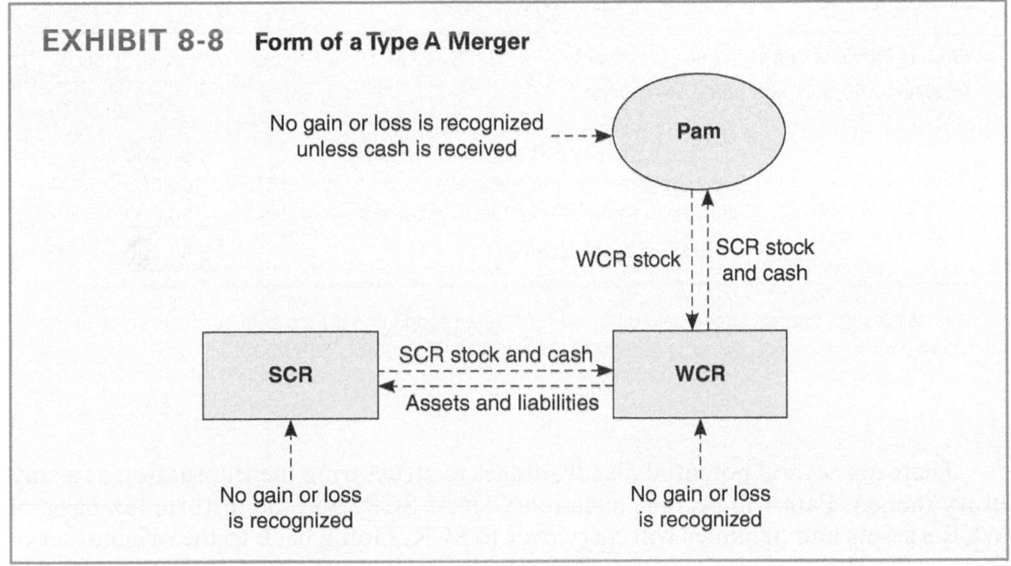

[41] *Gregory v. Helvering,* 293 U.S. 465 (1935).

[42] "A reorganizations" are so named because they are described in §368(a)(1)(*A*). Likewise, B and C reorganizations are described in subparagraphs (B) and (C).

Example 8-22

What if: Assume WCR will merge into SCR in a Type A reorganization. Under the terms of the deal, SCR will pay Pam $300,000 in SCR stock, after which WCR will merge into SCR. Pam's tax basis in her WCR stock is $50,000. What amount of gain will Pam realize on the exchange of her WCR stock for SCR stock?

Answer: $250,000 ($300,000 − $50,000)

What amount of gain will Pam recognize on the exchange of her WCR stock for SCR stock?

Answer: $0. Because Pam receives only SCR stock, she defers the entire $250,000 gain realized.

What is Pam's tax basis in her SCR stock?

Answer: $50,000. Because Pam defers the entire gain, her tax basis in the SCR stock is a substituted basis from her WCR stock. This preserves the gain deferred for future recognition if Pam sold her SCR stock in the future for its fair market value of $300,000.

What are SCR's tax bases in the assets it receives from WCR in the merger?

Answer: SCR receives a carryover tax basis in each of the assets received (e.g., the tax basis of the goodwill and customer list will be zero).

Example 8-23

What if: Suppose instead Pam wants some cash as well as SCR stock in the transaction. What is the maximum amount of cash Pam can receive from SCR and not violate the COI rule as illustrated in the regulations?

Answer: $180,000 ($300,000 × 60%). Pam can receive a maximum of 60 percent of the consideration in cash and not violate the COI rule under the regulations.

What if: Assume Pam receives $100,000 plus $200,000 in SCR stock in exchange for all of her WCR stock in a Type A merger. What amount of gain will Pam *realize* on the exchange?

Answer: $250,000 ($300,000 − $50,000)

What amount of gain will Pam *recognize* on the exchange?

Answer: $100,000. Pam must recognize gain in an amount that is the lesser of the gain realized or the boot received. Pam defers recognizing $150,000 gain.

What is Pam's tax basis in her SCR stock?

Answer: $50,000, computed as follows:

	Adjusted basis of WCR stock exchanged	$ 50,000
+	Gain recognized on the exchange	100,000
−	Fair market value of boot (cash) received	100,000
	Tax basis of stock received	$ 50,000

This calculation preserves the gain deferred for future recognition if Pam sold her SCR stock in the future for its fair market value of $200,000 ($200,000 − $50,000 = $150,000).

There are several potential disadvantages to structuring the transaction as a statutory merger. Pam will become a shareholder of SCR, and the historic tax basis of WCR's assets and liabilities will carry over to SCR. Going back to the original set of facts in the above example, Pam will not owe any tax on the transaction but she will not receive any cash. Finally, WCR will cease to exist as a separate corporation. Jim

EXHIBIT 8-9 Form of a Type A Forward Triangular Merger

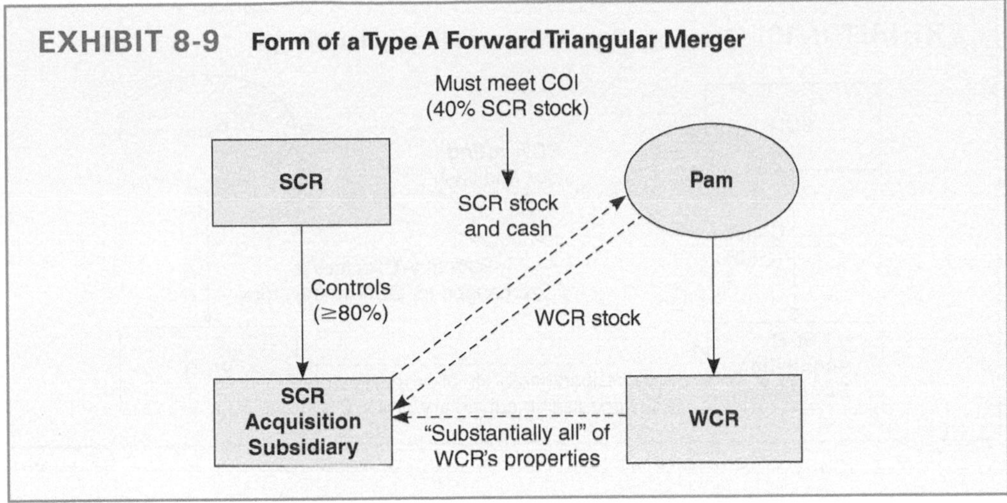

and Ginny expressed a desire to operate WCR as an independent company. To accomplish this, SCR will have to transfer the WCR assets and liabilities to a newly created subsidiary under §351. SCR will incur the additional cost of retitling the assets a second time and pay any state transfer tax on the transfer of the assets. This latter cost can be avoided by employing a variation of a Type A reorganization called a *forward (upstream) triangular merger.*

Forward Triangular Type A Merger In a forward triangular merger, SCR creates a subsidiary corporation (called, perhaps, SCR Acquisition Subsidiary) that holds SCR stock. WCR then merges into the subsidiary with Pam receiving the SCR stock in exchange for her WCR stock. When the dust clears, WCR assets and liabilities are isolated in a wholly owned subsidiary of SCR. Exhibit 8-9 provides an illustration of the "fictional" form of a forward triangular Type A merger for determining the tax consequences to the parties to the transaction.

This type of merger is a common vehicle for effecting mergers when the parent corporation stock is publicly traded or the parent corporation is a holding company. For a forward triangular merger to be effective, the transaction must satisfy the requirements to be a straight Type A merger and one additional requirement: SCR's acquisition subsidiary must acquire "substantially all" of WCR's properties in the exchange. The IRS interprets "substantially all" to mean 90 percent of the fair market value of WCR's net properties ($300,000), and 70 percent of the fair market value of WCR's gross properties ($335,000). The technical tax rules that apply to determine the tax basis of WCR's assets after the merger are complex and beyond the scope of this text.

Reverse Triangular Type A Merger Another variation of a Type A reorganization is the *reverse (downstream) triangular merger.* Suppose that WCR holds valuable assets that cannot be easily transferred to another corporation (perhaps employment contracts or licenses). In this scenario, it would not be prudent to dissolve WCR because these valuable assets would be lost. In a reverse triangular merger, SCR still creates a subsidiary corporation that holds SCR stock. However, it is the acquisition subsidiary that merges into WCR with Pam receiving the SCR stock in exchange for her WCR stock. When the dust clears, WCR is still intact, albeit as a wholly owned subsidiary of SCR. Reverse triangular Type A mergers are desirable because the transaction preserves the target corporation's existence. Exhibit 8-10 provides an illustration of the "fictional" form of a reverse triangular Type A merger for determining the tax consequences to the parties to the transaction.

EXHIBIT 8-10 Form of a Type A Reverse Triangular Merger

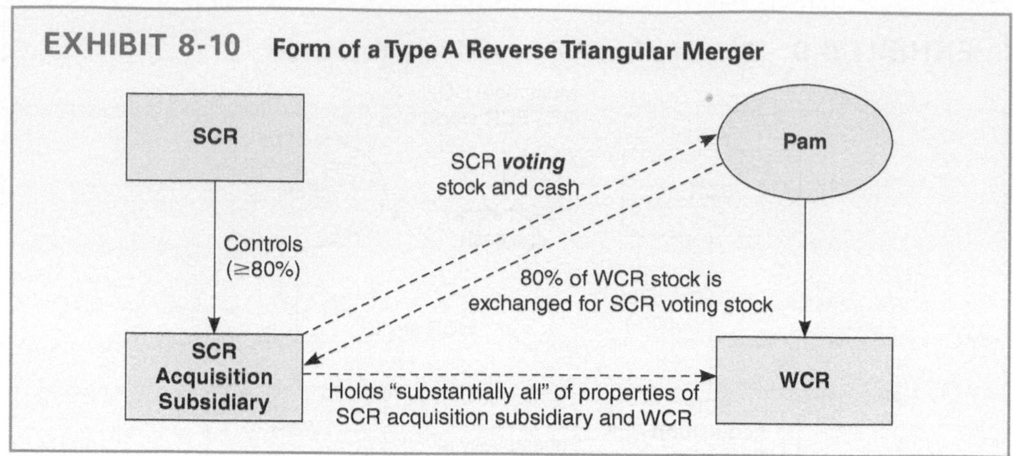

THE KEY FACTS

Forms of a Tax-Deferred Stock Acquisition

- Stock-for-stock B reorganization
  - The acquiring corporation must exchange solely voting stock for stock of the target corporation.
  - The acquiring corporation must control (own 80 percent or more of) the target corporation after the transaction.
  - The target corporation shareholders take a substituted tax basis in the acquiring corporation stock received in the exchange.
  - The acquiring corporation takes a carryover tax basis in the target corporation stock received in the exchange.

There are three additional requirements that must be met to satisfy the requirements for tax deferral in a reverse triangular merger. First, WCR must hold "substantially all" of the properties of both WCR and the SCR Acquisition Subsidiary. Second, Pam must transfer in the exchange an amount of stock in WCR that constitutes control of WCR (80 percent or more of WCR stock). Finally, Pam must receive SCR *voting stock* in return for her WCR stock that constitutes control of WCR in the exchange. For example, if the SCR Acquisition Subsidiary acquires 100 percent of WCR's stock in the exchange, at least 80 percent of the consideration the SCR Acquisition Subsidiary pays Pam must be in the form of SCR voting stock.

This last requirement often presents too difficult a hurdle to overcome in acquisitions in which the acquiring corporation wants to use a combination of cash and stock to acquire the target corporation. Publicly traded companies are very sensitive to the amount of stock they use in an acquisition because of the potential negative effect it can have on the company's earnings per share (i.e., issuing additional stock increases the denominator in the earnings per share computation). The technical tax rules that apply to determine the tax basis of WCR's assets after the merger are complex and beyond the scope of this text.

The Walt Disney Company acquired Pixar in a reverse triangular merger. Disney's acquisition subsidiary merged into Pixar, after which the former shareholders of Pixar received Disney stock in exchange for their Pixar stock.

Type B Stock-for-Stock Reorganizations

Type B reorganizations (cell 2) often are referred to as **stock-for-stock acquisitions.** The requirements to meet a tax-deferred Type B reorganization are very restrictive. In particular, SCR must acquire *control* (80 percent or more ownership) of WCR using *solely* SCR *voting* stock. Additional consideration of as little as $1 can taint the transaction and cause it to be fully taxable to Pam. Not surprisingly, Type B reorganizations are rare among publicly traded companies. Exhibit 8-11 provides an illustration of the form of a Type B merger.

In a Type B reorganization, Pam will defer recognition of any gain or loss realized and take a substituted basis in the SCR stock she receives. SCR takes a *carryover basis* (from Pam) in the WCR stock received. In the case of publicly traded companies, this requires the acquiring corporation to determine the tax basis of each share of stock it receives from thousands or even millions of shareholders of the target corporation. In such cases, the IRS allows the acquiring corporation to determine its stock basis using statistical sampling.

EXHIBIT 8-11 Form of a Type B Reorganization

SCR
Solely SCR voting stock
WCR stock
Pam
SCR "controls" WCR immediately after the exchange
WCR

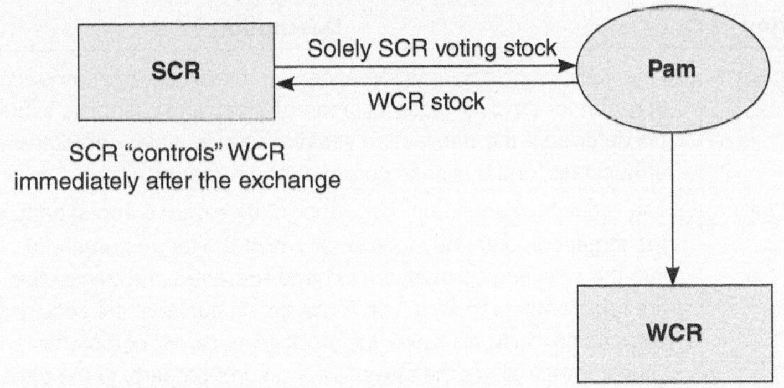

Example 8-24

What if: Let's say SCR will exchange SCR voting stock for all of Pam's WCR stock in a Type B stock-for-stock reorganization. Pam's tax basis in her WCR stock is $50,000. The fair market value of the SCR stock is $300,000. What amount of gain will Pam *realize* on the exchange of her WCR stock for SCR stock?

Answer: $250,000 ($300,000 – $50,000)

What amount of gain will Pam *recognize* on the exchange of her WCR stock for SCR stock?

Answer: $0. Because Pam receives only SCR stock, she defers the entire $250,000 gain realized.

What is Pam's tax basis in her SCR stock?

Answer: $50,000. Because Pam defers the entire gain, her tax basis in the SCR stock is a substituted basis from her WCR stock. This preserves the gain deferred for future recognition if Pam sold her SCR stock in the future for its fair market value of $300,000.

What are SCR's tax bases in the WCR stock received in the exchange?

Answer: SCR receives a substituted tax basis equal to Pam's basis in her WCR stock.

What are WCR's tax bases in the assets after the exchange?

Answer: WCR retains a carryover tax basis in each of the assets (e.g., the tax basis of the goodwill and customer list will be zero).

What if: Suppose Pam received $10,000 plus $290,000 of SCR stock in the transaction. How does this change in facts affect Pam's tax consequences?

Answer: The entire gain realized of $250,000 is recognized. For a Type B reorganization to be tax-deferred, Pam cannot receive any cash. Given her desire to move to Colorado, this limitation likely will be a deal breaker.

There are many variations of Type A and Type B acquisitions and other tax-deferred asset-type acquisitions that we do not discuss in this chapter because of complexity. Suffice it to say that tax experts in mergers and acquisitions have a toolbox of ideas and alternatives that allow for a multiplicity of ways to structure a transaction and achieve tax deferral to the parties to the reorganization. For the novice entering this field of taxation, this can be both exhilarating and exasperating. Our goal in this section is to provide you with a glimpse of this intricate area of taxation. A summary of the tax-deferred reorganizations discussed above along with the other forms of tax-deferred reorganizations is provided in Exhibit 8-12.

EXHIBIT 8-12 Summary of Tax-Deferred Corporate Reorganizations

Form of Reorganization	Description
Statutory Merger Type A	One corporation acquires the assets and liabilities of another corporation in return for stock or a combination of stock and cash. The acquisition is tax-deferred if the transaction satisfies the continuity of interest, continuity of business, and business purpose requirements.
Forward Triangular Type A	The acquiring corporation uses stock of its *parent* corporation to acquire the target corporation's stock, after which the target corporation merges into the acquiring corporation. To be tax-deferred, the transaction must meet the requirements to be a Type A merger. In addition, the acquiring corporation must use *solely* the stock of its parent corporation and acquire "substantially all" of the target corporation's property in the transaction.
Reverse Triangular Type A	The acquiring corporation uses stock of its parent corporation to acquire the target corporation's stock, after which the acquiring corporation merges into the target corporation (which becomes a subsidiary of the parent corporation). To be tax-deferred, the transaction must satisfy three requirements: (1) the surviving corporation must hold "substantially all" of the properties of both the surviving and the merged corporations; (2) the target shareholders must transfer in the exchange an amount of stock in the target that constitutes control of the target (80 percent or more of the target's stock); and (3) the target shareholders must receive parent corporation voting stock in return.
Type B	The acquiring corporation uses its voting stock (or the voting stock of its parent corporation) to acquire control (80 percent voting power and 80 percent of nonvoting stock) of the target corporation. To be tax-deferred, the target shareholders must receive *solely* voting stock of the acquiring corporation.
Type C	The acquiring corporation uses its voting stock (or voting stock of its parent corporation) to acquire "substantially all" of the target corporation's assets. The end result of a Type C reorganization resembles a Type A reorganization. The major difference between a Type C reorganization and a Type A reorganization is that state law governs the form of the Type A merger, while the Internal Revenue Code governs the form of the Type C reorganization.
Type D	A corporation transfers all or part of its assets to another corporation, and immediately after the transfer the shareholders of the transferor corporation own at least 50 percent of the voting power or value of the transferee corporation (nondivisive Type D). A corporation transfers all or part of its assets to another corporation, and immediately after the transfer the shareholders of the transferor corporation own at least 80 percent of the transferee corporation (divisive Type D).
Type E	Type E reorganizations are often referred to as recapitalizations. Stock in the corporation (e.g., common) is exchanged for a different class of stock (e.g., preferred) or securities (debt). Recapitalizations can range from an amendment in the corporate charter to a change in the redemption price or liquidating value of stock to an actual exchange of stock between the corporation and its shareholder(s).
Type F	Type F reorganizations are described as a "mere change in identity, form, or place of organization" of a single corporation. A corporation uses a Type F reorganization to change its corporate name or its state (country) of incorporation.
Type G	Type G reorganizations are often referred to as bankruptcy reorganizations. In a Type G reorganization, the corporation transfers all or a part of its assets to another corporation in a Title 11 case, and the stock of the corporation receiving the assets is distributed in a transaction that is tax-deferred.

The tax law also allows corporations to divide by transferring stock of a subsidiary to shareholders in a pro rata distribution (spin-off) or a non-pro rata distribution (split-off).[43] The technical details of these transactions are beyond the scope of this text.

COMPLETE LIQUIDATION OF A CORPORATION

LO 8-5

continued from page 8-23. . .

After several years of trying to get 360 Air off the ground, it became clear to Jim, Ginny, and even Al that there was not enough demand for snowboarding products in East Lansing to make their business venture profitable. Reluctantly, the three owners decided to liquidate the corporation. Once again, they summoned their tax adviser, Louis Tully, to help them understand the tax consequences of liquidating the corporation. Louis constructed the company's tax accounting balance sheet, which is reproduced below.

	FMV	Adjusted Basis	Difference
Cash	$138,000	$138,000	
Receivables	2,000	2,000	
Inventory	10,000	12,000	$ (2,000)
Building	150,000	48,000	102,000
Land	200,000	100,000	100,000
Total	$500,000	$300,000	$200,000

The parties agreed that 360 Air would sell off the remaining inventory and the land and building, and collect the remaining receivables. After the sale, 360 Air would pay taxes of $70,000 (assuming a tax rate of 35 percent) on the gains and divide the remaining $430,000 in cash pro rata between the three shareholders (50 percent to Al, 40 percent to Jim, and 10 percent to Ginny). ■

As the storyline indicates, the owners of a corporation may decide at some point to discontinue the corporation's business activities. This decision may be made because the corporation is not profitable, the officers and shareholders wish to change the organizational form of the business (e.g., to a flow-through entity), or the owners want to consolidate operations (e.g., a subsidiary is liquidated into the parent corporation).

A complete liquidation occurs when a corporation acquires all of its stock from all of its shareholders in exchange for "all" of its net assets, after which time the corporation ceases to do business. For tax purposes, a corporation files Form 966 to inform the IRS of its intention to liquidate its tax existence. The form should be filed within 30 days after the owners (board of directors) resolve to liquidate the corporation.

[43]§355.

Tax Consequences to the Shareholders in a Complete Liquidation

The tax consequences to the shareholders in a complete liquidation depend on (1) whether the shareholder is incorporated and (2) ownership percentage in the corporation. In general, all *noncorporate* shareholders receiving liquidating distributions have a fully taxable transaction.[44] The shareholders treat the property received as in "full payment in exchange for the stock" transferred. The shareholder computes capital gain or loss by subtracting the stock's tax basis from the money and fair market value of property received in return. If a shareholder assumes the corporation's liabilities on property received as a liquidating distribution, the amount realized in the computation of gain or loss is reduced by the amount of the liabilities assumed. The shareholder's tax basis in the property received equals the property's fair market value.

Example 8-25

Ginny received cash of $43,000 representing her 10 percent ownership in the company after all debts were paid. Ginny's tax basis in the 360 Air stock is $60,000.

What amount of gain or loss will Ginny *realize* on the exchange of her 360 Air stock for 360 Air assets?

Answer: $17,000 capital loss ($43,000 – $60,000).

What amount of loss will Ginny *recognize* on the exchange?

Answer: $17,000. The entire amount could be deductible to the extent of Ginny's capital gains.

Example 8-26

What if: Suppose that rather than sell the land, 360 Air distributed the land with $15,000 cash to Al, representing his 50 percent interest in the net fair market value of the company. Al's tax basis in the 360 Air stock is $100,000.

What amount of gain or loss will Al *realize* on the exchange of his 360 Air stock for 360 Air assets?

Answer: $115,000 capital gain [($200,000 + $15,000) – $100,000].

What amount of gain will Al *recognize* on the exchange?

Answer: $115,000. The entire amount is taxable.

What is Al's tax basis in the cash and land he receives in the liquidation?

Answer: $215,000. Al receives a tax basis in the assets he receives equal to their fair market values.

Example 8-27

As a result of the complete liquidation of 360 Air, Jim received $172,000, cash representing his 40 percent ownership. His tax basis in 360 Air is $240,000, an amount equal to the cash he contributed when the corporation was formed.

[44]§331.

What amount of gain or loss will Jim *realize* on the exchange of his 360 Air stock for 360 Air assets?

Answer: $68,000 net capital loss ($172,000 − $240,000).

What amount of loss will Jim *recognize* on the exchange?

Answer: $68,000. The entire amount could be deductible to the extent of Jim's capital gains. Otherwise, Jim can deduct a maximum of $3,000 of net capital loss and carry the unused capital loss forward.

Corporate shareholders are also taxed on liquidating distributions unless the corporation owns 80 percent or more of the stock (voting power and value). Corporate shareholders owning 80 percent or more of the stock (voting power and value) of the liquidating corporation do not recognize gain or loss on the receipt of liquidating distributions.[45] This nonrecognition treatment is mandatory. The tax basis in the property transferred carries over to the recipient.[46] This deferral provision allows a group of corporations under common control to reorganize their organizational structure without tax consequences.

Example 8-28

What if: Suppose 360 Air was a 100 percent-owned subsidiary of SCR, and SCR liquidated the company into itself. SCR has a tax basis in its 360 Air stock of $300,000.

What amount of gain or loss will SCR *realize* on the complete liquidation of 360 Air stock for 360 Air assets?

Answer: $200,000 net capital gain ($500,000 − $300,000).

What amount of gain will SCR *recognize* on the exchange?

Answer: $0. The gain is not recognized because SCR owns 80 percent or more of 360 Air.

What is SCR's tax basis in the assets and liabilities it receives in the liquidation?

Answer: 360 Air's tax basis in the assets and liabilities will not change. SCR will inherit a carryover tax basis in 360 Air's assets and liabilities.

THE KEY FACTS

Tax Consequences of a Complete Liquidation

- Shareholders other than corporations that own 80 percent or more of the liquidating corporation's stock recognize gain and usually loss in a complete liquidation of the corporation.
- Corporations that own 80 percent or more of the liquidating corporation's stock do not recognize gain and usually loss in a complete liquidation of the corporation.
- Shareholders recognizing gain or loss take a tax basis in property received in the complete liquidation equal to its fair market value.
- Corporate shareholders that defer recognizing gain or loss take a tax basis in property received in the complete liquidation equal to its carryover basis.

Tax Consequences to the Liquidating Corporation in a Complete Liquidation

The tax consequences to the liquidating corporation depend on the tax treatment applied to the shareholder to whom the property was distributed.

Taxable Liquidating Distributions Typically, a liquidating corporation recognizes all gains and certain losses on taxable distributions of property to shareholders.[47] The liquidating corporation does not recognize *loss* if the property is distributed to a *related party* and either (1) the distribution is non-pro rata, or (2) the asset distributed is *disqualified property*.[48] A *related person* generally is defined as a shareholder

[45]§332(a).
[46]§334(b)(1).
[47]§336(a).
[48]§336(d)(1).

who owns more than 50 percent of the stock of the liquidating corporation. *Disqualified property* is property acquired within five years of the date of distribution in a tax-deferred §351 transaction or as a nontaxable contribution to capital.

Example 8-29

360 Air made taxable liquidating distributions to Jim, Ginny, and Al during the current year. Jim owns 50 percent of the stock, Ginny owns 10 percent, and Al owns 40 percent. Assume for purposes of this example that 360 Air made a pro rata distribution of all of the assets to its three shareholders. The company's tax accounting balance sheet at the time of the distribution is reproduced below:

	FMV	Adjusted Basis	Difference
Cash	$138,000	$138,000	
Receivables	2,000	2,000	
Inventory	10,000	12,000	$ (2,000)
Building	150,000	48,000	102,000
Land	200,000	100,000	100,000
Total	$500,000	$300,000	$200,000

What amount of gain or loss does 360 Air recognize as a result of the distribution?

Answer: $200,000. 360 Air recognizes all gains and losses on the distribution of its assets in the following amounts and character:

	Gain (Loss) Recognized	Character
Inventory	$ (2,000)	Ordinary
Building	102,000	Ordinary (§291) and §1231
Land	100,000	§1231
Net gain	$200,000	

Note that the gain or loss on the complete liquidation is identical to gains and losses that would result if 360 Air had sold all of its assets at fair market value.

Example 8-30

What if: Assume Jim owned 60 percent of the stock, and 360 Air distributed all of the inventory to Jim in a non-pro rata distribution. The company's tax accounting balance sheet at the time of the distribution is reproduced below:

	FMV	Adjusted Basis	Difference
Cash	$138,000	$138,000	
Receivables	2,000	2,000	
Inventory	10,000	12,000	$ (2,000)
Building	150,000	48,000	102,000
Land	200,000	100,000	100,000
Total	$500,000	$300,000	$200,000

What amount of gain or loss does 360 Air recognize as a result of the distribution?

Answer: $202,000 gain. 360 Air recognizes all gains but cannot recognize the inventory loss because the distribution is non-pro rata and the loss property is distributed to a related person (Jim owns more than 50 percent of the stock).

	Gain (Loss) Recognized	Character
Inventory	$ 0	
Building	102,000	Ordinary (§291) and §1231
Land	100,000	§1231
Net gain	$202,000	

What if: Assume 360 Air distributed all of the inventory to Ginny in a non-pro rata distribution. What amount of gain or loss does 360 Air recognize as a result of the distribution?

Answer: $200,000. 360 Air can now recognize the $2,000 loss on the distribution of the inventory because the property was not distributed to a related person.

A second loss disallowance rule applies to built-in loss that arises with respect to property acquired in a §351 transaction or as a contribution to capital. A loss on the complete liquidation of such property is not recognized if the property distributed was acquired in a §351 transaction or as a contribution to capital, and a *principal purpose* of the contribution was to recognize a loss by the liquidating corporation.[49] This rule prevents a built-in loss existing at the time of the distribution (basis in excess of fair market value) from being recognized by treating the basis of the property distributed as being its fair market value at the time it was contributed to the corporation. This prohibited tax avoidance purpose is presumed if the property transfer occurs within two years of the liquidation. This presumption can be overcome if the corporation can show that there was a corporate business purpose for contributing the property to the corporation.

This provision is designed as an *anti-stuffing* provision to prevent shareholders from contributing property with built-in losses to a corporation shortly before a liquidation to offset gain property distributed in the liquidation. Earlier in this chapter you learned that Congress added a similar built-in loss disallowance rule that applies to §351 transfers.[50] Under this provision, if the *aggregate* adjusted tax basis of property transferred to a corporation by a shareholder in a §351 transfer exceeds the aggregate fair market value of the assets, the aggregate tax basis of the assets in the hands of the transferee corporation cannot exceed their aggregate fair market value. The loss disallowance rule that relates to liquidating distributions of built-in loss property received in a §351 transaction applies on an asset by asset basis to those assets that retained their built-in loss when contributed to the corporation.

Example 8-31

What if: Suppose Al transferred a building and land to 360 Air in return for 50 percent of the corporation's stock (50 shares) in a transaction that qualified under §351. The property transferred to the corporation had the following fair market values and adjusted bases:

	FMV	Adjusted Basis
Building	$ 75,000	$100,000
Land	200,000	100,000
Total	$275,000	$200,000

(continued on page 8-38)

[49]§336(d)(2).

[50]§362(e)(2).

In this case, the aggregate fair market value of the property transferred to the corporation exceeds the aggregate adjusted basis of the property. As a result, the building will retain its carryover basis of $100,000 and subsequent built-in loss of $25,000.

If the building and land are distributed to Al in complete liquidation of his ownership of 360 Air stock within two years of the §351 transaction, will 360 Air be able to deduct the $25,000 loss on the distribution of the building?

Answer: It depends. Because the liquidating distribution is made within two years of the §351 transaction, the presumption is that Al contributed the property to 360 Air for tax avoidance purposes (i.e., to allow the corporation to deduct the loss). The corporation can rebut this presumption by demonstrating that the contribution of the property by Al had a corporate business purpose at the time of the §351 transaction.

Nontaxable Liquidating Distributions The liquidating corporation does not recognize gain or loss on tax-free distributions of property to an 80 percent corporate shareholder.[51] If any one of the shareholders receives tax deferral in the liquidation, the liquidating corporation cannot recognize any *loss,* even on distributions to shareholders who receive taxable distributions.[52] There are exceptions to this rule that are beyond the scope of this text.

Example 8-32

What if: Assume 360 Air was a 100 percent-owned subsidiary of SCR, and SCR liquidated the company into itself. SCR has a tax basis in its 360 Air stock of $300,000. The company's tax accounting balance sheet at the time of the distribution is reproduced below:

	FMV	Adjusted Basis	Difference
Cash	$138,000	$138,000	
Receivables	2,000	2,000	
Inventory	10,000	12,000	$ (2,000)
Building	150,000	48,000	102,000
Land	200,000	100,000	100,000
Total	$500,000	$300,000	$200,000

What amount of gain or loss does 360 Air *recognize* as a result of the liquidation?

Answer: $0. 360 Air does not recognize any gain or loss on the liquidation because SCR is not taxed on the liquidating distribution.

What if: Suppose 360 Air was 80 percent owned by SCR and 20 percent owned by Jim. 360 Air distributed the inventory plus $90,000 to Jim in complete liquidation of his stock. Can 360 Air recognize the $2,000 inventory loss?

Answer: No. 360 Air cannot recognize the loss even though Jim is not a related party and has a taxable distribution. When one shareholder is not taxable on a liquidating distribution (SCR), the liquidating corporation cannot recognize any losses on the distribution of property to any shareholder.

Liquidation-related expenses, including the cost of preparing and effectuating a plan of complete liquidation, are deductible by the liquidating corporation on its final Form 1120. Deferred or capitalized expenditures such as organizational expenditures also are deductible on the final tax return.

[51]§337(a).

[52]§336(d)(3).

CONCLUSION

In this chapter we discussed some of the important tax rules that apply during the life cycle of a C corporation. As the storyline indicates, forming a corporation generally does not create any tax to any of the parties to the transaction. Gain or loss realized by the shareholders on the transfer of property to the corporation is deferred until a later date, either when the shareholder sells his ownership interest or the corporation liquidates. Subsequent acquisitions of new businesses or dispositions of existing businesses also can be achieved in a tax-deferred manner. However, failure to meet all of the requirements can convert a tax-deferred transaction into a taxable transaction. A complete liquidation of a corporation generally is a fully taxable transaction to the shareholders and the liquidating corporation, except in the case where a subsidiary is liquidated into its parent corporation.

Summary

Review the taxation of property dispositions. LO 8-1

- A person realizes gain or loss as a result of engaging in a transaction, which is defined as an exchange of property rights with another person.
- Gain or loss realized is computed by subtracting the adjusted basis of property transferred in the exchange from the amount realized in the exchange.
- The amount realized is computed as cash received plus the fair market value of other property received plus any liabilities assumed by the transferee on the property transferred, reduced by selling expenses and any liabilities assumed by the transferor on property received in the exchange.
- The general tax rule is that gain or loss realized is recognized (included in the computation of taxable income) unless a specific tax rule exempts the gain or loss from being recognized (permanently) or defers such recognition until a future date.

Compute the tax consequences to the parties to a tax-deferred corporate formation. LO 8-2

- Section 351 applies to transactions in which one or more persons transfer property to a corporation in return for stock, and immediately after the transfer, these same persons control the corporation to which they transferred the property.
- If a transaction meets these requirements, the transferors of property (shareholders) do not recognize (defer) gain or loss realized on the transfer of the property to the corporation.
    - Shareholders contributing property to a corporation in a §351 transaction compute gain or loss realized by subtracting the adjusted basis of the property they contribute to the corporation from the fair market value of the consideration they receive in return (amount realized).
    - Gain, but not loss, is recognized when property other than the corporation's stock (boot) is received in the exchange.
    - Gain is recognized in an amount equal to the *lesser of* the gain realized or the fair market value of boot received.
    - The tax basis of stock received in the exchange equals the tax basis of the property transferred, less any liabilities assumed by the corporation on the property contributed (substituted basis).
    - The shareholder's stock basis is increased by any gain recognized and reduced by the fair market value of any boot received.
- The corporation receiving property for its stock in a §351 exchange does not recognize (excludes) gain or loss realized on the transfer.
    - The tax basis of the property received by the corporation equals the property's tax basis in the transferor's hands (carryover basis).
    - The asset's tax basis is increased by any gain recognized by the shareholder on the transfer of the property to the corporation.

LO 8-3 Identify the different forms of taxable and tax-deferred acquisitions.

- Corporations can be acquired in taxable asset or stock purchases.
- Corporations can be acquired in tax-deferred asset or stock purchases.
- To be tax-deferred, an acquisition must meet certain IRC and judicial requirements to be a reorganization.
  - The judicial requirements, now summarized in the regulations, require continuity of interest, continuity of business enterprise, and business purpose.
- In a Type A tax-deferred acquisition, the target corporation's assets and liabilities are merged into the acquiring corporation (stock-for-assets exchange).
  - Type A acquisitions involving publicly traded corporations often use an acquisition subsidiary (triangular merger) to acquire the target corporation's assets and liabilities.
- In a Type B tax-deferred acquisition, the shareholders of the target corporation exchange their stock for stock of the acquiring corporation (stock-for-stock exchange).
  - Type B acquisitions prohibit the use of cash in the exchange.

LO 8-4 Determine the tax consequences to the parties to a corporate acquisition.

- Shareholders participating in a taxable asset or stock transaction compute gain or loss realized by subtracting the adjusted basis of the stock they surrender to the acquiring corporation from the fair market value of the consideration they receive in the exchange.
- Shareholders participating in a tax-deferred reorganization defer gain and loss realized in the exchange unless cash (boot) is received.
  - Shareholders receiving boot recognize gain, but not loss, in an amount equal to the lesser of the gain realized or the fair market value of the boot received.
- The corporation does not recognize gain on the distribution of its own stock in exchange for property in a reorganization.
- The stock received in return for stock in a tax-deferred reorganization has a tax basis equal to the tax basis of the stock surrendered in the exchange (substituted basis).
- The shareholder's stock basis is increased by any gain recognized and reduced by cash or other boot received.
- The assets transferred to the corporation in a tax-deferred reorganization carry over the tax basis of the shareholders contributing the property (carryover basis).

LO 8-5 Calculate the tax consequences that apply to the parties to a complete liquidation of a corporation.

- Noncorporate shareholders receiving a distribution in complete liquidation of their corporation recognize gain and (usually) loss in the exchange.
- Tax deferral is extended to corporate shareholders owning 80 percent or more of the liquidating corporation.
- The liquidating corporation recognizes gain and (usually) loss on the distribution of property to those shareholders who are taxable on the distribution.
- The liquidating corporation cannot deduct losses on property distributed in the following three situations:
  - The loss property is distributed to a related person and is non-pro rata.
  - The loss property was contributed to the corporation in a §351 transaction and the principle purpose of the contribution was tax avoidance.
  - One of the persons receiving a liquidating distribution was not taxable on the distribution (an 80 percent or more corporate shareholder).
- The liquidating corporation does not recognize gain or loss on the distribution of property to a corporate shareholder that is not taxable on the distribution.
- The tax basis of each asset received by the shareholder in a taxable complete liquidation equals the asset's fair market value on the date of the distribution.
- The tax basis of each asset received by an 80 percent or more corporate shareholder in a tax-deferred complete liquidation carries over from the liquidating corporation.

KEY TERMS

adjusted tax basis (8-3)
amount realized (8-3)
boot (8-7)
bright line tests (8-26)
carryover basis (8-14)
consolidation (8-27)
continuity of business enterprise (COBE) (8-27)
continuity of interest (COI) (8-26)
contribution to capital (8-18)
merger (8-27)
person (8-5)
realization (8-2)
reorganization (8-26)
§338 election (8-25)
§338(h)(10) election (8-25)
stock-for-stock acquisition (8-30)
substituted basis (8-9)
tax accounting balance sheet (8-22)

DISCUSSION QUESTIONS

1. Discuss the difference between gain realization and gain recognition in a property transaction. LO 8-1
2. What information must a taxpayer gather to determine the *amount realized* in a property transaction? LO 8-1
3. Distinguish between exclusion and deferral as it relates to a property transaction. LO 8-1
4. Contrast how a taxpayer's tax basis in property received in a property transaction will be affected if the transaction results in gain exclusion versus gain deferral. LO 8-1
5. What information must a taxpayer gather to determine the *adjusted basis* of property exchanged in a property transaction? LO 8-1
6. Why does Congress allow tax deferral on the formation of a corporation? LO 8-2
7. List the key statutory requirements that must be met before a corporate formation is tax-deferred under §351. LO 8-2
8. What is the definition of *control* for purposes of §351? Why does Congress require the shareholders to control a corporation to receive tax deferral? LO 8-2
9. What is a *substituted basis* as it relates to stock received in exchange for property in a §351 transaction? What is the purpose of attaching a substituted basis to stock received in a §351 transaction? LO 8-2
10. Explain whether the receipt of boot by a shareholder in a §351 transaction causes the transaction to be fully taxable. LO 8-2
11. Explain whether a corporation's assumption of shareholder liabilities will always constitute boot in a §351 transaction. LO 8-2
12. How does the tax treatment differ in cases where liabilities are assumed with a tax avoidance purpose versus where liabilities assumed exceed basis? When would this distinction cause a difference in the tax consequences of the transactions? LO 8-2
13. What is a *carryover basis* as it relates to property received by a corporation in a §351 transaction? What is the purpose of attaching a carryover basis to property received in a §351 transaction? LO 8-2
14. Under what circumstances does property received by a corporation in a §351 transaction not receive a carryover basis? What is the reason for this rule? LO 8-2
15. How does a corporation depreciate an asset received in a §351 transaction in which no gain or loss is recognized by the transferor of the property? LO 8-2
16. Explain if the tax consequences are the same whether a shareholder contributes property to a corporation in a §351 transaction or as a capital contribution. LO 8-2
17. Why might a corporation prefer to characterize an instrument as debt rather than equity for tax purposes? Are the holders of the instrument indifferent as to its characterization for tax purposes? LO 8-2
18. Under what conditions is it advantageous for a shareholder to hold §1244 stock? Why did Congress bestow these tax benefits on holders of such stock? LO 8-2
19. Why does the acquiring corporation usually prefer to buy the target corporation's assets directly in an acquisition? LO 8-3

LO 8-3 20. Why do the shareholders of the target corporation usually prefer to sell the stock of the target corporation to the acquiring corporation?

LO 8-3 21. What is the congressional purpose for allowing tax deferral on transactions that meet the definition of a corporate reorganization?

LO 8-3 22. Why do publicly traded corporations use a triangular form of Type A reorganization in acquiring other corporations?

LO 8-3 23. What are the key differences in the tax law requirements that apply to forward versus reverse triangular mergers?

LO 8-3 24. What are the key differences in the tax law requirements that apply to a Type A stock-for-assets acquisition versus a Type B stock-for-stock acquisition?

LO 8-4 25. How does the form of a regular §338 election compare and contrast to a §338(h)(10) election?

LO 8-4 26. What tax benefits does the buyer hope to obtain by making a §338 or §338(h)(10) election?

LO 8-4 27. In a stock acquisition, why is there a difference between the *tax basis of assets* held by an acquired corporation and the *tax basis of the shares* held by a corporate acquirer? Why is this difference important?

LO 8-4 28. What is the presumption behind the continuity of ownership interest (COI) requirement in a tax-deferred acquisition? How do the target shareholders determine if COI is met in a Type A reorganization?

LO 8-4 29. W Corporation will acquire all of the assets and liabilities of Z Corporation in a Type A merger, after which W Corporation will sell off all of its assets and liabilities and focus solely on Z Corporation's business. Explain whether the transaction will be taxable because W Corporation fails the *continuity of business enterprise test.*

LO 8-4 30. Compare how a shareholder computes her tax basis in stock received from the acquiring corporation in a straight Type A merger versus a Type B merger.

LO 8-5 31. Explain whether all shareholders receive the same tax treatment in a complete liquidation of a corporation.

LO 8-5 32. Explain whether a corporate shareholder recognizes gains and losses on the receipt of distributions of property from the complete liquidation of a subsidiary corporation.

LO 8-5 33. Under what circumstances does a corporate shareholder receive tax deferral in a complete liquidation?

LO 8-5 34. Under what circumstances will a liquidating corporation be allowed to recognize loss in a non-pro rata distribution?

LO 8-5 35. Compare and contrast the built-in loss duplication rule as it relates to §351 with the built-in loss disallowance rule as it applies to a complete liquidation.

PROBLEMS

All applicable problems are available with McGraw-Hill's *Connect® Accounting*.

LO 8-2 36. Ramon incorporated his sole proprietorship by transferring inventory, a building, and land to the corporation in return for 100 percent of the corporation's stock. The property transferred to the corporation had the following fair market values and adjusted bases:

	FMV	Adjusted Basis
Inventory	$ 10,000	$ 4,000
Building	50,000	30,000
Land	100,000	50,000
Total	$160,000	$84,000

The fair market value of the corporation's stock received in the exchange equaled the fair market value of the assets transferred to the corporation by Ramon.

a) What amount of gain or loss does Ramon *realize* on the transfer of the property to his corporation?
b) What amount of gain or loss does Ramon *recognize* on the transfer of the property to his corporation?
c) What is Ramon's basis in the stock he receives in his corporation?

37. Carla incorporated her sole proprietorship by transferring inventory, a building, and land to the corporation in return for 100 percent of the corporation's stock. The property transferred to the corporation had the following fair market values and adjusted bases: LO 8-2 planning

	FMV	Adjusted Basis
Inventory	$ 20,000	$ 10,000
Building	150,000	100,000
Land	250,000	300,000
Total	$420,000	$410,000

The corporation also assumed a mortgage of $120,000 attached to the building and land. The fair market value of the corporation's stock received in the exchange was $300,000.

a) What amount of gain or loss does Carla *realize* on the transfer of the property to the corporation?
b) What amount of gain or loss does Carla *recognize* on the transfer of the property to her corporation?
c) What is Carla's basis in the stock she receives in her corporation?
d) Would you advise Carla to transfer the building and land to the corporation? What tax benefits might she and the corporation receive if she kept the building and land and leased it to the corporation?

38. Ivan incorporated his sole proprietorship by transferring inventory, a building, and land to the corporation in return for 100 percent of the corporation's stock. The property transferred to the corporation had the following fair market values and adjusted bases: 

	FMV	Adjusted Basis
Inventory	$ 10,000	$15,000
Building	50,000	40,000
Land	60,000	30,000
Total	$120,000	$85,000

The fair market value of the corporation's stock received in the exchange equaled the fair market value of the assets transferred to the corporation by Ivan. The transaction met the requirements to be tax-deferred under §351.

a) What amount of gain or loss does Ivan *realize* on the transfer of the property to his corporation?
b) What amount of gain or loss does Ivan *recognize* on the transfer of the property to his corporation?
c) What is Ivan's basis in the stock he receives in his corporation?
d) What is the corporation's adjusted basis in each of the assets received in the exchange?
e) Would the stock held by Ivan qualify as §1244 stock? Why would this fact be important if he sold his stock at a loss at some future date?

LO 8-2

39. Zhang incorporated her sole proprietorship by transferring inventory, a building, and land to the corporation in return for 100 percent of the corporation's stock. The property transferred to the corporation had the following fair market values and adjusted bases:

	FMV	Adjusted Basis
Inventory	$ 20,000	$ 10,000
Building	150,000	100,000
Land	230,000	300,000
Total	$400,000	$410,000

The corporation also assumed a mortgage of $100,000 attached to the building and land. The fair market value of the corporation's stock received in the exchange was $300,000. The transaction met the requirements to be tax-deferred under §351.

a) What amount of gain or loss does Zhang *realize* on the transfer of the property to her corporation?
b) What amount of gain or loss does Zhang *recognize* on the transfer of the property to her corporation?
c) What is Zhang's tax basis in the stock she receives in the exchange?
d) What is the corporation's adjusted basis in each of the assets received in the exchange?

Assume the corporation assumed a mortgage of $500,000 attached to the building and land. Assume the fair market value of the building is now $250,000 and the fair market value of the land is $530,000. The fair market value of the stock remains $300,000.

e) How much, if any, gain or loss does Zhang recognize on the exchange assuming the revised facts?
f) What is Zhang's tax basis in the stock she receives in the exchange?
g) What is the corporation's adjusted basis in each of the assets received in the exchange?

LO 8-2
planning

40. Sam and Devon agree to go into business together selling college-licensed clothing. According to the agreement, Sam will contribute inventory valued at $100,000 in return for 80 percent of the stock in the corporation. Sam's tax basis in the inventory is $60,000. Devon will receive 20 percent of the stock in return for providing accounting services to the corporation (these qualified as organizational expenditures). The accounting services are valued at $25,000.

a) What amount of income gain or loss does Sam *realize* on the formation of the corporation? What amount, if any, does he *recognize*?
b) What is Sam's tax basis in the stock he receives in return for his contribution of property to the corporation?
c) What amount of income gain or loss does Devon *realize* on the formation of the corporation? What amount, if any, does he *recognize*?
d) What is Devon's tax basis in the stock he receives in return for his contribution of services to the corporation?

Assume Devon received 25 percent of the stock in the corporation in return for his services.

e) What amount of gain or loss does Sam *recognize* on the formation of the corporation?
f) What is Sam's tax basis in the stock he receives in return for his contribution of property to the corporation?

g) What amount of income, gain, or loss does Devon *recognize* on the formation of the corporation?

h) What is Devon's tax basis in the stock he receives in return for his contribution of services to the corporation?

i) What tax advice could you give Sam and Devon to change the tax consequences?

41. Jekyll and Hyde formed a corporation (Halloween Inc.) on October 31 to develop a drug to address split personalities. Jekyll will contribute a patented formula valued at $200,000 in return for 50 percent of the stock in the corporation. Hyde will contribute an experimental formula worth $120,000 and medical services in exchange for the remaining stock. Jekyll's tax basis in the patented formula is $125,000, whereas Hyde has a basis of $15,000 in his experimental formula.

LO 8-2

a) Describe the tax consequences of the transaction.

b) Prepare the §351 statement that must be included with the return.

42. Ron and Hermione formed Wizard Corporation on January 2. Ron contributed cash of $200,000 in return for 50 percent of the corporation's stock. Hermione contributed a building and land with the following fair market values and adjusted bases in return for 50 percent of the corporation's stock:

LO 8-2

	FMV	Tax-Adjusted Basis
Building	$ 75,000	$ 20,000
Land	175,000	80,000
Total	$250,000	$100,000

To equalize the exchange, Wizard Corporation paid Hermione $50,000 in addition to her stock.

a) What amount of gain or loss does Ron *realize* on the formation of the corporation? What amount, if any, does he *recognize*?

b) What is Ron's tax basis in the stock he receives in return for his contribution of property to the corporation?

c) What amount of gain or loss does Hermione *realize* on the formation of the corporation? What amount, if any, does she *recognize*?

d) What is Hermione's tax basis in the stock she receives in return for her contribution of property to the corporation?

e) What adjusted basis does Wizard Corporation take in the land and building received from Hermione?

Assume Hermione's adjusted basis in the land was $200,000.

f) What amount of gain or loss does Hermione *realize* on the formation of the corporation? What amount, if any, does she *recognize*?

g) What adjusted basis does Wizard Corporation take in the land and building received from Hermione?

Assume Hermione's adjusted basis in the land was $250,000.

h) What amount of gain or loss does Hermione *realize* on the formation of the corporation? What amount, if any, does she *recognize*?

i) What adjusted basis does Wizard Corporation take in the land and building received from Hermione?

j) What election can Hermione and Wizard Corporation make to allow Wizard Corporation to take a carryover basis in the land?

LO 8-2 planning

43. This year, Jack O. Lantern incurred a $60,000 loss on the worthlessness of his stock in the Creepy Corporation (CC). The stock, which Jack purchased in 2005, met all of the §1244 stock requirements at the time of issue. In December of this year, Jack's wife, Jill, also incurred a $75,000 loss on the sale of Eerie Corporation (EC) stock that she purchased in July 2005 and which also satisfied all of the §1244 stock requirements at the time of issue. Both corporations are operating companies.
   a) How much of the losses incurred on the two stock sales can Jack and Jill deduct this year, assuming they do not have capital gains in the current or prior years?
   b) Assuming they did not engage in any other property transactions this year, how much of a net capital loss will carry over to next year for Jack and Jill?
   c) What would be the tax treatment for the losses if Jack and Jill reported only $60,000 of taxable income this year, excluding the securities transactions?
   d) What tax planning suggestions can you offer the Lanterns to increase the tax benefits of these losses?

LO 8-2

44. Breslin Inc. made a capital contribution of investment property to its 100 percent owned subsidiary, Crisler Company. The investment property had a fair market value of $3,000,000 and a tax basis to Breslin of $2, 225,000.
   a) What are the tax consequences to Breslin Inc. on the contribution of the investment property to Crisler Company?
   b) What is the tax basis of the investment property to Crisler Company after the contribution to capital?

LO 8-3 research

45. On February 4, 2013, Verint Systems Inc. acquired Comverse Technology Inc. in a tax-deferred acquisition. The Form 8-K for Comverse (ticker CMVT, cik 803014) describes the transaction and was filed with the SEC on August 13, 2012. You can access the Form 8-K at the SEC's Investor website (http://www.sec.gov/edgar/searchedgar/webusers.htm). Read "Item 1.01, Entry into a Material Definitive Agreement," and determine which form of merger was used to affect the acquisition.

LO 8-3 research

46. On March 1, 2013, Leucadia National Corporation acquired Jefferies Group LLC. in a tax-deferred acquisition. The Form 8-K for Jefferies (ticker JEF, cik 1084580) describes the transaction and was filed with the SEC on November 13, 2012. You can access the Form 8-K at the SEC's Investor website (http://www.sec.gov/edgar/searchedgar/webusers.htm). Read "Item 1.01, Entry into a Material Definitive Agreement," and determine which form of merger was used to affect the acquisition.

LO 8-4

47. Amy and Brian were investigating the acquisition of a tax accounting business, Bottom Line Inc. (BLI). As part of their discussions with the sole shareholder of the corporation, Ernesto Young, they examined the company's tax accounting balance sheet. The relevant information is summarized as follows:

	FMV	Adjusted Basis	Appreciation
Cash	$ 10,000	$ 10,000	
Receivables	15,000	15,000	
Building	100,000	50,000	$ 50,000
Land	225,000	75,000	150,000
Total	$350,000	$150,000	$200,000
Payables	$ 18,000	$ 18,000	
Mortgage*	112,000	112,000	
Total	$130,000	$130,000	

*The mortgage is attached to the building and land.

Ernesto was asking for $400,000 for the company. His tax basis in the BLI stock was $100,000. Included in the sales price was an unrecognized customer list valued at $100,000. The unallocated portion of the purchase price ($80,000) will be recorded as goodwill.

a) What amount of gain or loss does BLI recognize if the transaction is structured as a direct asset sale to Amy and Brian? What amount of corporate-level tax does BLI pay as a result of the transaction, assuming a tax rate of 34 percent?

b) What amount of gain or loss does Ernesto recognize if the transaction is structured as a direct asset sale to Amy and Brian, and BLI distributes the after-tax proceeds (computed in question a) to Ernesto in liquidation of his stock?

c) What are the tax benefits, if any, to Amy and Brian as a result of structuring the acquisition as a direct asset purchase?

48. Using the same facts in problem 47, assume Ernesto agrees to sell his stock in BLI to Amy and Brian for $400,000. LO 8-4

a) What amount of gain or loss does BLI recognize if the transaction is structured as a stock sale to Amy and Brian? What amount of corporate-level tax does BLI pay as a result of the transaction, assuming a tax rate of 34 percent?

b) What amount of gain or loss does Ernesto recognize if the transaction is structured as a stock sale to Amy and Brian?

c) What are the tax benefits, if any, to Amy and Brian as a result of structuring the acquisition as a stock sale?

49. Rather than purchase BLI directly (as in problems 47 and 48), Amy and Brian will have their corporation, Spartan Tax Services (STS), acquire the business from Ernesto in a tax-deferred Type A merger. Amy and Brian would like Ernesto to continue to run BLI, which he agreed to do if he could obtain an equity interest in STS. As part of the agreement, Amy and Brian propose to pay Ernesto $200,000 plus voting stock in STS worth $200,000. Ernesto will become a 10 percent shareholder in STS after the transaction. LO 8-4

a) Will the continuity of ownership interest (COI) requirements for a straight Type A merger be met? Explain.

b) What amount of gain or loss does BLI recognize if the transaction is structured as a Type A merger? What amount of corporate-level tax does BLI pay as a result of the transaction, assuming a tax rate of 34 percent?

c) What amount of gain or loss does Ernesto recognize if the transaction is structured as a Type A merger?

d) What is Ernesto's tax basis in the STS stock he receives in the exchange?

e) What are the tax bases of the BLI assets held by STS after the merger?

50. Robert and Sylvia propose to have their corporation, Wolverine Universal (WU), acquire another corporation, EMU Inc., in a tax-deferred triangular Type A merger using an acquisition subsidiary of WU. The sole shareholder of EMU, Edie Eagle, will receive $250,000 plus $150,000 of WU voting stock in the transaction. LO 8-4

a) Can the transaction be structured as a forward triangular Type A merger? Explain why or why not.

b) Can the transaction be structured as a reverse triangular Type A merger? Explain why or why not.

51. Robert and Sylvia propose to have their corporation, Wolverine Universal (WU), acquire another corporation, EMU Inc., in a stock-for-stock Type B acquisition. LO 8-4

The sole shareholder of EMU, Edie Eagle, will receive $400,000 of WU voting stock in the transaction. Edie's tax basis in her EMU stock is $100,000.

a) What amount of gain or loss does Edie recognize if the transaction is structured as a stock-for-stock Type B acquisition?
b) What is Edie's tax basis in the WU stock she receives in the exchange?
c) What is the tax basis of the EMU stock held by WU after the exchange?

LO 8-5

52. Shauna and Danielle decided to liquidate their jointly owned corporation, Woodward Fashions Inc. (WFI). After liquidating its remaining inventory and paying off its remaining liabilities, WFI had the following tax accounting balance sheet:

	FMV	Adjusted Basis	Appreciation
Cash	$200,000	$200,000	
Building	50,000	10,000	$ 40,000
Land	150,000	90,000	60,000
Total	$400,000	$300,000	$100,000

Under the terms of the agreement, Shauna will receive the $200,000 cash in exchange for her 50 percent interest in WFI. Shauna's tax basis in her WFI stock is $50,000. Danielle will receive the building and land in exchange for her 50 percent interest in WFI. Danielle's tax basis in her WFI stock is $100,000. Assume for purposes of this problem that the cash available to distribute to the shareholders has been reduced by any tax paid by the corporation on gain recognized as a result of the liquidation.

a) What amount of gain or loss does WFI recognize in the complete liquidation?
b) What amount of gain or loss does Shauna recognize in the complete liquidation?
c) What amount of gain or loss does Danielle recognize in the complete liquidation?
d) What is Danielle's tax basis in the building and land after the complete liquidation?

LO 8-5

53. Tiffany and Carlos decided to liquidate their jointly owned corporation, Royal Oak Furniture (ROF). After liquidating its remaining inventory and paying off its remaining liabilities, ROF had the following tax accounting balance sheet:

	FMV	Adjusted Basis	Appreciation (Depreciation)
Cash	$200,000	$200,000	
Building	50,000	10,000	$ 40,000
Land	150,000	200,000	(50,000)
Total	$400,000	$410,000	$(10,000)

Under the terms of the agreement, Tiffany will receive the $200,000 cash in exchange for her 50 percent interest in ROF. Tiffany's tax basis in her ROF stock is $50,000. Carlos will receive the building and land in exchange for his 50 percent interest in ROF. His tax basis in the ROF stock is $100,000. Assume for purposes of this problem that the cash available to distribute to the shareholders has been reduced by any tax paid by the corporation on gain recognized as a result of the liquidation.

a) What amount of gain or loss does ROF recognize in the complete liquidation?
b) What amount of gain or loss does Tiffany recognize in the complete liquidation?
c) What amount of gain or loss does Carlos recognize in the complete liquidation?
d) What is Carlos's tax basis in the building and land after the complete liquidation?

Assume Tiffany owns 40 percent of the ROF stock and Carlos owns 60 percent. Tiffany will receive $160,000 in the liquidation and Carlos will receive the land and building plus $40,000.

e) What amount of gain or loss does ROF recognize in the complete liquidation?
f) What amount of gain or loss does Tiffany recognize in the complete liquidation?
g) What amount of gain or loss does Carlos recognize in the complete liquidation?
h) What is Carlos's tax basis in the building and land after the complete liquidation?

54. Jefferson Millinery Inc. (JMI) decided to liquidate its wholly owned subsidiary, 8 Miles High Inc. (8MH). 8MH had the following tax accounting balance sheet: LO 8-5

	FMV	Adjusted Basis	Appreciation
Cash	$200,000	$200,000	
Building	50,000	10,000	$ 40,000
Land	150,000	90,000	60,000
Total	$400,000	$300,000	$100,000

a) What amount of gain or loss does 8MH recognize in the complete liquidation?
b) What amount of gain or loss does JMI recognize in the complete liquidation?
c) What is JMI's tax basis in the building and land after the complete liquidation?

55. Jefferson Millinery Inc. (JMI) decided to liquidate its wholly owned subsidiary, 8 Miles High Inc. (8MH). 8MH had the following tax accounting balance sheet: LO 8-5

	FMV	Adjusted Basis	Appreciation
Cash	$200,000	$200,000	
Building	50,000	10,000	$ 40,000
Land	150,000	200,000	(50,000)
Total	$400,000	$410,000	$(10,000)

a) What amount of gain or loss does 8MH recognize in the complete liquidation?
b) What amount of gain or loss does JMI recognize in the complete liquidation?
c) What is JMI's tax basis in the building and land after the complete liquidation?

COMPREHENSIVE PROBLEMS

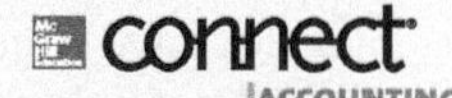

All applicable problems are available with McGraw-Hill's *Connect® Accounting*.

56. Several years ago, your client, Brooks Robinson, started an office cleaning service. His business was very successful, owing much to his legacy as the greatest defensive third baseman in major league history and his nickname, "The Human Vacuum Cleaner." Brooks operated his business as a sole proprietorship and used the cash method of accounting. Brooks was advised by his attorney that it is too risky to operate his business as a sole proprietorship and that he should incorporate to limit his liability. Brooks has come to you for advice on the tax implications of incorporation. His balance sheet is presented below. Under the terms of the incorporation, Brooks would transfer the assets to the corporation in return for 100 percent of the company's common stock. The corporation would also assume the company's liabilities (payables and mortgage).

Balance Sheet

	Adjusted Basis	FMV
Assets		
Accounts receivable	$ 0	$ 5,000
Cleaning equipment (net)	25,000	20,000
Building	50,000	75,000
Land	25,000	50,000
Total assets	$100,000	$150,000
Liabilities		
Accounts payable	$ 0	$ 10,000
Salaries payable	0	5,000
Mortgage on land and building	35,000	35,000
Total liabilities	$ 35,000	$ 50,000

a) How much gain or loss does Brooks *realize* on the transfer of each asset to the corporation?
b) How much, if any, gain or loss (on a per asset basis) does Brooks *recognize*?
c) How much gain or loss, if any, must the corporation recognize on the receipt of the assets of the sole proprietorship in exchange for the corporation's stock?
d) What tax basis does Brooks have in the corporation's stock?
e) What is the corporation's tax basis in each asset it receives from Brooks?
f) How would you answer the question in (b) if Brooks had taken back a 10-year note worth $25,000 plus stock worth $75,000 plus the liability assumption?
g) Will Brooks be able to transfer the accounts receivable to the corporation and have the corporation recognize the income when the receivable is collected?
h) Brooks was depreciating the equipment (200 percent declining balance) and building (straight-line) using MACRS when it was held inside the proprietorship. How will the corporation depreciate the equipment and building? Assume Brooks owned the equipment for four years (seven-year property) and the building for six years.
i) Will the corporation be able to deduct the liabilities when paid? Will it matter which accounting method (cash or accrual) the corporation uses?
j) Would you advise Brooks to transfer the land and building to the corporation? What other tax strategy might you suggest to Brooks with respect to the realty?

57. Your client, Midwest Products Inc. (MPI), is a closely held, calendar-year, accrual-method corporation located in Fowlerville, Michigan. MPI has two operating divisions. One division manufactures lawn and garden furniture and decorative objects (furniture division), while the other division manufactures garden tools and hardware (tool division). MPI's single class of voting common stock is owned as follows:

	Shares	Adjusted Basis	FMV
Iris Green	300	$2,000,000	$3,000,000
Rose Ruby	100	1,200,000	1,000,000
Lily White	100	800,000	1,000,000
Totals	500	$4,000,000	$5,000,000

The three shareholders are unrelated.

Outdoor Living Company (OLC), a publicly held, calendar-year corporation doing business in several midwestern states, has approached MPI about acquiring its furniture division. OLC has no interest in acquiring the tool division, however. OLC's management has several strong business reasons for the acquisition, the most important of which is to expand the company's market into Michigan. Iris, Rose, and Lily are amenable to the acquisition provided it can be accomplished in a tax-deferred manner.

OLC has proposed the following transaction for acquiring MPI's furniture division. On April 30 of this year, OLC will create a 100 percent-owned subsidiary, OLC Acquisition Inc. (OLC-A). OLC will transfer to the subsidiary 60,000 shares of OLC voting common stock and $2,000,000. The current fair market value of the OLC voting stock is $50 per share ($3,000,000 in total). Each of the three MPI shareholders will receive a pro rata amount of OLC stock and cash.

As part of the agreement, MPI will sell the tool division before the acquisition, after which MPI will merge into OLC-A under Michigan and Ohio state laws (a forward triangular Type A merger). Pursuant to the merger agreement, OLC-A will acquire all of MPI's assets, including 100 percent of the cash received from the sale of the tool division ($2,000,000), and will assume all of MPI's liabilities. The cash from the sale of the tool division will be used to modernize and upgrade much of the furniture division's production facilities. OLC's management is convinced that the cash infusion, coupled with new management, will make MPI's furniture business profitable. OLC management has no plans to liquidate OLC-A into OLC at any time subsequent to the merger. After the merger, OLC-A will be renamed Michigan Garden Furniture Inc.

a) Determine whether the proposed transaction meets the requirements to qualify as a tax-deferred forward triangular Type A merger. Consult Rev. Rul. 88-48 and Rev. Rul. 2001-25 in thinking about the premerger sale of the tool division assets.
b) Could the proposed transaction qualify as a reverse triangular Type A merger if OLC-A merged into MPI? If not, how would the transaction have to be restructured to meet the requirements to be a reverse triangular merger?

58. Rex and Felix are the sole shareholders of the Dogs and Cats Corporation (DCC). After several years of operations, they decided to liquidate the corporation and operate the business as a partnership. Rex and Felix hired a lawyer to draw up the legal papers to dissolve the corporation, but they need some tax advice from you, their trusted accountant. They are hoping you will find a way for them to liquidate the corporation without incurring any corporate-level tax liability.

The DCC's tax accounting balance sheet at the date of liquidation is as follows:

	Adjusted Basis	FMV
Assets		
Cash	$ 30,000	$ 30,000
Accounts receivable	10,000	10,000
Inventory	10,000	20,000
Equipment	30,000	20,000
Building	15,000	30,000
Land	5,000	40,000
Total assets	$100,000	$150,000
Liabilities		
Accounts payable		$ 5,000
Mortgage payable—Building		10,000
Mortgage payable—Land		10,000
Total liabilities		$ 25,000
Shareholders' Equity		
Common stock—Rex (80%)	$ 60,000	$100,000
Common stock—Felix (20%)	30,000	25,000
Total shareholders' equity	$ 90,000	$125,000

a) Compute the gain or loss recognized by Rex, Felix, and DCC on a complete liquidation of the corporation assuming each shareholder receives a pro rata distribution of the corporation's assets and assumes a pro rata amount of the liabilities.

b) Compute the gain or loss recognized by Rex, Felix, and DCC on a complete liquidation of the corporation assuming Felix receives $25,000 in cash and Rex receives the remainder of the assets and assumes all of the liabilities.

Assume Felix received the accounts receivable and equipment and assumed the accounts payable.

c) Will Felix recognize any income when he collects the accounts receivable?

d) Will Felix be able to take a deduction when he pays the accounts payable?

Assume Rex is a corporate shareholder of DCC.

e) Compute the gain or loss recognized by Rex, Felix, and DCC on a complete liquidation of the corporation assuming each shareholder receives a pro rata distribution of the corporation's assets and assumes a pro rata amount of the liabilities.

f) Compute the gain or loss recognized by Rex, Felix, and DCC on a complete liquidation of the corporation assuming Felix receives $25,000 in cash and Rex receives the remainder of the assets and assumes all of the liabilities.

Assume the equipment was contributed by Rex to DCC in a §351 transaction two months prior to the liquidation. At the time of the contribution, the property's fair market value was $25,000.

g) Would the tax result change if the property was contributed one year ago? Two years ago? Three years ago?

LO 8-5

59. Cartman Corporation owns 90 shares of SP Corporation. The remaining 10 shares are owned by Kenny (an individual). After several years of operations, Cartman decided to liquidate SP Corporation by distributing the assets to Cartman and Kenny. SP reported the following balance sheet at the date of liquidation:

	Adjusted Basis	FMV
Cash	$12,000	$ 12,000
Accounts receivable	8,000	8,000
Stock investment	2,000	10,000
Land	40,000	70,000
Total assets	$62,000	$100,000
Common stock—Cartman (90%)	$10,000	$ 90,000
Common stock—Kenny (10%)	7,000	10,000
Total shareholder equity	$ 17,000	$100,000

a) Compute the gain or loss recognized by SP, Cartman, and Kenny on a complete liquidation of the corporation, where SP distributes $10,000 of cash to Kenny and the remaining assets to Cartman.

b) Compute the gain or loss recognized by SP and Kenny on a complete liquidation of the corporation, where SP distributes the stock investment to Kenny and the remaining assets to Cartman. Assume that SP's tax rate is zero.

c) What form needs to be filed with the liquidation of SP?

chapter 9

Forming and Operating Partnerships

Learning Objectives

Upon completing this chapter, you should be able to:

LO 9-1 Determine whether a flow-through entity is taxed as a partnership or S corporation, and distinguish the entity approach from the aggregate approach for taxing partnerships.

LO 9-2 Resolve tax issues applicable to partnership formations and other acquisitions of partnership interests, including gain recognition to partners and tax basis for partners and partnerships.

LO 9-3 Determine the appropriate accounting periods and methods for partnerships.

LO 9-4 Calculate and characterize a partnership's ordinary business income or loss and its separately stated items and demonstrate how to report these items to partners.

LO 9-5 Explain the importance of a partner's tax basis and the adjustments that affect it.

LO 9-6 Apply the basis, at-risk, and passive activity loss limits to losses from partnerships.

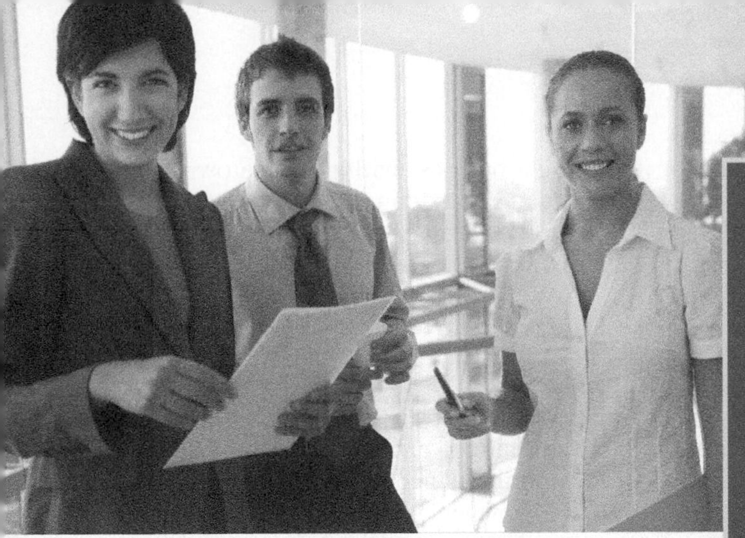

© PhotoAlto

Storyline Summary

Nicole Johnson

Location:	Salt Lake City, Utah
Status:	Managing member of Color Comfort Sheets LLC
Filing status:	Married to Tom Johnson
Marginal tax rate:	35 percent unless otherwise stated

Sarah Walker

Location:	Salt Lake City, Utah
Status:	Managing member of Color Comfort Sheets LLC
Filing status:	Married to Blaine Walker
Marginal tax rate:	28 percent unless otherwise stated

Chanzz Inc.

Location:	Salt Lake City, Utah
Business:	Managing sports franchises
Status:	Nonmanaging member of Color Comfort Sheets LLC
Filing status:	C Corporation with a June 30 year-end
Marginal tax rate:	35 percent

In Chapter 4, we introduced you to Nicole Johnson, who decided to turn her sheet-making hobby into a full-time business called Color Comfort Sheets (CCS). Early in 2014, after deciding to organize her new enterprise as a limited liability company (LLC), she turned her attention to raising capital for the business from other investors and a bank loan. Although Nicole's limited savings would clearly not be enough to get CCS started, she was willing to contribute a parcel of land in the industrial section of town that she had inherited five years ago from her grandfather. Her friend and mentor, Sarah Walker, offered to contribute both her time and money to help CCS get off the ground.

With Sarah on board, things seemed to be coming together nicely for Nicole. However, the amount her bank was willing to loan was not enough to fully capitalize CCS, and Nicole and Sarah were unable to invest any more cash into the business to make up the shortfall. Hoping to obtain the additional funding they needed, Nicole and Sarah visited Chance Armstrong, a successful local sports-team owner who had a reputation for being willing to take a chance on new ventures. After listening to Nicole and Sarah's proposal, Chance agreed to invest the additional cash needed to fully fund CCS. Rather than use his personal funds, however, Chance planned to have his closely held corporation, Chanzz Inc., invest in CCS. Unlike Nicole and Sarah, who would take an active role in managing CCS, Chanzz Inc.—with everyone's agreement—would not play a part. By the end of March, CCS had cash, land on which to build its manufacturing facility and offices, and owners who were excited and willing to work hard to make it a successful company.

to be continued . . .

In this chapter, we review the options for operating a business with multiple owners as a **flow-through entity.** In addition, we explain the basic tax consequences of forming and operating business entities taxed as partnerships by examining the specific tax consequences of forming and operating Color Comfort Sheets as a limited liability company (LLC).

LO 9-1

FLOW-THROUGH ENTITIES OVERVIEW

Income earned by flow-through entities is usually not taxed at the entity level. Instead, the *owners* of flow-through entities are taxed on the share of entity-level income allocated to them. Thus, unlike income earned by **C corporations,** income from flow-though entities is taxed only once—when it "flows through" to owners of these entities.[1]

Flow-through entities with multiple owners are governed by two somewhat different sets of rules in our tax system.[2] Unincorporated business entities such as **general partnerships, limited partnerships,** and **limited liability companies (LLC)** are generally treated as partnerships under the rules provided in **Subchapter K** of the Internal Revenue Code.[3] In contrast, corporations whose owners elect to treat them as flow-through entities are classified as such under the rules in **Subchapter S.** These corporations are called **S corporations.**

There are many similarities and a few important differences between the tax rules for partnerships and S corporations. Our focus in this chapter and the next is on the tax rules for partnerships. Then, in Chapter 11, we turn our attention to the tax treatment of S corporations and their shareholders.

TAXES IN THE REAL WORLD Hedge Funds

One can scarcely read the financial press these days without encountering some reference to hedge funds. Hedge funds are private investment funds that have grown in popularity in recent years to the point where they were estimated to have $1.5 trillion in assets under management at the beginning of 2009.[4] According to a study by the Joint Committee on Taxation, most hedge funds are organized as partnerships and their investors are taxed as limited partners.[5]

Aggregate and Entity Concepts

When Congress adopted Subchapter K in 1954, it had to decide whether to follow an **entity approach** and treat tax partnerships as entities separate from their partners, or to apply an **aggregate approach** and treat them simply as an aggregation of the partners' separate interests in the assets and liabilities of the partnership. In the end, Congress decided to apply both concepts in formulating partnership tax law. For instance, one of the most basic tenets of partnership tax law—that partnerships don't pay taxes—reflects the aggregate approach. However, Congress also adopted other partnership tax rules that fall more squarely on the side of the entity approach. For example, the requirement that partnerships, rather than partners, make most tax elections represents the entity concept. Throughout this chapter and the following chapter, we highlight examples where one or the other basic approaches underlies a specific partnership tax rule.

[1]The "check the box" rules determine how various legal entities should be classified for tax purposes. See the discussion in Chapter 4 for a more detailed explanation of these rules.

[2]Unincorporated entities with one individual owner are taxed as *sole proprietorships.* The tax rules relevant to sole proprietorships are discussed in Chapter 1. In addition to sole proprietorships, other specialized forms of flow-through entities such as real estate investment trusts and regulated investment companies are authorized by the Code. A discussion of these entities is beyond the scope of this chapter.

[3]Publicly traded partnerships may be taxed as corporations. The tax treatment of publicly traded partnerships is more fully developed in Chapter 4.

[4]"*Hedge Funds 2009,*" International Financial Services London (www.ifsl.org.uk), July 4, 2009.

[5]"*Present Law and Analysis Relating to Tax Treatment of Partnership Carried Interests and Related Issues, Part I*" (JCX-62-07), September 4, 2007.

PARTNERSHIP FORMATIONS AND ACQUISITIONS OF PARTNERSHIP INTERESTS

LO 9-2

Acquiring Partnership Interests When Partnerships Are Formed

When a partnership is formed, and afterwards, partners may transfer cash, other tangible or intangible property, and services to it in exchange for an equity interest called a **partnership interest.** Partnership interests represent the bundle of economic rights granted to partners under the partnership agreement (or operating agreement for an LLC).[6] These rights include the right to receive a share of the partnership net assets if the partnership were to liquidate, called a **capital interest,** and the right or obligation to receive a share of *future* profits *or future* losses, called a **profits interest.**[7] It is quite common for partners contributing property to receive both capital and profits interests in exchange. Partners who contribute services instead of property frequently receive only profits interests. The distinction between capital and profits interests is important because the tax rules for partnerships are sometimes applied to them differently.

THE KEY FACTS

Property Contributions

- Partners don't generally recognize gain or loss when they contribute property to partnerships.
- Initial tax basis for partners contributing property = basis of contributed property − debt securing contributed property + partnership debt allocated to contributing partner + gain recognized.
- Contributing partner's holding period in a partnership interest depends on the type of property contributed.

Contributions of Property

Partnership formations are similar to other tax-deferred transactions such as like-kind exchanges and corporate formations, because realized gains and losses from the exchange of contributed property for partnership interests are either fully or partially deferred for tax purposes depending on the specifics of the transaction. The rationale for permitting taxpayers to defer realized gains or losses on property contributed to partnerships is identical to the rationale for permitting tax deferral when corporations are formed.[8] From a practical perspective, the tax rules in this area allow entrepreneurs to organize their businesses without having to pay taxes. In addition, these rules follow the aggregate theory of partnership taxation because they recognize that partners contributing property to a partnership still own the contributed property, albeit a smaller percentage, since other partners will also indirectly own the contributed property through their partnership interests.

Gain and loss recognition. As a general rule, neither partnerships nor partners recognize gain or loss when they contribute property to partnerships.[9] This applies to property contributions when a partnership is initially formed and to subsequent property contributions. In this context, the term *property* is defined broadly to include a wide variety of both tangible and intangible assets but not services. The general rule facilitates contributions of property with **built-in gains** (fair market value is greater than tax basis) but discourages contributions of property with **built-in losses** (fair market value is less than tax basis). In fact, partners holding property with built-in losses are usually better off selling the property, recognizing the related tax loss, and contributing the cash from the sale to the partnership so it can acquire property elsewhere.

Example 9-1

What if: Assume Nicole contributes land to CCS with a fair market value of $120,000 and an adjusted basis of $20,000. What amount of gain or loss would she recognize on the contribution?

Answer: None. Under the general rule for contributions of appreciated property, Nicole will not recognize any of the $100,000 built-in gain from her land.

(continued on page 9-4)

[6]The partnership books reflect partners' shares of the partnership's net assets in their individual capital accounts.

[7]An interest in the future profits or losses of a partnership is customarily referred to as a profits interest rather than a profits/loss interest.

[8]Chapter 8 discusses the tax rules related to corporate formations.

[9]§721.

What if: Suppose Chanzz Inc. contributed equipment with a fair market value of $120,000 and a tax basis of $220,000 to CCS. What amount of the gain or loss would Chanzz Inc. recognize on the contribution?

Answer: None. Chanzz Inc. would not recognize any of the $100,000 built-in loss on the equipment. However, if Chanzz Inc. sold the property to an unrelated party and contributed $120,000 in cash instead of the equipment, it could recognize the $100,000 built-in tax loss. If, for some reason, the equipment Chanzz planned to contribute was uniquely suited to CCS's operations, Chanzz could obtain the same result by selling the equipment to Sarah, who would then contribute the equipment to CCS rather than her planned $120,000 cash contribution.

Partner's initial tax basis. Among other things, partners need to determine the tax basis in their partnership interests to properly compute their taxable gains and losses when they sell their partnership interests. A partner's tax basis in her partnership interest is her **outside basis.** In contrast, the partnership's basis in its assets is its **inside basis.** As we progress through this and the next chapter, you'll see other important reasons for calculating a partner's outside tax basis.

Determining a partner's initial tax basis in a partnership interest acquired by contributing property and/or cash is relatively straightforward if the partnership doesn't have any debt. Partners will simply have a basis in their partnership interest equivalent to the tax basis of the property and cash they contributed.[10] This rule ensures that realized gains and losses on contributed property are merely deferred until either the contributing partner sells her partnership interest or the partnership sells the contributed property.

Example 9-2

What if: Assume that Sarah contributed $120,000 to CCS in exchange for her partnership interest and that CCS had no liabilities. What is Sarah's outside basis in her partnership interest after the contribution?

Answer: Sarah's basis is $120,000, the amount of cash she contributed to CCS.

What if: Assume Nicole contributed land with a fair market value of $120,000 and an adjusted basis of $20,000 and CCS had no liabilities. What is Nicole's initial tax basis in CCS?

Answer: Nicole's basis is $20,000, the basis of the property she contributed to CCS. If Nicole immediately sold her interest in CCS for $120,000 (the value of the land she contributed), she would recognize gain of $100,000—exactly the amount she would have recognized if she had sold the land instead of contributing it to CCS.

When partnerships have debt, a few additional steps are required to determine a partner's tax basis in her partnership interest. First, each partner must include her share of the partnership's debt in calculating the tax basis in her partnership interest because partnership tax law treats each partner as borrowing her proportionate share of the partnership's debt and then contributing the borrowed cash to acquire her partnership interest.[11] You can understand the necessity for this basis increase by recalling that the basis of any purchased asset increases by the amount of any borrowed funds used to purchase it.

Partnerships may have either **recourse debt** or **nonrecourse debt** or both, and the specific approach to allocating partnership debt to individual partners differs for each. The fundamental difference between the two types of debt lies in the legal responsibility partners assume for ultimately paying the debt. Recourse debts are those for which partners have economic risk of loss—that is, they may have to legally satisfy

[10]§722.

[11]§752(a).

the debt with their own funds. For example, the unsecured debts of general partnerships, such as payables, are recourse debt because general partners are legally responsible for the debts of the partnership. Recourse debt is usually allocated to the partners who will ultimately be responsible for paying it.[12] The partners must consider their partner guarantees, other agreements, and state partnership or LLC statutes in making this determination.

Nonrecourse debts, in contrast, don't provide creditors the same level of legal recourse against partners. Nonrecourse debts such as mortgages are typically secured by real property and only give lenders the right to obtain the secured property in the event the partnership defaults on the debt. Because partners are responsible for paying nonrecourse debts only to the extent the partnership generates sufficient profits, such debts are generally allocated according to partners' profit-sharing ratios. (We discuss an exception to this general rule later in the chapter.[13]) The *basic* rules for allocating recourse and nonrecourse debt are summarized in Exhibit 9-1.

EXHIBIT 9-1 Basic Rules for Allocating Partnership Debt to Partners

Type of Debt	Allocation Method
Recourse	Allocated to partners with ultimate responsibility for paying debt
Nonrecourse	Allocated according to partners' profit-sharing ratios

The legal structure of entities taxed as partnerships also influences the way partners characterize and allocate partnership debt. Recourse debts in limited partnerships are typically allocated only to general partners, because, as we discuss in Chapter 4, limited partners are legally protected from a limited partnership's recourse debt holders.[14] Limited partners, however, may be allocated recourse debt if they forgo their legal protection by guaranteeing some or all of the recourse debt. Similarly, LLC members generally treat LLC debt as nonrecourse because they, like corporate shareholders, are shielded from the LLC's creditors. However, like limited partners, LLC members may treat debt as recourse debt to the extent they contractually assume risk of loss by agreeing to be legally responsible for paying the debt.[15]

Example 9-3

In reality, Sarah and Chanzz Inc. initially each contributed $120,000 and CCS borrowed $60,000 from a bank when CCS was formed. The bank required Nicole, Sarah, and Chanzz Inc. to personally guarantee the bank loan. The terms were structured so the members would each be responsible for a portion of the debt equal to the percentage of CCS losses allocated to each member (one-third each) and would have no right of reimbursement from either CCS or the other members of CCS. How much of the $60,000 bank debt was allocated to each member?

(continued on page 9-6)

[12]Reg. §1.752-2. Under the regulations, partners' obligations for paying recourse debt are determined by assuming a hypothetical, worst-case scenario where partnership assets (including cash) become worthless, and the resulting losses are then allocated to partners. The partners who legally would be responsible for partnership recourse debts under this scenario must be allocated the recourse debt. A detailed description of this approach for allocating recourse debt is beyond the scope of this book.

[13]Reg. §1.752-3 provides the rules for allocating nonrecourse debt, some of which are beyond the scope of this text.

[14]Recall from Chapter 4 that, in limited partnerships, general partners' liability is unlimited, whereas limited partners' liability is usually limited to the amount they have invested.

[15]It's actually quite common for banks and other lenders to require LLC members to personally guarantee loans made to LLCs.

Answer: Each member was allocated $20,000. The debt is treated as recourse debt because they are personally guaranteeing it. Because each guarantees one-third of the debt, the $60,000 debt is allocated equally among them.

What if: Assuming the $60,000 bank loan is CCS's only debt, what is Sarah's initial basis in her CCS interest after taking her share of CCS's bank debt into account?

Answer: Sarah's basis is $140,000 ($120,000 + $20,000) and consists of her cash contribution plus her share of CCS's $60,000 bank loan.

Another step is needed to determine a partner's outside basis when the partnership assumes *debt of the partner* secured by property the partner contributes to the partnership. Essentially, the contributing partner must treat her debt relief as a deemed cash distribution from the partnership that reduces her outside basis.[16] If the debt securing the contributed property is nonrecourse debt, the amount of the debt in excess of the basis of the contributed property is allocated solely to the contributing partner, and the remaining debt is allocated to all partners according to their profit-sharing ratios.[17]

Example 9-4

Nicole actually contributed $10,000 of cash and land with a fair market value of $150,000 and adjusted basis of $20,000 to CCS when it was formed. The land was encumbered by a $40,000 nonrecourse mortgage executed three years before. Recalling that CCS already had $60,000 in bank debt before Nicole's contribution, what tax bases do Nicole, Sarah, and Chanzz Inc. *initially* have in their CCS interests?

Answer: Their bases are $36,666, $146,666, and $146,666, respectively. Nicole, Sarah, and Chanzz Inc. would determine their initial tax bases as illustrated in the table below:

Description	Nicole	Sarah	Chanzz Inc.	Explanation
(1) Basis in contributed land	$20,000			
(2) Cash contributed	10,000	$120,000	$120,000	Example 9-3.
(3) Members' share of $60,000 recourse bank loan	20,000	20,000	20,000	Example 9-3.
(4) Nonrecourse mortgage in excess of basis in contributed land	20,000			Nonrecourse debt > basis is allocated only to Nicole.
(5) Remaining nonrecourse mortgage	6,666	6,666	6,666	33.33% × [$40,000 − (4)].
(6) Relief from mortgage debt	(40,000)			
The member's initial tax basis in CCS	36,666	146,666	146,666	Sum of (1) through (6).

Although in many instances partners don't recognize gains on property contributions, there is an important exception to the general rule that may apply when property secured by debt is contributed to a partnership. In these situations, the contributing partner recognizes gain *only if* the cash deemed to have been received from

[16]§752(b).

[17]Reg. §1.752-3(a)(2).

a partnership distribution exceeds the contributing partner's tax basis in her partnership interest prior to the deemed distribution.[18] Any gain recognized is generally treated as capital gain.[19]

Example 9-5

What if: Assume Sarah and Chanzz Inc., but *not* Nicole, personally guarantee all $100,000 of CCS's debt ($60,000 bank loan + $40,000 mortgage on land). How much gain, if any, would Nicole recognize on her contribution to CCS and what would be the basis in her CCS interest?

Answer: Nicole would recognize $10,000 gain and have a $0 basis, computed as follows:

Description	Amount	Explanation
(1) Basis in contributed land	$20,000	Example 9-4.
(2) Cash contributed	10,000	Example 9-4.
(3) Nicole's share of debt	0	Sarah and Chanzz guaranteed all of CCS's debt.
(4) Debt relief	(40,000)	Nicole was relieved of mortgage on land.
(5) Debt relief in excess of basis in contributed land and cash	(10,000)	Sum of (1) through (4).
(6) Capital gain recognized	10,000	(5) with opposite sign.
Nicole's initial tax basis in CCS	0	(5) + (6).

Partner's holding period in partnership interest. Because a partnership interest is a capital asset, its holding period determines whether gains or losses from the disposition of the partnership interest are short-term or long-term capital gains or losses. The length of a partner's holding period for a partnership interest acquired by contributing property depends on the nature of the assets the partner contributed. When partners contribute capital assets or §1231 assets (assets used in a trade or business and held for more than one year), the holding period of the contributed property "tacks on" to the partnership interest.[20] Otherwise, it begins on the day the partnership interest is acquired.

Example 9-6

What if: Assume Nicole contributed land (no cash) that she had held for five years in exchange for her partnership interest. One month after contributing the property, she sold her partnership interest and recognized a capital gain. Is the gain long-term or short-term?

Answer: The gain is long-term because the five-year holding period of the land is tacked on to Nicole's holding period for her partnership interest. She is treated as though she held the partnership interest for five years and one month at the time she sold it.

Partnership's tax basis and holding period in contributed property. Just as partners must determine their initial outside basis in their partnership interests after contributing property, partnerships must establish their inside basis in the contributed property.

[18]§731(a). However, §707(a)(2)(B) provides that deemed cash received from the relief of debt should be considered as sale proceeds rather than a distribution when circumstances indicate the relief of debt constitutes a disguised sale. Further discussion of disguised sale transactions is beyond the scope of this book.

[19]§731(a). This is equivalent to increasing what would have been a negative basis by the recognized gain to arrive at a zero basis. This mechanism ensures that partners will be left with an initial tax basis of zero any time they recognize gain from a property contribution.

[20]Reg. §1.1223-1(a).

Measuring both the partner's outside basis and the partnership's inside basis is consistent with the entity theory of partnership taxation. To ensure built-in gains and losses on contributed property are ultimately recognized if partnerships sell contributed property, partnerships generally take a basis in the property equal to the contributing partner's basis in the property at the time of the contribution.[21] Like the adjusted basis of contributed property, the holding period of contributed assets also carries over to the partnership.[22] In fact, the only tax attribute of contributed property that *doesn't* carry over to the partnership is the character of contributed property. Whether gains or losses on dispositions of contributed property are capital or ordinary usually depends on the manner in which the partnership uses contributed property.[23]

Example 9-7

What if: Assume CCS used the land Nicole contributed in its business for one month and then sold it for its fair market value of $150,000. What is the amount and character of the gain CCS would recognize on the sale (see Example 9-4)?

Answer: CCS recognizes $130,000 of §1231 gain. Nicole's basis in the land prior to the formation of CCS was $20,000. Because CCS receives a carryover basis in the land of $20,000, it recognizes $130,000 of gain when the land is sold for $150,000 ($110,000 in cash and $40,000 of debt relief minus $20,000 basis in land). Also, because CCS used the land in its business and because Nicole's five-year holding period carries over to CCS, the land qualifies as a §1231 asset to CCS, and CCS recognizes §1231 gain when the land is sold. Note that $130,000 of gain is recognized regardless of whether Nicole sells the land and contributes cash to CCS, or CCS sells the land shortly after it is contributed.

In addition to tracking the inside basis of its assets for tax purposes, partnerships not required to produce GAAP financial statements may decide to use inside tax basis, as well as tax income and expense recognition rules, to maintain their books. Under this approach, a new partnership would prepare its initial balance sheet using the tax basis for its assets. In addition, it would create a **tax capital account** for each new partner, reflecting the tax basis of any property contributed (net of any debt securing the property) and cash contributions. Because each new partner's tax capital account measures that partner's equity in the partnership using tax accounting rules, it will later be adjusted to include the partner's share of earnings and losses, contributions, and distributions.

Besides satisfying bookkeeping requirements, a partnership's tax basis balance sheet can provide useful tax-related information. For example, we can calculate each partner's share of the inside basis of partnership assets by adding the partner's share of debt to her **capital account.** Interestingly, partners who acquire their interests by contributing property (without having to recognize any gain) will have an *outside basis* equal to their share of the partnership's total inside basis. However, as we discuss more fully in the next chapter, partners' inside and outside bases will likely be different when they purchase existing partnership interests.

As another alternative to maintaining **GAAP capital accounts,** partnerships may also maintain their partner's capital accounts using accounting rules prescribed in the §704(b) tax regulations.[24] Partners set up **§704(b) capital accounts** in much the same

[21]§723.

[22]§1223(2).

[23]§702(b). However, §724 provides some important exceptions to this general rule for certain receivables, inventory, and capital loss property.

[24]Reg. §1.704-1(b)(2)(iv).

way as tax capital accounts, except that §704(b) capital accounts reflect the fair market value rather than the tax basis of contributed assets. Once a partnership begins operations, it can adjust §704(b) capital accounts so they continue to reflect the fair market value of partners' capital interests as accurately as possible. Partnerships may prefer this approach over simply maintaining tax capital accounts because §704(b) capital accounts may be a better measure of the true value of partners' capital interests.

continued from page 9-1...

Before forming CCS, its members agreed to keep its books using the tax basis of contributed assets and tax income and expense recognition rules. After receiving the cash and property contributions from its members and borrowing $60,000 from Nicole's bank, CCS prepared the tax basis balance sheet in Exhibit 9-2.

to be continued...

EXHIBIT 9-2 Color Comfort Sheets LLC

Balance Sheet
March 31, 2014

	Tax Basis	§704(b)/FMV*
Assets:		
Cash	$310,000	$310,000
Land	20,000	150,000
Totals	$330,000	$460,000
Liabilities and Capital:		
Long-term debt	$100,000	$100,000
Capital-Nicole	(10,000)	120,000
Capital-Sarah	120,000	120,000
Capital-Chanzz Inc.	120,000	120,000
Totals	$330,000	$460,000

*The §704(b)/FMV balance sheet is also provided to illustrate the difference in the two approaches to maintaining partners' capital accounts.

Contribution of Services So far we've assumed partners receive their partnership interests in exchange for contributed property. They may also receive partnership interests in exchange for services they provide to the partnership. For example, an attorney or other service provider might accept a partnership interest in lieu of cash payment for services provided as part of a partnership formation. Similarly, ongoing partnerships may compensate their employees with partnership interests, to reduce compensation-related cash payments and to motivate employees to behave more like owners. Unlike property contributions, services contributed in exchange for partnership interests may create immediate tax consequences to both the contributing partner *and* the partnership, depending on the nature of the partnership interest received.[25]

[25]Rev. Proc. 93-27, 1993-2 CB 343 and Rev. Proc. 2001-43, 2001-2 CB 191. In 2005, the IRS issued Prop. Reg. §1.704-1, which will change certain elements of current tax law when it is adopted as a final regulation. The concepts and examples discussed here are consistent with both current law and the proposed regulation.

continued from page 9-9. . .

Once CCS was organized in March 2014, it built a small production facility on the commercial land Nicole had contributed, purchased and installed the equipment needed to produce sheets, and hired and trained workers—all before the actual production and marketing of the sheets. After production began on July 1, 2014, CCS started selling its sheets to local specialty bedding stores, but the local market was limited. To create additional demand for their product, the members of CCS decided to draw on Sarah's marketing expertise to develop an advertising campaign targeted at home and garden magazines. All members of CCS agreed Sarah would receive, on December 31, 2014, an additional *capital interest* in CCS with a liquidation value of $20,000 *and* an increase in her profit-and-loss-sharing ratio from 33.33 percent to 40 percent (leaving the other members each with a 30 percent share of profits and losses), to compensate her for the time she would spend on this additional project. At this point, CCS's debt remained at $100,000.

to be continued . . .

Capital interests. Partners who receive unrestricted capital interests in exchange for services have the right to receive a share of the partnership's capital if it liquidates.[26] Because capital interests represent a current economic entitlement amenable to measurement, partners receiving capital interests for services must treat the amount they would receive if the partnership were to liquidate, or **liquidation value**[27] of the capital interest, as ordinary income.[28] In addition, the **service partner's** tax basis in the capital interest he receives will equal the amount of ordinary income he recognizes, and his holding period will begin on the date he receives the capital interest. The partnership either deducts or capitalizes the value of the capital interest, depending on the nature of the services the partner provides. For example, a real estate partnership would capitalize the value of a capital interest compensating a partner for architectural drawings used for a real estate development project.[29] Conversely, the same partnership would deduct the value of a capital interest compensating a partner for providing property management services. When the partnership deducts the value of capital interests used to compensate partners for services provided, it allocates the deduction only to the partners not providing services, or **nonservice partners,** because the deduction is related to the segment of the partnership tax year ending immediately before the admission of the new service partner.[30]

Example 9-8

What if: What are the tax consequences to Sarah and CCS if Sarah receives a capital interest (no profits interest) with a $20,000 liquidation value for her services?

Answer: As summarized below, Sarah has $20,000 of ordinary income, and CCS receives a $20,000 ordinary deduction. However, this deduction must be split equally between Nicole and Chanzz Inc. because, in effect, they transferred a portion of their capital to Sarah.

[26]Certain restrictions, such as vesting requirements, may be placed on partnership interests received for services. We limit our discussion here to unrestricted partnership interests.

[27]The proposed regulations in this area also allow the parties in this transaction to use the fair market value of partnership interests as a measure of value rather than liquidation value.

[28]The ordinary income recognized by the service partner is treated as a "guaranteed payment" by the service partner. Guaranteed payments are discussed more fully later in this chapter.

[29]§263(a).

[30]The preamble to Prop. Reg. §1.721-1(b) applies the varying interest rule of §706(d)(1) to the admission of a service partner.

Description	Sarah	Nicole	Chanzz Inc.	Explanation
(1) Ordinary income	$20,000			Liquidation value of capital interest.
Ordinary deduction		($10,000)	($10,000)	Capital shift from nonservice partners. (1) × .5

THE KEY FACTS

Other Acquisitions of Partnership Interests

- Contributing partner's tax basis and holding period in contributed property carries over to the partnership.
- If service partners report ordinary income, the partnership either expenses or capitalizes the amount depending on the nature of the services provided.
- The tax basis of a purchased partnership interest = purchase price + partnership debt allocated to partner, and the holding period begins on the purchase date.

Profits interests. It's fairly common for partnerships to compensate service partners with profits rather than capital interests. Profits interests are fundamentally different from capital interests, because the only economic benefit they provide is the right to share in the future profits of the partnership. Unlike capital interests, they have no liquidation value at the time they are received. Nonservice partners generally prefer to compensate service partners with profits interests because they don't have to forgo their current share of capital in the partnership and may not ever have to give up anything if the partnership is ultimately unprofitable. Thus, a profits interest is more risky than a capital interest from the perspective of the service partner.

The tax rules applicable to profits interests differ from those pertaining to capital interests due to the fundamental economic differences between them. Because there is no immediate liquidation value associated with a profits interest, the service partner typically will not recognize income and the nonservice partners will not receive deductions.[31] However, future profits and losses attributable to the profits interest are allocated to the service partner (and away from the nonservice partners) as they are generated. In addition, the partnership must adjust debt allocations based on profit-and-loss-sharing ratios to reflect the service partner's new or increased share of profits and losses.

Example 9-9

What if: Assuming Sarah received only a profits interest for her services instead of the capital interest she received in Example 9-8, what are the tax consequences to Sarah, Nicole, Chanzz Inc., and CCS?[32]

Answer: Sarah would not be required to recognize any income, and CCS would not deduct or capitalize any costs. As CCS generates future profits, Sarah will receive a greater share of the profits than she would have otherwise received, and the other two members will receive a correspondingly smaller share. In addition, with the increase in Sarah's profit-and-loss-sharing ratios from 33.33 percent to 40 percent, debt allocations among the partners will change to reflect Sarah's additional entitlement. Note that the debt allocations affect each partner's outside basis. The change in debt allocations is reflected in the table below:

Description	Sarah	Nicole	Chanzz Inc.	Explanation
(1) Increase in debt allocation	$5,334			Loss-sharing ratio increases from 33.33 percent to 40 percent or 6.67 percent [$60,000 recourse bank loan × 6.67% increase in loss-sharing ratio] + [$20,000 nonrecourse mortgage not allocated solely to Nicole × 6.67% increase in profit-sharing ratio].
Decrease in debt allocation		($2,667)	($2,667)	(1) × .5

[31]Rev. Proc. 93-27 indicates that income is recognized by the service partner "if the profits interest relates to a substantially certain and predictable stream of income," if the partner disposes of the profits interest within two years, or "the profits interest is a limited partnership interest in a publicly traded partnership."

[32]It is common for partnerships to grant a profits interest without an accompanying capital interest.

Example 9-10

What are the tax consequences to Sarah, Nicole, and Chanzz Inc. associated with the capital interest (liquidation value of $20,000) and profits interest Sarah receives for her services?

Answer: The tax consequences associated with giving Sarah *both* a capital and profits interest are summarized in the table below:

Description	Sarah	Nicole	Chanzz Inc.	Explanation
(1) Ordinary income	$20,000			Liquidation value of capital interest.
Ordinary deduction		($10,000)	($10,000)	Capital shift from nonservice partners. (1) × .5
(2) Increase in debt allocation	5,334			Loss-sharing ratio increases from 33.33 percent to 40 percent or 6.67 percent [$60,000 recourse bank loan × 6.67% increase in loss-sharing ratio] + [$20,000 nonrecourse mortgage not allocated solely to Nicole × 6.67% increase in profit-sharing ratio].
Decrease in debt allocation		(2,667)	(2,667)	(2) × .5

Organization, Start-up, and Syndication Costs When partnerships are formed, they typically incur some costs that must be capitalized rather than expensed for tax purposes, because they will benefit the partnership over its entire lifespan. This category of expenses includes **organization costs** associated with legally forming a partnership (such as attorneys' and accountants' fees), **syndication costs** to promote and sell partnership interests, and **start-up costs** that would normally be deducted as operating expenses except that they are incurred before the start of active trade or business. However, with the exception of syndication costs,[33] which are not deductible, the partnership may elect to amortize these costs. Chapter 2 provides additional detail about immediately expensing or amortizing business organization and start-up costs.

Acquisitions of Partnership Interests

After a partnership is formed and begins operating, new or existing partners can acquire partnership interests in exchange for contributing property and/or services, in which case the tax rules previously discussed in the context of forming a partnership still apply. Or new partners may purchase partnership interests from existing partners. Partners who purchase their partnership interests don't have to be concerned with recognizing taxable income when they receive their interests. However, in each of these scenarios they must still determine the initial tax basis and holding period in their partnership interests. Exhibit 9-3 summarizes the rules for determining the tax basis of partnership interests when they are received in exchange for contributed property or services, or when they are purchased.

[33]Syndication costs are typically incurred by partnerships whose interests are marketed to the public. Thus, syndication expenses are unusual in closely held partnerships.

EXHIBIT 9-3 Summary of Partner's Outside Basis and Holding Period by Acquisition Method

Acquisition Method	Outside Basis	Holding Period
Contribute Property	Equals basis of contributed property − debt relief + debt allocation + gain recognized.	If property contributed is a capital or §1231 asset, holding period includes holding period of contributed property. Otherwise begins on date interest received.
Contribute Services	Equals liquidation value of capital interest + debt allocation. Equals debt allocation if only profits interest received.	Begins on date interest received.
Purchase	Equals cost basis[34] + debt allocation	Begins on date interest purchased.

Example 9-11

CCS had overall operating losses from July 1, 2014 (when it began operating), through June 30, 2015. Because of the losses, Chanzz Inc. decided to sell its 30 percent interest in CCS (Chanzz Inc.'s original 33.33 percent interest in CCS was reduced to 30 percent at the end of 2014 when Sarah's interest was increased to compensate her for services provided) on July 1, 2015, to Greg Randall who, like Chanzz Inc., will be a nonmanaging member and guarantee a portion of CCS debt. Greg paid Chanzz Inc. $100,000 for its interest in CCS and was allocated a 30 percent share of CCS debt (CCS's debt remained at $100,000 on July 1, 2015). What is Greg's basis and holding period in CCS?

Answer: Greg's basis of $124,000 in CCS includes the $100,000 amount he paid to purchase the interest plus his $24,000 share of CCS's total $80,000 debt available to be allocated to all members ($60,000 recourse bank loan and $20,000 of nonrecourse mortgage remaining after allocating the first $20,000 to Nicole). Greg's holding period in his CCS interest begins on July 1, 2015.

PARTNERSHIP ACCOUNTING PERIODS, METHODS, AND TAX ELECTIONS

LO 9-3

A newly formed partnership must adopt its required tax year-end and decide whether it intends to use either the cash or accrual method as its overall method of accounting. As discussed in Chapter 1, an entity's tax year-end determines the cutoff date for including income and deductions in a particular return, and its overall accounting method determines when income and deductions are recognized for tax purposes. Partnerships must frequently make other tax-related elections as well.

Tax Elections

New partnerships determine their accounting periods and make tax elections including the election of overall accounting method, the election to expense a portion of organization and start-up costs, and the election to expense tangible personal property. Who formally makes all these elections? In theory, either the partnership or the partners themselves could do so. With just a few exceptions, the partnership tax rules rely on the entity theory of partnership taxation and make the partnership responsible for tax elections.[35] In many instances, the partnership does so in conjunction with filing its annual return. For example, it selects an accounting method

[34]§742.

[35]§703(b). Certain elections are made at the partner level.

and determines whether to elect to amortize start-up or organization costs by simply applying its elections in calculating ordinary business income on its first return. The partnership makes other tax elections by filing a separate document with the IRS, such as Form 3115 when it elects to change an accounting method.

Example 9-12

How will CCS elect its overall accounting method after it begins operations?

Answer: Nicole, Sarah, and Chanzz Inc. may jointly decide on an overall accounting method or, in their LLC operating agreement, they may appoint one of the members to be responsible for making this and other tax elections. Once they have made this decision, *CCS* makes the election by simply using the chosen accounting method when preparing its first information return.

Accounting Periods

THE KEY FACTS

Partnership Accounting Periods, Methods, and Tax Elections

- Partnerships are responsible for making most tax elections.
- A partnership's taxable year is the majority interest taxable year, the common taxable year of the principal partners, or the taxable year providing the least aggregate deferral to the partners.
- Partnerships are generally eligible to use the cash method unless they have average gross receipts greater than $5 million and have corporate partners.

Required Year-Ends Because partners include their share of partnership income or loss in their taxable year ending with the partnership taxable year, or within which the partnership taxable year falls, any partnership tax year other than that of the partners will result in some degree of tax deferral for some or all of the partners.[36] Exhibit 9-4 reflects the tax deferral a partner with a calendar year-end would receive if the corresponding partnership had a January 31 year-end.

EXHIBIT 9-4 Partner Defers 11 Months of Income for 1 Year

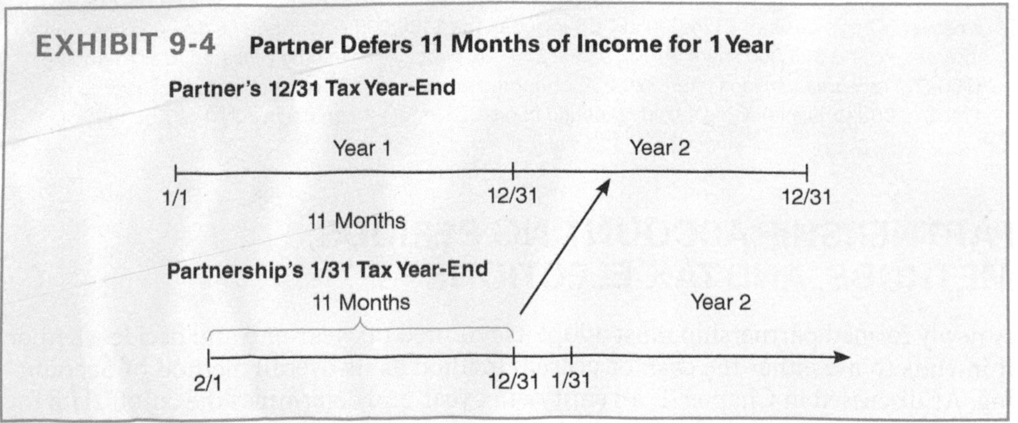

Because the partner reports the partnership's year 1 income earned from February 1 until January 31 in the partner's second calendar year (the year within which the partnership's January 31 year-end falls), the partner defers reporting for one year the 11 months of income she was allocated from February 1 through December 31 of her first calendar year.

The government's desire to reduce the aggregate tax deferral of partners (the sum of the deferrals for each individual partner) provides the underlying rationale behind the rules requiring certain partnership taxable year-ends. Partnerships are generally required to use one of three possible tax year-ends.[37] As illustrated in Exhibit 9-5, they must follow a series of steps to determine the appropriate year-end.

The first potential required tax year is the **majority interest taxable year,** the taxable year of one or more partners who together own more than 50 percent of the capital and

[36]§706(a).

[37]Under certain circumstances, other alternative taxable years may be available to partnerships. See Rev. Proc. 2002-38, 2002-1 CB 1037 and §444 for additional information concerning these options.

EXHIBIT 9-5 Steps to Determine a Partnership's Year-End

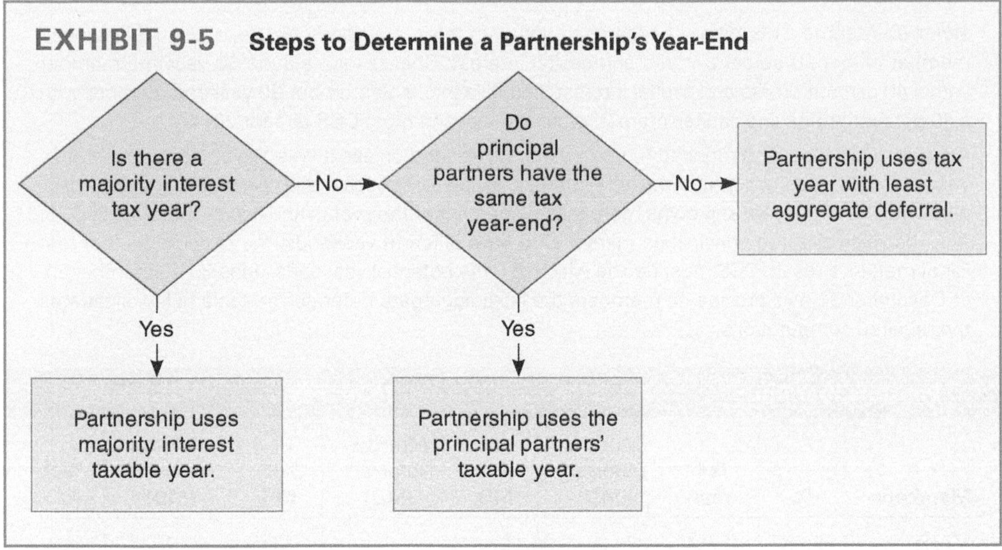

profits interests in the partnership.[38] However, there may not be a majority interest taxable year when several partners have different year-ends. For example, if a partnership has two partners with 50 percent capital and profits interests and each has a different tax year, there will be no majority interest taxable year. In that case, the partnership next applies the principal partners test to determine its year-end.

Under the **principal partners** test, the required tax year is the taxable year the principal partners *all* have in common. For this purpose, principal partners are those who have 5 percent or more interest in the partnership profits and capital.[39] Consider a partnership with two calendar-year partners, each with a 20 percent capital and profits interest, and thirty additional fiscal year-end partners, each with less than a 5 percent capital and profits interest. In this scenario, the required taxable year of the partnership is a calendar year corresponding with the taxable year of the partnership's only two principal partners. If, as in the earlier example, the partnership had two 50 percent capital and profits partners with different tax years, it would then use the tax year providing the "least aggregate deferral" to the partners, unless it is eligible to elect an alternative year-end.[40]

The tax year with the **least aggregate deferral** is the one among the tax years of the partners that provides the partner group as a whole with the smallest amount of aggregate tax deferral. Under this approach, we measure the total tax deferral achieved under each potential tax year mathematically by weighting each partner's months of deferral under the potential tax year by each partner's *profits* percentage and then summing the weighted months of deferral for all the partners.

Example 9-13

When CCS began operating in 2014, it had two calendar year-end members, Nicole and Sarah, and one member with a June 30 year-end, Chanzz Inc. What tax year-end must CCS use for 2014?

Answer: CCS was required to use the calendar year as its taxable year unless it was eligible for an alternative year-end. Although Chanzz Inc. had a June 30 taxable year, Nicole and Sarah both had calendar year-ends. Because Nicole and Sarah each initially own 33.33 percent of the capital and profits of CCS, and together they own greater than 50 percent of the profits and capital of CCS, the calendar year is the required taxable year for CCS because it is the majority interest taxable year.

(continued on page 9-16)

[38]§706(b)(1)(B)(i).
[39]§706(b)(3).
[40]Reg. §1.706-1(b)(3).

What if: Assume CCS initially began operating with three members: Nicole, a calendar year-end member with a 20 percent profits and capital interest; Chanzz Inc., a June 30 year-end member with a 40 percent profits and capital interest; and Telle Inc., a September 30 year-end member with a 40 percent profits and capital interest. What tax year-end must CCS use for 2014?

Answer: CCS would be required to use a June 30 year-end unless it was eligible for an alternative year-end. CCS does not have a majority interest taxable year because no partner or group of partners with the same year-end owns more than 50 percent of the profits and capital interests in CCS. Also, because all three principal partners in CCS have different year-ends, the principal partner test is not met. As a result, CCS must decide which of three potential year-ends, June 30, September 30, or December 31, will provide its members the least aggregate deferral. The table below illustrates the required computations:

Possible Year-Ends			12/31 Year-End		6/30 Year-End		9/30 Year-End	
Members	**%**	**Tax Year**	**Months Deferral* (MD)**	**% × MD**	**Months Deferral* (MD)**	**% × MD**	**Months Deferral* (MD)**	**% × MD**
Nicole	20%	12/31	0	0	6	1.2	3	.6
Chanzz Inc.	40	6/30	6	2.4	0	0	9	3.6
Telle Inc.	40	9/30	9	3.6	3	1.2	0	0
Total aggregate deferral				6		**2.4**		4.2

*Months deferral equals number of months between the proposed year-end and partner's year-end.

June 30 is the required taxable year-end because it provides members with the least aggregate tax deferral (2.4 is less than 6 and 4.2).

Accounting Methods

Although partnerships may use the accrual method freely, they may not use the cash method under certain conditions because it facilitates the deferral of income and acceleration of deductions. For example, partnerships with C corporation partners are generally not eligible to use the cash method.[41] However, if partnerships' average annual gross receipts for the three prior taxable years do not exceed $5 million, partnerships with C corporation partners may use the cash method if they otherwise qualify.[42] It should also be noted that entities generally eligible to use the overall cash method of accounting must nevertheless use the accrual method to account for the purchase and sale of inventory unless they meet certain exceptions provided by the IRS.[43]

Example 9-14

When CCS began operations, its members decided it should elect the cash method of accounting if eligible to do so. Would having a corporate member—Chanzz Inc.—prevent it from electing the cash method?

Answer: No. Although Chanzz Inc. was a founding member of CCS, its ownership share didn't affect the partnership's eligibility to use the cash method since CCS's average annual gross receipts were less than $5 million. If Chanzz Inc. had remained a member of CCS, the cash method might have been unavailable in future years if average annual gross receipts exceeded $5 million.

[41]§448(a)(2). In addition, §448(a)(3) prohibits partnerships classified as "tax shelters" from electing the cash method.

[42]§448(b)(3). If a partnership has not been in existence for at least three years, this test is applied based on the number of years it has been in existence.

[43]For example, Rev. Proc. 2001-10 2001-1 CB 272 exempts taxpayers with average annual gross receipts of $1 million or less from having to use the accrual method to account for the purchase and sale of inventory.

REPORTING THE RESULTS OF PARTNERSHIP OPERATIONS

LO 9-4

The first section in the Internal Revenue Code dealing with partnerships states emphatically that partnerships are flow-through entities: "A partnership as such shall not be subject to the income tax imposed by this chapter. Persons carrying on business as partners shall be liable for income tax only in their separate or individual capacities."[44] This feature of partnership taxation largely explains the popularity of partnerships over corporations, whose shareholders are subject to a double tax—once when the income is earned and again when it is distributed to shareholders as a dividend or when the shares are sold.

TAXES IN THE REAL WORLD Publicly Traded Partnerships

Would it surprise you to know that many private equity firms are organized as partnerships for tax purposes? Even more surprising may be the fact that several well-known private equity funds—including Fortress, KKR, and Blackstone—are publicly traded. Publicly traded firms are typically taxed as corporations even if they are legally structured as partnerships or, in the case of these private equity firms, as limited partnerships. However, relying on a provision in the tax code, they were able to maintain their tax status as partnerships after their public offerings.[45] Thus, investors purchasing shares in these private equity funds are buying investments subject to only one level of taxation but that, like shares in a corporation, can be readily traded in a public securities market.

Ordinary Business Income (Loss) and Separately Stated Items

Although partnerships are not taxpaying entities, they are required to file information returns annually. They also distribute information to each partner detailing the amount *and* character of items of income and loss flowing through the partnership.[46] Partners must report these income and loss items on their tax returns even if they don't receive cash distributions from the partnership during the year.

When gathering this information for their partners, partnerships must determine each partner's share of **ordinary business income (loss)** and **separately stated items.** Partnership ordinary business income (loss) is all partnership income (loss) exclusive of any separately stated items of income (loss). Separately stated items share one common characteristic—they are treated differently from a partner's share of ordinary business income (loss) for tax purposes. To better understand why certain items must be separately disclosed to partners, consider how two particular separately stated items, dividend income and capital losses, might affect an individual partner's tax liability. Qualified dividend income allocated to individual partners is taxed at either a 0 percent, 15 percent, or 20 percent rate, depending on individual partners' tax brackets.[47] In a similar vein, individual partners without capital gains during the year may deduct up to $3,000 in capital losses against their ordinary income, while other individual partners with capital gains may deduct more.[48] If a partnership's dividends and capital losses were simply buried in the computation of its overall income or loss for the year, the partner would be unable to apply these specific tax rules to her unique situation and determine her correct tax liability.

The Code specifically enumerates several common separately stated items, including short-term capital gains and losses, long-term capital gains and losses, §1231

THE KEY FACTS

Reporting the Results of Partnership Operations

- Partnerships file annual information returns reporting their ordinary business income (loss) and separately stated items.
- Ordinary business income (loss) = partnership overall income or loss exclusive of separately stated items.
- Separately stated items change partners' tax liabilities when they are separately stated.

[44]§701.
[45]§7704.
[46]Other items, such as tax credits, may also flow through the partnership to partners.
[47]§1(h).
[48]§1211.

gains and losses, charitable contributions, and dividends.[49] Many more items are considered under regulations issued by the IRS.[50] Exhibit 9-6 lists several other common separately stated items.

EXHIBIT 9-6 Common Separately Stated Items

- Interest income
- Guaranteed payments
- Net earnings (loss) from self-employment
- Tax-exempt income
- Net rental real estate income
- Investment interest expense
- §179 deduction

Example 9-15

After constructing a building and purchasing equipment in its first year of operations ending on December 31, 2014, CCS invested $15,000 of its remaining idle cash in stocks and bonds. CCS's books reflected an overall loss for the year of $80,000. Included in the $80,000 loss were $2,100 of dividend income, $1,200 of short-term capital gains, and a $20,000 deduction for the capital interest given to Sarah at the end of 2014 (see Example 9-10). How much ordinary business loss and what separately stated items are allocated to the CCS members for the taxable year ended December 31, 2014?

Answer: As reflected in the table below, CCS has $63,300 of ordinary business loss. In addition, it has $2,100 of dividend income, $1,200 in short-term capital gains, and $20,000 of ordinary deduction (related to the capital interest Sarah received) that are separately stated items. To Nicole, Sarah, and Chanzz Inc., CCS would report $21,100 of ordinary business loss, $700 of dividend income, and $400 of short-term capital gain. In addition, CCS would report $20,000 of ordinary income to Sarah for the capital interest she received, and a $10,000 deduction to Nicole and Chanzz Inc. reflecting the amount of partnership capital they relinquished.

Description	**CCS**	**Nicole** $\left(\frac{1}{3}\right)$	**Sarah** $\left(\frac{1}{3}\right)$	**Chanzz Inc.** $\left(\frac{1}{3}\right)$
2014 overall net loss	($80,000)			
Less:				
Dividends	2,100			
Short-term capital gains	1,200			
Ordinary deduction for Sarah's capital interest	(20,000)			
Ordinary business loss	(63,300)	(21,100)	(21,100)	(21,100)
Separately stated Items				
Dividends	2,100	700	700	700
Short-term capital gains	1,200	400	400	400
Ordinary income for capital interest to Sarah	20,000		20,000	
Ordinary deduction for capital interest to Sarah	(20,000)	(10,000)		(10,000)

Nicole and Sarah will treat their shares of CCS's ordinary business loss as an *ordinary* loss and include it along with their shares of dividend income and short-term capital gain in their individual tax

[49]§702.

[50]Reg. §1.702-1(a).

returns for the year.[51] Chanzz Inc. will also include its share of these items in its annual tax return. But, because Chanzz is a corporation, different tax rules apply to its share of dividend income and short-term capital gains. For example, Chanzz will be entitled to the dividends received deduction, while Nicole and Sarah will pay tax on their share of dividend income at a 15 percent rate since their marginal rates on ordinary income are above 15 percent.

Notice that the character of separately stated items is determined at the partnership level rather than at the partner level.[52] This treatment reflects the entity theory.

Example 9-16

What if: Assume Chanzz Inc. is an investments dealer rather than a sports franchise operator. How would Chanzz Inc. classify its share of the $1,200 gain from the securities sold by CCS during 2014?

Answer: Chanzz Inc. would classify the $1,200 as short-term capital gains. Because the securities CCS sold were capital assets to it, the gain on the sale is a capital gain even though the securities are inventory (an ordinary asset) to Chanzz Inc. That is, we determine the character of the income at the partnership level, not the partner level.

Guaranteed Payments In addition to dividends, capital gains, and other routine separately stated items, **guaranteed payments** are also very common items reported separately to the partners who receive them. As their name suggests, guaranteed payments are fixed amounts paid to partners regardless of whether the partnership shows a profit or loss for the year.[53] We can think of them—and some partnerships treat them—as economically equivalent to cash salary payments made to partners for services provided.[54] Specifically, they are typically deducted in computing a partnership's ordinary income or loss for the year. Though included in a partnership's ordinary business income (loss) computation, guaranteed payments must, nevertheless, be separately stated to the partners who receive them. This separate reporting serves the same purpose as providing W-2 forms to employees. Because guaranteed payments are similar to salary payments, partners treat them as ordinary income.

continued from page 9-10. . .
Because Sarah received an additional capital interest for marketing services she provided at the end of 2014, she held a 40 percent capital and profits interest and Nicole and Chanzz Inc. each held a 30 percent capital and profits interests at the beginning of 2015. After Sarah's initial work in formulating a marketing strategy in 2014, Nicole suggested they hire a permanent employee to oversee product marketing. However, because they were unable to find a suitable candidate, Sarah continued to shoulder the product marketing responsibilities in addition to her normal role as a managing member of CCS. To compensate Sarah for her additional workload, all members of CCS agreed to pay Sarah a $10,000 guaranteed payment for her marketing efforts in 2015. Exhibit 9-7 provides CCS's income statement for 2015. ■

[51]Nicole and Sarah would report their share of ordinary business loss on Schedule E, their share of dividend income on Schedule B, and their share of short-term capital gain on Schedule D of Form 1040.

[52]§702(b).

[53]§707(c).

[54]Fringe benefits that partners receive for services provided such as medical insurance and group-term life insurance are also treated as guaranteed payments. In addition to compensating partners for services provided, guaranteed payments are also made to partners for the use of capital.

EXHIBIT 9-7 Color Comfort Sheets LLC

Income Statement December 31, 2015	
Sales revenue	$40,000
Cost of goods sold	(20,000)
Employee wages	(50,000)
Depreciation expense	(18,000)
Guaranteed payments	(10,000)
Miscellaneous expenses	(2,800)
Dividend income	500
Long-term capital gains	300
Overall net loss	($60,000)

Example 9-17

Given CCS's operating results for *2015* presented in Exhibit 9-7, how much ordinary business loss and what separately stated items will it report on its return for the year? How will it allocate these amounts to its members?

Answer: The table below displays CCS's ordinary business loss and separately stated items and the allocation of these amounts to CCS's members:

Description	CCS	Nicole 30%	Sarah 40%	Chanzz Inc. 30% × 6/12*	Greg 30% × 6/12*
Sales revenue	$40,000				
Cost of goods sold	(20,000)				
Employee wages	(50,000)				
Depreciation expense	(18,000)				
Guaranteed payment to Sarah	(10,000)				
Miscellaneous expenses	(2,800)				
Ordinary business loss	(60,800)	($18,240)	($24,320)	($9,120)	($9,120)
Separately stated to partners					
Dividends	500	150	200	75	75
Long-term capital gains	300	90	120	45	45
Guaranteed payment			10,000		

*As we noted in Example 9-11, Chanzz Inc. sold out to Greg Randall on July 1, 2015. Therefore, the items related to Chanzz Inc.'s original 30 percent interest must be allocated between Chanzz Inc. and Greg Randall.[55]

THE KEY FACTS

Guaranteed Payments and Self-Employment Income

- Guaranteed payments are separately stated items, are treated as ordinary income by partners receiving them, and are either capitalized or expensed by partnerships.
- Guaranteed payments for services are always treated as self-employment income.
- Shares of ordinary business income (loss) are always treated as self-employment income (loss) by general partners and never treated as self-employment income (loss) by limited partners.
- Shares of ordinary business income (loss) may or may not be treated by LLC members as self-employment income (loss), depending on the extent of their involvement with the LLC.

Self-Employment Tax Individual partners, like sole proprietors, may be responsible for paying **self-employment taxes** in addition to income taxes on their share of earned income from partnerships.[56] The degree to which partners are responsible for self-employment taxes depends on their legal status as general partners, limited partners, or LLC members and their business activities. General partners report guaranteed payments for services they provide and their share of ordinary business income (loss) as self-employment income (loss) because they are actively involved in managing the partnership. Limited partners, on the other hand, are generally not allowed under state law to participate in the management of limited partnerships. Therefore, their share of ordinary business income (loss) is conceptually more like investment income than trade or business income. As a result, it is not subject to self-employment

[55]We assume here that the items are allocated based on the number of months the interest was held. See Chapter 10 for additional detail regarding methods to account for partners' varying interests in a partnership when a partnership interest is sold.

[56]Chapter 4 more fully discuss earned income and related self-employment taxes.

tax. However, if limited partners receive guaranteed payments for services provided to the partnership, they treat those payments as self-employment income.

Because LLC members may either be managing or nonmanaging members, the approach to taxing their share of ordinary business income (loss) for self-employment tax purposes ought to depend to some degree on their level of involvement in the LLC.[57] Tax rules in this area were developed before the popularity of LLCs, however, so no authoritative rules currently exist to help LLCs decide whether to characterize their members' shares of ordinary business income (loss) as self-employment income (loss). However, a proposed regulation issued by the IRS and later withdrawn can assist partnerships in drawing the line between aggressive and conservative positions in this area.[58] It provides that LLC members who have personal liability for the debts of the LLC by reason of being an LLC member, who have authority to contract on behalf of the LLC, *or* who participate more than 500 hours in the LLC's trade or business during the taxable year should be classified as general partners when applying the self-employment tax rules.

The lack of authoritative guidance in this area has resulted in a predictable diversity of practice. Some taxpayers and their advisers ignore the proposed regulation and claim that managing members of LLCs are similar to limited partners and shouldn't have to pay self-employment taxes at all.[59] Others follow the spirit of the proposed regulation and take the approach that managing members are similar to general partners and should pay self-employment tax on part or all of their share of ordinary business income (loss), depending on their level of involvement in the LLC.[60]

Example 9-18

For *2015*, should CCS classify Sarah's $10,000 guaranteed payment as self-employment income?

Answer: Yes. The law is clear with respect to guaranteed payments to LLC members—they are always treated as self-employment income.

Using the proposed regulation, will CCS classify Sarah's $24,320 (see Example 9-17) share of ordinary business loss for *2015* as a self-employment loss?

Answer: Yes. Under the proposed regulations, an LLC member who has personal liability for LLC debts or the ability to contract on behalf of the LLC, or who spends more than 500 hours participating in the business of the LLC, is classified as a general partner when applying the self-employment tax rules. Given Sarah's status as a managing member of CCS, at least one but probably all three criteria for classifying her share of CCS's ordinary business loss as self-employment loss will apply. Although these rules have not been finalized and are therefore not authoritative, the IRS would likely follow them because they represent its current thinking on the matter. Applying the law this way, CCS will report a $14,320 self-employment loss [($24,320) share of ordinary business loss + $10,000 guaranteed payment] as a separately stated item to Sarah so she can properly compute her self-employment tax liability on her individual return.

Example 9-19

Using the proposed regulation, will CCS classify Nicole's $18,240 (see Example 9-17) share of ordinary business loss for *2015* as self-employment loss?

Answer: Yes. Because Nicole, like Sarah, is involved in the day-to-day management of CCS, it will classify her entire share of ordinary business loss as self-employment loss, consistent with its classification of Sarah's share of ordinary business loss, and report the amount as a separately stated item to Nicole.

(continued on page 9-22)

[57]Guaranteed payments to LLC members are clearly subject to self-employment tax because they are similar to salary payments.

[58]Proposed Reg. §1.1402(a)-2.

[59]This argument may be difficult to sustain for professional service firms. The Tax Court, in *Renkemeyer, Campbell & Weaver, LLP, et al. v. Commissioner,* 136 TC 137 (2011), decided to treat law partners in a law firm organized as an LLP as subject to self-employment taxes.

[60]Nonmanaging LLC members are so similar to limited partners that taxpayers and their advisers typically treat them as if they were limited partners for self-employment tax purposes.

Under the proposed regulation, will CCS treat Greg's $9,120 share of ordinary business loss for *2015* as self-employment loss?

Answer: Yes. CCS will treat Greg's share of ordinary business loss as self-employment loss because he has guaranteed a portion of CCS's debt. CCS's total self-employment loss is $41,680 consisting of Sarah's $14,320 self-employment loss, Nicole's $18,240 self-employment loss, and Greg's $9,120 self-employment loss.

Net Investment Income Tax

An individual partner's share of gross income from interest, dividends, annuities, royalties, or rents is included in the partner's net investment income when calculating the net investment income tax (also known as the Medicare Contribution Tax on net investment income).[61] In addition, the partner's share of income from a trade or business that is a passive activity, income from a trade or business of trading financial instruments or commodities, and any net gain from disposing of property (other than property used in a trade or business that is not a passive activity) is also included in the partner's net investment income.[62]

Allocating Partners' Shares of Income and Loss

Partnership tax rules provide partners with tremendous flexibility in allocating overall profit and loss as well as specific items of profit and loss to partners, as long as partners agree to the allocations and they have "substantial economic effect." Partnership allocations designed to accomplish business objectives other than reducing taxes will generally have substantial economic effect.[63] If they are not defined in the partnership agreement or do not have substantial economic effect, allocations to partners must be made in accordance with the "partners' interests in the partnership."[64] According to tax regulations, the partners' interests in the partnership are a measure of the partners' economic arrangement, and should be determined by considering factors such as their capital contributions, distribution rights, and interests in economic profits and losses (if different from their interests in taxable income and loss). Partnership allocations inconsistent with partners' capital interests or overall profit-and-loss-sharing ratios are called **special allocations.**

Although special allocations are made largely at the discretion of partners, certain special allocations of gains and losses from the sale of partnership property are mandatory. Specifically, when property contributed to a partnership with built-in gains (fair market value greater than tax basis) or built-in losses (tax basis greater than fair market value) is subsequently sold, the partnership must allocate, to the extent possible, the built-in gain or built-in loss (at the time of the contribution) solely to the contributing partner and then allocate any remaining gain or loss to all the partners in accordance with their profit-and-loss-sharing ratios.[65] This rule prevents contributing partners from shifting their built-in gains and built-in losses to other partners.

[61]The tax imposed is 3.8% of the lesser of (a) net investment income or (b) the excess of modified adjusted gross income over $250,000 for married-joint filers and surviving spouses, $125,000 for married separate filers, and $200,000 for other taxpayers. Modified adjusted gross income equals adjusted gross income increased by income excluded under the foreign earned income exclusion less any disallowed deductions associated with the foreign earned income exclusion. §1411.

[62]For purposes of computing the net investment income tax, a partner's status as either active or passive with respect to an activity is determined according to the §469 passive activity loss rules explained later in this chapter. §1411(c)(2)(A).

[63]Reg. §1.704-1 defines the requirements allocations must satisfy to have substantial economic effect.

[64]§704(b).

[65]§704(c). In addition to requiring built-in gains and losses to be specially allocated to contributing partners, §704(c) also requires depreciation to be specially allocated to noncontributing partners. Tax regulations permit partners to choose among several methods for making these required special allocations. Further discussion of these methods is beyond the scope of this book.

Example 9-20

What if: Assume that at the beginning of 2015, Nicole and Sarah decide to organize CCS's marketing efforts by region. Nicole will take responsibility for marketing in the western United States, and Sarah will take responsibility for marketing in the eastern United States. All members agree that CCS's provision for allocating profits and losses in the operating agreement should be amended to provide Nicole and Sarah with better incentives. Specifically, CCS would like to allocate the first 20 percent of profits or losses from each region to Nicole and Sarah. Then, it will allocate any remaining profits or losses from each region among the members in proportion to their capital interests and profits interests at the end of 2015—40 percent to Sarah and 30 percent each to Nicole and Greg. Will CCS's proposed special allocation of profits and losses be accepted by the IRS?

Answer: Yes. Since CCS is a partnership for federal income tax purposes, it can make special allocations to members, and because they are designed to accomplish a business objective other than tax reduction, the IRS will accept them.[66]

What if: Assume the land Nicole contributed to CCS with a fair market value of $150,000 and tax basis of $20,000 was sold by CCS for $150,000 of consideration almost immediately after it was contributed. How would the resulting $130,000 gain be allocated among the members of CCS?

Answer: Nicole's built-in gain of $130,000 at the time of contribution must be allocated exclusively to her to prevent it from being shifted to other CCS members. Shifting the gain to other members could lower the overall tax liability of the CCS members if Sarah and Greg's marginal tax rates are lower than Nicole's marginal tax rate.

What if: Suppose CCS held the land Nicole contributed for one year and then sold it on March 31, 2015, for $180,000 instead of $150,000. How should the resulting $160,000 gain be allocated to Nicole, Sarah, and Chanzz Inc.?

Answer: The allocations are $139,000 to Nicole, $12,000 to Sarah, and $9,000 to Chanzz Inc., as reflected in the table below:

Description	CCS	Nicole 30%	Sarah 40%	Chanzz Inc. 30%
Total gain from sale of land	$160,000			
Less:				
Special allocation to Nicole of built-in gain	(130,000)	$130,000		
Post-contribution appreciation in land	30,000	9,000	$12,000	$9,000
Total gain allocations		139,000	12,000	9,000

Partnership Compliance Issues

Although partnerships don't pay taxes, they are required to file **Form 1065,** U.S. Return of Partnership Income (shown in Exhibit 9-8), with the IRS by the 15th day of the 4th month after their year-end (April 15 for a calendar year-end partnership). Partnerships may receive an automatic five-month extension to file by filing **Form 7004** with the IRS before the original due date of the return.[67] Page 1 of Form 1065 details the calculation of the partnership's ordinary business income (loss) for the year, and page 3, **Schedule K,** lists the partnership's ordinary business income (loss) and separately stated items. In addition to preparing Form 1065, the partnership is also responsible for preparing a Schedule K-1 for each partner detailing her individual share of the partnership's ordinary business income (loss) and separately stated items for the year. Once prepared, Schedule K-1s are included with Form 1065 when it is

[66]Reg. §1.704-1(b)(5), Example 10, suggests that this type of special allocation would not violate the substantial economic effect rules.

[67]Under §6698, late filing penalties apply if the partnership fails to file by the normal or extended due date for the return. The penalty is $195 times the number of partners in the partnership times the number of months (or fraction thereof) the return is late up to a maximum of 12 months.

EXHIBIT 9-8 (PART I) **Page 1 Form 1065**
CCS's 2015 Ordinary Business Loss (on 2014 forms)

Form **1065** Department of the Treasury Internal Revenue Service

U.S. Return of Partnership Income

For calendar year 2014, or tax year beginning ________, 2014, ending ________, 20____ .
▶ Information about Form 1065 and its separate instructions is at *www.irs.gov/form1065.*

OMB No. 1545-0123 **2014**

A Principal business activity Manufacturing	Type or Print	Name of partnership Color Comfort Sheets	D Employer identification number 00072359
B Principal product or service Textile Products		Number, street, and room or suite no. If a P.O. box, see the instructions. 375 East 450 South	E Date business started April 1, 2014
C Business code number 314000		City or town, state or province, country, and ZIP or foreign postal code Salt Lake City, UT 84608	F Total assets (see the instructions) $ 370,000

G Check applicable boxes: (1) ☐ Initial return (2) ☐ Final return (3) ☐ Name change (4) ☐ Address change (5) ☐ Amended return
(6) ☐ Technical termination - also check (1) or (2)
H Check accounting method: (1) ☑ Cash (2) ☐ Accrual (3) ☐ Other (specify) ▶
I Number of Schedules K-1. Attach one for each person who was a partner at any time during the tax year ▶ 4
J Check if Schedules C and M-3 are attached . . . ☐

Caution. *Include **only** trade or business income and expenses on lines 1a through 22 below. See the instructions for more information.*

Income	1a	Gross receipts or sales	1a	40,000		
	b	Returns and allowances	1b			
	c	Balance. Subtract line 1b from line 1a			1c	40,000
	2	Cost of goods sold (attach Form 1125-A)			2	20,000
	3	Gross profit. Subtract line 2 from line 1c			3	20,000
	4	Ordinary income (loss) from other partnerships, estates, and trusts (attach statement)			4	
	5	Net farm profit (loss) (attach Schedule F (Form 1040))			5	
	6	Net gain (loss) from Form 4797, Part II, line 17 (attach Form 4797)			6	
	7	Other income (loss) (attach statement)			7	
	8	**Total income (loss).** Combine lines 3 through 7			8	20,000
Deductions (see the instructions for limitations)	9	Salaries and wages (other than to partners) (less employment credits)			9	50,000
	10	Guaranteed payments to partners			10	10,000
	11	Repairs and maintenance			11	
	12	Bad debts			12	
	13	Rent			13	
	14	Taxes and licenses			14	
	15	Interest			15	
	16a	Depreciation (if required, attach Form 4562)	16a	18,000		
	b	Less depreciation reported on Form 1125-A and elsewhere on return	16b		16c	18,000
	17	Depletion **(Do not deduct oil and gas depletion.)**			17	
	18	Retirement plans, etc.			18	
	19	Employee benefit programs			19	
	20	Other deductions (attach statement)			20	2,800
	21	**Total deductions.** Add the amounts shown in the far right column for lines 9 through 20			21	80,800
	22	**Ordinary business income (loss).** Subtract line 21 from line 8			22	(60,800)

Sign Here Under penalties of perjury, I declare that I have examined this return, including accompanying schedules and statements, and to the best of my knowledge and belief, it is true, correct, and complete. Declaration of preparer (other than general partner or limited liability company member manager) is based on all information of which preparer has any knowledge.

▶ Signature of general partner or limited liability company member manager ▶ Date

May the IRS discuss this return with the preparer shown below (see instructions)? ☐ **Yes** ☐ **No**

Paid Preparer Use Only	Print/Type preparer's name	Preparer's signature	Date	Check ☐ if self-employed	PTIN
	Firm's name ▶			Firm's EIN ▶	
	Firm's address ▶			Phone no.	

For Paperwork Reduction Act Notice, see separate instructions. Cat. No. 11390Z Form **1065** (2014)

filed, and Schedule K-1s are also separately provided to all partners (each partner receives a Schedule K-1 with her income and loss allocations). Exhibit 9-8, parts I through III, displays CCS's information return, showing the operating results we summarized in Example 9-17 and Sarah's actual schedule K-1, reflecting the facts and conclusions in Examples 9-17 and 9-18.[68]

[68]We use 2014 forms because 2015 forms were unavailable at the time the book was published.

EXHIBIT 9-8 (PART II) **Page 3 Form 1065**
CCS's 2015 Schedule K (on 2014 forms)

Form 1065 (2014) Page 4

Section	Line	Schedule K — Partners' Distributive Share Items		Line	Total amount
Income (Loss)	1	Ordinary business income (loss) (page 1, line 22)		1	(60,800)
	2	Net rental real estate income (loss) (attach Form 8825)		2	
	3a	Other gross rental income (loss)	3a		
	b	Expenses from other rental activities (attach statement)	3b		
	c	Other net rental income (loss). Subtract line 3b from line 3a		3c	
	4	Guaranteed payments		4	10,000
	5	Interest income		5	
	6	Dividends: a Ordinary dividends		6a	500
		b Qualified dividends	6b 500		
	7	Royalties		7	
	8	Net short-term capital gain (loss) (attach Schedule D (Form 1065))		8	
	9a	Net long-term capital gain (loss) (attach Schedule D (Form 1065))		9a	300
	b	Collectibles (28%) gain (loss)	9b		
	c	Unrecaptured section 1250 gain (attach statement)	9c		
	10	Net section 1231 gain (loss) (attach Form 4797)		10	
	11	Other income (loss) (see instructions) Type ▶		11	
Deductions	12	Section 179 deduction (attach Form 4562)		12	
	13a	Contributions		13a	
	b	Investment interest expense		13b	
	c	Section 59(e)(2) expenditures: (1) Type ▶ (2) Amount ▶		13c(2)	
	d	Other deductions (see instructions) Type ▶		13d	
Self-Employment	14a	Net earnings (loss) from self-employment		14a	(41,680)
	b	Gross farming or fishing income		14b	
	c	Gross nonfarm income		14c	20,000
Credits	15a	Low-income housing credit (section 42(j)(5))		15a	
	b	Low-income housing credit (other)		15b	
	c	Qualified rehabilitation expenditures (rental real estate) (attach Form 3468, if applicable)		15c	
	d	Other rental real estate credits (see instructions) Type ▶		15d	
	e	Other rental credits (see instructions) Type ▶		15e	
	f	Other credits (see instructions) Type ▶		15f	
Foreign Transactions	16a	Name of country or U.S. possession ▶			
	b	Gross income from all sources		16b	
	c	Gross income sourced at partner level		16c	
		Foreign gross income sourced at partnership level			
	d	Passive category ▶ e General category ▶ f Other ▶		16f	
		Deductions allocated and apportioned at partner level			
	g	Interest expense ▶ h Other ▶		16h	
		Deductions allocated and apportioned at partnership level to foreign source income			
	i	Passive category ▶ j General category ▶ k Other ▶		16k	
	l	Total foreign taxes (check one): ▶ Paid ☐ Accrued ☐		16l	
	m	Reduction in taxes available for credit (attach statement)		16m	
	n	Other foreign tax information (attach statement)			
Alternative Minimum Tax (AMT) Items	17a	Post-1986 depreciation adjustment		17a	
	b	Adjusted gain or loss		17b	
	c	Depletion (other than oil and gas)		17c	
	d	Oil, gas, and geothermal properties—gross income		17d	
	e	Oil, gas, and geothermal properties—deductions		17e	
	f	Other AMT items (attach statement)		17f	
Other Information	18a	Tax-exempt interest income		18a	
	b	Other tax-exempt income		18b	
	c	Nondeductible expenses		18c	
	19a	Distributions of cash and marketable securities		19a	
	b	Distributions of other property		19b	
	20a	Investment income		20a	500
	b	Investment expenses		20b	
	c	Other items and amounts (attach statement)			

Form **1065** (2014)

EXHIBIT 9-8 (PART III) **2015 Schedule K-1 for Sarah Walker (on 2014 forms) CCS Operates as an LLC**

651113

[x] Final K-1 [ ] Amended K-1 OMB No. 1545-0123

Schedule K-1 (Form 1065) **2014**

Department of the Treasury
Internal Revenue Service

For calendar year 2014, or tax year beginning ________, 2014 ending ________, 20____

Partner's Share of Income, Deductions, Credits, etc. ▶ See back of form and separate instructions.

Part I Information About the Partnership

A Partnership's employer identification number

B Partnership's name, address, city, state, and ZIP code
Color Comfort Sheets
375 East 450 South
Salt Lake City, UT 84608

C IRS Center where partnership filed return
Ogden

D [ ] Check if this is a publicly traded partnership (PTP)

Part II Information About the Partner

E Partner's identifying number
429-88-3426

F Partner's name, address, city, state, and ZIP code
Sarah Walker
549 Laurel Lane
Holiday, UT 84609

G [x] General partner or LLC member-manager [ ] Limited partner or other LLC member

H [x] Domestic partner [ ] Foreign partner

I1 What type of entity is this partner? Individual

I2 If this partner is a retirement plan (IRA/SEP/Keogh/etc.), check here [ ]

J Partner's share of profit, loss, and capital (see instructions):

	Beginning	Ending
Profit	40 %	40 %
Loss	40 %	40 %
Capital	40 %	40 %

K Partner's share of liabilities at year end:

Nonrecourse	$ 12,000
Qualified nonrecourse financing	$ 8,000
Recourse	$ 24,000

L Partner's capital account analysis:

Beginning capital account	$
Capital contributed during the year	$
Current year increase (decrease)	$
Withdrawals & distributions	$ ( )
Ending capital account	$

[ ] Tax basis [ ] GAAP [ ] Section 704(b) book
[ ] Other (explain)

M Did the partner contribute property with a built-in gain or loss?
[ ] Yes [x] No
If "Yes," attach statement (see instructions)

Part III Partner's Share of Current Year Income, Deductions, Credits, and Other Items

1	Ordinary business income (loss)	(24,320)
2	Net rental real estate income (loss)	
3	Other net rental income (loss)	
4	Guaranteed payments	10,000
5	Interest income	
6a	Ordinary dividends	200
6b	Qualified dividends	200
7	Royalties	
8	Net short-term capital gain (loss)	
9a	Net long-term capital gain (loss)	120
9b	Collectibles (28%) gain (loss)	
9c	Unrecaptured section 1250 gain	
10	Net section 1231 gain (loss)	
11	Other income (loss)	
12	Section 179 deduction	
13	Other deductions	
14	Self-employment earnings (loss)	
	A	(14,320)
	C	8,000
15	Credits	
16	Foreign transactions	
17	Alternative minimum tax (AMT) items	
18	Tax-exempt income and nondeductible expenses	
19	Distributions	
20	Other information	
	A	200

*See attached statement for additional information.

For IRS Use Only

For Paperwork Reduction Act Notice, see Instructions for Form 1065. IRS.gov/form1065 Cat. No. 11394R Schedule K-1 (Form 1065) 2014

PARTNER'S ADJUSTED TAX BASIS IN PARTNERSHIP INTEREST

LO 9-5

Earlier in this chapter, we discussed how partners measure their initial tax basis in their partnership interests when they contribute property or services to partnerships in exchange for their partnership interests, or when they purchase partnership interests from an existing partner. Unlike the basis in a stock or other similar investment, which is usually fixed, the basis in a partnership is dynamic and must be *adjusted* as the partnership generates income and losses, changes its debt levels, and makes distributions to partners. These annual adjustments to a partner's tax basis are required to ensure partners don't double-count taxable income/gains and deductible expenses/losses, either when they sell their partnership interests or when they receive partnership distributions. They also ensure tax-exempt income and nondeductible expenses are not ultimately taxed or deducted.

Partners make the following adjustments to the basis in their partnership interests, annually:

- Increase for actual and deemed cash contributions to the partnership during the year.[69]
- Increase for partner's share of ordinary business income and separately stated income/gain items.
- Increase for partner's share of tax-exempt income.
- Decrease for actual and deemed[70] cash distributions[71] during the year.
- Decrease for partner's share of nondeductible expenses (fines, penalties, etc.).
- Decrease for partner's share of ordinary business loss and separately stated expense/loss items.

Partners first adjust their bases for items that increase basis, then for distributions, then by nondeductible expenses, and then by deductible expenses and losses to the extent any basis remains after prior adjustments.[72] Basis adjustments that decrease basis may never reduce a partner's tax basis below zero.[73]

Example 9-21

Given the events that affected CCS and its members during *2014*, what tax basis did Nicole, Sarah, and Chanzz Inc. have in their ownership interests at the end of 2014?

Answer: Their bases in CCS were $4,000, $152,000, and $114,000, respectively. Their individual tax basis calculations at the end of 2014 are illustrated in the table below:

Description	Nicole	Sarah	Chanzz Inc.	Explanation
(1) Initial tax basis (including debt)	$36,666	$146,666	$146,666	Example 9-4.
(2) Dividends	700	700	700	Example 9-15.
(3) Short-term capital gains	400	400	400	Example 9-15.
(4) Debt reallocation (deemed cash contribution/distribution)	(2,666)	5,334	(2,666)	Example 9-10.

(continued on page 9-28)

THE KEY FACTS

Partner's Basis Adjustments

- A partner will increase the tax basis in her partnership interest for:
  - Contributions.
  - Share of ordinary business income.
  - Separately stated income/gain items.
  - Tax-exempt income.
- A partner will decrease the tax basis in her partnership interest for:
  - Cash distributions.
  - Share of nondeductible expenses.
  - Share of ordinary business loss.
  - Separately stated expense/loss items.
- A partner's tax basis may not be negative.

[69]Recall that partners are deemed to have made a cash contribution to the partnership when they are allocated an additional share of partnership debt.

[70]Recall that partners are deemed to have received a cash distribution from the partnership when they are relieved of partnership debt.

[71]Property distributions to partners are also treated as basis reductions. We discuss property distributions at length in Chapter 10.

[72]Reg. §1.704-1(d)(2).

[73]§705(a)(2).

Description	Nicole	Sarah	Chanzz Inc.	Explanation
(5) Sarah's capital interest	(10,000)	20,000	(10,000)	Examples 9-10, 9-15.
(6) CCS's ordinary business loss	(21,100)	(21,100)	(21,100)	Example 9-15.
Tax basis on 12/31/14	$ 4,000	$152,000	$114,000	Sum of (1) through (6).

What if: Suppose Sarah sold her LLC interest but forgot to include her share of short-term capital gains when computing her basis to determine her gain on the sale. What are the tax consequences of Sarah's mistake?

Answer: Sarah would be double-taxed on the amount of the short-term capital gain. She was initially taxed on her share of the short-term capital gain allocation, and she would be taxed a second time when she recognized $400 more gain on the sale than had she included her share of the gain in her basis.

What if: Assume Sarah was allocated $700 of tax-exempt municipal bond income instead of dividend income. What would happen if she neglected to increase her basis in CCS by the $700 tax-exempt income?

Answer: If Sarah were to sell her interest in CCS for a price reflecting the tax-exempt income received, she would, in effect, be converting tax-exempt income into taxable income.

Example 9-22

In addition to the other events of *2015,* CCS increased its debt from $100,000 to $130,000 in the second half of the year. The $30,000 increase was attributable to accounts payable owed to suppliers. Unlike the case of the $60,000 bank loan, the members did not guarantee any of the accounts payable. Therefore, the accounts payable are considered nonrecourse debt because CCS is an LLC. Given this information, what are Nicole's, Sarah's, and Greg's tax bases in CCS at the end of *2015?*

Answer: Their bases are $0, $140,000, and $124,000, respectively. Nicole, Sarah, and Greg would determine their tax basis in CCS at the end of *2015* as illustrated in the table below:

Description	Nicole 30%	Sarah[74] 40%	Greg 30%	Explanation
(1) Tax basis on 1/1/15	$4,000	$152,000		Example 9-21.
(1) Greg's purchase of Chanzz Inc.'s interest			$124,000	Example 9-11.
(2) Dividends	150	200	75	Example 9-17.
(3) Long-term capital gains	90	120	45	Example 9-17.
(4) Increase in nonrecourse debt from accounts payable (deemed cash contribution)	9,000	12,000	9,000	$30,000 × member's profit-sharing ratio.
(5) CCS's ordinary business loss	(18,240)	(24,320)	(9,120)	Example 9-17.
Preliminary tax basis	(5,000)	140,000	124,000	Sum of (1) through (5).
Tax basis on 12/31/15	0*	140,000	124,000	*Nicole's basis can't go below zero.

Cash Distributions in Operating Partnerships

Even after a partnership has been formed, partners are likely to continue to receive actual and deemed cash distributions. For example, excess cash may be distributed to partners to provide them with cash flow to pay their taxes or simply for consumption,

[74]Recall that Sarah received a $10,000 cash guaranteed payment for services she performed in 2015. Cash guaranteed payments generally don't have a direct impact on the recipient partner's tax basis because they are similar to salary payments.

and deemed cash distributions occur as partnerships pay down their debts. The principles underlying the calculation of a partner's tax basis highlight the fact that partners are taxed on income as the partnership earns it instead of when it distributes it. If cash is distributed when partners have a positive tax basis in their partnership interests, the distribution effectively represents a distribution of profits that have been previously taxed, a return of capital previously contributed by the partner to the partnership, a distribution of cash the partnership has borrowed, or some combination of the three. Thus, as long as a cash distribution does not exceed a partner's tax basis before the distribution, it reduces the partner's tax basis but is not taxed. However, as we highlighted in our discussion of property contributions earlier in this chapter, cash distributions (deemed or actual) in excess of a partner's basis are taxable gains and are generally treated as capital gains.[75]

Example 9-23

What if: In Example 9-22, we determined that Sarah's basis in her partnership interest was $140,000. Assume that in addition to the facts provided in that example, Sarah received a $10,000 distribution in *2015*. What will her tax basis be at the end of the year?

Answer: Sarah's tax basis will be $130,000. After making only her positive adjustments for the year (positive adjustments come before negative adjustments such as distributions), she has a basis of $164,320, which is greater than the $10,000 distribution. Thus, the distribution would not have been taxable because it did not exceed her basis. Sarah would have also reduced her basis by the $10,000 distribution in addition to the $24,320 reduction for her share of the ordinary business loss, leaving her with an ending basis of $130,000 ($164,320 − $10,000 − $24,320).

What problem would be created if Sarah did not reduce her basis by the $10,000 distribution?

Answer: After she receives a $10,000 distribution, the value of Sarah's interest will decrease by $10,000. If she didn't reduce her tax basis by the distribution, selling her interest would produce a $10,000 artificial tax loss.

LOSS LIMITATIONS

LO 9-6

While partners generally prefer not to invest in partnerships with operating losses, these losses generate current tax benefits when partners can deduct them against other sources of taxable income. Unlike capital losses, which are of limited usefulness if taxpayers don't also have capital gains, ordinary losses from partnerships are deductible against any type of taxable income. However, they are deductible on the partner's tax return only when they clear three separate hurdles: (1) tax basis, (2) at-risk amount, and (3) passive activity loss hurdles. We discuss each hurdle below.

Tax Basis Limitation

A partner's basis limits the amount of partnership losses the partner can use to offset other sources of income. In theory, a partner's basis represents the amount a partner has invested in a partnership (or may have to invest to satisfy her debt obligations). As a result, partners may not utilize partnership losses in excess of their investment or outside basis in their partnership interests. Any losses allocated in excess of their basis must be suspended and carried forward indefinitely until they have sufficient basis to utilize the losses.[76] Any suspended losses remaining when partners sell or otherwise dispose of their interests are lost forever. Among other things, partners may create additional tax basis in the future by making capital contributions, by guaranteeing more partnership debt, and by helping their partnership to become profitable.

[75]§731.
[76]§704(d).

Example 9-24

In Example 9-22 we discovered Nicole was allocated $5,000 of ordinary loss in excess of her tax basis for 2015, leaving her with a basis of zero at the end of 2015. What does Nicole do with this loss?

Answer: Nicole will carry forward all $5,000 of ordinary loss in excess of her tax basis indefinitely until her tax basis in CCS becomes positive. To the extent her tax basis increases in the future, the tax basis limitation will no longer apply to her ordinary loss. Even then, however, the at-risk and/or passive activity loss hurdles may ultimately apply to constrain her ability to deduct the loss on her future tax returns.

What if: Assuming Nicole is allocated $4,000 of income from CCS in 2016, how much of her $5,000 suspended loss will clear the tax basis hurdle in *2016*?

Answer: Nicole's basis will initially increase by $4,000. Then she can apply $4,000 of her suspended loss against this basis increase, leaving her tax basis at zero and holding a remaining suspended loss of $1,000. The $4,000 loss clearing the tax basis hurdle must still clear the at-risk and passive activity loss hurdles before Nicole can deduct it on her return.

THE KEY FACTS

Loss Limitations

- Partnership losses in excess of a partner's tax basis are suspended and carried forward until additional basis is created.
- Remaining partnership losses are further suspended by the at-risk rules to the extent a partner is allocated nonrecourse debt not secured by real property.
- If a partner is not a material participant or the partnership is involved in rental activities, losses remaining after application of the tax basis and at-risk limitations may be used only against other passive income or when the partnership interest is sold.

At-Risk Limitation

The at-risk hurdle or limitation is more restrictive than the tax basis limitation, because it excludes a type of debt normally included in a partner's tax basis. We have already highlighted the distinction between recourse and nonrecourse debt and noted that partners allocated recourse debt have economic risk of loss, while partners allocated nonrecourse debt have no risk of loss. Instead, the risk of loss on nonrecourse debt is borne by lenders. The **at-risk rules** in §465 were adopted to limit the ability of partners to use nonrecourse debt as a means of creating tax basis to use losses from tax shelter partnerships expressly designed to generate losses for the partners. The at-risk rules limit partners' losses to their amount "at risk" in the partnership—their **at-risk amount.** Generally, a partner's at-risk amount is the same as her tax basis except that, with one exception, the partner's share of certain nonrecourse debts is not included in the at-risk amount. Specifically, the only nonrecourse debts considered to be at risk are nonrecourse real estate mortgages from commercial lenders that are unrelated to borrowers. This type of debt is called **qualified nonrecourse financing.**[77] In addition to qualified nonrecourse financing, partners are considered to be at risk to the extent of cash and the tax basis of property contributed to the partnership. Further, partners are at risk for any partnership recourse debt allocated to them.

Partners apply the at-risk limitation after the tax basis limitation. Any partnership losses that would otherwise have been allowed under the tax basis limitation are further limited to the extent they exceed a partner's at-risk amount. Losses limited under the at-risk rules are carried forward indefinitely until the partner generates additional at-risk amounts to utilize the losses, or until they are applied to reduce any gain from selling the partnership interest.

Example 9-25

In Example 9-22, we discovered Nicole was allocated an ordinary business loss of $18,240. In Example 9-24, we learned that of this loss, $13,240 cleared the tax basis hurdle and $5,000 did not. How much of the $13,240 ordinary business loss that clears the tax basis hurdle will clear the at-risk hurdle?

Answer: $4,240. The table below summarizes and compares Nicole's calculations to determine her tax basis and at-risk limitations for *2015:*

[77]§465(b)(6).

Example	Description	Tax Basis	At-Risk Amount	Explanation
9-22	(1) Nicole's tax basis on 1/1/15	$ 4,000	$4,000	Nicole's tax basis and at-risk amount are the same because she was only allocated recourse debt and qualified nonrecourse financing.
9-22	(2) Dividends	150	150	
9-22	(3) Long-term capital gains	90	90	
9-22	(4) Nonrecourse accounts payable	9,000	0	
	(5) Tax basis and at-risk amount before ordinary business loss	13,240	4,240	Sum of (1) through (4).
9-22	(6) Ordinary business loss	(18,240)		
	(7) Loss clearing the tax basis hurdle	(13,240)		Loss limited to (5).
	Loss suspended by tax basis hurdle	(5,000)		(6) − (7).
	(8) Loss clearing tax basis hurdle		(13,240)	(7).
	(9) Loss clearing at-risk hurdle		**(4,240)**	Loss limited to (5).
	Loss suspended by at-risk hurdle		(9,000)	(8) − (9).

Although Nicole's $9,000 share of the nonrecourse accounts payable added in *2015* and her investment income of $990 allow her to create enough tax basis in *2015* to get $13,240 of her $18,240 ordinary business loss past the tax basis limitation, she is not at risk with respect to her $9,000 share of accounts payable because an LLC's accounts payable are general nonrecourse debt. Therefore, $9,000 of the $13,240 ordinary business loss clearing the tax basis hurdle is suspended under the at-risk limitation. As a result, Nicole has two separate losses to carry forward: a $5,000 ordinary loss limited by her tax basis and a $9,000 ordinary loss limited by the at-risk rules, leaving $4,240 of ordinary loss that overcomes both the tax basis and at-risk hurdles.

Passive Activity Loss Limitation

Prior to 1986, partners with sufficient tax basis and at-risk amounts were able to utilize ordinary losses from their partnerships to offset portfolio income (i.e., interest, dividends, and capital gains), salary income, and self-employment income from partnerships and other trades or businesses. During this time, a partnership tax shelter industry thrived by marketing to wealthy investors partnership interests designed primarily to generate ordinary losses they could use to shield other income from tax. To combat this practice, Congress introduced the **passive activity loss (PAL) rules.**[78] These rules were enacted as a backstop to the at-risk rules and are applied after the tax basis and at-risk limitations. Thus, depending on their situation, partners may have to overcome *three separate hurdles* before finally reporting partnership ordinary losses on their returns. In a nutshell, the passive activity loss rules limit the ability of partners in rental real estate partnerships and other partnerships they don't actively manage (passive activities) from using their ordinary losses from these activities (remaining after the application of the tax basis and at-risk limitations) to reduce other sources of taxable income.

[78]§469. The passive activity loss rules apply primarily to individuals but also to estates, trusts, closely held C corporations, and personal service corporations.

Passive Activity Defined The passive activity rules define a passive activity as "any activity which involves the conduct of a trade or business,[79] and in which the taxpayer does not materially participate." According to the Code and Treasury regulations, participants in rental activities, including rental real estate[80] and limited partners without management rights, are automatically deemed to be passive participants. In addition, participants in all other activities are passive unless their involvement in an activity is "regular, continuous, and substantial." Clearly, these terms are quite subjective and difficult to apply. Fortunately, regulations provide more certainty in this area by enumerating seven separate tests for material participation.[81] An individual other than a limited partner can be classified as a material participant in an activity by meeting any *one* of the seven tests in Exhibit 9-9.

EXHIBIT 9-9 Tests for Material Participation

1. The individual participates in the activity more than 500 hours during the year.
2. The individual's activity constitutes substantially all the participation in such activity by individuals.
3. The individual participates more than 100 hours during the year and the individual's participation is not less than any other individual's participation in the activity.
4. The activity qualifies as a "significant participation activity" (individual participates for more than 100 hours during the year) and the aggregate of all other "significant participation activities" is greater than 500 hours for the year.
5. The individual materially participated in the activity for any 5 of the preceding 10 taxable years.
6. The activity involves personal services in health, law, accounting, architecture, and so on, and the individual materially participated for any three preceding years.
7. Taking into account all the facts and circumstances, the individual participates on a regular, continuous, and substantial basis during the year.

Income and Loss Baskets Under the passive activity loss rules, each item of a partner's income or loss from all sources for the year is placed in one of three categories or "baskets." Losses from *the passive basket* are not allowed to offset income from other baskets. The three baskets are (see Exhibit 9-10):

1. *Passive activity income or loss*—income or loss from an activity, including partnerships, in which the taxpayer is not a material participant.
2. *Portfolio income*—income from investments, including capital gains and losses, dividends, interest, annuities, and royalties.
3. *Active business income*—income from sources, including partnerships, in which the taxpayer is a material participant. For individuals, this includes salary and self-employment income.

The impact of segregating a partner's income in these baskets is to limit her ability to apply passive activity losses against income in the other two baskets. In effect, passive activity losses are suspended and remain in the passive income or loss basket until the taxpayer generates current-year passive income, either from the passive activity producing the loss or from some other passive activity, or until the taxpayer sells the activity that generated the passive loss. On the sale, in addition to reporting gain or loss from the sale of the property, the taxpayer will be allowed to deduct suspended passive losses as ordinary losses.

[79]The term *trade or business* is also deemed to include property held for the production of income such as rental property.

[80]§469(b)(7) provides an important exception to the general rule that all real estate activities are passive. To overcome this presumption, taxpayers must spend more than half their time working in trades or businesses materially participating in real estate activities and more than 750 hours materially participating in real estate activities during the year. This exception benefits partners that spend a substantial amount of time in partnership activities like real estate development and construction. Moreover, §469(i) permits individual taxpayers to treat up to $25,000 of losses from rental real estate as active losses each year.

[81]Reg. §1.469-5T.

EXHIBIT 9-10 Income and Loss Baskets

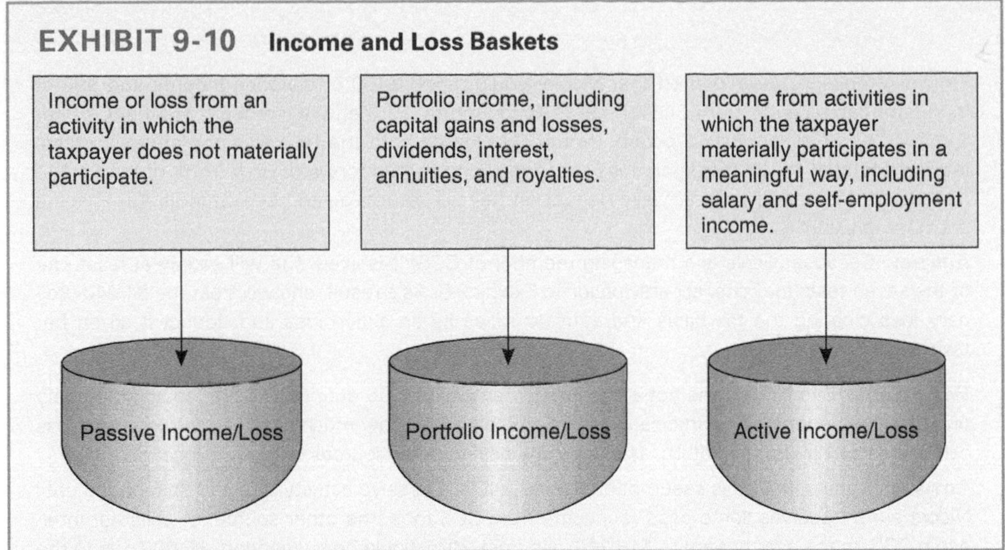
Income or loss from an activity in which the taxpayer does not materially participate.
Portfolio income, including capital gains and losses, dividends, interest, annuities, and royalties.
Income from activities in which the taxpayer materially participates in a meaningful way, including salary and self-employment income.
Passive Income/Loss
Portfolio Income/Loss
Active Income/Loss

ETHICS

Several years ago, Lou, together with his friend Carlo, opened an Italian restaurant in their neighborhood. The venture was formed as an LLC with Lou receiving a 75 percent ownership interest and Carlo receiving the remaining 25 percent ownership interest. While Lou was primarily responsible for operating the restaurant, Carlo only came in on weekends because he held a full-time job elsewhere. To document the time he spent in the restaurant, Carlo recorded the number of hours he worked in a logbook at the end of every shift. This year, because of a downturn in the local economy, the restaurant showed a loss for the first time ever. To be able to deduct his share of this loss when he files his tax return, Carlo would like to establish that he worked more than 500 hours during the year and is therefore a material participant in the restaurant. His logbook shows that he worked for 502 hours during the year; however, he rounded up to the nearest hour at the end of every shift to simplify his recordkeeping. For example, if he worked four hours and 25 minutes during a shift, he would have written five hours in the logbook. Should Carlo claim that he is a material participant on the basis of the hours recorded in his logbook and deduct his share of the loss? What would you do?

Example 9-26

As indicated in Example 9-22, Greg was allocated a $9,120 ordinary loss for *2015* and had a $124,000 tax basis at year-end *after* adjusting his tax basis for the loss. Given that Greg was allocated $9,000 of nonrecourse debt from accounts payable during *2015,* what is Greg's at-risk amount at the end of the year?

Answer: $115,000. Greg's at-risk amount is calculated by subtracting his $9,000 share of nonrecourse debt from his $124,000 tax basis.

Given Greg's status as a silent or nonmanaging member of CCS, how much of his $9,120 ordinary loss can he deduct in *2015* if he has no other sources of passive income?

Answer: None. Because Greg's tax basis and at-risk amount are large relative to his $9,120 ordinary loss, the tax basis and at-risk hurdles don't limit his loss. However, Greg's $9,120 loss would be classified as a passive loss and suspended until Greg received passive income from another source—hopefully CCS—or until he disposes of his interest in CCS.

What could Greg do to deduct any losses from CCS in the future?

Answer: He could satisfy one of the seven tests in Exhibit 9-9 to be classified as a material participant in CCS, thereby converting his future CCS losses from passive to active losses. Or he could become a passive participant in some other activity producing trade or business income that could be offset by any future passive losses from CCS.

Example 9-27

From Example 9-25 we learned that Nicole would report $150 of dividend income and $90 of long-term capital gains from CCS on her *2015* tax return. Further, we learned that $4,240 of her $18,240 *2015* ordinary loss allocation from CCS cleared both the tax basis and at-risk hurdles, leaving a total of $14,000 ordinary loss suspended and carried forward. How much of the $4,240 of ordinary loss can Nicole actually deduct on her tax return, given her status as a managing member of CCS?

Answer: Because Nicole is a managing member of CCS, it is likely she will satisfy at least one of the seven tests for material participation in Exhibit 9-9. As a result, she will treat the $4,240 ordinary loss clearing the tax basis and at-risk hurdles as an active loss and deduct it all on her tax return.

What if: Assume Nicole was not a managing member of CCS during *2015* and could not satisfy one of the seven material participation tests in Exhibit 9-9. How much of the $4,240 ordinary loss can she deduct on her tax return, assuming she has no other sources of passive income?

Answer: None. Under this assumption, the $4,240 is a passive activity loss and suspended until Nicole either receives some passive income from CCS (or some other source) or sells her interest in CCS. In the end, her entire $18,240 loss from *2015* would be suspended: $5,000 due to the tax basis limitation, $9,000 due to the at-risk limitation, and $4,240 due to the passive activity loss limitation.

CONCLUSION

This chapter explained the relevant tax rules pertaining to forming and operating partnerships. Specifically, we introduced important tax issues arising from partnership formations, including partner gain or loss recognition and calculating inside and outside basis. In addition, we explained accounting periods and methods, allocations of partners' ordinary income (loss) and separately stated items, basis adjustments, and loss limitation rules in the context of an operating partnership. Although it would seem that partnership tax law should be relatively straightforward given that partnerships don't pay taxes, by now you may have come to realize quite the opposite is true. The next chapter continues our discussion of partnership tax law with a focus on dispositions of partnership interests and partnership distributions.

Summary

LO 9-1 Determine whether a flow-through entity is taxed as a partnership or S corporation, and distinguish the entity approach from the aggregate approach for taxing partnerships.

- Unincorporated business entities with more than one owner are taxed as partnerships.
- Shareholders of certain corporations may elect to have them treated as flow-through entities by filing an S election with the IRS.
- Though partnerships and S corporations are both flow-through entities, the tax rules that apply to them differ.
- Partnership tax rules reflect both the aggregate and entity concepts.

LO 9-2 Resolve tax issues applicable to partnership formations and other acquisitions of partnership interests, including gain recognition to partners and tax basis for partners and partnerships.

- As a general rule, partners don't recognize gain or loss when they contribute property to partnerships in exchange for a partnership interest.

- Partnership recourse debt is allocated to partners with ultimate responsibility for paying the debt, and nonrecourse debt is allocated to partners using profit-sharing ratios.
- Partners contributing property encumbered by debt may have to recognize gain, depending on the basis of the property and the amount of the debt.
- Partners contributing property to a partnership will have an initial tax basis in their partnership interest equal to the basis of contributed property less any debt relief plus their share of any partnership debt and any gain they recognize.
- Partners receiving partnership interests by contributing capital assets or §1231 assets have a holding period in their partnership interest that includes the holding period of the contributed property. If they contribute any other type of property instead, their holding period begins on the date the partnership interest is received.
- Partnerships with contributed property have a tax basis and holding period in the property equal to the contributing partner's tax basis and holding period.
- Partners who receive capital interests in exchange for services must report the liquidation value of the capital interest as ordinary income, and the partnership either deducts or capitalizes an equivalent amount depending on the nature of the services provided.
- Partners who receive profits interests in exchange for services don't report any income. However, they share in any subsequent partnership profits and losses.
- Partners who purchase partnership interests have a tax basis in their interests equal to the purchase price plus their shares of partnership debt, and their holding periods begin on the date of purchase.

Determine the appropriate accounting periods and methods for partnerships. LO 9-3

- Partnerships, rather than individual partners, are responsible for making most tax elections.
- The Code mandates that partners include their share of income (loss) or other partnership items for "any taxable year of the partnership ending within or with the taxable year of the partner."
- Partnerships must use a tax year-end consistent with the majority interest taxable year, the taxable year of the principal partners, or the year-end providing the least aggregate deferral for the partners.
- Partnerships with average annual gross receipts over $5 million that have corporate partners may not use the cash method of accounting. Otherwise, partnerships may use either the cash or accrual method of accounting.

Calculate and characterize a partnership's ordinary business income or loss and its separately stated items, and demonstrate how to report these items to partners. LO 9-4

- Partnerships must file Form 1065, U.S. Return of Partnership Income, with the IRS annually and must provide each partner with a Schedule K-1 detailing the partner's share of ordinary business income (loss) and separately stated items.
- Separately stated items include short-term and long-term capital gains and losses, dividends, §1231 gains and losses, and other partnership items that may be treated differently at the partner level.
- The character of separately stated items is determined at the partnership rather than at the partner level.
- Guaranteed payments are typically fixed payments made to partners for services provided to the partnership. They are treated as ordinary income by partners who receive them and are either deducted or capitalized by the partnership depending on the nature of services provided.
- Guaranteed payments to any type of partner (or LLC member) and general partners' shares of ordinary business income (loss) are treated as self-employment income (loss).
- Limited partners' shares of ordinary business income (loss) are not treated as self-employment income (loss).
- Though the tax law is uncertain in this area, all or a portion of LLC members' shares of ordinary business income (loss) should be classified as self-employment income (loss) if members are significantly involved in managing the LLC.

- Partnerships provide a great deal of flexibility because they may specially allocate their income, gains, expenses, losses, and other partnership items, as long as the allocations have "substantial economic effect" or are consistent with partners' interests in the partnership. Special allocations of built-in gain or loss on contributed property to contributing partners are mandatory.

LO 9-5 Explain the implications of a partner's tax basis and the adjustments that affect it.

- Partners must make specified annual adjustments to the tax basis in their partnership interests to ensure that partnership taxable income/gain or deductible expense/loss items are not double taxed or deducted twice, and that partnership tax-exempt income or nondeductible expense is not taxed or deducted.
- Partners increase the tax basis in their interests by their actual or deemed cash contributions, shares of ordinary business income, separately stated income/gain items, and shares of tax-exempt income.
- Partners decrease the tax basis in their interests by their actual or deemed cash distributions, shares of ordinary business loss, separately stated expense/loss items, and shares of nondeductible expenses.
- A partner's tax basis may never be reduced below zero.
- Cash distributions that are less than a partner's tax basis immediately before the distribution are not taxable. However, cash distributions in excess of a partner's tax basis immediately before the distribution are generally taxable as capital gain.

LO 9-6 Apply the basis, at-risk, and passive activity loss limits to losses from partnerships.

- In order for losses to provide tax benefits to partners, partnership losses must clear the tax basis, at-risk, and passive activity loss hurdles (in that order).
- Partnership losses in excess of a partner's tax basis are suspended and may be utilized only when additional tax basis is created.
- Losses clearing the tax basis hurdle may be utilized only to the extent of the partner's at-risk amount. A partner's at-risk amount generally equals her tax basis (before any reduction for current year losses) less her share of nonrecourse debt that is not secured by real estate.
- If a partner is not a material participant in the partnership or if the partnership is involved in rental activities, losses clearing the basis and at-risk hurdles may be reported on the partner's tax return only when she has passive income from the partnership (or other sources) or when she sells her partnership interest.

KEY TERMS

aggregate approach (9-2)
at-risk amount (9-30)
at-risk rules (9-30)
built-in gain (9-3)
built-in loss (9-3)
C corporations (9-2)
capital account (9-8)
capital interest (9-3)
entity approach (9-2)
flow-through entities (9-2)
Form 1065 (9-23)
Form 7004 (9-23)
GAAP capital accounts (9-8)
general partnership (9-2)
guaranteed payments (9-19)
inside basis (9-4)
least aggregate deferral (9-15)
limited liability companies (LLC) (9-2)
limited partnership (9-2)
liquidation value (9-10)
majority interest taxable year (9-14)
nonrecourse debt (9-4)
nonservice partner (9-10)
ordinary business income (loss) (9-17)
organization costs (9-12)
outside basis (9-4)
partnership interest (9-3)
passive activity loss (PAL) rules (9-31)
principal partner (9-15)
profits interest (9-3)
qualified nonrecourse financing (9-30)
recourse debt (9-4)
S corporations (9-2)
Schedule K (9-23)
§704(b) capital accounts (9-8)
self-employment taxes (9-20)
separately stated items (9-17)
service partner (9-10)
special allocations (9-22)
start-up costs (9-12)
Subchapter K (9-2)
Subchapter S (9-2)
syndication costs (9-12)
tax capital accounts (9-8)

DISCUSSION QUESTIONS

1. What is a *flow-through entity,* and what effect does this designation have on how business entities and their owners are taxed? LO 9-1
2. What types of business entities are taxed as flow-through entities? LO 9-1
3. Compare and contrast the aggregate and entity concepts for taxing partnerships and their partners. LO 9-1
4. What is a partnership interest, and what specific economic rights or entitlements are included with it? LO 9-2
5. What is the rationale for requiring partners to defer most gains and all losses when they contribute property to a partnership? LO 9-2
6. Under what circumstances is it possible for partners to recognize gain when contributing property to partnerships? LO 9-2
7. What is *inside basis* and *outside basis,* and why are they relevant for taxing partnerships and partners? LO 9-2
8. What is recourse and nonrecourse debt, and how is each generally allocated to partners? LO 9-2
9. How does the amount of debt allocated to a partner affect the amount of gain a partner recognizes when contributing property secured by debt? LO 9-2
10. What is a tax basis capital account, and what type of tax-related information does it provide? LO 9-2
11. Distinguish between a capital interest and a profits interest, and explain how partners and partnerships treat each when exchanging them for services provided. LO 9-2
12. How do partners who purchase a partnership interest determine the tax basis and holding period of their partnership interests? LO 9-2
13. Why do you think partnerships, rather than the individual partners, are responsible for making most of the tax elections related to the operation of the partnership? LO 9-3
14. If a partner with a taxable year-end of December 31 is in a partnership with a March 31 taxable year-end, how many months of deferral will the partner receive? Why? LO 9-3
15. In what situation will there be a common year-end for the principal partners when there is no majority interest taxable year? LO 9-3
16. Explain the least aggregate deferral test for determining a partnership's year-end and discuss when it applies. LO 9-3
17. When are partnerships eligible to use the cash method of accounting? LO 9-3
18. What is a partnership's ordinary business income (loss) and how is it calculated? LO 9-4
19. What are some common separately stated items, and why must they be separately stated to the partners? LO 9-4
20. Is the character of partnership income/gains and expenses/losses determined at the partnership or partner level? Why? LO 9-4
21. What are guaranteed payments and how do partnerships and partners treat them for income and self-employment tax purposes? LO 9-4
22. How do general and limited partners treat their share of ordinary business income for self-employment tax purposes? LO 9-4
23. What challenges do LLCs face when deciding whether to treat their members' shares of ordinary business income as self-employment income? LO 9-4
24. How much flexibility do partnerships have in allocating partnership items to partners? LO 9-4

LO 9-4 25. What are the basic tax-filing requirements imposed on partnerships?

LO 9-5 26. In what situations do partners need to know the tax basis in their partnership interests?

LO 9-5 27. Why does a partner's tax basis in her partnership interest need to be adjusted annually?

LO 9-5 28. What items will increase a partner's basis in her partnership interest?

LO 9-5 29. What items will decrease a partner's basis in her partnership interest?

LO 9-6 30. What hurdles (or limitations) must partners overcome before they can ultimately deduct partnership losses on their tax returns?

LO 9-6 31. What happens to partnership losses allocated to partners in excess of the tax basis in their partnership interests?

LO 9-6 32. In what sense is the at-risk loss limitation rule more restrictive than the tax basis loss limitation rule?

LO 9-6 33. How do partners measure the amount they have at risk in the partnership?

LO 9-6 34. In what order are the loss limitation rules applied to limit partner's losses from partnerships?

LO 9-6 35. How do partners determine whether they are passive participants in partnerships when applying the passive activity loss limitation rules?

LO 9-6 36. Under what circumstances can partners with passive losses from partnerships deduct their passive losses?

PROBLEMS

All applicable problems are available with McGraw-Hill's *Connect® Accounting*.

LO 9-2 37. Joseph contributed $22,000 in cash and equipment with a tax basis of $5,000 and a fair market value of $11,000 to Berry Hill Partnership in exchange for a partnership interest.

a) What is Joseph's tax basis in his partnership interest?
b) What is Berry Hill's basis in the equipment?

LO 9-2 38. Lance contributed investment property worth $500,000, purchased three years ago for $200,000 cash, to Cloud Peak LLC in exchange for an 85 percent profits and capital interest in the LLC. Cloud Peak owes $300,000 to its suppliers but has no other debts.

a) What is Lance's tax basis in his LLC interest?
b) What is Lance's holding period in his interest?
c) What is Cloud Peak's basis in the contributed property?
d) What is Cloud Peak's holding period in the contributed property?

LO 9-2 39. Laurel contributed equipment worth $200,000, purchased 10 months ago for $250,000 cash and used in her sole proprietorship, to Sand Creek LLC in exchange for a 15 percent profits and capital interest in the LLC. Laurel agreed to guarantee all $15,000 of Sand Creek's accounts payable, but she did not guarantee any portion of the $100,000 nonrecourse mortgage securing Sand Creek's office building. Other than the accounts payable and mortgage, Sand Creek does not owe any debts to other creditors.

a) What is Laurel's initial tax basis in her LLC interest?
b) What is Laurel's holding period in her interest?
c) What is Sand Creek's initial basis in the contributed property?
d) What is Sand Creek's holding period in the contributed property?

40. Harry and Sally formed the Evergreen Partnership by contributing the following assets in exchange for a 50 percent capital and profits interest in the partnership: LO 9-2 planning

	Basis	Fair Market Value
Harry:		
Cash	$ 30,000	$ 30,000
Land	100,000	120,000
Totals	$130,000	$150,000
Sally:		
Equipment used in a business	200,000	150,000
Totals	$200,000	$150,000

a) How much gain or loss will Harry recognize on the contribution?
b) How much gain or loss will Sally recognize on the contribution?
c) How could the transaction be structured a different way to get a better result for Sally?
d) What is Harry's tax basis in his partnership interest?
e) What is Sally's tax basis in her partnership interest?
f) What is Evergreen's tax basis in its assets?
g) Following the format in Exhibit 9-2, prepare a tax basis balance sheet for the Evergreen partnership showing the tax capital accounts for the partners.

41. Cosmo contributed land with a fair market value of $400,000 and a tax basis of $90,000 to the Y Mountain Partnership in exchange for a 25 percent profits and capital interest in the partnership. The land is secured by $120,000 of nonrecourse debt. Other than this nonrecourse debt, Y Mountain Partnership does not have any debt. LO 9-2
a) How much gain will Cosmo recognize from the contribution?
b) What is Cosmo's tax basis in his partnership interest?

42. When High Horizon LLC was formed, Maude contributed the following assets in exchange for a 25 percent capital and profits interest in the LLC: LO 9-2

	Basis	Fair Market Value
Maude:		
Cash	$ 20,000	$ 20,000
Land*	100,000	360,000
Totals	$120,000	$380,000

*Nonrecourse debt secured by the land equals $160,000

James, Harold, and Jenny each contributed $220,000 in cash for a 25 percent profits and capital interest.
a) How much gain or loss will Maude and the other members recognize?
b) What is Maude's tax basis in her LLC interest?
c) What tax basis do James, Harold, and Jenny have in their LLC interests?
d) What is High Horizon's tax basis in its assets?
e) Following the format in Exhibit 9-2, prepare a tax basis balance sheet for the High Horizon LLC showing the tax capital accounts for the members.

LO 9-2

43. Kevan, Jerry, and Dave formed Albee LLC. Jerry and Dave each contributed $245,000 in cash. Kevan contributed the following assets:

	Basis	Fair Market Value
Kevan:		
Cash	$ 15,000	$ 15,000
Land*	120,000	440,000
Totals	$135,000	$455,000

*Nonrecourse debt secured by the land equals $210,000

Each member received a one-third capital and profits interest in the LLC.

a) How much gain or loss will Jerry, Dave, and Kevan recognize on the contributions?
b) What is Kevan's tax basis in his LLC interest?
c) What tax basis do Jerry and Dave have in their LLC interests?
d) What is Albee LLC's tax basis in its assets?
e) Following the format in Exhibit 9-2, prepare a tax basis balance sheet for the Albee LLC showing the tax capital accounts for the members. What is Kevan's share of the LLC's inside basis?
f) If the lender holding the nonrecourse debt secured by Kevan's land required Kevan to guarantee 33.33 percent of the debt and Jerry to guarantee the remaining 66.67 percent of the debt when Albee LLC was formed, how much gain or loss will Kevan recognize?
g) If the lender holding the nonrecourse debt secured by Kevan's land required Kevan to guarantee 33.33 percent of the debt and Jerry to guarantee the remaining 66.67 percent of the debt when Albee LLC was formed, what are the members' tax bases in their LLC interests?

LO 9-2

research

44. Jim has decided to contribute some equipment he previously used in his sole proprietorship in exchange for a 10 percent profits and capital interest in Fast Choppers LLC. Jim originally paid $200,000 cash for the equipment. Since then, the tax basis in the equipment has been reduced to $100,000 because of tax depreciation, and the fair market value of the equipment is now $150,000.

a) Must Jim recognize any of the potential §1245 recapture when he contributes the machinery to Fast Choppers? [*Hint:* See §1245(b)(3).]
b) What cost recovery method will Fast Choppers use to depreciate the machinery? [*Hint:* See §168(i)(7).]
c) If Fast Choppers were to immediately sell the equipment Jim contributed for $150,000, how much gain would Jim recognize and what is its character? [*Hint:* See §1245 and 704(c).]

LO 9-2

research

45. Ansel purchased raw land three years ago for $200,000 to hold as an investment. After watching the value of the land drop to $150,000, he decided to contribute it to Mountainside Developers LLC in exchange for a 5 percent capital and profits interest. Mountainside plans to develop the property and will treat it as inventory, like all the other real estate it holds.

a) If Mountainside sells the property for $150,000 after holding it for one year, how much gain or loss does it recognize and what is the character of the gain or loss? [*Hint:* See §724.]
b) If Mountainside sells the property for $125,000 after holding it for two years, how much gain or loss does it recognize and what is the character of the gain or loss?
c) If Mountainside sells the property for $150,000 after holding it for six years, how much gain or loss does it recognize and what is the character of the gain or loss?

46. Claude purchased raw land three years ago for $1,500,000 to develop into lots and sell to individuals planning to build their dream homes. Claude intended to treat this property as inventory, like his other development properties. Before completing the development of the property, however, he decided to contribute it to South Peak Investors LLC when it was worth $2,500,000, in exchange for a 10 percent capital and profits interest. South Peak's strategy is to hold land for investment purposes only and then sell it later at a gain. LO 9-2 research
   a) If South Peak sells the property for $3,000,000 four years after Claude's contribution, how much gain or loss is recognized and what is its character? [*Hint:* See §724.]
   b) If South Peak sells the property for $3,000,000 five and one-half years after Claude's contribution, how much gain or loss is recognized and what is its character?

47. Reggie contributed $10,000 in cash and a capital asset he had held for three years with a fair market value of $20,000 and tax basis of $10,000 for a 5 percent capital and profits interest in Green Valley LLC. LO 9-2 research
   a) If Reggie sells his LLC interest 13 months later for $30,000 when the tax basis in his partnership interest is still $20,000, how much gain does he report and what is its character?
   b) If Reggie sells his LLC interest two months later for $30,000 when the tax basis in his partnership interest is still $20,000, how much gain does he report and what is its character? [*Hint*: See Reg. §1.1223-3.]

48. Connie recently provided legal services to the Winterhaven LLC and received a 5 percent interest in the LLC as compensation. Winterhaven currently has $50,000 of accounts payable and no other debt. The current fair market value of Winterhaven's capital is $200,000. LO 9-2
   a) If Connie receives a 5 percent capital interest only, how much income must she report and what is her tax basis in the LLC interest?
   b) If Connie receives a 5 percent profits interest only, how much income must she report and what is her tax basis in the LLC interest?
   c) If Connie receives a 5 percent capital and profits interest, how much income must she report and what is her tax basis in the LLC interest?

49. Mary and Scott formed a partnership that maintains its records on a calendar-year basis. The balance sheet of the MS Partnership at year-end is as follows: LO 9-2

	Basis	Fair Market Value
Cash	$ 60	$ 60
Land	60	180
Inventory	72	60
	$192	$300
Mary	$ 96	$150
Scott	96	150
	$192	$300

At the end of the current year, Kari will receive a one-third capital interest only in exchange for services rendered. Kari's interest will not be subject to a substantial risk of forfeiture and the costs for the type of services she provided are typically not capitalized by the partnership. For the current year, the income and expenses from operations are equal. Consequently, the only tax consequences for the year are those relating to the admission of Kari to the partnership.

   a) Compute and characterize any gain or loss Kari may have to recognize as a result of her admission to the partnership.
   b) Compute Kari's basis in her partnership interest.

c) Prepare a balance sheet of the partnership immediately after Kari's admission showing the partners' tax capital accounts and capital accounts stated at fair market value.

d) Calculate how much gain or loss Kari would have to recognize if, instead of a capital interest, she received a profits interest.

LO 9-2

50. Dave LaCroix recently received a 10 percent capital and profits interest in Cirque Capital LLC in exchange for consulting services he provided. If Cirque Capital had paid an outsider to provide the advice, it would have deducted the payment as compensation expense. Cirque Capital's balance sheet on the day Dave received his capital interest appears below:

	Basis	Fair Market Value
Assets:		
Cash	$150,000	$ 150,000
Investments	200,000	700,000
Land	150,000	250,000
Totals	$500,000	$1,100,000
Liabilities and capital:		
Nonrecourse debt	100,000	100,000
Lance*	200,000	500,000
Robert*	200,000	500,000
Totals	$500,000	$1,100,000

*Assume that Lance's basis and Robert's basis in their LLC interests equal their tax basis capital accounts plus their respective shares of nonrecourse debt.

a) Compute and characterize any gain or loss Dave may have to recognize as a result of his admission to Cirque Capital.

b) Compute each member's tax basis in his LLC interest immediately after Dave's receipt of his interest.

c) Prepare a balance sheet for Cirque Capital immediately after Dave's admission showing the members' tax capital accounts and their capital accounts stated at fair market value.

d) Compute and characterize any gain or loss Dave may have to recognize as a result of his admission to Cirque Capital if he receives only a profits interest.

e) Compute each member's tax basis in his LLC interest immediately after Dave's receipt of his interest if Dave receives only a profits interest.

LO 9-2

51. Last December 31, Ramon sold the 10 percent interest in the Del Sol Partnership that he had held for two years to Garrett for $400,000. Prior to selling his interest, Ramon's basis in Del Sol was $200,000, which included a $100,000 share of nonrecourse debt allocated to him.

a) What is Garrett's tax basis in his partnership interest?

b) If Garrett sells his partnership interest three months after receiving it and recognizes a gain, what is the character of his gain?

LO 9-3

52. Broken Rock LLC was recently formed with the following members:

Name	Tax Year-End	Capital/Profits %
George Allen	December 31	33.33%
Elanax Corp.	June 30	33.33%
Ray Kirk	December 31	33.34%

What is the required taxable year-end for Broken Rock LLC?

53. Granite Slab LLC was recently formed with the following members: LO 9-3

Name	Tax Year-End	Capital/Profits %
Nelson Black	December 31	22.0%
Brittany Jones	December 31	24.0
Lone Pine LLC	June 30	4.5
Red Spot Inc.	October 31	4.5
Pale Rock Inc.	September 30	4.5
Thunder Ridge LLC	July 31	4.5
Alpensee LLC	March 31	4.5
Lakewood Inc.	June 30	4.5
Streamside LLC	October 31	4.5
Burnt Fork Inc.	October 31	4.5
Snowy Ridge LP	June 30	4.5
Whitewater LP	October 31	4.5
Straw Hat LLC	January 31	4.5
Wildfire Inc.	September 30	4.5

What is the required taxable year-end for Granite Slab LLC?

54. Tall Tree LLC was recently formed with the following members: LO 9-3

Name	Tax Year-End	Capital/Profits %
Eddie Robinson	December 31	40%
Pitcher Lenders LLC	June 30	25
Perry Homes Inc.	October 31	35

What is the required taxable year-end for Tall Tree LLC?

55. Rock Creek LLC was recently formed with the following members: LO 9-3

Name	Tax Year-End	Capital/Profits %
Mark Banks	December 31	35%
Highball Properties LLC	March 31	25
Chavez Builders Inc.	November 30	40

What is the required taxable year-end for Rock Creek LLC?

56. Ryan, Dahir, and Bill have operated Broken Feather LLC for the last four years using a calendar year-end. Each has a one-third interest. Since they began operating, their busy season has run from June through August, with 35 percent of their gross receipts coming in July and August. The members would like to change their tax year-end and have asked you to address the following questions: LO 9-3

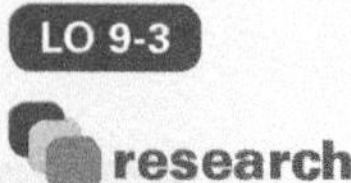

a) Can they change to an August 31 year-end and, if so, how do they make the change? [*Hint:* See Rev. Proc. 2002-38, 2002-1 CB 1037.]

b) Can they change to a September 30 year-end and, if so, how do they make the change? [*Hint:* See §444.]

57. Ashlee, Hiroki, Kate, and Albee LLC each own a 25 percent interest in Tally Industries LLC, which generates annual gross receipts of over $10 million. Ashlee, Hiroki, and Kate manage the business, but Albee LLC is a nonmanaging member. Although Tally Industries has historically been profitable, for the last three years losses have been allocated to the members. Given these facts, the members want to know whether Tally Industries can use the cash method of accounting. Why or why not? [*Hint:* See §448(b)(3).] LO 9-3

LO 9-4

58. Turtle Creek Partnership had the following revenues, expenses, gains, losses, and distributions:

Sales revenue	$ 40,000
Long-term capital gains	2,000
Cost of goods sold	(13,000)
Depreciation—MACRS	(3,000)
Amortization of organization costs	(1,000)
Guaranteed payments to partners for general management	(10,000)
Cash distributions to partners	(2,000)

a) Given these items, what is Turtle Creek's ordinary business income (loss) for the year?

b) What are Turtle Creek's separately stated items for the year?

LO 9-4

59. Georgio owns a 20 percent profits and capital interest in Rain Tree LLC. For the current year, Rain Tree had the following revenues, expenses, gains, and losses:

Sales revenue	$ 70,000
Gain on sale of land (§1231)	11,000
Cost of goods sold	(26,000)
Depreciation—MACRS	(3,000)
§179 deduction*	(10,000)
Employee wages	(11,000)
Fines and penalties	(3,000)
Municipal bond interest	6,000
Short-term capital gains	4,000
Guaranteed payment to Sandra	(3,000)

*Assume the §179 property placed in service limitation does not apply.

a) How much ordinary business income (loss) is allocated to Georgio for the year?

b) What are Georgio's separately stated items for the year?

LO 9-4

research

60. Richard Meyer and two friends from law school recently formed Meyer and Associates as a limited liability partnership (LLP). Income from the partnership will be split equally among the partners. The partnership will generate fee income primarily from representing clients in bankruptcy and foreclosure matters. While some attorney friends have suggested that partners' earnings will be self-employment income, other attorneys they know from their local bar association meetings claim just the opposite. After examining relevant authority, explain how you would advise Meyer and Associates on this matter. [*Hint:* See §1402(a)(13) and *Renkemeyer, Campbell & Weaver LLP v. Commissioner,* 136 T.C. 137 (2011).]

LO 9-4

61. The partnership agreement of the G&P general partnership states that Gary will receive a guaranteed payment of $13,000, and that Gary and Prudence will share the remaining profits or losses in a 45/55 ratio. For year 1, the G&P partnership reports the following results:

Sales revenue	$ 70,000
Gain on sale of land (§1231)	8,000
Cost of goods sold	(38,000)
Depreciation—MACRS	(9,000)
Employee wages	(14,000)
Cash charitable contributions	(3,000)
Municipal bond interest	2,000
Other expenses	(2,000)

a) Compute Gary's share of ordinary income (loss) and separately stated items to be reported on his year 1 Schedule K-1, including his self-employment income (loss).

b) Compute Gary's share of self-employment income (loss) to be reported on his year 1 Schedule K-1, assuming G&P is a limited partnership and Gary is a limited partner.

c) What do you believe Gary's share of self-employment income (loss) to be reported on his year 1 Schedule K-1 should be, assuming G&P is an LLC and Gary spends 2,000 hours per year working there full time?

62. Hoki Poki, a cash-method general partnership, recorded the following items for its current tax year: LO 9-4 research

Rental real estate income	$ 2,000
Sales revenue	70,000
§1245 recapture income	8,000
Interest income	2,000
Cost of goods sold	(38,000)
Depreciation—MACRS	(9,000)
Supplies expense	(1,000)
Employee wages	(14,000)
Investment interest expense	(1,000)
Partner's medical insurance premiums paid by Hoki Poki	(3,000)

As part of preparing Hoki Poki's current year return, identify the items that should be included in computing its ordinary business income (loss) and those that should be separately stated. [*Hint:* See Schedule K-1 and related preparer's instructions at www.irs.gov.]

63. On the last day of its current tax year, Buy Rite LLC received $300,000 when it sold a machine it had purchased for $200,000 three years ago to use in its business. At the time of the sale, the basis in the equipment had been reduced to $100,000 due to tax depreciation taken. How much did the members' self-employment earnings from Buy Rite increase when the equipment was sold? [*Hint:* See §1402(a)(3).] LO 9-4 research

64. Jhumpa, Stewart, and Kelly are all one-third partners in the capital and profits of Firewalker general partnership. In addition to their normal share of the partnership's annual income, Jhumpa and Stewart receive an annual guaranteed payment of $10,000 to compensate them for additional services they provide. Firewalker's income statement for the current year reflects the following revenues and expenses: LO 9-4

Sales revenue	$340,000
Interest income	3,300
Long-term capital gains	1,200
Cost of goods sold	(120,000)
Employee wages	(75,000)
Depreciation expense	(28,000)
Guaranteed payments	(20,000)
Miscellaneous expenses	(4,500)
Overall net income	$ 97,000

a) Given Firewalker's operating results, how much ordinary business income (loss) and what separately stated items [including the partners' self-employment earnings (loss)] will it report on its return for the year?

b) How will it allocate these amounts to its partners?

c) How much self-employment tax will each partner pay assuming none has any other source of income or loss?

LO 9-4

65. This year, Darrel's distributive share from Alcove Partnership includes $6,000 of interest income, $3,000 of dividend income, and $70,000 ordinary business income.
    a) Assume that Darrel materially participates in the partnership. How much of his distributive share from Alcove Partnership is potentially subject to the net investment income tax?
    b) Assume that Darrel does not materially participate in the partnership. How much of his distributive share from Alcove Partnership is potentially subject to the net investment income tax?

LO 9-4

66. This year, Alex's distributive share from Eden Lakes Partnership includes $8,000 of interest income, $4,000 of net long-term capital gains, $2,000 net section 1231 gain from the sale of property used in the partnership's trade or business, and $83,000 of ordinary business income.
    a) Assume that Alex materially participates in the partnership. How much of his distributive share from Eden Lakes Partnership is potentially subject to the net investment income tax?
    b) Assume that Alex does not materially participate in the partnership. How much of his distributive share from the Eden Lakes partnership is potentially subject to the net investment income tax?

LO 9-4
research

67. Lane and Cal each own 50 percent of the profits and capital of HighYield LLC. HighYield owns a portfolio of taxable bonds and municipal bonds, and each year the portfolio generates approximately $10,000 of taxable interest and $10,000 of tax-exempt interest. Lane's marginal tax rate is 35 percent while Cal's marginal tax rate is 15 percent. To take advantage of the difference in their marginal tax rates, Lane and Cal want to modify their operating agreement to specially allocate all of the taxable interest to Cal and all of the tax-exempt interest to Lane. Until now, Lane and Cal had been allocated 50 percent of each type of interest income.
    a) Is HighYield's proposed special allocation acceptable under current tax rules? Why or why not? [*Hint:* See Reg. §1.704-1(b)(2)(iii)(b) and §1.704-1(b)(5) Example (5).]
    b) If the IRS ultimately disagrees with HighYield's special allocation, how will it likely reallocate the taxable and tax-exempt interest among the members? [*Hint:* See Reg. §1.704-1(b)(5) Example (5)(ii).]

LO 9-5

68. Larry's tax basis in his partnership interest at the beginning of the year was $10,000. If his share of the partnership debt increased by $10,000 during the year and his share of partnership income for the year is $3,000, what is his tax basis in his partnership interest at the end of the year?

LO 9-5

69. Carmine was allocated the following items from the Piccolo LLC for last year:

    Ordinary business loss
    Nondeductible penalties
    Tax-exempt interest income
    Short-term capital gain
    Cash distributions

    Rank these items in terms of the order they should be applied to adjust Carmine's tax basis in Piccolo for the year (some items may be of equal rank).

LO 9-5

70. Oscar, Felix, and Marv are all one-third partners in the capital and profits of Eastside General Partnership. In addition to their normal share of the partnership's annual income, Oscar and Felix receive annual guaranteed payments of $7,000 to compensate them for additional services they provide. Eastside's

income statement for the current year reflects the following revenues and expenses:

Sales revenue	$420,000
Dividend income	5,700
Short-term capital gains	2,800
Cost of goods sold	(210,000)
Employee wages	(115,000)
Depreciation expense	(28,000)
Guaranteed payments	(14,000)
Miscellaneous expenses	(9,500)
Overall net income	$ 52,000

In addition, Eastside owed creditors $120,000 at the beginning of the year but managed to pay down its debts to $90,000 by the end of the year. All partnership debt is allocated equally among the partners. Finally, Oscar, Felix and Marv had a tax basis of $80,000 in their interests at the beginning of the year.

a) What tax basis do the partners have in their partnership interests at the end of the year?

b) Assume the partners began the year with a tax basis of $10,000 and all the debt was paid off on the last day of the year. How much gain will the partners recognize when the debt is paid off? What tax basis do the partners have in their partnership interests at the end of the year?

71. Pam, Sergei, and Mercedes are all one-third partners in the capital and profits of Oak Grove General Partnership. Partnership debt is allocated among the partners in accordance with their capital and profits interests. In addition to their normal share of the partnership's annual income, Pam and Sergei receive annual guaranteed payments of $20,000 to compensate them for additional services they provide. Oak Grove's income statement for the current year reflects the following revenues and expenses: LO 9-5

Sales revenue	$476,700
Dividend income	6,600
§1231 losses	(3,800)
Cost of goods sold	(245,000)
Employee wages	(92,000)
Depreciation expense	(31,000)
Guaranteed payments	(40,000)
Miscellaneous expenses	(11,500)
Overall net income	$ 60,000

In addition, Oak Grove owed creditors $90,000 at the beginning and $150,000 at the end of the year, and Pam, Sergei, and Mercedes had a tax basis of $50,000 in their interests at the beginning of the year. Also, on December 31 of the current year, Sergei and Mercedes agreed to increase Pam's capital and profits interest from 33.33 percent to 40 percent in exchange for additional services she provided to the partnership. The current liquidation value of the additional capital interest Pam received is $40,000.

a) What tax basis do the partners have in their partnership interests at the end of the year?

b) If, in addition to the expenses listed above, the partnership donated $12,000 to a political campaign, what tax basis do the partners have in their partnership interests at the end of the year assuming the liquidation value of the additional capital interest Pam received at the end of the year remains at $40,000?

LO 9-6 research

72. Laura Davis is a member in a limited liability company that has historically been profitable but is expecting to generate losses in the near future because of a weak local economy. In addition to the hours she works as an employee of a local business, she currently spends approximately 150 hours per year helping to manage the LLC. Other LLC members each work approximately 175 hours per year in the LLC, and the time Laura and other members spend managing the LLC has remained constant since she joined the company three years ago. Laura's tax basis and amount at-risk are large compared to her share of projected losses; however, she is concerned that her ability to deduct her share of the projected losses will be limited by the passive activity loss rules.
   a) As an LLC member, will Laura's share of losses be presumed to be passive as they are for limited partners? Why or why not? [*Hint:* See §469(h)(2), *Garnett v. Commissioner,* 132 T.C. 368 (2009), and Prop. Reg. § 1.469-5(e)(3)(i).]
   b) Assuming Laura's losses are not presumed to be passive, is she devoting sufficient time to the LLC to be considered a material participant? Why or why not?
   c) What would you recommend to Laura to help her achieve a more favorable tax outcome?

LO 9-6

73. Alfonso began the year with a tax basis in his partnership interest of $30,000. His share of partnership debt at the beginning and end of the year consists of $4,000 of recourse debt and $6,000 of nonrecourse debt. During the year, he was allocated $40,000 of partnership ordinary business loss. Alfonso does not materially participate in this partnership and he has $1,000 of passive income from other sources.
   a) How much of Alfonso's loss is limited by his tax basis?
   b) How much of Alfonso's loss is limited by his at-risk amount?
   c) How much of Alfonso's loss is limited by the passive activity loss rules?

LO 9-6

74. Jenna began the year with a tax basis of $45,000 in her partnership interest. Her share of partnership debt consists of $6,000 of recourse debt and $10,000 of nonrecourse debt at the beginning of the year and $6,000 of recourse debt and $13,000 of nonrecourse debt at the end of the year. During the year, she was allocated $65,000 of partnership ordinary business loss. Jenna does not materially participate in this partnership and she has $4,000 of passive income from other sources.
   a) How much of Jenna's loss is limited by her tax basis?
   b) How much of Jenna's loss is limited by her at-risk amount?
   c) How much of Jenna's loss is limited by the passive activity loss rules?

LO 9-5 LO 9-6 research

75. Juan Diego began the year with a tax basis in his partnership interest of $50,000. During the year, he was allocated $20,000 of partnership ordinary business income, $70,000 of §1231 losses, $30,000 of short-term capital losses, and received a cash distribution of $50,000.
   a) What items related to these allocations does Juan Diego actually report on his tax return for the year? [*Hint:* See Reg. §1.704-1(d)(2) and Rev. Rul. 66-94.]
   b) If any deductions or losses are limited, what are the carryover amounts and what is their character? [*Hint:* See Reg. §1.704-1(d).]

LO 9-6

76. Farell is a member of Sierra Vista LLC. Although Sierra Vista is involved in a number of different business ventures, it is not currently involved in real estate either as an investor or as a developer. On January 1, year 1, Farell has a $100,000 tax basis in his LLC interest that includes his $90,000 share of Sierra Vista's general debt obligations. By the end of the year, Farell's share of Sierra Vista's general debt obligations has increased to $100,000. Because of the time

he spends in other endeavors, Farell does not materially participate in Sierra Vista. His share of the Sierra Vista losses for year 1 is $120,000. As a partner in the Riverwoods Partnership, he also has year 1, Schedule K-1 passive income of $5,000.

a) Determine how much of the Sierra Vista loss Farell will currently be able to deduct on his tax return for year 1, and list the losses suspended due to tax basis, at-risk, and passive activity loss limitations.
b) Assuming Farell's Riverwoods K-1 indicates passive income of $30,000, determine how much of the Sierra Vista loss he will ultimately be able to deduct on his tax return for year 1, and list the losses suspended due to tax basis, at-risk, and passive activity loss limitations.
c) Assuming Farell is deemed to be an active participant in Sierra Vista, determine how much of the Sierra Vista loss he will ultimately be able to deduct on his tax return for year 1, and list the losses suspended due to tax basis, at-risk, and passive activity loss limitations.

LO 9-6

research

77. Jenkins has a one-third capital and profits interest in the Maverick General Partnership. On January 1, year 1, Maverick has $120,000 of general debt obligations and Jenkins has a $50,000 tax basis (including his share of Maverick's debt) in his partnership interest. During the year, Maverick incurred a $30,000 nonrecourse debt that is not secured by real estate. Because Maverick is a rental real estate partnership, Jenkins is deemed to be a passive participant in Maverick. His share of the Maverick losses for year 1 is $75,000. Jenkins is not involved in any other passive activities, and this is the first year he has been allocated losses from Maverick.

a) Determine how much of the Maverick loss Jenkins will currently be able to deduct on his tax return for year 1, and list the losses suspended due to tax basis, at-risk, and passive activity loss limitations.
b) If Jenkins sells his interest on January 1, year 2, what happens to his suspended losses from year 1? [*Hint:* See §706(c)(2)(A), Reg. §1.704-1(d)(1), Prop. Reg. §1.465-66(a), and *Sennett v. Commissioner* 80 TC 825 (1983).]

LO 9-6

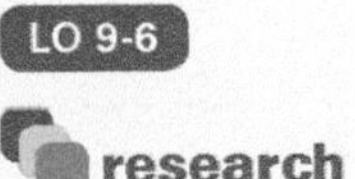

78. Suki and Steve own 50 percent capital and profits interests in Lorinda LLC. Lorinda operates the local minor league baseball team and owns the stadium where the team plays. Although the debt incurred to build the stadium was paid off several years ago, Lorinda owes its general creditors $300,000 (at the beginning of the year) that is not secured by firm property or guaranteed by any of the members. At the beginning of the current year, Suki and Steve had a tax basis of $170,000 in their LLC interests, including their share of debt owed to the general creditors. Shortly before the end of the year they each received a $10,000 cash distribution, even though Lorinda's ordinary business loss for the year was $400,000. Because of the time commitment to operate a baseball team, both Suki and Steve spent more than 1,500 hours during the year operating Lorinda.

a) Determine how much of the Lorinda loss Suki and Steve will each be able to deduct on their current tax returns, and list their losses suspended by the tax basis, at-risk, and passive activity loss limitations.
b) Assume that some time before receiving the $10,000 cash distribution, Steve is advised by his tax adviser that his marginal tax rate will be abnormally high during the current year because of an unexpected windfall. To help Steve utilize more of the losses allocated from Lorinda in the current year, his adviser recommends refusing the cash distribution and personally guaranteeing $100,000 of Lorinda's debt, without the right to be reimbursed by Suki. If Steve follows his adviser's recommendations, how much additional

Lorinda loss can he deduct on his current tax return? How does Steve's decision affect the amount of loss Suki can deduct on her current return and the amount and type of her suspended losses?

LO 9-6

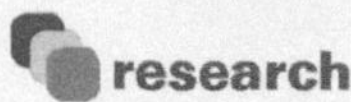

79. Ray and Chuck own 50 percent capital and profits interests in Alpine Properties LLC. Alpine builds and manages rental real estate, and Ray and Chuck each work full time (over 1,000 hours per year) managing Alpine. Alpine's debt (both at the beginning and end of the year) consists of $1,500,000 in nonrecourse mortgages obtained from an unrelated bank and secured by various rental properties. At the beginning of the current year, Ray and Chuck each had a tax basis of $250,000 in his LLC interest, including his share of the nonrecourse mortgage debt. Alpine's ordinary business losses for the current year totaled $600,000, and neither member is involved in other activities that generate passive income.
    a) How much of each member's loss is suspended because of the tax basis limitation?
    b) How much of each member's loss is suspended because of the at-risk limitation?
    c) How much of each member's loss is suspended because of the passive activity loss limitation? [*Hint:* See §469(b)(7).]

COMPREHENSIVE PROBLEMS

All applicable problems are available with McGraw-Hill's *Connect® Accounting*.

80. Aaron, Deanne, and Keon formed the Blue Bell General Partnership at the beginning of the current year. Aaron and Deanne each contributed $110,000 and Keon transferred an acre of undeveloped land to the partnership. The land had a tax basis of $70,000 and was appraised at $180,000. The land was also encumbered with a $70,000 nonrecourse mortgage for which no one was personally liable. All three partners agreed to split profits and losses equally. At the end of the first year, Blue Bell made a $7,000 principal payment on the mortgage. For the first year of operations, the partnership records disclosed the following information:

Sales revenue	$470,000
Cost of goods sold	410,000
Operating expenses	70,000
Long-term capital gains	2,400
§1231 gains	900
Charitable contributions	300
Municipal bond interest	300
Salary paid as a guaranteed payment to Deanne (not included in expenses)	3,000

    a) Compute the adjusted basis of each partner's interest in the partnership immediately after the formation of the partnership.
    b) List the separate items of partnership income, gains, losses, and deductions that the partners must show on their individual income tax returns that include the results of the partnership's first year of operations.
    c) Using the information generated in answering parts (a) and (b), prepare Blue Bell's page 1 and Schedule K to be included with its Form 1065 for its first year of operations, along with Schedule K-1 for Deanne.
    d) What are the partners' adjusted bases in their partnership interests at the end of the first year of operations?

81. The TimpRiders LP has operated a motorcycle dealership for a number of years. Lance is the limited partner, Francesca is the general partner, and they share capital and profits equally. Francesca works full-time managing the partnership. Both the partnership and the partners report on a calendar-year basis. At the start of the current year, Lance and Francesca had bases of $10,000 and $3,000, respectively, and the partnership did not carry any debt. During the current year, the partnership reported the following results from operations:

Net sales	$650,000
Cost of goods sold	500,000
Operating expenses	160,000
Short-term capital loss	2,000
Tax-exempt interest	2,000
§1231 gain	6,000

On the last day of the year, the partnership distributed $3,000 each to Lance and Francesca.

a) What outside basis do Lance and Francesca have in their partnership interests at the end of the year?
b) How much of their losses are currently not deductible by Lance and Francesca because of the tax basis limitation?
c) To what extent does the passive activity loss limitation apply in restricting their deductible losses for the year?
d) Using the information provided, prepare TimpRiders' page 1 and Schedule K to be included with its Form 1065 for the current year. Also, prepare a Schedule K-1 for Lance and Francesca.

82. LeBron, Dennis, and Susan formed the Bar T LLC at the beginning of the current year. LeBron and Dennis each contributed $200,000 and Susan transferred several acres of agricultural land she had purchased two years earlier to the LLC. The land had a tax basis of $50,000 and was appraised at $300,000. The land was also encumbered with a $100,000 nonrecourse mortgage (i.e., qualified nonrecourse financing) for which no one was personally liable. The members plan to use the land and cash to begin a cattle-feeding operation. Susan will work full-time operating the business, but LeBron and Dennis will devote less than two days per year to the operation.

All three members agree to split profits and losses equally. At the end of the first year, Bar T had accumulated $40,000 of accounts payable jointly guaranteed by LeBron and Dennis and had made a $9,000 principal payment on the mortgage. None of the members have passive income from other sources.

For the first year of operations, the partnership records disclosed the following information:

Sales revenue	$620,000
Cost of goods sold	380,000
Operating expenses	670,000
Dividends	1,200
Municipal bond interest	300
Salary paid as a guaranteed payment to Susan (not included in expenses)	10,000
Cash distributions split equally among the members at year-end	3,000

a) Compute the adjusted basis of each member's interest immediately after the formation of the LLC.

b) When does each member's holding period for his or her LLC interest begin?

c) What is Bar T's tax basis and holding period in its land?

d) What is Bar T's required tax year-end?

e) What overall methods of accounting were initially available to Bar T?

f) List the separate items of partnership income, gains, losses, deductions, and other items that will be included in each member's Schedule K-1 for the first year of operations. Use the proposed self-employment tax regulations to determine each member's self-employment income or loss.

g) What are the members' adjusted bases in their LLC interests at the end of the first year of operations?

h) What are the members' at-risk amounts in their LLC interests at the end of the first year of operations?

i) How much loss from Bar T, if any, will the members be able to deduct on their individual returns from the first year of operations?

chapter

10 Dispositions of Partnership Interests and Partnership Distributions

Learning Objectives

Upon completing this chapter, you should be able to:

LO 10-1 Determine the tax consequences to the buyer and seller of the disposition of a partnership interest, including the amount and character of gain or loss recognized.

LO 10-2 List the reasons for distributions, and compare operating and liquidating distributions.

LO 10-3 Determine the tax consequences of proportionate operating distributions.

LO 10-4 Determine the tax consequences of proportionate liquidating distributions.

LO 10-5 Explain the significance of disproportionate distributions.

LO 10-6 Explain the rationale for special basis adjustments, determine when they are necessary, and calculate the special basis adjustment for dispositions and distributions.

© PhotoAlto

Storyline Summary

Taxpayer:	Color Comfort Sheets LLC
Location:	Salt Lake City, Utah
Owners and interests:	Nicole Johnson, managing member—30 percent interest
	Sarah Walker, managing member—40 percent interest
	Greg Randall, nonmanaging member—30 percent interest

In January 2016,* Nicole and Sarah sit in the Color Comfort Sheets LLC (CCS), office discussing the current state of business affairs over a cup of coffee. They both agree they are not doing as well as they had hoped after two years of running the business. Their main topic of discussion this morning is how to turn the business around. Both women know the viability of the business is at stake if they can't figure out how to make it profitable . . . and soon.

As Nicole and Sarah brainstorm various ideas, Nicole's administrative assistant interrupts to announce a phone call from Noprah Winsted, the media mogul. Nicole takes the call. On her top-rated television talk show Noprah occasionally promotes products to her viewers based on her successful experience with the product. Apparently, one of Noprah's viewers sent her a set of Color Comfort sheets. Noprah is so happy with the product that she wants to promote the sheets on her show in about two weeks. Nicole and Sarah are, of course, thrilled with this news. Products Noprah has endorsed in the past have become wildly successful. The focus of Nicole and Sarah's meeting changes dramatically. Now they have to figure out how they can gear up for an immediate increase in production. Nicole and Sarah's analysis of the accounting records reveals that CCS is in a precarious cash position—the business is down to its last $10,000.

Nicole and Sarah immediately call Greg to fill him in on the news. Greg is as thrilled as they are to hear that Noprah will promote their sheets and agrees to kick in an additional $30,000. Nicole

*To allow the storyline to continue from the previous example, this chapter begins in 2016. We assume the 2015 tax laws apply for 2016 and subsequent years.

says that she will contribute $30,000 and Sarah antes up another $40,000.

The following couple of weeks fly by in a whirlwind of work—phone calls, meetings with bankers, and production scheduling. After the show airs, Nicole and Sarah sit down to talk about the show and the CCS product promotion. Noprah's special guest for the show had been popular film star, Tom Hughes, promoting his soon-to-be-released movie *Global Warfare.* Tom had been good-natured and actually shown interest in the sheets. During the show, he announced he would order a set as soon as the broadcast was over. Nicole and Sarah anticipate orders will roll in. Sure enough, before Noprah had even said goodbye to her studio audience, CCS's website traffic picked up and the phone lines were hopping with new orders.

By the end of 2016, CCS's financial situation has completely turned around; business is booming, the accounting records show a healthy profit, and the partners feel comfortable the trend will continue. Greg decides it is time to talk to Nicole and Sarah about cashing out his investment.

to be continued . . .

This chapter explores the tax consequences associated with selling partnership interests and with distributing partnership assets to partners.

LO 10-1 BASICS OF SALES OF PARTNERSHIP INTERESTS

As we've seen in previous chapters, owners of various business entities receive returns on their investments, either when the business makes distributions or upon the sale of their business interest. Corporate shareholders may sell their stock to other investors or back to the corporation. Likewise, partners may dispose of their interest in several ways: sell to a third party, sell to another partner, or transfer the interest back to the partnership. The payments in a disposition (sale) can come from either another owner of the partnership or a new investor; in either case, the sale proceeds come from outside the partnership.

Selling a **partnership interest** raises unique issues because of the flow-through nature of the entity. For example, is the interest a separate asset, or does the disposition represent the sale of the partner's share of each of the partnership's assets? (See Chapter 9 for a discussion of the entity and aggregate approaches to taxation of flow-through entities.) If the tax rules follow an entity approach, the interest is considered a separate asset and a sale of the partnership interest would be very similar to the sale of corporate stock. That is, the partner would simply recognize capital gain or loss on the sale, based on the difference between the sales price and the partner's tax basis in the partnership interest.

Alternatively, if the tax rules use the aggregate approach, the disposition represents a sale of the partner's share of each of the partnership's assets. This approach adds some complexity because of the differing character and holding periods of the partnership assets—ordinary, capital, and §1231. The selling partner also has the additional task of allocating the sales proceeds among the underlying assets in order to determine the gain or loss on each.

Rather than strictly following one approach, the tax rules end up being a mixture of the two approaches. When feasible, the entity approach controls; however, if the result distorts the amount or character of income, then the aggregate approach dominates. We discuss the tax consequences of sales of partnership interests by first taking the perspective of the seller (partner), then of the buyer (new investor).

Seller Issues

The seller's primary tax concern in a partnership interest sale is calculating the amount and character of gain or loss on the sale. The selling partner determines the gain or loss as the difference between the amount realized and her **outside basis** in the partnership.[1] Because the selling partner is no longer responsible for her share of the partnership liabilities, any debt relief increases the amount the partner *realizes* from the sale under general tax principles.

Example 10-1

Last year Chanzz Inc. sold its 30 percent interest in CCS on June 30 to Greg Randall, a wealthy local businessman, to limit its exposure to any further losses. Greg anticipated that CCS would become profitable in the near future and paid Chanzz Inc. $100,000 for its interest in CCS. Chanzz's share of CCS liabilities as of June 30 was $24,000. Chanzz Inc.'s basis in its CCS interest at the sale date was $105,000 (including its share of CCS's liabilities). What amount of gain did Chanzz recognize on the sale?

Answer: $19,000 gain, computed as follows:

Description	Amount	Explanation
(1) Cash and fair market value of property received	$100,000	
(2) Debt relief	24,000	
(3) Amount realized	$124,000	(1) + (2).
(4) Basis in CCS interest	105,000	
Recognized gain	$ 19,000	(3) − (4).

THE KEY FACTS

Sale of Partnership Interest

- **Seller issues**
  Gain or loss calculation
  Amount realized:
  Cash and fair market value of property received plus
  Debt relief
  Less: Basis in partnership interest
  Equals: Realized gain or loss
  - Tax year closes with respect to selling partner.
- **Buyer issues**
  - Outside basis—cost of the partnership interest plus share of partnership's liabilities.
  - Inside basis—selling partner's inside basis at sale date.
  - No changes to partnership asset bases (unless §754 election is in effect).

The character of the gain or loss from a sale of a partnership interest is generally capital, because partnership interests are capital assets.[2] However, a portion of the gain or loss will be ordinary if a seller realizes any gain or loss attributable to **unrealized receivables** or **inventory items.**[3] Practitioners often refer to these assets that give rise to ordinary gains and losses as **hot assets.**[4] Let's discuss that term further, because these assets are central to determining the tax treatment of many transactions in this chapter.

Hot Assets As you might expect, unrealized receivables include the right to receive payment for (1) "goods delivered, or to be delivered"[5] or (2) "services rendered, or to be rendered."[6] For cash-method taxpayers, unrealized receivables include amounts earned but not yet received (accounts receivable). Accrual-method taxpayers,

[1]Partners determine their outside basis as discussed in the previous chapter. Importantly, the outside basis includes the selling partner's share of distributive income for the year to the date of the sale.

[2]§731 and §741.

[3]§751(a). Partnerships are required to provide Form 8308 to all the parties to the sale as well as to the IRS. Selling partners include with their tax returns this form as well as a statement detailing the calculation of any ordinary gain from the sale of their interest.

[4]There are actually two definitions of *inventory items* in §751. Section 751(a) inventory items are defined in §751(d) to include *all* inventory items. However, under §751(b), the definition includes only *substantially appreciated* inventory. For purposes of determining the character of gain or loss from the sale of partnership interests, the term *inventory items* includes all inventory as in §751(a). However, these two definitions have created some confusion when using the term *hot assets.* In this chapter, we use the term *hot assets* to refer to unrealized receivables and all inventory items as in §751(a). The definition under §751(b) becomes more relevant when determining the tax treatment in a disproportionate distribution (discussed only briefly later in the chapter).

[5]§751(c)(1).

[6]§751(c)(2).

however, do not consider accounts receivable as unrealized receivables because they have already realized and recognized these items as ordinary income. Unrealized receivables also include items the partnership would treat as ordinary income if it sold the asset for its fair market value, such as depreciation recapture under §1245.[7]

Inventory items include classic inventory, defined as property held for sale to customers in the ordinary course of business, but also, more broadly, any assets that are *not* capital assets or §1231 assets.[8] Under this definition, assets such as equipment or real estate used in the business but not held for more than a year and all accounts receivable are considered inventory. This broad definition means cash, capital assets, and §1231 assets are the only properties not considered inventory.[9]

Example 10-2

CCS's balance sheet as of the date of Chanzz's sale of its CCS interest to Greg follows:

Color Comfort Sheets LLC
June 30, 2015

	Tax Basis	FMV
Assets:		
Cash	$ 27,000	$ 27,000
Accounts receivable	0	13,000
Investments	15,000	12,000
Inventory	1,000	1,000
Equipment (cost = $100,000)	80,000	86,000
Building	97,000	97,000
Land	20,000	150,000
Totals	$240,000	$386,000
Liabilities and capital:		
Long term debt	$100,000*	
Capital—Nicole	(49,000)	
—Sarah	108,000	
—Chanzz	81,000	
Totals	$240,000	

*Of the $100,000 of long-term debt, $20,000 is allocated solely to Nicole. The remaining $80,000 is allocated to all three owners according to their profit-sharing ratios.

Which of CCS's assets are considered hot assets under §751(a)?

Answer: The hot assets are accounts receivables of $13,000 and $6,000 depreciation recapture (§1245) potential ($86,000 – $80,000) in the equipment. The accounts receivable is an unrealized receivable because CCS has not included it in income for tax purposes under CCS's cash accounting method. The depreciation recapture is also considered an unrealized receivable under §751(a). Inventory would be considered a hot asset; however, because the tax basis and fair market value are equal, it will not affect the character of any gain recognized on the sale.

[7]§751(c).

[8]§751(d)(1).

[9]This broad definition of inventory includes all unrealized receivables except for recapture. Recapture items are excluded from the definition of inventory items simply because recapture is not technically an asset; rather, it is merely a portion of gain that results from the sale of property. Recapture is, however, considered an unrealized receivable (i.e., hot asset) under §751(a). This idea is important in determining whether inventory is substantially appreciated for purposes of determining the §751 assets for distributions as we discuss later in the chapter.

Example 10-3

Review CCS's balance sheet as of the end of 2016.

Color Comfort Sheets LLC
December 31, 2016

	Tax Basis	FMV
Assets:		
Cash	$390,000	$ 390,000
Accounts receivable	0	40,000
Inventory	90,000	200,000
Investments	60,000	105,000
Equipment (cost = $200,000)	150,000	200,000
Building (cost = $100,000)	90,000	100,000
Land—original	20,000	160,000
Land—investment	140,000	270,000
Totals	$940,000	$1,465,000
Liabilities and capital:		
Accounts payable	$ 80,000	
Long-term debt		
Mortgage on original land	40,000	
Mortgage on investment land	120,000	
Capital—Nicole	119,000	
—Sarah	332,000	
—Greg	249,000	
Totals	$940,000	

What amount of CCS's assets are considered to be hot assets as of December 31, 2016?

Answer: The hot assets include inventory with a fair market value of $200,000, unrealized receivables of $50,000 of depreciation recapture potential on the equipment, and $40,000 of accounts receivable.

When a partner sells her interest in a partnership that holds hot assets, she modifies her calculation of the gain or loss to ensure the portion that relates to hot assets is properly characterized as ordinary income. The process for determining the gain or loss follows:

Step 1: Determine the total gain or loss by subtracting outside basis from the amount realized.

Step 2: Calculate the partner's share of gain or loss from hot assets as if the partnership sold these assets at their fair market value. This represents the ordinary portion of the gain or loss.

Step 3: Finally, subtract the ordinary portion of the gain or loss obtained in Step 2 from the total gain or loss from Step 1. This remaining amount is the capital gain or loss from the sale.[10, 11]

[10]The partner must also determine if any portion of the capital gain or loss relates to collectibles (28 percent capital gain property) or to unrecaptured §1250 gains. This is typically referred to as the *look-through rule*.

[11]Any capital gain from the sale of a partnership interest is subject to the 3.8% Net Investment Income Tax unless the gain is allocable to trade or business assets held by the partnership that generate trade or business income not subject to the tax. See Prop. Reg. §1.1411-7 for a detailed discussion of this concept.

Example 10-4

In Example 10-1, Chanzz sold its interest in CCS to Greg Randall for $100,000 cash on June 30, 2015. As a result, Chanzz recognized a gain of $19,000 on the sale. What is the character of Chanzz's gain?

Answer: $5,700 of ordinary income and $13,300 of capital gain, determined as follows:

Step 1: Determine the total gain or loss: $19,000 from Example 10-1.

Step 2: Determine the ordinary gain or loss from hot assets:

Asset	(1) Basis	(2) FMV	(3) Gain/Loss (2) − (1)	Chanzz's Share 30% × (3)
Accounts receivable	$ 0	$13,000	$13,000	$3,900
Equipment	80,000	86,000	6,000	1,800
Total ordinary income				$5,700

Step 3: Determine the capital gain or loss:

Description	Amount	Explanation
(1) Total gain	$19,000	From Step 1.
(2) Ordinary income from §751(a)	5,700	From Step 2.
Capital gain	$13,300	(1) − (2).

Example 10-5

What if: Assume the same facts as in Example 10-4, except Greg is willing to pay Chanzz only $82,800 cash for its interest in CCS. What is the amount and character of Chanzz's gain or loss?

Answer: $5,700 of ordinary income and capital loss of $3,900, determined as follows:

Step 1: Determine the total gain or loss:

Description	Amount	Explanation
(1) Cash and fair market value of property received	$ 82,800	
(2) Debt relief	24,000	Chanzz's share of CCS's allocable debt (30% × $80,000).
(3) Amount realized	$106,800	(1) + (2).
(4) Basis in CCS interest	105,000	
Gain recognized	$ 1,800	(3) − (4).

Step 2: Determine the ordinary gain or loss from hot assets:

Asset	(1) Basis	(2) FMV	(3) Gain/Loss (2) − (1)	Chanzz's Share 30% × (3)
Accounts receivable	$ 0	$13,000	$13,000	$3,900
Equipment	80,000	86,000	6,000	1,800
Total ordinary income				$5,700

Step 3: Determine the capital gain or loss:

Description	Amount	Explanation
(1) Total gain	$ 1,800	From Step 1.
(2) Ordinary income from §751(a)	5,700	From Step 2.
Capital loss	$(3,900)	(1) − (2).

ETHICS

Sarah recently sold her partnership interest for significantly more than her tax basis in the interest. Two separate appraisals were commissioned at the time of the sale to estimate the value of the partnership's hot assets and other assets. The first appraisal estimates the value of the hot assets at approximately $750,000, while the second appraisal estimates the value of these assets at approximately $500,000. Given that the partnership's inside basis for its hot assets is $455,000, Sarah intends to use the second appraisal to determine the character of the gain from the sale of her partnership interest. Is it appropriate for Sarah to ignore the first appraisal when determining her tax liability from the sale of her partnership interest?

Buyer and Partnership Issues

A new investor in a partnership is of course concerned with determining how much to pay for the partnership interest. However, his primary tax concerns are about his inside and outside bases in the partnership. In general, for a sale transaction, the new investor's outside basis will be equal to his cost of the partnership interest.[12] To the extent that the new investor shares in the partnership liabilities, his share of partnership liabilities increases his outside basis.

Example 10-6

When Greg Randall acquired Chanzz's 30 percent interest in CCS for $100,000 on June 30, 2015 (see Example 10-1), he guaranteed his share of CCS's debts just as Chanzz had done. As a result, Greg will be allocated his share of CCS's allocable debt in accordance with his 30 percent profit-sharing ratio. What is the outside basis of Greg's acquired interest?

Answer: $124,000, determined as follows:

Description	Amount	Explanation
(1) Initial tax basis	$100,000	Cash paid to Chanzz.
(2) Share of CCS's liabilities	24,000	30% × CCS's allocable debt of $80,000.
Outside basis	$124,000	(1) + (2).

The partnership experiences very few tax consequences when a partner sells her interest.[13] The sale does not generally affect a partnership's **inside basis** in its assets.[14] The new investor typically "steps into the shoes" of the selling partner to determine his share of the partnership's inside basis of the partnership assets. Consequently, the new

[12]§1012. The outside basis will depend, in part, on how the new investor obtains the interest. For example, a gift generally results in a carryover basis whereas an inherited interest typically results in a basis equal to the fair market value as of the date of the decedent's death.

[13]Later in the chapter, we discuss situations in which the new investor's share of the partnership's asset bases are adjusted after a sale of a partnership interest under §754. Throughout this section, we assume that the partnership does not have a §754 election in effect.

[14]§743.

investor's share of inside basis is equal to the selling partner's share of inside basis at the sale date. Recall from the preceding chapter that each partner has a tax capital account that reflects the tax basis of property and cash contributed by the partner, the partner's share of earnings and losses, and distributions to the partner. In a sale of a partnership interest, the selling partner's tax capital account carries over to the new investor.[15]

Example 10-7

Refer to Example 10-2 for CCS's balance sheet as of June 30, 2015. What is Greg's share of CCS's inside basis immediately after purchasing Chanzz's 30 percent interest in CCS?

Answer: Greg's share is $105,000: the sum of Chanzz's tax capital account of $81,000 and its share of CCS's liabilities of $24,000. Greg simply steps into Chanzz's place after the acquisition. In the preceding example, we determined Greg's outside basis to be $124,000. A sale of a partnership interest often results in a difference between the new investor's inside and outside bases because the outside basis is the price paid based on fair market value and the inside basis is the share of tax basis in the partnership assets.

Varying Interest Rule If a partner's interest in a partnership increases or decreases during the partnership's tax year, the partnership income or loss allocated to the partner for the year must be adjusted to reflect her *varying interest* in the partnership.[16] Partners' interests increase when they contribute property or cash to a partnership[17] or purchase a partnership interest. Conversely, partners' interests decrease when they receive partnership distributions[18] or sell all or a portion of their partnership interests. Upon the sale of a partnership interest, the partnership tax year closes for the *selling* partner only. Regulations allow partners to choose between two possible methods for allocating income or loss to partners when their interests change during the year.[19] The first method allows the partnership to prorate income or loss to partners with varying interests, while the second method sanctions an interim closing of the partnership's books.[20]

Example 10-8

CCS had a $60,000 overall operating loss for the 2015 calendar year. The issue of how to allocate the 2015 loss between Chanzz Inc. and Greg was easily resolved because CCS's operating agreement specifies the proration method to allocate income or loss when members' interests in CCS change during the year. How much of CCS's 2015 loss will Chanzz be allocated under the proration method?

Answer: Chanzz takes a loss of $9,000, which includes its share of CCS's loss but for only one-half the year ($60,000 × 30% share × 6/12 months) and will report it on its tax return.[21] On the sale date, Chanzz decreases its basis in CCS by the $9,000 loss to determine its adjusted basis to use in calculating its gain or loss on the sale of its interest.

[15]An exception occurs when the selling partner contributed property with a built-in loss to the partnership. Only the contributing partner is entitled to that loss [see Chapter 9 and §704(c)(1)(C)]. Therefore, when a new investor buys a partnership interest from a partner that contributed built-in loss property, the new investor reduces his inside basis by the amount of the built-in loss at the contribution date.

[16]§706(d)(1).

[17]If all partners simultaneously contribute property or cash with a value proportionate to their interests, their relative interests will not change.

[18]If all partners receive distributions with a value proportionate to their interests, their relative interests will not change.

[19]Reg. §1.706-1(c).

[20]If within a 12-month period, there is a sale of 50 percent or more of the total capital and profits interest in the partnership, the partnership is terminated. When this occurs, the partnership tax year is closed for all partners, not just the selling partners. See §708(b).

[21]Prop. Reg. §1.706-1(c) requires the calendar-day convention when using the proration method. For the sake of mathematical simplicity, we use number of months here and elsewhere in the chapter when applying the proration method.

Example 10-9

What if: If CCS's overall loss through June 30 was $20,000, how much of the $60,000 overall loss for 2015 will Chanzz and Greg Randall be allocated under an interim closing of the books?

Answer: CCS will allocate $6,000 of loss (30% × $20,000) to Chanzz and $12,000 of loss (30% × $40,000) to Greg.

TAXES IN THE REAL WORLD Changing the Way Companies Dispose of a Business

Corporate takeovers seemed to be the transaction du jour during the 1990s, but many practitioners are predicting joint ventures will be the defining deal for the current decade. We see regular articles in *The Wall Street Journal* describing how firms are starting up joint ventures or strategic alliances—or exiting them. For example, McGraw-Hill and the CME Group recently brought the S&P 500 index and the Dow Jones Industrial Average under the same roof by forming a new LLC called S&P/Dow Jones Indices. To form the new joint venture, McGraw-Hill contributed its Standard & Poor's index business and CME group contributed its Dow Jones index business. In the end, McGraw-Hill owned 73 percent and the CME Group owned 27 percent of the new venture.

The increase in the number of joint ventures and their possible dissolution or disposition brings an increasing need to understand the partnership tax rules and regulations. More than ever before, corporate tax executives find they must advise senior management on the opportunities and pitfalls of structuring joint ventures and investments as partnerships or LLCs under Subchapter K of the Internal Revenue Code.

BASICS OF PARTNERSHIP DISTRIBUTIONS

LO 10-2

Like shareholders receiving corporate dividend distributions, partners often receive distributions of the partnership profits, known as **operating distributions.** Recall that owners of flow-through entities are taxed currently on their business income regardless of whether the business distributes it. As a result, partners may require cash distributions in order to make quarterly estimated tax payments on their share of business income. Usually, the general partners (or managing members of LLCs) determine the amount and timing of distributions; however, the partnership (operating) agreement may stipulate some distributions.

Partners may also receive **liquidating distributions.** Because the market for partnership interests is much smaller than for publicly traded stock, partners may have a difficult time finding buyers for their interests. Partnership agreements also often limit purchasers of an interest to the current partner group, to avoid adding an unwanted partner. If the current partner group either cannot or does not want to purchase the interest, the partnership can instead distribute assets to terminate a partner's interest. These liquidating distributions are similar to corporate redemptions of a shareholder's stock. They can also terminate the partnership. We first explore the tax consequences of operating distributions, and then examine the tax treatment for liquidating distributions.

LO 10-3

Operating Distributions

A distribution from a partnership is an operating distribution when the partners continue their interests afterwards. Operating distributions are usually paid to distribute the business profits to the partners but can also reduce a partner's ownership. The partnership may distribute money or other assets. Let's look at the tax consequences of distributions of money, and then the tax consequences of property other than money.

THE KEY FACTS

Operating Distributions

- **Gain or loss recognition:** Partners generally do not recognize gain or loss. One exception occurs when the partnership distributes money only and the amount is greater than the partner's outside basis.

(continued)

Operating Distributions of Money Only The general rule for operating distributions states that the partnership does not recognize gain or loss on the distribution of property or money.[22,23] Nor do the general tax rules require a partner to recognize gain or loss when she receives distributed property or money.[24] The partner simply reduces her (outside) basis in the partnership interest by the amount of the distribution. In doing so, she retains any gain or loss on her share of partnership assets represented by her outside basis.[25] In general, the partnership's basis in its remaining assets remains unchanged.[26]

Example 10-10

- **Basis of distributed assets:** Partners generally take a carryover basis in the distributed assets. If the partnership distribution includes other property and the combined inside bases is greater than the partner's outside basis, the bases of the other property distributed will be reduced.
- **Remaining outside basis:** In general, partners reduce outside basis by money and other property distributed.

What if: Suppose CCS makes its first distribution to the owners on December 31, 2016: $250,000 each to Nicole and Greg and $333,333 to Sarah. After taking into account their distributive share of CCS's income for the year, the owners have the following predistribution bases in their CCS interests:

Owner	Outside Basis
Nicole	$205,000
Sarah	420,000
Greg	334,000

What are the tax consequences (gain or loss and basis in CCS interest) of the distribution to Sarah?

Answer: Sarah does not recognize any gain or loss on the distribution. She reduces her outside basis from $420,000 to $86,667 ($420,000 − $333,333) after the distribution.

The general rule of no gain is impractical when the partner receives a greater amount of money than her outside basis. She cannot defer gain to the extent of the excess amount because the outside basis is insufficient for a full reduction. Therefore, the partner reduces her outside basis to zero[27] and recognizes gain (generally capital) to the extent the amount of money distributed is greater than her outside basis.[28] A partner *never* recognizes a loss from an *operating* distribution.

Example 10-11

What if: Suppose that in the December 31, 2016, distribution Nicole's distribution consists of $250,000 cash. Her outside basis is $205,000 before the distribution. What are Nicole's gain or loss and basis in her CCS interest after the distribution?

Answer: Nicole has $45,000 capital gain and $0 basis in CCS. Because she receives only money in the distribution, she decreases her outside basis to $0 and must recognize a $45,000 capital gain ($250,000 distribution less $205,000 basis). She recognizes gain because she receives a cash distribution in excess of her outside basis.

Operating Distributions That Include Property Other Than Money If a partnership makes a distribution that includes property *other than money,* the partners face the problem of reallocating their outside basis between the distributed assets (including

[22]For distribution purposes, money includes cash, deemed cash from reductions in a partner's share of liabilities, and the fair market value of marketable securities.

[23]§731(b).

[24]§731.

[25]The basis adjustment is a primary mechanism used to meet the overall tax objective of maintaining the partner's economic interest in the underlying partnership assets. We will see its use many times throughout this chapter.

[26]However, if the partnership has a §754 election in effect or if there is a substantial basis reduction, the partnership basis of its remaining assets must be adjusted following a distribution according to §734(a) and §755.

[27]§733.

[28]§731(a)(1).

money) and their continuing partnership interests.[29] Under the general rule, the partner takes a basis in the distributed property equal to the partnership basis in the property. This is called a **carryover basis.**[30] The tax rules define the order in which to allocate outside basis to the bases of distributed assets. First, the partner allocates the outside basis to any money received and then to other property as a carryover basis. The remainder is the partner's outside basis after the distribution.

Example 10-12

What if: Suppose CCS's December 31, 2016, distribution to Sarah consists of $133,333 cash and investments (other than marketable securities), with a fair market value of $200,000 and an adjusted basis of $115,000. Sarah has a predistribution outside basis of $420,000. What are the tax consequences (Sarah's gain or loss, basis of distributed assets, and outside basis of CCS interest, and CCS's gain or loss) of the distribution?

Answer: Sarah recognizes no gain or loss on the distribution. To determine her bases in the distributed assets, she first allocates $133,333 to the cash and then takes a carryover basis in the investments so her basis in the investments is $115,000. Sarah reduces her outside basis by $248,333 ($133,333 cash + $115,000 basis of investments). Her outside basis after the distribution is $171,667 ($420,000 − $248,333). CCS does not recognize any gain or loss on the distribution.

When the partnership distributes property (other than money) with a basis that exceeds the remaining outside basis (after the allocation to any money distributed), the partner assigns the remaining outside basis to the distributed assets,[31] and the partner's outside basis is reduced to zero.[32] The first allocation of outside basis goes to money, then to hot assets, and finally to other property.[33] In this case, the partner's basis in the property received in the distribution will be less than the property's basis in the hands of the partnership.

Example 10-13

What if: Suppose Nicole's December 31, 2016, distribution consists of $150,000 cash and investments (other than marketable securities) with a fair market value of $100,000 and an adjusted basis of $90,000. Her outside basis is $205,000 before the distribution. What are Nicole's tax consequences (gain or loss, basis of distributed assets, outside basis in CCS interest) of the distribution?

Answer: Nicole recognizes no gain or loss and takes a basis of $55,000 in the investments. Her outside basis in CCS is $0, computed as follows:

Description	Amount	Explanation
(1) Nicole's outside basis	$205,000	
(2) Cash distribution	150,000	
(3) Remaining basis	55,000	(1) − (2); remaining outside basis to be allocated to the distributed investments.
(4) Inside basis of investments	90,000	
(5) Basis in investments	55,000	Lesser of (3) or (4).
Nicole's outside basis in CCS	0	(3) − (5).

[29]In this context, money includes marketable securities [§731(c)(1)(A)]. The special rules in §731(c) for the treatment of distributed marketable securities are beyond the scope of this book.

[30]§732(a).

[31]§732(a)(2).

[32]§733.

[33]If multiple assets are distributed, then the outside basis will be allocated in accordance with §732(c). We discuss these rules later in conjunction with liquidating distributions.

Because a partner's outside basis includes her share of the partnership liabilities, the outside basis must reflect any changes in a partner's share of partnership debt resulting from a distribution. In essence, a partner treats a reduction of her share of debt as a distribution of money.[34] If the partner increases her share of debt, the increase is treated as a cash contribution to the partnership.

Example 10-14

What if: Suppose Greg receives land held for investment with a fair market value of $250,000 (adjusted basis is $140,000) as his distribution from CCS on December 31, 2016. He agrees to assume the $120,000 mortgage on the land after the distribution. His outside basis is $334,000 before considering the distribution. What are the tax consequences (gain or loss, basis of distributed assets, outside basis in her CCS interest) of the distribution to Greg?

Answer: Greg does not recognize any gain or loss on the distribution. His basis in the land is $140,000 and his outside basis in CCS is $278,000, determined as follows:

Description	Amount	Explanation
(1) Greg's predistribution outside basis	$334,000	
(2) Mortgage assumed by Greg	120,000	
(3) Greg's predistribution share of mortgage	36,000	(2) × 30% ownership.
(4) Deemed cash contribution from debt assumption	84,000	(2) − (3).
(5) Greg's outside basis after debt changes	418,000	(1) + (4).
(6) Greg's basis in distributed land	**140,000**	**Carryover basis from CCS.**
Greg's post-distribution outside basis	**278,000**	**(5) − (6).**

Greg must first consider the effects of changes in debt before determining the effects of the distribution. The tax rules treat him as making a net contribution of $84,000 cash to the partnership, the difference between the full mortgage he assumes and his predistribution share of the debt. Greg then allocates $140,000 of his outside basis to the land and reduces his outside basis accordingly.

LO 10-4

Liquidating Distributions

In contrast to operating distributions in which the partners retain a continuing interest in the partnership, liquidating distributions terminate a partner's interest in the partnership. If the current partners do not have sufficient cash or inclination to buy out the terminating partner, the partnership agreement usually allows the partnership to close out the partner's interest. At some point, all the partners may agree to terminate the partnership, either because they have lost interest in continuing it or it has not been profitable. In such cases, the partnership may distribute all its assets to the partners in complete partnership liquidation. This process is analogous to a complete corporate liquidation (discussed in Chapter 8).

The tax issues in liquidating distributions for partnerships are basically twofold: (1) to determine whether the terminating partner recognizes gain or loss and (2) to reallocate his or her entire outside basis to the distributed assets. The rationale behind the rules for liquidating distributions is simply to replace the partner's outside basis with the underlying partnership assets distributed to the terminating partner. Ideally, there would be no gain or loss on the distribution, and the asset bases would be the same in the partner's hands as they were inside the partnership. Of course, this case rarely occurs. The rules therefore are designed to determine when gain or loss must be recognized and to allocate the partner's outside basis to the distributed assets.

[34]§752(b).

Gain or Loss Recognition in Liquidating Distributions In general, neither partnerships nor partners recognize gain or loss from liquidating distributions. However, there are exceptions. For example, when a terminating partner receives more money in the distribution than her outside basis, she will recognize gain.[35] See Example 10-11 for an illustration in the context of operating distributions.

In contrast to operating distributions, a partner may recognize a *loss* from a liquidating distribution, but only when two conditions are met. These conditions are (1) the distribution includes only cash, unrealized receivables, and/or inventory; *and* (2) the partner's outside basis is greater than the sum of the *inside bases* of the distributed assets.[36] The loss on the distribution is a capital loss to the partner.

Commonly, the terminating partner's share of partnership debt decreases after a liquidating distribution. Any reduction in the partner's share of liabilities is considered a distribution of money to the partner and reduces the outside basis available for allocation of basis to other assets, including inventory and unrealized receivables.

Example 10-15

What if: Suppose on January 1, 2017, CCS liquidates Greg's interest in the LLC by distributing to him cash of $206,000 and inventory with a fair market value of $96,000 (adjusted basis is $43,000). Greg's share of CCS's liabilities as of the liquidation is $66,000. On January 1, 2017, Greg's outside basis in CCS is $334,000, including his share of CCS's liabilities. What is Greg's gain or loss on the liquidation of his CCS interest?

Answer: Greg recognizes a capital loss of $19,000 on the liquidation, computed as follows:

Description	Amount	Explanation
(1) Outside basis before distribution	$334,000	
(2) Debt relief	66,000	Deemed cash distribution.
(3) Outside basis after considering debt relief	$268,000	(1) − (2).
(4) Basis of property distributed (cash + inventory)	249,000	
Gain (loss) on distribution	$(19,000)	(4) − (3).

Greg recognizes a loss because he meets the two necessary conditions: (1) he receives only cash and inventory in the distribution *and* (2) the sum of the adjusted bases of the distributed assets is less than his basis in his CCS interest ($249,000 asset bases versus $268,000 CCS basis).

THE KEY FACTS

Gain or Loss Recognition in Liquidating Distributions

- **Generally:** Partners and partnerships do not recognize gain or loss.
- **Exceptions:**
  - **Gain:** Partner recognizes gain when partnership distributes money and the amount exceeds the partner's outside basis in the partnership interest.
  - **Loss:** Partner recognizes loss when two conditions are met: (1) Distribution consists of only cash and hot assets, and (2) the partner's outside basis exceeds the sum of the bases of the distributed assets.

Basis in Distributed Property A key theme of the partnership tax rules is the idea that the partnership acts merely as a conduit for the partners' business activities. Thus, the rules attempt to keep the basis of the assets the same regardless of whether the partner or the partnership has possession of them. Moving assets in and out of the partnership should therefore have few tax consequences. The primary objective of the basis rules in liquidating distributions is to allocate the partner's entire outside basis in the partnership to the assets the partner receives in the liquidating distribution. The allocation essentially depends on two things: (1) the partnership's bases in distributed assets relative to the partner's outside basis and (2) the type of property distributed—whether it is money, hot assets, or other property. For purposes of distributions, hot assets include unrealized receivables and inventory, as we've previously defined. We discuss each of the possible scenarios in Exhibit 10-1 in turn.

[35]These rules are very similar to those for operating distributions. When a partner receives money only in complete termination of the partnership interest, any gain on distribution cannot be deferred through a basis adjustment. Therefore, the partner recognizes the gain.

[36]§731(a)(2).

EXHIBIT 10-1 Alternative Scenarios for Determining Basis in Distributed Property

Type of Property Distributed	Partner's outside basis is *greater* than inside bases of distributed assets	Partner's outside basis is *less* than inside bases of distributed assets
Money only	Scenario 1	Scenario 3
Money and hot assets	Scenario 1	Scenario 4
Other property included in distribution[37]	Scenario 2	Scenario 5

Partner's Outside Basis Is Greater Than Inside Basis of Distributed Assets

Scenario 1: Distributions of money, inventory, and/or unrealized receivables. If the partnership distributes only money, inventory, and/or unrealized receivables (ordinary income property) and the partner's outside basis is greater than the sum of the inside bases of the distributed assets, the partner recognizes a capital loss.[38] The partner assigns a basis to the assets equal to the partnership basis in the assets and the remaining outside basis determines the recognized loss. To prevent a partner from converting a capital loss from her investment into an ordinary loss, the tax law prohibits increasing her basis in unrealized receivables and inventory and requires the partner to recognize a capital loss.[39]

Example 10-16

What if: Suppose Greg has an outside basis of $334,000, including his share of liabilities of $66,000. In a liquidating distribution, he receives $159,000 cash and inventory with a fair market value and basis of $49,000. Will Greg recognize a gain or loss? Why or why not?

Answer: Yes, Greg will recognize a capital loss of $60,000 on the liquidation computed as follows:

Description	Amount	Explanation
(1) Outside basis before distribution	$334,000	
(2) Debt relief	66,000	Deemed cash distribution.
(3) Outside basis after considering debt relief	$268,000	(1) − (2).
(4) Basis of property distributed (cash + inventory)	208,000	
Gain (loss) on distribution	$ (60,000)	(4) − (3).

In this case, Greg is unable to defer his loss without changing its character. Greg clearly cannot adjust the basis in the cash to defer the loss. *If* he increases his basis in the distributed inventory, he could defer the loss. However, this would produce an ordinary loss of $60,000 when Greg sells the inventory.[40] To prevent the conversion of a capital loss to an ordinary loss, Greg recognizes a $60,000 capital loss.

Scenario 2: Other property included in distributions. Recall that in this scenario the liquidating partner must reallocate all her outside basis to the distributed assets. We determined in Scenario 1 that when the partnership distributes only money and/or

[37]This category includes distributions that include other property in addition to or instead of either money or unrealized receivables or inventory. For example, the distributions in this category can include any combination of money, unrealized receivables, and inventory as long as other property is also distributed.

[38]§731(a)(2).

[39]§732(c)(1) and §731(a)(2).

[40]If the inventory distributed to Greg is also considered inventory in his hands, the eventual sale of the inventory will generate ordinary income. If the inventory is a capital asset to Greg, a sale of the asset within five years of the distribution will generate ordinary income. After five years, the gain or loss would be capital.

hot assets and the distributed asset bases are less than the partner's outside basis, it was impossible to allocate the entire outside basis to the distributed assets without changing the character of a resulting loss. Thus, a partner never increases the bases of hot assets. However, when the partnership distributes other property, in addition to money and/or hot assets, the partner can adjust the basis of the *other* property without converting ordinary gains and losses to capital, and the liquidating partner will not recognize any gain or loss from the distribution.

Example 10-17

What if: Suppose CCS has no liabilities or hot assets and distributes $50,000 in cash and land with a fair market value of $160,000 and an adjusted basis of $20,000 to Greg in complete liquidation of his CCS interest. Greg has an outside basis of $268,000 prior to the distribution. What is Greg's recognized gain or loss on the distribution?

Answer: Greg does not recognize any gain or loss. He receives money and other property with a total basis of $70,000, which is less than his outside basis of $268,000. Greg first reduces his outside basis by the amount of money he receives, and he assigns his remaining outside basis to the land as follows:

Description	Amount	Explanation
(1) Outside basis before distribution	$268,000	
(2) Basis allocated to money distributed	50,000	
Remaining outside basis assigned to land	$218,000	(1) − (2).

Note that Greg increases the basis of the other property received in liquidation (land) from $20,000 to $218,000 in order to allocate his entire outside basis to the distributed assets. In some cases, "other" property might include personal assets for which the partner may never be able to recover the basis increase.

Example 10-17 illustrates the required basis increase in a very simple situation. In reality, liquidating distributions may include several types of assets. In these situations, to allocate the outside basis to the distributed assets, the partner completes the following, more detailed process:[41]

Step 1: The partner first assigns a basis to any money, inventory, and unrealized receivables equal to the partnership's basis in these assets. The partner also assigns a basis to the other distributed property in an amount equal to the partnership's basis in those assets.

Step 2: The partner then allocates the remaining outside basis (full outside basis less the amounts assigned in Step 1) to the other distributed property that has unrealized appreciation to the extent of that appreciation. Thus, if an asset has an adjusted basis to the partnership of $500 and a fair market value of $700, the partner will allocate the first $200 of remaining basis to that asset.[42]

Step 3: The partner allocates any remaining basis to all other property in proportion to the relative *fair market values* of the other property.

$$\text{Basis allocation} = \text{Remaining basis} \times \frac{\text{FMV}_{\text{asset}}}{\text{Sum of FMV}_{\text{distributed other property}}}$$

[41]§732(c)(2).

[42]If the remaining outside basis is insufficient to allocate the full amount of appreciation to the distributed assets in this step, then the partner will allocate the remaining basis in this step to the appreciated assets based on their relative appreciation.

Example 10-18

What if: Suppose CCS makes the following distribution to Greg in liquidation of his CCS interest:

Asset	CCS Tax Basis	Fair Market Value
Cash	$181,000	$181,000
Investment A	5,000	12,000
Investment B	10,000	13,000
Inventory	43,000	96,000

Greg's basis in his CCS interest as of the liquidation is $334,000, including his $66,000 share of CCS's liabilities. What is Greg's recognized gain or loss on the distribution? What is Greg's basis in the distributed assets following the liquidation?

Answer: Greg recognizes no gain or loss on the distribution. Greg's bases in the distributed assets are:

Cash	$181,000
Investment A	21,120
Investment B	22,880
Inventory	43,000
Total	$268,000

Because Greg receives other property in the distribution and the distributed asset bases are less than Greg's outside basis (Scenario 2), he will allocate his outside basis as follows:

First, Greg determines his allocable basis:

Description	Amount	Explanation
(1) Basis in CCS before distribution	$334,000	
(2) Debt relief	66,000	Greg's 30 percent share of CCS's debt.
Allocable basis	$268,000	(1) − (2).

Next, Greg allocates his remaining CCS basis of $268,000 to the distributed assets by following the three-step allocation process.

Description	Amount	Explanation
Step 1:		
(1) Allocable basis	$268,000	See above.
(2) Basis assigned to cash	181,000	
(3) Basis assigned to inventory	43,000	
(4) Initial basis assigned to investment A	5,000	
(5) Initial basis assigned to investment B	10,000	
(6) Remaining allocable CCS basis	$ 29,000	(1) − (2) − (3) − (4) − (5).
Step 2:		
(7) Additional basis assigned to investment A	$ 7,000	Unrealized appreciation on investment A from example. FMV of $12,000 less basis of $5,000.
(8) Additional basis assigned to investment B	3,000	Unrealized appreciation on investment B from example. FMV of $13,000 less basis of $10,000.
(9) Remaining allocable CCS basis after Step 2	$ 19,000	(6) − (7) − (8).

Step 3:

(10) Additional basis allocated to other property: investment A.	$9,120	Basis allocation = $19,000 × ($12,000/$25,000) = $9,120.
(11) Additional basis allocated to other property: investment B.	$9,880	Basis allocation = $19,000 × ($13,000/$25,000) = $9,880

In Step 3, Greg allocates the remaining basis to the distributed investments based on their relative fair market values using:

$$\text{Basis allocation} = \text{Remaining basis} \times \frac{\text{FMV}_{\text{asset}}}{\text{Sum of FMV}_{\text{distributed other property}}}$$

Thus, Greg's bases in the investments are:

Description	Inv. A	Explanation	Inv. B	Explanation
(12) Initial basis assignment	$ 5,000	From (4) above)	$10,000	From (5) above.
(13) Basis assigned in Step 2	7,000	From (7) above)	3,000	From (8) above.
(14) Basis assigned in Step 3	9,120	From (10) above)	9,880	From (11) above.
Greg's bases in investments	$21,120	(12) + (13) + (14).	$22,880	(12) + (13) + (14).

Partner's Outside Basis Is Less Than Inside Basis of Distributed Assets

Scenario 3: Distributions of money only. A partner recognizes a gain (generally capital) if the partnership distributes money (only) that exceeds the partner's outside basis. The gain equals the excess amount received over the outside basis. Example 10-11 illustrates the tax consequences for this scenario in the context of an operating distribution.

Scenario 4: Distributions of money, inventory, and/or unrealized receivables. In liquidating distributions where the partner's outside basis is less than the inside basis of the distributed assets and the partnership distributes money and any property other than money, the partner reduces the basis in the distributed assets other than money but does not recognize gain or loss. Because the tax law does not restrict *reducing* bases of ordinary income assets, distributions of hot assets and other property will cause reductions in basis. However, the tax law does prescribe a particular sequence for the required reductions.

If the partnership distributes only money, inventory, and unrealized receivables, the partner reduces the basis of the hot assets distributed (assuming money doesn't exceed basis). The required decrease in the basis of the distributed assets is equal to the difference between the partner's outside basis and the partnership's inside basis in the distributed assets. The partner first assigns her outside basis to the assets received in an amount equal to the assets' inside bases (allocating to money first). Then the partner allocates the required *decrease* to the assets with unrealized depreciation, to eliminate any existing losses built into the distributed assets.[43] Finally, the partner allocates any remaining required decrease to the distributed assets in proportion to their *adjusted bases* (AB), after considering the previous steps using the following equation:

$$\text{Basis allocation} = \text{Required decrease} \times \frac{\text{AB}_{\text{asset}}}{\text{Sum of AB}_{\text{distributed assets}}}$$

[43]If the required decrease is insufficient to allocate the full amount of depreciation to the distributed assets in this step, then the partner will allocate the remaining required decrease in this step to the depreciated assets based on their relative unrealized depreciation.

Example 10-19

What if: Suppose CCS makes the following distribution to Greg in liquidation of his CCS interest:

Asset	CCS Tax Basis	Fair Market Value
Cash	$256,000	$256,000
Inventory A	50,000	129,000
Inventory B	25,000	17,000
Total	$331,000	

Greg's basis in his CCS interest as of the liquidation is $334,000, including his $66,000 share of CCS's liabilities. What is Greg's recognized gain or loss on the distribution? What is Greg's basis in the distributed assets following the liquidation?

Answer: Greg does not recognize any gain or loss. His basis in the cash is $256,000 and his basis in inventory A is $8,955 and his basis in inventory B is $3,045, computed as follows:

First, Greg reduces his outside basis in CCS by his $66,000 debt relief, such that his outside basis allocable to distributed assets is $268,000 ($334,000 − $66,000). He must allocate this remaining basis to the distributed assets using the following steps:

Description	Amount	Explanation
Step 1:		
(1) Allocable basis	$268,000	Basis in CCS of $334,000 − debt relief of $66,000.
(2) Basis assigned to cash	256,000	
(3) Initial basis assigned to inventory A	50,000	
(4) Initial basis assigned to inventory B	25,000	
(5) Required decrease	63,000	(2) + (3) + (4) − (1). Initial assignment of basis exceeds Greg's allocable CCS basis.
Step 2:		
(6) Required decrease to inventory B	8,000	Unrealized depreciation on inventory B from example. FMV of $17,000 less basis of $25,000.
(7) Remaining required decrease	55,000	(5) − (6).
(8) Interim adjusted basis of inventory B	17,000	(4) − (6).
Step 3:		
(9) Required decrease to inventory A	41,045	Basis reduction = $55,000 × ($50,000/$67,000).
(10) Required decrease to inventory B	13,955	Basis reduction = $55,000 × ($17,000/$67,000).
Final basis of inventory A	8,955	(3) − (9).
Final basis of inventory B	3,045	(8) − (10).

In Step 3, Greg decreases the basis of the inventory in proportion to its relative adjusted bases determined in Step 2 using the following allocation:

$$\text{Basis allocation} = \text{Required decrease} \times \frac{AB_{asset}}{\text{Sum of } AB_{distributed\ assets}}$$

Example 10-20

What if: Suppose CCS makes the following distribution to Greg in liquidation of his CCS interest:

Asset	CCS Tax Basis	Fair Market Value
Cash	$242,000	$242,000
Accounts receivable	0	12,000
Inventory	74,000	120,000
Total	$316,000	

Greg's basis in his CCS interest as of the liquidation is $334,000, including his share ($66,000) of CCS's liabilities. What is Greg's recognized gain or loss on the distribution? What is Greg's basis in the assets he receives in the liquidating distribution?

Answer: Greg does not recognize any gain or loss on the liquidation. His asset bases are:

Cash	$242,000
Accounts receivable	0
Inventory	26,000
Total	$268,000

Greg computes the basis as follows:

As a preliminary step to the allocation, he reduces his outside basis in CCS by his $66,000 debt relief, leaving an allocable outside basis of $268,000 ($334,000 − $66,000). He allocates this basis to the distributed assets using the following steps:

Description	Amount	Explanation
Step 1:		
(1) Allocable basis	$268,000	Basis in CCS of $334,000 − debt relief of $66,000.
(2) Basis assigned to cash	242,000	
(3) Initial basis assigned to accounts receivable	0	
(4) Initial basis assigned to inventory	74,000	
(5) Required decrease	48,000	(2) + (3) + (4) − (1). Initial assignment of basis exceeds Greg's allocable CCS basis.
Step 2: N/A because no assets have unrealized depreciation.		
Step 3:		
(6) Required decrease to accounts receivable	0	Basis reduction = $48,000 × ($-0-/$74,000).
(7) Required decrease to inventory	48,000	Basis reduction = $48,000 × ($74,000/$74,000).
Final basis of accounts receivable	0	(3) − (6).
Final basis of inventory	26,000	(4) − (7).

In Step 3, Greg decreases the basis of the accounts receivable and inventory in proportion to their relative adjusted bases using the following allocation:

$$\text{Basis reduction} = \text{Required decrease} \times \frac{AB_{\text{asset}}}{\text{Sum of } AB_{\text{distributed assets}}}$$

Note that in this scenario, the tax rules re-characterize a portion ($48,000) of Greg's ultimate gain from capital gain to ordinary income. The sum of the bases of the distributed assets ($316,000) exceeds Greg's allocable outside basis ($268,000) by $48,000. Absent the allocation rules illustrated in Example 10-20, this would have been a capital gain to Greg. Instead, as we discuss below, the basis decrease to the hot assets will cause Greg to recognize any gain as ordinary upon sale of these assets.

Scenario 5: Other property included in distributions. In our final scenario, the partnership distributes other property in addition to or instead of money and/or inventory and unrealized receivables, and the partner's outside basis is less than the combined inside bases of the distributed property. The terminating partner does not recognize gain or loss; rather, he decreases the basis in the other property distributed. The process for assigning basis to the distributed assets is similar to the method we described above, although the required basis decrease is focused on the other property rather than the hot assets.[44] The procedure is as follows:

Step 1: The partner first assigns a basis to any money, inventory, and unrealized receivables equal to the partnership's basis in these assets. The partner also assigns a basis to any other property equal to the partnership's basis in the other property distributed.

Step 2: The partner then allocates the required decrease (outside basis less partnership adjusted basis in distributed assets) to the other property that has unrealized depreciation to the extent of that depreciation to eliminate inherent losses. Thus, if an asset has an adjusted basis to the partnership of $700 and a fair market value of $600, the asset's basis is first reduced by $100 (unrealized depreciation).

Step 3: If any required decrease remains after accounting for the inherent losses in the distributed assets, the partner then allocates it to all other property in proportion to their *adjusted bases*. The adjusted bases used in this step are the bases from Step 2. We can determine the allocation as follows:

$$\text{Basis reduction} = \text{Required decrease} \times \frac{AB_{\text{asset}}}{\text{Sum of } AB_{\text{all distributed other property}}}$$

Example 10-21

What if: Suppose CCS makes the following distribution to Greg in liquidation of his CCS interest:

Asset	CCS Tax Basis	Fair Market Value
Cash	$187,000	$187,000
Investment A	10,000	7,000
Investment B	10,000	18,000
Inventory	70,000	102,000
Total	$277,000	

Greg's basis in his CCS interest as of the liquidation is $334,000, including his $66,000 share of CCS's liabilities of $66,000. What is Greg's recognized gain or loss on the distribution? What is Greg's basis in the distributed assets following the liquidation?

[44]§732(c)(3).

Answer: Greg does not recognize any gain or loss. His asset bases are as follows:

Cash	$187,000
Investment A	4,530
Investment B	6,470
Inventory	70,000
Total	$268,000

Greg's basis in these assets is determined as follows:

Greg first determines his allocable basis of $268,000 by reducing his CCS basis ($334,000) for the deemed cash distribution relating to his $66,000 share of the reduction in CCS's debt.

Description	Amount	Explanation
Step 1:		
(1) Allocable basis	$268,000	Basis in CCS of $334,000 − debt relief of $66,000.
(2) Basis assigned to cash	187,000	
(3) Initial basis assigned to investment A	10,000	
(4) Initial basis assigned to investment B	10,000	
(5) Initial basis assigned to inventory	70,000	
(6) Required decrease	9,000	(2) + (3) + (4) + (5) − (1). Initial assignment of basis exceeds Greg's allocable CCS basis.
Step 2:		
(7) Required decrease to investment A	3,000	Unrealized depreciation on investment A from example. FMV of $7,000 less basis of $10,000.
(8) Remaining required decrease	6,000	(6) − (7).
(9) Interim basis of investment A	7,000	(3) − (7).
Step 3:		
(10) Required decrease to investment A	2,470	Basis reduction = $6,000 × ($7,000/$17,000).
(11) Required decrease to investment B	3,530	Basis reduction = $6,000 × ($10,000/$17,000).
Final basis of investment A	4,530	(9) − (10).
Final basis of investment B	6,470	(4) − (11).

In Step 3, Greg decreases the basis of the other property (investments A and B) in proportion to their relative adjusted bases using the following allocation:

$$\text{Basis reduction} = \text{Required decrease} \times \frac{AB_{\text{asset}}}{\text{Sum of } AB_{\text{all distributed other property}}}$$

Character and Holding Period of Distributed Assets For both operating and liquidating distributions, the character of the distributed assets usually stays the same for the partner as it was in the partnership, in order to prevent conversion of ordinary income to capital gain for both operating and liquidating distributions. The principal purpose of these rules is to prevent the partner from converting partnership ordinary income into capital gain simply by distributing assets. Thus, if a partner sells certain assets with ordinary character after the distribution, the partner will recognize ordinary income from the sale.[45] These assets include inventory [§751(d)] and unrealized receivables [§751(c)]. For inventory items, the ordinary income "taint" will remain for five years after the distribution. For unrealized receivables, a subsequent sale at any time after the distribution will result in ordinary income. The reverse is not true, however. If a partnership distributes a capital asset that will be inventory to a terminating partner, the partner will have ordinary income from an eventual sale, not capital gain or loss. To ensure the character of any distributed long-term capital gain property retains its character to the partner, the partner's holding period generally includes the partnership's holding period.[46]

Example 10-22

Greg has decided to cash out his investment in CCS in order to invest in another project in which he can more actively participate. After speaking to Nicole and Sarah about the options, the three owners decide Greg can cash out using one of two options.

Option 1: CCS will liquidate Greg's interest by distributing cash of $242,000; accounts receivable worth $12,000 (adjusted basis is $0); and inventory worth $120,000 (adjusted basis is $74,000).

Option 2: Nicole and Sarah will purchase Greg's interest in CCS. Nicole agrees to purchase two-thirds of Greg's interest for $249,333 cash and Sarah purchases the remaining one-third for $124,667 cash.

Greg's basis in his 30 percent CCS interest is $334,000, including his share of CCS's liabilities of $66,000. Either event would occur on January 1, 2017, when CCS's balance sheet is as follows:

Color Comfort Sheets LLC
January 1, 2017

	Tax Basis	FMV
Assets:		
Cash	$390,000	$ 390,000
Accounts receivable	0	40,000
Inventory	90,000	200,000
Investments	60,000	105,000
Equipment (cost = $200,000)	150,000	200,000
Building (cost = $100,000)	90,000	100,000
Land—original	20,000	160,000
Land—investment	140,000	270,000
Totals	$940,000	$1,465,000
Liabilities and capital:		
Accounts payable	$ 80,000	
Long-term debt	0	
Mortgage on original land	40,000	
Mortgage on investment land	120,000	
Capital—Nicole	119,000	
—Sarah	332,000	
—Greg	249,000	
Totals	$940,000	

[45]§735(a).
[46]§735(b).

What are the tax consequences (amount and character of recognized gain or loss, basis in assets) for Greg under each option?

Answer: *Option 1:* Greg recognizes no gain or loss on the liquidation. His bases in the distributed assets are:

Cash	$242,000
Accounts receivable	0
Inventory	26,000
Total	$268,000

Option 2: Greg recognizes ordinary income of $60,000 and a capital gain of $46,000.

We determine these tax consequences as follows:

Option 1: The distribution allows Greg to defer recognizing any gain or loss on the liquidation. Example 10-20 provides the details of the analysis. Greg has debt relief in an amount equal to his share of CCS's liabilities ($66,000). The debt relief is treated as a distribution of cash, so Greg reduces his outside basis by this amount from $334,000 to $268,000. The difference between the sum of the adjusted bases of the distributed property and his outside basis is $48,000 ($316,000 − $268,000) and represents a required *decrease* to the bases of assets distributed in liquidation. Greg follows the prescribed method illustrated in Example 10-20 to determine his asset bases.

The basis reduction for these assets allows Greg to defer recognizing a $48,000 gain on the liquidation. The cost to accomplish the deferral is that if Greg sells the inventory and the accounts receivable immediately after the distribution, he will recognize ordinary income of $106,000 as follows:

Amount realized:		
Cash (equal to FMV of accounts receivable	$ 12,000	
and inventory)	120,000	$132,000
Less: Adjusted basis		
Accounts receivable	0	
Inventory	26,000	26,000
Ordinary Income		$106,000

The $106,000 ordinary income is $48,000 greater than the inherent gain on these assets of $58,000 ($132,000 − $74,000) had the partnership sold the assets. If Greg selects Option 1, he will not recognize income on the liquidation until he sells the inventory and collects (or sells) the accounts receivable, thereby leaving himself flexibility on the timing of gain recognition.

Option 2: In this option, Greg sells his CCS interest to Nicole and Sarah and receives cash of $374,000. Greg determines his total gain or loss as follows:

Amount realized:		
Cash	$374,000	
Debt relief	66,000	$440,000
Less: Basis in CCS interest		334,000
Realized and recognized gain		$106,000

Next, Greg determines the character of the gain from the sale by first identifying the gain related to hot assets.

Hot Asset − CCS	(1) Basis	(2) FMV	(3) Gain/Loss (2) − (1)	Greg's Share 30% × (3)
Accounts receivable	$ 0	$ 40,000	$ 40,000	$12,000
Inventory	90,000	200,000	110,000	33,000
Equipment	150,000	200,000	50,000	15,000
Total ordinary income				$60,000

(continued on page 10-24)

The final step for Greg is to determine the capital gain or loss by subtracting the ordinary portion from the total gain.

Total gain	$106,000
Less: ordinary income from §751(a)	(60,000)
Capital gain	$ 46,000

If he chooses Option 2, Greg will recognize $60,000 of ordinary income and $46,000 of capital gain in 2017.

Example 10-23

Given the tax consequences to Greg in the previous example, should he have CCS liquidate his interest (Option 1) or sell his interest (Option 2)?

Answer: Under Option 1 (the liquidation), Greg is able to defer all recognition of gain until he later sells the distributed assets. This provides him flexibility in when he pays tax on the liquidation. However, when he recognizes any income upon subsequent sales, the character of the income will be ordinary and taxed at ordinary rates. Under Option 2, Greg must recognize income immediately upon the sale: $60,000 of ordinary income and $46,000 of capital gain. He has no future tax liability related to the transaction. The capital gain will be taxed at a maximum of 15 percent (the regular maximum tax rate for long-term capital gains). An additional consideration is that under Option 2 Greg receives cash, rather than a mixture of cash and other assets. If he wants to immediately invest the proceeds in another venture, he may prefer a pure cash payment.

continued from page 10-2. . .

Greg takes the liquidation option (Option 1) offered by CCS to avoid recognizing a gain currently. Although this option doesn't give him as much cash as a sale would have, Greg figures it is enough for another investment and he can avoid paying tax this year.

For the first time, CCS has only two owners—Nicole and Sarah. After liquidating Greg's interest, Nicole's interest has increased to 43 percent and Sarah's to 57 percent. Both women are happy with that outcome, though sorry to lose Greg's interest in the business. ■

LO 10-5

DISPROPORTIONATE DISTRIBUTIONS

Up to this point in the chapter, all our distribution examples have represented the partner's pro rata share of the partnership's ordinary assets and other property, as specified in the partnership agreement based on the partner's capital interests. In practice, distributions may not always reflect each partner's proportionate share.[47] Both operating and liquidating distributions can be **disproportionate distributions.** Without going into all the details of these complex rules, let's briefly discuss the implications of distributions in which partners receive either more or less of their share of the so-called hot assets [assets defined in IRC §751(b) as **substantially appreciated**

[47]A thorough discussion of these issues is beyond the scope of this chapter. Therefore, we will abbreviate our discussion just to give a flavor for the issues and consequences of these disproportionate distributions.

inventory and unrealized receivables].[48] Note that the definition of hot assets for purposes of disproportionate distributions includes only *substantially appreciated* inventory, not all inventory as is the case under §751(a), the definition we used to characterize the gain in dispositions of partnership interests. Inventory is considered substantially appreciated if its fair market value is more than 120 percent of its basis.

Suppose a partner receives less than her share of hot assets in a liquidating distribution. This may occur, for example, if a partner receives only cash in a liquidating distribution from a partnership with hot assets. Rather than applying the rules we discussed above, the disproportionate distribution rules require the partner to treat the distribution as a sale or exchange.[49] Basically, the rules treat the partner as having sold her share of hot assets to the partnership in exchange for "cold" [non-§751(b)] assets. This deemed sale generates an ordinary gain or loss to the partner on the deemed sale, essentially equal to her share of the appreciation or depreciation in the portion of hot assets not distributed to her. On the other hand, the partnership is deemed to have purchased the hot assets from the partner in exchange for cold assets. Therefore, the *partnership* recognizes a capital or §1231 gain or loss equal to the remaining partners' inherent gain or loss in the distributed cold assets. The effects are reversed if a partner receives more than her share of the partnership's hot assets.[50] The rules guarantee that partners cannot convert ordinary income into capital gain through distributions. Thus, they require that partners will ultimately recognize their share of the partnership ordinary income regardless of the form of their distributions.

THE KEY FACTS

Disproportionate Distributions

- **When?**
  When distribution changes a partner's relative ownership of partnership hot assets.
- **Why?**
  To prevent partners from converting ordinary income into capital gains through distributions.
- **How?**
  Partner and partnership must treat distribution as a sale or exchange, which may result in recognition of gain (or loss).

Example 10-24

What if: Suppose CCS distributes $374,000 in cash to Greg Randall on January 1, 2017, in complete liquidation of Greg's 30 percent interest in CCS. Greg's basis in his CCS interest before the distribution is $334,000. Assume CCS's balance sheet is as follows:

Color Comfort Sheets LLC
December 31, 2016

	Tax Basis	FMV
Assets:		
Cash	$700,000	$ 700,000
Inventory	240,000	440,000
Totals	$940,000	$1,140,000
Liabilities and capital:		
Liabilities	$240,000	
Capital—Nicole	119,000	
—Sarah	332,000	
—Greg	249,000	
Totals	$940,000	

(continued on page 10-26)

[48]Unrealized receivables includes the accounts receivable of a cash-method taxpayer, the excess of the fair market value over basis of accounts receivable for accrual-method taxpayers, and recapture of depreciation under §1245. The definition of substantially appreciated inventory is broader than simply goods primarily held for sale to customers. It also includes property that would not be classified as capital assets or §1231 assets if sold by the partnership. As a result, receivables are included as "inventory."

[49]§751(b).

[50]The partner would generally recognize capital gain on the deemed sale and the partnership would recognize ordinary income.

Is this distribution disproportionate? What are the implications of the distribution?

Answer: From CCS's balance sheet as of December 31, 2016, the fair market value of Greg's share of hot assets for purposes of disproportionate distributions [§751(b)] is $132,000 ($72,000 adjusted basis). This figure includes 30 percent of the fair market value of CCS's inventory of $440,000. Since Greg receives only cash in the distribution, he has not received a proportionate share of CCS's hot assets. Thus, the distribution will be a disproportionate one.

The tax law treats Greg as having sold his share of the hot assets for cold assets, and he will recognize ordinary income equal to his share of the appreciation on the hot assets not distributed, $60,000 ($132,000 − $72,000). CCS does not recognize any gain or loss because it has no appreciation in the assets (cash) used to "purchase" the hot assets.

LO 10-6

SPECIAL BASIS ADJUSTMENTS

Recall that when a partner sells her partnership interest, the partnership's inside basis is generally unaffected by the sale. This creates a discrepancy between the new investor's outside basis (cost) and her share of the partnership's inside basis, which artificially changes the potential income or loss at the partnership level. For example, earlier in the chapter Greg Randall purchased Chanzz's 30 percent interest in CCS for $82,800 (Example 10-5). Greg's outside basis after the acquisition is $106,800, reflecting the cash payment of $82,800 and his share of CCS's debt at the time of the acquisition, $24,000. However, Greg's share of CCS's inside basis in its assets is $105,000 (see Example 10-7). This is the outcome because the sale does not affect CCS's inside basis and Greg simply steps into Chanzz's shoes for determining his share of the inside basis. The discrepancy reflects Chanzz's unrecognized share of appreciation of CCS's assets (that Greg paid full value for) as of the sale date and causes Greg to be temporarily overtaxed when CCS sells these appreciated assets.

Example 10-25

What if: Suppose that immediately after Greg acquires his 30 percent interest in CCS for $82,800, CCS sells its accounts receivable for their fair market value of $13,000 (adjusted basis is $0). (See Example 10-2 for CCS's balance sheet as of June 30, 2015, the acquisition date.) What is the amount and character of gain Greg recognizes on the sale?

Answer: When CCS sells the accounts receivable, it recognizes $13,000 of ordinary income, of which $3,900 (30 percent) is allocated to Greg. However, when Chanzz sold its interest to Greg, Chanzz was already taxed on the $3,900 allocated portion of that ordinary income under §751(a), and Greg paid full value for his interest in the receivables when he acquired his 30 percent interest in CCS. This means Greg will be taxed on the $3,900 again in 2015, and his outside basis increases by $3,900. Because Greg paid fair market value for his share of the receivables, he should not have any income when they are sold at fair market value. Eventually, when Greg disposes of his CCS interest, his ultimate gain (or loss) on the disposition will be $3,900 less, because of the increase to his outside basis from this additional income; meanwhile, he is overtaxed on the receivables. Greg must report ordinary income today for an offsetting capital loss (or reduced capital gain) in the future when he disposes of his interest.

The tax rules allow the partnership to make an election for a **special basis adjustment** to eliminate discrepancies between the inside and outside bases and correct the artificial income or loss at the partnership level.[51] For the most part, basis discrepancies arise in two situations: following *sales* of partnership interests, and following *distributions* where a partner receives more (and in cases of a liquidating distribution,

[51]§754. The election is made by including a written statement with the partnership return when filed for the year the election is to take effect.

less) than her share of the inside basis in the partnership property and the partner recognizes a gain or loss on the distribution. Once a partnership makes a §754 election, the partnership is required to make the special basis adjustment for all subsequent sales of partnership interest and partnership distributions. The election can be revoked only with permission from the IRS.

Even without a §754 election in effect, the partnership must adjust its bases if the partnership has a **substantial built-in loss** at the time a partner sells her partnership interest. A substantial built-in loss exists if the partnership's aggregate adjusted basis in its property exceeds the property's fair market value by more than $250,000 when a transfer of an interest occurs.[52] An analogous event—a **substantial basis reduction**—may occur for distributions, which also triggers a mandatory basis adjustment.

Although the election is made under §754, the actual authorization of the special basis adjustment is governed by two separate code sections depending on which situation gives rise to the adjustment: (1) sale of partnership interest [§743(b)], or (2) distributions [§734(b)]. These two sections determine how much of an adjustment will be made, and §755 then stipulates how the adjustment is allocated among the partnership assets.

THE KEY FACTS

Special Basis Adjustments

- **When?**
  Elective with a §754 election in effect and:
  (1) When a new investor purchases a partnership interest, or
  (2) When a partner recognizes a gain or loss in a distribution, or
  (3) When a partner takes a basis in distributed property that differs from the partnership basis in the property.
- **Mandatory:**
  (1) When a partner sells a partnership interest and the partnership has a substantial built-in loss at the time of sale, or
  (2) When a partnership has a substantial basis reduction from a distribution.
- **Why?**
  To prevent partners from being temporarily overtaxed or undertaxed after a partnership interest is transferred or after a distribution occurs.

EXHIBIT 10-2 Special Basis Adjustments

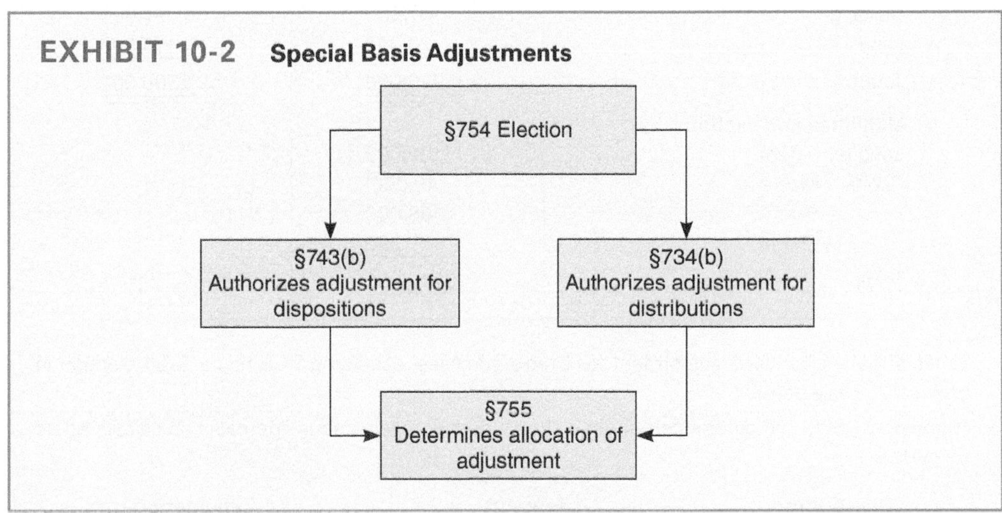

Special Basis Adjustments for Dispositions

The special basis adjustment the partnership makes when a partner sells her partnership interest is designed to give the new investor a share in the partnership assets equal to his outside basis. The basis adjustment in these cases applies *only* to the new investor. The inside bases of the continuing partners remain unchanged, so their income and losses will continue to be accurately allocated. The adjustment is equal to the difference between the new investor's outside basis and his share of inside basis.[53] The new investor's outside basis is generally equal to the cost of his partnership interest plus his share of partnership liabilities.[54] The special basis adjustment must

[52]§743(d)(1). In this context, a transfer generally refers to sales, exchanges, or transfers at death, not gift transfers.

[53]§743(b).

[54]A partner's share of inside basis is also labeled *previously taxed capital* [§1.743-1(d)]. The technical calculation is determined as follows (but generally equals the partner's tax capital account):

(1) the amount of cash the partner would receive on liquidation after an hypothetical sale of all the partnership assets for their fair market value after the sale of the partnership interest, plus

(2) the amount of taxable loss allocated to the partner from the hypothetical sale, less

(3) the amount of taxable gain allocated to the partner from the hypothetical sale.

then be allocated to the assets under allocation rules in §755, which are beyond the scope of this text.

Example 10-26

On June 30, 2015, Greg acquired Chanzz's 30 percent interest in CCS for $82,800. CCS's balance sheet as of the sale date is as follows:

Color Comfort Sheets LLC June 30, 2015	Tax Basis	FMV
Assets:		
Cash	$ 27,000	$ 27,000
Accounts receivable	0	13,000
Investments	15,000	12,000
Inventory	1,000	1,000
Equipment (cost = $100,000)	80,000	86,000
Building	97,000	97,000
Land	20,000	150,000
Totals	$240,000	$386,000
Liabilities and capital:		
Long term debt	$100,000	
Capital—Nicole	(49,000)	
—Sarah	108,000	
—Chanzz	81,000	
Totals	$240,000	

What is the special basis adjustment for Greg's purchase, assuming CCS had a §754 election in effect at the sale date?

Answer: $1,800, the difference between Greg's outside basis and inside basis, is calculated as follows:

Description	Amount	Explanation
(1) Cash purchase price	$ 82,800	
(2) Greg's share of CCS debt	24,000	$80,000 × 30%.
(3) Initial basis in CCS	$106,800	(1) + (2).
(4) Greg's inside basis	105,000	Chanzz's tax capital ($81,000) plus share of CCS debt ($24,000) (See Example 10-7).
Special basis adjustment	$ 1,800	(3) − (4).

When a new investor's special basis adjustment is allocated to depreciable or amortizable assets, the new investor will benefit from additional depreciation or amortization. In some cases, the amounts can be quite substantial, and a new investor may be willing to pay more for a partnership interest when the partnership has a §754 election in place than for one without it.

Special Basis Adjustments for Distributions

A similar potential problem exists when the partnership distributes assets to the partners that represent more (or, in some cases, less) than their share of the inside basis in the partnership assets. This usually occurs when a partner recognizes a gain or loss on a distribution or when a partner's basis in the distributed property is different from the partnership's basis in the property. In contrast to the special basis adjustment for sales of partnership interests, the special basis adjustment for distributions affects the common basis of *partnership* property and not merely one partner's basis.

The special basis adjustment can either increase or decrease the basis in the partnership assets. A **positive basis adjustment** will *increase* the basis in the partnership assets (1) when a partner receiving distributed property recognizes a gain on the distribution (for instance, in operating distributions where the partner receives money in excess of her outside basis), and (2) when a partner receiving distributed property takes a basis in the property less than the partnership's basis in the property. The positive adjustment will equal the sum of the gain recognized by the partners receiving distributed property and the amount of the basis reduction.

In Example 10-11, CCS distributed $250,000 cash to Nicole on December 31, 2016, as part of an operating distribution. Because Nicole's outside basis before the distribution was $205,000 and she received only money in the distribution, Nicole was required to recognize a $45,000 gain on the distribution. If CCS had a §754 election in effect, it would have a positive special basis adjustment from the distribution of $45,000.

A **negative basis adjustment** will *decrease* the basis in partnership assets (1) when a partner receiving distributed property in a liquidating distribution recognizes a loss on the distribution, and (2) when a partner receiving distributed property takes a basis in the property greater than the partnership's basis in the property.

The negative adjustment will equal the sum of the recognized loss and the amount of the basis increase made by the partners receiving the distribution. Recall from our previous discussion of distributions that negative adjustments can occur only in liquidating distributions. Only then does a partner recognize a loss or increase the distributed property basis from that of the partnership's basis.

In Example 10-15, CCS liquidated Greg's 30 percent interest by distributing cash of $206,000 and inventory with a fair market value of $96,000 (adjusted basis is $43,000). Because Greg's outside basis after considering his debt relief ($268,000) was greater than the sum of the bases of the property distributed ($249,000), Greg recognized a loss of $19,000 on the liquidation. If CCS had a §754 election in effect at the time of this liquidation, CCS would have a negative basis adjustment of $19,000.

As in the case of partnership dispositions, the allocation of the special basis adjustment among the partnership's assets for distributions is intended to offset any inequitable gain or loss the partners would have realized absent the adjustment. The process of allocating the adjustment for distributions is prescribed in §755, and these procedures are beyond the scope of this text.

CONCLUSION

The tax rules for partnership dispositions and distributions are among the most complex in the Internal Revenue Code. This chapter provided an overview of these rules and in some cases plunged into the complexity. We discussed the calculation of gains and losses from the sale of a partnership interest, as well as the basis implications of the purchase to a new investor. In doing so, we discussed how *hot assets* might affect the gain or loss. The chapter also explained the basic rules for determining the tax treatment of partnership distributions.

We illustrated how partnership elections might affect the partnership's basis in assets following partnership interest dispositions or distributions. In general, the tax rules are designed to avoid having business owners make decisions based on tax rules rather than on business principles; however, making this goal a reality provides for some challenging applications.

Summary

LO 10-1 Determine the tax consequences to the buyer and seller of the disposition of a partnership interest, including the amount and character of gain or loss recognized.

- Sellers are primarily concerned about their realized and recognized gain or loss on the sale of their partnership interest.
- Sellers' debt relief is included in the amount realized from the sale.
- Buyers' main tax concerns are determining their basis in the partnership interest they acquire and their inside bases of the partnership assets.
- A buyer's outside basis after an acquisition is generally his cost plus his share of partnership liabilities. A buyer's inside basis is generally the same as the seller's inside basis at the sale date.
- The sale of a partnership interest does not generally affect a partnership's inside basis.
- A partnership's tax year closes for the selling partner upon the sale of a partnership interest.
- Hot assets include unrealized receivables and inventory items.
- Unrealized receivables include the rights to receive payment for goods delivered or to be delivered, or services rendered or to be rendered, as well as items that would generate ordinary income if the partnership sold the asset for its fair market value, such as depreciation recapture.
- There are actually two definitions of inventory items. The first under §751(a) applies to sales of partnership interests and includes all classic inventory items and assets that are *not* capital or §1231 assets. The second definition of inventory [§751(b)] applies primarily to distributions and includes only substantially appreciated inventory.
- Sellers classify gains and losses from the sale of partnership interests as ordinary to the extent the gain relates to hot assets.
- Hot assets are also important to determine whether a distribution is proportionate or disproportionate.

LO 10-2 List the reasons for distributions, and compare operating and liquidating distributions.

- Distributions from a flow-through entity are one mechanism to return business profits or capital to the owners of the entity.
- Distributions may also be used to liquidate an owner's interest in the business or to completely terminate the business.
- Operating distributions include distributions in which the owner retains an interest in the business.
- The purpose of liquidating distributions is to terminate an owner's interest in the business.

LO 10-3 Determine the tax consequences of proportionate operating distributions.

- Partnerships do not generally recognize gain or loss on the distribution of property.
- Most operating distributions do not result in gain or loss to the partner receiving the distribution. Gains and losses are deferred through basis adjustments to the distributed assets and basis of the partnership interest.
- A partner recognizes a gain from an operating distribution if she receives a distribution of money that exceeds the basis in her partnership interest.
- Partners never recognize losses from operating distributions.

LO 10-4 Determine the tax consequences of proportionate liquidating distributions.

- The tax issues in liquidating distributions are primarily twofold: (1) determining whether the liquidating partner recognizes a gain or loss, and (2) allocating the liquidating partner's basis in her partnership interest to the distributed assets.
- A partner recognizes a gain only when the partnership distributes more money than her basis in the partnership interest.
- A partner recognizes a loss only when the partnership distributes cash and hot assets and the partner's basis in the partnership interest is greater than the sum of the bases of the distributed assets.

- In all other cases, a partner does not recognize gains or losses from a liquidating distribution; rather, she will simply reallocate her basis in the partnership interest to the distributed assets.
- The key to the allocation process is to focus on two factors: (1) the type of property distributed, and (2) whether the total basis in distributed assets is larger or smaller than the partner's basis in the partnership interest.
- The character of the distributed assets usually stays the same to the partner as in the partnership.

Explain the significance of disproportionate distributions. LO 10-5

- Disproportionate distributions occur when the assets distributed in either operating or liquidating distributions do not represent the partner's proportionate share of the partnership's hot and cold assets.
- A disproportionate distribution causes a shift in the proportion of ordinary income and capital gain income from the partnership. Therefore, the rules require the partner to treat a disproportionate distribution as a sale or exchange.
- If a partner receives more cold assets than her proportionate share in a distribution, she will generally recognize ordinary income in an amount equal to the appreciation of hot assets not distributed to her. If a partner receives more hot assets than her proportionate share, she will recognize capital gain equal to the appreciation of cold assets not distributed to her.
- The disproportionate distribution rules ensure that partners cannot convert ordinary income into capital gain through distributions.

Explain the rationale for special basis adjustments, determine when they are necessary, and calculate the special basis adjustment for dispositions and distributions. LO 10-6

- Discrepancies between a partner's inside and outside basis may cause a partner to be overtaxed or undertaxed, at least temporarily. Special basis adjustment rules allow the partnership to eliminate discrepancies between inside and outside bases to correct the artificial income or loss at the partnership level.
- Basis discrepancies may occur following the acquisition of a partnership interest and following distributions where a partner receives more or less than her share of the inside basis in the partnership property.
- When a new investor purchases a partnership interest, she may make a special basis adjustment equal to the difference between her outside basis and her share of inside basis if the partnership has a §754 election in effect.
- A special basis adjustment is mandatory even without a §754 election in effect when a partner sells a partnership interest and the partnership has a substantial built-in loss at the time of the sale.
- When a partner recognizes a gain from a distribution or takes a basis in distributed property less than the partnership's basis in the property, the partnership will have a positive special basis adjustment to increase the partnership asset bases.
- When a partner recognizes a loss from a liquidating distribution or takes a basis in distributed property greater than the partnership's basis in the property, the partnership will have a negative special basis adjustment to decrease the partnership asset bases.

KEY TERMS

carryover basis (10-11)
disproportionate distributions (10-24)
hot assets (10-3)
inside basis (10-7)
inventory items (10-3)
liquidating distributions (10-9)
negative basis adjustment (10-29)
operating distributions (10-9)
outside basis (10-3)
partnership interest (10-2)
positive basis adjustment (10-29)
special basis adjustment (10-26)
substantial basis reduction (10-27)
substantial built-in loss (10-27)
substantially appreciated inventory (10-24)
unrealized receivables (10-3)

DISCUSSION QUESTIONS

LO 10-1 1. Joey is a 25 percent owner of Loopy LLC. He no longer wants to be involved in the business. What options does Joey have to exit the business?

LO 10-1 2. Compare and contrast the aggregate and entity approaches for a sale of a partnership interest.

LO 10-1 3. What restrictions might prevent a partner from selling his partnership interest to a third party?

LO 10-1 4. Explain how a partner's debt relief affects his amount realized in a sale of partnership interest.

LO 10-1 5. Under what circumstances will the gain or loss on the sale of a partnership interest be characterized as ordinary rather than capital?

LO 10-1 6. What are *hot assets* and why are they important in the sale of a partnership interest?

LO 10-1 7. For an accrual-method partnership, are accounts receivable considered unrealized receivables? Explain.

LO 10-1 8. Can a partnership have unrealized receivables if it has no accounts receivable?

LO 10-1 9. How do hot assets affect the character of gain or loss on the sale of a partnership interest?

LO 10-1 10. Under what circumstances can a partner recognize both gain and loss on the sale of a partnership interest?

LO 10-1 11. Absent any special elections, what effect does a sale of partnership interest have on the partnership?

research LO 10-1 12. Generally, a selling partner's capital account carries over to the purchaser of the partnership interest. Under what circumstances will this not be the case?

LO 10-2 13. What distinguishes operating from liquidating distributions?

LO 10-3 14. Under what circumstances will a partner recognize a gain from an operating distribution?

LO 10-3 15. Under what circumstances will a partner recognize a loss from an operating distribution?

LO 10-3 16. In general, what effect does an operating distribution have on the partnership?

LO 10-3 17. If a partner's outside basis is less than the partnership's inside basis in distributed assets, how does the partner determine his basis of the distributed assets in an operating distribution?

LO 10-4 18. Under what conditions will a partner recognize gain in a liquidating distribution?

LO 10-4 19. Under what conditions will a partner recognize loss in a liquidating distribution?

LO 10-4 20. Describe how a partner determines his basis in distributed assets in cases in which a partnership distributes only money, inventory, and/or unrealized receivables in a liquidating distribution.

LO 10-4 21. How does a partner determine his basis in distributed assets when the partnership distributes other property in addition to money and hot assets?

LO 10-5 planning 22. SBT partnership distributes $5,000 cash and a parcel of land with a fair market value of $40,000 and a $25,000 basis to the partnership to Sam (30 percent partner). What factors must Sam and SBT consider in determining the tax treatment of this distribution?

LO 10-5 23. Discuss the underlying concern to tax policy makers in distributions in which a partner receives more or less than his share of the partnership hot assets.

LO 10-5 24. In general, how do the disproportionate distribution rules ensure that partners recognize their share of partnership ordinary income?

planning LO 10-6 25. Why would a new partner who pays more for a partnership interest than the selling partner's outside basis want the partnership to elect a special basis adjustment?

26. List two common situations that will cause a partner's inside and outside basis to differ. LO 10-6
27. Explain why a partnership might not want to make a §754 election to allow special basis adjustments. LO 10-6
28. When might a new partner have an upward basis adjustment following the acquisition of a partnership interest? LO 10-6
29. Are special basis adjustments mandatory? If so, when? LO 10-6

PROBLEMS

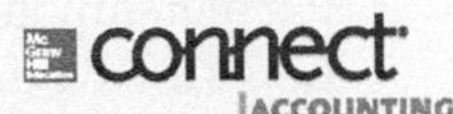

All applicable problems are available with McGraw-Hill's *Connect® Accounting*.

30. Jerry is a 30 percent partner in the JJM Partnership when he sells his entire interest to Lucia for $56,000 cash. At the time of the sale, Jerry's basis in JJM is $32,000. JJM does not have any debt or hot assets. What is Jerry's gain or loss on the sale of his interest? LO 10-1
31. Joy is a 30 percent partner in the JOM Partnership when she sells her entire interest to Hope for $72,000 cash. At the time of the sale, Joy's basis in JOM is $44,000 (which includes her $6,000 share of JOM liabilities). JOM does not have any hot assets. What is Joy's gain or loss on the sale of her interest? LO 10-1
32. Allison, Keesha, and Steven each own equal interests in KAS Partnership, a calendar-year-end, cash-method entity. On January 1 of the current year, Steven's basis in his partnership interest is $27,000. During January and February, the partnership generates $30,000 of ordinary income and $4,500 of tax-exempt income. On March 1, Steven sells his partnership interest to Juan for a cash payment of $45,000. The partnership has the following assets and no liabilities at the sale date: LO 10-1

	Tax Basis	FMV
Cash	$30,000	$30,000
Land held for investment	30,000	60,000
Totals	$60,000	$90,000

a) Assuming KAS's operating agreement provides for an interim closing of the books when partners' interests change during the year, what is Steven's basis in his partnership interest on March 1 just prior to the sale?
b) What is the amount and character of Steven's recognized gain or loss on the sale?
c) What is Juan's initial basis in the partnership interest?
d) What is the partnership's basis in the assets following the sale?

33. Grace, James, Helen, and Charles each own equal interests in GJHC Partnership, a calendar-year-end, cash-method entity. On January 1 of the current year, James's basis in his partnership interest is $62,000. For the taxable year, the partnership generates $80,000 of ordinary income and $30,000 of dividend income. For the first five months of the year, GJHC generates $25,000 of ordinary income and no dividend income. On June 1, James sells his partnership interest to Robert for a cash payment of $70,000. The partnership has the following assets and no liabilities at the sale date: LO 10-1

	Tax Basis	FMV
Cash	$ 27,000	$ 27,000
Land held for investment	80,000	100,000
Totals	$107,000	$127,000

a) Assuming GJHC's operating agreement provides that the proration method will be used to allocate income or loss when partners' interests change during the year, what is James's basis in his partnership interest on June 1 just prior to the sale?
b) What is the amount and character of James's recognized gain or loss on the sale?
c) If GJHC uses an interim closing of the books, what is the amount and character of James's recognized gain or loss on the sale?

LO 10-1

34. At the end of last year, Lisa, a 35 percent partner in the five-person LAMEC Partnership, has an outside basis of $60,000, including her $30,000 share of LAMEC debt. On January 1 of the current year, Lisa sells her partnership interest to MaryLynn for a cash payment of $45,000 and the assumption of her share of LAMEC's debt.
    a) What is the amount and character of Lisa's recognized gain or loss on the sale?
    b) If LAMEC has $100,000 of unrealized receivables as of the sale date, what is the amount and character of Lisa's recognized gain or loss?
    c) What is MaryLynn's initial basis in the partnership interest?

LO 10-1

35. Marco, Jaclyn, and Carrie formed Daxing Partnership (a calendar-year-end entity) by contributing cash 10 years ago. Each partner owns an equal interest in the partnership. Marco, Jaclyn, and Carrie each have an outside basis in his/her partnership interest of $104,000. On January 1 of the current year, Marco sells his partnership interest to Ryan for a cash payment of $137,000. The partnership has the following assets and no liabilities as of the sale date:

	Tax Basis	FMV
Cash	$ 18,000	$ 18,000
Accounts receivable	0	12,000
Inventory	69,000	81,000
Equipment	180,000	225,000
Stock investment	45,000	75,000
Totals	$312,000	$411,000

The equipment was purchased for $240,000, and the partnership has taken $60,000 of depreciation. The stock was purchased seven years ago.
    a) What are the *hot assets* [§751(a)] for this sale?
    b) What is Marco's gain or loss on the sale of his partnership interest?
    c) What is the character of Marco's gain or loss?
    d) What are Ryan's inside and outside bases in the partnership on the date of the sale?

LO 10-1

36. Franklin, Jefferson, and Washington formed the Independence Partnership (a calendar-year-end entity) by contributing cash 10 years ago. Each partner owns an equal interest in the partnership. Franklin, Jefferson, and Washington each have an outside basis in his partnership interest of $104,000. On January 1 of the current year, Franklin sells his partnership interest to Adams for a cash payment of $122,000. The partnership has the following assets and no liabilities as of the sale date:

	Tax Basis	FMV
Cash	$ 18,000	$ 18,000
Accounts receivable	0	12,000
Inventory	69,000	81,000
Equipment	180,000	225,000
Stock investment	45,000	30,000
Totals	$312,000	$366,000

The equipment was purchased for $240,000, and the partnership has taken $60,000 of depreciation. The stock was purchased seven years ago.

a) What is Franklin's overall gain or loss on the sale of his partnership interest?

b) What is the character of Franklin's gain or loss?

37. Travis and Alix Weber are equal partners in the Tralix Partnership, which does not have a §754 election in place. Alix sells one-half of her interest (25 percent) to Michael Tomei for $30,000 cash. Just before the sale, Alix's basis in her entire partnership interest is $75,000, including her $30,000 share of the partnership liabilities. Tralix's assets on the sale date are as follows: LO 10-1

	Tax Basis	FMV
Cash	$ 40,000	$ 40,000
Inventory	30,000	90,000
Land held for investment	80,000	50,000
Totals	$150,000	$180,000

a) What is the amount and character of Alix's recognized gain or loss on the sale?

b) What is Alix's basis in her remaining partnership interest?

c) What is Michael's basis in his partnership interest?

d) What is the effect of the sale on the partnership's basis in the assets?

38. Newton is a one-third owner of ProRite Partnership. Newton has decided to sell his interest in the business to Betty for $50,000 cash plus the assumption of his share of ProRite's liabilities. Assume Newton's inside and outside basis in ProRite are equal. ProRite shows the following balance sheet as of the sale date: LO 10-1

	Tax Basis	FMV
Assets:		
Cash	$ 80,000	$ 80,000
Receivables	25,000	25,000
Inventory	40,000	85,000
Land	30,000	20,000
Totals	$175,000	$210,000
Liabilities and capital:		
Liabilities	$ 60,000	
Capital—Newton	38,333	
—Barbara	38,334	
—Liz	38,333	
Totals	$175,000	

What is the amount and character of Newton's recognized gain or loss?

39. Coy and Matt are equal partners in the Matcoy Partnership. Each partner has a basis in his partnership interest of $28,000 at the end of the current year, prior to any distribution. On December 31, they each receive an operating distribution. Coy receives $10,000 cash. Matt receives $3,000 cash and a parcel of land with a $7,000 fair market value and a $4,000 basis to the partnership. Matcoy has no debt or hot assets. LO 10-3

a) What is Coy's recognized gain or loss? What is the character of any gain or loss?

b) What is Coy's ending basis in his partnership interest?

c) What is Matt's recognized gain or loss? What is the character of any gain or loss?

d) What is Matt's basis in the distributed property?

e) What is Matt's ending basis in his partnership interest?

LO 10-3 40. Justin and Lauren are equal partners in the PJenn Partnership. The partners formed the partnership seven years ago by contributing cash. Prior to any distributions, the partners have the following bases in their partnership interests:

Partner	Outside Basis
Justin	$22,000
Lauren	22,000

On December 31 of the current year, the partnership makes a pro rata operating distribution of:

Partner	Distribution
Justin	Cash $25,000
Lauren	Cash $18,000
	Property $7,000 (FMV)
	($2,000 basis to partnership)

a) What is the amount and character of Justin's recognized gain or loss?
b) What is Justin's remaining basis in his partnership interest?
c) What is the amount and character of Lauren's recognized gain or loss?
d) What is Lauren's basis in the distributed assets?
e) What is Lauren's remaining basis in her partnership interest?

LO 10-3 41. Adam and Alyssa are equal partners in the PartiPilo Partnership. The partners formed the partnership three years ago by contributing cash. Prior to any distributions, the partners have the following bases in their partnership interests:

Partner	Outside Basis
Adam	$12,000
Alyssa	12,000

On December 31 of the current year, the partnership makes a pro rata operating distribution of:

Partner	Distribution
Adam	Cash $16,000
Alyssa	Cash $8,000
	Property $8,000 (FMV)
	($6,000 basis to partnership)

a) What is the amount and character of Adam's recognized gain or loss?
b) What is Adam's remaining basis in his partnership interest?
c) What is the amount and character of Alyssa's recognized gain or loss?
d) What is Alyssa's basis in the distributed assets?
e) What is Alyssa's remaining basis in her partnership interest?

LO 10-3 42. Karen has a $68,000 basis in her 50 percent partnership interest in the KD Partnership before receiving a current distribution of $6,000 cash and land with a fair market value of $35,000 and a basis to the partnership of $18,000.
a) What is the amount and character of Karen's recognized gain or loss?
b) What is Karen's basis in the land?
c) What is Karen's remaining basis in her partnership interest?

LO 10-3 43. Pam has a $27,000 basis (including her share of debt) in her 50 percent partnership interest in the Meddoc partnership before receiving any distributions. This year Meddoc makes a current distribution to Pam of a parcel of land with a $40,000 fair market value and a $32,000 basis to the partnership. The land is encumbered with a $15,000 mortgage (the partnership's only liability).

a) What is the amount and character of Pam's recognized gain or loss?
b) What is Pam's basis in the land?
c) What is Pam's remaining basis in her partnership interest?

44. Two years ago, Kimberly became a 30 percent partner in the KST Partnership with a contribution of investment land with a $10,000 basis and a $16,000 fair market value. On January 2 of this year, Kimberly has a $15,000 basis in her partnership interest and none of her precontribution gain has been recognized. On January 2, Kimberly receives an operating distribution of a tract of land (not the contributed land) with a $12,000 basis and an $18,000 fair market value. LO 10-3 research
a) What is the amount and character of Kimberly's recognized gain or loss on the distribution?
b) What is Kimberly's remaining basis in KST after the distribution?
c) What is KST's basis in the land Kimberly contributed after Kimberly receives this distribution?

45. Rufus is a one-quarter partner in the Adventure Partnership. On January 1 of the current year, Adventure distributes $13,000 cash to Rufus in complete liquidation of his interest. Adventure has only capital assets and no liabilities at the date of the distribution. Rufus's basis in his partnership interest is $18,500. LO 10-4
a) What is the amount and character of Rufus's recognized gain or loss?
b) What is the amount and character of Adventure's recognized gain or loss?
c) If Rufus's basis is $10,000 at the distribution date rather than $18,500, what is the amount and character of Rufus's recognized gain or loss?

46. The Taurin Partnership (calendar-year-end) has the following assets as of December 31 of the current year: LO 10-4

	Tax Basis	FMV
Cash	$ 45,000	$ 45,000
Accounts receivable	15,000	30,000
Inventory	81,000	120,000
Totals	$141,000	$195,000

On December 31, Taurin distributes $15,000 of cash, $10,000 (FMV) of accounts receivable, and $40,000 (FMV) of inventory to Emma (a one-third partner) in termination of her partnership interest. Emma's basis in her partnership interest immediately prior to the distribution is $40,000.
a) What is the amount and character of Emma's recognized gain or loss on the distribution?
b) What is Emma's basis in the distributed assets?
c) If Emma's basis before the distribution was $55,000 rather than $40,000, what is Emma's recognized gain or loss and what is her basis in the distributed assets?

47. Melissa, Nicole, and Ben are equal partners in the Opto Partnership (calendar-year-end). Melissa decides she wants to exit the partnership and receives a proportionate distribution to liquidate her partnership interest on January 1. The partnership has no liabilities and holds the following assets as of January 1: LO 10-4

	Tax Basis	FMV
Cash	$18,000	$18,000
Accounts receivable	0	24,000
Stock investment	7,500	12,000
Land	30,000	36,000
Totals	$55,500	$90,000

Melissa receives one-third of each of the partnership assets. She has a basis in her partnership interest of $25,000.

a) What is the amount and character of any recognized gain or loss to Melissa?
b) What is Melissa's basis in the distributed assets?
c) What are the tax implications (amount and character of gain or loss and basis of assets) to Melissa if her outside basis is $11,000 rather than $25,000?
d) What is the amount and character of any recognized gain or loss from the distribution to Opto?

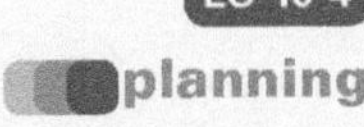

LO 10-4 planning

48. Lonnie Davis has been a general partner in the Highland Partnership for many years and is also a sole proprietor in a separate business. To spend more time focusing on his sole proprietorship, he plans to leave Highland and will receive a liquidating distribution of $50,000 in cash and land with a fair market value of $100,000 (tax basis of $120,000). Immediately before the distribution, Lonnie's basis in his partnership interest is $350,000, which includes his $50,000 share of partnership debt. The Highland Partnership does not hold any hot assets.

a) What is the amount and character of any gain or loss to Lonnie?
b) What is Lonnie's basis in the land?
c) What is the amount and character of Lonnie's gain or loss if he holds the land for 13 months as investment property and then sells it for $100,000?
d) What is the amount and character of Lonnie's gain or loss if he places the land into service in his sole proprietorship and then sells it 13 months later for $100,000?
e) Do your answers to parts (c) and (d) suggest a course of action that would help Lonnie to achieve a more favorable tax outcome?

LO 10-4

49. AJ is a 30 percent partner in the Trane Partnership, a calendar-year-end entity. On January 1, AJ has an outside basis in his interest in Trane of $73,000, which includes his share of the $50,000 of partnership liabilities. Trane generates $42,000 of income during the year and does not make any changes to its liabilities. On December 31, Trane makes a proportionate distribution of the following assets to AJ to terminate his partnership interest:

	Tax Basis	FMV
Inventory	$55,000	$65,000
Land	30,000	25,000
Totals	$85,000	$90,000

a) What are the tax consequences (gain or loss, basis adjustments) of the distribution to Trane?
b) What is the amount and character of any recognized gain or loss to AJ?
c) What is AJ's basis in the distributed assets?
d) If AJ sells the inventory four years after the distribution for $70,000, what is the amount and character of his recognized gain or loss?

LO 10-4

50. David's basis in the Jimsoo Partnership is $53,000. In a proportionate liquidating distribution, David receives cash of $7,000 and two capital assets: land 1 with a fair market value of $20,000 and a basis to Jimsoo of $16,000; and land 2 with a fair market value of $10,000 and a basis to Jimsoo of $16,000. Jimsoo has no liabilities.

a) How much gain or loss will David recognize on the distribution? What is the character of any recognized gain or loss?
b) What is David's basis in the distributed assets?
c) If the two parcels of land had been inventory to Jimsoo, what are the tax consequences to David (amount and character of gain or loss and basis in distributed assets)?

51. Megan and Matthew are equal partners in the J & J Partnership (calendar-year-end entity). On January 1 of the current year, they decide to liquidate the partnership. Megan's basis in her partnership interest is $100,000 and Matthew's is $35,000. The two partners receive identical distributions, with each receiving the following assets:

	Tax Basis	FMV
Cash	$30,000	$30,000
Inventory	5,000	6,000
Land	500	1,000
Totals	$35,500	$37,000

a) What is the amount and character of Megan's recognized gain or loss?
b) What is Megan's basis in the distributed assets?
c) What is the amount and character of Matthew's recognized gain or loss?
d) What is Matthew's basis in the distributed assets?

52. Bryce's basis in the Markit Partnership is $58,000. In a proportionate liquidating distribution, Bryce receives the following assets: LO 10-4

	Tax Basis	FMV
Cash	$ 8,000	$ 8,000
Land A	20,000	45,000
Land B	20,000	25,000

a) How much gain or loss will Bryce recognize on the distribution? What is the character of any recognized gain or loss?
b) What is Bryce's basis in the distributed assets?

53. Danner Inc. has a $395,000 capital loss carryover that will expire at the end of the current tax year if it is not used. Also, Danner Inc. has been a general partner in the Talisman Partnership for three years and plans to end its involvement with the partnership by receiving a liquidating distribution. Initially, all parties agreed that Danner Inc.'s liquidating distribution would include $50,000 in cash and land with a fair market value of $400,000 (tax basis of $120,000). Immediately before the distribution, Danner's basis in its partnership interest is $150,000, which includes its $100,000 share of partnership debt. The Talisman Partnership does not hold any hot assets. LO 10-4

a) What is the amount and character of any gain or loss to Danner Inc.?
b) What is Danner Inc.'s basis in the land?
c) Can you suggest a course of action that would help Danner Inc. avoid the expiration of its capital loss carryover?

54. Bella Partnership is an equal partnership in which each of the partners has a basis in his partnership interest of $10,000. Bella reports the following balance sheet: LO 10-1 LO 10-5 planning

	Tax Basis	FMV
Assets:		
Inventory	$20,000	$30,000
Land	10,000	15,000
Totals	$30,000	$45,000
Liabilities and capital:		
Capital—Toby	$10,000	
—Kaelin	10,000	
—Andrew	10,000	
Totals	$30,000	

a) Identify the *hot assets* if Toby decides to sell his partnership interest. Are these assets "hot" for purposes of distributions?

b) If Bella distributes the land to Toby in complete liquidation of his partnership interest, what tax issues should be considered?

LO 10-1 LO 10-6

55. Michelle pays $120,000 cash for Brittany's one-third interest in the Westlake Partnership. Just prior to the sale, Brittany's basis in Westlake is $96,000. Westlake reports the following balance sheet:

	Tax Basis	FMV
Assets:		
Cash	$ 96,000	$ 96,000
Land	192,000	264,000
Totals	$288,000	$360,000
Liabilities and capital:		
Capital—Amy	$ 96,000	
—Brittany	96,000	
—Ben	96,000	
Totals	$288,000	

a) What is the amount and character of Brittany's recognized gain or loss on the sale?

b) What is Michelle's basis in her partnership interest? What is Michelle's inside basis?

c) If Westlake were to sell the land for $264,000 shortly after the sale of Brittany's partnership interest, how much gain or loss would the partnership recognize?

d) How much gain or loss would Michelle recognize?

e) Suppose Westlake has a §754 election in place. What is Michelle's special basis adjustment? How much gain or loss would Michelle recognize on a subsequent sale of the land in this situation?

LO 10-4 LO 10-6

56. Cliff's basis in his Aero Partnership interest is $11,000. Cliff receives a distribution of $22,000 cash from Aero in complete liquidation of his interest. Aero is an equal partnership with the following balance sheet:

	Tax Basis	FMV
Assets:		
Cash	$22,000	$22,000
Investment	8,800	8,800
Land	2,200	35,200
Totals	$33,000	$66,000
Liabilities and capital:		
Capital—Chris	$11,000	
—Cliff	11,000	
—Cooper	11,000	
Totals	$33,000	

a) What is the amount and character of Cliff's recognized gain or loss? What is the effect on the partnership assets?

b) If Aero has a §754 election in place, what is the amount of the special basis adjustment?

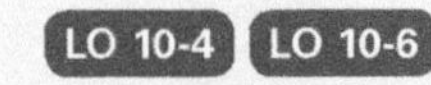

57. Erin's basis in her Kiybron Partnership interest is $3,300. Erin receives a distribution of $2,200 cash from Kiybron in complete liquidation of her interest. Kiybron is an equal partnership with the following balance sheet:

	Tax Basis	FMV
Assets:		
Cash	$2,200	$2,200
Stock (investment)	1,100	2,200
Land	6,600	2,200
Totals	$9,900	$6,600
Liabilities and capital:		
Capital—Erin	$3,300	
—Carl	3,300	
—Grace	3,300	
Totals	$9,900	

a) What is the amount and character of Erin's recognized gain or loss? What is the effect on the partnership assets?
b) If Kiybron has a §754 election in place, what is the amount of the special basis adjustment?

58. Helen's basis in Haywood partnership is $270,000. Haywood distributes all the land to Helen in complete liquidation of her partnership interest. The partnership reports the following balance sheet just before the distribution:

	Tax Basis	FMV
Assets:		
Cash	$220,000	$220,000
Stock (investment)	480,000	220,000
Land	110,000	220,000
Totals	$810,000	$660,000
Liabilities and capital:		
Capital—Charles	$270,000	
—Esther	270,000	
—Helen	270,000	
Totals	$810,000	

a) What is the amount and character of Helen's recognized gain or loss? What is the effect on the partnership assets?
b) If Haywood has a §754 election in place, what is the amount of the special basis adjustment?

COMPREHENSIVE PROBLEMS

All applicable problems are available with McGraw-Hill's *Connect® Accounting*.

59. Simon is a 30 percent partner in the SBD Partnership, a calendar-year-end entity. As of the end of this year, Simon has an outside basis in his interest in SBD of $188,000, which includes his share of the $60,000 of partnership liabilities. On December 31, SBD makes a proportionate distribution of the following assets to Simon:

	Tax Basis	FMV
Cash	$ 40,000	$ 40,000
Inventory	55,000	65,000
Land	30,000	45,000
Totals	$125,000	$150,000

a) What are the tax consequences (amount and character of recognized gain or loss, basis in distributed assets) of the distribution to Simon if the distribution is an operating distribution?
b) What are the tax consequences (amount and character of recognized gain or loss, basis in distributed assets) of the distribution to Simon if the distribution is a liquidating distribution?
c) Compare and contrast the results from parts (a) and (b).

planning 60. Paolo is a 50 percent partner in the Capri Partnership and has decided to terminate his partnership interest. Paolo is considering two options as potential exit strategies. The first is to sell his partnership interest to the two remaining 25 percent partners, Giuseppe and Isabella, for $105,000 cash and the assumption of Paolo's share of Capri's liabilities. Under this option, Giuseppe and Isabella would each pay $52,500 for half of Paolo's interest. The second option is to have Capri liquidate his partnership interest with a proportionate distribution of the partnership assets. Paolo's basis in his partnership interest is $110,000, including Paolo's share of Capri's liabilities. Capri reports the following balance sheet as of the termination date:

	Tax Basis	FMV
Assets:		
Cash	$ 80,000	$ 80,000
Receivables	40,000	40,000
Inventory	50,000	80,000
Land	50,000	60,000
Totals	$220,000	$260,000
Liabilities and capital:		
Liabilities	$ 50,000	
Capital—Paolo	85,000	
—Giuseppe	42,500	
—Isabella	42,500	
Totals	$220,000	

a) If Paolo sells his partnership interest to Giuseppe and Isabella for $105,000, what is the amount and character of Paolo's recognized gain or loss?
b) Giuseppe and Isabella each have a basis in Capri of $55,000 before any purchase of Paolo's interest. What are Giuseppe's and Isabella's basis in their partnership interests following the purchase of Paolo's interest?
c) If Capri liquidates Paolo's partnership interest with a proportionate distribution of the partnership assets ($25,000 deemed cash from debt relief, $15,000 of actual cash, and half of the remaining assets), what is the amount and character of Paolo's recognized gain or loss?
d) If Capri liquidates Paolo's interest, what is Paolo's basis in the distributed assets?
e) Compare and contrast Paolo's options for terminating his partnership interest. Assume Paolo's marginal tax rate is 35 percent, and his capital gains rate is 15 percent.

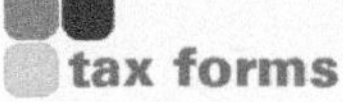
tax forms 61. Carrie D'Lake, Reed A. Green, and Doug A. Divot share a passion for golf and decide to go into the golf club manufacturing business together. On January 2, 2015, D'Lake, Green, and Divot form the Slicenhook Partnership, a general partnership. Slicenhook's main product will be a perimeter-weighted titanium driver with a patented graphite shaft. All three partners plan to actively

participate in the business. The partners contribute the following property to form Slicenhook:

Partner	Contribution
Carrie D'Lake	Land, FMV $460,000 Basis $460,000, Mortgage $60,000
Reed A. Green	$400,000
Doug A. Divot	$400,000

Carrie had recently acquired the land with the idea that she would contribute it to the newly formed partnership. The partners agree to share in profits and losses equally. Slicenhook elects a calendar-year-end and the accrual method of accounting.

In addition, Slicenhook received a $1,500,000 recourse loan from BigBank at the time the contributions were made. Slicenhook uses the proceeds from the loan and the cash contributions to build a state-of-the-art manufacturing facility ($1,200,000), purchase equipment ($600,000), and produce inventory ($400,000). With the remaining cash, Slicenhook invests $45,000 in the stock of a privately owned graphite research company and retains $55,000 as working cash.

Slicenhook operates on a just-in-time inventory system so it sells all inventory and collects all sales immediately. That means that at the end of the year, Slicenhook does not carry any inventory or accounts receivable balances. During 2015, Slicenhook has the following operating results:

Sales		$1,126,000
Cost of goods sold		400,000
Interest income from tax-exempt bonds		900
Qualified dividend income from stock		1,500
Operating expenses		126,000
Depreciation (tax)		
§179 on equipment	$39,000	
Equipment	81,000	
Building	24,000	144,000
Interest expense on debt		120,000

The partnership is very successful in its first year. The success allows Slicenhook to use excess cash from operations to purchase $15,000 of tax-exempt bonds (you can see the interest income already reflected in the operating results). The partnership also makes a principal payment on its loan from Big Bank in the amount of $300,000 and a distribution of $100,000 to each of the partners on December 31, 2015.

The partnership continues its success in 2016 with the following operating results:

Sales		$1,200,000
Cost of goods sold		420,000
Interest income from tax-exempt bonds		900
Qualified dividend income from stock		1,500
Operating expenses		132,000
Depreciation (tax)		
Equipment	147,000	
Building	30,000	177,000
Interest expense on debt		96,000

The operating expenses include a $1,800 trucking fine that one of its drivers incurred for reckless driving and speeding and meals and entertainment expense of $6,000.

By the end of 2016, Reed has had a falling out with Carrie and Doug and has decided to leave the partnership. He has located a potential buyer for his partnership interest, Indie Ruff. Indie has agreed to purchase Reed's interest in Slicenhook for $730,000 in cash and the assumption of Reed's share of Slicenhook's debt. Carrie and Doug, however, are not certain that admitting Indie to the partnership is such a good idea. They want at least to consider having Slicenhook liquidate Reed's interest on January 1, 2017. As of January 1, 2017, Slicenhook has the following assets:

	Tax Basis	FMV
Cash	$ 876,800	$ 876,800
Investment—tax exempts	15,000	18,000
Investment stock	45,000	45,000
Equipment—net of dep.	333,000	600,000
Building—net of dep.	1,146,000	1,440,000
Land	460,000	510,000
Total	$2,875,800	$3,489,800

Carrie and Doug propose that Slicenhook distribute the following to Reed in complete liquidation of his partnership interest:

	Tax Basis	FMV
Cash	$485,000	$485,000
Investment stock	45,000	45,000
Equipment—$200,000 cost net of dep.	111,000	200,000
Total	$641,000	$730,000

Slicenhook has not purchased or sold any equipment since its original purchase just after formation.

a) Determine each partner's recognized gain or loss upon formation of Slicenhook.
b) What is each partner's initial tax basis in Slicenhook on January 2, 2015?
c) Prepare Slicenhook's opening tax basis balance sheet as of January 2, 2015.
d) Using the operating results, what are Slicenhook's ordinary income and separately stated items for 2015 and 2016? What amount of Slicenhook's income for each period would each of the partner's receive?
e) Using the information provided, prepare Slicenhook's page 1 and Schedule K to be included with its Form 1065 for 2015. Also, prepare a Schedule K-1 for Carrie.
f) What are Carrie's, Reed's, and Doug's bases in their partnership interest at the end of 2015 and 2016?
g) If Reed sells his interest in Slicenhook to Indie Ruff, what is the amount and character of his recognized gain or loss? What is Indie's basis in the partnership interest?
h) What is Indie's inside basis in Slicenhook? What effect would a §754 election have on Indie's inside basis?
i) If Slicenhook distributes the assets proposed by Carrie and Doug in complete liquidation of Reed's partnership interest, what is the amount and character of Reed's recognized gain or loss? What is Reed's basis in the distributed assets?
j) Compare and contrast Reed's options for terminating his partnership interest. Assume Reed's marginal ordinary rate is 35 percent, and his capital gains rate is 15 percent.

KAPLAN CPA SIMULATIONS

KAPLAN CPA REVIEW

Please visit the *Connect Library* to access the following Kaplan CPA Simulation:

The simulation for **MST Consulting Services** covers corporate tax and partnerships.

chapter

11 S Corporations

Learning Objectives

Upon completing this chapter, you should be able to:

LO 11-1 Describe the requirements and process to elect S corporation status.

LO 11-2 Explain the events that terminate the S corporation election.

LO 11-3 Describe operating issues relating to S corporation accounting periods and methods, and explain income and loss allocations and separately stated items.

LO 11-4 Explain stock-basis calculations, loss limitations, determination of self-employment income, and fringe benefit rules that apply to S corporation shareholders.

LO 11-5 Apply the tax rules for S corporation operating distributions and liquidating distributions.

LO 11-6 Describe the taxes that apply to S corporations, estimated tax requirements, and tax return filing requirements.

© PhotoAlto

Storyline Summary

Nicole Johnson, Sarah Walker, and Chance Armstrong

Location:	Salt Lake City, Utah
Status:	Shareholders of newly formed Color Comfort Sheets Inc. (CCS)
Situation:	Formed CCS as a corporation and have elected to have the entity taxed as an S corporation.

In Chapter 4, we met Nicole Johnson, who turned her sheet-making hobby into a full-time business called Color Comfort Sheets (CCS). In this chapter, we assume Nicole formed CCS as a corporation, intending to elect S corporation tax status.

When starting the business, Nicole had cash to contribute to CCS but not enough to meet initial needs. She convinced her friend Sarah Walker to invest in CCS and, fortunately, after listening to Nicole and Sarah's proposal, local sports team owner Chance Armstrong also agreed to invest. Nicole and Sarah would take an active role in managing CCS; Chance would not. Nicole contributed a parcel of land and cash in exchange for one-third of CCS's stock. Sarah and Chance each contributed cash for one-third of the stock. With funding in place, CCS began operating on January 1, 2014. However, with the excitement (and turmoil) of starting the new business, it took Nicole, Sarah, and Chance a while to talk with their accountant about electing S corporation status. After several discussions, they filed their S election on May 1, 2014. ■

In this chapter, we discuss the tax and nontax characteristics of an **S corporation,** a hybrid entity that shares some characteristics with C corporations and some with partnerships.[1] S corporations are incorporated under state law and thus have the same legal protections as C corporations. They are governed by the same corporate tax rules that apply in the organization, liquidation, and reorganization of C corporations. However, unlike a C corporation, an S corporation is a flow-through entity and shares many tax similarities with partnerships. For example, basis calculations for S corporation shareholders and partners are similar, the income or loss of an S corporation flows through to its owners, and distributions are generally not taxed to the extent of the owner's basis.

Throughout this chapter, we highlight the tax similarities between S corporations and C corporations and between S corporations and partnerships, while focusing on the unique rules that apply to S corporations. These are more complex for S corporations that were once C corporations with **earnings and profits (E&P).**

LO 11-1

S CORPORATION ELECTIONS

Formations

The same rules for forming and contributing property govern S and C corporations. As discussed in Chapter 8, §351 and related provisions apply when one or more persons transfer property to a corporation (C or S) in return for stock, and immediately after the transfer, these persons control the corporation. These rules allow shareholders meeting the requirements to defer gains they realize when they transfer appreciated property to the corporation in exchange for stock. Note that similar rules apply to formations and property contributions to partnerships under §721. One important difference, however, is that partnership tax rules do not impose a control requirement to defer gains (see Chapter 9 for partnership contributions).

THE KEY FACTS

S Corporation Qualification Requirements

- Only U.S. citizens or residents, estates, certain trusts, and certain tax-exempt organizations may be S corporation shareholders.
- S corporations may have no more than 100 shareholders.
- For purposes of the 100-shareholder limit, family members and their estates count as only one shareholder.

S Corporation Qualification Requirements

Unlike C corporations and partnerships, S corporations are limited as to type and number of owners (shareholders).[2] Only U.S. citizens or residents, estates, certain trusts, and certain tax-exempt organizations may be shareholders, no corporations or partnerships.[3] S corporations may have no more than 100 shareholders; family members and their estates count as one. Family members include a common ancestor and her lineal descendants and their spouses (or former spouses). Thus, great-grandparents, grandparents, parents, children, grandchildren, great-grandchildren, and the respective spouses are family members for this purpose. A practical implication of these limits is that large, publicly traded corporations cannot elect to be treated as S corporations.

[1]S corporations get their name from **Subchapter S** of the Internal Revenue Code, which includes code sections 1361–1379.

[2]§1361.

[3]Grantor trusts, qualified Subchapter S trusts, electing small business trusts, certain testamentary trusts, and voting trusts can own S corporation stock. A discussion of these trusts is beyond the scope of this chapter. Eligible tax-exempt shareholders include qualified retirement plan trusts or charitable, religious, educational, etc., organizations that are tax-exempt under §501.

Example 11-1

What if: Suppose CCS was formed with Nicole Johnson, Sarah Walker, and Chanzz Inc., a corporation owned by Chance Armstrong, as shareholders. Would CCS be eligible to elect S corporation status?

Answer: No. Because one of its shareholders is a corporation (Chanzz Inc.), CCS would not be eligible to elect S corporation status.

What if: Suppose Nicole, Sarah, and Chance recruited 97 U.S. residents to become shareholders of CCS. Meanwhile, Nicole gave several of her CCS shares to her grandfather and his bride as a wedding gift. After the transfer, CCS had 102 shareholders. Can CCS elect S corporation status?

Answer: Yes. Nicole (descendant of common ancestor), her grandfather (common ancestor), and her grandfather's wife (spouse of common ancestor) are treated as *one* shareholder for purposes of the 100-shareholder limit.

S Corporation Election

An eligible corporation must make an affirmative election to be treated as an S corporation.[4] In addition to meeting the shareholder requirements above, it must:

- Be a domestic corporation (created or organized in the United States or under U.S. law or the law of any state in the United States).
- Not be a specifically identified ineligible corporation.[5]
- Have only one class of stock.

A corporation is considered to have only one class of stock if all of its outstanding shares provide identical distribution and liquidation rights. Differences in voting powers are permissible. In general, debt instruments do not violate the single class of stock requirement unless they are treated as equity elsewhere under the tax law.[6] In addition, §1361 provides safe-harbor rules to ensure that debt obligations are not recharacterized as a second class of stock.[7]

THE KEY FACTS

S Corporation Election

- An eligible corporation must make an affirmative election to be treated as an S corporation.
- Eligible corporations meet the type and number of shareholder requirements, are domestic corporations, are not specifically identified as ineligible corporations, and have only one class of stock.
- To elect S corporation status, the corporation makes a formal election using Form 2553.

Example 11-2

What if: Suppose Nicole was a resident of Toronto, Canada, and while she formed CCS in Canada under Canadian law, she still planned to do business in the United States. Is CCS eligible to elect S corporation status in the United States?

Answer: No. CCS would not be eligible for S corporation treatment because it was neither organized in the United States nor formed under U.S. laws.

What if: Suppose Nicole resided in Seattle and formed CCS under the state laws of Washington but planned to do a significant amount of business in Canada. Would CCS be eligible to elect S corporation status?

Answer: Yes, because CCS was formed under the laws of a U.S. state.

[4]§1362(a).

[5]Ineligible corporations include financial institutions using the reserve method of accounting under §585, insurance companies, corporations allowed a tax credit for income from Puerto Rico and from U.S. possessions under §936, corporations previously electing Domestic International Sales Corporation status, and corporations treated as a taxable mortgage pool.

[6]See §385 for factors considered in determining whether debt should be considered as equity for tax purposes.

[7]§1361(c)(5)(A) provides that straight debt issued during an S corporation year (i.e., not during a C corporation year) will not be treated as a second class of stock. §1361(c)(5)(A) defines straight debt as debt characterized by a written unconditional promise to pay on demand or on a specified date a sum certain in money if (1) the interest rate and interest payment dates are not contingent on profits, the borrower's discretion, or similar factors; (2) the debt is not convertible into stock; and (3) the creditor is an individual (other than a nonresident alien), an estate, a qualified trust, or a person who is actively and regularly engaged in the business of lending money.

To formally elect S corporation status effective as of the beginning of the current tax year, the corporation uses Form 2553, either in the prior tax year or on or before the 15th day of the third month of the current tax year.[8] Elections made after the 15th day of the third month of a year are effective at the beginning of the following year. All shareholders on the date of the election must consent to the election.

Example 11-3

What if: Suppose Nicole formed CCS as a C corporation in 2014 with a calendar tax year and finally got around to electing S corporation status on February 20, 2015. What is the earliest effective date of the S election?

Answer: January 1, 2015.

What if: Suppose Nicole formed CCS as a C corporation in 2014 with a calendar tax year and made the S election on March 20, 2015. When is the S election effective?

Answer: It is effective January 1, 2016, because Nicole made the election after March 15, 2015.

Even when the corporation makes the election on or before the 15th day of the third month of its tax year, the election will not be effective until the subsequent year if (1) the corporation did not meet the S corporation requirements for each day of the current tax year before it made the S election, or (2) one or more shareholders who held the stock in the corporation during the current year and before the S corporation election was made did not consent to the election (e.g., a shareholder disposes of his stock in the corporation in the election year before the election is made and fails to consent to the S election).[9]

Example 11-4

What if: Suppose in 2014 Nicole formed CCS as a C corporation (calendar tax year) with Nicole, Sarah, and Chanzz Inc. (a corporation) as shareholders. On January 2, 2015, Chanzz Inc. sold all its shares to Chance Armstrong. On January 31, 2015, CCS filed an S corporation election, with Nicole, Sarah, and Chance all consenting to the election. What is the earliest effective date of the S election?

Answer: January 1, 2016. Because CCS had an ineligible shareholder (Chanzz Inc.) during 2015, the election is not effective until the beginning of 2016.

What if: Suppose in 2014 Nicole formed CCS as a C corporation (calendar tax year) with Nicole, Sarah, and Chance as shareholders. On January 30, 2015, Chance sold his shares to Nicole. On February 15, 2015, CCS filed an S election, with Nicole and Sarah consenting to the election. Chance, however, did not consent to the election. What is the earliest effective date of the S election?

Answer: January 1, 2016. Because Chance was a shareholder until January 30, 2015, and he did not consent to the S election in 2015, the S election is not effective until the beginning of 2016, the year after the election.

The timing of the election may be especially important for C corporations with net operating losses. The reason: Net operating losses attributable to C corporation years generally cannot be carried over to the S corporation. Thus, it may be beneficial to delay the S election until the corporation has utilized its net operating losses.[10]

[8]§1362(b). When the IRS determines that taxpayers have reasonable cause for making late elections, it has the authority to treat late elections as timely [§1362(b)(5)]. Rev. Proc. 2013-30 provides a simplified method to provide relief for late elections by submitting the Form 2553 to the IRS with a statement that explains (a) that there was either reasonable cause for the late election or the late election was inadvertent and (b) that the taxpayer acted diligently to correct the mistake upon discovery.

[9]§1362(b)(2). Requiring all shareholders who own stock in an S corporation during the year to consent to the election ensures that shareholders who dispose of their stock before the election do not suffer adverse tax consequences from an election to which they did not consent.

[10]Later in this chapter we discuss one exception to the rule that disallows net operating loss carryovers from C corporation to S corporation years. See the discussion of the S corporation built-in gains tax.

S CORPORATION TERMINATIONS

LO 11-2

Once the S election becomes effective, the corporation remains an S corporation until the election is terminated. The termination may be voluntary or involuntary.

Voluntary Terminations

The corporation can make a *voluntary revocation* of the S election if shareholders holding more than 50 percent of the S corporation stock (including nonvoting shares) agree.[11] It files a statement with the IRS revoking the election made under §1362(a) and stating the effective date of the revocation and the number of shares issued and outstanding. In general, voluntary revocations made on or before the 15th day of the third month of the year are effective as of the beginning of the year. A revocation after this period is effective the first day of the following tax year. Alternatively, a corporation may specify the termination date as long as the date specified is on or after the date the revocation is made.[12]

Example 11-5

What if: Suppose CCS was initially formed as an S corporation with a calendar year-end. After a couple of years, things were going so well that Nicole and Sarah (each one-third shareholders) wanted to terminate the S election and take CCS public. However, Chance (also a one-third shareholder) was opposed to the S election termination. Can Nicole and Sarah terminate the S election without Chance's consent?

Answer: Yes. To revoke the election, Nicole and Sarah need to own more than 50 percent of the shares, and together they own 66.7 percent.

What if: If Nicole and Sarah file the revocation on February 15, 2016, what is the effective date of the S corporation termination (assuming they do not specify one)?

Answer: January 1, 2016. If they file the S corporation revocation after March 15, 2016, it becomes effective January 1, 2017. Alternatively, CCS could have specified an effective date of the S corporation's termination (in 2016 or after) as long as it was on or after the date the revocation was made.

ETHICS

Suppose Chance Armstrong is a French citizen but U.S. resident. Chance's mother has recently been diagnosed with a terminal illness, and Chance has decided to move back to France to take care of his mother and her affairs. Chance anticipates that he will live in France for several years and that he no longer would be considered a U.S. resident. If you were Sarah or Nicole, how would you react to Chance's decision to move? Would you ignore the impact Chance's move may have on CCS's S corporation status? Would you pressure Chance to sell his CCS stock to you?

Involuntary Terminations

Involuntary terminations can result from failure to meet requirements (by far the most common reason) or from an excess of passive investment income.

Failure to Meet Requirements A corporation's S election is automatically terminated if the corporation fails to meet the requirements. The termination is effective on the date it fails the S corporation requirements. If the IRS deems the termination inadvertent, it may allow the corporation to continue to be treated as an S corporation if, within a reasonable period after the inadvertent termination, the corporation takes the necessary steps to meet the S corporation requirements.[13]

[11]§1362(d)(1)(B).
[12]§1362(d)(1)(D).
[13]§1362(f).

Example 11-6

What if: Suppose CCS was formed as a calendar-year S corporation with Nicole Johnson, Sarah Walker, and Chance Armstrong as equal shareholders. On June 15, 2015, Chance sold his CCS shares to his solely owned C corporation, Chanzz Inc. Is CCS's S election still in effect at the beginning of 2016? If not, when was it terminated?

Answer: No, the election was automatically terminated on June 15, 2015, when Chanzz Inc. became a shareholder because S corporations may not have corporate shareholders.

Excess of Passive Investment Income If an S corporation has *earnings and profits* from a previous C corporation year (or through a reorganization with a corporation that has earnings and profits), its election is terminated if the S corporation has passive investment income in excess of 25 percent of gross receipts for three consecutive years. If the S corporation never operated as a C corporation or does not have C corporation earnings and profits (either by prior distribution of C corporate earnings and profits, or simply by not having earnings and profits at the effective date of the S election), this provision does not apply.

For purposes of the passive investment income test, **gross receipts** is the total amount of revenues received (including net capital gains from the sale of capital assets and gain (not offset by losses) from the sale of stock and securities) or accrued under the corporation's accounting method, *not* reduced by returns, allowances, cost of goods sold, or deductions. **Passive investment income (PII)** includes royalties, rents, dividends, interest, annuities, and gains from the sales or exchanges of stock or securities.[14] S corporation election terminations due to excess passive investment income are effective on the first day of the year following the third consecutive tax year with excess passive investment income.

Example 11-7

What if: Suppose CCS was initially formed as an S corporation with a calendar year-end. During its first three years, it reported passive investment income in excess of 25 percent of its gross receipts. Is CCS's S election terminated under the excess passive investment income test? If so, what is the effective date of the termination?

Answer: No, the excess passive investment income test does not apply to CCS in this situation because CCS has never operated as a C corporation; consequently, it does not have C corporation earnings and profits.

What if: Suppose CCS was initially formed as a C corporation with a calendar year-end. After its first year of operations (very profitable), CCS elected S corporation status, effective January 1, 2015. During 2016, 2017, and 2018, it reported passive investment income in excess of 25 percent of its gross receipts and had undistributed earnings and profits from its C corporation year. Is CCS's S election terminated under the excess passive investment income test? If so, what is the effective date of the termination?

Answer: Yes, it is terminated. Because CCS has C corporation earnings and profits from 2014 and excess passive investment income for three consecutive years as an S corporation, its S election is terminated effective on January 1, 2019.

Short Tax Years

S corporation election terminations frequently create an S corporation *short tax year* (a reporting year less than 12 months) and a C corporation short tax year. The corporation must then allocate its income for the full year between the S and the C corporation years, using the number of days in each short year (the daily method). Or it may use the

[14]PII excludes certain rents (e.g., rents derived from the active trade or business of renting property, produced film rents, income from leasing self-produced tangible property, temporary parking fees, etc.).

corporation's normal accounting rules to allocate income to the actual period in which it was earned (the specific identification method).[15] Both short tax year returns are due on the corporation's customary tax return due date (with normal extensions available).

Example 11-8

What if: Suppose CCS was formed as a calendar-year S corporation with Nicole Johnson, Sarah Walker, and Chance Armstrong as equal shareholders. On June 15, 2015, Chance sold his CCS shares (one-third of all shares) to his solely owned C corporation, Chanzz Inc., terminating CCS's S election on June 15, 2015. Assume CCS reported the following business income for 2015:

Period	Income
January 1 through June 14 (165 days)	$100,000
June 15 through December 31 (200 days)	265,000
January 1 through December 31, 2015 (365 days)	$365,000

If CCS uses the daily method of allocating income between the S corporation short tax year (January 1–June 14) and the C corporation short tax year (June 15–December 31), how much income will it report on its S corporation short tax year return and its C corporation short tax year return for 2015?

Answer: S corporation short tax year = $165,000 ($365,000/365 days × 165 days); C corporation short tax year = $200,000 ($365,000/365 days × 200 days).

What if: If CCS uses the specific identification method to allocate income, how much will it allocate to the S corporation short year and C corporation short year?

Answer: S corporation short tax year, $100,000; C corporation short tax year, $265,000.

Note that if the entity wanted to minimize the income subject to taxation as a C corporation, it would use the daily method of allocating income.

THE KEY FACTS

S Terminations and Reelections

- The S election may be revoked by shareholders holding more than 50 percent of the S corporation stock (including nonvoting shares).
- A corporation's S election is automatically terminated if (1) the S corporation fails to meet the S corporation requirements, or (2) the S corporation has earnings and profits from a previous C corporation year and has passive investment income in excess of 25 percent of gross receipts for three consecutive years.
- A corporation losing its S corporation status must wait until the beginning of the fifth year after the election was terminated to elect S corporation status again.

S Corporation Reelections

After terminating or voluntarily revoking S corporation status, the corporation may elect it again, but it generally must wait until the beginning of the fifth tax year *after* the tax year in which it terminated the election.[16] Thus, if the election was terminated effective the first day of the tax year, the corporation must wait five full years to again become an S corporation.

Example 11-9

What if: Let's return to the facts of the previous example. CCS was formed as a calendar-year S corporation with Nicole Johnson, Sarah Walker, and Chance Armstrong as equal shareholders. On June 15, 2015, Chance sold his CCS shares (one-third of all shares) to his solely owned C corporation, Chanzz Inc., terminating CCS's S election on June 15, 2015. Absent permission from the IRS (see text below), what is the earliest date CCS may again elect to be taxed as an S corporation?

Answer: January 1, 2020. This is the fifth tax year after the year in which the termination became effective.

What if: Assume on February 1, 2015, CCS voluntarily elected to revoke its S corporation status effective January 1, 2016. Absent IRS permission, what is the earliest CCS may again elect to be taxed as an S corporation?

Answer: January 1, 2021. This is the fifth year after the year in which the termination became effective.

[15]Use of the specific identification method requires that all shareholders at any time during the S corporation short year and the shareholders on the first day of the C corporation short year consent to the election using the specific identification method [§1362(e)(3)(A)]. However, an S corporation must use the specific identification method to allocate income between the short years (the per day allocation method is not allowed) if there is a sale or exchange of 50 percent or more of the corporation's stock during the year [§1362(e)(6)(D)].

[16]§1362(g).

The IRS may consent to an earlier election under a couple of conditions: (1) if the corporation is now owned more than 50 percent by shareholders who were not owners at the time of termination, or (2) if the termination was not reasonably within the control of the corporation or shareholders with a substantial interest in the corporation and was not part of a planned termination by the corporation or shareholders. Given the potential adverse consequences of an S election termination, the corporation should carefully monitor compliance with the S corporation requirements.

LO 11-3

OPERATING ISSUES

THE KEY FACTS

Operating Issues

- S corporations are generally required to adopt a calendar tax year.
- S corporations allocate profits and losses to shareholders pro rata, based on the number of outstanding shares each shareholder owns on each day of the tax year.
- S corporations determine each shareholder's share of ordinary business income (loss) and separately stated items.
- Ordinary business income (loss) is all income (loss) exclusive of any separately stated items of income (loss). Separately stated items are tax items that are treated differently than a shareholder's share of ordinary business income (loss) for tax purposes.

Accounting Methods and Periods

Like partnerships, S corporations determine their accounting periods and make accounting method elections at the entity level. An S corporation makes most of its elections (like the §179 election) in conjunction with filing its annual tax return, and some by filing a separate request with the IRS. (For example, an application to change accounting methods is filed on Form 3115, separate from the S corporation's tax return.) For an S corporation previously operating as a C corporation, all prior accounting methods carry over to the S corporation.

Recall that both C corporations and partnerships face restrictions on using the cash method. S corporations do not. They may choose the cash, accrual, or hybrid method unless selling inventory is a material income-producing factor for them. In that case they must account for gross profit (sales minus cost of goods sold) using the accrual method, even if they are otherwise cash-method taxpayers. Hence, they would use the hybrid method.

Tax laws also specify permissible tax years for S corporations, but they are a little less cumbersome than for partnerships. S corporations must use a calendar year-end unless they can establish a business purpose for an alternative year-end or a natural business year-end. (For example, a business that receives 25 percent or more of gross receipts for the previous three years in the last two months of the year-end requested would qualify for a noncalendar year-end.)[17]

Income and Loss Allocations

S corporations, like partnerships, are flow-through entities, and thus their profits and losses flow through to their shareholders annually for tax purposes. As we discussed in Chapter 9, partnerships have considerable flexibility in making special profit and loss allocations to their partners. In contrast, S corporations must allocate profits and losses pro rata, based on the number of outstanding shares each shareholder owns on each day of the tax year.[18]

An S corporation generally allocates income or loss items to shareholders on the last day of its tax year.[19] If a shareholder sells her shares during the year, she will report her share of S corporation income and loss allocated to the days she owned the stock (including the day of sale) using a pro rata allocation. If *all shareholders with changing ownership percentages* during the year agree, the S corporation can instead use its normal accounting rules to allocate income and loss (and other separately stated items, discussed below) to the specific periods in which it realized income and losses.

[17]§1378(b). In addition, S corporations, like partnerships, have the option of electing an alternative taxable year under §444.

[18]§1366(a), §1377(a).

[19]§1366(a).

Example 11-10

What if: Assume CCS was formed as a calendar-year S corporation with Nicole Johnson, Sarah Walker, and Chance Armstrong as equal (one-third) shareholders. On June 14, 2015, Chance sold his CCS shares to Nicole. CCS reported the following business income for 2015:

Period	Income
January 1 through June 14 (165 days)	$100,000
June 15 through December 31 (200 days)	265,000
January 1 through December 31, 2015 (365 days)	$365,000

How much 2015 income is allocated to each shareholder if CCS uses the daily method of allocating income?

Answer: Nicole's allocation is $188,333; Sarah's is $121,667; and Chance's is $55,000, calculated as follows.

	(1) January 1–June 14	(2) June 15–December 31	(1) + (2) Total 2015 Allocation
Nicole	$55,000	$133,333	**$188,333**
	($365,000/365 × 165 × 1/3)	($365,000/365 × 200 × 2/3)	
Sarah	$55,000	$66,667	**121,667**
	($365,000/365 × 165 × 1/3)	($365,000/365 × 200 × 1/3)	
Chance	$55,000	$0	**55,000**
	($365,000/365 × 165 × 1/3)		
Totals	$165,000	$200,000	$365,000

How much 2015 income is allocated to each shareholder if CCS uses its normal accounting rules to allocate income to the specific periods in which it was actually earned?

Answer: Nicole's allocation is $210,000 ($100,000 × 1/3 + $265,000 × 2/3); Sarah's is $121,667 ($365,000 × 1/3); and Chance's is $33,333 ($100,000 × 1/3).

Separately Stated Items

Like partnerships, S corporations are required to file tax returns (Form 1120S) annually. In addition, on Form 1120S, Schedule K-1, they supply information to each shareholder detailing the amount *and* character of items of income and loss flowing through the S corporation.[20] Shareholders must report these income and loss items on their tax returns even if they do not receive cash distributions during the year.

S corporations determine each shareholder's share of ordinary business income (loss) and separately stated items. Like partnerships, **ordinary business income (loss)** (also referred to as non-separately stated income or loss) is all income (loss) exclusive of any separately stated items of income (loss). **Separately stated items** are tax items that are treated differently from a shareholder's share of ordinary business income (loss) for tax purposes. The character of each separately stated item is determined at the S corporation level rather than at the shareholder level. The list of common separately stated items for S corporations is similar to that for partnerships, with a couple of exceptions. (For example, S corporations do not report self-employment income and do not have guaranteed payments.) Exhibit 11-1 lists several common separately stated items. See Form 1120S, Schedule K-1 (and related instructions) for a comprehensive list of separately stated items.

[20]Other items, such as tax credits and informational items such as AMT adjustments, also flow through from the S corporation to its shareholders and are reported to shareholders on Form 1120S, Schedule K-1.

EXHIBIT 11-1 Common Separately Stated Items

- Short-term capital gains and losses
- Long-term capital gains and losses
- Section 1231 gains and losses
- Dividends
- Interest income
- Charitable contributions
- Tax-exempt income
- Net rental real estate income
- Investment interest expense
- Section 179 deduction
- Foreign taxes

S corporations may hold stock in C corporations, and any dividends S corporations receive will flow through to their shareholders. However, S corporations are not entitled to claim the dividends received deduction (see Chapter 5 for a discussion of the dividends received deduction).

Assuming CCS operated as a C corporation in 2014 and an S corporation in 2015, Exhibit 11-2 presents the results of operations. CCS's S election was not effective until January 1, 2015, because the shareholders filed the S election after the required date for it to be effective in 2014.

EXHIBIT 11-2

Color Comfort Sheets
Income Statement
December 31, 2014 and 2015

	2014, C Corporation	2015, S Corporation
Sales revenue	$220,000	$520,000
Cost of goods sold	(50,000)	(115,000)
Salary to owners Nicole and Sarah	(70,000)	(90,000)
Employee wages	(45,000)	(50,000)
Depreciation expense	(15,000)	(20,000)
Miscellaneous expenses	(4,000)	(5,000)
Interest income	3,000	6,000
Dividend income	1,000	3,000
Overall net income	$ 40,000	$249,000

Example 11-11

Assume CCS was a C corporation for tax purposes in 2014 and an S corporation for 2015. Based on its operating results in Exhibit 11-2, how much ordinary business income and separately stated items are allocated to CCS's shareholders for 2014?

Answer: $0 ordinary business income and $0 separately stated items. Because CCS is a C corporation in 2014, its income does *not* flow through to its shareholders.

Based on the information in Exhibit 11-2, how much ordinary business income and separately stated items are allocated to CCS's shareholders for 2015?

Answer: See the following table for the allocations:

Description	CCS	Allocations Nicole 1/3	Sarah 1/3	Chance 1/3
2015 overall net income	$249,000			
Less:				
Dividends	3,000			
Interest income	6,000			
Ordinary business income	240,000	**$80,000**	**$80,000**	**$80,000**
Separately Stated Items:				
Interest income	6,000	**2,000**	**2,000**	**2,000**
Dividends	3,000	**1,000**	**1,000**	**1,000**

Nicole, Sarah, and Chance will treat their shares of CCS's ordinary business income as *ordinary* income and include it, along with their shares of interest and dividend income, in their individual tax returns for the year.[21]

Shareholder's Basis

LO 11-4

Just as partners must determine their bases in their partnership interests, S corporation shareholders must determine their bases in the S corporation stock to determine the gain or loss they recognize when they sell the stock, the taxability of distributions, and the deductibility of losses.

Initial Basis An S corporation shareholder calculates his *initial basis* upon formation of the corporation, like C corporation shareholders. (See Chapter 8 for a review.) Specifically, the shareholder's basis in stock received in the exchange equals the tax basis of the property transferred, less any liabilities assumed by the corporation on the property contributed (*substituted basis*). The shareholder's stock basis is increased by any gain recognized; it is reduced by the fair market value of any property received other than stock.[22] If, on the other hand, the shareholder purchased the S corporation stock from another shareholder or the corporation, the new shareholder's basis is simply the purchase price of the stock.[23]

Example 11-12

At the beginning of 2014, Nicole contributed $30,000 of cash and land with a fair market value of $130,000 and an adjusted basis of $125,000 to CCS. The land was encumbered by a $40,000 mortgage executed three years before. Sarah and Chance each contributed $120,000 of cash to CCS. What tax bases do Nicole, Sarah, and Chance have in their CCS stock at the beginning of 2014?

Answer: Nicole's basis is $115,000 ($30,000 cash + $125,000 adjusted basis of land − $40,000 mortgage assumed); Sarah's basis is $120,000; and Chance's is $120,000.

[21]Nicole, Sarah, and Chance would report their share of ordinary business income on Schedule E and their share of interest and dividend income on Schedule B of Form 1040.

[22]§358. This assumes the shareholder meets the §351 requirements. If the shareholder's exchange with the corporation does not meet these requirements, the shareholder's basis in the stock is its fair market value.

[23]If the shareholder acquires the stock by gift, her basis in the stock is the lesser of the donor's basis (increased for any gift taxes paid on the stock's appreciation) or the fair market value of the stock. In contrast, if the shareholder acquires the stock by bequest, her basis in the stock is the stock's fair market value on the date of the decedent's death adjusted to reflect any income in respect of the decedent.

Annual Basis Adjustments While C corporation rules govern the initial stock basis of an S corporation shareholder, subsequent calculations more closely resemble the partnership rules. Specifically, an S corporation shareholder's stock basis is dynamic and must be *adjusted* annually to ensure that (1) taxable income/gains and deductible expenses/losses are *not* double-counted by shareholders either when they sell their shares or receive S corporation distributions (e.g., because shareholders are taxed on the S corporation's income annually, they should not be taxed again when they receive distributions of the income) and (2) tax-exempt income and nondeductible expenses are not ultimately taxed or deducted.

THE KEY FACTS

S Corporation Shareholder's Basis Adjustments

- A shareholder will increase the tax basis in her stock for:
  - Contributions.
  - Share of ordinary business income.
  - Separately stated income/gain items.
  - Tax-exempt income.
- A shareholder will decrease the tax basis in her stock for:
  - Cash distributions.
  - Share of nondeductible expenses.
  - Share of ordinary business loss.
  - Separately stated expense/loss items.
- A shareholder's tax basis may not be negative.

S corporation shareholders make the following adjustments to their stock basis annually, in the order listed:

- Increase for any contributions to the S corporation during the year.
- Increase for shareholder's share of ordinary business income and separately stated income/gain items (including tax-exempt income).
- Decrease for distributions during the year.
- Decrease for shareholder's share of nondeductible expenses (fines, penalties).
- Decrease for shareholder's share of ordinary business loss and separately stated expense/loss items.[24]

As with a partnership, adjustments that decrease basis may never reduce an S corporation shareholder's tax basis below zero.[25]

S corporation shareholders are not allowed to include any S corporation debt in their stock basis. Recall that partners *are* allowed to include their share of partnership debt in their basis. One implication of this difference is that, everything else equal, an S corporation shareholder's basis will be lower than a partner's basis, due to the exclusion of debt (however, see the discussion of *debt basis* for S corporation shareholders below).

Example 11-13

Given the shareholders' 2014 bases in their CCS stock from the previous example (Nicole, $115,000; Sarah, $120,000; and Chance, $120,000), what basis does each have at the end of 2015, after taking into account the information in Exhibit 11-2 (but before taking into account any distributions, which are discussed below)?

Answer: Nicole, $198,000; Sarah, $203,000; and Chance, $203,000, computed as follows:

Description	Nicole	Sarah	Chance	Explanation
(1) Initial tax basis	$115,000	$120,000	$120,000	Example 11-12.
(2) Ordinary business income	80,000	80,000	80,000	Example 11-11.
(3) Interest income	2,000	2,000	2,000	Example 11-11.
(4) Dividends	1,000	1,000	1,000	Example 11-11.
Tax basis in stock at end of 2015	$198,000	$203,000	$203,000	(1) + (2) + (3) + (4).

Note the shareholders do not include any portion of CCS's debt in their stock basis.

What if: Suppose that, in addition to the amounts in Exhibit 11-2, CCS also recognized $1,200 of tax-exempt interest income in 2015. Nicole's share of this separately stated item is $400. Taking this allocation into account, what is Nicole's stock basis at the end of 2015?

Answer: It is $198,400 ($198,000 + $400). The tax-exempt income allocated to Nicole as a separately stated item increases her tax basis to ensure that she is never taxed on her share of the tax-exempt income.

[24]Reg. §1.1367-1(g) allows a shareholder to elect to decrease basis by ordinary business losses and separately stated expense/loss items *before* decreasing basis by nondeductible expenses by attaching a statement to the shareholder's tax return. This election is advantageous because loss/expense deductions are limited to a shareholder's basis, and this election results in a higher basis limitation for deductible loss/expense items.

[25]§1367(a)(2).

Loss Limitations

S corporations have loss-limitation rules similar to those for partnerships. For an S corporation shareholder to deduct it, a loss must clear three separate hurdles: (1) tax basis, (2) at-risk amount, and (3) passive activity.[26]

Tax Basis Limitation S corporation shareholders may not deduct losses in excess of their stock basis. Recall they are not allowed to include debt in their basis; partners are. This restriction makes it more likely that the tax basis limitation will apply to S corporation shareholders than to similarly situated partners. Losses not deductible due to the tax basis limitation are not necessarily lost. Rather, they are suspended until the shareholder generates additional basis. The carryover period for the suspended loss is indefinite. However, if the shareholder sells the stock before creating additional basis, the suspended loss disappears unused.

Example 11-14

What if: Suppose at the beginning of 2016, Nicole's basis in her CCS stock was $14,000. During 2016, CCS reported a $60,000 ordinary business loss and no separately stated items. How much of the ordinary loss is allocated to Nicole?

Answer: The loss allocation is $20,000 ($60,000 × 1/3).

How much of the $20,000 loss clears the tax basis hurdle for deductibility in 2016?

Answer: The amount of Nicole's basis in her CCS stock, or $14,000. The remaining $6,000 of loss does not clear the tax basis hurdle; it is suspended until Nicole generates additional basis.

Shareholders can mitigate the disadvantage of not including S corporation debt in their stock basis—by loaning money directly to their S corporations. These loans create **debt basis,** separate from the stock basis. Losses are limited first to the shareholders' tax bases in their shares *and then* to their bases in any direct loans made to their S corporations.[27] Specifically, if the total amount of items (besides distributions) that decrease the shareholder's basis for the year exceeds the shareholder's stock basis, the excess amount decreases the shareholder's debt basis. Like stock basis, debt basis cannot be decreased below zero. In subsequent years, any net increase in basis for the year *first restores the shareholder's debt basis* (up to the outstanding debt amount) and then the shareholder's stock basis. If the S corporation repays the debt owed to the shareholder before the shareholder's debt basis is restored, any loan repayment in excess of the shareholder's debt basis will trigger a taxable gain to the shareholder.

Example 11-15

What if: Suppose at the beginning of 2016, Nicole's basis in her CCS stock was $14,000. During 2016, Nicole loaned $8,000 to CCS, and CCS reported a $60,000 ordinary business loss and no separately stated items. How much of the $20,000 ordinary loss allocated to Nicole clears the tax basis hurdle for deductibility in 2016?

Answer: All $20,000. The first $14,000 of the loss reduces her stock basis to $0, and the remaining $6,000 reduces her debt basis to $2,000 ($8,000 − $6,000).

(continued on page 11-14)

[26]S corporations are also subject to the hobby loss rules in §183 that limit loss deductions for activities not engaged in for profit.

[27]§1366(d)(1)(B). These must be direct loans to the corporation. Thus, shareholders do not get debt basis when they guarantee a loan of the S corporation, although they would to the extent they had to "make good" on their guarantee obligation. At that point, the shareholders would get stock basis (if they have no right to repayment from the S corporation) or debt basis (if they have a right to repayment from the S corporation).

THE KEY FACTS

Loss Limitations

- S corporation losses in excess of a shareholder's tax basis and at-risk amount are suspended and carried forward until additional basis and amounts at risk are created.
- Upon S election termination, shareholders may create additional stock basis during the post-termination transition period to utilize losses limited by the basis or at-risk rules.
- The passive activity loss rules limit the ability of S corporation shareholders to deduct losses of the S corporation unless the shareholders are involved in actively managing the business.

What if: Suppose in 2017, CCS allocated $9,000 of ordinary business income to Nicole and no separately stated items. What are Nicole's CCS stock basis and debt basis at the end of 2017?

Answer: Her stock basis is $3,000; her debt basis is $8,000. The income first restores debt basis to the outstanding debt amount and then increases her stock basis.

At-Risk Limitation Like partners in partnerships, S corporation shareholders are subject to the *at-risk* rules. They may deduct S corporation losses only to the extent of their **at-risk amount** in the S corporation, as defined in §465. With one notable exception, an S corporation shareholder's at-risk amount is the sum of her stock and debt basis. The primary exception relates to nonrecourse loans and is designed to ensure that shareholders only are deemed at risk when they have an actual risk of loss. Specifically, an S corporation shareholder taking out a nonrecourse loan to make a capital contribution (either cash or other property) to the S corporation generally creates stock basis (equal to the basis of property contributed) in the S corporation but only increases her amount at risk by the net fair market value of her property, if any, used as collateral to secure the nonrecourse loan.[28] The collateral's net fair market value is determined at the loan date. Likewise, if the shareholder takes out a nonrecourse loan to make a direct *loan* to the S corporation, the loan creates debt basis, but only increases her amount at risk by the net fair market value of her property, if any, used as collateral to secure the nonrecourse loan. When the stock basis plus debt basis is different from the at-risk amount, S corporation shareholders apply the tax basis loss limitation first, and then the at-risk limitation. Losses limited under the at-risk rules are carried forward indefinitely until the shareholder generates additional at-risk amounts to utilize them or sells the S corporation stock.

Post-Termination Transition Period Loss Limitation The voluntary or involuntary termination of a corporation's S election creates a problem for shareholders with suspended losses due to the basis and at-risk rules. The reason: These losses are generally not deductible after the S termination date. Shareholders can obtain some relief provided by §1366(d)(3), which allows them to treat any suspended losses existing at the S termination date as occurring on the last day of the **post-termination transition period (PTTP).** In general, the PTTP begins on the day after the last day of the corporation's last taxable year as an S corporation and ends on the later of (a) one year after the last S corporation day or (b) the due date for filing the return for the last year as an S corporation (including extensions).[29]

This rule allows the shareholder to create additional stock basis (by making additional capital contributions) during the PTTP and to utilize suspended losses based on her *stock* basis (not her debt basis) at the end of the period. Any suspended losses utilized at the end of the PTTP reduce the shareholder's basis in her stock. Any losses not utilized at the end of the period are lost forever.

Example 11-16

What if: Suppose CCS terminated its S election on July 17, 2016. At the end of the S corporation's short tax year ending on July 17, Nicole's stock basis and at-risk amounts were both zero (she has never had debt basis), and she had a suspended loss of $15,000. In 2017, Nicole made additional capital contributions of $10,000 on February 20 and $7,000 on September 6. When does the PTTP end for CCS? How much loss may Nicole deduct, and what is her basis in the CCS stock at the end of the PTTP?

[28]§465(b)(2)(B). In some circumstances (beyond the scope of this text), shareholders do not create stock basis (or debt basis) for contributions (or shareholder loans to the S corporation) that are funded by nonrecourse loans.

[29]§1377(b)(1)(A). §1377(b) indicates that the PTTP also includes the 120-day period beginning on the date of a determination (not the date of the actual termination) that the corporation's S election had terminated for a previous taxable year.

Answer: For loss deduction purposes, CCS's PTTP ends on September 15, 2017. That date represents (b) in the "later of (a) or (b)" alternative—(a) one year after the last S corporation day, which would be July 17, 2017, or (b) the due date for filing the return for the last year as an S corporation, including extensions, which would be September 15, 2017, assuming CCS extends its tax return. (Note the short tax year S corporation return is due the same time as the short tax year C corporation return.) Nicole may deduct the entire $15,000 suspended loss because her basis at the end of the PTTP and before the loss deduction is $17,000. (That amount is calculated as a carryover basis of $0 on the last S corporation day plus $17,000 capital contributions during the PTTP.) Nicole's basis in CCS stock after the loss deduction is $2,000 ($17,000 basis at the end of the PTTP less the $15,000 loss deduction).

What if: Suppose Nicole made her second capital contribution on October 22 instead of September 6. How much loss can Nicole deduct, and what is her basis in CCS stock at the end of the PTTP?

Answer: The loss deduction is $10,000: Nicole's stock basis at the end of the PTTP and before her loss deduction is only $10,000 because the $7,000 contribution occurred after the end of the PTTP. Nicole's basis in the CCS stock at the end of the PTTP and after the loss deduction is zero ($10,000 basis less $10,000 loss deduction). Her basis then increases to $7,000 on October 22, but the $5,000 suspended loss is lost forever.

Passive Activity Loss Limitation S corporation shareholders, just like partners, are subject to the **passive activity loss rules.** There are no differences in the application of these rules for S corporations; the definition of a passive activity, the tests for material participation, the income and loss baskets, and the passive activity loss carryover rules described in Chapter 9 are exactly the same. Thus, as in partnerships, the passive activity loss rules limit the ability of S corporation shareholders to deduct losses unless they are involved in actively managing the business.[30]

Example 11-17

What if: Suppose in 2017, CCS incurred an ordinary business loss and allocated the loss equally to its shareholders. Assuming Nicole, Sarah, and Chance all had adequate stock basis and at-risk amounts to absorb the losses, which of the three shareholders would be least likely to deduct the loss due to the passive activity limitation rules?

Answer: Chance. Because he is not actively involved in managing CCS's business activities, any loss allocated to him is a passive activity loss.

Self-Employment Income

You might wonder whether an S corporation shareholder's allocable share of ordinary business income (loss) is classified as self-employment income for tax purposes. The answer is no, even when the shareholder actively works for the S corporation.[31]

When a shareholder does work as an employee of and receive a salary from an S corporation, the S corporation treats this salary payment like that made to any other employee: For Social Security taxes, it withholds 6.2% of the shareholder's salary or wages subject to the wage limitation, and for Medicare taxes, it withholds 1.45% of the shareholder's salary or wages up to $200,000 and 2.35% (1.45% plus .9% additional Medicare tax) on any shareholder salary or wages above $200,000.[32] In addition, the S corporation must pay its portion of the Social Security tax (6.2% of the shareholder's salary or wages) and Medicare tax (1.45% of the shareholder's salary or wages, regardless of the amount of salary or wages).

Because of this stark contrast in the treatment of ordinary business income and shareholder salaries, S corporation shareholders may desire to avoid payroll taxes by

[30]§469.

[31]Rev. Rul. 59-221, 1955-1 CB 225.

[32]Although employee liability for the .9% additional Medicare tax varies based on filing status ($250,000 combined salary or wages for married filing joint; $125,000 salary or wages for married filing separate; $200,000 salary or wages for all other taxpayers), employers are required to withhold the additional .9% Medicare tax on salary or wages above $200,000 irrespective of the taxpayer's filing status.

limiting or even eliminating their salary payments. However, if they work as employees, they are required to pay themselves a reasonable salary for the services they perform. If they pay themselves an unreasonably low salary, the IRS may attempt to reclassify some or all of the S corporation's ordinary business income as shareholder salary!

TAXES IN THE REAL WORLD S Corporation Salary in Question

In 2011, *The Wall Street Journal* reported that over the past 15 years when executive pay skyrocketed, the salaries of S corporation owners declined from 52 percent of the corporation's income in 1995 to 39 percent of the corporation's income in 2007. Over the same period, S corporation income doubled, while S corporation owner salary increased only 26 percent to an average salary of $38,400. Why the low pay? To avoid payroll taxes on salary, of course. The IRS, however, is wise to this strategy and has made this issue a top priority in auditing S corporations. In a recent 8th Circuit Court case, *Watson P.C. v. U.S.*, the IRS argued that the $24,000 salary to a 20-year CPA/S corporation owner was far too low. In this case, Mr. Watson received a $24,000 salary for his work for his CPA firm while receiving profit distributions of $203,651 and $175,470 from his S corporation in 2003 and 2004, respectively. The IRS contended that Mr. Watson's true pay was $91,044 for each year—and the 8th Circuit Court agreed with the IRS and district court, ruling that Mr. Watson owed extra tax plus interest and penalties. Factors indicating that Mr. Watson's salary was too low included the following: he was an exceedingly qualified accountant with an advanced degree and 20 years of experience; he worked 35 to 45 hours per week as a primary earner in a reputable firm, which had earnings much greater than comparable firms; the firm had significant gross earnings; and his salary was unreasonably low compared to other accountants and to the distributions he received.

Source: Watson, P.C. v. U.S. (8 Cir., 2012) 109 AFTR 2d 2012-1059; Laura Saunders, "The IRS Targets Income Tricks," *WSJ.com*, January 22, 2011.

3.8% Net Investment Income Tax

Just like partners in a partnership, S corporation shareholders are subject to the 3.8 percent Net Investment Income tax on their share of an S corporation's gross income from interest, dividends, annuities, royalties, rents, a trade or business that is a passive activity or a trade or business of trading financial instruments or commodities, and any net gain from disposing of property (other than property held in a trade or business in which the Net Investment Income tax does not apply), less any allowable deductions from these items.[33,34] Likewise, any gain from the sale of S corporation stock (or distributions in excess of basis) is subject to the Net Investment Income tax to the extent it is allocable to assets held by the S corporation that would have generated a net gain subject to the Net Investment Income tax if all S corporation assets were sold at fair market value.[35]

Fringe Benefits

True to their hybrid status, S corporations are treated in part like C corporations and in part like partnerships with respect to tax deductions for qualifying employee fringe benefits.[36] For shareholder-employees who own 2 percent or less of the entity, the S corporation receives C corporation tax treatment. That is, it gets a tax deduction for qualifying fringe benefits, and the benefits are nontaxable to *all* employees. For

[33]Interest, dividend, annuity, royalty, and rent income derived in the *ordinary* course of a trade or business that is not passive and does not involve financial instrument or commodity trading is exempt from the Net Investment Income tax.

[34]The tax imposed is 3.8 percent of the lesser of (a) net investment income or (b) the excess of modified adjusted gross income over $250,000 for married-joint filers and surviving spouses, $125,000 for married separate filers, and $200,000 for other taxpayers. Modified adjusted gross income equals adjusted gross income increased by income excluded under the foreign earned income exclusion less any disallowed deductions associated with the foreign earned income exclusion.

[35]See Prop. Reg. §1.1411-7.

[36]Qualifying fringe benefits are nontaxable to the employee. Other fringe benefits (nonqualifying) are taxed as compensation to employees.

shareholder-employees who own more than 2 percent of the S corporation, it receives partnership treatment.[37] That is, it gets a tax deduction, but the otherwise qualifying fringe benefits are taxable to the more than 2 percent shareholder-employees.[38]

Fringe benefits taxable to this group include employer-provided health insurance[39] (§106), group-term life insurance (§79), meals and lodging provided for the convenience of the employer (§119), and benefits provided under a cafeteria plan (§125). Examples of benefits that are nontaxable to more than 2 percent shareholder-employees (and partners in a partnership) include employee achievement awards (§74), qualified group legal services plans (§120), educational assistance programs (§127), dependent care assistance programs (§129), no-additional-cost services (§132), qualified employee discounts (§132), working condition fringe benefits (§132), *de minimis* fringe benefits (§132), on-premises athletic facilities (§132), and medical savings accounts (§220).

DISTRIBUTIONS

LO 11-5

S corporations face special rules when accounting for distributions (operating distributions of cash or other property and liquidating distributions).[40]

Operating Distributions

The rules for determining the shareholder-level tax consequences of operating distributions depend on the S corporation's history; specifically whether, at the time of the distribution, it has accumulated *earnings and profits* from a previous year as a C corporation. (See Chapter 7 for a discussion of C corporation earnings and profits.) We consider both situations—with and without accumulated earnings and profits.

S Corporation with No C Corporation Accumulated Earnings and Profits

Two sets of historical circumstances could apply here: (1) An entity may have been an S corporation since inception, or (2) it may have been converted from a C corporation but does not have C corporation accumulated earnings and profits at the time of the distribution. In both cases, as long as there are no C corporation accumulated earnings and profits, the rules for accounting for the distribution are very similar to those applicable to distributions to partners. That is, shareholder distributions are tax-free to the extent of the shareholders' stock basis (determined after increasing the stock basis for income allocations for the year[41]). If a distribution exceeds the shareholder's stock basis, the shareholder has a capital gain equal to the excess distribution amount.

Example 11-18

What if: Suppose CCS has been an S corporation since its inception. On June 1, 2017, CCS distributed $30,000 to Nicole. Her basis in her CCS stock on January 1, 2017, was $20,000. For 2017, Nicole was allocated $15,000 of ordinary income from CCS and no separately stated items. What is the amount and character of income Nicole recognizes on the distribution, and what is her basis in her CCS stock after the distribution?

Answer: Nicole has $0 income from the distribution and $5,000 basis in stock after the distribution ($35,000 − $30,000). Her stock basis for determining the taxability of the distribution was $35,000, or her beginning basis of $20,000 plus the $15,000 income allocation for the year (which is taxable to Nicole).

(continued on page 11-18)

[37]§1372(a).

[38]The §318 attribution rules apply (see Chapter 7) for purposes of determining who is a more than 2 percent shareholder.

[39]Note, however, that more than 2 percent shareholders are allowed to deduct their insurance costs as *for* AGI deductions [§162(l)].

[40]The §302 stock redemption rules that determine whether a distribution in redemption of a shareholder's stock should be treated as a distribution or a sale or exchange apply to both C corporations and S corporations. See discussion on redemptions in Chapter 7.

[41]§1368(d).

THE KEY FACTS

Cash Operating Distributions for S Corporations

- For S corporations without E&P: Distributions are tax-free to the extent of the shareholder's stock basis. If a distribution exceeds the shareholder's stock basis, the shareholder has a capital gain equal to the excess distribution amount.
- For S corporations with E&P: Distributions are deemed to be paid from (1) the AAA account (tax-free to the extent of basis and taxed as capital gain thereafter), (2) existing accumulated E&P (taxable as dividends), and (3) the shareholder's remaining basis in the S corporation stock, if any (tax-free to the extent of basis and taxed as capital gain thereafter).

What if: Assume the same facts except that CCS distributed $40,000 to Nicole rather than $30,000. What is the amount and character of income Nicole recognizes on the distribution, and what is her basis in her CCS stock after the distribution?

Answer: Nicole has a $5,000 long-term capital gain (she has held her CCS stock more than one year) and $0 basis in her stock (the distribution reduced her stock basis to $0).

What if: Suppose CCS began in 2014 as a C corporation and elected to be taxed as an S corporation in its second year of operations. In 2014, it distributed all its earnings and profits as a dividend, so it did not have any earnings and profits at the end of 2014. In 2015, it distributed $30,000 to Nicole when her basis in her stock was $35,000. What is the amount and character of income she recognizes on the distribution, and what is her basis in her CCS stock after the distribution?

Answer: Nicole has $0 income on the distribution and $5,000 basis in stock after the distribution ($35,000 − $30,000). Because CCS did not have C corporation earnings and profits at the time of the distribution, her outcome is the same as if CCS had been taxed as an S corporation since inception.

S Corporations with C Corporation Accumulated Earnings and Profits

When an S corporation has accumulated earnings and profits (E&P) from prior C corporation years, the distribution rules are a bit more complex. These rules are designed to ensure that shareholders cannot avoid the dividend tax on dividend distributions out of C corporation accumulated E&P by simply electing S corporation status and then distributing the accumulated E&P. For S corporations in this situation, the tax laws require the corporation to maintain an **accumulated adjustments account (AAA)** to determine the taxability of S corporate distributions. The AAA represents the cumulative income or losses *for the period the corporation has been an S corporation.* It is calculated as:

The beginning of year AAA balance
+ Separately stated income/gain items (excluding tax-exempt income)
+ Ordinary income
− Separately stated losses and deductions
− Ordinary losses
− Nondeductible expenses that are not capital expenditures (except deductions related to generating tax-exempt income)
− Distributions out of AAA[42]
= End of year AAA balance

Unlike a shareholder's stock basis, the AAA may have a negative balance. However, the *reduction for distributions* may not cause the AAA to go negative or to become more negative. Also, unlike stock basis, the AAA is a corporate-level account rather than a shareholder-specific account.

Example 11-19

CCS was originally formed as a C corporation and reported 2014 taxable income (and earnings and profits) of $40,000 (see Exhibit 11-2). Effective the beginning of 2015, it elected to be taxed as an S corporation. In 2015, CCS reported $249,000 of overall income (including separately stated items—see Exhibit 11-2). What is the amount of CCS's AAA for 2015 before considering the effects of distributions?

[42]If the current year income and loss items net to make a negative adjustment to the AAA, the net negative adjustments from these items is made to the AAA *after* any AAA reductions for distributions (i.e., the reduction in AAA for distributions is made before the net negative adjustment for current year income and loss items). §1368(e)(1)(C).

Answer: $249,000, computed as follows:

Description	Amount	Explanation
(1) Separately stated income	$ 9,000	$6,000 interest income + $3,000 dividend (see Exhibit 11-2).
(2) Ordinary business income	240,000	Example 11-11.
AAA before distributions	$249,000	(1) + (2).

What if: Assume that during 2015, CCS distributed $300,000 to its shareholders. What is CCS's AAA at the end of 2015?

Answer: AAA is $0, because the distribution cannot cause AAA to be negative.

What if: Instead of reporting $249,000 of income during 2015, assume that during 2015 CCS reported an ordinary business loss of $45,000, a separately stated charitable contribution of $5,000, and a $6,000 distribution to its shareholders. What is CCS's AAA at the end of 2015?

Answer: AAA is negative $50,000. CCS decreases its AAA by the $45,000 business loss and the $5,000 charitable contribution. AAA before distributions is negative $50,000. CCS does not decrease AAA by the $6,000 distribution because the distribution cannot cause AAA to be negative or make it more negative.

S corporation distributions are deemed to be paid from the following sources in the order listed:[43]

1. The AAA account (to the extent it has a positive balance).[44]
2. Existing accumulated earnings and profits from years when the corporation operated as a C corporation.
3. The shareholder's stock basis.[45]

S corporation distributions from the AAA (the most common distributions) are treated the same as distributions when the S corporation does not have E&P. They are nontaxable to the extent of the shareholder's basis, and they create capital gains if they exceed the shareholder's stock basis. If an S corporation makes a distribution from accumulated E&P, the distribution is taxable to shareholders as a dividend. (See Chapter 7 for the calculation of corporate E&P.) Once an S corporation's accumulated E&P is fully distributed, the remaining distributions reduce the shareholder's remaining basis in the S corporation stock (if any) and are nontaxable. Any excess distributions are treated as capital gain.

[43]S corporations may elect to have distributions treated as being first paid out of existing accumulated earnings and profits from C corporation years to avoid the excess net passive income tax. We discuss the excess net passive income tax later in the chapter.

[44]Prior to 1983, S corporations' shareholders were taxed on undistributed taxable income as a deemed distribution. This undistributed income is referred to as *previously taxable income (PTI)*. For S corporations with PTI, distributions are considered to be paid out of PTI (if there is any remaining that has not been distributed) after any distributions out of their AAA. These distributions are also nontaxable to the extent of basis and reduce both the shareholder's basis and PTI.

[45]Technically, the distributions come from the Other Adjustments Account (OAA) and then any remaining shareholder equity accounts (e.g., common stock, paid-in capital). The OAA starts at zero at the S corporation's inception, is increased for tax-exempt income, and is decreased by expenses related to tax-exempt income, any federal taxes paid that are attributable to a C corporation tax year, and any S corporate distributions after the AAA and accumulated E&P have been reduced to zero. As with the AAA, the reduction for distributions may not cause the OAA to go negative or to increase a negative balance. Because from the shareholder's perspective distributions out of the OAA and equity accounts both reduce the shareholder's stock basis, we do not discuss the OAA or other equity accounts in detail.

Example 11-20

What if: Assume at the end of 2015, before considering distributions, CCS's AAA was $24,000 and its accumulated E&P from 2014 was $40,000. Also assume Nicole's basis in her CCS stock is $80,000. If CCS distributes $60,000 on July 1 ($20,000 to each shareholder), what is the amount and character of income Nicole must recognize on her $20,000 distribution, and what is her stock basis in CCS after the distribution?

Answer: $12,000 dividend income and $72,000 stock basis after the distribution, computed as follows:

Description	Amount	Explanation
(1) Total distribution	$60,000	
(2) CCS's AAA beginning balance	24,000	
(3) Distribution from AAA	24,000	Lesser of (1) or (2).
(4) Distribution in excess of AAA	36,000	(1) − (3).
(5) Nicole's share of AAA distribution	8,000	(3) × 1/3 (nontaxable reduction of stock basis).
(6) Nicole's beginning stock basis	80,000	
(7) Nicole's ending stock basis	**72,000**	(6) − (5).
(8) CCS's E&P balance	40,000	
(9) Dividend distribution (from E&P)	36,000	Lesser of (4) or (8).
Nicole's share of dividend	**12,000**	(9) × 1/3.

Property Distributions At times, S corporations distribute appreciated property to their shareholders. When they do so, S corporations recognize gain as though they had sold the appreciated property for its fair market value just prior to the distribution.[46] (This rule contrasts with the partnership provisions for property distributions but is consistent with the C corporation rules.) Shareholders who receive the distributed property recognize their distributive share of the deemed gain and increase their stock basis accordingly. On the other hand, S corporations do not recognize losses on distributions of property whose value has declined.

For the shareholder, the amount of a property distribution is the fair market value of the property received (minus any liabilities the shareholder assumes on the distribution). The rules we described above apply in determining the extent to which the amount of the distribution is a tax-free reduction of basis, a capital gain for a distribution in excess of basis, or a taxable dividend to the shareholder.[47] (See the rules for the taxability of distributions for S corporations with and without C corporation accumulated earnings and profits.) Shareholders take a fair market value basis in the property received in the distribution.

Example 11-21

What if: Assume that at the end of 2016, CCS distributes long-term capital gain property (fair market value of $24,000, basis of $15,000) to each shareholder (aggregate property distribution of $72,000 with an aggregate basis of $45,000). At the time of the distribution, CCS has no corporate E&P and Nicole has a basis of $10,000 in her CCS stock. How much gain, if any, does CCS recognize on the distribution? How much income does Nicole recognize as a result of the distribution?

[46]§311(b). In addition, the S corporation may incur entity-level tax if the distributed property had built-in gains related to when the corporation converted to an S corporation. We discuss the built-in gains tax later in the chapter.

[47]Note that while S corporation shareholders reduce their stock basis by the fair market value of the property received, partners receiving property distributions from partnerships generally reduce the basis in their partnership interests by the adjusted basis of the distributed property.

Answer: CCS recognizes $27,000 of long-term capital gain and Nicole recognizes $14,000 of long-term capital gain, computed as follows:

Description	Amount	Explanation
(1) FMV of distributed property	$72,000	
(2) CCS's basis in distributed property	45,000	
(3) CCS's LTCG gain on distribution	**27,000**	(1) − (2).
(4) Nicole's share of LTCG from CCS	9,000	(3) × 1/3.
(5) Nicole's stock basis after gain allocation	19,000	$10,000 beginning basis + (4).
(6) Distribution to Nicole	24,000	(1) × 1/3.
(7) Nicole's stock basis after distribution	0	(5) − (6) limited to $0.
(8) LTCG to Nicole on distribution in excess of stock basis	5,000	(6) in excess of (5).
Nicole's total LTCG on distribution	**14,000**	(4) + (8).

THE KEY FACTS

Property Distributions

- S corporations recognize gains but not losses when they distribute property to their shareholders.
- For shareholders, the amount of the distribution is the fair market value of the property received (minus any liabilities the shareholder assumes on the distribution).
- The rules for determining the taxability of property distributions at the shareholder level are the same as those for cash distributions.
- Shareholders take a fair market value basis in the property received in the distribution.

Post-Termination Transition Period Distributions Recall the special tax rules relating to suspended losses at the S corporation termination date. Similarly, §1371(e) provides for special treatment of any S corporation distribution *in cash* after an S election termination and during the post-termination transition period (PTTP). Such cash distributions are tax-free to the extent they do not exceed the corporation's AAA balance and the individual shareholder's basis in the stock.

The PTTP for post-termination distributions is generally the same as the PTTP for deducting suspended losses, discussed above. For determining the taxability of distributions, the PTTP generally begins on the day after the last day of the corporation's last taxable year as an S corporation; it ends on the later of (a) one year after the last S corporation day or (b) the due date for filing the return for the last year as an S corporation (including extensions).[48]

Liquidating Distributions

Liquidating distributions of a shareholder interest in an S corporation follow corporate tax rules rather than partnership rules. For a complete liquidation of the S corporation, the rules under §§331 and 336 (discussed in Chapter 8) govern the tax consequences. S corporations generally recognize gain *or* loss on each asset they distribute in liquidation (recall that S corporations recognize gain but not loss on operating distributions of noncash property). These gains and losses are allocated to the S corporation shareholders, increasing or decreasing their stock basis. In general, shareholders recognize gain on the distribution if the value of the property exceeds their stock basis; they recognize loss if their stock basis exceeds the value of the property.

Example 11-22

What if: Assume that at the end of 2017, CCS liquidates by distributing long-term capital gain property (fair market value of $20,000, basis of $12,000) to each shareholder (aggregate property distribution of $60,000 with an aggregate basis of $36,000). At the time of the distribution, CCS has no corporate E&P and Nicole has a basis of $25,000 in her CCS stock. How much gain or loss, if any, does CCS recognize on the distribution? How much gain or loss does Nicole recognize as a result of the distribution?

(continued on page 11-22)

[48]§1377(b)(1)(A). For purposes of the taxability of distributions, the PTTP also includes: (1) the 120-day period that begins on the date of any determination (court decision, closing agreement, and so on) from an IRS audit that occurs after the S election has been terminated and adjusts the corporation's income, loss, or deduction during the S period; and (2) the 120-day period beginning on the date of a determination (not the date of the actual termination) that the corporation's S election had terminated for a previous taxable year [§1377(b)(1)(B) and (C)].

Answer: CCS recognizes $24,000 of long-term capital gain and Nicole recognizes $5,000 of net long-term capital loss, computed as follows:

Description	Amount	Explanation
(1) FMV of distributed property	$60,000	
(2) CCS's basis in distributed property	36,000	
(3) CCS's LTCG gain on distribution	24,000	(1) − (2).
(4) Nicole's share of LTCG from CCS	8,000	(3) × 1/3.
(5) Nicole's stock basis after gain allocation	33,000	$25,000 beginning basis + (4).
(6) Distribution to Nicole	20,000	(1) × 1/3.
(7) Nicole's LTCL on liquidating distribution	(13,000)	(6) − (5).
Nicole's NLTCL on distribution	(5,000)	(4) + (7).

LO 11-6

S CORPORATION TAXES AND FILING REQUIREMENTS

Although S corporations are flow-through entities generally not subject to tax, three potential taxes apply to S corporations that previously operated as C corporations: the **built-in gains tax, excess net passive income tax,** and **LIFO recapture tax.** The built-in gains tax is the most common of the three and will be our starting point.

THE KEY FACTS

Built-in Gains Tax

- The built-in gains tax applies only to S corporations that have a net unrealized built-in gain at the time they converted from C corporations and that recognize net built-in gains during the built-in gains tax recognition period.
- The net unrealized built-in gain represents the net gain (if any) that the corporation would recognize if it sold each asset at its fair market value.
- Recognized built-in gains (losses) include the gain (loss) for any asset sold during the year [limited to the unrealized gain (loss) for the specific asset at the S conversion date].
- The net recognized built-in gain is limited to the lesser of (a) the net recognized built-in gain less any NOL and capital loss carryovers, (b) the net unrealized built-in gain not yet recognized, and (c) the corporation's taxable income for the year using the C corporation tax rules.

Built-in Gains Tax

Congress enacted the built-in gains tax to prevent C corporations from avoiding corporate taxes on sales of appreciated property by electing S corporation status. The built-in gains tax applies only to an S corporation that has a *net unrealized built-in gain* at the time it converts from a C corporation. Further, for the built-in gains tax to apply, the S corporation, must subsequently *recognize* net built-in gains during the **built-in gains tax recognition period.**[49] The built-in gains tax recognition period is the first 5 years a corporation operates as an S corporation for asset sales in 2011 through 2014 (first 7 years for asset sales in 2009 and 2010; first 10 years for asset sales in other years).[50]

What exactly is a **net unrealized built-in gain?** Measured on the first day of the corporation's first year as an S corporation, it represents the net gain (if any) the corporation would recognize if it sold each asset at its fair market value. For this purpose, we net gains and losses to determine whether indeed there is a net unrealized gain at the conversion date. The corporation's accounts receivable and accounts payable are also part of the computation: Under the cash method, accounts receivable are gain items and accounts payable are loss items. If the S corporation has a net unrealized gain at conversion, it must compute its net recognized built-in gains for each tax year during the applicable built-in gain recognition period to determine whether it is liable for the built-in gains tax.

Example 11-23

CCS uses the accrual method of accounting. At the beginning of 2015, it owned the following assets (but leased its manufacturing facility and its equipment):

Asset	Fair Market Value (FMV)	Adjusted Basis (AB)	Built-in Gain (Loss)
Cash	$ 80,000	$ 80,000	$ 0
Accounts receivable	20,000	20,000	0
Inventory (FIFO)	130,000	110,000	20,000
Land	100,000	125,000	(25,000)
Totals	$330,000	$335,000	$ (5,000)

[49]§1374.

[50]At press time, the built-in gains tax recognition period is scheduled to expand to 10 years for asset sales in 2015.

What is CCS's net unrealized built-in gain when it converts to an S corporation on January 1, 2015?

Answer: CCS has $0 net unrealized built-in gain. It has a net unrealized built-in loss, so it is not subject to the built-in gains tax.

What if: Suppose CCS's inventory is valued at $155,000 instead of $130,000. What is its net unrealized built-in gain?

Answer: It is $20,000. The $45,000 built-in gain on the inventory is netted against the $25,000 built-in loss on the land.

Recognized built-in gains for an S corporation year include (1) the gain for any asset sold during the year (limited to the unrealized gain for the specific asset at the S conversion date) and (2) any income received during the current year attributable to pre-S corporation years (such as collection on accounts receivable for cash-method S corporations). Likewise, recognized built-in losses for a year include (1) the loss for any asset sold during the year (limited to the unrealized loss for the specific asset at the S conversion date) and (2) any deduction during the current year attributable to pre-S corporation years (such as deductions for accounts payable for cash-method S corporations). The net recognized built-in gain for any year is limited to *the least of:*

1. The net of the recognized built-in gains and losses for the year.
2. The net unrealized built-in gains as of the S election date less the net recognized built-in gains in previous years. (This restriction ensures the net recognized built-in gains during the recognition period do not exceed the net unrealized gain at the S conversion date.)
3. The corporation's taxable income for the year, using the C corporation tax rules exclusive of the dividends received deduction and net operating loss deduction.

If taxable income limits the net recognized built-in gain for any year [item (3) above], we treat the excess gain as a recognized built-in gain in the next tax year, *but only if* the next tax year is in the built-in gains tax recognition period. After the net recognized built-in gain to be taxed has been determined using the limitations above, it should be reduced by any net operating loss (NOL) or capital loss carryovers from prior C corporation years.[51] This base is then multiplied by the highest corporate tax rate (currently 35 percent) to determine the built-in gains tax. The built-in gains tax paid by the S corporation is allocated to the shareholders as a loss. The character of the allocated loss (ordinary, capital, §1231) depends on the nature of assets that give rise to the built-in gain tax. Specifically, the loss is allocated proportionately among the character of the recognized built-in gains resulting in the tax.[52] For planning purposes, it is important to consider when to recognize built-in losses to reduce the S corporation's exposure to the built-in gains tax. That is, the S corporation could seek to recognize built-in losses in years with recognized built-in gains, in order to avoid the built-in gains tax.

Example 11-24

What if: Suppose CCS had a net unrealized built-in gain of $20,000. In addition to other transactions in 2015, CCS sold inventory it owned at the beginning of the year; that inventory had built-in gain at the beginning of the year of $40,000 (FMV $150,000; cost basis $110,000). If CCS had been a C corporation in 2015, its taxable income would have been $200,000. How much built-in gains tax must CCS pay in 2015?

Answer: It must pay $7,000 ($20,000 × 35%) in built-in gains tax. CCS must pay a 35 percent tax on the least of (a) $40,000 (recognized built-in gain on inventory), (b) $20,000 (initial net unrealized gain), and (c) $200,000 (taxable income computed as if CCS was a C corporation for 2015). It will reduce the amount of ordinary business income it would otherwise allocate to its shareholders by $7,000—the amount of the built-in gains tax—because the entire amount of the tax is due to inventory sales.

What if: Assume the same facts as above (an initial net unrealized gain of $20,000) except CCS sold two assets that had built-in gains at the time CCS became an S corporation. CCS sold a capital

(continued on page 11-24)

[51]Capital loss carryovers only reduce built-in gains that are capital gains.

[52]§1366(f)(2).

asset with a built-in gain of $10,000 and inventory with a built-in gain of $40,000. CCS would still pay a $7,000 built-in gains tax. This tax would be allocated as a loss to its shareholders. What is the character of the $7,000 loss?

Answer: It is a $1,400 capital loss [$7,000 × (10,000 capital gain/$50,000 total recognized built in gain)] and a $5,600 ordinary loss [$7,000 × ($40,000 ordinary income from inventory sale/$50,000 total recognized built-in gain)].

What if: Assume that in addition to the initial facts in the example, CCS also had a net operating loss from 2014 (the year it operated as a C corporation) of $15,000. How much built-in gains tax will CCS have to pay in 2015?

Answer: It will pay $1,750 ($5,000 × 35%). CCS is allowed to offset $15,000 of the $20,000 recognized portion of the initial net unrealized gain by its $15,000 net operating loss carryover from 2014.

What if: Suppose CCS had a net unrealized built-in gain of $20,000. In addition to other transactions in 2015, CCS sold inventory it owned at the beginning of the year; that inventory had built-in gain at the beginning of the year of $40,000 (FMV $150,000; AB $110,000). If CCS had been a C corporation in 2015, its taxable income would have been $4,000. How much built-in gains tax would CCS have to pay in 2015?

Answer: $1,400 ($4,000 × 35%). CCS must pay a 35 percent tax on the least of (a) $40,000 (recognized built-in gain on inventory), (b) $20,000 (initial net unrealized gain), and (c) $4,000 (taxable income computed as if CCS was a C corporation for 2015). Because the tax was limited due to the taxable income limitation, the excess gain of $16,000 ($20,000 recognized built-in gain minus $4,000 gain on which CCS paid tax) is treated as a recognized built-in gain in 2016.

THE KEY FACTS

Excess Net Passive Income Tax

- The excess net passive income tax applies only to S corporations that previously operated as C corporations *and* at the end of the year have accumulated earnings and profits from a prior C corporation year.
- This tax applies when passive investment income exceeds 25 percent of gross receipts.
- Passive investment income includes royalties, rents, dividends, interest (including tax-exempt interest), and annuities.

Excess Net Passive Income Tax

If an S corporation previously operated as a C corporation *and* has accumulated earnings and profits at the end of the year from a prior C corporation year, it may be subject to the *excess net passive income tax*.[53] Congress created this tax to encourage S corporations to distribute their accumulated earnings and profits from prior C corporation years. It does not apply to S corporations that never operated as a C corporation, or to S corporations without earnings and profits from prior C corporation years.

The tax is levied on the S corporation's **excess net passive income,** computed as follows:

$$\text{Excess net passive income} = \text{Net passive investment income} \times \frac{\text{Passive investment income} - (25\% \times \text{Gross receipts})}{\text{Passive investment income}}$$

Note that an S corporation has excess net passive income only when (1) it has net passive investment income and (2) its passive investment income exceeds 25 percent of its gross receipts. For purposes of determining excess net passive income, *gross receipts* is the total amount of revenues (including passive investment income) received or accrued under the corporation's accounting method, and not reduced by returns, allowances, cost of goods sold, or deductions. Gross receipts include net capital gains from the sales or exchanges of capital assets and gains from the sales or exchanges of stock or securities (losses do not offset gains). As defined previously in the chapter, passive investment income includes royalties, rents, dividends, interest (including tax-exempt interest), annuities, and gains from the sales or exchanges of stock or securities. **Net passive investment income** is passive investment income decreased by any expenses connected with producing that income.

The excess net passive income tax is imposed on excess net passive income at the highest corporate tax rate (currently 35 percent). For purposes of computing the tax, excess net passive income is limited to taxable income computed as if the corporation were a C corporation (excluding net operating losses). The formula for determining the tax is:

$$\text{Excess net passive income tax} = 35\% \times \text{Excess net passive income}$$

[53]§1375.

Each item of passive investment income that flows through to shareholders is reduced by an allocable share of the excess net passive income tax. The portion of the tax allocated to each item of passive investment income is the amount of the item divided by the total amount of passive investment income.

The IRS may waive the excess net passive income tax in some circumstances, for example if the S corporation determined in good faith it did not have accumulated earnings and profits at the end of the tax year and within a reasonable period distributed earnings and profits it identified later.[54]

Example 11-25

During 2015 CCS reported the following income (see Exhibit 11-2):

	2015 (S Corporation)
Sales revenue	$520,000
Cost of goods sold	(115,000)
Salary to owners Nicole and Sarah	(90,000)
Employee wages	(50,000)
Depreciation expense	(20,000)
Miscellaneous expenses	(5,000)
Interest income	6,000
Dividend income	3,000
Overall net income	$249,000

What are CCS's passive investment income, net passive investment income, and gross receipts for 2015?

Answer: The amounts are $9,000 passive income ($6,000 interest income + $3,000 dividends); $9,000 net passive investment income (because CCS has $0 expenses in producing passive investment income); and $529,000 gross receipts ($520,000 sales revenue + $3,000 dividends + $6,000 interest income).

What is CCS's excess net passive income tax in 2015, if any?

Answer: Zero. CCS has accumulated earnings and profits from 2014 (see Exhibit 11-2), but it owes zero excess net passive income tax because its passive investment income is less than 25 percent of its gross receipts [$9,000 < $132,250 ($529,000 × 25%)].

What if: Suppose CCS has passive investment income of $180,000 ($120,000 interest + $60,000 dividends), expenses associated with the passive investment income of $20,000, and gross receipts of $700,000 ($520,000 + $180,000). Also, if CCS were a C corporation, its taxable income would have been $249,000; assume it had accumulated earnings and profits of $40,000. What is CCS's excess net passive income tax, if any? What effect, if any, would the excess net passive income tax have on interest and dividends allocated to the shareholders?

Answer: The base for the tax is limited to the lesser of (a) excess net passive income of $4,444 [($180,000 passive investment income minus $20,000 expenses associated with passive investment income) × ($180,000 − $700,000 × 25%)/$180,000] or $249,000 (CCS's taxable income if it had been a C corporation). Thus, the base for the tax is limited to $4,444, and the tax is $1,555 (35% × $4,444).

Interest and dividends allocated to the shareholders will be reduced by the excess net passive income tax. The interest income allocated to shareholders will be reduced by $1,037 [$1,555 tax × ($120,000 interest/$180,000 total passive investment income)], and dividend income will be reduced by $518 [$1,555 tax × ($60,000 dividend/$180,000)].

What if: Suppose CCS has passive investment income of $180,000, expenses associated with the passive investment income of $20,000, and gross receipts of $700,000 ($520,000 + $180,000). Also, if CCS were a C corporation, its taxable income would have been $2,000; assume it had accumulated earnings and profits of $40,000. What is CCS's excess net passive income tax, if any?

(continued on page 11-26)

[54]§1375(d).

Answer: The base for the tax is limited to the lesser of (a) excess net passive investment income of $4,444 [$160,000 × ($180,000 − 25% × $700,000)/$180,000] or (b) $2,000 (taxable income if CCS had been a C corporation). So the tax is $700 (35% × $2,000).

Remember, if an S corporation pays the net excess passive income tax for three years in a row, its S election will be terminated by the excess passive income test.

LIFO Recapture Tax

C corporations that elect S corporation status and use the LIFO inventory method are subject to the *LIFO recapture tax*. The purpose of this tax is to prevent former C corporations from avoiding built-in gains tax by using the LIFO method of accounting for their inventories. Specifically, a LIFO method corporation would not recognize built-in gains unless the corporation invaded its LIFO layers during the built-in gains tax recognition period.

The LIFO recapture tax requires the C corporation to include the **LIFO recapture amount** in its gross income in the last year it operates as a C corporation.[55] That amount equals the excess of the inventory basis computed using the FIFO method over the inventory basis computed using the LIFO method at the end of the corporation's last tax year as a C corporation. In addition to being included in gross income (and taxed at the C corporation's marginal tax rate), the LIFO recapture amount also increases the corporation's adjusted basis in its inventory at the time it converts to an S corporation. The basis increase reduces the amount of net unrealized gain subject to the built-in gains tax.

The corporation pays the LIFO recapture tax (technically a C corporation tax) in four annual installments. The first installment is due on or before the due date (not including extensions) of the corporation's last *C corporation* tax return. The final three annual installments are due each year on or before the due date (not including extensions) of the *S corporation*'s tax return.

The LIFO recapture tax does not preclude the S corporation from using the LIFO method, but it obviously does accelerate the gain attributable to differences between LIFO and FIFO for inventory existing at the time of the S corporation election.

Example 11-26

What if: Suppose CCS uses the LIFO method of accounting for its inventory. Assume that at the end of 2014, the basis of the inventory under the LIFO method was $90,000. Under the FIFO method, the basis of the inventory would have been $100,000. Finally, regular taxable income in 2014 was $40,000. What amount of LIFO recapture tax must CCS pay?

Answer: CCS must pay $1,500 [($100,000 FIFO inventory basis − $90,000 LIFO inventory basis) × 15 percent]. The 15 percent tax rate is the marginal rate at which the additional $10,000 of income would have been taxed in 2014 under the corporate tax rate schedule. CCS would increase its basis in its inventory by $10,000 to $100,000 as of the end of 2014, its last year as a C corporation. This would reduce the unrealized net built-in gain on the inventory.

When is CCS required to pay the tax?

Answer: CCS must pay $375 by March 16, 2015; March 15, 2016; March 15, 2017; and March 15, 2018. March 15 is the annual tax return due date without extensions (see discussion below).

What if: Assume the same facts as above except CCS's regular taxable income from 2014 was $700,000. What amount of LIFO recapture tax is CCS required to pay?

Answer: CCS must pay $3,400 [($100,000 FIFO inventory basis − $90,000 LIFO inventory basis) × 34 percent]. The 34 percent tax rate is the marginal rate at which the additional $10,000 of income would have been taxed in 2014 under the corporate tax rate schedule. CCS must pay $850 by March 16, 2015; March 15, 2016; March 15, 2017; and March 15, 2018.

[55]§1363(d).

EXHIBIT 11-3, PART I CCS's Form 1120S, page 1

Form **1120S**

Department of the Treasury
Internal Revenue Service

U.S. Income Tax Return for an S Corporation

▶ **Do not file this form unless the corporation has filed or is attaching Form 2553 to elect to be an S corporation.**
▶ **Information about Form 1120S and its separate instructions is at *www.irs.gov/form1120s*.**

OMB No. 1545-0123

2014

For calendar year 2014 or tax year beginning , 2014, ending , 20

A S election effective date **January 1, 2015**	Name **Color Comfort Sheets**	D Employer identification number **24-4681012**
B Business activity code number (see instructions) **314000**	TYPE OR PRINT — Number, street, and room or suite no. If a P.O. box, see instructions. **375 East 450 South**	E Date incorporated **January 1, 2014**
C Check if Sch. M-3 attached ☐	City or town, state or province, country, and ZIP or foreign postal code **Salt Lake City, UT 84103**	F Total assets (see instructions) $ **370,000**

G Is the corporation electing to be an S corporation beginning with this tax year? ☑ Yes ☐ No If "Yes," attach Form 2553 if not already filed

H Check if: **(1)** ☐ Final return **(2)** ☐ Name change **(3)** ☐ Address change **(4)** ☐ Amended return **(5)** ☐ S election termination or revocation

I Enter the number of shareholders who were shareholders during any part of the tax year ▶

Caution. Include **only** trade or business income and expenses on lines 1a through 21. See the instructions for more information.

Income	1a	Gross receipts or sales	1a	520,000		
	b	Returns and allowances	1b			
	c	Balance. Subtract line 1b from line 1a			1c	520,000
	2	Cost of goods sold (attach Form 1125-A)			2	115,000
	3	Gross profit. Subtract line 2 from line 1c			3	405,000
	4	Net gain (loss) from Form 4797, line 17 (attach Form 4797)			4	
	5	Other income (loss) (see instructions—attach statement)			5	
	6	**Total income (loss).** Add lines 3 through 5 ▶			6	405,000
Deductions (see instructions for limitations)	7	Compensation of officers (see instructions—attach Form 1125-E)			7	90,000
	8	Salaries and wages (less employment credits)			8	50,000
	9	Repairs and maintenance			9	
	10	Bad debts			10	
	11	Rents			11	
	12	Taxes and licenses			12	
	13	Interest			13	
	14	Depreciation not claimed on Form 1125-A or elsewhere on return (attach Form 4562)			14	20,000
	15	Depletion **(Do not deduct oil and gas depletion.)**			15	
	16	Advertising			16	
	17	Pension, profit-sharing, etc., plans			17	
	18	Employee benefit programs			18	
	19	Other deductions (attach statement)			19	5,000
	20	**Total deductions.** Add lines 7 through 19 ▶			20	165,000
	21	**Ordinary business income (loss).** Subtract line 20 from line 6			21	240,000
Tax and Payments	22a	Excess net passive income or LIFO recapture tax (see instructions)	22a			
	b	Tax from Schedule D (Form 1120S)	22b			
	c	Add lines 22a and 22b (see instructions for additional taxes)			22c	
	23a	2014 estimated tax payments and 2013 overpayment credited to 2014	23a			
	b	Tax deposited with Form 7004	23b			
	c	Credit for federal tax paid on fuels (attach Form 4136)	23c			
	d	Add lines 23a through 23c			23d	
	24	Estimated tax penalty (see instructions). Check if Form 2220 is attached ▶ ☐			24	
	25	**Amount owed.** If line 23d is smaller than the total of lines 22c and 24, enter amount owed			25	
	26	**Overpayment.** If line 23d is larger than the total of lines 22c and 24, enter amount overpaid			26	
	27	Enter amount from line 26 **Credited to 2015 estimated tax** ▶		**Refunded** ▶	27	

Sign Here

Under penalties of perjury, I declare that I have examined this return, including accompanying schedules and statements, and to the best of my knowledge and belief, it is true, correct, and complete. Declaration of preparer (other than taxpayer) is based on all information of which preparer has any knowledge.

▶ Signature of officer Date ▶ Title

May the IRS discuss this return with the preparer shown below (see instructions)? ☐ Yes ☐ No

Paid Preparer Use Only

Print/Type preparer's name	Preparer's signature	Date	Check ☐ if self-employed	PTIN
Firm's name ▶			Firm's EIN ▶	
Firm's address ▶			Phone no.	

For Paperwork Reduction Act Notice, see separate instructions. Cat. No. 11510H Form **1120S** (2014)

EXHIBIT 11-3, PART II CCS's 2015 partial Schedule K (on 2014 forms)

Schedule K		Shareholders' Pro Rata Share Items				Total amount
Income (Loss)	1	Ordinary business income (loss) (page 1, line 21)			1	240,000
	2	Net rental real estate income (loss) (attach Form 8825)			2	
	3a	Other gross rental income (loss)	3a			
	b	Expenses from other rental activities (attach statement)	3b			
	c	Other net rental income (loss). Subtract line 3b from line 3a			3c	
	4	Interest income			4	6,000
	5	Dividends: **a** Ordinary dividends			5a	3,000
		b Qualified dividends	5b	3,000		
	6	Royalties			6	
	7	Net short-term capital gain (loss) (attach Schedule D (Form 1120S))			7	
	8a	Net long-term capital gain (loss) (attach Schedule D (Form 1120S))			8a	
	b	Collectibles (28%) gain (loss)	8b			
	c	Unrecaptured section 1250 gain (attach statement)	8c			
	9	Net section 1231 gain (loss) (attach Form 4797)			9	
	10	Other income (loss) (see instructions) . . Type ▶			10	

> **THE KEY FACTS**
>
> **S Corporation Estimated Tax and Filing Requirements**
>
> - S corporations owing the built-in gains tax or excess net passive investment income tax (but not the LIFO recapture tax) must pay the tax based on estimated tax rules similar to C corporations.
> - S corporations file Form 1120S to report the results of their operations for the year. They request a filing extension on Form 7004.

Estimated Taxes

The estimated tax rules for S corporations generally follow the rules for C corporations: S corporations with a federal income tax liability of $500 or more due to the built-in gains tax or excess net passive income tax must estimate their tax liability for the year and pay it in four quarterly estimated installments. However, an S corporation is not required to make estimated tax payments for the LIFO recapture tax.[56]

Filing Requirements

S corporations are required to file **Form 1120S,** U.S. Income Tax Return for an S Corporation, with the IRS by the 15th day of the third month after the S corporation's year end (e.g., March 15 for a calendar-year-end S corporation). S corporations may receive an automatic, six-month extension by filing **Form 7004** with the IRS prior to the original due date of the return.[57] Thus, the extended due date of an S corporation tax return is generally September 15.

Exhibit 11-3 presents page 1 of CCS's Form 1120S (for its 2015 activities), CCS's partial Schedule K, and Nicole's K-1 (we use 2014 forms because 2015 forms were unavailable at the time this book went to press). Note the K-1 from the 1120S is different from the K-1 of the 1065. In contrast to the 1065 Schedule K-1, the 1120S Schedule K-1 does not report self-employment income, does not allocate entity-level debt to shareholders, and does not allow for shareholders to have profit-and-loss-sharing ratios that are different from shareholders' percentage of stock ownership.

[56]Rev. Proc. 94-61, IRB 1994-38,56.

[57]Under §6698, late-filing penalties apply if the S corporation fails to file by the normal or extended due date for the return.

EXHIBIT 11-3, PART III Nicole's 2015 Schedule K-1 (on 2014 forms)

671113

☐ Final K-1 ☐ Amended K-1 OMB No. 1545-0123

Schedule K-1 (Form 1120S) **2014**
Department of the Treasury
Internal Revenue Service

For calendar year 2014, or tax year beginning ________, 2014 ending ________, 20____

Shareholder's Share of Income, Deductions, Credits, etc. ▶ See back of form and separate instructions.

Part I Information About the Corporation

A Corporation's employer identification number
24-4681012

B Corporation's name, address, city, state, and ZIP code

Color Comfort Sheets
375 East 450 South
Salt Lake City, UT 84103

C IRS Center where corporation filed return
Ogden, UT

Part II Information About the Shareholder

D Shareholder's identifying number
123-45-8976

E Shareholder's name, address, city, state, and ZIP code

Nicole Johnson
811 East 8320 South
Sandy, UT 84094

F Shareholder's percentage of stock ownership for tax year . . . . 33.333333 %

For IRS Use Only

Part III Shareholder's Share of Current Year Income, Deductions, Credits, and Other Items

1	Ordinary business income (loss) 80,000	13	Credits	
2	Net rental real estate income (loss)			
3	Other net rental income (loss)			
4	Interest income 2,000			
5a	Ordinary dividends 1,000			
5b	Qualified dividends 1,000	14	Foreign transactions	
6	Royalties			
7	Net short-term capital gain (loss)			
8a	Net long-term capital gain (loss)			
8b	Collectibles (28%) gain (loss)			
8c	Unrecaptured section 1250 gain			
9	Net section 1231 gain (loss)			
10	Other income (loss)	15	Alternative minimum tax (AMT) items	
11	Section 179 deduction	16	Items affecting shareholder basis	
12	Other deductions			
		17	Other information	
		A		3,000

* See attached statement for additional information.

For Paperwork Reduction Act Notice, see Instructions for Form 1120S. IRS.gov/form1120s Cat. No. 11520D **Schedule K-1 (Form 1120S) 2014**

COMPARING C AND S CORPORATIONS AND PARTNERSHIPS

Exhibit 11-4 compares tax consequences for C corporations, S corporations, and partnerships discussed in this chapter.

EXHIBIT 11-4 Comparison of Tax Consequences for C and S Corporations and Partnerships

Tax Characteristic	C Corporation	S Corporation	Partnership/LLC
Forming or contributing property to an entity	No gain or loss on contribution of appreciated or depreciated property if transferors of property have control (as defined in §351) after transfer.	Same as C corporation.	Same as C and S corporations except no control requirement (§721 applies to partnerships).
Type of owner restrictions	No restrictions	Only individuals who are U.S. citizens or residents, certain trusts, and tax-exempt organizations.	No restrictions
Number of owner restrictions	No restrictions	Limited to 100 shareholders. (Family members and their estates count as one shareholder.)	Must have more than one owner.
Election	Default status if corporation under state law.	Must formally elect to have corporation taxed as S corporation.	Default status if unincorporated and have more than one owner.
Income and loss allocations	Not allocated to shareholders.	Income and loss flow through to owners based on ownership percentages.	Income and loss flow through to owners but may be allocated based on something other than ownership percentages (special allocations).
Entity debt included in stock (or partnership interest) basis	No	Generally no. However, loans made from shareholder to corporation create debt basis. Losses may be deducted to extent of stock basis and then debt basis.	Yes. All entity liabilities are allocated to basis of partners.
Loss limitations	Losses remain at corporate level.	Losses flow through but subject to basis limitation, at-risk limitation, and passive activity limitations.	Same as S corporations.
Self-employment income status of ordinary income allocations	Not applicable	Not self-employment income.	May be self-employment income depending on partner's status.

EXHIBIT 11-4 *(concluded)*

Tax Characteristic	C Corporation	S Corporation	Partnership/LLC
Salary to owners permitted	Yes	Yes	Generally, no. Salary-type payments are guaranteed payments subject to self-employment tax.
Fringe benefits	Can pay nontaxable fringe benefits to owners.	Can pay nontaxable fringe benefits to owners who own 2 percent or less of stock.	May not pay nontaxable fringe benefits to owners.
Operating distributions: owner tax consequences	Taxable as dividends to extent of earnings and profits.	Generally not taxable to extent of owner's basis.	Same as S corporations.
Operating distributions: Entity tax consequences	Gain on distribution of appreciated property; no loss on distribution of depreciated property.	Same as C corporations.	Generally no gain or loss on distribution of property.
Liquidating distributions	Corporation and shareholders generally recognize gain or loss on distributions.	Same as C corporations.	Partnership and partners generally do not recognize gain or loss on liquidating distributions.
Entity-level taxes	Yes, based on corporate tax rate schedule.	Generally no, but may be required to pay built-in gains tax, excess passive investment income tax, or LIFO recapture tax if converting from C to S corporation.	No
Tax year	Last day of any month or 52/53-week year.	Generally calendar year.	Based on tax year of owners.

CONCLUSION

This chapter highlighted the rules specific to S corporations and compared S corporations to C corporations and partnerships. S corporations are a true hybrid entity: They share characteristics with C corporations (the legal protection of a corporation and the tax rules that apply in organizing and liquidating a corporation). They also share characteristics with partnerships (the flow through of the entity's income and loss to its owners, ability to make tax-free distributions to the extent of the owner's basis, and basis calculations for owners).

Although many S corporation attributes follow from the C corporation or partnership rules, several specific attributes unique to S corporations may be particularly important in choosing an entity form or operating an S corporation in a tax-efficient manner. These attributes include unique S corporation taxes, the rules for how debt enters into the basis calculations and loss limitation rules for S corporations, and the rules for how distributions are taxed for S corporations previously operating as C corporations.

Summary

LO 11-1 Describe the requirements and process to elect S corporation status.

- Shareholders of S corporations are able to defer realized gains when they contribute property to the corporation if they have control of the corporation after the contribution.
- S corporations are limited in the type of owners they may have. Only individuals who are U.S. citizens or residents, certain trusts, and certain tax-exempt organizations may be shareholders of S corporations.
- S corporations may have no more than 100 shareholders. For this purpose, family members and their estates count as one shareholder. Family members include a common ancestor and her lineal descendants and their spouses (or former spouses).
- S corporations may have only one class of stock. The stock may have differences in voting rights between shares, but all stock must have identical rights with respect to corporate distribution and liquidation proceeds.
- The S corporation election is made on Form 2553. All shareholders on the date of the election must consent to the election.
- To be effective for the current year, the election must be filed in the prior tax year or on or before the 15th day of the third month of the year. Even then, the election may not be effective in certain circumstances.

LO 11-2 Explain the events that terminate the S corporation election.

- The S corporation election may be voluntarily revoked by shareholders owning more than 50 percent of the S corporation stock. In general, revocations made on or before the 15th day of the third month of the year are effective as of the beginning of the year and revocations after that date are effective on the first day of the next year. Alternatively, the shareholders may choose an alternate date that is not before the revocation election is filed.
- An S corporation's election is automatically terminated on the date it fails to meet the S corporation requirements.
- If an S corporation has earnings and profits from a previous C corporation year, its S election is terminated if it has passive investment income in excess of 25 percent of gross receipts for three consecutive years.
- When an S corporation election is terminated mid-year, the corporation files a short year tax return for the period it was an S corporation and a short year tax return for the portion of the year it was a C corporation. It can allocate the income on a per day basis or it may specifically identify the income to each period.
- When an S corporation's S election is terminated, it may not re-elect S status until the beginning of the fifth tax year after the tax year in which the election was terminated.

LO 11-3 Describe operating issues relating to S corporation accounting periods and methods, and explain income and loss allocations and separately stated items.

- When C corporations elect to become S corporations, all prior accounting methods carry over to the S corporation.
- S corporations are generally required to use a calendar tax year.
- Income and losses are allocated to S corporation shareholders pro rata based on the number of outstanding shares each shareholder owns on each day of the tax year or, with shareholder consent, it may use its normal accounting rules to allocate income and loss to the shareholders.
- S corporations determine their ordinary business income and separately stated items for the year and allocate these to the shareholders during the year.
- Separately stated items are tax items treated differently at the shareholder level than a shareholder's share of ordinary business income.

Explain stock-basis calculations, loss limitations, determination of self-employment income, and fringe benefit rules that apply to S corporation shareholders. LO 11-4

- An S corporation's shareholder's initial basis in her stock is generally the basis of the property contributed to the corporation minus liabilities assumed by the corporation on the contribution.
- S corporation shareholders adjust their stock basis annually. They increase it for (in this order) contributions to the S corporation during the year and the shareholder's share of ordinary business income and separately stated income/gain items. They decrease it for distributions during the year, the shareholder's share of nondeductible expenses, and the shareholder's share of ordinary business loss and separately stated expense/loss items. The basis may not be reduced below zero.
- S corporation shareholders are not allowed to include the S corporation's debt in their stock basis. However, they are allowed to create *debt basis* for the amount of loans they make directly to the S corporation. Debt basis can absorb S corporation losses (see below).
- For an S corporation shareholder to deduct them, S corporation losses must clear three separate hurdles: (1) tax basis limitation in stock (and debt), (2) at-risk amount limitation, and (3) passive activity loss limitation.
- Losses suspended at a particular level remain suspended until the shareholder creates additional tax basis or at-risk amounts, clears the passive loss hurdle, or sells her stock in the S corporation.
- If a shareholder's stock and debt basis is reduced by loss allocations and then increased by subsequent income allocations, the income allocation first increases the debt basis to the debt's outstanding amount before increasing the stock basis.
- When an S corporation's S election is terminated, S shareholders can deduct their share of S corporation losses on the last day of the post-termination transition period as long as the losses are able to clear the three loss limitation hurdles.
- Allocation of ordinary business income is not self-employment income to S corporation shareholders.
- If S corporation shareholders are employees of the corporation, their wages are subject to employment taxes.
- S corporation shareholders are subject to the Net Investment Income tax on their share of an S corporation's gross income from interest, dividends, annuities, royalties, rents, a trade or business that is a passive activity or a trade or business of trading financial instruments or commodities, and generally any net gain from disposing of property, less any allowable deductions from these items.
- Many fringe benefits that are nontaxable to other S corporation employees are taxable to employees who own more than 2 percent of the S corporation.

Apply the tax rules for S corporation operating distributions and liquidating distributions. LO 11-5

- Operating distributions from S corporations without accumulated earnings and profits from C corporation years are nontaxable to the extent of the shareholder's basis and then taxable as capital gain to the extent they exceed the shareholder's stock basis.
- Operating distributions from S corporations with accumulated earnings and profits from C corporation years are a nontaxable reduction in stock basis to the extent of the S corporation's accumulated adjustments account, a dividend to the extent of the corporation's earnings and profits, and then a nontaxable return of capital to the extent of the stock basis. Amounts in excess of the stock basis are capital gain.
- The accumulated adjustments account represents the cumulative income or losses for the period the corporation has been an S corporation.
- When S corporations distribute appreciated property to shareholders they must recognize gain on the distribution (the gain is allocated to the shareholders). When they distribute loss property, they are not allowed to deduct the losses. In either case, the fair market value of the property (reduced by liabilities) is the amount of the distribution to the shareholders.

- When an S election is terminated, cash distributions during the post-termination transition period are tax-free to the shareholder to the extent of the S corporation's accumulated adjustments account and the shareholder's stock basis.
- S corporations making liquidating distributions recognize gain or loss on the distributions. The gains or losses are allocated to the shareholders. The shareholders compare the amount received in the liquidating distribution to their stock basis to determine if they recognize gain or loss on the distributions.

LO 11-6 Describe the taxes that apply to S corporations, estimated tax requirements, and tax return filing requirements.

- S corporations that were formerly C corporations may be required to pay the built-in gains tax. The tax applies if the S corporation had a net unrealized built-in gain at the time it converted to an S corporation. It must pay the tax when it recognizes these net built-in gains during its first five years operating as an S corporation in 2011 through 2014 (first seven years in 2009 and 2010; first ten years in all other years).
- The base for the tax is limited to the least of (1) the net of the recognized built-in gains and losses for the year, (2) the net unrealized built-in gains as of the date of the S election date less the net recognized built-in gains in previous years, and (3) the corporation's taxable income for the year using the C corporation tax rules (excluding the dividends received deduction and NOL deduction). The base is then reduced by any net operating loss (NOL) or capital loss carryovers from prior C corporation years.
- S corporations that were formerly C corporations and have C corporation earnings and profits must pay the excess net passive income tax when their passive investment income exceeds 25 percent of their gross receipts.
- The formula for the tax is 35 percent (the highest corporate tax rate) × (net passive investment income × [passive investment income − (25% × gross receipts)]/passive investment income).
- C corporations that elect to be taxed as S corporations and that use the LIFO method of accounting for inventories must pay the LIFO recapture tax. The tax is the C corporation's marginal tax rate times the excess of the inventory valued under the LIFO method over the inventory valued under the FIFO method at the time the S election became effective. The corporation pays one-quarter of the tax on its final C corporation tax return and the final three installments on its S corporation tax return for the first three years it is an S corporation.
- S corporations that must pay the built-in gains tax or the excess passive income tax generally must pay estimated taxes in four quarterly installments. They are not required to make estimated tax payments for the LIFO recapture tax.
- S corporations file Form 1120S by the 15th day of the third month after the tax year-end (generally March 15).
- S corporations may receive a six-month extension by filing Form 7004.
- On Form 1120S, S corporations report ordinary business income and separately stated items on Schedule K. Each shareholder's portion of items on the Schedule K is reported to the shareholder on her Schedule K-1.

KEY TERMS

accumulated adjustments account (AAA) (11-18)
at-risk amount (11-14)
built-in gains tax (11-22)
built-in gains tax recognition period (11-22)
debt basis (11-13)
earnings and profits (E&P) (11-2)
excess net passive income (11-24)
excess net passive income tax (11-22)
Form 1120S (11-28)
Form 7004 (11-28)
gross receipts (11-6)
LIFO recapture amount (11-26)
LIFO recapture tax (11-22)
net passive investment income (11-24)
net unrealized built-in gain (11-22)
ordinary business income (loss) (11-9)
passive activity loss rules (11-15)
passive investment income (PII) (11-6)
post-termination transition period (PTTP) (11-14)
S corporation (11-2)
separately stated items (11-9)
Subchapter S (11-2)

DISCUSSION QUESTIONS

1. In general terms, how are C corporations different from and similar to S corporations? LO 11-1
2. What are the limitations on the number and type of shareholders an S corporation may have? How are these limitations different from restrictions on the number and type of shareholders C corporations or partnerships may have? LO 11-1
3. Why can't large, publicly traded corporations be treated as S corporations? LO 11-1
4. How do the tax laws treat family members for purposes of limiting the number of owners an S corporation may have? LO 11-1
5. Super Corp. was organized under the laws of the state of Montana. It issued common voting stock and common nonvoting stock to its two shareholders. Is Super Corp. eligible to elect S corporation status? Why or why not? LO 11-1
6. Karen is the sole shareholder of a C corporation she formed last year. If she elects S corporation status this year on February 20, when will the election become effective and why? What if she had made the election on March 20? LO 11-1
7. JB Corporation is a C corporation owned 80 percent by Jacob and 20 percent by Bauer. Jacob would like JB to make an S election but Bauer is opposed to the idea. Can JB elect to be taxed as an S corporation without Bauer's consent? Explain. LO 11-1
8. In what circumstances could a calendar-year C corporation make an election on February 1, year 1, to be taxed as an S corporation in year 1 but not have the election effective until year 2? LO 11-1
9. Theodore, Alvin, and Simon are equal shareholders of Timeless Corp. (an S corporation). Simon wants to terminate the S election, but Theodore and Alvin disagree. Can Simon unilaterally elect to have the S election terminated? If not, what would Simon need to do to have the S election terminated? LO 11-2
10. Juanita is the sole shareholder of Belize Corporation (a calendar-year S corporation). She is considering revoking the S election. It is February 1, year 1. What options does Juanita have for timing the effective date of the S election revocation? LO 11-2
11. Describe the circumstances in which an S election may be involuntarily terminated. LO 11-2
12. Describe a situation in which a former C corporation that elected to be taxed as an S corporation may have its S election automatically terminated, but a similarly situated corporation that has always been taxed as an S corporation would not. LO 11-2
13. When a corporation's S election is terminated mid-year, what options does the corporation have for allocating the annual income between the S corporation short year and the C corporation short year? LO 11-2
14. On June 1, year 1, Jasper Corporation's S election was involuntarily terminated. What is the earliest Jasper may be taxed as an S corporation again? Are there any exceptions to the general rule? Explain. LO 11-2
15. Apple Union (AU), a C corporation with a March 31 year-end, uses the accrual method of accounting. If AU elects to be taxed as an S corporation, what will its year-end and method of accounting be (assuming no special elections)? LO 11-3
16. Compare and contrast the method of allocating income or loss to owners for partnerships and for S corporations. LO 11-3
17. Why must an S corporation report separately stated items to its shareholders? How is the character of a separately stated item determined? How does the S corporation report this information to each shareholder? LO 11-3
18. How do S corporations report dividends they receive? Are they entitled to a dividends received deduction? Why or why not? LO 11-3

LO 11-4 19. Shawn receives stock in an S corporation when it is formed by contributing land with a tax basis of $50,000 and encumbered by a $20,000 mortgage. What is Shawn's initial basis in his S corporation stock?

LO 11-4 20. Why is a shareholder's basis in an S corporate stock adjusted annually?

LO 11-4 21. What adjustments are made annually to a shareholder's basis in S corporation stock and in what order? What impact do these adjustments have on a subsequent sale of stock?

LO 11-4 22. Can a shareholder's basis in S corporation stock ever be adjusted to a negative number? Why or why not?

LO 11-4 23. Describe the three hurdles a taxpayer must pass if he wants to deduct a loss from his share in an S corporation.

LO 11-4 24. Is a shareholder allowed to increase her basis in her S corporation stock by her share of the corporation's liabilities, as partners are able to increase the basis of their ownership interest by their share of partnership liabilities? Explain.

LO 11-4 25. How does a shareholder create *debt basis* in an S corporation? How is debt basis similar and dissimilar to stock basis?

LO 11-4 26. When an S corporation shareholder has suspended losses due to the tax basis or at-risk limitation, is he allowed to deduct the losses if the S corporation status is terminated? Why or why not?

LO 11-4 27. When considering C corporations, the IRS checks to see whether salaries paid are too large. In S corporations, however, it usually must verify that salaries are large enough. Account for this difference.

LO 11-4 28. How does the tax treatment of employee fringe benefits reflect the hybrid nature of the S corporation?

LO 11-4 29. If a corporation has been an S corporation since inception, describe how its operating distributions to its shareholders are taxed to the shareholders.

LO 11-4 30. How are the tax consequences of a cash distribution different from those of a noncash property distribution to both the corporation and the shareholders?

LO 11-5 31. What role does debt basis play in determining the taxability of operating distributions to shareholders?

LO 11-5 32. What does the accumulated adjustments account represent? How is it adjusted year by year? Can it have a negative balance?

LO 11-5 33. If an S corporation with accumulated E&P makes a distribution, from what accounts (and in what order) is the distribution deemed to be paid from?

LO 11-5 34. Under what circumstances could a corporation with earnings and profits make a tax-free distribution to its shareholders after the S election termination?

LO 11-5 35. How do the tax consequences of S corporation liquidating distributions differ from the tax consequences of S corporation operating distributions at both the corporate and shareholder levels?

LO 11-6 36. When is an S corporation required to pay a built-in gains tax?

LO 11-6 37. When is an S corporation required to pay the excess net passive income tax?

LO 11-6 38. Is the LIFO recapture tax a C corporation tax or an S corporation tax? Explain.

LO 11-6 39. When must an S corporation make estimated tax payments?

LO 11-6 40. On what form does an S corporation report its income to the IRS? When is the tax return due? What information does the S corporation provide to shareholders to allow them to complete their tax returns?

LO 11-6 41. Compare and contrast S corporations, C corporations, and partnerships in terms of tax consequences at formation, shareholder restrictions, income allocation, basis calculations, compensation to owners, taxation of distributions, and accounting periods.

PROBLEMS

connect ACCOUNTING

All applicable problems are available with McGraw-Hill's *Connect® Accounting*.

42. Julie wants to create an S corporation called J's Dance Shoes (JDS). Describe how the items below affect her eligibility for an S election. LO 11-1
    a) Because Julie wants all her shareholders to have an equal say in the future of JDS, she gives them equal voting rights and decides shareholders who take a more active role in the firm will have priority in terms of distribution and liquidation rights.
    b) Julie decides to incorporate under the state laws of Utah, since that is where she lives. Once she gets her business up and running, however, she plans on doing extensive business in Mexico.
43. Lucy and Ricky Ricardo live in Los Angeles, California. After they were married, they started a business named ILL Corporation (a C corporation). For state law purposes, the shares of stock in ILL Corp. are listed under Ricky's name only. Ricky signed the Form 2553 electing to have ILL taxed as an S corporation for federal income tax purposes, but Lucy did not sign. Given that California is a community property state, is the S election for ILL Corp. valid? LO 11-1 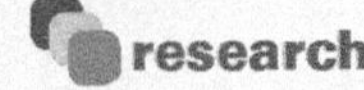
44. Jane has been operating Mansfield Park as a C corporation and decides she would like to make an S election. What is the earliest the election will become effective under each of these alternative scenarios? LO 11-1
    a) Jane is on top of things and makes the election on January 1, 2015.
    b) Jane is mostly on top of things and makes the election on January 15, 2015.
    c) Jane makes the election on February 10, 2015. She needed a little time to convince a C corporation shareholder to sell its stock to a qualifying shareholder. That process took all of January, and she was glad to have it over with.
    d) Jane makes the election on March 14, 2015.
    e) Jane makes the election on February 5, 2015. One of the shareholders refused to consent to the S election. He has since sold his shares (on January 15, 2015) to another shareholder who consented to the election.
45. Missy is one of 100 unrelated shareholders of Dalmatian, an S corporation. She is considering selling her shares. Under the following alternative scenarios, would the S election be terminated? Why or why not? LO 11-2
    a) Missy wants to sell half her shares to a friend, a U.S. citizen, so they can rename their corporation 101 Dalmatians.
    b) Missy's mother's family wants to be involved with the corporation. Missy splits half her shares evenly among her aunt, uncle, grandfather, and two cousins.
    c) Missy sells half her Dalmatian stock to her husband's corporation.
46. Cathy, Heathcliff, and Isabelle are equal shareholders in Wuthering Heights (WH), an S corporation. Heathcliff has decided he would like to terminate the S election. In the following alternative scenarios, indicate whether the termination will occur and indicate the date if applicable (assume no alternative termination dates are selected). LO 11-2
    a) Cathy and Isabelle both decline to agree to the termination. Heathcliff files the termination election anyway on March 14, 2015.
    b) Isabelle agrees with the termination, but Cathy strongly disagrees. The termination is filed on February 16, 2015.

c) The termination seems to be the first thing all three could agree on. They file the election to terminate on March 28, 2015.

d) The termination seems to be the first thing all three could agree on. They file the election to terminate on February 28, 2015.

e) Knowing the other two disagree with the termination, on March 16, 2015, Heathcliff sells one of his 50 shares to his maid, who recently moved back to Bulgaria, her home country.

LO 11-2

47. Assume the following S corporations and gross receipts, passive investment income, and corporate E&P. Will any of these corporations have its S election terminated due to excessive passive income? If so, in what year? All became S corporations at the beginning of year 1.

a) Clarion Corp.

Year	Gross Receipts	Passive Investment Income	Corporate Earnings and Profits
1	$1,353,458	$250,000	$321,300
2	1,230,389	100,000	321,300
3	1,139,394	300,000	230,000
4	1,347,039	350,000	100,000
5	1,500,340	400,000	0

b) Hanson Corp.

Year	Gross Receipts	Passive Investment Income	Corporate Earnings and Profits
1	$1,430,000	$247,000	$138,039
2	700,380	200,000	100,000
3	849,000	190,000	100,000
4	830,000	210,000	80,000
5	1,000,385	257,390	80,000

c) Tiffany Corp.

Year	Gross Receipts	Passive Investment Income	Corporate Earnings and Profits
1	$1,000,458	$250,000	$0
2	703,000	300,480	0
3	800,375	400,370	0
4	900,370	350,470	0
5	670,000	290,377	0

d) Jonas Corp.

Year	Gross Receipts	Passive Investment Income	Corporate Earnings and Profits
1	$1,100,370	$250,000	$500
2	998,000	240,000	400
3	800,350	230,000	300
4	803,000	214,570	200
5	750,000	200,000	100

48. Hughie, Dewey, and Louie are equal shareholders in HDL, an S corporation. HDL's S election terminates under each of the following alternative scenarios. When is the earliest it can again operate as an S corporation? LO 11-2

a) The S election terminates on August 1, year 2, because Louie sells half his shares to his uncle Walt, a citizen and resident of Scotland.

b) The S election terminates effective January 1, year 3, because on August 1, year 2, Hughie and Dewey vote (2 to 1) to terminate the election.

49. Winkin, Blinkin, and Nod are equal shareholders in SleepEZ, an S corporation. In the conditions listed below, how much income should each report from SleepEZ for 2015 under both the daily allocation and the specific identification allocation method? Refer to the following table for the timing of SleepEZ's income. LO 11-3

Period	Income
January 1 through March 15 (74 days)	$125,000
March 16 through December 31 (291 days)	345,500
January 1 through December 31, 2015 (365 days)	$470,500

a) There are no sales of SleepEZ stock during the year.

b) On March 15, 2015, Blinkin sells his shares to Nod.

c) On March 15, 2015, Winkin and Nod each sell their shares to Blinkin.

Use the following information to complete problems 50 and 51:

UpAHill Corporation (an S Corporation)
Income Statement
December 31, Year 1 and Year 2

	Year 1	Year 2
Sales revenue	$175,000	$310,000
Cost of goods sold	(60,000)	(85,000)
Salary to owners Jack and Jill	(40,000)	(50,000)
Employee wages	(15,000)	(20,000)
Depreciation expense	(10,000)	(15,000)
Miscellaneous expenses	(7,500)	(9,000)
Interest income	2,000	2,500
Dividend income	500	1,000
Overall net income	$ 45,000	$134,500

50. Jack and Jill are owners of UpAHill, an S corporation. They own 25 and 75 percent, respectively. LO 11-3

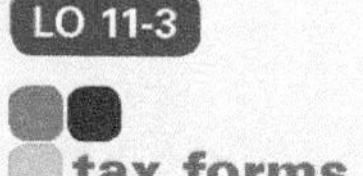

a) What amount of ordinary income and separately stated items are allocated to them for years 1 and 2 based on the information above?

b) Complete UpAHill's Form 1120S, Schedule K, for year 1.

c) Complete Jill's 1120S, Schedule K-1, for year 1.

51. Assume Jack and Jill, 25 and 75 percent shareholders in UpAHill Corporation, have tax bases in their shares at the beginning of year 1 of $24,000 and $56,000, respectively. Also assume no distributions were made. Given the income statement above, what are their tax bases in their shares at the end of year 1? LO 11-3 LO 11-4

Use the following information to complete problems 52 and 53:

Falcons Corporation (an S Corporation)
Income Statement
December 31, Year 1

	Year 1	Year 2
Sales revenue	$300,000	$430,000
Cost of goods sold	(40,000)	(60,000)
Salary to owners Julio and Milania	(40,000)	(80,000)
Employee wages	(25,000)	(50,000)
Depreciation expense	(20,000)	(40,000)
Section 179 expense	(30,000)	(50,000)
Interest income	12,000	22,500
Municipal bond income	1,500	4,000
Government fines	0	(2,000)
Overall net income	$158,500	$174,500
Distributions	$ 30,000	$ 50,000

LO 11-3

tax forms

52. Julio and Milania are owners of Falcons Corporation, an S corporation. They each own 50 percent of Falcons Corporation. In year 1, Julio and Milania received distributions of $20,000 and $10,000, respectively, from Falcons Corporation.
    a) What amount of ordinary income and separately stated items are allocated to them for year 1 based on the information above?
    b) Complete Falcons' Form 1120S, Schedule K for year 1.
    c) Complete Julio's 1120S, Schedule K-1 for year 1.

LO 11-3

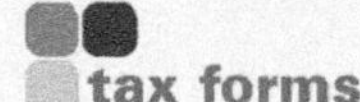

53. In year 2, Julio and Milania received distributions of $20,000 and $30,000, respectively, from Falcons Corporation.
    a) What amount of ordinary income and separately stated items are allocated to them for year 2 based on the information above?
    b) Complete Falcons Form 1120S, Schedule K for year 2.
    c) Complete Milania's 1120S, Schedule K-1 for year 2.

LO 11-4

54. Harry, Hermione, and Ron formed an S corporation called Bumblebore. Harry and Hermione both contributed cash of $25,000 to get things started. Ron was a bit short on cash but had a parcel of land valued at $60,000 (basis of $50,000) that he decided to contribute. The land was encumbered by a $35,000 mortgage. What tax bases will each of the three have in his or her stock of Bumblebore?

LO 11-4

55. Jessica is a one-third owner in Bikes-R-Us, an S corporation that experienced a $45,000 loss this year (year 1). If her stock basis is $10,000 at the beginning of the year, how much of this loss clears the hurdle for deductibility (assume at-risk limitation equals the tax basis limitation)? If she cannot deduct the whole loss, what happens to the remainder? Is she able to deduct her entire loss if she sells her stock at year-end?

LO 11-4

56. Assume the same facts as in the previous problem, except that at the beginning of year 1 Jessica loaned Bikes-R-Us $3,000. In year 2, Bikes-R-Us reported ordinary income of $12,000. What amount is Jessica allowed to deduct in year 1? What are her stock and debt bases in the corporation at the end of year 1? What are her stock and debt bases in the corporation at the end of year 2?

57. Birch Corp., a calendar-year corporation, was formed three years ago by its sole shareholder, James, who has operated it as an S corporation since its inception. Last year, James made a direct loan to Birch Corp. in the amount of $5,000. Birch Corp. has paid the interest on the loan but has not yet paid any principal. (Assume the loan qualifies as debt for tax purposes.) For the year, Birch experienced a $25,000 business loss. What amount of the loss clears the tax basis limitation, and what is James's basis in his Birch Corp. stock and Birch Corp. debt in each of the following alternative scenarios? LO 11-4
   a) At the beginning of the year, James's basis in his Birch Corp. stock was $45,000 and his basis in his Birch Corp. debt was $5,000.
   b) At the beginning of the year, James's basis in his Birch Corp. stock was $8,000 and his basis in his Birch Corp. debt was $5,000.
   c) At the beginning of the year, James's basis in his Birch Corp. stock was $0 and his basis in his Birch Corp. debt was $5,000.

58. Timo is the sole owner of Jazz Inc., an S corporation. On October 31, 2015, Timo executed an unsecured demand promissory note of $15,000 and transferred the note to Jazz (Jazz could require Timo to pay it $15,000 on demand). When Timo transferred the note to Jazz, his tax basis in his Jazz stock was zero. On January 31, 2016, Timo paid the $15,000 to Jazz as required by the promissory note. For the taxable year ending December 31, 2015, Jazz incurred a business loss of $12,000. How much of the loss clears the stock and debt basis hurdles for deductibility? LO 11-4 research

59. Chandra was the sole shareholder of Pet Emporium that was originally formed as an S corporation. When Pet Emporium terminated its S election on August 31, 2014, Chandra had a stock basis and an at-risk amount of zero. Chandra also had a suspended loss from Pet Emporium of $9,000. What amount of the suspended loss is Chandra allowed to deduct, and what is her basis in her Pet Emporium stock at the end of the post-termination transition period under the following alternative scenarios (assume Pet Emporium files for an extension to file its tax returns)? LO 11-4
   a) Chandra makes capital contributions of $7,000 on August 30, 2015, and $4,000 on September 14, 2015.
   b) Chandra makes capital contributions of $5,000 on September 1, 2015, and $5,000 on September 30, 2015.
   c) Chandra makes a capital contribution of $10,000 on August 31, 2015.
   d) Chandra makes a capital contribution of $10,000 on October 1, 2015.

60. Neil owns stock in two S corporations, Blue and Green. He actively participates in the management of Blue but maintains ownership in Green only as a passive investor. Neil has no other business investments. Both Blue and Green anticipate a loss this year, and Neil's basis in his stock of both corporations is zero. All else equal, if Neil plans on making a capital contribution to at least one of the corporations this year, to which firm should he contribute in order to increase his chances of deducting the loss allocated to him from the entity? Why? LO 11-4

61. In the past several years, Shakira had loaned money to Shakira Inc. (an S corporation) to help the corporation keep afloat in a downturn. Her stock basis in the S corporation is now zero, and she had deducted $40,000 in losses that reduced her debt basis from $100,000 to $60,000. Things appear to be turning around this year, and Shakira Inc. repaid Shakira $20,000 of the $100,000 outstanding loan. What is Shakira's income, if any, on the partial loan repayment? LO 11-4

LO 11-4 62. Adam Fleeman, a skilled carpenter, started a home improvement business with Tom Collins, a master plumber. Adam and Tom are concerned about the payroll taxes they will have to pay. Assume they form an S corporation and each earns a salary of $80,000 from the corporation; in addition, they expect their share of business profits to be $60,000 each. How much Social Security tax and Medicare tax (or self-employment tax) will Adam, Tom, and their corporation have to pay on their salary and profits?

planning LO 11-4 63. Using the facts in problem 62, could Adam and Tom lower their payroll tax exposure if they operated their business as a partnership? Why or why not?

LO 11-4 64. This year, Justin B.'s share of S corporation income includes $4,000 of interest income, $5,000 of dividend income, and $40,000 of net income from the corporation's professional service business activity.

a) Assume that Justin B. materially participates in the S corporation. How much of his S corporation income is potentially subject to the Net Investment Income tax?

b) Assume that Justin B. does not materially participate in the S corporation. How much of his S corporation income is potentially subject to the Net Investment Income tax?

LO 11-4 65. Friends Jackie (0.5 percent owner), Jermaine (1 percent owner), Marlon (2 percent owner), Michael (86 percent owner), and Tito (10.5 percent owner) are shareholders in Jackson 5 Inc. (an S corporation). As employees of the company, they each receive health insurance ($10,000 per year benefit), dental insurance ($2,000 per year benefit), and free access to a workout facility located at company headquarters ($500 per year benefit). What are the tax consequences of these benefits for each shareholder and for Jackson 5 Inc.?

LO 11-5 66. Maple Corp., a calendar-year corporation, was formed three years ago by its sole shareholder, Brady, who immediately elected S corporation status. On December 31 of the current year, Maple distributed $30,000 cash to Brady. What is the amount and character of gain Brady must recognize on the distribution in each of the following alternative scenarios?

a) At the time of the distribution, Brady's basis in his Maple Corp. stock was $35,000.

b) At the time of the distribution, Brady's basis in his Maple Corp. stock was $8,000.

c) At the time of the distribution, Brady's basis in his Maple Corp. stock was $0.

LO 11-5 67. Oak Corp., a calendar-year corporation, was formed three years ago by its sole shareholder, Glover, and has always operated as a C corporation. However, at the beginning of this year, Glover made a qualifying S election for Oak Corp., effective January 1. Oak Corp. did not have any C corporation earnings and profits on that date. On June 1, Oak Corp. distributed $15,000 to Glover. What is the amount and character of gain Glover must recognize on the distribution, and what is his basis in his Oak Corp. stock in each of the following alternative scenarios?

a) At the time of the distribution, Glover's basis in his Oak Corp. stock was $35,000.

b) At the time of the distribution, Glover's basis in his Oak Corp. stock was $8,000.

c) At the time of the distribution, Glover's basis in his Oak Corp. stock was $0.

68. Janna has a tax basis of $15,000 in her Mimikaki stock (Mimikaki has been an S corporation since inception). In 2015, Janna was allocated $20,000 of ordinary income from Mimikaki. What is the amount and character of gain she recognizes from end of the year distributions in each of the following alternative scenarios, and what is her stock basis following each distribution? LO 11-5
   a) Mimikaki distributes $10,000 to Janna.
   b) Mimikaki distributes $20,000 to Janna.
   c) Mimikaki distributes $30,000 to Janna.
   d) Mimikaki distributes $40,000 to Janna.
69. Assume the following year 2 income statement for Johnstone Corporation, which was a C corporation in year 1 and elected to be taxed as an S corporation beginning in year 2. Johnstone's earnings and profits at the end of year 1 were $10,000. Marcus is Johnstone's sole shareholder. What is Johnstone's accumulated adjustments account at the end of year 2, and what amount of dividend income does Marcus recognize on the year 2 distribution in each of the following alternative scenarios? LO 11-5

Johnstone Corporation
Income Statement
December 31, Year 2

	Year 2 (S Corporation)
Sales revenue	$150,000
Cost of goods sold	(35,000)
Salary to owners	(60,000)
Employee wages	(50,000)
Depreciation expense	(4,000)
Miscellaneous expenses	(4,000)
Interest income	10,000
Overall net income	$ 7,000

   a) Johnstone distributed $6,000 to Marcus in year 2.
   b) Johnstone distributed $10,000 to Marcus in year 2.
   c) Johnstone distributed $16,000 to Marcus in year 2.
   d) Johnstone distributed $26,000 to Marcus in year 2.
70. At the end of the year, before distributions, Bombay (an S corporation) has an accumulated adjustments account balance of $15,000 and accumulated E&P of $20,000 from a previous year as a C corporation. During the year, Nicolette (a 40 percent shareholder) received a $20,000 distribution (the remaining shareholders received $30,000 in distributions). What is the amount and character of gain Nicolette must recognize from the distribution? What is her basis in her Bombay stock at the end of the year (assume her stock basis is $40,000 after considering her share of Bombay's income for the year but before considering the effects of the distribution)? LO 11-5
71. Pine Corp., a calendar-year corporation, was formed three years ago by its sole shareholder, Connor, who has always operated it as a C corporation. However, at the beginning of this year, Connor made a qualifying S election for Pine Corp., effective January 1. Pine Corp. reported $70,000 of C corporation earnings and profits on the effective date of the S election. This year (its first S corporation LO 11-5

year), Pine reported business income of $50,000. Connor's basis in his Pine Corp. stock at the beginning of the year was $15,000. What is the amount and character of gain Connor must recognize on the following alternative distributions, and what is his basis in his Pine Corp. stock at the end of the year?

a) Connor received a $40,000 distribution from Pine Corp. at the end of the year.

b) Connor received a $60,000 distribution from Pine Corp. at the end of the year.

c) Connor received a $130,000 distribution from Pine Corp. at the end of the year.

d) Connor received a $150,000 distribution from Pine Corp. at the end of the year.

LO 11-5

72. Carolina Corporation, an S corporation, has no corporate E&P from its years as a C corporation. At the end of the year, it distributes a small parcel of land to its sole shareholder, Shadiya. The fair market value of the parcel is $70,000 and its tax basis is $40,000. Shadiya's basis in her stock is $14,000. Assume Carolina Corporation reported zero taxable income before considering the tax consequences of the distribution.

a) What amount of gain or loss, if any, does Carolina Corporation recognize on the distribution?

b) How much gain must Shadiya recognize (if any) as a result of the distribution, what is her basis in her Carolina Corporation stock after the distribution, and what is her basis in the land?

c) What is your answer to part (a) if the fair market value of the land is $25,000 rather than $70,000?

d) What is your answer to part (b) if the fair market value of the land is $25,000 rather than $70,000?

LO 11-5

73. Last year, Miley decided to terminate the S corporation election of her solely owned corporation on October 17, 2014 (effective immediately), in preparation for taking it public. At the time of the election, the corporation had an accumulated adjustments account balance of $150,000 and $450,000 of accumulated E&P from prior C corporation years, and Miley had a basis in her S corporation stock of $135,000. During 2015, Miley's corporation reported $0 taxable income or loss. Also, during 2015 the corporation made distributions to Miley of $80,000 and $60,000. How are these distributions taxed to Miley assuming the following?

a) Both distributions are in cash, and the first was paid on June 15 and the second on November 15.

b) Both distributions are in cash, and the first was paid on June 15 and the second on September 30.

c) The same facts in part (b) except the June 15 distribution was a property (noncash) distribution (fair market value of distributed property equal to basis).

LO 11-6

74. Alabama Corporation, an S corporation, liquidates this year by distributing a parcel of land to its sole shareholder, Mark Ingram. The fair market value of the parcel is $50,000 and its tax basis is $30,000. Mark's basis in his stock is $25,000.

a) What amount of gain or loss, if any, does Alabama Corporation recognize on the distribution?

b) How much gain must Mark recognize (if any) as a result of the distribution and what is his basis in the land?

c) What is your answer to part (a) if the fair market value of the land is $20,000 rather than $50,000?

d) What is your answer to part (b) if the fair market value of the land is $20,000 rather than $50,000?

75. Rivendell Corporation uses the accrual method of accounting and has the following assets as of the end of 2014. Rivendell converted to an S corporation on January 1, 2015. LO 11-6

Asset	Adjusted Basis	FMV
Cash	$ 40,000	$ 40,000
Accounts receivable	30,000	30,000
Inventory	130,000	60,000
Land	100,000	125,000
Totals	$300,000	$255,000

a) What is Rivendell's net unrealized built-in gain at the time it converted to an S corporation?
b) Assuming the land was valued at $200,000, what would be Rivendell's net unrealized gain at the time it converted to an S corporation?
c) Assuming the original land value but that the inventory was valued at $85,000, what would be Rivendell's net unrealized gain at the time it converted to an S corporation?

76. Virginia Corporation is a calendar-year corporation. At the beginning of 2015, its election to be taxed as an S corporation became effective. Virginia Corp.'s balance sheet at the end of 2014 reflected the following assets (it did not have any earnings and profits from its prior years as a C corporation). LO 11-6

Asset	Adjusted Basis	FMV
Cash	$ 20,000	$ 20,000
Accounts receivable	40,000	40,000
Inventory	90,000	200,000
Land	150,000	175,000
Totals	$300,000	$435,000

In 2015, Virginia reported business income of $50,000 (this would have been its taxable income if it were still a C corporation). What is Virginia's built-in gains tax in each of the following alternative scenarios?

a) During 2015, Virginia sold inventory it owned at the beginning of the year for $100,000. The basis of the inventory sold was $55,000.
b) Assume the same facts as part (a), except Virginia had a net operating loss carryover of $24,000 from its time as a C corporation.
c) Assume the same facts as part (a), except that if Virginia were a C corporation, its taxable income would have been $1,500.

77. Tempe Corporation is a calendar-year corporation. At the beginning of 2015, its election to be taxed as an S corporation became effective. Tempe Corp.'s balance sheet at the end of 2014 reflected the following assets (it did not have any earnings and profits from its prior years as a C corporation): LO 11-6

Asset	Adjusted Basis	FMV
Cash	$ 20,000	$ 20,000
Accounts receivable	40,000	40,000
Inventory	160,000	200,000
Land	150,000	120,000
Totals	$370,000	$380,000

Tempe's business income for the year was $40,000 (this would have been its taxable income if it were a C corporation).

a) During 2015, Tempe sold all of the inventory it owned at the beginning of the year for $210,000. What is its built-in gains tax in 2015?

b) Assume the same facts as in part (a), except that if Tempe were a C corporation, its taxable income would have been $7,000. What is its built-in gains tax in 2015?

c) Assume the original facts except the land was valued at $140,000 instead of $120,000. What is Tempe's built-in gains tax in 2015?

LO 11-6

78. Wood Corporation was a C corporation in 2014 but elected to be taxed as an S corporation in 2015. At the end of 2014, its earnings and profits were $15,500. The following table reports Wood's (taxable) income for 2015 (its first year as an S corporation).

Wood Corporation
Income Statement
December 31, 2015

Sales revenue	$150,000
Cost of goods sold	(35,000)
Salary to owners	(60,000)
Employee wages	(50,000)
Depreciation expense	(4,000)
Miscellaneous expenses	(4,000)
Interest income	8,000
Dividend income	2,000
Overall net income	$ 7,000

What is Wood Corporation's excess net passive income tax for 2015?

LO 11-6

79. Calculate Anaheim Corporation's excess net passive income tax in each of the following alternative scenarios:

a) Passive investment income, $100,000; expenses associated with passive investment income, $40,000; gross receipts, $120,000; taxable income if C corporation, $40,000; corporate E&P, $30,000.

b) Passive investment income, $100,000; expenses associated with passive investment income, $70,000; gross receipts, $120,000; taxable income if C corporation, $1,200; corporate E&P, $30,000.

c) Passive investment income, $100,000; expenses associated with passive investment income, $40,000; gross receipts, $120,000; taxable income if C corporation, $40,000; corporate E&P, $0.

LO 11-5 LO 11-6

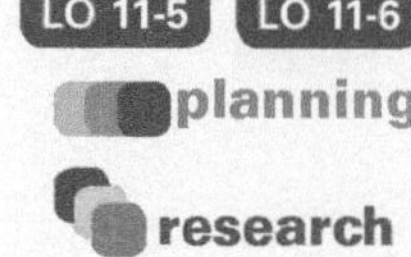

80. Mark is the sole shareholder of Tex Corporation. Mark first formed Tex as a C corporation. However, in an attempt to avoid having Tex's income double taxed, Mark elected S corporation status for Tex several years ago. On December 31, 2015, Tex reports $5,000 of earnings and profits from its years as a C corporation and $50,000 in its accumulated adjustments account from its activities as an S corporation (including its 2015 activities). Mark discovered that for the first time Tex was going to have to pay the excess net passive income tax. Mark wanted to avoid having to pay the tax but he determined the only way to avoid the tax was to eliminate Tex's E&P by the end of 2015. He determined that, because of the distribution ordering rules (AAA first), he would need to have Tex immediately (in 2015) distribute $55,000 to him. This would clear out Tex's

accumulated adjustments account first and then eliminate Tex's C corporation earnings and profits in time to avoid the excess net passive income tax. Mark was not sure Tex could come up with $55,000 of cash or property in time to accomplish his objective. Does Mark have any other options to eliminate Tex's earnings and profits without first distributing the balance in Tex's accumulated adjustments account?

81. Farve Inc. recently elected S corporation status. At the time of the election, the company had $10,000 of accumulated earnings and profits, and a net unrealized gain of $1,000,000 associated with land it had invested in (although some parcels had an unrealized loss). In the next couple of years, most of the income the company expects to generate will be in the form of interest and dividends (approximately $200,000 per year). However, in the future, the company will want to liquidate some of its current holdings in land and possibly reinvest in other parcels. What strategies can you recommend for Farve Inc. to help reduce its potential tax liability as an S corporation? LO 11-6 planning

82. Until the end of year 0, Magic Carpets (MC) was a C corporation with a calendar year. At the beginning of year 1 it elected to be taxed as an S corporation. MC uses the LIFO method to value its inventory. At the end of year 0, under the LIFO method, its inventory of rugs was valued at $150,000. Under the FIFO method, the rugs would have been valued at $170,000. How much LIFO recapture tax must MC pay, and what is the due date of the first payment under the following alternative scenarios? LO 11-6
    a) Magic Carpets' regular taxable income in year 0 was $65,000.
    b) Magic Carpets' regular taxable income in year 0 was $200,000.

COMPREHENSIVE PROBLEMS

All applicable problems are available with McGraw-Hill's *Connect® Accounting.*

83. Knowshon, sole owner of Moreno Inc., is contemplating electing S status for the corporation. Provide recommendations related to Knowshon's election under the following alternative scenarios: planning
    a) At the end of the current year, Moreno Inc. has a net operating loss of $800,000 carryover. Beginning next year, the company expects to return to profitability. Knowshon projects that Moreno will report profits of $400,000, $500,000, and $600,000 over the next three years. What suggestions do you have regarding the timing of the S election? Explain.
    b) How would you answer part (a) if Moreno Inc. had been operating profitably for several years and thus had no net operating loss?
    c) While several of Moreno Inc.'s assets have appreciated in value (to the tune of $2,000,000), the corporation has one property—some land in a newly identified flood zone—that has declined in value by $1,500,000. Knowshon plans on selling the loss property in the next year or two. Assume that Moreno does not have a net operating loss. What suggestions do you have for timing the sale of the flood zone property and why?

84. Barry Potter and Winnie Weasley are considering making an S election on March 1, 2015, for their C corporation, Omniocular. However, first they want to consider the implications of the following information: planning
    - Winnie is a U.S. citizen and resident.
    - Barry is a citizen of the United Kingdom, but a resident of the United States.

- Barry and Winnie each own 50 percent of the voting power in Omniocular. However, Barry's stock provides him with a claim on 60 percent of the Omniocular assets in liquidation.
- Omniocular was formed under Arizona state law, but it plans on eventually conducting some business in Mexico.

a) Is Omniocular eligible to elect S corporation status? If so, when is the election effective?

For the remainder of the problem, assume Omniocular made a valid S election effective January 1, 2015. Barry and Winnie each own 50 percent of the voting power and have equal claim on Omniocular's assets in liquidation. In addition, consider the following information:

- Omniocular reports on a calendar tax year.
- Omniocular's earnings and profits as of December 31, 2014, were $55,000.
- Omniocular's 2014 taxable income was $15,000.
- Omniocular's assets at the end of 2014 are as follows:

Omniocular Assets
December 31, 2014

Asset	Adjusted Basis	FMV
Cash	$ 50,000	$ 50,000
Accounts receivable	20,000	20,000
Investments in stocks and bonds	700,000	700,000
Investment in land	90,000	100,000
Inventory (LIFO)	80,000*	125,000
Equipment	40,000	35,000
Totals	$980,000	$1,030,000

*$110,000 under FIFO accounting.

- On March 31, 2015, Omniocular sold the land for $42,000.
- In 2015, Omniocular sold all the inventory it had on hand at the beginning of the year. This was the only inventory it sold during the year.

Other Income/Expense Items for 2015

Sales revenue	$155,000
Salary to owners	(50,000)
Employee wages	(10,000)
Depreciation expense	(5,000)
Miscellaneous expenses	(1,000)
Gain on sale of machinery	12,000
Interest income	40,000
Dividend income	65,000

- Assume that if Omniocular were a C corporation for 2015, its taxable income would have been $88,500.

b) How much LIFO recapture tax is Omniocular required to pay and when is it due?

c) How much built-in gains tax, if any, is Omniocular required to pay?

d) How much excess net passive income tax, if any, is Omniocular required to pay?

e) Assume Barry's basis in his Omniocular stock was $40,000 on January 1, 2015. What is his stock basis on December 31, 2015?

For the following questions, assume that after electing S corporation status Barry and Winnie had a change of heart and filed an election to terminate Omniocular's S election, effective August 1, 2016.

- In 2016, Omniocular reported the following income/expense items:

	January 1—July 31, 2016 (213 days)	August 1—December 31, 2016 (153 days)	January 1—December 31, 2016
Sales revenue	$80,000	$185,000	$265,000
Cost of goods sold	(40,000)	(20,000)	(60,000)
Salaries to Barry and Winnie	(60,000)	(40,000)	(100,000)
Depreciation expense	(7,000)	(2,000)	(9,000)
Miscellaneous expenses	(4,000)	(3,000)	(7,000)
Interest income	6,000	5,250	11,250
Overall net income (loss)	($25,000)	$125,250	$100,250

f) For tax purposes, how would you recommend Barry and Winnie allocate income between the short S corporation year and the short C corporation year if they would like to minimize double taxation of Omniocular's income?

g) Assume in part (f) that Omniocular allocates income between the short S and C corporation years in a way that minimizes the double taxation of its income. If Barry's stock basis in his Omniocular stock on January 1, 2016, is $50,000, what is his stock basis on December 31, 2016?

h) When is the earliest tax year in which Omniocular can be taxed as an S corporation again?

85. Abigail, Bobby, and Claudia are equal owners in Lafter, an S corporation that was a C corporation several years ago. While Abigail and Bobby actively participate in running the company, Claudia has a separate day job and is a passive owner. Consider the following information for 2015:

- As of January 1, 2015, Abigail, Bobby, and Claudia each have a basis in Lafter stock of $15,000 and a debt basis of $0. On January 1, the stock basis is also the at-risk amount for each shareholder.
- Bobby and Claudia also are passive owners in Aggressive LLC, which allocated business income of $14,000 to each of them in 2015. Neither has any other source of passive income (besides Lafter, for Claudia).
- On March 31, 2015, Abigail lends $5,000 of her own money to Lafter.
- Anticipating the need for basis to deduct a loss, on April 4, 2015, Bobby takes out a $10,000 loan to make a $10,000 contribution to Lafter. Bobby uses his automobile ($12,000 fair market value) as collateral.
- Lafter has an accumulated adjustments account balance of $45,000 as of January 1, 2015.
- Lafter has C corporation earnings and profits of $15,000 as of January 1, 2015.
- During 2015, Lafter reports a business loss of $75,000, computed as follows:

Sales revenue	$90,000
Cost of goods sold	(85,000)
Salary to Abigail	(40,000)
Salary to Bobby	(40,000)
Business (loss)	($75,000)

- Lafter also reported $12,000 of tax-exempt interest income.

a) What amount of Lafter's 2015 business loss of $75,000 are Abigail, Bobby, and Claudia allowed to deduct on their individual tax returns? What are each owner's stock basis and debt basis (if applicable) and each owner's at-risk amount with respect to the investment in Lafter at the end of 2015?

- During 2016, Lafter made several changes to its business approach and reported $18,000 of business income, computed as follows:

Sales revenue	$208,000
Cost of goods sold	(90,000)
Salary to Abigail	(45,000)
Salary to Bobby	(45,000)
Marketing expense	(10,000)
Business income	$ 18,000

- Lafter also reported a long-term capital gain of $24,000 in 2016.
- Lafter made a cash distribution on July 1, 2016, of $20,000 to each shareholder.

b) What amount of gain/income does each shareholder recognize from the cash distribution on July 1, 2016?

tax forms

86. While James Craig and his former classmate Paul Dolittle both studied accounting at school, they ended up pursuing careers in professional cake decorating. Their company, Good to Eat (GTE), specializes in custom-sculpted cakes for weddings, birthdays, and other celebrations. James and Paul formed the business at the beginning of 2015, and each contributed $50,000 in exchange for a 50 percent ownership interest. GTE also borrowed $200,000 from a local bank. Both James and Paul had to personally guarantee the loan. Both owners provide significant services for the business. The following information pertains to GTE's 2015 activities:

- GTE uses the cash method of accounting (for both book and tax purposes) and reports income on a calendar-year basis.
- GTE received $450,000 of sales revenue and reported $210,000 of cost of goods sold (it did not have any ending inventory).
- GTE paid $30,000 compensation to James, $30,000 compensation to Paul, and $40,000 of compensation to other employees (assume these amounts include applicable payroll taxes if any).
- GTE paid $15,000 of rent for a building and equipment, $20,000 for advertising, $14,000 in interest expense, $4,000 for utilities, and $2,000 for supplies.
- GTE contributed $5,000 to charity.
- GTE received a $1,000 qualified dividend from a great stock investment (it owned 2 percent of the corporation distributing the dividend) and it recognized $1,500 in short-term capital gain when it sold some of the stock.
- On December 1, 2015, GTE distributed $20,000 to James and $20,000 to Paul.

Required:

a) Assume James and Paul formed GTE as an S corporation.

- Complete GTE's Form 1120S, page 1; Form 1120 S, Schedule K; and Paul's Form 1120S, Schedule K-1 (note that you should use 2014 tax forms).
- Compute the tax basis of Paul's stock in GTE at the end of 2015.
- What amount of Paul's income from GTE is subject to FICA or self-employment taxes?

- What amount of income, including its character, will Paul recognize on the $20,000 distribution he receives on December 1?
- What amount of tax does GTE pay on the $1,000 dividend it received?

b) Assume James and Paul formed GTE as an LLC.

- Complete GTE's Form 1065, page 1; Form 1065, Schedule K; and Paul's Form 1065, Schedule K-1 (note that you should use 2014 tax forms).
- Compute the tax basis of Paul's ownership interest in GTE at the end of 2015.
- What amount of Paul's income from GTE is subject to FICA or self-employment taxes?
- What amount of income, including its character, will Paul recognize on the $20,000 distribution he receives on December 1?
- What amount of tax does GTE pay on the $1,000 dividend it received?

c) Assume James and Paul formed GTE as a C corporation.

- Complete GTE's Form 1120, page 1 (note that you should use the 2014 tax form).
- Compute the tax basis of Paul's stock in GTE at the end of 2015.
- What amount of Paul's income from GTE is subject to FICA or self-employment taxes?
- What amount of income, including its character, will Paul recognize on the $20,000 distribution he receives on December 1?
- What amount of tax does GTE pay on the $1,000 dividend it received?

chapter

12 State and Local Taxes

Learning Objectives

Upon completing this chapter, you should be able to:

LO 12-1 Describe the primary types of state and local taxes.

LO 12-2 Determine whether a business has sales and use tax nexus and calculate its sales tax withholding responsibilities.

LO 12-3 Identify whether a business has income tax nexus and determine its state income tax liabilities.

© Design Pics/Monkey Business

Storyline Summary

Ken Brody

Location:	Idaho
Status:	Sole owner of Wild West River Runners
Situation:	Ken owns retail stores in Idaho and Wyoming that sell merchandise locally; a Wyoming-based Internet store; and provides services in Idaho, Tennessee, Washington, and Wyoming. He must determine the company's state and local tax liabilities.

Ken Brody owns Wild West River Runners Incorporated (Wild West), an Idaho corporation. Wild West offers both guided white-water rafting adventures and retail sales of related equipment. It provides white-water rafting adventures in Idaho, Tennessee, Washington, and Wyoming; operates retail stores in Idaho and Wyoming; and runs an Internet-based retail store from Wyoming. Wild West's retail stores sell only locally (they never ship merchandise), but the salesclerks often refer customers to the Internet store (www.wildwestriverrunners.com). Most employees are seasonal (i.e., teachers or college students). During the off-season, a few guides make sales visits with Ken and operate the retail stores. Also during the off-season, Ken attends the annual Raft and River show for 10 days each year in Phoenix, Arizona, and travels the country promoting Wild West's guided river adventures.

Wild West's federal taxable income for the current year is $53,289, and it must determine its state and local tax liabilities. Because Wild West operates a multistate business, it must determine its sales and use tax withholding responsibilities and identify the states in which it must file returns. Once it makes these determinations, it must compute taxable income for each relevant state. ■

Like a lot of other businesses, Wild West is a multistate operation. From a business perspective, multistate businesses have access to a larger economic base than those operating in a single state. However, with this economic opportunity comes complexity and additional tax burdens.

LO 12-1

STATE AND LOCAL TAXES

The primary purpose of state and local taxes is to raise revenue to finance state governments. All 50 states and the District of Columbia have some combination of three primary revenue sources: sales and use tax, income or franchise tax, and property tax.[1]

This chapter focuses on sales and use taxes (excise taxes levied on the sale or use of tangible personal property within a state) and taxes based on *net* income (income taxes).[2]

Like federal tax law, state tax law includes the following:

- Legislative law (state constitution and tax code).
- Administrative law (regulations and rulings).
- Judicial law (state and federal tax cases).

While taxpayers deal with a single federal tax code, there are different tax codes for each state in which they are required to pay taxes. This makes state tax research particularly challenging. State tax agencies (such as the California Franchise Tax Board and New York Department of Finance and Taxation) administer the law and promulgate regulations for their particular states.[3] State and federal courts interpret the law when a state's tax authority and taxpayers cannot agree on its interpretation or constitutionality. Because of constitutionality questions, judicial law plays a significantly more important role in state tax law than in federal tax law.

It is impractical, if not impossible, to study each individual state statute in one text. Instead, this chapter addresses the most important state and local tax principles at a conceptual level.

The most important question Wild West, or any other taxpayer, must answer is whether it is subject to a state's taxing regime. The answer depends on the taxpayer's state of commercial domicile and whether the taxpayer has nexus in that state. **Commercial domicile** is the state where a business is headquartered and directs its operations; this location may be different from the place of incorporation.[4] A business must always collect sales tax and pay income tax in the state where it is domiciled. **Nondomiciliary businesses** (businesses not domiciled or headquartered in a state) are subject to tax only where they have nexus. **Nexus** is the sufficient (or minimum) connection between a business and a state that subjects the business to the state's tax system. The requirement for establishing nexus with a state depends on whether the tax is a sales and use tax, an income tax, or a nonincome-based tax. The nexus standard varies because the financial and administrative burdens vary across taxes. Sellers collect sales tax out of administrative convenience, but the sales tax burden belongs to the buyer in most states. In contrast, income tax is both owed and paid by the taxpayer earning the income.

[1]State and local jurisdictions may also tax or levy the following: personal property, capital stock, business licensing, transfer taxes, incorporation, excise, severance, payroll, disability, unemployment, fuel, and telecommunication.

[2]This chapter discusses income and franchise taxes interchangeably. Franchise taxes are imposed for the right to conduct business within a state. Most franchise taxes (such as the California Franchise Tax) are net income based.

[3]A great resource for guidance and forms from specific states can be found on the Federation of Tax Administrator's website: www.taxadmin.org/fta/link/forms.html.

[4]Some companies (e.g., Hewlett-Packard) are incorporated in one state (e.g., Delaware) but domiciled or headquartered in another (e.g., California). These companies pay taxes in both states (although sometimes just a capital stock tax applies in the state of incorporation if there are no activities other than incorporation within a state).

Wild West's commercial domicile is Idaho because it is headquartered there, and it must collect and remit Idaho sales tax and pay Idaho income tax. Yet, as detailed in Exhibit 12-1, it has activities and sales in other states, and therefore must collect sales and use tax and pay income tax in the states in which it has nexus.

EXHIBIT 12-1 Wild West's Activities and Sales by State

Wild West In-State Activities

State	Sale of Goods	Sale of Services	Employees	Property	Commercial Domicile
Arizona	✓				
California	✓				
Colorado	✓				
Idaho	✓	✓	✓	✓	✓
Tennessee	✓	✓	✓	✓	
Washington	✓	✓	✓	✓	
Wyoming	✓	✓	✓	✓	

Wild West Sales

State	Goods	Services	Total
Arizona	$ 89,242	$ 0	$ 89,242
California	132,045	0	132,045
Colorado	75,002	0	75,002
Idaho	167,921	625,003	792,924
Tennessee	45,331	357,061	402,392
Washington	41,982	377,441	419,423
Wyoming	185,249	437,755	623,004
Totals	$736,772	$1,797,260	$2,534,032

When a business sells tangible personal property, which is included in a state's sales tax base, in a state, it must collect and remit the **sales tax** on a periodic basis if it has nexus in that state.[5] Exhibit 12-2 provides an overview of who bears the burden

EXHIBIT 12-2 State Sales and Use Tax Process

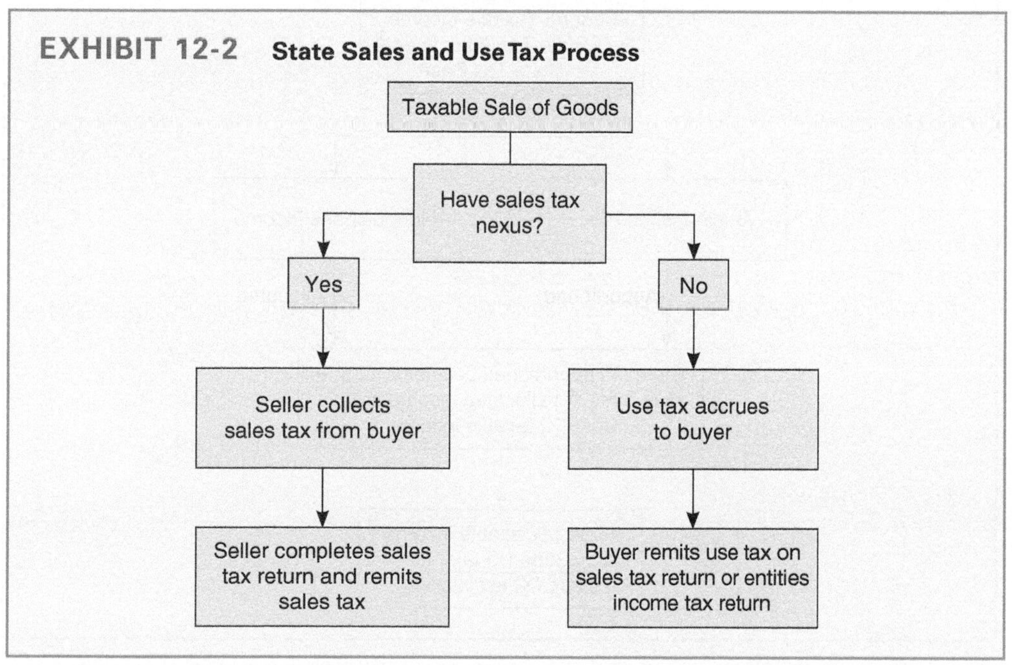

[5]Businesses remit their sales and use tax liability on a monthly, quarterly, or annual basis depending on the size of the liability and the state law thresholds.

(who must pay and who must collect and remit the tax) of sales and use taxes. Sales tax liability accrues on certain sales of tangible personal property within the state. For example, Wild West's Idaho retail store collects sales tax on goods sold in Idaho stores and remits the tax to the Idaho Department of Revenue. **Use tax** liability accrues in the state where purchased property will be used when no sales tax was paid. The use tax only occurs when a seller in one state ships goods to a customer in a different state and the seller is not required to collect the sales tax (the seller does not have sales and use tax nexus in the state in which the goods are shipped to). For example, Colorado customers ordering through Wild West's Wyoming Internet store (which has no Colorado sales tax nexus) are required to accrue and remit the Colorado use tax (usually through their personal income tax returns).[6] Businesses with sales and use tax nexus in a state are responsible for remitting the sales tax even when they fail to collect it.

Businesses engaged in **interstate commerce** must also deal with income-tax related issues. If a business meets certain requirements creating income tax nexus, it may be required to remit income tax to that state. The general process of determining a business's state income tax liability is highlighted in Exhibit 12-3. We compute the **state tax base** by making adjustments to federal taxable income. The adjustments are necessary to account for differences between federal income tax laws and state income tax laws. Then we divide the state tax base into **business income** and **nonbusiness income.** Business income (income from business activities) is subject to **apportionment** among states where nexus exists, based on the extent of the business's activities and property in various states. Nonbusiness income (all income except business income—generally investment income) is subject to **allocation** (assignment) directly to the business's state of commercial domicile. For states in which the business has nexus, state taxable income is the sum of the business income apportioned to that state plus the nonbusiness income allocated to that state. The business computes its state tax liability for that particular state by multiplying state taxable income by the state's tax rate.

Let's now look in more depth at sales and use tax and net income-based taxes, the nexus requirements, and the calculation of each tax.

EXHIBIT 12-3 State Income Tax Process

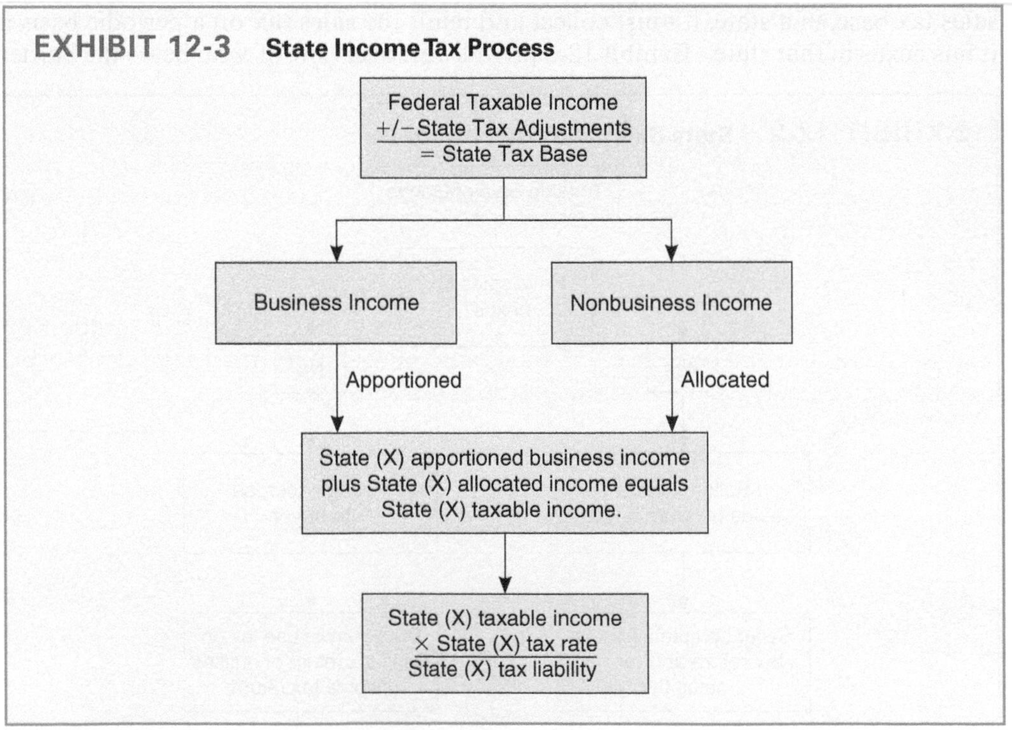

[6]Use tax is paid by individuals completing the use tax liability line on their individual tax return. Alternatively, business entities collecting and remitting sales tax include the use tax on their sales tax return.

SALES AND USE TAXES

LO 12-2

Forty-five states and the District of Columbia impose sales and use taxes; Alaska, Delaware, Montana, New Hampshire, and Oregon do not. Sales tax must be collected on the state's sales tax base. Generally, sales of tangible personal property are subject to the tax. Most states also tax restaurant meals, rental car usage, hotel room rentals (often at higher tax rates than general sales), and some services (which vary by state). Purchases of inventory for resale are exempt from the sales tax. For example, Wild West's rafting equipment purchases for resale are exempt from sales tax because inventory is taxed when sold, but its office furniture purchases for use in the business are taxable because they represent final sales. Taxable items that are included in the sales tax base vary from state to state. Many states exempt food (except prepared restaurant food) because taxing food is considered to be regressive; that is, it imposes a proportionally higher tax burden on lower-income taxpayers that spend a greater proportion of their income on food and other necessities. Most states also exempt sales of real property, intangible property, and services. However, many states are expanding the types of services subject to sales tax in order to increase their sales tax revenue.[7]

THE KEY FACTS

Sales Tax Nexus

- Nexus is the sufficient connection between a business and a state that allows a state to levy a tax on the business.
- Sales tax nexus is established through physical presence of salespeople or property in a state.

TAXES IN THE REAL WORLD Is It Candy or Is It Food?

Items subject to the sales and use tax vary from state to state. Historically, New York taxed the sale of large marshmallows but exempted the sale of small marshmallows. Large and small marshmallows were treated differently because large marshmallows were considered to be candy, which was included in the sales tax base, while small marshmallows were considered to be a food ingredient and therefore excluded from the sales tax base.

The Washington state legislature passed a law subjecting candy to sales taxes in 2010. Any item containing flour is considered a food item, not candy. As a result, Twix bars were exempt while Starburst candy was subject to sales tax. Within the year, Washington voters repealed the tax on candy and the sales tax on bottled water and soda through a ballot initiative.

Sales and Use Tax Nexus

Have you ever wondered why sometimes you pay tax on goods purchased over the Internet and sometimes you don't? The answer is nexus. A business is required to collect sales tax from customers in a state only if it has sales and use tax nexus with that state. For example, if you purchased this textbook from your local campus bookstore you paid tax (unless your state exempts educational materials), but if you purchased the book from Amazon.com you didn't pay sales tax unless you live in Washington and a few other states.[8] Exhibit 12-4 explains Amazon's position on sales tax collection and indicates that they could have a substantial sales tax liability if a state successfully asserts that the position was wrong.

Businesses that establish sales and use tax nexus with a state but fail to properly collect sales tax can create significant liabilities that may need to be disclosed for financial reporting purposes.[9] As a result, understanding when a business has nexus can be extremely important for profitability, business modeling, and compliance.

[7]For example, Connecticut taxes services such as tax preparation.

[8]Items sold by Amazon.com LLC or its subsidiaries and shipped to destinations in the following states are subject to sales tax withholding: Arizona, California, Connecticut, Florida, Georgia, Indiana, Kansas, Kentucky, Maryland, Massachusetts, Minnesota, Nevada, New Jersey, New York, North Carolina, North Dakota, Pennsylvania, Tennessee, Texas, Virginia, Washington, West Virginia, and Wisconsin. http://www.amazon.com/gp/help/customer/display.html/ref=help_search_1-2?ie=UTF8&nodeld=468512&qid=1414725266&sr=1-2, accessed October 30, 2014.

[9]Sales tax liabilities are ASC 450 contingencies. Amazon indicated a $407 million potential liability associated with sales taxes.

EXHIBIT 12-4 Excerpt from Amazon's 2013 Annual Report

From the Form 10-K

We Do Not Collect Sales or Consumption Taxes in Some Jurisdictions

U.S. Supreme Court decisions restrict the imposition of obligations to collect state and local sales taxes with respect to remote sales. However, an increasing number of states have considered or adopted laws that attempt to impose obligations on out-of-state retailers to collect taxes on their behalf. We support a Federal law that would allow states to require sales tax collection under a nationwide system. More than half of our revenue is already earned in jurisdictions where we collect sales tax or its equivalent. A successful assertion by one or more states or foreign countries requiring us to collect taxes where we do not do so could result in substantial tax liabilities, including for past sales, as well as penalties and interest.

Businesses create sales tax nexus (the sufficient connection with a state that requires them to collect sales tax) when they have a *physical presence* in the state. Businesses have a physical presence in the state if (1) salespeople (or independent contractors representing a business) enter a state to obtain sales or if (2) tangible property (such as a company-owned truck making deliveries) is located within a state.[10] One important planning strategy is that, because nexus is determined on a legal entity basis, nexus can be limited by creating a separate legal entity.

The physical presence requirement is a judicial interpretation of the Commerce clause of the U.S. Constitution. Designed to encourage interstate commerce, this clause gives Congress power "To regulate Commerce with foreign Nations, and among the several States, and with the Indian Tribes." Because Congress has never exercised its right, the courts have determined the sales tax nexus threshold. In *National Bellas Hess,* the Supreme Court held that an out-of-state mail-order company did not have a sales tax collection responsibility because it lacked physical presence (even though it mailed catalogs and advertised in the state).[11] The mail-order industry used this decision as a competitive advantage for several decades. In *Quill,* the Supreme Court reaffirmed that out-of-state (nondomiciliary) businesses must have a physical presence in the state before the state may require a business to collect sales tax from in-state customers.[12]

Example 12-1

Wild West sends promotional brochures from Idaho to its Colorado clients. Wild West generated sales of $75,002 to Colorado customers, but it has never collected Colorado sales and use tax or filed a Colorado sales and use tax return. Wild West has neither employees nor property in Colorado. Does it have sales and use tax nexus in Colorado?

Answer: No. Wild West lacks the physical presence required for Colorado nexus and therefore doesn't have Colorado sales and use tax collection responsibility.

What if: Assume that in addition to mailing promotional brochures, Ken visits Colorado on promotional trips. Does Wild West have sales and use tax nexus in Colorado under these circumstances?

Answer: Yes. The physical presence of Wild West's representatives, even for promotional trips, creates Colorado sales and use tax nexus.

[10]*Scripto, Inc. v. Carson, Sherriff,* et al., 362 U.S. 207 (1960). Scripto hired independent salesmen to represent the company in Florida. The Supreme Court held that these salesmen were agents of Scripto, who established the physical presence necessary to create nexus.

[11]*National Bellas Hess, Inc. v. Department of Revenue of the State of Illinois,* 386 U.S. 753 (1967).

[12]*Quill Corporation, Petitioner v. North Dakota,* 504 U.S. 298 (1992).

What if: Assume Wild West's representatives (independent contractors), rather than employees, visit Colorado retail stores to solicit additional sales orders. Does Wild West have sales and use tax nexus in Colorado under these circumstances?

Answer: Yes. The physical presence of Wild West's representatives creates Colorado sales and use tax nexus. Thus, the result is the same for employees or independent contractors.

TAXES IN THE REAL WORLD E-Commerce Sales and Use Tax

Businesses selling products over the Internet have been able to avoid collecting sales and use tax because sales tax nexus is created through physical presence in the state of the buyer. In fact, Internet sales represent billions of dollars annually. As a result, the physical presence nexus standard has cost states substantial sales tax revenue. In 2008, New York implemented the so-called Amazon rule that requires Internet-based retailers to collect and remit New York sales tax if they have in-state affiliates referring customers to websites; the rule is estimated to increase state revenues by $50 million per year. As you might expect, because this law—often referred to as *click-through nexus*—is potentially inconsistent with the Supreme Court's decision in *Quill,* Amazon has filed suit against the state of New York. During 2011, 15 states considered legislation to expand sales and use taxes beyond physical presence. Eight states have now implemented similar laws.

In 2010, Colorado took a different strategy by requiring out-of-state retailers to provide the names, addresses, and taxable purchases of Colorado residents rather than requiring the retailer to collect the sales and use tax. In 2012, this law was determined to be unconstitutional.

Congress is also currently considering three bills that would change the sales and use tax nexus requirements: the Main Street Fairness Act (S. 1452 and H.R. 2701), the Marketplace Equity Act (H.R. 3179), and the Marketplace Fairness Act (S. 1832).

Notwithstanding *Quill* (discussed earlier), it appears that large retailers are losing ground in the nexus fight. In 2011, Amazon agreed to start collecting sales tax in California beginning in 2013. While Amazon originally led the fight against sales and use tax nexus, it has changed its position by announcing it would support a federal law implementing a nationwide system. One question is whether Amazon has changed its policy because it believes the legal position to be unsupportable, because it is changing its business model and no longer seeks the competitive advantage of not collecting sales and use taxes, or whether it wishes to prevent others from entering its markets now that it has established itself as the market leader in online sales. Only time will tell how this story will end.

Sales and Use Tax Liability

Typically, sellers with nexus collect customers' sales tax liabilities. For example, Wild West collects sales tax on river rafting equipment it sells from its retail store but not on river guiding *services* it provides. If the seller doesn't have nexus, then the customer is responsible for remitting a use tax (at the same tax rate as sales tax) to the state in which the property is used. If the buyer is charged a sales tax in another state, the buyer will have a use tax liability for an incremental amount if the state where the property is used has a higher sales tax rate.

Example 12-2

Wild West received $3,500 from a customer named Casey Jarvie residing in Sacramento, California. Of this amount, $500 was for personal rafting equipment shipped to Sacramento, where the sales tax rate is 7.75 percent. The remaining $3,000 was payment for a four-day river raft adventure on the Salmon River in Idaho. Wild West has neither salespeople nor property in California. Does Wild West have a responsibility to collect sales tax from Casey?

Answer: No. Wild West lacks physical presence and does not have sales and use tax nexus in California; therefore, it has no California sales tax collection requirement.

(continued on page 12-8)

Because Wild West has no sales tax collection responsibility, does Casey have a use tax liability to the state of California? If so, in what amount?

Answer: Yes. Casey is responsible for remitting $38.75 of use tax ($500 × 7.75%) on his personal California state income tax return for the purchase and use of the personal rafting equipment in California. He is not required to pay California use tax on the river raft adventure purchase, because Wild West provided out-of-state *services* (no sales tax is due on the services in Idaho either).

What if: If Casey had Wild West hold the goods until he arrived in Burley, Idaho, to pick them up at the time of the trip (assume the sales tax rate in Burley, Idaho, is 6 percent), would Wild West have sales tax collection responsibility? If so, what is the sales tax amount?

Answer: Yes. Because Wild West has physical presence in Idaho, it is required to collect $30 ($500 × 6%) of sales tax and remit it to Idaho. Casey would also have an $8.75 California use tax liability ($38.75 reduced by the $30.00 remitted to Idaho) in this scenario.

ETHICS

Jill is a Virginia resident who purchased $1,500 of personal property items from Overstock.com and other Internet retailers during the year. While completing her personal tax return using a popular software package, Jill was asked to report her online purchases. After entering these purchases, she noticed that $75 of "use tax" was added to her state tax liability. Jill has never paid this in the past. She decided to delete the online purchase information she had previously entered. What do you think of Jill's failure to report her Virginia use tax?

Large companies must often file sales and use tax returns in all 45 states that have sales and use taxes and the District of Columbia.[13] This administrative burden is further complicated by the fact that there are over 7,500 tax jurisdictions (including counties, cities, school districts, and other divisions) imposing sales and use taxes, and several hundred rates change annually at various times during the year.[14] The sales and use tax administrative burden can also be large for small businesses. For example, a local pizzeria that delivers can sometimes be subject to a half-dozen sales tax rates if it crosses city, county, or school district boundaries.

ETHICS

In 2010, Colorado became the first state to require nondomiciliary businesses without sales tax nexus to report all the necessary information to the Colorado Department of Revenue so that Colorado can collect its use tax from its resident individuals and domiciliary businesses. Assume you are responsible for sales tax issues for an online retailer from another state. You believe that the Colorado tax is unconstitutional based on a seminar you attended and the advice of your accounting firm. Would you recommend that your company comply with the Colorado law? Would your opinion change if the court placed an injunction prohibiting the state from enforcing the new law?

[13]Some counties or political subdivisions of states without state sales taxes impose a county or local sales tax (such as Kenal Peninsula Borough in Alaska).

[14]Software companies provide sales and use tax solutions that help companies with the administrative burden. However, they generally fail to indemnify or compensate businesses against errors in their software that result in uncollected sales taxes, which creates a liability for the business.

Example 12-3

Recall from Exhibit 12-1 that Wild West has sales in Arizona, California, Colorado, Idaho, Tennessee, Washington, and Wyoming. Also, recall that it has property and employees in Idaho, Tennessee, Washington, and Wyoming. In which states does Wild West have sales and use tax nexus and, therefore, sales tax collection responsibility?

Answer: Wild West's physical presence of employees and real and personal property creates sales and use tax nexus in Idaho, Tennessee, Washington, and Wyoming.

How much sales and use tax must Wild West remit? Assume the following sales tax rates: Idaho (6.00 percent); Tennessee (9.25 percent); Washington (7.70 percent); and Wyoming (6.00 percent).

Answer: It must remit $28,616, computed as follows:

State	(1) Taxable Sales	(2) Rate	(1) × (2) Sales Tax Due
Idaho	$167,921	6.00%	$10,075
Tennessee	45,331	9.25	4,193
Washington	41,982	7.70	3,233
Wyoming	185,249	6.00	11,115
Totals	$440,483		$28,616

Remember, services are not generally subject to sales tax.

TAXES IN THE REAL WORLD Groupon

Have you ever bought a restaurant meal from Groupon? Did you know there is a tax issue complicating these types of purchases? Suppose you pay $25 for a $50 voucher good at your favorite restaurant. You just scored a great deal. Groupon collects the $25 and pays the restaurant $12.50. You show up, order $50 worth of food, and the server brings you the bill. How much sales tax should the restaurant collect from you on the prepared food (which is a taxable item)? You received $50 worth of prepared foods (one possible tax base), but you only paid $25 (another possible tax base), and the restaurant only received $12.50 (a third possible tax base). What is the nature of the $12.50 retained by Groupon? Did they provide a good (taxable) or a service (not taxable)? Most restaurants currently collect tax on the entire $50 benefit you received. They probably collected too much tax, but only time will tell.

LO 12-3

INCOME TAXES

Forty-six states impose an income tax on corporations; Nevada, South Dakota, Washington, and Wyoming do not.[15] Forty-three states tax income from partnerships and S corporations. This chapter focuses on corporations, but the same principles apply to flow-through entities.[16] Businesses must pay income tax in their state of commercial domicile (where they are headquartered). For example, Wild West is both incorporated and domiciled in Idaho and is therefore subject to Idaho's income tax regime. Until a few decades ago, many businesses believed they were virtually exempt from state income taxes in states other than their state of commercial

[15]Several states (such as California and New York) impose a franchise tax rather than an income tax. Since franchise taxes are generally based upon net income, they are essentially the same as income taxes.

[16]Actually, these states tax individuals, including the income that flows through from partnerships and S corporations (although New Hampshire and Tennessee tax only dividends and interest); Alaska, Florida, Nevada, South Dakota, Texas, Washington, and Wyoming do not.

domicile. However, in *Complete Auto Transit,* the Supreme Court spelled out four criteria for determining whether states can tax nondomiciliary companies and whether the tax imposed is discriminatory against nondomiciliary (domiciled in another state) businesses.[17] First, a sufficient connection or nexus must exist between the state and the business. Second, a state may tax only a fair portion of a business's income. Businesses must be able to divide or apportion income among the states where nexus exists. Third, the tax cannot be constructed to discriminate against nonresident businesses. For example, states cannot impose a higher tax rate on nondomiciliary businesses than domiciliary businesses. Fourth, the taxes paid must be fairly related to the services the state provides. For example, businesses have access to a state's courts, economic base, infrastructure, and so forth.

To determine their state income tax liabilities, businesses must answer the following questions:

- In which states is the business required to file tax returns (in which states does it have nexus)?
- If the business is related to other entities, should it file separate state tax returns, or should it include the activities of the related entities on its state tax returns?
- What adjustments to federal taxable income must the business make to determine state taxable income for each state in which it is required to file?
- If income is taxable (nexus exists) in more than one state, how is income divided among the various states in which the business is required to file tax returns?

Income Tax Nexus

Businesses must file income tax returns in states where they have income tax nexus. However, the determination of whether the business has established income tax nexus within a state depends on the nature of its business's activities in the state. Thus, the rules for determining income tax nexus are not necessarily the same as those for determining sales and use tax nexus. Physical presence creates income tax nexus for service providers, sellers of real property, and businesses licensing intangibles. However, physical presence does not necessarily create nexus for sellers of tangible personal property if their activities within a state are limited to "protected" activities as described by **Public Law 86-272.**

Public Law 86-272 In *Northwestern States Portland Cement,* the Supreme Court allowed Minnesota to tax an Iowa-based business.[18] By passing Public Law 86-272 in response, Congress placed limits on states' power to impose income taxes on nondomiciliary businesses. Businesses are protected from income tax nexus in a particular state if (and only if) *all* the following apply:

- The tax is based on net income (not gross receipts or revenue).
- The taxpayer sells only tangible personal property in that state.
- The taxpayer's in-state activities are limited to solicitation of sales (see next page for the definition of *solicitation*).
- The taxpayer participates in interstate commerce.
- The taxpayer is nondomiciliary.
- The taxpayer approves orders outside the state.
- The taxpayer delivers goods from outside the state.

[17]*Complete Auto Transit, Inc. v. Brady,* 430 U.S. 274 (1977).

[18]*Northwestern Cement Co. v. Minnesota,* 358 U.S. 450 (1959). Widespread alarm from the business community following the case led to an intense lobbying effort, and seven months later Congress enacted Public Law 86-272.

Businesses wishing to avoid nexus for taxes based on net income must sell only tangible personal property within the state.[19] Providing services along with property violates the criteria and creates nexus. For example, providing installation services with tangible personal property exceeds solicitation; in-state activities must be limited to solicitation of sales (discussed further in the next section). Only nondomiciliary companies engaging in interstate commerce are protected. Orders taken or received in-state must be sent out of state—say to regional sales offices or headquarters—for approval. The acceptance of orders in the state, or even the power to accept orders, exceeds the protection of Public Law 86-272 and would result in the business being subject to an income tax. Accepted orders must be delivered by common carrier.[20] Delivery using the seller's truck violates the criteria and creates nexus, except as permitted by state law (New Jersey, Rhode Island, and South Carolina are among the states that list delivery by private vehicles as a protected activity).

Example 12-4

What if: Assume that Wild West sends employees to Oregon to visit retail stores and solicit orders of rafting equipment only. Does the presence of Wild West's employees in Oregon create income tax nexus in Oregon?

Answer: No. The physical presence of representatives soliciting sales of tangible personal property is a protected activity under Public Law 86-272. Thus, no income tax nexus for Wild West in Oregon is created. Note, however, that this physical presence *would* create sales and use tax nexus for any sales generated by Wild West in Oregon, unless they have a valid reseller's certificate.

What if: Assume that Ken or other Wild West sales representatives entered Oregon to solicit customers for both rafting equipment and white-water adventures. Does the presence of Wild West's employees create income tax nexus in Oregon?

Answer: Yes. Solicitation of *services* is not a protected activity under Public Law 86-272. Thus, soliciting services creates income tax nexus for Wild West in Oregon and creates an income tax filing requirement.

Solicitation. Public Law 86-272 protects **solicitation** of tangible personal property but doesn't clearly define solicitation. In *Wisconsin v. Wrigley,* however, the Supreme Court addressed the definition.[21] Wrigley had sales representatives and a regional manager in Wisconsin. Sales meetings were held both in the manager's basement and in a rented hotel space. The sales reps had company cars, a stock of gum, display racks, and promotional literature. The sales activities included handing out promotional materials, free samples, and free display racks; replacing stale gum; handling billing disputes; and occasionally filling orders from their stock of gum and issuing an agency stock check (a bill) to customers. All other orders were sent to Illinois for acceptance and were filled by common carrier from outside the state. The Supreme Court determined the following activities meet the definition of solicitation:

- Soliciting by any form of advertising.
- Carrying samples and promotional materials for display or distribution without charge.
- Passing inquiries or complaints to the home office.
- Checking customer's inventory for reorder.

[19]Taxes calculated based on gross receipts or other bases are not protected by Public Law 86-272.

[20]*Common carrier* is a general term referring to delivery businesses (such as FedEx, UPS, DHL, or USPS).

[21]*Wisconsin Department of Revenue v. William Wrigley, Jr. Co.*, 505 US 214 (1992).

- Maintaining a sample room for two weeks or less; this is known as the **trade show rule.**
- Recruiting, training, and evaluating sales reps using homes or hotels.
- Owning or furnishing personal property and autos used in sales activities.

The Supreme Court held the following activities do *not* meet the definition of solicitation and, therefore, create income tax nexus with the state in which they take place:

- Making repairs.
- Collecting delinquent accounts.
- Investigating creditworthiness.
- Installing or supervising the installation of property.
- Training for employees other than sales reps.
- Approving or accepting orders.
- Repossessing property.
- Securing deposits.
- Maintaining an office other than in-home.

TAXES IN THE REAL WORLD Warranty

One of the biggest current issues for out-of-state retailers is the manner in which warranty work is performed. For example, assume you buy a new laptop for school from an online retailer because the price is unbeatable. Two months later you are told by customer support that the hard drive needs to be replaced and you need to ship the computer to Austin, Texas, for repair. You respond that you cannot go a week without your computer, so the retailer agrees to have a local shop do the repair for you. Many companies wrongly assume that hiring an independent representative to do in-state warranty work does not create nexus. The hiring of the independent contractor is an agency relationship that creates nexus for the out-of-state retailer. The Multistate Tax Commission issued guidance (MTC Nexus Bulletin 95-1) on this issue more than a decade ago—and taxpayers challenging this ruling have lost time and time again. Retailers with these issues quickly find themselves liable for both current and past income as well as sales and use taxes.

If sales reps know and understand these solicitation rules, they can help businesses avoid nexus in states where they want to avoid it.

Example 12-5

Assume that Wild West's Oregon sales reps give store employees free white-water gloves and pass on complaints to the home office. Do these activities create nexus for Wild West in Oregon?

Answer: No. Giving samples (without charge) and passing on complaints, suggestions, and customer inquiries are protected sales activities under Public Law 86-272. Therefore, Wild West is protected from Oregon income tax nexus.

What if: While in Oregon, several sales reps accepted checks for down payments on merchandise, repaired faulty merchandise, and performed credit checks. Do these activities create nexus in Oregon for Wild West?

Answer: Yes. Each of these activities is an unprotected sales activity, and any or all will create Oregon income tax nexus for Wild West.

Does a one-time sales activity violation create income tax nexus? Technically, yes. However, the *Wrigley* decision indicates that *de minimis* (immaterial) activities may be excluded. The determination of whether an activity is *de minimis* is a subjective one, based on relevant facts and circumstances.

Example 12-6

Assume that Wild West's sales reps occasionally investigate creditworthiness and occasionally repossess property in Oregon. Can Wild West avoid income tax nexus?

Answer: Possibly. Wild West must argue that these unprotected activities are *de minimis* because they were not material to its overall operations within Oregon.

Income Tax Nexus for Other Business Types or Nonincome-Based Taxes

Public Law 86-272 does not protect service providers, sellers of real property, or businesses licensing intangibles. Further, it does not protect businesses from nonincome-based taxes. Establishing income tax nexus for nonprotected activities, and nexus for nonincome-based taxes, requires a physical presence just like establishing sales and use tax nexus. The two most notable nonincome-based taxes are the Texas Margin Tax and the Washington Business and Occupation (B&O) tax. While nonincome-based taxes are beyond the scope of this chapter, a realization that a different nexus standard exists is vitally important.

Example 12-7

What if: Assume that Ken and other Wild West employees visit Colorado retail stores and hold slideshows about summer rafting trips. After the slideshows, Ken and the other guides interact with and gather information from potential white-water rafting customers. Do these solicitation activities create income tax nexus?

Answer: Yes. Because white-water rafting trips are services rather than tangible personal property, the physical presence of Wild West employees creates income tax nexus in Colorado.

Example 12-8

What if: Assume that Wild West sends employees into Texas to visit retail stores and solicit orders of rafting equipment. Texas instituted a new tax, the Margin Tax, beginning in 2008. The tax is calculated on the lesser of gross margin or 70 percent of sales revenue. Would the presence of Wild West employees create nexus for the Texas Margin Tax?

Answer: Yes. Because the tax is nonincome-based (it is not based on *net* income), Wild West is not protected by Public Law 86-272. Therefore, physical presence of salespeople soliciting sales of tangible personal property creates nexus (but it would *not* have created nexus if the tax were based on net income).

THE KEY FACTS

Income Tax Nexus

- Income tax nexus requirements vary depending on whether the business sells tangible personal property, services, or intangibles.
- Sellers of tangible personal property are protected from nexus under Public Law 86-272.
  - Physical presence is protected as long as in-state activities are limited to solicitation.
- Sellers of intangibles, real property, and services establish nexus through physical presence of sales personnel or property.
- Several states are now asserting economic nexus.

Economic Income Tax Nexus As we have discussed, businesses generally must have a physical presence in a state to establish income tax nexus with that state (Public Law 86-272 is the exception). However, many states are currently asserting a business without a physical presence in the state may establish income tax nexus if it has an economic presence in the state.[22] South Carolina was the first state to pursue economic nexus. South Carolina disallowed the royalty expenses of Toys 'R' Us South Carolina to Geoffrey (a related Delaware holding company) rather than

[22]The Supreme Court's *Quill* decision created doubt on the standard for income tax nexus because in defining sales tax nexus it said that "nexus for other taxes may be different," which the states have interpreted as meaning that physical presence may not be required for other types of taxes. Several recent cases have given de facto income tax nexus to businesses without the requisite physical presence [*Geoffrey, Inc. v. South Carolina Tax Commission,* S.C. Sup. Ct., 313 S.C. (1992); *Lanco, Inc. v. Director, Division of Taxation,* NJ Sup. Ct., Dkt. No.A-89-05 (2006); and *Tax Commissioner of West Virginia v. MBNA America Bank, N.A.,* 640 SE 2d 226 (WV 2006)].

subject Geoffrey to the South Carolina income tax. States asserting **economic nexus** claim they provide an infrastructure of phone and Internet connections to consumers (an economic base) that nonresident companies use to solicit business (this claim is analogous to providing roads for salespeople to visit the state's customers). For example, West Virginia asserted an income tax liability on a business (MBNA Bank) that merely solicited credit card customers through advertising and phone calls without having physical presence (employees or property) in the state. The West Virginia Supreme Court upheld the assertion, and the U.S. Supreme Court denied MBNA's *writ of certiorari*. However, most experts believe West Virginia's law to be unconstitutional, and the U.S. Supreme Court's refusal to hear the case was designed to urge Congress to resolve the uncertainty surrounding nexus issues.

Example 12-9

What if: Assume that Wild West's Internet store receives and fills an order from a West Virginia customer. Wild West has no physical presence in West Virginia. Does Wild West have West Virginia income tax nexus?

Answer: Perhaps. West Virginia's assertion of economic nexus does not require physical presence. Therefore, Wild West could have economic income tax nexus, which would require it to file an income tax return in West Virginia.

TAXES IN THE REAL WORLD Factor Presence

While several states have asserted economic nexus through state courts, the Multistate Tax Commission adopted the Factor Presence Nexus Standard in 2002 (MTC Policy Statement 02-02). This policy asserts that if any taxpayer exceeds any of the following criteria, substantial nexus is established:

- $50,000 of property
- $50,000 of payroll
- $500,000 of sales, or
- 25 percent of total property, payroll, or sales

A number of states have recently asserted this standard (or a variation) through either legislation or regulation: California, Colorado, Ohio, Oklahoma, and Washington. If upheld, this standard will change the game by making Public Law 86-272 irrelevant, and it should make all companies not filing income tax returns in a state nervous.

Now that we've explored income tax nexus, let's determine Wild West's income tax nexus and filing requirements.

Example 12-10

Wild West is domiciled in Idaho and has physical presence through property and employees whose activities exceed protected solicitation in Idaho, Tennessee, Washington, and Wyoming. Recall from Example 12-4 that Wild West has sales in the following states: Arizona, California, Colorado, Idaho, Tennessee, Washington, and Wyoming. Where does Wild West have income tax nexus?

Answer: Wild West has income tax nexus in Idaho, Tennessee, Washington, and Wyoming. Nexus in Idaho because of commercial domicile, physical presence of retail stores (where orders are accepted), and provision of services. Nexus in Tennessee, Washington, and Wyoming because of physical presence of retail stores (where orders are accepted) or provision of services. Where does Wild West have an income tax filing requirement?

Answer: Wild West will be required to file income tax returns in Idaho and Tennessee. Washington and Wyoming do not have a corporate income tax. Instead, Washington has a gross receipts tax (Business & Occupation tax). Wyoming does not tax corporations. As a result, Wild West will also file a Washington gross receipts return, as we discuss later.

Entities Included on Income Tax Return

When a business operates as more than one legal entity, how it files its tax return(s) becomes an issue. Some states require a **separate tax return** for each entity with income tax nexus in the state, and others require a **unitary tax return** (one return) for a group of related entities.[23]

Separate Tax Returns "Separate-return" states require only those businesses with nexus in a state to file an income tax return. This is generally true even when a group of companies file a federal consolidated tax return.[24] Traditionally, most states east of the Mississippi River (except Illinois) were separate-return states.

Example 12-11

Wild West has nexus in Tennessee (a separate-return state) because its employees provide services within the state and it owns property there. Must Wild West file a separate Tennessee income tax return?

Answer: Yes. Wild West must file a separate Tennessee income tax return because it has nexus in Tennessee.

What if: Assume that Wild West splits into two separate corporations: one that runs retail stores (Wild West Retail) and one that provides the guided rafting services (Wild West Services). How would the split affect Wild West's Tennessee income tax filing requirements?

Answer: Wild West would file two separate income tax returns: one for Wild West Retail and one for Wild West Services. Both companies would have nexus in Tennessee because Wild West Retail's stores do more than solicit sales of tangible personal property and Wild West Service's activities are not protected activities under Public Law 86-272.

THE KEY FACTS

Entities Included on a Tax Return

- Separate-return states require a separate return for each entity that has nexus in the state.
- Unitary states require members of a unitary group to file a single tax return reflecting the combined income of the unitary group.
  - Any of three factors determine a unitary group: functional integration, centralization of management, and economies of scale.

While separate tax returns are simple, the income reported on separate tax returns is potentially subject to manipulation through related-entity transactions (transfer pricing, for example). Another important planning technique is the use of *passive investment companies* (PICs). A company simply creates a subsidiary and transfers ownership of its trademarks and patents to a state that does not tax royalties, interest, and other similar types of intangible income. Then the new PIC charges a royalty for use of the intangible, which generates a deductible business expense in the state used and creates income in a little or no taxed state like Delaware or Nevada. States have implemented laws to fight this type of planning, but seven states have adopted unitary filing to avoid this issue. These "tax planning" opportunities are not available if the related entities are required to file a unitary tax return.

Unitary Tax Returns States west of the Mississippi River (and Illinois) are unitary return states. However, since 2004, Massachusetts, Michigan, New York, Ohio, Texas, Vermont, and Wisconsin have adopted unitary returns. Whether a business must file one tax return with other businesses or entities depends on whether these businesses are considered to be a "unitary" group of entities.

[23]The separate versus unitary discussion is a complex and controversial discussion even at the graduate tax level. However, a basic understanding of the terminology and concepts can be useful for all accounting professionals.

[24]Some states allow combined reporting, a setting where more than one corporation files together on the same income tax return. However, the tax is calculated as if each corporation filed a separate return and was taxed separately.

In *Mobil,* the Supreme Court identified the following three factors that can be used to determine whether a group of businesses is unitary:

- Functional integration (vertical or horizontal integration or knowledge transfer).
- Centralization of management (interlocking directors, common officers, or rotation of management between companies).
- Economies of scale (group discounts or other efficiencies due to size).[25]

The unitary concept considers the integration and flow of value, rather than the business's legal form and ownership structure, in determining which companies file a tax return together. Taxpayers must consider each of the three factors to determine whether two (or more) businesses will be treated as one for state tax purposes.

The important concept here is that companies filing a federal consolidated tax return can be separated, and companies not filing a federal consolidated tax return can become a unitary group.[26] A unitary tax return group includes all members meeting the unitary criteria—whether they have nexus or not.[27] Unitary businesses usually have a flow of value between the various businesses. For example, raw materials or components can flow between businesses or one entity may borrow funds from another. The unitary concept pervades activities in the entire income tax system, including computing taxable income, computing apportionment percentages (discussed later in the chapter), and determining tax return filing requirements. The primary difference between separate and unitary states is that separate states tax the entire apportioned income of each separate business unit with nexus while unitary states tax the entire unitary group using a smaller apportioned percentage.

Example 12-12

What if: As in the previous example, assume that Wild West is divided into two separate corporations: Wild West Retail (WWR) and Wild West Services (WWS). Ken owns and manages both companies. The rafting services company purchases all of its rafting equipment from the retail stores company. Guides for the rafting company stop at the retail store before trips so customers can purchase any necessary gear, and the store refers customers looking for guided rafting to the rafting company. Assume the two companies use the same marketing and accounting firms and receive discounts for having multiple bank accounts and insurance policies. Using the *Mobil* factors (functional integration, centralization of management, and economies of scale), are WWR and WWS part of a unitary group?

Answer: Yes. WWR and WWS would likely be considered a unitary group and thus would combine income and file a single tax return. The two companies likely share some integration in that their customer bases have significant overlap, and WWR purchases its equipment from WWS. They share centralization of management in that both are owned and operated by the same individual (Ken). The two companies have some economies of scale because they receive discounts for using the same accounting, banking, insurance, and marketing vendors. Businesses do not have to meet all three factors to be considered a unitary group, but WWR and WWS probably do. As a result, WWR and WWS would likely file a unitary (single) Idaho income tax return.

State Taxable Income

Companies doing business in multiple states must determine tax return due dates, procedures for filing tax return extensions, and other administrative requirements

[25]In *Mobil Oil Corp. v. Vermont Tax Commissioner,* 445 U.S. 425 (1980), the U.S. Supreme Court held that the income of a multistate business can be apportioned if its intrastate and out-of-state activities form a part of a unitary business.

[26]In some cases, different divisions of a single corporation can be separated and in others a partnership and corporation can be joined.

[27]Entities without nexus usually have apportionment factors that are zero. While their incomes increase the unitary group's income, their zero apportionment factors decrease the apportionment factors to the state. Therefore, the inclusion of entities without nexus is usually considered to be nondiscriminatory.

specific to each state. Businesses must also calculate state taxable income for each state in which they must file tax returns. Federal taxable income is generally the starting point for computing state taxable income. Just as corporations reconcile from book income to taxable income (see Chapter 5), businesses must reconcile from federal taxable income to state taxable income. This requires them to identify **federal/state adjustments** (differences) for *each specific state* before apportioning the income to a particular state where they have income tax nexus.

Rather than starting from scratch, many states conform to the federal tax law in some way. Most states "piggyback" their state tax laws on the federal tax laws (state tax codes generally follow the Internal Revenue Code).[28] Idaho generally conforms to the current Code. Consequently, Wild West will not report many federal/state adjustments. Other states adopt a specific version of the Code (the Code as of a specific date). California recently adopted the Code as of January 1, 2009 (previously it used the Code as of January 1, 2006), and Texas uses the Code as of January 1, 2007. This method requires more federal/state adjustments, because every subsequent change to the Internal Revenue Code results in less conformity between the state law and the federal tax law.

Because states cannot tax federal interest income (interest from Treasury notes, for example), all states require a negative adjustment (reduction in federal income in adjusting to state income) for federal interest income. Most states require a positive adjustment for state income taxes, because they *do not* allow businesses to deduct state income taxes, and they require a positive adjustment for state and local bond interest income if the bond is from another state (they tax out-of-state bond interest income).[29]

States' tax instruction booklets generally describe common federal/state tax adjustments applicable for that state, but these descriptions are often incomplete, and particularly problematic for states with low federal tax conformity. While it is impractical to identify all potential federal/state adjustments, Exhibit 12-5 provides a list of common federal/state adjustments and identifies each as positive adjustments (state income increasing) or negative adjustments (state income decreasing).

EXHIBIT 12-5 Common Federal/State Adjustments

Positive Adjustments (Increasing Taxable Income)

State and local income taxes
State and local bond interest income from bonds in other states
Federal dividends received deduction
Federal income tax refunds (only in states where federal tax is allowed as a deduction)
Intercompany expenses associated with related parties (for separate-return states)*
MACRS depreciation over state depreciation
Federal bonus depreciation
Federal domestic production activities deduction

Negative Adjustments (Decreasing Taxable Income)

U.S. obligation interest income (T-bills, notes, and bonds)
State dividends received deduction
Foreign dividend gross up
Subpart F income
State income tax refunds included on federal return
State depreciation over federal depreciation

*Approximately 20 separate-return states require a positive adjustment of intercompany royalties, interest, and other expenses between related parties. The disallowance prevents companies from extracting profits from high-tax states and placing them in low- or no-tax states.

[28]Also, states may conform or not conform to administrative authority such as Treasury Regulations, Revenue Procedures, and Revenue Rulings.

[29]Thirty-three of the 46 states with an income tax require a positive adjustment for state and local expenses deducted on the federal return.

Example 12-13

Wild West properly included, deducted, or excluded the following items on its federal tax return in the current year:

Item	Amount	Federal Treatment
Idaho income tax	$27,744	Deducted on federal return.
Tennessee income tax	18,152	Deducted on federal return.
Washington gross receipts tax	6,201	Deducted on federal return.
Idaho bond interest income	5,000	Excluded from federal return.
Federal T-note interest income	1,500	Included on federal return.
Domestic production activities deduction (DPAD)	7,304	Deducted on federal return.

Given federal taxable income of $53,289, what is Wild West's state tax base for Idaho and for Tennessee?

Answer: The Idaho state tax base is $97,685; for Tennessee it is $109,989. Bases are calculated as follows:

Federal Taxable Income	Idaho	Tennessee	Source
Wild West	$53,289	$ 53,289	Storyline
Positive Adjustments			
Idaho income tax	$27,744	$ 27,744	Idaho tax is not deducted.
Tennessee income tax	18,152	18,152	Tennessee tax is not deducted.
Washington gross receipts tax	0	0	Washington tax is not a positive adjustment because it is not an income-based tax.
State bond interest	0	5,000	States exempt their own interest only.
DPAD	0	7,304	Idaho conforms to federal law, Tennessee does not.
Total positive adjustments	$45,896	$ 58,200	
Negative Adjustments			
Federal interest	$ 1,500	$ 1,500	Federal interest is not taxable for state purposes.
Total negative adjustments	$ 1,500	$ 1,500	
State tax base	$97,685	$109,989	Federal + Positive − Negative.

Dividing State Tax Base among States

All state taxable income is taxed in the state of commercial domicile unless the business is taxable in more than one state. An interstate business must separate its business income (earned from business operations) from nonbusiness income (primarily from investments, including rents and royalties). The business must fairly *apportion* its business income among the states in which it conducts business, whereas it *allocates* or assigns nonbusiness income to a specific state (usually the state of commercial domicile).[30]

[30]The Multistate Tax Commission has provided guidance on the division of income between states in Article IV of its Compact. The Compact can be found at www.mtc.gov. Also, see the Uniform Division of Income Tax Purposes Act that many states have adopted.

Business Income Business income includes all revenues earned in the ordinary course of business—sales less cost of goods sold and other expenses. Business income is fairly apportioned or divided across the states with nexus.[31] If a business has nexus with a state, it may apportion income to that state—even if the state does not actually impose a tax.[32]

Example 12-14

Recall from the preceding example that Idaho and Tennessee state tax bases were $97,685 and $109,989, respectively. Wild West's federal tax return shows the following items of investment income: dividends of $6,000, interest income of $16,005 (which includes $14,505 of bank interest and $1,500 of federal government interest but excludes $5,000 from Idaho bond interest), and rental income of $18,000. What is Wild West's business income for Idaho and Tennessee?

Answer: Idaho and Tennessee business income amounts are $59,180 and $66,484, respectively, and calculated as follows:

	Idaho	Tennessee	Explanation
(1) State tax base	$97,685	$109,989	Example 12-13.
(2) Dividends	$ 6,000	$ 6,000	Federal tax return.
(3) Interest income	14,505	19,505	$14,505 (bank interest) + $5,000 of Idaho bond interest (for Tennessee only).
(4) Rental income	18,000	18,000	Federal tax return.
(5) Nonbusiness income	$38,505	$ 43,505	(2) + (3) + (4).
Business income	$59,180	$ 66,484	(1) − (5).

Apportionment formula. States determine the apportionment formula for income, and most rely on three factors: sales, payroll, and property. For each state in which it establishes income tax nexus, the business determines the factors as the ratio of (1) total sales, payroll, or property in a specific state to (2) total sales, payroll, or property everywhere. For example, the sales factor is:

$$\text{Sales factor in state } X = \frac{\text{Total sales in state } X}{\text{Total sales in all states}}$$

The sales factor includes all gross business receipts net of returns, allowances, and discounts.[33] The general rules for determining the amount of sales to include in the sales factor calculation are:

- Sales of tangible personal property are sourced (included) to the destination state (the location where the property is delivered to and used in).
- If the business does not have nexus in the destination state, sales are generally "thrown back" to the state from which the property is shipped; this is called the **throwback rule.**[34] For example, if Wild West ships goods from Idaho to

[31]*Complete Auto Transit, Inc. v. Brady,* 430 U.S. 274 (1977).

[32]Creating nexus in states without an income tax creates "nowhere income"—income that is not taxed anywhere.

[33]There is some variation in the sales factor among states.

[34]Some states don't have a throwback rule and some states such as California have a double-throwback rule. This rule applies to drop shipments from a state without nexus. For example, if a California company ships goods from Arizona into Colorado and has nexus in neither Arizona nor Colorado, the sales are thrown back from Colorado into Arizona and then thrown back again from Arizona to California.

Montana where it does not have nexus the sales are treated as if they are Idaho sales.

- Dock sales should be sourced to the good's ultimate destination (sales picked up by an out-of-state buyer at the seller's in-state dock rather than being shipped to the buyer's out-of-state location).
- Sales of services are sourced in the state where the services are performed (Illinois is an exception to this rule, but the list of market states is growing).
- Government sales are sourced in the state from which they were shipped.

TAXES IN THE REAL WORLD The Complexities in Sourcing Receipts from the Sale of Other Than Tangible Personal Property

The last 10 to 15 years have seen a shift from the equally weighted three-factor formula to adopting a single sales factor formula for apportionment purposes. As a result, the computation of the sales factor has gained importance for taxpayers and tax administrators alike. The increased significance of the sales factor coupled with an economic shift towards intangibles and services has shifted the focus of apportionment to sourcing receipts from sales other than sales of tangible personal property. Sales of other than the sale of tangible personal property historically have not been sourced on a destination basis. Rather, most states have generally adopted a method that assigns the sales to the state in which the income producing activity/cost of performance was performed. . . . Recently, states have moved towards a market state or destination approach for sourcing such receipts.

Source: Marilyn A. Wethekam, *Journal of State Taxation*, September–October 2010, p. 39.

Example 12-15

Recall from Exhibit 12-1 that Wild West reported sales of $2,534,032. The sales are split between goods and services and sourced by state as follows:

Wild West Sales			
State	**Goods**	**Services**	**Total**
AZ	$ 89,242	$ 0	$ 89,242
CA	132,045	0	132,045
CO	75,002	0	75,002
ID	**167,921**	**625,003**	**792,924**
TN	**45,331**	**357,061**	**402,392**
WA	41,982	377,441	419,423
WY	185,249	437,755	623,004
Totals	**$736,772**	**$1,797,260**	**$2,534,032**

Recall from Example 12-10 that Wild West has nexus in Idaho, Tennessee, Washington, and Wyoming. Washington has a gross receipts tax and Wyoming does not tax corporations. What are the sales apportionment factors for Idaho and Tennessee?

Answer: The apportionment factors for Idaho and Tennessee are 31.29 percent and 15.88 percent, respectively, calculated from figures in the Total column in the sales table above:

Idaho $$\frac{\$792,924}{\$2,534,032} = 31.29\%$$

Tennessee $$\frac{\$402,392}{\$2,534,032} = 15.88\%$$

Note the AZ, CA, and CO sales are thrownback to Wyoming because the sales were made through the Internet store.

Payroll is generally defined as total compensation paid to employees.[35] The payroll factor is calculated as follows:

- Payroll includes salaries, commissions, bonuses, and other forms of compensation.
- Payroll does not include amounts paid to independent contractors.
- Payroll for each employee is apportioned to a single state (payroll for employees who work in more than one state is sourced to the state where they perform the majority of services).

Example 12-16

Wild West's payments for wages are $737,021, sourced to the states as follows:

Payroll State	Wild West Wages
Idaho	**$201,032**
Tennessee	**148,202**
Washington	115,021
Wyoming	272,766
Total	**$737,021**

What are the payroll apportionment factors for Idaho and Tennessee?

Answer: The payroll apportionment factors for Idaho and Tennessee are 27.28 percent and 20.11 percent, respectively, calculated from the payroll table above:

Idaho $$\frac{\$201,032}{\$737,021} = 27.28\%$$

Tennessee $$\frac{\$148,202}{\$737,021} = 20.11\%$$

Property generally includes both real and tangible personal property, but not intangible property.[36] The general rules for determining the property factors are

- Use the average property values for the year [(beginning + ending)/2].
- Value property at historical cost rather than adjusted basis (do not subtract accumulated depreciation in determining value).

[35]The payroll definition varies by state.

[36]Property definitions may vary slightly by state.

- Include property in transit (such as inventory) in the state of destination.
- Include only business property (values of rented investment properties are excluded).
- Include rented or leased property by multiplying the annual rent by 8 and adding this value to the average owned-property factor.[37]

Example 12-17

The historical cost of Wild West's property (before subtracting accumulated depreciation) owned at the beginning and end of the year and rented during the year, by state, is as follows:

Property			
State	**Beginning**	**Ending**	**Rented**
Idaho	$1,042,023	$1,203,814	$36,000
Tennessee	502,424	531,984	0
Washington	52,327	65,829	60,000
Wyoming	1,420,387	1,692,373	0
Total	$3,017,161	$3,494,000	$96,000

What are the property apportionment factors for Idaho and Tennessee?

Answer: The property apportionment factors for Idaho and Tennessee are 35.07 percent and 12.85 percent, respectively, computed as follows:

Property and Rents Total					
	Owned Property			**Rented**	
State	**Beginning**	**Ending**	**Average**	**Rents × 8**	**Total**
Idaho	**$1,042,023**	**$1,203,814**	**$1,122,919**	**$288,000**	**$1,410,919**
Tennessee	**502,424**	**531,984**	**517,204**		**517,204**
Washington	52,327	65,829	59,078	$480,000	539,078
Wyoming	1,420,387	1,692,373	1,556,380		1,556,380
Total	**$3,017,161**	**$3,494,000**	**$3,255,581**		**$4,023,581**

$$\text{Idaho} \quad \frac{\$1{,}410{,}919}{\$4{,}023{,}581} = 35.07\%$$

$$\text{Tennessee} \quad \frac{\$517{,}204}{\$4{,}023{,}581} = 12.85\%$$

The average amount for each state from the subtotal property table is added to the inclusion amount from the subtotal rent table to reach the total property numerator for each state.

Historically, most states have used an equally weighted three-factor apportionment formula. This method adds together the sales, payroll, and property factors and divides the total by three to arrive at the apportionment factor (percentages) for each state. In recent years, many states have shifted to a double-weighted sales factor (doubling the sales factor, adding the payroll and property factors, and dividing the total by four). Both Idaho and Tennessee use the double-weighted sales factor for apportionment. Recently, some states have moved to a single-weighted sales

[37]The annual rent is multiplied by 8 to approximate the value of the rental property.

factor that eliminates the payroll and property factors altogether. California requires corporations to use a single-weighted sales factor beginning in 2013. All else equal, increasing the weight of the sales factor in the apportionment formula tends to decrease taxes on in-state businesses and increase taxes on out-of-state businesses. The reason is that in-state businesses tend to have higher payroll and property factors relative to their sales factor in the state, and out-of-state businesses tend to have higher sales factors than payroll and property factors.

TAXES IN THE REAL WORLD Apportionment: The Gillette Decision

The California Supreme Court on January 16, 2013, agreed to review the California Court of Appeal decision in *Gillette Co. v. Franchise Tax Board.*

In *Gillette,* the California Court of Appeal held that a taxpayer could apportion its income to California using the Multistate Tax Compact's evenly weighted three-factor formula, despite statutory language mandating the use of a three-factor, double-weighted sales formula for most corporations for the years at issue.

The court's ruling was based entirely on case law regarding interstate compacts and its view that when California became a signatory to the Multistate Tax Compact, it entered into a binding agreement with other signatory states that—absent repeal of the Compact in its entirety—obligated it to offer multistate taxpayers the option of using the Compact's allocation and apportionment provisions.

This ruling will have a large impact on whether companies are forced to use unfavorable state laws which typically require out of state companies to apportion income based solely on the sales factor or to choose a more favorable three-factor methodology which reduces the tax burden. The Michigan Supreme Court ruled for IBM in a similar case. Decisions are now pending in California, Oregon, Texas, and Minnesota, although *Gillette Co. v. Franchise Tax Board* is the most anticipated decision.

Example 12-18

Wild West must apportion its business income to Idaho and Tennessee. Its Idaho sales, payroll, and property factors are 31.29 percent, 27.28 percent, and 35.07 percent, respectively. Its Tennessee sales, payroll, and property factors are 15.88 percent, 20.11 percent, and 12.85 percent, respectively. These factors are aggregated from Examples 12-15 through 12-17. What are Wild West's apportionment factors in both states if they use a double-weighted sales factor?

Answer: The apportionment factors for Idaho and Tennessee are 31.23 percent and 16.18 percent, respectively.

Factor	Idaho	Tennessee	Explanation
(1) Sales	31.29%	15.88%	
(2) Sales	31.29	15.88	
(3) Payroll	27.28	20.11	
(4) Property	35.07	12.85	
Apportionment factor	31.23	16.18	[(1) + (2) + (3) + (4)]/4.

What if: Assume Tennessee uses an equally weighted three-factor apportionment formula. What are Wild West's apportionment factors?

Answer: The apportionment factor for Tennessee is 16.28 percent. Tennessee's apportionment factor would now be calculated as follows:

Factor	Tennessee	Explanation
(1) Sales	15.88%	
(2) Payroll	20.11	
(3) Property	12.85	
Apportionment factor	16.28	[(1) + (2) + (3)]/3.

Nonbusiness Income We've said nonbusiness income is all income except business income. Here are common types of nonbusiness income, and the rules for allocating them to specific states:[38]

- Allocate interest and dividends to the state of commercial domicile (except interest on working capital, which is business income).
- Allocate rental income to the state where the property generating the rental income is located.
- Allocate royalties to the state where the property is used (if the business has nexus in that state; if not, allocate royalties to the state of commercial domicile).
- Allocate capital gains from investment property to the state of commercial domicile.
- Allocate capital gains from selling rental property to the state where the rental property was located.

Example 12-19

Wild West reports nonbusiness income as follows:

Wild West			
	Idaho	**Tennessee**	
Dividends	$ 6,000	$ 6,000	From Example 12-14.
Interest	14,505	19,505	From Example 12-14.
Rental income	18,000	18,000	From Example 12-14.
Allocable total	$38,505	$43,505	

Wild West's commercial domicile is in Idaho. Its rental income is for real property located in Wyoming. To which state(s) should the firm allocate its nonbusiness income?

Answer: Wild West should allocate its nonbusiness income as follows:

Wild West		
Idaho	$20,505	$6,000 dividends + $14,505 interest income.
Nevada	0	
Tennessee	0	
Washington	0	
Wyoming	18,000	Rental income.
Total	$38,505	

State Income Tax Liability

It is relatively easy to calculate a business's state taxable income and state tax after separating business and nonbusiness income, apportioning business income, and allocating nonbusiness income. Specifically, calculate state taxable income by multiplying business income by the apportionment factor and then adding any nonbusiness income allocated to the state.

[38]Multistate Tax Compact, Article IV, Division of Income, Paragraph 4.

Example 12-20

What if: Assume Idaho and Tennessee have a flat income tax rate of 7.6 percent and 6.5 percent, respectively. What is Wild West's income tax liability for Idaho and Tennessee?

Answer: Its liabilities are $2,963 and $699 in Idaho and Tennessee, respectively, computed as follows:

Description	Idaho	Tennessee	Explanation
(1) State tax base	$97,685	$109,989	Example 12-14.
(2) Allocable income	($38,505)	($43,505)	Example 12-19.
(3) Business income	$59,180	$ 66,484	(1) − (2).
(4) Apportionment factor	31.23%	16.18%	Example 12-18.
(5) Apportioned income	$18,482	$ 10,757	(3) × (4).
(6) Allocable income	$20,505	$ 0	Example 12-19.
(7) State taxable income	$38,987	$ 10,757	(5) + (6).
(8) Tax rate	7.6%	6.5%	
Tax liability	$ 2,963	$ 699	(7) × (8).

THE KEY FACTS

Dividing Income among States with Nexus

- Business income is apportioned based on some combination of the following factors:
  - Sales
  - Payroll
  - Property
- Nonbusiness income is allocated.
  - Investment income is allocated to the state of commercial domicile.
  - Rents and royalties are generally allocated to the state where the property is used.

Non (Net) Income-Based Taxes

Several states have nonincome-based taxes. Washington has the Business & Occupation Tax, which is a gross receipts tax. Texas has the Margin Tax (many states are treating the Texas Margin Tax as a tax based on net income), the lesser of a gross margin tax or gross receipts tax. As we discussed earlier, Public Law 86-272 doesn't apply to nexus for nonincome-based taxes such as gross receipts taxes or property taxes; these are deductible for calculating taxable income for net income-based taxes.

Example 12-21

Wild West has nexus in Washington and is subject to that state's Business and Occupation (B&O) tax. The tax is .471 percent of gross receipts for retailers and 1.5 percent of gross receipts on services. Wild West's gross receipts from retail sales and services are $41,982 and $377,441, respectively (from Exhibit 12-1). Calculate Wild West's B&O tax.

Answer: Wild West's B&O tax is $5,860, calculated as follows:

Activity	(1) Receipts	(2) Rate	(1) × (2) Tax
Retailing	$ 41,982	0.471%	$ 198
Services	377,441	1.500	5,662
B&O tax			$5,860

CONCLUSION

In this chapter we discussed the fundamentals of state and local taxation with an emphasis on nexus, sales and use tax, and net income-based corporate taxes. State and local taxes currently make up a significant portion of many businesses' total tax burden and also consume a significant portion of the tax department's time.

Sales and use tax nexus is established through physical presence. Companies selling tangible personal property must collect sales tax from their customers (where nexus exists) and remit it to the various states. Income tax nexus requirements vary based on the type of goods or services provided by a business. Tangible personal property sales are protected from income tax nexus by Public Law 86-272 if certain criteria are met. For all other sales, nexus is created by physical presence, although some states are defining the concept of income tax nexus based on economic rather than physical presence.

Businesses subject to multijurisdictional taxation—taxation by more than one government—have many issues in common. A business located in San Diego, California, but also doing business in Tucson, Arizona, will be subject to California and Arizona tax. If it also does business in Rosarito, Mexico, it will be subject to both U.S. and Mexico taxes. State and local taxation and international taxation bring up many of the same issues. For both, businesses must determine which jurisdiction has the right to tax a transaction (nexus) and determine how to divide income among different jurisdictions. The next chapter examines multinational taxation.

Summary

LO 12-1 Describe the primary types of state and local taxes.

- The primary purpose of state and local taxes is to raise revenue.
- Like federal tax law, state tax law is comprised of legislative, administrative, and judicial law.
- Judicial law plays a more important role in state tax law than federal tax law because constitutionality is a primary concern for state tax laws.
- The most important question any taxpayer must answer is whether it is subject to a state's taxing regime.
- Nexus is the connection between a business and a state sufficient to subject the business to the state's tax system.
- When a business sells tangible personal property, either sales or use tax is due. If the seller has nexus, the seller must collect and remit the tax to the state. Otherwise, the buyer is responsible for paying the use tax.
- Businesses engaged in interstate commerce that have nexus must pay income tax.

LO 12-2 Determine whether a business has sales and use tax nexus and calculate its sales tax withholding responsibilities.

- Forty-five states and the District of Columbia impose sales and use taxes.
- The items subject to sales and use tax vary from state to state.
- Businesses are required to collect sales tax on sales only if they have sales and use tax nexus with that state.
- For nondomiciliary businesses, sales and use tax nexus is created through a physical presence (having salespeople or tangible property within the state, for example).

LO 12-3 Identify whether a business has income tax nexus and determine its state income tax liabilities.

- Forty-six states impose an income tax on corporations, and 43 states tax the owners of partnerships and S corporations.
- Businesses must pay income tax in their state of commercial domicile, and nondomiciliary firms are subject to tax if they have nexus in the state.
- Businesses divide or apportion their income among the states where they have established nexus.
- Nexus requirements vary based on the nature of the business's activities: physical presence creates income tax nexus for service providers, sellers of real property, and businesses licensing intangibles; Public Law 86-272 protects solicitation of tangible personal property from nexus.
- Some states require a separate income tax return for each entity with nexus, and others require a unitary (a single) tax return for a group of related entities as long as one of the entities has established nexus in the state.

- Businesses must calculate state taxable income for each state in which they must file a tax return—this requires businesses to identify federal/state adjustments.
- Firms adjust federal taxable income to arrive at their state taxable base.
- The state taxable base of an interstate business is separated into business and nonbusiness income: business income is apportioned across states using a general formula, and nonbusiness income is allocated to specific states using specific rules.
- Business income is apportioned using some variation of sales, payroll, and property factors.

KEY TERMS

allocation (12-4)
apportionment (12-4)
business income (12-4)
commercial domicile (12-2)
economic nexus (12-14)
federal/state adjustments (12-17)
interstate commerce (12-4)
nexus (12-2)
nonbusiness income (12-4)
nondomiciliary business (12-2)
Public Law 86-272 (12-10)
sales tax (12-3)
separate tax return (12-15)
solicitation (12-11)
state tax base (12-4)
throwback rule (12-19)
trade show rule (12-12)
unitary tax return (12-15)
use tax (12-4)

DISCUSSION QUESTIONS

1. Why do states and local jurisdictions assess taxes? LO 12-1
2. Compare and contrast the relative importance of judicial law to state and local and federal tax law. LO 12-1
3. Describe briefly the nexus concept and explain its importance to state and local taxation. LO 12-1
4. What is the difference, if any, between the state of a business's commercial domicile and its state of incorporation? LO 12-1
5. What types of property sales are subject to sales tax and why might a state choose to exclude the sales of certain types of property? LO 12-1
6. In what circumstances would a business be subject to income taxes in more than one state? LO 12-1
7. Describe how the failure to collect sales tax can result in a larger tax liability for a business than failing to pay income taxes. LO 12-1
8. Discuss why restaurant meals, rental cars, and hotel receipts are often taxed at a higher-than-average sales tax rate. LO 12-2
9. Compare and contrast general sales and use tax nexus and the new "Amazon" rule creating nexus in New York. LO 12-2
10. What is the difference between a sales tax and a use tax? LO 12-2
11. Renée operates Scandinavian Imports, a furniture shop in Olney, Maryland, that ships goods to customers in all 50 states. Scandinavian Imports also appraises antique furniture and has recently conducted in-home appraisals in the District of Columbia, Maryland, Pennsylvania, and Virginia. Online appraisals have been done for customers in California, Minnesota, New Mexico, and Texas. Determine where Scandinavian Imports has sales and use tax nexus. LO 12-2
12. Web Music, located in Gardnerville, Nevada, is a new online music service that allows inexpensive legal music downloads. Web Music prides itself on having the fastest download times in the industry. It achieved this speed by leasing server space from 10 regional servers dispersed across the country. Discuss where Web Music has sales and use tax nexus. LO 12-2
13. Discuss possible reasons why the Commerce clause was included in the U.S. Constitution. LO 12-2

LO 12-2 14. Describe the administrative burden businesses face in collecting sales taxes.

LO 12-3 15. Compare and contrast the rules determining where domiciliary and nondomiciliary businesses must file state income tax returns.

LO 12-3 16. Lars operates Keep Flying Incorporated, a used airplane parts business, in Laramie, Wyoming. Lars employs sales agents that visit mechanics in all 50 states to solicit orders. All orders are sent to Wyoming for approval, and all parts are shipped via common carrier. The sales agents are always on the lookout for wrecked, abandoned, or salvage aircraft with rare parts because they receive substantial bonuses for purchasing and salvaging these parts and shipping them to Wyoming. Discuss the states where Keep Flying has income tax nexus.

LO 12-3 17. Explain changes in the U.S. economy that have made Public Law 86-272 partially obsolete. Provide an example of a company that Public Law 86-272 works well for and one that it does not work well for.

LO 12-3 18. Climb Higher is a distributor of high-end climbing gear located in Paradise, Washington. Its sales personnel regularly perform the following activities in an effort to maximize sales:

- Carry swag (free samples) for distribution to climbing shop employees.
- Perform credit checks of new customers to reduce delivery time of first order of merchandise.
- Check customer inventory for proper display and proper quantities.
- Accept returns of defective goods.

Identify which of Climb Higher's sales activities are protected and unprotected from nexus under the *Wrigley* Supreme Court decision.

LO 12-3 19. Describe a situation in which it would be advantageous for a business to establish income tax nexus in a state.

LO 12-3 20. States are arguing for economic nexus; provide at least one reason for and one against the validity of economic nexus.

LO 12-3 21. Explain the difference between separate-return states and unitary-return states.

LO 12-3 22. Explain the rationale for the factors (functional integration, centralization of management, and economies of scale) that determine whether two or more businesses form a unitary group under the *Mobil* decision.

LO 12-3 23. Compare and contrast the reasons why book/tax and federal/state adjustments are necessary for interest income.

LO 12-3 24. Compare and contrast the ways a multistate business divides business and nonbusiness income among states.

LO 12-3 25. Contrast the treatment of government sales and dock sales for the sales apportionment factor.

LO 12-3 26. Most states have increased the weight of the sales factor for the apportionment of business income. What are some possible reasons?

LO 12-3 27. Compare and contrast federal/state tax differences and book/federal tax differences.

PROBLEMS

All applicable problems are available with McGraw-Hill's *Connect®* *Accounting*.

LO 12-2 28. Crazy Eddie Incorporated manufactures baseball caps and distributes them across the northeastern United States. The firm is incorporated and headquartered in New York and sells to customers in Connecticut, Delaware, Massachusetts, New Jersey, New York, Ohio, and Pennsylvania. It has sales reps only where discussed in the scenarios below. Determine the states in which Crazy Eddie has sales and use tax nexus given the following:

a) Crazy Eddie is incorporated and headquartered in New York. It also has property, employees, salespeople, and intangibles in New York.
b) Crazy Eddie has a warehouse, personal property, and employees in Connecticut.
c) Crazy Eddie has two customers in Delaware. Crazy Eddie receives orders over the phone and ships goods to its Delaware customers using FedEx.
d) Crazy Eddie has independent sales representatives in Massachusetts who distribute baseball-related items for over a dozen companies.
e) Crazy Eddie has salespeople who visit New Jersey. They follow procedures that comply with Public Law 86-272 by sending orders to New York for acceptance. The goods are shipped to New Jersey by FedEx.
f) Crazy Eddie provides graphic design services to another manufacturer located in Ohio. While the services are performed in New York, Crazy Eddie's designers visit Ohio at least quarterly to deliver the new designs and receive feedback.
g) Crazy Eddie receives online orders from its Pennsylvania clients. Because the orders are so large, the goods are delivered weekly on Crazy Eddie's trucks.

29. Brad Carlton operates Carlton Collectibles, a rare-coin shop in Washington, D.C., that ships coins to collectors in all 50 states. Carlton also provides appraisal service upon request. During the last several years the appraisal work has been done either in the D.C. shop or at the homes of private collectors in Maryland and Virginia. Determine the jurisdictions in which Carlton Collectibles has sales and use tax nexus. LO 12-2

30. Melanie operates Mel's Bakery in Foxboro, Massachusetts, with retail stores in Connecticut, Maine, Massachusetts, New Hampshire, and Rhode Island. Mel's also ships specialty breads nationwide upon request. Determine Mel's sales tax collection responsibility and calculate the sales tax liability for Massachusetts, Connecticut, Maine, New Hampshire, Rhode Island, and Texas, using the following information: LO 12-2
a) The Massachusetts stores earn $500,000 in sales. Massachusetts's sales tax rate is 5 percent; assume it exempts food items.
b) The Connecticut retail stores have $400,000 in sales ($300,000 from in-store sales and $100,000 from catering) and $10,000 in delivery charges for catering activities. Connecticut sales tax is 6 percent and excludes food products but taxes prepared meals (catering). Connecticut also imposes sales tax on delivery charges on taxable sales.
c) Mel's Maine retail store has $250,000 of sales ($200,000 for take-out and $50,000 of in-store sales). Maine has a 5 percent sales tax rate and a 7 percent sales tax rate on prepared food; it exempts other food purchases.
d) The New Hampshire retail stores have $250,000 in sales. New Hampshire is one of five states with no sales tax. However, it has a room and meals tax rate of 8 percent. New Hampshire considers any food or beverage served by a restaurant for consumption on or off the premises to be a meal.
e) Mel's Rhode Island stores earn $300,000 in sales. The Rhode Island sales tax rate is 7 percent and its restaurant surtax is 1 percent. Rhode Island considers Mel's a restaurant because its retail store has seating.
f) One of Mel's best customers relocated to Texas, which imposes an 8.25 percent state and local sales tax rate but exempts bakery products. This customer entertains guests regularly and ordered $5,000 of food items this year.

31. Cuyahoga County, Ohio, has a sales tax rate of 7.75 percent. Determine the state, local, and transit (a local transportation district) portions of the rate. You can find resources on the State of Ohio website, including the following link: http://www.tax.ohio.gov/portals/0/tax_analysis/tax_data_series/sales_and_use/salestaxmapcolor.pdf LO 12-2

LO 12-2

32. Kai operates the Surf Shop in Laie, Hawaii, which designs, manufacturers, and customizes surfboards. Hawaii has a 4 percent excise tax rate, technically paid by the seller. However, the state also allows "tax on tax" to be charged, which effectively means a customer is billed 4.166 percent of the sales price. Determine the sales and use tax the Surf Shop must collect and remit—or that the customer must pay—for each of the following orders:
    a) Bronco, a Utah customer, places an Internet order for a $1,000 board that will be shipped to Provo, Utah, where the local sales tax rate is 6.25 percent.
    b) Nick, an Alabama resident, comes to the retail shop on vacation and has a $2,000 custom board made. Nick uses the board on vacation and then has the Surf Shop ship it to Tuscaloosa, Alabama, where the sales tax rate is 8.5 percent.
    c) Brady, a Michigan resident, places an order for a $2,000 custom board at the end of his vacation. Upon completion, the board will be shipped to Ann Arbor, Michigan, where the sales tax rate is 7 percent.
    d) Bo, a Nebraska resident, sends his current surfboard to the Surf Shop for a custom paint job. The customization services come to $800. The board is shipped to Lincoln, Nebraska, where the sales tax rate is 7 percent.

LO 12-2
planning

33. Last year, Lane, a Los Angeles, California, resident, began selling autographed footballs through Trojan Victory (TV) Incorporated, a California corporation. TV has never collected sales tax. Last year it had sales as follows: California ($100,000), Arizona ($10,000), Oregon ($15,000), New York ($50,000), and Wyoming ($1,000). Most sales are made over the Internet and shipped by common carrier. Determine how much sales tax should TV have collected in each of the following situations:
    a) California treats the autographed football as tangible personal property subject to an 8.25 percent sales tax rate. Answer for California.
    b) California treats the autographed football as part tangible personal property ($50,000) and part services ($50,000), and tangible personal property is subject to an 8.25 percent sales tax rate. Answer for California.
    c) TV has no property or other physical presence in New York (10.25 percent) or Wyoming (5 percent). Answer for New York and Wyoming.
    d) TV has Lane deliver a few balls to fans in Arizona (5.6 percent sales tax rate) and Oregon (no sales tax) while attending football games there. Answer for Arizona and Oregon.
    e) Related to part (d), can you make any suggestions that would decrease TV's Arizona sales tax liability?

LO 12-2

34. Armstrong Incorporated, a Texas corporation, runs bicycle tours in several states. Armstrong also has a Texas retail store and an Internet store that ships to out-of-state customers. The bicycle tours operate in Colorado, North Carolina, and Texas, where Armstrong has employees and owns and uses tangible personal property. Armstrong has real property only in Texas and logs the following sales:

Armstrong Sales

State	Goods	Services	Total
Arizona	$ 34,194	$ 0	$ 34,194
California	110,612	0	110,612
Colorado	25,913	356,084	381,997
North Carolina	16,721	225,327	242,048
Oregon	15,431	0	15,431
Texas	241,982	877,441	1,119,423
Totals	$444,853	$1,458,852	$1,903,705

Assume the following tax rates: Arizona (5.6 percent), California (7.75 percent), Colorado (8 percent), North Carolina (6.75 percent), Oregon (8 percent), and Texas (8.5 percent). How much sales and use tax must Armstrong collect and remit?

35. Kashi Corporation is the U.S. distributor of fencing (sword fighting) equipment imported from Europe. It is incorporated in Virginia and headquartered in Arlington, Virginia; it ships goods to all 50 states. Kashi's employees attend regional and national fencing competitions where they maintain temporary booths to market their goods. Determine whether Kashi has income tax nexus in the following situations: LO 12-3 planning

a) Kashi is incorporated and headquartered in Virginia. It also has property, employees, salespeople, and intangibles in Virginia. Determine whether Kashi has nexus in Virginia.

b) Kashi has employees who live in Washington, D.C., and Maryland but perform all their employment-related activities in Virginia. Does Kashi have nexus in Washington, D.C., and Maryland?

c) Kashi has two customers in North Dakota. It receives their orders over the phone and ships goods to them using FedEx. Determine whether Kashi has nexus in North Dakota.

d) Kashi has independent sales representatives in Illinois who distribute fencing and other sports-related items for many companies. Does Kashi have nexus in Illinois?

e) Kashi has salespeople who visit South Carolina for a regional fencing competition for a total of three days during the year. They send all orders to Virginia for credit approval and acceptance, and Kashi ships the goods into South Carolina by FedEx. Determine whether Kashi has nexus in South Carolina.

f) Kashi has sales reps who visit California for a national fencing competition and several regional competitions for a total of 17 days during the year. They send all orders to Virginia for credit approval and acceptance. The goods are shipped by FedEx into California. Does Kashi have nexus in California?

g) Kashi receives online orders from its Pennsylvania client. Because the orders are so large, the goods are delivered weekly on Kashi's trucks. Does Kashi have nexus in Pennsylvania?

h) In addition to shipping goods, Kashi provides fencing lessons in Virginia and Maryland locations. Determine whether Kashi has nexus in Virginia and Maryland.

i) Given that Kashi ships to all 50 states, are there locations that would decrease Kashi's overall state income tax burden if nexus were created there?

36. Gary Holt LLP provides tax and legal services regarding the tax-exempt bond issues of state and local jurisdictions. Gary typically provides the services from his New York offices. However, for large issuances he and his staff occasionally travel to another state to complete the work. Determine whether the firm has income tax nexus in the following situations: LO 12-3

a) Gary Holt LLP is a New York partnership and headquartered in New York. It also has property and employees in New York. Does it have income tax nexus in New York?

b) Gary Holt LLP has employees who live in New Jersey and Connecticut and perform all their employment-related activities in New York. Does it have income tax nexus in New Jersey and/or Connecticut?

c) Gary Holt LLP has two customers in California. Gary personally travels there to finalize the Alameda County bond issuance. Does it have income tax nexus in California?

LO 12-3

37. Root Beer Inc. (RBI) is incorporated and headquartered in Seattle, Washington. RBI runs an Internet business, makerootbeer.com, and sells bottling equipment and other supplies for making homemade root beer. It also has an Oregon warehouse from which it ships goods. Determine whether RBI has income tax nexus in the following situations:
    a) Root Beer is incorporated and headquartered in Washington and has property and employees in Oregon and Washington. Determine whether RBI has nexus in Oregon and Washington.
    b) Root Beer has hundreds of customers in California but no physical presence (no employees or property). Does it have nexus in California?
    c) Root Beer has 500 New York customers but no physical presence (no employees or property). Remember New York has the new Amazon rule. Determine whether RBI has nexus in New York.

LO 12-3

38. Rockville Enterprises manufactures woodworking equipment and is incorporated and based in Evansville, Indiana. Its real property is all in Indiana. Rockville employs a large sales force that travels throughout the United States. Determine whether each of the following is a protected activity in nondomiciliary states under Public Law 86-272:
    a) Rockville advertises using television, radio, and newspapers in Wisconsin.
    b) Rockville's employees in Illinois check the credit of potential customers.
    c) Rockville maintains a booth at an industry tradeshow in Arizona for 10 days.
    d) Sales representatives check the inventory of a Tennessee customer to make sure it has enough in stock and that the stock is properly displayed.
    e) Rockville holds a management seminar executive retreat for corporate executives over four days in Florida.
    f) Sales representatives supervise the repossession of inventory from a customer that is not making payments on time in Maine.
    g) Rockville provides automobiles to Idaho and Montana sales representatives.
    h) An Alabama sales representative accepts a customer deposit on a large order.
    i) Colorado sales reps carry display racks and promotional materials that they place in customers' retail stores without charge.

LO 12-3 research

39. Software Incorporated is a sales and use tax software vendor that provides customers with a license to download and use its software on their machines. Software retains ownership of the software. It has customers in New Jersey and West Virginia. Does Software have economic nexus in these states because of the following decisions: *Lanco, Inc. v. Director, Division of Taxation,* NJ Sup. Ct., Dkt. No.A-89-05 (2006), and *Tax Commissioner of West Virginia v. MBNA America Bank, N.A.*, 640 SE 2d 226 (WV 2006)?

LO 12-3 research

40. Peter Inc., a Kentucky corporation, owns 100 percent of Suvi Inc., a Mississippi corporation. Peter and Suvi file a consolidated federal tax return. Peter has income tax nexus in Kentucky and South Carolina; Suvi in Mississippi and South Carolina. Kentucky, Mississippi, and South Carolina are separate-return states. In which states must Pete and Suvi file tax returns? Can they file a consolidated return in any states? Explain. (*Hint:* Use South Carolina Form SC 1120 and the related instructions.)

LO 12-3 research

41. Use California Publication 1061 (2013) to identify the various tests California uses to determine whether two or more entities are part of a unitary group.

42. Bulldog Incorporated is a Georgia corporation. It properly included, deducted, or excluded the following items on its federal tax return in the current year: LO 12-3 research tax forms

Item	Amount	Federal Treatment
Georgia income taxes	$25,496	Deducted on federal return.
Tennessee income taxes	13,653	Deducted on federal return.
Washington gross receipts tax	3,105	Deducted on federal return.
Georgia bond interest income	10,000	Excluded from federal return.
Federal T-note interest income	4,500	Included on federal return.
Domestic production activities deduction (DPAD)	15,096	Deducted on federal return.

Use Georgia's Corporate Income Tax Form 600 and Instructions to determine what federal/state adjustments Bulldog needs to make for Georgia. Bulldog's federal taxable income was $194,302. Calculate its Georgia state tax base. Complete Schedule 1, Page 1, of Form 600 for Bulldog.

43. Herger Corporation does business in California, Nevada, and Oregon, and has nexus in these states as well. Herger's California state tax base was $921,023 after making the required federal/state adjustments. Herger's federal tax return contains the following items: LO 12-3

Item	Amount
Federal T-note interest income	$ 5,000
Nevada municipal bond interest income	3,400
California municipal bond interest income	6,000
Interest expense related to T-note interest income	1,400
Royalty income	100,000
Travel expenses	9,025

Determine Herger's business income.

44. Bad Brad sells used semitrucks and tractor trailers in the Texas panhandle. Bad Brad has sales as follows: LO 12-3

Bad Brad	
State	**Sales**
Colorado	$ 234,992
Oklahoma	402,450
New Mexico	675,204
Texas	1,085,249
Totals	$2,397,895

Bad Brad is a Texas corporation. Answer the questions in each of the following alternative scenarios.

a) Bad Brad has nexus in Colorado, Oklahoma, New Mexico, and Texas. What are the Colorado, Oklahoma, New Mexico, and Texas sales apportionment factors?
b) Bad Brad has nexus in Colorado and Texas. Oklahoma and New Mexico sales are shipped from Texas (a throwback state). What are the Colorado and Texas sales apportionment factors?
c) Bad Brad has nexus in Colorado and Texas. Oklahoma and New Mexico sales are shipped from Texas (a throwback state); $200,000 of Oklahoma sales were to the federal government. What are the Colorado and Texas sales apportionment factors?
d) Bad Brad has nexus in Colorado and Texas. Oklahoma and New Mexico sales are shipped from Texas (assume Texas is a nonthrowback state). What are the Colorado and Texas sales apportionment factors?

LO 12-3 45. Nicole's Salon, a Louisiana corporation, operates beauty salons in Arkansas, Louisiana, and Tennessee. These salons' payroll by state are as follows:

Nicole's Salon	
State	**Payroll**
Arkansas	$ 130,239
Louisiana	309,192
Tennessee	723,010
Total	$1,162,441

What are the payroll apportionment factors for Arkansas, Louisiana, and Tennessee in each of the following alternative scenarios?

a) Nicole's Salon has nexus in Arkansas, Louisiana, and Tennessee.
b) Nicole's Salon has nexus in Arkansas, Louisiana, and Tennessee, but $50,000 of the Arkansas amount is paid to independent contractors.

LO 12-3 46. Delicious Dave's Maple Syrup, a Vermont corporation, has property in the following states:

	Property	
State	**Beginning**	**Ending**
Maine	$ 923,032	$ 994,221
Massachusetts	103,311	203,109
New Hampshire	381,983	283,021
Vermont	873,132	891,976
Total	$2,281,458	$2,372,327

What are the property apportionment factors for Maine, Massachusetts, New Hampshire, and Vermont in each of the following alternative scenarios?

a) Delicious Dave's has nexus in each of the states.
b) Delicious Dave's has nexus in each of the states, but the Maine total includes $400,000 of investment property that Delicious rents out (unrelated to its business).
c) Delicious Dave's has nexus in each of the states, but also pays $50,000 to rent property in Massachusetts.

LO 12-3 47. Susie's Sweet Shop has the following sales, payroll, and property factors:

	Iowa	Missouri
Sales	69.20%	32.01%
Payroll	88.00	3.50
Property	72.42	24.04

What are Susie's Sweet Shop's Iowa and Missouri apportionment factors under each of the following alternative scenarios?

a) Iowa and Missouri both use a three-factor apportionment formula.
b) Iowa and Missouri both use a four-factor apportionment formula that double-weights sales.
c) Iowa uses a three-factor formula and Missouri uses a single-factor apportionment formula (based solely on sales).

48. Brady Corporation is a Nebraska corporation, but owns business and investment property in surrounding states as well. Determine the state where each item of income is allocated. 
    a) $15,000 of dividend income.
    b) $10,000 of interest income.
    c) $15,000 of rental income for South Dakota property.
    d) $20,000 of royalty income for intangibles used in South Dakota (where nexus exists).
    e) $24,000 of royalty income from Kansas (where nexus does not exist).
    f) $15,000 of capital gain from securities held for investment.
    g) $30,000 of capital gain on real property located in South Dakota.
49. Ashton Corporation is headquartered in Pennsylvania and has a state income tax base there of $500,000. Of this amount, $50,000 was nonbusiness income. Ashton's Pennsylvania apportionment factor is 42.35 percent. The nonbusiness income allocated to Pennsylvania was $32,000. Assuming a Pennsylvania corporate tax rate of 8.25 percent, what is Ashton's Pennsylvania state tax liability? LO 12-3

COMPREHENSIVE PROBLEMS

All applicable problems are available with McGraw-Hill's *Connect® Accounting*.

50. Do you know what cloud computing is? Cloud computing is the use of hosted computer facilities through the Internet. Gmail, RIA Checkpoint, and even your iPhone are some applications of cloud computing. LO 12-3

    a) If HP provides a customized bundle of servers, storage, network and security software, and business application software to a customer in Washington State, how is it taxed?
    b) Is HP leasing tangible personal property, which is taxable, or providing a nontaxable service?
    c) Is the buyer of HP's product subject to Washington sales and use tax?
    d) Is HP subject to Washington's B&O tax?
51. Sharon Inc. is headquartered in State X and owns 100 percent of Carol, Joscy, and Janice Corps, which form a single unitary group. Assume sales operations are within the solicitation bounds of Public Law 86-272. Each of the corporations has operations in the following states:

Domicile State	Sharon Inc. State X (throwback)	Carol Corp State Y (throwback)	Josey Corp State Z (nonthrowback)	Janice Corp State Z (nonthrowback)
Dividend income	$ 1,000	$ 200	$ 300	$ 500
Business income	50,000	30,000	10,000	10,000
Sales: State X	70,000	10,000	10,000	10,000
State Y		40,000	5,000	
State Z		20,000	20,000	10,000
State A	20,000			
State B	10,000			10,000
Property: State X	50,000	20,000		10,000
State Y		80,000		
State Z			25,000	20,000
State A	50,000			
Payroll: State X	10,000	10,000		
State Y		40,000		
State Z			3,000	10,000
State A				10,000

Compute the following for State X assuming a tax rate of 15 percent.

a) Calculate the State X apportionment factor for Sharon Inc., Carol Corp., Josey Corp., and Janice Corp.
b) Calculate the business income apportioned to State X.
c) Calculate the taxable income for State X for each company.
d) Determine the tax liability for State X for the entire group.

52. Happy Hippos (HH) is a manufacturer and retailer of New England crafts headquartered in Camden, Maine. HH provides services and has sales, employees, property, and commercial domicile as follows:

Happy Hippos In-State Activities

State	Sales	Employees	Property	Services	Commercial Domicile
Connecticut	✓	✓		✓	
Maine	✓	✓	✓	✓	✓
Massachusetts	✓	✓			
New Hampshire	✓				
Rhode Island	✓	✓			
Vermont	✓	✓	✓	✓	

Happy Hippos sales of goods and services by state are as follows:

Happy Hippos Sales

State	Goods	Services	Total
Connecticut	$ 78,231	$ 52,321	$130,552
Maine	292,813	81,313	374,126
Massachusetts	90,238		90,238
New Hampshire	129,322		129,322
Rhode Island	98,313		98,313
Vermont	123,914	23,942	147,856
Totals	$812,831	$157,576	$970,407

HH has federal taxable income of $282,487 for the current year. Included in federal taxable income are the following income and deductions:

- $12,000 of Vermont rental income.
- City of Orono, Maine, bond interest of $10,000.
- $10,000 of dividends.
- $2,498 of state tax refund included in income.
- $32,084 of state net income tax expense.
- $59,234 of federal depreciation.

Maine state depreciation for the year was $47,923, and Maine doesn't allow deductions for state net income taxes.

The employees present in Connecticut, Massachusetts, and Rhode Island are salespeople who perform only activities protected by Public Law 86-272.

Each of the states is a separate-return state.

HH's payroll is as follows:

Payroll	
State	**Wages**
Connecticut	$ 94,231
Maine	392,195
Massachusetts	167,265
Rhode Island	92,391
Vermont	193,923
Total	$940,005

HH's property is as follows:

Property			
State	**Beginning**	**Ending**	**Rented**
Maine	$ 938,234	$ 937,652	
Vermont	329,134	428,142	$12,000
Total	$1,267,368	$1,365,794	$12,000

a) Determine the states in which HH has sales and use tax nexus.
b) Calculate the sales tax HH must remit assuming the following sales tax rates:
   - Connecticut (6 percent)
   - Maine (8 percent)
   - Massachusetts (7 percent)
   - New Hampshire (8.5 percent)
   - Rhode Island (5 percent)
   - Vermont (9 percent)
c) Determine the states in which HH has income tax nexus.
d) Determine HH's state tax base for Maine, assuming federal taxable income of $282,487.
e) Calculate business and nonbusiness income.
f) Determine HH's Maine apportionment factors using the three-factor method (assume that Maine is a throwback state).
g) Calculate HH's business income apportioned to Maine.
h) Determine HH's allocation of nonbusiness income to Maine.
i) Determine HH's Maine taxable income.
j) Calculate HH's Maine net income tax liability assuming a Maine income tax rate of 5 percent.

chapter

13 The U.S. Taxation of Multinational Transactions

Learning Objectives

Upon completing this chapter, you should be able to:

LO 13-1 Understand the basic U.S. framework for taxing multinational transactions and the role of the foreign tax credit limitation.

LO 13-2 Apply the U.S. source rules for common items of gross income and deductions.

LO 13-3 Recall the role of income tax treaties in international tax planning.

LO 13-4 Identify creditable foreign taxes and compute the foreign tax credit limitation.

LO 13-5 Distinguish between the different forms of doing business outside the United States and list their advantages and disadvantages.

LO 13-6 Comprehend the basic U.S. anti-deferral tax regime and identify common sources of subpart F income.

© Jose Luis Pelaez Inc/Blend Images LLC

Storyline Summary

Detroit Doughnut Depot

Privately held company located in Detroit, Michigan
Operated as a C corporation for U.S. tax purposes
Makes and sells fresh baked goods, homemade sandwiches, and premium coffee and tea drinks

Lily Green

Owner of Detroit Doughnut Depot (3D)

Filing status:	Married filing jointly
Dependents:	Two children
Marginal tax rate:	28 percent

Lily Green was excited about the growth of her coffee and baked goods business since she opened her store in downtown Detroit in 2005. From its humble beginnings, the Detroit Doughnut Depot (3D) had attracted a solid base of loyal customers who appreciated the freshness and organic ingredients that set the company's products apart from its competitors. Many of Lily's customers were commuters from nearby Windsor, Canada. They often asked Lily if she ever considered opening a store in Windsor, where they thought she would find a receptive customer base. Lily was intrigued by the idea of "going global" with her business, but she knew she needed to find someone to help her understand the U.S. and Canadian income tax implications of expanding her business to Windsor. Her first questions dealt with how and when she would be subject to Canadian tax and whether her Canadian activities also would be subject to U.S. tax.

to be continued . . .

Lily Green is about to join a growing trend of expansion by U.S. businesses into international markets. In 1983, gross receipts of non-U.S. subsidiaries of U.S. multinational corporations totaled approximately $720 billion; by 2010, that number exceeded $6 trillion, a more than eightfold increase.[1] Before-tax profits increased from $57 billion in 1983 to more than $1 trillion in 2010. Companies such as Google Inc. and McDonald's Corporation report a significant amount of revenue from international operations. For example, Google Inc. reported revenue from its international operations of $33.1 billion in 2013, approximately 56 percent of its total revenue.[2] McDonald's Corporation reported $28.1 billion of revenues in 2013, more than two-thirds of which came from outside the United States.

As dramatic as the outflow of investment from the United States has been, the inflow of investment by non-U.S. businesses and individuals into the United States has been just as impressive. According to the U.S. Bureau of Economic Analysis, the total amount of foreign-owned assets in the United States increased by more than 1,000 percent between 1989 and 2013 to $26.5 trillion.[3] U.S. subsidiaries of non-U.S. companies currently employ 5.6 million Americans.[4] Familiar non-U.S. headquartered companies with large U.S. operations include BP Global (United Kingdom), Toyota Motor Corporation (Japan), Honda Motor Corporation (Japan), Nissan Group (Japan), Nestle S.A. (Switzerland), Sony Corporation (Japan), GlaxoSmithKline PLC (United Kingdom), Volkswagen AG (Germany), Samsung Group (South Korea), BMW AG (Germany), Bridgestone Corporation (Japan), Bayer AG (Germany), and Philips Electronics N.V. (Netherlands).

This chapter provides a basic overview of the U.S. tax consequences related to transactions that span more than one national tax jurisdiction (in our storyline, the United States and Canada). We focus primarily on the U.S. tax rules that apply to **outbound transactions,** where a U.S. person engages in a transaction that occurs outside the United States or involves a non-U.S. person.[5] We also discuss briefly the U.S. tax rules that apply to **inbound transactions,** where a non-U.S. person engages in a transaction that occurs within the United States or involves a U.S. person. Most of the U.S. income tax rules that apply to multinational transactions are found in subchapter N of the Internal Revenue Code (§861–§999).

LO 13-1

THE U.S. FRAMEWORK FOR TAXING MULTINATIONAL TRANSACTIONS

When a U.S. person engages in a transaction that involves a country outside the United States, there arises the issue as to which tax authority or authorities have jurisdiction (i.e., the legal right) to tax that transaction. All governments (national, state, and local) must adopt a basis on which to claim the right to tax income. The criteria they choose to assert their right to tax a person or transaction is called **nexus.** At the national level, governments most often determine nexus by either the geographic source of the income **(source-based jurisdiction)** or the taxpayer's citizenship or residence **(residence-based jurisdiction).**

Once nexus is established, a government must decide how a person's income and expenses are to be allocated and apportioned to its tax jurisdiction. Under a

[1]Bureau of Economic Analysis, *U.S. Direct investment Abroad: Financial and Operating Data for U.S. Multinational Companies,* available at www.bea.gov.

[2]As a reference point, Google Inc. reported a *loss* of $42.3 million in 2005 from international operations.

[3]Bureau of Economic Analysis, *U.S. Net International Investment Position: End of Fourth Quarter and Year 2013.* Available at www.bea.gov.

[4]Organization for International Investment, data available at www.ofii.org.

[5]As used in this chapter, a "person" includes an individual, corporation, partnership, trust, estate, or association. Section 7701(a)(1). The "United States," as used in this context, includes only the 50 states and the District of Columbia. §7701(a)(9).

residence-based approach, a country taxes the worldwide income of the person earning the income. Under a source-based approach, a country taxes only the income earned within its boundaries. When applying a source-based approach, a government must develop source rules to allocate and apportion income and expenses to its jurisdiction. Within the United States, states use apportionment formulas that take into account sales, property, and payroll, or some combination of these factors, to apportion income and expenses to its tax jurisdiction.[6]

Income earned by a citizen or resident of one country that has its source in another country potentially can be taxed by both countries. The country where the taxpayer resides can assert residence-based jurisdiction, whereas the country where the income is earned can apply geographic source-based jurisdiction. To alleviate (mitigate) such double taxation and to promote international commerce, governments often allow their residents a tax credit for foreign income taxes paid on *foreign source* income. National governments also enter into bilateral income tax treaties with other national governments to mitigate the double taxation of income earned by residents of one country in the other country. Under a treaty, both countries may agree not to tax income earned within their boundaries by a resident of the other country.

The United States applies both residence-based jurisdiction and source-based jurisdiction in asserting its right to tax income. The U.S. government taxes *citizens* and *residents* on their worldwide income, regardless of source (residence-based jurisdiction).[7] In contrast, the U.S. government only taxes *nonresidents* on income that is "U.S. source" or is connected with the operation of a U.S. trade or business (source-based jurisdiction).

THE KEY FACTS

Basic Framework for U.S. Taxation of Multinational Transactions

- The United States taxes citizens and residents on their worldwide income and nonresidents on their U.S. source income.
- A noncitizen is treated as a U.S. resident for income tax purposes if the individual is a permanent resident (has a green card) or meets a substantial presence test.
- Nonresident income is characterized as either ECI or FDAP income.
  - ECI is taxed on a net basis using the U.S. graduated tax rates.
  - FDAP is taxed on a gross basis through a flat withholding tax.
- The U.S. allows citizens and residents a tax credit for foreign income taxes paid on foreign source income.
- The foreign tax credit is limited to the percentage of foreign source taxable income to taxable income times the precredit income tax on total taxable income.

U.S. Taxation of a Nonresident

U.S. source income earned by a nonresident is classified into two categories for U.S. tax purposes: (1) **effectively connected income** (ECI) and (2) **fixed and determinable, annual or periodic income** (FDAP). Income that is effectively connected with a U.S. trade or business is subject to *net taxation* (i.e., gross income minus deductions) at the U.S. graduated tax rates. A nonresident reports such income and related deductions on a U.S. tax return, either a Form 1120F for a corporation or a Form 1040NR for an individual. FDAP income, which is generally passive income such as dividends, interest, rents, or royalties, is subject to a *withholding tax* regime applied to *gross income.* The payor of the FDAP income withholds the tax at the statutory rate (30 percent under U.S. tax law) or less under a treaty arrangement and remits it to the government. The recipient of the FDAP income usually does not have to file a tax return and does not reduce the FDAP income by any deductions. Most countries, including Canada, apply a similar tax regime to U.S. persons earning income within their jurisdiction.[8]

Example 13-1

Lily decided to open a store in Windsor, Canada, from which she will sell baked goods and sandwiches made in her U.S. store and transported daily across the border. She elected to operate the store as a **branch** (an unincorporated division) of Detroit Doughnut Depot (3D) for Canadian tax purposes. Will 3D be subject to tax in Canada on any taxable income it earns through its Windsor store?

Answer: Yes. 3D will have nexus in Canada because it operates a business there (residence-based jurisdiction). As a result, Canada and the Province of Ontario will tax the branch's Canadian-source taxable income.

(continued on page 13-4)

[6]See Chapter 12 for a more thorough discussion of how states apportion income.

[7]The United States is the only country that applies full worldwide taxation based on citizenship as well as residency.

[8]Canada applies a 25 percent withholding tax rate on dividends, rents, and royalties unless reduced under a treaty. Canada does not impose a withholding tax on interest paid to a nonresident dealing at arm's length with the lender.

How will Canada tax 3D's Canadian-source taxable income?

Answer: Canada will apply the appropriate corporate tax rate(s) to the branch's taxable income (gross income less deductions). For 2015, the general Canadian corporate tax rate is a flat 15 percent after abatements. The province of Ontario also will impose an income tax of 10 percent on the branch's taxable income.

What if: Assume 3D does not operate a business in Canada but owns 5 percent of the stock in a Canadian company that pays the company a C$100 dividend each year.[9] How will Canada tax 3D on the dividend income it receives from its investment in the stock of a Canadian company?

Answer: Canada will apply a flat withholding tax on the gross amount of the dividend.[10]

Definition of a Resident for U.S. Tax Purposes

An individual who is not a U.S. citizen is characterized for U.S. tax purposes as either a **resident alien** or a **nonresident alien.** An individual becomes a U.S. resident by satisfying one of two tests found in the IRC.[11] Under the first test, sometimes referred to as the *green card test,* an individual is treated as a resident if he or she possesses a permanent resident visa ("green card") at any time during the calendar year. Under the second test, sometimes referred to as the *substantial presence test,* an individual becomes a U.S. resident when he or she is *physically present* in the United States for 31 days or more during the current calendar year, *and* the number of days of physical presence during the current calendar year plus one-third times the number of days of physical presence during the first preceding year plus one-sixth times the number of days of physical presence during the second preceding year equals or exceeds 183 days.[12] As we will discuss later in the chapter, these rules often are modified by treaties between the United States and other countries to limit instances where an individual might be taxed as a resident by more than one country.

As always, there are a number of exceptions to the physical presence test. For example, international students and teachers generally are exempt from the physical presence test for five and two years, respectively. Individuals who are present in the United States during the current year for less than 183 days and who establish that they have a "closer connection" to another country can elect to be exempt from the physical presence test.[13] Other exemptions apply to unexpected medical conditions that arise while an individual is in the United States and to commuters from Canada and Mexico who have a U.S. employer.

The residence of a corporation for U.S. tax purposes generally is determined by the entity's country of incorporation. For example, the parent company of Tyco International Ltd. is incorporated in Switzerland, although it is managed in the United States. For U.S. tax purposes, the parent company of Tyco is treated as a nonresident corporation, although its U.S. subsidiaries and U.S. branches are treated as U.S. residents. Some countries, such as the United Kingdom and Ireland, determine a corporation's residence based on where central management of the company is located. The U.K. government would treat the parent company of Tyco as a U.S. resident because the company is managed in the United States.

[9]The national currency of Canada is the Canadian dollar, abbreviated C$.

[10]Under the U.S.-Canada income tax treaty, the withholding tax on this dividend is 15 percent.

[11]§7701(b).

[12]For purposes of this test, a full day is considered any part of a day.

[13]An individual usually satisfies the closer connection test by demonstrating that he or she has a "tax home" in another country. A "tax home" is defined as the taxpayer's regular place of business or *regular place of abode.*

Example 13-2

What if: Assume for quality control purposes that Lily decided to do all of the baking for her Windsor store in Detroit. Every morning a Windsor employee drives a van to Detroit and picks up the baked goods for sale in Windsor. One of her employees, Stan Lee Cupp, made the 2-hour trip on 132 different days during 2015. He was not physically present in the United States prior to 2015. Will Stan be considered a U.S. resident in 2015 applying only the substantial presence test?

Answer: No. Although he is physically present in the United States for more than 30 days in 2015, Stan does not satisfy the 183-day test when applying the formula [132 + (1/3 × 0) + (1/6 × 0) = 132].

What if: Assume Stan continues to be physically present in the United States for 132 days in 2016 and 2017. Will Stan be considered a U.S. resident in 2016 or 2017 applying only the substantial presence test?

Answer:

2016: No. He does not satisfy the 183-day test when applying the formula [132 + (1/3 × 132) + (1/6 × 0) = 176].

2017: Yes. He now satisfies the 183-day test when applying the formula [132 + (1/3 × 132) + (1/6 × 132) = 198].

Does Stan qualify for any exceptions that allow him to avoid being treated as a U.S. resident in 2017?

Answer: Yes. Stan can avoid being a U.S. resident under the closer connection test because he was physically present in the United States for less than 183 days in 2017 and his tax home is in Canada. If Stan is in the United States for 183 days or more, he will have to rely on the U.S.-Canada income tax treaty to avoid being considered a U.S. resident for income tax purposes (to be discussed in more detail later in the chapter).

Overview of the U.S. Foreign Tax Credit System

The United States mitigates the double taxation of foreign source income by allowing citizens and residents to claim a **foreign tax credit** (FTC) for foreign income taxes paid on their *foreign source* income. The goal of the FTC is to keep a U.S. taxpayer's worldwide *effective tax rate* (total income taxes paid/taxable income) from exceeding the U.S. statutory tax rate. The United States attempts to achieve this result through the **foreign tax credit limitation,** which is computed as follows:

$$\frac{\text{Foreign source taxable income}}{\text{Total taxable income}} \times \text{Precredit U.S. tax on total taxable income}$$

Currently, the foreign tax credit limitation is computed separately for two categories of foreign source income—passive category income and general category income. (Special rules apply to income resourced by treaty and income earned in designated countries.) We discuss the type of income put in each category in more detail later in this chapter. A taxpayer can carry any unused (excess) FTC for the current year back to the previous tax year and then forward to the next ten future tax years.

Example 13-3

Lily's store in Windsor was an immediate success and reported taxable income on its Canadian operations of C$20,000 for 2015. 3D paid a combined national and provincial income tax of C$5,000 on its taxable income (at a flat tax rate of 25 percent). Because 3D operates the Windsor store as a branch, it also must report the income on its U.S. corporate income tax return along with taxable income from its Detroit operations. Assuming a translation rate of C$1:US$1, 3D reports the Canadian taxable income on its U.S. tax return as $20,000 and reports the Canadian income taxes as $5,000.

(continued on page 13-6)

3D reported U.S. taxable income of $80,000. The company's U.S. income tax on $100,000 of taxable income is $22,250 before any credit for the income taxes paid to Canada (see the corporate tax rate schedule on the inside back cover).

Using the above facts, what is the foreign tax credit limitation that applies to 3D's Canadian income taxes for 2015?

Answer: $4,450, computed as $20,000/$100,000 × $22,250,

where:

$20,000 = Foreign source taxable income
$100,000 = Total taxable income
$22,250 = Precredit U.S. tax on total taxable income

What is 3D's net U.S. tax after subtracting the available foreign tax credit?

Answer: $17,800, computed as $22,250 − $4,450. 3D has an excess foreign tax credit of $550 ($5,000 − $4,450) that it can carry forward for ten years.

What is 3D's effective tax rate on its total taxable income for 2015?

Answer: 22.8 percent, computed as ($5,000 + $17,800)/$100,000.

What if: Suppose the United States did not give 3D a foreign tax credit or a deduction for the Canadian taxes it paid on the Windsor operations. What would have been 3D's effective tax rate on its total taxable income for 2015?

Answer: 27.25 percent, computed as ($5,000 + $22,250)/$100,000.

What if: Assume 3D earned all of its $100,000 taxable income in the United States and paid no Canadian income taxes. What would have been the company's effective tax rate on its total taxable income for 2015?

Answer: 22.25 percent, computed as $22,250/$100,000.

What if: Assume 3D paid Canadian income taxes of C$4,000 for 2015 (a flat tax rate of 20 percent). What would have been its net U.S. tax after subtracting the available foreign tax credit?

Answer: $18,250, computed as $22,250 − $4,000.

What would have been 3D's effective tax rate on its total taxable income for 2015?

Answer: 22.25 percent, computed as ($4,000 + $18,250)/$100,000. In this example, 3D receives a full credit for the Canadian taxes in 2015 because the Canadian tax rate is less than the average U.S. tax rate. The company's effective tax rate on its total taxable income is the same as if it had earned all of the income in the United States.

LO 13-2

U.S. SOURCE RULES FOR GROSS INCOME AND DEDUCTIONS

Many of the U.S. tax rules that apply to multinational transactions require taxpayers to determine the jurisdictional (geographic) source (U.S. or foreign) of their gross income.[14] The source rules determine whether income and related deductions are from sources within or without the United States. All developed countries have source-of-income rules, although most practitioners consider the U.S. rules to be the most complex in the world.

The U.S. source-of-income rules are important to *non-U.S. persons* because they limit the scope of U.S. taxation to only their U.S. source income. For *U.S. persons,* the primary purpose of the U.S. source-of-income rules is to calculate *foreign source taxable income* in the numerator of the foreign tax credit limitation. The United States imposes a tax on the worldwide income of U.S. persons, regardless of its source or the U.S. person's residence. The United States cedes *primary jurisdiction* to foreign governments to

[14]The U.S. federal income tax source rules are found in §861–§865 and the accompanying regulations.

tax U.S. persons on income earned outside the United States while retaining the *residual* right to tax foreign source income to the extent it has not been "fully taxed" by the foreign government. The net result is that the United States taxes foreign source income earned by U.S. persons at a rate that theoretically reflects the difference between the U.S. tax rate and the foreign tax rate imposed on the income.

U.S. persons must understand the source-of-income rules in other situations. For example, U.S. citizens and residents employed outside the United States may be eligible to exclude a portion of their *foreign source earned income* from U.S. taxation under §911.[15] In addition, U.S. persons that pay U.S.-source FDAP income to foreign payees (e.g., interest or dividends) usually are required to withhold U.S. taxes on such payments.[16]

The source-of-income rules are definitional in nature; they do not impose a tax liability, create income, or allow a deduction. Although the primary focus of the source rules is on where the economic activity that generates income takes place, the U.S. government also uses the source rules to advance a variety of international tax policy objectives.

THE KEY FACTS

Source Rules

- The source rules determine if income or deductions are treated as U.S. source or foreign source.
- For a U.S. taxpayer, the source rules primarily determine foreign taxable income in the calculation of the foreign tax credit limitation.
- For a non-U.S. taxpayer, the source rules determine what income is subject to U.S. taxation.

Source of Income Rules

The Internal Revenue Code defines eight classes of gross income from sources within the United States[17] and eight classes of gross income from sources without the United States.[18] A summary of the general rules that apply to common sources of income follows. A detailed discussion of all of the exceptions to these rules is beyond the scope of this text.

Interest As a general rule, the taxpayer looks to the *residence* of the party *paying* the interest (the borrower) to determine the geographic source of interest received. A borrower's residence is determined at the time the interest is paid. Factors that determine an individual's residence include the location of the individual's family; whether the person buys a home, pays foreign taxes, and becomes involved in social and community affairs; and the length of time spent in a country. Under these general rules, interest income is U.S. source if it is paid by the United States or the District of Columbia, a noncorporate U.S. resident, or a U.S. corporation. Although interest income paid by a U.S. bank to a nonresident (e.g., an international student attending your university) is U.S.-source income, such interest is exempt from U.S. withholding or other income taxation.[19] This exception is designed to attract foreign capital to U.S. banks.

Example 13-4

3D was dissatisfied with the 1 percent interest rate it received on its checking account at Bank of America in Detroit. Lily's investment adviser suggested the company invest $50,000 in 5-year bonds issued by the Canadian government with an interest rate of 3 percent. During 2015, 3D received C$1,500 in interest from the bonds. Per the U.S.-Canada treaty, the Canadian government did not withhold taxes on the payment. Assume the translation rate is C$1:US$1.

What is the source, U.S. or foreign, of the interest Lily receives on the bonds?

Answer: Foreign source. The source of interest income depends on the residence of the borrower at the time the interest is paid. The Canadian government is considered a resident of Canada for U.S. source rule purposes.

[15]If certain conditions are met, a U.S. individual can exclude up to $100,800 of earned income from U.S. taxation in 2015 plus additional earnings equal to excess "foreign housing expenses" under §911.

[16]§1441.

[17]§861(a).

[18]§862(a).

[19]§871(i)(2)(A) and §881(d).

Dividends In general, the source of dividend income is determined by the *residence* of the corporation paying the dividend. Residence usually is determined by the corporation's country of incorporation or organization (in some countries, such as the United Kingdom, a corporation's residence is determined by where its central management is located).

Example 13-5

As part of diversifying its investment portfolio, 3D purchased 200 shares of Scotiabank (Bank of Nova Scotia, Canada). In 2015, Scotiabank paid 3D dividends of C$400. Scotiabank withheld C$60 in taxes (15 percent) on the payment. Assume the translation rate is C$1:US$1.

What is the source, U.S. or foreign, of the dividend 3D receives on the stock?

Answer: Foreign source. The source of dividend income depends on the residence of the payor of the dividend. Scotiabank is headquartered in Toronto, Canada, and is a resident of Canada for U.S. source rule purposes.

Compensation for Services The source of compensation received for "labor or personal services" is determined by the *location* where the service is performed. The IRS and the courts have held that the term includes activities of employees, independent contractors, artists, entertainers, athletes, and even corporations offering "personal services" (e.g., accounting). The Code provides a limited **commercial traveler exception,** in which personal service compensation earned by nonresidents within the U.S. is *not* treated as U.S. source if the individual meets the following criteria:

- The individual was present in the United States for not more than 90 days during the current taxable year;[20]
- Compensation for the services does not exceed $3,000; and
- The services are performed for a nonresident alien, foreign corporation, or foreign partnership or for the foreign office of a domestic corporation.[21]

The United States frequently alters the limitations on length of stay and compensation through treaty agreements. In most cases, the 90-day limit is extended to 183 days, and no dollar limit is put on the amount of compensation received.

Compensation for services performed within and outside the United States must be allocated between U.S. and foreign sources. An individual who receives compensation, other than compensation in the form of fringe benefits, as an employee for labor or personal services performed partly within and partly outside the United States is required to source such compensation on a *time basis*. An individual who receives compensation as an employee for labor or personal services performed partly within and partly outside the United States in the form of fringe benefits (e.g., additional amounts paid for housing or education) is required to source such compensation on a *geographic basis* (i.e., determined by the employee's principal place of work).

Example 13-6

What if: Assume for quality control purposes that Lily decided to do all of the baking for her Windsor store in Detroit. Every morning a Windsor employee would drive a truck to Detroit and pick up the baked goods for sale in Windsor. One of her employees, Stan Lee Cupp, made the 2-hour trip on 120 different days during 2015 (240 hours spent in the U.S.). 3D paid Stan a salary of C$50,000 during 2015. He worked a total of 1,920 hours during 2015. Assume the translation rate is C$1:US$1. How much U.S. source compensation does Stan have in 2015? Base your computation on hours worked.

[20]For purposes of this test, a full day is considered to be any part of a day.

[21]§861(a)(3)(A)–(C).

Answer: $6,250 (C$50,000 × 240/1,920 × $1). Stan sources his salary for U.S. tax purposes based on where he performed the services. Using hours worked, Stan spent 12.5 percent of his time performing services in the United States (240/1,920).

Using only the exception found in the IRC, will Stan be subject to U.S. tax on his U.S.-source wages in 2015?

Answer: Yes. Stan fails the commercial traveler exception. He is in the United States for more than 90 days during 2015.

What if: Assume Stan limits his trips to 90 days during 2015 (180 hours spent in the U.S.). Using only the IRC exception, will Stan be subject to U.S. tax on his U.S.-source salary in 2015?

Answer: Yes. Stan still fails the commercial traveler exception. Although he is in the United States for not more than 90 days, his U.S.-source salary is $4,688 (C$50,000 × 180/1,920 × $1), which exceeds $3,000.

As we discuss later in the chapter, the U.S.-Canada income tax treaty significantly liberalizes the commercial traveler exception to allow Stan to spend more time in the U.S. without being taxed by the U.S. government on his U.S. source wages.

TAXES IN THE REAL WORLD Taxing Professional Golfers

One of the issues that the IRS has struggled with is whether to characterize fees paid to foreign professional golf and tennis players pursuant to on-court endorsement contracts (e.g., wearing a company's logo or using its equipment) as income from royalties or income from personal services, or both. Two recent Tax Court cases involving well-known professional golfers illustrate the complexities of this issue.

The first case involved Retief Goosen, a PGA tour member and winner of the 2001 U.S. Open Championship.[1] Mr. Goosen was a citizen of South Africa and a resident of the United Kingdom, but he spent most of his time competing in the United States and Europe.

Mr. Goosen entered into several endorsement and appearance agreements with sponsors that allowed the sponsor to use his name and likeness to advertise and promote the sponsor's products or in connection with advertising and promoting a specific tournament or event. The "on-course" endorsement agreements required him to wear or use the sponsor's products during golf tournaments whereas the "off-course" endorsement agreements did not have this requirement.

Mr. Goosen reported all his prize money from golf tournaments and appearance fees in the United States as "effectively connected" income taxable in the United States. He characterized his endorsement fees from on-course endorsements as 50 percent royalty income and 50 personal services income. He sourced the personal services income from the on-course endorsement fees to the United States based on the number of days he played within the United States over the total number of days he played golf for the year. Mr. Goosen characterized his endorsement fees from the off-course endorsement agreements as 100 percent royalty income. The IRS argued that the sponsors primarily paid Mr. Goosen to perform personal services, which included playing golf and carrying or wearing the sponsors' products.

The Tax Court awarded a partial victory to both parties. The Court found that Mr. Goosen's name had a value beyond his golf skills and abilities for which his sponsors paid a substantial amount of money for the right to use his name and likeness. The sponsors also valued Goosen's play at tournaments, as evidenced by the fact that the sponsors conditioned the full endorsement fee on his playing in 36 tournaments a year. The court thus held that his performance of services and the use of his name and likeness were equally important and characterized 50 percent of the endorsement fees from the on-course endorsement agreements as royalty income and 50 percent of the fees as personal services income.

The Court held that Mr. Goosen's earnings from playing golf in the United States was effectively connected U.S. source income. The on-course endorsement and appearance fees

[1] *Reteif Goosen v. Commissioner,* 136 T.C. No. 27 (June 9, 2011).

(continued on page 13-10)

and his on-course royalty income also were held to be U.S. source effectively connected income to the extent they were sourced as U.S. source income because payment depended on whether he played a specified number of tournaments. Both categories of income were taxed at the regular U.S. graduated tax rates.

The Court held that income Mr. Goosen received from off-course endorsement agreements did not depend on whether he played in golf tournaments. Thus, the income was not effectively connected with a U.S. trade or business and was thus subject to a 30 percent withholding tax to the extent it was treated as U.S. source income.

The second case involved Sergio Garcia, a Spanish citizen but a resident of Switzerland.[2] The IRS again argued that the "vast majority" of his endorsement income should be treated as personal service income and subject to U.S. taxation at the regular tax rates. Mr. Garcia characterized 85 percent of his endorsement income as royalty income, which was not subject to U.S. taxation under the U.S.-Swiss income tax treaty. The Tax Court judge held that 65 percent of the endorsement income should be characterized as royalty income. It is interesting to note that the Tax Court apportioned a higher percentage of Mr. Garcia's income as royalties because he was designated as a "Global Icon" by the golf company that paid him the endorsement fees. The same company regarded Mr. Goosen as a "brand ambassador" and paid him less than Mr. Garcia because the company valued Mr. Garcia's "flash, looks and maverick personality" more than Mr. Goosen's "cool 'Iceman' demeanor."

[2]*Sergio Garcia v. Commissioner*, 140 T.C. No 6 (March 14, 2013).

Rents and Royalties Rent has its source where the property generating the rent is located. Royalty income has its source where the intangible property or rights generating the royalty is used. Royalties include payments related to intangibles such as patents, copyrights, secret processes and formulas, goodwill, trademarks, trade brands, and franchises. An intangible is "used" in the country that protects the owner against its unauthorized use.

Example 13-7

3D rented its Windsor store for C$2,500 per month, for a total of C$30,000 in 2015. Under the U.S.-Canada income tax treaty, 3D must withhold U.S. taxes at a 30 percent rate on rent payments that flow from the United States to Canada if the rent is U.S.-source income. Will 3D have to withhold taxes on the rent payments it makes in 2015?

Answer: No. The rent is considered foreign source income because the store that is rented is located in Canada.

Gain or Loss from Sale of Real Property In general, gain or loss from the sale of realty has its source where the property sold is located.

Gain or Loss from Sale of Purchased Personal Property Under the general rule, gain or loss from the sale of purchased personal (nonrealty) property[22] has its source based on the *seller's residence*. There are many exceptions to this general rule. In particular, gross income (sales minus cost of goods sold) from the sale of purchased *inventory* is sourced where *title passes*. Title is deemed to pass at the time when, and the place where, the seller's rights, title, and interest in the property are transferred to the buyer.

[22]Personal property under the source rules includes stock of a corporation. Sales of intangible property such as a patent, copyright, secret process, goodwill, trademark, trade brand, or franchise are subject to different source rules.

Inventory Produced within the United States and Sold Outside the United States (§863 Sales) Taxable income derived from the production of *inventory* within the United States and the sale of that inventory outside the United States has special apportionment rules found in regulations issued by the U.S. Treasury.[23] These regulations provide taxpayers with three elective methods for apportioning gross income (defined in these regulations as sales minus cost of goods sold) between U.S. and foreign sources, the one most frequently used being the *50/50 method.*

Under the 50/50 method, the taxpayer sources one-half of the gross income from sales based on where the assets that produce the inventory are located and sources the other half based on where title passes to the inventory. Gross income from sales of inventory that is produced in the United States and sold outside the United States, with title passing outside the United States, is sourced 50 percent U.S. source and 50 percent foreign source.

The 50/50 method provides U.S. producers with the opportunity to "create" foreign source income on export sales. This foreign source income generally is not taxed by the country in which the product is sold, unless the U.S. producer has a physical presence in the foreign country. Adding zero-taxed foreign source income to the numerator of the FTC limitation ratio increases the foreign tax credit amount, which is especially helpful when the taxpayer is in an excess foreign tax credit position.

Example 13-8

Return to the facts in Example 13-3. Lily's store in Windsor reported taxable income on its Canadian operations of C$20,000 for 2015. Detroit Doughnut Depot (3D) paid a combined national and provincial income tax of C$5,000 on its taxable income (at a flat tax rate of 25 percent). 3D reported the Canadian taxable income on its U.S. tax return as $20,000 and reported the Canadian income taxes as $5,000. 3D's Detroit operations reported U.S. taxable income of $80,000. 3D's precredit U.S. tax liability was $22,250 on taxable income of $100,000. As computed in Example 13-3, 3D's FTC is limited to $4,450 ($20,000/$100,000 × $22,250), resulting in an excess FTC of $550 in 2015. 3D's tax adviser suggested that the company could eliminate ("absorb") some of the excess credit by selling additional baked goods it produced in Detroit to grocery stores in Windsor, with shipping terms as FOB: Destination (i.e., title to the goods passes in Canada).

What if: Assume 3D is able to generate additional sales in excess of cost of goods sold of C$10,000 by selling more baked goods to Windsor grocery stores in 2015, and the sales qualify as §863(b) sales. Canada does not impose any Canadian tax on the sales because they were not made out of the Windsor store. 3D's taxable income increases to $110,000, and its precredit U.S. tax increases to $26,150. What is 3D's FTC limitation for 2015 under this change in facts?

Answer: $5,943, computed as $25,000/$110,000 × $26,150,

where:

$25,000 = Foreign source taxable income

$110,000 = Total taxable income

$26,150 = Precredit U.S. tax on total taxable income

3D increases the numerator in the FTC limitation ratio by $5,000 (50% × $10,000) because title passes in Canada. The denominator increases by $10,000, the additional taxable income generated by the §863(b) sales. 3D can now claim the entire FTC of $5,000 on its 2015 tax return.

[23]The regulations are issued under §863(b), which is what gives these sales their name.

Source of Deduction Rules

After determining the source of gross income as being from U.S. or foreign sources, a taxpayer may be required to **allocate** and **apportion** allowable deductions to gross income from each geographical source to compute taxable income from U.S. and foreign sources. For a U.S. taxpayer, this allocation and apportionment process determines the foreign source deductions that are subtracted from foreign source gross income in computing foreign source taxable income in the numerator of the FTC limitation computation. A non-U.S. taxpayer with gross income that is effectively connected with a U.S. trade or business must determine the U.S. source deductions that are subtracted from U.S. gross income to compute U.S. taxable income.

U.S. and non-U.S. taxpayers can have different motivations in seeking to deduct (or not deduct) expenses from either foreign source or U.S. source gross income. A U.S. taxpayer seeking to maximize the foreign tax credit limitation will want to allocate as few deductions to foreign source gross income as possible, the goal being to make the ratio of foreign source taxable income to total taxable income as close to 100 percent as possible (or whatever ratio is needed to absorb any excess credits). Non-U.S. taxpayers operating in a low-tax-rate country (a tax rate less than the U.S. rate) have a tax incentive to allocate as many deductions to U.S. source income as possible to minimize their U.S. tax liability. Non-U.S. taxpayers operating in a high-tax-rate country (a tax rate greater than the U.S. rate) have a worldwide tax incentive to allocate as many deductions to foreign source income as possible to minimize their worldwide tax liability.

ETHICS

International Contractors, Inc. has been hired by the U.S. government to build roads and bridges in Irock, a country with which the United States recently signed a treaty. To facilitate the issuance of visas and licenses to begin construction, an official from the Irock government asked for 100 "facilitating payments" (otherwise known as "grease payments") of $5,000 each from the company. These payments were customary in Irock and did not violate Irock law. The company intended to deduct the $500,000 payment in its financial statements. It was not clear if these payments violated the Foreign Corrupt Practices Act. To avoid IRS and possible Department of Justice scrutiny, the company's tax director suggested that the payment be described as "taxes and licenses" on the tax return (line 17 of Form 1120) without further details. What do you think of the tax director's advice? What tax and other consequences might result from taking this advice?

General Principles of Allocation and Apportionment The IRC provides very broad language in describing how to allocate deductions to U.S. and foreign source gross income. The regulations attempt to match deductions with the gross income such deductions were incurred to produce.[24] Matching usually is done based on the "factual relationship" of the deduction to gross income. Deductions that can be directly associated with a particular item of income (e.g., machine depreciation with manufacturing gross profit) are referred to as **definitely related deductions.** Deductions not directly associated with a particular item of gross income (e.g., medical expenses, property taxes, standard deduction) are referred to as **not definitely related deductions** and are allocated to all gross income.

[24]Reg. §1.861-8 provides the general rules for allocating and apportioning deductions to U.S. and foreign source gross income.

The regulations require the taxpayer to first allocate (associate) deductions to the class or classes of gross income such deductions were incurred to produce. The taxpayer then apportions the deduction between, in most cases, foreign source and U.S. source gross income. The regulations allow the taxpayer to apportion deductions using a method that reflects the factual relation between the deduction and the grouping of gross income. Examples include units sold, gross sales or receipts, and gross income.

Example 13-9

Return to the facts in Example 13-3. Lily's store in Windsor reported taxable income on its Canadian operations of C$20,000 for 2015. For U.S. tax purposes, foreign source gross income was $25,000. 3D paid a combined national and provincial income tax of C$5,000 on its taxable income (at a flat tax rate of 25 percent). The company reported the $20,000 taxable income on its U.S. corporate income tax return along with $80,000 of taxable income from its Detroit operations. 3D's U.S. income tax on $100,000 of taxable income is $22,250 before any credit for the income taxes paid to Canada. Included in the computation of taxable income was a deduction of $30,000 for advertising that 3D incurred to promote its stores in Detroit and Windsor. 3D elected to apportion the advertising deduction based on sales. For 2015, Detroit sales were $400,000 and Windsor sales were $100,000. How much of the $30,000 advertising deduction does 3D apportion to its foreign source taxable income for FTC purposes?

Answer: $6,000, computed as $100,000/$500,000 × $30,000,

where:

$100,000 = Canadian sales
$500,000 = Total sales
$30,000 = Advertising deduction

Using the above facts, what is the foreign tax credit limitation that applies to 3D's Canadian income taxes for 2015?

Answer: $4,227, computed as ($25,000 − $6,000)/$100,000 × $22,250,

where:

$25,000 = Foreign source gross income
$6,000 = Apportioned advertising deduction
$100,000 = Total taxable income
$22,250 = Precredit U.S. tax on total taxable income

Apportioning some of the advertising deduction to the numerator of 3D's FTC limitation ratio reduces the amount of foreign income taxes that are creditable in 2015.

Special Apportionment Rules Special apportionment rules apply to nine categories of deductions, most notably interest, research and experimentation, state and local income taxes, losses on property disposition, and charitable contributions.[25] These special apportionment rules are very complicated, and the details are beyond the scope of this text. The basic rules for interest expense and research and experimentation are discussed below.

Interest expense is allocated to all gross income using as a basis the assets that generated such income. Interest can be apportioned based on average tax book value or average fair market value for the year. Assets are attributed to income based on the source and type of income they generate, have generated, or may reasonably be

[25]The other deductions are stewardship expenses attributable to dividends received, supportive expenses, net operating losses, and legal and accounting fees.

expected to generate. Taxpayers may switch to the fair market value method at any time, but a switch back to the tax book value method requires permission from the commissioner. A taxpayer using the tax book value method can elect to use the alternative depreciation system on U.S. assets solely for purposes of apportioning interest expense.

Example 13-10

Expanding on the facts in Example 13-9, 3D borrowed $100,000 from Bank of America in Detroit and paid interest expense of $6,000 in 2015. 3D elected to apportion this interest expense between U.S. and foreign source income using average tax book value. 3D's U.S. assets had an average tax book value of $250,000 in 2015, and its foreign assets had an average tax book value of $50,000 in 2015. How much of the $6,000 interest deduction does 3D apportion to its foreign source taxable income for FTC purposes?

Answer: $1,000, computed as $50,000/$300,000 × $6,000,

where:

$50,000 = Average tax book value of Canadian assets
$300,000 = Total average tax book value of all of 3D's assets
$6,000 = Interest expense

Taking into account the apportioned advertising deduction and interest deduction, what is the foreign tax credit limitation that applies to 3D's Canadian income taxes for 2015?

Answer: $4,005, computed as ($25,000 − $6,000 − $1,000)/$100,000 × $22,250,

where:

$25,000 = Foreign source gross income
$6,000 = Apportioned advertising expense
$1,000 = Apportioned interest expense
$100,000 = Total taxable income
$22,250 = Precredit U.S. tax on total taxable income

Allocation of a portion of the interest expense to the numerator of 3D's FTC limitation ratio further reduces the amount of foreign taxes that are creditable in 2015.

Research and experimental (R&E) expenditures must be apportioned between U.S. and foreign source income using either a sales method or a gross income method. Taxpayers can apportion a percentage of R&E based on where the research is conducted. The amount that can be sourced under this exclusive apportionment method is 50 percent if the sales method is elected and 25 percent if the gross income method is elected.

Example 13-11

Expanding on the facts in Example 13-9 and Example 13-10, 3D incurred $8,000 of research and experimentation (R&E) expenses in developing new flavors of doughnuts and coffee. 3D incurred these expenses in its Detroit bakery and deducted the amount in computing its taxable income. 3D elected to apportion this R&E expense between U.S. and foreign source income using the sales method. For 2015, Detroit sales were $400,000 and Windsor sales were $100,000. How much of the $8,000 R&E expense does 3D apportion to its foreign source taxable income for FTC purposes?

Answer: $800, computed as $100,000/$500,000 × $4,000,

where:

$100,000 = Canadian sales

$500,000 = Total sales

$4,000 = R&E expense not exclusively apportioned to U.S. sources

3D apportions 50 percent of the $8,000 to U.S. source taxable income under the exclusive apportionment method. The remaining $4,000 is apportioned between U.S. and foreign source income based on sales.

Taking into account the apportioned advertising deduction, interest expense, and R&E expense, what is the foreign tax credit limitation that applies to 3D's Canadian income taxes for 2015?

Answer: $3,827, computed as ($25,000 − $6,000 − $1,000 − $800)/$100,000 × $22,250,

where:

$25,000 = Foreign source gross income

$6,000 = Apportioned advertising expense

$1,000 = Apportioned interest expense

$800 = Apportioned R&E expense

$100,000 = Total taxable income

$22,250 = Precredit U.S. tax on total taxable income

Allocation of a portion of the R&E expense to the numerator of 3D's FTC limitation ratio further reduces the amount of foreign taxes that are creditable in 2015.

What if: Assume 3D elected to use the gross income method to apportion R&E. For 2015, gross income from Detroit sales was $100,000 and gross income from Windsor sales was $25,000. How much of the $8,000 R&E expense does 3D apportion to its foreign source taxable income for FTC purposes?

Answer: $1,200, computed as $25,000/$125,000 × $6,000,

where:

$25,000 = Foreign source gross income

$125,000 = Total gross income

$6,000 = R&E expense not exclusively apportioned to U.S. sources

3D apportions 25 percent of the $8,000 to U.S. source taxable income under the exclusive apportionment method ($2,000). The remaining $6,000 is apportioned between U.S. and foreign source income based on gross income.

THE KEY FACTS

Treaties

- Treaties are designed to encourage cross-border trade by reducing the double taxation of such income by the countries that are party to the treaty.
- Treaties define when a resident of one country has nexus in the other country.
- Treaties reduce or eliminate the withholding tax imposed on cross-border payments such as interest, dividends, and royalties.

The foreign tax credit limitation is computed on Form 1118 (corporations) or Form 1116 (individuals). Exhibit 13-1 presents a completed Form 1118 for the cumulative facts in Examples 13-9, 13-10, and 13-11.

TREATIES

LO 13-3

A tax treaty is a bilateral agreement between two contracting countries in which each agrees to modify its own tax laws to achieve reciprocal benefits. The general purpose of an income tax treaty is to eliminate or reduce the impact of double taxation so that residents paying taxes to one country will not have the full burden of taxes in the other country. The United States signed its first income tax treaty with France in 1939. The United States now has income tax treaties with 67 countries.

EXHIBIT 13-1 Form 1118: Foreign Tax Credit Corporations, Schedules A, B, F, and H for 3D Corporation, cumulative facts from Examples 13-9, 13-10, and 13-11

Form **1118** (Rev. December 2014) Department of the Treasury Internal Revenue Service

Foreign Tax Credit—Corporations

► Information about Form 1118 and its separate instructions is at www.irs.gov/form1118.
► Attach to the corporation's tax return.

For calendar year 20 , or other tax year beginning , 20 , and ending , 20

OMB No. 1545-0123

Name of corporation: **Detroit Doughnut Depot** | Employer identification number

Use a **separate** Form 1118 for each applicable category of income listed below. See **Categories of Income** in the instructions. Also, see **Specific Instructions.** Check only one box on each form.

☐ Passive Category Income ☐ Section 901(j) Income: Name of Sanctioned Country ► ______
☑ General Category Income ☐ Income Re-sourced by Treaty: Name of Country ► ______

Schedule A **Income or (Loss) Before Adjustments** *(Report all amounts in U.S. dollars. See **Specific Instructions.**)*

Gross Income or (Loss) From Sources Outside the United States (*INCLUDE* Foreign Branch Gross Income here *and* on Schedule F)

	1. Foreign Country or U.S. Possession (Enter two-letter code; see instructions. Use a separate line for each.) *	2. Deemed Dividends (see instructions) (a) Exclude gross-up	2. (b) Gross-up (sec. 78)	3. Other Dividends (a) Exclude gross-up	3. (b) Gross-up (sec. 78)	4. Interest	5. Gross Rents, Royalties, and License Fees	6. Gross Income From Performance of Services	7. Other (attach schedule)	8. Total (add columns 2(a) through 7)
A	CN								25,000	25,000
B										
C										
D										
E										
F										
Totals (add lines A through F)									25,000	25,000

* For section 863(b) income, NOLs, income from RICs, and high-taxed income, use a single line (see instructions).

Deductions (*INCLUDE* Foreign Branch Deductions here *and* on Schedule F)

	9. Definitely Allocable Deductions — Rental, Royalty, and Licensing Expenses: (a) Depreciation, Depletion, and Amortization	(b) Other Expenses	(c) Expenses Related to Gross Income From Performance of Services	(d) Other Definitely Allocable Deductions	(e) Total Definitely Allocable Deductions (add columns 9(a) through 9(d))	10. Apportioned Share of Deductions Not Definitely Allocable (enter amount from applicable line of Schedule H, Part II, column (d))	11. Net Operating Loss Deduction	12. Total Deductions (add columns 9(e) through 11)	13. Total Income or (Loss) Before Adjustments (subtract column 12 from column 8)
A				6,000	6,000	1,800		7,800	17,200
B									
C									
D									
E									
F									
Totals				6,000	6,000	1,800		7,800	17,200

For Paperwork Reduction Act Notice, see separate instructions. Cat. No. 10900F Form **1118** (Rev. 12-2014)

Form 1118 (Rev. 12-2014) Page **2**

Schedule B **Foreign Tax Credit** *(Report all foreign tax amounts in U.S. dollars.)*

Part I—Foreign Taxes Paid, Accrued, and Deemed Paid *(see instructions)*

2. Foreign Taxes Paid or Accrued (attach schedule showing amounts in foreign currency and conversion rate(s) used)

	1. Credit is Claimed for Taxes (check one): ☑ Paid — Date Paid	☐ Accrued — Date Accrued	Tax Withheld at Source on: (a) Dividends	(b) Interest	(c) Rents, Royalties, and License Fees	Other Foreign Taxes Paid or Accrued on: (d) Section 863(b) Income	(e) Foreign Branch Income	(f) Services Income	(g) Other	(h) Total Foreign Taxes Paid or Accrued (add columns 2(a) through 2(g))	3. Tax Deemed Paid (from Schedule C—Part I, column 12, Part II, column 8(b), and Part III, column 8)
A	various						5,000			5,000	
B											
C											
D											
E											
F											
Totals (add lines A through F)							5,000			5,000	

Part II—Separate Foreign Tax Credit *(Complete a **separate** Part II for **each** applicable category of income.)*

1a	Total foreign taxes paid or accrued (total from Part I, column 2(h))	5,000	
b	Foreign taxes paid or accrued by the corporation during prior tax years that were suspended due to the rules of section 909 and for which the related income is taken into account by the corporation during the current tax year (see instructions)		
2	Total taxes deemed paid (total from Part I, column 3)	5,000	
3	Reductions of taxes paid, accrued, or deemed paid (enter total from Schedule G)	( )	
4	Taxes reclassified under high-tax kickout		
5	Enter the sum of any carryover of foreign taxes (from Schedule K, line 3, column (xiv) and from Schedule I, Part III, line 3) plus any carrybacks to the current tax year		
6	Total foreign taxes (combine lines 1a through 5)		5,000
7	Enter the amount from the applicable column of Schedule J, Part I, line 11 (see instructions). If Schedule J is **not** required to be completed, enter the result from the "Totals" line of column 13 of the applicable Schedule A		17,200
8a	Total taxable income from all sources (enter taxable income from the corporation's tax return)	100,000	
b	Adjustments to line 8a (see instructions)	0	
c	Subtract line 8b from line 8a		100,000
9	Divide line 7 by line 8c. Enter the resulting fraction as a decimal (see instructions). If line 7 is greater than line 8c, enter 1		.172
10	Total U.S. income tax against which credit is allowed (regular tax liability (see section 26(b)) minus American Samoa economic development credit)		22,250
11	Credit limitation (multiply line 9 by line 10) (see instructions)		3,827
12	**Separate foreign tax credit** (enter the smaller of line 6 or line 11 here and on the appropriate line of Part III)		3,827

Part III—Summary of Separate Credits (Enter amounts from Part II, line 12 for **each** applicable category of income. **Do not** include taxes paid to sanctioned countries.)

1	Credit for taxes on passive category income		
2	Credit for taxes on general category income	3,827	
3	Credit for taxes on income re-sourced by treaty (combine all such credits on this line)		
4	Total (add lines 1 through 3)		3,827
5	Reduction in credit for international boycott operations (see instructions)		
6	**Total foreign tax credit** (subtract line 5 from line 4). Enter here and on the appropriate line of the corporation's tax return		3,827

Form **1118** (Rev. 12-2014)

EXHIBIT 13-1 Form 1118: Foreign Tax Credit Corporations, Schedules A, B, F, and H for 3D Corporation, cumulative facts from Examples 13-9, 13-10, and 13-11 (*concluded*)

Form 1118 (Rev. 12-2014)

Schedule F **Gross Income and Definitely Allocable Deductions for Foreign Branches**

	1. Foreign Country or U.S. Possession (Enter two-letter code from Schedule A, column 1. Use a separate line for each.)	2. Gross Income	3. Definitely Allocable Deductions
A	CN	25,000	6,000
B			
C			
D			
E			
F			
Totals (add lines A through F)* ▶		25,000	6,000

* **Note:** *The Schedule F totals are not carried over to any other Form 1118 Schedule. (These totals were already included in Schedule A.) However, the IRS requires the corporation to complete Schedule F under the authority of section 905(b).*

Form 1118 (Rev. 12-2014) Page **10**

Schedule H **Apportionment of Deductions Not Definitely Allocable** *(complete only once)*

Part I—Research and Development Deductions

	(a) Sales Method				(b) Gross Income Method – Check method used: ☐ Option 1 ☐ Option 2				(c) Total R&D Deductions Not Definitely Allocable (enter the sum of all amounts entered in all applicable "R&D Deductions" columns)
	Product line #1 (SIC Code:)*		Product line #2 (SIC Code:)*		Product line #1 (SIC Code:)*		Product line #2 (SIC Code:)*		
	(i) Gross Sales	(ii) R&D Deductions	(iii) Gross Sales	(iv) R&D Deductions	(v) Gross Income	(vi) R&D Deductions	(vii) Gross Income	(viii) R&D Deductions	
1 Totals (see instructions)	500,000	8,000							
2 Total to be apportioned		4,000							
3 Apportionment among statutory groupings:									
a General category income	100,000	800							800
b Passive category income									
c Section 901(j) income*									
d Income re-sourced by treaty*									
4 Total foreign (add lines 3a through 3d)	100,000	800							800

* **Important:** See ***Computer-Generated Schedule H*** in instructions. Form **1118** (Rev. 12-2014)

Form 1118 (Rev. 12-2014) Page **11**

Schedule H **Apportionment of Deductions Not Definitely Allocable** *(continued)*

Part II—Interest Deductions, All Other Deductions, and Total Deductions

	(a) Average Value of Assets—Check method used: ☐ Fair market value ☑ Tax book value ☐ Alternative tax book value		(b) Interest Deductions		(c) All Other Deductions Not Definitely Allocable	(d) Totals (add the corresponding amounts from column (c), Part I; columns (b)(iii) and (b)(iv), Part II; and column (c), Part II). Enter each amount from lines 3a through 3d below in column 10 of the corresponding Schedule A.
	(i) Nonfinancial Corporations	(ii) Financial Corporations	(iii) Nonfinancial Corporations	(iv) Financial Corporations		
1a Totals (see instructions)	300,000		6,000			
b Amounts specifically allocable under Temp. Regs. 1.861-10T(e)						
c Other specific allocations under Temp. Regs. 1.861-10T						
d Assets excluded from apportionment formula						
2 Total to be apportioned (subtract the sum of lines 1b, 1c, and 1d from line 1a)	300,000		6,000			
3 Apportionment among statutory groupings:						
a General category income	50,000		1,000			1,000
b Passive category income						
c Section 901(j) income*						
d Income re-sourced by treaty*						
4 Total foreign (add lines 3a through 3d)	50,000		1,000			1,000

* **Important:** See ***Computer-Generated Schedule H*** in instructions. Form **1118** (Rev. 12-2014)

Exhibit 13-2 provides a list of the countries with which the United States has income tax treaties. U.S. treaties generally do not affect the U.S. taxation of U.S. citizens, residents, and domestic corporations because such taxpayers are taxed on a worldwide basis.

EXHIBIT 13-2 Countries with Which the U.S. Has Income Tax Treaties

Australia	India	Philippines
Austria	Indonesia	Poland
Bangladesh	Ireland	Portugal
Barbados	Israel	Romania
Belgium	Italy	Russian Federation
Bulgaria	Jamaica	Slovak Republic
Canada	Japan	Slovenia
China, Peoples Republic of	Kazakhstan	South Africa
Commonwealth of Independent States[a]	Korea, Republic of	Spain
Cyprus	Latvia	Sri Lanka
Czech Republic	Lithuania	Sweden
Denmark	Luxembourg	Switzerland
Egypt	Malta	Thailand
Estonia	Mexico	Trinidad and Tobago
Finland	Morocco	Tunisia
France	Netherlands	Turkey
Germany	New Zealand	Ukraine
Greece	Norway	United Kingdom
Hungary	Pakistan	Venezuela
Iceland		

[a]Armenia, Azerbaijan, Belarus, Georgia, Krygyzstan, Moldova, Takikistan, Turkmenistan, and Uzbekistan.

U.S. taxpayers can benefit from treaties that reduce the tax on designated items or classes of income. For example, most U.S. treaties provide a low withholding tax rate or an exemption from tax on various types of investment income (interest, dividends, gains from sale of stock, and royalties) that otherwise would be subject to a high withholding tax.[26] For individuals, U.S. treaties often provide exemption from taxation by the host country on wages or self-employment income earned in the treaty country, provided the individual does not spend more than 183 days in that other country. U.S. businesses generally are not taxed on business profits earned in the host treaty country unless they conduct that business through a **permanent establishment.** A permanent establishment generally is a fixed place of business such as an office or factory, although employees acting as agents can create a permanent establishment. Treaties also provide "tiebreaker" rules for determining the country in which an individual will be considered a resident for treaty purposes.

Example 13-12

What if: Lily was trying to determine if 3D would be subject to Canadian taxation under two different scenarios: (1) open a store in Windsor and operate it as a branch of 3D or (2) make the baked goods in Detroit and ship them to Windsor-area grocery stores using the company's van. Article VII of the U.S.-Canada income tax treaty states that the business profits of a U.S. resident are taxed in Canada only if the business operates in Canada through a permanent establishment. Article V defines a permanent establishment as including a place of management, a branch, an office, a factory, and a

[26]Absent a treaty, the United States imposes a withholding tax rate of 30 percent on payments of FDAP income to nonresidents.

workshop. Under the U.S.-Canada treaty, will 3D be subject to Canadian tax on taxable income earned through its Windsor store?

Answer: Yes. A branch is defined as a permanent establishment. Canada can tax 3D's Canadian-source taxable income under Article VII of the U.S.-Canada treaty.

Under the U.S.-Canada treaty, will 3D be subject to Canadian tax on taxable income earned by selling goods to grocery stores in Windsor directly?

Answer: No. 3D does not have a permanent establishment in Canada on these sales. Canada will not tax income from these sales under Article VII of the U.S.-Canada treaty.

Example 13-13

What if: Assume for quality control purposes that Lily decided to do all of the baking for her Windsor store in Detroit. Every morning a Windsor employee drives a van to Detroit and picks up the baked goods for sale in Windsor. One of her employees, Stan Lee Cupp, made the 2-hour trip on 200 different days during 2015. Article IV of the U.S.-Canada income tax treaty states where an individual is considered a resident of both countries under their respective tax laws, the individual will be considered a resident of the country in which he or she has a permanent home. Stan has a home only in Canada, and Canada still considers him to be a Canadian resident. Will Stan be considered a U.S. resident in 2015 applying only the substantial presence test?

Answer: Yes. Stan is physically present in the United States for more than 30 days in 2015 and satisfies the 183-day test when applying the formula [200 + (1/3 × 0) + (1/6 × 0) = 200].

Will Stan be considered a U.S. resident in 2015 applying the U.S.-Canada treaty?

Answer: No. Under the tiebreaker rules in the U.S.-Canada treaty, Stan is considered to be a resident of Canada only for income tax purposes because that is where he has his permanent home. The United States can tax Stan only on income that is considered to be from U.S. sources.

Example 13-14

What if: Assume that Stan made the 2-hour trip from Windsor to Detroit and back on 120 different days during 2015 (240 hours). 3D paid Stan a salary of C$50,000 during 2015. He worked a total of 240 days (1,920 hours) during 2015. Article XV of the U.S.-Canada income tax treaty states that a Canadian resident will be subject to U.S. tax on his U.S.-source compensation only if the compensation exceeds $10,000 or the individual is present in the United States for more than 183 days. Under the U.S.-Canada treaty, will Stan be subject to Canadian tax on his U.S.-source compensation in 2015?

Answer: No. Stan is exempt from U.S. tax on this compensation because under the apportionment rules for compensation discussed previously in Example 13-6, he has only $6,250 of U.S. compensation, computed as (240/1,920) × $50,000,

where:

240 = Number of hours worked in the United States

1,920 = Total number of hours worked

$50,000 = Total compensation in U.S. dollars

What if: Assume Stan received compensation of $86,000 in 2015. Under the U.S.-Canada treaty, will Stan be subject to Canadian tax on his U.S.-source compensation in 2015?

Answer: Yes. Although Stan was in the United States for less than 184 days, his U.S. source compensation is $10,750, computed as (240/1,920) × $86,000.

LO 13-4

FOREIGN TAX CREDITS

THE KEY FACTS

Foreign Tax Credits

- Only income taxes can be claimed as a credit on a U.S. tax return.
- A U.S. corporation owning 10 percent or more of a foreign corporation is eligible for an indirect FTC for taxes paid by the foreign corporation on dividends paid.
- The current year foreign tax credit cannot exceed the FTC limitation.
- The FTC limitation is applied to two separate categories (baskets) of foreign source income: passive and general.

The United States taxes the worldwide income of U.S. corporations, partnerships, trusts and estates, U.S. citizens, and resident aliens. As we have discussed, U.S. persons earning foreign source income may be subject to multiple taxation on such income by the United States and the country in which the individual resides or where the income is earned. For example, a U.S. citizen who is a resident of Great Britain and earns income in France may be subject to tax by all three governments. Without any relief from such multiple taxation, U.S. taxpayers would have little incentive to do business outside the United States.

FTC Limitation Categories of Taxable Income

The United States alleviates the multiple taxation of foreign source income earned by U.S. persons by allowing a tax credit for income taxes paid on such foreign source income. The foreign tax credit allowed in the current year is subject to a foreign tax credit limitation,[27] computed by multiplying the ratio of foreign source taxable income to total taxable income times precredit U.S. tax, as follows:

$$\frac{\text{Foreign source taxable income}}{\text{Total taxable income}} \times \text{Precredit U.S. tax}$$

The United States continuously struggles with whether, and to what extent, U.S. taxpayers should be required to segregate foreign source income subject to different tax rates and compute a separate FTC limitation for each category of income. Since 1976, the United States has required persons claiming the foreign tax credit to segregate foreign source income by category of income. Practitioners often refer to each income category as an **FTC basket.** Currently, the two primary categories of FTC income are **passive category income** and **general category income.**[28] The "basket" approach limits blending opportunities (high-tax foreign source income and low-tax foreign source income) to income that is of the same character.

Passive Category Income Passive category income generally is investment-type income that traditionally is subject to low foreign taxes (usually in the form of withholding taxes). Passive category income includes interest, certain dividends, rents, royalties, and annuities. Dividends received from 10–50 percent owned joint ventures and from more than 50 percent owned subsidiaries are subject to "look-through" rules. Under these rules, the dividend recipient characterizes the dividend for FTC basket purposes based on the source(s) of income from which the dividend is paid.

General Category Income Income not treated as passive category income is defined as general category income. General category income includes gross income from an active trade or business, financial services income, and shipping income.

The application of the FTC limitation formula can result in an excess credit if the taxpayer's creditable foreign taxes exceed the FTC limitation amount. The United States allows taxpayers to carry back an excess FTC one year and carry forward an excess credit ten years. Current year foreign tax credits are absorbed before any carryovers, which are absorbed on a first-in first-out basis.

[27]§904(d).
[28]§904(d).

Example 13-15

What if: Suppose 3D's branch operations in Windsor generated $20,000 of taxable income and paid Canadian tax of C$5,000. The branch income meets the definition of general category income for FTC purposes. In addition, 3D received a dividend of C$1,000 from its stock investment in Scotiabank. Under the U.S.-Canada treaty, Scotiabank withheld C$150 in taxes (15 percent) on the payment. The withholding tax is eligible for the foreign tax credit, and the dividend meets the definition of passive category income for FTC purposes. 3D has total taxable income of $100,000 in 2015 and has a precredit U.S. income tax of $22,250. In computing its FTC for 2015, can 3D combine the branch income with the dividend in calculating its FTC limitation?

Answer: No. The branch income and dividend cannot be "blended" because they are in different income categories for FTC limitation purposes.

How much of the C$5,150 in Canadian taxes can 3D claim as a FTC in 2015?

Answer: $4,600 ($4,450 + $150).

3D must compute separate FTC limitations for the branch income and dividend, as follows:

Branch income: $20,000/$100,000 × $22,250 = $4,450

Dividend income: $1,000/$100,000 × $22,250 = $223

3D can take a credit for the full amount of the withholding tax on the dividend ($150) but only a partial credit on the branch income. The separate basket approach prevents 3D from blending its high-tax income with its low-tax income.

What happens to the excess credit of $550 ($5,000 − $4,450) on the branch income?

Answer: 3D can carry back the excess FTC one year and then carry forward any remaining FTC for ten years.

What if: Assume the branch income and dividend are both general category income. How much of the C$5,150 of Canadian taxes can 3D take as a credit in 2015?

Answer: $4,673 computed as $21,000/$100,000 × $22,250,

where:

$21,000 = Foreign source taxable income

$100,000 = Total taxable income

$22,250 = Precredit U.S. tax on total taxable income

The low tax dividend income absorbs an additional $73 of branch foreign taxes. The addition of the $1,000 dividend to the branch FTC limitation increases the FTC ratio from 20 percent to 21 percent. This one percent increase in the ratio increases the FTC limitation by $223 (1% × $22,250). The FTC on the dividend is $150, leaving an excess $73 to apply against the branch FTC.

Creditable Foreign Taxes

The foreign tax credit is available only for foreign taxes the United States considers to be *income* taxes "in the U.S. sense." In general, a tax "resembles" the U.S. concept of an income tax when it is applied to net income.[29] Taxes that do not qualify as income taxes include property taxes, customs taxes, sales taxes, and value-added taxes. U.S. taxpayers can deduct noncreditable foreign taxes. On an annual basis, U.S. taxpayers also can elect to deduct foreign income taxes in lieu of claiming the credit. This election might make sense if the taxpayer does not expect to be able to use the credit during the ten-year carryforward period. Foreign taxes generally are translated into U.S. dollars using the average exchange rate for the year, regardless of when the

[29]There has been much litigation and many IRS rulings over whether a tax paid to another country qualifies as an income tax "in the U.S. sense."

tax is actually paid.[30] U.S. taxpayers can elect to translate withholding taxes using the exchange rate on the day the tax is withheld. This election makes translation of the withholding tax consistent with the translation of the payment (dividend, interest, royalty) into U.S. dollars, which is done using the exchange rate on the date of payment (referred to as the **spot rate**).

Direct Taxes Direct foreign income taxes are income taxes paid directly by the U.S. taxpayer.[31] For example, income taxes paid by 3D to the Canadian government on its branch operations in Windsor would be direct foreign income taxes and eligible for a credit on the company's U.S. tax return.

In Lieu of Taxes Taxes that do not qualify as income taxes can still be creditable if they are imposed "in lieu of" an income tax.[32] The most common example is a withholding tax imposed on gross income such as dividends, interest, and royalties. These taxes technically do not meet the definition of an income tax because they are imposed on gross, rather than net, income. However, most governments impose these taxes for administrative purposes in lieu of requiring the recipient of the income to file an income tax return.

Indirect (Deemed Paid) Taxes Indirect taxes are foreign income taxes imposed on the income of a U.S.-owned **foreign subsidiary** or **foreign joint venture.**[33] These taxes are not considered direct taxes because they are not paid by the U.S. parent company or investor. Had the U.S. corporation conducted its foreign operations through a branch, the before-tax income of the branch would be reported on the corporation's U.S. tax return and a direct FTC would be claimed for any income taxes paid by the branch. The income of a foreign subsidiary is not reported on the U.S. tax return until it is distributed to the U.S. parent as a dividend or other payment. The dividend amount is net of the foreign income taxes imposed on that income.[34]

To put the U.S. tax consequences of a dividend distribution on equal footing with branch income, the United States allows certain U.S. corporations to "impute" a foreign tax credit for the income taxes paid by the foreign subsidiary on the dividend distributed. The U.S. corporation must "gross up" the dividend by the amount of the credit.[35] This gross up causes the U.S. corporation to report the pretax income of the subsidiary related to the dividend distributed, similar to what would have been reported had the subsidiary been operated as a branch.

Example 13-16

What if: Let's say 3D operates its Windsor operations as a branch. The branch reported taxable income of C$20,000 for 2015 on which it paid a combined national and provincial income tax of C$5,000. Not including the branch income, 3D had taxable income of $80,000 from its U.S. operations in 2015. What amount of taxable income does 3D report on its U.S. tax return in 2015?

Answer: $100,000. 3D includes the branch income with its U.S. taxable income.

[30]§986(a)(1)(A).

[31]Direct foreign income taxes are creditable under §901.

[32]In lieu of income taxes are creditable under §903.

[33]Indirect foreign income taxes are creditable under §902 or §960.

[34]As discussed in Chapter 7, dividends are payments out of earnings and profits, which is after-tax economic income of a corporation.

[35]§78.

What amount of foreign taxes are creditable for foreign tax credit purposes?

Answer: $5,000. The Canadian income taxes paid on the branch operations are considered a direct FTC because 3D pays the tax directly.

What if: Suppose 3D operates its Windsor operations as a subsidiary. The subsidiary reported taxable income of C$20,000 for 2015 on which it paid a combined national and provincial income tax of C$5,000. Assume for purposes of this example only that for U.S. tax purposes the subsidiary's earnings and profits is $15,000, computed as C$20,000 − C$5,000.[36] At the end of 2015, the subsidiary distributed all of its E&P to 3D as a dividend. Not including the dividend income, 3D had taxable income of $80,000 from its U.S. operations in 2015. Assume Canada did not impose a withholding tax on the dividend. What amount of foreign taxes are creditable for foreign tax credit purposes?

Answer: $5,000. 3D receives a deemed paid credit equal to the income taxes paid by the subsidiary on the dividend received.

What amount of taxable income does 3D report on its U.S. tax return as a result of the dividend in 2015?

Answer: $20,000. 3D grosses up the $15,000 dividend by the deemed paid credit of $5,000. The amount of taxable income reported from the dividend equals the taxable income reported from the branch operations.

Most subsidiaries and joint ventures do not pay out all of their current E&P as a dividend in the year earned. When a subsidiary distributes a portion of its total E&P as a dividend, the deemed paid credit is computed on a "blended" basis based on total income taxes paid on total E&P accumulated since 1987.[37] The amount of foreign income taxes deemed paid by the U.S. corporate shareholder on the receipt of a dividend is computed as follows:

$$\frac{\text{Dividends paid from post-1986 earnings and profits}}{\text{Total post-1986 earnings and profits}} \times \text{Post-1986 foreign taxes}$$

The post-1986 E&P is computed using the corporation's **functional currency** unless the corporation keeps its books in U.S. dollars.[38] The foreign corporation maintains its pool of post-1986 foreign income taxes in U.S. dollars.

Example 13-17

What if: Assume 3D organized its Windsor operations as a Canadian subsidiary of 3D, Canadian Doughnut Depot Company (CDD). CDD reported taxable income of C$20,000 for 2015, on which it paid a combined national and provincial income tax of C$5,000. Because CDD operates as a Canadian corporation, the Canadian taxable income is not reported on 3D's U.S. corporate income tax return (CDD is a nonresident with no U.S.-source income). Also assume for purposes of this example only, that CDD has post-1986 earnings and profits (E&P) of C$15,000, all of which is characterized as general category income. During 2015, CDD paid a dividend of C$6,000 to 3D. CDD withheld a Canadian withholding tax of C$300 (5 percent). Not including the dividend, 3D had taxable income of $142,000 in 2015. What is 3D's deemed paid credit on the dividend received from CDD in 2015?

(continued on page 13-24)

[36]§964 requires a U.S. parent company to compute E&P for its foreign subsidiaries under U.S. tax rules. These rules are discussed in detail in Chapter 7.

[37]This computation was changed in the Tax Reform Act of 1986. Distributions received from E&P accumulated prior to 1987 are treated as being paid out of the E&P for the year distributed assuming a LIFO assumption.

[38]§986(b). *Functional currency* is the currency in which the corporation conducts its transactions.

Answer: $2,000, computed as C$6,000/C$15,000 × $5,000,

where:

C$6,000 = Dividend paid to 3D in CDD's functional currency

C$15,000 = Post-1986 earnings and profits in CDD's functional currency

$5,000 = Post-1986 foreign taxes in U.S. dollars

What amount of creditable foreign taxes does 3D have in 2015?

Answer: $2,300, computed as $2,000 + withholding taxes of $300.

What amount of gross income does 3D report as a result of the dividend from CDD?

Answer: $8,000, computed as $6,000 + $2,000. 3D must gross up the dividend ($6,000) by the deemed paid credit ($2,000) to compute the taxable income it reports from receiving the dividend. 3D's total taxable income for 2015 is $150,000 ($142,000 + $8,000), and its precredit U.S. tax is $41,750, [($50,000 × .15) + ($25,000 × .25) + ($25,000 × .34) + ($50,000 × .39)].

Assuming no deductions are subtracted from the foreign source gross income created by the dividend, what is 3D's FTC limitation for 2015?

Answer: $2,227, computed as $8,000/$150,000 × $41,750,

where:

$8,000 = Foreign source taxable income from the dividend

$150,000 = Total taxable income

$41,750 = Precredit U.S. tax on total taxable income

3D has an excess FTC of $73 ($2,300 − $2,227).

A U.S. corporation must own directly 10 percent or more of the foreign corporation paying the dividend to be eligible for the deemed paid credit.[39]

Example 13-18

What if: Assume 3D only owned 50 percent of CDD. CDD reported taxable income of C$20,000 for 2015 on which it paid a combined national and provincial income tax of C$5,000. For U.S. tax purposes, CDD has post-1986 earnings and profits (E&P) of C$15,000, all of which is characterized as general category income. During 2015 CDD paid a dividend of C$3,000 to 3D. CDD withheld a Canadian withholding tax of C$150 (5 percent). Not including the dividend, 3D had taxable income of $142,000 in 2015. What is 3D's deemed paid credit on the dividend received from CDD in 2015?

Answer: $1,000, computed as C$3,000/C$15,000 × $5,000,

where:

C$3,000 = Dividend paid to 3D in CDD's functional currency

C$15,000 = Post-1986 earnings and profits in CDD's functional currency

$5,000 = Post-1986 foreign taxes in U.S. dollars

What amount of creditable foreign taxes does 3D have in 2015?

Answer: $1,150, computed as $1,000 + withholding taxes of $150.

What amount of gross income does 3D report as a result of the dividend from CDD?

Answer: $4,000, computed as $3,000 + $1,000.

[39]Dividends paid to the foreign corporation from other foreign corporations can also be eligible for the deemed paid credit if certain direct and indirect ownership tests are met. This topic is beyond the scope of this text.

PLANNING FOR INTERNATIONAL OPERATIONS

LO 13-5

continued from page 13-1 . . .
After operating her Windsor store as a branch for the first year, Lily began to wonder if there were more tax-efficient ways to operate her Canadian operations. She was concerned that while the branch was easy to organize and operate, it might not provide the best tax advantages. Lily's tax adviser told her that Canada imposes a 10 percent "branch profits tax" on after-tax profits that exceed $500,000. Although the Windsor operations were a long way from reaching that level of profits, she hoped one day that she would reach that level of profitability. In addition, she wondered if it might be an advantage to have her Canadian operations identified as a Canadian company. Lily's tax adviser mentioned that operating as a Canadian corporation would provide deferral of her Canadian profits from U.S. taxation and would allow for some "transfer pricing" on the "sale" of her baked goods from the United States to Canada. ■

The organizational form through which a U.S. person does business or invests outside the United States affects the timing and scope of U.S. taxation of foreign source income or loss reported by the business or investment. U.S. corporations conducting international operations directly (branch) or through a flow-through entity (partnership) are subject to U.S. tax or receive a U.S. tax benefit currently on income or loss from those operations. Foreign source income earned by a foreign corporation owned by U.S. persons (e.g., a Canadian subsidiary of a U.S. corporation) generally is not subject to U.S. taxation until such income is repatriated to the U.S. shareholder as a dividend, interest, rent, royalty, or management fee (i.e., U.S. taxation of such income is deferred to a future period).

The organizational form chosen can help a U.S. person reduce worldwide taxation through the following means:

- Defer U.S. taxation of foreign source income not repatriated to the United States.
- Maximize the foreign tax credit limitation on distributions.
- Reduce foreign taxes in high-tax jurisdictions through tax-deductible payments (e.g., rent, interest, royalties, and management fees) to lower-tax jurisdictions.
- Take advantage of tax incentives provided by host jurisdictions (e.g., a tax holiday on profits for a specified time period).
- Use transfer pricing to shift profits from a high-tax jurisdiction to a low-tax jurisdiction.
- Take advantage of tax treaties to reduce withholding taxes on cross-border payments.

Hybrid entities such as limited liability companies can provide the U.S. investor with the legal advantages of corporate form (limited liability, continuity of life, transferability of interests) and the tax advantages of partnership or branch form (flow-through of losses and flow-through of foreign taxes to individual investors).

Each organizational form offers a U.S. person investing abroad with advantages and disadvantages. Most U.S. businesses operate abroad through either a subsidiary or hybrid entity. Corporation status provides the U.S. investor with protection against liabilities of the subsidiary, entitles the subsidiary to treaty benefits in its dealings outside the country of incorporation, and insulates its business income from U.S. taxation until such income is repatriated back to the United States. Conversely, losses incurred in the subsidiary are not currently deductible on the investor's U.S. tax return.

THE KEY FACTS

Organizational Forms for Conducting International Operations

- A U.S. taxpayer doing business outside the United States can choose between a branch, partnership, corporation, or hybrid entity.
- A **hybrid entity** is an entity that is treated as a flow-through entity for U.S. tax purposes and a corporation for foreign tax purposes (or vice versa).
- A U.S. taxpayer elects the U.S. tax status of a hybrid entity by "checking the box" on Form 8832.
- Per se entities are not eligible for the check-the-box election.

Check-the-Box Hybrid Entities

Through regulations, the U.S. Treasury allows U.S. taxpayers to elect the *U.S. tax status* of eligible entities by "checking the box" on Form 8832. Where the U.S. person owns 100 percent of the entity, the taxpayer can choose corporation status or branch status (the latter often is referred to as a **disregarded entity** because it is disregarded for U.S. tax purposes). Where more than one U.S. person owns the entity, the taxpayers can choose corporation status or partnership status. Such an entity is referred to as a hybrid entity. A multiple-person-owned hybrid entity for which corporation status is elected is referred to as a **reverse hybrid entity.** Certain designated "per se" foreign entities are not eligible for this elective treatment. These ineligible entities tend to be entities that can be publicly traded in their host countries (e.g., a German A.G., Dutch N.V., U.K. PLC, Spanish S.A., and a Canadian Corporation). The entire list is printed in the Instructions to Form 8832. In Canada, a U.S. corporation or individual must operate through an unlimited liability company (ULC) organized under the laws of Nova Scotia, Alberta, or British Columbia to achieve the benefits of operating through a hybrid entity.

Hybrid entities offer U.S. investors much flexibility in avoiding the U.S. "anti-deferral" rules found in subpart F, which we discuss in the next section. However, there are drawbacks to operating through a hybrid entity. In particular, a hybrid entity organized outside the United States may not be eligible for treaty benefits because it is not recognized as a resident of the United States by the host country. For example, the U.S.-Canada treaty does not extend treaty benefits to distributions from a ULC to its U.S. investors. Distributions from a Nova Scotia ULC to its U.S. parent company in the form of dividends or royalties will be subject to a 25 percent withholding tax instead of a 5 percent or 10 percent withholding tax, respectively, under the U.S.-Canada treaty. Exhibit 13-3 lists the advantages and disadvantages of operating outside the United States through different organizational forms.

Example 13-19

Lily expects her Canadian operations to be profitable for the foreseeable future. She has plans to expand her operations throughout the province of Ontario and hopefully throughout all of Canada. Lily is trying to decide whether she should change the organizational form of her Canadian operations from a branch to a corporation or perhaps a hybrid entity. Can Lily organize her Canadian operations as a hybrid entity in Ontario for U.S. tax purposes?

Answer: No. Hybrid entities (unlimited liability companies) can only be organized in Canada in the provinces of Nova Scotia, Alberta, and British Columbia.

What are the primary income tax reasons for organizing the Canadian operations as a corporation for U.S. tax purposes?

Answer: There are several. Operating as a corporation allows for deferral from U.S. taxation on income earned by the Canadian operations until it is distributed to 3D as a dividend. In addition, 3D can loan money or lease its trademarks to the Canadian corporation and transfer income from Canada to the United States in the form of tax-deductible interest or royalties.

Are there any compelling nontax reasons for organizing the Canadian operations as a corporation for U.S. tax purposes?

Answer: Yes. Corporate form limits 3D's liability in Canada to its Canadian assets. In addition, operating as a corporation allows the company to hold itself out as a Canadian business to its customers and borrow money directly from Canadian banks.

EXHIBIT 13-3 Advantages and Disadvantages of Operating Outside the United States in Different Organizational Forms

Branch

Advantages

- Foreign losses are currently deductible on the U.S. tax return.
- Foreign taxes imposed on income earned through the branch are eligible for the direct foreign tax credit.
- A branch qualifies as a permanent establishment and is eligible for treaty benefits.

Disadvantages

- Profits are subject to immediate U.S. taxation.
- The U.S. corporation must have 100 percent control over its international operations (joint ventures are not available).

Subsidiary

Advantages

- Separate entity status insulates the U.S. parent corporation against certain types of liabilities.
- Certain earnings are deferred from U.S. taxation until repatriation.
- Certain payments (management fees, royalties) made to the U.S. parent corporation may only be deductible in the host country if the payor is a corporation.

Disadvantages

- Losses are not deductible on the U.S. tax return for tax purposes.
- Certain foreign source income may be subject to the subpart F rules, which increases the administrative costs of operating as a subsidiary.

Hybrid entity treated as a flow-through entity

Advantages

- Foreign losses are currently deductible on the U.S. tax return.
- Foreign taxes imposed on income earned through the branch are eligible for the direct foreign tax credit.
- The U.S. corporation can operate as a joint venture.
- Certain payments (management fees, royalties, interest) made to the U.S. parent corporation are deductible in the foreign jurisdiction.

Disadvantages

- Profits are subject to immediate U.S. taxation.
- Dividend, interest, and royalty payments to the United States are not eligible for reduced treaty withholding taxes.

When drawing an organizational chart of a multinational company, the different organizational forms are often designated with different symbols. Exhibit 13-4 provides the symbols for each of the common organizational forms used by U.S. taxpayers to do business outside the United States and their tax status for U.S. tax purposes (we refer back to this exhibit in Exhibit 13-5).

U.S. ANTI-DEFERRAL RULES

LO 13-6

Deferral of U.S. taxation on all foreign source income earned through a foreign subsidiary would invite tax-planning strategies that shift income to low-tax countries to minimize worldwide taxation. U.S. individuals and corporations could transfer investment assets to subsidiaries located in low- (no-) tax countries **(tax havens)** and earn low-tax or tax-exempt income until such time as it was repatriated to the United States.

The United States has debated whether to allow full deferral on all foreign earnings since 1937, when the U.S. government enacted its first "anti-deferral"

EXHIBIT 13-4 Symbols for Different Organizational Forms and Their U.S. Tax Status

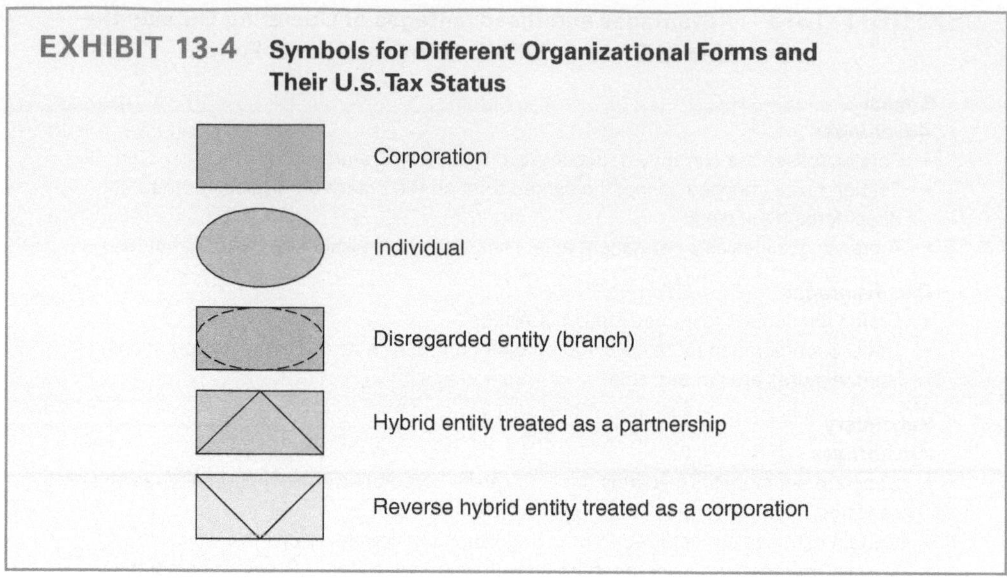

THE KEY FACTS

U.S. Anti-Deferral Rules

- Income described in subpart F of subchapter N of the IRC defines income that is not eligible for deferral from U.S. taxation when earned by a foreign corporation.
- Subpart F income generally includes foreign personal holding company income and foreign base company sales income.
- Subpart F applies only to U.S. shareholders of a CFC.
- *De minimus* and full inclusion rules apply to limit or expand whether a CFC's income is subject to the deemed dividend regime.

rules applying to foreign personal holding companies. Congress, with urging from President Kennedy, enacted more expansive anti-deferral rules in subpart F of subchapter N of the Internal Revenue Code in 1962.[40]

In a nutshell, subpart F requires certain *U.S. shareholders* in a **controlled foreign corporation** (CFC) to include in their gross income currently their pro rata share of specified categories of "tainted" income earned by the CFC during the current year **(subpart F income)** regardless of whether such income is repatriated as a dividend (the income is treated as if it was paid out to the shareholders as a deemed dividend at the end of the CFC's taxable year). The deemed dividend is translated into U.S. dollars using the average exchange rate for the year. The technical rules that determine the amount of the deemed dividend to be included in income are among the most complex provisions in the Internal Revenue Code.

Definition of a Controlled Foreign Corporation

A controlled foreign corporation is defined as any foreign corporation in which *U.S. shareholders* collectively own *more than* 50 percent of the total combined voting power of all classes of stock entitled to vote or the total value of the corporation's stock on *any day* during the CFC's tax year.[41] For purposes of subpart F, a *U.S. shareholder* is any *U.S. person* who owns or is deemed to own 10 percent or more of all classes of stock entitled to vote.[42] The term *United States person* means a citizen or resident of the United States, a domestic partnership, a domestic corporation, or any U.S. estate or trust, but it excludes certain residents of U.S. possessions.

Constructive ownership rules are used in the calculation of both the 50 percent test for determining CFC status and the 10 percent test for determining who is a U.S. shareholder.[43] These rules are similar to the constructive ownership rules found in subchapter C (Chapter 7) and include family attribution (spouse, children, grandchildren, and parents), entity-to-owner attribution, and owner-to-entity attribution. A detailed discussion of the other attribution rules is beyond the scope of this text.

[40]§§951–964.

[41]§957(a).

[42]§951(b).

[43]§958(b).

Example 13-20

What if: Assume Lily decided to partner with a Canadian investor, Maurice Richard, to expand her operations into Quebec through a Canadian corporation to be called Quebec Doughnut Depot (QDD). As part of the creation of QDD, Maurice contributed enough cash to the corporation to become a 50 percent shareholder in the company, with Lily owning the remaining 50 percent. Will QDD be a controlled foreign corporation (CFC) for U.S. tax purposes?

Answer: No. Lily is the only U.S. person who qualifies as a U.S. shareholder for purposes of determining if QDD is a CFC for U.S. tax purposes. Because Lily only owns 50 percent of QDD (not *more* than 50 percent), the corporation is not considered a CFC.

What if: Suppose Lily organized QDD with her husband, Red, and Maurice, with each owning one-third of the company's stock. Will QDD be a CFC for U.S. tax purposes?

Answer: Yes. Lily and Red are both U.S. persons who qualify as a U.S. shareholder for purposes of determining if QDD is a CFC for U.S. tax purposes (they each own at least 10 percent of the QDD stock). Because they collectively own more than 50 percent of QDD, the corporation is a CFC.

What if: Suppose Lily organized QDD with her husband, Red, and Maurice, with Lily owning 49 percent, Red owning 2 percent, and Maurice owning 49 percent of the company's stock. Will QDD be a CFC for U.S. tax purposes?

Answer: Yes. Lily is deemed to own Red's 2 percent stock interest in QDD under the family attribution rules, making her a U.S. shareholder owning 51 percent of QDD's stock.

Definition of Subpart F Income

Subpart F income generally can be characterized as low-taxed passive income or as "portable" income earned by a CFC. Passive income, otherwise referred to as **foreign personal holding company income,** includes interest, dividends, rents, royalties, annuities, gains from the sales of certain foreign property, foreign currency exchange rate gains, net income from certain commodities transactions, and income equivalent to interest. There are complex exceptions involving payments between CFCs in the same country, export financing interest, and rents and royalties derived in the active conduct of a trade or business. In addition, for tax years 2006–2014, subpart F income does not include dividends, interest, rents, and royalties received by one CFC from a related CFC to the extent the payment is attributable to non-subpart F income of the payor (the taxpayer "looks through" the payment to the income from which it was paid).

Example 13-21

What if: Assume, as in Example 13-17, that 3D organized its Windsor operations as a wholly owned Canadian subsidiary, Canadian Doughnut Depot Company (CDD). CDD reported taxable income from its bakery operations of C$75,000 in 2015. CDD also purchased 1,000 shares of stock (less than 1 percent) in Thorntons PLC, a United Kingdom corporation that makes fine chocolate. During 2015, CDD received dividends of £1,000, which translated into C$1,500.[44] Thorntons withheld £100 (C$150) of U.K. taxes on the payment (a 10 percent withholding tax under the U.K.-Canada treaty). Does the dividend from Thorntons to CDD constitute subpart F income to 3D in 2015?

Answer: Yes. Dividends from investments in corporations that are owned less than 10 percent by 3D are considered foreign personal holding company income under subpart F.

[44]The currency of the United Kingdom is the pound sterling, abbreviated £.

Also included in subpart F income is foreign base company sales income, which is defined as income derived by a CFC from the sale or purchase of personal property (e.g., inventory) to (or from) a related person, and the property is manufactured and sold outside the CFC's country of incorporation.[45] Similar rules apply to foreign base company services income.

This category of subpart F income was added because many countries offer incentives to multinational corporations to locate holding companies or sales companies within their borders by imposing no or a low tax on investment income or export sales. These companies are referred to as base companies because they operate primarily as profit centers and are located in a different country than where the economic activity (manufacture, sales, or service) takes place.

Without any anti-deferral rules, a U.S. multinational corporation could shift profits to a foreign base company by selling goods to the base company at an artificially low transfer price. The base company could then resell the goods at a higher price to the ultimate customer in a different country. The profit earned by the base company would be subject to the lower (or no) tax imposed by the tax haven country. The base company thus becomes a depository for the multinational company's excess funds, which can be invested in an active business or passive investment assets outside the United States.

Example 13-22

What if: Assume in 2016 that 3D set up a corporation in the Cayman Islands through which it intended to transfer its products from the United States to its operations in Canada. Under this plan, 3D would "sell" its products, made in the United States, to the subsidiary in the Cayman Islands at a low transfer price, after which the Cayman Islands subsidiary would resell the products to CDD at a high transfer price. The goal would be to locate as much profit as possible in a low-tax country (the Cayman Islands has no corporate income tax). Will profit from the sale of goods from the Cayman Islands subsidiary to CDD constitute subpart F income to 3D in 2016?

Answer: Yes. The Cayman Islands profit is considered foreign base company sales income under subpart F because the goods are manufactured outside the Cayman Islands by a related party (3D) and sold outside the Cayman Islands to a related party (CDD). 3D will be treated has having received a deemed dividend of the profit from the Cayman Islands subsidiary.

There are several exceptions that serve to exclude all or a portion of a CFC's subpart F income from current taxation to the U.S. shareholders. A *de minimis rule* excludes all gross income from being treated as foreign base company income if the sum of the CFC's gross foreign base company income is less than the lesser of 5 percent of gross income or $1 million. A *full inclusion rule* treats all of the CFC's gross income as foreign base company income if more than 70 percent of the CFC's gross income is foreign base company income. In addition, a taxpayer can *elect* to exclude "high-tax" subpart F income from the deemed dividend rules. High-tax subpart F income is taxed at an effective tax rate that is 90 percent or more of the highest U.S. statutory rate. For a U.S. corporation, the rate currently is 31.5 percent (90% × 35%). The calculation of the effective tax rate is complex and beyond the scope of this text.

[45]§954(d).

Example 13-23

Return to the facts in Example 13-21, in which CDD reported taxable income from its bakery operations of C$75,000 in 2015 and received dividends of £1,000 from Thorntons PLC, which translated into C$1,500. Assume CDD has gross income of C$125,000 in 2015. In the previous example, we determined that the dividend constitutes subpart F income for U.S. tax purposes. Will 3D have a deemed dividend of this subpart F income in 2015?

Answer: No. The dividend is less than the lesser of 5 percent of CDD's gross income ($6,250) or $1 million and is not subject to the deemed dividend rules under the *de minimus* rule.

The subpart F rules apply only in years in which a corporation is a CFC for an uninterrupted period of 30 days or more during its taxable year. Only those U.S. shareholders who own stock in the CFC on the last day in the CFC's taxable year are treated as having received their pro rata share of any subpart F deemed dividend.

The computation of the deemed dividend under subpart F is exceptionally complicated and requires the CFC to allocate both deductions and taxes paid to subpart F gross income. The formula for this computation can be found in worksheets in the Instructions to Form 5471. In addition, the U.S. shareholder receives a deemed paid foreign tax credit similar to the indirect foreign tax credit available on actual dividend distributions.[46]

Earnings of the CFC treated as a deemed dividend under subpart F becomes *previously taxed income* and subsequently can be distributed to the shareholders without being included in the recipient's gross income a second time.

Planning to Avoid Subpart F Income

U.S. multinational corporations expanding outside the United States often use hybrid entities as a tax-efficient means to avoid the subpart F rules. Tax aligning a U.S. corporation's international supply chain has become a frequent objective in international tax planning. Accomplishing this goal requires the formation of a foreign holding company (Foreign HoldCo) treated as a corporation for U.S. tax purposes (and thus eligible for deferral from U.S. taxation). The holding company owns the stock of hybrid entities set up to conduct each of the components of the company's foreign operations: financing (FinanceCo), manufacturing (OpCo), distribution (DistribCo), and intellectual property (IPCo). The holding company is strategically located in a country that lightly taxes dividend income paid by the hybrid entities. The hybrid entities also are strategically located in countries that tax the income from such operations (e.g., interest or royalties paid by the operating company to the finance company or intellectual property company) at a low tax rate. For instance, Ireland taxes manufacturing and intellectual property income at 12.5 percent. By conducting these operations through hybrid entities, transactions between the entities (e.g., a payment of interest, rents, or royalties from one entity to another), which otherwise would create subpart F income, are ignored for U.S. tax purposes but respected for foreign tax purposes because the hybrid entity is treated as a corporation in the country in which it is organized. This allows for the free flow of cash between foreign operations without the intrusion of the U.S. tax laws and the reduction of taxes in high-tax countries through cross-border payments that are deductible in the country in which the hybrid entity is located. Exhibit 13-5 provides a template for such an international operation.[47]

[46]§960.

[47]In hearings held on May 21, 2013, Senator Carl Levin accused Apple, Inc. of avoiding billions of U.S. taxes by structuring its overseas operations to route royalty income to low-tax jurisdictions. See http://www.hsgac.senate.gov/subcommittees/investigations/hearings/offshore-profit-shifting-and-the-us-tax-code_-part-2 for more details.

EXHIBIT 13-5 A Tax-Aligned International Supply Chain (see Exhibit 13-4 for explanation of symbols)

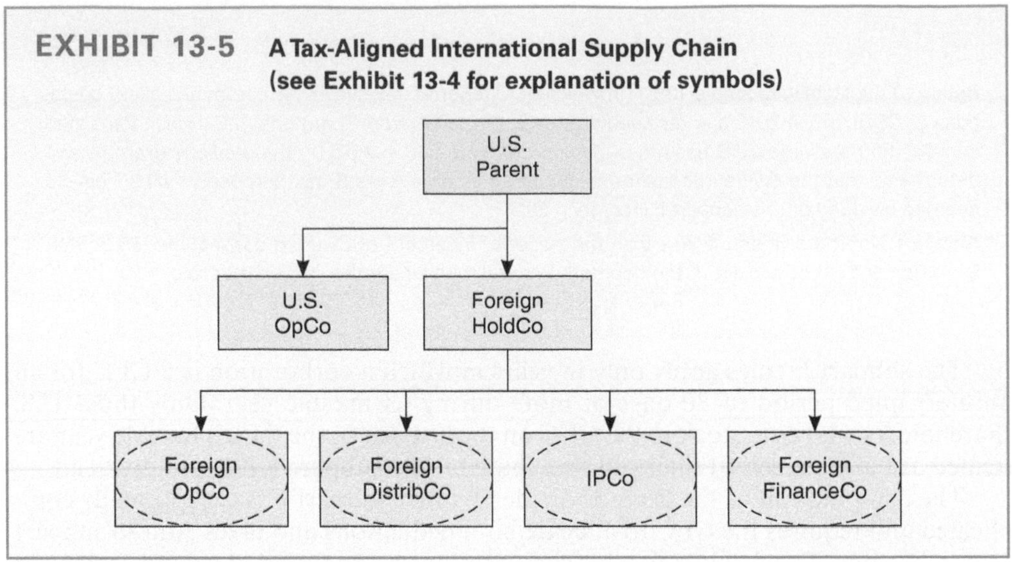

TAXES IN THE REAL WORLD Setting Sail for Low-Tax Jurisdictions

In January 2012, Aon Corporation, a U.S. global corporation providing risk management and human resource services, announced it was moving its corporate residence from Delaware to London, England. The company stated that the move was motivated by the desire to achieve greater access to emerging markets and take better advantage of the strategic proximity of the London market as one of the key international hubs of insurance and risk brokerage.

In addition, the company predicted that the move also would have several near- and long-term financial benefits, in particular, lower corporate tax rates and the ability to access cash located offshore without the imposition of the U.S. tax rate on the repatriation. Specifically, the company stated they believed "*the merger should significantly improve our ability to maintain a competitive global tax rate because the U.K. has implemented a dividend exemption system that generally does not subject non-U.K. earnings to U.K. tax when such earnings are repatriated to the U.K. in the form of dividends from non-U.K. subsidiaries*." Further, the company stated that a reduction in its global tax rate over the long-term would allow it to remain competitive with their global competitors.

In the transaction, the Aon shareholders exchanged their common stock in Aon for common stock in a newly formed English public-limited company. Such an exchange would be tax-free if the new corporation was located in the United States. However, under the "anti-inversion" rules, this cross-border exchange is taxable to the shareholders realizing gain, but not loss, on the exchange. In addition, the U.S. can treat the English corporation as a domestic corporation if the company does not have substantial business activities in its place of incorporation.

This transaction illustrates the incentive for U.S. companies to relocate in lower tax jurisdictions that have a dividend exemption system, which allows the company to repatriate foreign earnings without the imposition of host country taxation. It also illustrates the countermoves enacted by the U.S. government to prevent domestic companies from inverting tax-free.

One of the concerns expressed by the company was the potential backlash from its U.S. customers, who might perceive the company as not paying its fair share of U.S. taxes. Apparently, the shareholders valued tax savings more than reputation, as the vote was 98 percent in favor of the move.

Since Aon's announcement to move its worldwide headquarters to the United Kingdom, several other U.S.-headquartered companies also have "expatriated" to Europe. In 2012, at least six other U.S. corporations moved their parent company to the United Kingdom (Rowan Cos.), Ireland (Jazz Pharmaceuticals, Eaton Corp.), Switzerland (Pentair), the Netherlands (Sara Lee), and Australia (Tronox).

In 2013, Perrigo Co., a Michigan-based provider of healthcare products, merged with Elan Corp. PLC to form a new Irish-headquartered company. In the press conference, management stated that by being headquartered in Ireland, the company would reduce its effective tax rate from 27 percent in 2013 to 17 percent. Based on 2013 pretax income of $605 million, the tax rate reduction would have increased after-tax net income by $61 million, or $0.65 per share. Several inversions are pending in 2015, including Burger King's merger with Tim Horton to invert to Canada! President Obama and members of Congress have expressed opposition to these inversions and are considering what actions to take to prevent them.

PROPOSALS FOR CHANGE

In March 2014, President Obama proposed significant changes to the U.S. international tax laws that were intended to raise $276.3 billion in additional tax revenues over the period 2015–2024. Under one proposal, U.S. multinational corporations would be required to defer deducting interest expenses related to foreign source income until such income was recognized as income in the United States (e.g., as a repatriated dividend). In addition, a U.S. company's direct and deemed-paid foreign tax credits would be computed based on the average rate of foreign tax paid on total foreign earnings. This would result in a blending of high- and low-tax foreign tax credit pools to compute an average global effective tax rate computation. A third proposal would be to treat "excessive returns" on income from intangibles shifted out of the United States as subpart F (nondeferred) income. These proposals are highly controversial and are opposed by the majority of U.S. multinational companies. Many U.S. multinational companies are lobbying Congress through coalitions to reduce the corporate tax rate to make operating in the United States more competitive with other industrialized countries.

Rep. Dave Camp, former chair of the House Ways and Means Committee, released the Tax Reform Act of 2014 in February 2014, which proposed to lower the corporate tax rate from 35 percent to 25 percent by 2019 and transition the current worldwide tax regime to a "participation exemption" tax system that would exempt 95 percent of a U.S. corporation's international earnings from U.S. taxation when repatriated. In return, U.S. corporations would be deemed to repatriate their deferred foreign earnings to the United States and pay tax at a rate of either 8.75 percent (if cash) or 3.5 percent (other), payable in up to eight equal installments, with interest.[48] Although comprehensive international tax reform is a much discussed topic, it is difficult to predict what form, if any, such reform will take now that Rep. Paul Ryan chairs the Ways and Means Committee.

CONCLUSION

In this chapter we discussed some of the important U.S. tax rules that apply to U.S. persons who expand their business operations outside the United States. As the storyline indicates, a U.S. business that wants to expand its markets outside the United States must decide on an organizational form through which to conduct its business. Establishing a physical presence in another country generally subjects the profits of the business to taxation in the host country and potentially in the United States as well. Treaties between the United States and other countries can provide beneficial tax treatment to a U.S. company's operations, employees, and cross-border payments. Where a cross-border transaction is subject to both foreign and U.S. taxation, the United States provides relief in the form of a foreign tax credit for foreign income taxes paid on foreign income that is reported on a U.S. tax return. These credits can be reduced by the foreign tax credit limitation. By operating through a foreign corporation, a U.S. business can defer U.S. taxation on foreign source income until such income is repatriated to the United States. Certain types of income are not subject to deferral if earned through a CFC. The use of hybrid entities outside the United States provides U.S. companies with the ability to shift income and move cash across jurisdictions without being subject to deemed dividends under subpart F.

[48]For a more detailed discussion of international tax proposals on the table, see Michael P. Donohoe, Gary A. McGill, and Edmund Outslay, "Back to the Drawing Board: The Structural and Accounting Consequences of a Switch to a Territorial Tax System," *National Tax Journal,* September 2013.

Summary

LO 13-1 Understand the basic U.S. framework for taxing multinational transactions and the role of the foreign tax credit limitation.

- Countries most often determine nexus by either the geographic source of the income (source-based jurisdiction) or the taxpayer's citizenship or residence (residence-based jurisdiction).
  - Under a residence-based approach, a country taxes the worldwide income of the person earning the income.
  - Under a source-based approach, a country taxes only the income earned within its boundaries.
- The U.S. government taxes citizens and residents on their worldwide income, regardless of source (residence-based jurisdiction).
  - An individual who is not a citizen will be treated as a U.S. resident for income tax purposes if he or she is considered a permanent resident (has a green card) or satisfies a substantial presence test.
- The U.S. government only taxes nonresidents on income that is "U.S. source" or is connected with the operation of a U.S. trade or business (source-based jurisdiction).
- To alleviate (mitigate) potential double taxation and to promote international commerce, governments often allow their residents a tax credit for foreign income taxes paid on foreign source income.

LO 13-2 Apply the U.S. source rules for common items of gross income and deductions.

- The U.S. source rules determine whether income and related deductions are from sources within or without the United States.
  - The U.S. source-of-income rules are important to non-U.S. persons because they limit the scope of U.S. taxation of their worldwide income.
  - For U.S. persons, the primary purpose of the U.S. source-of-income rules is to calculate foreign source taxable income in the numerator of the foreign tax credit limitation.
- The Internal Revenue Code defines eight classes of gross income from sources within the United States and eight classes of gross income from sources without the United States.
  - As a general rule, the taxpayer looks to the borrower's residence to determine the geographic source of interest received.
  - In general, the source of dividend income is determined by the residence of the corporation paying the dividend.
  - The source of compensation received for labor or personal services is determined by the location where the service is performed.
  - Rent has its source where the property generating the rent is located.
  - Royalty income has its source where the intangible property or rights generating the royalty is used.
- After determining the source of gross income as being from U.S. or foreign sources, a taxpayer may be required to allocate and apportion allowable deductions to gross income from each geographical source to compute taxable income from U.S. and foreign sources.
  - The IRC provides very broad language in describing how to allocate deductions to U.S. and foreign source gross income.
  - The regulations attempt to match deductions with the gross income such deductions were incurred to produce, usually based on the "factual relationship" of the deduction to gross income.
  - Special apportionment rules apply to nine categories of deductions, most notably interest, research and experimentation, state and local income taxes, losses on property disposition, and charitable contributions.

Recall the role of income tax treaties in international tax planning. LO 13-3

- A tax treaty is a bilateral agreement between two contracting countries in which each agrees to modify its own tax laws to achieve reciprocal benefits.
- The general purpose of an income tax treaty is to eliminate or reduce (mitigate) the impact of double taxation so that residents paying taxes to one country will not have the full burden of taxes in the other country.
- The United States currently has income tax treaties with 67 countries.
- Most U.S. treaties provide a low withholding tax rate or an exemption from tax on various types of investment income (interest, dividends, gains from sale of stock, and royalties) that would otherwise be subject to a high withholding tax.

Identify creditable foreign taxes and compute the foreign tax credit limitation. LO 13-4

- The foreign tax credit is available only for foreign taxes the United States considers to be income taxes.
- Creditable foreign income taxes can be direct, indirect, or "in lieu of" income taxes.
- Taxpayers must compute a separate FTC limitation for each category ("basket") of foreign source taxable income.
  - Passive category income generally is investment-type income that traditionally is subject to low foreign taxes (usually in the form of withholding taxes).
  - Income not treated as passive category income is defined to be general category income. General category income includes gross income from an active trade or business, financial services income, and shipping income.
  - A taxpayer computes the FTC limitation by multiplying the ratio of foreign source taxable income to total taxable income times precredit U.S. tax, as follows:

$$\frac{\text{Foreign source taxable income}}{\text{Total taxable income}} \times \text{Precredit U.S. tax}$$

Distinguish between the different forms of doing business outside the United States and list their advantages and disadvantages. LO 13-5

- A U.S. person can do business outside the United States through a branch, partnership, corporation, or hybrid entity.
- A hybrid entity is an entity that is treated as a flow-through entity for U.S. tax purposes and a corporation for foreign tax purposes (or vice versa).
- A U.S. taxpayer elects the U.S. tax status of a hybrid entity by "checking the box" on Form 8832.
  - Certain designated per se foreign entities are not eligible for this elective treatment.

Comprehend the basic U.S. anti-deferral tax regime and identify common sources of subpart F income. LO 13-6

- Subpart F requires certain U.S. shareholders in a controlled foreign corporation (CFC) to include in their gross income currently their pro rata share of specified categories of "tainted" income earned by the CFC during the current year (*subpart F income*).
- A controlled foreign corporation is defined as any foreign corporation in which U.S. shareholders collectively own more than 50 percent of the total combined voting power of all classes of stock entitled to vote or the total value of the corporation's stock on any day during the CFC's tax year.
  - Constructive ownership rules are used in the calculation of both the 50 percent test for determining CFC status and the 10 percent test for determining who is a U.S. shareholder.
- Subpart F income generally can be characterized as low-taxed passive income or "portable" income earned by a CFC.
  - Foreign personal holding company income includes interest, dividends, rents, royalties, and gains from the sales of certain foreign property.
  - Foreign base company sales income is income derived by a CFC from the sale or purchase of personal property to (or from) a related person and the property is manufactured and sold outside the CFC's country of incorporation.

- There are several exceptions that serve to exclude all or a portion of a CFC's subpart F income from current taxation to the U.S. shareholders.
  - A *de minimis rule* excludes all gross income from being treated as foreign base company income if the sum of the CFC's gross foreign base company income is less than the lesser of 5 percent of gross income or $1 million.
  - A *full inclusion rule* treats all of the CFC's gross income as foreign base company income if more than 70 percent of the CFC's gross income is foreign base company income.

KEY TERMS

allocate (13-12)
apportion (13-12)
branch (13-3)
commercial traveler exception (13-8)
controlled foreign corporation (13-28)
definitely related deductions (13-12)
disregarded entity (13-26)
effectively connected income (13-3)
fixed and determinable, annual or periodic income (13-3)
foreign joint venture (13-22)
foreign personal holding company income (13-29)
foreign subsidiary (13-22)
foreign tax credit (13-5)
foreign tax credit limitation (13-5)
FTC basket (13-20)
functional currency (13-23)
general category income (13-20)
hybrid entity (13-26)
inbound transaction (13-2)
nexus (13-2)
nonresident alien (13-4)
not definitely related deductions (13-12)
outbound transaction (13-2)
passive category income (13-20)
permanent establishment (13-18)
residence-based jurisdiction (13-2)
resident alien (13-4)
reverse hybrid entity (13-26)
source-based jurisdiction (13-2)
spot rate (13-22)
subpart F income (13-28)
tax haven (13-27)

DISCUSSION QUESTIONS

LO 13-1 1. Distinguish between an outbound transaction and an inbound transaction from a U.S. tax perspective.

LO 13-1 2. What are the major U.S. tax issues that apply to an inbound transaction?

LO 13-1 3. What are the major U.S. tax issues that apply to an outbound transaction?

LO 13-1 4. How does a residence-based approach to taxing worldwide income differ from a source-based approach to taxing the same income?

LO 13-1 5. Henri is a resident of the United States for U.S. tax purposes and earns $10,000 from an investment in a French company. Will Henri be subject to U.S. tax under a residence-based approach to taxation? A source-based approach?

LO 13-1 6. What are the two categories of income that can be taxed by the United States when earned by a nonresident? How does the United States tax each category of income?

LO 13-1 7. Maria is not a citizen of the United States, but she spends 180 days per year in the United States on business-related activities. Under what conditions will Maria be considered a resident of the United States for U.S. tax purposes?

LO 13-1 8. Natasha is not a citizen of the United States, but she spends 200 days per year in the United States on business. She does not have a green card. True or False: Natasha will always be considered a resident of the United States for U.S. tax purposes because of her physical presence in the United States. Explain.

LO 13-1 9. Why does the United States allow U.S. taxpayers to claim a credit against their precredit U.S. tax for foreign income taxes paid?

10. What role does the foreign tax credit limitation play in U.S. tax policy? LO 13-1
11. Why are the income source rules important to a U.S. citizen or resident? LO 13-2
12. Why are the income source rules important to a U.S. nonresident? LO 13-2
13. Carol receives $500 of dividend income from Microsoft Inc., a U.S. company. True or False: Absent any treaty provisions, Carol will be subject to U.S. tax on the dividend regardless of whether she is a resident or nonresident. Explain. LO 13-2
14. Pavel, a citizen and resident of Russia, spent 100 days in the United States working for his employer, Yukos Oil, a Russian corporation. Under what conditions will Pavel be subject to U.S. tax on the portion of his compensation earned while working in the United States? LO 13-2
15. What are the potential U.S. tax benefits from engaging in a §863(b) sale? LO 13-2
16. True or False: A taxpayer will always prefer deducting an expense against U.S. source income and not foreign source income when filing a tax return in the United States. Explain. LO 13-2
17. Distinguish between *allocation* and *apportionment* in sourcing deductions in computing the foreign tax credit limitation. LO 13-2
18. Distinguish between a *definitely related deduction* and a *not definitely related deduction* in the allocation and apportionment of deductions to foreign source taxable income. LO 13-2
19. Briefly describe the two different methods for apportioning interest expense to foreign source taxable income in the computation of the foreign tax credit limitation. LO 13-2
20. Briefly describe the two different methods for apportioning R&E to foreign source taxable income in the computation of the foreign tax credit limitation. LO 13-2
21. IBM incurs $250 million of R&E in the United States. How does the "exclusive apportionment" of this deduction differ depending on the R&E apportionment method chosen in the computation of the foreign tax credit limitation? LO 13-2
22. What is the primary goal of the United States in negotiating income tax treaties with other countries? LO 13-3
23. What is a *permanent establishment,* and why is it an important part of most income tax treaties? LO 13-3
24. Why is a treaty important to a nonresident investor in U.S. stocks and bonds? LO 13-3
25. Why is a treaty important to a nonresident worker in the United States? LO 13-3
26. Why does the United States use a "basket" approach in the foreign tax credit limitation computation? LO 13-4
27. True or False: All dividend income received by a U.S. taxpayer is classified as passive category income for foreign tax credit limitation purposes. Explain. LO 13-4
28. True or False: All foreign taxes are creditable for U.S. tax purposes. Explain. LO 13-4
29. What is an "indirect credit" for foreign tax credit purposes? What is the tax policy reason for allowing such a credit? LO 13-4
30. What is a functional currency? What role does it play in the computation of an indirect credit for foreign tax credit purposes? LO 13-4
31. What is a hybrid entity for U.S. tax purposes? Why is a hybrid entity a popular organizational form for a U.S. company expanding its international operations? What are the potential drawbacks to using a hybrid entity? LO 13-5
32. What is a "per se" entity under the check-the-box rules? LO 13-5

LO 13-6 33. What are the requirements for a foreign corporation to be a *controlled foreign corporation* for U.S. tax purposes?

LO 13-6 34. Why does the United States not allow deferral on all foreign source income earned by a controlled foreign corporation?

LO 13-6 35. True or False: A foreign corporation owned equally by 11 U.S. individuals can never be a controlled foreign corporation? Explain.

LO 13-6 36. What is foreign base company sales income? Why does the United States include this income in its definition of subpart F income?

LO 13-6 37. True or False: Subpart F income is always treated as a deemed dividend to the U.S. shareholders of a controlled foreign corporation. Explain.

LO 13-6 38. True or False: Non-subpart F income always qualifies for tax deferral until it is repatriated back to the United States. Explain.

PROBLEMS

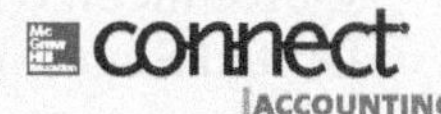

All applicable problems are available with McGraw-Hill's *Connect*® *Accounting*.

LO 13-1 39. Camille, a citizen and resident of Country A, received a $1,000 dividend from a corporation organized in Country B. Which statement best describes the taxation of this income under the two different approaches to taxing foreign income?

a) Country B will not tax this income under a residence-based jurisdiction approach but will tax this income under a source-based jurisdiction approach.

b) Country B will tax this income under a residence-based jurisdiction approach but will not tax this income under a source-based jurisdiction approach.

c) Country B will tax this income under both a residence-based jurisdiction approach and a source-based jurisdiction approach.

d) Country B will not tax this income under either a residence-based jurisdiction approach or a source-based jurisdiction approach.

LO 13-1 40. Spartan Corporation, a U.S. corporation, reported $2 million of pretax income from its business operations in Spartania, which were conducted through a foreign branch. Spartania taxes branch income at 25 percent, and the United States taxes corporate income at 35 percent.

a) If the United States provided no mechanism for mitigating double taxation, what would be the total tax (U.S. and foreign) on the $2 million of branch profits?

b) Assume the United States allows U.S. corporations to exclude foreign source income from U.S. taxation. What would be the total tax on the $2 million of branch profits?

c) Assume the United States allows U.S. corporations to claim a deduction for foreign income taxes. What would be the total tax on the $2 million of branch profits?

d) Assume the United States allows U.S. corporations to claim a credit for foreign income taxes paid on foreign source income. What would be the total tax on the $2 million of branch profits? What would be your answer if Spartania taxed branch profits at 40 percent?

LO 13-1 41. Guido is a citizen and resident of Belgium. He has a full-time job in Belgium and has lived there with his family for the past ten years. In 2013, Guido came to the United States for the first time. The sole purpose of his trip was business. He intended to stay in the United States for only 180 days, but he ended up staying for 210 days because of unforeseen problems with his business. Guido came to the United States again on business in 2014 and stayed for 180 days. In 2015 he came back to the United States on business and stayed for 70 days. Determine if Guido meets the U.S. statutory definition of a resident alien in 2013, 2014, and 2015 under the substantial presence test.

42. Use the facts in problem 41. If Guido meets the statutory requirements to be considered a resident of both the United States and Belgium, what criteria does the U.S.-Belgium treaty use to "break the tie" and determine Guido's country of residence? Look at Article 4 of the 2007 U.S.-Belgium income tax treaty, which you can find on the IRS website, www.irs.gov. LO 13-1 research

43. How does the U.S.-Belgium treaty define a *permanent establishment* for determining nexus? Look at Article 5 of the 2007 U.S.-Belgium income tax treaty, which you can find on the IRS website, www.irs.gov. LO 13-1 research

44. Mackinac Corporation, a U.S. corporation, reported total taxable income of $5 million. Taxable income included $1.5 million of foreign source taxable income from the company's branch operations in Canada. All of the branch income is general category income. Mackinac paid Canadian income taxes of $600,000 on its branch income. Compute Mackinac's allowable foreign tax credit. Assume a U.S. corporate tax rate of 34 percent. LO 13-1

45. Waco Leather Inc., a U.S. corporation, reported total taxable income of $5 million. Taxable income included $1.5 million of foreign source taxable income from the company's branch operations in Mexico. All of the branch income is general category income. Waco paid Mexican income taxes of $420,000 on its branch income. Compute Waco's allowable foreign tax credit. Assume a U.S. corporate tax rate of 34 percent. LO 13-1

46. Petoskey Stone Inc., a U.S. corporation, received the following sources of income during the current year. Identify the source of each item as either U.S. or foreign. LO 13-2
   a) Interest income from a loan to its German subsidiary.
   b) Dividend income from Granite Corporation, a U.S. corporation.
   c) Royalty income from its Irish subsidiary for use of a trademark.
   d) Rent income from its Canadian subsidiary of a warehouse located in Wisconsin.

47. Carmen SanDiego, a U.S. citizen, is employed by General Motors Corporation, a U.S. corporation. On April 1, 2015, GM relocated Carmen to its Brazilian operations for the remainder of 2015. Carmen was paid a salary of $120,000 and was employed on a 5-day week basis. As part of her compensation package for moving to Brazil, Carmen also received a housing allowance of $25,000. Carmen's salary was earned ratably over the 12-month period. During 2015 Carmen worked 260 days, 195 of which were in Brazil and 65 of which were in Michigan. How much of Carmen's total compensation is treated as foreign source income for 2015? Why might Carmen want to maximize her foreign source income in 2015? LO 13-2

48. John Elton is a citizen and bona fide resident of Great Britain (United Kingdom). During the current year, John received the following income: LO 13-2
   - Compensation of $30 million from performing concerts in the United States.
   - Cash dividends of $10,000 from a French corporation stock.
   - Interest of $6,000 on a U.S. corporation bond.
   - Interest of $2,000 on a loan made to a U.S. citizen residing in Australia.
   - Gain of $80,000 on the sale of stock in a U.S. corporation.

Determine the source (U.S. or foreign) of each item of income John received.

Income	Source
Income from concerts	
Dividend from French corporation	
Interest on a U.S. corporation bond	
Interest of $2,000 on a loan made to a U.S. citizen residing in Australia	
Gain of $80,000 on the sale of stock in a U.S. corporation	

49. Spartan Corporation, a U.S. company, manufactures green eyeshades for sale in the United States and Europe. All manufacturing activities take place in Michigan. During the current year, Spartan sold 10,000 green eyeshades to European customers at a price of $10 each. Each eyeshade costs $4 to produce. All of Spartan's production assets are located in the United States. For each independent scenario, determine the source of the gross income from sale of the green eyeshades.
    a) Spartan ships its eyeshades F.O.B., place of destination.
    b) Spartan ships its eyeshades F.O.B., place of shipment.

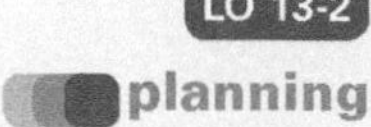

50. Falmouth Kettle Company, a U.S. corporation, sells its products in the United States and Europe. During the current year, selling, general, and administrative (SG&A) expenses included:

Personnel department	$ 500
Training department	350
President's salary	400
Sales manager's salary	200
Other general and administrative	550
Total SG&A expenses	$2,000

Falmouth had $12,000 of gross sales to U.S. customers and $3,000 of gross sales to European customers. Gross income (sales minus cost of goods sold) from domestic sales was $3,000 and gross profit from foreign sales was $1,000. Apportion Falmouth's SG&A expenses to foreign source income using the following methods:
    a) Gross sales.
    b) Gross income.
    c) If Falmouth wants to maximize its foreign tax credit limitation, which method produces the better outcome?

51. Owl Vision Corporation (OVC) is a North Carolina corporation engaged in the manufacture and sale of contact lenses and other optical equipment. The company handles its export sales through sales branches in Belgium and Singapore. The average tax book value of OVC's assets for the year was $200 million, of which $160 million generated U.S. source income and $40 million generated foreign source income. The average fair market value of OVC's assets was $240 million, of which $180 million generated U.S. source income and $60 million generated foreign source income. OVC's total interest expense was $20 million.
    a) What amount of the interest expense will be apportioned to foreign source income under the tax book value method?

b) What amount of the interest expense will be apportioned to foreign source income under the fair market value method?

c) If OVC wants to maximize its foreign tax credit limitation, which method produces the better outcome?

52. Freon Corporation, a U.S. corporation, manufactures air-conditioning and warm-air heating equipment. Freon reported gross sales from this product group of $50,000,000, of which $10,000,000 was foreign source. The gross profit percentage for domestic sales was 15 percent, and the gross profit percentage from non-U.S. sales was 20 percent. Freon incurred R&E expenses of $6,000,000, all of which were conducted in the United States. LO 13-2 planning

a) What amount of the R&E expense will be apportioned to foreign source income under the sales method?

b) What amount of the R&E expense will be apportioned to foreign source income under the gross income method?

c) If Freon wants to maximize its foreign tax credit limitation, which method produces the better outcome?

53. Colleen is a citizen and bona fide resident of Ireland. During the current year, she received the following income: LO 13-3 research

- Cash dividends of $2,000 from a U.S. corporation's stock.
- Interest of $1,000 on a U.S. corporation bond.
- Royalty of $100,000 from a U.S. corporation for use of a patent she developed.
- Rent of $3,000 from U.S. individuals renting her cottage in Maine.

Identify the U.S. withholding tax rate on the payment of each item of income under the U.S.-Ireland income tax treaty and cite the appropriate treaty article. You can access the 1997 U.S.-Ireland income tax treaty on the IRS website, www.irs.gov.

Income	Withholding Tax Rate	Treaty Article
Cash dividends of $2,000		
Interest of $1,000		
Royalty of $100,000		
Rent of $3,000		

54. Gameco, a U.S. corporation, operates gambling machines in the United States and abroad. Gameco conducts its operations in Europe through a Dutch B.V., which is treated as a branch for U.S. tax purposes. Gameco also licenses game machines to an unrelated company in Japan. During the current year, Gameco paid the following foreign taxes, translated into U.S. dollars at the appropriate exchange rate: LO 13-4

Foreign Taxes	Amount (in $)
National income taxes	1,000,000
City (Amsterdam) income taxes	100,000
Value-added tax	150,000
Payroll tax (employer's share of social insurance contributions)	400,000
Withholding tax on royalties received from Japan	50,000

Identify Gameco's creditable foreign taxes.

55. Sombrero Corporation, a U.S. corporation, operates through a branch in Espania. Management projects that the company's pretax income in the next taxable year will be $100,000, $80,000 from U.S. operations and $20,000 from LO 13-4

the branch. Espania taxes corporate income at a rate of 45 percent. The U.S. corporate tax rate is 35 percent.

a) If management's projections are accurate, what will be Sombrero's excess foreign tax credit in the next taxable year? Assume all of the income is general category income.

b) Management plans to establish a second branch in Italia. Italia taxes corporate income at a rate of 30 percent. What amount of income will the branch in Italia have to generate to eliminate the excess credit generated by the branch in Espania?

LO 13-4

56. Chapeau Company, a U.S. corporation, operates through a branch in Champagnia. The source rules used by Champagnia are identical to those used by the United States. For 2015, Chapeau has $2,000 of gross income, $1,200 from U.S. sources and $800 from sources within Champagnia. The $1,200 of U.S. source income and $700 of the foreign source income are attributable to manufacturing activities in Champagnia (general category income). The remaining $100 of foreign source income is passive category interest income. Chapeau had $500 of expenses other than taxes, all of which are allocated directly to manufacturing income ($200 of which is apportioned to foreign sources). Chapeau paid $150 of income taxes to Champagnia on its manufacturing income. The interest income was subject to a 10 percent withholding tax of $10. Assume the U.S. tax rate is 35 percent. Compute Chapeau's allowable foreign tax credit in 2015.

LO 13-4

57. Paton Corporation, a U.S. corporation, owns 100 percent of the stock of Tappan Ltd, a British corporation, and 100 percent of the stock of Monroe N.V., a Dutch corporation. Monroe has post-1986 undistributed earnings of €600 and post-1986 foreign income taxes of $400. Tappan has post-1986 undistributed earnings of £800 and post-1986 foreign income taxes of $200. During the current year, Tappan paid Paton a dividend of £100, and Monroe paid Paton a dividend of €100. The dividends were exempt from withholding tax under the U.S.-UK and U.S.-Netherlands income tax treaties. The exchange rates are as follows: €1:$1.50 and £1:$2.00.

a) Compute Paton's deemed paid credit on the dividends it received from Tappan and Monroe.

b) Assume this is Paton's only income and compute the company's net U.S. tax after allowance of any foreign tax credits.

LO 13-4
planning

58. Hannah Corporation, a U.S. corporation, owns 100 percent of the stock of its two foreign corporations, Red S.A. and Cedar A.G. Red and Cedar derive all of their income from active foreign business operations. Red operates in a low-tax jurisdiction (20 percent tax rate), and Cedar operates in a high-tax jurisdiction (50 percent tax rate). Red has post-1986 foreign income taxes of $200 and post-1986 undistributed earnings of 800u. Cedar has post-1986 foreign income taxes of $500 and post-1986 undistributed earnings of 500q. No withholding taxes are imposed on any dividends that Hannah receives from Red or Cedar. The exchange rate between all three currencies is 1:1. Assume a U.S. corporate tax rate of 35 percent. Under the look-through rules, all dividend income is treated as general category income.

a) Compute the effect of an 80u dividend from Red on Hannah's net U.S. tax liability.

b) Can you offer Hannah any suggestions regarding how it might eliminate the residual U.S. tax due on an 80u dividend from Red? Be specific in terms of the exact amounts involved in any planning opportunities you identify.

LO 13-5

59. Identify the "per se" companies for which a check-the-box election cannot be made for U.S. tax purposes in the countries listed below. Consult the Instructions

to Form 8832, which can be found on the "Forms and Instructions" site on the IRS website, www.irs.gov. research

a) Japan
b) Germany
c) Netherlands
d) United Kingdom
e) People's Republic of China

60. Eagle Inc., a U.S. corporation, intends to create a *limitada* in Brazil in 2015 to manufacture pitching machines. The company expects the operation to generate losses of US$2,500,000 during its first three years of operations. Eagle would like the losses to flow through to its U.S. tax return and offset its U.S. profits. LO 13-5 research
   a) Can Eagle "check the box" and treat the *limitada* as a disregarded entity (branch) for U.S. tax purposes? Consult the Instructions to Form 8832, which can be found on the "Forms and Instructions" site on the IRS website, www.irs.gov.
   b) Assume management's projections were accurate and Eagle deducted $75,000 of branch losses on its U.S. tax return from 2015–2017. At 01/01/18, the fair market value of the *limitada*'s net assets exceeded Eagle's tax basis in the assets by US$5 million. What are the U.S. tax consequences of checking the box on Form 8832 and converting the *limitada* to a corporation for U.S. tax purposes?

61. Identify whether the corporations described below are controlled foreign corporations. LO 13-6
   a) Shetland PLC, a UK corporation, has two classes of stock outstanding, 75 shares of class AA stock and 25 shares of class A stock. Each class of stock has equal voting power. Angus owns 35 shares of class AA stock and 20 shares of class A stock. Angus is a U.S. citizen who resides in England.
   b) Tony and Gina, both U.S. citizens, own 5 percent and 10 percent, respectively, of the voting stock of DaVinci S.A., an Italian corporation. Tony and Gina are also equal partners in Roma Corporation, an Italian corporation that owns 50 percent of the DaVinci stock.
   c) Pierre, a U.S. citizen, owns 45 of the 100 shares outstanding in Vino S.A., a French corporation. Pierre's father, Pepe, owns 8 shares in Vino. Pepe also is a U.S. citizen. The remaining 47 shares are owned by non-U.S. individuals.

62. USCo owns 100 percent of the following corporations: Dutch N.V., Germany A.G., Australia PLC, Japan Corporation, and Brazil S.A. During the year, the following transactions took place: LO 13-6
   a) Germany A.G. owns an office building that it leases to unrelated persons. Germany A.G. engaged an independent managing agent to manage and maintain the office building and performs no activities with respect to the property.
   b) Dutch N.V. leased office machines to unrelated persons. Dutch N.V. performed only incidental activities and incurred nominal expenses in leasing and servicing the machines. Dutch N.V. is not engaged in the manufacture or production of the machines and does not add substantial value to the machines.
   c) Dutch N.V. purchased goods manufactured in France from an unrelated contract manufacturer and sold them to Germany A.G. for consumption in Germany.
   d) Australia PLC purchased goods manufactured in Australia from an unrelated person and sold them to Japan Corporation for use in Japan.

   Determine whether the above transactions result in subpart F income to USCo.

LO 13-6

63. USCo manufactures and markets electrical components. USCo operates outside the United States through a number of CFCs, each of which is organized in a different country. These CFCs derived the following income for the current year:
   a) F1 has gross income of $5 million, including $200,000 of foreign personal holding company interest and $4.8 million of gross income from the sale of inventory that F1 manufactured at a factory located within its home country.
   b) F2 has gross income of $5 million, including $4 million of foreign personal holding company interest and $1 million of gross income from the sale of inventory that F2 manufactured at a factory located within its home country.

   Determine the amount of income that USCo must report as a deemed dividend under subpart F in each scenario.

COMPREHENSIVE PROBLEMS

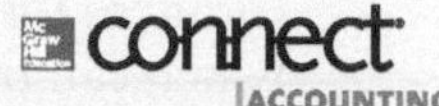

All applicable problems are available with McGraw-Hill's *Connect® Accounting*.

64. Spartan Corporation manufactures quidgets at its plant in Sparta, Michigan. Spartan sells its quidgets to customers in the United States, Canada, England, and Australia.

   Spartan markets its products in Canada and England through branches in Toronto and London, respectively. Title transfers in the United States on all sales to U.S. customers and abroad (FOB: destination) on all sales to Canadian and English customers. Spartan reported total gross income on U.S. sales of $15,000,000 and total gross income on Canadian and U.K. sales of $5,000,000, split equally between the two countries. Spartan paid Canadian income taxes of $600,000 on its branch profits in Canada and U.K. income taxes of $700,000 on its branch profits in the U.K. Spartan financed its Canadian operations through a $10 million capital contribution, which Spartan financed through a loan from Bank of America. During the current year, Spartan paid $600,000 in interest on the loan.

   Spartan sells its quidgets to Australian customers through its wholly owned Australian subsidiary. Title passes in the United States (FOB: shipping) on all sales to the subsidiary. Spartan reported gross income of $3,000,000 on sales to its subsidiary during the year. The subsidiary paid Spartan a dividend of $670,000 on December 31 (the withholding tax is 0 percent under the U.S.-Australia treaty). Spartan was deemed to have paid Australian income taxes of $330,000 on the income repatriated as a dividend.
   a) Compute Spartan's foreign source gross income and foreign tax (direct and withholding) for the current year.
   b) Assume 20 percent of the interest paid to Bank of America is allocated to the numerator of Spartan's FTC limitation calculation. Compute Spartan Corporation's FTC limitation using your calculation from question a and any excess FTC or excess FTC limitation (all of the foreign source income is put in the general category FTC basket).

65. Windmill Corporation manufactures products in its plants in Iowa, Canada, Ireland, and Australia. Windmill conducts its operations in Canada through a 50 percent owned joint venture, CanCo. CanCo is treated as a corporation for U.S. and Canadian tax purposes. An unrelated Canadian investor owns the remaining 50 percent. Windmill conducts its operations in Ireland through a wholly owned subsidiary, IrishCo. IrishCo is a controlled foreign corporation for U.S. tax purposes. Windmill conducts its operations in Australia through a wholly owned hybrid entity (KiwiCo) treated as a branch for U.S. tax purposes and a corporation for Australian tax purposes. Windmill also owns a 5 percent interest in a Dutch corporation (TulipCo).

During 2015, Windmill reported the following foreign source income from its international operations and investments.

	CanCo	IrishCo	KiwiCo	TulipCo
Dividend income				
Amount	$45,000	$28,000		$20,000
Withholding tax	2,250	1,400		3,000
Interest income				
Amount	30,000			
Withholding tax	0	0		
Branch income				
Taxable income			$93,000	
AUS income taxes			31,000	

Notes to the table:
1. CanCo and KiwiCo derive all of their earnings from active business operations.
2. The dividend from CanCo carries with it a deemed paid credit (§78 gross-up) of $30,000.
3. The dividend from IrishCo carries with it a deemed paid credit (§78 gross-up) of $4,000.

a) Classify the income received by Windmill and any associated §78 gross-up into the appropriate FTC baskets.
b) Windmill has $1,250,000 of U.S. source gross income. Windmill also incurred SG&A of $300,000 that is apportioned between U.S. and foreign source income based on the gross income in each basket. Assume KiwiCo's gross income is $93,000. Compute the FTC limitation for each basket of foreign source income. The corporate tax rate is 35 percent.

66. Euro Corporation, a U.S. corporation, operates through a branch in Germany. During 2015 the branch reported taxable income of $1,000,000 and paid German income taxes of $300,000. In addition, Euro received $50,000 of dividends from its 5 percent investment in the stock of Maple Leaf Company, a Canadian corporation. The dividend was subject to a withholding tax of $5,000. Euro reported U.S. taxable income from its manufacturing operations of $950,000. Total taxable income was $2,000,000. Precredit U.S. taxes on the taxable income were $680,000. Included in the computation of Euro's taxable income were "definitely allocable" expenses of $500,000, 50 percent of which were related to the German branch taxable income.

Complete pages 1 and 2 of Form 1118 for just the general category income reported by Euro. You can use the fill-in form available on the IRS website, www.irs.gov.

67. USCo, a U.S. corporation, has decided to set up a headquarters subsidiary in Europe. Management has narrowed its location choice to either Spain, or Ireland, or Switzerland. The company has asked you to research some of the income tax implications of setting up a corporation in these three countries. In particular, management wants to know what tax rate will be imposed on corporate income earned in the country and the withholding rates applied to interest, dividends, and royalty payments from the subsidiary to the USCo.

To answer the tax rate question, consult KPMG's *Corporate and Indirect Tax Survey 2014,* which you can access at http://www.kpmg.com/Global/en/IssuesAndInsights/ArticlesPublications/Documents/corporate-indirect-tax-rate-survey-2014.pdf. To answer the withholding tax questions, consult the treaties between the United States and Spain, Ireland, and Switzerland, which you can access at www.irs.gov (type in "treaties" as your search word).

chapter

14 Transfer Taxes and Wealth Planning

Learning Objectives

Upon completing this chapter, you should be able to:

LO 14-1 Outline the basic structure of federal transfer taxes and describe the valuation of property transfers.

LO 14-2 Summarize the operation of the federal gift tax and the calculation of the federal gift tax.

LO 14-3 Describe the federal estate tax, and compute taxable transfers at death and the federal estate tax.

LO 14-4 Apply fundamental principles of wealth planning and explain how income and transfer taxation interact to affect wealth planning.

© BananaStock/Jupiterimages

Storyline Summary

Taxpayers:	Bob and Harry Smith, brothers, ages 69 and 63, respectively Frank's Frozen Pizza Inc. (FFP) is a family business.
Description:	Bob, recently deceased, was a widower and has a son, Nate (age 28). Harry is married to Wilma, age 38, and has a daughter, Dina (age 35), a son-in-law, Steve, and a grandson, George (age 6).
Location:	Ann Arbor, Michigan
Employment status:	Bob and Harry inherited shares in FFP in 1990. Bob and Harry have been employees of FFP. Bob retired from FFP and died earlier this year. Harry is planning to retire as CEO of FFP.
Current situation:	Nate is Bob's executor.

Harry and Bob Smith were brothers and owners of a small privately held corporation, Frank's Frozen Pizzas Inc. (FFP). Their father, Frank, established the business 35 years ago, and Harry and Bob each inherited half of FFP's outstanding shares upon Frank's death. At the time of Frank's death in 1990, FFP shares were worth about $1 million, but the firm is now debt-free and has a value of $9 million. FFP's success didn't come easy. Over the years Harry and Bob were employed as executive officers and worked long, hard hours. After the death of his wife in 1995, Bob retired on his FFP pension. Over the years both Harry and Bob have transferred some of their FFP shares to other family members. Bob has given 20 percent of the shares in FFP to his son, Nate, and Harry has transferred a like amount to a trust established for Dina (his daughter) and George (his grandson).

Harry recently decided that he wants to retire from FFP and spend more time traveling and enjoying his family. Harry believes that Nate would like to assume responsibilities as CEO, and Dina has agreed to support Nate's decisions. Harry plans to begin an orderly transfer of his FFP stock to Dina to provide a future source of support for her and George. Besides his FFP stock, Harry has accumulated considerable personal assets to help maintain his lifestyle during retirement. Although Wilma, Harry's wife, owns significant assets, Harry also wants to provide for her support after his death. Finally, while Harry believes taxes and lawyers are necessary evils, he wants to avoid any unnecessary fees or taxes associated with the transfer of his assets. Hence, Harry would like advice on how to make his gifts in the most tax-efficient manner.

to be continued . . .

LO 14-1

INTRODUCTION TO FEDERAL TRANSFER TAXES

This chapter explains the structure of the federal transfer taxes. We begin by outlining transfer taxes and then proceed to describing in detail the federal gift tax. Finally, we describe the federal estate tax and introduce the principles of wealth planning.

Beginnings

In 1916 Congress imposed an estate tax on transfers of property at death. Transfers at death are dictated by the **last will and testament** of the deceased and such transfers are called **testamentary transfers.** The transfer tax system was expanded in 1924 to include a gift tax on lifetime transfers called **intervivos transfers** (from the Latin meaning "during the life of"). Eventually, a generation-skipping tax was also added to prevent tax avoidance by transferring assets to younger generations (transfers to grandchildren rather than to children).[1] Together, this trio of taxes represents one way of reducing the potential wealth society's richest families might accumulate over several generations. (Remember, neither gifts nor inheritances are included in recipients' gross income.)

TAXES IN THE REAL WORLD Perfect Timing

Roger Milliken died on December 30, 2010, just two days before the estate tax was revived. Milliken was 95 years old and had directed his family's business for 71 years as President and CEO of Milliken & Company. Milliken's estate, estimated under $1 billion, was subject to probate in Spartanburg County, South Carolina. In his 111-page will, described by the Spartanburg Journal Watchdog, Milliken established multiple trusts and directed that the family business would remain privately owned. Moreover, Milliken instructed trustees that no change of tax laws would warrant deviating from his intentions. In a two-page letter, Milliken expressed the hope that income from the trust would enable his descendants to pursue careers. To qualify for income from the trusts, Milliken's children must be 40 years old at which time they will be eligible to receive 10 percent of the trust's income. The distribution increases to 50 percent at age 44 and to all of the net income by the age of 49. Milliken also expressed hope that money from the trusts would enable his children and grandchildren to achieve true self-fulfillment and happiness.

Common Features of Integrated Transfer Taxes

The two primary federal transfer taxes, the estate tax and the gift tax, were originally enacted separately and operated independently. In 1976 they were *unified* into a transfer tax scheme that applies a progressive tax rate schedule to cumulative transfers. In other words, the estate and gift taxes now are integrated into a common formula.

This integrated formula takes into account the cumulative effect of transfers in previous periods when calculating the tax on a transfer in a current period. Likewise, it takes lifetime transfers into account to determine the tax on assets transferred at death. As you'll see in the tax formulas, we add the taxable transfers in prior years to the current-year transfers and compute the tax on total (cumulative) transfers. Then, we subtract the tax on the earlier transfers from the total tax, to avoid taxing the earlier gifts twice. This calculation is designed to increase the likelihood that the most current transfers will be taxed at a higher marginal tax rate. However, the effect of this feature has been sharply reduced by recent reductions in the top tax rates. Exhibit 14-1 presents the unified transfer tax rate schedule for estate and gift taxes.

The second common feature of the integrated transfer taxes is the **unified credit.** The unified credit was enacted in 1977, and it applies to both the gift tax and the estate tax.

[1]The estate tax was optional for decedents dying in 2010. In lieu of the estate tax, executors could opt to have the adjusted tax basis of the assets in gross estate carry over to the heirs of the decedent. The estate tax is back in place for decedents dying subsequent to 2010.

EXHIBIT 14-1 Unified Transfer Tax Rates*

Tax Base equal to or over	Not over	Tentative tax	plus	of amount over
0	$ 10,000	0	18%	0
$ 10,000	20,000	$ 1,800	20	$ 10,000
20,000	40,000	3,800	22	20,000
40,000	60,000	8,200	24	40,000
60,000	80,000	13,000	26	60,000
80,000	100,000	18,200	28	80,000
100,000	150,000	23,800	30	100,000
150,000	250,000	38,800	32	150,000
250,000	500,000	70,800	34	250,000
500,000	750,000	155,800	37	500,000
750,000	1,000,000	248,300	39	750,000
1,000,000		345,800	40	1,000,000

THE KEY FACTS

Common Features of the Unified Transfer Taxes

- Property transfers, whether made by gift or at death, are subject to transfer tax using a progressive tax rate schedule.
- The unified credit exempts cumulative transfers of up to $5.43 million ($10.86 million for married taxpayers).
- Each transfer tax allows a deduction for transfers to charities and surviving spouses (the charitable and marital deductions, respectively).

The credit is designed to prevent the application of transfer tax to taxpayers who either would not accumulate a relatively large amount of property transfers during their lifetime and/or would not have a relatively large transfer passing to heirs upon their death. The amount of cumulative taxable transfers a person can make without exceeding the unified credit was originally called the **exemption equivalent.** The exemption equivalent is now called the *applicable exclusion amount,* but we continue to refer to it as the exemption equivalent.

Exhibit 14-2 presents the exemption equivalent amounts for both the estate and gift taxes since 1986. The exemption equivalent was the same amount for gift and estate tax purposes until 2004, at which time the gift tax was frozen at $1,000,000 exemption equivalent. In 2011, the exemption equivalent for the gift tax was reunified with the estate tax and, beginning in 2012, the exemption equivalent is adjusted annually for inflation.

The amount of the unified credit depends on both the transfer tax rate and the exemption equivalent at the time of the transfer. Because both the tax rate and the exemption equivalent change over time, the unified credit is best understood by converting the exemption equivalent into a tax credit using the current tax rate schedule. For example, the exemption equivalent was $5 million for transfers made in 2011, and the unified credit at this time was determined by the tax rate schedule in effect in 2011.

EXHIBIT 14-2 The Exemption Equivalent or Applicable Exclusion Amount

Year of Transfer	Gift Tax	Estate Tax
1986	$ 500,000	$ 500,000
1987–1997	600,000	600,000
1998	625,000	625,000
1999	650,000	650,000
2000–2001	675,000	675,000
2002–2003	1,000,000	1,000,000
2004–2005	1,000,000	1,500,000
2006–2008	1,000,000	2,000,000
2009–2010*	1,000,000	3,500,000
2011	5,000,000	5,000,000
2012	5,120,000	5,120,000
2013	5,250,000	5,250,000
2014	5,340,000	5,340,000
2015	5,430,000	5,430,000

*The unified credit and exemption is zero for taxpayers who opt out of the estate tax in 2010.

In contrast, the exemption equivalent is $5.43 million for transfers made in 2015, and under the unified tax rate schedule the unified credit is $2,117,800.

A third common feature of the unified tax system is the application of two common deductions. Each transfer tax provides an unlimited charitable deduction for charitable contributions and a generous **marital deduction** for transfers to a spouse. The marital deduction allows almost unfettered transfers between spouses, treating a married couple as virtually a single taxpayer.

A final important feature of the transfer taxes is the valuation of transferred property. Property transferred via gift or otherwise is valued at fair market value. While fair market value is simple in concept, it is very complicated to apply. For purposes of the transfer taxes, fair market value is defined by the **willing-buyer, willing-seller rule** as follows:

> The price at which such property would change hands between a willing buyer and a willing seller, neither being under any compulsion to buy or to sell, and both have reasonable knowledge of the relevant facts.

Fair market value is determined based on the facts and circumstances for each individual property. Determining value is relatively simple for properties that have an active market. For example, stocks and bonds traded on exchanges or over-the-counter are valued at the mean of the highest and lowest selling prices. Unfortunately, the valuation of many other properties, especially realty, is very difficult. The large number of court cases resolving contentious values testifies to the difficulties in applying the willing-buyer, willing-seller rule.

LO 14-2 THE FEDERAL GIFT TAX

The gift tax is levied on individual taxpayers for all taxable gifts made during a calendar year. As we'll explain shortly, each *individual* (married couples cannot elect joint filing for gift tax returns) who makes a gift in excess of the annual exclusion amount must file a gift tax return (Form 709) by April 15 of the following year.[2] Exhibit 14-3 presents the complete formula for the federal gift tax in two parts. In the first part, we calculate taxable gifts for each donee, and in the second, we calculate the gift tax using aggregate taxable gifts to all donees. We begin the first part by identifying transfers that constitute gifts.

EXHIBIT 14-3 The Federal Gift Tax Formula

	***Part 1:* Calculate taxable gifts for each individual donee:**
	Current Gifts
Minus	½ of split gifts (included in spouse's current gifts)
Plus	½ of split gifts by spouse
Minus	Annual exclusion ($14,000 per donee)
Minus	Marital and charitable deductions
Equals	Current taxable gifts
	***Part 2:* Sum taxable gifts for all donees and calculate tax:**
	Total Current Taxable Gifts
Plus	Prior taxable gifts
Equals	Cumulative taxable gifts
Times	Current tax rates
Equals	Cumulative tax
Minus	Current tax on prior taxable gifts
Minus	Remaining unified credit
Equals	Gift Tax Payable

[2]A gift tax return reporting taxable gifts must be filed by April 15th following year-end if a taxpayer has made *any* taxable gifts during the current calendar year *or wishes to elect* gift-splitting. When taxpayers request extensions for their individual income tax returns, they also receive a six-month extension for filing their gift tax returns.

Transfers Subject to Gift Tax

The gift tax is imposed on lifetime transfers of property for less than adequate consideration. Typically, a gift is made in a personal context such as between family members. The satisfaction of an obligation is not considered a gift. For example, tuition payments for a child's education satisfy a support obligation. On the other hand, transfers motivated by affection or other personal motives, including transfers associated with marriage, are gratuitous and subject to the tax. The gift tax is imposed once a gift has been completed, and this occurs when the **donor** relinquishes control of the property and the **donee** accepts the gift.[3] For example, deposits made to a joint bank account are not completed gifts because the donor (depositor) can withdraw the deposit at any time. The gift will be complete at the time the *donee* withdraws cash from the account.

THE KEY FACTS

Gifts Excluded from the Gift Tax

- Incomplete and revocable gifts.
- Payments for support obligations or debts.
- Contributions to political parties or candidates.
- Medical and educational expenses paid on behalf of an unrelated individual.

TAXES IN THE REAL WORLD Love and Taxes

The small claims division of the Tax Court was asked to determine whether payments between former lovers constituted gifts or compensation. Jue-Ya Yang lived with her boyfriend, Howard Shih, who was an artist and calligrapher. While they were romantically involved, Mr. Shih made payments to Ms. Yang and later deducted these payments as wages.

Ms. Yang admitted doing housekeeping and cooking, but she argued that the payments were gifts. Mr. Shih's testimony about the romantic relationship was evasive. He admitted on cross-examination that while their relationship was more than a professional one, Mr. Shih could not even recall taking Ms. Yang out on dates. The court concluded that Mr. Shih's testimony was untrue and held that the payments were gifts made because of love and affection.

Source: Jue-Ya Yang, TC Summary Opinion 2008-156 (12-15-08).

In some instances a donor may relinquish some control over transferred property but retain other powers that can influence the enjoyment or disposition of the property. If the retained powers are important, then the transfer will not be a complete gift.[4] For example, a transfer of property to a trust will not be a complete gift if the grantor retains the ability to revoke the transfer. If the grantor releases the powers, then the gift will generally be complete at that time because the property is no longer subject to the donor's control. For example, a distribution of property from a revocable trust is a completed gift because the grantor no longer has the ability to revoke the distribution.

Example 14-1

On July 12th of this year Harry transferred $250,000 of FFP stock to a new trust. He gave the trustee directions to pay income to Dina for the next 20 years and then remit the remainder to her son George. Harry named a bank as trustee but retained the power to revoke the trust in case he should need additional assets after retirement. Is the transfer of the stock a completed gift?

Answer: No. Harry retains sufficient control that the transfer of the stock to the trust is an incomplete gift.

What if: Suppose that $15,000 of trust income were distributed to Dina at year-end. Is the transfer of the cash to Dina a completed gift?

Answer: Yes. With the payment Harry has relinquished control over the $15,000, and thus, it is a completed gift.

What if: Suppose that Harry releases his power to revoke the trust at a time when the shares of FPP in the trust are valued at $225,000. Would this release cause the transfer of the stock to be a completed gift and, if so, what is the amount of the gift?

Answer: Yes. By releasing his powers Harry has relinquished control over the entire trust, and the value of the trust at that time ($225,000) would be a completed gift.

[3]If a donee refuses or disclaims a gift under §2518, the gift is not complete.

[4]§2514 addresses the treatment of general powers of appointment.

There are several important exceptions to the taxation of completed gifts. For example, political contributions are not gifts. Also, the payment of medical or educational expenses on behalf of another individual is not considered a gift if the payments are made directly to the health care provider or to the educational institution. To avoid confusing a division of property with a gift, we treat a transfer of property in conjunction with a divorce as nongratuitous (it is treated as a transfer for adequate consideration) if the property is transferred within three years of the divorce under a written property settlement.

In addition, special rules apply to transfers of certain types of property. To make a completed gift of a life insurance policy, the donor must give the donee all the incidents of ownership, including the power to designate beneficiaries. An individual who creates a joint tenancy (either a tenancy in common or joint tenancy with right of survivorship) with someone who does not provide adequate consideration is deemed to make a gift at that time. The gift is the amount necessary to pay for the other party's interest in the property. For example, suppose the donor pays $80,000 toward the purchase of $100,000 in realty held as equal tenants in common with the donee (i.e., the donee provides only $20,000 of the purchase). The donor is deemed to make a gift of $30,000 to the donee, the difference between the value of the joint interest ($100,000 ÷ 2 = $50,000) and the consideration provided by the donee ($20,000).

ETHICS

Rudy is a retired engineer who has three adult daughters and several grandchildren. This year Carol, his youngest daughter, approached Rudy for a $40,000 business loan. Although Carol had no collateral for the loan and did not sign any written promise to repay the money, Rudy still transferred the funds to her account. Do you think that Rudy should file a gift tax return for the transfer? Suppose that Rudy has no intention of demanding repayment, but has not told anyone of his intention. Any difference?

Example 14-2

This year Harry helped purchase a residence for use by Dina and her husband Steve. The price of the residence was $250,000, and the title named Harry and Steve joint tenants with the right of survivorship. Harry provided $210,000 of the purchase price and Steve the remaining $40,000. Has Harry made a completed gift and, if so, in what amount?

Answer: Yes, Harry made a complete gift to Steve of $85,000, calculated by subtracting the amount paid by Steve from the price of his ownership interest ($125,000 minus $40,000).

What if: Suppose Steve didn't provide any part of the purchase price. What is the amount of the gift?

Answer: Harry made a complete gift to Steve of half the purchase price, $125,000.

Valuation Gifts are taxed at the fair market value of the donated property on the date the gift becomes complete. Remember, that despite the valuation of a gift at fair market value, the donee generally takes a carryover basis for income tax purposes.[5]

Valuation of remainders and other temporal interests. Assigning value to unique property is difficult enough, but sometimes we must also assign a value to a stream of payments over time or a payment to be made in the future. The right to currently enjoy property or receive income payments from property is called a **present interest.** In contrast, the right to receive income or property in the future is called a **future interest.** A present right to possess and/or collect income from property may not be

[5]The carryover basis may be increased for any gift tax paid (after 1976) on the appreciation of the property.

permanent; if granted for a specific period of time or until the occurrence of a specific event, it is a **terminable interest.** For example, the right to receive income payments from property for 10 years is a terminable interest. A right to possess property and/or receive income for the duration of someone's life is called a **life estate.** The person whose life determines the duration of the life estate is called the life tenant.

At the end of a terminable interest, the property will pass to another owner, the person holding the future interest. In a **reversion,** it returns to the original owner. If it goes to a new owner, the right to the property is called a **remainder** and the owner is called a **remainderman.** For example, the right to own property after a 10-year income interest has ended is a future interest held by the remainderman. The right to property after the termination of a life estate is also called a remainder.

Future interests are common when property is placed in a trust. **Trusts** are legal entities established by a person called the **grantor.** Trusts are administered by a **trustee** and generally contain property called the trust **corpus.** The trustee has a **fiduciary duty** to manage the property in the trust for the benefit of a **beneficiary** or beneficiaries. This duty requires the trustee to administer the trust in an objective and impartial manner and not favor one beneficiary over another.

Since a future interest is essentially a promise of a future payment, we estimate the value of the remainder by discounting the future payment to a present value using a market rate of interest. For example, suppose property worth $100 is placed in a trust with the income to be paid to an income beneficiary each year for 10 years, after which time the property accumulated in the trust will be distributed. The remainder is a future interest with a value we estimate by calculating the present value of a payment of $100 in 10 years as follows:

$$\text{Value of remainder interest} = \frac{\text{Future payment}}{(1 + r)^n}$$

where r is the market rate of interest, and n is the number of years. The interest rate used for this calculation is published monthly by the Treasury as the §7520 rate.[6] If the §7520 rate is 6 percent, we calculate the value of a remainder of $100 placed in trust for 10 years as follows:

$$\text{Value of remainder interest} = \frac{\$100}{(1 + .06)^{10}} = \frac{\$100}{(1.791)} = \$55.83$$

The value of property consists of the present interest (the right to income) and the future interest (the remainder). Hence, once we have estimated the value of the remainder, we compute the value of the income interest as the difference between the value of the remainder and the total value of the property.

$$\begin{aligned}\text{Value of income interest} &= \text{Total value} - \text{Value of remainder}\\ &= \$100 - \$55.83\\ &= \$44.17\end{aligned}$$

If the terminable interest is a life estate, the valuation of the remainder is a bit more complicated, because payment of the remainder is delayed by the duration of the life estate. To estimate this delay, we base the calculation upon the number of years the life tenant is expected to live. To facilitate the calculation, the regulations provide a table that calculates the discount rate by including the life tenant's age. Exhibit 14-4 includes a portion of the table from the regulation with interest rates by column and the age of the life tenant by row.

THE KEY FACTS

Valuation of Remainders and Income Interests

- Future interests are valued at present value, calculated by estimating the time until the present interest expires.
- The present value calculation uses the §7520 interest rate published by the Treasury.
- If the present interest is measured by a person's life (a life estate), then we estimate the delay by reference to the person's life expectancy as published in IRS tables.
- We value a present interest such as an income interest or life estate by subtracting the value of the remainder interest from the total value of the property.

[6]The §7520 rate is 120 percent of the applicable federal midterm rate in effect during the month of the transaction.

EXHIBIT 14-4 Discount Factors for Estimating the Value of Remainders

Regulation Section 20.2031-7(d)(7)
Table S.—Based on Life Table 2000CM Single Life Remainder Factors
Applicable After May 1, 2009
[Interest rate]

Age	4.2%	4.4%	4.6%	4.8%	5.0%	5.2%	5.4%	5.6%	5.8%	6.0%
0	.06083	.05483	.04959	.04501	.04101	.03749	.03441	.03170	.02931	.02721
1	.05668	.05049	.04507	.04034	.03618	.03254	.02934	.02652	.02403	.02183
2	.05858	.05222	.04665	.04178	.03750	.03373	.03042	.02750	.02492	.02264
3	.06072	.05420	.04848	.04346	.03904	.03516	.03173	.02871	.02603	.02366
4	.06303	.05634	.05046	.04530	.04075	.03674	.03319	.03006	.02729	.02483
5	.06547	.05861	.05258	.04726	.04258	.03844	.03478	.03153	.02866	.02610
6	.06805	.06102	.05482	.04935	.04453	.04026	.03647	.03312	.03014	.02749
35	.19692	.18423	.17253	.16174	.15178	.14258	.13408	.12621	.11892	.11217
36	.20407	.19119	.17931	.16833	.15818	.14879	.14009	.13204	.12457	.11764
37	.21144	.19838	.18631	.17515	.16481	.15523	.14635	.13811	.13046	.12335
38	.21904	.20582	.19357	.18222	.17170	.16193	.15287	.14444	.13661	.12932
86	.79825	.79044	.78278	.77524	.76783	.76055	.75340	.74636	.73944	.73264
87	.80921	.80176	.79443	.78722	.78014	.77316	.76630	.75956	.75292	.74638
88	.81978	.81268	.80569	.79880	.79203	.78536	.77880	.77234	.76598	.75971
89	.82994	.82317	.81651	.80995	.80349	.79712	.79085	.78467	.77859	.77259

Example 14-3

Harry transferred $500,000 of FFP stock to the DG Trust, whose trustee is directed to pay income to Dina for her life and, upon Dina's death, pay the remainder to George (or his estate). At time of the gift, Dina was 35 years old and the §7520 interest rate was 5.8 percent. What are the values of the gift of the life estate and of the remainder interest?

Answer: Harry made a $59,460 gift of the remainder to George and $440,540 of the life estate to Dina. Under Table S (see Exhibit 14-4), the percentage of the property that represents the value of George's remainder is 0.11892. Thus, George's remainder is valued at $59,460 ($500,000 × 0.11892). Dina's life estate is the remaining value of $440,540 ($500,000 − $59,460).

The Annual Exclusion One of the most important aspects of the gift tax is the **annual exclusion,** which operates to eliminate "small" gifts from the gift tax base. The amount of the exclusion has been revised upwards periodically over the years and is now indexed for inflation.[7] In 2015 it is $14,000.

The annual exclusion is available to offset gifts made to *each* donee regardless of the number of donees in any particular year. For example, a donor could give $14,000 in cash to each of 10 donees every year without exceeding the annual exclusion. One important limitation to the annual exclusion is that it applies only to gifts of *present* interests; that is, a gift of a future interest is not eligible for an annual exclusion.

Example 14-4

When Harry transferred $500,000 of FFP stock to the DG Trust (Example 14-3), he simultaneously made two taxable gifts, a life estate to Dina and a remainder to George. What is the amount of the taxable gift of the life estate to Dina and the remainder interest to George, after taking the exclusion amount into account?

[7]The exclusion is indexed for inflation in such a way that the amount of the exclusion only increases in increments of $1,000. The annual exclusion was $10,000 from 1981 through 2001, but was $11,000 for 2002 through 2005, $12,000 for 2006 through 2008, $13,000 for 2009 through 2012, and $14,000 since 2012.

Answer: Dina's life estate is a present interest and would qualify for the annual exclusion. However, George's remainder is a future interest and will not qualify for the annual exclusion. Harry would file a Form 709 to report total taxable gifts of $486,000 consisting of a $426,540 taxable gift to Dina ($440,540 less the annual exclusion of $14,000) and a taxable gift of $59,460 to George (no annual exclusion is available for a future interest).

	Dina	George	Harry's Gift Tax Return
Current gifts	$440,540	$59,460	$500,000
Annual exclusion	−14,000	−0	−14,000
Taxable gifts	$426,540	$59,460	$486,000

THE KEY FACTS

Annual Exclusion

- Most gifts are eligible for an annual exclusion of $14,000 per donee per year.
- Gifts of present interests qualify for the exclusion.
- Gifts of future interests placed in trust for a minor can also qualify for the exclusion.

Most gifts will only qualify for an annual exclusion if the donee has a present interest (the ability to immediately use the property or the income from it). However, a special exception applies to future interests given to minors (under the age of 21). Gifts in trust for a minor are future interests if the minor does not have the ability to access the income or property until reaching the age of majority. These gifts will still qualify for the annual exclusion as long as the property can be used to support the minor and any remaining property is distributed to the child once he or she reaches age 21.[8]

Example 14-5

Harry transferred $48,500 of cash to the George Trust. The trustee of the George Trust has the discretion to distribute income or corpus (principal) for George's benefit and is required to distribute all assets to George (or his estate) not later than George's 21st birthday. Is this gift eligible for the annual exclusion? If so, what is the amount of the taxable gift?

Answer: Yes, Harry will be entitled to an annual exclusion for the transfer despite the fact that George's interest is a future one, because the gift is in trust for the support of a minor and the property must distribute the assets to George once he reaches age 21. The amount of the gift is $48,500 reduced to a taxable gift of $34,500 after application of the $14,000 annual exclusion.

Taxable Gifts

In part 1 of the formula in Exhibit 14-3, **current gifts** are accumulated for each donee, and this amount includes all gifts completed during the calendar year for each individual. Current gifts do not include transfers exempted from the tax, such as political contributions. We make several adjustments to calculate current **taxable gifts** for each donee. As we've seen, each taxpayer is allowed an annual exclusion applied to the cumulative gifts of present interests made during the year to *each* donee. Next, if a married couple elects to split gifts (discussed below), half of each gift is included in current gifts of each spouse. The marital deduction for gifts to spouses and the charitable deduction for gifts to charity are the last adjustments to calculate taxable gifts for each donee. We discuss each in turn.

Gift-Splitting Election Married couples have the option to *split gifts,* allowing them to treat *all* gifts made in a year as if each spouse had made one-half of each gift. In a **community property state,** both spouses automatically own equal shares in most property acquired during the marriage.[9] Hence, when they make a gift of community property the transfer is divided between them equally. In **common-law states,** one spouse can own a disproportionate amount of property because he or she earns most of the income. The gift-splitting election provides a mechanism for married couples in common-law states to achieve the same result as couples receive automatically in community property states.[10]

[8]The courts have created another exception to the present interest rule called *Crummey power.* A discussion of this exception is beyond the scope of this text.

[9]Depending upon state law, the ownership of property acquired by either spouse prior to a marriage is not automatically divided equally between the spouses. In other words, property owned prior to the marriage is not necessarily community property and continues to belong to the original owner.

[10]There are nine community property states: Arizona, California, Idaho, Louisiana, Nevada, New Mexico, Texas, Washington, and Wisconsin.

Example 14-6

Wilma and Harry live in Michigan, a common-law state. For the holidays Wilma gave cash gifts of $30,000 to Steve and $41,000 to Dina. Wilma and Harry did not elect to split gifts. What is the amount of Wilma's taxable gifts?

Answer: $43,000. After using her annual exclusion (both gifts are present interests), Wilma has made taxable gifts of $16,000 to Steve ($30,000 − $14,000) and $27,000 to Dina ($41,000 − $14,000).

What if: Suppose Wilma and Harry elect gift-splitting this year. How would your answer change?

Answer: Both Wilma and Harry made taxable gifts of $7,500. Under gift-splitting, Wilma and Harry are each treated as making a gift of $15,000 to Steve and $20,500 to Dina. After the annual exclusion, both Wilma and Harry made a $1,000 taxable gift to Steve [($30,000 ÷ 2) − $14,000 = $1,000]. In addition, both Wilma and Harry made a $6,500 taxable gift to Dina [($41,000 ÷ 2) − $14,000 = $6,500].

What if: Suppose Wilma and Harry lived in Texas (a community property state), and Wilma made the same gifts from community property.

Answer: Both Wilma and Harry made a taxable gift of $7,500. Under state law, each spouse is automatically treated as gifting half the value of any gifts made from community property. After the annual exclusion, both Wilma and Harry made a $1,000 taxable gift to Steve [($30,000 ÷ 2) − $14,000], and each made a $6,500 taxable gift to Dina [($41,000 ÷ 2) − $14,000].

Besides increasing the application of the annual exclusion, a gift-splitting election also increases the likelihood that taxable gifts will be taxed at lower tax rates or offset by unified credits. To utilize gift-splitting, each spouse must be a citizen or resident of the United States, be married at the time of the gift, and not remarry during the remainder of the calendar year. Both spouses must consent to the election by filing a timely gift tax return. Taxpayers make this election annually and can apply it to all gifts completed by either spouse during the calendar year. As a result of the election, both spouses share a joint and several liability for any gift tax due.

THE KEY FACTS

Marital Deduction

- Deduct gifts of property to a spouse in computing taxable gifts.
- Transfers of terminable interests in property, such as a life estate, will not generally qualify for the deduction.
- The deduction is limited to the value of property included in taxable gifts.

Marital Deduction The marital deduction was originally enacted to equalize the treatment of spouses residing in common-law states. In community property states, the ownership of most property *acquired* during a marriage is automatically divided between the spouses. In common-law states, one spouse can own a disproportionate amount of property if he or she earns most of the income. Absent the marital deduction, in a common-law state, a transfer between the spouses to equalize the ownership of property would be treated as a taxable gift. However, because transfers to spouses are eligible for a marital deduction, no taxable gift results from such a transfer.

The marital deduction is subject to two limits. First, the amount is limited to the value of the gift after the annual exclusion. Second, transfers of **nondeductible terminable interests** do not qualify for a marital deduction. A nondeductible terminable interest is a property interest transferred to the spouse that terminates when some event occurs or after a specified amount of time, when the property is transferred to another.

Example 14-7

After his decision to retire, Harry gave Wilma a piece of jewelry that is a family heirloom valued at $50,000. What is the amount of this taxable gift?

Answer: Zero. This gift will qualify for an annual exclusion, and the value after subtracting the annual exclusion qualifies for the marital deduction. The taxable gift is calculated below:

Current gift	$50,000
Less: Annual exclusion	−14,000
Less: Marital deduction	−36,000
Taxable gift	$ 0

What if: Suppose Harry transferred $200,000 to a trust with directions to pay income to Wilma for her life (a life estate). After Wilma's death, the corpus of the trust would then pass to Dina (the remainder). What is the amount of this taxable gift if Wilma is age 38 at the time and the §7520 interest rate is 5 percent?

Answer: The total taxable gift is $186,000. This transfer is actually two gifts, a gift of a present interest to Wilma (a life estate) and a future interest to Dina (the remainder). The gift of the remainder is valued at $34,340 using Wilma's age and the §7520 interest rate from the table in Exhibit 14-4 ($200,000 × 0.17170). The remainder does not qualify for an annual exclusion because it is a future interest. The gift of the life estate is a present interest valued at $165,660 ($200,000 − $34,340), and it qualifies for the annual exclusion. The taxable gifts are calculated below:

	Dina (remainder)	Wilma (life estate)
Current gifts	$34,340	$165,660
Less: Annual exclusion (life estate)	−0	−14,000
Less: Marital deduction	−0	−0
Taxable gift	$34,340	$151,660

When the life estate is given to a spouse, it does not qualify for the marital deduction because it will terminate upon a future event (Wilma's death) and then pass to another person (Dina).

The limitation on the deductibility of terminable interests ensures that property owned by a married couple is subject to a transfer tax when the property is eventually transferred from the couple (as opposed to between the spouses). If a life estate were eligible for a marital deduction, it would not be taxed at the time of the gift nor would any value be taxed upon Wilma's death (the life estate disappears with her death). Hence, a marital deduction is available only for spousal transfers that will eventually be included in the recipient spouse's estate.[11]

There is an exception to the general prohibition against claiming a marital deduction for a transfer of a terminable interest called a **QTIP.** QTIP is the acronym for **qualified terminable interest property.** The QTIP exception provides that an intervivos transfer of an income interest for life to a spouse (or surviving spouse for a testamentary transfer-discussed later) qualifies for a marital deduction if the transfer meets two criteria.[12] First, the spouse must be entitled to all of the income from the property payable at least annually, and second, no person has the power to appoint any part of the property to anyone other than the spouse until the death of the spouse. For qualifying transfers, the executor or donor can elect to claim the marital deduction for part or all of the entire value of the property. If a marital deduction is claimed, then the value of the property will either be a taxable gift if subsequently transferred by the spouse or will be included in the estate of the surviving spouse upon her subsequent demise. In other words, the value of the QTIP will be taxed to the recipient spouse eventually because the transfer was initially deducted as a QTIP.

Charitable Deduction The amount of the charitable deduction is also limited to the value of the gift after the annual exclusion. Requirements for an organization to qualify for the gift tax charitable deduction are quite similar to those for the income tax deduction (the entity must be organized for religious, charitable, scientific, educational, or other public purposes, including governmental entities). Unlike the income tax deduction, however, the charitable deduction has no percentage limitation. In addition, as long as the qualifying charity receives the donor's entire interest in the property, no gift tax return need be filed (assuming the donor has no other taxable gifts). Finally, a transfer to a charity also qualifies for an income tax deduction (subject to the AGI limits on the income tax charitable deduction).

[11]The limit is analogous to nondeductible terminable interests for the estate tax marital deduction.

[12]The QTIP exceptions for the gift and estate taxes are provided in §2523(f) and §2056(b)(7), respectively.

Example 14-8

Harry donated $155,000 in cash to State University. What is the amount of the taxable gift?

Answer: Zero. The gift qualifies for the charitable gift tax deduction, as calculated below.

Current gift	$155,000
Less: Annual exclusion	−14,000
Less: Charitable deduction	−141,000
Taxable gift	$ 0

Note that Harry can also claim an income tax deduction for the transfer.

Computation of the Gift Tax

Part 2 of the formula in Exhibit 14-3 provides the method of calculating the gift tax. It begins by summing the taxable gifts made for all donees during a calendar year.

Example 14-9

Harry and Wilma did not make any gifts from community property and did not elect to gift-split this year (see Example 14-6). What is the amount of Harry's current taxable gifts this year?

Answer: Harry made $591,500 of taxable gifts, calculated using Part 1 of the formula in Exhibit 14-3 as follows:

Gifted Property	Donee	Value	Example #
1. Residence	Steve	$ 85,000	14-2
Less: Annual exclusion		−14,000	
2. DG Trust—life estate	Dina	440,540	14-3
Less: Annual exclusion		−14,000	
3. DG Trust—remainder	George	59,460	14-3
4. George Trust	George	48,500	14-5
Less: Annual exclusion		−14,000	
5. Jewelry	Wilma	50,000	14-7
Less: Annual exclusion		−14,000	
Less: Marital deduction	Wilma	−36,000	
6. Donation	State University	155,000	14-8
Less: Annual exclusion		−14,000	
Less: Charitable deduction	State U	−141,000	
Harry's current taxable gifts		$591,500	

The amounts of the marital and charitable deductions are limited to the value of the property included in taxable gifts.

Will Wilma be required to file a gift tax return this year? If so, what is the amount of her taxable gifts?

Answer: Wilma must also file a gift tax return this year because her current gifts exceed the annual exclusion. Wilma's taxable gifts sum to $43,000, calculated as follows:

Gifted Property	Donee	Value	Example #
Cash gift	Steve	$30,000	14-6
Less: Annual exclusion		−14,000	
Holiday gift	Dina	41,000	14-6
Less: Annual exclusion		−14,000	
Wilma's current taxable gifts		$43,000	

What if: What is the amount of Harry and Wilma's taxable gifts if they elect to gift-split?

Answer: Harry and Wilma each made $310,250 of taxable gifts, calculated as follows:

				Gift Splitting	
	Harry	**Wilma**	**Donee**	**Harry**	**Wilma**
Harry's gift of a residence	85,000		Steve	42,500	42,500
Less: Annual exclusion	−14,000			−14,000	
Wilma's cash gift		30,000	Steve	15,000	15,000
Less: Annual exclusion		−14,000			−14,000
Harry's transfer to DG trust	440,540		Dina	220,270	220,270
Less: Annual exclusion	−14,000			−14,000	
Wilma's holiday gifts		41,000	Dina	20,500	20,500
Less: Annual exclusion		−14,000			−14,000
DG Trust—remainder	59,460			29,730	29,730
George Trust	48,500			24,250	24,250
Less: Annual exclusion	−14,000			−14,000	−14,000
Harry's gift of jewelry	50,000		Wilma	50,000	
Less: Annual exclusion	−14,000			−14,000	
Less: Marital deduction	−36,000			−36,000	
Donation to State U	155,000		State U	77,500	77,500
Less: Annual exclusion	−14,000			−14,000	−14,000
Less: Charitable deduction	−141,000			−63,500	−63,500
Total	591,500	43,000		310,250	310,250

Note that absent gift-splitting, Harry and Wilma made taxable gifts totaling $634,500 ($591,500 + $43,000), but under gift-splitting that reduced to $620,500 ($310,250 + $310,250) because Wilma was able to use an additional $14,000 annual exclusion for her portion of the gift to the George Trust. Neither Harry nor Wilma was able to use any additional annual exclusions for the gifts to Steve and Dina because they had already used annual exclusions to these two donees. If they elect to gift-split, Harry and Wilma will be jointly and severally liable for the gift taxes.

Prior Taxable Gifts We compute the gift tax on cumulative taxable gifts by adding prior taxable gifts to current taxable gifts. The purpose of adding gifts from previous periods is to increase the tax base and thereby increase the marginal tax rate applying to current gifts. To prevent double taxation of prior taxable gifts, we subtract the gift tax on prior taxable gifts from the tax on total transfers. Note the tax on prior taxable gifts is the tax we computed on prior transfers under the *current* rate schedule (the tax actually paid in a prior year is not relevant).

Unified Credit The last adjustment in the formula is the unused portion of the unified credit. We've seen that the unified credit eliminates the gift tax for individuals who do not transfer a relatively large cumulative amount of property during their lifetime. The unified credit was originally the same for both the gift and estate taxes, but it has been adjusted many times and the exemption equivalent for the gift tax is $5.43 million (see Exhibit 14-2). A gift tax return must be filed by each individual (no joint filing) who has made taxable gifts during the calendar year or who elects to split gifts, even if no tax is due because of the unified credit.

Example 14-10

Harry made a taxable gift of $1,000,000 in 2007. At that time, the exemption equivalent for the gift tax was $1 million, so Harry did not pay any gift taxes on the transfer. Otherwise, Harry has not made any taxable gifts before this year. What should Harry report this year as his cumulative taxable gifts, gift tax on cumulative taxable gifts, gift tax on current taxable gifts, credit for current tax on prior taxable gifts, and gift tax due?

(continued on page 14-14)

Answer: Harry should report cumulative taxable gifts of $1,591,500, gift tax on cumulative gifts of $582,400 and no gift tax due this year. The calculation is as follows:

Current taxable gifts	$ 591,500	
Prior taxable gifts	1,000,000	
Cumulative taxable gifts	$1,591,500	
Tax on cumulative taxable gifts		$582,400
Less: Current tax on prior taxable gifts ($1 million)		−345,800
Tax on current taxable gifts		$236,600
Unified credit on current taxable gifts		−236,600
Gift tax due		$ 0

Harry used $1 million of his exemption equivalent in 2007, and this year he used another $591,500. Hence, at the end of 2015, Harry has $3,838,500 of exemption equivalent remaining ($5,430,000 − $1,000,000 − $591,500).

What if: Suppose that Harry made a taxable gift of $3,500,000 in 2007, and at that time, the exemption equivalent was $1 million. What should Harry report this year as his cumulative taxable gifts, gift tax on cumulative taxable gifts, gift tax on current taxable gifts, credit for current tax on prior taxable gifts, and gift tax due?

Answer: Harry should report cumulative taxable gifts of $4,091,500 and gift tax on cumulative gifts of $1,582,400. The calculation is as follows:

Current taxable gifts	$ 591,500	
Prior taxable gifts	3,500,000	
Cumulative taxable gifts	$4,091,500	
Tax on cumulative taxable gifts		$1,582,400
Less: Current tax on prior taxable gifts ($3.5 million)		−1,345,800
Tax on current taxable gifts		236,600
Unified credit on current taxable gifts		−236,600
Gift tax due		$ 0

Note that Harry is in the top marginal gift tax rate and that $591,500 times 40% equals $236,600. Note also that at the end of 2015, Harry would have $3,838,500 of exemption equivalent remaining ($5,430,000 − $1,000,000 − $591,500).

What is Wilma's gift tax due?

Wilma's current taxable gifts	$43,000	
Prior taxable gifts	+0	
Cumulative taxable gifts	$43,000	
Tax on cumulative taxable gifts		$8,920
Less: Current tax on prior taxable gifts		−0
Tax on current taxable gifts		$8,920
Unified credit on current taxable gifts		−8,920
Gift tax due		$ 0

Wilma has used $43,000 of her exemption equivalent. Hence, at the end of 2015, Wilma has $5,297,000 of exemption equivalent remaining.

The gift tax formula requires donors to keep track of the portion of the exemption equivalent they used to offset prior taxable gifts, in order to prevent multiple applications of the credit. We compute the gift tax on previous gifts using the current tax rate schedule but, this amount does *not* represent the amount of gift tax paid—just the gifts previously subject to tax. The unused portion of the unified credit then reduces the total gift tax to reach the gift tax due. We must track the amount of unified credit used to offset prior gifts from each period, because the gift tax on previous periods ignores the amount of gift tax actually paid. Exhibit 14-5 presents the first page of the 2014 gift tax return Form 709 for Harry Smith (Form 709 for 2015 was not available from the IRS as of press date).

EXHIBIT 14-5 Page 1 of Form 709 Gift Tax Return for Harry Smith

Form **709**

Department of the Treasury
Internal Revenue Service

United States Gift (and Generation-Skipping Transfer) Tax Return

► **Information about Form 709 and its separate instructions is at *www.irs.gov/form709*.**

(For gifts made during calendar year 2014)

► **See instructions.**

OMB No. 1545-0020

2014

1 Donor's first name and middle initial	2 Donor's last name	3 Donor's social security number
HARRY	SMITH	000-00-0000
4 Address (number, street, and apartment number)		5 Legal residence (domicile)
2813 ELMWOOD		WASHTENAW, MICHIGAN
6 City or town, state or province, country, and ZIP or foreign postal code		7 Citizenship (see instructions)
ANN ARBOR, MICHIGAN 48109		USA

Part 1—General Information

		Yes	No
8	If the donor died during the year, check here ► ☐ and enter date of death ______ , ______ .		
9	If you extended the time to file this Form 709, check here ► ☐		
10	Enter the total number of donees listed on Schedule A. Count each person only once ►		
11a	Have you (the donor) previously filed a Form 709 (or 709-A) for any other year? If "No," skip line 11b	✓	
b	Has your address changed since you last filed Form 709 (or 709-A)?		✓
12	**Gifts by husband or wife to third parties.** Do you consent to have the gifts (including generation-skipping transfers) made by you and by your spouse to third parties during the calendar year considered as made one-half by each of you? (see instructions.) (If the answer is "Yes," the following information must be furnished and your spouse must sign the consent shown below. **If the answer is "No," skip lines 13–18.**)		✓
13	Name of consenting spouse — 14 SSN		
15	Were you married to one another during the entire calendar year? (see instructions)		
16	If 15 is "No," check whether ☐ married ☐ divorced or ☐ widowed/deceased, and give date (see instructions) ►		
17	Will a gift tax return for this year be filed by your spouse? (If "Yes," mail both returns in the same envelope.)	✓	
18	**Consent of Spouse.** I consent to have the gifts (and generation-skipping transfers) made by me and by my spouse to third parties during the calendar year considered as made one-half by each of us. We are both aware of the joint and several liability for tax created by the execution of this consent. **Consenting spouse's signature ►** **Date ►**		
19	Have you applied a DSUE amount received from a predeceased spouse to a gift or gifts reported on this or a previous Form 709? If "Yes," complete Schedule C		✓

Part 2—Tax Computation

1	Enter the amount from Schedule A, Part 4, line 11	1	591,500
2	Enter the amount from Schedule B, line 3	2	1,000,000
3	Total taxable gifts. Add lines 1 and 2	3	1,591,500
4	Tax computed on amount on line 3 (see *Table for Computing Gift Tax* in instructions)	4	582,400
5	Tax computed on amount on line 2 (see *Table for Computing Gift Tax* in instructions)	5	345,800
6	Balance. Subtract line 5 from line 4	6	236,600
7	Applicable credit amount. If donor has DSUE amount from predeceased spouse(s), enter amount from Schedule C, line 4; otherwise, see instructions	7	2,117,800
8	Enter the applicable credit against tax allowable for all prior periods (from Sch. B, line 1, col. C)	8	345,800
9	Balance. Subtract line 8 from line 7. Do not enter less than zero	9	1,772,000
10	Enter 20% (.20) of the amount allowed as a specific exemption for gifts made after September 8, 1976, and before January 1, 1977 (see instructions)	10	
11	Balance. Subtract line 10 from line 9. Do not enter less than zero	11	1,772,000
12	Applicable credit. Enter the smaller of line 6 or line 11	12	236,600
13	Credit for foreign gift taxes (see instructions)	13	0
14	Total credits. Add lines 12 and 13	14	236,600
15	Balance. Subtract line 14 from line 6. Do not enter less than zero	15	0
16	Generation-skipping transfer taxes (from Schedule D, Part 3, col. H, Total)	16	
17	Total tax. Add lines 15 and 16	17	0
18	Gift and generation-skipping transfer taxes prepaid with extension of time to file	18	
19	If line 18 is less than line 17, enter **balance due** (see instructions)	19	
20	If line 18 is greater than line 17, enter **amount to be refunded**	20	

Attach check or money order here.

Sign Here

Under penalties of perjury, I declare that I have examined this return, including any accompanying schedules and statements, and to the best of my knowledge and belief, it is true, correct, and complete. Declaration of preparer (other than donor) is based on all information of which preparer has any knowledge.

May the IRS discuss this return with the preparer shown below (see instructions)? ☐ Yes ☐ No

► Signature of donor — Date

Paid Preparer Use Only

Print/Type preparer's name	Preparer's signature	Date	Check ☐ if self-employed	PTIN
Firm's name ►			Firm's EIN ►	
Firm's address ►			Phone no.	

For Disclosure, Privacy Act, and Paperwork Reduction Act Notice, see the instructions for this form. Cat. No. 16783M Form **709** (2014)

continued from page 14-1. . .
Early this year Bob was injured in an auto accident. Unable to recover from his injuries, he died after two days in the hospital. Bob is survived by his son, Nate, who is also the executor of Bob's estate. Nate is now collecting his father's assets, and he would like help in preparing Bob's federal estate tax return. ■

LO 14-3

THE FEDERAL ESTATE TAX

The estate tax is designed to tax the value of property owned or controlled by an individual at death, the decedent. Because federal gift and estate taxes are integrated, taxable gifts affect the tax base for the estate tax. Exhibit 14-6 presents the estate tax formula.

EXHIBIT 14-6 The Federal Estate Tax Formula

	Gross estate
Minus	Expenses, debts, and losses
Equals	Adjusted gross estate
Minus	Marital and charitable deductions
Equals	Taxable estate
Plus	Adjusted taxable gifts
Equals	Estate tax base
Times	Current tax rates
Equals	Tentative tax
Minus	Gift taxes paid on adjusted taxable gifts
Minus	Unified credit
Equals	Estate Tax Payable

The Gross Estate

Property possessed by or owned (titled) by a decedent at the time of death is generally referred to as the **probate estate,** because the transfer of this property is carried out by a probate court. **Probate** is the process of gathering property possessed by or titled in the name of a decedent at the time of death, paying the debts of the decedent, and transferring the ownership of any remaining property to the decedent's **heirs.** Property in the probate estate can include cash, stocks, jewelry, clothing, and realty owned by or titled in the name of the deceased at the time of death.

The **gross estate** is broader than the probate estate. The gross estate consists of (1) the fair market value of property possessed or owned by a decedent at death *plus* (2) the value of certain automatic property transfers that take effect at death.[13] Property transfers that take effect only at death are not in the probate estate because the transfer takes place just as death occurs. Hence, the probate court does not need to affect a transfer. However, as discussed below, property subject to certain types of automatic transfers is specifically included in the gross estate because the automatic transfer is a substitute for a testamentary transfer.

Example 14-11

What if: Nate took an inventory of his father's property in preparation for distributing assets according to Bob's will. Nate must report this preliminary inventory of personal and investment property to the probate court; it includes the following:

[13]§2033. The principle of increasing the gross estate for transfers taking effect at death began with *gifts in contemplation of death.* So-called deathbed gifts were a device used to avoid the estate tax in the years before enactment of the gift tax.

	Fair Market Value
Auto	$ 33,000
Clothes, furniture, and personal effects	48,000
Smith painting (original cost/initial estimated value)	25,000
Checking and savings accounts	75,250
FFP stock	9,500,000
Residence	400,000
Other investments	8,200
Total	$10,089,450

What amount of this property is included in Bob's gross estate?

Answer: Bob's gross estate includes the value of *all* the above property, or $10,089,450, because he owned these assets at his death (i.e. these assets are included on Bob's probate estate).

What if: Suppose Bob was also entitled to a pension distribution of $15,000 but had not yet received the check at his time of death. Would this value also be included in Bob's probate estate and therefore gross estate?

Answer: Yes. Although Bob had not received the check, he was legally entitled to the property at the time of his death, and therefore it will be included in both his probate estate and gross estate.

Specific Inclusions Besides property in the probate estate, the gross estate also includes property transferred automatically at the decedent's death. These automatic transfers can occur without the help of a probate court because the ownership transfers by law at the time of death.

Certain automatic property transfers are specifically included in the gross estate because, while the decedent didn't own the property at death, Congress deemed that the decedent controlled the ultimate disposition of the property. That is, the decedent effectively determined who would receive the property at the time of death. A common example is property held in **joint tenancy with right of survivorship,** which legally transfers to the surviving tenant upon the joint tenant's death. Joint bank accounts are commonly owned in joint ownership with right of survivorship. In contrast, tenants in common hold divided rights to property and have the ability to transfer these rights during their life or upon death. Property held by tenants in common, such as real estate, does not automatically transfer at death and thus must be transferred via probate. Although the decedent's interest in jointly owned property (with the right of survivorship) ceases at death, the value of the interest the decedent held in this property is still included in the gross estate.[14]

Example 14-12

Nate and his father jointly own two parcels of real estate not included in the inventory above. One parcel is a vacation home in Colorado. Nate owns this property jointly with Bob and the title is held in joint ownership with the right of survivorship. Will this property be included in Bob's probate estate and/or gross estate?

Answer: The property will *not* be included in Bob's *probate* estate, but it will be included in Bob's *gross* estate. When Bob died, Nate automatically became the sole owner of the property without going through probate. However, the property will be included in Bob's gross estate because it is an automatic transfer that is specifically included in the gross estate by law.

[14]§2040. There are a number of other transfers that are specifically included in the gross estate. For example, §2036 to §2039 and §2041 address transfers with retained life estates, transfers taking place at death, revocable transfers, annuities, and powers of appointment. A discussion of these provisions is beyond the scope of this text.

The second parcel is real estate in west Texas that Nate and Bob hold as equal tenants in common. Will it be necessary to probate this parcel of real estate to transfer ownership of Bob's share to the beneficiary named in Bob's will?

Answer: Yes. The value of Bob's one-half interest in the west Texas real estate is also included in his gross estate.

Another example of an automatic transfer is insurance on the life of the decedent. Proceeds of life insurance paid due to the death of the decedent are specifically included in the gross estate if either of two conditions is met. The proceeds are included in the gross estate if (1) the decedent owned the policy or had "incidents" of ownership such as the right to designate the beneficiary or (2) the decedent's estate or **executor** is the beneficiary of the insurance policy (that is, the executor must use the insurance proceeds to discharge the obligations of the estate).

Example 14-13

Bob owned and paid annual premiums on an insurance policy that, on his death, was to pay the beneficiary of his choice $500,000. Bob named Nate the beneficiary, and the insurance company paid Nate $500,000 after receiving notification of Bob's death. Will Bob's gross estate include the value of the insurance proceeds paid to Nate?

Answer: Yes. The $500,000 of insurance proceeds is specifically included in Bob's estate despite the fact that it was paid directly to Nate and did not go through probate.

What if: Suppose Bob transferred ownership of the policy to Nate four years prior to his death. Nate had the power to designate the beneficiary of the policy, and he also paid the annual premiums. Will Bob's gross estate include the value of the insurance proceeds paid to Nate?

Answer: No. Bob had no incidents of ownership at his death (Nate controlled who is paid the proceeds upon Bob's death), and the proceeds were not paid to his estate.

Jointly owned property. The proportion of the value of jointly owned property included in the gross estate depends upon the type of ownership. When a decedent's interest is a **tenancy in common** (i.e., there is no right of survivorship), a proportion of the value of the property is included in the gross estate that matches the decedent's ownership interest. For example, consider a decedent who owned a one-third interest in property as a tenant in common. If the entire property is worth $120,000 at the decedent's death, then $40,000 is included in his gross estate.

The amount includible for property held as joint tenancy with the right of survivorship depends upon the marital status of the owners. When property is jointly owned by a husband and wife with the right of survivorship, *half the value* of the property is automatically included in the estate of the first spouse to die.[15] For *unmarried* co-owners, the value included in the decedent's gross estate is determined by the decedent's contribution to the total cost of the property. For example, consider a decedent who provided two-thirds of the total cost of property held as joint tenants with the right of survivorship. If the entire property is worth $240,000 at the decedent's death, then two-thirds ($160,000) is included in his gross estate.

Example 14-14

Bob and Nate originally purchased the Colorado vacation home seven years ago for $20,000 and held it as joint tenants with the right of survivorship. This property is not included in the list of property in Bob's probate estate because the title passes automatically to Nate upon Bob's death. Bob provided $15,000 of the purchase price, and Nate provided the remaining $5,000. The property was worth $400,000 at Bob's death. How much is included in his gross estate?

[15]In some states joint tenancy with a right of survivorship between spouses is referred to as a **tenancy by the entirety.**

Answer: Bob's gross estate includes $300,000. For property held in joint tenancy with the right of survivorship, the amount included in the gross estate is equal to the proportion of the purchase price provided by the decedent. Bob provided 75 percent ($15,000 ÷ $20,000 = 75%). Hence, his gross estate will include $300,000 (75% × $400,000) of the value of the vacation home.

What if: Suppose Bob was married and owned the home with his wife as joint tenants with the right of survivorship. What amount would be included in Bob's gross estate?

Answer: The amount included in the estate is half the value of any property held with the surviving spouse as joint tenants with the right of survivorship, $200,000 in this case.

The west Texas land Bob and Nate owned is valued at $500,200. They owned it as tenants in common, with Bob holding a one-quarter interest and Nate holding the rest. What amount is included in Bob's gross estate?

Answer: The amount included in the estate is $125,050 ($500,200 × 25%), because Bob owned a one-quarter interest in the property.

Exhibit 14-7 summarizes the rules for determining the value of jointly owned property included in a decedent's gross estate.

EXHIBIT 14-7 Amount of Jointly Owned Property Included in Gross Estate

Ownership Form	Marital Status of Co-owners	Amount in Gross Estate
Community property (discussed below)	Married	Half the fair market value
Joint tenancy with right of survivorship	Married	Half the fair market value
Joint tenancy with right of survivorship	Unmarried	Percentage of fair market value determined by decedent's contribution to total cost of the property
Tenancy in common	Married or unmarried	Percentage of fair market value determined by decedent's interest in the property

Transfers within three years of death. Certain transfers, such as transfers of insurance policies, made within three years of the decedent's death are also included in the decedent's gross estate, valued as of the time of death. Without this provision, a simple but effective estate tax planning technique would be to transfer ownership in an insurance policy just prior to the decedent's death. This strategy, called *deathbed gifts,* would reduce the decedent's transfer taxes on the life insurance by the difference between its proceeds from the policy (the value at death) and its value on the date transferred.

Only certain transfers are specifically included under this provision, and they are often difficult to identify. Gift taxes paid on any taxable gifts during the three-year period preceding the donor's death are also included in the decedent's gross estate. This gross-up provision prevents donors from escaping estate tax on the amount of gift taxes paid within three years of death. In other words, the amount of gift taxes paid are included in the estate because these amounts would have been included in the estate had the decedent kept the property until death.

Example 14-15

What if: Suppose Bob owned a life insurance policy, and he transferred all incidents of ownership in the policy to his son one year before dying from a fatal disease. Would the life insurance proceeds be included in Bob's gross estate?

Answer: Yes. Bob's estate would include proceeds of the policy (grossed up for the gift taxes paid on the transfer), because Bob transferred the incidents of ownership within three years of his death.

Valuation Property is included in the gross estate at the *fair market value* on the date of the decedent's death. Virtually all the factors (and controversies) regarding valuation that we've already discussed with the gift tax also apply to the valuation of property for estate tax purposes.

Example 14-16

At his death Bob owned an original landscape painting made in the late 1800s by one of his ancestors, Tully Smith. Bob purchased the Smith painting for $25,000 in 1980, and last year an expert estimated it was worth $210,000. Nate now has the painting appraised by another expert, who estimates its value at $250,000 based upon a painting by the same artist that sold at auction last month. What value should be placed on the painting for inclusion in the gross estate?

Answer: Nate should value the painting at $250,000 according to its specific characteristics and attributes (such as age, condition, history, authenticity, and so forth). Of course, the IRS might disagree with this value and seek to value the painting at a higher value.

THE KEY FACTS

Valuation of Assets

- Property is included in the estate at its fair market value at the date of the decedent's death.
- The executor can elect to value the estate on an alternate valuation date, six months after death, if it reduces the gross estate and estate tax.

The executor of an estate, however, can elect—irrevocably—to have all the property in the gross estate valued on an **alternative valuation date.** The alternative date for valuing the estate is six months after the date of death or on the date of sale or distribution of the property (if this occurs before the end of the six-month period). This election is available only if it reduces the value of the gross estate and the combined estate and generation-skipping taxes.[16]

Example 14-17

What if: Bob's shares of FPP are included in his estate at a value of $9.5 million. Suppose the value of the shares plummeted to $5 million several months after Bob's death. Could Nate as executor of Bob's estate opt to value these shares at the lower cost for estate tax purposes?

Answer: Nate could elect to value the shares on the alternate valuation date, six months after Bob's death. However, to qualify for this election, he must value *all* property in the estate on the alternate date, and the election must reduce the value of the entire gross estate as well as the combined estate and generation-skipping taxes.

Example 14-18

At the time of his death Bob owned a reversion in a trust he established for his niece, Dina. Under the terms of the trust, Dina is entitled to income for her life (a life estate), and Bob (or his heir) is entitled to the reversion. At the time of Bob's death, the trust assets were valued at $100,000, Dina was 35, and the §7520 interest rate was 6 percent. Should this reversion be included in Bob's gross estate and, if so, what value is placed on the future interest?

Answer: Bob's reversion interest is included in his estate because this is a property right he owned at his death. Under Table S in the regulations (Exhibit 14-4), based upon Dina's age and the current interest rate at the time of Bob's death, the percentage of the property that represents the value of Bob's reversion is 0.11217. Thus, his reversion is valued at $11,217 ($100,000 × 0.11217).

What if: Suppose the trust was established for George, age 6. Would this influence the value of Bob's reversion interest?

Answer: Yes. Under Table S in the regulations and based upon George's age and the current interest rate, the portion of the property that represents the value of Bob's reversion is 0.02749. Thus, Bob's reversion is valued at $2,749 ($100,000 × 0.02749).

[16]§2032A. An executor can also elect to value certain realty used in farming or in connection with a closely held business at a special use valuation. Special use valuation allows realty to be valued at a current use that does not result in the best or highest fair market value. This election is available when the business is conducted by the decedent's family, constitutes a substantial portion of the gross estate, and the property passes to a qualifying heir of the decedent.

Gross Estate Summary So far we've seen that the decedent's gross estate consists of the assets subject to probate as well as certain assets transferred outside probate. These latter assets include property owned by the decedent in joint tenancy with the right of survivorship as well as life insurance. The gross estate also includes certain property transferred by the decedent within three years of death and certain future interests owned by the decedent.

Example 14-19

Given previous examples, what is the value of Bob's gross estate?

Answer: It is $11,251,458, calculated as follows:

Property	Value	Example
Auto	$ 33,000	14-11
Personal effects	48,000	14-11
Smith painting	250,000	14-16
Checking and savings accounts	75,250	14-11
FPP shares	9,500,000	14-11
Residence	400,000	14-11
Other investments	8,200	14-11
Life insurance proceeds	500,000	14-13
Colorado vacation home	300,000	14-12 and 14-14
West Texas land	125,050	14-12 and 14-14
Reversion interest in Dina Trust	11,217	14-18
Gross estate	$11,250,717	

The Taxable Estate

Referring to the estate tax formula in Exhibit 14-6, we calculate the taxable estate in two steps. The first consists of reducing the gross estate by deductions allowed for administrative expenses, debts of the decedent, and losses incurred during the administration of the estate. These deductions are allowed because Congress intends to tax the *net* amount transferred to beneficiaries. This step results in the **adjusted gross estate.** In the second step, we allow deductions for transfers to a decedent's spouse (the marital deduction) and to charities (the charitable deduction). These deductions result in the **taxable estate.** We discuss each type of deduction next.

Administrative Expenses, Debts, Losses, and State Death Taxes Debts included in or incurred by the estate, such as mortgages and accrued taxes, are deductible. Expenses incurred in administering the estate are also deductible, such as executor's fees, attorneys' fees, and the like. Funeral expenses are deductible, including any reasonable expenditure allowed under local law. Casualty and theft losses are deductible without any floor limitation. These losses must be incurred during the administration of the estate, otherwise the deduction belongs to the new owner of the property. Finally, death taxes imposed by the state are also deductible.[17]

Example 14-20

Nate paid $6,685 in funeral expenses for his father's services, and during the administration of his father's estate he paid executor's fees of $4,032 and attorney's fees of $9,500. In addition, Nate discovered Bob owed debts totaling $100,500. Since Michigan has no state death or inheritance taxes, no amounts were owed to the state. What is Bob's adjusted gross estate (gross estate minus expenses and debts)?

(continued on page 14-22)

[17]§2053, §2054, and §2058 address expenses, losses, and state death taxes, respectively.

Answer: It is $11,130,000, calculated as follows:

Gross estate		$11,250,717
Funeral expenses	$ 6,685	
Executor's fees and expenses	4,032	
Attorney's fees	9,500	
Debts of the decedent	100,500	
Total expenses and debts		−120,717
Adjusted gross estate		$11,130,000

The estate may collect income earned during its administration and, therefore, the estate will need to file an estate *income* tax return. The executor has the option of deducting administration expenses (but not funeral expenses) and casualty and theft losses on the estate tax return or on the estate's *income* tax return. While no double deduction is available, the choice is relatively simple. If the estate owes no estate taxes, then the executor should claim the deduction on the estate income tax return. If the estate owes estate taxes, the marginal estate tax rate is likely to be higher than the marginal income tax rate. Hence, it should probably claim the deduction on the estate tax return.

What if: Suppose that during the administration of Bob's estate a storm damaged the Colorado vacation home. Bob's share of the casualty loss to the home was $25,000. Would this be deductible in calculating Bob's taxable estate?

Answer: Yes, although the executor can choose to deduct this loss on either the estate tax return or the estate's *income* tax return for the period that included the casualty. If the deduction is claimed on the estate tax return, the loss deduction is not subject to any floor limitations (such as the per casualty floor limitation and the 10 percent of AGI limits imposed on casualty losses claimed in individual income tax returns).

THE KEY FACTS

Estate Tax Deductions

- Estate tax deductions include the debts of the decedent, funeral expenses, and the costs of administering the estate, including casualty losses.
- The value of property interests bequeathed to a surviving spouse is deductible if the interest is not terminable.
- The value of property bequeathed to a qualified charity is deductible.

Marital and Charitable Deductions To avoid taxing a married couple's estate twice, Congress provides a deduction for bequests to a surviving spouse. To qualify for the marital deduction, the transferred property must be included in the estate of the deceased spouse. That is, the surviving spouse must receive the property from the decedent and control its ultimate disposition. For example, property that passes to the surviving spouse as a result of joint tenancy with the right of survivorship qualifies for the marital deduction, as would a direct bequest from the decedent. However, property rights that are terminable do not generally qualify for the marital deduction. For example, suppose the decedent bequeaths the surviving spouse the right to occupy the decedent's residence until such time as the spouse remarries. The value of the right to possess the residence is a terminable interest and is not eligible for the marital deduction. In general, the estate tax marital deduction is unlimited in amount, so no tax is imposed even on a decedent who leaves her entire estate to a spouse.[18]

Charitable contributions of property are also deductible without any limitation. Charities are defined to include the usual public organizations (corporations organized exclusively for religious, charitable, scientific, literary, or educational purposes) but exclude certain nonprofit cemetery organizations. Interestingly, foreign charities qualify for the charitable deduction under the estate and gift tax but not under the income tax. No deduction is allowed unless the charitable bequest is specified under

[18]*Qualified terminable interest properties* (*QTIPs* for short) are an exception to the nondeductibility of terminable interest property where the executor agrees to have qualifying terminable interests included in the estate of the surviving spouse. A detailed discussion of this exception is beyond the scope of this text.

the last will and testament or is a transfer of property by the decedent before his death that is subsequently included in the decedent's estate. The amount of any bequest must be mandatory, although another person such as the executor can be given discretion to identify the charitable organization.

Example 14-21

Not long after Bob's death, Nate gathered the Smith family for a reading of Bob's will. The will was relatively simple because Bob was unmarried at the time of his death. Bob had an adjusted gross estate of $11,130,000 and left all his property to Nate, with two exceptions. Bob bequeathed his remainder interest in the Dina Trust (value of $11,958) to Dina, and he bequeathed the Smith painting (value of $250,000) to the Midwest Museum in Ann Arbor (a qualified charity). Is either of these bequests deductible in calculating Bob's taxable estate? What is Bob's taxable estate?

Answer: The bequest to the museum qualifies for the charitable deduction because the museum is a qualified charity. Since Bob was unmarried at his death, none of the bequests qualify for the marital deduction. Bob's taxable estate is $10,880,000 calculated as follows:

Adjusted gross estate	$11,130,000
Charitable deduction	−250,000
Taxable estate	$10,880,000

What if: Suppose Bob was married at the time of his death and left a portion of his FPP stock, valued at $4.5 million, to his surviving spouse. What amount of this transfer, if any, would qualify for the marital deduction?

Answer: Bob's estate would be entitled to a marital deduction of $4.5 million, the value of the entire spousal bequest. In the extreme, if Bob had left *all his property* to his spouse, then his taxable estate would be reduced to zero.

Computation of the Estate Tax

Three additional steps are necessary to calculate the estate tax liability from the taxable estate. First, we increase the taxable estate by **adjusted taxable gifts** to determine the estate tax base. Next, we compute the tentative tax on the estate tax base, and finally, we reduce the tentative tax by credits. These credits are primarily composed of the tax on adjusted taxable gifts and the unified credit.

Adjusted Taxable Gifts Adjusted taxable gifts are taxable gifts other than transfers already included in the gross estate. The objective of adding previously taxed transfers to the taxable estate is to allow the estate tax base to reflect all transfers, both intervivos and testamentary. Under a progressive tax rate schedule, this adjustment is designed to increase the marginal tax rate on the estate. Adjusted taxable gifts themselves, however, are not subject to tax in the estate formula. To prevent double taxation of prior taxable gifts, we reduce the tentative estate tax by a credit for the taxes that would have been payable on the adjusted taxable gifts under the current tax rate schedule. Thus, although prior gifts have a direct effect on the magnitude of cumulative taxable transfers, the estate tax is imposed only on cumulative transfers under the *current* rate schedule.

Example 14-22

After reviewing all Bob's records, Nate determined he had made only one taxable gift of FPP stock in 2009. This transfer resulted in a taxable gift of $1 million. Because the unified credit offset the entire gift tax on this transfer, Bob did not pay any gift taxes at that time. What is the amount of cumulative transfers subject to estate tax, and what is Bob's gross estate tax (tax prior to credits)?

(continued on page 14-24)

Answer: Bob's estate includes $11,880,000 of cumulative taxable transfers and Bob's gross estate tax is $4,697,800. Despite the fact that Bob didn't pay any gift taxes on the prior gift because of the unified credit, the transfer still operates to increase the amount of taxable transfers subject to the top marginal estate tax rate. Bob's gross estate tax is calculated as follows:

Adjusted taxable gifts	$ 1,000,000	Prior gift
Taxable estate	10,880,000	Taxable transfers in estate
Cumulative transfers	$11,880,000	Total taxable transfers
Tentative tax	$ 4,697,800	Tax on all transfers
Current tax on adjusted taxable gifts	−0	Tax due to 2009 gift
Gross estate tax	$ 4,697,800	Tax prior to credits

What if: Suppose Bob had not made any taxable gifts prior to his death. Would this fact reduce his estate tax? What is his gross estate tax in this circumstance?

Answer: Without the gift of stock Bob's estate tax would be significantly lower, because adding adjusted taxable gifts operates to increase the estate's marginal tax rate. Bob's gross estate tax would be $4,297,800, calculated as follows:

Adjusted taxable gifts	$ 0
Taxable estate	10,880,000
Cumulative transfers	$10,880,000
Tentative tax	$ 4,297,800
Taxes payable on adjusted taxable gifts	−0
Gross estate tax	$ 4,297,800

Note that Bob's gross estate tax has decreased by $400,000. This is the amount of incremental tax on the $1 million increase in the cumulative transfer because of the prior transfer.

What if: Suppose that Bob's 2009 taxable gift was $4 million. Because the gift tax exemption equivalent in 2009 was only $1.0 million, Bob would have paid gift tax on this transfer. What is the amount of the credit for taxable payable on adjusted taxable gifts and how does this prior taxable transfer affect Bob's gross estate tax?

Answer: Because Bob paid a gift tax on the transfer, his estate is allowed a $1,200,000 credit for taxes payable on adjusted taxable gifts. This credit represents the tax (under the current rate schedule) on the taxable transfer ($4 million) after reduction for the current tax on the exemption equivalent at the time of the prior transfer ($1.0 million).

Current tax on adjusted taxable gifts	$1,545,800
Unified credit ($1.0 million at current tax rate)	−345,800
Current taxes payable on adjusted taxable gifts	$1,200,000

Note that the credit is 40 percent of the gift in excess of the exemption equivalent ($4,000,000 − $1,000,000 = $3,000,000). The $4 million prior taxable transfer is included in the calculation of Bob's cumulative taxable transfers and the gross estate tax is calculated as before.

Adjusted taxable gifts	$ 4,000,000
Taxable estate	10,880,000
Cumulative transfers	$14,880,000

Tentative transfer tax	$ 5,897,800
Taxes payable on adjusted taxable gifts	−1,200,000
Gross estate tax	$ 4,697,800

Hence, the adjusted taxable gift increases the amount of Bob's estate subject to the top estate tax rate, but is not subject to additional transfer tax at the time of Bob's death.

Unified Credit Besides subtracting the credit for tax on adjusted taxable gifts, we reduce the gross estate tax by several other credits.[19] The most important is the unified credit, because it eliminates the estate tax on cumulative transfers up to the exemption equivalent (currently $5.43 million). Hence, estate taxes are only imposed on relatively large estates. The objective of the unified credit is to prevent the application of transfer tax to taxpayers who either would not accumulate a relatively large amount of property transfers during their lifetime and/or would not have a relatively large value of assets to pass to heirs upon their death.

The unified credit for a surviving spouse is increased by the amount of the deceased spouse's unused unified credit. For example, in 2015 a spouse whose deceased spouse died without using any unified credit is entitled to an exemption equivalent of $10.86 million.

Besides eliminating transfer taxes for relatively small cumulative transfers, the exemption equivalent also acts as the transfer requirement for filing an estate return. That is, an estate tax return (Form 706) must be filed if the gross estate plus adjusted taxable gifts equals or exceeds the exemption equivalent. Exhibit 14-8 presents the first page of 2015 Form 706 for Bob Smith. The deadline for the estate tax return is nine months after the decedent's death.[20]

THE KEY FACTS

Adjusted Taxable Gifts and the Unified Credit

- Adjusted taxable gifts are added to the taxable estate in calculating cumulative taxable transfers.
- Lifetime gifts are not subject to double tax because the tax on cumulative transfers is reduced for taxes on adjusted taxable gifts.
- The unified credit eliminates transfer taxes on estates with relatively small cumulative lifetime and testamentary transfers (total transfers under the exemption equivalent).
- Credit is applied after reducing the total tax on cumulative transfers for taxes payable on adjusted taxable gifts.

Example 14-23

Bob died on February 7 of this year. What amount of estate tax must be paid on his estate, given his prior taxable gift of $1 million? What is the due date for Bob's estate tax return?

Answer: Estate tax of $2,580,000 is due after applying the unified credit, computed as follows:

Tentative tax	$4,697,800
Taxes payable on adjusted taxable gifts	−0
Less: Unified credit	2,117,800
Estate tax due	$2,580,000

Bob's executor must file the estate tax return (Form 706 in Exhibit 14-8) or request an extension of time within nine months of Bob's death (by November 7 of this year).

What if: Suppose that Bob did not make any taxable gifts during his life. What amount of estate tax would be owed upon his death?

Answer: Bob's estate would only owe $2,180,000, computed as follows:

Tentative tax	$4,297,800
Taxes payable on adjusted taxable gifts	−0
Less: Unified credit	2,117,800
Estate tax due	$2,180,000

[19]There are other credits that could also apply, but these are beyond the scope of this text. The credit for taxes on prior transfer is designed to adjust the tax for property that was subjected to estate tax within the last 10 years. There is also a credit for pre-1977 gift taxes paid on certain pre-1977 gifts that must be included in the gross estate. Both of these credits are equitable adjustments for potential multiple transfer taxes associated with sequential deaths and multiple inclusions, respectively. Prior to 2005, there was a credit for state death taxes.

[20]There is an automatic six-month extension to file the estate tax return. However, an estimate of the tax due must be paid on the due date of the return.

EXHIBIT 14-8 Page 1 of Form 706 Estate Tax Return for Bob Smith

Form **706** (Rev. August 2013) Department of the Treasury Internal Revenue Service

United States Estate (and Generation-Skipping Transfer) Tax Return

▶ Estate of a citizen or resident of the United States (see instructions). To be filed for decedents dying after December 31, 2012.
▶ Information about Form 706 and its separate instructions is at *www.irs.gov/form706*.

OMB No. 1545-0015

Part 1—Decedent and Executor

1a Decedent's first name and middle initial (and maiden name, if any): BOB	1b Decedent's last name: SMITH		2 Decedent's social security no.: 000 00 0000
3a City, town, or post office; county; state or province; country; and ZIP or foreign postal code.: ANN ARBOR, WASHTENAW COUNTY MICHIGAN 48109	3b Year domicile established: 1990	4 Date of birth: 1940	5 Date of death: 2015
6a Name of executor (see instructions): NATE SMITH	6b Executor's address (number and street including apartment or suite no.; city, town, or post office; state or province; country; and ZIP or foreign postal code) and phone no.: 6500 TRAIL RD, ANN ARBOR, MICHIGAN 48109		Phone no. (000) 000-0000
6c Executor's social security number (see instructions): 000 00 0000			

6d If there are multiple executors, check here ☐ and attach a list showing the names, addresses, telephone numbers, and SSNs of the additional executors.

7a Name and location of court where will was probated or estate administered: WASHTENAW COUNTY PROBATE COURT — 7b Case number: 00-12345

8 If decedent died testate, check here ▶ ☐ and attach a certified copy of the will. 9 If you extended the time to file this Form 706, check here ▶ ☐

10 If Schedule R-1 is attached, check here ▶ ☐ 11 If you are estimating the value of assets included in the gross estate on line 1 pursuant to the special rule of Reg. section 20.2010-2T(a) (7)(ii), check here ▶ ☐

Part 2—Tax Computation

1	Total gross estate less exclusion (from Part 5—Recapitulation, item 13)			1	11,251,458
2	Tentative total allowable deductions (from Part 5—Recapitulation, item 24)			2	371,458
3a	Tentative taxable estate (subtract line 2 from line 1)			3a	10,880,000
b	State death tax deduction			3b	0
c	Taxable estate (subtract line 3b from line 3a)			3c	10,880,000
4	Adjusted taxable gifts (see instructions)			4	1,000,000
5	Add lines 3c and 4			5	11,880,000
6	Tentative tax on the amount on line 5 from Table A in the instructions			6	4,697,800
7	Total gift tax paid or payable (see instructions)			7	0
8	Gross estate tax (subtract line 7 from line 6)			8	4,697,800
9a	Basic exclusion amount	9a	5,340,000		
9b	Deceased spousal unused exclusion (DSUE) amount from predeceased spouse(s), if any (from Section D, Part 6—Portability of Deceased Spousal Unused Exclusion).	9b	0		
9c	Applicable exclusion amount (add lines 9a and 9b)	9c	5,340,000		
9d	Applicable credit amount (tentative tax on the amount in 9c from Table A in the instructions)	9d	2,117,800		
10	Adjustment to applicable credit amount (May not exceed $6,000. See instructions.)	10	0		
11	Allowable applicable credit amount (subtract line 10 from line 9d)			11	2,117,800
12	Subtract line 11 from line 8 (but do not enter less than zero)			12	2,580,000
13	Credit for foreign death taxes (from Schedule P). (Attach Form(s) 706-CE.)	13			
14	Credit for tax on prior transfers (from Schedule Q)	14			
15	Total credits (add lines 13 and 14)			15	0
16	Net estate tax (subtract line 15 from line 12)			16	2,580,000
17	Generation-skipping transfer (GST) taxes payable (from Schedule R, Part 2, line 10)			17	
18	Total transfer taxes (add lines 16 and 17)			18	2,580,000
19	Prior payments (explain in an attached statement)			19	
20	Balance due (or overpayment) (subtract line 19 from line 18)			20	2,580,000

Under penalties of perjury, I declare that I have examined this return, including accompanying schedules and statements, and to the best of my knowledge and belief, it is true, correct, and complete. Declaration of preparer other than the executor is based on all information of which preparer has any knowledge.

Sign Here

▶ Signature of executor ▶ Date

▶ Signature of executor ▶ Date

Paid Preparer Use Only

Print/Type preparer's name	Preparer's signature	Date	Check ☐ if self-employed	PTIN
Firm's name ▶			Firm's EIN ▶	
Firm's address ▶			Phone no.	

For Privacy Act and Paperwork Reduction Act Notice, see instructions. Cat. No. 20548R Form **706** (Rev. 8-2013)

WEALTH PLANNING CONCEPTS

LO 14-4

Wealth planning coordinates both income and transfer tax strategies with nontax objectives. Before we explore transfer tax strategies, recall the third transfer tax, the generation-skipping tax, and the potential for income taxation of fiduciary entities such as estates and trusts. While these topics are certainly not unimportant, we note them only in passing because their complexity is beyond the scope of this text.

> **THE KEY FACTS**
>
> **Basic Wealth Planning Techniques**
>
> - A serial gift strategy saves gift taxes by converting a potentially large taxable transfer into multiple smaller transfers that qualify for the annual exclusion.
> - Bypass provisions in a will or bypass trusts reduce estate taxes by using the unified credit of the deceased spouse, transferring some property to beneficiaries other than the surviving spouse.
> - Testamentary transfers allow a step-up in tax basis to fair market value, thereby eliminating income tax on unrealized appreciation.
> - Lifetime gifts eliminate transfer taxes on post-gift appreciation.

The Generation-Skipping Tax

The **generation-skipping tax (GST)** is a supplemental tax designed to prevent the avoidance of transfer taxes (both estate and gift tax) through transfers that skip a generation of recipients. For example, a grandparent could give a life estate in property to a child, with the remainder to a grandchild. When the child dies and the grandchild inherits the property, no transfer tax is imposed because nothing remains in the child's estate (the life estate terminates at death). In this way, the grandparent pays one transfer tax (on the initial gift) to transfer the property down two generations.

The GST is triggered by the transfer of property to someone more than one generation younger than the donor or decedent—a grandchild rather than a child. A transfer to a grandchild is not subject to GST, however, if the grandchild's parents are dead. The GST is very complex and can be triggered directly by transfers or indirectly by a termination of an interest. Fortunately, the GST is not widely applicable because it does not apply to transfers that qualify for an annual gift tax exclusion and each donor/decedent is entitled to a relatively generous aggregate exemption ($5.43 million in 2015).

Income Tax Considerations

A **fiduciary** entity is a legal entity that takes possession of property for the benefit of a person. An **estate** is a fiduciary that comes into existence upon a person's death to transfer the decedent's real and personal property. Likewise, a *trust* is also a fiduciary whose purpose is to hold and administer the corpus for other persons *(beneficiaries)*. While an estate exists only temporarily (until the assets of the decedent are distributed), a trust may have a prolonged or even indefinite existence. Because fiduciaries can exist for many years, special rules govern the taxation of income realized on property they hold. These rules are complex and relate to how fiduciaries account for income under state law. A detailed discussion is beyond the scope of this text, but we can provide a useful general outline.

The trust or testamentary instrument (or, in the absence of an instrument, state law) determines how income and expenses are allocated between beneficiaries—fiduciary accounting income belongs to income beneficiaries and corpus (principal) belongs to the remainderman. For example, an instrument may allocate gains on the sale of assets to corpus and rental receipts to trust accounting income. Likewise, depreciation expense may be allocated to accounting income whereas repairs may be allocated to corpus. Accounting income is important because it determines how much income the fiduciary can (or must) distribute. Trusts and estates may have discretion whether to accumulate income within the fiduciary (for future distribution) or make current distributions.[21] Income retained by the fiduciary is taxed as income to the fiduciary, and consequently, the fiduciary must file an income tax return. In contrast, income distributed currently by the fiduciary is taxed as income to the beneficiary. To accomplish this flow-through of income, fiduciaries are granted an income tax deduction for current distributions of income and this deduction depends, in part, on accounting income.

[21]Regulations under §§ 651–652 make a distinction between simple trusts and complex trusts. **Simple trusts** must distribute all trust accounting income currently (and cannot make charitable contributions) whereas **complex trusts** are not required by the trust instrument to distribute income currently.

To better understand how taxable income is divided between a fiduciary and its beneficiaries, it is helpful to first summarize the formula for determining a fiduciary's taxable income.[22] With few exceptions, the formula for calculating a fiduciary's taxable income is analogous to the individual income tax formula. Gross income for a fiduciary is determined in the same manner as gross income for an individual. For example, trusts are generally taxed on realized income, but they can exclude certain items from gross income, such as municipal interest, and make elections to defer certain items, such as installment gains. A fiduciary can also deduct expenses similar to an individual. For example, a fiduciary can deduct trade or business expenses, interest, taxes, casualty losses, charitable contributions, and miscellaneous itemized deductions. Although a fiduciary is not entitled to a standard deduction (i.e., there is no distinction between deductions for AGI and itemized deductions), miscellaneous itemized deductions for a fiduciary are still subjected to a 2 percent limitation calculated using a hypothetical AGI. A fiduciary is also allowed a personal exemption, $600 for an estate and $300 for a trust that distributes all income currently, and $100 for other trusts. Lastly, a fiduciary is allowed a deduction for distributions of income to beneficiaries. It is this **distribution deduction** that operates to eliminate the potential for double taxation of income.

The maximum amount of the distribution deduction (and the maximum aggregate amount of gross income reportable by beneficiaries) is determined by reference to **distributable net income (DNI).** DNI is calculated by adjusting taxable income for the fiduciary, but unfortunately, this calculation is circular. That is, taxable income for a fiduciary depends upon the distribution deduction, which in turn depends upon DNI, which in turn depends upon taxable income. Moreover, the calculation of fiduciary taxable income is further complicated by items such as net operating losses, net capital losses, charitable contributions, multiple beneficiaries, and discretionary (versus mandatory) distributions. Suffice it to say that the calculation of income tax for a fiduciary can be a very complicated matter.

While granting a fiduciary discretion over distributions complicates the calculation of taxable income, it might appear that this discretion also provides an opportunity to split income (by creating yet another taxpayer). However, the fiduciary income tax rates are generally as high as or higher than the tax rates for individual beneficiaries. Hence, the potential income tax benefits from splitting income between fiduciaries and beneficiaries are typically negligible.

Transfer Tax Planning Techniques

Transfer tax planning strategies are the same as those employed for income tax planning: timing, shifting, and conversion. Like income tax planning, wealth planning is primarily concerned with accomplishing the client's goals in the most efficient and effective manner after considering *both* tax and nontax costs. For the most part, wealth planning is directed to maximizing after-tax wealth to be transferred from an older generation to a younger generation. A critical constraint in this process, however, is determining how tax strategies can achieve the client's ultimate (nontax) goals. Before attempting to integrate tax and nontax considerations, let's survey a few basic techniques for transfer tax planning.

Serial Gifts

A **serial gift** strategy converts a large taxable transfer into a tax-exempt transfer by dividing the transfer into multiple intervivos gifts. As long as the gifts qualify as present interests and do not exceed the annual exclusion, the transfers are exempt from all transfer taxes. Although serial gifts are an easy and low-cost planning strategy, this technique is limited in scope because only $14,000 ($28,000 if married) can be transferred each year tax-free to any specific donee. Hence, serial gifts can move significant amounts of wealth only if employed by multiple donors over multiple years and multiple donees.

[22]Subchapter J (§§ 641–692) contains the provisions governing income taxation of fiduciaries.

Example 14-24

Suppose Harry and Wilma decide to begin transferring wealth to Dina and George. To what extent can serial gifts accomplish this goal without triggering gift taxes?

Answer: Harry and Wilma could make annual gifts of $14,000 each to Dina and George. These gifts would remove $56,000 per year from the Smiths' estate without triggering any transfer taxes (gift tax or generation-skipping tax). They could include any type of property as long as Dina and George can presently enjoy the property or income generated by it.

Bypass Provisions In retirement, many individuals are concerned about keeping sufficient wealth to support a comfortable lifestyle for themselves and a surviving spouse. Indeed, it is common for a spouse to leave all of his or her property to the surviving spouse for this very reason. This type of plan will avoid all estate taxes on the estate of the first spouse to die (assuming the estate contains no terminable interests). However, it may not minimize total transfer taxes when we consider the estates of *both* spouses. The deceased spouse who leaves all property to the surviving spouse has no taxable estate (because of the marital deduction) and his or her unified credit goes unused. A **bypass provision** in the will of the deceased spouse will use the unified credit by transferring some property to beneficiaries other than the surviving spouse. The usefulness of bypass provisions as estate saving devices was eroded by the legislation passed in December 2010, the **deceased spousal unused exclusion** (DSUE) amount. The ability of a surviving spouse to utilize a deceased spouse's unused unified credit essentially fulfills the same objective as a bypass provision. Example 14-25 generates a comparison of the tax savings from a bypass provision (Alternative 1) to the savings from a DSUE (Alternative 2).

Example 14-25

What if: Suppose that Harry and Wilma have made no taxable gifts and Harry dies with a taxable estate of $30 million. Several years later, Wilma dies holding only the property she inherited from Harry. To isolate the estate tax savings, let's also assume that after Harry's death Wilma consumes any income from the property, and the value of the property remains constant. In addition, let's ignore the time value of money and assume no adjustments for inflation. Compare the total amount of transfer taxes for Harry and Wilma under two alternatives. In the first alternative, assume that Harry uses a bypass provision to bequeath $5.43 million to Dina and the rest to Wilma. In the second alternative, assume that Harry leaves all his property to Wilma and she uses Harry's unused unified credit under a DSUE provision. How much more total transfer taxes will be paid a DSUE than using a bypass provision?

Answer: The bypass provision results in exactly the same tax at the DSUE provision as calculated below:

	Alternative 1 Bypass	Alternative 2 DSUE
Harry's gross estate	$ 30,000,000	$ 30,000,000
Marital deduction	−24,570,000	−30,000,000
Harry's taxable estate	$ 5,430,000	$ 0
Harry's gross estate tax	$ 2,117,800	$ 0
Unified credit	−2,117,800	− 0
Harry's estate tax due	$ 0	$ 0
Wilma's taxable estate	$ 24,570,000	$ 30,000,000
Wilma's gross estate tax	$ 9,773,800	$ 11,945,800
Wilma's unified credit	−2,117,800	−4,298,800
Wilma's estate tax	$ 7,656,000	$ 7,656,000

A bypass provision will not save taxes over the DSUE because the unified credit is calculated by combining spouses' unused exemption equivalents. In Alternative 2 in Example 14-25 Wilma's estate is able to claim a unified credit based on a exemption equivalent of $10.86 million. However, one important difference is that, absent special provisions in the will, any property transferred via a bypass provision will not be available to support the surviving spouse. Hence, taxpayers should consider a bypass provision only after estimating the amount of support required by the surviving spouse. A handy alternative to a bypass provision is a testamentary transfer that qualifies for a QTIP. Because an executor can elect to take the marital deduction for any portion of a QTIP transfer, it can be used to minimize combined estate taxes for a couple.

Example 14-26

What if: Suppose that Harry wanted to have all $30 million of his estate available to support Wilma, but also wanted to use the marital deduction to minimize total estate taxes. Harry could have a QTIP provision in his will that transfers all $30 million to a trust with the income to be payable annually to Wilma. In addition, Wilma has a testamentary power to appoint the trust property. What is the total estate tax if the executor elects to claim a $24.75 million marital deduction for the QTIP transfer?

Answer: $7,728,000 per the following computation:

	QTIP
Harry's gross estate	$30,000,000
Marital deduction	−24,860,000
Taxable transfer	$ 5,430,000
Harry's gross estate tax	$ 2,117,800
Unified credit	−2,117,800
Harry's estate tax due	$ 0
Wilma's estate	$24,570,000
Wilma's gross estate tax	$ 9,773,800
Wilma's unified credit	−2,117,800
Wilma's estate tax	$ 7,656,000

The Step-Up in Tax Basis Timing is an important component in tax planning. Generally, a good tax strategy delays payment of tax, thereby reducing the present value of the tax paid. While deferral is important, transfer tax planning must also consider the potential appreciation of assets transferred, and the effect of the income tax that could apply if and when the appreciation is realized. Gifted property generally retains the donor's basis in the property (the donee takes a **carryover basis**), whereas inherited property takes a tax basis of fair market value. The advantage of gifting property is that the donor eliminates the transfer tax on any additional future appreciation on the gifted property. The disadvantage is that the unrealized appreciation of the gifted property will eventually be taxed (although at the donee's income tax rate). Thus, gifting appreciating property reduces future transfer taxes but at the cost of additional future income taxes imposed on the donee. In contrast, for inherited property, past appreciation (up to the date of death) will never be subject to income tax but instead is subject to transfer tax at the time of the transfer.

Example 14-27

What if: Harry currently owns 30 percent of the outstanding shares of FFP. These shares have a basis of $300,000 but are worth in excess of $2.7 million. Suppose Harry intends to transfer his FPP shares to his daughter Dina who, in turn, intends to sell them after Harry's death. To what extent should income tax considerations influence whether Harry transfers these shares via intervivos gift or testamentary transfer? Estimate the total tax savings if Harry delays the transfer of the shares until his death three years hence. Assume that the transfer (whether by gift or inheritance) will be taxed at the top transfer rate of 40 percent, while when Dina sells the shares in three years the gain will be taxed at a capital gains tax rate of 20 percent. Let's also assume that the FPP shares will not appreciate and the prevailing interest rate is 6 percent.

Answer: The total tax savings is $686,260 if Harry delays the transfer until his death rather than gifting the shares to Dina immediately. See the following discussion and computations:

	Gift	Inheritance	Explanation
Gift tax paid	$1,080,000		40% times $2.7 million
Time value of gift tax	× 1.191		$(1.06)^3$
Future value of gift tax	$1,286,260		Value of gift tax paid
Estate tax paid		$1,080,000	40% times $2.7 million
Dina's capital gain tax 15%	$ 480,000	0	Gain of $2.4 million on gift due to carryover basis
Total taxes paid	$1,766,260	$1,080,000	$686,260 of tax savings

If a sale is planned, then the step-up in tax basis becomes critical to avoid being taxed on the accumulated appreciation. In this scenario, a testamentary transfer provides a step-up in tax basis and delays payment of the transfer tax for three years.

What if: Suppose Dina has no interest in selling the family business and intends to eventually transfer the shares to George. Moreover, suppose Harry believes the FFP shares will appreciate to $3.5 million within three years. To what extent should income tax considerations influence whether Harry transfers these shares immediately via intervivos gift or in three years via testamentary transfer? Estimate the total tax savings if Harry transfers the shares immediately rather than delaying the transfer until his death.

Answer: The tax savings is $113,740 if Harry transfers property immediately rather than delaying the transfer until his death. See the following discussion and computations:

	Gift	Inheritance	Explanation
Gift tax paid	$1,080,000		40% times $2.7 million
Time value of gift tax	× 1.191		$(1.06)^3$
Future value of gift tax	$1,286,260		Value of gift tax paid
Estate tax paid		$1,400,000	40% times $3.5 million
Total taxes paid	$1,286,260	$1,400,000	$113,740 of tax savings

If Dina plans to hold the shares indefinitely and the property is rapidly appreciating, then an intervivos gift avoids having future appreciation taxed in Harry's estate. Although a gift of the shares would accelerate the imposition of transfer taxes, any unused unified credit could minimize the amount of taxes due on the transfer. In this scenario, an intervivos transfer reduces total transfer taxes even though the gift tax is paid three years before an estate tax would be due.

Timing becomes critical in determining how to trade off income tax savings (the step-up in tax basis) against transfer tax costs (paying gift tax now or paying estate taxes on additional appreciation later). Most tax advisors will suggest that elderly clients sell business assets or investments with unrealized losses, because upon death the basis of these assets will be adjusted downward to fair market value. In other words, the adjustment to basis can be a step-down as well as a step-up, and a sale prevents the elimination of the loss deduction.

Integrated Wealth Plans

A client can have many nontax goals associated with the ultimate disposition of wealth, and some are very personal. It is often difficult to ascertain and prioritize them for planning purposes. However, an effective wealth plan must identify and integrate these personal objectives with tax costs. Often, the primary nontax objective of wealth planning is to preserve value during the transfer of control (management) of business assets. Thus, an essential nontax element of any effective wealth plan is to identify a safe mechanism to support the older generation in a specific lifestyle while transferring control to the younger generation.

Trusts are common vehicles for tax planning, in large part because these fiduciaries can be structured to achieve a great variety of tax and nontax objectives, including the support of specific beneficiaries.[23] The trustee is responsible for managing property in the trust, but the grantor also gives the trustee discretionary powers to provide flexibility. These powers can include the discretion to distribute income or corpus among beneficiaries. In addition grantors can retain powers, including the ability to revoke the trust, select the trustee (original or successor), terminate beneficial interests, and add to the corpus. The most important aspect of an irrevocable trust is that the provisions (including powers and guidelines for the exercise of discretionary powers) cannot be changed once the trust instrument has been executed.

Specific types of trusts are common to many wealth transfer plans. For example, a **bypass trust** is used in lieu of a bypass provision in the will to maximize the unified credit of the first spouse to die. This is accomplished by leaving the surviving spouse with a terminable interest (e.g., a life estate in investment property) that won't qualify for the marital deduction in the amount of the exemption equivalent. A **life insurance trust** is funded with an irrevocable transfer of a life insurance policy, and the trustee is given the power to name beneficiaries and redesignate them in case of divorce or death. Upon the death of the grantor, the amount of the policy is paid into the trust but not included in the grantor's estate. Moreover, an immediate cash distribution from the trust is not taxable income to the beneficiaries.

Example 14-28

Harry is planning to purchase a $2 million life insurance policy. He wants to use the proceeds to support Wilma after his death and have any remaining funds paid to his surviving children. How would Harry structure a bypass trust to accomplish these goals?

Answer: Harry should transfer the policy to an irrevocable trust that directs the trustee to hold the policy and pay the premiums until Harry's death. At that time, the trustee should be directed to invest the $2 million proceeds and pay income to Wilma for the remainder of her life or until she remarries. At that time, the trust will terminate and pay the remainder to Harry's surviving children or their estates.

What if: Suppose Harry transfers the policy to an irrevocable trust and dies four years later. Will the use of this bypass trust trigger any estate taxes at that time?

Answer: Harry's transfer of the policy to the trust will be a taxable gift today to the extent of the value of the transfer. However, the $2 million proceeds from the policy will not be included in Harry's estate upon his death.

[23]Trusts are also popular because the trust property transfers outside probate, thereby avoiding both the costs and the publicity associated with probate.

Donors often use partnerships to transfer assets and for the control of a business in a systematic manner that also provides them with income and security. One specific form of partnership, the **family limited partnership,** divides a family business into various ownership interests, representing control of operations and future income and appreciation of the assets. These limited partnerships were sometimes used to transfer appreciation to members of a younger generation while allowing the older generation to effectively retain control of the business. Obviously, the intent of the estate and gift taxes is to recognize transfers of assets that also represent control of the assets. Hence, it was not surprising that Congress revised the law to restrict the ability of family limited partnerships to effectively transfer appreciation in business assets and operations to younger generations without also transferring control.

CONCLUSION

In this chapter we learned to identify taxable transfers whether made at death (testamentary transfers) or during life (intervivos transfers). We also learned how to calculate estate and gift taxes, and we introduced some fundamental transfer tax planning techniques. The simplest and most effective wealth planning technique is serial giving. As long as the gifts are restricted to present interests under the annual exclusion, serial giving avoids all transfer taxes. Other methods, such as bypass trusts and family limited partnerships, can also be effective under the proper circumstances. In all cases, however, wealth planning should be carefully coordinated with other needs and objectives.

Summary

Outline the basic structure of federal transfer taxes and describe the valuation of property transfers. LO 14-1

- Congress imposes a tax on transfers of property whether the transfer is a gift or occurs at death.
- The unified transfer tax scheme provides for a progressive tax rate schedule that applies to cumulative transfers. That is, transfers in all prior periods are taken into account when calculating the tax for a transfer in a current period.
- The unified credit offsets transfer tax on cumulative lifetime transfers (the exemption equivalent) of $5.43 million for gifts and transfers at death.
- Each transfer tax shares two common deductions, an unlimited deduction for charitable contributions and a marital deduction that allows almost unfettered transfers between spouses.
- Property transfers are valued at fair market value defined as the value paid by a willing buyer to a willing seller. The determination of fair market value often depends upon the facts and circumstances surrounding the property.

Summarize the operation of the federal gift tax and the calculation of the federal gift tax. LO 14-2

- Lifetime transfers of property for no (or inadequate) consideration are taxed as gifts if the transfer is complete and irrevocable.
- Contributions to political parties or candidates, and medical and educational expenses paid on behalf of an unrelated individual, are excluded from gift taxation.
- Gifts are taxed at the fair market value of the donated property on the date the gift becomes complete, and small gifts are reduced by the annual exclusion ($14,000) if they are present interests.
- With gift-splitting, married couples can elect to treat all gifts made in a year as if each spouse made one-half of each gift.

- Calculate taxable gifts by adjusting current gifts for exclusions and gift-splitting, and then deducting the marital deduction (for qualifying gifts to a spouse) and the charitable deduction.
- Transfers of terminable interests in property, such as a life estate, will not generally qualify for the marital deduction.
- Compute the gift tax on cumulative taxable gifts by adding prior taxable gifts to current taxable gifts.
- Reduce the gift tax on cumulative gifts by the gift tax on prior taxable gifts calculated, after applying the unified credit actually used in prior periods.
- Then reduce the gift tax by the *unused* portion of the unified credit.
- The generation-skipping tax is a supplemental tax designed to prevent the avoidance of transfer taxes (both estate and gift tax) through transfers that skip a generation of recipients.

Describe the federal estate tax, and compute taxable transfers at death and the federal estate tax.

- The gross estate includes property owned by the decedent at death (the probate estate) and certain property transfers taking effect at death.
- Property the decedent owned jointly is included in the gross estate. The value of the decedent's interest is included when property is held in joint tenancy, whereas half the value of the property is included when held with a spouse in joint tenancy with the right of survivorship.
- Temporal interests begin or end with the passage of time. The value of a future interest, such as a remainder, can be determined from IRS tables, and the value of a present interest, such as a life estate, is calculated at the difference between the value of the future interest and the current value of the property.
- The gross estate is reduced by administrative expenses, debts of the decedent, and losses incurred during the administration of the estate, resulting in the adjusted gross estate.
- The adjusted gross estate is reduced for certain transfers to a surviving spouse (the marital deduction) and for transfers to charities (the charitable deduction), resulting in the taxable estate.
- The taxable estate is increased by adjusted taxable gifts to determine cumulative transfers, and the tentative estate tax calculated using this tax base represents transfer tax on total transfers.
- Calculate the estate tax due by reducing the tentative tax by the estate tax calculated using adjusted taxable gifts and the unified credit.

LO 14-4

Apply fundamental principles of wealth planning and explain how income and transfer taxation interact to affect wealth planning.

- Trusts and estates are fiduciary taxpayers taxed on accumulated (undistributed) income via a fiduciary income tax return.
- Because fiduciary income tax rates are generally as high as or higher than the tax rates for individual beneficiaries, the income tax benefits from splitting income between fiduciaries and beneficiaries are typically negligible.
- A serial gift strategy saves gift taxes by converting a potentially large taxable transfer into a tax-exempt transfer of multiple smaller gifts that qualify for the annual exclusion of the donor.
- Bypass provisions in a will or bypass trusts reduce estate taxes by using the unified credit of the deceased spouse through a transfer of some property to beneficiaries other than the surviving spouse.
- Testamentary transfers allow a step-up in tax basis to fair market value, thereby eliminating the income tax on unrealized appreciation. In contrast, appreciation of property transferred via intervivos transfers may be eventually realized and taxed as income. However, a gift eliminates transfer taxes on expected future appreciation.

KEY TERMS

adjusted gross estate (14-21)
adjusted taxable gifts (14-23)
alternative valuation date (14-20)
annual exclusion (14-8)
beneficiary (14-7)
bypass provision (14-29)
bypass trust (14-32)
carryover basis (14-30)
common-law states (14-9)
community property states (14-9)
complex trust (14-27n)
corpus (14-7)
current gifts (14-9)
deceased spousal unused exclusion (14-29)
distributable net income (DNI) (14-28)
distribution deduction (14-28)
donee (14-5)
donor (14-5)
estate (14-27)
executor (14-18)
exemption equivalent (14-3)
family limited partnership (14-33)
fiduciary (14-27)
fiduciary duty (14-7)
future interest (14-6)
generation-skipping tax (GST) (14-27)
gift (14-5)
grantor (14-7)
gross estate (14-16)
heirs (14-16)
intervivos transfers (14-2)
joint tenancy with right of survivorship (14-2)
last will and testament (14-2)
life estate (14-7)
life insurance trust (14-32)
marital deduction (14-4)
nondeductible terminable interests (14-10)
present interest (14-6)
probate (14-16)
probate estate (14-16)
qualified terminable interest property (QTIP) (14-11)
remainder (14-7)
remainderman (14-7)
reversion (14-7)
serial gift (14-28)
simple trust (14-27n)
taxable estate (14-21)
taxable gifts (14-9)
tenancy by the entirety (14-18n)
tenancy in common (14-18)
terminable interest (14-7)
testamentary transfers (14-2)
trust (14-7)
trustee (14-7)
unified credit (14-2)
willing-buyer (14-4)
willing-seller rule (14-4)

DISCUSSION QUESTIONS

1. Identify the features common to the gift tax formula and the estate tax formula. LO 14-1
2. Explain why Congress felt it necessary to enact a gift tax to complement the estate tax. LO 14-1
3. Describe the unified credit and the purpose it serves in the gift and estate tax. LO 14-1
4. Fred is retired and living on his pension. He has accumulated almost $1 million of property he would like to leave to his children. However, Fred is afraid much of his wealth will be eliminated by the federal estate tax. Explain whether this fear is well founded. LO 14-1
5. Define fair market value for transfer tax purposes. LO 14-1
6. Describe the requirements for a complete gift, and contrast a gift of a present interest with a gift of a future interest. LO 14-2
7. Describe a property transfer or payment that is not, by definition, a transfer for inadequate consideration. LO 14-2
8. Describe a situation in which a transfer of cash to a trust might be considered an incomplete gift. LO 14-2
9. Identify two types of transfers for inadequate consideration that are specifically excluded from imposition of the gift tax. LO 14-2
10. Under what circumstances will a deposit of cash to a bank account held in joint tenancy be considered a completed gift? LO 14-2
11. Explain how a purchase of realty could result in a taxable gift. LO 14-2
12. Describe the conditions for using the annual exclusion to offset an otherwise taxable transfer. LO 14-2
13. List the conditions for making an election to split gifts. LO 14-2

LO 14-2 14. Describe the limitations on the deduction of transfers to charity.

LO 14-2 15. Explain the purpose of adding prior taxable gifts to current taxable gifts and show whether these prior gifts could be taxed multiple times over the years.

LO 14-3 16. Explain why the gross estate includes the value of certain property transferred by the decedent at death, such as property held in joint tenancy with the right of survivorship, even though this property is not subject to probate.

LO 14-3 17. Identify the factors that determine the proportion of the value of property held in joint tenancy with the right of survivorship that will be included in a decedent's gross estate.

LO 14-3 research 18. Harold owns a condo in Hawaii that he plans on using for the rest of his life. However, to ensure his sister Maude will own the property after his death, Harold deeded the remainder of the property to her. He signed the deed transferring the remainder in July 2009 when the condo was worth $250,000 and his life estate was worth $75,000. In January 2011 Harold died, at which time the condo was worth $300,000. What amount, if any, is included in Harold's gross estate? Explain.

LO 14-3 19. Paul is a widower with several grown children. He is considering transferring his residence into a trust for his children and retaining a life estate in it. Comment on whether this plan will prevent the value of the home from being included in Paul's gross estate when he dies.

LO 14-3 20. Explain how a remainder and an income interest are valued for transfer tax purposes.

LO 14-3 21. Explain why the fair market value of a life estate is more difficult to estimate than an income interest.

LO 14-3 22. Describe a reason why transfers of terminable interests should not qualify for the marital deduction.

LO 14-3 23. True or False: Including taxable gifts when calculating the estate tax subjects these transfers to double taxation. Explain.

LO 14-3 24. People sometimes confuse the unified credit with the exemption equivalent. Describe how these terms differ.

LO 14-4 25. Describe a reason why a generation-skipping tax was necessary to augment the estate and gift taxes.

LO 14-4 26. Explain why an effective wealth transfer plan necessitates cooperation between lawyers, accountants, and investment advisors.

LO 14-4 27. Describe how to initiate the construction of a comprehensive and effective wealth plan.

LO 14-4 28. List two questions you might pose to a client to find out whether a program of serial gifts would be an advantageous wealth transfer plan.

LO 14-4 29. A client in good health wants to support the college education of her teenage grandchild. The client holds various properties but proposes to make a gift of cash in the amount of the annual exclusion. Explain to the client why a direct gift of cash may not be advisable and what property might serve as a reasonable substitute.

LO 14-4 30. An elderly client has a life insurance policy worth $40,000 that upon her death pays $250,000 to her sole grandchild (or his estate). The client retains ownership of the policy. Outline for her the costs and benefits of transferring ownership of the policy to a life insurance trust.

LO 14-4 31. Describe the conditions in which a married couple would benefit from the use of a bypass provision or a bypass trust.

LO 14-4 32. Under what conditions can a executor or trustee elect to claim a marital deduction for a transfer of a terminable interest to a spouse?

LO 14-4 33. Explain how a transfer of property as a gift may have income tax implications to the donee.

PROBLEMS

All applicable problems are available with McGraw-Hill's *Connect® Accounting*.

34. Raquel transferred $100,000 of stock to a trust, with income to be paid to her nephew for 18 years and the remainder to her nephew's children (or their estates). Raquel named a bank as independent trustee but retained the power to determine how much income, if any, will be paid in any particular year. Is this transfer a complete gift? Explain. LO 14-2

35. This year Gerry's friend, Dewey, was disabled. Gerry paid $15,000 to Dewey's doctor for medical expenses and paid $12,500 to State University for college tuition for Dewey's son. Has Gerry made taxable gifts and, if so, in what amounts? LO 14-2

36. This year Dan and Mike purchased realty for $180,000 and took title as equal tenants in common. However, Mike was able to provide only $40,000 of the purchase price and Dan the remaining $140,000. Has Dan made a complete gift to Mike and, if so, in what amount? LO 14-2

37. Last year Nate opened a savings account with a deposit of $15,000. The account was in the name of Nate and Derrick, joint tenancy with the right of survivorship. Derrick did not contribute to the account, but this year he withdrew $5,000. Has Nate made a complete gift and, if so, what is the amount of the taxable gift and when was the gift made? LO 14-2

38. Barry transfers $1,000,000 to an irrevocable trust with income to Robin for her life and the remainder to Maurice (or his estate). Calculate the value of the life estate and remainder if Robin's age and the prevailing interest rate result in a Table S discount factor for the remainder of 0.27. LO 14-2

39. This year Jim created an irrevocable trust to provide for Ted, his 32-year-old nephew, and Ted's family. Jim transferred $70,000 to the trust and named a bank as the trustee. The trust was directed to pay income to Ted until he reaches age 35, and at that time the trust is to be terminated and the corpus is to be distributed to Ted's two children (or their estates). Determine the amount, if any, of the current gift and the taxable gift. If necessary, you may assume the relevant interest rate is 6 percent and Jim is unmarried. LO 14-2

40. This year Colleen transferred $100,000 to an irrevocable trust that pays equal shares of income annually to three cousins (or their estates) for the next eight years. At that time, the trust is terminated and the corpus of the trust reverts to Colleen. Determine the amount, if any, of the current gifts and the taxable gifts. If necessary, you may assume the relevant interest rate is 6 percent and Colleen is unmarried. What is your answer if Colleen is married and she elects to gift-split with her spouse? LO 14-2

41. Sly is a widower and wants to make annual gifts of cash to each of his four children and six grandchildren. How much can Sly transfer to his children this year if he makes the maximum gifts eligible for the annual? What is the amount of the total transfer if Sly is married and elects to gift splitting, assuming his spouse makes no other gifts? LO 14-2

42. Jack and Liz live in a community property state and their vacation home is community property. This year they transferred the vacation home to an irrevocable trust that provides their son, Tom, a life estate in the home and the remainder to their daughter, Laura. Under the terms of the trust, Tom has the right to use the vacation home for the duration of his life, and Laura will automatically own the property after Tom's death. At the time of the gift the home was valued at $500,000, Tom was 35 years old, and the §7520 rate was 5.4 percent. What is the amount, if any, of the taxable gifts? Would your answer be different if the home were not community property and Jack and Liz elected to gift-split? LO 14-2

LO 14-2 43. David placed $80,000 in trust with income to Steve for his life and the remainder to Lil (or her estate). At the time of the gift, given the prevailing interest rate, Steve's life estate was valued at $65,000 and the remainder at $15,000. What is the amount, if any, of David's taxable gifts?

LO 14-2 44. Stephen transferred $15,000 to an irrevocable trust for Graham. The trustee has the discretion to distribute income or corpus for Graham's benefit but is required to distribute all assets to Graham (or his estate) not later than Graham's 21st birthday. What is the amount, if any, of the taxable gift?

LO 14-2 45. For the holidays, Marty gave a watch worth $25,000 to Emily and jewelry worth $40,000 to Natalie. Has Marty made any taxable gifts this year and, if so, in what amounts? Does it matter if Marty is married to Wendy and they live in a community property state?

LO 14-2 46. This year Jeff earned $850,000 and used it to purchase land in joint tenancy with a right of survivorship with Mary. Has Jeff made a taxable gift to Mary and, if so, in what amount? What is your answer if Jeff and Mary are married?

LO 14-2 47. Laura transfers $500,000 into trust with the income to be paid annually to her spouse, William, for life (a life estate) and the remainder to Jenny. Calculate the amount of the taxable gifts from the transfers.

LO 14-2 48. Red transferred $5,000,000 of cash to State University for a new sports complex. Calculate the amount of the taxable gift.

LO 14-2 49. In 2010 Casey made a taxable gift of $5 million to both Stephanie and Linda (a total of $10 million in taxable gifts). Calculate the amount of gift tax due this year and Casey's unused exemption equivalent under the following alternatives.

a) This year Casey made a taxable gift of $1 million to Stephanie. Casey is not married, and the 2010 gift was the only other taxable gift he has ever made.

b) This year Casey made a taxable gift of $5 million to Stephanie. Casey is not married, and the 2010 gift was the only other taxable gift he has ever made.

c) This year Casey made a gift worth $5 million to Stephanie. Casey is married to Helen in a common law state, and the 2010 gift was the only other taxable gift he or Helen has ever made. Casey and Helen elect to gift split.

LO 14-3 tax forms 50. Tom Hruise was an entertainment executive who had a fatal accident on a film set. Tom's will directed his executor to distribute his cash and stock to his wife, Kaffie, the real estate to his church, The First Church of Methodology, and the remainder of his assets were to be placed in trust for his three children. Tom's estate consisted of the following:

Assets:	
Personal assets	$ 800,000
Cash and stock	24,000,000
Intangible assets (film rights)	71,500,000
Real estate	15,000,000
	$111,300,000
Liabilities:	
Mortgage	$ 3,200,000
Other liabilities	4,100,000
	$ 7,300,000

a) Tom made a taxable gift of $8 million in 2011. Compute the estate tax for Tom's estate.

b) Fill out lines 1 through 12 in part 2 of Form 706 for Tom's estate.

LO 14-3 51. Hal and Wendy are married, and they own a parcel of realty, Blackacre, as joint tenants with the right of survivorship. Hal owns an additional parcel of realty, Redacre, in his name alone. Suppose Hal should die when Blackacre is worth $800,000 and Redacre is worth $750,000. What value of realty would be included in Hal's probate estate, and what value in Hal's gross estate?

52. Walter owns a whole-life insurance policy worth $52,000 that directs the insurance company to pay the beneficiary $250,000 on Walter's death. Walter pays the annual premiums and has the power to designate the beneficiary of the policy (it is currently his son, James). What value of the policy, if any, will be included in Walter's estate upon his death? LO 14-3

53. Many years ago James and Sergio purchased property for $450,000. Although they are listed as equal co-owners, Sergio was able to provide only $200,000 of the purchase price. James treated the additional $25,000 of his contribution to the purchase price as a gift to Sergio. If the property is worth $900,000 at Sergio's death, what amount would be included in Sergio's estate if the title to the property was tenants in common? What if the title were joint tenancy with right of survivorship? LO 14-3

54. Terry transferred $500,000 of real estate into an irrevocable trust for her son, Lee. The trustee was directed to retain income until Lee's 21st birthday and then pay him the corpus of the trust. Terry retained the power to require the trustee to pay income to Lee at any time, and the right to the assets if Lee predeceased her. What amount of the trust, if any, will be included in Terry's estate? LO 14-3

55. Last year Robert transferred a life insurance policy worth $45,000 to an irrevocable trust with directions to distribute the corpus of the trust to his grandson, Danny, upon his graduation from college, or to Danny's estate upon his death. Robert paid $15,000 of gift tax on the transfer of the policy. Early this year, Robert died and the insurance company paid $400,000 to the trust. What amount, if any, is included in Robert's gross estate? LO 14-3

56. Willie purchased a whole-life insurance policy on his brother, Benny. Under the policy, the insurance company will pay the named beneficiary $100,000 upon the death of the insured, Benny. Willie names Tess the beneficiary, and upon Benny's death, Tess receives the proceeds of the policy, $100,000. Identify and discuss the transfer tax implications of this arrangement. LO 14-3 research

57. Jimmy owns two parcels of real estate, Tara and Sundance. Tara is worth $240,000 and Sundance is worth $360,000. Jimmy plans to bequeath Tara directly to his wife Lois and leave her a life estate in Sundance. What amount of value will be included in Jimmy's gross estate and taxable estate should he die now? LO 14-3

58. Roland had a taxable estate of $5.5 million when he died this year. Calculate the amount of estate tax due (if any) under the following alternatives. LO 14-3
    a) Roland's prior taxable gifts consist of a taxable gift of $1 million in 2005.
    b) Roland's prior taxable gifts consist of a taxable gift of $1.5 million in 2005.
    c) Explain how the tax calculation would change if Roland made a $1 million taxable gift in the year prior to his death.

59. Brad and Angelina are a wealthy couple who have three children, Fred, Bridget, and Lisa. Two of the three children, Fred and Bridget, are from Brad's previous marriages. On Christmas this year, Brad gave each of the three children a cash gift of $10,000, and Angelina gave Lisa an additional cash gift of $40,000. Brad also gave stock worth $40,000 (adjusted basis of $10,000) to the Actor's Guild (an "A" charity). LO 14-3 tax forms
    a) Brad and Angelina have chosen to split gifts. Calculate Brad's gift tax. Assume that Angelina has no previous taxable gifts, but Brad reported previous taxable gifts of $2 million in 2009 when he used $345,800 of unified credit and paid $435,000 of gift taxes.
    b) Fill out parts 1 and 4 of Form 709 for Brad.

60. Jones is seriously ill and has $6 million of property that he wants to leave to his four children. He is considering making a current gift of the property (rather than leaving the property to pass through his will). Assuming any taxable transfer will be subject to the highest transfer tax rate, determine how much gift tax Jones will owe if he makes the transfers now. How much estate tax will Jones save if he dies after three years, during which time the property appreciates to $6.8 million? LO 14-4 planning

LO 14-4 61. Angelina gave a parcel of realty to Julie valued at $210,000 (Angelina purchased the property five years ago for $88,000). Compute the amount of the taxable gift on the transfer, if any. Suppose several years later Julie sold the property for $215,000. What is the amount of her gain or loss, if any, on the sale?

LO 14-4 research 62. Several years ago Doug invested $21,000 in stock. This year he gave his daughter Tina the stock on a day it was valued at $20,000. She promptly sold it for $19,500. Determine the amount of the taxable gift, if any, and calculate the amount of taxable income or gain, if any, for Tina. Assume Doug is not married and does not support Tina, who is 28.

LO 14-4 63. Roberta is considering making annual gifts of $14,000 of stock to each of her four children. She expects to live another five years and to leave a taxable estate worth approximately $8 million. She requests that you justify the gifts by estimating her estate tax savings from making the gifts.

LO 14-4 64. Harold and Maude are married and live in a common-law state. Neither have made any taxable gifts and Maude owns (holds title) all their property. She dies with a taxable estate of $15 million and leaves it all to Harold. He dies several years later, leaving the entire $15 million to their three children. Calculate how much estate tax would have been saved if Maude had used a bypass provision in her will to direct $9 million to her children and the remaining $6 million to Harold. Ignore the time value of money and all credits in this problem except for the unified credit.

COMPREHENSIVE PROBLEMS

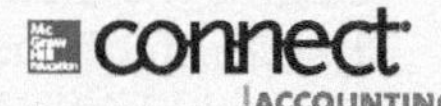

All applicable problems are available with McGraw-Hill's *Connect® Accounting*.

planning 65. Suppose Vince dies this year with a gross estate of $15 million and no adjusted prior gifts. Calculate the amount of estate tax due (if any) under the following *alternative* conditions:

a) Vince leaves his entire estate to his spouse, Millie.
b) Vince leaves $10 million to Millie and the remainder to charity.
c) Vince leaves $10 million to Millie and the remainder to his son, Paul.
d) Vince leaves $10 million to Millie and the remainder to a trust whose trustee is required to pay income to Millie for her life and the remainder to Paul.

66. Hank is a single individual who possesses a life insurance policy worth $300,000 that will pay his two children a total of $800,000 upon his death. This year Hank transferred the policy and all incidents of ownership to an irrevocable trust that pays income annually to his two children for 15 years and then distributes the corpus to the children in equal shares.

a) Calculate the amount of gift tax due (if any) on the gift. Assume that Hank has made only one prior taxable gift of $5 million in 2011.
b) Calculate the amount of cumulative taxable transfers for estate tax purposes if Hank dies this year but after the date of the gift. At the time of his death, Hank's probate estate is $10 million divided in equal shares between his two children.

67. Jack is single and he made his first taxable gift of $1,000,000 in 2008. Jack made no further gifts until 2009, at which time he gave $1,750,000 to each of his three children and an additional $1,000,000 to State University (a charity). The annual exclusion in 2009 was $13,000. Recently Jack has been in poor health and would like you to estimate his estate tax should he die this year. Jack estimates his taxable estate (after deductions) will be worth $5.4 million at his death.

68. Montgomery has decided to engage in wealth planning and has listed the value of his assets below. The life insurance has a cash surrender value of $120,000, and the proceeds are payable to Montgomery's estate. The trust is an irrevocable trust created by Montgomery's brother 10 years ago and contains assets currently valued at $800,000. The income from the trust is payable to Montgomery's faithful butler, Walen, for his life, and the remainder is payable to Montgomery or his estate. Walen is currently 37 years old, and the §7520 interest rate is currently 5.4 percent. Montgomery is unmarried and plans to leave all his assets to his surviving relatives.

Property	Value	Adjusted Basis
Auto	$ 20,000	$ 55,000
Personal effects	75,000	110,000
Checking and savings accounts	250,000	250,000
Investments	2,500,000	770,000
Residence	1,400,000	980,000
Life insurance proceeds	1,000,000	50,000
Real estate investments	5,125,000	2,800,000
Trust	800,000	80,000

a) Calculate the amount of the estate tax due (if any), assuming Montgomery dies this year and has never made any taxable gifts.
b) Calculate the amount of the estate tax due (if any), assuming Montgomery dies this year and made one taxable gift in 2006. The taxable gift was $1 million, and Montgomery used his unified credit to avoid paying any gift tax.
c) Calculate the amount of the estate tax due (if any), assuming Montgomery dies this year and made one taxable gift in 2006. The taxable gift was $1 million, and Montgomery used his unified credit to avoid paying any gift tax. Montgomery plans to bequeath his investments to charity and leave his remaining assets to his surviving relatives.

Appendix A

Tax Forms

All tax forms can be obtained from the IRS website: www.irs.gov.

Form **1065** Department of the Treasury Internal Revenue Service

U.S. Return of Partnership Income

For calendar year 2014, or tax year beginning ______________, 2014, ending ______________, 20 ______.

▶ Information about Form 1065 and its separate instructions is at *www.irs.gov/form1065.*

OMB No. 1545-0123

2014

A Principal business activity	Type or Print	Name of partnership	D Employer identification number
B Principal product or service		Number, street, and room or suite no. If a P.O. box, see the instructions.	E Date business started
C Business code number		City or town, state or province, country, and ZIP or foreign postal code	F Total assets (see the instructions) $

G Check applicable boxes: **(1)** ☐ Initial return **(2)** ☐ Final return **(3)** ☐ Name change **(4)** ☐ Address change **(5)** ☐ Amended return

(6) ☐ Technical termination - also check (1) or (2)

H Check accounting method: **(1)** ☐ Cash **(2)** ☐ Accrual **(3)** ☐ Other (specify) ▶ ______________

I Number of Schedules K-1. Attach one for each person who was a partner at any time during the tax year ▶ ______________

J Check if Schedules C and M-3 are attached . . . . . ☐

Caution. *Include* ***only*** *trade or business income and expenses on lines 1a through 22 below. See the instructions for more information.*

Income	1a	Gross receipts or sales	1a			
	b	Returns and allowances	1b			
	c	Balance. Subtract line 1b from line 1a			1c	
	2	Cost of goods sold (attach Form 1125-A)			2	
	3	Gross profit. Subtract line 2 from line 1c			3	
	4	Ordinary income (loss) from other partnerships, estates, and trusts (attach statement)			4	
	5	Net farm profit (loss) (attach Schedule F (Form 1040))			5	
	6	Net gain (loss) from Form 4797, Part II, line 17 (attach Form 4797)			6	
	7	Other income (loss) (attach statement)			7	
	8	**Total income (loss).** Combine lines 3 through 7			8	
Deductions (see the instructions for limitations)	9	Salaries and wages (other than to partners) (less employment credits)			9	
	10	Guaranteed payments to partners			10	
	11	Repairs and maintenance			11	
	12	Bad debts			12	
	13	Rent			13	
	14	Taxes and licenses			14	
	15	Interest			15	
	16a	Depreciation (if required, attach Form 4562)	16a			
	b	Less depreciation reported on Form 1125-A and elsewhere on return	16b		16c	
	17	Depletion **(Do not deduct oil and gas depletion.)**			17	
	18	Retirement plans, etc.			18	
	19	Employee benefit programs			19	
	20	Other deductions (attach statement)			20	
	21	**Total deductions.** Add the amounts shown in the far right column for lines 9 through 20			21	
	22	**Ordinary business income (loss).** Subtract line 21 from line 8			22	

Sign Here

Under penalties of perjury, I declare that I have examined this return, including accompanying schedules and statements, and to the best of my knowledge and belief, it is true, correct, and complete. Declaration of preparer (other than general partner or limited liability company member manager) is based on all information of which preparer has any knowledge.

▶ Signature of general partner or limited liability company member manager ▶ Date

May the IRS discuss this return with the preparer shown below (see instructions)? ☐ **Yes** ☐ **No**

Paid Preparer Use Only

Print/Type preparer's name	Preparer's signature	Date	Check ☐ if self-employed	PTIN
Firm's name ▶			Firm's EIN ▶	
Firm's address ▶			Phone no.	

For Paperwork Reduction Act Notice, see separate instructions. Cat. No. 11390Z Form **1065** (2014)

Form 1065 (2014) Page 2

Schedule B Other Information

		Yes	No
1	What type of entity is filing this return? Check the applicable box: a ☐ Domestic general partnership b ☐ Domestic limited partnership c ☐ Domestic limited liability company d ☐ Domestic limited liability partnership e ☐ Foreign partnership f ☐ Other ▶		
2	At any time during the tax year, was any partner in the partnership a disregarded entity, a partnership (including an entity treated as a partnership), a trust, an S corporation, an estate (other than an estate of a deceased partner), or a nominee or similar person?		
3	At the end of the tax year:		
a	Did any foreign or domestic corporation, partnership (including any entity treated as a partnership), trust, or tax-exempt organization, or any foreign government own, directly or indirectly, an interest of 50% or more in the profit, loss, or capital of the partnership? For rules of constructive ownership, see instructions. If "Yes," attach Schedule B-1, Information on Partners Owning 50% or More of the Partnership		
b	Did any individual or estate own, directly or indirectly, an interest of 50% or more in the profit, loss, or capital of the partnership? For rules of constructive ownership, see instructions. If "Yes," attach Schedule B-1, Information on Partners Owning 50% or More of the Partnership		
4	At the end of the tax year, did the partnership:		
a	Own directly 20% or more, or own, directly or indirectly, 50% or more of the total voting power of all classes of stock entitled to vote of any foreign or domestic corporation? For rules of constructive ownership, see instructions. If "Yes," complete (i) through (iv) below		

(i) Name of Corporation	(ii) Employer Identification Number (if any)	(iii) Country of Incorporation	(iv) Percentage Owned in Voting Stock

		Yes	No
b	Own directly an interest of 20% or more, or own, directly or indirectly, an interest of 50% or more in the profit, loss, or capital in any foreign or domestic partnership (including an entity treated as a partnership) or in the beneficial interest of a trust? For rules of constructive ownership, see instructions. If "Yes," complete (i) through (v) below		

(i) Name of Entity	(ii) Employer Identification Number (if any)	(iii) Type of Entity	(iv) Country of Organization	(v) Maximum Percentage Owned in Profit, Loss, or Capital

		Yes	No
5	Did the partnership file Form 8893, Election of Partnership Level Tax Treatment, or an election statement under section 6231(a)(1)(B)(ii) for partnership-level tax treatment, that is in effect for this tax year? See Form 8893 for more details		
6	Does the partnership satisfy **all four** of the following conditions?		
a	The partnership's total receipts for the tax year were less than $250,000.		
b	The partnership's total assets at the end of the tax year were less than $1 million.		
c	Schedules K-1 are filed with the return and furnished to the partners on or before the due date (including extensions) for the partnership return.		
d	The partnership is not filing and is not required to file Schedule M-3 If "Yes," the partnership is not required to complete Schedules L, M-1, and M-2; Item F on page 1 of Form 1065; or Item L on Schedule K-1.		
7	Is this partnership a publicly traded partnership as defined in section 469(k)(2)?		
8	During the tax year, did the partnership have any debt that was cancelled, was forgiven, or had the terms modified so as to reduce the principal amount of the debt?		
9	Has this partnership filed, or is it required to file, Form 8918, Material Advisor Disclosure Statement, to provide information on any reportable transaction?		
10	At any time during calendar year 2014, did the partnership have an interest in or a signature or other authority over a financial account in a foreign country (such as a bank account, securities account, or other financial account)? See the instructions for exceptions and filing requirements for FinCEN Form 114, Report of Foreign Bank and Financial Accounts (FBAR). If "Yes," enter the name of the foreign country. ▶		

661113

☐ Final K-1 ☐ Amended K-1

OMB No. 1545-0092

Schedule K-1 (Form 1041)
Department of the Treasury
Internal Revenue Service

2014

For calendar year 2014, or tax year beginning ________, 2014, and ending ________, 20 ____

Beneficiary's Share of Income, Deductions, Credits, etc.

▶ **See back of form and instructions.**

Part I Information About the Estate or Trust

A Estate's or trust's employer identification number

B Estate's or trust's name

C Fiduciary's name, address, city, state, and ZIP code

D ☐ Check if Form 1041-T was filed and enter the date it was filed ________

E ☐ Check if this is the final Form 1041 for the estate or trust

Part II Information About the Beneficiary

F Beneficiary's identifying number

G Beneficiary's name, address, city, state, and ZIP code

H ☐ Domestic beneficiary ☐ Foreign beneficiary

Part III Beneficiary's Share of Current Year Income, Deductions, Credits, and Other Items

1	Interest income	11	Final year deductions
2a	Ordinary dividends		
2b	Qualified dividends		
3	Net short-term capital gain		
4a	Net long-term capital gain		
4b	28% rate gain	12	Alternative minimum tax adjustment
4c	Unrecaptured section 1250 gain		
5	Other portfolio and nonbusiness income		
6	Ordinary business income		
7	Net rental real estate income	13	Credits and credit recapture
8	Other rental income		
9	Directly apportioned deductions		
		14	Other information
10	Estate tax deduction		

*See attached statement for additional information.

Note. A statement must be attached showing the beneficiary's share of income and directly apportioned deductions from each business, rental real estate, and other rental activity.

For IRS Use Only

Form **1120**
Department of the Treasury
Internal Revenue Service

U.S. Corporation Income Tax Return

For calendar year 2014 or tax year beginning ________, 2014, ending ________, 20 ____

▶ Information about Form 1120 and its separate instructions is at *www.irs.gov/form1120.*

OMB No. 1545-0123

2014

A Check if:
1a Consolidated return (attach Form 851) ☐
b Life/nonlife consolidated return ☐
2 Personal holding co. (attach Sch. PH) ☐
3 Personal service corp. (see instructions) ☐
4 Schedule M-3 attached ☐

TYPE OR PRINT
Name
Number, street, and room or suite no. If a P.O. box, see instructions.
City or town, state, or province, country and ZIP or foreign postal code

B Employer identification number
C Date incorporated
D Total assets (see instructions)
$

E Check if: **(1)** ☐ Initial return **(2)** ☐ Final return **(3)** ☐ Name change **(4)** ☐ Address change

Income	1a	Gross receipts or sales	1a			
	b	Returns and allowances	1b			
	c	Balance. Subtract line 1b from line 1a			1c	
	2	Cost of goods sold (attach Form 1125-A)			2	
	3	Gross profit. Subtract line 2 from line 1c			3	
	4	Dividends (Schedule C, line 19)			4	
	5	Interest			5	
	6	Gross rents			6	
	7	Gross royalties			7	
	8	Capital gain net income (attach Schedule D (Form 1120))			8	
	9	Net gain or (loss) from Form 4797, Part II, line 17 (attach Form 4797)			9	
	10	Other income (see instructions—attach statement)			10	
	11	**Total income.** Add lines 3 through 10 ▶			11	
Deductions (See instructions for limitations on deductions.)	12	Compensation of officers (see instructions—attach Form 1125-E) ▶			12	
	13	Salaries and wages (less employment credits)			13	
	14	Repairs and maintenance			14	
	15	Bad debts			15	
	16	Rents			16	
	17	Taxes and licenses			17	
	18	Interest			18	
	19	Charitable contributions			19	
	20	Depreciation from Form 4562 not claimed on Form 1125-A or elsewhere on return (attach Form 4562)			20	
	21	Depletion			21	
	22	Advertising			22	
	23	Pension, profit-sharing, etc., plans			23	
	24	Employee benefit programs			24	
	25	Domestic production activities deduction (attach Form 8903)			25	
	26	Other deductions (attach statement)			26	
	27	**Total deductions.** Add lines 12 through 26 ▶			27	
	28	Taxable income before net operating loss deduction and special deductions. Subtract line 27 from line 11			28	
	29a	Net operating loss deduction (see instructions)	29a			
	b	Special deductions (Schedule C, line 20)	29b			
	c	Add lines 29a and 29b			29c	
Tax, Refundable Credits, and Payments	30	**Taxable income.** Subtract line 29c from line 28 (see instructions)			30	
	31	Total tax (Schedule J, Part I, line 11)			31	
	32	Total payments and refundable credits (Schedule J, Part II, line 21)			32	
	33	Estimated tax penalty (see instructions). Check if Form 2220 is attached ▶ ☐			33	
	34	**Amount owed.** If line 32 is smaller than the total of lines 31 and 33, enter amount owed			34	
	35	**Overpayment.** If line 32 is larger than the total of lines 31 and 33, enter amount overpaid			35	
	36	Enter amount from line 35 you want: **Credited to 2015 estimated tax ▶**		**Refunded ▶**	36	

Sign Here

Under penalties of perjury, I declare that I have examined this return, including accompanying schedules and statements, and to the best of my knowledge and belief, it is true, correct, and complete. Declaration of preparer (other than taxpayer) is based on all information of which preparer has any knowledge.

▶ Signature of officer | Date | ▶ Title

May the IRS discuss this return with the preparer shown below (see instructions)? ☐ **Yes** ☐ **No**

Paid Preparer Use Only

Print/Type preparer's name	Preparer's signature	Date	Check ☐ if self-employed	PTIN
Firm's name ▶			Firm's EIN ▶	
Firm's address ▶			Phone no.	

Form **1120S**

Department of the Treasury
Internal Revenue Service

U.S. Income Tax Return for an S Corporation

▶ Do not file this form unless the corporation has filed or is attaching Form 2553 to elect to be an S corporation.
▶ Information about Form 1120S and its separate instructions is at *www.irs.gov/form1120s.*

OMB No. 1545-0123

2014

For calendar year 2014 or tax year beginning , 2014, ending , 20

	TYPE OR PRINT	
A S election effective date	Name	D Employer identification number
B Business activity code number (see instructions)	Number, street, and room or suite no. If a P.O. box, see instructions.	E Date incorporated
C Check if Sch. M-3 attached ☐	City or town, state or province, country, and ZIP or foreign postal code	F Total assets (see instructions) $

G Is the corporation electing to be an S corporation beginning with this tax year? ☐ Yes ☐ No If "Yes," attach Form 2553 if not already filed

H Check if: **(1)** ☐ Final return **(2)** ☐ Name change **(3)** ☐ Address change **(4)** ☐ Amended return **(5)** ☐ S election termination or revocation

I Enter the number of shareholders who were shareholders during any part of the tax year . . . . ▶

Caution. Include **only** trade or business income and expenses on lines 1a through 21. See the instructions for more information.

Income	1a	Gross receipts or sales	1a			
	b	Returns and allowances	1b			
	c	Balance. Subtract line 1b from line 1a			1c	
	2	Cost of goods sold (attach Form 1125-A)			2	
	3	Gross profit. Subtract line 2 from line 1c			3	
	4	Net gain (loss) from Form 4797, line 17 (attach Form 4797)			4	
	5	Other income (loss) (see instructions—attach statement)			5	
	6	**Total income (loss).** Add lines 3 through 5 ▶			6	
Deductions (see instructions for limitations)	7	Compensation of officers (see instructions—attach Form 1125-E)			7	
	8	Salaries and wages (less employment credits)			8	
	9	Repairs and maintenance			9	
	10	Bad debts			10	
	11	Rents			11	
	12	Taxes and licenses			12	
	13	Interest			13	
	14	Depreciation not claimed on Form 1125-A or elsewhere on return (attach Form 4562)			14	
	15	Depletion **(Do not deduct oil and gas depletion.)**			15	
	16	Advertising			16	
	17	Pension, profit-sharing, etc., plans			17	
	18	Employee benefit programs			18	
	19	Other deductions (attach statement)			19	
	20	**Total deductions.** Add lines 7 through 19 ▶			20	
	21	**Ordinary business income (loss).** Subtract line 20 from line 6			21	
Tax and Payments	22a	Excess net passive income or LIFO recapture tax (see instructions)	22a			
	b	Tax from Schedule D (Form 1120S)	22b			
	c	Add lines 22a and 22b (see instructions for additional taxes)			22c	
	23a	2014 estimated tax payments and 2013 overpayment credited to 2014	23a			
	b	Tax deposited with Form 7004	23b			
	c	Credit for federal tax paid on fuels (attach Form 4136)	23c			
	d	Add lines 23a through 23c			23d	
	24	Estimated tax penalty (see instructions). Check if Form 2220 is attached ▶ ☐			24	
	25	**Amount owed.** If line 23d is smaller than the total of lines 22c and 24, enter amount owed			25	
	26	**Overpayment.** If line 23d is larger than the total of lines 22c and 24, enter amount overpaid			26	
	27	Enter amount from line 26 **Credited to 2015 estimated tax ▶**		**Refunded ▶**	27	

Sign Here

Under penalties of perjury, I declare that I have examined this return, including accompanying schedules and statements, and to the best of my knowledge and belief, it is true, correct, and complete. Declaration of preparer (other than taxpayer) is based on all information of which preparer has any knowledge.

▶ Signature of officer | Date | ▶ Title

May the IRS discuss this return with the preparer shown below (see instructions)? ☐ Yes ☐ No

Paid Preparer Use Only

Print/Type preparer's name	Preparer's signature	Date	Check ☐ if self-employed	PTIN
Firm's name ▶			Firm's EIN ▶	
Firm's address ▶			Phone no.	

671113

☐ Final K-1 ☐ Amended K-1 OMB No. 1545-0123

Schedule K-1 (Form 1120S) **2014**
Department of the Treasury
Internal Revenue Service

For calendar year 2014, or tax year beginning ____________, 2014 ending ____________, 20____

Shareholder's Share of Income, Deductions, Credits, etc.

▶ See back of form and separate instructions.

Part I Information About the Corporation

A Corporation's employer identification number

B Corporation's name, address, city, state, and ZIP code

C IRS Center where corporation filed return

Part II Information About the Shareholder

D Shareholder's identifying number

E Shareholder's name, address, city, state, and ZIP code

F Shareholder's percentage of stock ownership for tax year . . . . ____________ %

For IRS Use Only

Part III Shareholder's Share of Current Year Income, Deductions, Credits, and Other Items

1	Ordinary business income (loss)	13	Credits
2	Net rental real estate income (loss)		
3	Other net rental income (loss)		
4	Interest income		
5a	Ordinary dividends		
5b	Qualified dividends	14	Foreign transactions
6	Royalties		
7	Net short-term capital gain (loss)		
8a	Net long-term capital gain (loss)		
8b	Collectibles (28%) gain (loss)		
8c	Unrecaptured section 1250 gain		
9	Net section 1231 gain (loss)		
10	Other income (loss)	15	Alternative minimum tax (AMT) items
11	Section 179 deduction	16	Items affecting shareholder basis
12	Other deductions		
		17	Other information

* See attached statement for additional information.

SCHEDULE M-3 (Form 1120)

Department of the Treasury
Internal Revenue Service

Net Income (Loss) Reconciliation for Corporations With Total Assets of $10 Million or More

► Attach to Form 1120 or 1120-C. ► Information about Schedule M-3 (Form 1120) and its separate instructions is available at *www.irs.gov/form1120.*

OMB No. 1545-0123

2014

Name of corporation (common parent, if consolidated return) | **Employer identification number**

Check applicable box(es): (1) ☐ Non-consolidated return (2) ☐ Consolidated return (Form 1120 only)

(3) ☐ Mixed 1120/L/PC group (4) ☐ Dormant subsidiaries schedule attached

Part I Financial Information and Net Income (Loss) Reconciliation (see instructions)

1a Did the corporation file SEC Form 10-K for its income statement period ending with or within this tax year?

☐ **Yes.** Skip lines 1b and 1c and complete lines 2a through 11 with respect to that SEC Form 10-K.

☐ **No.** Go to line 1b. See instructions if multiple non-tax-basis income statements are prepared.

b Did the corporation prepare a certified audited non-tax-basis income statement for that period?

☐ **Yes.** Skip line 1c and complete lines 2a through 11 with respect to that income statement.

☐ **No.** Go to line 1c.

c Did the corporation prepare a non-tax-basis income statement for that period?

☐ **Yes.** Complete lines 2a through 11 with respect to that income statement.

☐ **No.** Skip lines 2a through 3c and enter the corporation's net income (loss) per its books and records on line 4a.

2a Enter the income statement period: Beginning MM/DD/YYYY Ending MM/DD/YYYY

b Has the corporation's income statement been restated for the income statement period on line 2a?

☐ **Yes.** (If "Yes," attach an explanation and the amount of each item restated.)

☐ **No.**

c Has the corporation's income statement been restated for any of the five income statement periods immediately preceding the period on line 2a?

☐ **Yes.** (If "Yes," attach an explanation and the amount of each item restated.)

☐ **No.**

3a Is any of the corporation's voting common stock publicly traded?

☐ **Yes.**

☐ **No.** If "No," go to line 4a.

b Enter the symbol of the corporation's primary U.S. publicly traded voting common stock . . . . . ☐☐☐☐☐

c Enter the nine-digit CUSIP number of the corporation's primary publicly traded voting common stock . . . . . ☐☐☐☐☐☐☐☐☐

4a	Worldwide consolidated net income (loss) from income statement source identified in Part I, line 1 .	4a	
b	Indicate accounting standard used for line 4a (see instructions): (1) ☐ GAAP (2) ☐ IFRS (3) ☐ Statutory (4) ☐ Tax-basis (5) ☐ Other (specify) ________		
5a	Net income from nonincludible foreign entities (attach statement)	5a	( )
b	Net loss from nonincludible foreign entities (attach statement and enter as a positive amount) . . .	5b	
6a	Net income from nonincludible U.S. entities (attach statement)	6a	( )
b	Net loss from nonincludible U.S. entities (attach statement and enter as a positive amount)	6b	
7a	Net income (loss) of other includible foreign disregarded entities (attach statement)	7a	
b	Net income (loss) of other includible U.S. disregarded entities (attach statement)	7b	
c	Net income (loss) of other includible entities (attach statement)	7c	
8	Adjustment to eliminations of transactions between includible entities and nonincludible entities (attach statement)	8	
9	Adjustment to reconcile income statement period to tax year (attach statement)	9	
10a	Intercompany dividend adjustments to reconcile to line 11 (attach statement)	10a	
b	Other statutory accounting adjustments to reconcile to line 11 (attach statement)	10b	
c	Other adjustments to reconcile to amount on line 11 (attach statement)	10c	
11	**Net income (loss) per income statement of includible corporations.** Combine lines 4 through 10 .	11	

Note. Part I, line 11, must equal Part II, line 30, column (a) or Schedule M-1, line 1 (see instructions).

12 Enter the total amount (not just the corporation's share) of the assets and liabilities of all entities included or removed on the following lines.

	Total Assets	Total Liabilities
a Included on Part I, line 4 . . . . . ►		
b Removed on Part I, line 5 . . . . . ►		
c Removed on Part I, line 6 . . . . . ►		
d Included on Part I, line 7 . . . . . ►		

Schedule M-3 (Form 1120) 2014 Page **2**

Name of corporation (common parent, if consolidated return)	**Employer identification number**

Check applicable box(es): **(1)** ☐ Consolidated group **(2)** ☐ Parent corp **(3)** ☐ Consolidated eliminations **(4)** ☐ Subsidiary corp **(5)** ☐ Mixed 1120/L/PC group

Check if a sub-consolidated: **(6)** ☐ 1120 group **(7)** ☐ 1120 eliminations

Name of subsidiary (if consolidated return)	**Employer identification number**

Part II Reconciliation of Net Income (Loss) per Income Statement of Includible Corporations With Taxable Income per Return (see instructions)

	Income (Loss) Items (Attach statements for lines 1 through 12)	(a) Income (Loss) per Income Statement	(b) Temporary Difference	(c) Permanent Difference	(d) Income (Loss) per Tax Return
1	Income (loss) from equity method foreign corporations				
2	Gross foreign dividends not previously taxed . . .				
3	Subpart F, QEF, and similar income inclusions . .				
4	Section 78 gross-up				
5	Gross foreign distributions previously taxed . . .				
6	Income (loss) from equity method U.S. corporations				
7	U.S. dividends not eliminated in tax consolidation .				
8	Minority interest for includible corporations . . .				
9	Income (loss) from U.S. partnerships				
10	Income (loss) from foreign partnerships				
11	Income (loss) from other pass-through entities . .				
12	Items relating to reportable transactions				
13	Interest income (see instructions)				
14	Total accrual to cash adjustment				
15	Hedging transactions				
16	Mark-to-market income (loss)				
17	Cost of goods sold (see instructions)	( )			( )
18	Sale versus lease (for sellers and/or lessors) . . .				
19	Section 481(a) adjustments				
20	Unearned/deferred revenue				
21	Income recognition from long-term contracts . .				
22	Original issue discount and other imputed interest .				
23a	Income statement gain/loss on sale, exchange, abandonment, worthlessness, or other disposition of assets other than inventory and pass-through entities				
b	Gross capital gains from Schedule D, excluding amounts from pass-through entities				
c	Gross capital losses from Schedule D, excluding amounts from pass-through entities, abandonment losses, and worthless stock losses				
d	Net gain/loss reported on Form 4797, line 17, excluding amounts from pass-through entities, abandonment losses, and worthless stock losses				
e	Abandonment losses				
f	Worthless stock losses (attach statement)				
g	Other gain/loss on disposition of assets other than inventory				
24	Capital loss limitation and carryforward used . . .				
25	Other income (loss) items with differences (attach statement)				
26	**Total income (loss) items.** Combine lines 1 through 25				
27	**Total expense/deduction items** (from Part III, line 38)				
28	Other items with no differences				
29a	Mixed groups, see instructions. All others, combine lines 26 through 28				
b	PC insurance subgroup reconciliation totals . . .				
c	Life insurance subgroup reconciliation totals . . .				
30	**Reconciliation totals.** Combine lines 29a through 29c				

Note. Line 30, column (a), must equal Part I, line 11, and column (d) must equal Form 1120, page 1, line 28.

Schedule M-3 (Form 1120) 2014

Schedule M-3 (Form 1120) 2014 Page 3

Name of corporation (common parent, if consolidated return)	Employer identification number

Check applicable box(es): (1) ☐ Consolidated group (2) ☐ Parent corp (3) ☐ Consolidated eliminations (4) ☐ Subsidiary corp (5) ☐ Mixed 1120/L/PC group

Check if a sub-consolidated: (6) ☐ 1120 group (7) ☐ 1120 eliminations

Name of subsidiary (if consolidated return)	Employer identification number

Part III Reconciliation of Net Income (Loss) per Income Statement of Includible Corporations With Taxable Income per Return—Expense/Deduction Items (see instructions)

Expense/Deduction Items	(a) Expense per Income Statement	(b) Temporary Difference	(c) Permanent Difference	(d) Deduction per Tax Return
1 U.S. current income tax expense				
2 U.S. deferred income tax expense				
3 State and local current income tax expense				
4 State and local deferred income tax expense				
5 Foreign current income tax expense (other than foreign withholding taxes)				
6 Foreign deferred income tax expense				
7 Foreign withholding taxes				
8 Interest expense (see instructions)				
9 Stock option expense				
10 Other equity-based compensation				
11 Meals and entertainment				
12 Fines and penalties				
13 Judgments, damages, awards, and similar costs				
14 Parachute payments				
15 Compensation with section 162(m) limitation				
16 Pension and profit-sharing				
17 Other post-retirement benefits				
18 Deferred compensation				
19 Charitable contribution of cash and tangible property				
20 Charitable contribution of intangible property				
21 Charitable contribution limitation/carryforward				
22 Domestic production activities deduction				
23 Current year acquisition or reorganization investment banking fees				
24 Current year acquisition or reorganization legal and accounting fees				
25 Current year acquisition/reorganization other costs				
26 Amortization/impairment of goodwill				
27 Amortization of acquisition, reorganization, and start-up costs				
28 Other amortization or impairment write-offs				
29 Reserved				
30 Depletion				
31 Depreciation				
32 Bad debt expense				
33 Corporate owned life insurance premiums				
34 Purchase versus lease (for purchasers and/or lessees)				
35 Research and development costs				
36 Section 118 exclusion (attach statement)				
37 Other expense/deduction items with differences (attach statement)				
38 **Total expense/deduction items.** Combine lines 1 through 37. Enter here and on Part II, line 27, reporting positive amounts as negative and negative amounts as positive				

Schedule M-3 (Form 1120) 2014

Form **706** (Rev. August 2013)
Department of the Treasury
Internal Revenue Service

United States Estate (and Generation-Skipping Transfer) Tax Return

▶ Estate of a citizen or resident of the United States (see instructions). To be filed for decedents dying after December 31, 2012.
▶ Information about Form 706 and its separate instructions is at *www.irs.gov/form706*.

OMB No. 1545-0015

Part 1—Decedent and Executor

1a Decedent's first name and middle initial (and maiden name, if any)	1b Decedent's last name		2 Decedent's social security no.
3a City, town, or post office; county; state or province; country; and ZIP or foreign postal code.	3b Year domicile established	4 Date of birth	5 Date of death
6a Name of executor (see instructions)	6b Executor's address (number and street including apartment or suite no.; city, town, or post office; state or province; country; and ZIP or foreign postal code) and phone no.		
6c Executor's social security number (see instructions)	Phone no.		

6d If there are multiple executors, check here ☐ and attach a list showing the names, addresses, telephone numbers, and SSNs of the additional executors.

7a Name and location of court where will was probated or estate administered	7b Case number

8 If decedent died testate, check here ▶ ☐ and attach a certified copy of the will. 9 If you extended the time to file this Form 706, check here ▶ ☐

10 If Schedule R-1 is attached, check here ▶ ☐ 11 If you are estimating the value of assets included in the gross estate on line 1 pursuant to the special rule of Reg. section 20.2010-2T(a) (7)(ii), check here ▶ ☐

Part 2—Tax Computation

1	Total gross estate less exclusion (from Part 5—Recapitulation, item 13)			1	
2	Tentative total allowable deductions (from Part 5—Recapitulation, item 24)			2	
3a	Tentative taxable estate (subtract line 2 from line 1)			3a	
b	State death tax deduction			3b	
c	Taxable estate (subtract line 3b from line 3a)			3c	
4	Adjusted taxable gifts (see instructions)			4	
5	Add lines 3c and 4			5	
6	Tentative tax on the amount on line 5 from Table A in the instructions			6	
7	Total gift tax paid or payable (see instructions)			7	
8	Gross estate tax (subtract line 7 from line 6)			8	
9a	Basic exclusion amount	9a			
9b	Deceased spousal unused exclusion (DSUE) amount from predeceased spouse(s), if any (from Section D, Part 6—Portability of Deceased Spousal Unused Exclusion)	9b			
9c	Applicable exclusion amount (add lines 9a and 9b)	9c			
9d	Applicable credit amount (tentative tax on the amount in 9c from Table A in the instructions)	9d			
10	Adjustment to applicable credit amount (May not exceed $6,000. See instructions.)	10			
11	Allowable applicable credit amount (subtract line 10 from line 9d)			11	
12	Subtract line 11 from line 8 (but do not enter less than zero)			12	
13	Credit for foreign death taxes (from Schedule P). (Attach Form(s) 706-CE.)	13			
14	Credit for tax on prior transfers (from Schedule Q)	14			
15	Total credits (add lines 13 and 14)			15	
16	Net estate tax (subtract line 15 from line 12)			16	
17	Generation-skipping transfer (GST) taxes payable (from Schedule R, Part 2, line 10)			17	
18	Total transfer taxes (add lines 16 and 17)			18	
19	Prior payments (explain in an attached statement)			19	
20	Balance due (or overpayment) (subtract line 19 from line 18)			20	

Under penalties of perjury, I declare that I have examined this return, including accompanying schedules and statements, and to the best of my knowledge and belief, it is true, correct, and complete. Declaration of preparer other than the executor is based on all information of which preparer has any knowledge.

Sign Here

▶ Signature of executor ▶ Date

▶ Signature of executor ▶ Date

Paid Preparer Use Only

Print/Type preparer's name	Preparer's signature	Date	Check ☐ if self-employed	PTIN
Firm's name ▶			Firm's EIN ▶	
Firm's address ▶			Phone no.	

Form 706 (Rev. 8-2013)

Estate of:	Decedent's social security number

Part 3—Elections by the Executor

Note. For information on electing portability of the decedent's DSUE amount, including how to opt out of the election, see Part 6—Portability of Deceased Spousal Unused Exclusion.

Note. Some of the following elections may require the posting of bonds or liens.

Please check "Yes" or "No" box for each question (see instructions).

			Yes	No
1	Do you elect alternate valuation?	1		
2	Do you elect special-use valuation? If "Yes," you must complete and attach Schedule A-1	2		
3	Do you elect to pay the taxes in installments as described in section 6166? If "Yes," you must attach the additional information described in the instructions. **Note. By electing section 6166 installment payments, you may be required to provide security for estate tax deferred under section 6166 and interest in the form of a surety bond or a section 6324A lien.**	3		
4	Do you elect to postpone the part of the taxes due to a reversionary or remainder interest as described in section 6163?	4		

Part 4—General Information

Note. Please attach the necessary supplemental documents. **You must attach the death certificate.** (See instructions)

Authorization to receive confidential tax information under Reg. section 601.504(b)(2)(i); to act as the estate's representative before the IRS; and to make written or oral presentations on behalf of the estate:

Name of representative (print or type)	State	Address (number, street, and room or suite no., city, state, and ZIP code)

I declare that I am the ☐ attorney/ ☐ certified public accountant/ ☐ enrolled agent (check the applicable box) for the executor. I am not under suspension or disbarment from practice before the Internal Revenue Service and am qualified to practice in the state shown above.

Signature	CAF number	Date	Telephone number

1 Death certificate number and issuing authority (attach a copy of the death certificate to this return).

2 Decedent's business or occupation. If retired, check here ▶ ☐ and state decedent's former business or occupation.

3a Marital status of the decedent at time of death:

☐ Married ☐ Widow/widower ☐ Single ☐ Legally separated ☐ Divorced

3b For all prior marriages, list the name and SSN of the former spouse, the date the marriage ended, and whether the marriage ended by annulment, divorce, or death. Attach additional statements of the same size if necessary.

4a Surviving spouse's name	4b Social security number	4c Amount received (see instructions)

5 Individuals (other than the surviving spouse), trusts, or other estates who receive benefits from the estate (do not include charitable beneficiaries shown in Schedule O) (see instructions).

Name of individual, trust, or estate receiving $5,000 or more	Identifying number	Relationship to decedent	Amount (see instructions)
All unascertainable beneficiaries and those who receive less than $5,000 ▶			
Total			

If you answer "Yes" to any of the following questions, you must attach additional information as described.		Yes	No
6	Is the estate filing a protective claim for refund? If "Yes," complete and attach two copies of Schedule PC for each claim.		
7	Does the gross estate contain any section 2044 property (qualified terminable interest property (QTIP) from a prior gift or estate)? (see instructions)		
8a	Have federal gift tax returns ever been filed? If "Yes," attach copies of the returns, if available, and furnish the following information:		
b	Period(s) covered / c Internal Revenue office(s) where filed		
9a	Was there any insurance on the decedent's life that is not included on the return as part of the gross estate?		
b	Did the decedent own any insurance on the life of another that is not included in the gross estate?		

Form 706 (Rev. 8-2013)

Estate of: | **Decedent's social security number**

Part 4—General Information *(continued)*

	If you answer "Yes" to any of the following questions, you must attach additional information as described.	Yes	No
10	Did the decedent at the time of death own any property as a joint tenant with right of survivorship in which **(a)** one or more of the other joint tenants was someone other than the decedent's spouse, and **(b)** less than the full value of the property is included on the return as part of the gross estate? If "Yes," you must complete and attach Schedule E		
11a	Did the decedent, at the time of death, own any interest in a partnership (for example, a family limited partnership), an unincorporated business, or a limited liability company; or own any stock in an inactive or closely held corporation?		
b	If "Yes," was the value of **any** interest owned (from above) discounted on this estate tax return? If "Yes," see the instructions on reporting the total accumulated or effective discounts taken on Schedule F or G		
12	Did the decedent make any transfer described in sections 2035, 2036, 2037, or 2038? (see instructions) If "Yes," you must complete and attach Schedule G		
13a	Were there in existence at the time of the decedent's death any trusts created by the decedent during his or her lifetime?		
b	Were there in existence at the time of the decedent's death any trusts not created by the decedent under which the decedent possessed any power, beneficial interest, or trusteeship?		
c	Was the decedent receiving income from a trust created after October 22, 1986, by a parent or grandparent?		
	If "Yes," was there a GST taxable termination (under section 2612) on the death of the decedent?		
d	If there was a GST taxable termination (under section 2612), attach a statement to explain. Provide a copy of the trust or will creating the trust, and give the name, address, and phone number of the current trustee(s).		
e	Did the decedent at any time during his or her lifetime transfer or sell an interest in a partnership, limited liability company, or closely held corporation to a trust described in lines 13a or 13b?		
	If "Yes," provide the EIN for this transferred/sold item. ▶		
14	Did the decedent ever possess, exercise, or release any general power of appointment? If "Yes," you must complete and attach Schedule H		
15	Did the decedent have an interest in or a signature or other authority over a financial account in a foreign country, such as a bank account, securities account, or other financial account?		
16	Was the decedent, immediately before death, receiving an annuity described in the "General" paragraph of the instructions for Schedule I or a private annuity? If "Yes," you must complete and attach Schedule I		
17	Was the decedent ever the beneficiary of a trust for which a deduction was claimed by the estate of a predeceased spouse under section 2056(b)(7) and which is not reported on this return? If "Yes," attach an explanation		

Part 5—Recapitulation.

Note. If estimating the value of one or more assets pursuant to the special rule of Reg. section 20.2010-2T(a)(7)(ii), enter on both lines 10 and 23 the amount noted in the instructions for the corresponding range of values. (See instructions for details.)

Item no.	Gross estate		Alternate value	Value at date of death
1	Schedule A—Real Estate	1		
2	Schedule B—Stocks and Bonds	2		
3	Schedule C—Mortgages, Notes, and Cash	3		
4	Schedule D—Insurance on the Decedent's Life (attach Form(s) 712)	4		
5	Schedule E—Jointly Owned Property (attach Form(s) 712 for life insurance)	5		
6	Schedule F—Other Miscellaneous Property (attach Form(s) 712 for life insurance)	6		
7	Schedule G—Transfers During Decedent's Life (att. Form(s) 712 for life insurance)	7		
8	Schedule H—Powers of Appointment	8		
9	Schedule I—Annuities	9		
10	Estimated value of assets subject to the special rule of Reg. section 20.2010-2T(a)(7)(ii)	10		
11	Total gross estate (add items 1 through 10)	11		
12	Schedule U—Qualified Conservation Easement Exclusion	12		
13	Total gross estate less exclusion (subtract item 12 from item 11). Enter here and on line 1 of Part 2—Tax Computation	13		

Item no.	Deductions		Amount
14	Schedule J—Funeral Expenses and Expenses Incurred in Administering Property Subject to Claims	14	
15	Schedule K—Debts of the Decedent	15	
16	Schedule K—Mortgages and Liens	16	
17	Total of items 14 through 16	17	
18	Allowable amount of deductions from item 17 (see the instructions for item 18 of the Recapitulation)	18	
19	Schedule L—Net Losses During Administration	19	
20	Schedule L—Expenses Incurred in Administering Property Not Subject to Claims	20	
21	Schedule M—Bequests, etc., to Surviving Spouse	21	
22	Schedule O—Charitable, Public, and Similar Gifts and Bequests	22	
23	Estimated value of deductible assets subject to the special rule of Reg. section 20.2010-2T(a)(7)(ii)	23	
24	Tentative total allowable deductions (add items 18 through 23). Enter here and on line 2 of the Tax Computation	24	

Form **709**

Department of the Treasury
Internal Revenue Service

United States Gift (and Generation-Skipping Transfer) Tax Return

▶ Information about Form 709 and its separate instructions is at *www.irs.gov/form709.*

(For gifts made during calendar year 2014)
▶ **See instructions.**

OMB No. 1545-0020

2014

Part 1—General Information

1 Donor's first name and middle initial	2 Donor's last name	3 Donor's social security number
4 Address (number, street, and apartment number)		5 Legal residence (domicile)
6 City or town, state or province, country, and ZIP or foreign postal code		7 Citizenship (see instructions)

		Yes	No
8	If the donor died during the year, check here ▶ ☐ and enter date of death ____________ , ______.		
9	If you extended the time to file this Form 709, check here ▶ ☐		
10	Enter the total number of donees listed on Schedule A. Count each person only once ▶		
11a	Have you (the donor) previously filed a Form 709 (or 709-A) for any other year? If "No," skip line 11b		
b	Has your address changed since you last filed Form 709 (or 709-A)?		
12	**Gifts by husband or wife to third parties.** Do you consent to have the gifts (including generation-skipping transfers) made by you and by your spouse to third parties during the calendar year considered as made one-half by each of you? (see instructions.) (If the answer is "Yes," the following information must be furnished and your spouse must sign the consent shown below. **If the answer is "No," skip lines 13–18.**)		
13	Name of consenting spouse — 14 SSN		
15	Were you married to one another during the entire calendar year? (see instructions)		
16	If 15 is "No," check whether ☐ married ☐ divorced or ☐ widowed/deceased, and give date (see instructions) ▶		
17	Will a gift tax return for this year be filed by your spouse? (If "Yes," mail both returns in the same envelope.)		
18	**Consent of Spouse.** I consent to have the gifts (and generation-skipping transfers) made by me and by my spouse to third parties during the calendar year considered as made one-half by each of us. We are both aware of the joint and several liability for tax created by the execution of this consent.		
	Consenting spouse's signature ▶ **Date ▶**		
19	Have you applied a DSUE amount received from a predeceased spouse to a gift or gifts reported on this or a previous Form 709? If "Yes," complete Schedule C		

Part 2—Tax Computation

1	Enter the amount from Schedule A, Part 4, line 11	1	
2	Enter the amount from Schedule B, line 3	2	
3	Total taxable gifts. Add lines 1 and 2	3	
4	Tax computed on amount on line 3 (see *Table for Computing Gift Tax* in instructions)	4	
5	Tax computed on amount on line 2 (see *Table for Computing Gift Tax* in instructions)	5	
6	Balance. Subtract line 5 from line 4	6	
7	Applicable credit amount. If donor has DSUE amount from predeceased spouse(s), enter amount from Schedule C, line 4; otherwise, see instructions	7	
8	Enter the applicable credit against tax allowable for all prior periods (from Sch. B, line 1, col. C) .	8	
9	Balance. Subtract line 8 from line 7. Do not enter less than zero	9	
10	Enter 20% (.20) of the amount allowed as a specific exemption for gifts made after September 8, 1976, and before January 1, 1977 (see instructions)	10	
11	Balance. Subtract line 10 from line 9. Do not enter less than zero	11	
12	Applicable credit. Enter the smaller of line 6 or line 11	12	
13	Credit for foreign gift taxes (see instructions)	13	
14	Total credits. Add lines 12 and 13	14	
15	Balance. Subtract line 14 from line 6. Do not enter less than zero	15	
16	Generation-skipping transfer taxes (from Schedule D, Part 3, col. H, Total)	16	
17	Total tax. Add lines 15 and 16	17	
18	Gift and generation-skipping transfer taxes prepaid with extension of time to file	18	
19	If line 18 is less than line 17, enter **balance due** (see instructions)	19	
20	If line 18 is greater than line 17, enter **amount to be refunded**	20	

Attach check or money order here.

Sign Here

Under penalties of perjury, I declare that I have examined this return, including any accompanying schedules and statements, and to the best of my knowledge and belief, it is true, correct, and complete. Declaration of preparer (other than donor) is based on all information of which preparer has any knowledge.

May the IRS discuss this return with the preparer shown below (see instructions)? ☐ Yes ☐ No

Signature of donor | Date

Paid Preparer Use Only

Print/Type preparer's name	Preparer's signature	Date	Check ☐ if self-employed	PTIN
Firm's name ▶			Firm's EIN ▶	
Firm's address ▶			Phone no.	

For Disclosure, Privacy Act, and Paperwork Reduction Act Notice, see the instructions for this form. Cat. No. 16783M Form **709** (2014)

SCHEDULE A Computation of Taxable Gifts (Including transfers in trust) (see instructions)

A Does the value of any item listed on Schedule A reflect any valuation discount? If "Yes," attach explanation . . . . Yes ☐ No ☐

B ☐ ◄ Check here if you elect under section 529(c)(2)(B) to treat any transfers made this year to a qualified tuition program as made ratably over a 5-year period beginning this year. See instructions. Attach explanation.

Part 1—Gifts Subject Only to Gift Tax. Gifts less political organization, medical, and educational exclusions. (see instructions)

A Item number	B • Donee's name and address • Relationship to donor (if any) • Description of gift • If the gift was of securities, give CUSIP no. • If closely held entity, give EIN	C	D Donor's adjusted basis of gift	E Date of gift	F Value at date of gift	G For split gifts, enter 1/2 of column F	H Net transfer (subtract col. G from col. F)
1							
Gifts made by spouse —*complete **only** if you are splitting gifts with your spouse and he/she also made gifts.*							

Total of Part 1. Add amounts from Part 1, column H . . . . ►

Part 2—Direct Skips. Gifts that are direct skips and are subject to both gift tax and generation-skipping transfer tax. You must list the gifts in chronological order.

A Item number	B • Donee's name and address • Relationship to donor (if any) • Description of gift • If the gift was of securities, give CUSIP no. • If closely held entity, give EIN	C 2632(b) election out	D Donor's adjusted basis of gift	E Date of gift	F Value at date of gift	G For split gifts, enter 1/2 of column F	H Net transfer (subtract col. G from col. F)
1							
Gifts made by spouse —*complete **only** if you are splitting gifts with your spouse and he/she also made gifts.*							

Total of Part 2. Add amounts from Part 2, column H . . . . ►

Part 3—Indirect Skips. Gifts to trusts that are currently subject to gift tax and may later be subject to generation-skipping transfer tax. You must list these gifts in chronological order.

A Item number	B • Donee's name and address • Relationship to donor (if any) • Description of gift • If the gift was of securities, give CUSIP no. • If closely held entity, give EIN	C 2632(c) election	D Donor's adjusted basis of gift	E Date of gift	F Value at date of gift	G For split gifts, enter 1/2 of column F	H Net transfer (subtract col. G from col. F)
1							
Gifts made by spouse —*complete **only** if you are splitting gifts with your spouse and he/she also made gifts.*							

Total of Part 3. Add amounts from Part 3, column H . . . . ►

(If more space is needed, attach additional statements.)

Part 4—Taxable Gift Reconciliation

1	Total value of gifts of donor. Add totals from column H of Parts 1, 2, and 3		1	
2	Total annual exclusions for gifts listed on line 1 (see instructions)		2	
3	Total included amount of gifts. Subtract line 2 from line 1		3	
Deductions (see instructions)				
4	Gifts of interests to spouse for which a marital deduction will be claimed, based on item numbers ______________ of Schedule A	4		
5	Exclusions attributable to gifts on line 4	5		
6	Marital deduction. Subtract line 5 from line 4	6		
7	Charitable deduction, based on item nos. ________ less exclusions	7		
8	Total deductions. Add lines 6 and 7		8	
9	Subtract line 8 from line 3		9	
10	Generation-skipping transfer taxes payable with this Form 709 (from Schedule D, Part 3, col. H, Total)		10	
11	**Taxable gifts.** Add lines 9 and 10. Enter here and on page 1, Part 2—Tax Computation, line 1		11	

Terminable Interest (QTIP) Marital Deduction. (see instructions for Schedule A, Part 4, line 4)

If a trust (or other property) meets the requirements of qualified terminable interest property under section 2523(f), and:

a. The trust (or other property) is listed on Schedule A, and

b. The value of the trust (or other property) is entered in whole or in part as a deduction on Schedule A, Part 4, line 4, then the donor shall be deemed to have made an election to have such trust (or other property) treated as qualified terminable interest property under section 2523(f).

If less than the entire value of the trust (or other property) that the donor has included in Parts 1 and 3 of Schedule A is entered as a deduction on line 4, the donor shall be considered to have made an election only as to a fraction of the trust (or other property). The numerator of this fraction is equal to the amount of the trust (or other property) deducted on Schedule A, Part 4, line 6. The denominator is equal to the total value of the trust (or other property) listed in Parts 1 and 3 of Schedule A.

If you make the QTIP election, the terminable interest property involved will be included in your spouse's gross estate upon his or her death (section 2044). See instructions for line 4 of Schedule A. If your spouse disposes (by gift or otherwise) of all or part of the qualifying life income interest, he or she will be considered to have made a transfer of the entire property that is subject to the gift tax. See *Transfer of Certain Life Estates Received From Spouse* in the instructions.

12 Election Out of QTIP Treatment of Annuities

☐ ◀ Check here if you elect under section 2523(f)(6) **not** to treat as qualified terminable interest property any joint and survivor annuities that are reported on Schedule A and would otherwise be treated as qualified terminable interest property under section 2523(f). See instructions. Enter the item numbers from Schedule A for the annuities for which you are making this election ▶ ______________

SCHEDULE B Gifts From Prior Periods

If you answered "Yes," on line 11a of page 1, Part 1, see the instructions for completing Schedule B. If you answered "No," skip to the Tax Computation on page 1 (or Schedules C or D, if applicable). Complete Schedule A before beginning Schedule B. See instructions for recalculation of the column C amounts. Attach calculations.

A Calendar year or calendar quarter (see instructions)	B Internal Revenue office where prior return was filed	C Amount of applicable credit (unified credit) against gift tax for periods after December 31, 1976	D Amount of specific exemption for prior periods ending before January 1, 1977	E Amount of taxable gifts
1 Totals for prior periods	1			

2	Amount, if any, by which total specific exemption, line 1, column D is more than $30,000	2	
3	Total amount of taxable gifts for prior periods. Add amount on line 1, column E and amount, if any, on line 2. Enter here and on page 1, Part 2—Tax Computation, line 2	3	

(If more space is needed, attach additional statements.)

Form 709 (2014) Page 4

SCHEDULE C Deceased Spousal Unused Exclusion (DSUE) Amount

Provide the following information to determine the DSUE amount and applicable credit received from prior spouses. Complete Schedule A before beginning Schedule C.

A Name of Deceased Spouse (dates of death after December 31, 2010 only)	B Date of Death	C Portability Election Made? Yes	No	D If "Yes," DSUE Amount Received from Spouse	E DSUE Amount Applied by Donor to Lifetime Gifts (list current and prior gifts)	F Date of Gift(s) (enter as mm/dd/yy for Part 1 and as yyyy for Part 2)
Part 1—DSUE RECEIVED FROM LAST DECEASED SPOUSE						
Part 2—DSUE RECEIVED FROM PREDECEASED SPOUSE(S)						

TOTAL (for all DSUE amounts applied from column E for Part 1 and Part 2)

1	Donor's basic exclusion amount (see instructions)	1	
2	Total from column E, Parts 1 and 2	2	
3	Add lines 1 and 2	3	
4	Applicable credit on amount in line 3 (See *Table for Computing Gift Tax* in the instructions). Enter here and on line 7, Part 2—Tax Computation	4	

SCHEDULE D Computation of Generation-Skipping Transfer Tax

Note. Inter vivos direct skips that are completely excluded by the GST exemption must still be fully reported (including value and exemptions claimed) on Schedule D.

Part 1—Generation-Skipping Transfers

A Item No. (from Schedule A, Part 2, col. A)	B Value (from Schedule A, Part 2, col. H)	C Nontaxable Portion of Transfer	D Net Transfer (subtract col. C from col. B)
1			
Gifts made by spouse (for gift splitting only)			

(If more space is needed, attach additional statements.)

Form **709** (2014)

Appendix B

Tax Terms Glossary

§83(b) election a special tax election that employees who receive restricted stock or other property with ownership restrictions can make to accelerate income recognition from the normal date when restrictions lapse to the date when the restricted stock or other property is granted. The election also accelerates the employer's compensation deduction related to the restricted stock or other property.

§1231 assets depreciable or real property used in a taxpayer's trade or business owned for more than one year.

§1231 look-back rule a tax rule requiring taxpayers to treat current year net §1231 gains as ordinary income when the taxpayer has deducted a §1231 loss as an ordinary loss in the five years preceding the current tax year.

§1245 property tangible personal property and intangible property subject to cost recovery deductions.

§1250 property real property subject to cost recovery deductions.

§162(m) limitation the $1 million deduction limit on nonperformance based salary paid to certain key executives.

§179 election an incentive for small businesses that allows them to immediately expense a certain amount of tangible personal property placed in service during the year.

§197 purchased intangibles intangible assets that are purchased that must be amortized over 180 months regardless of their actual useful lives.

§263A Cost (or UNICAP) certain book expenses that must be capitalized into inventory for tax purposes.

§291 depreciation recapture the portion of a corporate taxpayer's gain on real property that is converted from §1231 gain to ordinary income.

§338 election an election by a corporate buyer of 80-percent-or-more of a corporation's stock to treat the acquisition as an asset acquisition and not a stock acquisition.

§338(h)(10) election a joint election by the corporate buyer and corporate seller of the stock of a subsidiary of the seller to treat the acquisition as a sale of the subsidiary's assets by the seller to the buyer.

§481 adjustment a change to taxable income associated with a change in accounting methods.

§7520 rate an interest rate set at 120 percent of the applicable federal midterm rate (published monthly by the Treasury) and used to calculate the value of temporal interests.

12-month rule regulation that allows prepaid business expenses to be currently deducted when the contract does not extend beyond 12 months and the contract period does not extend beyond the end of the tax year following the year of the payment.

704(b) capital accounts partners' capital accounts maintained using the accounting rules prescribed in the Section 704(b) regulations. Under these rules, capital accounts reflect the fair market value of property contributed to and distributed property from partnerships.

A

Accelerated Cost Recovery System (ACRS) the depreciation system enacted by Congress in 1981 that is based on the concept of set recovery periods and accelerated depreciation methods.

Accounting method the procedure for determining the taxable year in which a business recognizes a particular item of income or deduction thereby dictating the timing of when a taxpayer reports income and deductions.

Accounting period a fixed period in which a business reports income and deductions, generally referred to as a tax year.

Accrual method a method of accounting that generally recognizes income in the period earned and recognizes deductions in the period that liabilities are incurred.

Accrued market discount a ratable amount of the market discount at the time of purchase (based on the number of days the bond is held over the number of days until maturity when the bond is purchased) that is treated as interest income when a bond with market discount is sold before it matures.

Accumulated adjustments account (AAA) an account that reflects the cumulative income or loss for the time the corporation has been an S corporation.

Accumulated earnings and profits undistributed earnings and profits from years prior to the current year.

Accumulated earnings tax a tax assessed on corporations that retain earnings without a business reason to do so.

Acquisition subsidiary a subsidiary used by the acquiring corporation in a triangular merger to acquire the target corporation.

Active participant in a rental activity an individual who owns at least 10% of a rental property and participates in the process of making management decisions, such as approving new tenants, deciding on rental terms, and approving repairs and capital expenditures.

Ad valorem tax a tax based on the value of property.

Adjusted basis *see* adjusted tax basis.

Adjusted current earnings (ACE) a version of a corporation's current year earnings that more closely represents a corporation's economic income for the year than do regular taxable income or alternative minimum taxable income.

Adjusted gross estate gross estate reduced by administrative expenses, debts of the decedent, and losses, and state death taxes.

Adjusted tax basis the taxpayer's acquisition basis (for example, cost) plus capital improvements less depreciation or amortization.

Adjusted taxable gifts cumulative taxable gifts from previous years other than gifts already included in the gross estate valued at date of gift values.

Aggregate approach a theory of taxing partnerships that ignores partnerships as entities and taxes partners as if they directly owned partnership net assets.

All-events test requires that income or expenses are recognized when (1) all events have occurred that determine or fix the right to receive the income or liability to make the payments and (2) the amount of the income or expense can be determined with reasonable accuracy.

Allocate as used in the sourcing rules, the process of associating a deduction with a specific item or items of gross income for purposes of computing foreign source taxable income.

Allocation the method of dividing or sourcing nonbusiness income to specific states.

Allowance method bad debt expense is based on an estimate of the amount of the bad debts in accounts receivable at year-end.

Alternative minimum tax a tax on a broader tax base than the base for the "regular" tax; the additional tax paid when the tentative minimum tax (based on the alternative minimum tax base) exceeds the regular tax (based on the regular tax base). The alternative minimum tax is designed to require taxpayers to pay some minimum level of tax even when they have low or no regular taxable income as a result of certain tax breaks in the tax code.

Alternative minimum tax adjustments adjustments (positive or negative) to regular taxable income to arrive at the alternative minimum tax base.

Alternative minimum tax base (AMT base) alternative minimum taxable income minus the alternative minimum tax exemption.

Alternative minimum tax exemption a deduction to determine the alternative minimum tax base that is phased out based on alternative minimum taxable income.

Alternative minimum tax system a secondary or parallel tax system calculated on an *alternative* tax base that more closely reflects economic income than the regular income tax base. The system was designed to ensure that taxpayers generating economic income pay some *minimum* amount of income tax each year.

Alternative valuation date the date nine months after the decedent's date of death.

Amortization the method of recovering the cost of intangible assets over a specific time period.

Amount realized the value of everything received by the seller in a transaction (cash, FMV of other property, and relief of liabilities) less selling costs.

Annual exclusion amount of gifts allowed to be made each year per donee (regardless of the number of donees) to prevent the taxation of relatively small gifts ($14,000 per donee per year in 2014).

Annualized income method a method for determining a corporation's required estimated tax payments when the taxpayer earns more income later in the year than earlier in the year. Requires corporations to base their first and second required estimated tax installments on their income from the first three months of the year, their third installment based on their taxable income from the first six months of the year, and the final installment based on their taxable income from the first nine months of the year.

Applicable tax rate the tax rate or rates used to measure a company's deferred tax asset or liability. In general, it is the enacted tax rate that is expected to apply to taxable income in the period in which the deferred tax asset or liability is expected to be recovered or settled. For U.S. tax purposes, the applicable tax rate is the regular tax rate.

Apportion as used in the sourcing rules, the process of calculating the amount of a deduction that is associated with a specific item or items of gross income for purposes of computing foreign source taxable income.

Apportionment the method of dividing business income of an interstate business among the states where nexus exists.

Arm's-length amount price in transactions among unrelated taxpayers, where each transacting party negotiates for his or her own benefit.

Arm's-length transaction transactions among unrelated taxpayers, where each transacting party negotiates for his or her own benefit.

Articles of incorporation a document, filed by a corporation's founders with the state describing the purpose, place of business, and other details of the corporation.

Articles of organization a document, filed by a limited liability company's founders with the state, describing the purpose, place of business, and other details of the company.

Asset and liability approach the approach taken by ASC Topic 740 that focuses on computing a company's current taxes payable (refundable) and deferred tax assets and liabilities on the balance sheet. The income tax provision recorded on the income statement is the amount needed to adjust the beginning of the year balance sheet amounts to the end of the year balance sheet amounts.

Assignment of income doctrine the judicial doctrine holding that earned income is taxed to the taxpayer providing the service, and that income from property is taxed to the individual who owns the property when the income accrues.

At-risk amount an investor's risk of loss in a worst-case scenario. In a partnership, an amount generally equal to a partner's tax basis exclusive of the partner's share of nonrecourse debt.

At-risk rules tax rules limiting losses flowing through to partners or S corporation shareholders to their at-risk amount.

B

Bargain element (of stock options) the difference between the fair market value of the employer's stock and the amount employees pay to acquire the employer's stock.

Beneficiary person for whom trust property is held and administered.

Bonus depreciation additional depreciation allowed in the acquisition year for new tangible personal property with a recovery period of 20 years or less.

Book equivalent of taxable income a company's pretax income from continuing operations adjusted for permanent differences.

Book or financial reporting income the income or loss corporations report on their financial statements using applicable financial accounting standards.

Book–tax difference a difference in the amount of an income item or deduction item taken into account for book purposes compared to the amount taken into account for the same item for tax purposes.

Boot property given or received in an otherwise nontaxable transaction such as a like-kind exchange that may trigger gain to a party to the transaction.

Branch an unincorporated division of a corporation.

Bright line tests technical rules found in the tax law that provide the taxpayer with objective tests to determine the tax consequences of a transaction.

Brother-sister controlled group a form of controlled group consisting of two or more corporations if five or fewer individuals collectively own more than 50 percent of the voting power or stock value of the corporation on the last day of the year.

Built-in gain the difference between the fair market value and tax basis of property owned by an entity when the fair market value exceeds the tax basis.

Built-in gains tax a tax levied on S corporations that were formerly C corporations. The tax applies to net unrealized built-in gains at the time the corporation converted from a C corporation to the extent the gains are recognized during the built-in gains tax recognition period. The applicable tax rate is 35 percent.

Built-in gains tax recognition period the first 5 years a corporation operates as an S corporation after converting from a C corporation for asset sales in 2011, 2012, and 2013 (first 7 years for asset sales in 2009 and 2010; first 10 years for assets sales in other years).

Built-in loss the difference between the fair market value and tax basis of property owned by an entity when the tax basis exceeds the fair market value.

Business activity a profit-motivated activity that requires a relatively high level of involvement or effort from the taxpayer to generate income.

Business income income derived from business activities.

Business purpose doctrine the judicial doctrine that allows the IRS to challenge and disallow business expenses for transactions with no underlying business motivation.

Business tax credits nonrefundable credits designed to provide incentives for taxpayers to hire certain types of individuals or to participate in certain business activities.

Bypass provision a provision in the will of a deceased spouse that transfers property to nonspousal beneficiaries to maximize the value of the decedent's unified credit.

Bypass trust a trust used in lieu of a bypass provision to transfer property to nonspousal beneficiaries to maximize the value of the unified credit of the first spouse to die.

C

C corporation a corporate taxpaying entity with income subject to taxation. Such a corporation is termed a "C" corporation because the corporation and its shareholders are subject to the provisions of subchapter C of the Internal Revenue Code.

Capital account an account reflecting a partner's share of the equity in a partnership. Capital accounts are maintained using tax accounting methods or other methods of accounting, including GAAP, at the discretion of the partnership.

Capital asset in general, an asset other than an asset used in a trade or business or an asset such as an account or note receivable acquired in a business from the sale of services or property.

Capital gain property any asset that would have generated a long-term capital gain if the taxpayer had sold the property for its fair market value.

Capital interest an economic right attached to a partnership interest giving a partner the right to receive cash or property in the event the partnership liquidates. A capital interest is synonymous with the liquidation value of a partnership interest.

Capital loss carryback the amount of a corporation's net capital loss from one year that it uses to offset net capital gains in any of the three preceding tax years.

Capital loss carryover the amount of a corporation's or an individual's net capital loss from one year that it may use to offset net capital gains in future years.

Capitalization recording an expenditure as an asset on the balance sheet rather than expensing it immediately.

Carryover basis the basis of an asset the transferee takes in property received in a nontaxable exchange. The basis of the asset carries over from the transferor to the transferee.

Cash method the method of accounting that recognizes income in the period in which cash, property, or services are received and recognizes deductions in the period paid.

Cash surrender value the amount, if any, the owner of a life insurance policy receives when the policy is cashed in before the death of the insured individual.

Cash tax rate the tax rate computed by dividing a company's taxes paid during the year by its pretax income from continuing operations.

Certificate of deposit an interest-bearing debt instrument offered by banks and savings and loans. Money removed from the CD before maturity is subject to a penalty.

Certificate of limited partnership a document limited partnerships must file with the state to be formerly recognized by the state. The document is similar to articles of incorporation or articles or organization.

Character of income determines the rate at which income will be taxed. Common income characters (or types of income) include tax-exempt, ordinary, and capital.

Charitable contribution deduction modified taxable income taxable income for purposes of determining the 10% of taxable income deduction limitation for corporate charitable contributions. Computed as taxable income before deducting (1) any charitable contributions, (2) the dividends received deduction, (3) net operating loss carrybacks, and (4) the domestic production activities deduction.

Combined controlled group a form of a controlled group consisting of three or more corporations each of which is a member of either a parent-subsidiary or brother-sister controlled group and one of the corporations is the parent in the parent-subsidiary controlled group and also is in a brother-sister controlled group.

Commercial domicile the state where a business is headquartered and directs operations; this location may be different from the place of incorporation.

Commercial traveler exception a statutory exception that exempts nonresidents from U.S. taxation of compensation from services if the individual is in the United States 90 days or less and earns compensation of $3,000 or less.

Common-law states the 41 states that have not adopted community property laws.

Community-property states nine states (Arizona, California, Idaho, Louisiana, Nevada, New Mexico, Texas, Washington, and Wisconsin) that automatically equally divide the ownership of property acquired by either spouse during a marriage.

Community property systems systems in which state laws dictate how the income and property is legally shared between a husband and a wife.

Complex trust a trust that is not required by the trust instrument to distribute income currently.

Conglomerate a group of corporations in different businesses under common ownership.

Consolidation the combining of the assets and liabilities of two or more corporations into a new entity.

Constructive dividend a payment made by a corporation to a shareholder that is recharacterized by the IRS or courts as a dividend even though it is not characterized as such by the corporation.

Constructive ownership rules that cause stock not owned by a taxpayer to be treated as owned by the taxpayer for purposes of meeting certain stock ownership tests.

Constructive receipt doctrine the judicial doctrine that provides that a taxpayer must recognize income when it is actually or constructively received. Constructive receipt is deemed to have occurred if the income has been credited to the taxpayer's account or if the income is unconditionally available to the taxpayer, the taxpayer is aware of the income's availability, and there are no restrictions on the taxpayer's control over the income.

Continuity of business enterprise (COBE) a judicial (now regulatory) requirement that the acquiring corporation continue the target corporation's historic business or continue to use a "significant" portion of the target corporation's historic business assets to be tax-deferred.

Continuity of interest (COI) a judicial (now regulatory) requirement that the transferors of stock in a reorganization collectively retain a continuing ownership (equity) interest in the target corporation's assets or historic business to be tax-deferred.

Contribution to capital a shareholder's or other person's contribution of cash or other property to a corporation without receipt of an additional equity interest in the corporation.

Controlled foreign corporation a foreign corporation that is more than 50 percent owned by U.S. shareholders.

Controlled group a group of corporations owned by the same individual shareholders; it can either be brother-sister corporations or parent-subsidiary corporations.

Corporation business entities recognized as separate entities from their owners under state law.

Corpus the principal or property transferred to fund a trust or accumulated in the trust.

Cost depletion the method of recovering the cost of a natural resource that allows a taxpayer to estimate or determine the number of units that remain in the resource at the beginning of the year and allocate a pro rata share of the remaining basis to each unit of the resource that is extracted or sold during the year.

Cost recovery the method by which a company expenses the cost of acquiring capital assets. Cost recovery can take the form of depreciation, amortization, or depletion.

Coupon rate the interest rate expressed as a percentage of the face value of the bond.

Covenant not to compete a contractual promise to refrain from conducting business or professional activities similar to those of another party.

Current earnings and profits a year-to-year calculation maintained by a corporation to determine if a distribution is a dividend. Earnings and profits is computed for the current year by adjusting taxable income to make it more closely resemble economic income.

Current gifts gifts completed during the calendar year that are not already exempted from the gift tax.

Current income tax expense or benefit the amount of taxes paid or payable (refundable) in the current year.

Current tax liability or asset the amount of taxes payable or refundable in the current year.

D

Debt basis the outstanding principal of direct loans from an S corporation shareholder to the S corporation. Once taxpayers deduct losses to the extent of their stock basis, they may deduct losses to the extent of their debt basis. When the debt basis has been reduced by losses, it is restored by income/gain allocations.

Deductible temporary differences book-tax differences that will result in tax deductible amounts in future years when the related deferred tax asset is recovered.

Deferral items, deferred income, or deferrals realized income that will be taxed as income in a subsequent year.

Deferral method recognizes income from advance payments for goods by the earlier of (1) when the business would recognize the income for tax purposes if it had not received the *advance* payment or (2) when it recognizes the income for financial reporting purposes.

Deferred like-kind exchange a like-kind exchange where the taxpayer transfers like-kind property before receiving the like-kind property in exchange. The property to be received must be identified within 45 days and received within 180 days of the transfer of the property given up.

Deferred tax asset the expected future tax benefit attributable to deductible temporary differences and carryforwards.

Deferred tax liability the expected future tax cost attributable to taxable temporary differences.

Defined benefit plan employer-provided qualified plans that spell out the specific benefit employees will receive on retirement.

Defined contribution plan employer-provided qualified plans that specify the maximum annual contributions employers and/or employees may contribute to the plan.

Definitely related deductions deductions that are associated with the creation of a specific item or items of gross income.

Depletion the cost recovery method to allocate the cost of natural resources as they are removed.

Depreciation the cost recovery method to allocate the cost of tangible personal and real property over a specific time period.

Depreciation recapture the conversion of §1231 gain into ordinary income on a sale (or exchange) based on the amount of accumulated depreciation on the property at the time of sale or exchange.

Direct conversion when a taxpayer receives noncash property as a replacement for property damaged or destroyed in an involuntary conversion rather than a cash payment.

Direct write-off method required method for deducting bad debts for tax purposes. Under this method, businesses deduct bad debt only when the debt becomes wholly or partially worthless.

Disproportionate distributions partnership distributions that change the partners' relative ownership of hot assets.

Disregarded entities unincorporated entities with one owner that are treated as flow-through entities for U.S. income tax purposes.

Dividends distributions to shareholders of money or property from the corporation's earnings and profits.

Dividends received deduction a corporate deduction for part or all of a dividend received from other taxable, domestic corporations.

Document perfection program a program under which all tax returns are checked for mathematical and tax calculation errors.

Domestic production activities deduction (DPAD) a deduction for businesses that manufacture goods in the United States.

Donee person receiving a gift.

Donor person making a gift.

Double taxation the tax burden when an entity's income is subject to two levels of tax. Income of C corporations is subject to double taxation. The first level of tax is at the corporate level and the second level of tax on corporate income occurs at the shareholder level. Income of flow-through entities is generally not subject to double taxation.

DRD modified taxable income taxable income for purposes of applying the taxable income limitation for the dividends received deduction. Computed as the dividend receiving corporation's taxable income before deducting the dividends received deduction, any net operating loss deduction, the domestic production activities deduction, and capital loss carrybacks.

E

Earnings and profits a measure of a corporation's earnings that is similar to its economic earnings. Corporate dividends are taxable to shareholders to the extent they come from earnings and profits.

Economic nexus the concept that businesses without a physical presence in the state may establish income tax nexus in the state through an economic presence there.

Enacted tax rate the statutory tax rate that will apply in the current or a future period.

Entity approach a theory of taxing partnerships that treats partnerships as entities separate from partners.

Estate fiduciary legal entity that comes into existence upon a person's death and is empowered by the probate court to gather and transfer the decedent's real and personal property.

Excess net passive income net passive investment income × passive investment income in excess of 25% of the S corporation's gross receipts divided by its passive investment income.

Excess net passive income tax a tax levied on an S corporation that has accumulated earnings and profits from years in which it operated as a C corporation if the corporation reports excess net passive income.

Exchanged basis the basis of an asset received in a nontaxable exchange. An exchanged basis is generally the basis of the asset given up in a nontaxable exchange. Exchanged basis may also be referred to as a *substituted basis.*

Executor the person who takes responsibility for collecting the assets of the decedent, paying the decedent's debts, and distributing the remaining assets to the rightful heirs.

Exemption equivalent the amount of cumulative taxable transfers a taxpayer can make without exceeding the unified credit.

Exercise date the date employees use their stock options to acquire employer stock at a discounted price.

Exercise price the price at which holders of stock options may purchase stock in the corporation issuing the option.

F

Family limited partnership a partnership designed to save estate taxes by dividing a family business into various ownership interests representing control of operations and future income and appreciation of the assets.

Favorable book-tax difference a book-tax difference that requires a subtraction from book income in determining taxable income.

Federal/state adjustments amounts added to or subtracted from federal taxable income when firms compute taxable income for a particular state.

Federal short-term interest rate the quarterly interest rate used to determine the interest charged for tax underpayments (federal short-term rate plus 3 percent).

Fiduciary a person or legal entity that takes possession of property for the benefit of beneficiaries.

Fiduciary duty a requirement that a fiduciary act in an objective and impartial manner and not favor one beneficiary over another.

FIFO *see* first-in, first-out (FIFO) method.

Fiscal year a year that ends on a day other than December 31.

First-in, first-out (FIFO) method an accounting method that values the cost of assets sold under the assumption that the assets are sold in the order purchased (i.e., first purchased, first sold).

Fixed and determinable, annual or periodic income U.S. source passive income earned by a nonresident.

Flat tax a tax in which a single tax rate is applied throughout the tax base.

Flexible spending account a plan that allows employees to contribute before-tax dollars that may be used for unreimbursed medical expenses or dependent care.

Flipping a term used to describe the real estate investment practice of acquiring a home, repairing or remodeling the home, and then immediately, or soon thereafter, selling it (presumably at a profit).

Floor limitation a minimum amount that an expenditure (or credit or other adjustment to taxable income) must meet before any amount is allowed.

Flow-through entities legal entities like partnerships, limited liability companies, and S corporations that do not pay income tax. Income and losses from flow-through entities are allocated to their owners.

Foreign joint venture a 50 percent or less owned foreign entity.

Foreign personal holding company income a category of foreign source passive income that includes interest, dividends, rents, royalties, and gains from sale of assets.

Foreign subsidiary a more than 50 percent owned foreign corporation.

Foreign tax credit a credit for income taxes paid to a foreign jurisdiction.

Foreign tax credit limitation the limit put on the use of creditable foreign taxes for the current year.

Form 1065 the form partnerships file annually with the IRS to report partnership ordinary income (loss) and separately stated items for the year.

Form 1120S the form S corporations file annually with the IRS to report S corporation ordinary income (loss) and separately stated items for the year.

Form 7004 the form C corporations, partnerships, and S corporations file to receive an automatic extension to file their annual tax return.

Forward triangular merger an acquisition in which the acquired (target) corporation merges into an acquisition subsidiary of the acquiring corporation, after which the acquired corporation becomes part of the acquisition subsidiary of the acquiring corporation.

FTC basket a category of income that requires a separate FTC limitation computation.

Full-inclusion method the method for accounting for advance payments for goods that requires that businesses immediately recognize advance payments as taxable income.

Full-month convention a convention that allows owners of intangibles to deduct an entire month's amortization in the month of purchase and month of disposition.

Functional currency the currency of the primary economic environment in which an entity operates (that is the currency of the jurisdiction in which an entity primarily generates and expends cash).

Future interest the right to receive property in the future.

G

GAAP capital accounts partners' capital accounts maintained using generally accepted accounting principals.

General category income foreign source income that is not considered passive category income for foreign tax credit purposes (generally income from an active trade or business).

General partnership a partnership with partners who all have unlimited liability with respect to the liabilities of the entity.

Generation-skipping tax (GST) supplemental transfer tax designed to prevent the avoidance of estate and gift taxes through transfers that skip a generation of recipients.

Gift a transfer of property where no, or inadequate, consideration is paid for the property.

Golsen rule the rule that states that the U.S. Tax Court will abide by the circuit court's rulings that has appellate jurisdiction for a case.

Goodwill the value of an acquired business in excess of the fair market value of identifiable assets.

Grantor person creating a trust.

Gross estate property owned by the decedent at death and certain property transfers taking effect at death.

Gross income realized income reduced for any excluded or deferred income.

Gross receipts (for purposes of net passive investment income tax calculation) the total amount of revenues (including passive investment income) received or accrued under the corporation's accounting method, not reduced by returns, allowances, cost of goods sold, or deductions. Gross receipts include net capital gains from the sales or exchanges of capital assets and gains from the sales or exchanges of stock or securities (losses do not offset gains).

Group-term life insurance term life insurance provided by an employer to a group of employees.

Guaranteed payments payments made to partners or LLC members that are guaranteed because they are not contingent on partnership profits or losses. They are economically similar to shareholder salary payments.

H

Half-year convention a depreciation convention that allows owners of tangible personal property to take one-half of a year's worth of depreciation in the year of purchase and in the year of disposition regardless of when the asset was actually placed in service or sold.

Heirs persons who inherit property from the deceased.

Hot assets unrealized receivables or inventory items defined in §751(a) that give rise to ordinary gains and losses. The exact definition of hot assets depends on whether it is in reference to dispositions of a partnership interest or distributions.

Hybrid entity an entity for which an election is available to choose the entity's tax status for U.S. tax purposes.

I

Impermissible accounting method an accounting method prohibited by tax laws.

Indirect conversion the receipt of money or other property as a replacement for property that was destroyed or damaged in an involuntary conversion.

Inheritance a transfer of property when the owner is deceased (the transfer is made by the decedent's estate).

Initial public offering the first sale of stock by a company to the public.

Inside tax basis the tax basis of an entity's assets and liabilities.

Installment sale a sale for which the taxpayer receives payment in more than one period.

Institutional shareholder an entity with large amounts to invest in corporate stock, such as investment companies, mutual funds, brokerages, insurance companies, pension funds, investment banks, and endowment funds.

Intangible assets assets that do not have physical characteristics. Examples include goodwill, covenants not to compete, organizational expenditures, and research and experimentation expenses.

Interstate commerce business conducted between parties in two or more states.

Intervivos transfers gifts made by a donor during his or her lifetime.

Inventory items (for sale of partnership interest purposes) classic inventory defined as property held for sale to customers in the ordinary course of business, but also assets that are not capital assets or §1231 assets, which would produce ordinary income if sold by the entity. There are actually two definitions of inventory items in §751. §751(a) inventory items are defined in §751(d) to include all inventory items. The §751(b) definition includes only substantially appreciated inventory.

Investment interest expense interest paid on borrowings or loans that are used to fund portfolio investments. Individuals are allowed an itemized deduction for qualified investment interest paid during the year.

Involuntary conversion a direct or indirect conversion of property through natural disaster, government condemnation, or accident that allows a taxpayer to defer realized gain if certain requirements are met.

J

Joint tenancy with the right of survivorship title to property that provides the co-owners with equal rights to it and that automatically transfers to the survivor at the death of a co-owner.

L

Last will and testament the document that directs the transfer of ownership of the decedent's assets to the heirs.

Least aggregate deferral an approach to determine a partnership's required year-end if a majority of the partners don't have the same year-end and if the principal partners don't have the same year-end. As the name implies, this approach minimizes the combined tax deferral of the partners.

Life estate the right to possess property and/or collect income from property for the duration of someone's life.

Life insurance trust a trust funded with an irrevocable transfer of a life insurance policy and that gives the trustee the power to re-designate beneficiaries.

LIFO last-in, first-out method; an accounting method that values the cost of assets sold under the assumption that assets are sold in the reverse order in which they are purchased (i.e., last purchased, first sold).

LIFO recapture amount the excess of a C corporation's inventory basis under the FIFO method in excess of the inventory basis under the LIFO method in its final tax year as a C corporation before it becomes an S corporation.

LIFO recapture tax a tax levied on a C corporation that elects to be taxed as an S corporation when it is using the LIFO method for accounting for inventories.

Like-kind exchange a nontaxable (or partially taxable) trade or exchange of assets that are similar or related in use.

Limited liability company (LLC) a type of flow-through entity for federal income tax purposes. By state law, the owners of the LLC have limited liability with respect to the entity's debts or liabilities. Limited liability companies are taxed as partnerships for federal income tax purposes.

Limited partnership a partnership with at least one general partner with unlimited liability for the entity's debts and at least one limited partner with liability limited to the limited partner's investment in the partnership.

Liquidating distributions a distribution that terminates an owner's interest in the entity.

Liquidation value the amount a partner would receive if the partnership were to sell all its assets, pay its debts, and distribute its remaining assets to the partners in exchange for their partnership interests.

Listed property business assets that are often used for personal purposes. Depreciation on listed property is limited to the business use portion of the asset.

Long-term capital gain property property that would generate long-term capital gain if it were sold. This includes capital assets held for more than a year.

Long-term capital gains or losses gains or losses from the sale of capital assets held for more than 12 months.

Luxury automobile an automobile on which the amount of annual depreciation expense is limited because the cost of the automobile exceeds a certain threshold. The definition excludes vehicles with gross vehicle weight exceeding 6,000 pounds.

M

M adjustments *see* Schedule M adjustments.

Majority interest taxable year the common tax year of a group of partners who jointly hold greater than 50% of the profits and capital interests in the partnership.

Marital deduction the deduction for transfers of qualified property to a spouse.

Medicare tax the Medical Health Insurance (MHI) tax. This tax helps pay medical costs for qualifying individuals. The Medicare tax rate for employees is 1.45% on salary or wages up to $200,000 ($125,000 for married filing separate; $250,000 of combined salary or wages for married filing joint) and is 2.35% on salary or wages in excess of $200,000 ($125,000 for married filing separate; $250,000 of combined salary or wages for married filing joint). For employers, the Medicare tax rate is 1.45% of employee salary or wages, regardless of the amount of salary or wages. Self-employed taxpayers pay both the employee and employer Medicare tax.

Merger the acquisition by one (acquiring) corporation of the assets and liabilities of another (target) corporation. No new entity is created in the transaction.

Mid-month convention a convention that allows owners of real property to take one-half of a month's depreciation during the month when the property was placed in service and in the month it was disposed of.

Mid-quarter convention a depreciation convention for tangible personal property that allows for one-half of a quarter's worth of depreciation in the quarter of purchase and in the quarter of disposition. This convention must be used when more than 40% of tangible personal property is placed into service in the fourth quarter of the tax year.

Minimum tax credit credit available in certain situations for the alternative minimum tax paid. The credit can be used only when the regular tax exceeds the tentative minimum tax.

Modified Accelerated Cost Recovery System (MACRS) the current tax depreciation system for tangible personal and real property. Depreciation under MACRS is calculated by finding the depreciation method, the recovery period, and the applicable convention.

N

Negative basis adjustment (for special basis adjustment purposes) the sum of the recognized loss and the amount of the basis increase made by an owner receiving the distribution.

Net long-term capital gain the net gain resulting when taxpayers combine long-term capital gains and losses for the year.

Net long-term capital loss the net loss resulting when taxpayers combine long-term capital gains and losses for the year.

Net operating loss (NOL) the excess of allowable deductions over gross income.

Net operating loss carryback the amount of a current year net operating loss that is carried back to offset income in a prior year.

Net operating loss carryover the amount of a current year net operating loss that is carried forward for up to 20 years to offset taxable income in those years.

Net passive investment income passive investment income less any expenses connected with producing it.

Net short-term capital gain the net gain resulting when taxpayers combine short-term capital gains and losses for the year.

Net short-term capital loss the net loss resulting when taxpayers combine short-term capital gains and losses for the year.

Net unearned income unearned income in excess of a specified threshold amount of a child under the age of 19 or under the age of 24 if a full-time student.

Net unrealized built-in gain the net gain (if any) an S corporation that was formerly a C corporation would recognize if it sold each asset at its fair market value. It is measured on the first day of the corporation's first year as an S corporation.

Nexus the connection between a business and a tax jurisdiction sufficient to subject the business to the tax jurisdiction's tax system. Also, the connection that is required to exist between a jurisdiction and a potential taxpayer such that the jurisdiction asserts the right to impose a tax.

Nonbusiness income all income except for business income—generally investment income and rental income.

Nondeductible terminable interests transfers of property interests to a spouse that do not qualify for a marital deduction, because the interest of the spouse terminates when some event occurs or after a specified amount of time and the property is then transferred to another person.

Nondomiciliary business a business operating in a state other than its commercial domicile.

Nonperformance based compensation compensation paid to an employee that does not depend on the employee's performance or the corporation's performance or success. It usually is straight salary.

Nonqualified deferred compensation compensation provided for under a nonqualified plan allowing employees to defer compensation to a future period.

Nonqualified stock option a type of stock option requiring employees to treat the bargain element from options exercised as ordinary income in the tax year options are exercised. Correspondingly, employers may deduct the bargain element as compensation expense in the tax year options are exercised.

Nonrecaptured net §1231 losses a net §1231 loss that is deducted as an ordinary loss in one year and has not caused subsequent §1231 gain to be taxed as ordinary income.

Nonrecognition provisions tax laws that allow taxpayers to permanently exclude income from taxation or to defer recognizing realized income until a subsequent period.

Nonrecognition transaction a transaction where at least a portion of the realized gain or loss is not currently recognized.

Nonrecourse debt debt for which no partner bears any economic risk of loss. Mortgages on real property are a common form of nonrecourse debt.

Nonresident alien an individual who does not meet the criteria to be treated as a resident for U.S. tax purposes.

Nonservice partner a partner who receives a partnership interest in exchange for property rather than services.

Nontaxable fringe benefit an employer provided benefit that may be excluded from an employee's income.

Not definitely related deductions deductions that are not associated with a specific item or items of gross income in computing the foreign tax credit limitation.

O

Operating distributions payments to the owners from an entity that represent a distribution of entity profits. Distributions generally fall into the category of operating distributions when the owners continue their interests in the entity after the distribution.

Ordinary asset an asset created or used in a taxpayer's trade or business (e.g., accounts receivable or inventory) that generates ordinary income (or loss) on disposition.

Ordinary business income (loss) a partnership's or S corporation's remaining income or loss after separately stated items are removed. It is also referred to as nonseparately stated income (loss).

Ordinary income property property that if sold would generate income taxed at ordinary rates.

Ordinary and necessary an expense that is normal or appropriate and that is helpful or conducive to the business activity.

Organization costs costs associated with legally forming a partnership (such as attorneys' and accountants' fees).

Organizational expenditures expenses that are (1) connected directly with the creation of a corporation or partnership, (2) chargeable to a capital account, and (3) generally amortized over 180 months (limited immediate expensing may be available).

Outbound transaction a transaction conducted outside the United States by a U.S. person that is subject to U.S. taxation.

Outside tax basis an investor's tax basis in the stock of a corporation or the interest in a partnership or LLC.

P

PAL an acronym for "passive activity loss." Losses allocated to partners who are not material participants in the partnership are passive activity losses.

Parent-subsidiary controlled group a form of controlled group consisting of one corporation that owns at least 80% of the voting power or stock value of another corporation on the last day of the year.

Partial liquidation a distribution made by a corporation to shareholders that results from a contraction of the corporation's activities.

Partnership agreement an agreement among the partners in a partnership stipulating the partners' rights and responsibilities in the partnership.

Partnership interest an intangible asset reflecting the economic rights a partner has with respect to a partnership including the right to receive assets in liquidation of the partnership called a capital interest and the right to be allocated profits and losses called a profits interest.

Passive activity an activity in which the taxpayer does not materially participate.

Passive activity income or loss income or loss from an activity in which the taxpayer does not materially participate.

Passive activity loss rules tax rules designed to limit taxpayers' ability to deduct losses from activities in which they don't materially participate against income from other sources.

Passive category income foreign source personal holding company income such as interest, dividends, rents, royalties, annuities, and gains from sale of certain assets that is combined in computing the FTC limitation.

Passive investment income (PII) royalties, rents, dividends, interest (including tax exempt interest), annuities, and gains from the sales or exchanges of stock or securities.

Passive investments direct or indirect investments (other than through a C corporation) in a trade or business or rental activity in which the taxpayer does not materially participate.

Payment liability liabilities of accrual method businesses for which economic performance occurs when the business actually *pays* the liability for, among others: worker's compensation; tort; breach of contract or violation of law; rebates and refunds; awards, prizes, and jackpots; insurance, warranties, and service contracts provided *to* the business; and taxes.

Percentage depletion a method of recovering the cost of a natural resource that allows a taxpayer to recover or expense an amount based on a statutorily determined percentage.

Permanent book-tax differences items of income or deductions for either book purposes or for tax purposes during the year but not both. Permanent differences do not reverse over time so over the long run the total amount of income or deduction for the item is different for book and tax purposes.

Permanent establishment generally, a fixed place of business through which an enterprise carries out its business. Examples include a place of management, a branch, an office, and a factory.

Permissible accounting method accounting method allowed under the tax law. Permissible accounting methods are adopted the first time a taxpayer uses the method on a tax return.

Person an individual, trust, estate, partnership, association, company, or corporation.

Personal expenses expenses incurred for personal motives. Personal expenses are not deductible for tax purposes.

Personal holding companies closely held corporations generating primarily investment income.

Personal holding company tax penalty tax on the undistributed income of a personal holding company.

Personal property all tangible property other than real property.

Positive basis adjustment (for special basis adjustment purposes) the sum of the gain recognized by the owners receiving distributed property and the amount of any required basis reduction.

Post-termination transition period (PTTP) the period that begins on the day after the last day of a corporation's last taxable year as an S corporation and generally ends on the later of (a) one year after the last S corporation day, or (b) the due date for filing the return for the last year as an S corporation (including extensions).

Present interest right to presently enjoy property or receive income from the property.

Principal partner a partner having a 5% interest or more in partnership capital or profits.

Private activity bond a bond issued by a municipality but proceeds of which are used to fund privately owned activity.

Probate the process in the probate court of gathering property possessed by or titled in the name of a decedent at the time of death, paying the debts of the decedent and transferring the ownership of any remaining property to the decedent's heirs.

Probate estate property possessed by or titled in the name of a decedent at the time of death.

Procedural regulations regulations that explain Treasury Department procedures as they relate to administering the Code.

Production of income a for-profit activity that doesn't rise to the level of a trade or business.

Profits interest an interest in a partnership giving a partner the right to share in future profits but not the right to share in the current value of a partnership's assets. Profits interests are generally not taxable in the year they are received.

Public Law 86-272 federal law passed by Congress that provides additional protection for sellers of tangible personal property against income tax nexus.

Publicly state traded corporations corporations whose stock is publicly traded on a stock exchange.

Q

Qualified moving expense reimbursement a nontaxable fringe benefit that allows employers to pay moving-related expenses on behalf of employees.

Qualified nonrecourse financing nonrecourse debt secured by real property from a commercial lender unrelated to the borrower.

Qualified production activities income (QPAI) the *net* income from selling or leasing property that was manufactured in the United States.

Qualified replacement property property acquired to replace property damaged or destroyed in an involuntary conversion. It must be of a similar or related use to the original property even if the replacement property is real property (rental real estate for rental real estate).

Qualified retirement plans employer-sponsored retirement plans that meet government-imposed funding and anti-discrimination requirements.

R

Real property land and structures permanently attached to land.

Real property tax a tax on the fair market value of land and structures permanently attached to land.

Realization gain or loss that results from an exchange of property rights in a transaction.

Realization principle the proposition that income only exists when there is a transaction with another party resulting in a measurable change in property rights.

Realized gain or loss the difference between the amount realized and the adjusted basis of an asset sold or otherwise disposed of.

Reasonable in amount an expenditure is reasonable when the amount paid is not extravagant nor exorbitant.

Recognition gain or loss included in the computation of taxable income.

Recourse debt debt held by a partnership for which at least one partner has economic risk of loss.

Recovery period a length of time prescribed by statute in which business property is depreciated or amortized.

Remainder the right to ownership of a property that transfers to a new owner, the remainderman, following a temporary interest.

Remainderman the person entitled to a remainder interest.

Reorganization a tax-deferred transaction (acquisition, disposition, recapitalization, or change of name or place of incorporation) that meets one of the seven statutory definitions found in §368(a)(1).

Research and experimentation costs expenses for research including costs of research laboratories (salaries, materials, and other related expenses). Taxpayers can elect to amortize research and development costs over not less than 60 months from the time benefits are first derived from the research.

Residence-based jurisdiction taxation of income based on the taxpayer's residence.

Resident alien an individual who is not a U.S. citizen but is treated as a resident for U.S. tax purposes.

Reverse hybrid entity a "check-the-box" entity owned by multiple persons for which corporation status is elected.

Reverse triangular merger an acquisition in which an acquisition subsidiary of the acquiring corporation merges into the acquired (target) corporation, after which the acquired corporation becomes a subsidiary of the acquiring corporation.

Reversion terms by which ownership of property returns to the original owner following a temporary interest.

S corporation a corporation under state law that has elected to be taxed under the rules provided in subchapter S of the Internal Revenue Code. Under subchapter S, an S corporation is taxed as a flow-through entity.

Sales tax a tax imposed on the retail sales of goods (plus certain services). Retailers are responsible for collecting and remitting the tax; typically sales tax is collected at the point of sale.

Schedule C a schedule on which a taxpayer reports the income and deductions for a sole-proprietorship.

Schedule K a schedule filed with a partnership's annual tax return listing its ordinary income (loss) and its separately stated items.

Schedule M adjustments book-tax differences that corporations report on the Schedule M-1 or M-3 of Form 1120 as adjustments to book income to reconcile to taxable income.

Schedule M-1 a schedule on Form 1120 that reconciles book income to taxable income before special deductions. Book-tax differences are reported in a general way.

Schedule M-3 a schedule on Form 1120 that reconciles book income to taxable income for corporations and partnerships with total assets of $10 million or more. The schedule M-3 includes much more detail than the Schedule M-1, including identifying whether each book-tax difference is a temporary difference or a permanent book-tax difference.

Security a financial instrument including an equity interest in business organizations and creditor interests such as savings accounts, notes, and bonds.

Self-employment taxes Social Security and Medicare taxes paid by the self-employed on a taxpayer's net earnings from self-employment. For self-employed taxpayers, the terms "self-employment tax" and "FICA tax" are synonymous.

Separate tax return a state tax return methodology requiring that each related entity with nexus files a separate tax return.

Separately stated items income, expenses, gains, losses, credits, and other items that are excluded from a partnership's or S corporation's operating income (loss) and disclosed to partners in a partnership or shareholders of an S corporation separately because their tax effects may be different for each partner or shareholder.

Serial gift transfer tax strategy that uses the annual exclusion to convert a potentially large taxable transfer into a tax-exempt transfer by dividing it into multiple intervivos gifts spread over several periods or donees.

Service partner partners who receive their partnership interest by contributing services rather than cash or property.

Single member LLC a limited liability company with only one member. Single member LLCs with individual owners are taxed as sole proprietorships and as disregarded entities otherwise.

Sole proprietorship a business entity that is not legally separate from the individual owner of the business. The income of a sole proprietorship is taxed and paid directly by the owner.

Solicitation selling activities or activities ancillary to selling that are protected under Public Law 86-272.

Source-based jurisdiction taxation of income based on where the income is earned.

Special allocations allocations of income, gain, expense, or loss, etc., that are allocated to the owners of an entity in a manner out of proportion with the owners' interests in the entity. Special allocations can be made by entities treated as partnerships for federal income tax purposes.

Special basis adjustment an optional (sometimes mandatory) election to adjust the entity asset bases as a result of an owner's disposition of an interest in the entity or of distributions from the entity to its owners.

Specific identification method an elective method for determining the cost of an asset sold. Under this method, the taxpayer specifically chooses the assets that are to be sold.

Split-gift election election that allows spouses to treat all gifts made in a year as if each spouse made one-half of each gift.

Spot rate the foreign currency exchange rate on a specific day.

Start-up costs expenses that would be classified as business expenses except that the expenses are incurred before the business begins. These costs are generally capitalized and amortized over 180 months, but limited immediate expensing may be available.

State tax a tax imposed by one of the 50 U.S. states.

Stock dividend a dividend made by a corporation of its own stock.

Stock-for-stock acquisition an exchange of solely voting stock by the acquiring corporation in exchange for stock of the target corporation, after which the acquiring corporation controls (owns 80-percent-or-more of) the target corporation. Often referred to as a "Type B reorganization."

Stock redemption a property distribution made to shareholders in return for some or all of their stock in the distributing corporation that is not in partial or complete liquidation of the corporation.

Stock split a stock redemption in which a corporation exchanges a ratio of shares of stock (e.g., 2 for 1) for each share held by the shareholder.

Strike price *see* exercise price.

Structural tax rate the tax rate computed by dividing a company's income tax provision adjusted for nonrecurring permanent differences by its pretax income from continuing operations.

Subchapter K the portion of the Internal Revenue Code dealing with partnerships tax law.

Subchapter S the portion of the Internal Revenue Code containing tax rules for S corporations and their shareholders.

Subpart F income income earned by a controlled foreign corporation that is not eligible for deferral from U.S. taxation.

Substantial basis reduction negative basis adjustment of more than $250,000 resulting from a distribution from an entity taxed as a partnership to its owners.

Substantial built-in loss exists when a partnership's adjusted basis in its property exceeds the property's fair market value by more than $250,000 when a transfer of an interest occurs.

Substantially appreciated inventory (for partnership disproportionate distributions purposes) inventory with a fair market value that exceeds its basis by more than 120%.

Substituted basis the transfer of the tax basis of stock or other property given up in an exchange to stock or other property received in return.

Syndication costs costs partnerships incur to promote the sale of partnership interests to the public. Syndication expenses must be capitalized and are not amortizable.

T

Tacks the adding on of the transferor's holding period of property to the transferee in a tax-deferred exchange.

Tax a payment required by a government that is unrelated to any specific benefit or service received from the government.

Tax accounting balance sheet a balance sheet that records a company's assets and liabilities at their tax bases instead of their financial accounting bases.

Tax base the item that is being taxed (e.g., purchase price of a good, taxable income, etc.).

Tax basis the amount of a taxpayer's unrecovered cost of or investment in an asset. *See also* adjusted tax basis.

Tax bracket a range of taxable income taxed at a specified rate.

Tax capital accounts partners' capital accounts initially determined using the tax basis of contributed property and maintained using tax accounting income and expense recognition principles.

Tax carryforwards tax deductions or credits that cannot be used on the current year tax return and that can be carried forward to reduce taxable income or taxes payable in a future year.

Tax contingency reserve a company's reserve for taxes it has not paid, but it may pay in the future, for uncertain tax positions taken on the current and prior year income tax returns.

Tax shelter an investment or other arrangement designed to produce tax benefits without any expectation of economic profits.

Tax year a fixed period in which a business reports income and deductions, generally referred to as an accounting period.

Taxable estate adjusted gross estate reduced by the marital deduction and the charitable deduction.

Taxable fringe benefit a noncash fringe benefit provided by employers to an employee that is included in taxable income (e.g., auto allowance or group-term life over $50,000).

Taxable gifts the amount left after adjusting current gifts for gift splitting, annual exclusions, the marital deduction, and the charitable deduction.

Taxable temporary differences book-tax differences that will result in taxable amounts in future years when the related deferred tax liability is settled.

Temporary book-tax differences book-tax differences that reverse over time such that, over the long-term, corporations recognize the same amount of income or deductions for the items on their financial statements as they recognize on their tax returns.

Tenancy by the entirety ownership by husband and wife similar to joint tenancy with right of survivorship.

Tenancy in common ownership in which owners hold divided rights to property and have the ability to transfer these rights during their life or upon their death.

Tentative minimum tax the tax on the AMT tax base under the alternative minimum tax system.

Terminable interest a right to property that terminates at a specified time or upon the occurrence of a specified event, such as a life estate.

Testamentary transfers transfers that take place upon the death of the donor.

Third-party intermediaries people or organizations that facilitate the transfer of property between taxpayers in a like-kind exchange. Typically, the intermediary receives the cash from selling the property received from the taxpayer and uses it to acquire like-kind property identified by the taxpayer.

Throwback rule the rule that sales into a state without nexus are included with sales from the state the property was shipped from.

Trade show rule a rule that permits businesses to have physical presence at conventions and trade shows, generally up to two weeks a year, without creating nexus.

Traditional 401(k) a popular type of defined contribution plan with before-tax employee and employer contributions and taxable distributions.

Transfer taxes taxes on the transfer of wealth from one taxpayer to another. The estate and gift taxes are two examples of transfer taxes.

Travel expenses expenditures incurred while "away from home overnight," including the cost of transportation, meals, lodging, and incidental expenses.

Triple i agreement a 10-year agreement filed with the IRS in which the taxpayer agrees to notify the IRS that he or she has acquired a prohibited interest after waiving the family attribution rules in a complete redemption.

Trust fiduciary entity created to hold and administer the property for other persons according to the terms of a trust instrument.

Trustee the person responsible for administering a trust.

U

Uncertain tax positions a tax return position for which a corporation does not have a high degree of certainty as to its tax consequences.

Unfavorable book-tax difference any book-tax difference that requires an add back to book income in computing taxable income. This type of adjustment is unfavorable because it increases taxable income relative to book income.

Unified credit amount of credit based on the exemption equivalent designed to prevent transfer taxation of smaller cumulative transfers.

Uniform cost capitalization rules (UNICAP rules) specify that inventories must be accounted for using full absorption rules to allocate the indirect costs of productive activities to inventory.

Unitary tax return a state tax return methodology requiring the activities of a group of related entities to be reported on a single tax return. The criteria for determining whether a group of entities must file a unitary tax return are functional integration, centralization of management, and economies of scale.

Unrealized receivables any rights to receive payment for (1) goods delivered, or to be delivered, or (2) services rendered, or to be rendered. Unrealized receivables also include other assets to the extent that they would produce ordinary income if sold for their fair market value.

Unrecaptured §1250 gain a gain from the sale of real estate held by a noncorporate taxpayer for more than one year in a trade or business or as rental property attributable to tax depreciation deducted at ordinary tax rates. This gain is taxable at a maximum 25% capital gains rate.

Unrecognized tax benefit a reserve for tax benefits related to a tax position for which the corporation does not have a high degree of certainty as to its sustainability on audit or in a court of law.

Use tax a tax imposed on the retail price of goods owned, possessed, or consumed within a state that were *not* purchased within the state.

V

Valuation allowance the portion of a deferred tax asset for which management determines it is more likely than not that a tax benefit will not be realized on a future tax return.

Vest to become legally entitled to receive a particular benefit without risk of forfeiture; to gain ownership.

Vesting date the date on which the taxpayer becomes legally entitled to receive a particular benefit without risk of forfeiture.

Vesting period period of employment over which employees earn the right to own and exercise stock options.

W

Willing-buyer, willing-seller rule the guideline for determining fair market value as "the price at which such property would change hands between a willing buyer and a willing seller, neither being under any compulsion to buy or to sell, and both have reasonable knowledge of the relevant facts."

Appendix C

Ten additional Comprehensive Tax Return problems—covering individual, corporation, partnership and S corporation tax returns, can be found in the *Connect Library*.

Comprehensive Tax Return Problems

CORPORATE TAX RETURN PROBLEM 1

Required:

- Complete Alvin's Music Inc.'s (AMI) 2014 Form 1120, Schedule D, and Schedule G (if applicable) using the information provided below.
- Neither Form 4562 for depreciation nor Form 4797 for the sale of the equipment is required. Include the amount of tax depreciation and the tax gain on the equipment sale given in the problem (or determined from information given in the problem) on the appropriate lines on the first page of Form 1120.
- Assume that AMI does not owe any alternative minimum tax.
- If any information is missing, use reasonable assumptions to fill in the gaps.
- The forms, schedules, and instructions can be found at the IRS website (www.irs.gov). The instructions can be helpful in completing the forms.

Facts:

Alvin's Music Inc. (AMI) was formed in 2006 by Alvin Jones and Theona Smith. Alvin and Theona officially incorporated their store on June 12, 2007. AMI sells (retail) all kinds of music-related products including musical instruments, sheet music, CDs, and DVDs. Alvin owns 60 percent of the outstanding common stock of AMI and Theona owns the remaining 40 percent.

- AMI is located at 355 Music Way, East Palo Alto, CA 94303.
- AMI's Employer Identification Number is 29-5748859.
- AMI's business activity is retail sales of music-related products. Its business activity code is 451140.
- Officers of the corporation are as follows:
  - Alvin is the chief executive officer and president (Social Security number 123-45-6789).
  - Theona is the executive vice president (Social Security number 978-65-4321).
  - Gwen Givens is the vice president over operations (Social Security number 789-12-3456).
  - Carlson Bannister is the secretary (Social Security number 321-54-6789).
- All officers devote 100 percent of their time to the business and all officers are U.S. citizens.

- Neither Gwen nor Carlson owns any stock in AMI.
- AMI uses the accrual method of accounting and has a calendar year-end.
- AMI made four equal estimated tax payments of $70,000 each. Its tax liability last year was $175,000. If it has overpaid its federal tax liability, AMI would like to receive a refund.
- AMI paid a dividend of $80,000 to its shareholders on December 1. AMI had ample earnings and profits (E&P) to absorb the distribution.

The following is AMI's audited income statement for 2014:

AMI Income Statement For year ending December 31, 2014	
Revenue from sales	$3,420,000
Sales returns and allowances	(40,000)
Cost of goods sold	(834,000)
Gross profit from operations	$2,546,000
Other income:	
Capital gains	$ 8,000
Gain from disposition of fixed assets	2,000
Dividend income	12,000
Interest income	15,000
Gross Income	$2,583,000
Expenses:	
Compensation	$(1,300,000)
Depreciation	(20,000)
Bad debt expense	(15,000)
Meals and entertainment	(5,000)
Maintenance	(5,000)
Charitable donations	(27,000)
Property taxes	(45,000)
State income taxes	(60,000)
Other taxes	(56,000)
Interest	(62,000)
Advertising	(44,000)
Professional services	(32,000)
Pension expense	(40,000)
Supplies	(6,000)
Other expenses	(38,000)
Total expenses	(1,755,000)
Income before taxes	828,000
Federal income tax expense	(260,000)
Net Income after taxes	$ 568,000

Notes:

1. AMI has a capital loss carryover to this year from last year in the amount of $5,000.
2. AMI's inventory-related purchases during the year were $1,134,000. AMI values its inventory based on cost using the FIFO inventory cost flow method. Assume the rules of §263A do not apply to AMI.
3. Of the $15,000 interest income, $2,500 was from a City of Fremont bond that was used to fund public activities (issued in 2013), $3,500 was from a Pleasanton city bond used to fund private activities (issued in 2014), $3,000 was from a U.S. Treasury bond, and the remaining $6,000 was from a money market account.

4. AMI sold equipment for $10,000. It originally purchased the equipment for $12,000 and, through the date of the sale, had recorded a cumulative total of $4,000 of book depreciation on the asset and a cumulative total of $6,000 of tax depreciation. For tax purposes, the entire gain was recaptured as ordinary income under §1245.
5. AMI's dividend income came from Simon's Sheet Music. AMI owned 15,000 shares of the stock in Simon's Sheet Music (SSM) at the beginning of the year. This represented 15 percent of the SSM outstanding stock.
6. On July 22, 2014, AMI sold 2,500 shares of its Simon's Sheet Music Stock for $33,000. It had originally purchased these shares on April 24, 2010, for $25,000. After the sale, AMI owned 12.5 percent of Simon's Sheet Music.
7. AMI's compensation is as follows:
   - Alvin $210,000
   - Theona $190,000
   - Gwen $110,000
   - Carlson $90,000
   - Other $700,000
8. AMI wrote off $10,000 in accounts receivable as uncollectible during the year.
9. Regular tax depreciation was $31,000. None of the depreciation should be claimed on Form 1125A.
10. Of the $62,000 of interest expense, $56,000 was from the mortgage on AMI's building and the remaining $6,000 of interest is from business-related loans.
11. The pension expense is the same for both book and tax purposes.
12. Other expenses include $3,000 for premiums paid on term life insurance policies for which AMI is the beneficiary. The policies cover the lives of Alvin and Theona.

The following are AMI's audited balance sheets as of January 1, 2014, and December 31, 2014.

	2014	
	January 1	December 31
Assets		
Cash	$ 240,000	$ 171,000
Accounts receivable	600,000	700,000
Allowance for doubtful accounts	(35,000)	(40,000)
Inventory	1,400,000	1,700,000
U.S. government bonds	50,000	50,000
State and local bonds	140,000	140,000
Investments in stock	300,000	275,000
Building and other depreciable assets	1,500,000	1,600,000
Accumulated depreciation	(200,000)	(216,000)
Land	900,000	900,000
Other assets	250,000	270,000
Total assets	$5,145,000	$5,550,000
Liabilities and Shareholders' Equity		
Accounts payable	$ 250,000	$ 220,000
Other current liabilities	125,000	120,000
Mortgage	800,000	790,000
Other liabilities	200,000	162,000
Capital stock	600,000	600,000
Retained earnings	3,170,000	3,658,000
Total liabilities and shareholders' equity	$5,145,000	$5,550,000

CORPORATE TAX RETURN PROBLEM 2

Required:

- Complete Blue Catering Service Inc.'s (BCS) 2014 Form 1120, Schedule D, and Schedule G (if applicable) using the information provided below.
- Form 4562 for depreciation is not required. Include the amount of tax depreciation given in the problem on the appropriate line on the first page of Form 1120.
- Assume that BCS does not owe any alternative minimum tax.
- If any information is missing, use reasonable assumptions to fill in the gaps.
- The forms, schedules, and instructions can be found at the IRS website (www.irs.gov). The instructions can be helpful in completing the forms.

Facts:

Cara Siler, Janna Funk, and Valerie Cloward each own one-third of the common stock of Blue Catering Services Inc. (BCS). BCS was incorporated on February 4, 2008. It has only one class of stock outstanding and operates as a C corporation for tax purposes. BCS caters all types of social events throughout southern California.

- BCS is located at 540 Waverly Way, San Diego, CA 92101.
- BCS's Employer Identification Number is 38-4743474.
- BCS's business activity is catering food and services. Its business activity code is 722300.
- The shareholders also work as officers for the corporation as follows:
  - Cara is the chief executive officer and president (Social Security number 231-54-8976).
  - Janna is the executive vice president and chief operating officer (Social Security number 798-56-3241).
  - Valerie is the vice president of finance (Social Security number 879-21-4536).
- All officers devote 100 percent of their time to the business and all officers are U.S. citizens.
- BCS uses the accrual method of accounting and has a calendar year-end.
- BCS made four equal estimated tax payments of $20,000 each. Its tax liability last year was $70,000. If it has overpaid its federal tax liability, BCS would like to receive a refund.
- BCS paid a dividend of $30,000 to its shareholders on November 1. BCS had ample earnings and profits (E&P) to absorb the distribution.

The following is BCS's audited income statement for 2014:

BCS Income Statement For year ending December 31, 2014	
Revenue from sales	$1,800,000
Sales returns and allowances	(5,000)
Cost of goods sold	(350,000)
Gross profit from operations	$1,445,000
Other income:	
Capital loss	$ (15,000)
Dividend income	25,000
Interest income	10,000
Gross income	$1,465,000

BCS Income Statement For year ending December 31, 2014	
Expenses:	
Compensation	$ (950,000)
Depreciation	(10,000)
Bad debt expense	(15,000)
Meals and entertainment	(3,000)
Maintenance	(6,000)
Property taxes	(11,000)
State income taxes	(45,000)
Other taxes	(44,000)
Rent	(60,000)
Interest	(5,000)
Advertising	(52,000)
Professional services	(16,000)
Employee benefits	(32,000)
Supplies	(5,000)
Other expenses	(27,000)
Total expenses	(1,281,000)
Income before taxes	184,000
Federal income tax expense	(62,000)
Net income after taxes	$ 122,000

Notes:

1. BCS's inventory-related purchases during 2014 were $360,000. It values its inventory based on cost using the FIFO inventory cost flow method. Assume the rules of §263A do not apply to BCS.
2. Of the $10,000 interest income, $1,250 was from a City of Irvine bond that was used to fund public activities (issued in 2012), $1,750 was from an Oceanside city bond used to fund private activities (issued in 2011), $1,000 was from a U.S. Treasury bond, and the remaining $6,000 was from a money market account.
3. BCS's dividend income came from Clever Cakes Inc. (CC). BCS owned 10,000 shares of the stock in Clever Cakes at the beginning of the year. This represented 10 percent of SSM outstanding stock.
4. On October 1, 2014, BCS sold 1,000 shares of its CC stock for $25,000. It had originally purchased these shares on April 18, 2010, for $40,000. After the sale, BCS owned 9 percent of CC.
5. BCS's compensation is as follows:
   - Cara $150,000
   - Janna $140,000
   - Valerie $130,000
   - Other $530,000
6. BCS wrote off $25,000 in accounts receivable as uncollectible during the year.
7. BCS's regular tax depreciation was $28,000. None of the depreciation should be claimed on Form 1125A.
8. The $5,000 interest expense was from a business loan.
9. Other expenses include $6,000 for premiums paid on term life insurance policies for which BCS is the beneficiary. The policies cover the lives of Cara, Janna, and Valerie.

The following are BCS's audited balance sheets as of January 1, 2014, and December 31, 2014.

	2014 January 1	2014 December 31
Assets		
Cash	$ 180,000	$ 205,000
Accounts receivable	560,000	580,000
Allowance for doubtful accounts	(60,000)	(50,000)
Inventory	140,000	150,000
U.S. government bonds	20,000	20,000
State and local bonds	120,000	120,000
Investments in stock	400,000	360,000
Fixed assets	140,000	160,000
Accumulated depreciation	(50,000)	(60,000)
Other assets	20,000	21,000
Total assets	$1,470,000	$1,506,000
Liabilities and Shareholders' Equity		
Accounts payable	$ 280,000	$ 240,000
Other current liabilities	20,000	18,000
Other liabilities	40,000	26,000
Capital stock	400,000	400,000
Retained earnings	730,000	822,000
Total liabilities and shareholders' equity	$1,470,000	$1,506,000

PARTNERSHIP TAX RETURN PROBLEM 1

Required:

- For 2014, complete Aspen Ridge limited partnership's page 1 of Form 1065; complete Schedule K on page 4 of Form 1065; complete lines 1 and 2 of the Analysis of Net Income (Loss) at the top of page 5 of Form 1065; and complete Schedules M-1 and M-2 at the bottom of page 5 of Form 1065. Finally, complete Mark Sullivan's Schedule K-1.
- Form 4562 for depreciation is not required. Include any tax depreciation or Section 179 expense on the appropriate line of page 1 of Form 1065 or Schedule K.
- If any information is missing, use reasonable assumptions to fill in any gaps.
- The forms, schedules, and instructions can be found at the IRS website (www.irs.gov). The instructions can be helpful in completing the forms.

Facts:

The Aspen Ridge limited partnership was formed on April 1, 2009, by Mark Sullivan, its general partner, and two other limited partners when they each contributed an equal amount of cash to start the new enterprise. Aspen Ridge is an outdoor equipment retailer selling camping, fishing, skiing, and other outdoor gear to the general public. Mark has a 33.33% profits, loss, and capital interest and the limited partners hold the remaining 66.66% of the profits, loss, and capital interests. Their profits, loss, and capital interests have remained unchanged since the partnership was formed. Mark is actively involved in managing the business while the limited partners are simply investors.

- Aspen Ridge is located at 1065 North 365 South, Ogden, UT, 84401.
- The employer identification number for Aspen Ridge is 85-8976654.
- Aspen Ridge uses the accrual method of accounting and has a calendar year-end.
- Mark's address is 543 Wander Lane, Holliday, UT 84503 and his Social Security number is 445-27-3484.

The following is Aspen Ridge's 2014 income statement for books:

Aspen Ridge Income Statement For year ending December 31, 2014	
Sales	$965,500
Sales Returns and Allowances	(9,700)
Cost of Goods Sold	(538,200)
Gross Profit from Operations	$ 417,600
Other Income:	
Interest from money market account	$ 3,200
Gain from sale of photograph	34,000
Gross Income	$454,800
Expenses:	
Employee wages	$ 95,400
Interest on accounts payable	2,700
Payroll and property taxes	10,800
Supplies	4,300
Rent on retail building	18,500
Depreciation on furniture and fixtures	4,550
Advertising	8,300
Guaranteed payments to Mark Sullivan	35,000
Utilities	6,400
Accounting and legal services	4,400
Meals and entertainment	2,240
Charitable contribution to the Sierra Club	3,300
Miscellaneous expenses	5,750
Total Expenses	(201,640)
Net Income for Books	$ 253,160

Notes:

1. Aspen Ridge has total assets of $1,725,800 and total liabilities of $540,300 at the beginning of the year and total assets of $2,065,300 and total liabilities of $806,640 at the end of the year.
2. Partnership liabilities consist of accounts payable, and Mark, as general partner, is legally responsible for paying these liabilities if the partnership does not.
3. Two years ago, Aspen Ridge purchased an original Ansel Adams outdoor landscape photograph with the intent to display it permanently in the retail store. This year, however, the photograph was sold to a local ski lodge where it is now hangs on the wall. The $34,000 recognized gain from the sale is reflected in the income statement above.

4. For tax purposes, Aspen Ridge has consistently elected under Section 179 to expense any furniture or fixtures purchased every year since it was formed. As a result, it does not have a tax basis in any of its depreciable assets. This year, Aspen Ridge expensed $17,300 of signs and display cases for tax purposes.
5. On November 20th, Aspen Ridge distributed $180,000 ($60,000 per partner) to the partners.
6. Miscellaneous expenses include a $900 fine for violating a local signage ordinance.
7. Aspen Ridge maintains its books using generally accepted accounting principles.

PARTNERSHIP TAX RETURN PROBLEM 2

Required:

- Using the information provided below, complete Arlington Building Supply's (ABS) 2014 Form 1065 and Schedule D. Also complete Jerry Johnson and Steve Stillwell's Schedule K-1.
- Form 4562 for depreciation is not required. Use the amount of tax depreciation and §179 expense provided in the income statement and the information in #4 below to complete the appropriate lines on the first page and on Schedule K of Form 1065.
- Form 4797 for the sale of trade or business property is not required. Use the amount of gain and loss from the sale of the truck and forklifts in the income statement and the information provided in #4 and #5 below to complete the appropriate lines on the first page and on Schedule K of Form 1065.
- If any information is missing, use reasonable assumptions to fill in any gaps.
- The forms, schedules, and instructions can be found at the IRS website (www.irs.gov). The instructions can be helpful in completing the forms.

Facts:

On January 1, 2004, two enterprising men in the community, Jerry Johnson and Steve "Swiss" Stillwell, anticipated a boom in the local construction industry. They decided to sell their small businesses and pool their resources as general partners in establishing a retail outlet for lumber and other building materials, including a complete line of specialty hardware for prefab tree-houses. Their general partnership was officially formed under the name of Arlington Building Supply and soon became a thriving business.

- ABS is located at 2174 Progress Ave., Arlington, IL 64888.
- ABS's Employer Identification Number is 91-3697984.
- ABS's business activity is retail construction. Its business activity code is 444190.
- Both general partners are active in the management of ABS.
  - Jerry Johnson's Social Security number is 500-23-4976. His address is 31 W. Oak Drive, Arlington, IL 64888.
  - Steve Stillwell's Social Security number is 374-68-3842. His address is 947 E. Linder Street, Arlington, IL 64888.
- ABS uses the accrual method of accounting and has a calendar year-end.

The following is ABS's 2014 income statement:

ABS
Income Statement
For year ending December 31, 2014

Sales (on account)	$410,000	
Less: Sales returns	−20,000	
		$390,000
Cost of goods sold		−150,000
Gross profit on sales		$240,000
Operating expenses		
Salaries and wages (including partners' guaranteed payments)	$79,000	
Property taxes	1,600	
Payroll taxes	2,450	
Depreciation and 179 expense	40,062	
Advertising	2,000	
Bad debt expense	3,850	
Office expense	1,800	
Repairs	2,150	
Miscellaneous	450	
Fire insurance	4,850	138,212
Net operating income		$101,788
Other income		
Gain on sale of securities	$ 1,350	
Gain on sale of truck	16,399	
Dividend income	695	
Interest income	4,260	22,704
		$124,492
Other deductions		
Interest on mortgage	$ 5,400	
Interest on notes payable	2,250	
Charitable contributions	5,000	
Life insurance premiums	3,000	
Loss on sale of forklifts	466	16,116
NET INCOME		$108,376

Notes:

1. The partnership maintains its books according to the §704(b) regulations. Under this method of accounting, all book and tax numbers are the same except for life insurance premiums and tax-exempt interest.
2. The partners' percentage ownership of original contributed capital is 30 percent for Johnson and 70 percent for Stillwell. They agree that profits and losses will be shared according to this same ratio. Any additional capital contributions and withdrawals must be made in these same ratios.
3. For their services to the company, the partners will receive the following annual guaranteed payments:

Johnson	$28,000
Stillwell	$21,000

   Johnson is expected to devote all his time to the business, while Stillwell will devote approximately 75 percent of his.

4. Two forklifts were sold in September 2014. The old lifts were purchased new four years ago. Two new forklifts were purchased on September 1, 2014, for $32,000 and the partnership intends to immediately expense them under §179 (see depreciation and 179 expense in the income statement above).
5. The truck sold this year was purchased several years ago. $16,099 of the total gain from the sale of the truck should be recaptured as ordinary income under IRC §1245.
6. The partnership uses currently allowable tax depreciation methods for both regular tax and book purposes and has adopted a policy of electing not to claim bonus depreciation. Assume alternative minimum tax depreciation equals regular tax depreciation.
7. The partners decided to invest in a small tract of land with the intention of selling it about a year later at a substantial profit. On January 1, 2014, they executed a $50,000 note with the bank to obtain the $70,000 cash purchase price. Interest on the note is payable yearly, and the principal is due in 18 months. The first interest payment of $2,250 was made on December 30, 2014 (see interest on notes payable in income statement above).
8. The note payable to the bank as well as the accounts payable are treated by the partnership as recourse debt. Assume the total recourse debt is allocated $28,776 to Jerry and $70,224 to Steve.
9. Some years after the partnership was formed, a mortgage of $112,500 was obtained on the land and warehouse from Commerce State Bank. Principal payments of $4,500 must be paid each December 31, along with 8 percent interest on the outstanding balance (see interest on mortgage in income statement above). The holder of the note agreed therein to look only to the land and warehouse for his security in the event of default. Because this mortgage is nonrecourse debt, it should be allocated among the partners according to their profit sharing ratios.
10. The partnership values its inventory at lower of cost or market and uses the FIFO inventory method. Assume the rules of §263A do not apply to ABS.
11. During the year, the partnership bought 300 shares of ABC, Ltd., for $6,100 on February 8, 2014. All the shares were sold for $6,650 on April 2, 2014. ABS received a Form 1099-B indicating that the basis of the ABC shares was reported to the IRS.
12. Two hundred shares of XYZ Corporation were sold for $10,600 on September 13, 2014. The stock was purchased on December 1, 2008, and is not eligible for the 28 percent capital gains rate. ABS received a Form 1099-B indicating that the basis of the XYZ shares was reported to the IRS.
13. The following dividends were received:

XYZ (qualified)	$400
ABC, Ltd. (not qualified)	295
Total	$695

14. The partnership received interest income from the following sources:

Interest on Illinois municipal bonds	$3,200
Interest on savings	560
Interest on accounts receivable	500
Total	$4,260

15. The partnership donated $5,000 cash to the Red Cross.
16. Life insurance policies on the lives of Johnson and Stillwell were purchased in the prior year. The partnership will pay all the premiums and is the beneficiary of the policy. The premiums for the current year were $3,000 (see income statement above), and no cash surrender value exists for the first or second year of the policy.

17. The partners withdrew the following cash amounts from the partnership during the year (in addition to their guaranteed payments):

Johnson	$20,000
Stillwell	$35,000

The following are ABS's balance sheets as of January 1, 2014, and December 31, 2014.

		12/31/14		1/1/14
Assets				
Cash		$ 70,467		$ 43,042
Accounts receivable		76,000		57,000
Inventories		60,000		50,000
Investment in municipal bonds		50,000		50,000
Investment in XYZ common stock		40,200		50,000
Truck			$ 16,500	
Less accumulated depreciation			13,649	
				2,851
Machinery and equipment	$ 66,000		$ 50,000	
Less accumulated depreciation	58,697		34,376	
		7,303		15,624
Building	$120,000		$120,000	
Less accumulated depreciation	39,875		36,798	
		80,125		83,202
Land		90,000		20,000
TOTALS		$474,095		$371,719
Liabilities and Capital				
Accounts payable		$ 49,000		$ 45,500
Notes payable		50,000		0
Mortgage payable		63,000		67,500
Capital: Jerry Johnson		94,553		82,040
Steve Stillwell		217,542		176,679
TOTALS		$474,095		$371,719

S CORPORATION TAX RETURN PROBLEM

Required:

- Using the information provided below, complete Salt Source Inc.'s (SSI) 2014 Form 1120S. Also complete Kim Bentley's Schedule K-1.
- Form 4562 for depreciation is not required. Include the amount of tax depreciation given in the problem on the appropriate line on the first page of Form 1120S.
- If any information is missing, use reasonable assumptions to fill in the gaps.
- The forms, schedules, and instructions can be found at the IRS website (www.irs.gov). The instructions can be helpful in completing the forms.

Facts:

Salt Source Inc. (SSI) was formed as a corporation on January 5, 2011, by its two owners Kim Bentley and James Owens. SSI immediately elected to be taxed as an S corporation for federal income tax purposes. SSI sells salt to retailers throughout the Rocky Mountain region. Kim owns 70 percent of the SSI common stock (the only class of stock outstanding) and James owns 30 percent.

- SSI is located at 4200 West 400 North, Salt Lake City, UT 84116.
- SSI's Employer Identification Number is 87-5467544.

- SSI's business activity is wholesale sales. Its business activity code is 424990.
- Both shareholders work as employees of the corporation.
- Kim is the president of SSI (Social Security number 312-89-4567). Kim's address is 1842 East 8400 South, Sandy, UT 84094.
- James is the vice president of SSI (Social Security number 321-98-7645). James's address is 2002 East 8145 South, Sandy, UT 84094.
- SSI uses the accrual method of accounting and has a calendar year-end.

The following is SSI's 2014 income statement:

SSI Income Statement For year ending December 31, 2014	
Revenue from sales	$ 980,000
Sales returns and allowances	(10,000)
Cost of goods sold	(110,000)
Gross profit from operations	$ 860,000
Other income:	
Dividend income	$ 15,000
Interest income	5,000
Gross income	$ 880,000
Expenses:	
Compensation	$(600,000)
Depreciation	(10,000)
Bad debt expense	(14,000)
Meals and entertainment	(2,000)
Maintenance	(8,000)
Business interest	(1,000)
Property taxes	(7,000)
Charitable contributions	(10,000)
Other taxes	(30,000)
Rent	(28,000)
Advertising	(14,000)
Professional services	(11,000)
Employee benefits	(12,000)
Supplies	(3,000)
Other expenses	(21,000)
Total expenses	(771,000)
Net income	$ 109,000

Notes:

1. SSI's purchases during 2014 were $115,000. It values its inventory based on cost using the FIFO inventory cost flow method. Assume the rules of §263A do not apply to SSI.
2. Of the $5,000 interest income, $2,000 was from a West Jordan city bond used to fund public activities (issued in 2007) and $3,000 was from a money market account.
3. SSI's dividend income comes from publicly traded stocks that SSI has owned for two years.

4. SSI's compensation is as follows:
   - Kim $120,000
   - James $80,000
   - Other $400,000.
5. SSI wrote off $6,000 in accounts receivable as uncollectible during the year.
6. SSI's regular tax depreciation was $17,000. AMT depreciation was $13,000.
7. SSI distributed $60,000 to its shareholders.
8. SSI is not required to compute the amount in its accumulated adjustments account.

The following are SSI's book balance sheets as of January 1, 2014, and December 31, 2014.

	2014	
	January 1	December 31
Assets		
Cash	$ 90,000	$143,000
Accounts receivable	300,000	310,000
Allowance for doubtful accounts	(60,000)	(68,000)
Inventory	45,000	50,000
State and local bonds	38,000	38,000
Investments in stock	82,000	82,000
Fixed assets	100,000	100,000
Accumulated depreciation	(20,000)	(30,000)
Other assets	20,000	21,000
Total assets	$595,000	$646,000
Liabilities and Shareholders' Equity		
Accounts payable	$ 60,000	$ 55,000
Other current liabilities	5,000	8,000
Other liabilities	10,000	14,000
Capital stock	200,000	200,000
Retained earnings	320,000	369,000
Total liabilities and shareholders' equity	$595,000	$646,000

GIFT TAX RETURN PROBLEM

Lamar Grabowski is a prosperous rancher who lives in Crawford (Cherry County), Nebraska. Lamar is 60 years old and has been married to Elouisa (58 years old) for the past 37 years. Mildred and Charles are Lamar and Elouisa's adult children, ages 32 and 36, respectively. Over the years Lamar has considered making gifts to his children. Finally, in 2007 Lamar gave $250,000 each to Mildred and Charles. This year Lamar made the following gifts to Mildred and Charles:

Property	Recipient	Market Value	Adjusted Basis
Cash from joint savings account	Mildred Jones	$1,380,000	
100 acres of ranch land near Crawford	Charles Grabowski	1,640,000	$125,000

In addition to these gifts, this year Lamar also made a gift of 20,000 shares of Acme Inc. stock to State University (a qualified educational institution). The stock is listed on a national exchange (CUSIP = 000123TP) and was valued at $800,000 on the date of the gift. Lamar purchased the Acme stock 34 years ago for $25,000, and he inherited the ranch land from his father in 1992 when it was valued at $600,000. Lamar's cash gifts are made from Lamar and Elouisa's joint savings account, and although Elouisa is a professional accountant, she has not contributed to the joint savings account.

Lamar filed a timely gift tax return for the 2007 gifts offsetting a portion of each gift with his $12,000 annual exclusion and offsetting the remaining $147,640 of gift taxes with a portion of his unified credit. Lamar has engaged you to calculate the gift tax and prepare a draft of the 2014 gift tax return (pages 1–3). Lamar and Elouisa have indicated they would like to gift split.

ESTATE TAX RETURN PROBLEM

Clark Griswold is a wealthy engineer and inventor who retired to his residence in Fort Collins (Larimer County), Colorado. Clark is married to Ellen and they have two adult children, Russell and Audrey. Clark passed away on March 22 of this year at the age of 60, and his executor, Frank Shirley, has hired you to calculate the estate tax and prepare a draft of the 2014 estate tax return (pages 1 through 3). Clark's estate is being administered through the Larimer County Probate Court.

Frank has inventoried Clark's assets and has listed the value of his assets below. The auto, residence, and checking account were owned jointly (with the right of survivorship) with his wife. Clark also owned a whole life insurance policy with a cash surrender value of $50,000. Ellen and Clark's estate were listed as beneficiaries on the insurance policy with Ellen receiving $1 million and the estate receiving the remainder of the proceeds. The Ajax common stock, the real estate, and the patent were all owned by Clark rather than joint ownership. Frank also noted that the real estate is subject to an $800,000 mortgage. At his death Clark also owed $1,500 on his credit card.

Property	Value	Adjusted Basis
Auto	$ 20,000	$ 55,000
Personal effects	75,000	110,000
Checking account	250,000	250,000
30,000 shares of Ajax common stock	1,200,000	270,000
Residence	6,800,000	480,000
Life insurance	4,000,000	50,000
Real estate	3,500,000	2,100,000
Patent	4,225,000	100,000

Clark's will instructs Frank to distribute Clark's property as follows: Ellen inherits Clark's personal effects, Russell inherits the patent, and Audrey inherits 10,000 shares of the Ajax stock and the real estate. The will also instructs Frank to distribute 20,000 shares of the Ajax stock to State University (an educational institution), and after paying Clark's personal debts, the residual of the estate (if any) is divided equally between Russell and Audrey. The estate paid Clark's personal debts (credit card debt) and $4,300 of funeral expenses associated with Clark's burial. Finally, the estate paid Frank $27,000 in executor's fees associated with the administration of Clark's estate.

Clark's tax records indicate that in 2007 Clark gave $500,000 of Ajax stock to Russell and $500,000 of cash to Audrey. Clark filed a timely gift tax return (Form 709) and paid no gift taxes.

Appendix D

Code Index

Page numbers followed by n refer to footnotes.

Subject Index

Page numbers followed by n refer to footnotes.

B

C

D

E

F

G

H

I

J

K

L

P

Q

R

S

T